The Palgrave Handbook of Development Cooperation for Achieving the 2030 Agenda

"Why should countries help others to develop? How should their efforts be organized? This magisterial tome provides deep insights from almost 50 experts from around the world on the conceptual issues involved and public policy implications. The future of the planet and its soon-to-be 9 billion inhabitants depends on sustainable development. This book helps us understand how to get there."
—Homi Kharas, *Senior Fellow for Global Economy and Development, Center for Sustainable Development at The Brookings Institution*

"This book offers a sound and clear understanding of the narratives, norms, and institutions as far as development cooperation in the context of Agenda 2030 is concerned. The authors emphasize the role of collective action as a method to foster the attainment of global policy frameworks such as Agenda 2030 across national, regional, and global levels, and diverse policy areas. However, regardless of the mechanism set to attain the SDGs, they doubt that its attainment is still feasible due to the characteristics of power struggles and unresolved contestations surrounding this global development agenda. The authors do note the concrete and measurable goals, targets, and indicators that can be used to hold governments and non-governmental actors accountable, and yet warn that the negotiation process among the UN Member States is so politicized that it jeopardizes the success of the agenda.

The authors emphasize that Agenda 2030 and the Paris Agreement are the main global strategies to promote a sustainable society with an ecologically sound and economically viable future. With respect to Development Financing, they recognize ODA as an important resource for the poorest or most conflict-affected countries, however, warn that even if every donor met the 0.7 percent target, it would barely touch the trillions that have been variously estimated to be required to achieve SDGs. They question the modes of cooperation between the actors in the global North and South which still remains based on traditional patterns of cooperation. The authors argue for technical cooperation and transnational cooperation as an equitable mode of cooperation with more potential towards developing innovative solutions for sustainable development.

I consider this book as a very important contribution to the current debates on the future of development cooperation, especially as we embark in the uncertainties of a post-COVID19 era."
—Ibrahim Assane Mayaki, *Chief Executive Officer of the African Union Development Agency-NEPAD (AUDA-NEPAD)*

Sachin Chaturvedi · Heiner Janus ·
Stephan Klingebiel · Li Xiaoyun ·
André de Mello e Souza · Elizabeth Sidiropoulos ·
Dorothea Wehrmann
Editors

The Palgrave Handbook of Development Cooperation for Achieving the 2030 Agenda

Contested Collaboration

palgrave
macmillan

Editors
Sachin Chaturvedi
Research and Information System for
Developing Countries (RIS)
New Delhi, India

Stephan Klingebiel
German Development Institute /
Deutsches Institut für
Entwicklungspolitik (DIE)
Bonn, Germany

André de Mello e Souza
Institute for Applied Economic Research
Rio de Janeiro, Brazil

Dorothea Wehrmann
German Development Institute /
Deutsches Institut für
Entwicklungspolitik (DIE)
Bonn, Germany

Heiner Janus
German Development Institute /
Deutsches Institut für
Entwicklungspolitik (DIE)
Bonn, Germany

Li Xiaoyun
China Agricultural University
Beijing, China

Elizabeth Sidiropoulos
South African Institute of International Affairs
Wits University
Johannesburg, South Africa

ISBN 978-3-030-57937-1   ISBN 978-3-030-57938-8 (eBook)
https://doi.org/10.1007/978-3-030-57938-8

© The Editor(s) (if applicable) and The Author(s) 2021. This book is an open access publication.
Open Access This book is licensed under the terms of the Creative Commons Attribution 4.0 International License (http://creativecommons.org/licenses/by/4.0/), which permits use, sharing, adaptation, distribution and reproduction in any medium or format, as long as you give appropriate credit to the original author(s) and the source, provide a link to the Creative Commons license and indicate if changes were made.
The images or other third party material in this book are included in the book's Creative Commons license, unless indicated otherwise in a credit line to the material. If material is not included in the book's Creative Commons license and your intended use is not permitted by statutory regulation or exceeds the permitted use, you will need to obtain permission directly from the copyright holder.
The use of general descriptive names, registered names, trademarks, service marks, etc. in this publication does not imply, even in the absence of a specific statement, that such names are exempt from the relevant protective laws and regulations and therefore free for general use.
The publisher, the authors and the editors are safe to assume that the advice and information in this book are believed to be true and accurate at the date of publication. Neither the publisher nor the authors or the editors give a warranty, expressed or implied, with respect to the material contained herein or for any errors or omissions that may have been made. The publisher remains neutral with regard to jurisdictional claims in published maps and institutional affiliations.

Cover credit: sorendls/E+ collection/Getty Images

This Palgrave Macmillan imprint is published by the registered company Springer Nature Switzerland AG
The registered company address is: Gewerbestrasse 11, 6330 Cham, Switzerland

PREFACE

Global policy frameworks such as the 2030 Agenda for Sustainable Development and its 17 Sustainable Development Goals (SDGs) require collective action across national, regional, and global levels and different policy areas. At a time when multilateralism is increasingly being contested, it is crucial to develop constructive ways for intensifying cooperation across these levels to achieve the 2030 Agenda. In order to identify improved governance structures for SDG cooperation, our handbook contributes to a better understanding of contested narratives, norms, and institutions.

We are pleased to present this handbook—a collaborative effort of international researchers and practitioners across disciplines. The book features chapters that provide unique perspectives on the conceptual and practical challenges for achieving the SDGs. The findings are most relevant to the policy field of development cooperation, but they also address broader questions currently being discussed in global governance research. The chapters in this book examine different forms of cooperation and contestation but also exemplify that contestation does not necessarily result in gridlock. In line with the current debates on the 2030 Agenda, our authors were invited to present a diversity of perspectives, including critical views and disagreements. We believe that a key contribution of this handbook is to present different perspectives on how to govern the implementation of the SDGs. As a result, this handbook will hopefully advance discussions among both practitioners and researchers and lead to new commonly shared ideas.

The 2030 Agenda is a universal agenda that needs to be translated for, and implemented in, heterogeneous contexts across the world. Given these pluralistic settings, contributors to this handbook apply varying perspectives as well as normative assumptions, depending on the contexts they are analysing. Similarly, the chapters in this handbook are of different lengths to allow for a sound analysis of the different types of questions under investigation. This diversity notwithstanding, the introductory chapter serves to identify common analytical foundations and puts forward overarching findings and lessons learnt.

As editors, we compiled and discussed thematic areas and research topics that shape development cooperation as a policy field and which we consider to be of high relevance for the implementation of the 2030 Agenda. Based on this selection, we approached authors who are experts in the respective areas. We are thankful for the great efforts of all the authors, who dedicated their time to this project and open-mindedly considered all comments raised during two author workshops and several rounds of reviews for each chapter. We are also grateful to all reviewers who provided comments and suggestions on earlier drafts of the chapters and to all the experts who engaged in discussions during our author workshops. We would also like to express our appreciation for those who contributed to this book while working in challenging research environments.

This volume has its roots at the following institutions: the China Agricultural University, the German Development Institute/Deutsches Institut für Entwicklungspolitik (DIE), the Institute for Applied Economic Research, the Research and Information System for Developing Countries, and the South African Institute of International Affairs. We thank each of these institutions for their essential support. We also gratefully acknowledge financial support from the German Federal Ministry for Economic Cooperation and Development (BMZ), including through the Managing Global Governance (MGG) network at DIE.

We are happy to have worked on this project with Palgrave Macmillan and we thank Alina Yurova for her continued support and assistance in seeing this volume through to its finalisation. We are grateful to the three anonymous reviewers for their valuable feedback on the book proposal. Importantly, we thank Robert Furlong for being an excellent copy editor of the entire handbook. Finally, we thank Benjamin Heil, Cornelia Hornschild, Nora Pierau, and Jonas Willen at the German Development Institute for their essential support on editorial and administrative matters.

As is the usual practice, all errors remain solely the responsibility of the editors.

New Delhi, India	Sachin Chaturvedi
Bonn, Germany	Heiner Janus
Bonn, Germany	Stephan Klingebiel
Beijing, China	Li Xiaoyun
Rio de Janeiro, Brazil	André de Mello e Souza
Johannesburg, South Africa	Elizabeth Sidiropoulos
Bonn, Germany	Dorothea Wehrmann

Contents

1 Development Cooperation in the Context of Contested
   Global Governance   1
   Sachin Chaturvedi, Heiner Janus, Stephan Klingebiel,
   Li Xiaoyun, André de Mello e Souza, Elizabeth Sidiropoulos,
   and Dorothea Wehrmann

Part I Global Cooperation for Achieving the SDGs

2 Maximising Goal Coherence in Sustainable
   and Climate-Resilient Development? Polycentricity
   and Coordination in Governance   25
   Sander Chan, Gabriela Iacobuta, and Ramona Hägele

3 Development Finance and the 2030 Goals   51
   Emma Mawdsley

4 Transnational Science Cooperation for Sustainable
   Development   59
   Anna Schwachula

Part II Development Cooperation: Narratives and Norms

5 An Evolving Shared Concept of Development
   Cooperation: Perspectives on the 2030 Agenda   91
   Milindo Chakrabarti and Sachin Chaturvedi

6	The Globalisation of Foreign Aid: Global Influences and the Diffusion of Aid Priorities Liam Swiss	113
7	The Untapped Functions of International Cooperation in the Age of Sustainable Development Adolf Kloke-Lesch	127
8	The Difficulties of Diffusing the 2030 Agenda: Situated Norm Engagement and Development Organisations Lars Engberg-Pedersen and Adam Fejerskov	165
9	Diffusion, Fusion, and Confusion: Development Cooperation in a Multiplex World Order Paulo Esteves and Stephan Klingebiel	185
10	Conceptualising Ideational Convergence of China and OECD Donors: Coalition Magnets in Development Cooperation Heiner Janus and Tang Lixia	217

Part III Measurements of Development Cooperation: Theories and Frameworks

11	Measuring Development Cooperation and the Quality of Aid Ian Mitchell	247
12	Interest-Based Development Cooperation: Moving Providers from Parochial Convergence to Principled Collaboration Nilima Gulrajani and Rachael Calleja	271
13	Monitoring and Evaluation in South-South Cooperation: The Case of CPEC in Pakistan Murad Ali	289
14	The Implementation of the SDGs: The Feasibility of Using the GPEDC Monitoring Framework Debapriya Bhattacharya, Victoria Gonsior, and Hannes Öhler	309

15 Counting the Invisible: The Challenges and Opportunities of the SDG Indicator Framework for Statistical Capacity Development 329
Rolando Avendano, Johannes Jütting, and Manuel Kuhm

Part IV Institutional Settings for Development Cooperation

16 Building a Global Development Cooperation Regime: Failed but Necessary Efforts 349
André de Mello e Souza

17 Failing to Share the Burden: Traditional Donors, Southern Providers, and the Twilight of the GPEDC and the Post-War Aid System 367
Gerardo Bracho

18 Should China Join the GPEDC? Prospects for China and the Global Partnership for Effective Development Cooperation 393
Li Xiaoyun and Qi Gubo

19 South Africa in Global Development Fora: Cooperation and Contestation 409
Elizabeth Sidiropoulos

20 Middle Powers in International Development Cooperation: Assessing the Roles of South Korea and Turkey 435
R. Melis Baydag

Part V Aligning National Priorities with Development Cooperation/SDGs

21 The SDGs and the Empowerment of Bangladeshi Women 453
Naomi Hossain

22 Russia's Approach to Official Development Assistance and Its Contribution to the SDGs 475
Yury K. Zaytsev

| 23 | US Multilateral Aid in Transition: Implications for Development Cooperation
Tony Pipa | 499 |

Part VI The Contribution of SSC and Triangular Cooperation to the SDGs

24	"The Asian Century": The Transformational Potential of Asian-Led Development Cooperation Anthea Mulakala	519
25	South-South Development Cooperation as a Modality: Brazil's Cooperation with Mozambique Jurek Seifert	543
26	South Africa as a Development Partner: An Empirical Analysis of the African Renaissance and International Cooperation Fund Philani Mthembu	567
27	Triangular Cooperation: Enabling Policy Spaces Geovana Zoccal	583
28	Achieving the SDGs in Africa Through South-South Cooperation on Climate Change with China Moritz Weigel and Alexander Demissie	605
29	India as a Partner in Triangular Development Cooperation Sebastian Paulo	625

Part VII The Role of Non-state Actors to the SDGs

| 30 | Partnerships with the Private Sector: Success Factors and Levels of Engagement in Development Cooperation
Jorge A. Pérez-Pineda and Dorothea Wehrmann | 649 |
| 31 | The Role and Contributions of Development NGOs to Development Cooperation: What Do We Know?
Nicola Banks | 671 |

32	**Southern Think Tank Partnerships in the Era of the 2030 Agenda** Andrea Ordóñez-Llanos	689
33	**Conclusion: Leveraging Development Cooperation Experiences for the 2030 Agenda—Key Messages and the Way Forward** Sachin Chaturvedi, Heiner Janus, Stephan Klingebiel, Li Xiaoyun, André de Mello e Souza, Elizabeth Sidiropoulos, and Dorothea Wehrmann	705

Index   717

Notes on Contributors

Murad Ali is Assistant Professor of Development Studies at the University of Malakand in Pakistan. He completed his Ph.D. at Massey University in New Zealand in 2012 and his postdoctoral degree at the German Development Institute (DIE) in 2018. He is the author of *The Politics of US Aid to Pakistan: Aid Allocation and Delivery from Truman to Trump*, which was published by Routledge in 2019.

Rolando Avendano is an Economist at the Asian Development Bank (ADB). Prior to joining ADB, he worked for Partnership in Statistics for Development in the 21st Century (PARIS21), the OECD (Development Centre and Economics Department), and the University of Los Andes in Colombia. He holds a Ph.D. in economics from the Paris School of Economics.

Nicola Banks is a Senior Lecturer in global urbanism and urban development at the University of Manchester. Her research interests include the transformative potential of development NGOs, and she has recently conducted research mapping the United Kingdom's development NGO sector.

R. Melis Baydag is Research Associate and Ph.D. candidate at the Chair of International Politics, Ruhr-University Bochum, Germany. She previously worked as Guest Researcher at the German Development Institute (DIE). Her research interests include middle powers, international development cooperation, and societal approach.

Debapriya Bhattacharya is Distinguished Fellow at the Centre for Policy Dialogue; Chair of the Southern Voice network of think tanks; and a member of the Governing Board at BRAC International. He was the Former Ambassador and Permanent Representative of Bangladesh to WTO and UN Offices in Geneva; a Special Advisor on least-developed countries to the Secretary General of UNCTAD; and Executive Director of the Centre for Policy Dialogue. He studied in Dhaka, Moscow, and Oxford.

Gerardo Bracho is a Mexican Diplomat and an Associate Fellow at the Centre for Global Cooperation Research. He is the Mexican Delegate (development) at the OECD and has been Senior Advisor at the OECD-DAC and Deputy Director General at AMEXCID. He has published extensively on development issues.

Rachael Calleja is a Senior Research Associate at the Center for Global Development and a Research Fellow at the Norman Paterson School of International Affairs. Her research interests include aid effectiveness, donor motivations, and the management of development agencies. She holds a Ph.D. in international affairs from Carleton University, Canada.

Milindo Chakrabarti is Visiting Fellow at the Research and Information System for Developing Countries think tank in New Delhi, in addition to serving as a Full Professor at the Jindal School of Government and Public Policy, O.P. Jindal Global University in Sonipat, India. He is also an Adjunct Professor with the Natural Resources Institute of Manitoba University in Winnipeg Canada. His specialisations include development cooperation, programme evaluation, and development economics.

Sander Chan is a Political Scientist specialising in international environmental governance at the German Development Institute (DIE) and Adjunct Assistant Professor at the Copernicus Institute of Sustainable Development, Utrecht University. His research interests include global environmental politics, transnational actors in developing countries, development, and climate governance.

Sachin Chaturvedi is the Director General at the Research and Information System for Developing Countries think tank in New Delhi. He works on issues related to development economics, involving development finance, SDGs, and South–South cooperation, in addition to trade, investment, and innovation linkages, with a special focus on the World Trade Organization. He is also a member of the Board of Governors at the Reserve Bank of India.

Alexander Demissie is the Founding Director of The China Africa Advisory. His research interest is focussed on China–Africa relations, in particular on China–Ethiopia relations. He is also a Ph.D. researcher and a non-resident lecturer at the University of Bonn on topics surrounding China–Africa relations.

Lars Engberg-Pedersen is Head of the Research Unit and Senior Researcher at the Danish Institute for International Studies. He works on international development cooperation and global norms and has coordinated several research programmes. He has undertaken research on aid in fragile situations, aid management practices, and poverty reduction by local organisations, among other issues.

Paulo Esteves is an Associate Professor at the Institute of International Relations in Rio (IRI/PUC-Rio), the Director of the BRICS Policy Center, and a Research Fellow at the Institute for Advanced Sustainability Studies (Potsdam) and the National School of Public Administration (ENAP) in Brazil. He has published articles and book chapters in the area of international development. He was the President of the Brazilian Association of International Relations between 2011 and 2014.

Adam Moe Fejerskov is a Researcher at the Danish Institute for International Studies. His research addresses the dynamics of contemporary global development and international theory on norms and organisations. His newest books are *The Gates Foundation's Rise to Power* (2018) and *Rethinking Gender Equality in Global Governance: The Delusion of Norm Diffusion* (2019).

Victoria Gonsior is an Economist within the Development Planning and Research Unit at the Ministry of Planning and Economic Development in Sierra Leone. She participates in the Fellowship Programme of the Overseas Development Institute and worked previously as a Researcher at the German Development Institute (DIE).

Qi Gubo is a Professor and Rural Development Researcher at the China Institute for South–South Cooperation in Agriculture/College of Humanities and Development Studies at China Agricultural University. She received her Ph.D. in agricultural economics in 1996. Her main research interests are resource management and sustainable development, and international development cooperation.

Nilima Gulrajani is Senior Research Fellow at the Overseas Development Institute in London and an Associate at the Department of International Development at King's College. Previously, she was an Assistant Professor at the London School of Economics. She currently serves as an Associate Editor of the journal *Public Administration and Development*.

Ramona Hägele is a Researcher at the German Development Institute (DIE) with a focus on the water–energy–food nexus under conditions of climate change and the integrated implementation of the 2030 Agenda. Her main research interests are integrated water resources management and local water governance.

Naomi Hossain is a Political Sociologist currently at the Accountability Research Center at American University. She researches the politics of development, chiefly but not exclusively in Bangladesh, and has published on political elites, the social and political responses to crises, women's empowerment, and food riots.

Gabriela Iacobuta is a Researcher at the German Development Institute (DIE) within the "Environmental Governance" programme. The focus of her work is on the adoption and stringency of domestic climate change mitigation policies and measures around the world and the potential implications of these policies and measures to the implementation of the 2030 Agenda and its Sustainable Development Goals. She is currently also pursuing a Ph.D. at Wageningen University & Research, The Netherlands, on the same research topic.

Heiner Janus is a Researcher at the German Development Institute (DIE) in the programme "Inter- and Transnational Cooperation". He holds a Ph.D. from the University of Manchester's Global Development Institute. His research focusses on aid and development effectiveness and the role of rising powers in development cooperation.

Johannes Jütting Executive Head of the Partnership in Statistics for Development in the 21st Century (PARIS21), is a trained Development Economist with a Ph.D. from Humboldt University at Berlin in agricultural economics and expertise in various fields of development such as agriculture, health economics, institutional change, gender, employment, and social protection, as well as data and statistics.

Stephan Klingebiel has been serving as the Director of the UNDP (United Nations Development Programme) Seoul Policy Centre since mid-2019. He previously worked as the Chair of the programme "Inter- and Transnational Cooperation" of the German Development Institute (DIE). From 2007 to 2011, he was the Founding Director of the KfW Development Bank office in Kigali, Rwanda. He was a regular Guest Professor at Stanford University (2011–2019) and is a Senior Lecturer at the University of Marburg. The views expressed herein are those of the author and can in no way be taken to reflect the official views or positions of the United Development Programme.

Adolf Kloke-Lesch became Executive Director of the Sustainable Development Solutions Network in Germany in 2014. Prior to this, he served as Managing Director at the Deutsche Gesellschaft für Internationale Zusammenarbeit (2011/2012) and Director General at the German Federal Ministry for Economic Cooperation and Development (BMZ, 2007–2010). Before joining BMZ in 1978, he graduated from the Berlin Technical University, where he studied urban and regional planning.

Manuel Kuhm holds a B.Sc. in international economics from the University of Tübingen and is currently finishing his M.A. in development economics at the University of Passau. Previously, he worked for Partnership in Statistics for Development in the 21st Century (PARIS21) at the OECD's Statistics and Data Directorate. His research interests include statistical capacity development, innovative entrepreneurship, and digital technological change.

Tang Lixia Professor, is Deputy Dean at the China Institute for South–South Cooperation in Agriculture, China Agricultural University. She has been involved in several research projects on poverty analysis and livelihood development, social public policy analysis, international development aid, and Chinese engagements in Africa.

Emma Mawdsley is a Reader in Human Geography at the University of Cambridge and the Director of the Margaret Anstee Centre for Global Studies at Newnham College. She works on international development cooperation, with a particular focus on South–South partnerships and how the United Kingdom and other DAC donors are responding to this and other shifts in global development.

André de Mello e Souza is a Researcher at the Institute for Applied Economic Research (IPEA), a Brazilian governmental think tank. He earned a Ph.D. in political science from Stanford University in the United States. He previously worked as a Professor of International Relations at the Pontifical Catholic University of Rio de Janeiro.

Ian Mitchell is a Senior Fellow and Co-director of the "Development Policy and Leadership" programme at the Center for Global Development in Europe. He leads research on how governments' policies accelerate or inhibit development and poverty reduction—considering both the effectiveness of aid and policies including trade, migration, environment, and security. He is also an Associate Fellow at Chatham House and at the Institute for Fiscal Studies.

Philani Mthembu is Executive Director at the Institute for Global Dialogue. His recent publications include a book titled *China and India's Development Cooperation in Africa: The Rise of Southern Powers*, and he is co-editor of the books *From MDGs to Sustainable Development Goals: The Travails of International Development*, and *Africa and the World: Navigating Shifting Geopolitics*.

Anthea Mulakala leads The Asia Foundation's work on Asian Approaches to Development Cooperation, focussing on how Asian countries are shaping the global development cooperation landscape. Previously, she served as Country Representative Malaysia at the World Bank (Indonesia), at the Department for International Development (Bangladesh, Sri Lanka), and at South Asia Partnership (Canada).

Hannes Öhler is a Researcher at the German Development Institute (DIE) and works on issues related to development effectiveness, aid allocation, and private aid. He holds a Ph.D. in development economics from Heidelberg University and studied economics in Göttingen, Kiel, Innsbruck, and Verona.

Andrea Ordóñez-Llanos is Director of Southern Voice, a network of think tanks devoted to bringing research from the Global South to international debates on the development agenda. She is co-editor of the book *Southern Perspectives on the Post-2015 International Development Agenda*. Her work focusses on fostering better knowledge systems to support sustainable development.

Sebastian Paulo is a freelance researcher focussing on international development cooperation, global governance, and India's role as a global development partner. He has worked for various think tanks, including the Observer Research Foundation, the German Development Institute (DIE), and the OECD Development Centre.

Jorge A. Pérez-Pineda is an Economist at the National Autonomous University of Mexico (UNAM) and holds a Ph.D. in international economics and development from the Complutense University of Madrid. At the German Development Institute (DIE), he specialised in the area of global governance. He belongs to the National System of Researchers in Mexico (SNI 1) and networks such as REMECID, REEDES, NEST, and MGG. He is also a Research Professor at Anáhuac University México.

Tony Pipa is a Senior Fellow in Global Economy and Development at the Brookings Institution, where his research focusses on local leadership of the global sustainable development agenda; the effectiveness of multilateral aid; and place-based policies to strengthen the prosperity and resilience of marginalised communities.

Anna Schwachula studied literature and sociology at the University of Bonn and received a Ph.D. from Bremen University. In her dissertation, she focussed on science policy for cooperation with the Global South and impacts on sustainable development. She is a Researcher at the German Development Institute (DIE).

Jurek Seifert is a Development Cooperation Expert. He holds a Ph.D. from the University of Duisburg-Essen and has focussed on South–South cooperation, development effectiveness, and private-sector engagement. He has conducted research at the BRICS Policy Center in Rio de Janeiro, Brazil, and has worked in German development cooperation.

Elizabeth Sidiropoulos is the Chief Executive of the South African Institute of International Affairs. She has published on South Africa's development diplomacy and global governance engagement. She is co-editor of *Development Cooperation and Emerging Powers: New Partners or Old Patterns* (2012) and *Institutional Architecture and Development: Responses from Emerging Powers* (2015).

Liam Swiss is an Associate Professor of Sociology at Memorial University. He researches the role of foreign aid in international norm diffusion, the politics of Canadian aid policy, and women's political representation in the Global South. His book *The Globalization of Foreign Aid: Developing Consensus* was published by Routledge in 2018.

Dorothea Wehrmann holds a Ph.D. in political science and works as a Researcher at the German Development Institute (DIE). She studied social sciences, political communication, and interamerican studies. Her research areas include international and transnational cooperation in networks, private-sector engagement in development cooperation, and the politics of the polar regions.

Moritz Weigel is the Founding Director of The China Africa Advisory. His research interests include China–Africa relations and sustainable development. He has published extensively on South–South and triangular cooperation on climate change. He holds an M.A. in economics, political science, and modern China studies from the University of Cologne.

Li Xiaoyun is a Chair Professor (one of the few prominent professors) at China Agricultural University and Honorary Dean at the China Institute for South–South Cooperation in Agriculture. He is the Chair of the Network of Southern Think Tanks and Chair of the China International Development Research Network. His expertise mainly focusses on international development, aid, agriculture, and poverty reduction.

Yury K. Zaytsev is a Senior Research Fellow at the Russian Academy of National Economy and Public Administration. His expertise covers macroeconomic regulation; global economic governance; international investments; and international development assistance and cooperation. His professional experience deals with consulting projects for, among others, the World Bank, the Eurasian Development Bank, and CISCO Entrepreneur Institute.

Geovana Zoccal has been a Researcher Associate at the BRICS Policy Center since 2012. She received a Ph.D. (2018) and an M.A. (2013) in international relations at Pontifical Catholic University of Rio de Janeiro. She was the German Chancellor Fellow at the Alexander von Humboldt Foundation (2018–2019), based at the German Ministry for Economic Cooperation and Development (BMZ), and was a Visiting Fellow in 2017 at the Institute of Development Studies at the University of Sussex.

ABBREVIATIONS

2030 Agenda	United Nations 2030 Agenda for Sustainable Development
AAA	Accra Agenda for Action
AAAA	Addis Ababa Action Agenda
AAGC	Asia–Africa Growth Corridor
ABC	Brazilian Cooperation Agency/Agência Brasileira de Cooperação
ADAPT	Advanced Data Planning Tool
ADB	Asian Development Bank
AIIB	Asian Infrastructure Investment Bank
AMC	Advanced Market Commitment
AMEXCID	Mexican Agency for International Development Cooperation/Agencia Mexicana de Cooperación Internacional para el Desarrollo
ANC	African National Congress
APDev	Africa Platform for Development Effectiveness
APRM	African Peer Review Mechanism
ARF	African Renaissance and International Cooperation Fund
AS	Alliance for Sustainability
ASEAN	Association of Southeast Asian Nations
AU	African Union
BAPA	Buenos Aires Plan of Action
BAPA+40	Second High-Level United Nations Conference on South–South Cooperation/Buenos Aires Plan of Action plus 40
BBIN	Bangladesh, Bhutan, India, and Nepal
BEPS	Base Erosion and Profit-Shifting
BICS	Brazil, India, China, South Africa
BIMSTEC	Bay of Bengal Initiative for Multi-Sectoral Technical and Economic Cooperation
BMBF	German Federal Ministry of Education and Research/Bundesministerium für Bildung und Forschung
BMZ	German Federal Ministry for Economic Cooperation and Development/Bundesministerium für wirtschaftliche Zusammenarbeit und Entwicklung

BRI	Belt and Road Initiative
BRICS	Brazil, Russia, India, China, South Africa
CAP	Common African Position on the Post-2015 Development Agenda
CBDR	Common But Differentiated Responsibilities
CDB	China Development Bank
CDI	Commitment to Development Index
CGD	Center for Global Development
CIS	Commonwealth of Independent States
CPEC	China–Pakistan Economic Corridor
CRBC	China Road and Bridge Corporation
CRF	Country Results Framework
CRS	Common Reporting Standard
CSO	Civil Society Organisation
CSR	Corporate Social Responsibility
DAAD	German Academic Exchange Service/Deutscher Akademischer Austauschdienst
DAC	Development Assistance Committee
DAG	Development Assistance Group
DBSA	Development Bank of Southern Africa
DC	Development Cooperation
DD	DAC Donor
DFID	Department for International Development (United Kingdom)
DIE	German Development Institute/Deutsches Institut für Entwicklungspolitik
DIRCO	Department of International Relations and Cooperation (South Africa)
DPA	Development Partnership Administration
DPF	Development Partnership Fund (India–United Nations)
DRC	Democratic Republic of Congo
ECDC	Economic Cooperation Among Developing Countries
Embrapa	Brazilian Agricultural Research Corporation/Empresa Brasileira de Pesquisa Agropecuária
EP	Emerging Power
EU	European Union
EXIM	Export-Import
FAO	Food and Agriculture Organization of the United Nations
FDI	Foreign Direct Investment
FfD	Financing for Development Forum (United Nations)
FIDC	Forum for Indian Development Cooperation
Fiocruz	Oswaldo Cruz Foundation
FOCAC	Forum on China–Africa Cooperation
FONA	Research for Sustainable Development Framework Programme (BMBF)
FTA	Free Trade Agreement (Pakistan–China)
G7	Group of Seven
G20	Group of Twenty
GDP	Gross Domestic Product
GFCE	Global Forum on Cyber Expertise
GHG	Greenhouse Gas

GII	Gender Inequality Index
GIZ	German Corporation for International Cooperation/Deutsche Gesellschaft für Internationale Zusammenarbeit
GNI	Gross National Income
GNP	Gross National Product
GPEDC	Global Partnership for Effective Development Co-operation
GPG	Global Public Good
GPI	Global Partnership Initiative
HIC	High-Income Country
HLF	High Level Forum
HLG-PCCB	High-Level Group for Partnership, Coordination and Capacity-Building for Statistics for the 2030 Agenda
HLM	High-Level Meeting
HLP	High-Level Panel of Eminent Persons on the Post-2015 Development Agenda
HLPF	High-Level Political Forum on Sustainable Development
HOM	Head of Mission (United Nations)
HSS	Health System Strengthening
IATF	Inter-Agency Task Force on Financing for Development (United Nations)
IBRD	International Bank for Reconstruction and Development
IBSA	India, Brazil, and South Africa
IBSA Fund	India, Brazil, and South Africa Facility for Poverty and Hunger Alleviation
IDA	International Development Association
IDC	International Development Cooperation
IFF	Illicit Financial Flow
IFFIm	International Finance Facility for Immunisation
IGN	Inter-Governmental Negotiation
IMF	International Monetary Fund
IPCC	Intergovernmental Panel on Climate Change
IR	International Relations
IRENA	International Renewable Energy Agency
ISA	International Solar Alliance
IWRM	Integrated Water Resources Management
JCC	Joint Cooperation Committee (Pakistan)
JST	Joint Support Team
JWG	Joint Working Group
KP	Kyoto Protocol
LDC	Least-Developed Country
LIC	Low-Income Country
LOC	Line of Credit
M&E	Monitoring and Evaluation
MANAGE	National Institute of Agricultural Extension Management (India)
MDB	Multilateral Development Bank
MDG	Millennium Development Goal
MEA	Ministry of External Affairs (India)
MEE	Ministry of Ecology and Environment of the People's Republic of China

MIC	Middle-Income Country
MIKTA	Mexico, Indonesia, Korea, Turkey, Australia
MoF	Ministry of Finance
MoIs	Means of Implementation
MoU	Memorandum of Understanding
MPT	Middle Power Theory
MW	Megawatt
NDB	New Development Bank
NDC	Nationally Determined Contribution
NDP	National Development Plan
NDRC	National Development and Reform Commission (China)
NEPAD	New Partnership for Africa's Development
NeST	Network of Southern Think Tanks
NGO	Non-Governmental Organisation
NSC	North-South Cooperation
NSO	National Statistical Office
ODA	Official Development Assistance
OECD	Organisation for Economic Co-operation and Development
OPIC	Overseas Private Investment Corporation
OWG	Open Working Group of the General Assembly on Sustainable Development Goals
Oxfam GB	Oxfam Great Britain
PA Index	Principled Aid Index
PALOP	Portuguese-Speaking African Countries/Países Africanos de Língua Oficial Portuguesa
PARIS21	Partnership in Statistics for Development in the 21st Century
PBIG	Post-Busan Interim Group
PDR	Planning Development Reform (Pakistan)
PFSD	Partnerships for Sustainable Development
PIO	Public International Organisations
PPP	Public–Private Partnership
PPPD	Public–Private Partnership for Development
PROCID	Programa de Cooperación Internacional para el Desarrollo (Mexico)
PSE	Private-Sector Engagement Through Development Cooperation
QuODA	Quality of Official Development Assistance
RC	Recipient Country
SADC	Southern African Development Community
SADPA	South African Development Partnership Agency
SAP	Structural Adjustment Programme
SCO	Shanghai Cooperation Organisation
SDG	Sustainable Development Goal
SECI	Solar Energy Corporation of India
SEGIB	Ibero-American General Secretariat/Secretaría General Iberoamericana
SEZ	Special Economic Zone
SG	Secretary-General
SITA	Supporting Indian Trade and Investment for Africa
SPCI	Southern Climate Partnership Incubator
SSC	South–South Cooperation

SSCCC	South–South Cooperation on Climate Change
SSDC	South–South Development Cooperation
T20	Think 20
TCDC	Technical Cooperation Among Developing Countries
TERI	The Energy and Resources Institute
TMP	Theory of Middle Powers
TOSSD	Total Official Support for Sustainable Development
TrC	Triangular Cooperation
TT-SSC	Task Team on South–South Cooperation
UN DCF	United Nations Development Cooperation Forum
UN DESA	United Nations Department of Economic and Social Affairs
UN	United Nations
UNCTAD	United Nations Conference on Trade and Development
UNDP	United Nations Development Programme
UNEP	United Nations Environment Programme
UNESCAP	United Nations Economic and Social Commission for Asia and the Pacific
UNFCCC	United Nations Framework Convention on Climate Change
UNGA	United Nations General Assembly
UNICEF	United Nations Children's Fund
UNOSSC	United Nations Office for South–South Cooperation
UNPK	United Nations Peacekeeping
UNSDG	United Nations Sustainable Development Group
UNSC	United Nations Security Council
USAID	United States Agency for International Development
USG	Under-Secretary-General
VNR	Voluntary National Review
WBG	World Bank Group
WHO	World Health Organization
WP-EFF	Working Party on Aid Effectiveness (OECD)
WSSD	World Summit on Sustainable Development (Rio+10)
ZAR	South African Rand

List of Figures

Fig. 2.1	Complementary levels of coherence for implementing the Post-2015 Agenda (*Source* Adapted from OECD [2014, p. 15])	29
Fig. 7.1	"North-South" and "South-South" cooperation in the pre-2015 world (*Note* LIC [low-income country], MIC [middle-income country], WBG [World Bank Group], UNDG [United Nations Development Group], HIC [high-income country]. *Source* Author)	148
Fig. 7.2	Mutually transformative cooperation in the 2030 world (*Note* AIIB [Asian Infrastructure Investment Bank], ASEAN [Association of Southeast Asian Nations], HIC [high-income country], LIC [low-income country], MIC [middle-income country], WBG [World Bank Group], UNDG [United Nations Development Group], IMF [International Monetary Fund], OECD [Organisation for Economic Co-operation and Development], EU [European Union], SCO [Shanghai Cooperation Organisation], UNSDG [United Nations Sustainable Development Group]. *Source* Author)	150
Fig. 9.1	Formal model of the tripartite structure of contemporary international norms (*Source* Winston 2018)	189
Fig. 9.2	The proto-constitution of development cooperation clusters (1945–1961) (*Source* Authors)	192
Fig. 9.3	The establishment of the ODA normative framework (1961–1972) (*Source* Authors)	194
Fig. 9.4	Manufacturing the SSC normative framework (1961–1978) (*Source* Authors)	196
Fig. 9.5	Conditional official development assistance (*Source* Authors)	198
Fig. 9.6	From Paris to Nairobi: Diffusion strategies of aid effectiveness (*Source* Authors)	200
Fig. 9.7	Busan and the fusion attempt (*Source* Authors)	201
Fig. 9.8	TOSSD: The neutralisation of development flows (*Source* Authors)	205

LIST OF FIGURES

Fig. 11.1	Countries by absolute size of economy and relative average income level (*Notes* CDI refers to the [OECD] countries that the Center for Global Development (CGD) assessed in its 2018 Commitment to Development Index. The remaining G20 countries (in red) have been added to the 2020 edition as well as Chile, Israel and United Arab Emirates. *Source* Author's analysis; uses gross domestic product [GDP] and gross national income [2018 data] from the World Bank [2020])	249
Fig. 15.1	Survey results on regional disaggregation requirements. Question 12: Please indicate what types of data disaggregation require the most immediate support (*Source* PARIS21 2018b)	335
Fig. 21.1	Global Gender Gap Index rankings, South Asia, in 2018 (*Note* Lower scores indicate lower levels of gender inequality in the particular domain, that is, better scores. *Source* Author, based on data from the World Economic Forum [2018])	457
Fig. 22.1	Official development assistance provided by the Russian Federation in the period from 2005 to 2017 ($ millions) (*Source* Based on data provided by the OECD-DAC and the MoF of Russia [Knobel and Zaytsev 2018])	478
Fig. 22.2	Distribution of Russian ODA to bilateral and multilateral assistance ($ millions) (*Source* Based on data provided by the OECD-DAC and the MoF of Russia [Knobel and Zaytsev 2018])	480
Fig. 23.1	US ODA, 2005–2016 (*Source* Brookings analysis of OECD Creditor Reporting System [CRS] ODA data [For more information on the data analysis, see "Note about the individual projects (CRS) database" under OECD. Stat on the OECD International Development Statistics (IDS) online databases website: https://www.oecd.org/dac/stats/idsonline.htm])	502
Fig. 26.1	Allocation trends between 2003 and 2015 (*Source* Author, using data from annual reports of the ARF [2003–2015])	576
Fig. 26.2	Expenditure trends between 2003 and 2015 (*Source* Author, using data from annual reports of the ARF [2003–2015])	577
Fig. 28.1	"NDC-SDG Connections"—overview of linkages between African countries' NDCs and the SDGs (*Source* DIE [2019])	607
Fig. 28.2	Current and future spending scenarios on China's SSCCC (*Source* Weigel [2016])	611
Fig. 30.1	Concept of orchestration (*Source* Wehrmann [2018])	658
Fig. 31.1	Sources of income for British development NGOs (2009–2014) (*Source* Banks and Brockington 2018)	682

List of Tables

Table 1.1	Contested cooperation matrix: mapping the role of development cooperation for achieving the SDGs	12
Table 5.1	Features of GAVI	102
Table 5.2	Features of the International Solar Alliance	106
Table 5.3	Features of UNPK	109
Table 7.1	Functional mapping of externally oriented policies and the place of development cooperation	135
Table 7.2	Functional mapping of the means of implementation of the 2030 Agenda	138
Table 9.1	Effectiveness principles: From Paris to Busan	203
Table 10.1	Potential coalition magnet ideas in development cooperation	223
Table 11.1	SDG indicators focussed on international spillovers and cooperation	250
Table 11.2	Development contributions and policies	251
Table 11.3	Development contributions and impacts	252
Table 11.4	Policies that matter for international sustainable development	261
Table 12.1	Summary of dimensions, indicators, and data sources	279
Table 12.2	Change in PA Index scores between 2013 and 2017 by dimension and overall	281
Table 13.1	Analytical framework for assessing China–Pakistan development partnership	292
Table 13.2	A brief assessment of CPEC within the NeST framework	305
Table 14.1	GPEDC monitoring framework—effectiveness principles and indicators	313
Table 15.1	Survey results on regional SDG indicator prioritisation	335
Table 17.1	The burden-sharing game	374
Table 20.1	Comparing Korea (KR) and Turkey (TR)	443
Table 21.1	Gender Inequality Index, South Asia	464
Table 22.1	The amount of financial participation by Russia in international development institutions in 2017	481
Table 22.2	List of national goals of the Presidential May Decree of 2018	487
Table 26.1	ARF allocation and expenditure (2003–2015)	575

Table 28.1	Contested cooperation matrix for China's South-South cooperation on climate change with African countries	615
Table 30.1	Elements contributing to the success of partnerships	656

CHAPTER 1

Development Cooperation in the Context of Contested Global Governance

Sachin Chaturvedi, Heiner Janus, Stephan Klingebiel, Li Xiaoyun, André de Mello e Souza, Elizabeth Sidiropoulos, and Dorothea Wehrmann

1.1 Introduction

The 2030 Agenda for Sustainable Development has successfully set a normative framework that defines development as a universal aspiration for inclusiveness and sustainability. Furthermore, this global agreement contains concrete and measurable goals, targets, and indicators that can be used to hold governments and non-governmental actors accountable for achieving sustainable

---

S. Chaturvedi (✉)
Research and Information System for Developing Countries (RIS), New Delhi, India
e-mail: sachin@ris.org.in

H. Janus · S. Klingebiel · D. Wehrmann
German Development Institute / Deutsches Institut für Entwicklungspolitik (DIE), Bonn, Germany
e-mail: heiner.janus@die-gdi.de

S. Klingebiel
e-mail: stephan.klingebiel@die-gdi.de

D. Wehrmann
e-mail: dorothea.wehrmann@die-gdi.de

X. Li
China Agricultural University, Beijing, China
e-mail: xiaoyun@cau.edu.cn

© The Author(s) 2021
S. Chaturvedi et al. (eds.), *The Palgrave Handbook of Development Cooperation for Achieving the 2030 Agenda*,
https://doi.org/10.1007/978-3-030-57938-8_1

development (Fukuda-Parr and McNeill 2019). Particularly in the field of development cooperation, the 2030 Agenda has become the most prominent reference framework for policy-making and, even beyond the field of development cooperation, the 2030 Agenda is seen as enhancing international cooperation geared towards the global common good (Messner and Scholz 2018).

Yet, the negotiation process among United Nations (UN) member states was politicised (Kapto 2019) and the agenda has been characterised by power struggles (Burke and Rürup 2019) and unresolved contestations (McNeill 2019). Given the mostly incoherent and fragmented landscape of global cooperation, particularly in the field of development cooperation, it is uncertain whether the Sustainable Development Goals (SDGs) will be achieved. Although we see an opportunity for development cooperation actors to find better ways of coordinating across what we call "sites of contested cooperation" (Mello e Souza 2021; Janus and Tang 2021, Chapter 10), we observe the lack of a comprehensive assessment on the current state of different approaches to development cooperation and their potential contribution to the implementation of the 2030 Agenda (Fiddian-Qasmiyeh and Daley 2019a; Kragelund 2019). Against this backdrop, we ask: How can different narratives and norms in development cooperation be reconciled to achieve the 2030 Agenda? This central question guides the handbook.

In the handbook, we propose to answer this question in three main steps. First, we argue that we need a more detailed overview of the narratives and norms shaping distinct approaches in the policy field of development cooperation. Second, we strive for a better understanding of persisting and new institutional sites of contestation. Third, we explore how international governance structures can better address contestation and improve cooperation.

In recent years, development cooperation has been in search of a *new narrative* for underlying motives and rationales. The 2030 Agenda provides a comprehensive global framework that represents a broader consensus than previous frameworks (e.g. Millennium Declaration and the Millennium Development Goals, MDGs). However, a significant weakening of multilateral problem-solving approaches is challenging its implementation. The rise of nationalistic populism and "my country first" movements—not just in the

A. de Mello e Souza
Institute for Applied Economic Research, Rio de Janeiro, Brazil
e-mail: andre.souza@ipea.gov.br

E. Sidiropoulos
Wits University, South African Institute of International Affairs, Johannesburg, South Africa
e-mail: elizabeth.sidiropoulos@wits.ac.za

United States, the UK, and Central and Eastern Europe, but also across Asia and other regions—has strengthened anti-globalisation and pro-national interest narratives. This trend has also impacted domestic development agendas (Roberts 2018). Globalisation challenges, such as violent conflicts, increasing migration and numbers of refugees, as well as climate change as a global challenge, have turned discourses on development cooperation away from development-oriented motives towards the strategic interests of development cooperation providers, such as expanding their own political and economic opportunities (Mawdsley et al. 2018). Countries leverage foreign aid to influence UN decision-making processes, and newly designed migration compacts between the European Union and African partners serve as additional examples in this regard.

Along with changing narratives, development cooperation has been subject to increased *norm competition*. The norms and standards for implementing development interventions are more diversified with a changing institutional landscape of development cooperation (Bhattacharya and Llanos 2016; Fejerskov et al. 2017; Gray and Gills 2018). For many decades, the Organisation for Economic Co-operation and Development's (OECD) Development Assistance Committee (DAC) held the de facto monopoly in defining norms for development cooperation. As a reaction to the growing importance of South-South cooperation (SSC) providers, the DAC has revised its concept of official development assistance (ODA) and proposed an additional measurement for covering "Total Official Support for Sustainable Development". Meanwhile, providers of SSC and private actors have introduced alternative (and complementary) norms and standards that better reflect their requirements and values, such as "mutual benefits" and "horizontality" (Fourie et al. 2019; Hansen and Wethal 2015). In addition, emerging economies have created new international institutions such as the New Development Bank (NDB) and the Asian Infrastructure Investment Bank (AIIB) (Wang 2019). We are therefore witnessing an increasingly fragmented landscape of institutions, norms, and standards for implementing development interventions.

Norm competition also extends to *measuring the quality of development cooperation* at the level of providers, beneficiaries, and individual projects, as exemplified by different conceptual and analytical frameworks for, among other things, SSC (Besharati et al. 2017). Whereas previous policy debates focussed on "aid effectiveness" principles and project evaluation guidelines defined by the OECD-DAC, the current landscape has become more fragmented (Klingebiel et al. 2016). There is no universal framework for measuring the quality, impact, or results of development cooperation, and the SDGs have opened up new opportunities for different providers of development cooperation to present their respective strengths (Uchenna and Simplice 2018). Most development actors can easily align themselves with the SDGs because the 2030 Agenda does not provide specific guidance on defining the quality of development cooperation (Pérez-Pineda and Wehrmann 2021, Chapter 30; Rudolph 2017). At the project level, a wealth of new research, methods, and data has increased our knowledge of how development cooperation across the world can work. Yet, establishing universal standards and comparability across development interventions, as well as data availability and quality, remains a challenge (Ali 2021, Chapter 13; Keijzer 2016; Organisation for Economic Co-operation and Development 2018), also due to the inherently political nature of the different approaches being pursued (Fourie et al. 2019).

Apart from narratives and norms, we need a better understanding of persisting and new *sites of contestation* in development cooperation. These sites can include international and multilateral organisations, multi-stakeholder partnerships, bilateral and multilateral cooperation, or other development cooperation-related platforms. From a global governance perspective, the SDGs provide an inclusive multilateral umbrella that encompasses a range of these sites of contestation where various actors can engage across the policy field of development cooperation. Such a loose umbrella is useful because it provides an overarching supra-architecture for all types of cooperation. A major limitation, however, is that the SDG framework does not offer guidance on how different platforms can coordinate their contributions towards achieving the development goals in an integrated and holistic manner across local, national, regional, and international levels, as well as across all dimensions of sustainable development (Chan et al. 2021, Chapter 2; Kharas and Rogerson 2017). Moreover, the consensus reached on the SDGs is continually being contested due to changing political dynamics. As the rise of nationalist policies illustrates, international actors can quickly switch from supporting to undermining multilateralism.

Against this backdrop, we provide an overview of existing sites of contestation and newly emerging sites of contestation. There are several existing sites of contestation in the policy field of development cooperation. Most prominently, the UN Development Cooperation Forum (UN DCF) and the Global Partnership for Effective Development Co-operation (GPEDC) have worked alongside each other. The OECD and UN Development Programme jointly host the GPEDC. However, the partnership is still primarily associated with the 30 member countries of the OECD's Development Assistance Committee. In contrast, the UN DCF has a universal membership of the 193 UN member states. In recent years, the number of exchanges between both platforms has increased, but neither platform has become universally accepted as being effective for norm- and standard-setting in development cooperation. In addition, neither platform provides tangible inputs to the Financing for Development Forum of the UN, the official review mechanism of SDG 17, or the High-level Political Forum—the principal institutional platform for reviewing progress towards the SDGs. Other sites of contestation include, for instance, club governance formats such as the G20 development working group, the BRICS group (Brazil, Russia, India, China, and South Africa) (Lauria and Fumagalli 2019), the IBSA group (India, Brazil, and South Africa), and MIKTA, an informal grouping composed of Mexico, Indonesia, Korea, Turkey, and Australia formed in the margins of the UN General Assembly in 2013.

Since the 2030 Agenda and SDG negotiations were started in 2013, new sites of contestation have emerged in development cooperation. Most prominently, new development banks have been founded by emerging countries, for example, the BRICS's NDB and the AIIB. These banks were established partly because emerging countries did not see their interests being adequately represented and also due to their distrust of traditional global governance institutions, in particular the Bretton Woods Institutions (Wang 2015). Hence, the creation of new development banks is an example of counter-institutionalisation. Other examples for new sites of contestation include regional initiatives such as the Belt and Road Initiative and the Silk Road Fund by China, the "New Marshall Plan" for Africa, and the Asia-Africa Growth Corridor launched by India and Japan. These new sites of contestation are not explicitly geared towards the policy field of development cooperation—they all touch on trade and investment—but they do have fundamental impacts on how development cooperation is changing.

Apart from mapping the various sites of contestation in development cooperation, there is a need to explore how existing governance structures can be improved to deal with contestation and avoid gridlock (Hale et al. 2013). Achieving the SDGs will also depend on how successful development cooperation actors can be in advancing different types of cooperation and finding constructive ways of addressing contested responsibilities. Within the SDG framework, we find tentative examples of how this process might unfold. These examples fall into two categories: existing forms of cooperation that turn towards taking on greater responsibilities, and new forms of cooperation that are started because of the SDGs.

As examples for the first category of existing types of cooperation and governance mechanisms, we consider ODA providers who have taken on a holistic development cooperation perspective. Traditional ODA provision is geared towards tackling domestic problems in poorer countries in the form of North-South cooperation, including (the still relevant) challenge of poverty reduction. More recent debates on ODA, in addition, acknowledge universality and the role that ODA can play in promoting developmental policies in donor countries, as well as the role of ODA in providing global public goods (Janus et al. 2015; Kaul 2016; Paulo and Klingebiel 2016).[1] The traditional understanding of SSC, shaped by the Buenos Aires Plan of Action of 1978, focussed mostly on the provision of technical assistance, whereas new directions for SSC focus on analysing the expansion of the development finance, trade, and investment elements of SSC and their developmental effects (Fiddian-Qasmiyeh and Daley 2019b; Kragelund 2019; Mawdsley 2019; Mawdsley et al. 2019).

Examples for the second category of new types of cooperation and governance mechanisms can be found in the emergence of North-North and South-North cooperation as well as in the growing number and diversity of multi-actor partnerships (Beisheim and Liese 2014; Wehrmann 2018). Furthermore, there are reciprocal learning formats in which knowledge communities or communities of practice self-organise around sustainable development challenges. For instance, countries across all income groups (low-, middle-, and high-income) have formed alliances to promote voluntary sustainability standards. Another example is the Group of Friends of the Voluntary National Reviews, which advocates for rigorous reporting on the SDGs. Providing a better understanding of how new cooperation formats have emerged and which specific mechanisms have enabled existing cooperation formats to take on more responsibility is another main contribution of this book.

Across the individual chapters in this handbook, we bring all three components together—(i) mapping narratives and norms, (ii) identifying and investigating sites of contestation, and (iii) reflecting on better governance structures for SDG cooperation. Each chapter provides a unique perspective on these conceptual and practical challenges for development cooperation and adds to the overall tapestry of knowledge on the complex policy field we call development cooperation, in particular towards better understanding and addressing contested cooperation for achieving the SDGs.

1.2 Coordination and Responsibilities: The Twin Challenges of the SDGs

The guiding question of this handbook ("How can different narratives and norms in development cooperation be reconciled to achieve the 2030 Agenda?") builds on two challenges that we consider central for the implementation of the 2030 Agenda and that we understand as the twin challenges of the SDGs: How can different SDG-related policies be coordinated? And how can responsibilities be divided in a just manner?

Achieving the SDGs requires coordinating policies across different policy fields at different global levels. The *coordination challenges* in this context are grouped into three categories: interdependencies of policies, collective action problems, and disconnected national and global policy-making.

First, the 17 goals, 169 targets, and 232 indicators of the SDG framework form a complex web of *interdependencies* with potential synergies and trade-offs across different policies (Barbier and Burgess 2019). Research has produced the first conceptual tools for mapping these interconnections (Nilsson et al. 2016), including network analysis (Le Blanc 2015), but countries have not yet applied these tools to inform their decision-making. Instead, "there is a considerable risk that countries will adopt arbitrary or politically salient approaches to prioritisation and/or pursue the same 'siloed' approaches that have met with limited success in the past" (Allen et al. 2018, p. 422). The skills of governments to organise, manage, lead, and scale cross-sector cooperation are traditionally limited (Florini 2018). This problem is compounded by the extremely broad scope of the SDG agenda, which includes virtually all aspects of development. The agenda brings together a plethora of distinct actors and encourages the formation of new partnerships in development cooperation, but at the same time it allows stakeholders to justify and legitimise any policy or set of policies as contributing to such an agenda.

Second, due to the numerous *collective action problems* contained in the SDGs, multiple actors with divergent and often conflicting interests need to cooperate across multiple sectors and jurisdictional levels (Bowen et al. 2017). This coordination challenge has been conceptualised in different ways across economics (public choice theory, transaction costs, game theory) and political science (analysing voting or environmental policies, for instance). The core of collective action problems is that individual actors usually do not act in the common interest (Olson 2009), even if they will benefit, leading to coordination failures and suboptimal outcomes, in particular, underproviding global public goods (Bodenstein et al. 2017). In this way, the provision of global public goods such as a stable climate, safety from communicable diseases, global security, and financial stability mirrors collective action problems to be addressed when envisioning the implementation of the SDGs (Kaul 2018).

Third, *national and global level policy-making* are often disconnected. To date, national plans for achieving the SDGs appear to be shaped by path dependencies, rather than by systematic analyses of interlinkages between SDGs (Breuer et al. 2019; Tosun and Leininger 2017) and across national and global levels. Most SDG indicators measure progress at the national level, and less than 30 per cent of indicators measure a "transboundary" effect (Mitchell 2021, Chapter 11). Richer countries provide bilateral support to developing countries for achieving the SDGs, but global- and regional-level discussions on collective action as well as debates on domestic development issues in richer countries are largely neglected. Finally, multi-stakeholder approaches that cut across local, national, and cross-border levels are still developing and are contested (Wehrmann 2018).

In addition to these coordination challenges, the SDGs mask underlying *contested responsibilities*. Even though the SDGs are universal, it has not been specified how different actors should share responsibilities for implementing the SDGs. SDG 17, on the means of verification, addresses issues such as finance, trade, and technology, but it mostly reaffirms existing commitments. The goal promotes partnerships, including public-private and civil society partnerships, but it does not provide concrete guidance for how to establish these partnerships. From a critical perspective, SDG 17 reflects strong moral ambitions—similar to MDG 8 on the global partnership—but elicits weak normative commitments, leading to a situation of voluntarism in cooperation (Cooper and French 2018). Such voluntarism and self-organisation may again spur goal incoherence (Chan et al. 2021, Chapter 2).

According to Bexell and Jönsson (2017), responsibilities can further be broken down into three different types: cause, obligation, and accountability. The *causes* of responsibility remain largely hidden in the SDG documents, as questions on how power relations and historical circumstances determine current responsibilities are not addressed (Bexell and Jönsson 2017). Responsibility in terms of *obligation* is seemingly boundless, leading to countless goal conflicts and exacerbating the goal conflicts identified above. Crucially, the SDGs do not clarify how diverse needs—particularly those of low-income countries—will be met and how rich countries will be held responsible by SDG 17 to leverage their wealth and influence towards global sustainable development. Responsibility in the sense of *accountability* is largely based on voluntarism, and even seemingly objective technical discussions on numbers, indicators, and data are the product of power relations and unresolved contestation (Fukuda-Parr and McNeill 2019). Overall, the SDG framework, therefore, did not make progress towards defining what "common but differentiated responsibilities" (Pauw et al. 2015) mean in practice, but instead gave rise to open and hidden forms of contestation at all levels of SDG implementation.

We argue that these twin challenges of the SDGs—*unresolved coordination challenges* and *contested responsibilities*—will hinder the achievement of the 2030 Agenda. Making progress towards achieving the SDGs thus requires that governmental and non-governmental actors cooperate more and find constructive ways of addressing these twin challenges. Although these two challenges apply to the overall SDG framework and potentially all policy fields related to the SDGs, we specifically focus on the policy field of development cooperation.

1.3 The Policy Field of Development Cooperation

The policy field of development cooperation is central for addressing these twin challenges of the SDGs for three main reasons. First, development cooperation actors were critical drivers of the 2030 Agenda and have always been closely linked to development debates in the UN. Second, development cooperation is functionally geared towards solving coordination problems through different forms of cooperation, either bilaterally or multilaterally, by facilitating dialogue and aligning ideas and interests. Third, development cooperation and policies in this field have historically dealt with contested responsibilities—from its origins in colonial history to reconstruction efforts after the Second World War, and from different alliances during the Cold War to discussions on global responsibilities today.

From a research perspective, we understand development cooperation as an organisational field (DiMaggio and Powell 1983; Scott 2013). Fields can be described as having three features: "a constitutional object binding the different organizations together, power relations shaping interaction between the different organizations in the field, and emerging rules and principles that organizations are expected to adhere to in order to be considered legitimate" (Fejerskov 2016, p. 5). For the book, we understand development cooperation broadly as an organisational field encompassing all actors that proclaim contributions to development cooperation. Individual chapters of this handbook, however, will apply specific definitions of different types of development cooperation based on the respective author's understanding.

Broadly defined, development cooperation, therefore, includes ODA providers, SSC providers, developing countries, and non-governmental actors (including civil society, philanthropy, and businesses). Similarly, Fejerskov et al. (2017) list states, including new global powers, industrialising countries, and post-socialist states; and non-state actors, which include private foundations, celebrity organisations, religious organisations, corporations, and social enterprises, as well as novel forms of grassroots or do-it-yourself development endeavours. Listing these actors in a joint category, however, is contested because each actor—whether it is a government from the North or the South, or a private actor—has its own definition of development cooperation, which does not necessarily correspond with other competing definitions (Fourie et al. 2019; Kragelund 2019).

The problem with broad definitions of development cooperation, however, as Mthembu (2018) points out, is that they cease to have any real meaning when just about any economic transaction between different actors can be seen as development cooperation. Hence, researchers have proposed more specific definitions that are centred on the overarching objective of development cooperation. Alonso and Glennie (2015) suggest that development cooperation needs to: (i) specifically intend to support development, (ii) operate through actions that would not be promoted (or at least not in the same way) by the market alone, (iii) differentiate in favour of developing countries, particularly the poorest, in order to broaden their opportunities for progress, and (iv) be based on cooperative relationships that try to enhance developing-country ownership. Mitchell (2021, Chapter 11) alternatively proposes to define development cooperation as "a country's policies, and how these affect the current and future welfare and growth of other countries' people and economies". Finally, Mthembu (2018) argues that development cooperation from Southern powers should be defined as official transfers of money, goods, and services (that are concessional in nature) to developing countries specifically for their economic development and welfare.

Even with these mores specific definitions of development cooperation, we claim that measurability and comparability across different types of development cooperation remain a challenge (see Part III of handbook on measurements of development cooperation). Although measuring financial components of development cooperation can be straightforward, the measurement of technical cooperation and policy spillovers between countries of contributions towards global public goods are more challenging. Kaul (2018) provides an overview of how to define global public goods and how to conceptualise global public policy that provides global public goods. She notes that, so far, there exists no fully-fledged global public policy, neither on the theoretical nor practical level, except for some limited policy innovations. Nevertheless, policies directed towards the global common good are needed not only for the implementation of the 2030 Agenda but also, as Messner and Scholz highlight (2018), to stabilise globalisation and to achieve sustainable human development for most people.

Moreover, in the field of development cooperation, we observe simultaneous contestation and cooperation in an ongoing dynamic process: In recent years, development cooperation has undergone fundamental and dynamic changes. These changes have been spurred by internal and contextual factors, such as the financial crisis in 2007/2008, the rise of the digital economy, and the alignment of development goals with climate goals (TWI2050—The World in 2050 [2018]; United Nations Department of Economic and Social Affairs 2018; World Bank 2018).[2] In this context, a key trend affecting development cooperation has been the increasing global role of emerging economies and the disruption of established formats of cooperation (Chaturvedi et al. 2012; Zürn 2018b).

The growing contributions of SSC are often analysed alongside ODA, as defined by members of the OECD's DAC (Bergamaschi et al. 2017; Mawdsley et al. 2019). Others describe development cooperation between actors of the South in terms of a "new development compact" built on the principles of mutual gain, non-interference, and collective growth opportunities, and characterised by the absence of conditionalities (Chaturvedi 2016). According to a definition provided by IBSA, SSC is based on principles of "respect for national sovereignty; national ownership and independence; equality; non-conditionality; non-interference in domestic affairs; and mutual benefit"; IBSA partners claim that "SSC is completely different from the North–South/donor–donee cooperation, and that ODA templates are not a good basis for SSC" (Government of India 2018). However, common principles for effectiveness, differentiated assessment approaches, and the corresponding data for evaluation are still missing, limiting potentials for comparisons and knowledge transfers (Ali 2021, Chapter 13; Bhattacharya et al. 2021, Chapter 14). Others argue that such definitions and propositions on how the South should be analysed or mobilised would be "antithetical to the very foundations of the debates we and our contributors build upon in our respective modes of research and action" (Fiddian-Qasmiyeh and Daley 2019a, pp. 3–4).

From a global governance perspective,[3] there has been a more extensive variety of narratives and norms put forward by an increasing number of heterogeneous actors in development cooperation (Mawdsley et al. 2019). Also, beyond the field of development cooperation, scholars suggest that global politics are embedded in normative and institutional structures that are dominated by hierarchies and power inequalities, and therefore inherently lead to contestation, resistance, and distributional struggles (Morse and Keohane 2014; Zürn 2018a). In institutions (and partnerships), for example, norms and standards guiding cooperation are the result of negotiation processes that are determined by organisational contexts such as organisational structures, practices, and departmental and individual relationships (Tjosvold 1984). These negotiation processes among states and non-governmental actors within existing fora and in new fora are what we understand as sites of contested cooperation. These sites of contested cooperation also determine how partnerships (and institutions) collaborate to achieve the 2030 Agenda, how their distinct purposes may relate to and build on each other, and ultimately how responsibilities are defined.

Moreover, actors engage in parallel platforms of global and club governance for development cooperation, sometimes in direct or indirect contestation with one another. Existing development cooperation platforms, such as the UN DCF and the GPEDC, work alongside new platforms, such as the UN High-level Political Forum and the G20 Development Group (Bracho 2021, Chapter 17; Lauria and Fumagalli 2019). Against this backdrop, we characterise the current policy field of development cooperation as being shaped by multiple sites of *"contested cooperation"*.

1.4 Development Cooperation as an Example of Contested Global Governance

The policy field of development cooperation is central for addressing the twin challenges of the 2030 Agenda, but it is going through fundamental and dynamic changes that we characterise as "contested cooperation". Drawing on global governance research, we analyse contested cooperation for the specific case of development cooperation, but we also highlight broader implications for global governance challenges as such. "Global governance" can be understood as a normative concept for the search of more collective cross-border solutions, and therefore it relates closely to the twin challenges of the SDGs. Moreover, the main focus of global governance[4] research lies in analysing structures and regulations supporting collective approaches beyond the hegemonic dominance of power politics.

Research on the current state of international cooperation speaks of "contested multilateralism" (Morse and Keohane 2014) and "contested global governance" (Cooper 2014; Zürn 2018a). There are two main forms of *contestation*: "politicisation of international authorities" (also called regime-shifting or institution-shifting) and "counter-institutionalisation" (also called regime-creation or institution-creation) (Morse and Keohane 2014; Zürn 2018a). Applying these concepts to development cooperation, actors can therefore either challenge existing international institutions by working through them, or create new international institutions that better address their needs, and thereby further serve the purpose "to influence or replace the old ones" (Zürn 2018b, p. 12).[5]

According to Zürn (2018a), the politicisation of international institutions and counter-institutionalisation increase with the level and type of authority an institution has. The policy field of development cooperation—if narrowly defined as ODA only, for instance—typically involves little transfer of authority to international institutions and generally has lower salience in public debates than other policy areas such as trade or migration, for instance. Hence, we would expect moderate levels of contestation. However, if we assume a

Table 1.1 Contested cooperation matrix: mapping the role of development cooperation for achieving the SDGs

Contestation			
Cooperation		Institution-shifting	Institution-creation
	Established cooperation	**1. Updating international institutions** *Examples: Updating SSC definition (BAPA+40), updating ODA reporting system*	**2. Proliferating international institutions** *Examples: Creation of AIIB, NDB*
	New types of cooperation	**3. Collaborating in international institutions** *Examples: SDG Voluntary National Reviews in High-level Political Forum*	**4. Piloting collaboration** *Examples: Voluntary sustainability standards and accompanying platform*

Source Authors

broader definition of development cooperation that is closely integrated with other high-salience policy areas such as trade and investment, for instance, we could expect higher levels of contestation.

Therefore, the concept of contested cooperation describes the current development cooperation landscape that is shaped by ongoing processes of institution-shifting and institution-creation within established forms of development cooperation and new types of cooperation. As illustrated in Table 1.1, there are four main cases. In the first case, established types of cooperation and institution-shifting lead to actors "updating international institutions" (1). Examples for existing forms of cooperation are North-South cooperation, defined as ODA by the OECD-DAC, or longstanding types of SSC. With these established types of cooperation, OECD-DAC members, for example, politicise existing international institutions when they propose to change the reporting system of ODA towards accommodating their commercial interests. Correspondingly, providers of SSC might politicise the UN when they introduce new language on SSC in different international frameworks, such as the SDGs. Non-state actors can also contribute to institution-shifting in similar ways, either through influencing states to advocate on their behalf or by directly engaging. In the second case, existing forms of cooperation are combined with institution-creation, leading to what we call "proliferating international institutions" (2). Examples for contestation in the form of institution-creation are the NDB and the AIIB. Both incumbent and rising powers use counter-institutionalisation to challenge existing international institutions in development cooperation.

For cases three and four, we focus on new types of cooperation that are emerging in the SDG context, what we call "collaboration"[6] for achieving the SDGs. The literature on defining collaboration typically describes collaboration as a qualitatively more ambitious type of cooperation (Emerson et al. 2012; Phillips et al. 2000; Thomson and Perry 2006; Wood and Gray 1991). We are therefore interested in seeing more profound and complex forms of collaboration among development actors as new types of "SDG collaboration" emerge. In the third case of Table 1.1, we expect that, coupled with contestation in the form of institution-shifting, these new types of cooperation can lead to "collaboration in international institutions" (3). Potential examples for this case could be South-North and North-North cooperation, multi-stakeholder partnerships, and other new and innovative forms of cooperation. The Voluntary National Reviews of the SDGs provide a specific example in which different countries showcase new types of cooperation within the UN.

The fourth case occurs when new types of cooperation are coupled with institution-creation, leading to "piloting cooperation" (4). Here, actors collaborate outside existing institutions and create new institutions to match their innovative types of cooperation. One illustrative example in this regard is the introduction of voluntary national sustainability standards, in which all types of countries (high-, medium-, and low-income) collaborate to define good social and environmental practices for an industry or product outside of existing international institutions in a flexible issue-specific format. This handbook illustrates the outcomes of contested cooperation and discusses the consequences of contested cooperation in the context of the SDGs by applying an actor-based perspective. Whether contested cooperation ultimately leads to improvements or failure in achieving the SDGs will depend on the specific decision-space of actors within a given site of contestation. Potential outcomes range from radical shifts to marginal changes in the form of institutional layering (Streeck and Thelen 2009) to complete gridlock (Hale et al. 2013).

In sum, this handbook contributes to an evolving academic and policy debate on governance challenges and their interaction with development cooperation. More specifically, the chapters in this book relate to debates on: the rise of ideas (norm generation and diffusion) in international relations (global) collective action, innovations on (global) solutions, global public and common goods, and the changing contexts of development cooperation within the context of global governance. All chapters apply varying understandings of development cooperation and the different concepts derived at in and beyond global governance research, yet they all showcase examples of contestation. Hence, these varied approaches to development cooperation, whether broadly or narrowly defined, can be used as exciting case studies for displaying various examples of contestation across different levels of authority transfer and salience. Ultimately, a better understanding of these sites of contested cooperation will contribute towards better coordination of competing narratives and norms in development cooperation to achieve the 2030 Agenda.

1.5 Structure of the Book

This handbook contributes to a better understanding of contestations that limit cooperation in the field of development cooperation. The chapters identify avenues for enhanced cooperation to achieve the 2030 Agenda. To address the twin challenges of the SDGs—the lack of coordination and contested responsibilities—we draw on multiple perspectives to capture how the policy field of development cooperation is changing in complex ways. We apply the concept of contested cooperation as a guiding concept: All contributions reflect on examples of contestation and cooperation and address how development cooperation can better contribute towards achieving the 2030 Agenda and the SDGs.

To answer the guiding question of this handbook—"How can different narratives and norms in development cooperation be reconciled to achieve the 2030 Agenda?"—it is organised into seven parts. The first part relates to governance challenges affecting the implementation of the 2030 Agenda more generally and within the context of specific SDGs. The chapters in this part outline context-specific needs for improving governance structures to achieve global public and common goods in different policy sectors and under consideration of different economic potentials. The second and third parts provide an overview on the evolution of different narratives and norms in the policy field of development cooperation by discussing the main changes in the policy field over the last several years and their consequences for measuring development cooperation.

The main change reflected on is the shift of the underlying rationale of development cooperation, from needs-based (alleviating poverty, providing basic services, etc.) towards more interest-based cooperation (political and economic interests), including the provision of global public and common goods (enlightened self-interest). This changing rationale of development cooperation also affects the implementation of the 2030 Agenda. The chapters of the second and third parts, therefore, contribute to a better understanding of the limits and opportunities for cooperation based on the evolution of different narratives and norms in development cooperation. Overall, the chapters in this part reflect on the trends driving the long-term transformation of development cooperation as well as the current shifts in the development narrative from various angles.

The fourth part focusses on the subject of norm competition, with specific reference to global institutional platforms for development cooperation (UN, G20, OECD, etc.) to provide a better understanding of persisting and new sites of contestation and their different contexts. In parallel to global governance becoming multi-polar, the development cooperation landscape has proliferated, offering multiple platforms for engagement. Each platform has a distinct history, mandate, and specific set of norms that it endorses. For decades, the OECD defined aid as ODA, whereas SSC had a distinct and different set of norms. With the recent rise of new global institutions and platforms, competition between norms has increased, as has the number of sites of contested cooperation within and outside of established formats of cooperation. The chapters in this part highlight different elements of the ongoing norm competition across the institutional landscape of development cooperation.

In contrast to parts one to four, which mostly focus on conceptual and scholarly debates, parts five to seven deepen policy debates. These parts are particularly relevant for practitioners and researchers who engage in debates on the quality of aid and the adoption of "aid effectiveness" principles. Both have received significant attention in development cooperation over the past decades but have lost momentum recently. Part five, for example, focusses on competing norms and narratives at the global and national levels. The chapters in this part discuss how norms and narratives can be better reconciled to enhance the quality of development cooperation towards achieving the 2030 Agenda by identifying pathways for connecting negotiating processes, exchanging knowledge, and harmonising strategies. In a similar vein, parts six and seven shed light on the conceptual and practical challenges for development cooperation as well as the contributions of South-South and triangular cooperation and non-state actors to the 2030 Agenda.

Notes

1. Over the past 20 years, various scholars have shifted the discussion on the diverse nature of collective goods to the transnational level. Kaul et al. (2016) define global public goods (GPGs) as commodities that enjoy global application in terms of use, cost, or both. Others use the term "global common good" to address goals or parameters that are relevant to a global community (Messner and Scholz 2018). Both the term global common good and GPGs, as concepts, have been influential when considering the political economy of collective action on a transnational level. Development cooperation plays a vital role in providing GPGs, and thereby international provision competes with the allocation of development cooperation resources on the national level.
2. Academic and policy literature has analysed different elements of these changes, such as the proliferation of development actors (Zimmermann and Smith 2011) and the diversification of development finance (Prizzon et al. 2017). Other researchers have investigated how the underlying rationale of the policy field itself has been changing, for instance through concepts such as "beyond aid" (Janus et al. 2015), "the end of ODA" (Severino and Ray 2009), or "the post-aid world" (Mawdsley et al. 2014).
3. Understood as encompassing "the totality of institutions, policies, norms, procedures and initiatives through which States and their citizens try to bring more predictability, stability and order to their responses to transnational challenges" (United Nations 2014, p. vi). In academic debates, the term "global governance" points to the exercise of authority across national borders.
4. Debates on the meaning of global governance, however, are also contested in several ways (Weiss and Wilkinson 2018). Scholars such as Acharya (2018), for example, disentangle the concept of global governance in relation to identified

issue areas, areas within which intensified globalisation and the proliferation of collective action problems are central.
5. For this handbook, we do not prescribe an overarching definition of the term "institutions", given the large number of distinct rationalist or constructivist definitions of institutions. For the specific purpose of this introduction, however, we follow Duffield (2007, p. 8), who defines international institutions as "relatively stable sets of related constitutive, regulative, and procedural norms and rules that pertain to the international system, the actors in the system (including states as well as non-state entities), and their activities".
6. Cooperation occurs when participants agree on a shared problem that they try to solve through a division of labour, whereas collaboration refers to the process of working together to develop and sustain the solution of shared problems. Collaboration implies the sharing of risks, resources, responsibilities, and rewards, and it requires synchronised and coordinated activity (Camarihna-Matos and Afsarmanesh 2008). Cooperation and collaboration differ in terms of their depth of interaction, integration, commitment, and complexity, with cooperation falling at the low end of the continuum, and collaboration at the high end (Bryson et al. 2015). Collaboration is a process that evolves over time "in which autonomous actors interact through formal and informal negotiation, jointly creating rules and structures governing their relationships and ways to act or decide on the issues that brought them together; it is a process involving shared norms and mutually beneficial interactions" (Thomson and Perry 2006, p. 23). Thomson and Perry (2006, p. 23) argue that cooperation involves reciprocities and an exchange of resources that is not necessarily symmetrical and that "cooperation for a mutual goal moves this to collaboration".

REFERENCES

Acharya, A. (2018). *The end of American world order*. Hoboken, NJ: Wiley.
Ali, M. (2021). Monitoring and evaluation in South-South cooperation: The case of CPEC in Pakistan. In: Palgrave, this volume.
Allen, C., Metternicht, G., & Wiedmann, T. (2018). Prioritising SDG targets: Assessing baselines, gaps and interlinkages. *Sustainability Science, 14*(2), 1–18.
Alonso, J. A., & Glennie, J. (2015). *What is development cooperation?* https://www.un.org/en/ecosoc/newfunct/pdf15/2016_dcf_policy_brief_no.1.pdf.
Barbier, E. B., & Burgess, J. C. (2019). Sustainable development goal indicators: Analyzing trade-offs and complementarities. *World Development, 122,* 295–305.
Beisheim, E., & Liese, A. (Eds.). (2014). *Transnational partnerships—Effectively providing for sustainable development?* London: Palgrave Macmillan.
Bergamaschi, I., Moore, P., & Tickner, A. B. (Eds.). (2017). *South-South cooperation beyond the myths: Rising donors, new aid practices?* London: Palgrave Macmillan.
Besharati, N., Rawhani, C., & Rios, O. G. (2017). *A monitoring and evaluation framework for South-South cooperation*. https://saiia.org.za/wp-content/uploads/2017/05/saia_NeST-Working-Paper_20170515.pdf.
Bexell, M., & Jönsson, K. (2017). Responsibility and the United Nations' Sustainable Development Goals. *Forum for Development Studies, 44*(1), 13–29.
Bhattacharya, D., Gonsior, V., & Öhler, H. (2021). The implementation of the SDGs: The feasibility of using the GPEDC monitoring framework. In: Palgrave this volume.

Bhattacharya, D., & Llanos, A. O. (2016). *Southern perspectives on the post-2015 international development agenda*. London: Routledge.

Bodenstein, T., Faust, J., & Furness, M. (2017). European Union development policy: Collective action in times of global transformation and domestic crisis. *Development Policy Review, 35*(4), 441–453.

Bowen, K. J., Cradock-Henry, N. A., Koch, F., Patterson, J., Häyhä, T., Vogt, J., & Barbi, F. (2017). Implementing the "Sustainable Development Goals": Towards addressing three key governance challenges—collective action, trade-offs, and accountability. *Current Opinion in Environmental Sustainability, 26*, 90–96.

Bracho, G. (2021). Failing to share the burden: Traditional donors, Southern providers, and the twilight of the GPEDC and the post-war aid system. In: Palgrave, this volume.

Breuer, A., Janetschek, H., & Malerba, D. (2019). Translating Sustainable Development Goal (SDG) interdependencies into policy advice. *Sustainability, 11*(7), 2092.

Bryson, J. M., Crosby, B. C., & Stone, M. M. (2015). Designing and implementing cross-sector collaborations: Needed and challenging. *Public Administration Review, 75*(5), 647–663.

Burke, S., & Rürup, B. L. (2019). Political thriller exposes the underbelly of global goals. *Global Policy, 10*(S1), 137.

Camarihna-Matos, L. M., & Afsarmanesh, H. (2008). Concept of collaboration. In D. G. Putnik & M. M. Cunha (Eds.), *Encyclopedia of networked and virtual organizations* (pp. 311–315). Hershey, NY: IGI Global.

Chan, S., Iacobuta, G., & Haegele, R. (2021). Maximising goal coherence in sustainable and climate-resilient development? Polycentricity and coordination in governance. In: Palgrave this volume.

Chaturvedi, S. (2016). The development compact: A theoretical construct for South-South cooperation. *International Studies, 53*(1), 15–43.

Chaturvedi, S., Fues, T., & Sidiropoulos, E. (2012). *Development cooperation and emerging powers: New partners or old patterns?*. London: Zed Books.

Cooper, A. F. (2014). The G20 and contested global governance: BRICS, middle powers and small states. *Caribbean Journal of International Relations and Diplomacy, 2*(3), 87–109.

Cooper, N., & French, D. (2018). SDG 17: Partnerships for the goals—Cooperation within the context of a voluntarist framework. In D. French & L. J. Kotzé (Eds.), *Sustainable Development Goals: Law, theory and implementation* (pp. 271–304). Cheltenham: Edward Elgar Publishing.

DiMaggio, P. J., & Powell, W. W. (1983). The iron cage revisited: Institutional isomorphism and collective rationality in organizational fields. *American Sociological Review, 48*(2), 147–160.

Duffield, J. (2007). What are international institutions? *International Studies Review, 9*(1), 1–22.

Emerson, K., Nabatchi, T., & Balogh, S. (2012). An integrative framework for collaborative governance. *Journal of Public Administration Research and Theory, 22*(1), 1–29.

Fejerskov, A. M. (2016). Understanding the nature of change: How institutional perspectives can inform contemporary studies of development cooperation. *Third World Quarterly, 37*(12), 2176–2191.

Fejerskov, A. M., Lundsgaarde, E., & Cold-Ravnkilde, S. (2017). Recasting the "new actors in development" research agenda. *The European Journal of Development Research, 29*(5), 1070–1085.

Fiddian-Qasmiyeh, E., & Daley, P. (2019a). Introduction. Conceptualising the Global South and South-South encounters. In E. Fiddian-Qasmiyeh & P. Daley (Eds.), *Routledge handbook of South-South relations* (pp. 1–28). London and New York, NY: Routledge.

Fiddian-Qasmiyeh, E., & Daley, P. (2019b). *Routledge handbook of South-South relations*. London and New York, NY: Routledge.

Florini, A. (2018). Professionalizing cross-sector collaboration to implement the SDGs. In R. M. Desai, H. Kato, H. Kharas, & J. W. McArthur (Eds.), *From summits to solutions: Innovations in implementing the Sustainable Development Goals* (pp. 106–125). Washington, DC: The Brookings Institution.

Fourie, E., Nauta, W., & Mawdsley, E. (2019). Introduction. In E. Mawdsley, E. Fourie, & W. Nauta (Eds.), *Researching South-South development cooperation: The politics of knowledge production* (pp. 1–11). London and New York, NY: Routledge.

Fukuda-Parr, S., & McNeill, D. (2019). Knowledge and politics in setting and measuring the SDGs: Introduction to special issue. *Global Policy, 10*(S1), 5–15.

Government of India. (2018, June 5). *IBSA Declaration on South-South Cooperation*. https://www.mea.gov.in/bilateral-documents.htm?dtl/29955/IBSA_Declaration_on_SouthSouth_Cooperation.

Gray, K., & Gills, B. K. (Eds.). (2018). *Rising powers and South-South cooperation*. London: Routledge.

Hale, T., Held, D., & Young, K. (2013). *Gridlock: Why global cooperation is failing when we need it most*. Cambridge: Polity Press.

Hansen, A., & Wethal, U. (Eds.). (2015). *Emerging economies and challenges to sustainability: Theories, strategies, local realities*. London: Routledge.

Janus, H., Klingebiel, S., & Paulo, S. (2015). Beyond aid: A conceptual perspective on the transformation of development cooperation. *Journal of International Development, 27*(2), 155–169.

Janus, H., & Tang, L. (2021). Conceptualising ideational convergence of China and OECD donors: Coalition magnets in development cooperation. In: Palgrave this volume.

Kapto, S. (2019). Layers of politics and power struggles in the SDG indicators process. *Global Policy, 10*(S1), 134–136.

Kaul, I. (2016). *Global public goods*. Cheltenham: Edward Elgar.

Kaul, I., Blondin, D., & Nahtigal, N. (2016). Understanding global public goods: Where we stand and where to next. In I. Kaul (Ed.), *Global public goods* (pp. xiii–xcii). Cheltenham: Edward Elgar Publishing.

Kaul, I. (2018). Conceptualizing global public policy: A global public good perspective. In D. Stone & K. Moloney (Eds.), *The Oxford handbook of global policy and transnational administration*. Oxford: Oxford University Press.

Keijzer, N. (2016). Open data on a closed shop? Assessing the potential of transparency initiatives with a focus on efforts to strengthen capacity development support. *Development Policy Review, 34*(1), 83–100.

Kharas, H., & Rogerson, A. (2017). *Global development trends and challenges: Horizon 2025 revisited*. https://www.odi.org/sites/odi.org.uk/files/resource-documents/11873.pdf.

Klingebiel, S., Mahn, T., & Negre, M. (Eds.). (2016). *The fragmentation of aid: Concepts, measurements and implications for development cooperation*. London: Palgrave Macmillan.

Kragelund, P. (2019). *South-South development*. London: Routledge.

Lauria, V., & Fumagalli, C. (2019). BRICS, the Southern model, and the evolving landscape of development assistance: Toward a new taxonomy. *Public Administration and Development* (online version of record before inclusion in an issue). https://onlinelibrary.wiley.com/doi/full/10.1002/pad.1851.

Le Blanc, D. (2015). Towards integration at last? The Sustainable Development Goals as a network of targets. *Sustainable Development, 23*(3), 176–187.

Mawdsley, E. (2019). South-South cooperation 3.0? Managing the consequences of success in the decade ahead. *Oxford Development Studies, 47*(3), 1–16.

Mawdsley, E., Fourie, E., & Nauta, W. (2019). *Researching South-South development cooperation: The politics of knowledge production*. London: Routledge.

Mawdsley, E., Murray, W. E., Overton, J., Scheyvens, R., & Banks, G. (2018). Exporting stimulus and "shared prosperity": Reinventing foreign aid for a retroliberal era. *Development Policy Review, 36*(S1), O25–O43.

Mawdsley, E., Savage, L., & Kim, S. M. (2014). A "post-aid world"? Paradigm shift in foreign aid and development cooperation at the 2011 Busan High Level Forum. *The Geographical Journal, 180*(1), 27–38.

McNeill, D. (2019). The contested discourse of sustainable agriculture. *Global Policy, 10*(S1), 16–27.

Mello e Souza, A. (2021). Building a global development cooperation regime: Necessary but failed efforts. In: Palgrave this volume.

Messner, D., & Scholz, I. (2018). Globale Gemeinwohlorientierung als Fluchtpunkt internationaler Kooperation für nachhaltige Entwicklung – Ein Perspektivwechsel. *Zeitschrift Für Außen- Und Sicherheitspolitik, 11*(4), 561–572.

Mitchell, I. (2021). Measuring development cooperation and the quality of aid. In: Palgrave this volume.

Morse, J. C., & Keohane, R. O. (2014). Contested multilateralism. *The Review of International Organizations, 9*(4), 385–412.

Mthembu, P. (2018). Conceptual framework and the importance of consistent definitions. In P. Mthembu (Ed.), *China and India's development cooperation in Africa: The rise of Southern powers* (pp. 15–27). Cham: Springer International Publishing.

Nilsson, M., Griggs, D., & Visbeck, M. (2016). Policy: Map the interactions between Sustainable Development Goals. *Nature News, 534*(7607), 320.

Olson, M. (2009). *The logic of collective action* (p. 124). Cambridge, MA: Harvard University Press.

Organisation for Economic Co-operation and Development. (2018). *Development cooperation report 2018: Joining forces to leave no one behind*. Paris: OECD Publishing.

Paulo, S., & Klingebiel, S. (2016). *New approaches to development cooperation in middle-income countries—brokering collective action for global sustainable development* (Discussion Paper 8/2016). Bonn: German Development Institute/Deutsches Institut für Entwicklungspolitik (DIE).

Pauw, P., Bauer, S., Richerzhagen, C., Brandi, C., & Schmole, H. (2015). *Different perspectives on differentiated responsibilities* (Discussion Paper 6/2014). Bonn: German Development Institute/Deutsches Institut für Entwicklungspolitik (DIE).

Pérez-Pineda, J. A., & Wehrmann, D. (2021). Partnerships with the private sector: Success factors and levels of engagement in development cooperation. In: Palgrave this volume.

Phillips, N., Lawrence, T. B., & Hardy, C. (2000). Inter-organizational collaboration and the dynamics of institutional fields. *Journal of Management Studies, 37*(1), 23–43.

Prizzon, A., Greenhill, R., & Mustapha, S. (2017). An "age of choice" for external development finance? Evidence from country case studies. *Development Policy Review, 35*(S1), O29–O45.

Roberts, K. M. (2018). Populism and political representation. In C. Lancaster & N. van de Walle (Eds.), *The Oxford handbook of the politics of development*. Oxford: Oxford University Press.

Rudolph, A. (2017). *The concept of SDG-sensitive development cooperation: Implications for OECD-DAC members* (Discussion Paper 1/2017). Bonn: German Development Institute/Deutsches Institut für Entwicklungspolitik (DIE).

Scott, W. R. (2013). *Institutions and organizations: Ideas, interests, and identities*. Los Angeles, CA: Sage.

Severino, J.-M., & Ray, O. (2009). *The end of ODA: Death and rebirth of a global public policy* (Working Paper No. 167). Washington, DC: Center for Global Development.

Streeck, W., & Thelen, K. (2009). Institutional change in advanced political economies. In B. Hancké (Ed.), *Debating varieties of capitalism: A reader* (pp. 95–131). Oxford: Oxford University Press.

Thomson, A. M., & Perry, J. L. (2006). Collaboration processes: Inside the black box. *Public Administration Review, 66*(S1), 20–32.

Tjosvold, D. (1984). Cooperation theory and organizations. *Human Relations, 37*(9), 743–767.

Tosun, J., & Leininger, J. (2017). Governing the interlinkages between the Sustainable Development Goals: Approaches to attain policy integration. *Global Challenges, 1*(9), 1700036.

TWI2050—The World in 2050 (2018). *Transformations to achieve the Sustainable Development Goals*. Laxenburg, Austria: International Institute for Applied Systems Analysis.

Uchenna, E., & Simplice, A. (Eds.). (2018). *Financing sustainable development in Africa*. London: Palgrave Macmillan.

United Nations. (2014). *Global governance and global rules for development in the post-2015 era*. Policy Note. Committee for Development Policy. http://www.un.org/en/development/desa/policy/cdp/cdp_publications/2014cdppolicynote.pdf.

United Nations Department of Economic and Social Affairs. (2018). *Financing for development: Progress and prospects 2018*. Report of the Interagency Task Force on Financing for Development. https://www.un.org/development/desa/publications/financing-for-development-progress-and-prospects-2018.html.

Wang, H. (2015). *The Asian Infrastructure Investment Bank: A New Bretton Woods moment? A total Chinese triumph?* (CIGI Policy Brief No. 59). https://www.files.ethz.ch/isn/190852/policy_brief_no_59.pdf.

Wang, H. (2019). The New Development Bank and the Asian Infrastructure Investment Bank: China's ambiguous approach to global financial governance. *Development and Change, 50*(1), 221–244.

Wehrmann, D. (2018). *Incentivising and regulating multi-actor partnerships and private-sector engagement in development cooperation* (Discussion Paper 21/2018). Bonn: German Development Institute/ Deutsches Institut für Entwicklungspolitik (DIE).

Weiss, T. G., & Wilkinson, R. (Eds.). (2018). *International organization and global governance* (2nd ed.). London: Routledge.

Wood, D. J., & Gray, B. (1991). Toward a comprehensive theory of collaboration. *The Journal of Applied Behavioral Science, 27*(2), 139–162.

World Bank (2018). *Information and communications for development 2018: Data-driven development.* https://openknowledge.worldbank.org/handle/10986/30437.

Zimmermann, F., & Smith, K. (2011). More actors, more money, more ideas for international development co-operation. *Journal of International Development, 23*(5), 722–738.

Zürn, M. (2018a). Contested global governance. *Global. Policy, 9*(1), 138–145.

Zürn, M. (2018b). *A theory of global governance: Authority, legitimacy, and contestation.* Oxford: Oxford University Press.

Open Access This chapter is licensed under the terms of the Creative Commons Attribution 4.0 International License (http://creativecommons.org/licenses/by/4.0/), which permits use, sharing, adaptation, distribution and reproduction in any medium or format, as long as you give appropriate credit to the original author(s) and the source, provide a link to the Creative Commons license and indicate if changes were made.

The images or other third party material in this chapter are included in the chapter's Creative Commons license, unless indicated otherwise in a credit line to the material. If material is not included in the chapter's Creative Commons license and your intended use is not permitted by statutory regulation or exceeds the permitted use, you will need to obtain permission directly from the copyright holder.

PART I

Global Cooperation for Achieving the SDGs

CHAPTER 2

Maximising Goal Coherence in Sustainable and Climate-Resilient Development? Polycentricity and Coordination in Governance

Sander Chan, Gabriela Iacobuta, and Ramona Hägele

2.1 Introduction

The 2030 Agenda for Sustainable Development and the Paris Agreement—both, respectively, adopted and concluded in 2015—are the main global transformation strategies in terms of achieving a sustainable society with an ecologically sound and economically viable future. The 17 Sustainable Development Goals (SDGs) that accompany the 2030 Agenda demonstrate broad international agreement on the multifacetedness of sustainable development, as well as the interlinkages between the different areas of sustainability. The achievement of one SDG is likely to positively or negatively affect progress on a number of other SDGs (International Council for Science [ICSU] and

---

S. Chan (✉)
Global Center on Adaptation, Groningen, The Netherlands
e-mail: sander.chan@gca.org

Copernicus Institute of Sustainable Development, Utrecht University, Utrecht, The Netherlands

G. Iacobuta
Wageningen University & Research, Wageningen, The Netherlands
e-mail: gabriela.iacobuta@die-gdi.de

S. Chan · G. Iacobuta · R. Hägele
German Development Institute / Deutsches Institut für Entwicklungspolitik (DIE), Bonn, Germany
e-mail: ramona.haegele@die-gdi.de

© The Author(s) 2021
S. Chaturvedi et al. (eds.), *The Palgrave Handbook of Development Cooperation for Achieving the 2030 Agenda*,
https://doi.org/10.1007/978-3-030-57938-8_2

International Social Science Council 2015). In that regard, the highly transformative nature of SDG 13 on climate change means that this goal directly interacts with a large number of SDGs, and indirectly with all SDGs (Intergovernmental Panel on Climate Change [IPCC] 2018; von Stechow et al. 2016). This aspect is clearly reflected in countries' nationally determined contributions (NDCs), submitted under the Paris Agreement, where Dzebo et al. (2017) found numerous links between forwarded climate-related activities and the SDGs.

Given these strong interactions, a focus on goal coherence between climate action and sustainable development priorities appears to be well suited to advance policy coherence more broadly (Gomez-Echeverri 2018; Winkler et al. 2015), and it therefore stands as the main focus in this chapter. Hereby, climate action is understood as all efforts taken to reduce greenhouse gas emissions and strengthen resilience and adaptive capacity to climate-induced impacts (United Nations General Assembly [UNGA] 2015, p. 23); sustainable development action is referred to as all adopted measures to achieve economic, social, and environmental development "without compromising the ability of future generations to meet their own needs" (Brundtland et al. 1987, p. 41; UNGA 2015, p. 3). In that sense, sustainability is a state, whereas sustainable development is a process.

A consideration of coherence between the global challenges of climate-resilient and sustainable development is necessary for three reasons. Firstly, climate change would have widespread impacts across multiple SDGs in itself. Secondly, to keep global warming well below 2 °C, the world needs to undergo a deep socio-economic transformation (IPCC 2014). For this reason, SDG 13 on climate action is one of the goals of the 2030 Agenda that requires the most effort (Nicolai et al. 2015). Thirdly, efforts related to other SDGs are also likely to increase or reduce the level of greenhouse gas emissions (United Nations Environment Programme [UNEP] 2016) and affect the ability of communities to adapt to climate change. Hence, mainstreaming climate-development interactions throughout sustainable development processes is essential for policy coherence.

Interactions and coherence between climate and sustainable development and opportunities for policy integration have been studied for decades (Beg et al. 2002; Nordhaus 1977; Swart 2003). For instance, various scholars have conducted comprehensive assessments of multiple climate measures and development dimensions (IPCC 2014, 2018; Kok et al. 2008; von Stechow et al. 2015, 2016), or assessments of narrower development areas such as air quality (Bollen et al. 2010; Braspening et al. 2016), energy security (Bollen et al. 2010; Guivarch and Monjon 2015), energy poverty (Chakravarty and Tavoni 2013; Solaymani et al. 2015; Ürge-Vorsatz and Tirado Herrero 2012), or energy in general (McCollum et al. 2018; Nerini et al. 2018). Although climate action tends to have mostly positive impacts on sustainable development in the long term, trade-offs are also likely to occur (IPCC 2018), for instance higher biofuel demand could negatively impact food security and increase land competition (Hasegawa et al. 2018). Policy coherence that maximises synergies and limits trade-offs is therefore essential for an effective implementation.

This chapter brings together three governance discussions, namely on coherence in sustainable and climate-resilient development, emerging polycentricity, and coordination tools. It argues that the predominant focus in addressing polycentricity—by policy-makers and researchers alike—has so far been on addressing functional deficits, for example closing the global mitigation gap, or financing gaps. This remains true despite the increased level of attention being given to the polycentric nature of both sustainable development and climate governance. However, a focus on functional gaps does not help overcome goal incoherence—the imbalanced implementation of internationally agreed goals. In fact, the voluntariness and self-organisational nature of polycentric governance could actually increase the level of incoherence in implementation. Therefore, we argue that insights on the emerging polycentric structures in sustainability and climate governance should be combined with the growing knowledge on goal coherence. The combination of these fields of knowledge could inform supportive policies in development cooperation as well as orchestration frameworks that ensure greater coherence in the achievement of multiple goals.

This chapter proceeds with a discussion of coherence and coordination to realise broad sustainable development. Subsequently, we discuss the growing polycentricity of sustainable development and climate governance as well as the recent coordination efforts between state and non-state actions that do not necessarily improve goal coherence. Finally, we discuss novel tools that could improve coordination towards goal coherence.

2.2 Coherence

The term "coherence" has been widely—and loosely—used in policy and research, referring to a wide variety of understandings, including coherence between actors, between levels of governance, between various policies and goals, and between goals and resources (Carbone 2008; Collste et al. 2017; Organisation for Economic Co-operation and Development [OECD] 2014; Tosun and Lang 2017). Moreover, related terms have been used interchangeably—for instance "policy coherence" and "policy integration", and "coordination" and "collaboration"—without clear conceptual distinctions (Hoebink 2004; Matthews 2011; Rogge and Reichardt 2016). In this chapter, policy coherence for sustainable development is referred to as an "approach and policy tool to systematically integrate the social, economic and environmental dimensions of sustainable development at all stages of domestic and international policy making" (OECD 2018, p. 83). In this context, integration is achieved by fostering synergies and by identifying and reconciling trade-offs between competing goals and objectives of the three development dimensions and of national and international policies. Policy synergies occur when a mix of (two or more) policies complement each other in a way that enables greater achievements than the sum of individual policies, as the policies reinforce one another. Policies that lead to co-benefits beyond or in development areas outside of their main objective can also be seen as synergistic. For instance, a reduction in fossil fuel combustion to reduce greenhouse gas emissions would additionally improve air quality. Synergies may also emerge by improving education for girls (SDG 4), which will further enhance maternal health (SDG 3) and contribute to gender equality (SDG 5), poverty eradication (SDG 1), and economic growth (SDG 8) (Nilsson et al. 2016, p. 321). On the other hand, trade-offs occur when objectives or outcomes of a policy conflict with those of another policy. This could be the case of an energy tax that might meet the objective of improved energy efficiency but could increase the level of energy poverty in poor households. Similarly, improved access to energy for all (SDG 7) can negatively affect efforts for climate change mitigation (SDG 13). When trade-offs are present, they could be addressed with complementary measures that reduce negative impacts or through political compromises when no feasible measures are available to tackle the impacts. Unaddressed trade-offs are the main source of incoherence, as these would lead to policies cancelling out each other's benefits and to related governance inefficiency.

To achieve greater coherence, policy integration is essential to maximise synergies and avoid trade-offs between specific policy issue-areas (United Nations [UN] 2018, p. v). Such policy integration is characterised by purposeful interactions between actors from different sectors who create interdependencies through *cooperation* and *coordination* (Tosun and Lang 2017, pp. 554f.). In this sense, coordination refers to processes that bring together various institutions and actors to mutually formulate policies, standards, and procedures. Subsets of policy coordination are cooperation and collaboration, whereby policy cooperation is characterised by temporary and informal means of building relationships within and across institutions, and collaboration is based on voluntarism and driven by problem-solving (Bouckaert et al. 2010; Tosun and Lang 2017, p. 565).

To promote goal coherence and a successful implementation of all sustainable and climate-resilient development goals, institutions at all levels should agree on common approaches and cooperate to deal with interrelated problems (UN 2018, p. v). The achievement of goal coherence is dependent on multiple implementation levels and processes, such as adequate public administrative practices and the substantive engagement of various stakeholders, which can be referred to as "policy coherence".

Integrated policy-making is usually analysed from an institutional perspective by three dimensions of integration: horizontal integration across policy sectors, vertical integration across levels of government, and the engagement of all relevant stakeholders (Breuer et al. 2018; Giessen 2011a, b; Tosun and Lang 2017). Thus, stakeholders from the national, subnational, local, and societal levels need to align actions to achieve coherence (Beisheim and Simon 2016; ICSU 2017; UN 2018, p. vi). Referring to policy integration as a process occurring at a meta-level "involves the use of specific instruments designed to integrate a set of considerations, issues, and stakeholders across different policy domains" (Tosun and Lang 2017, p. 555). Moreover, the pursuit of policy coherence should be understood from a procedural as well as an outcome-oriented perspective (Rogge and Reichardt 2016, p. 1622). Successful integration is thus a situation in which policies have obtained the highest degree of coherence (UN 2018, p. v) through coordination, cooperation, and political leadership (Tosun and Lang 2017, p. 557).

The cross-cutting nature of the 17 SDGs of the 2030 Agenda requires governments to break out of both policy and institutional silos and to embrace broader governance participation to ensure both horizontal (across sectors) and vertical (across actors) policy coherence. Following the Organisation for Economic Co-operation and Development categorisation of key areas in which coherence needs to be enabled (see Fig. 2.1), the comprehensive implementation of the 2030 Agenda will need coherence between global and national goals; across international agendas and processes; between economic, social, and environmental policies; between different sources of finance; and between the diverse actions of multi-actors and stakeholders (OECD 2014). In order to address coherence on multiple levels, close coordination is required at all stages of policy-making, guided by adequate institutions and mechanisms. All key areas of coherence are also relevant to development cooperation.

This chapter recognises the multi-dimensionality of coherence, emphasising both *goal coherence as the objective* to maximise synergies and avoid trade-offs between potentially competing objectives and goals to realise sustainable development at large, as well as the need to *coordinate* the efforts by a large number of actors (at multiple levels of governance) to ensure the maximisation of *goal coherence as an outcome*. Scholars have asked whether coherence is at all

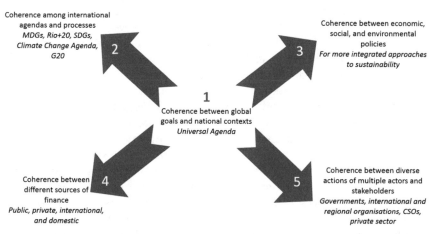

Fig. 2.1 Complementary levels of coherence for implementing the Post-2015 Agenda (*Source* Adapted from OECD [2014, p. 15])

possible in a complex Earth system that features many nonlinear interactions, and in pluralist governance contexts where a degree of incoherence seems inevitable, given the manifold interests and interpretations of what constitutes what is good (see Carbone 2008; Koulaimah-Gabriel 1999). However, we argue that even when complete goal coherence is not possible, the maximisation of coherence is desirable and necessary to realise sustainable development, and it can be partly realised through the integration of novel tools that identify how different goals are linked and what gaps are left by specific groups. Better identification of goal (in)coherence and gaps could also facilitate governance processes that build public support for cases where trade-offs are unavoidable.

2.3 Coordination

The *coordination* of efforts in sustainable development presents a problem that is related to goal (in)coherence, but it is even more about aligning a multiplicity of actors that contribute—or should contribute—to various aspects of sustainable development. Even if one assumes a limited number of national governments as the main actors in global sustainability politics—as is often the case in theories of international relations—goal coherence is not a very likely outcome. Countries are faced with different development realities in terms of state capacity, regime type, level of economic welfare, social equity, and human development. To further compound contested coordination and responsibilities, the number of actors beyond national governments—including civil society, businesses, and investors—that engage in sustainable development and climate governance is growing.

Although dispersed non-state and subnational efforts have left governance "fragmented", optimistic voices argue that "polycentric governance" could more effectively deliver on multiple goals and governance functions. A growing body of literature emphasises how decentralised and seemingly dispersed state and non-state efforts can address governance gaps (Bäckstrand et al. 2010; Haas 2004; Kropp and Türk 2017). For instance, private actors may be in a better position to devise sector-specific approaches; civil society organisations can effectively build constituencies to support specific sustainable development and climate actions; investors can leverage much-needed resources and help shift billions towards a sustainable and low-carbon economy; subnational and local communities can contribute to the achievement of global goals through concrete and context-specific projects; etc. One could argue that fragmentation of climate and sustainability actions could—perhaps somewhat counter-intuitively—improve the aggregate impact on global challenges. In large numbers and at sufficient scale, disperse and decentralised efforts could close the global climate mitigation gap, or sustainable development financing gaps. When climate and sustainable development challenges are closely interlinked in a mutually reinforcing manner, a good degree of goal coherence could thus be achieved without much coordination.

This theoretical possibility, however, is not supported by evidence. First, although the growing number of actors has often been hailed for their potential to solve global challenges, evidence of the effectiveness of (individual) non-state and subnational efforts is scattered and scarce. Moreover, even if these efforts are effective by any measurement, the scale of engagement by state and non-state actors is still insufficient to solve the most urgent sustainable development challenges (Chan et al. 2018). Second, coordination is increasingly a feature of emerging sustainability and climate governance systems; seemingly dispersed non-state efforts are linked among themselves and to international (and governmental) governance (Chan et al. 2019). What looks like a fragmented landscape of scattered sustainability and climate actions is in fact part of an emerging polycentric structure, as we discuss in the following section.

2.4 Emerging Polycentricity in Sustainable Development and Climate Governance

The overall narrative of the need for, and the emergence of, actors beyond states in sustainable development and climate governance is that traditional actors—in particular governments and international organisations—have failed, maybe not in terms of defining the goals or in setting up rules, but in terms of problem-solving (Beisheim and Simon 2016; Chan et al. 2015). Yet, the growing number of actors engaging in sustainability and climate actions still does not dissipate the calls for more and better coordination towards (coherently) realising sustainable development, as defined by the 2030 Agenda. One form of coordination could take the form of polycentric governance, wherein multiple non-hierarchical institutions are linked in order to more effectively address global sustainability and climate challenges.

Polycentric governance is characterised by the presence of multiple institutions, each with considerable autonomy to set their rules and norms in specific domains (e.g. Jordan et al. 2018; Ostrom 2010). The emergence of polycentricity, as noted by Pattberg et al. (2018), is not only observable from the growing number of institutions, but also (and particularly) from the increasing amount of interlinkages between different institutions. In the following, we note a particular—if stylised—pathway of emergence of polycentricity and the linkages that define it across both climate and sustainable development governance. Namely, (1) state-centred, hierarchical types of governance are increasingly seen as inefficient and ineffective in terms of problem-solving; (2) actors other than states develop initiatives that govern particular domains in conjunction with, or instead of, "traditional" public authorities; and (3) public actors, governments, and international organisations increasingly recognise the additionality of other actors as partners in governance, and they create linkages to more effectively fulfil governance functions such as implementing goals, co-producing norms, and standards, but also achieving political objectives (including the "rolling back of the state", the influencing of other governmental actors) and ulterior motives (e.g. "window-dressing").

2.4.1 Polycentricity in Climate Governance

With climate change, state-centred governance has long been the norm, despite obvious shortcomings. The epitome of a state-centred model for climate governance, arguably, was the Kyoto Protocol (KP), which divided responsibilities among developed countries to reduce emissions. However, most observers agree to the utter ineffectiveness of the KP (e.g. Vogler 2016). States simply retracted their participation in the KP when they failed to keep the terms (e.g. Canada, United States). In terms of problem-solving, the KP has done very little to reduce greenhouse gases. The failure to produce a climate agreement at the Copenhagen Climate Change Conference in 2009 not only demonstrated the failure to implement, but also the failure to reach further agreements. In the period between the 2009 Copenhagen and the 2015 Paris Climate Change Conferences, it became clear that, despite decades of negotiations, governments have largely failed to produce the necessary actions to halt global heating. If governments fail to take the necessary action, the only route may be one that predominantly features the contributions of the private sector and subnational entities. Indeed, scholars have noted the emergence of many non-state and subnational initiatives (e.g. Bulkeley et al. 2014; Hoffmann 2011). The proliferation of non-state and subnational climate actions has also been noted by international bureaucrats. For instance, at the start of her tenure as Executive Secretary of the United Nations Framework Convention on Climate Change (UNFCCC), Christiana Figueres initiated the "Momentum for Change Initiative", which, for the first time, engaged non-state and subnational contributions in the context of the UNFCCC. The basic idea of engaging non-state and subnational actors in climate governance was subsequently further developed (Chan et al. 2016). To prevent a lost decade for climate action between Copenhagen and a yet-to-be-negotiated new agreement, governments initiated a negotiations workstream on "Pre-2020 Ambition".

This resulted in a Pre-2020 agenda, which recognised and promoted the role of non-state actors to make additional contributions towards closing the global mitigation gap. Non-state and subnational engagement gained an increasingly programmatic form in the run-up to the 2015 Paris Climate Change Conference; under the Lima-Paris Action Agenda, the Peruvian and French presidencies of the Conference of the Parties—with the assistance of the UNFCCC secretariat—mobilised more than 70 large-scale mitigation (and some adaptation) initiatives. Throughout the period, the number of actors stepping up with climate actions increased dramatically (e.g. UNEP 2018). A multiplicity of actors have gained authority in limited domains, such as networks of cities and regions (such as Local Governments for Sustainability (ICLEI), the C40 Cities Climate Leadership Group, Under 2 MOU), sectoral coalitions (e.g. SloCat, We Mean Business), and public–private initiatives (e.g. Climate and Clean Air Coalition, Mission Innovation). Including the individual initiatives to take climate action, the UNFCCC currently registers more than 12,000 largely new institutions and actors.

The mere existence of many climate actions and the greater involvement of all types of stakeholders do not itself constitute a polycentric governance system. However, in the wake of the emergence of non-state and subnational climate actions, we also observe a tight coupling between hierarchies and some of the newer institutions (Keohane and Victor 2011), as well as a convergence between distinct sets of actors, for instance in carbon accounting standard-setting (Green 2013). At the global level of governance, United Nations (UN) climate conferences have increasingly become a meeting point and the "heartbeat" of climate action, as non-state and subnational actors organise their schedules and time their outputs around them. The resulting governance system is therefore not only characterised by multiple actors, but also a high degree of linking and convergence through shared events, timing, and joint production. Importantly, governments and international organisations themselves are increasingly acknowledging the central role that non-state and subnational actors could play, particularly in implementing climate goals, and have moved to create linking institutions. The 2015 Paris Climate Change Conference not only produced the accompanying universal climate agreement, but also a decision to link the sphere of non-state and subnational actions through, for example, technical examination processes; the (continued) recording of actions and their progress; and the programmatic mobilisation and high-level showcasing of actions under the leadership of newly installed "High-Level Climate Action Champions". In the light of the changed logic of the Paris Agreement, this linking departs from a strictly multilateral, state-centred governance model towards more hybrid and goal-driven governance (Falkner 2016). Non-state and subnational efforts are no longer seen as substitutive to governmental efforts because both contribute to the achievement of self-determined national targets (so-called nationally determined contributions).

Beyond the UNFCCC context, other institutions also link the governmental and transnational spheres of governance. For instance, the Initiative for Climate Action Transparency is developing guidance for governments to include non-state action in the formulation of their climate goals (Initiative for Climate Action Transparency 2018). Therefore, governance is not only the site of fragmentation and contestation, but also of new linking institutions emerging from the seeming complexity of climate governance; governance is becoming polycentric. The patterns and shape of that polycentric structure to some extent answers the (perceived) shortcomings of the "traditional" state-centred climate regime and is, arguably, more inclusive of different environmental and industrial regimes (including the Ozone Regime, and shipping and aviation), thereby bridging the shortcomings of overly compartmentalised formal international regimes. These emerging polycentric structures in climate governance can also be found in sustainable development governance, as we illustrate in the following section.

2.4.2 Polycentricity in Sustainable Development Governance

In sustainable development governance—despite covering a much larger and diverse set of problems—we also see the budding of a polycentric governance structure comprising growing linkages between the actions of non-state actors and governments and international organisations (see Frey and Sabbatino 2018). Since sustainable development subsumes many themes and subsystems of governance—for instance, food governance, energy governance, biodiversity governance, etc.—the measure of polycentricity across various sustainability governance subsystems varies. For instance, Pattberg et al. (2017) argue for the development of institutional linkages between state and non-state actors in global biodiversity governance, largely following the example of climate governance.

The autonomous contributions of stakeholders, or at least their potential, was already acknowledged at the 1992 United National Conference on Environment and Development (also known as the Earth Summit) (Pattberg et al. 2012). The political outcomes included the Rio Declaration on Environment and Development, which stated that participation by all concerned citizens at all levels can best handle environmental issues (Principle 10). Nonetheless, the 1992 Earth Summit is best remembered for some of its more "traditional" intergovernmental outcomes, in particular the Convention on Biological Diversity, the Framework Convention on Climate Change, and the Convention to Combat Desertification. However, by the time of the 2002 World Summit on Sustainable Development (WSSD, also known as Rio+10), there was a prominent idea that these international agreements had not sufficiently been delivered upon. A widely shared diagnosis of the implementation gap was that governmental approaches had largely failed, negotiations were largely deadlocked, overly bureaucratic international organisations were not up to their tasks, and many national governments were bogged down by a lack of political will, bad governance, and a lack of resources. Subsequently, the problem is not the absence of international norms, but the lack of implementation and capacity to implement. The suggestion of more governmental approaches or regulatory frameworks was met with stark opposition. For instance, the United States made clear that they would not consent to any new agreements. Rather than developing new international frameworks and agreements, the focus of WSSD was therefore on the implementation of existing agreements. This time, governments went a step further than just acknowledging the potential of non-state and networked institutions. The main outcomes of the WSSD, which were rather unique at the time, included "Partnerships for Sustainable Development" (PFSD) that involve non-state and subnational stakeholders in making additional contributions towards the realisation of global sustainable development and the Millennium Development Goals (precursors to the SDGs). By opening a registry for Partnerships for Sustainable Development, it recognised contributions by non-state and networked institutions and invited them to align activities in order to implement sustainable development. In a unique turn, the partnerships were presented as "type-2" official outcomes of the WSSD, complementing the more conventional intergovernmental political outcomes, which were dubbed "type-1". Initially presented as a success with the registration of more than 200 partnerships, the number of new registrations dwindled in later years. However, the agreement on the 2030 Agenda for Sustainable Development in 2015, which included the SDGs, gave new impetus to, once again, link the governmental and non-state and subnational spheres of governance. The SDGs themselves were the outcome of a constituency-based effort and advice from a governmentally nominated "Open Working Group". SDG 17 (Partnerships for the Goals) explicitly aims at the means of implementation and at revitalising the global partnership for sustainable development. This time, the new UN "Partnerships for SDGs" platform featured thousands of actions taken by a multiplicity of stakeholders, both individual and cooperative. Through events at the High-Level Political Forum as well as the Partnerships for SDGs platform, more participation is being encouraged. While it remains to be seen to which extent Partnerships for SDGs will contribute to the achievement of the goals, political controversy related to recognising them seems to have dissipated (see Mert 2009 on the institutionalisation of the partnership discourse). In particular, the private sector is not seen as a mere provider of resources, but also as development actor that provides leadership in tackling specific questions of sustainable development (Sachs 2012). This may be due to a growing acceptance of non-state and hybrid forms of governance, but also due to the fact that the SDGs were agreed upon in advance between governments. Moreover, in terms of linkages, we can clearly see increased linking between the non-state and subnational spheres of activities and the predominant process of sustainable development governance at the intergovernmental level around the 2030 Agenda and the High-Level Political Forum. In parallel to the Paris Agreement, the 2030 Agenda and the SDGs extended the need for development and sustainable goal achievement to developed countries—at least formally—thereby doing away with an implied hierarchical order that placed a large part of the burden for sustainable development on developing countries.

In sum, both in climate and sustainable development governance, we see a pattern towards growing linkages between actions and initiatives by non-state actors and governments and international organisations (see Frey and Sabbatino 2018). First, government-centred governance by itself is widely perceived as being ineffective and/or insufficient. Second, the number of non-state, subnational, and transnational initiatives has increased dramatically in order to respond to governmental shortfalls, and their contributions become more salient in view of governmental shortcomings. Moreover, actions across both the domains of climate and sustainable development governance are well connected, not only in terms of substantive linkages, but also institutionally, for example biodiversity governance (see Pattberg et al. 2017). There is increased linking between initiatives, as well as between initiatives and public actors (governments and international organisations). It is therefore important to raise the question about whether polycentric governance systems—while linking actors across various substantive domains—also effectively address problems of incoherence. However, evidence of the effectiveness of (individual) non-state and subnational efforts is scattered and scarce, and evidence of the greater effectiveness of non-state engagement in governance systems is even scarcer. The promise that actors across a polycentric governance landscape could effectively address specific functional gaps in governance has motivated many policy-makers and international organisations to seek improved engagement, building new institutions and processes that link the realms of state, non-state, and subnational sustainable development and climate actions (Cole 2015; Tosun and Leininger 2017). However, even if non-state and subnational efforts proved to effectively address functional deficits and even help resolve global challenges—for example closing the global mitigation gap, or financing gaps—goal coherence cannot be taken for granted. In the following section, we discuss the effectiveness and risks of polycentric governance in achieving goal coherence.

2.5 Polycentric Governance and Coherence

According to, for example, Ostrom (2010), the emergence of polycentric structures holds promise for more effective governance, even in the absence of a hierarchy and monocentric, state-centred coordination. Polycentric structures may increase the amount of communication among different parties, leading to mutual trust and increased levels of cooperation. Moreover, a polycentric structure provides opportunities to improve policies over time through learning and experimentation (Cole 2015). Indeed, the growing acknowledgement of a multiplicity of actors in global sustainability and climate governance rests on the several optimistic premises concerning the emergence of multiple autonomous—but interconnected—state and non-state actors in governance. For instance, Chan et al. (2019), describing stylised arguments often used to support non-state engagements, point out optimistic expectations that non-state actors can conjure a greater effect through their sheer numbers. They also improve representation, maximise synergies by focussing on win–win constellations, and create a self-perpetuating dynamic by diffusing new norms, building coalitions, and strengthening proactive actors. On the particular point of synergies, they highlight the prevalent argument that "[w]ithout climate-resilient and sustainable development, all stand to lose, and existing achievements are at risk. 'Everybody wins' captures the view that non-state actor engagement brings overall benefits through win–win constellations" (Chan et al. 2019, p. 3). At the same time, they point out that—in practice—not everybody wins; for instance, despite growth in the number of non-state actors, the large majority of them are based in the Global North (Bulkeley et al. 2014; Chan et al. 2018, 2019). Moreover, even if more actors from the Global South are involved, most transnational and non-state initiatives are led by North-based actors, raising doubts about whether the benefits of a polycentric governance system will proportionately accrue to developing countries.

In the following, we argue that emerging polycentric governance systems—and in particular the growing linkages between non-state and state actors—are seen as holding the potential to address governance gaps, but they do not address fundamental questions of incoherence. Rather, greater numbers of governance actors potentially increase the level of incoherence in terms of (1) unevenly addressing areas that have been identified as intergovernmental priorities; (2) unevenly distributed impacts of governance; and (3) largely ignoring trade-offs between goals within individual initiatives. These problems are compounded by two related characteristics of polycentric structures: a high degree of voluntariness and self-organisation.

Without aiming at a comprehensive overview, we contrast arguments that suppose a (theoretically) positive relation between polycentricity and coherence before providing evidence-based counterarguments.

First, one could argue that through multiple actors in polycentric structures, there is a greater functional alignment of capacities towards achieving goals. The possibility of self-organisation within a polycentric governance system allows new groupings, or "bricolages", that flexibly could further emancipation and transnational and regional cooperation (Mittelmann 2013). This was obviously the case when the WSSD referred to the PFSD as implementation instruments. Similarly, non-state and subnational climate actions are widely seen as contributions towards narrowing the global mitigation gap. However, the functionalist logic behind conceiving non-state and subnational efforts as "contributions" towards implementation is very limited, and it seemingly reduces their function to implementation. For this to happen, one needs to narrowly define non-state and subnational functions (mitigation, implementation) and ignore the political contingency of non-state and subnational choices. In this regard, the *absence* of non-state/subnational action should be considered equally as relevant, as this leads to uneven implementation—for example across various sustainability goals—leading to politically controversial outcomes and the incoherent implementation of goals.

Second, the current engagement of non-state and subnational actors is largely based on the idea of synergies of individual actions. For instance, Partnerships for SDGs and Pre-2020 Climate Action mostly include the "forerunners" within the private sector. Their actions are presented as a triple win (profit, planet, people), or wins across different substantive themes. However, this is not always the case. For instance, Mert and Dellas (2012) take the example of partnerships in the water sector, which seemingly align with the sustainability goals of the WSSD, namely improving public health and access to safe drinking water in developing countries. However, the chosen approaches and technologies have implications for environmental impact, maintenance and storage, equity of access, and self-reliance. For instance, partnerships that promote disinfection agents not only provide safe water, but also promote behavioural changes and the creation of a market for such products, the cost of which could again prove prohibitive for some of the most vulnerable communities (see Stockman et al. 2007).

Third, one could also argue that the broader inclusion of a multiplicity of actors will—through inclusive processes and deliberation—lead to acceptable courses of action, even if some compromises must be made and not all trade-offs can be completely avoided. The universal and global inclusion of stakeholders, however, cannot be guaranteed, even when some of the most prominent institutions linking non-state actions and intergovernmental processes—the aforementioned Partnerships for SDGs and Pre-2020 Climate Action—are being administered by the UN. In fact, multiple studies demonstrate that patterns of inclusion across sustainable development and climate governance are highly imbalanced (Bulkeley et al. 2014; Chan et al. 2018; Hsu et al. 2015; Pattberg et al. 2012). Consistently, we see the overrepresentation of already influential (North-based) actors. This raises the question of whether such imbalanced inclusion could lead to equitable outcomes and address trade-offs in a manner that could carry the broad consent of those affected.

Fourth, the broad engagement in sustainable and climate-resilient solutions is good for all, or at least avoids the counterfactual of non-action, which is definitely bad for all (see Chan et al. 2019). In that sense, polycentric structures, featuring many actions, are seen to not only stimulate solutions but also overall growth, which is considered to benefit all (e.g. through job and wealth creation). However, this reasoning falls within a growth paradigm that critical scholars and many practitioners and policy-makers have rejected. Latour (2018), for instance, eloquently argues that much of the political action under an assumption of modernisation simply does not add up in the context of a finite planet. Infinite growth is impossible, and the "earth/territory" for people to "land" on is rapidly disappearing. Critics of neoliberalism, similarly, have argued that the inclusion of multiple actors into a "green economy" merely increases the resilience of an otherwise exploitative economy (Spash 2012; cf. D'Amato et al. 2017).

Finally, one could argue that non-state and transnational norms could improve coherence by complementing international norms, or by providing them where they are lacking, for instance in carbon verification standards or in sustainable forestry (e.g. Pattberg 2007). Polycentric structures could allow for a more comprehensive governance by bringing such norms into governance areas that were previously not—or only partially—governed by governmental and intergovernmental regimes (see Morseletto 2019). However, despite linking among multiple stakeholders through networks, transnational and non-state norms may still not have sufficient authority to ensure coherence and predictability in a governance system. For instance, the success of initially widely accepted transnational standards for sustainable forestry by the Forest Stewardship Council has also inspired alternative and competing accountability systems, which could, again, challenge the Forest Stewardship Council (Chan and Pattberg 2008). Subsequently, there is no "stable" system of transnational governance that could reliably make up for the gaps left by governments and international regimes.

The above discussion does not assume the *absence* of coordination. In recent years, scholars have called for "frameworks" and "orchestration" to ensure better alignment between international goals and a large variety of non-state and subnational inputs (Abbott and Bernstein 2015; Chan et al. 2015). At the global level, programmatic efforts are taken to recognise and mobilise more—and to some extent more effective—transnational action. For instance, the aforementioned Lima-Paris Action Agenda and the Partnerships for SDGs platform mobilised and invited state and non-state initiatives, respectively, to demonstrate momentum towards a new climate agreement and to ensure a multiplicity of contributions towards the implementation of the SDGs. However, although such frameworks and programmatic efforts have taken shape internationally, they emphasise the need to respond to functional deficits, for example the engagement of more actors and their solutions; eliciting more quantitative financial or emission reduction commitments; or the provision of examples to follow. To ensure goal coherence, however, such a focus is too narrow. These frameworks use soft instrumentation, such as "recognition" and "visibility", that emphasise voluntariness and societal self-organisation. As a result, linkages between the governmental realm of climate and sustainability governance and non-state and subnational action primarily concerns "frontrunners" in specific areas of sustainable development. Although their potential to contribute to specific challenges is difficult to deny (Chan et al. 2018; Hsu et al. 2015; UNEP 2016, 2018), individual actors and groups focussing on particular functional needs on a voluntary basis are likely to be spread unevenly across multiple goals rather than preserve the integrity of the 2030 Agenda. Moreover, at the individual level of actions, actors are confronted with trade-offs and synergies in the approaches they choose. How efforts towards achieving one objective influence other objectives may be dealt with in very different ways, and often without a broader consultation with those affected. When trade-offs between goals are unavoidable, individual choices then lack social legitimacy. Without a better understanding of how a myriad of individual efforts deal with some of the most urgent trade-offs, it becomes difficult or impossible to preserve the integrity of a broader sustainability agenda and to maximise goal coherence.

We posit that existing frameworks and programmatic efforts have an important role to play in the preservation of the integrity of broad sustainable development—not only to tout synergic linkages between actors, goals, and sustainable development, but also to carefully consider goal incoherence and trade-offs between multiple sustainability objectives. While still acknowledging the impossibility of complete coherence, the maximisation of coherence could be helped by emerging approaches and tools, as we discuss in the following.

2.6 NOVEL TOOLS FOR IDENTIFYING (IN)COHERENCE

In recent years, a number of tools and approaches have been developed that can be used to increase policy coherence among multiple goals. Such tools can, for instance, map the co-impacts of individual actions in one area on other sustainable development areas, attempt to quantify these impacts based on varied indicators or a unifying indicator, or support decisions between multiple options based on a set of predefined criteria.

One way to improve *horizontal coordination* across actors for an enhanced policy coherence is to raise awareness of the links between different sustainable development objectives and how actions towards a specific objective may support or undermine another. For instance, potential interlinkages between various SDGs and targets can be identified from correlations with past data of respective indicators (Pradhan et al. 2017; Zhou and Moinuddin 2017). A method that is unconstrained by data availability, but requires an understanding of co-impacts, is Nilsson et al.'s (2016) seven-tier scoring approach of impacts that indicate to what extent different goals are directly or inversely linked in a manner that is inextricable or creates an enabling environment for co-impact. The International Science Council (Griggs et al. 2017) applies this method to demonstrate the interlinkages between a number of SDGs. However, such a broad mapping of SDGs does not take into account the different country contexts and how different settings may affect the occurrence or relative importance of specific impacts. A related approach that would also help the *vertical coordination* and alignment of national and subnational climate and sustainability actions with the global agenda would be that of Weitz et al. (2017), who translate this scoring approach to the country level by applying it to the Swedish sustainable development context. Moreover, by going beyond mapping primary impacts to secondary impacts, they identified key clusters of highly interconnected SDGs that could help further determine groups of stakeholders that could effectively cooperate on these focussed development areas. Another way to address narrower development areas is to concentrate on the impacts of one SDG or target. For instance, if the main goal is to increase climate action, then the impacts of possible actions for the achievement of SDG 13 should be mapped individually using existing tools (IPCC 2018; Tilburg et al. 2018).

Other tools that link climate and sustainable development can help coordination across various actors by identifying the gaps left by a certain group. For instance, the NDC-SDG Connections tool (Brandi et al. 2017) and ClimateWatch (Northrop et al. 2016) analyse countries' NDCs under the Paris Agreement to map climate activities that directly tackle other SDGs and the mentions of keywords that can be directly related to other SDGs, respectively. Non-state actors could use these tools to identify synergies between climate and sustainable development that remain untapped by the state, based on the NDCs.

Although mapping could effectively help identify linkages between sustainable development areas and relevant actors, it is much more difficult to gain an understanding of the magnitude of respective impacts. In this regard, integrated assessment models and cost–benefit analysis have been suggested, with the latter perhaps being more preferable from a perspective of goal coherence.

Cost–benefit analysis distinguished itself by defining the overall impacts of a policy or project through a single unit, as aggregate (net) costs and benefits to human well-being, usually through a financial indicator (financial cost–benefit analysis) or as a measure of utility (social cost–benefit analysis). In the case of sustainable development more broadly defined, the social cost–benefit analysis can provide the added value of quantifying and monetising many development aspects that are not directly linked to the market (Atkinson and Mourato 2006; Patassini 2005). However, relying on only one final number can conceal important distributional effects across different stakeholders—who bear the costs and who gain from the benefits—but also across the different areas of sustainable development, for example high benefits to poverty reduction but substantial costs to health.

Contrary to cost–benefit analyses, integrated assessment models can complement mapping exercises by providing impact evaluations in both monetary and physical terms across a variety of sustainable development areas (Collste et al. 2017). Although most scenarios defined in these models are set to optimise for minimum costs of implementation, prioritising the economic aspect over the social and environmental costs of outcomes, optimisation by social and environmental indicators is possible. The Intergovernmental Panel on Climate Change special report on 1.5 °C of global warming shines a light on sustainable development costs and benefits of climate change mitigation and presents these in both physical and monetary terms (IPCC 2018). For instance, health benefits of keeping global warming limited to 1.5 °C instead of 2 °C is estimated to amount to 110–190 million fewer deaths and annual monetary savings of $100 billion per year by 2030 (equivalent to 35 per cent of the investment needed for air pollution control) (Shindell et al. 2018). To overcome the prioritisation limitations of impact mapping and quantification exercises, multi-criteria decision-making tools could furthermore give insight by attaching different weights to affected sustainable development areas, often through consultations with multiple relevant actors. Such a combination of qualitative and quantitative data could also help to overcome limitations where quantitative physical or monetary data is unavailable (Cohen et al. 2018; Dubash et al. 2013).

Coming to a better understanding of the impacts of policies on different development areas by using the above tools can improve coherent outcomes of governance when they inform the directing of resources towards areas where trade-offs appear or where gaps are prevalent, while avoiding duplication of action—for instance, diverting part of the air pollution control investments away from the areas where climate policy will contribute as a co-benefit. However, we need to acknowledge that perfect coherence is impossible and that acceptable as well as legitimate outcomes in trade-off situations are necessary (e.g. Kuyper et al. 2017). The mere use of tools, even when they have improved significantly in recent years, cannot detract from the fact that decision-making at all levels is political. Especially in the case of trade-offs, participatory approaches are necessary to reach compromises and agree on priorities.

2.7 Conclusion: Implications for International and National Coordination and International Cooperation

Internationally, frameworks and programmatic efforts that promote non-state and subnational engagement could use tools in the assessment of the types of non-state and subnational sustainable development and climate actions. Generally, the assessment of non-state and subnational engagement—and the tracking of progress at UN-administered platforms, such as the Non-state Actor Zone for Climate Action and Partnerships for SDGs—has been fairly weak. To understand the overall impacts on sustainable development, it is not only necessary to understand the performance of individual initiatives vis-à-vis the goals they want to contribute, but also to take into account and understand the possible co-effects (synergies and trade-offs). Such an appraisal of systemic effects gives insight into whether a multiplicity of actors and actions improves or worsens overall coherence and the integrity of the 2030 Agenda. Using tools to understand synergies and trade-offs within a larger landscape of variegated actions could provide transparency about the most urgent trade-offs. Arguably, providing transparency is one of the stronger assets of the current Pre-2020 Climate Action and Partnerships for SDGs platforms. But mere transparency is not enough to address incoherence. Even using a very simple representation of frequencies of sustainability actions across the 17 SDGs on the Partnerships for SDGs platform reveals a vast underrepresentation of non-state and subnational actions addressing SDG 10 (Reduced inequalities). The problem with current frameworks and programmatic efforts that emphasise mere "visibility" and—to some extent—transparency, is that patterns of imbalanced implementation are not systematically informing, for instance, technical dialogues or the mobilisations of key actors. Subsequently, we believe it is necessary to follow up on such observations with targeted processes and dialogues to avoid trade-offs, where possible, and to make choices that can gain the consent of those most affected.

Nationally successful policy coherence cannot solely be achieved through sustainable development policies, but also through the coordination of human and institutional capacity (see Román et al. 2012). The implementation of the Paris Agreement and the 2030 Agenda is anchored nationally, respectively, through NDCs and national implementation plans. However, the two agendas often advance in parallel, where climate is broadly assigned to environmental ministries, while the 2030 Agenda becomes the responsibility of more central institutions at the cabinet level, such as president's or prime minister's office or the planning and finance ministries (Bouyé et al. 2018). The cross-cutting nature of the 17 SDGs requires governments to break out of silos and to embrace broader participation to ensure both horizontal (across sectors) and vertical (across actors) policy coherence. The key areas in which coherence needs to be enabled for the implementation of the 2030 Agenda are: coherence between global and national goals; coherence across international agendas and processes; coherence between economic, social, and environmental policies; coherence between different sources of finance; and coherence between diverse actions of multi-actors and stakeholders (OECD 2014). These dimensions of coherence must require close coordination at all stages of policy-making, guided by adequate institutions and mechanisms. Coherent implementation requires horizontal integration through coordination among line ministries, but it should also go beyond the state level and acknowledge the potential of a polycentric reality, ensuring the activation of multiple actors, including civil society, academia, businesses, and development organisations. A number of countries have designated new coordinating bodies for the implementation of the SDGs that go beyond horizontal participation across ministries and involve regional authorities and non-governmental actors (see Breuer et al. 2018; Chan et al. 2018; Tosun and Leininger 2017). For instance, the German Sustainable Development Strategy established mechanisms that facilitate coordination between authorities at the federal, regional, and municipal levels, such as the Sustainability Network of Lord Mayors, Regional Hubs for Sustainability Strategies (RENN), and the Federal-Länder Experience Pool. Going beyond regional and local authorities, the Czech Republic facilitates consultations and dialogue and incentivises SDG implementation action through a diverse group of stakeholders, including the private sector, civil society, and sectoral experts (OECD 2018). The potential contribution to implementation towards broad sustainable development is considerable and could be better realised through the use of recent tools for multi-criteria decision-making and country-specific mapping and cost–benefit analysis.

Finally, all key areas of coherence are also relevant to development cooperation. A strong indication for the needed scale of international cooperation could be derived from the overwhelming majority of developing countries that define conditional and unconditional climate targets, whereby the former are conditional on external support, technology transfer, innovation, and international financing. Although such means of implementation have always been central to international development cooperation, emerging polycentric governance structures also change the expectation patterns of developing countries. They not only make more ambitious targets dependent on traditional development aid between countries, but they also expect other stakeholders to play a role in a variety of functions, including the leveraging and provision of resources, services, and localised solutions. In climate governance, such shifting expectations also explain the fact that developing countries more often refer to the role of the private sector and non-state actors in their NDCs compared to those of other countries (Hsu et al. 2019). Similar anticipation of non-state contributions can be found in SDG strategies at the national level. For instance, already submitted "voluntary national reviews" have shown that some countries, such as Benin, are pursuing a procedural approach to policy integration, establishing bodies, and new procedures in order to coordinate and monitor SDG implementation. Such bodies are not only composed of governmental actors, but also international donors, civil society, businesses, and labour unions (Breuer et al. 2018; Tosun and Leininger 2017, p. 7). Interestingly, the simultaneous conditioning of policy targets and inviting state and non-state capacities could be seen as an implicit understanding of the current incoherence of sustainable development efforts in developing countries. Through a broader uptake of new tools to identify governance gaps and goal interlinkages, sources and thematic areas of incoherence could be better specified—beyond the summary formulations in NDCs and SDG-based national strategies. Similar to general national-level implementation, findings on specific implementation contexts allow for setting priorities on stimulating and leveraging transnational capacity-building for sustainable development in developing countries. A better understanding of factors that influence coherence also represents an important opportunity to improve both donor countries' and recipient countries' policies and to leverage the efforts of state and non-state actors across a polycentric governance landscape.

REFERENCES

Abbott, K. W., & Bernstein, S. (2015). The high-level political forum on sustainable development: Orchestration by default and design. *Global Policy, 6*(3), 222–233.

Atkinson, G., & Mourato, S. (2006). *Cost–benefit analysis and the environment: Recent developments*. Paris: Organisation for Economic Co-operation and Development.

Bäckstrand, K., Khan, J., Kronsell, A., & Lövbrand, E. (2010). The promise of new modes of environmental governance. In K. Bäckstrand, J. Khan, A. Kronsell, & E. Lövbrand (Eds.), *Environmental politics and deliberative democracy* (pp. 3–27). Northampton, MA: Edward Elgar.

Beg, N., Morlot, J. C., Davidson, O., Afrane-Okesse, Y., Tyani, L., Denton, F., et al. (2002). Linkages between climate change and sustainable development. *Climate Policy, 2*(2–3), 129–144.

Beisheim, M., & Simon, N. (2016). *Multi-stakeholder partnerships for implementing the 2030 Agenda: Improving accountability and transparency* (Analytical Paper for the 2016 ECOSOC Partnership Forum). Berlin: Stiftung Wissenschaft und Politik.

Bollen, J., Hers, S., & van der Zwaan, B. (2010). An integrated assessment of climate change, air pollution, and energy security policy. *Energy Policy, 38*(8), 4021–4030.

Bouckaert, G., Peters, B. G., & Verhoest, K. (2010). *The coordination of public sector organizations, shifting patterns of public management*. Basingstoke: Palgrave Macmillan.

Bouyé, M., Harmeling, S., & Schulz, N. S. (2018). *Connecting the dots: Elements for a joined-up implementation of the 2030 Agenda and Paris Agreement*. Bonn: Deutsche Gesellschaft für Internationale Zusammenarbeit.

Brandi, C., Dzebo, A., & Janetschek, H. (2017). *The case for connecting the implementation of the Paris Climate Agreement and the 2030 Agenda for Sustainable Development* (DIE Briefing Paper 21/2017). Bonn: German Development Institute/Deutsches Institut für Entwicklungspolitik (DIE).

Braspening, R. O., van den Berg, M., Klimont, Z., Deetman, S., Janssens-Maenhout, G., Muntean, M., et al. (2016). Exploring synergies between climate and air quality policies using long-term global and regional emission scenarios. *Atmospheric Environment, 140,* 577–591.

Breuer, A., Leininger, J., & Tosun, J. (2018, August 22–25). *Institutional design and policy coherence: National implementation approaches to the SDGs*. Presented at the panel "Organizational Coordination and Policy Integration I" at the ECPR General Conference, Universität Hamburg.

Brundtland, G., Khalid, M., Agnelli, S., Al-Athel, S. A., Chidzero, B., Fadika, L. M., et al. (1987). *Our common future: The World Commission on environment and development*. Oxford: Oxford University Press.

Bulkeley, H., Andonova, L. B., Betsill, M. M., Compagnon, D., Hale, T., Hoffmann, M. J., et al. (2014). *Transnational climate change governance*. New York, NY: Cambridge University Press.

Carbone, M. (2008). Mission impossible: The European Union and policy coherence for development. *Journal of European Integration, 30,* 323–342.

Chakravarty, S., & Tavoni, M. (2013). Energy poverty alleviation and climate change mitigation: Is there a trade off? *Energy Economics, 40*(1), S67–S73.

Chan, S., Boran, I., van Asselt, H., Iacobuta, G., Niles, N., Rietig, K., et al. (2019). Promises and risks of nonstate action in climate and sustainability governance. *Wiley Interdisciplinary Reviews: Climate Change, 10*(3), e572.

Chan, S., Brandi, C., & Bauer, S. (2016). Aligning transnational climate action with international climate governance: The road from Paris. *Review of European, Comparative & International Environmental Law, 25*(2), 238–247.

Chan, S., Falkner, R., Goldberg, M., & van Asselt, H. (2018). Effective and geographically balanced? An output-based assessment of non-state climate actions. *Climate Policy, 18*(1), 24–35.

Chan, S., & Pattberg, P. (2008). Private rule-making and the politics of accountability: Analyzing global forest governance. *Global Environmental Politics, 8*(3), 103–121.

Chan, S., van Asselt, H., Hale, T., Abbott, K. W., Beisheim, M., Hoffmann, M., et al. (2015). Reinvigorating international climate policy: A comprehensive framework for effective nonstate action. *Global Policy, 6*(4), 466–473.

Cohen, B., Blanco, H., Dubash, N. K., Dukkipati, S., Khosla, R., Scrieciu, S., et al. (2018). Multi-criteria decision analysis in policy-making for climate mitigation and development. *Climate and Development, 11*(3), 212–222.

Cole, D. H. (2015). Advantages of a polycentric approach to climate change policy. *Nature Climate Change, 5*(2), 114–118.

Collste, D., Pedercini, M., & Cornell, S. E. (2017). Policy coherence to achieve the SDGs: Using integrated simulation models to assess effective policies. *Sustainability Science, 12*(6), 921–931.

D'Amato, D., Droste, N., Chan, S., & Hofer, A. (2017). The green economy: Pragmatism or revolution? Perceptions of young researchers on social ecological transformation. *Environmental Values, 26*(4), 413–435.

Dubash, N. K., Raghunandan, D., Sant, G., & Sreenivas, A. (2013). Indian climate change policy: Exploring a co-benefits-based approach. *Economic and Political Weekly, 48*(22), 47–61.

Dzebo, A., Brandi, C., Janetschek, H., Savvidou, G., Adams, K., Chan, S., et al. (2017). *Exploring connections between the Paris Agreement and the 2030 Agenda for Sustainable Development* (SEI Policy Brief). Stockholm: Stockholm Environment Institute.

Falkner, R. (2016). The Paris Agreement and the new logic of international climate politics. *International Affairs, 92*(5), 1107–1125.

Frey, M., & Sabbatino, A. (2018). The role of the private sector in global sustainable development: The UN 2030 Agenda. In G. Grigore, A. Stancu, & D. McQueen (Eds.), *Corporate responsibility and digital communities* (pp. 187–204). Cham: Palgrave Macmillan.

Giessen, L. (2011a). Horizontal policy integration. In H. Schiffman & P. Robbins (Eds.), *Green issues and debates* (pp. 293–296). Thousand Oaks, CA: Sage.

Giessen, L. (2011b). Vertical policy integration. In H. Schiffman & P. Robbins (Eds.), *Green issues and debates* (pp. 486–489). Thousand Oaks, CA: Sage.

Gomez-Echeverri, L. (2018). Climate and development: Enhancing impact through stronger linkages in the implementation of the Paris Agreement and the Sustainable Development Goals (SDGs). *Philosophical Transactions of the Royal Society A: Mathematical, Physical and Engineering Sciences, 376*(2119), 1–17.

Green, J. F. (2013). *Rethinking private authority: Agents and entrepreneurs in global environmental governance*. Princeton, NJ: Princeton University Press.

Griggs, D. J., Nilsson, M., Stevance, A., & McCollum, D. (2017). *A guide to SDG interactions: From science to implementation*. Paris: International Council for Science.

Guivarch, C., & Monjon, S. (2015). Identifying the main uncertainty drivers of energy security in a low-carbon world: The case of Europe. *Energy Economics, 64*, 530–541.

Haas, P. M. (2004). Addressing the global governance deficit. *Global Environmental Politics, 4*(4), 1–15.

Hasegawa, T., Fujimori, S., Havlík, P., Valin, H., Bodirsky, B. L., Doelman, J. C., et al. (2018). Risk of increased food insecurity under stringent global climate change mitigation policy. *Nature Climate Change, 8*(8), 699–703.

Hoebink, P. (2004). Evaluating Maastricht's triple C: The "C" of coherence. In P. Hoebink (Ed.), *The Treaty of Maastricht and Europe's development co-operation* (pp. 183–218). Brussels and Amsterdam: European Union and Aksant.

Hoffmann, M. J. (2011). *Climate governance at the crossroads: Experimenting with a global response after Kyoto*. Oxford: Oxford University Press.

Hsu, A., Brandt, J., Widerberg, O., Chan, S., & Weinfurter, A. (2019). Exploring links between national climate strategies and non-state and subnational climate action in nationally determined contributions (NDCs). *Climate Policy*. https://doi.org/10.1080/14693062.2019.1624252.

Hsu, A., Moffat, A. S., Weinfurter, A. J., & Schwartz, J. D. (2015). Towards a new climate diplomacy. *Nature Climate Change, 5*(6), 501–503.

ICSU (International Council for Science). (2017). *A guide to SDG interactions: From science to implementation.* https://council.science/publications/a-guide-to-sdg-interactions-from-science-to-implementation.

ICSU, & International Social Science Council. (2015). *Review of targets for the Sustainable Development Goals: The science perspective.* http://www.icsu.org/publications/reports-and-reviews/review-of-targets-for-the-sustainable-development-goals-the-science-perspective-2015/SDG-Report.pdf.

Initiative for Climate Action Transparency. (2018). *Non-state and subnational action guidance. Guidance for integrating the impact of non-state and subnational mitigation actions into national greenhouse gas projections, targets and planning.* https://climateactiontransparency.org/wp-content/uploads/2018/08/ICAT-Non-State-and-Subnational-Action-Guidance-July-2018.pdf.

IPCC (Intergovernmental Panel on Climate Change). (2014). *Climate change 2014: Synthesis report. Contribution of working groups I, II and III to the fifth assessment report of the Intergovernmental Panel on Climate Change* (Core writing team, R. K. Pachauri & L. A. Meyer, Eds.). Geneva: Author.

IPCC. (2018). *Global warming of 1.5 °C: An IPCC special report on the impacts of global warming of 1.5 °C above pre-industrial levels and related global greenhouse gas emission pathways, in the context of strengthening the global response to the threat of climate change, sustainable development, and efforts to eradicate poverty* (V. Masson-Delmotte, P. Zhai, H. O. Pörtner, D. Roberts, J. Skea, P. R. Shukla, et al., Eds.). Geneva: Author.

Jordan, A., Huitema, D., Van Asselt, H., & Forster, J. (Eds.). (2018). *Governing climate change: Polycentricity in action?* Cambridge: Cambridge University Press.

Keohane, R. O., & Victor, D. G. (2011). The regime complex for climate change. *Perspectives on Politics, 9*(1), 7–23.

Kok, M., Metz, B., Verhagen, J., & Van Rooijen, S. (2008). Integrating development and climate policies: National and international benefits. *Climate Policy, 8*(2), 103–118.

Koulaimah-Gabriel, A. (1999). The EU and the developing world: Coherence between the Common Foreign and Security Policy and development co-operation. In J. Forster & O. S. Stokke (Eds.), *Policy coherence in development co-operation* (pp. 346–372). London: Frank Cass, in association with the European Association of Developmental Research and Training Institutes.

Kropp, C., & Türk, J. (2017). Bringing climate change down to Earth: Climate change governance from the bottom up. In A. Esguerra, N. Helmerich, & T. Risse (Eds.), *Sustainability politics and limited statehood* (pp. 179–210). Cham: Palgrave Macmillan.

Kuyper, J., Bäckstrand, K., & Schroeder, H. (2017). Institutional accountability of nonstate actors in the UNFCCC: Exit, voice, and loyalty. *Review of Policy Research, 34*(1), 88–109.

Latour, B. (2018). *Down to Earth: Politics in the new climatic regime.* Cambridge: Polity Press.

Matthews, F. (2011). The capacity to co-ordinate—Whitehall, governance and the challenge of climate change. *Public Policy Administration, 27*(2), 169–189.

McCollum, D. L., Echeverri, L. G., Busch, S., Pachauri, S., Parkinson, S., Rogelj, J., et al. (2018). Connecting the Sustainable Development Goals by their energy inter-linkages. *Environmental Research Letters, 13*(3), 1–23.

Mert, A. (2009). Partnerships for sustainable development as discursive practice: Shifts in discourses of environment and democracy. *Forest Policy and Economics, 11*(5–6), 326–339.

Mert, A., & Dellas, E. (2012). Technology transfer through water partnerships: A framework of assessment for legitimacy. In P. Pattberg, F. Biermann, A. Mert, & S. Chan (Eds.), *Public–private partnerships for sustainable development: Emergence, influence, and legitimacy* (pp. 209–238). Northampton, MA: Edward Elgar.

Mittelmann, J. H. (2013). Global bricolage: Emerging market powers and polycentric governance. *Third World Quarterly, 34*(1), 23–37.

Morseletto, P. (2019). Confronting the nitrogen challenge: Options for governance and target setting. *Global Environmental Change, 54*, 40–49.

Nerini, F. F., Tomei, J., To, L. S., Bisaga, I., Parikh, P., Black, M., et al. (2018). Mapping synergies and trade-offs between energy and the Sustainable Development Goals. *Nature Energy, 3*(1), 10–15.

Nicolai, S., Hoy, C., Berliner, T., & Aedy, T. (2015). *Projecting progress: Reaching the SDGs by 2030.* http://www.odi.org/sites/odi.org.uk/files/odi-assets/publications-opinion-files/9839.pdf.

Nilsson, M., Griggs, D., & Visbeck, M. (2016). Map the interactions between Sustainable Development Goals. *Nature, 534*(7607), 320–322.

Nordhaus, B. W. D. (1977). Economic growth and climate—The carbon dioxide problem. *The American Economic Review, 67*(1), 341–346.

Northrop, E., Biru, H., Lima, S., Bouye, M., & Song, R. (2016). *Examining the alignment between the intended nationally determined contributions and Sustainable Development Goals* (Working Paper). Washington, DC: World Resources Institute.

OECD (Organisation for Economic Co-operation and Development). (2014). *Better policies for development 2014: Policy coherence and illicit financial flows.* Paris: OECD Publishing.

OECD. (2018). *Policy coherence for sustainable development 2018: Towards sustainable and resilient societies.* Paris: OECD Publishing.

Ostrom, E. (2010). Beyond markets and states: Polycentric governance of complex economic systems. *American Economic Review, 100*(3), 641–672.

Patassini, D. (2005). *Beyond benefit cost analysis.* London: Routledge.

Pattberg, P. H. (2007). *Private institutions and global governance: The new politics of environmental sustainability.* Northampton, MA: Edward Elgar.

Pattberg, P. H., Biermann, F., Chan, S., & Mert, A. (2012). *Public–private partnerships for sustainable development: Emergence, influence and legitimacy.* Northampton, MA: Edward Elgar.

Pattberg, P. H., Chan, S., Sanderink, L., & Widerberg, O. (2018). Linkages: Understanding their role in polycentric governance. In A. Jordan, D. Huitema, H. van Asselt, & J. Forster (Eds.), *Governing climate change: Polycentricity in action?* (pp. 168–187). Cambridge: Cambridge University Press.

Pattberg, P. H., Kristensen, K., & Widerberg, O. (2017). *Beyond the CBD: Exploring the institutional landscape of governing for biodiversity* (Report R-17/06). Amsterdam: IVM Institute for Environmental Studies.

Pradhan, P., Costa, L., Rybski, D., Lucht, W., & Kropp, J. P. (2017). A systematic study of sustainable development goal (SDG) interactions. *Earth's Future, 5*(11), 1169–1179.

Rogge, K. S., & Reichardt, K. (2016). Policy mixes for sustainability transitions: An extended concept and framework for analysis. *Research Policy, 45*(8), 1620–1635.

Román, M., Linnér, B. O., & Mickwitz, P. (2012). Development policies as a vehicle for addressing climate change. *Climate and Development, 4*(3), 251–260.

Sachs, J. D. (2012). From millennium development goals to Sustainable Development Goals. *The Lancet, 379*(9832), 2206–2211.

Shindell, D., Faluvegi, G., Seltzer, K., & Shindell, C. (2018). Quantified, localized health benefits of accelerated carbon dioxide emissions reductions. *Nature Climate Change, 8*, 291–295.

Solaymani, S., Kardooni, R., Yusoff, S. B., & Kari, F. (2015). The impacts of climate change policies on the transportation sector. *Energy, 81*, 719–728.

Spash, C. L. (2012). Green economy, red herring. *Environmental Values, 21*(2), 95–99.

Stockman, L., Fischer, T., Deming, M., Ngwira, B., Bowie, C., Cunliffe, N., et al. (2007). Point-of-use water treatment and use among mothers in Malawi. *Emerging Infectious Diseases, 13*(7), 1077–1080.

Swart, R. (2003). Climate change and sustainable development: Expanding the options. *Climate Policy, 3*(1), 19–40.

Tosun, J., & Lang, A. (2017). Policy integration: Mapping the different concepts. *Policy Studies, 38*(6), 553–570.

Tosun, J., & Leininger, J. (2017). Governing the interlinkages between the Sustainable Development Goals: Approaches to attain policy integration. *Global Challenges, 1*(9), 1700036.

UN (United Nations). (2018). *Working together: Integration, institutions and the Sustainable Development Goals (World Public Sector report 2018)*. New York, NY: Division for Public Administration and Development Management.

UNEP (United Nations Environment Programme). (2016). *The emissions gap report 2016*. Nairobi: Author.

UNEP. (2018). *The emissions gap report 2018*. Nairobi: Author.

UNGA (United Nations General Assembly). (2015). *Transforming our world: The 2030 Agenda for sustainable development*. New York, NY: United Nations.

Ürge-Vorsatz, D., & Tirado Herrero, S. (2012). Building synergies between climate change mitigation and energy poverty alleviation. *Energy Policy, 49*, 83–90.

van Tilburg, X., Rawlins, J., Luijten, J., Roeser, F., Gonzales-Zuñiga, S., Lütke-hermöller, K., et al. (2018). *NDC update report. Special edition: Linking NDCs and SDGs*. http://ambitiontoaction.net/wp-content/uploads/2018/05/NDC-Upadate-Report-May-2018.pdf.

Vogler, J. (2016). *Climate change in world politics*. Basingstoke: Palgrave Macmillan.

Von Stechow, C., McCollum, D., Riahi, K., Minx, J. C., Kriegler, E., Van Vuuren, D. P., et al. (2015). Integrating global climate change mitigation goals with other sustainability objectives: A synthesis. *Annual Review of Environment and Resources, 40*, 363–394.

Von Stechow, C., Minx, J. C., Riahi, K., Jewell, J., McCollum, D. L., Callaghan, M. W., et al. (2016). 2 °C and SDGs: United they stand, divided they fall? *Environmental Research Letters, 11*(3), 1–15.

Weitz, N., Carlsen, H., Nilsson, M., & Skånberg, K. (2017). Towards systemic and contextual priority setting for implementing the 2030 Agenda. *Sustainability Science, 13*(2), 531–548.

Winkler, H., Boyd, A., Gunfaus, M. T., & Raubenheimer, S. (2015). Reconsidering development by reflecting on climate change. *International Environmental Agreements: Politics, Law and Economics, 15*(4), 369–385.

Zhou, X., & Moinuddin, M. (2017). *Sustainable Development Goals interlinkages and network analysis: A practical tool for SDG integration and policy coherence.* https://sdginterlinkages.iges.jp/files/IGES_Research%20Report_SDG%20Interlinkages_Printing%20Version.pdf.

Open Access This chapter is licensed under the terms of the Creative Commons Attribution 4.0 International License (http://creativecommons.org/licenses/by/4.0/), which permits use, sharing, adaptation, distribution and reproduction in any medium or format, as long as you give appropriate credit to the original author(s) and the source, provide a link to the Creative Commons license and indicate if changes were made.

The images or other third party material in this chapter are included in the chapter's Creative Commons license, unless indicated otherwise in a credit line to the material. If material is not included in the chapter's Creative Commons license and your intended use is not permitted by statutory regulation or exceeds the permitted use, you will need to obtain permission directly from the copyright holder.

CHAPTER 3

Development Finance and the 2030 Goals

Emma Mawdsley

3.1 Introduction

In August 2017, Achim Steiner, the recently appointed Administrator of the United Nations Development Programme (UNDP), addressed the annual conference of the European Association of Development Institutions, at Bergen, Norway. As the United Nation's (UN) leading development institution, the UNDP will play a particularly important role in pursuing the Sustainable Development Goals (SDGs) and the 2030 Agenda for Sustainable Development. Steiner was candid about some of the shortcomings of the SDGs, and he was all the more persuasive for that. His request to the large audience of international development academics and practitioners was that they actively, and critically, engage with the SDGs—whatever their faults, he argued, nothing better is going to come along.

In this short chapter, I pick up on one area that marks a key shift from the Millennium Development Goals (MDGs) and SDGs, namely financing. Accompanying the SDG process—their formulation, launch, and current operationalisation—has been a parallel set of multi-stakeholder meetings and debates over how to finance these hugely ambitious global goals, particularly in poorer countries. The slogan making the rounds is "from billions to trillions". Various forms of public and private finance were rallied for the MDGs (2000–2015), notably at the 2002 Monterrey Financing for Development conference. But the pre-eminent form of financing for the MDGs—and

E. Mawdsley (✉)
University of Cambridge, Cambridge, UK
e-mail: eem10@cam.ac.uk

© The Author(s) 2021
S. Chaturvedi et al. (eds.), *The Palgrave Handbook of Development Cooperation for Achieving the 2030 Agenda*,
https://doi.org/10.1007/978-3-030-57938-8_3

thus attendant pressures and politics—was centred around official development assistance (ODA) or "foreign aid", including debt relief. A variety of MDG-related donor meetings sought to encourage donors to reach their long-standing commitments to provide 0.7 per cent of gross national income in ODA. Few have ever met this target (the annual number varies slightly, but it was five in 2018), and it seems most unlikely that the majority ever will, under current definitions and trends. As the SDGs coalesced, however, their ambition and scale evidently rendered this 0.7 per cent target grossly inadequate. ODA continues to be recognised as an important resource, especially for the poorest and/or most conflict-affected countries, but even if every donor met the 0.7 per cent target, it would barely touch the trillions that have been variously estimated to be required to achieve the SDGs. SDG 13 (Take urgent action to combat climate change and its impacts) is estimated to require $100 billion annually by 2020 (Liverman 2018), while Schmidt-Traub (2015) calculates that an extra $1.4 trillion a year is necessary to pursue all 17 goals in the low- and lower-middle-income countries alone.

Various sources of SDG finance are under discussion, such as raising levels of domestic resource mobilisation. Combating tax evasion and limiting capital flight, for example, were discussed at the 2015 UN summit on Financing for Development at Addis Ababa, but this failed to produce an international tax body, or indeed to bring any new money to the table. Rather, the energy lies with the private sector, and here the debates and initiatives around financing the 2030 Agenda are stimulating, deepening, and consolidating existing trends around the private sector within international development. Private-sector representatives are being invited to drive and shape global development governance and policy by the UN and other multilaterals (e.g. Mader 2016) and national development agencies (e.g. Mawdsley 2015). Despite referencing small and medium-sized enterprises, private-sector voices are dominantly from transnational corporations and the financial sector. In 2017, the Blended Finance Taskforce was established by the UN's Business & Sustainable Development Commission to help mobilise this large-scale capital. In its flagship report, "Better Finance, Better World", produced in 2018, the task force aimed to identify key barriers to the effective use of blended finance and issued calls for action from leaders in the investment and development finance community (Blended Finance Taskforce 2018). Development institutions are increasingly seeking partnerships with venture capital, hedge funds, investment banks, sovereign wealth funds, credit rating agencies, global accountancy firms, and corporations, which are themselves increasingly governed by financial logics (Krippner 2011), in order to open up new circuits of financial investment, speculation, and extraction. The background against which this is happening is a shift away from the MDGs' focus on direct *poverty reduction*—however problematic that was—towards the central analytic of *economic growth*.

The logic runs that, given the staggering amounts required to meet the projected investment gap—particularly, but not only, in poorer countries—the role of ODA and other forms of public finance should be to "unlock", "catalyse", and "leverage" much larger flows of private finance for "development". This is seen to be especially relevant to middle-income countries, which have broader borrowing choices and less need for ODA than low-income countries. Donors are increasingly deploying the concept of "blended finance" and expanding their use of financial instruments such as debt and equity finance for public–private partnerships (PPPs). Donors now actively promote one of their role's as "de-risking investment" through various guarantees and finance deals, or as Carroll and Jarvis (2014) put it, public money is being used to "escort international capital into frontier and emerging markets" in the name of development. The UN, the Organisation for Economic Co-operation and Development (OECD), Bretton Woods Institutions, and their private-sector partners all talk the language of sustainable growth ultimately serving poverty reduction—for example, of aligning the global financial system to "long-term" perspectives (when examined, "long term" can be as short as one year for investors); of building green economies and infrastructure; with labour (supposedly) protected by renewed commitments to corporate social responsibility.

Liverman (2018, p. 173) observes:

> Rather than address the structural basis of poverty, hunger and inequality with roots in colonialism, the MDGs made developing countries responsible for addressing these problems, with a nod to the role of debt relief and aid in helping to meet the goals.

The failure to address the structural basis of poverty, inequality, and unsustainability is a criticism also made of the SDGs (Scheyvens et al. 2016), as weak accountability mechanisms favour existing models and vested interests (Donald and Way 2016). But it is the financing of the SDGs that is the focus here. The SDG "business model" is based on ever deeper integration and (supposed) alignment being projected between business, finance, development, and sustainability. But as Hickel (2015) observes, the SDGs seek to reduce inequality through income growth for the bottom 40 per cent, but without touching or redistributing the incomes of the top 1 per cent; SDG 17—to revitalise the global partnership for sustainable development—includes a target (17.10) that promotes universal open trading systems under the World Trade Organization and increasing exports from developing countries, for example. This is a model which has offered bare and highly precarious poverty reduction for some, and which has deepened global inequality.

The trend from the narrow construct of "ODA" to the broader category of "development finance" is not solely about the SDGs, but the 2030 Agenda provides a normalising narrative and, through the UN and other development organisations, the SDGs act as institutional interfaces for deepening state–private capital hybrid formations. This latest iteration of neoliberal development—in which the imperatives of finance play an even more prominent role than in earlier Washington and post-Washington Consensus ideologies and interventions—is expected to provide resources to scale, innovation, efficiency, and energy. The focus on infrastructure, land, and digital financial technologies (Gabor and Brooks 2017) are presented as essential drivers of growth, which will trickle down into poverty reduction. The growing turn towards state-supported development financing is not new, but it is certainly entering a different scale and phase. Donors and the mainstream international development community (now including Brazil, China, and India) are reorienting their narratives and practices to continue to serve capital, now in a qualitatively different conjuncture (Mawdsley 2015, 2018b). The "work" of the 1980s and 1990s (privatisation, land titling, deregulation, dismantling capital controls, and otherwise enhancing the free movement of capital) in the Global North and the Global South has led to vast over-accumulation of international capital, super-charged by booms and busts, including the 1997 Asian financial crisis, the 2001 dot com bubble, and the 2007/2008 global financial crisis. The "financing for development" agenda provides a legitimating veneer to the development industry's current "work" to create investment opportunities in "frontier" economies. In their analysis of the latest wave of donor-supported PPPs, for example, Bayliss and Van Waeyenberge (2018, p. 2) suggest:

> While earlier drives for privatisation in donor advocacy formally highlighted the potential efficiency gains deriving from increased private sector involvement in public service provision, the more recent wave of PPP advocacy is anchored almost entirely in arguments seeking to match a glut in global savings with the need to upscale public service provision in developing countries. This has created an increasingly financialised approach to infrastructure, as policy is framed in terms of investment opportunities for financial investors and institutional arrangements bearing on infrastructure provision are reconfigured to facilitate their entry into the sector.

For its many mainstream advocates—the UN, bilateral development agencies, philanthrocapitalist foundations, and private-sector partners—this is entirely desirable. Greater "financial inclusion" for individuals and communities, and financial-sector deepening for low- and middle-income countries, are all framed as unalloyed improvements. A Kenyan woman can now safely transfer money to a distant relative or trading partner in the blink of an eye through M-Pesa, whereas at the other end of the spectrum, blended finance from Northern and Southern partners is leading to a surge of infrastructure building around the world. New approaches to impact investment (Organisation for Economic Co-operation and Development 2019) and new instruments such as development impact bonds and weather index-based insurance are deepening financial logics in development narratives, institutional functioning, programmatic interventions, and stakeholder subjectivities. Not all of these claims can be, or should be, lightly dismissed. But critical scholars are raising a host of concerns (e.g. Brooks 2016; Storm 2018). Out of what is an increasingly rich and detailed literature, two are very briefly mentioned here.

The first concerns complexity, accountability, and transparency. Efforts to monitor these flows of public money into private-sector and financial partnerships by academics and civil society watchdogs are increasingly hampered by commercial privacy barriers. For example, an increasingly large share of bilateral ODA is being routed through national development finance institutions, which are tasked with supplying investment to the private sector to support development in poor and middle-income countries. This can be in the form of loans, equity investments, risk guarantee instruments, and so on. Unlike more "traditional" uses of ODA, these flows now "leveraging" or "catalysing" private-sector investment can be hidden behind layers of commercial privacy, or in some cases routed through highly secretive tax havens (European Network on Debt and Development, n.d.). Even ODA is going to become more difficult to record and follow. The OECD-Development Assistance Committee (DAC) has been leading dialogue among its members around "modernising ODA". Although some desirable reforms appear to be emerging, it is evident that ODA will also become considerably more complex to understand and track. These trends have considerable implications for the transparency and accountability of public money, and also for scrutinising the claims that various public–private development partnerships are leading to the inclusive and sustainable growth claimed by the SDGs.

A second concern is that of risk. Over-indebted farmers committing suicide in India, housing bubbles in Argentina, and the enduring (and inherent) volatility of the global financial market are all forms and scales of risk that are largely unacknowledged in the ebullient language of "fintech" and financial-sector deepening. Akyuz (2017) provides a searing critique of the growing risks of (over-)financialising the "periphery". At present, however, the international development community and its private-sector/financial partners appear to be complacent at best, and in denial at worst, about extending and deepening insufficiently regulated financial tools and markets. To take just one example, in 2017 the Business & Sustainable Development Commission (which is an extremely high-ranking and influential platform launched in 2016 that was explicitly framed around the SDGs) produced a report on "Ideas for Action for a Long-Term and Sustainable Financial System" (Business & Sustainable Development Commission 2017). The report's complacency about financialisation and risk is striking. Even as it seeks to better align the existing financial system with the aspirations of the SDGs, the report starts from the position that "global finance is highly regulated" (Business & Sustainable Development Commission 2017, p. 7). The only reference to systemic risk is a reassuring statement on the "progress" made since the 2008 financial crisis. All remaining references to risk are couched in terms of risks to *investors* (e.g. because of climate change, or the higher risks of investing in poorer countries). The risks to *borrowers* or to collateral populations in contexts of deepening financialisation—whether individuals, municipal authorities, or countries—are almost entirely absent from the report. This is an extraordinary omission.

Steiner asked critical scholars to engage constructively with the SDGs, and there are persuasive reasons to do so. But the SDGs do not simply rest on a disastrous economic system, they seek to legitimate it, accelerate it, and deepen it. The global goals cannot resolve the contradictions between economies, societies, and environments—indeed, ecological survival—under the hegemony of finance capital.

Note

1. This chapter is adapted from a commentary on Liverman (2018) published in *Dialogues in Human Geography* (Mawdsley 2018a). I am grateful to the editors and publishers of *DHG* for allowing me to publish it here with small amendments and adjustments; and to the editors and reviewers of this collection for their generosity and patience.

References

Akyuz, Y. (2017). *Playing with fire: Deepening financial integration and new vulnerabilities of the Global South*. Oxford: Oxford University Press.

Bayliss, K., & Van Waeyenberge, E. (2018). Unpacking the public–private partnership revival. *The Journal of Development Studies, 54*(4), 577–593.

Blended Finance Taskforce. (2018). *Better finance, better world: Consultation paper of the blended finance taskforce*. https://www.blendedfinance.earth/better-finance-better-world.

Brooks, S. H. (2016). Private finance and the post-2015 development agenda. *Development Finance Agenda, 1*(3), 24–27.

Business & Sustainable Development Commission. (2017). *Ideas for action for a long-term and sustainable financial system*. http://s3.amazonaws.com/aws-bsdc/BSDC_SustainableFinanceSystem.pdf.

Carroll, T., & Jarvis, D. S. L. (2014). *Financialisation and development in Asia*. London: Routledge.

Donald, K., & Way, S. (2016). Accountability for the sustainable development goals: A lost opportunity? *Ethics & International Affairs, 30*(2), 201–213. https://doi.org/10.1017/S0892679416000083.

European Network on Debt and Development. (n.d.). *Private finance*. https://eurodad.org/privatef.

Gabor, D., & Brooks, S. H. (2017). The digital revolution in financial inclusion: International development in the fintech era. *New Political Economy, 22*(4), 423–436.

Hickel, J. (2015, August 24). Why the new sustainable development goals won't make the world a fairer place. *The Conversation*. http://theconversation.com/why-the-new-sustainable-development-goals-wont-make-the-world-a-fairer-place-46374.

Krippner, G. (2011). *Capitalizing on crisis: The political origins of the rise of finance.* Cambridge, MA: Harvard University Press.

Liverman, D. M. (2018). Geographic perspectives on development goals: Constructive engagements and critical perspectives on the MDGs and the SDGs. *Dialogues in Human Geography, 8*(2), 168–185.

Mader, P. (2016). Card crusaders, cash infidels and the holy grails of digital financial inclusion. *Behemoth: A Journal on Civilisation, 9*(2), 50–81. https://doi.org/10.6094/behemoth.2016.9.2.916.

Mawdsley, E. (2015). DFID, the private sector, and the re-centring of an economic growth agenda in international development. *Global Society, 29*(3), 339–358.

Mawdsley, E. (2018a). "From billions to trillions": Financing the SDGs in a world "beyond aid". *Dialogues in Human Geography, 8*(2), 191–195.

Mawdsley, E. (2018b). The "Southernisation" of development? *Asia Pacific Viewpoint, 59*(2), 173–185.

Organisation for Economic Co-operation and Development. (2019). *Social impact investment 2019: The impact imperative for sustainable development.* https://www.oecd.org/dac/social-impact-investment-2019-9789264311299-en.htm.

Scheyvens, R., Banks, G., & Hughes, E. (2016). The private sector and the SDGs: The need to move beyond "business as usual". *Sustainable Development, 24*(6), 371–382.

Schmidt-Traub, G. (2015). *Investment needs to achieve the sustainable development goals: Understanding the billions and trillions.* http://unsdsn.org/wp-content/uploads/2015/09/151112-SDG-Financing-Needs.pdf.

Storm, S. (Ed.). (2018). Forum 2018. *Development and Change, 49*(2), 302–546.

Open Access This chapter is licensed under the terms of the Creative Commons Attribution 4.0 International License (http://creativecommons.org/licenses/by/4.0/), which permits use, sharing, adaptation, distribution and reproduction in any medium or format, as long as you give appropriate credit to the original author(s) and the source, provide a link to the Creative Commons license and indicate if changes were made.

The images or other third party material in this chapter are included in the chapter's Creative Commons license, unless indicated otherwise in a credit line to the material. If material is not included in the chapter's Creative Commons license and your intended use is not permitted by statutory regulation or exceeds the permitted use, you will need to obtain permission directly from the copyright holder.

CHAPTER 4

Transnational Science Cooperation for Sustainable Development

Anna Schwachula

4.1 INTRODUCTION

Transnational research cooperation between partners in the Global South and the Global North is an under-researched but relevant topic, often overlooked in the context of development cooperation and development research. In this contribution, I argue that changing ideas about development also require changes in the mode of inter- and transnational cooperation. With a shift towards "global development", the previous emphasis on necessary change in "developing countries" moved towards an emphasis on the need for transformation in *all* countries (Horner and Hulme 2017; Hulme 2016). If all nations are perceived as "developing countries" in certain aspects of social, economic, or ecological sustainable development, previous cooperation patterns, which often imply North-South knowledge hierarchies, have to be reassessed, and additional types of cooperation for global sustainable development should be examined.

Cooperation in research, or more generally in science,[1] between researchers in the Global North and South[2] can be considered, as such an additional type of transnational cooperation, beyond established approaches of technical development cooperation. Transnational research cooperation, as well as the policies that frame it nationally and globally, thus fall into the context of

---

A. Schwachula (✉)
German Development Institute / Deutsches Institut für Entwicklungspolitik (DIE), Bonn, Germany
e-mail: anna.schwachula@die-gdi.de

© The Author(s) 2021
S. Chaturvedi et al. (eds.), *The Palgrave Handbook of Development Cooperation for Achieving the 2030 Agenda*,
https://doi.org/10.1007/978-3-030-57938-8_4

the discussions around the future of development cooperation "beyond aid" (Horner and Hulme 2017; Janus et al. 2015).

However, so far, the potential of transnational research cooperation is little acknowledged, both within the community of development research and in global debates and governance mechanisms for sustainable development, such as the 2030 Agenda for Sustainable Development or the Global Partnership for Effective Development Co-operation (GPEDC). The role of science cooperation for sustainable development is much less recognised in development practice, policy, and research than the role of other types of knowledge cooperation, such as capacity development or knowledge transfer (see Sect. 4.2). I put forward, however, that transnational research cooperation for sustainable development should be endorsed by global agreements and national policies.

Transnational research cooperation can contribute to identifying and establishing potential pathways towards equitable sustainable development. In the ideal case, cooperative transnational and transdisciplinary research comes up with solutions that are relevant to stakeholders and can be implemented in and adapted to local contexts (Hirsch Hadorn et al. 2006; Lang et al. 2012).[3] Furthermore, jointly producing new knowledge as well as exchanging knowledge on equal terms should be emphasised as suitable modes of cooperation. Modes of equitable cooperation correspond more smoothly with the new paradigm of global sustainable development than traditional North-South knowledge transfer or capacity development.

Lastly, I argue that stronger global agreements might also contribute to better policy coherence for development at the national level, where transnational research cooperation may be part of science policy—as in the German case—which may have objectives that diverge from development policy. Put differently, in view of sustainability-oriented transnational research cooperation, the current gaps in global governance may aggravate policy incoherence on the national level, with potentially detrimental effects on sustainable development. Hence, this chapter also provides an illustration of the concepts of the challenge of *coordinating* policy-making on the national and global levels and of the *contested* objectives and responsibilities of different policy fields, which are introduced in the introduction to this handbook.

In this contribution, I elaborate on the role of knowledge (Sect. 4.2), science as a specific type of knowledge, and the role of research cooperation for sustainable development (Sect. 4.3) before I examine the role of national policies—along the example of German science and development policy—and global norms for transnational research cooperation between partners from the Global North and the Global South (Sect. 4.4). In Sect. 4.5, I draw some conclusions in view of the existing gaps in the framework of global governance for transnational research cooperation for sustainable development.

This contribution is based on empirical qualitative research on German science policy for cooperation between Germany and the Global South in sustainability research, carried out in the framework of my Ph.D. (Schwachula 2019).

4.2 Knowledge and Development

Without explicitly referring to knowledge as a driver of development or making its role explicit, development practice and development policy have been closely interlinked with knowledge since colonial times (Hornidge 2014a). This is a relevant fact, as I propose here to define science as a specific type of knowledge, distinguished from other types only through its specific rules of production (Knorr-Cetina 1999; Sismondo 2008). This perspective on knowledge and science as socially shared definitions of phenomena is grounded in a constructivist approach, more specifically in the Sociology of Knowledge Approach to Discourse (Keller 2005, 2013).

With science being perceived as a type of knowledge, it is therefore necessary to contemplate the role of knowledge in development in general, before scrutinising in depth the role of science cooperation between partners in the Global North and the Global South. Putting science into context seems particularly relevant, as the role of knowledge, and more so science, has been discussed controversially in view of development.

In an everyday understanding, knowledge is defined as internalised information and as an "understanding of or information about a subject that you get by experience or study, either known by one person or by people generally" ("Knowledge" 2018). In a more encompassing understanding, constructivist scholars propose to define knowledge as a socially shared and accepted perception of phenomena that is considered to be objective and valid, and therefore perceived as legitimate (Keller 2013). In pointing at the socially constructed nature of knowledge, the constructivist perspective substantially diverges from a positivist perception of objective reality.

In view of knowledge in the development context, the constructivist approach is helpful, as it emphasises the interconnections between knowledge and power, which are inherent in any context of cooperation between different partners in the Global North and South. "Knowledge" then "refers to everything which is supposed to 'exist' (including ideas, theories, everyday assumptions, language, incorporated routines and practices)" (Keller 2005, p. 6). Knowledge and power are connected through the embeddedness of knowledge in discourses and corresponding "dispositifs", that is, discourse-related institutions and structures (Foucault 1980; Keller 2013).

Among other effects, discursive power becomes evident in the validity, objectivity, truth, or value attributed to specific types of knowledge and the social groups creating this knowledge, while other types of knowledge are discredited. Institutionalised power and resources, such as financial, cultural, or social capital, influence whose knowledge is counted as legitimate and spread (Keller 2003, 2013). In view of the role of knowledge for development, this is essential, as the next section shows.

Next to knowledge that is counted in social terms as being essential, and therefore transmitted in formal education systems, different types of knowledge with different social attributions of credibility coexist. Knowledge spans from everyday, tacit lay knowledge to explicit, highly specialised forms of knowledge, such as scientific knowledge or traditional, local knowledge on specific aspects of our life world. The importance of these different knowledge types for development is increasingly being recognised (Arocena and Sutz 2012; Leach et al. 2012; Smith et al. 2014). Compared to other types of knowledge, scientific knowledge is often counted as the most neutral, objective, and therefore legitimate—even if, from a constructivist perspective, scientific knowledge is considered to be only one type of knowledge among others, differentiating itself only through its specific rules of production (Knorr-Cetina 1999; Sismondo 2008).[4]

4.2.1 Knowledge for Development: A Tense Relation

Since colonial times, the definition of development has been predominantly shaped in the Global North, at the expense of Southern perspectives. In consequence, the uneven distribution of power and accepted knowledge has also shaped development cooperation in practice (della Faille 2011; Escobar 1992; Esteva 2010; Gardner and Lewis 2000; Gore 2000; Nederveen Pieterse 2011; Ziai 2010, 2015). Development thinking was firmly based on the belief of the superiority of Western knowledge and the model of Western/Northern modernity, to be followed as a pathway to development, which was understood to be the modernisation of traditional societies. Modernity and development meant triggering economic growth and introducing modern institutions, values, and norms. In this development paradigm, non-Western knowledge was neglected and devalued (Cowen and Shenton 2003; Crewe and Harrison 1998). Modernisation theory and its assumptions of knowledge for development have been criticised for many years, among other reasons for being too simplistic (Chataway et al. 2006), too linear (Evers 2000), for implying an expert lay hierarchy (Illi 2001; Sillitoe 2000), or for maintaining North-South hierarchies and technological dependence (Shamsavari 2007).

In the Global South, some countries, such as Brazil, China, India, and Mexico, among others, have developed strong science systems—backed by public and private investments in research—and turned into global players in science production (UN Educational, Scientific and Cultural Organization 2015). At the same time, development policy and practice are opening up to different conceptualisations, including Southern knowledge and perspectives. For example, the concept of "Buen Vivir" as a Southern vision of development is widely known in the development community (Acosta Espinosa 2008). Moreover, the development paradigm, as such, is shifting towards more equitable knowledge/power relations, as evident in the increased focus on ownership, partnership, and the local suitability of interventions in North-South cooperation, a shift towards a global perspective on development, and the rise of South-South cooperation as an additional type of development cooperation (Janus et al. 2015).

While knowledge, power, and development are closely interrelated in determining the very idea of the latter, knowledge has also turned into a *subject* of development policy and practice. Institutions such as the World Bank (1999) firmly introduced "knowledge for development" on the agenda of development policy and practice (Evers et al. 2006), uncritically picturing knowledge as a panacea for development—that is, knowledge produced elsewhere to be used in the context of the Global South. Knowledge is viewed as a precondition and driver of (sustainable) development. Making knowledge useable for development consequently has turned into a normative goal pursued by many governments and institutions, often in view of the economic usability of knowledge (Hornidge 2012, 2014a).

Different scholars have contested the simplistic idea that knowledge is a silver bullet for development and have painted a more differentiated picture instead. While generally affirming the important role of knowledge in sustainable development, the scientific community acknowledges that, next to the inherent relation between knowledge and power, knowledge is surrounded by different types of social, legal, political, and technical boundaries (see among others, Evers 2000; Evers et al. 2006; Hornidge 2013). In addition, certain aspects of the concept of "knowledge for development" are debated—such as its best use (Narayanaswamy 2013); the role of local or indigenous knowledge; and the problems of conceptualising it as the opposite of scientific or expert knowledge (Agrawal 1995; Mosse 2001; Sillitoe 2000).

Even in a contested area such as knowledge and (or for) development, some things are not disputed, however. This includes the importance of primary and secondary education and the knowledge transmitted by it, including basic factual and practical types of knowledge as well as knowledge-related skills, such as literacy (Klochikhin 2012). The value attributed to basic education and knowledge is reflected in national development policies as well as their international framing: Transmitting knowledge through education was one of the Millennium Development Goals and included in the Sustainable Development Goals (SDGs) as well (United Nations [UN] 2015; UN Development Programme [UNDP] 2013).

Basic education is even used as an indicator for development: Both the Human Development Index as well as the Multidimensional Poverty Index include knowledge—measured through average and expected years of schooling—as indicators (UNDP 2018). Primary, secondary, and tertiary education as well as capacity development continue to be a focus of development policies worldwide. In Germany, for example, basic education is well-established as a subfield of national education policy as well as international development policy (German Federal Ministry of Education and Research [BMBF] 2016; German Federal Ministry for Economic Cooperation and Development [BMZ] 2015).

Next to the formal education system, knowledge cooperation may also take place in the form of *capacity development* or *knowledge transfer* in different sectors, for example, through vocational training in specific fields of expertise.

While the role of education and capacity development is mainly to *transmit* knowledge from one individual or institutional actor—often from a donor country—to another, more recently emphasis has also been put on knowledge *exchange*, with knowledge being shared among partners in both directions. Here, the focus ideally is on *mutual learning* (Arocena and Sutz 2010; Bradley 2007; Upreti 2011). The 2030 Agenda puts knowledge sharing at the heart of SDG 17. Online platforms such as the United Nation's (UN) SDG Knowledge Platform (UN Department of Economic and Social Affairs 2019) and the GPEDC Knowledge Platform (Global Partnership for Effective Development Co-operation [GPEDC] 2019) similarly target virtual knowledge sharing for sustainable development. According to Janus et al. (2015), next to perceiving development as a global phenomenon, it is a further feature of "beyond aid" to emphasise the role of knowledge exchange among partners from different societal sectors and different world regions. However, knowledge sharing is still to be differentiated from the joint production of *new* knowledge on specific phenomena, as enabled in research cooperation.

4.3 Transnational Research Cooperation for Sustainable Development

A further type of knowledge cooperation is the production of new scientific insights in research cooperation. Indeed, the idea of turning science into a lever of a development process can be traced back to colonial times (Smith 2009). In general, however, "science for development" meant that scientific knowledge produced in the Global North was to be used in development contexts of the Global South—the idea of science for development was thus coupled to the modernist ideas of knowledge and technology transfer from North to South (Hornidge 2014b). Until today, Southern scientific knowledge is not well represented in influential scientific journals, and Southern scientists are not sufficiently integrated in institutions supporting the scientific knowledge system, such as editorial boards (Cummings and Hoebink 2017). In consequence, Southern scientific perspectives are globally less visible. This exclusion from institutions of global science production and representation also entails that the research agendas on topics concerning the Global South are set in the Global North (Landau 2012).

Taking the interlinkages between knowledge production and power into consideration helps to explain why these skews in global knowledge production continue to exist. In a vicious circle, the science system favours Northern "experts" and scientific knowledge while excluding Southern knowledge, in consequence reinforcing dependencies and inequalities. However, countries of the Global South are increasingly interested in establishing their own science systems in the expectation of gaining the potential benefits of science on economic, social, and environmental development (Conway et al. 2010).[5]

At the same time, research cooperation among Southern and Northern partners on equal terms becomes more important. It is portrayed as a means of linking up to international state-of-the-art research, of accessing different bodies of knowledge, and of connecting with global scientific networks (Commission for Research Partnerships with Developing Countries [KFPE] 2010; Conway et al. 2010; The Royal Society 2011). Strong cooperation patterns have traditionally been in place among researchers in Northern countries. Cooperation between the Global North and the emerging powers of the Global South has become stronger in the last decades as well, with transnational cooperation framed through bilateral science agreements on the national level. To a lesser extent, research cooperation takes place between partners of the Global North and Southern countries classified as lower-middle-income or least-developed countries, within patterns of South-South research cooperation, or as trilateral cooperation (BMBF 2014a, 2016).

Cooperation in research can assume different shapes, ranging from short- or long-term staff exchanges and individual scholarships for international mobility to cooperation in joint international projects and institutional twinning or creating joint research institutions. Research cooperation, as such, differs from development cooperation in not having a predefined normative objective. It may cover all areas of science and research—from basic, disciplinary research to inter- and transdisciplinary cooperation in applied sciences. Research cooperation can be aimed at pure knowledge creation without any further objectives of knowledge application, but it might also target objectives *beyond* science, then being defined as applied research. Next to economic usability—often the primal aim of applied science and science policy—research may pursue other targets, such as ecological sustainability (Jahn 2013; Smith et al. 2010; Ziegler 1998), or social aspects of "development", such as contributing to social equity or making better political decisions (Ely et al. 2010; Gibbons et al. 1994; Jasanoff 2003; Nowotny et al. 2001; Sarewitz et al. 2004; Sismondo 2008).

4.3.1 Science and Sustainable Development

In most societies, "autonomous" and curiosity-driven types of science coexist with "relevant" and problem-focussed types of science (Kaldewey 2013). At the same time, the role of science in and for society in general—or sustainable development in particular—is being debated (Glerup and Horst 2014; also see Stock and Schneidewind 2014).

I would like to propose two potentially conducive relations between science and sustainable development: Science *on* sustainable development and science *for* sustainable development. These are closely related to the concepts of transformation science and transformative science (German Advisory Council on Global Change [WBGU] 2011, 2016), while extending their scope. Science *on* sustainable development encompasses all types of research in the field that create new insights on sustainable development. It fills knowledge gaps and scientifically analyses problems in all areas of sustainable development, such as the effects of climate change, natural resource depletion, social inequalities, interdependencies between dimensions of sustainable development, etc. Given the complexity of sustainable development, as such, many fields of basic and applied research potentially produce relevant knowledge on sustainable development. In addition, research on sustainable development also deals with potential social and technological transformation processes, examines path dependencies and barriers preventing transformations, builds scenarios for different pathways towards sustainability, etc. Progress monitoring and measuring or indicator development for sustainability-related global agreements, such as the Paris Climate Agreement and the 2030 Agenda, are further fields of research *on* sustainable development.

In contrast, science *for* sustainable development is solutions-oriented research that is potentially aimed at transformative change. Researchers engaged in this type of applied research develop different types of solutions or innovations on different scales to target different dimensions of sustainable development. While technical innovations are often prominent, solutions could equally address social practices or governance, including science-based policy advice for sustainable development. If science is viewed in terms of its relevance and applicability for sustainable development, a crucial element is to transform scientific knowledge into *impact* outside of science (Douthwaite et al. 2007; Sarewitz et al. 2004). The process of creating impact—thus describing the relation between science and societal aspects—can be illuminated through the concept of "innovation".

Until today, innovation is predominantly interpreted as an economy-related concept. For analysing science for sustainable development, more encompassing conceptualisations are more suitable, however. Innovation then refers to any novelty implemented in a specific context or to the process of its implementation. In this definition, innovation is not necessarily aimed at economic benefits (Röling 2009). Objects of innovation can be material phenomena, such as a technology, or non-material innovations, such as a new technique, organisational or process-related changes, or social processes (Ul Hassan et al. 2011). Potentially, science-based innovations thus may have various entry points to "the real world". Scientific results may be adopted in the form of an innovative technology, product, or process that leads, for example, to better medical treatments, enhanced food security, or improved adaptation to climate change (Arocena and Sutz 2012; Conway et al. 2010; Douthwaite 2002; Hornidge 2013; Röling 2009; Smith 2009; STEPS Centre 2010). Or they may inspire social innovation, for example, changing public perceptions and individual behaviour, or influencing social or economic policies and governance structures (Sumner et al. 2009).

Transdisciplinary knowledge creation is widely believed to be a mode of research that corresponds well to the objective of applied science for sustainable development. It has been put into practice in transnational research cooperation and, subsequently, the concept has been taken up in policy advice and by policy-makers as an adequate form of effective, science-based problem-solving (Jahn et al. 2012). As a mode of science, transdisciplinarity is recommended to—and applied within—the development research community as well as in sustainability research to create impact beyond publications or patents (KFPE 1998; Stöckli et al. 2012). Transdisciplinary approaches are characterised by problem-orientation, policy-orientation, and/or impact-orientation. In all stages of the research process, partners from academia, civil society, and policy are involved; this is perceived to ensure relevant and suitable results and solutions (Lang et al. 2012; Lyall 2008; Mollinga 2008; Pohl and Hirsch Hadorn 2008). The concept of transdisciplinarity entails the idea of respecting and appreciating diverse knowledge on equal footing. In view of North-South cooperation, symmetric partnerships between researchers from developed countries and developing countries that are based on mutual interest and ownership—including joint agenda-setting, decision-making, implementation, and management—are strived for, but also critically reflected on (see, among others, Bradley 2007; KFPE 1998; Stöckli et al. 2012; Wiesmann et al. 2011; Zingerli 2010). Transnational transdisciplinary cooperation may face difficulties in practice, for example, when certain partners lack adequate funding, or when different partners have different problem definitions. In addition to different socio-economic, institutional, and epistemic backgrounds, diverging research interests and a lack of methodologies on international cooperation can lead to reproducing (neo)colonial patterns or patronage relationships as well as enhancing power imbalances (Bradley 2007; Fuest 2005, 2007; Grosfoguel 2013; Maselli et al. 2006; Zingerli 2010). It is therefore necessary to align practices on the ground with the normative discourse on transdisciplinary partnerships. Although practice and theory thus may deviate, as in other types of cooperation, transnational transdisciplinary cooperation is still believed to be a valuable principle for coming up with implementable solutions as well as an even distribution of benefits stemming from the research process, thereby providing a fruitful mutual experience for all parties involved in the partnership (STEPS Centre 2010; Stöckli et al. 2012).

Next to the potential benefits, more reflexive accounts of the impacts of applied science on society also acknowledge the potential of negative or unintended consequences or trade-offs.[6] For example, science-based innovations leading to economic growth might aggravate inequality at the same time; medical research might not produce the expected impacts on reducing infection rates among certain social groups; or the introduction of a new drought-resistant crop variety might lead to abandoning a more nutritious one (Douthwaite et al. 2001; Sarewitz et al. 2004; Smith 2009).

The scope and the scale addressed through both the science *on* and *for* sustainable development may differ. In view of scope, research may focus on isolated dimensions of sustainable development, such as ecological problems, or it may investigate phenomena from a more encompassing perspective and consider social and economic aspects alongside ecological ones, thus displaying a larger conceptual scope. It may also focus on interconnections or trade-offs between dimensions of sustainable development. In view of scale, research perspectives may address an overarching systemic level, such as a country's innovation system, or it may address the transformation of society as a whole towards sustainability (Geels 2004; Geels and Schot 2007; WBGU 2011). On a smaller scale, research may also target problem analysis and find solutions to concrete sustainability issues at a context-dependent, problem-specific level (Rhodes and Sulston 2009; Sumner et al. 2009). The proposed categories, as often is the case, are not clear-cut but may overlap and blur. Nevertheless, they serve to distinguish between some characteristic features of research on and for sustainable development.

4.4 Governing Science in the Context of the 2030 Agenda

The role of science for and on sustainable development and research cooperation between partners of the Global North and the Global South in global governance as well as national German science policy are the subjects of this section. As shown in Sect. 4.3, science as a specific type of knowledge can be an important cornerstone of sustainable development. Inter- and transnational cooperation play an essential role in interlinking partners and bodies of knowledge globally.

National policies as well as internationally and globally agreed norms are necessary to guide its shape, however. Scholars point to the essential role that policies play in setting a future course for framing societal problems, solutions, and standpoints (Clay and Schaffer 1984). Due to the internationalisation of research and worldwide spread of the technologies produced, national science policies oriented towards international cooperation influence scientific networks and cooperation and become important next to policies focussed on the local or national level (European Commission 2009; Smith 2009; The Royal Society 2011).

At the same time, global norms and agreements in other fields of international cooperation, such as development cooperation, also potentially influence inter- and transnational research cooperation. Hence, norms, agreements, and policies themselves turn into topics of interest, as they set the conditions for cooperation in research to have positive impacts on society, such as sustainable development (Bucar 2010; STEPS Centre 2010).

4.4.1 German Policies for Science Cooperation Versus Policies for Development Cooperation

Transnational research cooperation between partners in the Global North and the Global South touches the political fields of both development policy and science policy. The German case provides an empirical illustration of the importance of the specific political framework of research cooperation between the Global North and South, which determines its potential effects. Although countries differ in view of their political institutions—and the findings therefore cannot be generalised—the separation of policy fields into science policy, on the one hand, and development policy, on the other, can be commonly observed. Along the German example, I argue that the coherence of science policy and development policy objectives on the country level might benefit from a closer focus of global governance mechanisms on the role of research cooperation between the Global South and North—and that it is therefore a worthwhile scientific endeavour to analyse the political context in different national political set-ups.

In the German context, the Federal Ministry of Education and Research (BMBF) is the largest provider of public funds for research cooperation between German researchers and partners in the Global South. Decisively setting the course of cooperation, the policies for research cooperation with developing countries or emerging economies are a field of science policy and not the policies of the Federal Ministry for Economic Cooperation and Development (BMZ). The same division of responsibilities holds true in the European Union (EU), which funds research cooperation between EU member states and developing countries and emerging economies within its Framework Programme for Research and Innovation, which is currently Horizon 2020 (BMBF 2008; European Commission 2015). In other European countries, such as Switzerland and France, the policies and funding for research cooperation are the shared responsibilities of both the ministries of science as well as the ministries of development cooperation (Institut de recherche pour le développement 2012; KFPE 2013).

In view of funding research cooperation with the Global South, the BMBF provides the largest amount of public funding in Germany. BMBF expenditures for cooperation with BRICS countries alone amounted to approximately €47 million in 2012 (BMBF 2014b). In view of BMBF funding for cooperation with other countries of the Global South, the only numbers available were those reported as official development assistance (ODA) expenditures, which increased from €112.7 million in 2012 (BMZ 2013) to €149.9 million in 2015 (Bohnet et al. 2018). Quite likely, these figures include activities of cooperation in education as well as research. Other official sources state that between 2011 and 2015, the BMBF allocated €206 million to cooperation with African partner countries (18. German Federal Parliament 2017). The BMBF's Subdepartment for Sustainability, Climate, Energy has the longest tradition of cooperating with countries of the Global South—both on a political level as well as in funding cooperative research. As with other BMBF research programmes, its framework programme Research for Sustainability Development (FONA) is primarily dedicated to supporting German researchers. Nevertheless, in the scope of the programme, many initiatives for cooperation between Germany and the Global South have been funded. The importance given to the international dimension of sustainability and environmental issues is shown in the high amount of expenditures for inter- and transnational cooperation, which amounted to 20 per cent of the total funds of FONA, €100 million per year, from 2010 to 2014 (Fischer and Mennicken 2013). Larger funding initiatives for research cooperation with partners in the Global South include funding initiatives on Integrated Water Resources Management (IWRM) (BMBF 2004a) and sustainable Megacities (BMBF 2004b), as well as the establishment of two Regional Climate Science Service Centres in Western and Southern Africa in 2010, now in their second funding phases (BMBF 2019).

The BMZ funds activities within higher education and research, including individual scholarships and university partnerships for science management, with approximately €50 million per year (18. German Federal Parliament 2017). The BMZ's policies for research cooperation, as part of the development policy portfolio, are often coupled with (higher) education (BMZ 2015). BMZ programmes instead target infrastructural measures and capacity development in the higher education sector. For example, the BMZ supports cooperation with higher education institutions in developing countries, aligning curricula to job market demands, sharpening research profiles, and fostering internationalisation. In addition, the BMZ funds some research through intermediary organisations, such as the German Academic Exchange Service (DAAD), the Alexander von Humboldt Foundation, and the Deutsche Gesellschaft für Internationale Zusammenarbeit (GIZ). For example, funded through the BMZ, the DAAD and GIZ cooperated with the Commission of the African Union to set up the Pan African University's Institute of Water and Energy Sciences. Aiming at fostering higher education, science, and technological development across Africa, the Pan African University established new institutes at existing research centres in addition to educating postgraduates as well as PhD candidates and conducting applied research (German Academic Exchange Service 2016; Gesellschaft für Internationale Zusammenarbeit 2016). Distinguishing more specifically between funding for higher education and funding for research, as such, shows that although higher education is funded comprehensively within the BMZ's portfolio, compared to other sources of research cooperation funding—and also compared to the BMZ's overall expenditures—its funds for research-related activities are small (BMBF 2014b).

4.4.2 Coherence of German Science Policy and Development Policy

Next to the source of funding for research cooperation between partners of the Global North and the Global South, the policy objectives of different ministries also vary. In view of the policies for research cooperation, the different institutional and discursive frameworks of the BMBF and the BMZ influence the objectives, mode, and target groups of cooperation. This is essential, also in view of policy coherence for development.

The BMBF, as such, is not primarily aimed at international policy-making, but rather focusses on the German national context in its policies and funding measures. Nevertheless, international cooperation is part of its policy spectrum. Across its departments, the BMBF funds international research cooperation within the scope of different strategies, within different funding initiatives, with different partner countries, on different topics, and with different objectives (BMBF 2014c). The motivation for funding research cooperation with developing and emerging countries is *not* predominantly a concern for global sustainable development. It is of equal importance to foster German interests, such as positioning Germany as a player on future markets or contributing to technology exports (Schwachula 2019).[7]

To ensure policy coherence, ministries are legally obliged to cooperate with the Joint Rules of Procedure of the Federal Ministries (Cabinet of Germany 2011). At the same time, the German constitution grants a high degree of autonomy to each ministry, which counteracts coherence. In this sense, the fate of the Internationalisation Strategy (BMBF 2008, 2016), which was issued by the BMBF but is inter-ministerial in scope, and the International Cooperation Action Plan (BMBF 2014a) is illustrative. Although on paper the documents set an overarching framework for funding international cooperation in education and research across the entire German government, the documents are not binding.

In addition, policy coherence is endangered by rivalries between ministries. Instead of viewing ministries as non-political entities of administration, the relations between the BMBF and the BMZ illustrate that policy-makers also defend their political turf, especially when policy fields overlap. Policies, programmes, and funding measures are the outcomes of previous processes of policy-making, and therefore they are the products of knowledge politics, of strategic or coincidental integration, or the inclusion of different actors in the policy process. They are subject to bureaucratic rules and regulations and coined by pre-existing norms, values, and beliefs, which finally crystallise in policies.

I argue that the causes of incoherent policies lie within the different logics and perspectives on cooperation with the Global South. Neither the processes of policy-making nor policy outcomes are reconciled, as the BMBF aims to maintain its own political autonomy, whereas the BMZ is not in a position to prescribe policy coherence for development (Schwachula 2019). Despite distancing itself from the policy rationales of the BMZ, however, the BMBF is able to report some of its activities as ODA, contributing 0.9 per cent of the German ODA quota, which ranked it fourth among the German federal ministries in 2015 (Bohnet et al. 2018).

4.4.3 Global Governance of Science for Sustainable Development

More traditional types of development cooperation are defined, negotiated, and aligned on the global level in view of their modes of cooperation, thematic responsibilities, and development targets, such as the SDGs. Hence, global governance structures are in place for development cooperation. In contrast to other types of cooperation, however, science cooperation between the Global North and South has received little attention in global governance and is barely regulated. Thus, research cooperation is nationally and internationally mostly "ungoverned", which is surprising in view of its high potential as a type of cooperation conducive to sustainable development and the SDGs, in particular. The existing institutions and norms of (sustainable) development on the global scale curiously still have not put North-South research cooperation into the spotlight.

International development agreements such as the Paris Declaration on Aid Effectiveness, its follow-up Accra Agenda for Action (Organisation for Economic Co-operation and Development [OECD] 2008), the Busan Partnership for Effective Development Co-operation (OECD 2011), and the following GPEDC set an overarching framework for national policies, such as the development policy of the BMZ, as well as for non-state action.

In contrast to development policy, the BMBF's science policy, which is directed at transnational cooperation, is *not* bound to fulfilling international agreements relating to sustainable development, such as the 2030 Agenda and its SDGs. Thus, international development targets and agreements are of subordinate importance for the political framing of science cooperation between the Global North and the Global South. BMBF funding for research on sustainable development, in cooperation with partners from the Global South, *may* be reported as part of German ODA—but it does not *have* to be. The BMBF could use at least part of its resources to fund entirely different research activities. International political agreements in the context of the G20 rarely address the role of science cooperation for sustainable development (Cabinet of Germany 2018).

Separate international and global policies or governance mechanisms for transnational research partnerships between the Global North and the Global South, as an equivalent to development cooperation, do not exist. In view of principles of cooperation and their conduciveness to sustainable development, transnational research cooperation in practice often takes place outside of global agreements. The 2030 Agenda, as such, does not specifically conceptualise knowledge or science cooperation as a contribution to development cooperation. In its portrayal of knowledge for development, the document remains ambiguous and vague. Although it portrays the SDGs as global, encompassing concerns, science is mainly portrayed in view of its economic viability, for example through technology development. Although SDG target 17.6 specifically calls for science cooperation—including North-South, South-South, and triangular cooperation—it only relates to technology development.

Next to technology development, the 2030 Agenda specifically refers to the accompanying task of research, such as developing indicators and monitoring implementation. In the agenda, the institutionalisation of an online platform for information on existing science and technology initiatives is called for (however, such a platform was only available in a test version at the time of research) (UN 2018a). Institutions surrounding the 2030 Agenda, such as the High-level Political Forum on Sustainable Development (HLPF), and the voluntary national reviews rely on scientific data collection for the SDGs. Results of a yearly UN-convened Multi-stakeholder Forum on Science, Technology and Innovation for the Sustainable Development Goals are fed into the HLPF (UN 2018b). The UN additionally mandates an international group of scientists with elaborating a science-based Global Sustainable Development Report for strengthening science-policy interfaces (UN 2018c).

Beyond technology development and accompanying research on sustainable development, however, the 2030 Agenda, as such, does not refer to transnational research cooperation as a beneficial type of partnership for encompassing sustainable development. Target 17.16, on multi-stakeholder partnerships, makes no reference to science, or to different types of knowledge at all (UN 2015). Cummings et al. therefore conclude "that there is a mismatch between the transformative vision and strategy within the SDGs and the non-transformative nature of the means of implementation and the goals and targets" and call for a more inclusive, pluralist perspective on knowledge for development (Cummings et al. 2018, p. 738).

The development-related agreements, institutions, and norms established by the members of the Organisation for Economic Co-operation and Development (OECD) do not cover the role of science, as such—more specifically, they also do not adequately cover the role of research cooperation between partners of the Global North and South. The Paris Declaration (2005) does not allude to science or research at all. The Accra Agenda for Action mentions research institutes only in the context of taking "an active role in dialogue on development policy and on the role of aid in contributing to countries' development objectives" (OECD 2008, p. 16). The Busan Partnership Agreement, while highlighting the role of new actors in cooperation and alluding to the importance of knowledge, does not consider the role of science beyond its role of monitoring and assessing the performance of development institutions (OECD 2011). Following up on the Busan Partnership Agreement, the GPEDC, as a shared initiative between the UN and the OECD, aims at effective partnerships for reaching the 2030 Agenda. It is based on four principles: joint ownership, focus on results, inclusive development partnerships, transparency and accountability (OECD and UNDP 2019). Although it promotes a "whole of society approach to development", the role of cooperation with research is neglected, whereas multi-stakeholder partnerships with civil society organisations and the private sector are specifically encouraged.

The GPEDC attributes a substantial role to monitoring, data, and evidence, and thus to research accompanying the implementation of the GPEDC's objectives (OECD and UNDP 2019). The GPEDC also acknowledges the important role of knowledge for development. As an objective, the work programme of 2017/2018 stated that knowledge sharing should be enabled by "[b]ringing together the learning, knowledge and technology available across constituencies to help scale development solutions at a faster pace" (GPEDC 2017, p. 5). Aiming at developing into a knowledge-sharing hub for development actors on different levels, the GPEDC also established an online knowledge platform as a "one-stop shop to evidence-based solutions, peer learning and networking to advance the effectiveness of all development efforts, for achievement of national priorities and the SDGs" (GPEDC 2019). However, researchers are not among the listed social actors for cooperating in development, nor is science included as a topic of discussion in view of its potential benefits.

The neglect of research cooperation in development norms and partnerships is mirrored in the low levels of research funding officially reported as ODA, although the OECD Development Assistance Committee's (DAC) reporting directives for ODA actually would allow research activities to be reported as ODA:

> Research includes financing by the official sector, whether in the donor country or elsewhere, of research into the problems of developing countries. This may be either (i) undertaken by an agency or institution whose main purpose is to promote the economic growth or welfare of developing countries, or (ii) commissioned or approved, and financed or part-financed, by an official body from a general purpose institution with the specific aim of promoting the economic growth or welfare of developing countries. (OECD-DAC Working Party on Development Finance Statistics 2018, p. 30)

Interestingly, thus, the OECD reporting guidelines deviate from the GPEDC's discourse by specifically mentioning research as a means of ODA. For both GPEDC documents as well as 2030 Agenda documents, it holds true that—beyond a very general reference to research for development, that is, research on the problems of the Global South, or technology-oriented research and innovation[8]—none of the documents or knowledge platforms suggest any rules or guidelines on the role of research, as such, or on principles of cooperation in transnational research. Accordingly, neither topics, nor principles, nor modes, nor partner regions of cooperation are regulated—none are incentivised, none are forbidden. Potentially, any researchers from the Global North may decide to cooperate with partners in the Global South on almost any given topic, in any given mode—and potentially also report it as ODA.

I argue that it is worthwhile to scrutinise the gaps in global governance for research cooperation between partners in the Global South and North, as they may aggravate policy incoherence on the national level. The example of

Germany illustrates that, without informal agreements or formal rules on the international or global level, science policy for international cooperation may pursue objectives that are detached from—and potentially even run contrary to—those of development policy. In addition, the lack of detailed criteria for reporting science cooperation may have detrimental effects: In practice, this leads to research partnerships that are reported as ODA while not meeting the partnership principles agreed upon, as I elaborate below.

In appraising the absence of regulations and norms—both formal and informal—for transnational research cooperation, the concept of freedom of research has to be taken into account, a freedom that is granted to research in most democratic national constitutions in the Global North as well as the Global South. Some philosophers of science even perceive the autonomy of science as being the crucial element of ensuring its creativity and productivity (Polanyi 2000). In the science systems of most countries, science policy enables curiosity-driven, autonomous research, while also guiding research towards specific societal aims.

Science is thus promoted as a means of reaching an objective *beyond* science, within other parts of society (Sarewitz et al. 2004; Sarewitz and Pielke 2007). In consequence, research cooperation is never entirely free of being governed. Research on some topics or locations is restricted or enabled by certain rules: For example, ethical principles for medical research, aimed at protecting the rights and lives of research participants, are internationally agreed upon (World Health Organization 2019). On topics such as nuclear research, transnational research cooperation is restricted due to security issues, for example, between EU countries and Iran (DLR Project Management Agency 2019).

However, governing science does not always imply that it is restricted. Conventions, rules, and norms may also *enable* or incentivise certain types of science or research cooperation. For example, in an attempt to enable scientific cooperation, the Arctic Council issued an agreement on research cooperation in and on the Arctic (Arctic Council 2017). In this light, global agreements may help guide transnational research cooperation between the Global South and the Global North towards becoming more conducive to sustainable development.

An explicit normative framework for research cooperation on the global level entailing principles of fair and successful cooperation, such as partnership, ownership, and benefit-sharing, might enhance policy coherence in, for example, the German case, where national science policies for transnational cooperation with the Global South are not aligned with policies for sustainable development. The field of science policy, even if it is oriented towards transnational cooperation with the Global South, is untouched by any global norms or regulations, thus it is open to deviations from globally agreed targets. In the German context, the bargaining power of actors within the BMBF, who pursue development-oriented targets of research policy, may be strengthened by integrating science cooperation among Northern and Southern partners more explicitly into the global development agenda. It would provide additional global legitimation for research policies targeting global development, which often compete against nationally oriented policy rationales. A focus on research partnerships on the global agenda might also strengthen the position of the BMZ or comparable development ministries where it concerns the enforcement of policy coherence of other political fields with developmental objectives.

The process of the policy design of older German funding initiatives for international cooperation, such as the IWRM initiative (BMBF 2004a) and the Megacities initiative (BMBF 2004b), illustrates why gaps in global governance mechanisms, in view of transnational research, may have detrimental effects. Both funding measures were aimed at cooperation with different partner countries in the Global South, ranging from Namibia, Uzbekistan, Mongolia, Brazil, Iran, and Peru to South Africa, among others. Despite their international focus, the funding programmes were unilaterally designed by the BMBF according to German research interests, and in the case of the IWRM initiative, also according to German business interests.[9] They were *not* co-designed or co-financed by partner countries. Hence, this exclusion of Southern partners in setting agendas and designing cooperation policies ran contrary to any principles of ownership and partnership, as specified in the GPEDC. Furthermore, the mode of agenda-setting as well as the funding modalities, which only allowed for minimal funds for Southern researchers, had severe consequences for the transnational research projects implemented. Effects ranged from practical problems, such as finding funding for researchers in the Southern partner country, to the ethical problem of repeating old patterns of cooperation between well-paid foreign experts and local researchers as mere recipients of knowledge—and in some cases the effects led to promoting technologies as a solution at the expense of social or other types of innovation (Schwachula 2019). Despite this mismatch with norms for development cooperation, research cooperation projects such as those in the IWRM and Megacities funding initiatives were reported as ODA. This phenomenon is not restricted to Germany; similar criticism has been voiced in view of the British Global Challenges Research Fund for not supporting equitable partnerships, despite being reported as ODA (Fransman and Newman 2019).

More recent science cooperation funding, such as the BMBF's German–African Regional Science Service Centres, offers examples of more inclusive agenda-setting and policy design. During the creation of these centres, the BMBF and the governments of Southern and West African countries negotiated on topics and funding before the large-scale projects were initiated in 2010. These projects were reported as ODA and also complied with internationally agreed partnership principles of development cooperation. This, however, was a lucky coincidence of voluntary alignment and cannot be attributed to a steering effect of the global governance framework, as such.

4.5 Conclusions

As argued throughout this contribution, research cooperation between the Global North and the Global South may be a complementary means of reaching the SDGs. It should therefore be raised onto the global development agenda. Providing a conducive normative framework for transnational research cooperation between partners of the Global South and North could also contribute to setting the conditions right for fair, fruitful, and thereby "successful" cooperation. Although the inclusion of different stakeholders—along with their perspectives and types of knowledge—is often portrayed as the most effective way of solution-oriented research, the appreciation of diverse bodies of knowledge is also a matter of mutual respect as an intrinsic value. In this sense, principles for transnational cooperation in research should extend beyond principles of effectiveness, as in the GPEDC's definition: Next to the *effective* production of relevant new knowledge, principles of research cooperation should also include the ideas of *fairness* and *equity* within the partnership (Fransman and Newman 2019). Beyond the impacts of creating new knowledge, adding fairness and equity as partnership principles can contribute to structural changes, such as more equity in the global system of knowledge production and representation, thereby also counteracting global inequalities, as such.

As shown in Sect. 4.3, in the context of sustainable development, science cooperation potentially is a form of knowledge cooperation among equal partners who jointly produce relevant new insights and generate innovations for sustainable development. It is important to point out that equity in this sense does not refer to the level of integration into the global system of science. This would require all partners to start from a level playing field, which at present is not given, due to the existing inequalities in the global system of science production and representation and different levels of access to funding. Fairness and equity as key elements of cooperation are rather an approach towards appreciating diverse stances, perspectives, and knowledge in research cooperation. Filling these principles with life means enabling all partners to partake in agenda-setting, decision-taking, and the process of research on equal footing, thereby fostering all partners to become independent players within the global system of science production and representation in the long run.

In contrast to knowledge transfer from Northern partners to Southern partners, cooperation in research offers the potential for cooperation on equal terms. It is therefore highly suitable to put the new global development paradigm into cooperation practice. However, although science cooperation between partners in the Global South and the Global North has a high potential for contributing to sustainable development, its potential is currently not being fully tapped. Without regulating modes of agenda-setting for research cooperation, and without incentivising cooperation on certain topics, national policy-makers for science cooperation may frame science and development issues and direct the flows of research funds according to political priorities—possibly negatively affecting the SDGs.

Despite a shifting paradigm towards "global development", entailing the idea that all types of knowledge and experiences count (Horner and Hulme 2017), technology transfer and capacity development continue to be the most common knowledge-related modes of cooperation, firmly grounded in the ongoing development norms, including the 2030 Agenda as well as the GPEDC. However, these activities essentially aim at knowledge flows from knowledgeable, that is, Northern partners, to those partners in the South who need to "catch up" knowledge-wise, thus following a Western or Northern model of development and modernity (Shamsavari 2007; Smith 2009). Hence, despite contrary global rhetoric, the idea of one-way knowledge transfer or capacity development, which is inherently based on the assumption of a superiority of Western or Northern knowledge, persists in development policy and practices.

However, we face times of shifting global power constellations, combined with an urgency of combating climate change and the necessity of turning towards more sustainable development pathways worldwide. In this regard, science cooperation seems to be an adequate cooperation pattern. Research cooperation may inspire leapfrogging developments in the Global South and lead to the development of alternative solutions for the Global North. In consequence, jointly producing new knowledge through research, as well as exchanging knowledge on equal terms, should receive much more attention as adequate types of knowledge cooperation for achieving sustainable development. If sustainable development is taken seriously as a global agenda, the mode of cooperation should mirror the fact that partners from all countries—as developing countries in certain aspects of social, economic, or ecological development—need access to new knowledge, and thus a one-way transfer of knowledge will not suffice. Instead, partners need to jointly create novel insights.

Specific topics of sustainable development that affect partners on both sides could present starting points for comparative research in international teams. Issues such as social inequality on different scales, carbon-neutral development, sustainable urban development, and sustainable production and consumption present challenges in most countries (WBGU 2011, 2016). Research cooperation on these topics might enhance mutual learning instead of repeating traditional patterns of cooperation; jointly developing pathways might enable sustainable development in all partner countries.

At the moment, the gaps in global governance in view of sustainability-oriented transnational research cooperation pose a risk rather than an opportunity: *First*, the gap negatively affects the coherence of development policy and research policy at the national level. *Second*, the gap enhances the risk of research cooperation reproducing antiquated patterns of North-South cooperation, thereby reifying global inequalities; *third*, the gap in global governance bears the risk of turning certain sustainability-related problems into global "orphan issues" that lack funding structures as well as powerful speakers raising these topics on the national science policy agenda; and *fourth*, the potential of research cooperation to develop innovative solutions for sustainable development is not being adequately tapped.

An agreement on transnational research cooperation between partners in the Global North and the Global South would therefore be beneficial. Such an agreement should *first*, enhance an equitable mode of cooperation among different stakeholders (inter- and transdisciplinary); *second*, enable science cooperation in view of sustainability topics on various scales (local and global; problem-specific or systemic entry points), and it should *third*, support open-ended, reflexive research for all kinds of solutions, ranging from social to technological innovations.

Notes

1. In this paper, the terms "research cooperation" and "science cooperation" are used interchangeably.
2. The term "Global South" is used here to depict the countries located mainly in the Global South that are enlisted as recipients of official development assistance (ODA) by the Organisation for Economic Co-operation and Development (OECD), which in turn draws on the World Bank's numbers on gross national income (OECD 2018).
3. Successful examples include different types of innovations stemming from transdisciplinary, transnational research cooperation projects focussed on sustainable urbanisation and sustainable water management between partners from Germany and the Global South. Solutions ranged from city development plans to decision support systems, governance schemes, eco-parks, water treatment facilities, and awareness-raising activities, among others (Schwachula 2019).
4. In this sense, Kuhn's seminal work on scientific "paradigms" (1962) as well as Foucault's work on "epistemes" (Foucault 2005 [1966]; 1972) show how scientific knowledge is enabled, limited, directed, interrupted, and re-interpreted through specific underlying meaning schemes; Knorr-Cetina (1999) demonstrates that different types and institutions of knowledge production disintegrate science into scattered disciplines with their own standards, definitions, modes, and world views.
5. It remains to be investigated if the rise of Southern scientific powers leads to changes within the global system of knowledge production in the long run, comparable to the changes occurring with the rise of Southern donors and South-South cooperation in technical development cooperation.
6. In the light of the potential positive or negative impacts of solution-oriented research, traditional indicators of research success, such as bibliometric data, are not adequate, as they do not measure any effects outside of the science system. Impact measurement of science, however, is difficult and still in an early stage (Douthwaite 2002; Douthwaite et al. 2007; Ely and Oxley 2014; Martin 2011; Maselli et al. 2006; STEPS Centre 2010; Sumner et al. 2009).
7. Based on a constructivist understanding, I consider policy and funding initiatives as concrete outcomes of knowledge exchange and negotiations among different actors, with different levels of power, pursuing different objectives in view of global, inter- and transnational cooperation in research.

8. As previously analysed, the OECD and the UN have a history of conceptualising science, technology, and innovation, mainly with regard to their economic viability (Schwachula et al. 2014).
9. Viewed from a development perspective, the practice of technology-export to the Global South through research cooperation (ODA-classified) might be categorised as "informal tied aid", which scholars perceive as being potentially harmful and a *hindrance* to sustainable development in developing countries (Carbone 2014).

REFERENCES

18. German Federal Parliament. (2017). *Unterrichtung durch die Bundesregierung: Strategie der Bundesregierung zur Internationalisierung von Bildung, Wissenschaft und Forschung* (Drucksache 18/ 11100). Berlin: Cabinet of Germany.

Acosta Espinosa, A. (2008). El buen vivir, una oportunidad por construir. *Ecuador Debate, 75*, 33–48.

Agrawal, A. (1995). Dismantling the divide between indigenous and scientific knowledge. *Development and Change, 26*(3), 413–439.

Arctic Council. (2017). *Agreement on enhancing international Arctic scientific cooperation.* https://oaarchive.arctic-council.org/handle/11374/1916.

Arocena, R., & Sutz, J. (2010). Weak knowledge demand in the South: Learning divides and innovation policies. *Science and Public Policy, 37*(8), 571–582.

Arocena, R., & Sutz, J. (2012). Research and innovation policies for social inclusion: An opportunity for developing countries. *Innovation and Development, 2*(1), 147–158.

BMBF (German Federal Ministry of Education and Research). (2004a). *Bekanntmachung von Richtlinien zur Förderung eines Ideenwettbewerbs zur Vorbereitung von Projekten im Rahmen des Förderschwerpunktes "Integriertes Wasserressourcen-Management (IWRM) einschließlich des notwendigen Technologie—und Know how-Transfers".* http://www.bmbf.de/foerderungen/2434.php.

BMBF. (2004b). *Bekanntmachung "Forschung für die nachhaltige Entwicklung der Megastädte von morgen".* https://www.bmbf.de/foerderungen/bekanntmachung-62.html.

BMBF. (2008). *Strengthening Germany's role in the global knowledge society. Strategy of the Federal Government for the internationalization of science and research.* Bonn and Berlin: Author.

BMBF. (2014a). *The BMBF's international cooperation action plan: Summary of the central points.* Berlin: Author.

BMBF (2014b). *Bundesbericht Forschung und Innovation 2014.* Bonn and Berlin: Author.

BMBF. (2014c). *Political staff and organization.* http://www.bmbf.de/en/5625.php.

BMBF. (2016). *Internationalisation of education, science and research. Strategy of the Federal Government.* Bonn and Berlin: Author.

BMBF. (2019). *Afrika: Partner im Kampf gegen den Klimawandel.* https://www.bmbf.de/de/afrika-partner-im-kampf-gegen-den-klimawandel-9250.html.

BMZ (German Federal Ministry for Economic Cooperation and Development). (2013). *Mittelherkunft der bi- und multilateralen ODA 2011–2012*. Bonn and Berlin: Author.

BMZ. (2015). *BMZ education strategy: Creating equitable opportunities for quality education*. Bonn and Berlin: Author.

Bohnet, M., Klingebiel, S., & Marschall, P. (2018). *Die Struktur der deutschen öffentlichen Entwicklungszusammenarbeit: Hintergründe, Trends und Implikationen für das BMZ und andere Bundesressorts* (Discussion Paper 15/2018). Bonn: Deutsches Institut für Entwicklungspolitik / German Development Institute (DIE).

Bradley, M. (2007). *North-South research partnerships: Challenges, responses and trends* (IDRC, Canadian Partnerships Working Paper 1). Ottawa, ON: International Development Research Centre.

Bucar, M. (2010). *Science and technology for development: Coherence of the common EU R&D policy with development policy objectives* (Discussion Paper 19/2010). Bonn: Deutsches Institut für Entwicklungspolitik / German Development Institute (DIE).

Cabinet of Germany. (2011). *Joint rules of procedure of the Federal Ministries—Gemeinsame Geschäftsordnung der Bundesministerien (GGO)*. Berlin: Federal Ministry of the Interior, Building and Community.

Cabinet of Germany. (2018). *Gruppe der Zwanzig: Wissenswertes rund um die G20*. Berlin: Federal Ministry of the Interior, Building and Community.

Carbone, M. (2014). Much ado about nothing? The European Union and the global politics of untying aid. *Contemporary Politics, 20*(1), 103–117.

Chataway, J., Smith, J., & Wield, D. (2006). *Science and technology partnerships for poverty alleviation in Africa* (ESRC Innogen Centre Working Paper 45). Edinburgh and Milton Keynes: ESRC Innogen Centre.

Clay, E. J., & Schaffer, B. (1984). *Room for manoeuvre: An exploration of public policy planning in agricultural and rural development*. Cranbury, NJ: Associated University Press.

Conway, G., Waage, J., & Delaney, S. (2010). *Science and innovation for development*. London: UK Collaborative on Development Sciences.

Cowen, M. P., & Shenton, R. R. (2003). *Doctrines of development*. New York, NY: Routledge.

Crewe, E., & Harrison, E. (1998). *Whose development? An ethnography of aid*. London and New York, NY: Zed Books.

Cummings, S., & Hoebink, P. (2017). Representation of academics from developing countries as authors and editorial board members in scientific journals: Does this matter to the field of development studies? *The European Journal of Development Research, 29*(2), 369–383.

Cummings, S., Regeer, B., de Haan, L., Zweekhorst, M., & Bunders, J. (2018). Critical discourse analysis of perspectives on knowledge and the knowledge society within the sustainable development goals. *Development Policy Review, 36*(6), 727–742.

Della Faille, D. (2011). Discourse analysis in international development studies: Mapping some contemporary contributions. *Journal of Multicultural Discourses, 6*(3), 215–235.

DLR Project Management Agency. (2019). *Iran: Überblick zur internationalen Kooperation*. https://www.kooperation-international.de/laender/asien/iran/zusammenfassung/ueberblick-zur-internationalen-kooperation/.

Douthwaite, B. (2002). *Enabling innovation: A practical guide to understanding and fostering technological change.* London and New York, NY: Zed Books.

Douthwaite, B., Alvarez, S., Cook, S., George, P., Howell, J., Mackay, R., et al. (2007). Participatory impact pathways analysis: A practical application of program theory in research-for-development. *The Canadian Journal of Program Evaluation, 22*(2), 127–159.

Douthwaite, B., deHaan, N., Manyong, V., & Keatinge, J. D. H. (2001). Blending "hard" and "soft" science: The "Follow the Technology" approach to catalyzing and evaluating technology change. *Conservation Ecology, 5*(2), Art. 13. https://www.ecologyandsociety.org/vol5/iss2/art13/manuscript.html.

Ely, A., Leach, M., Scoones, I., & Stirling, A. (2010). A new manifesto for innovation, sustainability and development—Response to Rhodes and Sulston. *European Journal of Development Research, 22*(4), 586–588.

Ely, A., & Oxley, N. (2014). *STEPS Centre research: Our approach to impact* (STEPS Working Paper 60). Brighton: STEPS Centre.

Escobar, A. (1992). Reflections on "development": Grassroots approaches and alternative politics in the third world. *Futures, 24*(5), 411–436.

Esteva, G. (2010). Development. In W. Sachs (Ed.), *The development dictionary: A guide to knowledge as power* (2nd ed., pp. 1–23). London and New York, NY: Zed Books.

European Commission. (2009). *Drivers of international collaboration in research.* In Technopolis Group and Manchester Institute of Innovation Research (Eds.). Brussels: Author.

European Commission (2015). *Horizon 2020.* http://ec.europa.eu/programmes/horizon2020/.

Evers, H.-D. (2000). *Epistemic cultures: Towards a new sociology of knowledge* (Department of Sociology Working Papers 151). Singapore: National University of Singapore.

Evers, H.-D., Gerke, S., & Menkhof, T. (2006). *Wissen und Entwicklung-Strategien für den Aufbau einer Wissensgesellschaft* (ZEF Policy Briefs 6). Bonn: Center for Development Research (ZEF).

Fischer, A., & Mennicken, L. (2013). *FONA international: Innovation und Umsetzung.* Presented at the 10. BMBF-Forum für Nachhaltigkeit, Leipzig. Bonn: Federal Ministry of Education and Research.

Foucault, M. (1972). *The archaeology of knowledge—l'archéologie du savoir.* New York, NY: Pantheon.

Foucault, M. (1980). *Power/knowledge: Selected interviews and other writings, 1972–1977.* C. Gordon (Ed.). New York, NY: Pantheon Books.

Foucault, M. (2005). *The order of things: An archaeology of the human sciences—les mots et les choses.* London and New York, NY: Routledge.

Fransman, J., & Newman, K. (2019). Rethinking research partnerships: Evidence and the politics of participation in research partnerships for international development. *Journal of International Development, 31*(7), 523–544.

Fuest, V. (2005). *Partnerschaft, Patronage oder Paternalismus? Eine empirische Analyse der Praxis universitärer Forschungskooperation mit Entwicklungsländern* (ZEF Working Paper Series 9). Bonn: Center for Development Research (ZEF).

Fuest, V. (2007). German-African research co-operation: Practices, problems and policies. *Africa Spectrum, 42*(3), 483–505.

Gardner, K., & Lewis, D. (2000). Dominant paradigms overturned or "business as usual"? Development discourse and the white paper on international development. *Critique of Anthropology, 20*(1), 15–29.

Geels, F. W. (2004). From sectoral systems of innovation to socio-technical systems: Insights about dynamics and change from sociology and institutional theory. *Research Policy, 33*(6–7), 897–920.

Geels, F. W., & Schot, J. (2007). Typology of sociotechnical transition pathways. *Research Policy, 36*(3), 399–417.

German Academic Exchange Service. (2016). *Pan African University (PAU)*. https://www.daad.de/en/information-services-for-higher-education-institutions/further-information-on-daad-programmes/pauwes/.

Gesellschaft für Internationale Zusammenarbeit. (2016). *Ein Wissenschaftsnetzwerk für Afrikas Entwicklung: Die Panafrikanische Universität*. https://www.giz.de/de/weltweit/26267.html.

Gibbons, M., Limoges, C., Nowotny, H., Schwartzman, S., Scott, P., & Trow, M. (1994). *The new production of knowledge: The dynamics of science and research in contemporary societies*. London: Sage.

Glerup, C., & Horst, M. (2014). Mapping "social responsibility" in science. *Journal of Responsible Innovation, 1*(1), 31–50.

Gore, C. (2000). The rise and fall of the Washington Consensus as a paradigm for developing countries. *World Development, 28*(5), 789–804.

GPEDC (Global Partnership for Effective Development Co-operation). (2017). *2017 and 2018 programme of work*. http://effectivecooperation.org/wp-content/uploads/2017/05/2017-18-Global-Partnership-Work-Programme.pdf.

GPEDC (2019). *GPEDC knowledge platform*. https://knowledge.effectivecooperation.org/.

Grosfoguel, R. (2013). The structure of knowledge in Westernized universities: Epistemic racism/sexism and the four genocides/epistemicides of the long 16th century. *Human Architecture: Journal of the Sociology of Self-Knowledge, 11*(1), 73–90.

Hirsch Hadorn, G., Bradley, D., Pohl, C., Rist, S., & Wiesmann, U. (2006). Implications of transdisciplinarity for sustainability research. *Ecological Economics, 60*(1), 119–128.

Horner, R., & Hulme, D. (2017). *Converging divergence? Unpacking the new geography of 21st century global development* (GDI Working Papers 2017–010). Manchester: University of Manchester.

Hornidge, A.-K. (2012). "Knowledge" in development discourse: A critical review. In A.-K. Hornidge & C. Antweiler (Eds.), *Environmental uncertainty and local knowledge: Southeast Asia as a laboratory of global ecological change* (pp. 21–54). Bielefeld: Transcript.

Hornidge, A.-K. (2013). "Knowledge", "knowledge society" & "knowledge for development": Studying discourses of knowledge in an international context. In R. Keller & I. Truschkat (Eds.), *Methodologie und Praxis der Wissenssoziologischen Diskursanalyse* (Vol. 1, pp. 397–424)., *Interdisziplinäre Perspektiven* Wiesbaden: Springer VS Verlag.

Hornidge, A.-K. (2014a). Wissensdiskurse: Normativ, faktisch, hegemonial. *Soziale Welt, 65*, 7–24.

Hornidge, A.-K. (2014b). *Discourses of knowledge: Normative, factual, hegemonic* (Habilitationsschrift). Bonn: Rheinische Friedrich-Wilhelms-Universität Bonn.

Hulme, D. (2016). *Should rich nations help the poor?* Cambridge and Malden, MA: Polity Press.

Illi, H. (2001). *Development experts at the interface: An inquiry into the knowledge dimension of allocative and strategic action in the arena of a German/Nepalese health development project.* Bielefeld: Sociology of Development Research Center, Bielefeld University.

Institut de recherche pour le développement. (2012). *IRD annual report.* Marseille: Author.

Jahn, T. (2013). Wissenschaft für eine nachhaltige Entwicklung braucht eine kritische Orientierung. *GAIA—Ecological Perspectives for Science and Society, 22*(1), 29–33.

Jahn, T., Bergmann, M., & Keil, F. (2012). Transdisciplinarity: Between mainstreaming and marginalization. *Ecological Economics, 79,* 1–10.

Janus, H., Klingebiel, S., & Paulo, S. (2015). Beyond aid: A conceptual perspective on the transformation of development cooperation. *Journal of International Development, 27*(2), 155–169.

Jasanoff, S. (2003). Technologies of humility: Citizen participation in governing science. *Minerva, 41*(3), 223–244.

Kaldewey, D. (2013). *Wahrheit und Nützlichkeit: Selbstbeschreibungen der Wissenschaft zwischen Autonomie und gesellschaftlicher Relevanz.* Bielefeld: Transcript.

Keller, R. (2003). Der Müll der Gesellschaft: Eine wissenssoziologische Diskursanalyse. In R. Keller, A. Hirseland, W. Schneider, & W. Viehöver (Eds.), *Handbuch Sozialwissenschaftliche Diskursanalyse (Band 2: Forschungspraxis)* (pp. 197–232). Opladen: Leske und Budrich.

Keller, R. (2005). Analysing discourse. An approach from the sociology of knowledge. *Forum Qualitative Sozialforschung / Forum: Qualitative Social Research, 6*(3), Art. 32.

Keller, R. (2013). *Doing discourse research: An introduction for social scientists.* Los Angeles, CA: Sage.

KFPE (Commission for Research Partnerships with Developing Countries). (1998). *Guidelines for research in partnership with developing countries: 11 principles.* Bern: Author.

KFPE. (2010). *Weshalb mehr Forschungskooperation mit den Ländern des Südens und Ostens?* (Diskussionspapiere der KFPE). Bern: Author.

KFPE. (2013). *Jahresbericht 2012 der KFPE.* https://naturwissenschaften.ch/organisations/kfpe/about_kfpe/annual_reports.

Klochikhin, E. A. (2012). Linking development and innovation: What does technological change bring to the society? *European Journal of Development Research, 24*(1), 41–55.

Knorr-Cetina, K. (1999). *Epistemic cultures: How the sciences make knowledge.* Cambridge, MA: Harvard University Press.

Knowledge (2018). In *Cambridge Dictionary.* https://dictionary.cambridge.org/dictionary/english/knowledge.

Kuhn, T. S. (1962). *The structure of scientific revolutions.* Chicago, IL: University of Chicago Press.

Landau, L. B. (2012). Communities of knowledge or tyrannies of partnership: Reflections on North-South research networks and the dual imperative. *Journal of Refugee Studies, 25*(4), 555–570.

Lang, D. J., Wiek, A., Bergmann, M., Stauffacher, M., Martens, P., Moll, P., ...Thomas, C. J. (2012). Transdisciplinary research in sustainability science: Practice, principles, and challenges. *Sustainability Science, 7*(1), 25–43.

Leach, M., Rockström, J., Raskin, P., Scoones, I., Stirling, A., Smith, A., ...Olsson, P. (2012). Transforming innovation for sustainability. *Ecology and Society, 17*(2), Art. 11.

Lyall, C. (2008). *A short guide to designing interdisciplinary research for policy and practice* (ISSTI Briefing Notes 6). Edinburgh: Institute for the Study of Science, Technology and Innovation.

Martin, B. R. (2011). The research excellence framework and the "impact agenda": Are we creating a Frankenstein monster? *Research Evaluation, 20*(3), 247–254.

Maselli, D., Lys, J.-A., & Schmid, J. (2006). *Improving impacts of research partnerships* (2nd ed.) (partially revised). Bern: Commission for Research Partnerships with Developing Countries (KFPE).

Mollinga, P. (2008). *The rational organisation of dissent: Boundary concepts, boundary objects and boundary settings in the interdisciplinary study of natural resources management* (ZEF Working Paper Series 33). Bonn: Center for Development Research (ZEF).

Mosse, D. (2001). "People's knowledge", participation and patronage: Operations and representations in rural development. In B. Cooke & U. Kothari (Eds.), *Participation: The new tyranny?* (pp. 16–35). London and New York, NY: Zed Books.

Narayanaswamy, L. (2013). Problematizing "knowledge-for-development". *Development and Change, 44*(5), 1065–1086.

Nederveen Pieterse, J. (2011). Discourse analysis in international development studies. *Journal of Multicultural Discourses, 6*(3), 237–240.

Nowotny, H., Scott, P., & Gibbons, M. (2001). *Re-thinking science: Knowledge and the public in an age of uncertainty*. Cambridge: Wiley.

OECD (Organisation for Economic Co-operation and Development). (2008). *The Paris declaration on aid effectiveness and the Accra Agenda for action*. http://www.oecd.org/dac/effectiveness/parisdeclarationandaccraagendaforaction.htm.

OECD. (2011). *The Busan partnership for effective development co-operation*. https://www.oecd.org/development/effectiveness/busanpartnership.htm.

OECD. (2018). *DAC list of ODA recipients*. http://www.oecd.org/dac/financing-sustainable-development/development-finance-standards/daclist.htm.

OECD-DAC Working Party on Development Finance Statistics (2018). *Converged statistical reporting directives for the creditor reporting system (CRS) and the annual DAC questionnaire*. https://one.oecd.org/document/DCD/DAC/STAT(2018)9/FINAL/en/pdf.

OECD & UNDP. (2019). *Making development co-operation more effective: 2019 progress report of the GPEDC (Part I and II)*. https://www.oecd-ilibrary.org/development/making-development-co-operation-more-effective_26f2638f-en.

Pohl, C., & Hirsch Hadorn, G. (2008). Methodological challenges of transdisciplinary research. *Natures Sciences Sociétés, 16*(2), 111–121.

Polanyi, M. (2000). The republic of science: Its political and economic theory. *Minerva, 38*, 1–21.

Rhodes, C., & Sulston, J. (2009). Scientific responsibility and development. *European Journal of Development Research, 22*(1), 3–9.

Röling, N. (2009). Conceptual and methodological developments in innovation. In P. C. Sanginha, A. Waters-Bayer, S. Kaaria, J. Njuki, & C. Wettasinha (Eds.), *Innovation Africa: Enriching farmers' livelihoods* (pp. 9–34). London: Earthscan.

Sarewitz, D., Foladori, G., Invernizzi, N., & Garfinkel, M. (2004). Science policy in its social context. *Philosophy Today, 48*(5), 67–83.

Sarewitz, D., & Pielke, R. A., Jr. (2007). The neglected heart of science policy: Reconciling supply of and demand for science. *Environmental Science & Policy, 10*(1), 5–16.

Schwachula, A. (2019). *Sustainable development in science policy-making: The German Federal Ministry of Education and Research's policies for international cooperation in sustainability research*. Bielefeld: Transcript.

Schwachula, A., Vila Seoane, M., & Hornidge, A.-K. (2014). *Science, technology and innovation in the context of development: An overview of concepts and corresponding policies recommended by international organisations* (ZEF Working Paper Series 132). Bonn: Center for Development Research (ZEF).

Shamsavari, A. (2007). *The technology transfer paradigm: A critique* (Economics Discussion Paper 4). Kingston upon Thames: Kingston University.

Sillitoe, P. (2000). Let them eat cake: Indigenous knowledge, science and the "poorest of the poor". *Anthropology Today, 16*(6), 3–7.

Sismondo, S. (2008). Science and technology studies and an engaged program. In E. Hackett, O. Amsterdamska, M. Lynch, & J. Wajcman (Eds.), *The handbook of science and technology studies* (pp. 13–31). London and Cambridge, MA: MIT Press.

Smith, J. (2009). *Science and technology for development*. London: Zed Books.

Smith, A., Fressoli, M., & Thomas, H. (2014). Grassroots innovation movements: Challenges and contributions. *Journal of Cleaner Production, 63*, 114–124.

Smith, A., Voß, J.-P., & Grin, J. (2010). Innovation studies and sustainability transitions: The allure of the multi-level perspective and its challenges. *Research Policy, 39*(4), 435–448.

STEPS Centre. (2010). *Innovation, sustainability, development: A new manifesto*. Brighton: STEPS Centre.

Stock, G., & Schneidewind, U. (2014, September 18). Streit ums Mitspracherecht. Ein Interview von Christiane Grefe und Andreas Sentker. *Die Zeit*, p. 41.

Stöckli, B., Wiesmann, U., & Lys, J.-A. (2012). *A guide for trans-boundary research partnerships: 11 Principles / 7 Questions*. Bern: Commission for Research Partnerships with Developing Countries (KFPE).

Sumner, A., Perkins, N.I., & Lindstrom, J. (2009). *Making science of influencing: Assessing the impact of development research* (IDS Working Papers 335). Brighton: Institute of Development Studies.

The Royal Society. (2011). *Knowledge, networks and nations: Global scientific collaboration in the 21st century*. London: Author.

Ul Hassan, M., Hornidge, A.-K., van Veldhuizen, L., Akramkhanov, A., Rudenko, I., & Djanibekov, N. (2011). *Follow the innovation—participatory testing and adaptation of agricultural innovations in Uzbekistan: Guidelines for researchers and practitioners*. Bonn: Center for Development Research (ZEF).

United Nations (UN). (2015). *Transforming our world: The 2030 Agenda for Sustainable Development.* http://www.un.org/sustainabledevelopment/sustainable-development-goals/.

UN. (2018a). *Sustainable development goals knowledge platform: technology facilitation mechanism.* https://sustainabledevelopment.un.org/tfm.

UN. (2018b). *Sustainable development goals knowledge platform: Multi-stakeholder forum on science, technology and innovation for the SDGs (STI Forum).* https://sustainabledevelopment.un.org/TFM/STIForum2019.

UN. (2018c). *Sustainable Development Goals Knowledge Platform: Global sustainable development report 2019.* https://sustainabledevelopment.un.org/globalsdreport/2019.

UN Department of Economic and Social Affairs. (2019). *Sustainable Development Goals Knowledge Platform.* https://sustainabledevelopment.un.org/.

UN Educational, Scientific and Cultural Organization. (2015). *UNESCO science report: Towards 2030* (UNESCO Science Report 2015). Paris: UNESCO Publishing.

UNDP (UN Development Programme). (2013). *The Millennium Development Goals: Eight goals for 2015.* http://www.undp.org/content/undp/en/home/mdgoverview.html.

UNDP. (2018). *Human development reports.* http://hdr.undp.org/en.

Upreti, B. (2011). Research partnerships and capacity development in the South: A social learning perspective. In U. Wiesmann & H. Hurni (Eds.), *Research for sustainable development: Foundations, experiences, and perspectives* (Perspectives of the Swiss National Centre of Competence in Research (NCCR) North-South, University of Bern, Vol. 6.) (pp. 73–90). Bern, Switzerland: Geographica Bernensia.

WBGU (German Advisory Council on Global Change). (2011). *World in transition—a social contract for sustainability.* Berlin: Author.

WBGU. (2016). *Humanity on the move: Unlocking the transformative power of cities.* Berlin: Author.

Wiesmann, U., Hurni, H., Ott, C., & Zingerli, C. (2011). Combining the concepts of transdisciplinarity and partnership in research for sustainable development. In U. Wiesmann & H. Hurni (Eds.), *Research for sustainable development: Foundations, experiences, and perspectives* (Perspectives of the Swiss National Centre of Competence in Research (NCCR) North-South, University of Bern) (Vol. 6, pp. 43–70). Bern, Switzerland: Geographica Bernensia.

World Bank. (1999). *World development report 1998–1999: Knowledge for development.* Washington, DC: Oxford University Press.

World Health Organization. (2019). *Ethical standards and procedures for research with human beings.* https://www.who.int/ethics/research/en/.

Ziai, A. (2010). Zur Kritik des Entwicklungsdiskurses. *Aus Politik und Zeitgeschichte, 10*(Entwicklungspolitik), 23–29.

Ziai, A. (2015). *The contribution of discourse analysis to development studies* (DPS Working Papers 1). Kassel: Department for Development and Postcolonial Studies.

Ziegler, H. (1998). Brauchen wir eine Wissenschaftspolitik? Eine Polemik. *Neue Gesellschaft Frankfurter Hefte, 8,* 714–720.

Zingerli, C. (2010). A sociology of international research partnerships for sustainable development. *European Journal of Development Research, 22*(2), 217–233.

Open Access This chapter is licensed under the terms of the Creative Commons Attribution 4.0 International License (http://creativecommons.org/licenses/by/4.0/), which permits use, sharing, adaptation, distribution and reproduction in any medium or format, as long as you give appropriate credit to the original author(s) and the source, provide a link to the Creative Commons license and indicate if changes were made.

The images or other third party material in this chapter are included in the chapter's Creative Commons license, unless indicated otherwise in a credit line to the material. If material is not included in the chapter's Creative Commons license and your intended use is not permitted by statutory regulation or exceeds the permitted use, you will need to obtain permission directly from the copyright holder.

PART II

Development Cooperation: Narratives and Norms

CHAPTER 5

An Evolving Shared Concept of Development Cooperation: Perspectives on the 2030 Agenda

Milindo Chakrabarti and Sachin Chaturvedi

5.1 INTRODUCTION

With a collective commitment to the Sustainable Development Goals (SDGs), the worlds of development cooperation, in general, and development finance, in particular, are keenly looking for new and innovative sources of financing for effective and timely outcomes. It is with this backdrop that the growing emphasis and discussions on inclusion—as encapsulated in the idea of "inclusive development"—are to be viewed. This commitment to the SDGs also brings a shift from quantitative to qualitative aspects of development goals along with cross-domain and cross-border connections.

This would require greater cohesion at the global level and breaking out of silos and narrow national growth strategies (e.g. the present debate on climate change mitigation strategy, or the re-emergence of protectionist trade policies being pursued by individual nations, triggering a potential trade war). Eventually, this may entail the recognition of appropriate institutional mechanisms in a spirit of collective action, as the implementation of the SDGs may require a set of global public goods (GPGs) for the effective delivery of quality goods and services, which somehow were met through a narrow focus on quantitative accomplishments in the time of the Millennium Development Goals.

M. Chakrabarti (✉) · S. Chaturvedi
Research and Information System for Developing Countries (RIS), New Delhi, India
e-mail: milindo.chakrabarti@ris.org.in

S. Chaturvedi
e-mail: sachin@ris.org.in; dgoffice@ris.org.in

The challenge to be settled during the coming days would be to identify an effective global institutional structure that could be proposed by the members of the G20. This structure to help implement the action plans for the 2030 Agenda for Sustainable Development may be designed by the G20 in close collaboration with non-G20 members. Although sustainable development is a universal developmental goal, there is a long history of "development cooperation" at work. However, as of today, three distinct models of "development cooperation" can be identified. They are (i) the official development assistance (ODA)-based model of North-South cooperation (NSC), led by the Organisation for Economic Co-operation and Development (OECD)/Development Assistance Committee, (ii) the South-led solidarity and sharing-based model of South-South cooperation (SSC), and (iii) the newly evolving model of triangular cooperation (TrC), which involves joining hands between two entities to provide development support to a third country. The exact identity of the entities that would provide development support has yet to be agreed upon. Furthermore, both NSC and SSC are based on a set of stated principles—at times to the extent of contradicting one another—and they are always posited as being complementary to each other. Any such stated set of driving principles for TrC has yet to emerge. Given these ground-level variations across the different models of development cooperation, it is pertinent to raise a fundamental question as to how development partnerships can be institutionalised around SDG 17, which calls for "Partnerships for the goals". Are the existing institutional models for development cooperation—NSC and SSC—sufficient to help achieve the other 16 goals? In case they are not, is the emerging model of TrC capable of filling the institutional vacuum? If TrC is also not expected to deliver, what alternative institutional framework could the G20 propose?

The present chapter is an endeavour to identify a new set of global institutional structures to effectively facilitate the achievement of some SDGs. The next section develops the analytical framework that helps conceptualise the three premises driving the process of development cooperation. The subsequent section advocates the usefulness of using a multi-modality approach in development cooperation, articulated in the literature as "development compact" (Chaturvedi 2016). Following that, the next section purports that most, if not all, of the SDGs create GPGs, in the sense that the achievement of the targets are neither rivalled in consumption nor do they exclude anyone from accruing the benefits of these targets. The spirit of "no one is left behind" aptly captures the GPG characteristics of the outcomes of achieving the targets. A few case studies were written to find the extent to which these premises were maintained in organising the provision of GPGs through the creation of new forms of global institutional structures. Issues as diverse as health care (GAVI, the Vaccine Alliance, involving SDGs 3, 4, and 17), peacekeeping (SDGs 16 and 17), and energy (International Solar Alliance, ISA, involving SDGs 7, 13, and 17) have been taken up. The case studies indicate that such institutional frameworks are often effective in creating access to resources, and thereby contribute to the creation of some specific types of GPGs. Broadly, it has been observed that successful collective actions were organised around issues that centred on a lack of access to particular resources, and that such actions involved multiple actors, including non-state ones.

5.2 Analytical Framework

The basis for this framework rests on contextualising cooperation against the background of the fundamental requirements for development. It is based on integrating three conceptual premises that underscore the global quest for sustainable development and coming up with an effective but new institutional mechanism that can create GPGs. These conceptual premises are based on a primary construct that development, or the lack of it, is characterised by the degree of access to resources. The underlying objective of "leaving no one behind" as a given target for the achievements of the SDGs is very much centred around the intention of providing better access to resources for all. The provision of GPGs is tantamount to lowering the access barriers for those who are lagging behind.

The resources that are used by any human being may be divided into four distinct components: natural resources—those supplied by nature; economic resources—those which are man-made and include produced resources, technology, and knowledge; political resources[1]—the power to negotiate the access regime for the first two types of resources; and social resources—social networks based on faith, belief systems, and kinships. The last two types of resources may be grouped under institutional resources. It is interesting to note that access to any of these resources is not independent of access to the rest of the resources. Access to natural resources is contingent upon access to economic, social, and political resources. The long history of colonialism may be cited as an attestation of the argument. Simultaneously, access to political resources is also conditioned by access to economic resources. The reverse is also tue, simultaneously. The variations in the degree of access to resources are observed at all levels—local, subnational, national, regional, and global—and thus explain the existence of developmental disparities at all of these levels. Given this primary construct, we would argue that development cooperation and the quest for sustainable development may be framed using the following three premises. We shall observe later that the idea of a development compact can also be meaningfully inferred to emerge from this theoretical framework. The premises are:

1. *Access to resources and capability*: The world is divided between those who enjoy greater access to value-added resources and those who have lower degrees of such access. The former is described as "developed" and the latter "developing". Such distinctions exist among "states" at an aggregative level and also among communities within a "state" at a disaggregated level[2] (Chakrabarti 2018).

2. *Role of prevailing institutional architecture in facilitating access*: Access to resources and the capability to add value to them are determined by the prevailing institutional architecture at the global, regional, and local levels, which, in turn, is indicative of one's access to political and social resources. The institutional architecture determines the rules of the game to be followed in the distribution of, access to, withdrawal of, management of, exclusion from, alienation of, and the making of alterations to resources. Whereas access refers to "the right to enter a defined physical property", withdrawal implies "the right to obtain the 'products' of a resource". Management takes care of "the right to regulate internal use patterns and transform the resource by making improvements", whereas alteration refers to "the right to change the set of goods and services provided by a resource". Finally, exclusion is "the right to determine who will have an access right, and how that right may be transferred", and alienation refers to "the right to sell or lease some or all rights". The rights beyond access play their respective roles in determining the capability of a community or a nation to add value to the resources they have access to (Schlager and Ostrom 1992, pp. 249–262).
3. *Focus on stakeholders*: There exist multiple groups of stakeholders—often with conflicting interests—keen on enjoying the aforesaid rights to resources and the capability to add value to them. Designing an appropriate institutional structure involves creating opportunities for collective action and balancing such interests across stakeholders to ensure the optimal utilisation of the resource in question. The collective action also involves costs to the participating stakeholders. They lose because of the institutional restrictions put on their behaviour in terms of access, withdrawal, management, alteration, exclusion, and alienation vis-à-vis the resource in question. On the other hand, collective inaction is often preferable, as it removes such restrictions vis-à-vis the behaviour of an individual, who can then enjoy complete behavioural freedom. However, there are situations when the cost of collective action becomes less than that of collective inaction. This premise is substantiated by the recent emergence of a global consensus towards the adoption of the SDGs. With the realisation that collective inaction would increase the vulnerability of human beings in terms of their social, economic, and ecological existence, all the countries across the world agreed to sign on the dotted lines and engage in effective collective action, even at the expense of curtailing their "national sovereignty" to a considerable degree.

5.3 THE DEVELOPMENT COMPACT

It may be pertinent to explore at this juncture as to how ODA—as extended by the members of the OECD and development cooperation—as practised within the ambit of SSC, would identify possible meeting points, and how theoretical and institutional frameworks would help delineate elements for different modalities (Chakrabarti 2016). The requirement of resources and the development of an appropriate access regime to such resources as well as their appropriate sources vis-à-vis domestic spending, concessional international funding, and/or private investments will depend on such institutional frameworks that are entwined with effective and operational models. Development cooperation may essentially be looked at as an effort to enhance access to resources and capacity for increased value addition for communities that are lagging behind, compared to others enjoying a larger domain of access.

All such activities involve invoking a better access protocol and can be classified under five heads of the "development compact": capacity-building, trade and investment, development finance, technology transfer, and grants. Capacity-building activities contribute to enhanced access to economic resources through human resource development, and thereby to increased capacity for enhanced value addition. Trade and investment, on the other hand, facilitate greater access to resources such as goods and services, along with access to markets beyond domestic boundaries. Technology transfer is akin to access to economic resources, which facilitates value addition. Development finance and grants facilitate access to financial resources, albeit indirectly, and provide access to economic resources.

Needless to say, even though we differentiate between these five modalities, they may not remain mutually exclusive while being used. Just as the access framework for the apparently distinct four resources we identified are intertwined, the different modalities under the development compact are also interlinked with one another. They may be used in several possible permutations and combinations to facilitate the process of "access" for those who have been lagging behind. Such possible variations in their relative importance when deciding on the appropriate access regime create space for multi-stakeholder governance systems for development. Compared to the greater emphasis on grants and loans in the OECD schema, the development compact—through its multi-modality approach, which facilitates access to political and social resources by augmenting the human-capital base of a country—appears to effectively handle the whole of the access system mentioned above. Increased opportunities for trade broaden access to social networks in the form of strengthening people-to-people connections. Opening up market access also helps to enhance social access. Increased cooperation in a horizontal space also contributes to collective efforts in enhancing the level of political access at the global level. Engaging actors beyond the state—including civil society organisations, academia, people's representatives, traders, policy-makers, among others—helps in formulating a multi-stakeholder governance mechanism for development, or sustainable development to be specific. In this process, these actors also facilitate the creation of positive externalities, which are enjoyed by all the participants. This reduces the cost of collective action involving different stakeholders, who often might have had conflicting interests in a particular resource governance regime in a prior situation of collective inaction.

A few comments linking GPGs with the SDGs are in order. The present chapter argues that almost all of the SDGs are linked to the provision of public goods and have a global imperative—they may be termed as facilitating GPGs. Public goods tend to be undersupplied and are required to be supplied in larger quantities on a global scale. However, on a cautionary note, it may be said that the issues of concern in achieving the 17 SDGs do not necessarily relate directly to the provision of GPGs alone. The SDGs—which are related to poverty, hunger, health and well-being, education, gender equity, sanitation, employment and economic growth, industrial activities, and reduced inequality—directly qualify to be considered as the creation of GPGs, as they involve the provision of global resources in order to achieve them so that no one is left behind. SDG 17, in the form of partnerships for the goals, clearly articulates the GPG aspect of the SDGs. However, apparently, some of the SDGs cannot be considered as providing GPGs. Rather, they are characteristically more akin to protecting global commons. The SDGs linked to the protection of global commons are those relating to life on land and below water as well as to climate action. Conceptually, whereas a public good suffers from the fate of the underprovision of resources to create them, commons are problematic because they tend to be overconsumed, as existing institutional mechanisms are not efficient enough to prevent their overconsumption, and consequently they suffer from the tendency of being overused. However, it requires the provision of considerable resources—economic, political, and social—and the facilitation of access to them by humanity to develop the necessary incentive–disincentive mechanisms that encourage the protection of global commons from the present state of overconsumption. The provision of such resources is akin to that required for the creation of GPGs.

5.4 A Few Case Studies

We share a few case studies that underscore the relevance of the conceptual framework elaborated in the section above. Whereas the first case study looks at the experiences of the workings of GAVI, the Vaccine Alliance (GAVI) in proving a GPG, the second one considers the case of ISA, which is being jointly promoted by India and France in an effort to simultaneously provide a GPG and protect a global common—the global climate. The final one relates to India's experiences in peacekeeping under United Nations (UN) supervision. The cases follow a common pattern in their elaborations. We identify the three premises already elaborated in the earlier sections, namely: increasing access as the focus of action, the institutional mechanism that was crafted to increase access, and the engagement of stakeholders in a polycentric set-up to institutionalise "increased" access to the resource in question. It is also noted that they all are related to one or more of the SDGs.

5.4.1 *GAVI, the Vaccine Alliance*

GAVI, which came into being in 2000, holds the special promise of health for all that we have been longing for. It covers SDG 3 (access to good health and well-being), SDG 6 (access to clean water and sanitation), and SDG 17 ("Partnerships for the goals").

5.4.1.1 *Objectives and Principles*
Why was there a need for GAVI? The *institutional structures* prevailing before GAVI had failed on several parameters, leading to the dire need for another intervention. The World Health Organization's (WHO) Expanded Programme on Immunization (EPI) barely registered any change in global immunisation rates. Later, the Universal Childhood Immunization campaign of WHO and the United Nations Children's Fund (UNICEF)—though showing commendable performance in terms of coverage and results—soon lost momentum after it began focussing on other priorities.

There were several reasons supporting the demand and necessity to come up with an institutional change to ensure better access to health-related resources.

First, a state of development can be measured by the degree of access to value-added resources. Access to the resources and processes that are required to reduce child mortality is necessary for sustainable development. A healthy population is the first prerequisite for having such capabilities. By exploring the synergies between public and private partners—which include governments of both developed and developing countries, civil society organisations, independent individuals, research and technical health institutes, in addition to the founder, the Bill & Melinda Gates Foundation—GAVI hopes to provide the people with opportunities to realise reduced levels of child mortality.

The second important component for access to resources in terms of sound institutional architecture has also been considered. GAVI tries to make these resources available through its participatory and collective approach of taking along most of the stakeholders in a process with a polycentric design. This effort by GAVI to supply the desired changes hinges on a unique approach that combines funding and partnership.

5.4.1.2 *Funding*
The Vaccine Alliance is funded through direct contributions (77 per cent) and innovative finance (23 per cent). Direct contributions include grants and agreements from donor governments, foundations, corporations, and organisations—in other words, they include support from both the public and private sectors. Innovative financing mechanisms include the International Finance Facility for Immunisation (IFFIm), the Pneumococcal Advance Market Commitment (AMC), the GAVI Matching Fund, and the loan buydown facility. They are also financed by public and private sources. In addition, the innovation ecosystem helps countries modernise their immunisation

delivery systems by sourcing proven high-impact technologies and "infusing" them with resources and expertise to take them to scale. GAVI-supported countries are also required to contribute a portion of the cost of purchasing their vaccines. The co-financing policy helps them to facilitate programme sustainability after GAVI's financial support ends.

5.4.1.3 Partnership

As stated above, in terms of providing financial resources, GAVI's partners include both governments and private-sector entities: 79 per cent of GAVI's funding is from governments committed to GAVI's mission of saving children's lives, whereas 21 per cent of contributions come from the private sector, which is emerging as a prominent component of GAVI's diversified financing strategy. Care should be taken to note that governments and private-sector entities contribute simultaneously to innovative financing mechanisms and also engage in direct contributions to the GAVI fund.

WHO has partnered to regulate vaccines and support country introductions, thereby strengthening immunisation coverage and data quality; UNICEF is in partnership to procure vaccines and support countries in maintaining their cold chains, improving access, and collecting data; the World Bank helps pioneer innovative finance mechanisms such as the IFFIm and the AMC; the Bill & Melinda Gates Foundation and other private-sector partners provide funding and expertise; implementing country governments join hands to identify their immunisation needs as well as to co-finance and implement vaccine programmes; civil society organisations help ensure that vaccines reach every child; vaccine manufacturers guarantee vaccine quality, supply, and affordability for developing countries; donor-country governments make long-term funding commitments; private-sector partners contribute resources, expertise, and innovation to help achieve GAVI's mission; research agencies help GAVI generate the evidence base and communicate the value of vaccines.

5.4.1.4 The Institutional Structure of GAVI

Health system strengthening (HSS) is the format by which GAVI addresses the bottlenecks in the health systems of the recipient countries. GAVI holds that strong health systems are essential in expanding and sustaining immunisation coverage. For instance, it employs a health workforce; improves the supply, distribution, and maintenance of vaccines; and works on the organisation and management of the procedures in order to strengthen the systems. There were 69 countries that had been approved for support in such a manner by the end of April 2017 (GAVI, the Vaccine Alliance [GAVI], n.d.-a).

GAVI works in a unique, circular way. The country receiving support is the starting point of the whole process. The implementing country puts forth new proposals and annual progress reports of its performance. These reports are reviewed together by the GAVI Secretariat, Vaccine Alliance partners, and the Independent Review Committee, which then give their recommendations to the GAVI Board on how the respective country delivery can be improved.

These recommendations are implemented through the provision of vaccines and HSS support by GAVI to the implementing country. The implementing country again submits the proposals and annual progress reports, which lead to another cycle.

A full country evaluation is the tool through which gaps in the systems of the implementing countries are identified, leading to further actions towards improvement. Huge financial flows committed by GAVI to the countries ensure the easing of financial constraints in the proposed plans.

Thus, GAVI replaces the "institutions of control" with the "institutions of collective action" and propounds the idea that the cost of coming together (collective action) is much less than the cost of working alone or not collaborating (collective inaction). It shows how a potentially effective model can be developed that benefits all of its stakeholders if they consciously decide to participate in collective action.

It can also be gauged through GAVI's resource mobilisation model, which is a form of TrC involving the co-financing efforts of the respective countries, aided by a strong donor base and market-shaping strategies. The promising initiatives in this direction have been IFFIm, which ensures the long-term predictability of financing by efficiently leveraging capital markets to shift funds to meet country demand; AMC, which accelerates the manufacturing and delivery of vaccines; and the GAVI Matching Fund, which maximises the value of giving for corporations as well as their customers and employees.

GAVI's co-financing policy works by identifying three phases of graduation of country ownership and the steps to sustainability. Countries are in the initial self-financing phase when per capita gross national income (GNI) is less than $1045, which leads to the second phase, when GNI is between $1045 and $1580 and consists of countries in the preparatory transition phase. Finally, the third phase is when per capita GNI is more than $1580 and countries are called to be in the accelerated transition phase. The first phase demands that countries pay $0.20 per dose, whereas the second phase asks for increases in co-payments of 15 per cent per year, and the third phase requires a steady increase in payments in order to reach sustainability after five years. Thus, the purpose of co-financing policy is to enhance ownership and put countries on a trajectory towards financial sustainability in preparation of phasing out GAVI support in accordance with increases in GNI per capita.

India is in the third phase of co-financing policy, whereby it began transitioning away from GAVI support in 2017, and thus expects to begin fully self-financing all of its vaccine programmes by 2021. GAVI is committed to assist India with up to $345 million during this period to strengthen its health systems as well as its supply of vaccines against pneumonia and rotavirus. Up until 29 March 2019, around $290 million was sanctioned out of the committed amount; around $179 million (61.72 per cent of the committed amount for the period between 2017 and 2023) has already been disbursed.

The Government of India is already prioritising reaching every child with vaccines with its new Mission Indradhanush initiative. With its HSS methods,

GAVI can push this cause even further and help India achieve its set targets. India is in immense need of such support given the fact that it is home to 4 million under-immunised children, which accounts for about a fifth of all GAVI-supported countries.

> GAVI and its partners will provide targeted support to help India's immunisation system identify and reach children who are not receiving vaccines, including exploring how India's vast number of polio workers can support uptake of other routine vaccines, such as the 5-in-1 pentavalent vaccine and these new vaccines. (GAVI 2016)

> [Sixty per cent] of all GAVI-procured vaccines are manufactured in India. Through the partnership, GAVI and the Government of India plan to work more closely together to help create a more sustainable global and domestic vaccine manufacturing base within India. This will be crucial to ensuring sufficient vaccine supplies are available for the 27 million children born in India every year, and children living in all 72 other GAVI-supported countries. (GAVI 2016)

India has committed $9 million to GAVI for the cycle between 2016 and 2020, which amounts to 0.11 per cent of the total commitments (GAVI, n.d.-b).

The GAVI model is an apparently successful display of putting the development priorities of developing countries at the centre (Brooks et al. 2017; Bustreo et al. 2015; Lee et al. 2013). It is a demand-driven model in which countries choose their own issues and decide where GAVI's support needs to be applied. GAVI provides completely untied aid, and up to 97 per cent of GAVI support is based on multi-year commitments. Also, there is active participation by civil society, specifically for scaling-up immunisation equity and coverage.

As per the latest information available at the GAVI website, against a target of immunising 300 million children by 2020, GAVI so far has achieved the immunisation of 198 million children, compared to having immunised 66 million children in 2018; 4.3 million future deaths have been averted through this effort, as compared to 1.7 million in 2018. The under-five mortality rate has dropped from 64 per 1000 in 2015 to 59 per 1000 in 2018, against a 2020 target of 58 per 1000. Future disability-adjusted life years averted currently stand at 203 million compared to 80 million in 2018 against a 2020 target of 250 million. What is further encouraging is the fact that the vaccination process was carried out in all of the countries that were no longer receiving GAVI support. Independent academic studies also support some of the findings. It has been observed that expanded access to, and free provision of, post-exposure prophylaxis through GAVI would prevent an additional 489,000 deaths between 2020 and 2035. Under this switch to efficient intradermal post-exposure prophylaxis regimens, total projected vaccine needs remain similar (about 73 million vials). Yet, 17.4 million more people are vaccinated, making this an extremely cost-effective method, with costs of $635 per death being averted and $33 per disability-adjusted life years averted (WHO Rabies Modelling Consortium 2019). A case study of GAVI's 15-year engagement with a vaccine against diphtheria, tetanus, pertussis, hepatitis B, and *haemophilus influenzae* type b (pentavalent) provides evidence of the benefits and potential risks of trying to influence markets (Malhame et al. 2019). As a recognition of GAVI's services, it was presented with the 2019 Lasker-Bloomberg Public Service Award.

As argued earlier, polycentric institutions represent a suitable combination of institutions at levels that take care of operational and governance issues. Such an approach has been initiated by GAVI, as the interests of its stakeholders intersect and overlap on the common goal of providing a given health service globally. The combination of long-term commitments in the form of technical expertise of the development community with the business know-how of the private sector—along with contributions of resources (financial and/or human) from other stakeholders according to their ability—is arranged to help achieve the long-term goal of immunisation with self-sufficiency.

It is not that GAVI has had a smooth road. There have been problems identified with even this institutional structure. GAVI has been questioned on several grounds in the Full Country Evaluation Reports by the independent evaluators as to: how demonstration projects could have been better designed to maximise learning for the national introduction of vaccines; how complex the nature of HSS procedures is; how there are a number of deficiencies in the design of GAVI HSS grants; how the oversized administrative and management burdens of GAVI grants and processes have further strained the limited programme capacity of EPI introduced by WHO long back; and how overly optimistic the application and implementation timelines are, to name a few. But having said that, the reason why GAVI still succeeds is the fact that it incorporates these suggestions into the following cycle of HSS for the country.

The case study presented on GAVI clearly indicates that a new institutional structure that cuts through hierarchical structures, with the nation states at the centre, can also be quite effective in ensuring greater access to resources and the capacity to add value to them. Examples in terms of the growth of the internet, success of peacekeeping operations, etc., also contribute meaningfully to arguments in favour of creating such multi-stakeholder institutions. A structured understanding of GAVI is given in Table 5.1.

5.4.2 International Solar Alliance

ISA is also a very effective example of efforts at developing a polycentric institution in providing access to energy to communities that are largely energy-deficient. It is an initiative to bring in effective collective action in facilitating increased access to energy; consequently, the adoption of SDGs also adds credence to the three premises elaborated upon earlier. ISA was jointly launched by India and France on 30 November 2015 at the UN Climate

Table 5.1 Features of GAVI

Elements of theoretical framework	Features of GAVI
Access to resources, capabilities, and modalities	• Pathways for sustainable, affordable health services and access to clean water and sanitation facilities • Reductions in the costs of finance and technology • Reduction in the levels of child mortality and consequent capacity-building, leading to enhancement in the quality of human capital
Institutional architecture	• Access to sound institutional architecture, which GAVI tries to make available through its participatory and collective approach of taking along most of the stakeholders in the process • To ensure efficient collective action, multi-stakeholder institutional structures are being created • Finances to be supported by multilateral, public, and philanthropic stakeholders and contributions from them
Focus on stakeholder	• Aspires to involve multiplicity of stakeholders • Potential stakeholders include governments, bilateral and multilateral organisations, industry, corporate enterprises, and philanthropic entities • Seeks cooperation with other stakeholders involved in this area/domain

Source Authors

Change Conference in Paris (COP 21). It is conceived to establish a common platform for cooperation among solar resource-rich countries (i.e. *Suryaputras* or sunshine countries) that are located fully or partially between the Tropics of Cancer and Capricorn to harness solar energy. In this context, sunshine countries share common challenges and opportunities as far as sustainable energy resources are concerned. ISA is intended to create opportunities for greater collaboration in technology, research and development, and capacity-building (Cernuschi et al. 2018). Part of ISA is still in its infancy, but the initiative merits attention also at the level of planning. The ISA Framework Agreement was opened for signatures during COP 22 at Marrakesh on 15 November 2016. There are 121 potential countries that are considered to be rich in solar power. Of them, 86 countries have signed and 68 countries have further ratified the ISA Framework Agreement as of 8 September 2020: 30 of them belong to the category of least-developed countries, while 37 are Small Island

Developing States. ISA partners include multilateral financial institutions such as the Asian Development Bank, the African Development Bank, the New Development Bank, the Asian Infrastructure and Investment Bank, the European Investment Bank, and the World Bank. Specialised international agencies such as the International Energy Agency (IEA), the International Renewable Energy Agency (IRENA), the Green Climate Fund, the Climate Parliament, and the Regions of Climate Action have also partnered with ISA. The United Nations Development Programme (UNDP) has also chipped in as a partner in this endeavour. The notable ones among the corporate partners are a number of energy-linked public-sector enterprises from India, in addition to private-sector entities such as Soft Bank in Japan and CLP in Hong Kong.

ISA is now an inter-governmental body registered with the UN under Article 102 of the UN Charter and headquartered in Gurugram, India.

5.4.2.1 Objectives and Principles
Some of the collective aspirations of this common platform are: reducing the costs of finance and technology for the immediate deployment of competitive solar generation; paving the way for future solar generation, storage, and good technologies for countries' individual needs; and increasing the utilisation and promotion of solar energy and solar applications in its member countries (Press Information Bureau [PIB] 2016e). Ghosh and Chawla (2016) call it a mission to take it from the lab to the streets. In this process, ISA also intends to create direct and indirect employment opportunities and increase economic activities in member countries (PIB 2016b). ISA aims to be a $1 trillion opportunity, and the Global Solar Council (GSC)[3] has committed to creating 25 million jobs in the solar space among ISA countries (PIB 2016a).

Its five-point plan of action includes:

- *Rural and decentralised applications*: Most Alliance member countries are agrarian economies. This programme aims to improve yields and economic benefits by providing reliable, affordable solar applications that are suited to needs and accessible to all farmers in various fields.
- *Access to affordable finance*: The financial cost is currently the major obstacle to the deployment of solar technologies, despite rapid technological progress. The countries taking part in the programme work on drawing up common principles for legislative and regulatory frameworks, and on risk-reduction instruments aimed at enhancing their chances of accessing finance.
- *Island and village solar mini-grids*: Islands and non-interconnected communities are among those most interested in renewables, and solar in particular. This programme aims to develop and replicate commercial models, adopt common standards, and launch calls for tenders for the installation of mini-grids.

- *Rooftop installations*: Thanks to its ability to generate small quantities of energy at multiple feed-in points, rooftop solar panels can produce decentralised energy, thus limiting the costs of upgrading grids and pooling electrical production variations across a large number of installations. This programme aims to lift barriers to its development.
- *Solar e-mobility*: Solar e-mobility technologies (including roads, vehicles, and scooters) are seeing very rapid development. This programme seeks to develop these applications and promote their deployment, including through energy storage, and to harmonise practices across the countries taking part in the programme.

5.4.2.2 The Institutional Structure of ISA

As mentioned earlier, ISA aims at involving a multiplicity of stakeholders. Apart from governments, stakeholders include bilateral and multilateral organisations, industry, corporate enterprises, and others. For instance, ISA is working in close cooperation with UNDP for the creation of complementary linkages; strategic cooperation in programmatic and technical expertise; the establishment of knowledge-management systems; and the strengthening of ISA's institutional structure (PIB 2016c). In addition, ISA is collaborating with the World Bank to promote solar energy globally by developing financial instruments, roadmaps to mobilise financing (including concessional financing), as well as technical assistance and knowledge transfer (PIB 2016d).

India has also committed to supporting ISA by hosting its Secretariat at the National Institute of Solar Energy campus in Gurgaon, India, for an initial period of five years. Thereafter, it is expected to generate its own resources and become self-financing (PIB 2016b).

Two programmes of ISA—Affordable Finance at Scale and Scaling Solar Applications for Agricultural Use—were launched in April 2016 and are intended to serve the primary interests of farming communities (PIB 2016f). Another such initiative is the Terrawatt Initiative, which is a global non-profit initiative that seeks to gather all relevant stakeholders through partnerships, memorandums of understanding, informal agreements, and workshops (Terrawatt Initiative 2016). Such programmes target the necessities of solar-rich countries.

Potential linkages to ISA are to be explored with the initiative Solar Guidelines India, which is under the Indo-German Energy Programme. This initiative is to act as the central information database of India's Ministry for New and Renewable Energy and the Solar Energy Corporation of India (SECI) for all stakeholders in the solar sector in India. It has been conceived in order to enable investment and stimulate the development of the India's solar sector (Solar Guidelines 2016).

As far as institutional mechanisms and governance structure are concerned, ISA is still in the development phase. It has established an assembly and a Secretariat. The second assembly was held in Delhi on 31 October 2019, whereas the Secretariat has been operating from Gurugram, India, since 2016. Among the recent initiatives taken up by ISA is the ISA Solar Cooling Initiative (also known as I-SCI), in collaboration with the University of Birmingham in the UK. The initiative aims to help member countries develop solar-energy-linked cold chains and cooling systems for agricultural use.

5.4.2.3 Contributions

In January 2018, India committed to setting up a $350 million solar development fund. In addition, nine companies and banks have agreed to develop and finance various solar projects, which include a $1 billion partnership corpus of the National Thermal Power Corporation and CLP India to the ISA. In addition, India has provided $62 million for the establishment of the ISA Secretariat. Heads of state and government from 23 member countries attended a day-long summit on 11 March 2018 in New Delhi to formally inaugurate the platform for the mass deployment of solar energy, especially in developing countries. India has already provided assistance worth $143 million for 13 solar projects that have been completed or are being implemented across the world. Continuing with this co-operative effort, India will be providing assistance to the tune of $1.4 billion for 27 new projects in 15 developing countries. These solar projects are in Bangladesh, Mali, Seychelles, Tanzania, Mali, Rwanda, Nigeria, Ghana, and Guinea. During the summit, France also committed €700 million to ISA.

It may be recalled that on 30 June 2016, the Alliance entered into an understanding with the World Bank to accelerate the mobilisation of finance for solar energy. The bank will have a major role in mobilising more than $1000 billion in the investments that will be needed by 2030 to meet ISA's goals of generating 1 TW of affordable solar energy.

As part of its plans to provide proactive leadership in the diffusion of solar energy, India also committed to provide 500 training slots (in solar technology) every year to ISA member countries.

The other recurring expenditures of ISA are intended to be met through membership fees; contributions from bilateral and multilateral agencies; other appropriate institutions; and also from interest earned from the corpus fund (PIB 2016b). As ISA requires massive investment for affordable solar energy by 2030, contributions from multiple stakeholders are an essential feature of the ISA financing mechanism.

The contributions from India to the development of ISA so far have taken several forms.

- The government of India will contribute $27 million to ISA for creating the corpus, building infrastructure, and paying recurring expenditures over a five-year duration from 2016–2017 to 2020–2021.

- SECI and the Indian Renewable Energy Development Agency have contributed $1 million each to create the ISA corpus fund.
- India's Ministry of External Affairs, through its Development Partnership Administration programme, has set aside $1.5–$2 billion as a line of credit facility to undertake solar projects in those African countries that have signed and ratified the ISA Framework Agreement.
- India is also committed to providing 500 training slots for member countries and starting a solar tech mission to lead research and development. So far, two such training programmes on Solar Energy for Master Trainers from ISA member countries have been organised under the Indian Technical and Economic Cooperation Programme, which involves more than 60 participants.

The French Agency for Development committed €700 million for solar projects by 2022, bringing its total commitment to €1 billion since the creation of ISA. A structured understanding of ISA is given in Table 5.2.

Table 5.2 Features of the International Solar Alliance

Elements of theoretical framework	*Features of ISA*
Access to resources, capabilities, and modalities	• Pathway for sustainable, affordable, and clean energy, and mitigating climate change concerns • Reductions in the costs of finance and technology • Capacity-building to enhance the quality of human capital
Institutional architecture	• To ensure efficient collective action, multi-stakeholder institutional structures are being created • Proposal for an assembly, a council, and a Secretariat • Finances to be supported through membership fees, interest earned, and contributions from various stakeholders
Focus on stakeholder	• Aspires to involve a multiplicity of stakeholders • Potential stakeholders include governments, bilateral and multilateral organisations, industry, and corporate enterprises • Seeks cooperation with other stakeholders involved in this area/domain

Source Authors

5.4.3 UN Peacekeeping

UN Peacekeeping (UNPK) can be cited as another endorsement of the access–institution–polycentricity model expounded in this chapter. In the self-help-based prevailing international system, the disastrous consequences of the two world wars provided valuable insights on the need for international peace and security. This was further necessitated by conflicts arising due to power struggles within and among states. However, there was no collective international mechanism to maintain peace in conflict zones before the UN initiated peacekeeping efforts in 1948 to maintain international peace and security. As a consequence of the two world wars, this state of affairs was felt to have changed, and collective action of a universal character began. Taking into account the contributions of UNPK, it was awarded the Nobel Peace Prize in 1988.

5.4.3.1 Objectives and Principles

Peace enables smooth access to resources and adds value that is conducive for development. As such, UN drew attention to the need for collective action through the means of peacekeeping, which is a strategy to maintain and preserve peace in conflict zones as well as to assist in implementing agreements achieved by stakeholders. Moreover, peace enables the conditions for the realisation of the SDGs in the contemporary context. In addition, the cost of collective action for peacekeeping is less than the cost of collective inaction.

UN peacekeepers are sent to diverse regions that range from regions where civil-war conditions prevail to places where there are no agreements, or agreements with negligible scope for commitment from the warring groups as far as the settlement of conflict is concerned. So far, 71 such missions have been initiated—13 of them are currently in operation (as of September 2020). In many cases, they are also sent to regions where constitutional authority either does not exist or exists with limited authority. In such diverse conditions, peacekeepers are required to keep hostile factions apart at a safe distance, safeguard humanitarian relief operations, monitor human rights violations, assist in mine clearance, monitor state boundaries or borders, provide police support to the citizens, assist in rebuilding logistical infrastructure such as roads, railways, and bridges, and support electoral processes.

UNPK involves global partnerships as well as collective action of a universal character, which is reflected in the composition of its various peacekeeping missions. UNPK missions consist of personnel from many countries in order to create conditions for lasting peace in the conflict zones. Due to the transformational nature of the international security environment, UNPK has evolved from a simple model of peacekeeping—involving only the military—into a complex, multi-dimensional peacekeeping model consisting of the military, police, and civilians working together for sustainable peace.

In addition, UNPK is guided by three basic principles: (i) consent of the parties, (ii) impartiality, and (iii) non-use of force, except in self-defence and defence of the mandate.

5.4.3.2 Institutional Structure

UNPK functions under a normative framework provided by the UN Charter, the UN Security Council (UNSC) mandates, international human rights laws, and international humanitarian laws. Though UNPK does not find explicit mention in the UN Charter, its legal basis is derived from the Charter itself. As mentioned in Chapter VI (Pacific Settlement of Disputes), Chapter VII (Action with Respect to the Peace, Breaches of the Peace and Acts of Aggression), and Chapter VII (Regional Arrangements) of the UN Charter, various arrangements provide the legal and institutional foundations for UNPK operations. Moreover, UNPK takes into account various dimensions mandated by international human rights laws and international humanitarian laws. In accordance with these provisions, UNPK operations are mandated by the UNSC in order to fulfil its primary authorised responsibility—as per the UN Charter—to maintain global peace and security. The UNSC consists of five permanent members—the victor nations of the Second World War—which hold veto power. Other members of the UNSC are the 10 non-permanent members, which are elected for two-year terms by the UN General Assembly (UNGA).

Once the mandate is formulated, the hierarchical authority, command, and control structure of UNPK is transferred to a multinational institution. At the headquarters level, the Under-Secretary-General (USG) for Peacekeeping Operations monitors all UNPK operations. The Head of Mission (HOM), who coordinates activities in the field, exercises operational authority in the field and reports to the Secretary-General (SG) through the USG for Peacekeeping Operations.

The existing and mandated institutional structures of UNPK in any particular country involve distinct layers of governance—operational, collective choice, and constitutional. Whereas the ground-level operations are coordinated and managed by operational-choice-level institutions staffed by personnel both from within and outside of the country, the collective-choice-level institutions maintain communication liaisons within the constitutional-choice-level structure.

5.4.3.3 Contributions

As UNPK is a collective action, its financing is the collective responsibility of all members of the UN, in accordance with Article 17 (Chapter IV) of the UN Charter. Accordingly, the UNGA has framed some general principles for financing UNPK operations through Resolution 55/235 of December 2000. Moreover, these provisions are also updated, as per requirements of various peacekeeping missions. As of 1 September 2019, there were 109,736 people serving in UN peacekeeping operations (85,674 uniformed people from 120 countries, 12,932 civilians, and 1230 volunteers) representing 122 countries. European nations contribute nearly 7000 units to this total. Pakistan, India, and Bangladesh are among the largest individual contributors, with more than 5000 units each. African nations contributed nearly half the total—more than 44,000 units. Approved resources for the period from 1 July 2018 until 30

June 2019 is about $6.69 billion. The annual budget of UNPK missions is 0.5 per cent of the global military budget, signifying the cost-effectiveness of the missions to ensure peace in disturbed regions.

UNPK keeps evolving according to emerging necessities. An Agenda for Peace—written by then-SG of the UN, Boutros Boutros-Ghali (Ghali 1992)—as well as the Report of the Panel on United Nations Peace Operations (Brahimi 2000) and the Report of the High-level Independent Panel on Peace Operations (United Nations 2015) reflect these realities and indicate a transformation in the approaches of UNPK. In this context, one remarkable aspect is that the overwhelming number of conflict zones where UNPK missions have taken place or are ongoing lie in the Global South. Moreover, most of the countries that contribute personnel to UNPK missions are from the South. Though it is being authorised by the UNSC and receiving financial contributions from every UN Member State, the actual implementation of missions on the ground relies on credible contributions from the South. This also points to the need for a greater role and engagement of the South in the decision-making processes of UNPK as well as the involvement of non-state actors, which requires both institutional and political changes. A structured understanding of UNPK is given in Table 5.3.

Table 5.3 Features of UNPK

Elements of theoretical framework	Features of UNPK
Access to resources, capabilities, and modalities	• Pathway for peace and prosperity of conflict-ridden nations and consequent enhancement in access to resources
	• Capacity-building to enhance the quality of human capital
Institutional architecture	• Financing is the collective responsibility of all members of the UN
	• A multi-stakeholder institutional structure involving the UN and local government. The HOM, who coordinates activities in the field, exercises operational authority in the field and reports to the SG/USG
Focus on stakeholder	• Aspires to involve a multiplicity of stakeholders
	• UNPK has evolved from a simple model of peacekeeping—involving only the military—into a complex, multi-dimensional peacekeeping model consisting of the military, police, and civilians working together for sustainable peace

Source Authors

5.5 By Way of Conclusion

The year 2015 marked a watershed in the annals of human history. All 193 countries in the world ratified the adoption of the 2030 Agenda for Sustainable Development and its 17 Sustainable Development Goals on 26 September during the UNGA Summit in New York. The goals are aimed at making a world where no one is left behind and built around the 5 P's—people, planet, prosperity, peace, and partnership—to set off an ambitious agenda that aims to tackle poverty, climate change, and inequality for all people in all countries. Sustained efforts have been called for to ensure that the goals are achieved by 2030. A list of 169 targets and 230 indicators has been prepared to guide each country towards achieving these goals within a given time frame.

The achievement of such ambitious goals would involve providing access to a host of resources to large segments of the global population. Such an access regime would require considerable resources—physical, financial, human, and, on top of those, institutional—in order to be created. In order to move forward on this track, member nations must explore ways and means to move in a collective manner and ensure greater inclusion. In the process, more GPGs would probably be created. As we found in the cases described above, it is possible to create access to desired resources for larger segments of humanity, even with the crafting of innovative institutional mechanisms that are not purely market-driven. Naidu et al. (2019) argue that

> [e]conomics does have its universals, of course, such as market-based incentives, clear property rights, contract enforcement, macroeconomic stability, and prudential regulation. These higher-order principles are associated with efficiency and are generally presumed to be conducive to superior economic performance. But these principles are compatible with an almost infinite variety of institutional arrangements with each arrangement producing a different distributional outcome and a different contribution to overall prosperity.

Polycentric institutions, as opposed to monocentric ones, can provide effective solutions for many of the vexing problems identified by the SDGs. The call to respect plurality will be difficult to ignore.

Notes

1. Access to such resources facilitates increased access to power-sharing, for example: leadership, governance, etc.
2. One such example is the process of colonisation, wherein some resource-poor colonisers could develop at the expense of the access to the resources of their colonies. In the process, the colonies became "developing" or "underdeveloped".
3. The GSC is an association of leading national and regional solar associations from both established and emerging markets in order to unify the solar power sector at an international level, share best practices, and accelerate global market developments. The GSC can complement ISA in its mission.

REFERENCES

Brahimi, L. (2000). *Report of the panel on United Nations peace operations* (A/55/305-S/2000/809). https://undocs.org/A/55/305.

Brooks, A., Habiman, D., & Huckerby, G. (2017). Making the leap into the next generation: A commentary on how Gavi, the Vaccine Alliance is supporting countries' supply chain transformations in 2016–2020. *Vaccine, 35*, 2110–2114.

Bustreo, F., Okwo-Bele, J. M., & Kamara, L. (2015). World Health Organization perspectives on the contribution of the Global Alliance for Vaccines and Immunization on reducing child mortality. *Archives of Disease in Childhood, 100*(Issue Suppl 1), s34–s37.

Cernuschi, T., Gaglione, S., & Bozzani, F. (2018). Challenges to sustainable immunization systems in Gavi transitioning countries. *Vaccine, 36*(45), 6858–6866.

Chakrabarti, M. (2016). *Development compact—The cornerstone of India's development cooperation: An "externalities" perspective* (Policy Brief No. 8). New Delhi: Forum for Indian Development Cooperation.

Chakrabarti, M. (2018). Lexicon and syntax: Sustainable Development Goals—An access perspective. *Development Cooperation Review, 1*(8), 28–31.

Chaturvedi, S. (2016). *The logic of sharing: Indian approach to South-South cooperation.* Delhi: Cambridge University Press.

GAVI (GAVI, the Vaccine Alliance). (2016, January 6). *Historic partnership between Gavi and India to save millions of lives.* https://www.gavi.org/news/media-room/historic-partnership-between-gavi-and-india-save-millions-lives.

GAVI. (n.d.-a). *Countries approved for support.* https://www.gavi.org/programmes-impact/our-impact/countries-approved-support.

GAVI. (n.d.-b). *Donor profiles.* https://www.gavi.org/investing/funding/donor-contributions-pledges/annual-contributions-and-proceeds/.

Ghali, B. B. (1992). *An agenda for peace: Preventive diplomacy, peacemaking and peace-keeping* (A/47/277-S/24111). Report of the Secretary-General. https://www.un.org/ruleoflaw/files/A_47_277.pdf.

Ghosh, A., & Chawla, K. (2016, August 26). Can the international solar alliance change the game? *The Hindu.* https://www.thehindu.com/opinion/columns/Can-the-international-solar-alliance-change-the-game/article14589187.ece.

Lee, L. A., Franzel, L., Atwell, J., Datta, S. D., Friberg, I. K., Goldie, S. J., et al. (2013). The estimated mortality impact of vaccinations forecast to be administered during 2011–2020 in 73 countries supported by the GAVI Alliance. *Vaccine, 31*(Supplement 2), B61–B72.

Malhame, M., Baker, E., Gandhi, G., Jones, A., Kalpaxis, P., Iqbal, R., et al. (2019). Shaping markets to benefit global health—A 15-year history and lessons learned from the pentavalent vaccine market. *Vaccine: X, 2*, 100033.

Naidu, S., Rodrik, D., & Zucman, G. (2019, February 15). Economics after neoliberalism. *Boston Review.* https://bostonreview.net/forum/suresh-naidu-dani-rodrik-gabriel-zucman-economics-after-neoliberalism.

PIB (Press Information Bureau). (2016a, April 22). *ISA trillion dollar opportunity to serve humanity.* Press Release. http://pib.nic.in/newsite/PrintRelease.aspx?relid=139091.

PIB. (2016b). International Solar Alliance (ISA). *PIB backgrounder.* http://www.pib.nic.in/newsite/backgrounders.aspx?relid=135761.

PIB. (2016c, April 23). *International Solar Alliance cell and UNDP declared cooperation for promoting solar energy.* Press Release. http://pib.nic.in/newsite/PrintRelease.aspx?relid=141095.

PIB. (2016d, June 30). *International Solar Alliance cell and World Bank signs declaration for promoting solar energy*. Press Release. http://pib.nic.in/newsite/PrintRelease.aspx?relid=146680.

PIB. (2016e, January 25). *International Solar Alliance will be the first international and inter-governmental organisation of 121 countries to have headquarters in India with United Nations as strategic partner*. Press Release. http://pib.nic.in/newsite/PrintRelease.aspx?relid=135794.

PIB. (2016f, April 23). *Shri Piyush Goyal jointly launches programmes under ISA along with Ms. Ségolène Royal, French Minister of Environment & President of COP21*. Press Release. http://pib.nic.in/newsite/PrintRelease.aspx?relid=140090.

Schlager, E., & Ostrom, E. (1992). Property-rights regimes and natural resources: A conceptual analysis. *Land Economics, 1992*(68), 249–262.

Solar Guidelines. (2016). *Solar Guidelines*. http://www.solarguidelines.in.

Terrawatt Initiative. (2016). *Terrawatt Initiative*. http://www.theterrawattinitiative.org.

United Nations. (2015). *Report of the High-level Independent Panel on Peace Operations on uniting our strengths for peace: Politics, partnership and people* (A/70/95-S/2015/466). https://www.un.org/en/ga/search/view_doc.asp?symbol=S/2015/446.

WHO Rabies Modelling Consortium. (2019). The potential impact of provision of rabies postexposure prophylaxis in Gavi-eligible countries: A modelling study. *Lancet Infect Dis, 19*(1), 102–111.

Open Access This chapter is licensed under the terms of the Creative Commons Attribution 4.0 International License (http://creativecommons.org/licenses/by/4.0/), which permits use, sharing, adaptation, distribution and reproduction in any medium or format, as long as you give appropriate credit to the original author(s) and the source, provide a link to the Creative Commons license and indicate if changes were made.

The images or other third party material in this chapter are included in the chapter's Creative Commons license, unless indicated otherwise in a credit line to the material. If material is not included in the chapter's Creative Commons license and your intended use is not permitted by statutory regulation or exceeds the permitted use, you will need to obtain permission directly from the copyright holder.

CHAPTER 6

The Globalisation of Foreign Aid: Global Influences and the Diffusion of Aid Priorities

Liam Swiss

6.1 Introduction

Although countries follow many different pathways to become aid donors—and we witness considerable heterogeneity among donors in terms of where, when, how, and on what they spend their aid funds—there remains a striking degree of similarity among donors. For instance, donors as different as Spain, Poland, Canada, and Japan all espouse some form of support for gender equality in their programming and policies. Many of these similarities derive from what has been referred to as an "emerging global consensus" around different development priorities, yet the processes by which donors come to look and act alike have received limited attention.

To examine this puzzle, this chapter explains why bilateral aid donors often look and act alike, despite their disparate national interests and histories—a phenomenon I have previously labelled "the globalisation of foreign aid" (Swiss 2018). I identify processes that drive this similarity or isomorphism of aid actors and the diffusion of aid priorities—processes that drive the globalisation of aid. Building on earlier research, in this chapter, I reflect on: (1) how the isomorphism of aid institutions and the homogenisation of aid policy represent the effects of these common processes of globalisation; (2) the implications of the globalisation of aid on the 2030 Agenda for Sustainable Development; and (3) how the globalisation of aid contributes to the thread of "contested cooperation" that is woven through this volume.

L. Swiss (✉)
Memorial University, St. John's, NL, Canada
e-mail: lswiss@mun.ca

© The Author(s) 2021
S. Chaturvedi et al. (eds.), *The Palgrave Handbook of Development Cooperation for Achieving the 2030 Agenda*,
https://doi.org/10.1007/978-3-030-57938-8_6

6.2 The Globalisation of Aid

Despite varied interests and motivations, aid donors often think and act alike on a wide array of development policies and programming priorities in the face of otherwise heterogeneous national interests, cultures, development contexts, and organisational structures. Donors frequently acknowledge the puzzling degree of similarity in their approaches—the isomorphism of their practices and institutions—as being reflective of an emerging "global consensus" on things development- or aid-related. My research into this phenomenon labels this "the globalisation of aid" and works to explain the puzzle by drawing upon sociological neo-institutionalism and World Society theory to show how this globalisation is due to the creation, circulation, and enactment of world-level models for how aid should be delivered and the priorities on which it should focus (Swiss 2018).

By exploring the globalisation of aid in two domains (gender and security) and across donors at two levels (globally and using a three-country comparison), my findings reveal processes that promote the globalisation of aid at the macro- and micro-levels. At both scales, these processes lead to isomorphism within the aid sector, despite the divergent national interests, histories, and contexts of various donor countries. Here, I focus more on the macro-level processes of globalisation that shape donor policies and priorities, and then briefly introduce the micro-level processes that operate within aid agencies to facilitate the globalisation of aid.

6.2.1 Macro-Level Globalisation Processes

The macro-level influences identified build upon the sociological neo-institutionalist World Society perspective advanced by John W. Meyer and his students (Boli and Thomas 1999b; Meyer et al. 1997; Schofer et al. 2012). A primary focus of World Society research is the explanation of isomorphism among different states and organisations. The empirical literature in this tradition has provided significant macro-sociological evidence of how the influence of global cultural models on states leads to isomorphism or globalisation. World Society researchers show that the increasing isomorphism of states in areas as varied as educational systems, environmentalism, human rights, and legal systems derives from the influence of global actors, treaties, meetings, and networks (Boyle et al. 2015; Cole and Ramirez 2013; Frank et al. 2009; Kim et al. 2013; Nugent and Shandra 2009; Schofer and Hironaka 2005; Schofer and Meyer 2005).

Key factors identified in this literature that are linked to the diffusion of common models and institutions include state ties to international non-governmental organisations, the timing of global conferences, and the ratification of various international treaties or agendas. The World Society perspective argues that the diffusion of common institutional models is associated with greater ties to such international actors and the timing of such global agenda-setting events. Likewise, mimicry and the influence of the behaviour of other states are also shown to be a strong factor in promoting the diffusion of global models. To this end, states are shown to be more likely to display isomorphic behaviour when they: (1) are influenced by the behaviour of other states; (2) are more embedded in global networks of international organisations; and (3) aim to comply with global agendas. It is these same three macro-level influences that I identify in my research on the globalisation of aid (Swiss 2011, 2012, 2014, 2016b, 2018) and review here.

1. *Influence of other donors: Mimicry and contagion*

Donors adopt and implement new policy and programming priorities by copying the work of other donors (Swiss 2014, 2018). As perceived donor leaders innovate and implement new policy and programming directions, other donors look to them to inspire their own policy reforms and programming decisions. This emulation of leading donors is in keeping with earlier theories of mimicry and their relationship to institutional isomorphism (DiMaggio and Powell 1983). For instance, Swiss (2018) shows that Sweden—perceived as a leader in gender equality programming in the mid-2000s—was an inspiration for Canadian reforms to their gender policy and practices in that period. Indeed, one could argue that Sweden's 2014 Feminist Foreign Policy (Ministry for Foreign Affairs Sweden 2018) played a significant role in influencing Canada's subsequent advent of its Feminist International Assistance Policy in 2017 (Brown and Swiss 2017; Tiessen and Swan 2018).

Mimicry, in the World Society literature, extends to what researchers refer to as model density—measured using the number of countries or organisations that have adopted a world-level model. In essence, the higher the number of countries that adopt a policy model, treaty, or other institutional forms, the greater the likelihood that other countries will do the same. Similar to contagion effects identified in other literatures, this density effect is evident in aid donors as well, with quantitative evidence showing that the more donor countries adopt a focus on women and gender, the more likely it is that others will do so as well (Swiss 2012). For instance, statistical modelling of the adoption of donor women/gender policies and units in the period from 1968 through 2003 reveals that for every four donors that adopted such policies, the chance of other donors following suit increased by more than 100 per cent (Swiss 2018). This herd mentality among donors demonstrates the clear role for mimicry and contagion in furthering the globalisation of aid.

2. *The DAC and beyond: International organisationsns*

Another key macro-level influence on the globalisation of aid is that of international and inter-governmental organisations (Boli and Thomas 1997, 1999a). In the case of Western bilateral donors, the critical organisation in this regard is the Organisation for Economic Co-operation and Development's (OECD)

Development Assistance Committee (DAC) (Eyben 2013; Kim and Lightfoot 2011; Swiss 2016a; Verschaeve and Orbie 2018). As has been shown in other sectoral contexts (Alasuutari 2011; Alasuutari and Rasimus 2009), the OECD and its bodies are venues for standards-setting and policy development and act as a forum for donor discussion. In my earlier research, I demonstrate how the DAC's GenderNet working group of donor representatives played a key role in the spread of policies on women in development among donors (Swiss 2012).

By holding donor meetings, developing guidelines, and actively policing DAC donor behaviour through its peer review processes, the DAC shapes donor norms and encourages donors to conform to a specified set of priorities and practices. Indeed, the peer review process has been shown to influence donors to match the "best practices" of other donors as they reform and refine their aid programmes (Ashoff 2013; Carroll and Kellow 2011; Pagani 2002; Verschaeve and Orbie 2016). This is not to say that the peer review process is omnipotent in shaping donor structures and behaviours. As Lim (2014) shows, the first DAC peer review after South Korea joined the DAC contributed to some change in Korea's development cooperation, but many recommendations were difficult to implement. Although peer review involves examination by donor peers from other countries, the process is facilitated through the DAC, and the body of DAC peer review reports over the years provides evidence of a clear role for the DAC in setting standards and encouraging their implementation, by old and new donors alike.

3. *The 2030 Agenda and the global goals: Conferences and treaties*

The final macro-level influence on the globalisation of aid is that of global-level conferences, treaties, and their associated agendas. In the World Society literature, these treaties, events, and their outcomes have been linked to the diffusion of a variety of policies, models, and institutional forms (Cole 2012, 2013a, b; Swiss 2009; Yoo 2011). For aid donors, these influences have been felt via world-level conferences such as the Beijing World Conference on Women (Hafner-Burton and Pollack 2002; Moser and Moser 2005; Swiss 2012, 2018), which influenced donor responses to gender and development, and more generally worked to shape the global women's movement. Similar conferences and their outcome documents, whether aid-focussed (i.e. the 2005 Paris Declaration on Aid Effectiveness) or not (i.e. the 2015 Paris Agreement on climate change), hold substantial sway with donors. For instance, following the 2005 Paris Declaration, donors quickly embraced aid effectiveness principles such as country concentration and donor collaboration, though the implementation of these principles, in practice, did not always conform to the intent of the declaration (Brown and Swiss 2013; Hyden 2008; Sjöstedt 2013).

Still, international declarations and agenda-setting conferences are key factors in explaining the globalisation of aid. Since 2000, we have seen this play out most clearly through, first, the Millennium Development Goals (MDGs), and now the Sustainable Development Goals (SDGs) of the 2030 Agenda. For instance, despite the sometimes uneven and problematic adoption of the MDGs by donors (Clemens et al. 2007; Easterly 2009; Thiele et al. 2007), we witness at least a rhetorical, if not practical, adoption of the MDGs as a key factor in shaping donor aid allocation and priorities in a number of areas. Clemens and co-authors discuss how, even if the MDGs were unlikely to be achieved through aid, having them as an aspirational or symbolic target was able to "galvanise" the aid community to act and devote more aid towards the MDG agenda (Clemens et al. 2005). My interviews with aid workers in three donor agencies (Canadian International Development Agency, Swedish International Development Cooperation Agency, and United States Agency for International Development) revealed this same influence, where having gender equality as MDG 3 was reported by donor officials as being a valuable tool for helping advance gender and development as a priority (Swiss 2018). Even though the SDGs of the 2030 Agenda are relatively new, it is likely that this latest set of goals will serve a similar role in shaping donor aid allocation and priorities (Sethi et al. 2017).

6.2.2 Micro-Level Globalisation Processes

At the micro-level, the globalisation of aid is discerned by examining processes and mechanisms enacted by the personnel and officials working within aid donor agencies and other development actors. Drawing upon the literature on policy and norm translation, Fejerskov (2018) identifies these processes as "micro-sociological processes of agency" through which aid officials act to translate and adapt ideas into aid agencies. Swiss (2018) highlights five such processes operating within aid agencies that work to connect them to the common policy and programming models which reflect the globalisation of aid: (1) internalisation and certification of models by referring to outside authority; (2) active connections between donors and local and international civil society groups engaged in development; (3) bureaucratic activism where donor officials champion or step outside of their formal duties to promote policy and programming reforms; (4) policy processes driven by the need to have a position on some new policy or issue area for an international or multi-donor meeting or conference; and (5) processes by which donor officials attempt to assert autonomy from their respective ministries of foreign affairs (when the donor agency is a separate entity). Each of these micro-level processes is used by donor officials to justify, explain, enact, and translate common aid priorities and policies across a wide range of donor actors.

6.2.3 Why the Globalisation of Aid Matters

While puzzling, the globalisation of aid might seem a trivial feature of the international aid community. Yet, I argue that these globalisation processes in the aid sector merit further self-critique from aid actors and greater attention from researchers because of three main concerns (Swiss 2018, p. 5).

1. **Constraints on acceptable priorities**: The globalisation of aid may constrain the potential range of development interventions deemed acceptable by donors and therefore limit recipient countries in how they structure their development interventions. For instance, if the majority of aid donors is primarily interested in supporting health-related development in a country, where does that country turn for support of its other development priorities such as climate change adaptation, renewable energy, or governance reform? More consensus among donors about the priorities of development globally may thus constrain the space for recipient countries to find development cooperation support outside that consensus.
2. **Less room for innovation**: The globalisation of aid can stymy innovation and new approaches—if a donor consensus exists around a given issue, it becomes more difficult to propose alternative approaches to these issues within aid agencies. The tendency for best practices in aid to lead to cookie-cutter or one-size-fits-all approaches to certain development challenges is emblematic of the risks to innovation or doing development differently. Indeed, even when innovation is encouraged via "grand challenges" or pilot initiatives, consensus begins to emerge around successful innovations, and donors quickly aim to "scale up" the innovation into the latest cookie-cutter solution.
3. **Reduced research and analysis**: The globalisation of aid leads to a reduced need for donors to undertake research and analysis linked to various priorities and contributes to a shift of donor focus to process rather than developmental concerns. If the globalisation of aid has led donors to adopt a relatively uniform set of aid priorities and approaches, a donor agency has less incentive to ensure that those priorities and approaches are informed directly by local context and development priorities. In this way, the globalisation of aid can contribute to approaches that see donors do development similarly in many contexts rather than valorising the local needs of societies and communities where they work. In extremis, this may lead donors to a focus that ignores local contexts and prioritises donor processes over the actual evidentiary basis for aid interventions.

Each of these limits and constraints underscores the potential downsides of a globalised aid community and reveals why it is important for aid researchers to consider isomorphism among aid agencies and their priorities as a potential risk to effective and appropriate aid. Unfortunately, these same possible negative effects of the globalisation of aid are also likely to shape how it influences the 2030 Agenda moving forward, the topic to which I turn in the next section.

6.3 Implications for the 2030 Agenda

The globalisation of aid is likely to advance in the context of the 2030 Agenda. SDG priorities will shape aid donors' programming and policies by narrowing their focus on the SDGs; however, this may be less evident than in the past under the MDGs because of the more than doubling of the number of goals. Indeed, with 17 SDGs, the scope of the SDGs may present donors with a wider array of policy and programming priorities to target. This may lead to the appearance of a less isomorphic aid field, but in reality, it might just present a more diverse set of targets at which donors will aim their efforts while still conforming to normative pressures to support the SDGs. The globalised aid consensus will include more potential choices but still constrain donors to work within the ambit of the SDGs.

Taken to its extreme, another potential risk of the globalisation of aid for the 2030 Agenda is that donors will overly focus their efforts on a narrow subset of the SDGs to the neglect of others. This may lead to a patchwork and uneven implementation of the 2030 Agenda. Indeed, with 17 goals, the ability of individual donors—or even donors collectively—to address all of the SDGs in a meaningful fashion is limited. This means that, as aid donor priorities coalesce around certain SDGs, the globalisation of aid may limit the potential to evenly implement the 2030 Agenda. In this respect, the contradiction of having a global agenda imposed through the SDGs that is simultaneously prescriptive but overbroad carries the risk of only a patchwork uptake of the agenda in a globalised aid context. For instance, there is good reason to expect that donors will dedicate more energy and resources to the achievement of certain SDGs and their related targets than others. The focus of SDG 1 on extreme poverty is more likely to attract donor attention and official development assistance (ODA) dollars than SDG 12 and its focus on responsible consumption and production. Add to this the challenge that donors do not always choose the most appropriate aid instruments and modalities to contribute to specific SDGs in a given country, and a globalised aid agenda in support of the SDGs heightens the risk of a mismatch between donor and recipient aims (Rudolph 2017).

Likewise, although there is a wider scope of the substantive development goals under the 2030 Agenda, the influence of SDG 17 to strengthen the implementation of global partnerships for sustainable development may work to constrain donor approaches for supporting the SDGs. By focussing donor efforts on a specified range of modalities such as the use of multi-stakeholder partnerships, support to capacity-building, or efforts to increase policy coherence, SDG 17 provides donors with an outside authority to refer to in justifying their programming decisions. The internalisation and certification process outlined above would serve in such cases for donor agency officials to legitimate their policy and programming plans by linking them to support for SDG 17. Although concentrating donor efforts to support the global goals would seem to be an inherently good thing for the achievement of the 2030 Agenda, it also runs the risk of having donors exclude alternative approaches to development that do not meet with the modalities outlined in SDG 17. In this way, the globalisation of aid can blinker aid donors in their programming choices and approaches to partnering. These effects of the globalisation of aid on the 2030 Agenda could play a role in stymying aid/donor innovation in attempting to achieve the SDGs. Although the breadth of SDG 17 and its manifold indicators suggests that almost "anything goes" in order for donors to contribute to the goal, the reality of the wide menu of modalities available to donors may play the opposite role in limiting donor interventions due to donors becoming overly focussed on one or another of the 19 targets of SDG 17.

Another implication of the globalisation of aid on the 2030 Agenda relates to non-DAC donors, South-South cooperation, and new donor countries. The same sorts of globalisation processes I discuss above in the DAC context have been shown to shape new and emerging donors in similar ways, though there still exist significant gaps between the development cooperation of established and emerging donors (Gulrajani and Swiss 2018, 2019). New donor countries respond to similar norms about how to be a donor country, as have the DAC donors, and recent research shows that these normative frameworks are in flux, possibly converging to a new set of ideas of what it means to be a donor, whether DAC or non-DAC (Gulrajani and Swiss 2019). If the globalisation of aid in the 2030 Agenda era brings both conventional ODA donors and South-South cooperation partners into a common set of priorities and practices, this may lead to greater coherence of development cooperation—in its many guises—in support of the SDGs and the broader 2030 Agenda. Although donor norms for ODA providers and South-South cooperation partners have not always aligned previously, a period of contested cooperation may see the globalisation of aid shape norms for both that become increasingly similar.

6.4 The Globalisation of Aid and Contested Cooperation

Whereas the globalisation of aid is likely more reflective of collaboration in the development assistance field, contestation can be viewed as a driver of new and emerging aid policy priorities and programming trends. This section considers the globalisation of aid's relationship to both collaboration and contestation and briefly suggests how it is implicated in this volume's arguments around "contested cooperation" in the 2030 Agenda era.

Collaboration leads to the globalisation of aid. As donors and other international actors convene to address particular development issues or challenges, the common approaches, priorities, and guidelines they devise contribute significantly to the globalisation of aid. This globalisation of aid—donors sharing common policies and priorities—contributes to what Gulrajani and Swiss identify as the norms of donorship (Gulrajani and Swiss 2018, 2019). These norms—the agenda of a globalised aid community—represent the result of collaboration among an array of aid actors, experts, researchers, and communities. Successful collaborations lead to shared understandings, the diffusion of common practices and models, and the isomorphism of aid actors and practices. Yet, it is clear that the aid sector and its practices can be fickle and ebb and flow through a series of "new and improved" policies and best practices on what seems like a more frequent schedule.

Here, I think it is important to consider the globalisation of aid not as a uniform adoption of one static approach to aid by donors, but instead as a dynamic series of such priorities, policies, and models that fall in and out of favour, not only because of collaboration in the aid sector, but also via contestation. Contestation, as many chapters in this volume illustrate, is a key part of the foreign aid sector globally. Despite the globalisation of aid, there is consistent contestation in the development assistance sector, which can lead to a heterogeneous adoption or implementation of norms and aid priorities (Cold-Ravnkilde et al. 2018). Indeed, even when donors arrive at a set of priorities around an issue such as aid effectiveness, gender, or security, the practices of aid are highly contested and sometimes diverge sharply from organisation to organisation, donor to donor (Brown and Swiss 2013). These gaps might be exaggerated by greater contestation in the donor space. More recently, conventional DAC donors have witnessed such contestation from emerging donors and providers of South-South cooperation (Gulrajani and Swiss 2018). Such contestation of the DAC status quo has been perceived in recent years via the growing role of the United Nations Development Cooperation Forum, despite some of its shortcomings (Verschaeve and Orbie 2016).

Contested cooperation, in this sense, represents the cyclical dynamic of the coming and going of vogues of aid priorities and practices that represent the globalisation of aid. The aid sector is embedded in the negotiation, adoption, and eventual rejection of globalised priorities and approaches, which are eventually contested and then jettisoned in favour of a new approach or fad that has evolved from contestation and collaboration by other aid actors. This contested cooperation framework—interacting with the globalisation processes I outline above—makes for a valuable lens through which to understand persistence and change in development cooperation.

Common aid models emerge from new collaboration, are contested between, through, and within aid agencies, and may eventually achieve a form of dominance that results in the seeming isomorphism and diffusion of aid priorities, which I argue represent the globalisation of aid. Arguably, the globalisation of aid, and the isomorphism and diffusion it represents, is a key outcome of the contested cooperation that this volume identifies in the global aid sector. With the 2030 Agenda, we are likely to witness these globalised outcomes around a variety of aid practices and priorities before the closing of the SDGs in 2030. Indeed, as the variety of actors involved in the contested cooperation that helps drive this process widens, the globalisation of aid will likely touch upon many more donors, development non-governmental organisations, and aid recipients as 2030 approaches.

REFERENCES

Alasuutari, P. (2011). The governmentality of consultancy and competition: The influence of the OECD. In G. Solinis & N. Baya-Laffite (Eds.), *Mapping out the research-policy matrix: Highlights from the first International forum on the social science-policy Nexus* (pp. 147–165). Paris: UNESCO Publishing.

Alasuutari, P., & Rasimus, A. (2009). Use of the OECD in justifying policy reforms: The case of Finland. *Journal of Power, 2*(1), 89–109.

Ashoff, G. (2013). *50 years of peer reviews by the OECD's Development Assistance Committee: An instrument of quality assurance and mutual learning* (DIE Briefing Paper 12/2013). Bonn: German Development Institute / Deutsches Institut für Entwicklungspolitik (DIE).

Boli, J., & Thomas, G. M. (1997). World culture in the world polity: A century of international non-governmental organization. *American Sociological Review, 62*(2), 171–190.

Boli, J., & Thomas, G. M. (1999a). INGOs and the organization of world culture. In J. Boli & G. M. Thomas (Eds.), *Constructing world culture: International nongovernmental organizations since 1875* (pp. 13–49). Stanford, CA: Stanford University Press.

Boli, J., & Thomas, G. M. (1999b). *Constructing world culture: International nongovernmental organizations since 1875.* Stanford, CA: Stanford University Press.

Boyle, E. H., Kim, M., & Longhofer, W. (2015). Abortion liberalization in world society, 1960–2009. *American Journal of Sociology, 121*(3), 882–913.

Brown, S., & Swiss, L. (2013). The hollow ring of donor commitment: Country concentration and the decoupling of aid effectiveness norms from donor practice. *Development Policy Review, 31*(6), 737–755.

Brown, S., & Swiss, L. (2017). Canada's feminist international assistance policy: Game-changer or fig leaf? In K. A. H. Graham & A. M. Maslove (Eds.), *How Ottawa spends, 2017–2018* (pp. 117–131). Ottawa, ON: School of Public Policy and Administration, Carleton University.

Carroll, P., & Kellow, A. (2011). *The OECD: A study of organisational adaptation.* Cheltenham: Edward Elgar Publishing.

Clemens, M. A., Kenny, C. J., & Moss, T. J. (2005). The millennium development goal aid targets, and the costs of over-expectations. *Sustainable Development Law & Policy, 6*(1), 58–84.

Clemens, M. A., Kenny, C. J., & Moss, T. J. (2007). The trouble with the MDGs: Confronting expectations of aid and development success. *World Development, 35*(5), 735–751.

Cold-Ravnkilde, S. M., Engberg-Pedersen, L., & Fejerskov, A. M. (2018). Global norms and heterogeneous development organizations: Introduction to special issue on new actors, old donors and gender equality norms in international development cooperation. *Progress in Development Studies, 18*(2), 77–94.

Cole, W. M. (2012). Human rights as myth and ceremony? Reevaluating the effectiveness of human rights treaties, 1981–2007. *American Journal of Sociology, 117*(4), 1131–1171.

Cole, W. M. (2013a). Strong walk and cheap talk: The effect of the international covenant of economic, social, and cultural rights on policies and practices. *Social Forces, 92*(1), 165–194.

Cole, W. M. (2013b). Government respect for gendered rights: The effect of the convention on the elimination of discrimination against women on women's rights outcomes, 1981–2004. *International Studies Quarterly, 57*(2), 233–249.

Cole, W. M., & Ramirez, F. O. (2013). Conditional decoupling assessing the impact of national human rights institutions, 1981 to 2004. *American Sociological Review, 78*(4), 702–725.

DiMaggio, P., & Powell, W. W. (1983). The iron cage revisited: Institutional isomorphism and collective rationality in organizational fields. *American Sociological Review, 48*(2), 147–160.

Easterly, W. (2009). How the millennium development goals are unfair to Africa. *World Development, 37*(1), 26–35.

Eyben, R. (2013). Struggles in Paris: The DAC and the purposes of development aid. *European Journal of Development Research, 25*(1), 78–91.

Fejerskov, A. M. (2018). Development as resistance and translation: Remaking norms and ideas of the Gates Foundation. *Progress in Development Studies, 18*(2), 126–143.

Frank, D. J., Hardinge, T., & Wosick-Correa, K. (2009). The global dimensions of rape-law reform: A cross-national study of policy outcomes. *American Sociological Review, 74*(2), 272–290.

Gulrajani, N., & Swiss, L. (2018). Donor proliferation to what ends? New donor countries and the search for legitimacy. *Canadian Journal of Development Studies / Revue canadienne d'études du développement*, 1–21. https://doi.org/10.1080/02255189.2019.1543652.

Gulrajani, N., & Swiss, L. (2019). Donorship in a state of flux. In I. Olivié & A. Pérez (Eds.), *Aid power and politics* (pp. 199–222). London: Routledge.

Hafner-Burton, E., & Pollack, M. A. (2002). Mainstreaming gender in global governance. *European Journal of International Relations, 8*(3), 339–373.

Hyden, G. (2008). After the Paris declaration: Taking on the issue of power. *Development Policy Review, 26*(3), 259–274.

Kim, S., & Lightfoot, S. (2011). Does "DAC-ability" really matter? The emergence of non-DAC donors: Introduction to policy arena. *Journal of International Development, 23*(5), 711–721.

Kim, M., Longhofer, W., Boyle, E. H., & Nyseth Brehm, H. (2013). When do laws matter? National minimum-age-of-marriage laws, child rights, and adolescent fertility, 1989–2007. *Law & Society Review, 47*(3), 589–619.

Lim, S. (2014). Compliance with international norms: Implementing OECD DAC principles in South Korea. *Globalizations, 11*(6), 859–874.

Meyer, J. W., Boli, J., Thomas, G. M., & Ramirez, F. O. (1997). World society and the nation-state. *American Journal of Sociology, 103*(1), 144–181.

Ministry for Foreign Affairs Sweden. (2018). *Handbook: Sweden's feminist foreign policy*. https://www.government.se/4abf3b/contentassets/fc115607a4ad4bca913cd8d11c2339dc/handbook-swedens-feminist-foreign-policy.

Moser, C., & Moser, A. (2005). Gender mainstreaming since Beijing: A review of success and limitations in international institutions. *Gender and Development, 13*(2), 11–22.

Nugent, C., & Shandra, J. M. (2009). State environmental protection efforts, women's status, and world polity: A cross-national analysis. *Organization & Environment, 22*(2), 208–229.

Pagani, F. (2002). Peer review as a tool for co-operation and change. *African Security Review, 11*(4), 15–24.

Rudolph, A. (2017). *The concept of SDG-sensitive development cooperation: Implications for OECD-DAC members* (DIE Discussion Paper 1/2017). Bonn: German Development Institute / Deutsches Institut für Entwicklungspolitik (DIE).

Schofer, E., & Hironaka, A. (2005). The effects of world society on environmental protection outcomes. *Social Forces, 84*(1), 25–47.

Schofer, E., Hironaka, A., Frank, D. J., & Longhofer, W. (2012). Sociological institutionalism and world society. In E. Amenta, K. Nash, & A. Scott (Eds.), *The Wiley-Blackwell companion to political sociology* (pp. 57–68). Malden, MA: Wiley-Blackwell.

Schofer, E., & Meyer, J. W. (2005). The worldwide expansion of higher education in the twentieth century. *American Sociological Review, 70*(6), 898–920.

Sethi, T., Custer, S., Turner, J., Sims, J., DiLorenzo, M., & Latourell, R. (2017). *Realizing agenda 2030: Will donor dollars and country priorities align with global goals? A baseline report*. Williamsburg, VA: AidData.

Sjöstedt, M. (2013). Aid effectiveness and the Paris declaration: A mismatch between ownership and results-based management? *Public Administration and Development, 33*(2), 143–155.

Swiss, L. (2009). Decoupling values from action: An event-history analysis of the election of women to parliament in the developing world, 1945–1990. *International Journal of Comparative Sociology, 50*(1), 69–95.

Swiss, L. (2011). Security sector reform and development assistance: Explaining the diffusion of policy priorities among donor agencies. *Qualitative Sociology, 34*(2), 371–393.

Swiss, L. (2012). The adoption of women and gender as development assistance priorities: An event history analysis of world polity effects. *International Sociology, 27*(1), 96–119.

Swiss, L. (2014). Mimicry and motives: Canadian aid allocation in longitudinal perspective. In S. Brown, D. R. Black, & M. den Heyer (Eds.), *Rethinking Canadian* (pp. 101–124). Ottawa, ON: University of Ottawa Press.

Swiss, L. (2016a). A sociology of foreign aid and the world society. *Sociology Compass, 10*(1), 65–73.

Swiss, L. (2016b). Space for gender equality in the security and development agenda? Insights from three donors. In S. Brown & J. Grävingholt (Eds.), *The securitization of foreign aid* (pp. 188–211). Basingstoke: Palgrave Macmillan.

Swiss, L. (2018). *The globalization of foreign aid: Developing consensus*. London: Routledge.

Thiele, R., Nunnenkamp, P., & Dreher, A. (2007). Do donors target aid in line with the millennium development goals? A sector perspective of aid allocation. *Review of World Economics, 143*(4), 596–630.

Tiessen, R., & Swan, E. (2018). Canada's feminist foreign policy promises: An ambitious agenda for gender equality, human rights, peace, and security. In N. Hillmer & P. Lagassé (Eds.), *Justin Trudeau and Canadian foreign policy* (pp. 187–205). Cham: Springer International Publishing.

Verschaeve, J., & Orbie, J. (2016). The DAC is dead, long live the DCF? A comparative analysis of the OECD Development Assistance Committee and the UN Development Cooperation Forum. *The European Journal of Development Research, 28*(4), 571–587.

Verschaeve, J., & Orbie, J. (2018). Ignoring the elephant in the room? Assessing the impact of the European Union on the Development Assistance committee's role in international development. *Development Policy Review, 36*(S1), O44–O58.

Yoo, E. (2011). International human rights regime, neoliberalism, and women's social rights, 1984–2004. *International Journal of Comparative Sociology, 52*(6), 503–528.

Open Access This chapter is licensed under the terms of the Creative Commons Attribution 4.0 International License (http://creativecommons.org/licenses/by/4.0/), which permits use, sharing, adaptation, distribution and reproduction in any medium or format, as long as you give appropriate credit to the original author(s) and the source, provide a link to the Creative Commons license and indicate if changes were made.

The images or other third party material in this chapter are included in the chapter's Creative Commons license, unless indicated otherwise in a credit line to the material. If material is not included in the chapter's Creative Commons license and your intended use is not permitted by statutory regulation or exceeds the permitted use, you will need to obtain permission directly from the copyright holder.

CHAPTER 7

The Untapped Functions of International Cooperation in the Age of Sustainable Development

Adolf Kloke-Lesch

7.1 Introduction: An Agenda That Calls for More

In this contribution, I challenge the traditional notion of development cooperation by using a functional approach to understanding externally oriented policies, apply this approach to assess whether the means of implementation (MoIs) incorporated in the 2030 Agenda for Sustainable Development are commensurate to its universal character, and elaborate key features of a truly universal concept of international cooperation for sustainable development. After the introduction setting the scene, the next part unpacks the traditional notion of development cooperation from a functional perspective, with a particular view on past contestations in political practice, in order to arrive at a more basic understanding of different forms and roles in the fields of international relations and cooperation. In the third part, this functional understanding is used to roughly compare the ambitions of the 2030 Agenda with the envisaged MoIs, with a particular view to implementation within "developed countries" as well as between them.[1] The fourth part takes an exemplary look at the ways international organisations and cooperation formats between "developed countries" have embraced and processed the agenda during the first four years since its adoption. The conclusion contrasts the development cooperation concept of the pre-2015 world with a concept of international cooperation required for the 2030 world.

A. Kloke-Lesch (✉)
Sustainable Development Solutions Network Germany (SDSN Germany),
Bonn, Germany
e-mail: kloke-lesch@sdsngermany.de

© The Author(s) 2021
S. Chaturvedi et al. (eds.), *The Palgrave Handbook of Development Cooperation for Achieving the 2030 Agenda*,
https://doi.org/10.1007/978-3-030-57938-8_7

127

The adoption of the universal 2030 Agenda for Sustainable Development with its 17 Sustainable Development Goals (SDGs) by a world leaders' summit at the United Nations (UN) in September 2015 marked both a big success of, and a great challenge to, development cooperation actors. Under its ambitious headline "Transforming our world", the 2030 Agenda presents itself as "a plan of action for people, planet and prosperity" (United Nations [UN] 2015c). The 2030 Agenda sets "universal and transformative Goals and targets" and stipulates a "Global Partnership for Sustainable Development" under which "all countries and all stakeholders [...] will implement this plan" (UN 2015c). Development cooperation actors need to learn from this success, fully embrace its implications, and transform themselves towards a truly universal international cooperation for sustainable development.

The 2030 Agenda was a success for development cooperation actors because they were able to leave their conceptual path-dependencies, epitomised by the eight Millenniums Development Goals (MDGs),[2] by joining the processes initiated by the UN Conference on Sustainable Development in 2012 (also known as Rio+20) and incorporating their ambitions, objectives, and approaches in the emerging new universal agenda of sustainable development.

This was by no means preordained. Just a few months before the Rio+20 conference, a High-Level Panel of Eminent Persons on the Post-2015 Development Agenda (HLP) was convened by the UN Secretary-General.[3] The HLP was, in the first place, understood as a parallel process to what later became the Open Working Group of the General Assembly on Sustainable Development Goals (OWG).[4]

The two processes differed markedly. The HLP worked for "a poverty/basic needs agenda, serving to coordinate international aid efforts", whereas the OWG aimed at "a sustainable development agenda incorporating poverty, environmental sustainability, economic development, and social equity" (Fukuda-Parr and McNeill 2019, p. 9). The terms of reference for the HLP even called on the panel "to advise the Secretary-General on how the SDGs relate to the broader Post-2015 development agenda". This mandate putting the post-2015 development agenda somewhere "above" the SDGs was soon to be overtaken by history, as the OWG became the one and only intergovernmental process shaping the new integrated agenda. The report of the HLP (High Level Panel 2013) acknowledged, and eventually supported, this comprehensive approach with, for example, the notion of "One World: One Sustainable Development Agenda". Hence, the HLP's report reflects the beginning of a real acceptance by many—in particular in the traditional development cooperation community—that a transformational agenda might be possible (Dodds et al. 2017). The 2030 Agenda can thus be seen as a result of a contestation of traditional narratives and norms of development policy and cooperation that led to the successful evolution of a new normative framework.

One of the major challenges presented by the 2030 Agenda to development cooperation as well as to other actors lies in the fact that its universal, integrated, and indivisible character constitutes sort of a Copernican turn in the thinking of (global) development that is not accompanied by a comparable overhaul of the institutional and instrumental set-up of the pre-2015 world. Surely, this would not constitute a fundamental problem for the implementation of the 2030 Agenda if the SDGs would only need to be achieved in the "developing countries". Quite the opposite is the case. As the SDGs are calling for actions by all and benefitting all (Von der Heijden et al. 2014), most of them can only be achieved globally if also achieved in and by the "developed countries".

However, the normative framework of the 2030 Agenda is barely recognised as a contestation or challenge also to the norms and institutions governing relations and cooperation between the "developed countries". This should be of serious concern since implementing the transformative 2030 Agenda within the framework of the pre-2015 institutions and instruments puts the world at risk of also ending up in a pre-2015 world again.

Therefore, both the scholarly and political debates on the international implementation of the 2030 Agenda (Cooper and French 2018; Stafford-Smith et al. 2017) should move beyond "North-South" and "South-South" cooperation and address the agenda's repercussions also on "North-North" cooperation. To this end, development studies, when shaping their role in the decades to come (Baud et al. 2019), also need to more fundamentally review—and most probably reframe—some of the basic tenets and terminologies they have stuck to for decades.[5]

In order to take a bird's eye view on the changing patterns and necessities of international cooperation, scholarly debates more than ever need to make dated as well as more recent diplomatic and bureaucratic terminologies their subjects by using their own conceptualities and terminologies instead of following or mirroring the political discourse. This is all the more needed and demanding, as multiple contestations to the paradigms of development and development cooperation have led to sort of a Babylonian Confusion aggravating the difficulties of understanding and working in a rapidly changing world. This contribution does not aim to resolve this. Rather, it should be read as a call to open a door to new thinking, research, and practice.

7.2 What *Is* Development Cooperation? A Functional Approach to External Policies

Throughout the past decades, a primarily normative conceptualisation of development cooperation has been one of its most distinctive features vis-à-vis other policy fields, which are basically defined or understood in functional terms. Nevertheless, also development cooperation is a manifestation of governmental functions. The underlying assumption of this functional approach is that in all states (as "political systems") "the same functions are performed [...] even though these functions may be performed with different frequencies, and by different kinds of structures" (Almond 1960, p. 11), and that this can also be applied to the external behaviour of states, which in the twenty-first century may go well beyond the function of "protecting the integrity of political systems from outside threats, or expanding into and attacking other societies" (Almond 1960, p. 5).

Thus, in order to arrive at a functional understanding of development cooperation, the core question is not "What is the *purpose* of development cooperation?" but rather "What *is* development cooperation?" (Kloke-Lesch 1998a, b).[6] The distinction between the basic (or abstract) function of a policy field on the one hand, and its (changing) substantial purposes (policy goals) on the other hand, is quite familiar in different policy fields. Foreign policy is essentially not understood, for example, as peace policy by definition, but rather in functional terms as the management and shaping of relations to other states ("Diplomacy *is* intermediation" [Haynal 2002, p. 34]). Nor is economic policy primarily conceived, for example, as growth policy, but rather as governments' actions influencing economic orders, processes, or structures.

By contrast, development cooperation has been normatively framed mainly by purpose, namely the promotion of economic and social development of "developing countries", with the MDGs having had narrowed this normative approach to the eradication of poverty (UN 2015a). The geographical limitation[7] to (changing) lists of "developing countries" is the inherently inevitable consequence of the underlying normative concept of development, followed by the membership of both the UN and the Development Assistance Committee (DAC) of the Organisation for Economic Co-operation and Development (OECD). Furthermore, for some decades (and for many actors and scholars still today), the measures and instruments used for this purpose have been equalled to aid, or at least have had to show a certain grant element, characterising the so-called donor–recipient relationship.

Contrary to this primarily normative conceptualisation, I am going to suggest a basically functional reading of "development cooperation" that is neither linked to a specific normative concept of development, nor to a limited group of countries in the first place: "development cooperation" as shaping conditions within (other) countries by using cooperative and promotional means. A functional understanding of development cooperation, as well as of external governmental activities at large, seems better suited to answer contestations that the policy field of development cooperation has repeatedly been faced with: contestations to the notion and norm of development itself, in relation to other policy fields, and by new actors and challenges that emerge over time, not least by the 2030 Agenda. After some sketchy observations on these contestations, the functional understanding of development cooperation within externally oriented policy fields is further explained and prepares for a functional assessment of the 2030 Agenda's means of implementation.

7.2.1 The Contested Notion of "Development"

Throughout the decades, development cooperation has mainly been based on a specific, normative notion of development itself (Kloke-Lesch 2019). These traditional discourses understand development mainly as a progressive ("positive"), primarily socio-economic process that needs to happen in the "developing countries" and had happened before in the "developed countries". Also, critical development studies (Veltmeyer and Wise 2018), which argue in favour of alternative development paths, tend to stick to a normative and geographically limited (or at least focussed) notion of development.[8] At the same time, calls to reconsider and abandon the term "development" are growing, as the term appears to produce more misunderstandings than solutions and to perpetuate the dichotomies of Self/Other or South/North (Schönberg 2019).

In order to break free of these basically normative connotations of "development" and get a better grip on the manifold processes under "accelerated globalisation", the concept of transformation studies tries to contribute towards a rethinking of international development (Alff and Hornidge 2019). Here, transformation is conceived as an open-ended and unpredictable process ("any process of change, including studying it, or attempts to actively shape it") with an emphasis on "the negotiation processes inherent to unfolding change, rather than about its ultimate result or outcome" not "being bound or fixed to particular places, regions or areas" (Alff and Hornidge 2019, p. 142), and thereby also challenging the traditional geographical limits of the notion of development. This challenge also sneaked into the renewed definition of development studies that evolved within the European Association of Development Research and Training Institutes, which mentions as one of the emerging novel concerns "poverty and social exclusion in industrialised countries" while maintaining development studies as "also characterised by normative and policy concerns" (Mönks et al. 2019).[9] Moving these argumentations even further, one could also turn to a more neutral understanding of the notion of "development" itself as a term covering the change ("developments") occurring or unfolding in any place.

On the normative side, the advent of the universal concept of sustainable development—with its economic, social, environmental, as well as political dimensions—constitutes a contestation to both the purpose and the geographical focus of the traditional concept of development: the 2030 Agenda claims that development everywhere needs to be sustainable. Thus, sustainable development as a concept cannot be confined to "developing countries", giving rise to doubts whether the notion of development can have any separate normative meaning at all alongside the notion of sustainable development. In the same vein, "the concept of the global common good as a normative and analytical framework for development research and policy and international cooperation for global sustainability" (Messner and Scholz 2018, p. 1) constitutes a fundamental change of perspective by moving the vanishing point of development and development cooperation beyond "developing countries" alone. These various contestations have contributed to an emerging shift "towards a new paradigm of global development" where the term "international development" and the accompanying concept of development cooperation from the "North" to the "South" became seen as "increasingly inappropriate for encompassing the various actors, processes and major challenges with which our world engages in the early 21st century" (Horner 2019). In this context, it is worth noting that the notion of global development is—and should always be—broader than a political product such as the 2030 Agenda with its SDGs, which by their very character are an expression of a political compromise struck in a given moment in history.[10]

7.2.2 Development Cooperation: Normative Overcharge and the Risk of Marginalisation

Based on a primarily normative concept of development, most development cooperation actors from the "North" have a penchant for occupying the high moral ground and deliberately trying to insulate themselves from political, economic, or other interests and concerns beyond their own remit all too easily denounced as selfish, amoral, or at least short-term, and denied having normative bearings of their own. This basically altruistic self-perception renders development cooperation quite a delicate position with regard to other policy fields. Since giving in to self-interest is seen as an aberration from the path of virtue and questioning their core identity, development cooperation actors hesitate to enter in a give-and-take situation with other departments.

In addition, aid that is also oriented towards securing domestic or national interests is seen as a detrimental ("not always the most efficient, nor the most effective") way to maximise global development ambitions (Gulrajani and Calleja 2019). This claim of maintaining the "integrity" or "purity" of development cooperation by the "North" as, for example, epitomised in the Principled Aid Index (Gulrajani and Calleja 2019), is an underestimated impediment when seeking political compromise. On the other hand, counting in self-interest and non-developmental normative concerns always has been—and continues to be—part of the political reality of development cooperation (Gulrajani and Calleja 2019; Mawdsley 2017). Denying this leads to the often observed hypocrisy in domestic and international development discourses, hampering the credibility more than the very fact itself.

Also, the suggestion to understand development cooperation quite broadly as "a country's policies and how these affect the current and future welfare and growth of other countries' people and economies" and to include actors "that do not have an explicit policy towards other countries […] because their policies – for example, on climate, migration, and trade—have a bearing on people elsewhere, regardless of their intent" (Mitchell 2021) can be seen as an acknowledgement of the realities of cooperation while maintaining a traditional normative orientation. The talk of win-win cooperation and enlightened self-interest tries to overcome this hypocrisy, but it does not change much the basic normative understanding of development cooperation.

It was after the end of the "East-West" conflict, in particular, that development cooperation actors hoped to break free of the geopolitical considerations infringing on their activities and focus on their core normative purpose, which inter alia led to the Millennium Declaration (UN 2000) and the MDGs. However, the two decades following the MDGs have shown something different and confronted a normatively overcharged notion of development cooperation with new contestations. Insulating development cooperation from infringements by other policy fields, while at the same time confronting them with far-reaching developmental demands, can lead to isolation and marginalisation of the policy field or, eventually, to its subordination to others.

7.2.3 Time and Again Too Narrow to Cope with New Challenges

Lastly and most importantly, a normative and geographically limited self-conceptualisation of development cooperation makes it difficult for development cooperation actors to deal with emerging new challenges and new actors. This could, for example, be observed after 1989, when Western donors started to support and promote transformation in Central and Eastern Europe and in the countries of the former Soviet Union by deploying institutions and instruments of development cooperation. This engagement of development cooperation actors was heavily contested, both from within and beyond the traditional development community, arguing that these countries were not "developing countries", the purpose of the engagement was not poverty reduction, and including them in the official development assistance (ODA) would crowd out traditional recipients.[11]

The primarily normative and geographically limited understanding of developing cooperation encapsulated in the ODA concept also holds sway over the discourses on the increased heterogeneity of "developing countries" (van Bergeijk and van Marrewijk 2013; Fialho and van Bergeijk 2017). There, it leads to calls to focus development cooperation on low-income countries, to graduate middle-income countries from the list of ODA recipients, and to "hand over" cooperation with them to departments beyond the aid agencies. A comparable debate runs about whether, or to what extent, support for global public goods such as climate or biodiversity (Kaul 2017), activities in the context of military interventions such as in Afghanistan or Iraq (Dalrymple 2016; Kisangani and Pickering 2015), or, more recently, measures in the context of migration (CSO Partnership 2017) should be considered part of development cooperation.

Furthermore, and not only in these topical contexts, foreign affairs as well as line ministries of DAC countries have created budget lines and set up operational structures to implement projects in "developing countries" and to fund respective multilateral institutions, thus bypassing aid departments and agencies, and furthering the "fragmentation of aid" (Klingebiel et al. 2016). To a significant extent, the emergence of these actors can be seen also as a reaction to the hesitation and refusal by traditional development actors to embrace new topics, for example in the areas mentioned above and the related concerns of other departments. Consequently, and although most of these activities are reported as ODA, aid departments are struggling to coordinate and embed them into their broader frameworks of development cooperation.

These contestations from within the individual DAC countries are accompanied and reinforced from beyond the DAC by the increasing relevance of other state actors and approaches often subsumed under "South-South" cooperation.[12] In its self-perception as well as in the UN, this type of cooperation is explicitly seen as distinct from ODA (UN 2019b) by following the idea of a mutually beneficial cooperation taking quite different, multimodal forms by linking financial and technical cooperation under concessionary terms with non-concessionary means, knowledge sharing, trade, and investment in all kinds of sectors.

The discussed concept of Total Official Support for Sustainable Development (TOSSD) can be understood as an attempt to develop an overarching framework for all external, officially supported finance for sustainable development (UN 2019a). "Southern" actors see this as the "Southernisation" of ODA and an attempt to measure "South-South" cooperation with a concept originally coming from the OECD. Still, the vanishing point also of the TOSSD concept lies in a group of countries categorised as "developing".

7.2.4 What Is Development Cooperation?

Given these changing conceptualisations and contestations of development cooperation, it seems useful to look for a more basic feature that is common to all the different manifestations: the function of development cooperation within the externally oriented policy fields (Kloke-Lesch 1998a, b). Such a basic feature needs to be embedded into a broader functional understanding of externally oriented governmental activities. For this, it seems helpful to develop a very basic mapping of the external functions of a state as a "political system", that is, the functions that relate to its external environment and are performed in order to maintain the system (see Table 7.1). These potential functions could be basically described as threefold: first, shaping relations *between* countries, second, shaping conditions *within* (other) countries, and third, shaping *global* conditions.

Shaping relations *between* countries is the most basic and oldest external function of states, including, on the one hand, the relations between the states (as "political systems") themselves (from mutual recognition and diplomacy through to the threat and use of military force), and on the other hand non-governmental relations between the countries, such as the interactions of economic and societal actors or individual persons (e.g. flow of people, goods,

Table 7.1 Functional mapping of externally oriented policies and the place of development cooperation

Fields of activity / Instruments	Shaping relations *between* countries	Shaping conditions *within* countries	Shaping *global* conditions
Regulation of governmental and non-governmental behaviour			
Promotion of non-governmental behaviour			
Inter-governmental cooperation			

	Core functions of development cooperation
	Related functions (policy coherence for development)

Source Author

services, capital, knowledge, and information). Traditionally, this function is exerted by a state primarily with a view to domestic and national purposes, while in principle respecting the concepts of sovereignty and non-interference with regard to other states.

However, as the internal developments of other countries sometimes matter, shaping the conditions *within* countries emerged as a second external function of states. This function can be exerted with high, low, or no respect for the principles of sovereignty and non-interference as well as on the basis, for example, of a request/invitation from the one state or a proposition by the other. It may relate to economic or social conditions (e.g. labour standards, security or human rights issues, or environmental as well as migration concerns).

Beyond the conditions *within* countries, there is increasing interest by states in shaping *global* conditions. This third external function of states relates to global public goods as well as other concerns that require more than measures just within countries (e.g. climate; oceans, including deep sea mining; biodiversity; global macroeconomic stability and a functioning trading system; health; air traffic security; space; and migration).

When exercising these functions, governments can use and combine a broad array of means. I suggest categorising them as regulatory, promotional, and cooperative. Regulatory means include laws and norms at the national and international levels. Promotional means refer in the first place to financial and other incentives for non-governmental actors (e.g. business, civil society organisations, individual persons) engaged in external activities. Cooperative means, in this context, are specifically understood as intended intergovernmental project and programme cooperation aiming at concrete, palpable outcomes.

All three external functions of a state can be performed in unilateral, bilateral, plurilateral, and multilateral ways. The motives can be selfish, altruistic, or enlightened. The objectives may lie at home or abroad. Furthermore, the functions can be intertwined. For example, countries can shape relations to other countries with the aim of changing conditions within these countries, or they can engage in shaping conditions within other countries while aiming at global conditions or pursuing domestic policy purposes.

When applying this understanding of external governmental activities, one can describe *the basic function of development cooperation as shaping conditions within (other) countries by using cooperative and promotional civilian means* (Kloke-Lesch 1998a, b). These instruments include, above all, (1) realising projects and programmes that are often accompanied by an active influence on the framework conditions in the respective countries and (2) promoting non-governmental activities in these countries. For this functional definition, it does not matter whether it is performed by a dedicated department ("aid agency") or by governmental entities scattered across departments. Furthermore, development policy in a broader sense would also try to influence the regulatory activities, for example by foreign affairs or trade departments, with a view to its pursued objectives ("policy coherence for development").

Thus, this functional role of development cooperation can come into play wherever, whenever, and for whatever reason it is politically desired and possible to influence conditions in specific countries using civilian means, from unilateral through to multilateral ones. Such a functional approach to development cooperation would not start with the question whether countries, or people in countries, are needy, but rather whether there is a necessity or interest felt to impact on developments in countries, irrespective of whether they are listed as "developing" or "developed" countries.

Depriving the notion of development cooperation of its traditional normative core and geographical focus is not meant to allow for policies not strongly rooted in the norms and values that are enshrined, for example, in international law and national constitutions (Burchi et al. 2018). On the contrary, a functional approach can be helpful in better analysing and understanding the realities and normative framings of international relations and cooperation under changing circumstances, in comparing the activities of different actors by using a uniform terminology, and in identifying necessary next steps when implementing a new, ambitious, and universal normative framework such as the 2030 Agenda for Sustainable Development.

7.2.5 Untapped Potential: A Functional Reading of the 2030 Agenda's Means of Implementation

The 2030 Agenda marks a fundamental turn from the concept of "international development" organised around the "North-South" binary, poverty eradication, and aid for "developing countries" to a universal concept of "global development" with sustainable development at its normative core and requiring a broad range of MoIs in and between all countries: domestic as well as international, non-financial as well as financial, concessional as well as non-concessional, and political as well as technical ones (Kloke-Lesch 2016).

Do the 2030 Agenda and the steps to implement it actually live up to its proclaimed universal ambitions? On the conceptual and normative levels, the broadening of the substantial purpose of development into sustainable development is spelt out throughout the document and has, in principle, been accepted globally. With regard to the universality of the agenda and the geographic shift from "developing countries" to all countries, as well as to global issues and global public goods, the picture is more nuanced. On the one hand, the agenda calls on all countries for implementation ("These are universal goals and targets which involve the entire world, developed and developing countries alike" [UN 2015c]), and almost all of the SDGs—including their substantial targets—are framed in a universal way. On the other hand, the document maintains the distinction between "developed" and "developing" countries and gives particular prominence to implementation in the latter, while calling on the former to support these endeavours. This lopsidedness gets stronger with respect to the means of implementation, which rely mainly on the Addis Ababa Action Agenda (AAAA) of the Third International Conference on Financing for Development (UN 2015b).

The AAAA is a product of the Financing for Development process, which predates the universal 2030 Agenda and has been limited to the implementation in "developing countries" (Kloke-Lesch 2016). The relation between the AAAA and the 2030 Agenda was a contested issue, in particular with regard to non-financial means of implementation, the role of the "common but differentiated responsibilities" principle beyond environmental issues, and to what extent the 2030 Agenda and the individual SDGs should contain specific means of implementation (Dodds et al. 2017). Eventually, the AAAA was declared an integral part of the 2030 Agenda and, in addition, means of implementation targets were included both under each SDG and SDG 17.

7.2.6 Lopsided Universality: A Functional Mapping of the Means of Implementation of the 2030 Agenda

When applying the functional understanding of external governmental activities, the 62 MoIs mentioned in the 2030 Agenda[13] (see Annex) can be understood as a regulatory framework geared towards the three fields of activities described (shaping relations *between* countries/shaping conditions *within* countries/shaping *global* conditions) by using the three basic kinds of means (*regulatory, promotional,* and *cooperative instruments*), leading to nine principle functional fields (plus the overarching MoI 17.14 on policy coherence for sustainable development). In Table 7.2, I assign each MoI to one

Table 7.2 Functional mapping of the means of implementation of the 2030 Agenda

Fields of activity / Instruments	Shaping relations *between* countries	Shaping conditions *within* countries	Shaping *global* conditions	Total
Regulation of governmental and non-governmental behaviour				19 (2/14/3) (0/0/18/1/0)
Promotion of non-governmental behaviour				23 (12/9/2) (0/0/4/3/16)
Intergovernmental cooperation				19 (0/17/2) (0/0/2/5/12)
Subtotal 1	0 0 3 1 10	0 0 15 6 16	0 0 6 2 2	61 (0/0/24/9/28)
Subtotal 2	14 (2/12/0)	40 (14/9/17)	7 (3/2/2)	61 (19/23/19)
Overarching		17.14		
Total		62 (0/0/25/9/28)		

Exclusively oriented towards "developed countries"	0
Universally oriented with an additional focus on "developed countries"	0
Universally oriented	25
Universally oriented with an additional focus on "developing countries"	9
Exclusively oriented towards "developing countries"	28

Source Author

of these fields according to its main focus. In addition, all MoIs are categorised according to their universality or focus on a type of country, leading to five categories: (1) exclusively oriented towards "developed countries", (2) universally oriented with an additional focus on "developed countries", (3) universally oriented, (4) universally oriented with an additional focus on "developing countries", and (5) exclusively oriented towards "developing countries". With all the reservations that these different kinds of rough categorisations and assignments entail, the analysis provides at least some general patterns that expose both the overall mindset that led to the MoIs of the 2030 Agenda and the blind spots or missing means of implementation.

With regard to fields of activities, the MoIs of the 2030 Agenda have a clear and strong focus on shaping conditions within countries. Two-thirds (40) focus on implementation within countries, whereas 14 address relations between countries, and only 7 relate to the shaping of global conditions. While a strong focus on domestic implementation is indispensable, the relatively lesser focus of the MoIs on global conditions is deplorable. Although this can be explained by the fact that the negotiations on the 2030 Agenda tried to avoid interfering with other processes, regimes, and institutions, such as the ones on climate or trade, it can also be seen as a missed opportunity for injecting a specific 2030 Agenda momentum into these areas and making them accountable to the 2030 Agenda processes. Regarding the types of instruments, the MoIs are quite evenly distributed between regulatory (19), promotional (23), and cooperative (19) instruments. The significantly strong showing of promotional instruments demonstrates the particular focus of the 2030 Agenda on the mobilisation of non-governmental actors, in particular from the business sector and civil society.

When checking the MoIs against the universal aspirations of the 2030 Agenda, three quite significant features emerge: (1) a first majority of the MoIs are framed in a universal way, addressing all countries, "developed" as well as "developing" countries alike; (2) a second, overlapping majority of the MoIs are exclusively, or with a special focus, geared towards "developing countries"; (3) not one of the MoIs is geared exclusively, or with a special focus, towards "developed countries".[14] More specifically: the first majority (34 out of 62) of the MoIs are framed in a universal way, including nine of them giving an additional reference to "developing countries". When taking the latter together with the 28 MoIs that refer exclusively to implementation in "developing countries", one arrives at a second majority (37 out of 62) of the MoIs geared at least partly towards the "developing countries", including those that call for support by "developed countries".

Furthermore, two other features are significant. First, all but one of the MoIs (18 out of 19) that address the regulation of governmental and non-governmental behaviour (including norm-setting) are framed in a strictly universal mode; most of them (14) are related to the domestic implementation in both "developed" and "developing" countries. Second, most of the MoIs that are geared towards the promotion of non-governmental behaviour (16 out of 23) and international cooperation (12 out of 19) have an exclusive focus on "developing countries", addressing primarily the external relations of, and the conditions within, these countries.

7.2.7 Unfinished Business: "Developed Countries" Are Not Left off the Hook

This two-faced character of the means of implementation of the 2030 Agenda—strongly universal on the one hand, and lopsided towards "developing countries" on the other hand when it comes to specifics—reveals that the Copernican turn in development thinking being ushered in by the 2030 Agenda is still incomplete with regard to implementation, institutions, and instruments. This incompleteness reflects the interests of, and power relations between, major groups of countries as well as institutional path-dependencies inherited from the pre-2015 world. As "developing countries" have become used to goals being set by the international community for their domestic development (such as the MDGs), this is in many ways quite a new experience for "developed countries", in particular when operating within a common framework with "developing countries". For "developing countries", internationally agreed goals—including their commitments to implement them via domestic actions—have been acceptable as long as they are accompanied (quid pro quo) by commitments, although often vague, from "developed countries" to support this implementation through aid and other means. "Developed countries" have more or less accepted these commitments but remained hesitant about accepting means to monitor and enforce their implementation, even more so if they relate to issues where their own domestic and the international development goals conflict (King 2016). Thus, this hesitation by "developed countries" tends to increase even further with the 2030 Agenda, as now monitoring and implementation relate also to issues that are traditionally seen as being primarily domestic ones, without prima facie significant external relevance.

In addition, the pre-existence of the traditional development cooperation architecture with its institutions and instruments rendered it quite easy to draw on them when designing the MoIs of the 2030 Agenda. At the same time, this tended to be reinforced by the institutional interests of actors within this architecture on both the "donor" and "recipient" sides. At the same time, a more detailed inclusion of means of implementation beyond the development cooperation architecture—for example in areas such as international human rights covenants, trade agreements, international finance, or even environmental conventions—was met with some hesitation from many sides, not least by institutional actors in these areas that wanted to avoid "subordination" to a framework not of their own making. Thus, it is quite plausible that the negotiations on the 2030 Agenda (Dodds et al. 2017) settled with a prevalence of MoIs related to "developing countries" and development cooperation but only included a few weaker hints to other institutional arenas.

However, although the MoIs do not make specific references to implementation in "developed countries", these are not released from their respective responsibilities. The letter and the spirit of the majority of the MoIs are truly universal and establish a responsibility, in the sense of "obligation" (Bexell and Jönsson 2017), also of "developed countries" to act on the SDGs domestically and in their relations with each other. Furthermore, the agenda itself calls on all countries to put "cohesive nationally owned sustainable development strategies" at the heart of the efforts and underscores "that, for all countries, public policies and the mobilization and effective use of domestic resources, […] are central" (UN 2015c).

This is all the more compelling with regard to the "developed countries". Their gross domestic product (GDP) amounts to roughly three-fifths of global GDP, and their trade and foreign direct investment just between them amount to roughly half of both. But it is not only these figures that matter due to their sheer size in addition to the spillover effects on other countries and the planet that go along with them (Schmidt-Traub et al. 2019). Also, the patterns of production and consumption, of trade and foreign direct investment, and, for example, of knowledge production and technological development that prevail within and between "developed countries" critically shape the global system and their interactions with other countries.

Furthermore, and most importantly, without being embraced also by the people of "developed countries" as a positive agenda that is beneficial to themselves as well, the 2030 Agenda will not get the required societal and political support. It is therefore of critical importance to link core societal concerns in "developed countries" to the SDGs and integrate them as guiding objectives in the respective domestic policies.

7.3 International Cooperation Still Largely Trapped in the Pre-2015 World

The first four years of implementing the 2030 Agenda have seen manifold initiatives in the fields of international cooperation and relations to embrace the agenda and translate it into action. However, the agenda's ambition that "all countries and all stakeholders [...] will implement this plan" (UN 2015c) has not been met, and "the transformation required to meet the Sustainable Development Goals by 2030 is not yet advancing at the speed or scale required", as put by UN Secretary-General António Guterres (UN 2019c). The reasons for this unsatisfactory picture have been subject to both scholarly and civil society debates highlighting, for example, the lack of governance and institutional mechanisms in domestic implementation (Kindornay 2019); the voluntarist character of the framework and a lack of both intensification and institutionalisation of cooperation (Cooper and French 2018); much too little attention on interlinkages and interdependencies among goals (Stafford-Smith et al. 2017) or on the underlying social structures, power relations, and governance arrangements (Martens 2019).

The functional mapping of the MoIs of the 2030 Agenda proposed in this contribution reveals an additional feature: the international implementation envisaged by the 2030 Agenda remains in many ways trapped in the development cooperation patterns of the pre-2015 world, focussed primarily on cooperative and promotional instruments geared towards shaping conditions in "developing countries". Regulatory and norm-setting MoIs—framed universally and addressing domestic implementation, also within "developed countries"—are not accompanied by cooperative and promotional means of implementation. MoIs addressing particularly the relations between "developed countries" are largely missing. The way international organisations and cooperation formats between "developed countries" have embraced and processed the agenda so far mainly mirrors this lopsided feature, but it also shows the first small and reluctant steps out of the pre-2015 trap.

7.3.1 *United Nations and Bretton Woods Institutions*

It was the UN performing its universal regulatory, primarily norm-setting function in shaping relations *between* countries, conditions *within* countries, as well as *global* conditions that led to the adoption of the 2030 Agenda. Many of the MoIs of the agenda are an expression of this function. However, the UN has few means at its disposal to enforce the norms set by the agenda. The only major institutional innovation to support the implementation of the 2030 Agenda is the United Nations High-level Political Forum on Sustainable Development (HLPF).[15] This intergovernmental body is to play a central role in the universal follow-up and review of the 2030 Agenda, including "voluntary national reviews" undertaken by both "developed" and "developing" countries and involving multiple stakeholders.[16]

However, there are concerns related to the quality of the reports and the underlying review processes (International Institute for Sustainable Development 2019; Kindornay 2019). Furthermore, the consequences of the reporting are unclear, raising the question of the reviews' relevance (Beisheim 2018). Another major limitation to the effectiveness of the HLPF is the fact that the organisations of the UN system, including the Bretton Woods institutions, and other organisations such as the World Trade Organisation are not accountable to the HLPF. They are just invited "to contribute within their respective mandates to the discussions of the forum" (UN 2013, p. 6). Thus, the HLPF as a truly universal body is admittedly a major achievement in itself, but it still lacks the means to live up to its mandate.

The universality of the SDGs and of the HLPF is also a challenge to the other parts of the UN system, with many struggling to overcome their path-dependencies inherited from the pre-2015 world. What used to be the United Nations Development System geared towards "developing countries" needed to turn itself into a United Nations *Sustainable* Development System, which carries not only many of the terminological but also political and practical questions (Burley and Lindores 2016), in particular to what extent activities geared to domestic implementation in "developed countries" should be included.

In the meantime, first steps could be observed. The United Nations Development Group was turned into the United Nations Sustainable Development Group. The UN's statistical work on the SDGs covers all countries, as do, in principle, major reports on the SDGs, such as the "Global Sustainable Development Report" (UN 2019d). The United Nations Department of Economic and Social Affairs (UN DESA), which traditionally has been the home base of "developing countries" in the UN (Janus and Weinlich 2018), is now taking first steps towards becoming the hub and home for the universal SDGs.

In this context, it is worthwhile to note, for example, that the "Financing for Sustainable Development Report 2019" (UN 2019a) was issued for the first time under this title (it was formerly known as the "Financing for Development Report"), paying tribute to the universality of the 2030 Agenda. The report also covers, at least to a certain extent, domestic issues "developed countries" are faced with when implementing the 2030 Agenda, such as rising inequalities and the gender pay gap, investment-to-GDP ratio, as well as public and private debt levels through to sustainable investment and just transitions. With regard to regulatory means, the report also covers, for example, the European Commission's legislative proposals that aim to establish a unified European classification system of sustainable economic activities ("taxonomy") and sees—with regard to integrated national financing frameworks for sustainable development—"clearly scope to do so in both developed and developing countries" (UN 2019a, p. 11). These first steps towards universality come as a pleasant difference to the OECD's "Global Outlook on Financing for Sustainable Development 2019" (Organisation for Economic Co-operation and Development [OECD] 2019c), which reduces its very topic to financing sustainable development in the "developing countries".

However, there is still some way to go from embracing the universality of the SDGs in the UN's conceptual, regulatory/norm-setting, and analytical work to doing so in its operational activities, which remain largely confined to shaping conditions within "developing countries". This requires further reforms, for example of UN DESA (Janus and Weinlich 2018), and may even need changes in mandates, for example of the UN's funds and programmes.

This feature becomes even clearer with the Bretton Woods institutions. Both the World Bank Group (WBG) and the International Monetary Fund (IMF) have a tendency of reductively speaking about the "2030 Development Agenda" instead of the 2030 Agenda for Sustainable Development and maintaining that they serve the SDGs by delivering on their core mandates, which actually predate the 2030 Agenda (International Monetary Fund [IMF] 2019a; World Bank Group 2016). Although the WBG claims to "continue to work in distinct, complementary ways across the full range of *low, middle, and high-income member countries* [...] allowing transfer of knowledge, experience, and resources across its entire membership", the role of the latter is only seen as to "provide the financial strength of the WBG institutions" (World Bank Group 2016, p. 3). Also, the IMF, whose mandate is—compared to the World Bank Group—truly universal, directs its support for the SDGs "primarily" towards "developing countries" (IMF 2019a, p. 2). With regard to climate change and the IMF, the picture looks a little bit different, as the IMF highlights its "unique role among UN agencies: given its focus on macro and fiscal policies, universal membership and regular interactions with finance ministries" and that it "has a role in providing analysis of (and guidance on) energy pricing and macro-fiscal policies consistent with countries' climate strategies submitted for the Paris Agreement" (IMF 2019b, p. 41). So far, this view has not been transferred to the 2030 Agenda. Thus, the potentially transformative power of the regulatory, promotional, and cooperative instruments of both institutions remains largely untapped with regard to high-income countries.

7.3.2 *OECD and European Union*

As the two major international or, respectively, supranational organisations, the OECD and the European Union (EU), which are comprised in the first place of high-income countries, are of critical importance for the implementation of the 2030 Agenda in and between "developed countries". Both committed themselves quite early to contribute towards achieving the SDGs, but they are still struggling to translate this commitment into their core operational activities beyond the realm of development cooperation.

As early as 2016, the OECD adopted an OECD Action Plan on the Sustainable Development Goals calling to "apply an SDG lens to the OECD's strategies and policy tools" (OECD 2016), followed by the adaption of the DAC mandate to the 2030 Agenda (DAC 2017). However, despite the many activities—in particular on measuring distance to the SDG targets in OECD member countries themselves (OECD 2019b) and on "policy coherence for sustainable development" (OECD 2019d)—the SDGs have not even been mentioned once in 30 of the 35 OECD Economic Surveys of member economies issued since 2016.[17] These OECD flagship products actually reflect the views and policies of both the OECD and the respective countries. Only the surveys on Slovenia (2017), The Netherlands (2018), and Poland (2018) included references to the 2030 Agenda or the SDGs in an at least somewhat systematic way.[18] The broad neglect of the 2030 Agenda by the Economic Surveys is particularly remarkable since these surveys cover quite a range of issues that are highly relevant for achieving the SDGs within the OECD countries.

A similar pattern could be observed with the EU. On the one hand, the EU championed the SDGs during the negotiation period and was quite quick in translating the 2030 Agenda into the new European Consensus on Development framing the agenda's "implementation [...] in partnership with all developing countries" (European Union [EU] 2017, p. 4). On the other hand, four years after the adoption of the 2030 Agenda, the EU was still reflecting whether the agenda should have a significant bearing at all on domestic European policies (European Commission 2019a; Kloke-Lesch 2018), for example through the EU's budget and regulatory work, which could significantly contribute to shaping conditions within member countries. Evidence shows that half of the member states have some sort of national sustainable development strategy that is actually operational (Niestroy et al. 2019), but that implementation at this level is not supported by community-level activities "to mainstream the SDGs in all policies, in particular through the better regulation tools, and other instruments such as structural funds" (Niestroy et al. 2019, p. 6). It was only recently that the elected president of the next European Commission committed to refocus the European Semester—a framework for the coordination of economic policies across the EU—into an instrument that integrates the SDGs (von der Leyen 2019).

7.3.3 G7 and G20

The Group of Seven (G7) and the Group of Twenty (G20), as global governance clubs made up by the major industrialised and emerging economies, could be places to address the implementation of the 2030 Agenda, both within and between these countries. Instead, the summit history since 2015 has shown a different picture.[19] The G7 have never endeavoured to systematically embrace the agenda as something of relevance for their domestic policies or their relations with each other. Already in 2015, and only a couple of months before the adoption of the 2030 Agenda, the G7 Summit in Elmau, Germany, positioned the agenda primarily in the traditional development cooperation context. The Ise-Shima/Japan Summit (2016) went one step further by committing "to advance the implementation of the 2030 Agenda, domestically and internationally" but failed to specify this beyond health as well as women's empowerment and gender equality. Thereafter, the G7 summits in 2017 (Taormina, Italy) and 2018 (Charlevoix, Canada) referred to the agenda only marginally and in relation to "developing countries". One could see this reluctance by the G7 as the result of a silent division of labour between G7 and G20 processes, but the developments in the G20 reveal similar patterns.

In distinction from the G7, the G20 brings together major "developed" and "developing" countries that could—and initially did—render it easier to embrace the 2030 Agenda as being relevant to the domestic policies of its members. Immediately after the SDG summit, the 2015 G20 Summit in Antalya, Turkey, committed to "develop an action plan in 2016 to further align our work with the 2030 Agenda". The G20 Action Plan on the 2030 Agenda for Sustainable Development was adopted by the 2016 G20 Summit (Hangzhou, China) and updated in all of the following summits (2017 Hamburg, Germany; 2018 Buenos Aires, Argentina; and 2019 Osaka, Japan). The Action Plan and its updates, including the joint OECD/UNDP report on the "G20 Contribution to the 2030 Agenda" (OECD and United Nations Development Programme 2019), are proof of the great potential the G20 holds in contributing to the implementation of the agenda—also within and between its members—through regulatory work, including norm-setting, and by initiating or promoting cooperation. However, this potential is left largely untapped. The G20's support for the agenda appears to be fading (Bauer et al. 2019). Updates are limited to collective actions, depend on voluntary inputs from responsible work streams, and resemble an inventory rather than a means of driving change. Actions reported are mainly linked to the provision of global public goods and support to "developing countries". Since the presentations on national actions by the G20 members in Annex B to the 2016 Action Plan have not been continued, the only G20 instrument to promote domestic implementation remains the Voluntary Peer Learning Mechanism and the documentation of its results in the updates. From a structural point of view, it is important to note that G20 leaders mandated the Development Working Group "to act as a coordinating body and policy resource for sustainable development across the G20" (G20 Action Plan) but failed to adapt its composition (and name) in line with the upgraded mandate. Composed in the first place of representatives from development cooperation departments (on the donors' as well as on the recipients' side), and without participation from departments that are responsible for the domestic implementation of the agenda in the G20 countries, the Development Working Group is in a very difficult position to impact both other G20 work streams and domestic implementation. Thus, the underlying common problem with the G20 and the G7 is a widespread and increasing defensiveness of their members and/or leaders to make domestic implementation of the agenda a common cause between them.

7.3.4 Bilateral Cooperation and Relations Between "Developed Countries"

There is little evidence whether, or to what extent, "developed countries" will introduce the 2030 Agenda as a formative feature into the bilateral relations between them. As a case in point, the EU and its member states—as a self-declared "global trail blazer in sustainable development" (European Commission 2019a, p. 31)—committed to advancing the implementation of the 2030 Agenda "globally through the full range of their external actions" (European Commission 2019b, p. 7) but focus, for example, their Joint Synthesis Report "Supporting the Sustainable Development Goals Across the World" (European Commission 2019b) exclusively on "developing countries". It is surprising that this report does not refer to the recent EU-Canada and EU-Japan partnership agreements. Both the Comprehensive Economic and Trade Agreement with Canada and the Economic Partnership Agreement with Japan have dedicated chapters on sustainable development. Both make explicit reference to the 2030 Agenda or the SDGs and the implementation within the respective countries; establish regulatory, promotional, as well as cooperative instruments with regard to trade and investment; and set up institutional structures and processes (e.g. Committees on Trade and Sustainable Development) to oversee their implementation.[20] The 2019 EU-Canada Summit committed, for example, to reinforce research and innovation cooperation to tackle societal challenges and promote sustainable development. For comparison: also the new Canada–United States–Mexico Agreement resolves to "further the aims of sustainable development" (preamble) and emphasises "the importance of green growth […] in achieving a competitive and sustainable North American economy" (Agreement on Environmental Cooperation), but it does not refer to the 2030 Agenda.[21] It is much too early to say whether the provisions in these different agreements will turn into something transformative compared to a low-ambition or mere do-no-harm approach.

The same applies to the new Treaty of Aachen between France and Germany, which also contains specific provisions on the 2030 Agenda, including the creation of a joint platform to deal with transformation processes in both societies.[22] Another example for introducing the SDGs into a cooperation format between "developed countries" can be found within the Arctic

Council, where "a closer and more visible tie-in between the Arctic Council's work and the SDGs" was discussed although only with the conclusion "that the Arctic Council could offer valuable guidance in the pursuit of the SDGs in the Arctic, while their implementation is a national responsibility" (Arctic Council 2018, pp. 9–10). Even if some of these small steps indicate a possible direction for the future, they cannot hide the fact that, so far, the 2030 Agenda has not made its way into mainstream relations and cooperation between "developed countries". This, however, needs to change if countries want to live up to the ambition of the agenda and address the emerging geoeconomics and geopolitics of sustainable development, as already becoming evident, for example, in the Arctic or with the ongoing energy transition (International Renewable Energy Agency 2019).

7.3.5 Conclusion: Towards Mutually Transformative Cooperation in the 2030 World

Mapping the MoIs of the 2030 Agenda from a functional perspective laid bare a gap between the universal ambitions of the agenda and its lopsided MoIs, which could also be observed during the first steps of implementing the agenda, in particular within and between "developed countries". As the implementation of the agenda within and between these countries is of outmost importance to its overall success, the function of development cooperation ("shaping conditions within (other) countries by using cooperative and promotional instruments") should be exerted also vis-à-vis "developed countries" wherever necessary, accompanied by regulatory instruments designed accordingly ("policy coherence for sustainable development"). For this to happen, the pre-2015 development cooperation model needs to transition into a model of mutually transformative cooperation for the 2030 world.

So far, development cooperation actors have answered to the 2030 Agenda mainly by adopting its terminology and using it as a reinforced narrative underpinning and incrementally broadening their pre-existing business models. The new DAC mandate, for example, speaks of supporting "developing countries" in their implementation of the 2030 Agenda and promoting the importance of global public goods and policy coherence for sustainable development in this regard (DAC 2017). The mandate commits to modernising ODA and improving the development cooperation architecture, but it does not question their basic features inherited from the pre-2015 world with respect to the universality of the 2030 Agenda.

The same phenomenon can be observed with "South-South" cooperation. The Buenos Aires Outcome Document of the Second High-level United Nations Conference on South-South Cooperation (BAPA+40) reaffirmed the basic features and principles of "South-South" cooperation such as mutual benefit, also predating the 2030 Agenda, and put them into relation with the implementation of the 2030 Agenda while also acknowledging "the need to enhance the development effectiveness of South-South and triangular cooperation" (UN 2019b, p. 3). The repeated and supportive reference to triangular cooperation[23] fails to be truly innovative by sticking to an approach aligned to the "requesting developing country" (UN 2019b, p. 8). Thus, the mutuality of cooperation remains confined to the "South-South" dimension, and the role of the "North" remains unidirectional.

Although these conceptual role-assignments are political and ideological constructs that are highly contested by the realities of both "North-South" and "South-South" cooperation (Bergamaschi et al. 2017; Mawdsley 2017), they still frame much of the debate and institutional framings. Figure 7.1 illustrates the main features of the pre-2015 model with, on the one hand, the

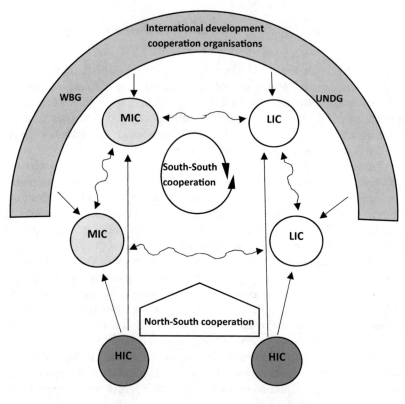

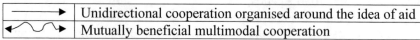

Fig. 7.1 "North-South" and "South-South" cooperation in the pre-2015 world (*Note* LIC [low-income country], MIC [middle-income country], WBG [World Bank Group], UNDG [United Nations Development Group], HIC [high-income country]. *Source* Author)

unidirectional "North-South" development cooperation basically organised around the idea of aid and, on the other hand, the "South-South" cooperation with mutually beneficial cooperation at its purported conceptual core.

However, under the new paradigm of global development (Horner 2019) being ushered in by the 2030 Agenda, also the concept of development cooperation needs to become global, both in political practice and in scholarly debates. As "the 2030 Agenda constitutes a new basis for international cooperation between all countries", it is evident that "all forms and forums of international cooperation must contribute to implement the 2030 Agenda" (Scholz et al. 2017). The agenda's concept of a Global Partnership for Sustainable Development brings about two significant openings in this regard, firstly by its universality in calling on all countries to implement it, and secondly by highlighting non-governmental actors, including particularly the private sector, and all types of resources in a way not seen before in a comparable document. The former requires "developed countries" to also transform their relations and cooperation with each other, while the latter both mirrors a recent trend in the "North-South" cooperation reflected in the beyond-aid debate (Janus et al. 2015) and allows for fully including "South-South" cooperation with its distinctive features of linking aid, trade, and investment in a mutually beneficial way.

Well thought through, this already entails three core ingredients of a cooperation model for the 2030 world: universality, multimodality, and mutuality. Universality requires incorporating "North-North" cooperation alongside "North-South" and "South-South" cooperation. Multimodality implies that cooperation modes previously confined to relations between specific groups of countries can be applied between all types of countries. Mutuality in a universal cooperation model extends beyond "South-South" and "North-North" cooperation and needs to be introduced well into "North-South" (or "South-North") cooperation. Furthermore, and most importantly, in a 2030 Agenda context, a universal, multimodal, and mutual cooperation needs to be transformational, leading to "transformationality" as a fourth ingredient.

Figure 7.2 illustrates key features of a cooperation model for the 2030 world linking all types of countries (exemplified as high-income, middle-income, and low-income countries) in basically the same ways with each other as well as with the international and supranational cooperation organisations, with mutually transformative cooperation at its core. This relates, on the one hand, to transforming existing cooperation between all types of countries and, on the other hand, introducing new transformative cooperation. Wherever necessary, states as well as international and supranational institutions should use not only regulatory but also promotional and cooperative instruments to shape conditions within—and relations between—countries of all income levels in ways conducive to achieving the SDGs.

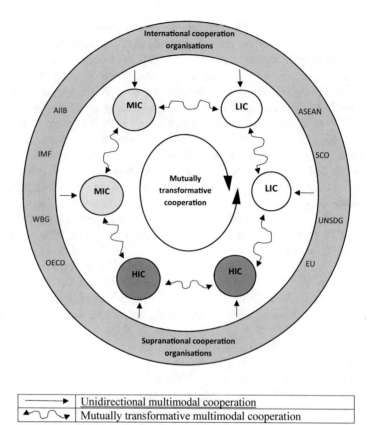

Fig. 7.2 Mutually transformative cooperation in the 2030 world (*Note* AIIB [Asian Infrastructure Investment Bank], ASEAN [Association of Southeast Asian Nations], HIC [high-income country], LIC [low-income country], MIC [middle-income country], WBG [World Bank Group], UNDG [United Nations Development Group], IMF [International Monetary Fund], OECD [Organisation for Economic Co-operation and Development], EU [European Union], SCO [Shanghai Cooperation Organisation], UNSDG [United Nations Sustainable Development Group]. *Source* Author)

Development cooperation actors (bi- and multilateral ones alike) from both the "North" and the "South" need to answer whether they want to be part of this new 2030 world of international cooperation by turning themselves into a universal means for delivering transformative change across countries at all levels of income or by just sticking to their normative, geographical, and institutional patterns inherited from the pre-2015 world. International cooperation actors from other governmental departments (both in the "North" and the "South") as well as international and supranational organisations need to decide whether to also introduce the transformative momentum of the 2030 Agenda into their cooperation with (other) "developed countries" or to confine this to their cooperation with (other) "developing countries". Both groups of actors have to face the challenge that, in a world of common and collective problems (Haddad 2013), it is increasingly inadequate and inappropriate to stick to a cooperation architecture that separates countries and actors instead of bringing them together as equals working and (re)searching for the global common good. Development cooperation actors as well as other actors should embrace this opportunity. The function of international cooperation in the 2030 world is to jointly deliver change, not aid.

Notes

1. I put the terms "developing countries" and "developed countries" into quotation marks throughout the text, as these terms have become highly inappropriate given the increasing differentiation between countries. The same applies to the terms "North" and "South". Towards the end of the chapter, I use the terms "high-income", "middle-income", and "low-income" countries to indicate a rough differentiation by income categories, although such a differentiation is still only based on one criterion. In its new Five-Year Strategy, the Overseas Development Institute (ODI) in London decided to "transition from using terms such as 'developing' and 'developed' that create false distinctions between countries, communities and the universal challenges we all face" (Overseas Development Institute 2018).
2. The MDGs were established on the basis of the United Nations Millennium Declaration, adopted in 2000 (UN 2000, 2015a).
3. The panel was part of the Secretary-General's post-2015 initiative mandated by the 2010 MDG summit (UN, n.d.-a).
4. The OWG was initiated by the Rio+20 conference (UN, n.d.-b).
5. This might also be helpful with resolving some of the other highly contested issues such as "beyond aid" (Janus et al. 2015), the diversity and comparability of "South-South" cooperation (Chaturvedi 2018), and the convergence of "North-South" and "South-South" cooperation (Chaturvedi 2016; Li 2018).
6. Here and in the following, this paper takes up and refines some observations and propositions the author elaborated on at the end of the 1990s (Kloke-Lesch 1998a, b).
7. I refer to geographies of development or development cooperation in a socio-economic sense, not in the sense of physical geographies.
8. Also, ethical approaches to development (Dower 2008; Drydyk 2017) tend to stick to a geographically confined approach.
9. EADI's elaborate definition of development studies covers definitions and goals, learning and teaching, and learning objectives (outcomes). The introductory definition reads as follows: "Development Studies (also known as 'international development studies' or 'international development') is a multi- and inter-disciplinary field of study rather than a single discipline. It seeks to understand the interplay between social, economic, political, technological, ecological, cultural and gendered aspects of societal change at the local, national, regional and global levels" (European Association of Development Research and Training Institutes 2017).

10. Therefore, development studies, also when turning into global development studies, need to maintain intellectual independence and "the SDGs should not become a straightjacket" for them (Melber 2017).
11. For some time (until 2005) the DAC tried to accommodate the difficulties by introducing the term "official aid" for countries and territories in transition (including Russia), which also included more advanced developing countries. Today, all the countries concerned (except Russia) are either on the DAC List of ODA recipients or have become—some after being on the list for some years—members of the EU (OECD, n.d.).
12. The increasingly relevant private philanthropic actors the Bill & Melinda Gates Foundation are left aside in this contribution but could be subsumed under the non-governmental actors that are potentially subject to regulatory and promotional functions of external governmental activities (see Table 7.1).
13. While focussing the analysis on the 62 explicit MoIs, it has to be acknowledged that many SDGs and their targets are, in fact, means themselves or intermediate goals contributing to the achievement of higher goals, rendering the distinction between goals and targets on the one hand, and MOI on the other hand, somehow artificial (Elder et al. 2016). In addition to the 62 explicit MoIs, 19 out of the (other) 107 SDG targets can be seen as process targets (Development Assistance Committee [DAC] 2016).
14. This is particularly surprising, as at least the targets under SDG 8 (Decent work and economic growth) and SDG 12 (Responsible consumption and production) call on "developed countries" to take the lead with improving global resource efficiency in consumption and production and endeavouring to decouple economic growth from environmental degradation, in accordance with the 10-Year Framework of Programmes on Sustainable Consumption and Production.
15. The HLPF was mandated in 2012 by the outcome document of the Rio+20 conference (UN 2012).
16. Until 2019 roughly 140 countries (out of them around 30 "developed countries") have submitted voluntary national reviews to the HLPF, indicating at least a certain interest in showing domestic efforts of implementation in both "developing" and "developed countries" (UN, n.d.-c).
17. The Economic surveys can be found on the OECD website at http://www.oecd.org/economy/surveys/.
18. The surveys on the Czech Republic (2018) and Denmark (2019) made just marginal references.
19. For the G7 and G20 Summit documents, turn to http://www.g7.utoronto.ca/ and http://www.g20.utoronto.ca/.
20. Also the EU-Mercosur Association Agreement is designed in a similar way. The EU agreements with Canada, Japan, and Mercosur can be found at https://eeas.europa.eu/headquarters/headquarters-homepage_en.
21. For a brief assessment of the Environmental Cooperation Agreement under CUSMA, see Cosbey (2019); the texts of the draft agreements can be found here: https://www.international.gc.ca/trade-commerce/trade-agreements-accords-commerciaux/agr-acc/cusma-aceum/text-texte/toc-tdm.aspx?lang=eng.
22. See https://www.auswaertiges-amt.de/blob/2179780/ccd486958222bd5a490d42c57dd7ed03/190118-download-aachenervertrag-data.pdf.

23. Triangular cooperation is conceptualised as a "collaboration in which traditional donor countries and multilateral organizations facilitate South-South initiatives" (UN Office for South-South Cooperation 2019).

Annex

	Annex: Means of implementation of the 2030 Agenda
SDG 1 No Poverty	**1.a** Ensure significant mobilization of resources from a variety of sources, including through enhanced development cooperation, in order to provide adequate and predictable means for developing countries, in particular least developed countries, to implement programmes and policies to end poverty in all its dimensions
	1.b Create sound policy frameworks at the national, regional and international levels, based on pro-poor and gender-sensitive development strategies, to support accelerated investment in poverty eradication actions
SDG 2 Zero Hunger	**2.a** Increase investment, including through enhanced international cooperation, in rural infrastructure, agricultural research and extension services, technology development and plant and livestock gene banks in order to enhance agricultural productive capacity in developing countries, in particular least developed countries
	2.b Correct and prevent trade restrictions and distortions in world agricultural markets, including through the parallel elimination of all forms of agricultural export subsidies and all export measures with equivalent effect, in accordance with the mandate of the Doha Development Round
	2.c Adopt measures to ensure the proper functioning of food commodity markets and their derivatives and facilitate timely access to market information, including on food reserves, in order to help limit extreme food price volatility
SDG 3 Good Health and Well-being	**3.a** Strengthen the implementation of the World Health Organization Framework Convention on Tobacco Control in all countries, as appropriate
	3.b Support the research and development of vaccines and medicines for the communicable and non-communicable diseases that primarily affect developing countries, provide access to affordable essential medicines and vaccines, in accordance with the Doha Declaration on the TRIPS Agreement and Public Health, which affirms the right of developing countries to use to the full the provisions in the Agreement on Trade-Related Aspects of Intellectual Property Rights regarding flexibilities to protect public health, and, in particular, provide access to medicines for all
	3.c Substantially increase health financing and the recruitment, development, training and retention of the health workforce in developing countries, especially in least developed countries and small island developing States
	3.d Strengthen the capacity of all countries, in particular developing countries, for early warning, risk reduction and management of national and global health risks
SDG 4 Quality Education	**4.a** Build and upgrade education facilities that are child, disability and gender sensitive and provide safe, non-violent, inclusive and effective learning environments for all
	4.b By 2020, substantially expand globally the number of scholarships available to developing countries, in particular least developed countries, small island developing States and African countries, for enrolment in higher education, including vocational training and information and communications technology, technical, engineering and scientific programmes, in developed countries and other developing countries
	4.c By 2030, substantially increase the supply of qualified teachers, including through international cooperation for teacher training in developing countries, especially least developed countries and small

	island developing States
SDG 5 Gender Equality	**5.a** Undertake reforms to give women equal rights to economic resources, as well as access to ownership and control over land and other forms of property, financial services, inheritance and natural resources, in accordance with national laws
	5.b Enhance the use of enabling technology, in particular information and communications technology, to promote the empowerment of women
	5.c Adopt and strengthen sound policies and enforceable legislation for the promotion of gender equality and the empowerment of all women and girls at all levels
SDG 6 Clean Water and Sanitation	**6.a** By 2030, expand international cooperation and capacity-building support to developing countries in water- and sanitation-related activities and programmes, including water harvesting, desalination, water efficiency, wastewater treatment, recycling and reuse technologies
	6.b Support and strengthen the participation of local communities in improving water and sanitation management
SDG 7 Affordable and Clean Energy	**7.a** By 2030, enhance international cooperation to facilitate access to clean energy research and technology, including renewable energy, energy efficiency and advanced and cleaner fossil-fuel technology, and promote investment in energy infrastructure and clean energy technology
	7.b By 2030, expand infrastructure and upgrade technology for supplying modern and sustainable energy services for all in developing countries, in particular least developed countries, small island developing States and landlocked developing countries, in accordance with their respective programmes of support
SDG 8 Decent Work and Economic Growth	**8.a** Increase Aid for Trade support for developing countries, in particular least developed countries, including through the Enhanced Integrated Framework for Trade-related Technical Assistance to Least Developed Countries
	8.b By 2020, develop and operationalize a global strategy for youth employment and implement the Global Jobs Pact of the International Labour Organization
SDG 9 Industry, Innovation, and Infrastructure	**9.a** Facilitate sustainable and resilient infrastructure development in developing countries through enhanced financial, technological and technical support to African countries, least developed countries, landlocked developing countries and small island developing States
	9.b Support domestic technology development, research and innovation in developing countries, including by ensuring a conducive policy environment for, inter alia, industrial diversification and value addition to commodities
	9.c Significantly increase access to information and communications technology and strive to provide universal and affordable access to the Internet in least developed countries by 2020
SDG 10 Reducing Inequality	**10.a** Implement the principle of special and differential treatment for developing countries, in particular least developed countries, in accordance with World Trade Organization agreements
	10.b Encourage official development assistance and financial flows, including foreign direct investment, to States where the need is greatest, in particular least developed countries, African countries, small island developing States and landlocked developing countries, in accordance with their national plans and programmes

7 THE UNTAPPED FUNCTIONS OF INTERNATIONAL COOPERATION ... 155

	10.c By 2030, reduce to less than 3 per cent the transaction costs of migrant remittances and eliminate remittance corridors with costs higher than 5 per cent
SDG 11 **Sustainable Cities and Communities**	**11.a** Support positive economic, social and environmental links between urban, peri-urban and rural areas by strengthening national and regional development planning
	11.b By 2020, substantially increase the number of cities and human settlements adopting and implementing integrated policies and plans towards inclusion, resource efficiency, mitigation and adaptation to climate change, resilience to disasters, and develop and implement, in line with the Sendai Framework for Disaster Risk Reduction 2015–2030, holistic disaster risk management at all levels
	11.c Support least developed countries, including through financial and technical assistance, in building sustainable and resilient buildings utilizing local materials
SDG 12 **Responsible Consumption and Production**	**12.a** Support developing countries to strengthen their scientific and technological capacity to move towards more sustainable patterns of consumption and production
	12.b Develop and implement tools to monitor sustainable development impacts for sustainable tourism that creates jobs and promotes local culture and products
	12.c Rationalize inefficient fossil-fuel subsidies that encourage wasteful consumption by removing market distortions, in accordance with national circumstances, including by restructuring taxation and phasing out those harmful subsidies, where they exist, to reflect their environmental impacts, taking fully into account the specific needs and conditions of developing countries and minimizing the possible adverse impacts on their development in a manner that protects the poor and the affected communities
SDG 13 Climate Action	**13.a** Implement the commitment undertaken by developed-country parties to the United Nations Framework Convention on Climate Change to a goal of mobilizing jointly $100 billion annually by 2020 from all sources to address the needs of developing countries in the context of meaningful mitigation actions and transparency on implementation and fully operationalize the Green Climate Fund through its capitalization as soon as possible
	13.b Promote mechanisms for raising capacity for effective climate change-related planning and management in least developed countries and small island developing States, including focusing on women, youth and local and marginalized communities
SDG 14 Life Below Water	**14.a** Increase scientific knowledge, develop research capacity and transfer marine technology, taking into account the Intergovernmental Oceanographic Commission Criteria and Guidelines on the Transfer of Marine Technology, in order to improve ocean health and to enhance the contribution of marine biodiversity to the development of developing countries, in particular small island developing States and least developed countries
	14.b Provide access for small-scale artisanal fishers to marine resources and markets
	14.c Enhance the conservation and sustainable use of oceans and their resources by implementing international law as reflected in the United Nations Convention on the Law of the Sea, which provides the legal framework for the conservation and sustainable use of oceans and their resources, as recalled in paragraph 158 of "The future we want"
SDG 15 Life On Land	**15.a** Mobilize and significantly increase financial resources from all sources to conserve and sustainably use biodiversity and ecosystems
	15.b Mobilize significant resources from all sources and at all levels to finance sustainable forest management and provide adequate incentives to developing countries to advance such management,

		including for conservation and reforestation
		15.c Enhance global support for efforts to combat poaching and trafficking of protected species, including by increasing the capacity of local communities to pursue sustainable livelihood opportunities
SDG 16 Peace, Justice, and Strong Institutions		**16.a** Strengthen relevant national institutions, including through international cooperation, for building capacity at all levels, in particular in developing countries, to prevent violence and combat terrorism and crime
		16.b Promote and enforce non-discriminatory laws and policies for sustainable development
SDG 17 Partnerships for the Goals		
	Finance	**17.1** Strengthen domestic resource mobilization, including through international support to developing countries, to improve domestic capacity for tax and other revenue collectio
		17.2 Developed countries to implement fully their official development assistance commitments, including the commitment by many developed countries to achieve the target of 0.7 per cent of gross national income for official development assistance (ODA/GNI) to developing countries and 0.15 to 0.20 per cent of ODA/GNI to least developed countries; ODA providers are encouraged to consider setting a target to provide at least 0.20 per cent of ODA/GNI to least developed countries
		17.3 Mobilize additional financial resources for developing countries from multiple sources
		17.4 Assist developing countries in attaining long-term debt sustainability through coordinated policies aimed at fostering debt financing, debt relief and debt restructuring, as appropriate, and address the external debt of highly indebted poor countries to reduce debt distress
		17.5 Adopt and implement investment promotion regimes for least developed countries
	Technology	**17.6** Enhance North-South, South-South and triangular regional and international cooperation on and access to science, technology and innovation and enhance knowledge sharing on mutually agreed terms, including through improved coordination among existing mechanisms, in particular at the United Nations level, and through a global technology facilitation mechanism
		17.7 Promote the development, transfer, dissemination and diffusion of environmentally sound technologies to developing countries on favourable terms, including on concessional and preferential terms, as mutually agreed
		17.8 Fully operationalize the technology bank and science, technology and innovation capacity-building mechanism for least developed countries by 2017 and enhance the use of enabling technology, in particular information and communications technology
	Capacity-building	**17.9** Enhance international support for implementing effective and targeted capacity-building in developing countries to support national plans to implement all the Sustainable Development Goals, including through North-South, South-South and triangular cooperation
	Trade	**17.10** Promote a universal, rules-based, open, non-discriminatory and equitable multilateral trading system under the World Trade Organization, including through the conclusion of negotiations under its Doha Development Agenda
		17.11 Significantly increase the exports of developing countries, in particular with a view to doubling the least developed countries' share of global exports by 2020

		**17.12** Realize timely implementation of duty-free and quota-free market access on a lasting basis for all least developed countries, consistent with World Trade Organization decisions, including by ensuring that preferential rules of origin applicable to imports from least developed countries are transparent and simple, and contribute to facilitating market access			
Systemic issues		**17.13** Enhance global macroeconomic stability, including through policy coordination and policy coherence			
		**17.14** Enhance policy coherence for sustainable development			
		**17.15** Respect each country's policy space and leadership to establish and implement policies for poverty eradication and sustainable development			
		**17.16** Enhance the Global Partnership for Sustainable Development, complemented by multi-stakeholder partnerships that mobilize and share knowledge, expertise, technology and financial resources, to support the achievement of the Sustainable Development Goals in all countries, in particular developing countries			
		**17.17** Encourage and promote effective public, public-private and civil society partnerships, building on the experience and resourcing strategies of partnerships			
		**17.18** By 2020, enhance capacity-building support to developing countries, including for least developed countries and small island developing States, to increase significantly the availability of high-quality, timely and reliable data disaggregated by income, gender, age, race, ethnicity, migratory status, disability, geographic location and other characteristics relevant in national contexts			
		**17.19** By 2030, build on existing initiatives to develop measurements of progress on sustainable development that complement gross domestic product, and support statistical capacity-building in developing countries			
Exclusively oriented towards so-called developed countries	Universally oriented with an additional focus on so-called developed countries	Universally oriented	Universally oriented with an additional focus on so-called developing countries	Exclusively oriented towards so-called developing countries
0	0	25	9	28

Source Author, based on UN (2015c)

References

Alff, H., & Hornidge, A.-K. (2019). "Transformation" in international development studies: Across disciplines, knowledge hierarchies and oceanic spaces. In I. Baud, E. Basile, T. Kontinen, & S. von Itter (Eds.), *Building development studies for the new millennium*. EADI Global Development Series (pp. 141–161). Basingstoke: Palgrave Macmillan.

Almond, G. (1960). Introduction: A functional approach to comparative politics. In G. A. Almond & J. S. Coleman (Eds.), *The politics of the developing areas* (pp. 3–64). Princeton, NJ: Princeton University Press.

Arctic Council. (2018, March 22–23). *Report: SAO plenary meeting*. https://oaarchive.arctic-council.org/handle/11374/2165.

Baud, I., Basile, E., Kontinen, T., & von Itter, S. (Eds.) (2019). *Building development studies for the new millennium* (EADI Global Development Series). Basingstoke: Palgrave Macmillan.

Bauer, S., Berger, A., & Iacubato, G. (2019). *With or without you: How the G20 could advance global action towards climate-friendly sustainable development* (Briefing Paper 10/2019). Bonn: German Development Institute / Deutsches Institut für Entwicklungspolitik (DIE).

Beisheim, M. (2018, October). *UN reforms for the 2030 Agenda—Are the HLPF's working methods and practices "fit for purpose"?* (SWP Research Paper 9). Berlin: Stiftung Wissenschaft und Politik.

Bergamaschi, I., Moore, P., & Tickner, A. B. (Eds.) (2017). *South-South cooperation beyond the myths: Rising donors, new aid practices?* London: Palgrave Macmillan.

Bexell, M., & Jönsson, K. (2017). Responsibility and the United Nations' Sustainable Development Goals. *Forum for Development Studies, 44*(1), 13–29.

Burchi, F., de Muro, P., & Kollar, E. (2018). Constructing well-being and poverty dimensions on political grounds. *Social Indicators Research, 137*(2), 441–462.

Burley, J., & Lindores, D. (2016). *The UN development system and its operational activities for development: Updating the definitions*. https://www.cbd.int/financial/doc/un-terminology2016.pdf.

Chaturvedi, S. (2016). The development compact: A theoretical construct for South-South cooperation. *International Studies, 53*(1), 15–43.

Chaturvedi, S. (2018). *South-South cooperation: Theoretical perspectives and empirical realities*. https://www.ssc-globalthinkers.org/node/160.

Cooper, N., & French, D. (2018). SDG 17: Partnerships for the Goals—Cooperation within the context of a voluntarist framework. In D. French & L. J. Kotzé (Eds.), *Sustainable Development Goals: Law, theory and implementation* (pp. 271–303). Cheltenham: Edward Elgar Publishing.

Cosbey, A. (2019, February). *Weighing up the environmental cooperation agreement under the Canada–United States–Mexico Agreement* (IISD Policy Brief). https://www.iisd.org/library/weighing-environmental-cooperation-agreement-under-canada-united-states-mexico-agreement.

CSO Partnership. (2017). *CSO recommendations on the DAC's new purpose code for the "facilitation of orderly, safe, regular and responsible migration and mobility"*. http://cso.csopartnership.org/6504-2/.

DAC (Development Assistance Committee). (2016, January). *An SDG-based results framework for development co-operation*. Draft note by the results team of the development co-operation directorate. https://www.oecd.org/dac/peer-reviews/SDG-based%20results%20framework.docx.
DAC. (2017, October 31). *DAC high-level communiqué*. https://www.oecd.org/dac/DAC-HLM-2017-Communique.pdf.
Dalrymple, S. (2016). *New aid rules allow for the inclusion of a wider set of peace and security activities*. http://devinit.org/post/new-aid-rules-allow-for-the-inclusion-of-a-wider-set-of-peace-and-security-activities/.
Dodds, F., Donoghue, D., & Roesch, J. (2017). *Negotiating the Sustainable Development Goals*. London: Routledge.
Dower, N. (2008). The nature and scope of development ethics. *Journal of Global Ethics, 4*(3), 183–193.
Drydyk, J. (2017). Ethical issues in development. In J. Grugel & D. Hammet (Eds.), *The Palgrave handbook of international development* (pp. 55–76). London: Palgrave Macmillan.
Elder, M., Bengtsson, M., & Akenji, L. (2016). An optimistic analysis of the means of implementation for Sustainable Development Goals: Thinking about goals as means. *Sustainability, 8*(9), 962.
EU. (2017). *The new European consensus on development—"our world, our dignity, our future"*. https://ec.europa.eu/europeaid/sites/devco/files/european-consensus-on-development-final-20170626_en.pdf.
European Association of Development Research and Training Institutes. (2017). *Definition of development studies*. https://www.eadi.org/typo3/fileadmin/Documents/Publications/EADI_Definition_Development_Studies_2017.pdf.
European Commission. (2019a). *Reflection paper: Towards a sustainable Europe by 2030*. https://ec.europa.eu/commission/sites/beta-political/files/rp_sustainable_europe_30-01_en_web.pdf.
European Commission. (2019b). *Supporting the Sustainable Development Goals across the world: Joint synthesis report of the European Union and its member states*. https://ec.europa.eu/europeaid/sites/devco/files/jsr-report-20190717_en.pdf.
Fialho, D., & van Bergeijk, P. A. G. (2017). The proliferation of developing country classifications. *The Journal of Development Studies, 53*(1), 99–115.
Fukuda-Parr, S., & McNeill, D. (2019). Knowledge and politics in setting and measuring the SDGs: Introduction to special issue. *Global Policy, 10*(1), 5–15.
Gulrajani, N., & Calleja, R. (2019). *The principled aid index* (Policy Briefing). London: Overseas Development Institute.
Haddad, L. (2013). *Development research: The shape of things to come?* http://www.developmenthorizons.com/2013/08/development-research-shape-of-things-to.html.
Haynal, G. (2002). *DOA: Diplomacy on the ascendant in the age of disintermediation*. https://scholarsprogram.wcfia.harvard.edu/files/fellows/files/haynal.pdf.
High Level Panel. (2013). *A new global partnership: Eradicate poverty and transform economies through sustainable development. The Report of the High-Level Panel of Eminent Persons on the Post-2015 Development Agenda (HLP)*. https://www.un.org/sg/sites/www.un.org.sg/files/files/HLP_P2015_Report.pdf.
Horner, R. (2019). Towards a new paradigm of global development? Beyond the limits of international development. *Progress in Human Geography*, 1–22. https://doi.org/10.1177/0309132519836158.

IMF (International Monetary Fund). (2019a). *Review of implementation of IMF commitments in support of the 2030 Agenda for Sustainable Development* (IMF Policy Paper). Washington, DC: Author.

IMF. (2019b). *Fiscal policies for Paris climate strategies—From principle to practice* (IMF Policy Paper). Washington, DC: Author.

International Institute for Sustainable Development. (2019). HLPF 2019 highlights. *Earth Negotiations Bulletin (ENB), 33*(51).

International Renewable Energy Agency. (2019). *A new world: The geopolitics of the energy transformation*. Abu Dhabi: Author.

Janus, H., Klingebiel, S., & Paulo, S. (2015). Beyond aid: A conceptual perspective on the transformation of development cooperation. *Journal of International Development, 27*(2), 155–169.

Janus, H., & Weinlich, S. (2018). *A mountain worth climbing: Reforming the UN Department of Economic and Social Affairs* (Briefing Paper 20/2018). Bonn: German Development Institute / Deutsches Institut für Entwicklungspolitik (DIE).

Kaul, I. (2017). *Providing global public goods—What role for the multilateral development banks?* (ODI Report). London: Overseas Development Institute.

Kindornay, S. (2019). *Progressing national SDG implementation: An independent assessment of the voluntary national review reports submitted to the United Nations High-level Political Forum in 2018*. Ottawa: Canadian Council for International Co-operation.

King, M. (2016). Broadening the global development framework post 2015: Embracing policy coherence and global public goods. *European Journal of Development Research, 28*(1), 13–29.

Kisangani, E. F., & Pickering, J. (2015). Soldiers and development aid. *Journal of Peace Research, 52*(2), 215–227.

Klingebiel, S., Mahn, T., & Negre, M. (Eds.). (2016). *The fragmentation of aid: Concepts, measurements and implications for development cooperation*. London: Palgrave Macmillan.

Kloke-Lesch, A. (1998a). Funktionale Positionsbestimmung der Entwicklungspolitik. *Internationale Politik und Gesellschaft, 3*(1998), 324–332.

Kloke-Lesch, A. (1998b). The position of development policy: A functional definition. In D. Messner (Ed.), *New perspectives of international and German development policy* (INEF-Report 33) (pp. 36–47). Duisburg: Institut für Entwicklung und Frieden.

Kloke-Lesch, A. (2016). The G20 and the Sustainable Development Goals (SDGs): Reflections on future roles and tasks. In Chongyang Institute for Financial Studies (Ed.), *G20 and global governance: Blue book of G20 Think Tank 2015–2016* (pp. 55–71). Beijing: CITIC Publ. Group.

Kloke-Lesch, A. (2018). Why is the EU failing to champion the SDGs? *Horizons: Journal of International Relations and Sustainable Development, 12*(2018), 144–159.

Kloke-Lesch, A. (2019). Globale Entwicklungspolitik: Politikberatung zwischen aid-community und global public goods. In S. Falk, M. Glaab, A. Römmele, H. Schober, & M. Thunert (Eds.), *Handbuch Politikberatung* (pp. 417–434). Wiesbaden: Springer.

Li, Y. (2018). *Assessment of South-South cooperation and the global narrative on the eve of BAPA + 40* (Research Paper 88). Geneva: South Centre.

Martens, J. (2019). Revisiting the hardware of sustainable development. In B. Adams, C. A. Billorou, R. Bissio, C. Y. Ling, K. Donald, J. Martens, & S. Prato (Eds.), *Reshaping governance for sustainability: Transforming institutions—Shifting power—Strengthening rights* (Global Civil Society Report on the 2030 Agenda and the SDGs, pp. 11–19). Bonn: Global Policy Forum Europe e.V.

Mawdsley, E. (2017). National interests and the paradox of foreign aid under austerity: Conservative governments and the domestic politics of international development since 2010. *The Geographical Journal, 183*(3), 223–232.

Melber, H. (2017). *Development studies and the SDGs—Mapping an agenda* (EADI Policy Paper Series). Bonn: European Association of Development Research and Training Institutes.

Messner, D., & Scholz, I. (2018). Globale Gemeinwohlorientierung als Fluchtpunkt internationaler Kooperation für nachhaltige Entwicklung – ein Perspektivwechsel. *Zeitschrift Für Außen- Und Sicherheitspolitik, 11*(4), 561–572.

Mitchell, I. (2021). Measuring development cooperation and the quality of aid. In S. Chaturvedi et al., (Eds.), *The Palgrave handbook of development cooperation for achieving the 2030 agenda: Contested collaboration* (pp. 247–270).

Mönks, J., Carbonnier, G., Mellet, A., & de Haan, L. (2019). Novel perceptions on development studies: International review and consultations towards a renewed vision. In I. Baud, E. Basile, T. Kontinen, & S. von Itter (Eds.), *Building development studies for the new millennium*. EADI Global Development Series (pp. 217–241). Basingstoke: Palgrave Macmillan.

Niestroy, I., Hege, E., Dirth, E., Zondervan, R., & Derr, K. (2019). *Europe's approach to implementing the Sustainable Development Goals: Good practices and the way forward.* http://www.europarl.europa.eu/thinktank/en/document.html?reference=EXPO_STU%282019%29603473.

OECD (Organisation for Economic Co-operation and Development). (2016a). *Better policies for 2030: An OECD action plan on the Sustainable Development Goals.* https://www.oecd.org/dac/Better%20Policies%20for%202030.pdf.

OECD. (2019b). *Measuring distance to the SDG targets 2019: An assessment of where OECD countries stand.* Paris: OECD Publishing.

OECD. (2019c). *Global outlook on financing for sustainable development 2019.* https://www.oecd.org/dac/financing-sustainable-development/development-finance-topics/Global-Outlook-on-Financing-for-SD-2019.pdf.

OECD. (2019d). *Policy coherence for sustainable development 2019.* https://www.oecd.org/gov/pcsd/policy-coherence-for-sustainable-development-highlights-2019.pdf.

OECD. (n.d.). *History of DAC Lists of aid recipient countries.* http://www.oecd.org/development/financing-sustainable-development/development-finance-standards/historyofdaclistsofaidrecipientcountries.htm#Concepts.

OECD & United Nations Development Programme (UNDP). (2019). *G20 contribution to the 2030 Agenda—Progress and way forward.* https://g20.org/pdf/documents/en/oecd-undp_report_g20_contribution_2030_agenda.pdf.

Overseas Development. (2018). *Five-year strategy.* https://www.odi.org/sites/odi.org.uk/files/long-form-downloads/strategy_booklet_final_web_0.pdf.

Schmidt-Traub, G., Hoff, H., & Bernlöhr, M. (2019, July 15). *International spillovers and the Sustainable Development Goals (SDGs)* (SDSN Policy Brief). Paris: Sustainable Development Solutions Network.

Scholz, I., Esteves, P., Yuefen, L., & Anbumozhi, V. (2017). *Reforming international cooperation towards transformative change.* https://www.g20-insights.org/policy_briefs/reforming-international-cooperation-towards-transformative-change/.

Schönberg, J. (2019). Imagining postcolonial development studies: Reflections on positionalities and research practices. In I. Baud, E. Basile, T. Kontinen, & S. von Itter (Eds.), *Building development studies for the new millennium.* EADI Global Development Series (pp. 97–116). Basingstoke: Palgrave Macmillan.

Stafford-Smith, M., Griggs, D., Gaffney, O., Ullah, F., Reyers, B., Kanie, N., et al. (2017). Integration: The key to implementing the Sustainable Development Goals. *Sustainability Science, 12*(6), 911–919.

UN (United Nations). (2000). *United Nations millennium declaration.* Resolution adopted by the General Assembly (A/RES/55/2). https://www.un.org/en/development/desa/population/migration/generalassembly/docs/globalcompact/A_RES_55_2.pdf.

UN. (2012, July 27). *The future we want.* Resolution adopted by the General Assembly (A/RES/66/288*). https://www.un.org/en/development/desa/population/migration/generalassembly/docs/globalcompact/A_RES_66_288.pdf.

UN. (2013, July 9). *Format and organizational aspects of the High-level Political Forum on Sustainable Development.* Resolution adopted by the General Assembly (A/RES/67/290). https://www.un.org/ga/search/view_doc.asp?symbol=A/RES/67/290&Lang=E.

UN. (2015a). *The Millennium Development Goals report 2015.* New York, NY: Author.

UN. (2015b). *Outcome Document of the Third International Conference on Financing for Development: Addis Ababa Action Agenda.* General Assembly (A/CONF.227/L.1). https://www.un.org/africarenewal/sites/www.un.org.africarenewal/files/N1521991.pdf.

UN. (2015c). *Transforming our world: The 2030 Agenda for Sustainable Development.* Resolution adopted by the General Assembly (A/RES/70/1). https://www.un.org/en/development/desa/population/migration/generalassembly/docs/globalcompact/A_RES_70_1_E.pdf.

UN. (2019a). *Financing for sustainable development report 2019: Inter-agency Task Force on Financing for Development.* New York, NY: Author.

UN. (2019b). *Buenos Aires Outcome Document of the Second High-level United Nations Conference on South-South Cooperation.* Resolution adopted by the General Assembly (A/73/L.80). https://digitallibrary.un.org/record/3799433.

UN. (2019c). *Special edition: Progress towards the Sustainable Development Goals. Report of the Secretary-General (E/2019/68).* https://unstats.un.org/sdgs/files/report/2019/secretary-general-sdg-report-2019-EN.pdf.

UN. (2019d). *Global Sustainable Development Report 2019.* New York, NY: Author.

UN. (n.d.-a). *The Secretary-General's High-Level Panel of Eminent Persons on the Post-2015 Development Agenda.* https://www.un.org/sg/en/management/hlppost2015.shtml.

UN. (n.d.-b). *Open Working Group on Sustainable Development Goals.* https://sustainabledevelopment.un.org/owg.html.

UN. (n.d.-c). *Voluntary national reviews.* https://sustainabledevelopment.un.org/vnrs/.

UN Office for South-South Cooperation. (2019). *About South-South and triangular cooperation.* https://www.unsouthsouth.org/about/about-sstc/.

Van Bergeijk, P. A. G., & van Marrewijk, C. (2013). Heterogeneity and development: An agenda. *The Journal of International Trade & Economic Development, 22*(1), 1–10.

Veltmeyer, H., & Wise, R. D. (Eds.). (2018). *Critical development studies: An introduction.* Black Point, Nova Scotia: Fernwood Publishing.

Von der Heijden, K., Olsen, S., & Scott, A. (2014). *From solidarity to universality—How global interdependence impacts the post-2015 development agenda* (Background Paper 1). London: Independent Research Forum.

Von der Leyen, U. (2019). *A union that strives for more—My agenda for Europe.* https://ec.europa.eu/commission/interim_en.

World Bank Group. (2016). *Forward look: A vision for the World Bank Group in 2030* (DC2016-0008). http://pubdocs.worldbank.org/en/545241485963738230/DC2016-0008.pdf.

Open Access This chapter is licensed under the terms of the Creative Commons Attribution 4.0 International License (http://creativecommons.org/licenses/by/4.0/), which permits use, sharing, adaptation, distribution and reproduction in any medium or format, as long as you give appropriate credit to the original author(s) and the source, provide a link to the Creative Commons license and indicate if changes were made.

The images or other third party material in this chapter are included in the chapter's Creative Commons license, unless indicated otherwise in a credit line to the material. If material is not included in the chapter's Creative Commons license and your intended use is not permitted by statutory regulation or exceeds the permitted use, you will need to obtain permission directly from the copyright holder.

CHAPTER 8

The Difficulties of Diffusing the 2030 Agenda: Situated Norm Engagement and Development Organisations

Lars Engberg-Pedersen and Adam Fejerskov

8.1 Introduction

The 2030 Agenda for Sustainable Development represents a milestone for global cooperation, whether we consider the process that led to its ratification or the breadth of its ambitions. The process shaping the 2030 Agenda has been far more inclusive and democratic than any other global political negotiation in the past, including the narrowly conceived Millennium Development Goals (MDGs). That is not to say it was devoid of conflict, contestation, or strong divergences along the way; the alternating inclusion and exclusion of specific goals, such as Sustainable Development Goal (SDG) 10 (Reduce inequality within and among countries), during the negotiations are a testament to such normative quarrels (Fukuda-Parr and McNeill 2019). The final outcome is an immensely ambitious and wide-ranging agenda for global development as we move towards 2030. It may be clearly underfinanced and suffer from inadequate attention to its actual implementation, yet in its normative form it represents a strong political guidepost, waging a clear battle with different ideologies and diverse national politics.

This chapter draws on Cold-Ravnkilde et al. (2018) and Fejerskov et al. (2019).

L. Engberg-Pedersen (✉) · A. Fejerskov
Danish Institute for International Studies, Copenhagen, Denmark
e-mail: lep@diis.dk

A. Fejerskov
e-mail: admo@diis.dk

© The Author(s) 2021
S. Chaturvedi et al. (eds.), *The Palgrave Handbook of Development Cooperation for Achieving the 2030 Agenda*,
https://doi.org/10.1007/978-3-030-57938-8_8

The challenge that lies ahead then—prompted by its universal nature—is to implement the agenda's rapid diffusion into national policies and reforms needed all over the world if the agreement is to ensure extensive transformation before its deadline. This is no easy task. The historical legacies of global normative agreements such as the 2030 Agenda—the ones both broad and narrow in scope—have taught us that global norms are rarely diffused or implemented straightforwardly and rarely bring about the forms of change written into their global agreements (Czarniawska and Joerges 1996; Engberg-Pedersen et al. 2019; Van der Vleuten et al. 2014; Zwingel 2016). Change may never come about, or it may arrive in a form far removed from what was imagined—for both good and bad. How can we explain these apparent challenges of spreading global norms across the world? In addition, is the 2030 Agenda faced with this very same problem? Whereas the answer to the first question requires quite a few more pages, the second question can be answered more certainly with a yes. Thus, an international agreement is far from enough to establish normative support everywhere; the politicians who pushed for the 2030 Agenda and the SDGs must contemplate how they can mobilise people in all corners of the world around these global norms. The adoption of the agenda in 2015 was actually only the end of the beginning. In order to realise the goals, a straightforward implementation is not to be expected, as the goals imply significant social, political, and economic changes that will challenge both vested interests and normative practices in different societies. Accordingly, pro-SDG politicians should foresee considerable obstacles and resistance. Moreover, there is the significant political challenge that the responsibility for implementing the agenda to some extent has been diluted. The primary responsible is, and should be, governments. But how do governments in countries without significant resources implement a highly ambitious agenda? Wealthy countries managed to avoid taking responsibility at the UN Conference on Financing for Development at Addis Ababa, where the question was supposed to find an answer. Thus, the inequalities between countries and the disparate capacities to address the SDGs are a fundamental condition for the subsequent discussion on norm engagement.

When endeavouring to make an argument for why the 2030 Agenda and the SDGs will not be easily diffused throughout the world and bring about the changes they are expected to from the outset, it is tempting to point to the political developments that have taken place since the agreement was negotiated. The election of Donald Trump and the return of American unilateralism, deteriorating US–China relations, Brexit, and European political chaos amidst an advancing, if economically weak, Russia, together indicate a rising nationalism. This phenomenon has also been witnessed in parts of South America, Africa, and Asia, stimulating conflicts between countries, interests, ideologies, and values rather than leading towards the partnership called for in the agreement. The improbability that the 2030 Agenda can be agreed upon in today's political climate is very real. Still, we argue, a solely political explanation for why the 2030 Agenda cannot easily be diffused—and even an agreement that builds on the contemporary rise of nationalism's preference for hard-boiled interests or right-wing populism's challenge to multilateralism and internationalism—is not adequate.

We argue in this chapter that the diffusion of the 2030 Agenda and the SDGs is not only challenging due to contemporary political circumstances, but also because of the fundamental situated nature of how actors engage with global norms. As attempts are made to integrate the SDGs in international, regional, or national politics, they are not merely carried from one place to another in a fixed and unbreakable form, despite them having been given formal numbers, targets, and indicators. This is not just because of their inconsistencies (see Fukuda-Parr and McNeill 2019; Gasper et al. 2019), but also because—as global norms are present at their core—they find themselves in muddy, multi-actor, and multi-level processes of interaction that occur whenever such norms are used, manipulated, bent, or betrayed by actors. The inter-subjective nature of global norms means that these are addressed, reproduced, or changed during social interactions and cannot be understood as existing outside such processes. They do not have any inherent energy that transports them across boundaries from one place to the other. Rather, actors relate to them in different situations—sometimes intentionally and sometimes not—both through discourses and practices. In doing so, they may be influenced by the norms, but they may also influence them in return and change their meaning. This situated understanding of norm engagement leads us to argue that the SDGs' potential for spreading and inducing change is as shaped by local cultural, social, and conjunctural factors as it is by political ones.

Part of this handbook's rationale is to analyse a growing normative competition and contestation between different groups of actors such as Organisation for Economic Co-operation and Development (OECD)/Development Assistance Committee (DAC) and non-OECD/DAC members, not least to underline an argument of how the SDGs are treated differently across the world. The situated understanding of norm engagement, as it is furthered here, contributes to this discussion with an argument that we should be careful in assuming that strongly diverging ways of interpreting, implementing, and advancing the SDGs only exist across regions or levels of development. The approach to the SDGs may be as different within these imagined groups as it may be between them. There is little homogeneity even among OECD development actors as to how the global norms of the 2030 Agenda should be interpreted, understood, and pursued.

In this chapter then, we attempt to unpack the question of why global norms such as the SDGs cannot be easily diffused across the world. First, we sketch out the basics of how a situated understanding of norm engagement can be conceptualised by confronting conventional perceptions of diffusion to show that global norms are made and remade as actors engage with them in different situations under different circumstances. Second, we extend that understanding to show that we do not have to draw up normative contestation between blocs of countries or regions to see differing views to, interpretations of, and attempts at implementing the 2030 Agenda. Even among OECD development organisations and donors, the situated nature of norms means that these are engaged with in strikingly diverse ways across different actors. We draw on the findings of a four-year research programme entitled Global Norms and Heterogeneous Development Organizations, in which seven major development partners were studied for the way they engage with global norms on gender equality and women's empowerment, which are today largely inscribed into SDG 5.[1] We end with a set of conclusions on where this leaves discussions on how the SDGs may be spread across the world and bring with them much needed transformation.

8.2 Situated Norm Engagement

The 2030 Agenda and its SDGs fundamentally represent what can be called prescriptive norms, understood as *acknowledged, but not necessarily accepted, understandings of collective ambitions* (Fejerskov et al. 2019). This way of understanding prescriptive norms emphasises their contested nature and draws attention to the distinction between formally acknowledging certain ideas and normatively internalising them. Actors may very well acknowledge particular collective ambitions without having any intentions of turning them into concrete policies. It may be politically expedient for governments to sign international agreements even though they do not subscribe to their contents. The factor that turns such internationally acknowledged ideas into global norms is that relevant actors who which to be seen as legitimate players in a field all refer to the ideas as being important. However, they are likely to interpret them differently, partly because they may not accept them, partly because they operate in different contexts. Despite the formally agreed ambitions of the SDGs, there is no single understanding of the norms inherent in them—across the globe or across history. Even when diplomats and politicians signed the 2030 Agenda, different interpretations of the document surely existed. However, this does not mean that any interpretation is valid—although there is substantial leeway, as we see below. Certain views and practices may be difficult to defend because they are widely perceived to contradict global norms.

Prescriptive norms are fundamentally of a political nature, as they typically address issues of resource allocation between different social groups. Global norms are often developed to challenge existing practices in different parts of the world, and if they are taken seriously in these societies, they will change who gains and who loses in specific situations. Thus, both the elaboration and implementation of global norms are political processes in which actors struggle to make particular ideas dominate social, political, and economic interactions. In an interdependent world where legitimacy is a key asset to furthering one's concerns, the competition for elaborating international prescriptive norms is fierce, as these norms constitute significant reference points in the struggle for influence.

A situated approach to global norms underlines the broader social processes of norm engagement and the discontinuous transformation that they imply. Norm engagement is a social process that is inseparable from situations, their history, and their likely future. Norms are shaped by actors and are not fixed structures to be carried around from one locality to the next. Rather, norms are in themselves social interactions and relations. Though some actors are influential and therefore seek to be norm entrepreneurs, whereas others have fewer opportunities and may be perceived as "norm receivers", the distinction is relative. In the end, global norms are intended to change the widespread practices undertaken by the actors who support them. Therefore, these actors are unlikely to just "receive" and accept global norms. It is argued that the more global norms challenge existing practices, the less they are likely to be accepted and integrated in societies (Merry and Levitt 2019). In such a situation, one may expect global norms to be either rejected or adapted to local conditions. In the latter case, they are changed by those who are expected to "receive" them. Though this change may not have global outreach, reinterpretations of global norms are far from uncommon. In the field of gender equality, several norms have changed over time. The protection of women in labour markets was once a global norm; today, however, it is viewed as a practice that marginalises women (Zwingel 2016). Likewise, the Beijing Platform for Action in 1995 conceptualised "women's empowerment" as a way to confront patriarchal practices, whereas different actors later interpreted it as an instrument to accelerate growth (Eyben and Napier-Moore 2009). Perceiving norms as fixed is "process-reduction", that is, making static in substantial ways that which is dynamic and unfolding. Regardless of the apparent strength of the SDGs, norms should not be seen as agents in themselves, but as ideas shaped and given meaning through interaction.

Thus, it varies greatly across actors how they engage with norms, just as it does from situation to situation, meaning that the same actor may approach the same set of ideas in different ways over time because of contextual changes. The social position of an actor significantly influences norm engagement and may define whether actors address norms at all, and whether their interpretations of a norm influence other actors, including in organisational contexts (Battilana et al. 2009). As social positions define access to networks and webs of social relations, they facilitate or prevent the influence of particular normative interpretations. Nevertheless, they do not determine how norms are interpreted, as even the marginalised have opportunities for resistance (Scott 1985).

Global norms are made, sustained, and changed inter-subjectively by actors engaged in political struggles. As such, these norms are the object of conflicts of interpretation rather than of continued homogenisation. Although the SDGs capture elements of many different norms and constitute a reference point for discussions in particular fields, they do not provide a fixed interpretation of a collective ambition to which actors respond passively through a logic of appropriateness. Actors continuously interpret, adapt, and change the

SDGs as they address them. Thus, every reference to the SDGs simultaneously works to strengthen them as an important normative issue and to adjust or change them in terms of their concrete contents. Sometimes, moreover, actors deliberately seek to resist global norms (Bloomfield and Scott 2017).

Other dimensions such as space and time also influence the way actors engage with the SDGs. The physical, social, or economic nature of any space shapes social interactions and norm engagement. Time and space confine what is perceived as legitimate human activity. All spaces produce certain shared understandings that help interpret action, but such understandings are never uniform. More or less different interpretations are likely to exist, given the diversity of individuals who—with different purposes, experiences, and expectations—share the space. This is evident when diplomats from different countries meet. Although they may have gone to the same universities, may have participated in the same international negotiations for years, and may all be acutely aware of the dos and don'ts at the negotiating table, they are likely to interpret the texts in front of them differently. Space does not determine understandings, but it helps in shaping them.

Temporality, or time, similarly influences norm engagement. The agentic dimension of social action is significantly shaped by the flow of time (Emirbayer and Mische 1998). Agency is informed by the past (habitual aspects), the present (contextualising past habits and future projects within the moment), and the future (capacity to imagine alternative possibilities). When engaging with the SDGs during social interactions, actors thus simultaneously revisit past patterns of thought and action, try to imagine future trajectories or imageries, and do so while confronted with the dilemmas, demands, and ambiguities of the present moment. Because the perceptions of the past, the present, and the future change over time, the same actors are likely to engage with particular ideas differently at different points in time. There is also a significant element of temporality to the SDGs because they are imaginations of the past, present, and, most importantly, the future. They are constructed as ideal states of what should be, reflecting inter-subjective hopes and desires based on past experiences and present challenges.

8.3 Development Organisations and the Diffusion of the SDGs

Closer to the reality of the 2030 Agenda, what does this somewhat abstract conceptualisation of situated norm engagement mean for the way the SDGs are engaged with and understood by development actors? To try and answer that question, we now draw on the findings from a four-year research project on how different development organisations respond to global normative pressures, primarily at the policy level (see Cold-Ravnkilde et al. 2018). Much like this handbook, the project worked from the fundamental observation that international development cooperation today is caught at the intersection of homogenising global forces and increasingly heterogeneous development organisations. What happens at this intersection? Do global norms diffuse and homogenise different development organisations "behind their back"? Do development organisations consciously translate global agreements into their own specific contexts, subverting or supporting the agreements accordingly?

To narrow the scope of analysis, the research project focussed on seven new and old development organisations, including Agencia Mexicana de Cooperación Internacional para el Desarrollo (AMEXCID) in Mexico, Danida[2] in Denmark, Islamic Relief Worldwide, Oxfam Great Britain (Oxfam GB), South Africa's development cooperation, the Bill and Melinda Gates Foundation, and the World Bank. The project explored how global normative pressures to address issues of gender equality and women's empowerment specifically, as an example of a strong global norm, affect these development organisations in terms of their policies and organisational cultures.

It is clear that development organisations respond markedly different to normative pressures, sometimes with effects on policies and core organisational goals, at other times with resistance or lip service that leaves organisational practices untouched, decoupling deed from word. Such processes take place through institutional negotiations, conflicts, and interpretations, in which individuals, groups, and departments contest for the dominant interpretations. It is also clear that distinctions between so-called new and old development organisations or donors, as well as between multilateral, bilateral, and private aid agencies, should not be exaggerated when it comes to matters of how they engage with global norms such as those of the SDGs. In some respects, there are astonishing similarities across these lines of difference. The way that gender equality is interpreted in distinct organisational cultures is rather similar in the World Bank, the Bill and Melinda Gates Foundation, and Islamic Relief Worldwide. Gender equality was taken on board with enthusiasm in all three organisations, but in ways that fit the dominating views in the respective organisations. The processes in Oxfam GB and the World Bank also resembled each other to the extent that they were rather introverted exercises that paid little attention to the views of their peers. AMEXCID, Islamic Relief Worldwide, and Danida were all concerned with gaining credibility through references to global gender equality norms; the difficulties involved in turning a strong formal commitment into concrete action are shared by Danida and South Africa's development cooperation, albeit for different reasons. These observations call for less rigid perceptions of aid agencies than those based on "newness" or whether organisations are international, national, or non-governmental.

The way global norms on gender equality have been addressed in these development organisations demonstrates that the scope for furthering global norms is heavily circumscribed by contingent and contextual factors. In certain situations, there is little or no room to move the agenda forward, and it may be counterproductive to insist on specific norms, as these will be undermined by rejecting their importance. In other situations, contingent events or unforeseen occurrences may suddenly pave the way for strong engagement with a global norm. This leads us to conceptualise a set of explanatory dimensions that greatly shape how global norms such as the SDGs are engaged with in development organisations under different situations. These are (i) organisational history, culture, and structures; (ii) actor strategies, emotions, and relationships; (iii) organisational uncertainty, pressures, and priorities; and (iv) the normative context and stakeholders. Global norm engagement in development organisations will always be shaped by these different factors, if to differing degrees—sometimes tipping engagements towards a rapid adoption of global norms, and at other times speaking against it. We expand on these in the following and discuss how they influence norm engagement in the seven development organisations.

8.3.1 Organisational History, Culture, and Structures

When global norms enter into organisational contexts, they do not encounter empty halls but layers of practices, rules, and ideas, all embedded in institutional history. Having a religious, entrepreneurial, banking, anti-apartheid, ministerial, or voluntary historical origin greatly shapes how global norms are conceptualised in organisations. The framing of the SDGs is thus highly dependent on how the organisational culture legitimises different arguments, ideas, and concerns. Over time, organisational cultures will develop relatively coherent meanings, beliefs, rituals, and images (Schein 1996; Scott 2014). Although far from unchangeable, uncontested, or unambiguous, these cultures become institutionalised in the organisation's mandate, history, iconography, and procedures. They shape the ways in which external demands, changes, and contexts are interpreted (Barnett and Finnemore 2004), and they make certain interpretations of global norms more feasible than others. This is not least because organisational cultures substantially shape the way staff relate to each other—both within departments and in intra-organisational relations with other departments—during which clashes over issues of power, authority, and both material and immaterial resources may occur.

Within the World Bank, the (re)turn to "gender equality as smart economics" around 2006 gained legitimacy and credibility by being framed in a way that was particularly appealing to the dominant logic of economists. Furthermore, the way in which gender equality was packaged using the image of women as active agents resonated in an organisation that was increasingly characterised by micro-economic thinking (Jones 2018). Similarly, norms on gender equality have had to assimilate to the dominant organisational culture in the Bill and Melinda Gates Foundation, which is characterised by quantitative impact measurements and technology-as-progress mantras (Fejerskov 2018a). The organisational history of the Bill and Melinda Gates Foundation means it is deeply embedded in private-sector practice and thought, with a strong belief in technology and measurability as cures to the illnesses of the world. Such cultures are not easily challenged or transformed. Elsewhere, Zilber (2002) has shown how, over the course of decades, organisational practices may remain the same, though the logics with which they are associated change on the surface. Such a decoupling between foreground discourses and background practices speaks to the persistent nature of organisational culture and history.

As organisations are formed to achieve certain goals, departmental structures are essentially set up to distribute roles, tasks, and activities to staff and units, as well as standardised and formalised coordination mechanisms to govern relations. The structures of development organisations are fundamental in shaping organisational narratives and practices. In particular, the organisation of policy-making units and implementing organs creates a separation of fundamentally different kinds of practices in different socio-economic contexts (Engberg-Pedersen 2014; Mosse 2005). Despite the formally one-dimensional relations between such units, organisational structures are characterised by a multiplicity of dimensions that shape narratives and practices by compartmentalising and separating organisational subcultures, resulting in different practices and beliefs. Accordingly, organisational structures are important in defining actors' access to—and possession of—the formal and informal authority with which they can initiate and influence processes of engaging with global norms.

8.3.2 Actor Strategies, Emotions, and Relationships

Actors are central in facilitating and shaping the spread of global norms across contexts. Individual actors can act and work to shape the implementation of a new idea, norm, or practice, and adoption will always be facilitated or blocked by human action, just as processes of institutionalisation and translation are shaped by it. However, organisational actors are faced with numerous challenges when they seek to initiate and influence processes of norm engagement. They may have to undermine existing logics and practices and legitimise new ones in the eyes of other organisational actors, or create hybrid forms in which new and old ideas are melded together—that is, if the SDGs do not resonate with existing activities or ideas in an organisation in the first place, the actors will have a very difficult time making a difference there (Merry and Levitt 2019). For the purpose of seeing their organisations engage with norms, actors need strategies. They need to mobilise different forms of material, political, and organisational resources, frame new organisational practices or rules inspired by the 2030 Agenda in an acceptable manner, and create resonances to inspire other organisational actors. Analysing the Women and Land project, funded by the Bill and Melinda Gates Foundation, Fejerskov (2018b) shows how actors become central as the project moves from the top layers of management in the Gates Foundation's headquarters through an intermediary organisational level to its implementation in concrete localities. Staff involved in implementation actively engage in reinterpretations of the meaning and objectives of the project to make it fit the context and resonate with ideas that are perceived to be legitimate.

To create a coherent vision for change that appeals to other organisational actors, including implementing staff (Battilana et al. 2009), actors may frame their change projects to align with the organisation's dominant values. They often do this while being confronted with "institutional defenders" (DiMaggio 1988), who benefit from the organisational status quo. Actors may construct imageries that lend coherence to new norms and ideas or create stories through which heroes and villains are defined. For staff members who do not possess formal authority, it is especially important to attract the intellectual attention of central managers and decision-makers in the organisation. The scope for conducting such normative work may relate to the actors' abilities, characteristics, or qualities (Beckert 1999), their social and organisational positions (Battilana et al. 2009), or the degree to which their organisation is receptive to change. Juul Petersen (2018) shows how the staff of Islamic Relief Worldwide actively make use of "double speak" to satisfy different audiences and organisational priorities by, for example, highlighting how particular verses in the Qur'an can support mainstream development approaches to gender equality. However, attempting to bridge different concerns in this way means diluting the contents of gender equality norms to make them acceptable to the more conservative constituents in the organisation.

The way norms "travel" into organisations is intertwined with emotions and relationships. In the institutional literature, little is known about how individuals experience institutions or the emotional aspects of engaging in institutional work (Barley 2008; Lawrence and Suddaby 2006). By contrast, other areas of contemporary social science and the humanities are devoting increased attention to emotions (or "affect") as part of a material (re)turn to the body (Massumi 2002; Rose 2013), even to the point of engaging in the neurosciences of emotions. In this interpretation, emotions are considered a set of automatically triggered brain–body behaviours and expressions that are inherently independent of intentions (Smail 2007). In other manifestations, the turn has served in part to challenge the (over)use of rationality in making over-flat accounts of what forms opinions, motivates action, and shapes judgement. In this line of thought, emotions should not be regarded as purely individual-level psychological factors that are divorced from individuals' social positions or rational cognitive processes (Voronov and Vince 2012).

The notion of emotions emphasises the importance of actors in organisations and sheds light on how an organisation's staff mobilises energy around a norm, which is necessary for it to mobilise attention (Benford and Snow 2000; Czarniawska and Joerges 1996). Adopting a "relational approach" to development, Anne-Marie Fechter (2012) considers relationships and emotions as essential attributes of development practices. In that sense, staff's personal relationships as well as their beliefs, values, and motivations are likely to affect how norms on gender equality travel and manifest themselves within development organisations (Mosse 2011). In Oxfam GB, staff members often hold strong beliefs about gender, resulting in fierce emotional contestations over gender programmes. Crewe (2018) shows that such contestations reflect not only a conflict between different feminist and non-feminist values, but also the antagonism between different organisational imperatives. However, the struggles are fuelled by deep personal commitments and alliances, which significantly influence policy outcomes.

8.3.3 *Organisational Pressures and Priorities*

Whenever actors engage with the SDGs in organisations, such interaction will be strongly influenced by organisational pressures and priorities at a given time and place. These pressures and priorities are management concerns and organisational threats and opportunities that staff feel override the more immediate daily purposes of their work. Particularly in relation to new projects and policy-making, organisational pressures and priorities tend to set a determining framework for organisational processes. They include what can be labelled as political opportunity structures—in which organisational leaders assess whether such windows of opportunity are central to their organisation—but threats to organisational survival and processes of organisational typically change the agendas of top leaders and managers. Thus, staff perceptions of formal and informal priorities influence whether and how norms on gender equality become a strong focus in concrete development programmes. When Warren Buffett decided to grant some $30 billion to the Bill and Melinda Gates Foundation in 2006, it considerably reframed the organisational context into which gender equality norms were travelling at the time (Fejerskov 2018a). In some organisations, the pressure for disbursement is significant, and gender equality is rarely a concern that can move a lot of money quickly. Conversely, in the case of Danida, when faced with continuous administrative cuts, a significant organisational priority shaping the context of a new gender equality policy was that it should require as little administrative capacity as possible (Engberg-Pedersen 2018).

Formal priorities in terms of development policies emphasising the SDGs may not automatically turn into a strong emphasis on the issue in concrete development programmes. For instance, Danida staff are very adept at sensing the "real" priorities of development ministers and top managers, regardless of official policies. Many Danish development ministers have repeatedly stated their support for gender equality, but several evaluations note the limited success of gender mainstreaming. Thus, the absence of the minister when a new gender policy is presented to the public sends a signal about how it is prioritised. Nonetheless, formal priorities may be important, especially if they are in line with staff perceptions of informal pressures and priorities.

Whereas some explanatory dimensions, such as organisational cultures and history, only experience incremental change over the course of years, if not decades, organisational pressures and priorities often go through rapid change as a consequence of changes in leadership, the influence of different stakeholders, and shifts in the normative environment. This is not least the case with public aid agencies, with elections being a frequent source of disruption in political priorities, and thus organisational pressures. In South Africa, departmental infighting over the establishment of an overarching organisational framework for development cooperation—the South African Development Partnership—as well as continuous (re)structuring processes within the Women's Ministry have contributed to a stronger gender push in South Africa's development cooperation being impeded (Cold-Ravnkilde 2019). In Oxfam GB, recent discussions on gender equality and its conceptualisation have been heavily influenced by both organisational restructuring and funding pressures. The Oxfam family is changing its organisational arrangements in a strategic process going up to 2020, which staff see as almost the only concern of top managers. At the same time, fundraising was challenged both politically and through increased competition. All this produced a conceptualisation of a gender-related programme being described as tumbleweed—blown in all directions and never settling down (Crewe 2018).

8.3.4 Normative Environment and Stakeholders

The notion of a normative environment refers to actors sharing organisational or social spheres with the organisation in question. It espouses specific values and influences the organisation and the actors within it through normative measures because actors in the normative environment do not have any relations of formal authority with the organisation. They may be part of a similar institutional or organisational field, but they also include others who are perceived as legitimate stakeholders, such as the media or academic environments. Normative actors encourage particular forms of action, logics, and goals, and they may accordingly favour particular kinds of translation, exerting indirect power through knowledge, legitimacy, or prestige.

Responses to such forms of pressure from the normative environment may, of course, take on many forms. Decoupling is a core argument of institutional thought (Meyer and Rowan 1977), in which organisations disconnect foreground (symbolic) changes from more structural or procedural changes in the organisation's machinery. Pressure from perhaps several different normative environments creates multiple, and often conflicting, demands to which the organisation is expected to respond in timely fashion—something that is not always possible. Moreover, public aid agencies are expected to respond simultaneously to the national political environment, which is more often than not of a fragmented nature, and the normative framework espoused by the international community of peer aid agencies. Defiance of pressure from the normative environment is an equally likely response, yet also one implying potentially significant consequences.

Often, different normative environments entail bridging very different, sometimes contradictory sets of norms in order to appeal to different audiences. In building its identity as a regional development partner, South Africa is navigating between the normative environments of liberal internationalists who believe that South Africa's regional leadership should be pursued through the promotion of human rights and democracy, and of constituents being primarily concerned about non-interference and anti-imperialist discourses. Moreover, historical contestations between feminists and nationalists over the meaning and interpretations associated with gender issues in South Africa continue to shape conflicts over gender norms between stakeholders both inside and outside the administration (Cold-Ravnkilde 2019). In the case of AMEXCID, debates around gender equality and women's rights are introduced and framed to simultaneously resonate and address a national feminicide (Sørensen 2018). By emphasising its own national historical experiences of (unsuccessfully) addressing violence against women, gender policy-making has come to form an important part of building AMEXCID's identity as a development partner in the region. Mexico's gender-related development activities emphasising South–South cooperation reflect an attempt to appeal to domestic constituencies, international donor communities, and targeted partner countries in the region (Sørensen 2018). Despite having similar characteristics as so-called emerging actors embedded in national contexts of feminicide pandemics, South Africa and AMEXCID have responded rather differently to international and domestic pressures to address gender norms in their respective development cooperation engagements. AMEXCID quite clearly commits itself to working to achieve global norms on gender equality, such as the MDGs and SDGs, including the goal of promoting gender equality and empowering women. Contrary to this, alignment with what is often conceived of as Western-imposed hegemony is contested in South Africa's normative environment, thus impeding the institutionalisation of gender norms into a strategic policy framework (Cold-Ravnkilde 2019).

8.4 Conclusion

The SDGs will undoubtedly influence discussions of development in the years to come. As analysed in this chapter, seven major aid agencies and partners have all embraced global norms on gender equality and women's empowerment, despite the substantially different histories, organisation, and orientations of these agencies. Contemporary development cooperation is heavily influenced by more than 40 years of international discussions and agreements on norms pertaining to gender equality. To be recognised as a legitimate player by peer organisations and development communities, even organisations established with a strong focus on financial issues (e.g. the World Bank), on technological development (e.g. the Bill and Melinda Gates Foundation), or on religious issues (e.g. Islamic Relief Worldwide) feel obliged to address gender equality norms. Despite a normative environment of feminicide epidemics in Mexico, also AMEXCID has taken up gender equality as an important political priority.

Nevertheless, the chapter questions the extent to which global norms are diffused as a recognisable, homogeneous understanding perceived in the same way across social contexts. As we have argued elsewhere (Fejerskov et al. 2019), there is a need to refocus theories on how global norms influence social action—from diffusion to the situations of norm engagement. Norms do not have an energy of their own enabling them to spread from place to place unaffected by social interaction. Rather, they are interpreted in substantially different ways, depending on the actors engaging with the norms and the situations in which this takes place. Thus, global social change does not necessarily move towards increased homogenisation as a consequence of international agreements on prescriptive norms. In the case of the aid agencies, their particular organisational histories, cultures, and structures are one aspect influencing how global norms on gender equality are addressed. Another is how organisational actors and norm entrepreneurs frame global norms within existing organisational concerns and manage to mobilise attention. Particular organisational pressures and priorities may also thoroughly circumscribe the extent to which and how global norms can be promoted in an aid agency. Finally, normative environments shape, stimulate, bias, and/or impede norm engagement. There are, accordingly, a host of factors that may influence how global norms are addressed in any particular situation, and it is unlikely that a particular understanding should prevail across time and space.

This creates a paradox. On the one hand, global norms such as the SDGs are likely to be taken up in discussions of development in most parts of the world. On the other hand, they will be reframed depending on the specific circumstances in different social settings. This means that development discussions will be characterised by tensions between broad global norms that allow for different interpretations and situation-specific factors, pulling the interpretations in very different directions. These interpretations will, subsequently, influence global negotiations whenever the SDGs are revisited. However, this is not to say that the SDGs are irrelevant. Rather, it is to argue that the SDGs do not uniformise development discussions around the world and that their influence depends on two interrelated issues, namely actors' political strengths and political contingencies. Strong actors and norm entrepreneurs advocating the SDGs may be able to shape political agendas, but they will typically have to adapt the goals to local circumstances if they meet resistance. However, even strong actors may get their wings clipped in the face of political contingencies drawing attention away from the SDGs. An example of this is the deteriorating political support for gender equality in Russia (Gradskova 2019). Despite increasing attention to gender equality during the 1990s and the first years of the new millennium, an alliance between the political regime and the Catholic Church has since emphasised the family above gender issues, implying, inter alia, a softening of the legal regulations addressing violence against women in the family. As noted in this chapter, organisational pressures and priorities may also change rapidly and influence the scope for norm engagement by organisational actors who would like to promote gender concerns.

Accordingly, the SDGs are fragile prescriptive norms that are constantly up for reinterpretation and whose impact on concrete policies and practices is highly dependent on actors and contingencies. As noted in the introduction to this book, development cooperation can be characterised as contested collaboration, not least because two tendencies point in directions undermining collective ambitions about global development: the increasing strength of emerging economies challenges the normative dominance of OECD countries, and the growing nationalism in many countries weakens the appetite for international cooperation. Does this mean that the SDGs were a short-lived attempt to agree on global development? Probably not. First, the 2030 Agenda is not the normative product of an exclusive group of OECD countries. Several powerful countries in all parts of the world have had to put up with one or two things to agree on the agenda. Influential actors in emerging economies and the Global South are pushing for normative developments and strengthened efforts to achieve the SDGs. Even the human rights agenda, which has often been criticised as a project of the Global North, was in the 1960s entirely dependent on support from former colonies (Jensen 2016). Thus, the 2030 Agenda enjoys widespread support, while the pockets of resistance are to be found in all parts of the world. Secondly, several global challenges (e.g. climate change) do not go away if you bury your head in the sand and refuse international cooperation. As they cannot be resolved by any individual country, these challenges are likely to enforce cooperation at some point if war and social collapse are to be avoided. An already established and legitimate framework for which goals should be pursued in that situation is likely to facilitate such cooperation. Thirdly, whereas governments and politicians have diverse interests, often of a short-term nature, populations generally value the fundamental focus of the SDGs on living conditions and well-being. Though the goals cover a vast terrain, they reflect a strong emphasis on issues that regularly come out on top of people's preferences, such as education, health, jobs (United Nations Development Group 2013). Moreover, the inclusive call for "leaving no one behind" has a strong appeal in most societies.

Thus, the SDGs have a significant potential for popular support that norm entrepreneurs may be able to mobilise. Politicians and policy-makers who seek to promote a focus on the SDGs should consider three issues. First, they need to be aware of and address the paradox between global norms and concrete realities. It is not useful to insist on a rigid interpretation of the SDGs when trying to convince others that the goals are relevant and appealing. The SDGs need to be seen as relevant in relation to both the development problems confronting societies around the world and the norms and values that people in different places nourish. This "bridging" is no easy task, but it will have to be taken seriously. Second, contingent challenges should be recognised. In Europe, refugees and Brexit have topped the political agenda recently, and it is often difficult to get completely different topics on the political agenda. SDG advocates should consider this and try to develop ways of framing the 2030 Agenda that speak to current political concerns while gradually moving attention towards the SDGs. Third, politicians supporting the SDGs should possibly turn more towards the public to exert pressure and build support for the 2030 Agenda over the long run rather than focus exclusively on short-term political struggles. Without a very strong platform, the latter is difficult to control, given that most politicians concentrate on immediate concerns in order to win upcoming elections. The political weakness of the SDGs is their long-term nature, but if they can be turned into pertinent concerns felt by people at large, they may substantially influence our future.

Notes

1. Articles analysing the case studies are published in two issues of *Progress in Development* (volume 18, issues 2 and 3, 2018).
2. Danida is the term used to describe the Danish Ministry of Foreign Affairs in relation to Danish development cooperation and is no longer used as an acronym, although it is derived from the Danish International Development Agency.

References

Barley, S. R. (2008). Coalface institutionalism. In R. Greenwood, C. Oliver, R. Suddaby, & K. Sahlin-Andersson (Eds.), *The Sage handbook of organizational institutionalism* (pp. 491–518). Los Angeles, CA: Sage.

Barnett, M., & Finnemore, M. (2004). *Rules for the world: International organizations in global politics*. London and Ithaca, NY: Cornell University Press.

Battilana, J., Leca, B., & Boxenbaum, E. (2009). How actors change institutions: Towards a theory of institutional entrepreneurship. *Academy of Management Annals, 3*(1), 65–107.

Beckert, J. (1999). Agency, entrepreneurs, and institutional change: The role of strategic choice and institutionalized practices in organizations. *Organization Studies, 20*(5), 777–799.

Benford, R. D., & Snow, D. A. (2000). Framing processes and social movements: An overview and assessment. *Annual Review of Sociology, 26,* 611–639.

Bloomfield, A., & Scott, S. V. (Eds.). (2017). *Norm antipreneurs and the politics of resistance to global normative change*. Abingdon: Routledge.

Cold-Ravnkilde, S. M. (2019). *Gender norm fragmentation in South Africa's development cooperation*. Manuscript in preparation.

Cold-Ravnkilde, S. M., Engberg-Pedersen, L., & Fejerskov, A. (2018). Global norms and heterogeneous development organizations: Introduction to special issue on new actors, old donors and gender equality norms in international development cooperation. *Progress in Development Studies, 18*(2), 77–94.

Crewe, E. (2018). Flagships and tumbleweed: A history of the politics of gender justice work in Oxfam GB 1986–2015. *Progress in Development Studies, 18*(2), 110–125.

Czarniawska, B., & Joerges, B. (1996). Travels of ideas. In B. Czarniawska & G. Sevón (Eds.), *Translating organizational change* (pp. 13–48). Berlin: Walter de Gruyter.

DiMaggio, P. (1988). Interest and agency in institutional theory. In L. G. Zucker (Ed.), *Institutional patterns and organizations: Culture and environment* (pp. 3–22). Cambridge, MA: Ballinger.

Emirbayer, M., & Mische, A. (1998). What is agency? *American Journal of Sociology, 103*(4), 962–1023.

Engberg-Pedersen, L. (2014). Bringing aid management closer to reality: The experience of Danish bilateral development cooperation. *Development Policy Review, 32*(1), 113–131.

Engberg-Pedersen, L. (2018). Do norms travel? The case of gender in Danish development cooperation. *Progress in Development Studies, 18*(3), 153–171.

Engberg-Pedersen, L., Fejerskov, A., & Cold-Ravnkilde, S. M. (Eds.). (2019). *Rethinking gender equality in global governance: The delusion of norm diffusion*. Basingstoke: Palgrave Macmillan.

Eyben, R., & Napier-Moore, R. (2009). Choosing words with care? Shifting meanings of women's empowerment in international development. *Third World Quarterly, 30*(2), 285–300.

Fechter, A.-M. (2012). The personal and the professional: Aid workers' relationships and values in the development process. *Third World Quarterly, 33*(8), 1387–1404.

Fejerskov, A. (2018a). *The Gates Foundation's rise to power: Private authority in global politics*. London and New York, NY: Routledge.

Fejerskov, A. (2018b). Development as resistance and translation: Remaking norms and ideas of the Gates Foundation. *Progress in Development Studies, 18*(2), 126–143.

Fejerskov, A. M., Engberg-Pedersen, L., & Cold-Ravnkilde, S. M. (2019). Rethinking the study of global gender equality norms: Towards a situated approach. In L. Engberg-Pedersen, A. M. Fejerskov, & S. M. Cold-Ravnkilde (Eds.), *Rethinking gender equality in global governance: The delusion of norm diffusion* (pp. 1–40). Basingstoke: Palgrave Macmillan.

Fukuda-Parr, S., & McNeill, D. (2019). Knowledge and politics in setting and measuring the SDGs: Introduction to special issue. *Global Policy, 10*(S1), 5–15.

Gasper, D., Shah, A., & Tankha, S. (2019). The framing of sustainable consumption and production in SDG 12. *Global Policy, 10*(S1), 83–95.

Gradskova, Y. (2019). Gender equality as a declaration: The changing environment of Nordic-Russian cooperation. In L. Engberg-Pedersen, A. M. Fejerskov, & S. M. Cold-Ravnkilde (Eds.), *Rethinking gender equality in global governance: The delusion of norm diffusion* (pp. 169–190). Basingstoke: Palgrave Macmillan.

Jensen, S. L. B. (2016). *The making of international human rights: The 1960s, decolonization, and the reconstruction of global values*. Cambridge: Cambridge University Press.

Jones, B. (2018). A more receptive crowd than before: Explaining the World Bank's gender turn in the 2000s. *Progress in Development Studies, 18*(3), 172–188.

Juul Petersen, M. (2018). Translating global gender norms in Islamic Relief Worldwide. *Progress in Development Studies, 18*(3), 189–207.

Lawrence, T. B., & Suddaby, R. (2006). Institutions and institutional work. In S. R. Clegg, C. Hardy, T. B. Lawrence, & W. R. Nord (Eds.), *Handbook of organization studies* (pp. 215–254). London: Sage.

Massumi, B. (2002). *Parables for the virtual: Movement, affect, sensation*. Durham and London: Duke University Press.

Merry, S. E., & Levitt, P. (2019). Remaking women's human rights in the vernacular: The resonance dilemma. In L. Engberg-Pedersen, A. M. Fejerskov, & S. M. Cold-Ravnkilde (Eds.), *Rethinking gender equality in global governance: The delusion of norm diffusion* (pp. 145–168). Basingstoke: Palgrave Macmillan.

Meyer, J. W., & Rowan, B. (1977). Institutionalized organizations: Formal structure as myth and ceremony. *American Journal of Sociology, 83*(2), 340–363.

Mosse, D. (2005). Global governance and the ethnography of international aid. In D. Mosse & D. Lewis (Eds.), *The aid effect: Giving and governing in international development* (pp. 1–36). London: Pluto Press.

Mosse, D. (Ed.). (2011). *Adventures in Aidland: The anthropology of professionals in international development*. Oxford and New York, NY: Berghahn Books.

Rose, N. (2013). The human sciences in a biological age. *Theory, Culture & Society, 30*(1), 3–34.

Schein, E. H. (1996). Culture: The missing concept in organization studies. *Administrative Science Quarterly, 41*(2), 229–240.

Scott, J. C. (1985). *Weapons of the weak: Everyday forms of peasant resistance*. London and New Haven, CT: Yale University Press.

Scott, W. R. (2014). *Institutions and organizations* (4th ed.). Thousand Oaks, CA: Sage.

Smail, D. (2007). *On deep history and the brain*. Berkeley, London, and Los Angeles, CA: University of California Press.

Sørensen, N. N. (2018). Diffusing gender equality norms in the midst of a feminicide pandemic: The case of AMEXCID and decentralized Mexican South-South cooperation. *Progress in Development Studies, 18*(2), 95–109.

United Nations Development Group. (2013). *A million voices: The world we want*. New York, NY: Author.

Van Der Vleuten, A., van Eerdewijk, A., & Roggeband, C. (Eds.). (2014). *Gender equality norms in regional governance: Transnational dynamics in Europe, South America and Southern Africa*. Basingstoke: Palgrave Macmillan.

Voronov, M., & Vince, R. (2012). Integrating emotions into the analysis of institutional work. *Academy of Management Review, 37*(1), 58–81.

Zilber, T. B. (2002). Institutionalization as an interplay between actions, meanings, and actors: The case of a rape crisis center in Israel. *The Academy of Management Journal, 45*(1), 234–254.

Zwingel, S. (2016). *Translating international women's rights: The CEDAW convention in context*. Basingstoke: Palgrave Macmillan.

Open Access This chapter is licensed under the terms of the Creative Commons Attribution 4.0 International License (http://creativecommons.org/licenses/by/4.0/), which permits use, sharing, adaptation, distribution and reproduction in any medium or format, as long as you give appropriate credit to the original author(s) and the source, provide a link to the Creative Commons license and indicate if changes were made.

The images or other third party material in this chapter are included in the chapter's Creative Commons license, unless indicated otherwise in a credit line to the material. If material is not included in the chapter's Creative Commons license and your intended use is not permitted by statutory regulation or exceeds the permitted use, you will need to obtain permission directly from the copyright holder.

CHAPTER 9

Diffusion, Fusion, and Confusion: Development Cooperation in a Multiplex World Order

Paulo Esteves and Stephan Klingebiel

9.1 Introduction

Development cooperation (DC) is undergoing fundamental changes for several reasons. Firstly, the narrative of DC is in flux. For many decades, the Organisation for Economic Co-operation and Development (OECD) approach to official development assistance (ODA) was the predominant narrative in this regard. However, the rise of South-South cooperation (SSC) is introducing a distinct concept of DC (Bracho 2017; Chaturvedi 2016; Zoccal Gomes and Esteves 2018), and multiple sites of "contested cooperation" (see the Introduction to this handbook) have become a key feature of the DC field. In addition, the 2030 Agenda for Sustainable Development and its Sustainable Development Goals (SDGs) provide a universal umbrella concept for "sustainable development" and "partnerships" in support of sustainable development. At the same time, OECD ODA providers are rephrasing their ODA approaches (e.g. stronger emphasis on co-benefits for ODA providers).

Secondly, we can observe several interrelated challenges concerning the DC system per se. At least three challenges need to be highlighted (Ashoff and Klingebiel 2014): (i) The fragmentation of actors and approaches is an

---

P. Esteves (✉)
Pontifícia Universidade Católica do Rio de Janeiro, Rio de Janeiro, Brazil

S. Klingebiel
German Development Institute / Deutsches Institut für Entwicklungspolitik (DIE), Bonn, Germany
e-mail: Stephan.klingebiel@die-gdi.de

© The Author(s) 2021
S. Chaturvedi et al. (eds.), *The Palgrave Handbook of Development Cooperation for Achieving the 2030 Agenda*,
https://doi.org/10.1007/978-3-030-57938-8_9

increasing trend and major feature of DC in several regards (increase of multilateral funds, philanthropic actors, increase of new funding instruments, etc.) (Klingebiel, Mahn, et al. 2016). The increase of actors might lead, for example, to a stronger need for coordination efforts; (ii) a list of principal–agent problems deriving from the complex constellation of actors in the DC system (in terms of "accountability", "ownership", etc.) (Keijzer et al. 2018; Martens et al. 2002; Ostrom et al. 2002); (iii) the potentially negative impacts of DC, especially on the governance and economy of partner countries (see, e.g., Brautigam and Knack 2004).

Several analytical pieces have discussed those structural changes and systemic challenges. Whereas former debates (roughly until 2005) mainly associated the DC narrative and systemic aspects with the OECD's approach to DC, a whole range of new analytical pieces are meanwhile looking at SSC and, to some extent, triangular approaches. Of course, SSC is not fundamentally a new development paradigm and operational approach. The Bandung Conference in 1955, other discussions on technical cooperation among developing countries (TCDC) in the 1960s and 1970s, and the Buenos Aires Plan of Action (1978) indicate that SSC is not a new type of international cooperation. However, what is different from the past is its dynamic increase in terms of volume, geographical coverage, and attractiveness as well as its implications and significance for DC in general.

One main implication of such changes is the search for, and debate on, norms guiding different types of DC. The predominant debates on DC until the beginning of the 2000s were mainly guided and influenced by the Development Assistance Committee (DAC) of the OECD and its member states. Ideas and norms originated mainly from the discussions of this specific club. This does not exclude, for example, debates and conclusions on DC norms in the context of the United Nations (UN) (e.g. the target that OECD countries should provide at least 0.7 per cent of their gross domestic product for ODA) or the inclusion of developing countries in the OECD Working Party on Aid Effectiveness (WP-EFF).[1] Nevertheless, DC was basically binarily coded: donors as providers of DC or ODA and developing countries at the receiving end.

The rise of SSC and the increasing attention paid to SSC has led to a significant shift. The former de facto monopoly situation of OECD providers of DC is over. SSC is an alternative option for countries looking for development finance and other types of development support. Moreover, SSC is a main instrument for the provider countries to increase their "soft power" potential (Nye 2011) and to influence global governance structures. At the same time, SSC providers were only partly successful in agreeing on their set of norms for SSC as a specific type of DC. For example, the BRICS (Brazil, Russia, India, China, and South Africa) countries were already able to organise discussions on SSC. However, they have not come up so far with a specific organisational understanding and definition of a set of norms.

Nonetheless, we are increasingly witnessing challenges based on the two distinct DC approaches. One challenge is stemming from a de facto disagreement between the main actors on a global platform for discussions, and subsequently on norms for DC. The transformation of the former OECD WP-EFF into the Global Partnership for Effective Development Co-operation (GPEDC), jointly managed by the OECD and the UN Development Programme (UNDP), is not accepted by the main providers of SSC (especially China, India, Brazil, and South Africa) (Klingebiel and Xiaoyun 2016). The UN Development Cooperation Forum (UN DCF) is a global dialogue platform on DC. However, this forum is not able to perform as a norm-sharpener in the field of DC (Janus et al. 2016). Thus, a functioning global platform on DC norms does not exist so far. Consequently, there exist mainly two distinct sets of norms for DC.

Against this background, the present chapter analyses changing norms for DC from the end of the Cold War to the establishment of the 2030 Agenda. We aim at identifying the diverging norms for ODA and SSC and the interrelationship between both norm systems. Thus, norm-making, norm-taking, and norm-diffusion of two competing norm clusters are key terms (which will be introduced later on) and offer crucial perspectives to our chapter.

9.2 Norms, Norm-Diffusion, and Norm Competition: The Case of Norms for Development Cooperation

In general terms, norms can be understood as "shared understandings that make behavioral claims" (Checkel 2001). DC is shaped by norms. ODA "being administered with the promotion of the economic development and welfare of developing countries as its main objective" (definition of ODA; see OECD, n.d.-a) and SSC being based on the principle of "solidarity"[2] are illustrations of concrete norms forming different types of DC. Those are concrete examples of how narratives and concepts of DC are translated into specific norms.

Academic debates on norms in international relations (IR) provide numerous insights (e.g. Gilardi 2013; Risse 2017). In development research and research on DC, only a few studies try to benefit explicitly from IR discussions on norms. The work of Cold-Ravnkilde et al. (2018) is one of the few examples of the application of academic debates, specifically for DC. More generally, Acharya (2004) approaches the debates about norm-diffusion being a main concept from a perspective of the Global South for explaining which and whose ideas matter in world politics. Transnational norm-diffusion is a crucial dimension for a number of the most important IR debates (Gilardi 2013). Overall, there are different phases of research on norms (Rosert 2012): At the beginning of the IR debates on norms, there was a clear focus on the evidence that norms exist and matter. In a second phase of the academic debates, the focus was on how norms influence and impact policies. A third dimension covered mainly the question of why norms might have different consequences on different actors or in different context settings. For the current phase, there is a strong interest in norm-diffusion and the relationship between competing norms. The implications of norms for IR are far-reaching. The "spread of ideas" is directly related to the question "Whose norms matter?" (Acharya 2004). Thus, the transnational diffusion of norms, ideas, and policies has a strong link to the ability of actors to shape (global) agendas. The ability to spread norms is therefore an element of power.

Norms can be typically viewed from a constructivist or rationalist perspective (see, e.g., Checkel 2001; Gilardi 2013; Payne 2001; Risse 2017; Rosert 2012). Constructivist theorists mainly focus on ideational building blocks and persuasive communication as a foundation for norm-building. Rationalist theorists would rather focus on material forces in achieving normative changes.

Norm-diffusion is highly relevant for development research and research on global agenda-setting abilities. Traditionally, countries of the Global South can be regarded as "norm-takers": They have to comply with certain conditions in order to be eligible for development assistance.

Norms for global governance structures were created in the past, mainly without a defined role for countries from the Global South. This applies, for instance, to decisions related to the G7 and the OECD. Thus, the definitions of norms on DC (more specifically with respect to ODA) were for almost 50 years provided by the OECD-DAC as the "norm-maker".

The main interest of the present contribution is to create a better understanding of norms in the field of DC. In this context, it is important to note that norms evolve. The role of actors might also change fundamentally. In academic literature, for instance, China's shift from being a "norm-taker" to a "norm-maker" on foreign aid has been one of the debates over the last decade (see, e.g., Reilly 2011). Nevertheless, we argue that norm-setting (creation of norms) and norm-diffusion (the process that is needed to spread norms) are intertwined processes, displacing and scrambling what would otherwise be considered as steady positions: norm-maker and norm-taker positions.

It is the intention of our chapter to make the most important norms as well as changes in norms visible. We mainly discuss those aspects based on a comparison between the OECD's approach to ODA and the approach of SSC partners.

For our approach, we refer to an emerging debate on "norm clusters". Winston (2018) has introduced the term as a new theoretical construct. She identifies inconsistencies between the accepted structure of contemporary international norms and the variety of accepted outcomes of norm-diffusion in the real world. Her proposal for a new conceptual structure is as follows: to restructure the concept of contemporary international norms itself into a looser and less determinate collection of interlocking normative components. In her view, a norm cluster consists of a bounded collection of interrelated and specific (i) problems, (ii) values, and (iii) behaviours.

Winston (2018, pp. 13ff.) uses the Non-Proliferation Treaty of the UN as an example. She identifies (i) the problem "Nuclear weapons exist", (ii) the value "Nuclear war is undesirable", and (iii) the behaviours "No

> If [problem], [value] suggests [behavior].

Fig. 9.1 Formal model of the tripartite structure of contemporary international norms (*Source* Winston 2018)

weapons transfer", "No weapons development", "No acceptance of transferred weapons", and "Reporting and verification".

Winston (2018) proposed a formal model for norms structuration based on three components (Fig. 9.1).

According to Winston, "A norm cluster is a bounded collection of interrelated specific problems, values, and behaviors that are understood to be similar enough that their adopters form a family group" (Winston 2018, p. 10). She assumes that, even in contexts where different problems are found and distinct values coexist, a norm may be created as "an 'appropriate' means of addressing the more general problem that motivates norm cluster adoption" (Winston 2018, p. 10).

We adopt Winston's model with two caveats. First, the model ignores power relations embedded within the process of norm-setting and norm-diffusion. As we argue, power is the missing link connecting values and what may be considered appropriate behaviour. Second, issues are framed as political problems by a specific set of values, and not the other way around.

In this section, we address the issue area of development. Let us assume, for instance, that within the development field, the lack of resources, capacities, or technology—or general dispossession, as we call it (or privation)—is a material condition or a social fact. Nevertheless, this material condition or social fact may be framed as a different problem, depending on the agent's set of values and relative position. Indeed, whereas for great powers the general issue of dispossession may be understood through the lenses of rivalry, influence, or national security, the same issue may be experienced by the dispossessed agents as a matter of autonomy, sovereignty, or self-reliance. Therefore, drawing on the Winston model, we understand that problems are not a priori givens, but rather social facts framed by values and relative positions, and then turned into problems.

Henceforth, we suggest the following model of norms structuration:

> If [issue], [value] frames [problems] suggesting [behaviour]

For the purpose of our analysis, we apply this approach to the policy field of DC. In our model of a norm cluster for DC, we identify joint "problem" and "value" statements for DC norms based on ODA and SSC. However, we identify "behaviours" that are only partly the same.

In the following parts of our chapter, we provide a more detailed justification for the previous proposal on how to apply the norm cluster approach. Especially, we are providing a norm cluster approach for DC for several phases. We start with the early years of the emergence of a concept of (Western) development assistance and early debates on SSC (1945–1961). We discuss changes over time before, in our conclusion, we reflect on the current phase since the Fourth High-Level Forum on Aid Effectiveness in Busan in 2011.

9.3 The Mirroring Constitution of Official Development Assistance and South-South Cooperation Norms

The concept of ODA was crafted after the Second World War. The Marshall Plan, the bipolar competition, and the decolonisation process framed the emerging norms governing the development assistance provided by developed countries. These norms were established mainly by the United States (largely visible in what is called the Truman Doctrine, as mainly conceptualised in 1947 and 1948) and throughout the interplay between the former European empires and their former colonies (Klingebiel 2014). The relevance of national liberation movements in the colonies is often underestimated. Fifteen years after the end of the Second World War, 40 nations and their 800 million inhabitants became independent. The history of European powers became no less knotted to these newly sovereign entities than it was during the colonial rule (Bayly 2004; Garavini 2012). Development and modernisation tied the European powers and their former colonies, generating not only one but two mirroring clusters of norms among donors and recipients from one side, and Southern partners from the other. These clusters were underpinned by specific understandings about what development meant.

As discussed above, drawing on Winston's norm clusters approach, the material fact of dispossession may originate from different political or social problems when framed by different agents. Dispossession would be a way to designate a situation of populations in former colonies as well as states' lack of capacities and resources. Nevertheless, the definition of a development challenge depends on the set of values and the relative position from where the problem is framed. Hence, the relative position frames the ways in which the problem is understood as well as the rules and behaviours suggested to address the problem.

During decolonisation, economic and social issues (dispossession) at the international system's periphery were framed in different ways by the European powers and the newly sovereign states. These distinct understandings would establish two clusters of norms: development assistance and SSC. This section addresses the mirroring constitution of these two clusters, taking as a point of departure the events after the Second World War.

In the developed world, the Marshall Plan and President Harry Truman's Doctrine to provide assistance to "developing countries" are considered very often to be the landmarks from which contemporary DC evolved (Zeiler 2015). Four arguments were mobilised to leverage domestic support for international assistance: the rivalry between the two superpowers, the need to keep a foot in former colonial territories, the eventual support from developing countries at the UN, and the economic gains achieved by means of export promotions and tied aid (Griffin 1991, p. 647).

International assistance was also a subject of debate within the post-colonial region. In 1954, China's Premier, Zhou Enlai, and India's prime minister, Jawaharlal Nehru, highlighted "equality and cooperation for mutual benefit" as one of the "Five Principles of Peaceful Coexistence" at the signing of the Sino-Indian Treaty of 1954 (Van Eekelen 1964). One year later, the final communiqué at the Bandung Conference incorporated the five principles as part of the "Ten Principles of Bandung". The 29 countries present at the Asian-African Conference distinguished international assistance provided by states "outside the region" and cooperation based on the principles of mutual interest and respect for national sovereignty (Jayaprakash 2005, para. 1). These principles included self-determination, respect for territorial integrity and sovereignty, non-interference, promotion of mutual interests, and cooperation (see Carbonnier et al. 2012; Dellios and Ferguson 2013; Huang 2018).

Even though they shared a common concern—dispossession—developed countries and former colonies framed it as two different political problems. From one side, the United States and former European empires saw the post-colonial region as a disputed territory with the Soviet Union or as a site where they should keep or recover their influence. Hence, DC was seen as a foreign policy tool to keep the soviets out and gain influence.

From the other side, dispossession was taken as a handicap that diminished the individual country's ability to make its own policies. DC should, then, be a tool to foster self-determination (and to support the emerging post-colonial elites) that is underpinned by a respect for sovereignty and guided by the principles of mutual interest and equality.

Figure 9.2 presents both clusters, highlighting the two relative positions from where the problems of development were framed. From one side, developed countries framed the issue of dispossession through security lenses. Dispossession was turned into underdevelopment—a condition from which discontent and potential allegiances with the soviet bloc could grow, becoming, therefore, a threat. Assistance would be a tool for developed countries to maintain influence, and ultimately their hierarchical position vis-à-vis the post-colonial world. From the other side, leaders in the post-colonial world understood dispossession within the light of the colonial experience. As a political problem, it would become an obstacle for self-determination. Cooperation among former colonies would be a path to assert the right for self-determination.

European countries and the United States started to discuss a joint initiative on development assistance in the late 1950s. The international norm-setting

Fig. 9.2 The proto-constitution of development cooperation clusters (1945–1961) (*Source* Authors)

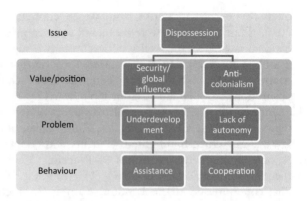

process was part of an institutional mushrooming both at the multilateral and national levels. At the national and multilateral levels, initiatives such as the establishment of cooperation agencies or clubs of agencies, such as the Development Assistance Group (DAG), created by the Organisation for European Economic Co-operation member states, are evidence of how development assistance was being consolidated as a legitimate answer to the challenges generated by the decolonisation process (see Bracho 2015; Führer 1996).

In 1961, the "Resolution of the Common Aid Effort" outlined the ODA framework and its differences vis-à-vis so-called other official flows or private finance. In so doing, it establishes a boundary between "business as usual" and development assistance "in the form of grants or loans on favorable terms […]". Furthermore, to DAG members, the resolution assigned the task of helping "the less-developed countries help themselves" (Organisation for Economic Co-operation and Development [OECD] 2006, p. 10).

The divisive line between DAG members and less-developed countries re-enacted the old lines that enabled colonialism and trusteeship, generating a privileged position for Western powers. As Bracho (2015) suggested, the old idea of responsibilities, which, for centuries, supported colonialism, was brought again to the table. As he pointed out, "the responsibilities remained; though it was now reformulated as a collective responsibility of the rich nations of the North to help the poor ones of the South reach development" (Bracho 2015, p. 2). The ODA framework established a divisive line between donors and recipients. Developed countries should establish a way to provide assistance on an "assured and continuing basis" (OECD 2006, p. 10).

As the title of the resolution suggests, the main question shifted to how Western powers would share the burden of international assistance (Bracho 2015, p. 5). After many recommendations, the DAC established the concept of ODA in 1972:

> ODA consists of flows to developing countries and multilateral institutions provided by official agencies, including state and local governments, or by their executive agencies, each transaction of which meets the following test: a) it is

administered with the promotion of the economic development and welfare of developing countries as its main objective, and b) it is concessional in character and contains a grant element of at least 25 percent (calculated at a rate of discount of 10 percent). (OECD, n.d.-a)

Even though the DAG was the main venue where the concept of ODA was being coined, the concept arose from the intersection between developing countries' demands and the developed countries' willingness to create a financial flow that would distinguish itself from trade and investment. The concept of ODA resulted from a "decade-long process of setting objectives for aid volume and terms" (Scott 2015, p. 21). This process was "both a collaboration and a tug-of-war between the DAC (representing the donors) and the UN (dominated by aid recipients)" (Scott 2015, p. 21).

Taking advantage of the UN Conference on Trade and Development's (UNCTAD) favoured environment, the developing world exerted significant pressure on the DAC countries for the adoption of softer and untied loans and the expansion of the maturity period. UNCTAD I strengthened the vocabulary around the idea of preferential treatment for developing countries beyond the field of trade and, by default, the responsibilities assigned to developed countries. At the end of UNCTAD I, the creation of the G77 was an important step in vocalising the demand for preferential treatment and a "necessary means for co-operation amongst the developing countries themselves" (Group of 77 1964).

Likewise, UNCTAD I and UNCTAD II became opportunities for developing countries to advocate the target of 1 per cent of the gross domestic product as the ODA contribution (Scott 2015). The inception of ODA was, therefore, instrumental for the establishment of the 0.7 target in 1970 and vice versa. UNCTAD was also a venue for developing countries to assert what they would expect from DAC members: (i) "financial and technical cooperation" for "strengthening the economic and political **independence**", (ii) "financial and technical assistance […] to ensure the steady and uninterrupted **growth of their national economy**", and (iii) such assistance **should not be subject to any political, economic, military, or other conditions** unacceptable to the developing countries (UN Conference on Trade and Development [UNCTAD] 1964, p. 44, authors' emphasis).

Confronting the pressure from developing countries and civil society organisations (CSOs), DAC countries agreed on the concept of ODA as a way to streamline aid flows, measuring and monitoring them against the intended target. Since 1972, ODA has provided the main normative framework for DC. The regulatory dimension of ODA encompasses at least four principles: (i) must have a developmental purpose; (ii) it is an official flow, and therefore mobilises public funds; (iii) must be concessional with a grant element; (iv) it is unidirectional (from developed countries to developing countries), not involving necessarily any expectation of reciprocity.

Developing countries were far from playing the role of norm-takers. As the debates from Bandung to UNCTAD show, a concessional flow attached to a given target was a demand of newly independent countries. Instead of the dyadic model of norm-makers and -takers, the case of ODA shows how a norm can be produced as a mirror effect, where two different positions with different rationales converge to the same set of principles and rules. Figure 9.3 summarises the process of ODA norm-setting.

Even considering that developed and developing countries were driven by these different sets of values and interests, the establishment of ODA as the North-South cooperation (NSC) normative framework was a decision taken by DAC members under growing pressure from developing countries. The establishment of ODA as a set of norms was one of these critical points when, as Winston (2018) perceived, different agents coalesced, generating a behavioural pattern for both developed and developing countries and engendering a cluster of norms.

ODA was perceived by developing countries as key for achieving de facto independence. Nevertheless, due to the structural asymmetries between donors and recipients, developing countries re-enacted the idea of DC among themselves at the two UNCTAD conferences (UNCTAD 1964). During three decades, concepts and approaches related to dependency theory influenced debates around TCDC and economic cooperation among developing countries (ECDC). TCDC and ECDC were still foreign policy tools, mobilised to cement coalitions among Southern countries as the G77.

The first conference on "Promoting and Implementing Technical Cooperation among Developing Countries (TCDC)" in Buenos Aires in 1978 was a critical juncture to turn "cooperation among developing countries" into what is now known as SSC. On the one hand, developing countries were

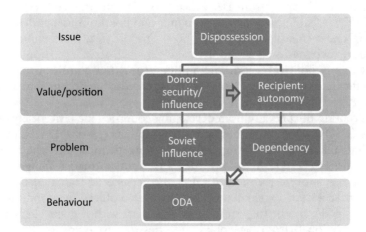

Fig. 9.3 The establishment of the ODA normative framework (1961–1972) (*Source* Authors)

still animated by the claims for the transformation of the structures of the international system that were manifested throughout the New International Economic Order resolution at the UN General Assembly. In this context, the claims for self-determination were supplemented with a general aspiration for self-reliance. Self-determination was seen as a juridical condition for autonomy—a necessary condition, but not a sufficient one. For achieving autonomy, any developing country should rely on its own capacities and on its partners within the South.

On the other hand, though, developing countries were starting to face the severe consequences of a broader economic crisis rooted in high levels of debt and debt-servicing, droughts, deterioration of commodity prices, and the oil prices shock. The expectations nurtured by the discourses of Southern leaders contrasted with the resources available for producing actual changes. At the Buenos Aires conference, the contrast between great aspirations and scarce political and economic resources became evident.

The final declaration presented TCDC as a "means of building communication and of promoting wider and more effective cooperation among developing countries […] experience for their mutual benefit and for achieving national and collective self-reliance which are essential for their social and economic development" (United Nations [UN] 2019, p. 6, para. 5). Building on the Bandung principles, the conference stressed the principles of sovereignty, non-intervention, and non-interference, and it presented TCDC as a modality of DC guided by the principles of horizontality (as opposed to the vertical relationship between donor and recipient) and mutual benefits (as opposed to the idea of responsibility and assistance). Nevertheless, the contrast between ODA and TCDC was balanced when the document further elaborated on the relationship between NSC and SSC: "TCDC is intended neither to replace the existing relationship between the North and the South nor indeed to be used as an argument against the continuation of North-South technical flows" (Talal 1978, p. 75).

While the conference in 1978 kept the main reformist tenets that had animated the debates around SSC, it also acknowledged ODA's centrality and stated the complementary nature of SSC vis-à-vis NSC: TCDC "will increase the absorptive capacity of developing countries for technical and other imports from developed countries" (UN 2019, p. 4). Such a statement consolidated the dual position of developing countries, as recipients of ODA and partners of SSC. Indeed, feeling the heat of the economic crises, developing countries urged the donors to increase ODA disbursement.

> Furthermore, the difficulties currently encountered by the world economy make it even more necessary for the developing countries to evolve strategies based on greater national and collective self-reliance, for which TCDC is an important instrument. This in no way reduces the **responsibility of developed countries to undertake the necessary policy measures. In particular, the increase of development assistance for accelerated development of developing countries**. (UN 2019, p. 6, authors' emphasis)

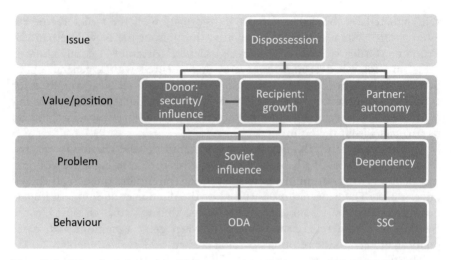

Fig. 9.4 Manufacturing the SSC normative framework (1961–1978) (*Source* Authors)

The Buenos Aires conference contributed towards reinforcing two normative clusters within the broader field of DC. Contrary to the conventional scholarship though, as we have argued, these two clusters have mutually constituted themselves as mirrors, reproducing each other—almost identical but still inverted. Despite many differences between these two clusters, the cornerstone of such inversion was actually the differential responsibilities assigned to developed and developing countries. Indeed, developed countries' responsibilities manifested themselves not only throughout the concessional nature and the grant element that defined ODA, or the preferential treatment in trade (which was outside the normative reach of ODA), but particularly through the idea of non-reciprocity or non-mutuality. Indeed, by inverting the ODA framework, SSC emphasised mutual benefits and the idea of reciprocity as the foundation of the relationships between Southern countries. Figure 9.4 summarises the constitution of the SSC cluster.

9.4 From Paris to Nairobi: The Emergence of SSC and the Diffusion of the Effectiveness Agenda

After Buenos Aires, in the context of a generalised debt crisis where developing countries missed the necessary resources for engaging in SSC in a significant way, ODA was consolidated as a quasi-monopolist set of practices. In terms of significance, SSC was hardly visible in developing countries. The Soviet Union had few countries with a special relationship and cooperation formats (e.g. with Cuba); however, Eastern forms of DC never gained momentum or relevance. Starting at the end of the 1970s, OECD donors adopted a two-pronged approach towards development assistance based on the combination of policies designed to fight poverty and the promotion of structural adjustments via conditional loans and grants. Even though conditionalities were always part of development assistance practices, they became an ubiquitous resource in the hands of traditional donors during the 1980s and 1990s (Stokke 1995).

After the end of the Cold War, the DC community faced a paradoxical situation. While the end of the East/West rivalry expanded the demand for development assistance (generating new recipients and new agendas), it impacted negatively on the supply side, diminishing the volume of ODA offered by DAC donors (Severino and Ray 2009). Freed from the threat represented by the Soviet Union, donors could focus on their own fiscal accounts. Cutting ODA became an easy way to produce more balanced sheets. At the same time, these donors had to redirect their efforts to normalise the economic and political situations in the former soviet bloc and stabilise conflict-affected countries, particularly in Africa. From being a tool designed to contain the advancement of the Soviet Union and keep influence over the former colonies, development assistance focussed now on institutional reforms and the governance agenda, aiming at integrating the periphery of the international system into the liberal-democratic and market-oriented world. Accordingly, the ODA agenda was broadened, encompassing comprehensive plans of market-oriented institutional reforms, democracy promotion, and sectoral programmes. The new agenda indicated a shift from security to "good governance"—and especially democracy—as a main development assistance goal.

Conditional development assistance became an ordinary tool for promoting economic and political reforms in the Global South, playing at least a three-fold role. First, the vocabulary of good governance could replace the security rhetoric that underpinned the expenditure in development assistance during the Cold War, building legitimacy among donors' constituencies. Second, it would help to integrate parts of the former soviet bloc into the international market. Finally, following the democratic peace credo, and in line with the idea of a "New World Order", conditional development assistance would contribute towards building a stable and peaceful world while promoting democracy.

Nevertheless, the decline of ODA provision between 1990 and 1997 illustrates the difficulties that such a model faced during that period. As the DAC report "Shaping the twenty-first Century: The Role of Development Co-operation" (OECD Development Assistance Committee [DAC] 1996) indicated, there was a "deep concern that domestic preoccupations and budgetary pressures in some Member countries could seriously jeopardize the international development co-operation effort at a critical juncture" (OECD-DAC 1996, p. 16). Nevertheless, facing significant fiscal constraints—polarised around the structuralist and monetarist positions and involved with structural adjustment programmes (SAPs), either voluntarily or under coercion—developing countries had little policy or fiscal spaces for engaging with SSC. For almost a decade, the DC arena was almost entirely occupied by ODA, as Fig. 9.5 tries to illustrate.

At the end of the 1990s, conditional ODA started to be contested, showing its first signs of exhaustion. Beyond the poor economic results, though, at the end of the decade, criticism against the conditional delivery model (Hermes and Lensink 2001) became pervasive. Three points were noteworthy: (i) a legitimacy gap generated by the imposition of policies by foreign powers; (ii) the selectivity of the conditional approach (Doornbos 2001; Pronk 2001); and, (iii) the sustainability gap broadened with the dismantling of national capacities for policy design and implementation across the developing world, perpetuating in many cases aid dependency.

The DAC report "Shaping the 21st Century" illustrated the limits of the conditional assistance practices paving the way towards a new agenda for DAC donors. The effectiveness agenda was finally codified at the Second High-Level Forum (HLF-2) in Paris in 2005, rebuilding DAC donors' own position within the DC field and aiming at obturating the gaps described above (Esteves and Assunção 2014).

In 2006, Richard Manning, chair of the DAC, published an article entitled "Will 'Emerging Donors' Change the Face of International Co-operation?" (Manning 2006). In that piece, Manning recognised the almost exclusive position taken by ODA donors after the end of the Cold War and, acknowledging the growing relevance of non-DAC development partners, suggested a new question: Will "non-DAC donors not apply DAC 'standards'?" (Manning 2006, p. 377). Looking at the evident trends, particularly with regard to China and India, Manning sketched a norm-diffusion strategy that started

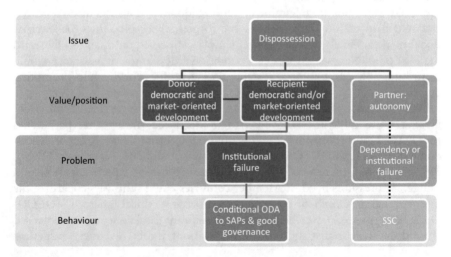

Fig. 9.5 Conditional official development assistance (*Source* Authors)

with the establishment of "links with these other donors – or in some cases rebuild links that have atrophied" (Manning 2006, p. 383). The strategy was based on mechanisms of socialisation and learning, opening existing venues for the so-called emerging donors, supporting the production of evidence-based knowledge, and opening new forms of collaboration with them. The first significant movement would take place at the DAC's Third High-Level Forum on Aid Effectiveness (HLF-3) in 2008.

Rather than only reviewing the progress made since the Paris Declaration, the HLF became itself an occasion for the diffusion of the Paris Agenda. The meeting resulted in the Accra Agenda for Action (AAA). Beyond the usual vocabulary, the AAA included references to civil society and—for the first time in a DAC HLF outcome document—to SSC. In 2009, a Task Team on South-South Cooperation (TT-SSC) was also created, recognising the need for greater dialogue with SSC providers. The TT-SSC was designed as a multi-stakeholder platform (including donors, middle-income countries, academia, civil society, and bilateral and multilateral agencies). The TT-SSC aimed at mapping, documenting, analysing, and discussing evidence on the synergies between aid effectiveness principles and SSC practices (Task Team on South-South Cooperation [TT-SSC] 2010b). It should also work on adapting the Paris and Accra principles for SSC, adding the so-called Southern perspectives to the effectiveness agenda and identifying complementarities and intersections between South-South and North-South cooperation. Between 2009 and 2010, the TT-SSC documented and analysed 110 cases presented and discussed at the High-Level Event on South-South Cooperation and Capacity Development held in Bogota (OECD 2010; TT-SSC 2010a). The efforts for gathering data and producing knowledge were followed with the creation of new sites and opportunities for interaction between traditional donors and SSC partners (SSCPs) where such findings could be presented and discussed. Moreover, traditional donors started to launch initiatives of triangular cooperation as a way to socialise and influence the newcomers (Zoccal Gomes and Esteves 2018).

The process of socialisation spawned some resistance, though. In 2008, the UN DCF met for the first time. Created within the framework of the UN Economic and Social Council, the HLF was set up to discuss trends and promote coherence between the various modalities of DC, with particular emphasis on SSC. Despite being relatively recent and meeting only every two years, the UN DCF was perceived as being a universal space that was more horizontal than the DAC club. Eyben and Savage (2012) further note that by framing its agenda under the HLF, SSCPs also presented a discursive challenge to the "aid effectiveness" promoted by the DAC, bringing to the fore the concept of "development effectiveness".

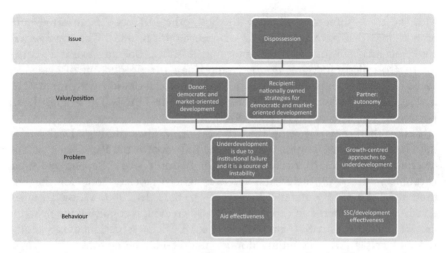

Fig. 9.6 From Paris to Nairobi: Diffusion strategies of aid effectiveness (*Source* Authors)

Marking the 30th anniversary of the Buenos Aires Plan of Action (1978), the 2009 High-level UN Conference on South-South Cooperation was held in Nairobi, Kenya. The Nairobi Final Document presents SSC as an essential tool for economic development, emphasising the sharing of challenges, difficulties, experiences, and innovative solutions. Principles such as the absence of conditionalities, sovereignty, and national ownership, which should be respected to ensure the effectiveness of SSC, were also pointed out. Like the UN DCF, the document also underscores the need to distinguish SSC from ODA, while challenging the effectiveness agenda by acknowledging "the need to enhance **the development effectiveness** of South-South cooperation" (UN 2009, para. 18, authors' emphasis).

The subtle challenge to the Paris Agenda is noteworthy. Nevertheless, in addition to reaffirming the complementarity between SSC and NSC, the document largely adopted the vocabulary of the Paris Agenda (ownership, mutual accountability, results management, transparency, alignment, etc.). However, there is no explicit reference to the Paris Agenda (Figs. 9.6 and 9.7).

9.5 Busan and Beyond: From Fusion to Confusion

DAC's diffusion strategy was summarised in the report "Investing in Development: A Common Cause in a Changing World", endorsed at the 2009 High-Level Meeting (HLM) in the midst of the financial crisis. As the report stated, "the objective of the exercise was to address how to sustain and increase the relevance of the Committee in the changing development landscape over the next ten to fifteen years by reviewing its role, structure, functioning and composition" (OECD-DAC 2009, p. 2). The report's recommendations included the following wording:

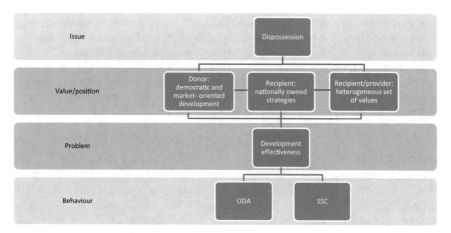

Fig. 9.7 Busan and the fusion attempt (*Source* Authors)

> The DAC must [...] extend and deepen inclusion of key development stakeholders in all areas of its work. It should invest heavily in **reaching out to and building effective relationships with other donors** and other key stakeholder groups. It should work pro-actively to **welcome new members.** (OECD-DAC 2009, p. 4, authors' emphasis)

At the governance structure, the recommendation was reflected almost immediately in the enlargement of the WP-EEF in order to include recipients and attract rising powers under the hybrid category of providers–recipients.[3] Furthermore, the WP-EEF established a TT-SSC, presented as "an inclusive platform to document and discuss how SSC practices enrich the aid effectiveness agenda" (OECD-DAC 2010, p. 2).

The outreach strategy to diffuse the principles of Paris included invitations to events convened either by the DAC or by its member states (Eyben 2012). Nevertheless, such spaces were still seen as carefully controlled by the convener. Thus, the challenge of upholding the credibility of the DAC as a policy space remained, as there were still restrictions on participation, especially given the legitimacy gained by one of its institutional competitors, the UN DCF (Eyben 2012, p. 85). While in 2008 Ghana had been chosen as the host country of the HLF-3, aiming to show openness regarding the participation of recipient countries, the next HLF took place in South Korea, which was a new DAC member seen as a bridge between the North and South, particularly between developed countries and emerging powers. In order to garner support from the latter group, the objectives of the conference were framed in terms of "development effectiveness". As Eyben (2012) duly noted, "development effectiveness" was kept as a buzzword, enabling the emergence of diverse meanings, adapted to the speaker's position:

> Development effectiveness as "results" reflected DAC donors' concerns about value for money at a time of cuts to domestic budgets. For centre-right donor governments, for whom private sector investment is the development driver, development effectiveness' meanings of "results" and "beyond aid" meanings could usefully be combined to achieve some common ground with the rising powers. Recipient government [...] also stressed that development as spurring investment and increasing productivity. (Eyben 2012, p. 88)

The vagueness of the concept not only enabled a conversation between different positions, but also created the possibility of amalgamating the two cluster of norms within a single framework. Indeed, while at first glance the focus on effectiveness could suggest the primacy of the DAC in setting the agenda, the displacement of the debate towards "development effectiveness" could be considered as evidence of SSCP agency. Unlike Nairobi, where traditional donors grabbed the opportunity to diffuse the Paris principles within the SSC agenda, in Busan—facing the growing fragmentation of the international DC field (Klingebiel, Mahn, et al. 2016)—they strove to generate a single cluster of norms.

Whereas Nairobi was about diffusion, Busan was about fusion. The fusion process encompassed four dimensions (Esteves and Assunção 2014). First, as discussed above, the conceptual framework for the new architecture around the Southern loosened agenda of development effectiveness in order to enable the conversation with emerging powers. Second and third, following the steps taken in Accra, there was recognition of SSC as a legitimate modality of DC and of CSOs and private agents as relevant partners. Finally, a new institutional architecture that could host all these agents and stakeholders was established: the GPEDC. As Bracho (2017) has pointed out, though, the key normative conundrum revolved around the concept of differential responsibilities. While traditional donors were trying to water down the principle of common but differentiated responsibilities (CBDR), SSCPs were conditioning their agreement with any final document to the upholding of differentiation (Bracho 2017).

Differential responsibilities were the normative cornerstone of all ODA frameworks. They had been recognised since their inception in the 1960s and manifested with the 0.7 target in the 1970s. Furthermore, the UN Conference on Environment and Development (Rio 1992) established the principle of CBDR. For many traditional donors, Busan was the opportunity to share the burden of funding international development with emerging powers. Hence, the wording suggested for the issue was "common goals and the aspiration in support of these over the long term" (Bracho 2017, p. 15).

Busan's main result was the beginning of a process that would lead to the establishment of the GPEDC (Abdel-Malek 2015). Beyond the DAC's distinctive club structure, the GPEDC intended to become a multi-stakeholder platform that would include, among governments, not only traditional donors and recipients but also major SSC providers. More than that, the platform was to mobilise private actors, philanthropy, and CSOs. The OECD and UNDP joint sponsorship supported the universalist claim embedded in the GPEDC's structure. Three meetings of the Interim Post-Busan Group, attended by Brazil, India, and China as observers, consolidated its structure. At the end of the process, the Interim Group assigned two seats to the new hybrid donor/recipient in the platform governance structure.

However, in the first HLM in Mexico (2014), Brazil, India, and China decided not to participate in the platform. Difficulties in maintaining the principle of differentiation of responsibilities aggravated the perception that the process was a continuation of the Paris Agenda and driven by the DAC rather than the foundation for a genuinely new framework capable of merging the two clusters of norms into one original framework. As demonstrated by Zoccal Gomes (2018), many Southern agents still perceived the significant presence of the Paris principles driving the process: "Even if these principles were no longer referred directly, they were regarded as the dominant principles of DAC practice" (Zoccal Gomes 2018, p. 173).

The absence of China and India and Brazil's presence only as an observer at the First High-Level Meeting of the Global Partnership in Mexico would point to the GPEDC's limits on merging the two clusters of standards. The absence of the three countries at the Second High-Level Meeting of the GPEDC in Nairobi would confirm these limits; in addition, South Africa also did not attend the HLM in Nairobi. Moreover, the failed attempt to merge the two clusters had at least five unforeseen consequences: (i) the weakening of the effectiveness agenda; (ii) ODA's decentring as a central practice in the field of international DC; (iii) the thinning of the very concept of ODA; (iv) the weakening of the notion of international responsibility; and finally, (v) the increased fragmentation of the field.

A simple process of tracing and contrasting the principles generated in Busan reveals the reproduction of the Paris Agenda as the cornerstone of what would be an allegedly unified cluster of norms (see Table 9.1). For many partners, SSC would become a development flow among developing countries, framed, though, by principles inherited from the DAC's own process. Instead

Table 9.1 Effectiveness principles: From Paris to Busan

Paris	Accra	Busan
Ownership	Ownership	Ownership of development priorities by developing countries
Management for results	Delivering results	Focus on results
	Inclusive partnerships	Inclusive development partnerships
Mutual accountability		Transparency and accountability to each other
Alignment	Capacity development	
Harmonisation		

Source Authors, based on the DAC's Paris Declaration, the Accra Agenda for Action, and the Busan Partnership for Effective Development Co-Operation of the foundation for a new cluster of norms, throughout the fusing of the existing clusters, Busan generated the expansion of the DAC's activities. In that sense, one may argue that the GPEDC works more like a tool or a platform for the DAC's outreach strategy than as a genuine governance scheme embedded in a universal cluster of norms. Indeed, while striving to keep its position, the DAC lost the opportunity to contribute towards reshaping the field around the concept of development effectiveness. Furthermore, as the GPEDC also kept the monitoring and assessment ambitions inherited and inspired by the DAC tradition, it ended up dismissing key SSC providers, particularly China and India.

The Busan HLF also fed a trend that had already been in place since the previous decade: the decentring of ODA as the normative foundation of DC (at least for developed countries). From one side, Accra traditional donors acknowledged, for the first time, the relevance of other sets of practices, such SSC, as being relevant for the field of international DC. From the other side, for developed countries, ODA had established the boundaries discriminating development flows from other activities such as trade and investment, the emergence of SSC providers, the growing relevance of the Financing for Development agenda; the pervasive discourse on development partnerships expelled ODA from the core of the field, turning it into one development flow among others. The OECD-DAC's work on a new tool for measurement, Total Official Support for Sustainable Development (TOSSD), illustrates this ODA decentring process. Paragraph 17 of the compendium states:

> The TOSSD measure will not supplant the ODA measure and should uphold internationally agreed standards in support of sustainable development. It will therefore be a separate, conceptually distinct statistical metric tailored to the SDG era – encompassing support for tackling global challenges and promoting development enablers, for mobilising private sector resources through official interventions and for monitoring the ambitious "billions to trillions" financing agenda set out in Addis Ababa. No TOSSD targets or associated commitments will be established. ODA will remain the cornerstone of OECD DAC members' accountability to the international development community – including the different commitments that have been undertaken in that regard. (OECD 2016, p. 10)

Nevertheless, the same document presents TOSSD as "an international data standard for measuring development finance, including relevant instruments, principles and standards, and investment aims (e.g. SDG achievement)" (OECD 2016, p. 11). As Chaturvedi et al. (2016) have pointed out, "TOSSD is a metric to simply capture broader resource flows, including and extending beyond ODA flows. Further, the use of an umbrella accounting mechanism to capture SSC can **neutralize** the distinction between North-South Cooperation (NSC) and South-South Cooperation (SSC)" (Chaturvedi et al. 2016, p. 2, authors' emphasis). Neutralisation is an accurate way to capture TOSSD's main effect; the compendium candidly represents such a process, clarifying the multiple intentions behind the development flows that are captured by the new metric: (i) the economic development of developing countries; (ii) other motivations (commercial, cultural, or political); and (iii) mutual benefits (including SSC flows). Figure 9.8 presents the DC field, reconfigured to the TOSSD metric accordingly.

During the public consultation process, the United States' laconic comment is revealing of how TOSSD dissolved the specificities of each development flow:

> The U.S. has concerns about including export credits under TOSSD. The inclusion of U.S. export credits under TOSSD would mischaracterize the underlying purpose and use of U.S. export credit financing, which are to promote the exports of, and create jobs in, the United States. (OECD, n.d.-b, p. 1)

Moreover, as discussed below, TOSSD mingles DC in general, and ODA in particular, into a broader spectrum of flows, keeping aside the specific responsibilities assigned to developed countries in promoting international development. Such concerns were vocalised by a vast array of institutions, including non-governmental organisations and think tanks such as OXFAM (2016), Reality of Aid (2016), and the German Development Institute (DIE) (Klingebiel, Mank, et al. 2016). Despite the peculiar ways with which the principle of mutual benefits was brought from the SSC vernacular to the TOSSD rationale (see Chaturvedi et al. 2016), the incorporation of such a principle, side by side with ODA, opened the door for any profitable initiatives being included as support for sustainable investment, as the DIE rightly pointed out:

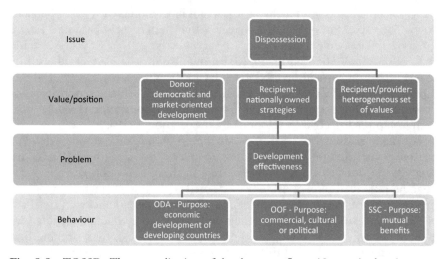

Fig. 9.8 TOSSD: The neutralisation of development flows (*Source* Authors)

Perhaps these "benefits" can be elaborated upon. Is this a reference to economic development and welfare as mentioned in the ODA definition (see the point made above) or does the word "benefits" open the door to corporations that seek profitable investment with side-benefits of development of one kind or another? Or both? (Klingebiel, Mank, et al. 2016)

After the difficulties in achieving the Busan HLF main goal, that is, fusing both clusters, the TOSSD process, as opened in 2016, illustrated another dynamic: confusion. In this context, confusion means some degree of anomy, or a trend towards anomy: a situation where agents behave unpredictably, taking each other's positions, challenging established norms, and stretching existing concepts.

Such confusion impacted directly upon the concept of ODA in at least two ways: first, as already revealed in the TOSSD compendium, taking advantage of the door opened by SDG 16, many traditional donors started to bring ODA resources to activities related to peace, security, and support for refugees in their own territories (Knoll and Sherriff 2017; Shenfeldt 2018; Singfield 2019). Even though one can argue that peace and security activities are a cornerstone for any developmental project, it is also possible to understand it as a way to stretch the very concept of ODA. Indeed, the DAC is currently discussing the limits of in-donor use of ODA funds and the ways to report them (Knoll and Sherriff 2017).

Such widening mobilisation of ODA resources also appears in so-called blended finance and in the emerging practices for fostering private-sector engagement in development issues. The OECD defines blended finance as the "strategic use of development finance for the mobilisation of additional finance towards sustainable development in developing countries" (OECD 2019). Development finance also includes ODA and its blending with other financial flows. The expansion of blended finance within the DC field became a reason for concern, not only for academics (Waeyenberge 2015), CSOs, and think tanks (Romero 2016; Wehrmann 2018), but also for the DAC itself. Not by chance, the DAC established its principles for blended finance (OECD-DAC 2018), and the GPEDC further elaborated a set of voluntary principles for Private-sector Engagement through Development Cooperation (PSE) (Global Partnership for Effective Development Co-operation 2019).

For many reasons, this turn towards the private sector is noteworthy. For our purposes, though, it is important to stress how traditional donors are opening the door to a substantive change in the ODA's normative foundation. As described above, ODA was defined as a flow characterised by the sole purpose of the "promotion of the economic development and welfare of developing countries". This definition implied both unidirectionality and non-reciprocity (from developed to developing countries). Even arguing that PSE in general and blended finance, in particular, are being oriented towards the promotion of the economic development and welfare of developing countries—which is far from self-evident, and the available data points in the other direction—when blended with private finance, ODA is neither unidirectional nor based on the principle of non-reciprocity. Moreover, these new practices seem to confirm how traditional donors are adopting, without necessarily saying it, the principle of mutual benefits, in tandem with what Chaturvedi et al. (2016) have called the "Southernisation" of DC.

9.6 Conclusion

The analysis of DC from the IR perspective of norms provides several insights. First, the two main existing sub-categories of DC—ODA and SSC—provide a highly relevant illustration of the academic discourse on norm-diffusion in IR. Despite the soft-power nature of DC, the debates on the dominating norms are highly controversial between ODA and SSC actors, not least for the period of time since the Busan HLF. DC is a symbolic policy field for international conflicts between main country groupings. It is at the same time an area to share international agendas and increase soft-power capacities, for example through reputation and international visibility.

Second, contrary to interpretations that consider developed countries as norm-makers and developing countries as norm-takers, our analysis provides evidence and highlights how Southern agents have influenced the processes of norm-setting and norm-diffusion for DC. Even though, for many decades, OECD countries and the DAC seem to be the sole "entrepreneurs", developing countries have played a significant role in setting DC norms. Indeed, as we argued in Sect. 9.2, the ideas of preferential treatment, concessionality, and the establishment of the 0.7 per cent target were nurtured and advocated by developing countries in UN fora such as UNCTAD and by their leading group, the G77. Likewise, as seen in Sect. 9.3, even when the OECD approach to make ODA a global norm was exercised through conditionalities or via SAPs during the 1980s and 1990s, the diffusion was a complex and recursive process rather than a linear pathway.

Even considering that the figures from SSC on volumes were not particularly relevant, SSC partners did not adopt the principles of good governance advocated by OECD donors. On the contrary, SSC practitioners not only kept the principle of non-interference but also added if not a principle, then at least a guideline supporting the practices of non-conditionality. Likewise, as ODA recipients, developing countries responded to the good governance principles and conditionalities for market-based solution in heterogeneous and almost always hybrid ways, as the cases of the BRICS countries show (Ban and Blyth 2013).

After 2005, the DAC and its member states adopted a softer model of the effectiveness agenda diffusion that was based on "socialisation" and "learning". Nevertheless, as we have argued, the ODA reform itself was an answer to a dynamic interplay between donors and recipients (which we designated as legitimacy, selectivity, and sustainability gaps). The principles of ownership and harmonisation that emerged from Paris—against the backdrop of emerging powers' growing footprint within the DC field—aimed to fill these gaps. These principles can hardly be seen as a copyrighted product, authored by development experts in Paris. The launch of the effectiveness agenda may also be considered a complex process of norm-setting rather than an agent-centred norm-making decision. This analysis may also contribute to development theory, as we discuss below.

Before that, though, there is a third analytical insight that may be noteworthy. The whole context of norms for DC has fundamentally changed because of the rise of SSC volumes and visibility. Even though SSC providers so far have not been able to define an explicit set of concrete SSC norms, the concept has gained a lot of momentum. The Second High-level UN Conference on South-South Cooperation in Buenos Aires (March 2019) (BAPA+40) showed that a global consensus on SSC is difficult to reach, and that a defining moment for SSC providers (it is even difficult to identify a concrete group of SSC providers) to come up with a measurable competing concept of DC has not been reached yet. Furthermore, for several SSC providers, it might be more useful to question and challenge OECD norms for DC, and then assert their uniqueness, rather than proposing a clear set of competing norms.

This leads us to our fourth conclusion. The current main diffusion approach to DC norms from a global perspective is more complex. Socialisation approaches to norm-diffusion seem to face at least two serious obstacles: one normative and the other institutional. From the normative point of view, while key SSC providers are unwilling to advance a serious debate around the concept of differential responsibilities, traditional donors are insisting on a burden-sharing rhetoric, which would ultimately water down all differentiation between ODA donors and SSC providers. The most visible proof of such a conundrum appears in the debates about quantification, monitoring, and reporting.

The fifth insight drawn in this section is related to Winston's (2018) concept of "norm cluster". The concept is very useful for identifying and understanding inconsistencies between the accepted outcomes of norm-diffusion in the real world. Her proposal for a new conceptual structure based on a bounded collection of interrelated specific (i) problems, (ii) values, and (iii) behaviours was a meaningful way to provide a research structure. Nevertheless, as we have argued, Winston's conceptual work must first take into account how social facts are framed into problems through the specific values rooted in agents' specific positions.

In the case analysed here, we have tried to demonstrate how, since the end of the Second World War, the social fact of dispossession was framed as a political problem in different ways by developed and developing countries. Furthermore, Winston's conceptual framework also underestimates the power relations embedded in the processes of setting what would be considered appropriate behaviour. As we have tried to demonstrate, the diffusion of power helps us understand how and why ODA, from 1945 to 2005, was consolidated as the normative framework in the field of DC, in spite of the attempts of developing countries to advance the alternative framework of SSC. Likewise, power relations also help us to understand how and why SSC has decentred ODA from its almost ubiquitous position since the beginning of the 2000s.

Sixth, in terms of future research, it is advisable for IR scholars working on norms to look out for DC case studies, given the high relevance of norm-diffusion issues. At the same time, it is recommendable for development research that focusses on different approaches to DC to use—to a much larger degree—analytical frameworks that come from the norms discourse.

Seventh, an obstacle for the significant process of socialisation is institutional. Currently, as the GPEDC was unable to attract key SSCPs, and as the UN DCF progressively loses relevance, there is no institutional arrangement mandated and endowed with the convening power for gathering traditional donors and SSCPs. The few initiatives for socialisation are confined to outreach or events on the margins of international conferences. Possibilities for "learning" are also rather limited: few SSC providers are explicitly looking for learning experiences; at the same time, traditional donors are looking to influence SSC approaches.

Nevertheless, the BAPA+40 process and its outcome document opened an unexpected door for learning and, perhaps, socialisation experiences: triangular cooperation. Further work needs to be done to understand the relevance of triangular cooperation. While scanning the outcome document, though, one may notice that the expression of "South-South and triangular cooperation" appears 56 times, indicating that statements about SSC also refer to triangular arrangements, most of which would include traditional donors. Moreover, paragraph 28 is entirely dedicated to triangular cooperation, recognising "that triangular cooperation is a modality that builds partnerships and trust, between all partners, and that combines diverse resources and capacities, under the ownership of the requesting developing country" (UN 2019, p. 8). Institutionally, the outcome document also recognises, specifically, the Global Partnership Initiative on Effective Triangular Cooperation in its efforts for mapping, documenting, and disseminating successful experiences.

Yet, although triangular cooperation may appear as an intersecting point where learning and eventually socialisation can take place, it is not enough to suggest a vigorous process of norm-setting and norm-diffusion. On the contrary, as the TOSSD concept shows, the OECD might be willing to adjust to some extent its norm set to SSC standards, but it will not do so via learning or socialisation, but rather through emulation and competition. The main diffusion mechanism of the current phase is "competition". Such a mechanism arises in interdependent, "less hierarchical and more decentralised" (Brake and Katzenstein 2013, p. 746) environments, such as markets. Hence, the competitive mechanism is framed, from one side, by the end of the unipolar moment and the emergence of alternative sources of political and economic power, and from the other side by the interactive dynamics of key competitors. The failure of the DAC's socialisation attempts of SSC providers has resulted in donors' own policy adjustments towards Southern norms and methods (Chaturvedi et al. 2016). The trouble with such a mechanism is precisely the externalities generated from rivals' policy adjustments (Braun and Gilardi 2006), spawning an adaptive and recursive process that may, likely, lead to a race-to-the-bottom. We have called such dynamics a situation that leads to an anomic environment.

Notes

1. The WP-EFFstarted as an OECD donor-only grouping in 2003 and evolved into a partnership of donors and developing countries in 2005 (see OECD-DAC 2010).
2. "South-South cooperation is a manifestation of solidarity among peoples…" (see UN Office for South-South Cooperation, n.d.).
3. "Since Accra, the current shape of the Working Party on Aid Effectiveness has changed in order to reflect the commitments. It is now led by two co-chairs; one from a developing country, another from a donor organisation. Its participants now include 24 aid-recipient countries; 8 countries which both provide and receive aid; 31 donors; 9 multilaterals; 6 civil society and other institutions (CSOs, parliamentarians)" (OECD-DAC 2010, p. 2).

References

Abdel-Malek, T. (2015). *The global partnership for effective development cooperation: Origins, actions and future prospects* (Studies 88). Bonn: German Development Institute / Deutsches Institut für Entwicklungspolitik (DIE).

Acharya, A. (2004). How ideas spread: Whose norms matter? Norm localization and institutional change in Asian regionalism. *International Organization, 58*(2), 239–275.

Ashoff, G., & Klingebiel, S. (2014). *Transformation of a policy area: Development policy is in a systemic crisis and faces the challenge of a more complex system environment* (Discussion Paper 9/2014). Bonn: German Development Institute/ Deutsches Institut für Entwicklungspolitik (DIE).

Ban, C., & Blyth, M. (2013). The BRICS and the Washington Consensus: An introduction. *Review of International Political Economy, 20*(2), 241–255.

Bayly, C. A. (2004). *The birth of the modern world 1780–1914: Global connections and comparisons*. London: Blackwell.

Bracho, G. (2015). *In search of a narrative for Southern providers: The challenge of the emerging countries to the development cooperation agenda* (Discussion Paper 1/2015). Bonn: German Development Institute / Deutsches Institut für Entwicklungspolitik (DIE).

Bracho, G. (2017). *The troubled relationship of the emerging powers and the effective development cooperation agenda: History, challenges and opportunities* (Discussion Paper 25/2017). Bonn: German Development Institute / Deutsches Institut für Entwicklungspolitik (DIE).

Brake, B., & Katzenstein, P. J. (2013). Lost in translation? Nonstate actors and the transnational movement of procedural law. *International Organization, 67*(4), 725–757.

Braun, D., & Gilardi, F. (2006). Taking "Galton's Problem" seriously towards a theory of policy diffusion. *Journal of Theoretical Politics, 18*(3), 298–322.

Brautigam, D. A., & Knack, S. (2004). Foreign aid, institutions, and governance in sub-Saharan Africa. *Economic Development and Cultural Change, 52*(2), 255–285.

Carbonnier, G., Thorndahl, M., & Arcand, J.-L. (2012). *International development policy: Aid, emerging economies and global policies*. Basingstoke: Palgrave Macmillan.

Chaturvedi, S. (2016). *The logic of sharing: Indian approach to South-South cooperation*. Cambridge: Cambridge University Press.

Chaturvedi, S., Chakrabarti, M., & Shiva, H. (2016). *TOSSD: Southernisation of ODA* (FIDC Policy Brief No. 9). New Delhi: Forum for Indian Development Cooperation.

Checkel, J. T. (2001). Why comply? Social learning and European identity change. *International Organization, 55*(3), 553–588.

Cold-Ravnkilde, S. M., Engberg-Pedersen, L., & Fejerskov, A. M. (2018). Global norms and heterogeneous development organizations: Introduction to special issue on new actors, old donors and gender equality norms in international development cooperation. *Progress in Development Studies, 18*(2), 77–94.

Dellios, R., & Ferguson, R. J. (2013). *China's quest for global order: From peaceful rise to harmonious world*. Lanham, MD: Lexington Books.

Doornbos, M. (2001). "Good governance": The rise and decline of a policy metaphor? *Journal of Development Studies, 31*(6), 93–108.

Esteves, P., & Assunção, M. (2014). South-South cooperation and the international development battlefield: Between the OECD and the UN. *Third World Quarterly, 35*(10), 1775–1790.

Eyben, R. (2012). Struggles in Paris: The DAC and the purposes of development aid. *European Journal of Development Research, 25*(1), 78–91.

Eyben, R., & Savage, L. (2012). Emerging and submerging powers: Imagined geographies in the new development partnership at the Busan Fourth High Level Forum. *Journal of Development Studies, 49*(4), 457–469.

Führer, H. (1996). *The story of official development assistance: A history of the Development Assistance Committee and the Development Co-operation Directorate in dates, names and figures*. Paris: Organisation for Economic Co-operation and Development.

Garavini, G. (2012). *After empires: European integration, decolonization, and the challenge from the Global South: 1957–1986*. Oxford: Oxford University Press.

Gilardi, F. (2013). Transnational diffusion: Norms, ideas, and policies. In W. Carlsnaes, T. Risse, & B. Simmons (Eds.), *Handbook of international relations* (pp. 453–477). London: Sage.

Global Partnership for Effective Development Co-operation. (2019). *Kampala principles on effective private-sector engagement in development co-operation*. https://effectivecooperation.org/wp-content/uploads/2019/06/Kampala-Principles-final.pdf.

Griffin, K. (1991). Foreign aid after the Cold War. *Development and Change, 22*(4), 645–685.

Group of 77. (1964). Joint declaration of the seventy-seven developing countries made at the conclusion of the United Nations Conference on Trade and Development. https://www.g77.org/doc/Joint%20Declaration.html.

Hermes, N., & Lensink, R. (2001). Changing the conditions for development aid: A new paradigm? *The Journal of Development Issues, 37*(6), 1–16.

Huang, M. (2018). *South-South cooperation and Chinese foreign aid*. New York, NY: Springer.

Janus, H., Klingebiel, S., & Mahn, T.C. (2016). *How to shape development cooperation? The Global Partnership and the Development Cooperation Forum* (Briefing Paper 3/2014). Bonn: German Development Institute / Deutsches Institut für Entwicklungspolitik (DIE).

Jayaprakash, N.D. (2005). India and the Bandung Conference of 1955–II. *People's Democracy (Weekly Organ of the Communist Party of India (Marxist)), XXIX*(23).

Keijzer, N., Klingebiel, S., Örnemark, C., & Scholtes, F. (2018). *Seeking balanced ownership in changing development cooperation relationships* (Report 2018:08). Stockholm: Expert Group for Aid Studies.

Klingebiel, S. (2014). *Development cooperation: Challenges of the new aid architecture*. Basingstoke: Palgrave Macmillan.

Klingebiel, S., Mahn, T., & Negre, M. (Eds.) (2016). *The fragmentation of aid: Concepts, measurements and implications for development cooperation*. Basingstoke: Palgrave Macmillan.

Klingebiel, S., Mank, I., Keijzer, N., Pauw, P., & Wolff, P. (2016). *TOSSD Compendium 2016—Contribution of the German Development Institute / Deutsches Institut für Entwicklungspolitik (DIE) to the Organisation for Economic Co-operation and Development (OECD) public consultation on the Total Official Support for Sustainable Development (TOSSD) Compendium 2016*. Bonn: German Development Institute / Deutsches Institut für Entwicklungspolitik (DIE).

Klingebiel, S., & Xiaoyun, L. (2016). *Crisis or progress? The Global Partnership for Effective Development Cooperation (GPEDC) after Nairobi* (The Current Column of 6 December 2016). Bonn: German Development Institute / Deutsches Institut für Entwicklungspolitik (DIE).

Knoll, A., & Sherriff, A. (2017). *Making waves: Implications of the irregular migration and refugee situation on official development assistance spending and practices in Europe—A study of recent developments in the EU institutions, Denmark, Germany, the Netherlands and Sweden*. Stockholm: EBA.

Manning, R. (2006). Will "emerging donors" change the face of international co-operation? *Development Policy Review, 24*(4), 371–385.

Martens, B., Mummert, U., Murrell, P., & Seabright, P. (2002). *The institutional economics of foreign aid*. Cambridge: Cambridge University Press.

Nye, J. S. (2011). *The future of power*. New York, NY: PublicAffairs.

OECD. (2006). *DAC in dates: The history of OECD's development assistance committee*. Paris: Development Co-operation Directorate, Organisation for Economic Co-operation and Development.

OECD (Organisation for Economic Co-operation and Development). (2010). *Bogota statement: Towards effective and inclusive development partnerships*. Paris: Organisation for Economic Co-operation and Development.

OECD. (2016). *TOSSD compendium for public consultation*. http://www.oecd.org/dac/financing-sustainable-development/TOSSD%20Compendium2016.pdf.

OECD. (2019). *Blended finance*. https://www.oecd.org/dac/financing-sustainable-development/development-finance-topics/blended-finance.htm.

OECD. (n.d.-a). *Official development assistance—Definition and coverage.* http://www.oecd.org/development/financing-sustainable-development/development-finance-standards/officialdevelopmentassistancedefinitionandcoverage.htm.
OECD. (n.d.-b). *Comments on TOSSD compendium.* http://www.oecd.org/dac/financing-sustainable-development/USA%20-%20comments%20on%20TOSSD%20Compendium.pdf.
OECD-DAC (Development Assistance Committee). (1996). *Shaping the 21st century: The contribution of development co-operation.* Paris: Organisation for Economic Co-operation and Development.
OECD-DAC. (2009). *Development Assistance Committee reflection exercise—Investing in development: A common cause in a changing world.* Paris: Organisation for Economic Co-operation and Development.
OECD-DAC. (2010). *The Working Party on Aid Effectiveness—Transforming global partnerships for development.* Paris: Organisation for Economic Co-operation and Development.
OECD-DAC. (2018). *OECD-DAC blended finance principles for unlocking commercial finance for the Sustainable Development Goals.* Paris: Organisation for Economic Co-operation and Development.
Ostrom, E., Gibson, C., Shivakumar, S., & Andersson, K. (2002). *Aid, incentives, and sustainability: An institutional analysis of development cooperation* (Sida Studies in Evaluation 02/01). Stockholm: Swedish International Development Cooperation Agency.
OXFAM. (2016). *Oxfam comments on Total Official Support for Sustainable Development (TOSSD) proposal, September 6, 2016.* London: OXFAM.
Payne, R. A. (2001). Persuasion, frames and norm construction. *European Journal of International Relations, 7*(1), 37–61.
Pronk, J. P. (2001). Aid as a catalyst. *Development and Change, 32*(4), 611–629.
Reality of Aid. (2016). *Reality of Aid's feedback on the OECD DAC's draft TOSSD compendium.* Quezon City: Reality of Aid.
Reilly, J. (2011). A norm-taker or a norm-maker? Chinese aid in Southeast Asia. *Journal of Contemporary China, 21*(73), 71–91.
Risse, T. (2017). *Domestic politics and norm diffusion in international relations.* London: Routledge.
Romero, M. J. (2016). Development finance takes "private turn": Implications and challenges ahead. *Development, 59*(1), 59–65.
Rosert, E. (2012). Fest etabliert und weiterhin lebendig: Normenforschung in den internationalen Beziehungen. *Zeitschrift Für Politikwissenschaft, 22*(4), 599–623.
Scott, S. (2015). *The accidental birth of "official development assistance"* (OECD Development Co-operation Working Papers, No. 24). Paris: Organisation for Economic Co-operation and Development.
Severino, J.-M., & Ray, O. (2009). *The end of ODA: Death and rebirth of a global public policy* (Working Paper 167). Washington, DC: Center for Global Development.
Shenfeldt, A. (2018). The European development response to the refugee and migration crisis. *International Organisations Research Journal, 13*(4), 195–212. https://doi.org/10.17323/1996-7845-2018-04-09.
Singfield, K.E. (2019). *Die deutsche Entwicklungsfinanzierungspolitik seit 2009* (Master's thesis). Cologne: Universität zu Köln.

Stokke, O. (1995). *Aid and political conditionality*. London and Portland, OR: F. Cass.

Talal, H. B. (1978). Statement by his Royal Highness Crown Prince Hassan Bin Talal of Jordan at a plenary meeting of the conference held on 31 August 1978. Report of the United Nations Conference on TCDC. https://undocs.org/pdf?symbol=en/A/CONF.79/13/Rev.1.

Task Team on South-South Cooperation (TT-SSC). (2010). *Boosting South-South cooperation in the context of aid effectiveness: Telling the story of partners involved in more than 110 cases of South-South and triangular cooperation*. Paris: Organisation for Economic Co-operation and Development.

TT-SSC.(2010b, March 24–26). Main conclusions of roundtable 3—Teaming up for South-South co-operation and capacity development: The role of triangular co-operation. High level event on South-South co-operation and capacity development, Bogota. http://api.ning.com/files/TqrIro7OEa6OVQym2xM4LkfmDMhsNX1QwApkeSM9ux53rwLs18s10QQ98jf0faYa3D92bR-yeFa95RLG4Ml97tlQKhAY8GvG/SummaryRT3_FINAL.pdf.

United Nations (UN). (2009). *Nairobi Outcome Document of the High-level United Nations Conference on South-South Cooperation*. https://digitallibrary.un.org/record/673444?ln=en.

UN. (2019). *Buenos Aires Outcome Document of the Second High-level United Nations Conference on South-South Cooperation (A/73/L.80)*. https://undocs.org/en/A/73/L.80.

UN Office for South-South Cooperation. (n.d.). About South-South and triangular cooperation. https://www.unsouthsouth.org/about/about-sstc/.

UNCTAD (UN Conference on Trade and Development). (1964). *Final act and report*. https://unctad.org/en/Docs/econf46d141vol1_en.pdf.

Van Eekelen, W. F. (1964). *Indian foreign policy and the border dispute with China*. The Hague: Martinus Nijhoff.

Waeyenberge, E. V. (2015). *The private turn in development finance* (Working Paper Series No. 140). London: Financialisation, Economy, Society and Sustainable Development.

Wehrmann, D. (2018). *Incentivising and regulating multi-actor partnerships and private-sector engagement in development cooperation* (Discussion Paper 21/2018). Bonn: German Development Institute / Deutsches Institut für Entwicklungspolitik (DIE).

Winston, C. (2018). Norm structure, diffusion, and evolution: A conceptual approach. *European Journal of International Relations, 24*(3), 638–661.

Zeiler, T. W. (2015). Genesis of a foreign aid revolution. In R. H. Geselbracht (Ed.), *Foreign aid and the legacy of Harry S. Truman* (pp. 33–42). Kirksville: Truman State University Press.

Zoccal Gomes, G. (2018). *Fronteiras Esgarçadas: Mobilização de capitais transformando fronteiras e prática dóxica da coope-ração internacional para o desenvolvimento* (doctoral thesis). Rio de Janeiro: Pontifícia Universidade Católica.

Zoccal Gomes, G., & Esteves, P. (2018). The BRICS effect: Impacts of South-South cooperation in the social field of international development cooperation. *IDS Bulletin, 49*(3), 129–144.

Open Access This chapter is licensed under the terms of the Creative Commons Attribution 4.0 International License (http://creativecommons.org/licenses/by/4.0/), which permits use, sharing, adaptation, distribution and reproduction in any medium or format, as long as you give appropriate credit to the original author(s) and the source, provide a link to the Creative Commons license and indicate if changes were made.

The images or other third party material in this chapter are included in the chapter's Creative Commons license, unless indicated otherwise in a credit line to the material. If material is not included in the chapter's Creative Commons license and your intended use is not permitted by statutory regulation or exceeds the permitted use, you will need to obtain permission directly from the copyright holder.

CHAPTER 10

Conceptualising Ideational Convergence of China and OECD Donors: Coalition Magnets in Development Cooperation

Heiner Janus and Tang Lixia

10.1 Introduction

China's continued economic growth and increasing level of engagement on the international stage have spurred an intense debate over China's role as a rising power in development cooperation. Academic literature has painted a nuanced picture of Chinese foreign aid, such as defining (Bräutigam 2011; Grimm et al. 2011; Li 2012), tracking (Kitano and Harada 2016), and assessing the allocation and effects of Chinese foreign aid (Strange et al. 2017). One dominating theme across this literature is a focus on the differences between Chinese and Organisation for Economic Co-operation and Development (OECD) development cooperation and the development cooperation of members of the OECD.[1] For instance, China does not define and assess its aid according to the OECD-Development Assistance Committee's (DAC) definition of official development assistance (ODA) but reports aid based on own standards (Bräutigam 2011).

China is usually portrayed as a challenger to the DAC donors and an alternative model (Hackenesch 2013; Kragelund 2015; Woods 2008; Zhang

---

H. Janus (✉)
German Development Institute / Deutsches Institut für Entwicklungspolitik (DIE), Bonn, Germany
e-mail: heiner.janus@die-gdi.de

L. Tang
China Institute for South-South Cooperation in Agriculture,
China Agricultural University, Beijing, China
e-mail: tanglx@cau.edu.cn

© The Author(s) 2021
S. Chaturvedi et al. (eds.), *The Palgrave Handbook of Development Cooperation for Achieving the 2030 Agenda*,
https://doi.org/10.1007/978-3-030-57938-8_10

et al. 2015). Debates on Chinese development cooperation also tend to be embedded in comparisons between DAC donors and "emerging donors" such as Brazil, India, South Africa, and China (Chin and Quadir 2012; Li and Carey 2014; Rowlands 2012). This literature assesses whether OECD-DAC and non-DAC donors such as China converge or diverge in terms of rhetoric, motives, norms (Reilly 2012), conditionality, thematic focus, institutional structures (Sidiropoulos et al. 2015), and modalities (Vazquez et al. 2016). Typically, these studies focus on explaining the differences between Chinese and OECD-DAC aid and often conclude that they are largely irreconcilable.

Despite long-standing differences between China and OECD donors, however, there has been a growing overlap between the aid activities of China and DAC donors across several areas of cooperation in recent years. On the one hand, OECD donors have increasingly pursued their national interests in development cooperation (Gulrajani 2017; Mawdsley 2017b). On the other hand, China has initiated a big push on global development. Most notably, China has launched the Belt and Road Initiative (BRI), also known as "the Silk Road of the 21st Century", massively increasing investments and its profile across Asia and Africa (Chun 2017). In addition, China has stepped up its engagement in multilateralism. During its G20 presidency in 2018, China championed the implementation of the 2030 Agenda for Sustainable Development, linking G20 and United Nations (UN) activities. Two new multilateral institutions—the New Development Bank ("BRICS [Brazil, Russia, India, China and South Africa] bank") and the Asian Infrastructure Investment Bank—are backed by China. Based on these observations of China's increased level of international engagement and the related literature on Chinese foreign aid, this chapter analyses potential areas of convergence between China and other international actors.

As a deliberate choice and in contrast to other academic literature, this analysis does not emphasise the differences between China and OECD-DAC donors but focuses on the concept of "ideational convergence" (Bickerton et al. 2015; Radaelli 2006). Ideational convergence is defined as the extent to which ideas held by different development actors become more similar over time. There are three main reasons for this approach. First, there is a gap in unpacking convergence in the literature, as most research focuses on the differences between China and other actors. In particular, there is an increasing level of convergence of ideas between China and OECD-DAC donors regarding international development that current political theories do not fully explain. Second, even within broad areas of convergence, there are nuanced differences that this analysis reveals. Third, for normative reasons, we believe that an increased understanding of convergence is needed to foster cooperation among different global development actors.

In addition, the analysis focuses on the international development discourse[2] and the importance of ideas for determining political outcomes, following a constructivist approach to international relations. This chapter emphasises the role of discourse, capturing both ideas and the interactive process by which ideas are conveyed, because discourse can help to explain how specific policies and initiatives are adopted and why political change occurs (Schmidt 2008). When viewing international development as a policy field, ideas are crucial for coordinated action by helping to organise coalitions around the shared goals and identities of different actors (Fligstein and McAdam 2012; Yanguas 2017). Although the "turn to ideas" (Jessop 2001; Schmidt 2008) has been ongoing in the political science literature, few of these ideational theories have been applied to study Chinese foreign engagement (Feng 2016; Wang and Blyth 2013).

For China as a development actor, a focus on ideas fits well because ideas formulated by the country's leadership are the cornerstone of its policy-making, including Chinese foreign aid. At the same time, policy-making in China is often characterised as a gradual, experimental, and adaptive process (Ang 2016; Qian 2017). Therefore, it is investigated whether the meaning of ideas and their interpretations change over time, especially in the Chinese policy discourse on foreign aid (Varrall 2013; Zhang et al. 2015). The key research question for this chapter is: How can the convergence of ideas in international development cooperation be conceptualised, and which specific ideas indicate a convergence on development thinking between China and OECD donors?

This analysis is structured in four parts. First, the theoretical background on ideas and institutions for explaining Chinese foreign aid is introduced. Next, the concept of "coalition magnets" is defined and the analytical framework is laid out. Third, three coalition magnets are identified: mutual benefit, development results, and the 2030 Agenda. For each of these coalition magnets, the potential of fostering joint OECD-DAC and Chinese engagement in development cooperation is explored. The final part contextualises the findings in the current development discourse and presents conclusions.

The chapter relies mainly on desk research with a focus on the academic and policy literature from OECD countries and China as well as interviews conducted in China with foreign aid experts from September to October 2017. Moreover, a wide range of official and unofficial sources was consulted to understand how development cooperation discourse is expressed, particularly in contemporary Chinese elite discourse. Official documents and grey literature allow for examining how Chinese elites interpret and elaborate on official Chinese government narratives, and how they seek to portray such narratives to domestic and foreign audiences.

10.2 Theoretical Background: Understanding China's Rise Through Ideas and Institutions

Chinese foreign policy has changed radically in recent years. In the 1990s, President Deng Xiaoping had characterised China's foreign policy strategy as "taoguang yanghui, yousuo zuowei" (keeping a low profile while trying to accomplish something) because of the radical shifts in the international order after the collapse of the Soviet Union (Lee 2016; Wang 2014). The United

States had become the global superpower, and China did not want to challenge them, and neither took on a leadership role in the "Global South". In the past two decades, Presidents Jiang Zemin and Hu Jintao followed this policy of maintaining a low profile in international relations and mainly concentrated on China's economic growth (Lee 2016). With President Xi Jinping, however, the world has witnessed a massive expansion of Chinese engagement abroad. Contrary to his predecessors, President Xi uses terms such as "China Path" or "China Dream" (Sørensen 2015) to suggest "a strong nation capable of global leadership and of representing an alternative model of governance that sets China apart from market-led capitalism or liberal democracy" (Shi-Kupfer et al. 2017, p. 9).

International relations theories analysing the increase in China's international efforts, including foreign aid, usually focus on national interest as the main driver. Typically, pursuing national interest within an anarchic system of sovereign nation states means increasing state power relative to other states, either through hard or "soft power" (Ding 2010; Nye 2004). Cooperation between China and other actors in this context is viewed as being driven purely by the pursuit of material self-interest and eventually leading to conflict (Allison 2017; Gilpin 1983; Mearsheimer 2010). However, these theories are insufficient to fully explain the rapid expansion of—and the changes in—Chinese development cooperation. For instance, soft power has limitations, both as a deliberate Chinese political strategy and as an analytical lens. Soft power is often used as an empty catch-all term with little analytical precision, neglecting the nuances of international engagement (Rawnsley 2016). Besides, soft power requires a specific context—typically a common rule-governed institutional setting and the presence of underlying mutual interest—in order to be utilised effectively as an explanatory factor (Kearn 2008). China's communication of its foreign policy, however, still targets a domestic audience and does not resonate abroad, leading to limited success of its soft power strategies (Gill and Huang 2006; Lee 2016; Shambaugh 2015).

Furthermore, Chinese efforts to protect global public goods such as the Paris Agreement, the Iran nuclear deal, or the global free trade regime cannot be solely explained as a strategy to expand power at the expense of other countries. Ideas of enlightened self-interest or global cooperation could provide a complementary explanation that has yet to be studied in greater detail (Anand 2004; Kaul et al. 1999; Kenny et al. 2018). Thus, applying an ideational framework to assess the power of ideas to form coalitions of political actors may help to explain the increased level of Chinese engagement in foreign aid. Another important argument for an ideational approach to studying China's foreign engagement is the role of ideas in its policy-making. As an authoritarian one-party state, ideas and discourses in China are key factors in determining political outcomes. Those presenting ideas in the Chinese academic literature often react to changes in the official policies of the Chinese Communist Party, which determines what "correct ideas" are (Chin et al. 2013).

Scholars have thus far not applied discursive frameworks widely in studying the Chinese domestic discourse. Rationalist international relations frameworks tend to view China as a monolithic actor, without unpacking domestic policy discourse. Our analysis builds on "discursive institutionalism" (Schmidt 2008, 2010), which is complementary to the new institutionalist approaches of historical institutionalism, rational choice institutionalism, and sociological institutionalism. A major criticism against these three institutionalisms is that institutions have become overly deterministic, and agents have mostly set preferences or are fixated by norms. Hay argues that

> actors as driven either by utility maximization in an institutionalized game scenario (rational choice institutionalism) or by institutionalized norms and cultural conventions (normative/sociological institutionalism) or, indeed, both (historical institutionalism), are unlikely to offer much analytical purchase on questions of complex post-formative institutional change. (Hay 2006a, p. 6)

Discursive institutionalism moves away from this static perspective of viewing institutions as largely constraining rules that are external to the actors. Instead, discursive institutionalism defines institutions as being simultaneously given (the context within which agents think, speak, and act) as well as contingent (as the results of agents' thoughts, words, and actions) (Schmidt 2008, p. 314). Hence, institutions are internal to the actors and serve both as structures that constrain behaviour and as constructs created and changed by those actors (Schmidt 2008, p. 314). Actors then engage through ideas and discourse with these institutions to maintain or change institutional outcomes or policies (Béland 2005). For the Chinese context, this discursive institutionalist approach offers a complementary perspective to the dominant rational choice heavy literature and explains how Chinese political behaviour and policy-making outcomes are driven by ideas rather than solely by self-interest (Campbell 2002).

Ideas themselves are increasingly crucial for understanding processes of political change. We define ideas as causal beliefs about economic, social, and political phenomena (Béland and Cox 2016). Ideas are cognitive products, meaning that they are interpretations of the material world in the mind, and ideas posit relationships (formal and informal) between things and events, and they are guides (causes) for actions (Béland and Cox 2010, pp. 3–4). Institutions are understood as "carriers of ideas" or "collective memories", following Schmidt (2011). Power[3] is understood as the ability to shape outcomes and reach particular goals (Béland and Cox 2016; Morriss 2006), which includes the dimension of ideational power (Carstensen and Schmidt 2016). Power is a key factor in this process of discourse when actors promote certain ideas at the expense of other ideas. Ideas and power can interact in various ways, for example through discourse.

For the analysis, the focus is placed on ideas that can serve as vehicles for collective action and coalition-building, and the role of policy entrepreneurs to use framing processes to influence discourse. Policy entrepreneurs are broadly defined as "people who are willing to invest resources of various kinds in hopes of a future return in the form of policies they favour" (Kingdon 1984, p. 143). These policy entrepreneurs could be political leaders, elected officials, party members, policy-makers, the media, interest groups, public intellectuals, opinion-makers, social movements, or ordinary people. Policy entrepreneurs use strategic framing, a process by which actors use their ideas and their power to influence discourse (Béland and Cox 2016, p. 432).

10.3 Analytical Framework: Ideas as Coalition Magnets

We adopt an ideational framework developed by Béland and Cox (2016), who argue that ideas can shape political power relations through their role as "coalition magnets", defined as the capacity of an idea to appeal to a diverse set of individuals and groups, and to be used strategically by policy entrepreneurs.

Béland and Cox (2016) highlight two critical characteristics of an idea that makes it attractive for policy entrepreneurs to employ as a coalition magnet. First, ambiguous and polysemic ideas that appeal to a range of heterogeneous actors for different reasons have a strong potential for becoming coalition magnets. The broader the idea, the easier it is for policy entrepreneurs to bring different constituencies together and transcend political divisions. Clearly defined and narrow ideas are typically less suited. Second, ideas need to be valent, meaning that they evoke emotional reactions that can be positive or negative and have low or high intensity. Particularly, ideas with a positive and high-intensity valence are likely to have strong coalition-building potential.

Once policy entrepreneurs determine to use a specific idea as a coalition magnet, they typically seek to create a new language that is unfamiliar to actors in a given policy debate, or they use existing language in a new and unfamiliar way. Next, key actors in the policy debate with decision-making authority need to embrace the idea and grant legitimacy to the given policy preference. Finally, different actors whose perceived interests had previously placed them at odds need to engage jointly with the particular issue in new ways, or actors that had previously not been engaged in a given issue need to do so. When these circumstances are in place, Béland and Cox (2016) argue that an idea can become a coalition magnet that policy entrepreneurs use to alter power relations and political outcomes. As an example of coalition magnet ideas, they analyse the ideas "sustainability", "solidarity", and "social inclusion".

The main limitations of the coalition magnet framework are similar to limitations of discursive institutionalism or constructivist ideational theories. Primarily, there is a risk that ideational theories ascribe a vague or almost meaningless role to institutions (Bell 2011), or what Hay (2006b) calls "ideational voluntarism". In particular, ideational theories need to address the structure-agency problem and determine the relationship between the ideational and the material. A series of methodological issues follow from this ontological challenge, as any ideational theory needs to clarify the relation between institutions, ideas, and policy outcomes. For the specific case of coalition magnet ideas, it is crucial to understand them as "ideas empowering actors" (Parsons 2016), whereby the challenge for the analysis is to track who champions the ideas, how their agendas relate to perceived problems, how these change over time, and to what extent actors have shared core understandings or different interpretations of a given idea.

The framework is applied to three ideas in international development cooperation—mutual benefit, development results, and the 2030 Agenda—to assess their potential as coalition magnets (Table 10.1). In the analysis, the ambiguity and valence of the idea are assessed first, and then the analysis shifts to which actors embrace the idea to grant it legitimacy, before turning to the question of whether policy entrepreneurs are already using the idea as a coalition magnet. The analysis does not, however, go beyond the analysing stage of agenda-setting in the policy process because the main focus lies on assessing the strengths and weaknesses of each policy idea with respect to fostering convergence between China and OECD-DAC development actors. However, coalitions may be fragile after the agenda-setting stage, especially

Table 10.1 Potential coalition magnet ideas in development cooperation

Idea	Mutual benefit	Development results	2030 Agenda
Articulation of idea	Principle of South-South cooperation and Chinese aid	Principle of OECD-DAC development cooperation	United Nations Development Agenda
Policy proposals (examples)	Chinese white papers on foreign aid	OECD-DAC managing for development results, results-based management	National plans for achieving Sustainable Development Goals (SDGs)
Scale of coalition	Mainly providers of South-South cooperation, increasingly popular among OECD-DAC donors	Mainly OECD-DAC donors, increasingly popular among South-South cooperation providers, including China	All international development actors

Source Authors, based on Béland and Cox (2016)

regarding implementation or other post-agenda-setting stages of the policy cycle (Howlett et al. 2009). Ultimately, coalition magnets can also become "empty signifiers" (Laclau 1996), ideas that bring disparate people together in a common cause but otherwise have no attachment to precise content. Still, coalition magnet ideas are not assumed to "float freely" but are anchored in transnational policy networks and different domestic structures that differ in terms of state–society relations as well as values and norms embedded in political cultures (Risse-Kappen 1994). This analysis, therefore, contextualises its findings against the background of global development discussions and domestic challenges that policy entrepreneurs face by analysing different types of discourse that link ideas with collective action (Schmidt 2011).

Three ideas are purposefully selected to cover different domains of aid policy-making (motives, implementation, goal system) and different associations in terms of actors that are predominantly linked to the specific idea. The first idea, mutual benefit, is being discussed in the context of the underlying motives of development cooperation and has been a cornerstone of Chinese foreign aid and South-South cooperation. For this idea, we also analyse to what extent OECD-DAC countries have used it. The second idea represents the implementation and management side of foreign aid, namely what is often termed "development results"—the idea that aid interventions should lead to measurable improvements in people's lives. This idea has been codified by OEDC-DAC donors in various policy documents, whereas China has only gradually moved into this direction. The third idea represents the goal system of international development, namely the 2030 Agenda, which was agreed in the UN in 2015 and theoretically applies to all development actors equally, including those from China and OECD-DAC countries.

10.4 Three Potential Coalition Magnets

10.4.1 Mutual Benefit

The idea of "mutual benefit", or "mutual interest" (Li et al. 2014), has a long history in development cooperation and is anchored in South-South cooperation and Chinese foreign aid. In the Bandung Conference of African and Asian states in 1955, participants endorsed five principles of peaceful coexistence—including the principle of equality and mutual benefit—which has its roots in the Soviet aid model (Johnston and Rudyak 2017). In 1964, Chinese Premier Zhou Enlai laid out eight principles for "China's Aid to Third World Countries", which again included "equality and mutual benefit" as the first principle. Since then, mutual benefit has been reaffirmed in numerous Chinese policy documents, such as the Chinese white papers on foreign aid in 2011 (China State Council 2011) and 2014 (China State Council 2014).

Mutual benefit is a highly polysemic idea, since its meaning is interpreted differently by various actors. In a Chinese context, "mutual benefit" is often mentioned along with "win-win outcomes" and is used across all areas of Chinese engagement with other countries, including political, economic, cultural, and security relations (Chen 2017). In the foreign aid context, mutual benefit is understood as a mix of trade, investment, and aid. Moreover, in the South-South rhetoric, mutual benefit is portrayed as a counter-model to the OECD-DAC approach (Grimm 2014). Here, the mutual benefit expresses a partnership among equals (horizontal cooperation) and not the benevolent gifts of an altruistic donor to a recipient country (vertical cooperation). Still, the question of how benefits are distributed precisely between China and its partners is usually not specified when mutual benefit is mentioned in Chinese policy documents. Besides, power relations between China and its partners can be skewed and unbalanced, even when benefits are mutual (Grimm 2014; Hackenesch 2013).

In development discourse, mutual benefit traditionally has not been seen as particularly valent. DAC donors emphasise developing country benefits such as poverty reduction or access to better services. Yet, donor motivations for aid allocation decisions have always been driven by a mix of interests (Hulme 2016) and mostly dominated by political and economic interests (Alesina and Dollar 2000; Berthélemy 2006). But own national interests of donors are often presented in direct contradiction to altruistic (also called benevolent or humanitarian) donor motives. This notion is based on research that indicates aid is less likely to be effective when given for strategic reasons as opposed to being allocated for developmental purposes (Dreher et al. 2016; Minoiu and Reddy 2010). In addition, mutual benefit contradicts efforts of OECD-DAC donors to "untie aid", and the official ODA definition highlights that interests related to commercial endeavours and poverty reduction should be separated.

In recent years, there has been a strong trend towards a more open acknowledgement of national interests in the development discourse and practices of OECD-DAC donors (Gulrajani 2017; Keijzer and Lundsgaarde 2017; Mawdsley 2017b). As a consequence, the legitimacy of acknowledging mutual benefit is increasing. Some see this trend mostly as a "shift in discourse communicating the goals of development cooperation to domestic audiences" (Keijzer and Lundsgaarde 2017, p. 7) and not a fundamental change. Since the financial crisis in 2009, however, national interests, such as security, political, and economic interests, have taken a front seat in aid discourse. As part of a trend towards "retroliberalism" (Mawdsley et al. 2016; Murray and Overton 2016), donors such as the United Kingdom, Australia, New Zealand, Canada, and the Netherlands have strengthened the private sector and export orientation of their aid. Another trend has been the rising number of refugees and migrants coming to Europe, which triggered massive shifts in the allocation of aid budgets. In Germany's aid budget, the "in-donor refugee costs" have increased from about 1 per cent in 2014 to almost 17 per cent in 2015 (Knoll and Sheriff 2017, p. 17).

One driver of the mutual interest trend is the rise of emerging economies, which are challenging the traditional OECD model of aid. The "BRICS effect" (Younis 2013) has contributed to OECD donors reconsidering their approaches to aid. Collier (2016) even states that a focus on mutual benefit in aid is ethical, arguing that the aid partnership will be more genuine and stable than under a purely charitable approach. Previously, Collier described how "Western aid would adopt a model close to Chinese aid" (Collier 2013, p. 15) in terms of linking public investments with private enterprises.

For China, the question is to what extent the interpretation of mutual benefit has changed since the 1950s. First, policy ideas in China are often announced in rather vague terms from the leadership and then later interpreted and implemented by a large staff of civil servants in a process that has been termed "directed improvisation" (Ang 2016), suggesting potential space for experimentation. Second, the interpretation of "orthodox" norms can change over time. One example is the evolution of the "win-win" idea, which has gone through multiple "historic leaps" and rounds of "new thinking", whereby the original, more narrow meaning has expanded to all types of engagement between China and other countries (Chen 2017). Another example is the Chinese norm of "non-interference", whereby China has softened its stance and become increasingly interventionist in the field of peace and security (Grimm 2014). A similar process of softening seems to be taking place for the idea of mutual benefit, whereby the distribution of benefits is slowly tilting towards the partner countries. In the context of China's BRI, for example, China is investing in many high-risk projects and regions, where the immediate benefits predominantly fall to the partners.

A further indication of a shift in the interpretation of mutual benefit was the introduction of the term "community of shared future for mankind" by President Xi in 2015. This principle has quickly risen to become one of the most influential ideas in Chinese foreign policy. Yang Jiechi, a high-ranking foreign policy official, stated that "a new form of international relations characterized by mutual respect, fairness, justice, and mutual benefit is the basic path toward a community of shared future for humanity" (Yang 2018). Although scholars warn about a "sinocentric" (Callahan 2013; Nordin and Weissmann 2017) world view of the Chinese leadership when it speaks about a "community of shared destiny", there has been a noticeable shift of Chinese discourse towards "actively shouldering our international responsibilities and obligations" (Chen 2017). Such thinking echoes debates on "global public goods" (Ahluwalia et al. 2016; Cepparulo and Giuriato 2016), in which national interests, such as protecting the global climate, health, and security regimes, are put in the context of collective development challenges.

This analysis indicates that mutual benefit has the potential to be strategically used by policy entrepreneurs to foster convergence around this idea. The idea is polysemic, as it covers multiple dimensions of Chinese foreign engagement, including foreign aid, and is understood differently across China, other South-South cooperation providers, developing countries, and OECD-DAC donors. The valence of mutual benefit has further shifted from generating a high negative-intensity reaction among OECD-DAC donors towards greater acceptance and endorsement. Next, mutual benefit has been legitimised by

China and OECD-DAC donors across different policy documents. Nevertheless, as of yet, policy entrepreneurs have not used mutual benefit as a coalition magnet to bring China, other South-South cooperation providers, developing countries, and OECD-DAC donors together. Discussions on common principles for foreign aid remain fragmented across different international platforms (Li et al. 2018; Mawdsley 2017a).

10.4.2 Development Results

The idea of development results entails the performance of foreign aid being continuously measured across multiple dimensions, including financial, economic, social, and environmental dimensions. Development results are firmly embedded in the OECD-DAC approach to foreign aid and date back to the 1960s, when "aid projects" (Baum and Tolbert 1985) were being implemented in increasingly formalised ways (e.g. through the introduction of the project cycle and project analysis). Later, in the 1980s, the "new public management" (Minogue et al. 1998) trend spread private-sector management approaches with the intent of making aid more market- and performance-orientated (Hood 1991; Turner et al. 2015). Today, the "results agenda" has firmly taken hold of many aspects of foreign aid (Eyben et al. 2015)—for instance as a principle for effective development cooperation—in the form of results frameworks for the management of aid organisations (Holzapfel 2016), results-based approaches for disbursing aid funds (Janus and Klingebiel 2014), and in the 2030 Agenda with its 17 goals and 169 indicators. In China, the Ministry of Commerce issued "Management Methods of Foreign Assistance Complete Projects" in 2009 and "Regulations on China's Foreign Aid Management" in 2014 (China Ministry of Commerce 2014) outlining an evaluation system of Chinese aid (Zhou 2016). In 2018, the Chinese government set up the China International Development Cooperation Agency to better manage its aid delivery (Zhou and Zhang 2018).

The development results idea in foreign aid can be polysemic because the critical question is: Whose results? Given a large number of aid stakeholders, such as donors, the donors' publics, recipient governments, and the recipient countries' publics, there can be diverging interests and power imbalances across the various relationships between these stakeholders. For instance, the drivers of the results trend among OECD-DAC countries are the interest to measure the effectiveness of foreign aid and the need to be accountable and report to aid constituents. In Chinese aid, too, the idea of development results can be polysemic, and results encompass those in the recipient countries as well as the results for China (Zhou 2016). Early mentions of results—such as Premier Zhou Enlai's eight principles of foreign aid in 1964 (Zhou 1964)—which include "quick results", are different from more recent documents on Chinese foreign aid that mention "substantial results" (China State Council 2011), "win-win results" (China State Council 2014), and "real results" (Xi 2017).

The idea of development results is typically seen as valent because achieving results is appealing to most stakeholders of foreign aid. However, the seemingly value-neutral results agenda among DAC donors can mask underlying political issues in administering aid, which has led to push back on the uncritical endorsement of the results agenda (Eyben et al. 2015; Paul 2015). DAC donors typically define results along a "results chain", in which only outcomes and impacts (improvements in people's lives) are viewed as results, and aid evaluations are made public to foster accountability. However, results frameworks that are used for reporting on foreign aid also include expenditures on administering aid, such as personnel costs for aid workers, and DAC donors have openly advocated integrating self-interest-oriented metrics into ODA reporting.

Still, the idea of development results enjoys high legitimacy, both in the DAC and in the Chinese context. The results agenda of DAC members and efforts to track the effectiveness of foreign aid and inform constituents remain high on the policy agenda. In political and formal terms, "managing for development results" is one of the five principles of the Paris Declaration on Aid Effectiveness (Organisation for Economic Co-operation and Development [OECD] 2005/2008). In South-South cooperation, which includes Chinese foreign aid, the Nairobi Outcome Document from 2009 and the 2019 outcome document of the High-level Conference on South-South Cooperation in Buenos Aires both affirm that the "impact of South-South cooperation should be assessed with a view to improving, as appropriate, its quality in a results-oriented manner" (United Nations General Assembly 2009, p. 4; 2019, p. 9).

A potential convergence around development results could, for instance, occur on a technical level of monitoring and evaluating foreign aid. Although the SDGs provide a potential guiding framework for reporting on development results, DAC donors aim to provide more nuanced information concerning results by differentiating results data in two main ways. First, they want to distinguish between three tiers: development results in the form of outcomes or impacts on the national and global levels, development cooperation results attributable to donors, and performance information on the organisations providing aid (OECD 2017; Zwart 2017). Second, DAC donors want to report disaggregated results information according to different purposes: accountability to constituents, communication for public relations, strategic direction, and learning for improving effectiveness. Yet, these discussions are ongoing, and balancing these different reporting purposes while presenting aid results according to the SDGs remains a challenge (Zwart 2017).

China, so far, has not participated in international fora for discussing results or evaluations as a donor country. As a donor, China offers little transparency regarding self-reported information on foreign aid, and information is not disaggregated on a country or project basis. In past years though, China has made significant moves towards a more systematic and open approach to reporting development results. First, the publication of white papers has provided more information, and now parts of China's aid portfolio are systematically monitored and evaluated using developmental criteria (Zhou 2016). Second, Chinese researchers are involved in numerous projects documenting the effects of aggregate Chinese aid and aid projects, with an increasing level of support from the Chinese government (Vazquez et al. 2016). Lastly, China has presented a detailed plan for implementing the SDGs and reported on progress towards achieving the SDGs, stating that

> China has pressed ahead with international cooperation under the Belt and Road Initiative, implemented a series of major result-oriented measures for international cooperation and stepped up assistance to other developing countries, particularly the LDCs [least-developed countries], making important contributions to regional and global implementation of the 2030 Agenda. (China Ministry of Foreign Affairs [MOFA] 2017, p. 73)

This analysis indicates that the development results idea (similar to mutual benefit) has the potential to be strategically used by policy entrepreneurs to foster convergence. The idea is polysemic, as it covers multiple dimensions and is understood differently across the various stakeholders. The valence of development results has traditionally been positive, and results reporting triggers high-intensity reactions. Next, development results have been legitimised by OECD-DAC donors and China across different policy documents. Nevertheless, policy entrepreneurs have not used development results as a coalition magnet so far to bring China, other South-South cooperation providers, developing countries, and OECD-DAC donors together.

10.4.3   2030 Agenda

The 2030 Agenda for Sustainable Development was agreed at the 2015 UN summit in New York and lays out a normative vision for global sustainable development (United Nations General Assembly 2015). It includes 17 goals across many different development dimensions and was carefully negotiated over several years and deliberated among all UN member states and other stakeholders. Thus, the 2030 Agenda is a highly valent and polysemic idea. It is valent because it is universally endorsed across the world and aspires to promote human development while safeguarding the planet. The idea of the 2030 Agenda is polysemic because no country is mandated to adopt each goal, but rather free to prioritise and implement certain parts of the agenda. Likewise, different actors are permitted to apply their own understandings of how the agenda should be achieved.

The legitimacy of the 2030 Agenda idea is unrivalled in development cooperation because it has been agreed by the UN, which has universal membership and is regarded as the most legitimate international organisation. Initially, the negotiation positions of China and OECD-DAC countries seemed to be quite far apart. In particular, there was the historical persistence of a North-South divide in the UN, often pinning OECD countries against the G77 and China, leading to gridlock across many areas of international cooperation (Fues and Ye 2014; Hale et al. 2013). Despite the adversarial starting position, there has been a high degree of convergence in positions between OECD countries and China, who have embraced the 2030 Agenda as a guiding framework for their development contributions, global policy discussions, and domestic policy-making.

China has actively engaged in the 2030 Agenda deliberations as a member of the Open Working Group—the official negotiation platform—and by publishing a position paper on the agenda (Fues and Ye 2014). Since 2015, China has introduced a National Plan on Implementation of the 2030 Agenda for Sustainable Development (China MOFA 2016) and published a "Progress Report on Implementation of the 2030 Agenda for Sustainable Development" (China MOFA 2017). Key Chinese planning documents such as the "Communiqué of the Fifth Plenary Meeting of the 18th Central Committee of the Chinese Communist Party" and the 13th Five-Year Plan reference the 2030 Agenda and tie it to domestic development strategies (Li and Zhou 2016, p. 67). OECD countries have similarly embraced the 2030 Agenda in their foreign and domestic policies, although to varying degrees (OECD 2016).

The vital area for potential convergence is the notion of "universality", meaning that the development goals do not just apply to developing countries but that all countries, including OECD countries, need to apply the goals to their domestic development. Next, the 2030 Agenda has contributed towards joining the policy communities around "sustainable development" with the policy communities around "human development", as they had been separated within the UN and bureaucratic structures internationally (Bexell and Jönsson 2017). Another area of strong convergence has been the combination of goals, instruments, and review frameworks in the 2030 Agenda, expressed in the Addis Ababa Action Agenda on financing for development, the SDGs, and the follow-up and review mechanisms. Finally, China and OECD countries have jointly embraced the 2030 Agenda across various international fora, such as the G20 (Dongxiao et al. 2017; Li and Zhou 2016).

In terms of challenges and nuanced divergence, the issues of responsibility and burden-sharing stand out (Bexell and Jönsson 2017). These discussions can be summarised under the label of common but differentiated responsibilities (CBDR), which stems from the 1992 Rio Declaration on Environment and Development. The CBDR principle, however, has been slow to change into an updated understanding of differentiated forms of responsibilities (Dongxiao et al. 2017). More recently, however, emerging economies such as China have started applying the "intended nationally determined contributions" principle—introduced in the context of the Paris Agreement—to the 2030 Agenda. Based on "self-differentiation" (Mbeva and Pauw 2016), China proclaims self-determined contributions for achieving the 2030 Agenda in a bottom-up way. But critically, China still views itself as "the world's largest developing country" (Chin 2012; China MOFA 2016) and a "responsible major developing country" (China MOFA 2017). China, therefore, holds two potentially conflicting identities, being a developing country and a main global economic power at the same time.

Compared to mutual benefit and development results, the 2030 Agenda possesses the most significant potential of becoming a coalition magnet idea, given its polysemic character and strong positive valence. Besides, the 2030 Agenda has unmatched global legitimacy as a new sustainable development paradigm that has been universally endorsed by all UN member states. Despite these favourable conditions, policy entrepreneurs again struggled in using the 2030 Agenda to foster greater convergence between OECD countries and China, especially concerning the burden-sharing discussion.

10.5 Contextualising Mutual Benefit, Development Results, and the 2030 Agenda in a Changing Global Development Landscape

Comparing the ideas, it can be observed that each idea has a strong potential to become a coalition magnet idea, as each idea is polysemic and valent, and has been legitimised through various policy documents from OECD countries as well as from China. Yet, none of the ideas has been strategically used by policy entrepreneurs to foster convergence and consensus between OECD countries and China. As a next step, we contextualise our findings in the current landscape of global development discussions and explore the challenges that prevent policy entrepreneurs from fostering convergence generally as well as individually for each of the three ideas. Based on this analysis, we explore tentative steps that policy entrepreneurs could take to foster convergence for each of the three coalition magnet ideas.

In terms of challenges that prevent convergence around coalition magnet ideas, one key global trend has been the rise of identity-based populist and nationalist political movements in OECD countries (Luce 2017; Schmidt 2017) as well as in China (Johnston 2017). Gills (2017, p. 157) states that populist political currents have been making "a 'nationalist' appeal to citizens, and rejecting alternative cosmopolitan responses to the tensions generated by an increasingly globalized world". Cosmopolitan ideas on greater multilateral cooperation, such as mutual benefit, development results, and the 2030 Agenda, are therefore facing a generally unfavourable policy environment and are likely to encounter strong political opposition. Policy entrepreneurs, therefore, need to use their political power and rhetorical skills in politically smart ways (Béland and Cox 2016) to bridge the divide between nationalistic populism and cosmopolitan ideas of multilateralism.

Based on discursive institutionalism, this gap in multilateralism is closely linked to the divide between what Schmidt (2008) calls the coordinative and the communicative spheres of discourse. In the coordinative sphere, experts conduct policy discussions among themselves, whereas the communicative sphere involves the general public (Schmidt 2008).[4] Each sphere requires distinctive discursive strategies (speaker, message, audience) to be successful in terms of achieving political change (Schmidt 2011). One key problem, however, has been that experts in the coordinative sphere have not sufficiently interacted with those in the communicative sphere, while the communicative sphere has been increasingly subject to the influence of technology and technological disruption (Schmidt 2017). As a result, public statements and practical policies keep diverging, as politicians make policy announcements that their administrations cannot deliver.

The main strategy for countering this trend is finding ways of coupling the coordinative and communicative spheres of discourse. Policy entrepreneurs need to disseminate their ideas across the coordinative policy sphere and the communicative politics sphere with tailored strategies to create new policy coalitions in national and international settings that may cut across political cleavages. We explore the concept of coupling the coordinative and communicative spheres of discourse by applying it to OECD countries and China for each of the three potential coalition magnet ideas. Therefore, we first reflect on the specific challenges to greater convergence for each idea and then sketch potential ways of bridging these challenges by coupling coordinative and communicative spheres of discourse.

For the potential coalition magnet idea of *mutual benefit*, two main obstacles prevent greater convergence. First, the strong emphasis on the commercial interests of OECD-DAC donors and China risks co-opting a developmental agenda for private gains. Already authors are warning that the main beneficiaries of mutual benefit-oriented aid in OECD-DAC countries are business elites and consultants (Mawdsley et al. 2016). Second, power relations in development cooperation are still largely skewed towards the aid provider, and the agency and voice of recipients are under threat. Previous efforts of OECD-DAC donors to self-discipline, for example through the Paris Declaration on Aid Effectiveness, have failed and lost their political support. An attempt by OECD-DAC donors to extend the ODA definition towards total official support for sustainable development in a non-inclusive and non-transparent process was perceived as an attempt to shirk existing donor commitments (Besharati 2017).

Going forward, policy entrepreneurs face the challenge of fostering more nuanced and transparent dialogue on the balance of *mutual benefit*, where the main problem is not the existence of national interests but their concealment. Keijzer and Lundsgaarde (2017) propose extending the monitoring and evaluation toolbox of ODA to better track benefits outside of the recipient country. Such a step would improve transparency and allow for a more honest dialogue on foreign aid. Chinese foreign aid already systematically monitors mutual benefit in select projects, although these evaluations have not yet been published (Zhou 2016). Hence, China could move towards a more transparent discussion of how benefits are distributed in its cooperation, for instance by making internal tendering processes more transparent and open for competition. Although the transparent evaluation of mutual benefit is a long-term objective for policy entrepreneurs, a more immediate step could be a discussion on global public goods and enlightened self-interest. Using the coalition magnet idea of mutual benefit in this way could foster greater convergence between OECD-DAC donors and China and help to couple the coordinative and communicative spheres of discourse between the international and national levels.

For the potential coalition magnet idea of *development results*, the main challenge is that OECD-DAC donors and China are falling behind on established metrics of aid effectiveness. For example, the share of country programmable aid[5] in bilateral ODA and the amount of ODA to LDCs[6] have declined in recent years (OECD 2017). A 2016 survey of 81 developing countries showed that only about half of all aid was spent through country systems (OECD and United Nations Development Programme 2016). These trends come at the expense of recipient countries. In the same way, developing countries that partner with China and its partners continue to have little insight and influence on the details of Chinese aid allocation and results reporting. Although China remains actively engaged with other providers of South-South cooperation to jointly develop own reporting standards for development results, this process has been moving slowly.

Going forward, the SDGs provide sufficient room for policy entrepreneurs to foster the convergence of DAC donors and China in terms of reporting *development results* and harmonising monitoring and evaluation approaches. DAC donors have to achieve greater coherence and transparency in differentiating tiers of results (development results, development cooperation results, and performance) as well as purposes of results reporting (accountability, communication, direction, and learning) while upholding established aid effectiveness standards. China could increase its engagement for further defining South-South cooperation principles and standards while continuing its move towards more transparent and disaggregated reporting on its foreign aid. Moving into these directions again would be a way for OECD donors and China to better bridge the growing divide between the coordinative and communicative spheres of discourse, domestically as well as internationally. Yanguas (2018) suggests that there is a need for a new "moral vision" (Lumsdaine 1993) for aid that is based on "humane internationalism" through a better understanding and acknowledgement of the politics of aid.

For the potential coalition magnet idea of the *2030 Agenda*, there is already a broad corridor of convergence. Yet, policy entrepreneurs face the challenge of working across global, regional, and national levels in coordinated ways, constantly reframing the idea of the 2030 Agenda according to these contexts and in ways that enable engagement and awareness among the broader public. This challenge of cultivating collective action across multiple sectors and scales is interconnected with the challenges of making difficult trade-offs across SDG goals and finding ways to hold societal actors accountable for their influence on the SDGs (Bowen et al. 2017). On top of addressing these interconnected governance challenges, policy entrepreneurs are confronted to link the coordinative sphere of discourse of policy construction with the communicative sphere of discourse of deliberation, contestation, and legitimisation (Schmidt 2017).

Going forward, there are many cases where policy entrepreneurs can use the coalition magnet idea of the 2030 Agenda to achieve political change and foster multilateral cooperation. China's SDG report already states that

> China has strengthened economic dialogue and policy coordination with major economies including the US [United States], the EU [European Union], the UK [United Kingdom], France, Germany, India, Japan and Russia with a view to facilitating steady growth of the world economy and improving the development environment for developing countries. (China MOFA 2017, p. 76)

These efforts could be strengthened in line with "reciprocal peer-learning" (Mahn 2017; Pisano and Berger 2016), a learning process among equals. To achieve this goal, policy entrepreneurs have to build upon outreach activities started during the SDG negotiations and mobilise support around a continued global public conversation on the 2030 Agenda.

Overall, we have shown that each idea—mutual benefit, development results, and the 2030 Agenda—faces slightly different challenges in terms of coupling the coordinative and communicative spheres of discourse in addition to the increasing level of divergence between national-level politics and multilateralism. However, we also have demonstrated that each idea is already well anchored on the global and national levels, and if they are used strategically by policy entrepreneurs, they could link international norms to domestic processes of political and social change. Policy entrepreneurs, whether they are political leaders or social activists, need to be grounded in a deep understanding of the domestic context of each country—where they want to achieve political outcomes—to couple the coordinative and communicative spheres of discourse.

10.6 Conclusion

We have shown that the concept of coalition magnet ideas is a useful framework for analysing the challenges of international development cooperation, particularly the positions of the OECD donors and China that are seemingly at odds. We have applied the framework to three ideas—mutual benefit, development results, and the 2030 Agenda—and have analysed how each idea could be strategically employed by policy entrepreneurs to foster convergence and political change. Furthermore, we have briefly outlined how policy entrepreneurs can be politically smart in fostering convergence in the current global context of development cooperation, linking the domestic and global levels of policy-making.

Based on our assessment of the three coalition magnet ideas, we draw the following conclusions about the role of ideas in fostering convergence among diverging policy preferences. First, coalition magnet ideas have the potential to bring DAC members and China together around policy prescriptions that fall into a broad corridor of national and international epistemic communities around respective coalition magnet ideas. For mutual benefit, we highlighted global public goods; for development results, we stressed nuanced results reporting; and for the 2030 Agenda, we identified reciprocal learning. Second, we sketched out how coalition magnet ideas can be effective tools for achieving policy change, even in a global environment that is characterised by nationalist tendencies. The key for policy entrepreneurs is to couple policy and communicative discourse through individually targeted policy messages.

Finally, our chapter is only a first general application of the concept of coalition magnet ideas to development cooperation in OECD-DAC countries and China. We have not focused on any discussions "beyond aid" (Janus et al. 2015; Lin and Wang 2016) for instance, which see development cooperation in a larger context of multilateral engagement across many policy areas and communities, such as private-sector actors or trade and investment relations. Hence, further research on mapping coalition magnets across different policy areas and forms of international cooperation could be the next step.

Second, we have not unpacked the detailed processes of how ideas become coalition magnet ideas at the domestic and international levels, beyond the stage of agenda-setting towards implementing policies that lead to actual political change. In particular, it would be pertinent to analyse to what extent policy entrepreneurs from OECD countries and China are able to couple the communicative and coordinative spheres of discourse across domestic and international audiences and epistemic communities. Thus, causal process tracing (Bennett and Checkel 2014; Jacobs 2013) of coalition magnet ideas on the domestic level could be a way to deepen our understanding of how some ideas become influential, while others do not. Third, the examples in this analysis focused on governmental actors driving political change from the top. Additional research could also consider the role of non-governmental actors and social mobilisation around coalition magnet ideas.

NOTES

1. We use the terms "OECD-DAC donors", "OECD donors", and "DAC donors" synonymously in this chapter to refer to the 30 countries that are members of the OECD-DAC and report their aid according to the official development assistance definition.
2. In addition to the definition of "discourse", based on discursive institutionalism, we understand "development discourse" according to Apthorpe and Des Gasper, who state that development discourse "as a field lacks clear boundaries, since development and development studies have none either, and further that the types of discourse in them are not all of one type" (Apthorpe and Gasper 2014, p. 168). In total, they differentiate between five different major uses of "development discourse", out of which "development policy discourse" and "discourse

of leading international development donors" are closest to the interests of this analysis.
3. For a more detailed analysis of power, including ideational power, see Blyth (2016), Carstensen and Schmidt (2016), Parsons (2016), and Widmaier (2016).
4. Similarly, Kingdon (1984) speaks about policy entrepreneurs being able to couple three streams—problem, policy, and political—through advocacy and brokerage during windows of opportunity.
5. Country programmable aid tracks the proportion of bilateral aid over which recipients have or could have significant say; 21 out 30 DAC member countries reduced their volume of country programmable aid between 2010 and 2015 (OECD 2017).
6. Since 2011, bilateral ODA flows to LDCs have fallen; 19 out of 30 DAC members provided less ODA to LDCs in 2015 than in 2010.

References

Ahluwalia, M. S., Summers, L., Velasco, A., Birdsall, C. N., & Morris, S. (2016). *Multilateral development banking for this century's development challenges*. Washington, DC: Center for Global Development.

Alesina, A., & Dollar, D. (2000). Who gives foreign aid to whom and why? *Journal of Economic Growth, 5*(1), 33–63.

Allison, G. (2017). *Destined for war: Can America and China escape Thucydides's trap?* Boston, MA: Houghton Mifflin Harcourt.

Anand, P. B. (2004). Financing the provision of global public goods. *The World Economy, 27*(2), 215–237.

Ang, Y. Y. (2016). *How China escaped the poverty trap*. London and Ithaca, NY: Cornell University Press.

Apthorpe, R., & Gasper, D. (2014). *Arguing development policy: Frames and discourses*. London and New York, NY: Routledge.

Baum, W., & Tolbert, S. (1985). Investing in development: Lessons of World Bank experience. *Finance and Development, 22*(4), 25.

Béland, D. (2005). Ideas and social policy: An institutionalist perspective. *Social Policy & Administration, 39*(1), 1–18.

Béland, D., & Cox, R. H. (2010). *Ideas and politics in social science research*. Oxford: Oxford University Press.

Béland, D., & Cox, R. H. (2016). Ideas as coalition magnets: Coalition building, policy entrepreneurs, and power relations. *Journal of European Public Policy, 23*(3), 428–445.

Bell, S. (2011). Do we really need a new "constructivist institutionalism" to explain institutional change? *British Journal of Political Science, 41*(4), 883–906.

Bennett, A., & Checkel, J. T. (2014). *Process tracing*. Cambridge: Cambridge University Press.

Berthélemy, J. C. (2006). Bilateral donors' interest vs. recipients' development motives in aid allocation: Do all donors behave the same? *Review of Development Economics, 10*(2), 179–194.

Besharati, N. A. (2017). *New development finance measure should be TOSSD out the window!* (Policy Insights 45). Johannesburg: South African Institute of International Affairs.

Bexell, M., & Jönsson, K. (2017). Responsibility and the United Nations' sustainable development goals. *Forum for Development Studies, 44*(1), 13–29.

Bickerton, C. J., Hodson, D., & Puetter, U. (2015). The new intergovernmentalism: European integration in the post-maastricht era. *JCMS: Journal of Common Market Studies, 53*(4), 703–722.

Blyth, M. (2016). The new ideas scholarship in the mirror of historical institutionalism: A case of old whines in new bottles? *Journal of European Public Policy, 23*(3), 464–471.

Bowen, K. J., Cradock-Henry, N. A., Koch, F., Patterson, J., Häyhä, T., Vogt, J., et al. (2017). Implementing the "Sustainable Development Goals": Towards addressing three key governance challenges—Collective action, trade-offs, and accountability. *Current Opinion in Environmental Sustainability, 26*, 90–96.

Bräutigam, D. (2011). Aid "with Chinese characteristics": Chinese foreign aid and development finance meet the OECD-DAC aid regime. *Journal of International Development, 23*(5), 752–764.

Callahan, W. A. (2013). *China dreams: 20 visions of the future*. Oxford: Oxford University Press.

Campbell, J. L. (2002). Ideas, politics, and public policy. *Annual Review of Sociology, 28*(1), 21–38.

Carstensen, M. B., & Schmidt, V. A. (2016). Power through, over and in ideas: Conceptualizing ideational power in discursive institutionalism. *Journal of European Public Policy, 23*(3), 318–337.

Cepparulo, A., & Giuriato, L. (2016). Responses to global challenges: Trends in aid-financed global public goods. *Development Policy Review, 34*(4), 483–507.

Chen, X. (2017). *Win-win cooperation: Formation, development and characteristics*. http://www.ciis.org.cn/english/2017-11/17/content_40072596.htm.

Chin, G. T. (2012). China as a "net donor": Tracking dollars and sense. *Cambridge Review of International Affairs, 25*(4), 579–603.

Chin, G., Pearson, M. M., & Yong, W. (2013). Introduction—IPE with China's characteristics. *Review of International Political Economy, 20*(6), 1145–1164.

Chin, G., & Quadir, F. (2012). Introduction: Rising states, rising donors and the global aid regime. *Cambridge Review of International Affairs, 25*(4), 493–506.

China MOFA. (2017). *China's progress report on implementation of the 2030 Agenda for Sustainable Development*. http://www.fmprc.gov.cn/web/ziliao_674904/zt_674979/dnzt_674981/qtzt/2030kcxfzyc_686343/P020170824650025885740.pdf.

China Ministry of Commerce. (2014). *Regulations on China's foreign aid management (trial)*. http://www.mofcom.gov.cn/article/b/c/201411/20141100799438.shtml. English: http://www.cn.undp.org/content/china/en/home/library/south-south-cooperation/measures-for-the-administration-of-foreign-aid-.html.

China MOFA (China Ministry of Foreign Affairs). (2016). *National plan on implementation of the 2030 Agenda for Sustainable Development*. http://www.fmprc.gov.cn/mfa_eng/zxxx_662805/W020161014332600482185.pdf.

China State Council. (2011). *China's foreign aid*. http://english.gov.cn/archive/white_paper/2014/09/09/content_281474986284620.htm.

China State Council. (2014). *China's foreign aid*. http://english.gov.cn/archive/white_paper/2014/08/23/content_281474982986592.htm.

Chun, Z. (2017). The Belt and Road Initiative and global governance in transition. *China Quarterly of International Strategic Studies, 3*(2), 175–191.

Collier, P. (2013). *Aid as a catalyst for pioneer investment* (WIDER Working Paper No. 2013/004). Helsinki: United Nations University World Institute for Development Economics Research.

Collier, P. (2016). *The ethical foundations of aid: Two duties of rescue* (BSG Working Paper 2016/016). Oxford: Blavatnik School of Government.

Ding, S. (2010). Analyzing rising power from the perspective of soft power: A new look at China's rise to the status quo power. *Journal of Contemporary China, 19*(64), 255–272.

Dongxiao, C., Esteves, P., Martinez, E., & Scholz, I. (2017). *Implementation of the 2030 Agenda by G20 members: How to address the transformative and integrated character of the SDGs by individual and collective action.* http://www.g20-insights.org/policy_briefs/implementation-2030-agenda-g20-members-address-transformative-integrated-character-sdgs-individual-collective-action/.

Dreher, A., Eichenauer, V. Z., & Gehring, K. (2016). Geopolitics, aid, and growth: The impact of UN security council membership on the effectiveness of aid. *The World Bank Economic Review, 32*(2), 268–286.

Eyben, R., Guijt, I., Roche, C., & Shutt, C. (2015). *The politics of evidence and results in international development: Playing the game to change the rules.* Rugby: Practical Action Publishing.

Feng, Y. (2016). *Ideas as domestic factors in the formation of China's multilateralist foreign policies: Cases of WTO, ASEAN+ 3 and SCO* (dissertation). Brussels: Université Libre de Bruxelles.

Fligstein, N., & McAdam, D. (2012). *A theory of fields.* Oxford: Oxford University Press.

Fues, T., & Ye, J. (2014). *The United Nations post-2015 agenda for global development: Perspectives from China and Europe.* Bonn: German Development Institute/Deutsches Institut für Entwicklungspolitik (DIE).

Gill, B., & Huang, Y. (2006). Sources and limits of Chinese "soft power". *Survival, 48*(2), 17–36.

Gills, B. (2017). The future of development from global crises to global convergence. *Forum for Development Studies, 44*(1), 155–161.

Gilpin, R. (1983). *War and change in world politics.* Cambridge: Cambridge University Press.

Grimm, S. (2014). China-Africa cooperation: Promises, practice and prospects. *Journal of Contemporary China, 23*(90), 993–1011.

Grimm, S., Rank, R., Schickerling, E., & McDonald, M. (2011). *Transparency of Chinese aid: An analysis of the published information on Chinese external financial flows.* Stellenbosch: Centre for Chinese Studies.

Gulrajani, N. (2017). Bilateral donors and the age of the national interest: What prospects for challenge by development agencies? *World Development, 96*, 375–389.

Hackenesch, C. (2013). Aid donor meets strategic partner? The European Union's and China's relations with Ethiopia. *Journal of Current Chinese Affairs, 42*(1), 7–36.

Hale, T., Held, D., & Young, K. (2013). *Gridlock: Why global cooperation is failing when we need it most.* Cambridge: Polity Press.

Hay, C. (2006a). Constructivist institutionalism. In S. A. Binder, R. A. W. Rhodes, & B. A. Rockman (Eds.), *The Oxford handbook of political institutions.* Oxford: Oxford University Press. https://doi.org/10.1093/oxfordhb/9780199548460.003.0004.

Hay, C. (2006b). Political ontology. In R. E. Goodin & C. Tilly (Eds.), *The Oxford handbook of contextual political analysis* (pp. 78–96). Oxford: Oxford University Press.

Holzapfel, S. (2016). Boosting or hindering aid effectiveness? An assessment of systems for measuring donor agency results. *Public Administration and Development, 36*(1), 3–19.

Hood, C. (1991). A public management for all seasons. *Public Administration, 69*(1), 3–19.

Howlett, M., Ramesh, M., & Perl, A. (2009). *Studying public policy: Policy cycles and policy subsystems* (Vol. 3). Oxford: Oxford University Press.

Hulme, D. (2016). *Should rich nations help the poor?* Hoboken, NJ: Wiley.

Jacobs, A. M. (2013). Process-tracing the effects of ideas. In A. Bennett & J. T. Checkel (Eds.), *Process tracing: From metaphor to analytic tool* (pp. 41–73). Cambridge: Cambridge University Press.

Janus, H., & Klingebiel, S. (2014). Results-based aid: Potential and limits of an innovative modality in development cooperation. *International Development Policy/Revue internationale de politique de développement, 5.2.* https://journals.opene dition.org/poldev/1746.

Janus, H., Klingebiel, S., & Paulo, S. (2015). Beyond aid: A conceptual perspective on the transformation of development cooperation. *Journal of International Development, 27*(2), 155–169.

Jessop, B. (2001). Institutional re(turns) and the strategic–relational approach. *Environment and Planning A, 33*(7), 1213–1235.

Johnston, A. I. (2017). Is Chinese nationalism rising? Evidence from Beijing. *International Security, 41*(3), 7–43.

Johnston, L., & Rudyak, M. (2017). China's "innovative and pragmatic" foreign aid: Shaped by and now shaping globalisation. In L. Song, R. Garnaut, C. Fang, & L. Johnston (Eds.), *China's new sources of economic growth: Vol. 2: Human capital, innovation and technological change* (pp. 431–452). Acton: Australian National University Press.

Kaul, I., Grunberg, I., & Stern, M. A. (1999). Global public goods: Concepts, policies and strategies. In I. Kaul & I. Grunberg (Eds.), *Global public goods: International cooperation in the 21st century* (pp. 450–508). Oxford and New York, NY: Oxford University Press.

Kearn, D. W., Jr. (2008). A hard case for soft power: China's rise and security in East Asia. *Journal of Asian Politics and History, 3*(5), 1–26.

Keijzer, N., & Lundsgaarde, E. (2017). *When unintended effects become intended: Implications of "mutual benefit" discourses for development studies and evaluation practices* (Working Paper). Nijmegen: Ministry of Foreign Affairs of the Netherlands, and Radboud University.

Kenny, C., Snyder, M., & Patel, D. (2018). *Measures of global public goods and international spillovers* (Working Paper No. 474). Washington, DC: Center for Global Development.

Kingdon, J. W. (1984). *Agendas, alternatives, and public policies* (Vol. 45). Boston, MA: Little, Brown.

Kitano, N., & Harada, Y. (2016). Estimating China's foreign aid 2001–2013. *Journal of International Development, 28*(7), 1050–1074.

Knoll, A., & Sheriff, A. (2017). *Making waves: Implications of the irregular migration and refugee situation on official development assistance spending and practices in Europe* (EBA reports 2017:01). Stockholm: The Expert Group for Aid Studies.

Kragelund, P. (2015). Towards convergence and cooperation in the global development finance regime: Closing Africa's policy space? *Cambridge Review of International Affairs, 28*(2), 246–262.

Laclau, E. (1996). *Emancipation(s)*. London and New York, NY: Verso.

Lee, P. S. (2016). The rise of China and its contest for discursive power. *Global Media and China, 1*(1–2), 102–120.

Li, X. (2012). *Agricultural development in China and Africa: A comparative analysis*. London: Routledge.

Li, X., Banik, D., Tang, L., & Wu, J. (2014). Difference or indifference: China's development assistance unpacked. *IDS Bulletin, 45*(4), 22–35.

Li, X., & Carey, R. (2014). *The BRICS and the international development system: Challenge and convergence?* (IDS Evidence Report 58). Brighton: Institute of Development Studies.

Li, X., Gu, J., Leistner, S., & Cabral, L. (2018). Perspectives on the global partnership for effective development cooperation. *IDS Bulletin, 49*(3), 145–166.

Li, X., & Zhou, T. (2016). Achieving the sustainable development goals: The role for the G20 from China's perspective. *China & World Economy, 24*(4), 55–72.

Lin, J. Y., & Wang, Y. (2016). *Going beyond aid: Development cooperation for structural transformation*. Cambridge: Cambridge University Press.

Luce, E. (2017). *The retreat of Western liberalism*. New York, NY: Atlantic Monthly Press.

Lumsdaine, D. H. (1993). *Moral vision in international politics: The foreign aid regime, 1949–1989*. Princeton, NJ: Princeton University Press.

Mahn, T. C. (2017). *Accountability for development cooperation under the 2030 Agenda* (Discussion Paper 10/2017). Bonn: German Development Institute/Deutsches Institut für Entwicklungspolitik (DIE).

Mawdsley, E. (2017a). Development geography 1: Cooperation, competition and convergence between "North" and "South". *Progress in Human Geography, 41*(1), 108–117.

Mawdsley, E. (2017b). National interests and the paradox of foreign aid under austerity: Conservative governments and the domestic politics of international development since 2010. *The Geographical Journal, 183*(3), 223–232.

Mawdsley, E., Murray, W. E., Overton, J., Scheyvens, R., & Banks, G. (2016). Exporting stimulus and "shared prosperity": Re-inventing foreign aid for a retroliberal era. *Development Policy Review, 36*(S1), O25–O43.

Mbeva, K., & Pauw, W. (2016). *Self-differentiation of countries' responsibilities* (Discussion Paper 4/2016). Bonn: German Development Institute/Deutsches Institut für Entwicklungspolitik (DIE).

Mearsheimer, J. J. (2010). The gathering storm: China's challenge to US power in Asia. *The Chinese Journal of International Politics, 3*(4), 381–396.

Minogue, M., Polidano, C., & Hulme, D. (1998). *Beyond the new public management*. Cheltenham: Edward Elgar.

Minoiu, C., & Reddy, S. G. (2010). Development aid and economic growth: A positive long-run relation. *The Quarterly Review of Economics and Finance, 50*(1), 27–39.

Morriss, P. (2006). Steven Lukes on the concept of power. *Political Studies Review, 4*(2), 124–135.

Murray, W. E., & Overton, J. (2016). Retroliberalism and the new aid regime of the 2010s. *Progress in Development Studies, 16*(3), 244–260.

Nordin, A. H., & Weissmann, M. (2017). Will Trump make China great again? The Belt and Road Initiative and international order. *International Affairs, 94*(2), 231–249.

Nye, J. S. (2004). *Soft power: The means to success in world politics.* New York, NY: Public Affairs.

OECD. (2016). *Better policies for 2030: An OECD action plan on the sustainable development goals.* http://www.oecd.org/dac/Better%20Policies%20for%202030.pdf.

OECD. (2017). *Development co-operation report 2017: Data for development.* Paris: OECD Publishing.

OECD (Organisation for Economic Co-operation and Development). (2005/2008). *The Paris Declaration on Aid Effectiveness and the Accra Agenda for Action.* https://www.oecd.org/dac/effectiveness/34428351.pdf.

OECD & United Nations Development Programme. (2016). *Making development co-operation more effective: 2016 progress report.* Paris: OECD Publishing.

Parsons, C. (2016). Ideas and power: Four intersections and how to show them. *Journal of European Public Policy, 23*(3), 446–463.

Paul, E. (2015). Performance-based aid: Why it will probably not meet its promises. *Development Policy Review, 33*(3), 313–323.

Pisano, U., & Berger, G. (2016). *Exploring peer learning to support the implementation of the 2030 Agenda for SD* (Quarterly Report 40). Vienna: European Sustainable Development Network.

Qian, Y. (2017). *How reform worked in China: The transition from plan to market.* Cambridge, MA: MIT Press.

Radaelli, C. M. (2006). Europeanization: Solution or problem? In M. Cini & A. K. Bourne (Eds.), *Palgrave advances in European Union studies* (pp. 56–76). New York, NY: Springer.

Rawnsley, G. D. (2016). Reflections of a soft power agnostic. In X. Zhang, H. Wasserman, & W. Mano (Eds.), *China's media and soft power in Africa* (pp. 19–31). New York, NY: Springer.

Reilly, J. (2012). A norm-taker or a norm-maker? Chinese aid in Southeast Asia. *Journal of Contemporary China, 21*(73), 71–91.

Risse-Kappen, T. (1994). Ideas do not float freely: Transnational coalitions, domestic structures, and the end of the Cold War. *International Organization, 48*(2), 185–214.

Rowlands, D. (2012). Individual BRICS or a collective bloc? Convergence and divergence amongst "emerging donor" nations. *Cambridge Review of International Affairs, 25*(4), 629–649.

Schmidt, V. A. (2008). Discursive institutionalism: The explanatory power of ideas and discourse. *Annual Review of Political Science, 11,* 303–326.

Schmidt, V. A. (2010). Taking ideas and discourse seriously: Explaining change through discursive institutionalism as the fourth "new institutionalism". *European Political Science Review, 2*(01), 1–25.

Schmidt, V. A. (2011). Speaking of change: Why discourse is key to the dynamics of policy transformation. *Critical Policy Studies, 5*(2), 106–126.

Schmidt, V. A. (2017). Britain-out and Trump-in: A discursive institutionalist analysis of the British referendum on the EU and the US presidential election. *Review of International Political Economy, 24*(2), 248–269.

Shambaugh, D. (2015). China's soft-power push: The search for respect. *Foreign Affairs, 94*(4), 99–107.

Shi-Kupfer, K., Ohlberg, M., Lang, S., & Lang, B. (2017). *Ideas and ideologies competing for China's political future* (MERICS Paper on China No. 5). Berlin: Mercator Institute for China Studies.

Sidiropoulos, E., Pineda, J. A. P., Chaturvedi, S., & Fues, T. (2015). *Institutional architecture and development: Responses from emerging powers*. Johannesburg: South African Institute of International Affairs.

Sørensen, C. T. (2015). The significance of Xi Jinping's "Chinese Dream" for Chinese foreign policy: From "Tao Guang Yang Hui" to "Fen Fa You Wei". *Journal of China and International Relations, 3*(1), 53–73.

Strange, A. M., Dreher, A., Fuchs, A., Parks, B., & Tierney, M. J. (2017). Tracking underreported financial flows: China's development finance and the aid–conflict nexus revisited. *Journal of Conflict Resolution, 61*(5), 935–963.

Turner, M., Hulme, D., & McCourt, W. (2015). *Governance, management and development: Making the state work*. Basingstoke: Palgrave Macmillan.

United Nations General Assembly. (2009). *The Nairobi outcome document of the High-Level United Nations Conference on South-South Cooperation*. https://digitallibrary.un.org/record/673444.

United Nations General Assembly. (2015). *Transforming our world: The 2030 Agenda for Sustainable Development*. https://www.unfpa.org/sites/default/files/resource-pdf/Resolution_A_RES_70_1_EN.pdf.

United Nations General Assembly. (2019). *Buenos Aires outcome document of the Second High-Level United Nations Conference on South-South Cooperation*. https://digitallibrary.un.org/record/3801900?ln=enbly.

Varrall, M. (2013). Chinese views on China's role in international development assistance. *Pacific Affairs, 86*(2), 233–255.

Vazquez, K., Xiaojin, M., & Yao, S. (2016). *Mix and match? How countries deliver development cooperation and lessons for China*. United Nations Development Programme and the Chinese Academy of International Trade and Economic Cooperation. http://dspace.jgu.edu.in:8080/jspui/bitstream/10739/1003/1/UNDP-CH-SSC-%20Mix%20and%20Match%20How%20Countries%20Deliver%20Development%20Cooperation%20and%20Lessons%20for%20China.pdf.

Wang, H. (2014). *From "taoguang yanghui" to "yousuo zuowei": China's engagement in financial minilateralism* (CIGI Papers No. 52). Waterloo: Centre for International Governance Innovation.

Wang, Q. K., & Blyth, M. (2013). Constructivism and the study of international political economy in China. *Review of International Political Economy, 20*(6), 1276–1299.

Widmaier, W. (2016). The power of economic ideas—Through, over and in—Political time: The construction, conversion and crisis of the neoliberal order in the US and UK. *Journal of European Public Policy, 23*(3), 338–356.

Woods, N. (2008). Whose aid? Whose influence? China, emerging donors and the silent revolution in development assistance. *International Affairs, 84*(6), 1205–1221.

Xi, J. (2017, October 18). Report at 19th Communist Party of China national congress. *China Daily*. http://www.chinadaily.com.cn/china/19thcpcnationalcongress/2017-11/04/content_34115212.htm.

Yang, J. (2018). The 19th CPC national congress and China's major country diplomacy in the new era. *QiuShi Journal, 10*(34). http://english.qstheory.cn/2018-02/11/c_1122395899.htm.

Yanguas, P. (2017). The role and responsibility of foreign aid in recipient political settlements. *Journal of International Development, 29*(2), 211–228.

Yanguas, P. (2018). *Why we lie about aid: Development and the messy politics of change*. London: Zed Books.

Younis, M. (2013). *Rising powers in international development—Report from the series of events held by IDS and partners in Johannesburg preceding the 5th BRICS summit in March 2013* (Evidence Report 24). https://opendocs.ids.ac.uk/opendocs/bitstream/handle/123456789/2948/ER24%20Final%20Online.pdf?sequence=1.

Zhang, Y., Gu, J., & Chen, Y. (2015). *Rising powers in international development—China's engagement in international development cooperation: The state of the debate* (Evidence Report 116). https://opendocs.ids.ac.uk/opendocs/bitstream/handle/123456789/5838/ER116_ChinasEngagementinInternationalDevelopmentCooperationTheStateoftheDebate.pdf?sequence=1&isAllowed=y.

Zhou, E. (1964). *The Chinese government's eight principles for economic aid and technical assistance to other countries*. http://digitalarchive.wilsoncenter.org/document/121560.

Zhou, T. (2016). *Evaluating South-South development cooperation: China's approach and trends*. Seoul: Korea Development Institute and The Asia Foundation.

Zhou, T., & Zhang, H. (2018). China's Belt and Road Initiative: An opportunity to re-energize South-South cooperation. *China Quarterly of International Strategic Studies, 4*(4), 559–576.

Zwart, R. (2017). *Strengthening the results chain: Synthesis of case studies of results-based management by providers* (OECD Development Policy Papers, No. 7). Paris: OECD Publishing.

Open Access This chapter is licensed under the terms of the Creative Commons Attribution 4.0 International License (http://creativecommons.org/licenses/by/4.0/), which permits use, sharing, adaptation, distribution and reproduction in any medium or format, as long as you give appropriate credit to the original author(s) and the source, provide a link to the Creative Commons license and indicate if changes were made.

The images or other third party material in this chapter are included in the chapter's Creative Commons license, unless indicated otherwise in a credit line to the material. If material is not included in the chapter's Creative Commons license and your intended use is not permitted by statutory regulation or exceeds the permitted use, you will need to obtain permission directly from the copyright holder.

PART III

Measurements of Development Cooperation: Theories and Frameworks

CHAPTER 11

Measuring Development Cooperation and the Quality of Aid

Ian Mitchell

11.1 Introduction

It is clear from other chapters of this book, in particular that of Gerardo Bracho, that the mechanisms for effective development cooperation between countries—either through the Global Partnership for Effective Development Cooperation (GPEDC), the Organisation for Economic Co-operation and Development (OECD), or the United Nations (UN)—are currently uncertain, or contested. But progress can be made on *measuring* what countries are doing in different areas of cooperation. One of the major constraints Bracho highlights to deeper collaboration relates to whether all countries have "the same responsibilities as traditional donors" in the effectiveness agenda and whether each should be "subject to practically the same scrutiny" (Bracho 2021, Chapter 17). However, even before we consider respective countries' responsibilities and scrutiny, we can at least try and measure the contributions of different countries to development on a consistent basis. Such a measurement would have value in a number of dimensions. First, it would enable countries to understand what they are contributing to development in absolute terms. Second, it enables comparison and learning between different approaches. Third, it can give a measure of the potential for improvement. Fourth, it can enable scrutiny of these areas to drive improvement, and finally, it can provide the underlying measures to enable contributions to be assessed against responsibilities. This chapter aims to take stock of our ability

---

I. Mitchell (✉)
Center for Global Development, London, UK
e-mail: imitchell@cgdev.org

to measure contributions to effective development cooperation across different countries.

What do we mean by "development cooperation"? The principle I use here is that "development cooperation" refers to a country's policies and how these affect the current and future welfare and growth of other countries' people and economies.[1] So, even countries that do not have an explicit policy towards other countries are included because their policies—for example, on climate, migration, and trade—have a bearing on people elsewhere, regardless of their intent. In this respect, all countries are global citizens and have a development impact that can be measured. This is consistent with the universality (i.e. applying to all) of the Sustainable Development Goals (SDGs) and the 2030 Agenda for Sustainable Development, which sets the framework on the goals, targets, and measures applying to, and agreed on, by all countries.

In order for development cooperation measurement to be meaningful, it needs to be undertaken with reference to the "size" of the country being measured. Taking greenhouse gas emissions as an example, it is clear that—all else being equal—a more populous country will emit a greater absolute volume, so measuring that country's effort will mean calculating a per head figure. Similar arguments can be made for "aid", which is measured relative to the size of the economy. Using measures relative to country size can enable comparisons between countries at different income and population levels. Of course, this means that absolute contributions of countries are ignored. So, although the United States is the largest absolute aid donor, its government gives relatively little compared to the size of its economy. The absolute contribution (see below) is what matters for global impact, but when it comes to the measurement and comparison of efforts, this must be scaled by an appropriate measure of the relevant size of the country.

Differences in citizens' footprints in individual countries notwithstanding, the largest (often the most populous) economies are likely to have the largest absolute spillovers on other countries—for that reason, their development cooperation should be of greatest interest to us. If the level of a country's income means it should take a greater responsibility for its impacts, then the top right of Fig. 11.1 illustrates those countries of greatest interest.

The chart demonstrates that the G20—formed broadly on the basis of the size of members' economies—is still essentially the largest economies,[2] and that the vast majority of countries with higher incomes are predominantly members of the OECD. Together, the G20 and OECD countries produce around 90 per cent of global GDP, and likely a similarly substantial portion of transboundary spillovers.

Note that we do not consider the actions of private actors in this analysis. This is not that the private sector is unimportant, but rather that country governments set the framework for the private sector and—in assessing development cooperation—we are concerned with what governments do, or do not

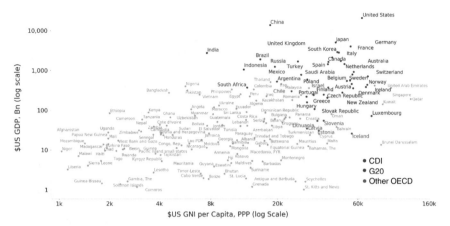

Fig. 11.1 Countries by absolute size of economy and relative average income level (*Notes* CDI refers to the [OECD] countries that the Center for Global Development (CGD) assessed in its 2018 Commitment to Development Index. The remaining G20 countries (in red) have been added to the 2020 edition as well as Chile, Israel and United Arab Emirates. *Source* Author's analysis; uses gross domestic product [GDP] and gross national income [2018 data] from the World Bank [2020])

do. However, the basic principle we discuss should also apply to companies—they should understand and measure where their activities in the market lead to spillover impacts on others outside the market. This would include energy companies quantifying their impacts on the climate, and tobacco companies quantifying their impacts on health. All companies should understand these impacts, as they are responsible for them. A promising initiative in this regard is the Global Reporting Initiative (2018), which helps to develop common standards for sustainability reporting. In my view, every company creating material spillovers should quantify these impacts in a move to "quantified corporate social responsibility".

But why do we need to measure development cooperation when we have the targets and indicators underpinning the SDGs? The 2030 Agenda and the SDGs are the globally agreed framework around development, but they are not focussed on what one country does for another, and they offer only a partial picture of development cooperation. The 17 SDGs are supported by targets and quantitative indicators. However, the clear majority of SDG indicators relate to national performance rather than transboundary or spillover effects (see Table 11.1). Of the 244 indicators supporting the SDGs, fewer than 30 per cent measure a "transboundary" effect. Even SDG 17 (Strengthen the means of implementation and revitalise the global partnership for sustainable development) has over a third of its 25 indicators focussed on national performance. The OECD has undertaken a similar exercise, focussing on the 169 targets in the SDGs. It finds that 169 (57 per cent) can be described as

Table 11.1 SDG indicators focussed on international spillovers and cooperation

	Total indicator measures[a]	Indicators that measure international: Spillover or cooperation	Cooperation only
All SDGs	244	70 (29%)	37 (15%)
SDG 17 (global partnership)	25	16 (64%)	6 (24%)

[a]This includes, respectively, 50 (all SDGs) and 6 (SDG 17) where no internationally established methodology or standards are yet available for the indicator. SDG 17 is to "Strengthen the means of implementation and revitalize the global partnership for sustainable development". "Cooperation" was defined as indicators measuring an international intent
Source Author

having transboundary elements (Organisation for Economic Co-operation and Development [OECD] 2019). These indicators and targets therefore provide only a partial picture of development cooperation.

So what can we measure on development cooperation now, and what more do we need? The remainder of this chapter looks at the scope of what we should measure, considers the state of the measures in each area, and concludes with where future collaboration is needed.

11.2 Framework for Measuring Development Cooperation

Here, I consider development cooperation in three different, perhaps overlapping, areas,[3] which I think is helpful conceptually. First, *development finance*—including aid and concessional finance—can be provided by a government to another country to support its development. Second, *policies with bilateral international impacts*—in particular those related to the exchange of goods, capital, people, and ideas (such as trade and migration policy)—have impacts both domestically and in other countries, often with mutual benefits. Third, countries' actions contribute to, or detract from, *global public goods* (GPGs) (or regional ones)—in particular, on climate, but also in areas such as security. My colleague at CGD Charles Kenny has generated an illustrative (rather than exhaustive) list of 72 GPGs and examined their spatial and temporal distribution (Kenny et al. 2018) (Table 11.2).

Table 11.2 Development contributions and policies

Area	Description	Policies[b]
Development finance and aid[a]	Finance from governments that is provided below market rates or in grants for other countries	Funding including: • Multilateral agencies • Bilateral aid and finance
Policies with international impacts	Policies that affect the cross-border exchange of goods, people, capital, ideas	• Trade • Migration • Investment • Technology
Global public goods	Contributions to international issues that are of benefit to all (or most) countries	• Climate • Security • Knowledge • Health

[a]Development finance/aid is also a type of policy in the second area—policy with international impact—but is defined distinctly here as being costly to the provider government (whereas this is not a condition in the second area)
[b]These form an illustrative—not exhaustive—list of policies and, as noted above, may fall into more than one area
Source Author

The distinction between these three groups relates to the focus of the impact. The first two groups both relate to policies that bilaterally affect other countries. The first group—development finance—is broken out separately, as often its intention is to (positively) impact another country. In addition, development finance is often seen as a critical limiting factor in development and receives significant attention in development and the literature. The second group relates to policies that have a direct effect on a partner country and may or may not have a positive effect or mutually beneficial effect. The third group has impacts—intended or otherwise—that are international but affect several countries simultaneously, or have the characteristics of public goods or bads (i.e. countries cannot be excluded from their impacts and cannot diminish them). Table 11.3 elaborates on these descriptions with the domestic and international impacts.

We now consider each of these areas, in turn, and consider the most important areas to measure.

Table 11.3 Development contributions and impacts

	Impacts (incl. spillovers)		
	Domestic	Partner country	Global
Aid and concessional finance	Costly[a]	Positive	Mixed
Policy with international impacts	Mixed	Mixed	Mixed
Global public goods	Costly[a]	Mixed	Positive

[a]Although domestic efforts on concessional finance and GPGs do have domestic benefits, these are usually outweighed by the domestic costs. Were this not the case, they would not be, respectively, concessional, or public goods

Source Author

11.3 Development Finance, Aid, and Measuring Quality

In this section, we look at (i) measures of quantity of concessional aid/finance, (ii) what we know about effective development finance and, (iii) what measures we have available on quality.

11.3.1 *Measuring Concessional Development Finance and Aid Quantity*

Measuring the quantity of aid—or concessional development finance—requires a common definition. Most efforts and our starting point are to concentrate on the (net) concessional element of governments' grants or loans to other countries. Calculating this requires data that is consistent between countries and a common methodology to establish how concessional the lending is. For the 30 members of the OECD's Development Assistance Committee (DAC), both of these exist in defining official development assistance (ODA) and "other official flows", though the methodology remains contentious and arguably does not provide a consistent guide to the concessionality of development finance (OECD-DAC 2018). Still, the original aim of the DAC—to agree on standards in order to enable a fair comparison between countries of different economic sizes in supporting development and provide countries with good incentives to do so (Scott 2015)—remains highly relevant.

Beyond the DAC, there is no common data nor an agreed methodology on calculating concessional finance. There are valuable efforts to consistently and comprehensively measure *all* financial flows—in particular, the task force on Total Official Support for Sustainable Development (OECD-DAC, n.d.). In February 2019, the task force published "emerging reporting instructions"— so usable measures are therefore some way off, and in any case, they would not identify the degree of concessionality in that finance and may not be available for all countries.

To calculate an estimate of government concessional finance provided by each country, there seem to be several possibilities. First, we could use government budgets to calculate the cost—to the taxpayer—of a country's aid and development finance efforts.[4] This would reliably estimate the financial effort a country is making to support development, but it relies on there being publicly available information—suitably disaggregated accounts—on a country's overseas activities. Second, an important element of concessional finance is the funds provided to international development organisations. This could be limited to those "multilateral" institutions with open, accessible accounts or, ideally, also include bilateral agencies—see McArthur and Rasmussen (2018), for example. Third, countries could be surveyed to provide their own estimates of concessional finance. Fourth, if government development finance, and its terms, could be measured, the degree of concessionality could be calculated or estimated (AidData produces figures for China on this basis). A new paper by me and my colleagues combines these latter three approaches to generate a new measure of "Finance for International Development" which enables more consistent comparisons across countries (Mitchell et al. 2020).

On the "quantity" of concessional development finance then, there seem to be some possibilities for making estimates. These will produce imperfect or incomplete figures, but these estimates will perhaps incentivise countries to do better, or ideally to come together and agree on common definitions.

11.3.2 What Does Effective Development Finance Look Like?

It is clear from evaluation evidence that aid and development finance can be transformationally positive or, conversely, completely wasted, or even damaging. Waste can occur in spite of good intentions, where interventions turn out to be less effective at reducing poverty than expected, as was the case with microfinance (Roodman 2012, p. 2), or because effectiveness is subordinated to geopolitical or commercial interests, for example in the famous case of the Pergau Dam (Lankester 2012). Aid might also have unintended effects: there is evidence that American food aid prolongs civil conflict (Nunn and Qian 2014). However, aid can also have enormous positive effects. In just under 20 years, Gavi, the Vaccine Alliance says it has treated 0.7 billion children and prevented 10 million deaths, generating savings of $18 in healthcare costs, lost wages, and lost productivity for each $1 spent (Gavi, the Vaccine Alliance, n.d.).

Countries discussed "aid effectiveness"—specifically the high-level principles and practices by which aid is allocated—and reached agreements in Rome (2003), Paris (2005), Accra (2008), and Busan (2011) (OECD, n.d.-a). Over the past decade, the context altered significantly with, for example: the agreement of the SDGs; the shift in the world's major economies and concentrations of extreme poverty; and aid providers changing the instruments they use. The principles (OECD, n.d.-b) agreed at Busan were:

- *Ownership* of development priorities by developing countries: Countries should define the development model that they want to implement.
- *A focus on results*: Having a sustainable impact should be the driving force behind investments and efforts in development policy-making.
- *Partnerships* for development: Development depends on the participation of all actors and recognises the diversity and complementarity of their functions.
- *Transparency and shared responsibility*: Development cooperation must be transparent and accountable to all citizens.

Busan also gave birth to the GPEDC.[5] The GPEDC now collects data with indicators[6] grouped under these four principles. The GPEDC's online platform enables comparisons between "development partners", but for some countries, the data is thin, or non-existent (e.g. in the 2017 results, China scored 100 per cent for indicator 1a—"proportion of new development interventions draw their objectives from country-led results frameworks"—but this is based on just one country's response). The GPEDC does not attempt to aggregate the indicators into themes, nor overall scores; nor does it rank agencies or countries. We return to measures that do attempt to compare, combine, and rank below.

What does research say about the impact of development finance and the practices that enhance its effectiveness? Much research focusses on GDP growth as the variable of interest, although it is clear that much aid is not targeted at that outcome—in particular, humanitarian aid, which covers 12.8 per cent of aid for DAC countries (OECD, n.d.-c), is most needed where economies are shrinking. Still, in the case of increased levels of education and health, we would expect some positive impact on GDP, and perhaps regression-based analysis can provide insights on effective aid. Howarth (2017) provides a good overview of this literature and concludes:

> [T]here is very little evidence to support the "hard" sceptical view that aid actively harms growth. It is, however, now understood that aid is subject to diminishing returns, and increasing it beyond a certain proportion of a recipient's GDP may have a harmful effect. Expectations about what aid can achieve have also become more realistic.

We are currently undertaking a literature review on the evidence on the determinants of effective aid that will consider issues such as using (recipient) country systems, recipient ownership, predictability, and transparency as traits of aid associated with higher impacts. Similarly, the evidence is clear that tying aid—that is, requiring aid to be spent only with providers from your own country—reduces its effectiveness,[7] but it still features prominently in aid providers' commitments (Meeks, n.d.).

Which of these principles or practices can and should be measured? And how important are they? Below we move on to efforts to measure and aggregate measures of quality that attempt to bring these together by donor or agency.

11.3.3 Data Sources for Measuring Development Finance Effectiveness

The evidence and theory about aid effectiveness is all very well, but what can we actually measure?

There are just three main sources that can be used to measure elements of development finance quality consistently across a wide range of countries (OECD-only measures are discussed below). These are:

- GPEDC survey—collected 10 indicators under four themes[8];
- Listening to Leaders survey—AidData's (2018) survey has been done twice, 2017 and 2014, and it provides data on the level of "helpfulness" and "influence" for providers of development cooperation;
- The International Aid Transparency Initiative—which is a standard for open data publishing that is available to all countries as well as non-state donors, and it enables some analysis of a large proportion of aid.

We have already seen that the information on the quantity of concessional finance is limited, and that these sources provide a relatively limited picture of the quality of development finance.

The GPEDC survey measures indicators of development finance effectiveness but, as noted above, the results are dependent on response rates. In the 2016 round, this led to patchy coverage, at least in terms of being able to assess some major countries providing assistance—for example, some of China's results were based on just one response (we are awaiting the details of the 2018 results). In addition, many Southern providers are averse to efforts to define, monitor, and compare development cooperation measures for both political and technical reasons (Besharati and MacFeely 2019). AidData's (2018) Listening to Leaders survey measures the views of leaders in low- and middle-income countries, but it is not a direct measure of aid effectiveness. The International Aid Transparency Initiative, which also feeds into the GPEDC's monitoring framework, improves transparency by hosting a machine-readable database of aid projects, and it gives cross-country comparisons of transparency in its published statistics. Publish What You Fund used this, along with other information, to create the Aid Transparency Index (Publish What You Fund 2018), which gives more detail on transparency for large donors. Transparency is likely to encourage scrutiny and lead to more effective behaviours, though it says little about the effectiveness of development finance more generally.

In addition to these measures, there are assessments being undertaken on the effectiveness of international organisations that receive aid. The

Multilateral Organisation Performance Assessment Network provides institutional scores in four areas of organisational effectiveness but also covers "results" (development effectiveness).[9] In addition, the Australian government (Australian Government & Australian AID 2012), the Ministry of Foreign Affairs of Denmark (2013), and the United Kingdom government (UK Government & Department for International Development 2011, 2013), among others, have undertaken and published their own reviews of multilateral organisations. Still, even if these reviews produce "ratings", they largely reflect qualitative analysis. Furthermore, they are limited to multilateral organisations and are not available for countries own ("bilateral") agencies. Still, to the extent that we know how much countries contribute to these organisations, we have some ways of assessing the "quality" of those contributions.

For OECD-DAC countries, and for the multilateral institutions that spend ODA, it is possible to calculate a number of aid effectiveness indicators using the OECD's "Creditor Reporting System". These indicators can relate to theory, evidence, or consensus about how they relate to quality. For these countries, the common reporting standard (CRS) provides a relatively comprehensive and comparable source of data at the project level to show where aid goes, the level of financial commitments and disbursements, what purposes it serves, and some descriptive information. However, it is up to the user of the data to conceptualise how these variables can be manipulated and analysed to produced aid quality indicators. Notably, many emerging development actors and providers of South-South cooperation do not report to the DAC, so CRS data is not available about them.

OECD-DAC countries also undertake systematic peer reviews, and these draw on quantitative measures as well as undertake qualitative assessments of development effectiveness. These are an important source of scrutiny, challenge, and mutual learning, and they often achieve high levels of engagement from ministers. Since the reviews follow a framework, it may be possible to systematically assess the findings across reviews—for example, on the elements of evaluation framework—and assign a quantitative score to the analysis.

So, for the 30 OECD-DAC countries and the group of around 13 countries that report to the DAC (OECD 2018a), relatively detailed data exists or can be feasibly created with publicly available data, but beyond these countries we have very limited quantitative information on the characteristics of their concessional development finance. Some admirable efforts have been made to use publicly available data to estimate the concessional element of development finance from Southern cooperation providers (United Nations Development Programme 2016) and also to identify six process and six outcome quality assessment guidelines. These are important efforts and, given the likely importance of transparency to effectiveness, Southern actors can surely accelerate progress towards the SDGs by providing common and consistent data on their concessional finance.

11.3.4 Quantifying Aid Quality

There have been relatively few attempts to quantitatively measure aid quality. Roodman (2013) developed a three-part aid quality measure that took a given quantity of aid and discounted it for tied aid, selectivity for less-poor and poorly governed recipient countries, and project proliferation. The resulting "quality-adjusted aid quantity" was used in the Commitment to Development Index through 2013. Easterly and Pfutze (2008) assessed and ranked 48 agencies quantitatively on aid "best practices" and included their own survey (with limited responses) regarding employment and administrative expenses to calculate overhead costs of agencies. Knack et al. (2010), in a World Bank policy research working paper, use a quantitative measure with 18 indicators using the Paris survey and OECD-DAC data. Birdsall and Kharas (2014) produced "QuODA", the quality of official development assistance, from 2010 (based on data from 2008), which put together 30 indicators of aid quality and grouped them under four themes that aligned with the Paris principles of aid effectiveness. This enabled agencies to compare their "scores" in each of these four areas. Subsequently, Barder et al. (2016) combined QuODA scores for bilateral and multilateral donors to produce an "Aid Quality Index", which was used in the Commitment to Development Index from 2014.

McKee and Mitchell (2018) produced an updated QuODA and were able to replicate or replace 24 indicators of aid effectiveness (see Annex A). Several of the original QuODA indicators were altered and replaced with GPEDC measures, which put a stronger emphasis on recipient views of aid (e.g. QuODA originally measured the effectiveness of recipients' evaluation systems, but in the updated version using GPEDC measures, it checks whether evaluations are planned with recipients). As before, QuODA was fed into the Commitment to Development Index as the measure of "aid quality", thereby giving even weight to each of the 24 indicators.

There are a number of significant limitations to these measures of aid quality including: heterogeneity in donor mandates and aid objectives whether there is any objective "optimum" allocation to aid recipients and whether fragmentation (allowing for greater competition and choice) or concentration (requiring less administrative burden) of donors is better for recipients (e.g. see Klingebiel et al. 2016). As noted above, there are limited direct links from measures of aid effectiveness to actual development impact. In the case of QuODA, a significant criticism is that it gives credit for aid going to poor and well-governed countries, but this runs counter to the need to give aid to fragile states, which are home to more than 60 per cent of the world's extreme poor, and this figure expected to rise further (OECD 2018b, p. 99). Indeed, this challenge also applies to a number of indicators, including those collected by the GPEDC, which tends to emphasise alignment to, or use of, recipient country systems and frameworks that may be weaker in fragile states.

11.3.5 Concluding on Measures of Aid Effectiveness

In terms of measuring aid quality, there is a stated international consensus on the principles of effective aid from 2011, but little sign that these are the foundation of aid allocation, nor of recent or high-level interest from governments. There are some areas where evidence gives a clear view of some types of aid being more effective, including: avoiding tied aid, giving transparently and predictably, and giving to poorer countries. Still, in other areas, there is a lack of evidence, and tensions between different priorities. For example, there is a tension between giving in well-governed countries versus fragile states, and there may be a tension between using recipient systems and preventing leakage, particularly in fragile states. There may also be a tension between impacts that are easier to measure precisely, and programmes aiming for more systemic change.

There are few individual or aggregate measures of aid quality covering all actors. Nonetheless, there would still be value in producing and, crucially, comparing them. These comparisons would enable providers to see how their own development finance compared to others, prompt questions about differences, and ultimately improve approaches through learning. For DAC donors, much greater detail is possible, and it seems right that countries with high incomes have greater responsibility and should be held to a higher level of accountability.

11.4 Policies with Bilateral International Impacts

In considering what countries can do in terms of development cooperation, the contribution of development finance and aid is only one part of the overall picture. "Beyond aid" there are a number of other policies that have a major bearing on development. This is often referred to as the "policy coherence for development" agenda, which emphasises the role of different policy areas in affecting development. Policies and their coherence for development are being recognised in achieving the SDGs (Knoll 2014). The role of policy beyond aid in development has long been recognised. Since 2003, the Commitment to Development Index, developed by David Roodman (2005) and Nancy Birdsall (and now directed by me with colleagues of the Center for Global Development), has identified policy areas that affect development. It now tracks countries' efforts in several policy areas, currently aid, environment, investment, migration, security, technology, and trade. Below, I expand on how policies matter in the flow of goods, people, finance, and ideas.

To illustrate the importance of policies beyond aid, consider China, which reduced the proportion of its population living on less than $1.90 per day from 66 to 0.7 per cent in only 25 years to 2015 (World Bank, n.d.-a), although it had benefitted from very little aid.[10] Crucial elements of this transformation included domestic market reform and access to global markets, including membership in the World Trade Organization (Subramanian and Wei 2003).

Trade policy, then, is a crucial determinant in development. The substantial liberalisation of trade policy and the reduction in agricultural subsidies over the past four decades are likely to have played a key role in providing an international trade environment conducive to development. Of course, the recent trade disputes between the United States and China, along with the United Kingdom stepping back from its deep trade relationship with the European Union, illustrate that this environment is under threat, or even in reverse. As emerging economies grow, their markets and trade policies will be increasingly important to the development of others.

Migration is an area that has traditionally received less attention as a policy for development, often due to concerns with "brain drain". My colleague Michael Clemens has refuted the idea that migration harms developing countries via a "brain drain" (Clemens 2009). He shows that 94 per cent of the countries that grew to middle-income status or higher between 1960 and 2013 also saw an increase in the proportion of their population emigrating (Clemens 2017, p. 5). Often the impacts on migrants themselves are forgotten in discussions of development and migration. Work by Clemens and Lant Pritchett shows that simply by moving from a poor country to a rich one, people can increase their incomes by 700–1000 per cent (Clemens 2011). This effect is a multiple of effective aid programmes (Pritchett 2016). The importance of migration is also illustrated through the sums of remittance flows to low- and middle-income countries: These amounted to $429 billion in 2016 (World Bank Group and Knomad 2018, p. 4)—almost four times the amount of ODA, and much more stable than private finance flows.

On ideas, countries' policies centred on spreading ideas and knowledge also matter. One element of this effort if focussed on research and development, which we consider under GPGs. Other areas that matter are policies around knowledge transfer, for example on intellectual property rights (Park and Lippoldt 2014).

On finance, we have considered in the section above the quantity and quality of government-led development finance. But policy also governs several other important areas—in particular, policy on international tax plays a role in a developing country's ability to raise tax revenue (domestic resource mobilisation). Countries also seek to influence or support private financial flows, for example with their investment policy and agreements. Work by the Research Centre for Policy Coherence and Development (CIECODE) (see Robinson et al. 2018, pp. 20–21) provides a framework for considering an equilibrium between ensuring that countries retain their right to regulate as they pursue public policy interests (including sustainable development objectives) while contributing to a favourable investment climate and protecting foreign investors from unjustified discrimination measures by the host state.

In summary, any assessment of countries' development contributions should take these policy areas into account.

11.5 Global Public Goods

GPGs can be described simply as "goods, whose benefits or costs are of nearly universal reach or potentially affecting anyone anywhere" (Kaul 2013). In economics, examples of pure public goods are those where someone cannot be prevented from consuming a good ("non-excludable") and where one person's consumption does not detract from another's ("non-rival"). Street lights have public good characteristics, and clean air is close to being a pure public good. GPGs are those public goods that are "global" or significantly transboundary. Examples include climate stability, security, and freedom from disease—we all benefit from these, but one country's activity affects their overall supply.

A country's contribution to GPGs is distinct from the policies in the prior section because one country's activities affect all (or many) countries simultaneously, whereas in the prior section we were concerned with bilateral policy impacts. GPGs therefore require global—rather than bilateral—collaboration, and incentives are more diffuse.

In terms of countries' contributions to GPGs, these can be positive or negative (and some activities—intentional or otherwise—create global public "bads" such as pollution). We can think of GPGs as assets that provide returns for a wide range of countries and people, but that countries can unilaterally add to, or deplete. The most obvious example is that of the climate. The Earth's atmosphere is an asset that benefits the entire planet (to different degrees) by protecting us from the sun's rays. Countries damage that asset when activity leads to greenhouse gas emissions, or they can contribute to that asset with forests, which absorb these gases and mitigate its depletion.

A key issue in accepting and allocating responsibility for maintaining GPGs is whether to consider the asset (i.e. the stock), or the current contributions to it (the flow). In this analysis, as we are concerned with current efforts, we focus on the latter, but it is clear that historic contributions are relevant in many cases, especially in assigning responsibility for enhancement or damage. Similarly, a country may contribute to a GPG by providing it directly, or by preserving it (which might include reducing or eliminating damaging activity).

Which GPGs should we be most concerned with? There is relatively little research assessing the value and importance of GPGs. Kenny et al. (2018) has produced a list and includes the categories of health (including vaccination); environment; economy; security; knowledge and technology; migration; and norms. I have attached a full list in Annex B. It is clear that countries' actions in many of these areas have the potential to affect millions of lives overseas.

An important research question is the relative importance—and valuation—of these GPGs. There appears to be little work attempting to compare, say, the value of undertaking vaccination with climate mitigation. There have been calls for multilateral and bilateral development agencies to fund more projects that address these and other GPGs. As this would involve some trade-off of

GPGs with other objectives—including poverty reduction—it is important for policy-makers to understand their relative value and effectiveness.

11.6 Conclusion

More effective development cooperation has the potential to lift large numbers of people out of extreme poverty. A common measurement between countries and institutions is extremely valuable in highlighting differences in approach, and it can proceed with or without targets, but it does rely on common standards and data. We can and should measure what we can now; if these comparisons are partial, this will signal clearly to policy-makers where better data is needed.

In this chapter, I have set out three main types of policy that matter for development, summarised in Table 11.4.

On development finance—including aid—there is a need for basic information on the quantity and terms of concessional finance. The Total Official Support for Sustainable Development measure is a helpful broader measure in development, but there remains a core question about how much concessional help is being funded by taxpayers, and it is important for recipients to understand whether any finance they receive is concessional or just effectively private lending through public bodies. New common standards and measures, which are not restricted to, or only led by, the OECD countries, are needed for all countries.

The political commitment to aid effectiveness and its measurement, at least in traditional OECD-DAC donors, has waned. The GPEDC, whose membership is broader, appears to lack buy-in from some key countries, although its data gathering is an important source of comparability in aid effectiveness, and it should be empowered and resourced to develop and extend its surveys.

Table 11.4 Policies that matter for international sustainable development

Policy area	Policies including
Development finance	Funding for: • Multilateral agencies • Bilateral aid and concessional finance
Policies with bilateral international impacts	• Trade • Migration • Investment • Technology
Global public goods	• Climate • Security • Knowledge • Health

Source Author

Countries will need to come together to agree how they will address effectiveness in the new environment where, for example, most of the extreme poor are potentially in fragile states. Without this focus on effectiveness, there is a risk that substantial sums of global aid are being used ineffectively, prolonging progress on the SDGs and keeping millions unnecessarily in poverty.

More generally, we need to be clear that concessional finance is not the only—or even perhaps the most important—policy supporting development. Policies around the flow of goods, people, and ideas are as important as those around capital. Similarly, GPGs receive too little attention, and little research exists that values these goods and considers the trade-offs between them and other areas. Common measures appear to be present in many of these issues.

The Center for Global Development will be continuing work in these areas, and it hopes to produce new measures of countries' commitments to development, which apply to a broader group of major economies, and to evolve its measures of development finance. We hope these will support governments and leaders to reinvigorate their commitments to effectiveness, and help build a new consensus on effective aid and development that will accelerate the achievement of the global goals.

Acknowledgements I'm very grateful for excellent advice and input to this chapter from Arthur Baker, Caitlin McKee, Stephan Kyburz, Lee Robinson, and Owen Barder. All views and any errors are mine.

Notes

1. A fuller definition of "development" in this section would be "activities that directly enhance welfare of people—particularly those in poverty or extreme poverty—in another country; and/or that is likely to lead to stronger economic, environmental, or social growth".This is a broad definition that, in principle, would encompass any policies or actions that affect other countries, including, for example, positions in international and regional fora. In practice, we are mainly concerned with those that have the biggest—or a material—impact on others. For example, a single vote at the UN or European Union would be unlikely to qualify as material, but failure to adopt certain international treaties would.
2. According to this measure, in 2017, several other countries would have qualified if the G20 was purely defined by GDP at market prices. For example, Nigeria, Iran, Poland, Switzerland, and Thailand have absolute GDPs higher than the smallest economy in the G20 (South Africa).
3. I explain the rationale for the groupings below. For a detailed description of the rationale and evidence supporting the impact of policies on development, see Robinson et al. (2018).
4. This suggestion was made by Pierre Jacquet in a December 2018 workshop at CGD on the future of measuring commitment to development.
5. The Global Partnership was created at the Fourth High-Level Forum on Aid Effectiveness in Busan in 2011 (GPEDC, n.d.-a).
6. For a current indicator framework, see the GPEDC (n.d.-b).

7. In 1968, the United Nations Conference on Trade and Development released a paper identifying and discussing the impact of tied aid. This report was followed by a condemnation of the practice by the Pearson Commission. Jepma (1991) found that the value of aid was reduced 13–23 per cent by the practice of tying. Despite recent progress, the OECD continues to push for untying aid (OECD, n.d.-d).
8. See the GPEDC (n.d.-b) for a current indicator framework.
9. "MOPAN assessments provide a snapshot of four dimensions of organisational effectiveness (strategic management, operational management, relationship management, and knowledge management), but also cover development effectiveness (results)" (Multilateral Organisation Performance Assessment Network, n.d.).
10. China received aid that grew from near zero in 1980 to a peak of 0.725 per cent of GDP in 1993 before falling to 0.146 per cent in 2000, and to 0.1 per cent in 2003 and below zero (i.e. a net donor) after 2010 (World Bank, n.d.-b).

ANNEX A. QUALITY OF OFFICIAL DEVELOPMENT ASSISTANCE (QuODA) INDICATORS

Below are the 24 indicators included in the 2018 update of QuODA. The last three columns identify where there is some support for the indicator. Full explanations of indicators and supporting sources are available in McKee and Mitchell (2018).

Theme	No.	Description	Source	Inclusion supported by		
				Academic	Recipients	Paris
Maximising efficiency	ME1	Allocation to poor countries	DAC	Y		
	ME2	Allocation to well-governed countries	DAC	Y		
	ME4	High country programmable aid share	DAC	Y		
	ME5	Focus/specialisation by recipient country	DAC	Y	Y	
	ME6	Focus/specialisation by sector	CRS		Y	
	ME7	Support of select global public good facilities	DAC	Y		
	ME8	Share of untied aid	CRS			Y
Fostering institutions	FI1	Share of aid to recipients' top development priorities	CRS; UN My World	Y	Y	

(continued)

(continued)

Theme	No.	Description	Source	Academic	Recipients	Paris
	FI3	Share of aid recorded in recipient budgets	GPEDC		Y	Y
	FI4	Interventions using obj. from recipient frameworks	GPEDC	Y		
	FI5	Use of recipient country systems	GPEDC		Y	Y
	FI7	Share of scheduled aid recorded as received by recipients	GPEDC		Y	Y
	FI8	Coverage of forward spending plans/aid predictability	GPEDC	Y	Y	
Reducing burden	RB1	Significance of aid relationships	DAC	Y		
	RB2	Fragmentation across donor agencies	CRS			
	RB3	Median project size	CRS		Y	
	RB4	Contribution to multilaterals	DAC			
Transparency and learning	TL1	Membership in IATI	IATI	Y		
	TL2	Info on development funding publicly accessible	GPEDC			
	TL3	Recording of project title and descriptions	CRS			
	TL4	Detail of project description	CRS			
	TL5	Reporting of aid delivery channel	CRS			
	TL6	Completeness of project-level commitment data	CRS		Y	
	TL8	Share of evaluations planned with recipient	GPEDC	Y		

ANNEX B. LIST OF GLOBAL PUBLIC GOODS

This annex provides a list of 39 *measurable* indicators of global public goods and six measures of other spillovers based on Kenny et al. (2018).

Health

1. Antibiotics use in agriculture
2. WHO International Health Regulations Score—this measures surveillance, response, and preparedness for disease in a country
3. Vaccinations—benefits to home country but global spillovers

Health spillovers:

- Exports of health-reducing products (such as tobacco)

Environment

4. Forests—a role in regulating environment. Forest area, protected areas such as national parks
5. Fish stocks agreements participation
6. Fuel subsidies
7. Meat production—contributes to greenhouse gas emissions, deforestation, water use
8. Treaties/conventions
9. Emissions of CO_2, anthropogenic sulphur dioxide
10. Consumption of chlorofluorocarbons
11. Ocean acidification
12. Freshwater shocks and use

Economy

13. Membership in WTO—influences global rule-setting and upholds a rules-based system
14. Trade barriers—tariffs, subsidies, NTBs, STRI
15. ODA—in particular, funding for GPGs
16. Member of IMF—similar rationale as WTO
17. (negatively)—in receipt of IMF loan—due to risk of cross-border contagion
18. Contribution to UN budget
19. Good business practices—prevent a race to the bottom. Participation in:

    (a) The inclusive framework on base erosion and profit-shifting

(b) Global forum on transparency and exchange of information for tax purposes
(c) Convention on mutual administrative assistance in tax matters
(d) Financial Secrecy Index

20. Crime and corruption—participation in:

    (a) UN Convention against Transnational Organized Crime
    (b) UN Convention against Corruption

Other economy spillovers:

- Foreign direct investment
- International Finance Corporation distance to frontier score—ease of doing business internationally

Security

21. Cultivation of drugs that have major security and health spillovers globally—cannabis, cocaine (coca bush), opiates (opium poppy)
22. Consumption of these drugs
23. Exports of arms—particularly to countries with low respect for civil and political rights
24. Number of WMDs (e.g. nuclear) held
25. Contribution to UN peacekeeping budget
26. Participation in arms conventions—ATT, CCM, NPT, CTBT, CWC, BWC
27. Ratification of ICC's Rome statute—ICC has brought cases of crimes against humanity
28. Global Cybersecurity Index value—a proxy for cybersecurity
29. Armed conflict-related deaths and terror-related deaths

Technology

30. Research and development expenditure
31. Total patent grants—patents encourage innovation
32. Scientific and technical journal articles
33. Internet access—in the form of internet exchange points—broader access facilitates greater global exchange of ideas and information

Migration

34. Refugees departing a country—scored negatively as a burden on the international system
35. Refugees entering a country

Other migration spillovers:

- Migrant stock
- Visa restrictions—make movement and integration difficult
- Remittances from a country

Norms

36. Participation in UN Convention on the Law of the Sea—the use of the sea and its resources
37. Basel convention on control of transboundary movements of hazardous wastes and disposal
38. Adoption of the metric system—to facilitate greater comparability across countries
39. International student ID card—to permit students from certain countries to access cultural institutions with student status in other countries

References

AidData. (2018). *The 2017 Listening to Leaders survey aggregate dataset*. https://www.aiddata.org/data/the-2017-listening-to-leaders-survey-aggregate-dataset.

Australian Government & Australian AID. (2012). *Australian multilateral assessment*. https://dfat.gov.au/about-us/publications/Documents/ama-full-report-2.pdf.

Barder, O., Krylova, P., & Talbot, T. (2016). *How much and how well: Revisiting the aid component of the Commitment to Development Index* (CGD Policy Paper 085). Washington, DC: Center for Global Development.

Besharati, N. A., & Macfeely, S. (2019, March). *Defining and quantifying South-South cooperation* (UNCTAD Research Paper No. 30). Geneva: United Nations.

Birdsall, N., & Kharas, H. (2014). *The quality of official development assistance (QuODA)*. 3rd ed. https://www.cgdev.org/sites/default/files/QUODA_final_revised_september.pdf.

Bracho, G. (2021). Failing to share the burden: Traditional donors, Southern providers, and the twilight of the GPEDC and the post-war aid system. In S. Chaturvedi et al. (Eds.), *The Palgrave Handbook of Development Cooperation for Achieving the 2030 Agenda* (pp. 367–391). Palgrave.

Clemens, M. A. (2009). *Think again: Brain drain*. https://www.cgdev.org/article/think-again-brain-drain-foreignpolicycom.

Clements, M. A. (2011). *Trillion-dollar bills on the sidewalk: Why don't more economists study emigration?* https://www.cgdev.org/blog/trillion-dollar-bills-sidewalk-why-don%E2%80%99t-more-economists-study-emigration.

Clemens, M.A. (2017). *Migration is a form of development: The need for innovation to regulate migration for mutual benefit* (Population Division Technical Paper No. 2017/8). New York, NY: United Nations Department of Economic and Social Affairs.

Easterly, W., & Pfutze, T. (2008, Spring). Where does the money go? Best and worst practices in foreign aid. *The Journal of Economic Perspectives, 22*(2), 29–52.

Gavi, the Vaccine Alliance. (n.d.). *Facts and figures*. https://www.gavi.org/about/mission/facts-and-figures/.

Global Reporting Initiative. (2018). GRI Standards Download Center. https://www.globalreporting.org/standards/gri-standards-download-center/.

GPEDC (Global Partnership for Effective Development Co-operation). (n.d.-a). *About the partnership*. http://effectivecooperation.org/about/about-the-partnership/.

GPEDC. (n.d.-b). *The monitoring framework of the global partnership*. http://effectivecooperation.org/wp-content/uploads/2015/05/GPEDC-Monitoring-Framework-10-Indicators.pdf.

Howarth, C. N. (2017). *Does development aid work?* https://www.academia.edu/36050294/Does_Development_Aid_Work.

Jepma, C. J. (1991). *The tying of aid*. Paris: Organisation for Economic Co-operation and Development.

Kaul, I. (2013). *Global public goods—A concept for framing the post-2015 agenda?* (DIE Discussion Paper 2/2013). Bonn: German Development Institute / Deutsches Institut für Entwicklungspolitik (DIE).

Kenny, C., Snyder, M., & Patel, D. (2018). *Measures of global public goods and international spillovers* (CGD Working Paper 474). Washington, DC: Center for Global Development.

Klingebiel, S., Mahn, T., & Negre, M. (Eds.). (2016). *The fragmentation of aid: Concepts, measurements and implications for development cooperation*. London: Palgrave Macmillan.

Knack, S., Rogers, H. F., & Eubank, N. (2010). Aid quality and donor rankings. *World Development, 39*(11), 1907–1917. https://www.sciencedirect.com/science/article/abs/pii/S0305750X11002038.

Knoll, A. (2014, June). *Bringing policy coherence for development into the post-2015 agenda* (ECDPM Discussion Paper 163). Maastricht: European Centre for Development Policy Management.

Lankester, T. (2012). *The politics and economics of Britain's foreign aid: The Pergau Dam affair*. London: Routledge.

McArthur, J. W., & Rasmussen, K. (2018). *Who funds which multilateral organizations?* https://www.brookings.edu/wp-content/uploads/2017/12/globalviews_who_funds_which_multilaterals.pdf.

McKee, C., & Mitchell, I. (2018). *Quality of official development assistance: QuODA 2018 methodology*. https://www.cgdev.org/sites/default/files/quoda-methodology-2018.pdf.

Meeks, P. (n.d.). *Unravelling tied aid*. https://eurodad.org/files/pdf/1546810-unravelling-tied-aid-1530880935.pdf.

Ministry of Foreign Affairs of Denmark. (2013). *Danish multilateral development cooperation analysis*. http://um.dk/da/~/media/UM/Danish-site/Documents/Danida/Samarbejde/Int-org/Danish%20Multilateral%20Development%20Cooperation%20Analysis.pdf.

Mitchell, I., Ritchie, E., & Rogerson, A. (2020). *Finance for international development* (CGD Working Paper 529). Washington, DC: Center for Global Development. https://www.cgdev.org/publication/finance-internationaldevelopment- fid.

Multilateral Organisation Performance Assessment Network. (n.d.). *Mission statement.* http://www.mopanonline.org/about/ourmission/.

Nunn, N., & Qian, N. (2014). U.S. food aid and civil conflict. *American Economic Review, 104*(6), 1630–1666.

OECD (Organisation for Economic Co-operation and Development). (2018a). *Development co-operation report 2018: Joining forces to leave no one behind.* Paris: OECD Publishing.

OECD. (2018b). *States of fragility 2018.* Paris: OECD Publishing.

OECD. (2019). *Measuring distance to the SDG targets 2019: An assessment of where OECD countries stand.* Paris: OECD Publishing.

OECD. (n.d.-a). *The high level fora on aid effectiveness: A history.* http://www.oecd.org/dac/effectiveness/thehighlevelforaonaideffectivenessahistory.htm.

OECD. (n.d.-b). *The Busan Partnership for Effective Development Co-operation.* http://www.oecd.org/development/effectiveness/busanpartnership.htm.

OECD. (n.d.-c). *Aid at a glance charts.* http://www.oecd.org/dac/financing-sustainable-development/development-finance-data/aid-at-a-glance.htm.

OECD. (n.d.-d). *Untied aid.* http://www.oecd.org/dac/financing-sustainable-development/development-finance-standards/untied-aid.htm.

OECD-DAC (Development Assistance Committee). (2018). *Note on the treatment of loan concessionality in DAC statistics.* http://www.oecd.org/dac/stats/concessionality-note.htm.

OECD-DAC. (n.d.). *International TOSSD task force.* http://www.oecd.org/dac/financing-sustainable-development/development-finance-standards/tossd-task-force.htm.

Park, W. G., & Lippoldt, D. C. (2014). Channels of technology transfer and intellectual property rights in developing countries. In S. Ahn, B. H. Hall, & K. Lee (Eds.), *Intellectual property for economic development* (pp. 33–89). Cheltenham, UK: Edward Elgar Publishing.

Pritchett, L. (2016, October 25). *The least you can do for global poverty is better than the best you can do.* https://www.cgdev.org/blog/least-you-can-do-global-poverty-better-best-you-can-do.

Publish What You Fund. (2018). *Aid Transparency Index 2018.* https://www.publishwhatyoufund.org/reports/2018-Aid-Transparency-Index.pdf.

Robinson, L., Käppeli, A., McKee, C., Mitchell, I., & Hillebrandt, H. (2018). *The Commitment to Development Index: 2018 edition* (Methodological Overview Paper). https://www.cgdev.org/sites/default/files/CDI-2018-methodology.pdf.

Roodman, D. (2005). *The Commitment to Development Index: 2005 edition.* https://www.cgdev.org/sites/default/files/archive/doc/cdi/technicaldescrip05.pdf.

Roodman, D. (2012). *Due diligence: An impertinent inquiry into microfinance* (CGD Brief). https://www.cgdev.org/sites/default/files/1425842_file_Roodman_Due_Diligence_brief_FINAL.pdf.

Roodman, D. (2013). *The Commitment to Development Index: 2013 edition.* https://www.cgdev.org/sites/default/files/archive/doc/CDI_2013/Index-technical-description-2013-final.pdf.

Scott, S. (2015). *The accidental birth of "official development assistance"* (OECD Development Co-operation Working Papers No. 24). Paris: OECD Publishing.

Subramanian, A., & Wei, S.-J. (2003, October). *The WTO promotes trade, strongly but unevenly* (NBER Working Paper No. 10024). Cambridge, MA: National Bureau of Economic Research.

UK Government & Department for International Development. (2011). *Multilateral aid review 2011.* https://assets.publishing.service.gov.uk/government/uploads/system/uploads/attachment_data/file/67583/multilateral_aid_review.pdf.

UK Government & Department for International Development. (2013). *Multilateral aid review update 2013.* https://assets.publishing.service.gov.uk/government/uploads/system/uploads/attachment_data/file/297523/MAR-review-dec13.pdf.

United Nations Development Programme. (2016). *Concessional financial flows among southern countries: Conceptualising design principles, operational modalities and an assessment framework.* https://www.undp.org/content/dam/undp/library/development-impact/SS%20Research%20Publications/11873%20-%20Concessional%20Financial%20Flows%20Among%20Southern%20Countries_Op%2008_Web%20Version(1).pdf.

World Bank. (2020). *World Development Indicators online database.* https://data.worldbank.org/data-catalog/world-development-indicators.

World Bank. (n.d.-a). *Poverty headcount ratio at $1.90 a day (2011 PPP) (% of population).* https://data.worldbank.org/indicator/SI.POV.DDAY?locations=CN.

World Bank. (n.d.-b). *Net ODA received (% of GNI).* https://data.worldbank.org/indicator/DT.ODA.ODAT.GN.ZS?locations=CN.

World Bank Group & Knomad. (2018). *Migration and remittances: Recent developments and outlook.* http://pubdocs.worldbank.org/en/992371492706371662/MigrationandDevelopmentBrief27.pdf.

Open Access This chapter is licensed under the terms of the Creative Commons Attribution 4.0 International License (http://creativecommons.org/licenses/by/4.0/), which permits use, sharing, adaptation, distribution and reproduction in any medium or format, as long as you give appropriate credit to the original author(s) and the source, provide a link to the Creative Commons license and indicate if changes were made.

The images or other third party material in this chapter are included in the chapter's Creative Commons license, unless indicated otherwise in a credit line to the material. If material is not included in the chapter's Creative Commons license and your intended use is not permitted by statutory regulation or exceeds the permitted use, you will need to obtain permission directly from the copyright holder.

CHAPTER 12

Interest-Based Development Cooperation: Moving Providers from Parochial Convergence to Principled Collaboration

Nilima Gulrajani and Rachael Calleja

12.1 Introduction

"I am unashamed about the need to ensure that our aid programme works for the UK", said UK Prime Minister Theresa May in a speech in South Africa in 2018 on her first trip to the continent (Gov.UK 2018). A net positive return to both donor and recipient is now a legitimate expectation and politically acceptable rationale for overseas aid provision. Among those states who do not view themselves in the ilk of traditional Western donors, securing "mutual interests" also provides a central motivation for development cooperation. For example, at the 2018 Forum on China-Africa Cooperation, United Nations (UN) Secretary-General António Guterres suggested "win-win" collaborations characterise the relation between China and Africa, citing climate change as an area that would "generate the future that we want" (UN News 2018).

A common dilemma for aid providers nowadays thus seems to be how to craft a development policy that balances domestic economic advantages, geopolitical priorities, and recipient needs (Milner and Tingley 2013). This chapter explores both the emergence and the effects of the discursive dominance of "national interest" logics within development assistance. We start first by exploring the literatures on donor motivations in political science that have

---

N. Gulrajani (✉)
Overseas Development Institute, London, UK
e-mail: n.gulrajani@odi.org.uk

R. Calleja
Center for Global Development (CGD Europe), London, UK
e-mail: rcalleja@CGDEV.org

© The Author(s) 2021
S. Chaturvedi et al. (eds.), *The Palgrave Handbook of Development Cooperation for Achieving the 2030 Agenda*,
https://doi.org/10.1007/978-3-030-57938-8_12

theorised the rationale for aid provision as either altruistic or selfish, suggesting that these are ideal types that frame the debate on why states engage in overseas development even as, in reality, they tend to be combined to different degrees at different moments in time. In Sect. 12.3, we delineate the growth of national interest logics in foreign aid over the last decade among all development cooperation providers. We introduce an analytical distinction between two narratives of interest-based development cooperation: a principled interest in furthering the security, stability, and prosperity of the world; and a parochial motivation serving short-term geopolitical or commercial gains. In Sect. 12.4, we present the conceptual foundation of the principled national interest as donor actions that align aid to needs, global collective action, and public spiritedness. In Sect. 12.5, we introduce the Principled Aid Index (PA Index) as one tangible effort to decode these dual meanings by measuring Northern donor efforts to allocate aid according to a principled national interest. In Sect. 12.6, we present the results of this benchmarking exercise. This is followed by a final section that recommends collaborative effort across Northern and Southern providers for advancing development cooperation that serves a principled national interest.

12.2 False Dichotomies? the Competing Rationales for Development Cooperation

Literature on foreign aid has long proposed two motivations for aid-giving, which reflect the differences between the realist and idealist theories of international relations. At one end of the spectrum, aid is provided as donors display their "mercantile", self-serving motives. On the other side, donors exhibit the moral values and humane principles of a "clergyman" (van Dam and van Dis 2014).

There is little doubt that foreign aid enables the pursuit, promotion, and defence of the national interests of the donor nation, and that it has done so for some time (Morgenthau 1962; see also McKinley and Little 1977, 1978a, b, 1979). No country would provide aid if it did not serve—or was at least benign to—its own concerns and priorities (Packenham 1966). At the same time, donors are clearly capable of generosity towards, and solidarity with, international causes and crises—this is perhaps most visible in the case of natural disasters and humanitarian assistance (Lumsdaine 1993; Lumsdaine and Schopf 2007; Pratt 2000). This suggests some amount of ebb and flow to donor motivations, with the possibility of movement and mixtures of actions chosen because they are predominantly morally right, and domestically desirable.

Historically, both of these broad motivations for giving foreign aid—to selflessly help the world's poorest and most vulnerable, and to promote the realist interests of the donor—have been presented as polar opposite rationales. At one level, there is a sense in this depiction of donor motivations that it is either parochial populism or principled poverty reduction, with both pulling in different directions. They illustrate the extremes from which all donors must ultimately choose their place. Yet, pure altruism and total self-interest represent two extreme ends of a spectrum of motivations; they are admittedly more ideal types than true depictions of any real case.[1] In reality, both motivations are likely to be present in most aid allocation decisions, and it is to be expected that the balance between the two will vary between different donor countries as well as over time (Lancaster 2007; Maizels and Nissanke 1984; Schraeder et al. 1998). The purposes of aid are always mixed and will always be as such.

If donor motivation varies, this begs the question: What are the causal pathways for its evolution and transformation? Research suggests it is the confluence of international and domestic forces that influences state behaviour. Domestic political economy variables, including the political party in power, the role of the media, and the structure of government, are all potential influences (Dietrich 2016; Fuchs et al. 2014; Lancaster 2007; Lundsgaarde 2012). A supportive domestic constituency also matters (Lancaster 2007; Yanguas 2018).

At the same time, global norms—common-sense standards of appropriate behaviour within international society—also influence donor motivations (Finnemore and Sikkink 2001; Fukuda-Parr and Shiga 2016; Gulrajani and Swiss 2017). Understandings of what is good, desirable, and appropriate in international development cooperation exert pressures on development actors and establish expectations that they will accept, comply, and participate according to these rules. Scripts and structures in the international system thus interact with discourses in domestic political life to influence the likelihood of principled or parochial development engagements (Lumsdaine 1993).

Ultimately, idealistic and pragmatic donor motivations are not mutually exclusive but positioned along a continuum with their relative emphasis in constant evolution. But while donors can be simultaneously altruistic and nationalistic, more often it is one of these motivations that dominate at any given moment in time. Donor motivation can thus be seen as a continuous variable comprised of shifting ratios of a "clergyman's idealism" and a "merchant's pragmatism" (van Dam and van Dis 2014). If these motivations are the inseparable and contradictory "yin and yang" of development cooperation providers that supply assistance, knowledge of where the balance sits in the current contemporary policy space and what the full range of motivations is across the universe of donors becomes analytically valuable.

12.3 Drivers of Convergence to Interest-Based Development Cooperation

While pure altruism and self-interest represent ideal-type motivations rather than true depictions of any real case, they give a sense of the extremes from which all aid providers must ultimately choose their place. Nowhere is the mixed motivational basis for development cooperation more obvious than in current development discourse, where the idea of an "enlightened" self-interest—where "win-wins" and "mutual benefits" are practically possible—is now a powerful political rationale for providing development assistance for both Northern and Southern actors (Keijzer and Lundsgaarde 2017, 2018; Kharas and Rogerson 2017). And yet, from the post-Cold War period to the Millennium Development Goals, a strong altruistic and solidaristic narrative provided the main orientation for development (Collier 2016; Mawdsley et al. 2017). What explains this change?

Domestic trends are certainly decentring the traditional Northern template of donorship between a modern "developed" donor and an "underdeveloped" recipient (Gulrajani 2017; Gulrajani and Swiss 2019). Fiscal austerity has heaped political pressure on the objectives and mandates of foreign aid, as donors are pushed to look "beyond aid" to meet the challenges of global inequality and poverty reduction (Gulrajani 2017). What little official development assistance (ODA) is left is now expected to service multiple policy areas, including the cultivation of diplomatic allies, incentivising foreign direct investment, and reducing the effects of global migratory pressures. Politicians placate constituencies opposed to overseas development spending in terms of the domestic gains that can be obtained. In the North, this is partly a response to queries about the effectiveness of aid to tackle the root causes of underdevelopment and the legacy of dependency and corruption it can leave in its wake, but also a liberal internationalist reaction to the domestic forces of populism that elevate domestic interests above international causes and challenges. In the South, the importance of reciprocity and mutual benefits has partly been a defensive response by elected leaders concerned by the optics of overseas development spending, given domestic underdevelopment (Mawdsley 2019).

A shifting geography of power and poverty is also pushing donors towards an interest-based approach to development cooperation. The proportion of people living in extreme poverty across the world is projected to fall from 11 per cent in 2013 to 5 per cent in 2030, and over the last 15 years, 35 low-income countries have achieved middle-income status (Manuel et al. 2018). To the extent that emerging markets represent lucrative investment and trading destinations, as well as geopolitically valuable allies in a fractured global system, development spending is once again becoming more openly and deeply intertwined with public diplomacy, which in turn shifts the normative meanings and purposes of aid (Gulrajani et al. 2019). Donors now see opportunities for trade and investment with the South, as well as question the value of delivering scarce concessional resources to states with the capacity to mobilise market-based resources.

Alongside, charitable motivations are viewed with suspicion from recipients that are now middle-income countries, countries that in many cases are providing cooperation themselves. The growing scale of development resources from non-Development Assistance Committee (DAC) providers (broadly comparable with what the DAC defines as ODA) has been estimated at $32 billion (gross) in 2014, representing 17 per cent of the current DAC total (Benn and Luijkx 2017).[2] South-South cooperation rests on principles of equal partnership, or horizontality, and is anchored to ideas of solidarity and reciprocity (Gulrajani and Swiss 2019). Embracing these norms is predicated on the rejection of relations between a generous "donor" and a poor "recipient" dominated by the altruistic act of "aid" that sustains the power of the provider and the inferiority of the receiver. Southern horizontality upholds the equality between an implicit acknowledgement of sovereign rights as well as a state's capacity to give as well as receive. This rejection of the charitable basis upon which donorship norms are founded is thus highly legitimate in the eyes of Southern recipients (Fukuda-Parr and Shiga 2016).

There is added incentive to abandon altruistic motivations as DAC donors compete with non-DAC providers for political influence, economic leverage, and commercial gain in aid-receiving states (Gulrajani and Swiss 2018). Among the DAC donors, there is a perception that the standards of accountability to which their cooperation is held (e.g. for ODA reporting, on transparency obligations, on effectiveness) are more stringent than for non-DAC providers (Bracho 2015). This is despite the fact that DAC members have always had room to pursue commercial and geopolitical ambitions through their aid policies and practices and have certainly done so in the past. What has changed, perhaps, is the reduced inhibition and discursive acceptability of framing donor assistance as offering a domestic return on investment. This has led some to suggest that traditional ODA is undergoing a process of "Southernisation" (Asmus et al. 2017; Bracho 2015; Fejerskov et al. 2017; Mawdsley 2018, 2019). As Southern providers fail to assume responsibilities and engage in "disloyal competition", traditional donors certainly appear to feel under less pressure to keep their own commitments.

Finally, the realities of a globalising world mean that the ills of underdevelopment—illegal financial flows, refugee movements, disease outbreaks, pollution, terrorism—are no longer confined to national borders. Globalised transmission chains and feedback loops mean that acts in remote locations to reduce famine, stop pandemics, or minimise inequality are conduits for domestic interests in robust border control, healthy communities, and economic trade and investment. At a time when conflicts, health pandemics, financial capital, and carbon emissions travel indiscriminately across national borders, there are long-run economic, environmental, and security benefits that accrue to the aid-providing nation when development is achieved, particularly in targeted geographic areas where spillover effects are large and directly affect the donor country (Blodgett Bermeo 2018; Kaul 2017). This is clearly different to the national interests motivating Western aid during the Cold War, when containment of communism was a primary objective and little concern was paid to how aid resources may or may not have contributed to development. The Sustainable Development Goals recognise that development is an expansive, universally shared mission, the achievement of which lies in the mutual interests of all countries (Keijzer and Lundsgaarde 2017). Survey data suggests that framing the rationale for aid provision as servicing mutual interests is indeed a qualified source of increased public support for aid (Bond 2016; van Heerde-Hudson et al. 2018; Wood and Hoy 2018).

Such trends are making the advancement of the national interest a legitimate discursive and normative framework for the development programmes of most bilateral aid providers (Carter 2016; Gulrajani 2017; Rabinowitz and Greenhill 2018). We believe this may be viewed as a degree of normative convergence across the North-South binary. Certainly, many have hinted at the minor variations in the moral narratives of each type of development cooperation provider, suggesting differences are not matters of fundamental principle but of interpretation (Chandy and Kharas 2011; Kragelund 2015; Mawdsley 2015). Although servicing the national interest should not be a necessary condition for everything an aid provider does (Carter 2016), the pressures and forces above justify development spending by highlighting some level of domestic return.

It is increasingly acceptable for providers to welcome domestic dividends from their development spending under the assumption that deriving such benefits does not undermine the primary purpose of economic development and welfare, which form the legal basis for investments qualifying as ODA in the first place (Keijzer and Lundsgaarde 2017). At the same time, there is little evidence to support political declarations that aid can always deliver benefits everywhere. Academic literature is certainly sceptical: selfish motives are found to result in suboptimal allocations, as aid is inefficiently assigned to states and sectors for reasons other than development (Girod 2008; Steele 2011). Aid to advance geopolitical interests has also been shown to be less effective (Dreher et al. 2016; Kilby and Dreher 2010; Stone 2010).

Conversely, where donors are shown to have little strategic interest in countries, the scope for development impact is higher (Girod 2012). We forget at our peril that state interests align with global development objectives to the extent that all states benefit from a safer and more prosperous world. Global interdependencies and interconnections have amplified the impact of development challenges that were once confined to state boundaries. The allocation of aid resources to advance this principled "national interest" is both "ethical" and in the "real long-term interests of rich countries" (Black 2016, p. 18; Pratt 1989). Unlike a narrow parochial national interest that colonises the purpose, modalities, and structure of development policy, domestic benefits from a principled national interest are indirect and accrue slowly over time.

A principled approach to the national interest is embodied in the maxim of "doing well by doing good". It is embedded in Tocqueville's ideal of "enlightened self-interest", whereby working for the collective good is viewed as a way of serving individual interests, allowing for greater compatibility between mercantile and moral motivations. At the same time, slippery use of the term "national interest" also means it can refer to activities that advance short-term direct benefits to the donor states—for example, more commercial contracts for domestic firms, greater opportunities to export, or more resources that never actually get sent to recipient countries. Distinguishing a principled from a parochial national interest is a way for citizens to hold donors to account for the kind of national interest they are advancing through their aid allocation. As one former Canadian foreign minister, Mitchell Sharp, once said: "If the primary purpose of our aid is to help ourselves, rather than to help others, we shall probably receive in return what we deserve, and a good deal less than we expect" (Black 2016, p. 22). A principled national interest is what all development cooperation providers should be striving towards.

12.4 A Principled National Interest: A Conceptual and Empirical Basis

The PA Index is an analytical tool created by the Overseas Development Institute that seeks to distinguish between a principled and a parochial national interest (Gulrajani and Calleja 2019). It allows for dual meanings of "aid in the national interest" to be untangled and provides a basis for comparing the type of national interest adopted by individual DAC donors. If we locate principled and parochial national interest narratives on opposite ends of a spectrum of motivations, then we can use aid allocation data to measure where donors sit on this spectrum. This requires a conceptual understanding of a principled national interest, which we argue is made up of three principles.

1. *Principle of need*: A principled national interest ensures that aid is provided to support vulnerable populations and areas where needs are the greatest. Countries have a "duty" to support those facing catastrophes or "mass despair"—including from life-threatening hunger, disease, and disaster (Collier 2016). In the long run, supporting vulnerable populations is in the national interest of donors (and their citizens), as such actions contribute to reducing the scope for political conflict, increasing human capital, supporting trade and investment, and ensuring that no one gets left behind. A principled approach is one that prioritises contributions to global development rather than short-term gains (Rabinowitz and Greenhill 2018).
2. *Principle of global cooperation*: A principled approach to the national interest prioritises actions that support global public goods, and international institutions and systems. Global public goods, such as clean air and the eradication of disease, benefit the Global North and South alike. These goods extend beyond national boundaries, are non-rival, and are often closely linked to poverty alleviation and sustainable development (consider climate change, for example). Supporting global collective action also extends to the provision of core financial support

for multilateral institutions, which are well placed to generate transformational change in North-South relations. Core funding, unlike earmarked resources, preserves the neutrality of multilateral institutions and provides funding to support predictable programming and organisational effectiveness (Gulrajani 2016).

3. *Principle of public spiritedness:* A principled national interest avoids the instrumentalisation of development assistance to advance short-term economic and political agendas over recipient needs or development outcomes. Instead, principled actions are those that remain focussed on global development objectives and outcomes. Indeed, aid that seeks to actively achieve domestic benefits for aid providers can incentivise donor moral hazard by focussing efforts on achieving short-term interests over development outcomes (Collier 2016). Such domestic benefits are Pareto suboptimal, as they reduce the prioritisation of long-term development results.

These principles frame the range of activities that can be considered emblematic of a principled national interest through supporting long-run prosperity and security for donors by advancing key developmental objectives. We use these principles as the conceptual basis for the PA Index, which tests the degree to which donors allocate aid in accordance with each principle using a series of 12 indicators (four per principle) to proxy the principles of need, cooperation, and public spiritedness.[3] The indicators are designed to capture different facets of donor allocations to measure the degree to which their actions are seen to promote a principled national interest. This not only provides a basis for comparing performance across DAC members, but it also allows for an assessment of how and whether donor rhetoric is reflected in reality. The full list of indicators and data sources used to compose the Index is available in Table 12.1.[4]

The indicators form the basis of the PA Index, which benchmarks the type of national interest adopted by 29 DAC donors in each year between 2013 and 2017. The Index aggregates indicator scores by principle to derive a score out of a maximum 10 points for each dimension.[5] The scores per principle are then summed to a total score out of a possible 30 points, with each principle considered to have an equal weight over the total score and degree of principledness attained by donors. In all cases, higher scores represent more principled performance.

Table 12.1 Summary of dimensions, indicators, and data sources

Principle	Indicator	Data source*
Needs	A. Targeting poverty: Share of ODA/gross national income targeted to least-developed countries	OECD CRS and DAC1
	B. Supporting displaced populations: Share of bilateral ODA to developing countries that cumulatively host 70 per cent of cross-border forcibly displaced populations	OECD CRS and UNHCR "Time Series" dataset
	C. Assisting conflict-affected states: Share of humanitarian ODA to countries with active violent conflicts	OECD CRS and UCDP/PRIO "Armed Conflict Database"
	D. Targeting gender inequality: Share of bilateral ODA to countries with the highest levels of gender inequality	OECD CRS and UNDP's GII
Global cooperation	A. Enhancing global trade prospects: Share of bilateral ODA to reduce trade-related constraints and build the capacity and infrastructure required to benefit from opening to trade	OECD CRS
	B. Providing core support for multilateral institutions: Share of ODA as core multilateral funding (minus core funding to European Union institutions)	OECD "Members' total use of multilateral system" and DAC1
	C. Tackling the effects of climate change: Share of total ODA (bilateral and imputed multilateral) for climate mitigation and adaptation	OECD Climate Finance Dataset, "Members' total use of multilateral system" and DAC1
	D. Constraining infectious diseases: Share of total ODA (bilateral and imputed multilateral) allocated to slow the spread of infectious diseases	OECD CRS and "Members' total use of multilateral system"
Public spiritedness	A. Minimising tied aid: Average share of formally and informally tied aid	OECD's CRS and OECD's "Report on the DAC untying recommendation"

(continued)

Table 12.1 (continued)

Principle	Indicator	Data source*
	B. Reducing alignment between aid spending and UN voting: Correlation between UN voting agreement across donors and recipients and bilateral ODA disbursements to recipients	OECD CRS and UN voting data (see Voeten et al. 2009)
	C. Delinking aid spending and arms exports: Correlation between donor arms exports to recipients and bilateral ODA disbursements to recipients	OECD CRS and UN Comtrade
	D. Localising aid: Share of bilateral ODA spent as country programmable aid (CPA) as well as humanitarian and food aid	OECD CPA dataset and CRS

Note on abbreviations Creditor Reporting System (CRS), Uppsala Conflict Data Program (UCDP), Peace Research Institute Oslo (PRIO), Gender Inequality Index (GII)
Source Adapted from Gulrajani and Calleja (2019)

12.5 Convergence and Changing National Interest Narratives

Using the PA Index, we test whether donors are increasingly pursuing a less principled approach to aid in the national interest by examining changes to donor scores over time. We begin by calculating the difference in scores between 2013 and 2017 for each donor. This provides a basic measure or trajectory of changes to donor allocations and provides an overall picture of which donors are becoming more or less principled. The results of this analysis are reported in Table 12.2.[6]

The results indicate that between 2013 and 2017, nine donors (Belgium, Denmark, Germany, Iceland, Japan, Netherlands, Slovak Republic, the United Kingdom, and the United States) declined overall on the PA Index, while the remaining 20 improved over the same period. The largest declines were in Belgium and the Slovak Republic, suggesting that the overall allocations of both countries in 2017 reflected less principled allocations than those a made a few years earlier. Alternatively, Greece and Norway show the largest net improvements over the period, indicating a possible tendency towards more principled behaviour.

Although these findings suggest that donors are becoming more—rather than less—principled, there are two points worth noting. First, although most donors show increasing scores over time, several show very minor changes in either direction. In these cases, performance could be considered flat rather than defining a trajectory of meaningful change. A good example is the case

Table 12.2 Change in PA Index scores between 2013 and 2017 by dimension and overall

	Overall	Needs	Global cooperation	Public spiritedness
Australia	0.77	-0.15	1.48	-0.57
Austria	0.71	1.33	-0.18	-0.44
Belgium	-3.55	-1.52	-1.51	-0.52
Canada	0.02	1.38	-0.40	-0.96
Czech Republic	0.59	1.18	-0.01	-0.57
Denmark	-1.50	0.86	-1.86	-0.50
Finland	0.37	-0.79	1.53	-0.37
France	3.70	0.97	3.27	-0.55
Germany	-1.00	0.23	-0.12	-1.11
Greece	7.24	3.79	0.59	2.86
Hungary	0.58	-0.19	-0.38	1.16
Iceland	-1.46	0.05	-0.75	-0.75
Ireland	2.48	1.87	0.67	-0.06
Italy	0.12	0.03	0.33	-0.24
Japan	-0.08	-2.42	2.41	-0.07
Korea	0.04	-0.56	-0.10	0.70
Luxembourg	2.61	0.49	2.46	-0.34
Netherlands	-1.68	0.14	-0.56	-1.26
New Zealand	1.70	0.30	0.20	1.20
Norway	4.40	1.04	2.49	0.88
Poland	0.94	2.63	0.29	-1.98
Portugal	2.34	1.50	1.48	-0.64
Slovak Republic	-3.47	-1.52	-0.13	-1.82
Slovenia	1.51	1.63	0.01	-0.13
Spain	1.21	0.00	1.69	-0.48
Sweden	2.19	0.87	1.13	0.19
Switzerland	2.06	0.92	1.23	-0.09
United Kingdom	-1.99	-0.08	-0.72	-1.19
United States	-1.19	-0.24	0.43	-1.38

Source Authors' calculations using PA Index dataset

of Canada, which shows an increase in its PA Index score of 0.02 between 2013 and 2017, or the equivalent of less than 1 per cent of its initial score of 22 in 2013. Although there is no cut-off for determining the level of change that can be considered meaningful, small changes in score are less likely to reflect deliberate policy changes towards more or less principled behaviour. Second, examining changes in overall donor performance could obscure trends in performance at the level of each principle. Given that the overall score of the PA Index is composed of the sum of scores across the three principles, donors that show opposite changes in scores across principles may see limited overall change once the scores are summed across dimensions.

Finally, looking at the results over time by principle, we find that although donors have tended to show improved performance on both the principles of needs and global cooperation, there is a striking deterioration in performance on the public spiritedness dimension almost across the board. Donor scores on the public spiritedness dimension fell by 6 per cent over 2013 values across the sample period, with an absolute decline in public spiritedness reported for 23 out of 29 donors. By contrast, donor scores on the needs and global cooperation dimensions increased by 10 per cent and 9 per cent, respectively, over 2013 values, with 20 donors improving their allocations towards needs and vulnerable populations and 17 donors strengthening support for global cooperation.

The combination of changes across the principles is counterintuitive, yet they have important implications for understanding convergence in donor behaviour in the context of narratives of aid in the national interest. On the one hand, the results provide strong support for the argument that donors are converging on an approach to the national interest that increasingly focusses on using aid to extract short-term political and economic gains through aligning allocations to easy domestic "wins". On the other, rising performance on the needs and cooperation principles suggests that the pursuit of domestic interests has not (as yet) deteriorated average donor support for vulnerable populations and global challenges.

The simultaneous convergence towards both types of behaviours could suggest that although donors acknowledge that the impact of developmental challenges can have consequences at home, they remain under pressure to show citizens that aid spending supports the domestic interest. This approach—which is somewhat akin to having one's cake and eating it too—risks undermining development results to attain short-term wins for constituents. For donors facing continued demands to show results to citizens, a key question is whether, and how, to change the domestic narrative to show citizens that the principled national interest can have a meaningful impact at home.

12.6 Building Normative Consensus for a Principled Approach Across the North-South Divide

The challenge of pursuing a principled over a parochial national interest is one faced by both Northern and Southern donors alike. In part, this is because both groups face a public communications challenge explaining and justifying overseas giving to their citizenry. Although our analysis has focussed on the types of narratives pursued by Northern donors, the ultimate objective of a principled national interest will have the greatest global outcomes when pursued by all development actors. Put differently, if principled actions are in the long-run interest of Northern and Southern actors alike, then the best chances of achieving development outcomes and promoting global prosperity, stability, and security are achieved when all actors are working towards the same goal.

To this end, we see three potential avenues for deepening collaboration towards a principled aid approach. First, there is a need to generate a consensus on the principled approach to the national interest that bridges the North-South divide. As donors continue to face pressure to instrumentalise aid in alignment with domestic commercial and strategic interests, a joint commitment made by both Northern and Southern donors to promote a principled national interest could provide impetus for collective action. Such a commitment could guide actions that result from formal donor fora, such as the 2019 BAPA+40 (Buenos Aires Plan of Action plus 40), which recently called for increased financial and technical cooperation, and greater collaboration between North and South through triangular cooperation (UN News 2019). It could also support efforts to finance sustainable development—including through the Financing for Development Forum—by ensuring that new mechanisms for development financing maintain their focus on achieving the Sustainable Development Goals. It can also be fostered through informal discussions and alliance-building, where the common shared interests of all development cooperation providers are recognised. Aligning scaled-up engagements to a principled rather than a parochial national interest can enable normative collaboration and ensure that development actions are focussed on supporting long-term global development outcomes.

Second, there is a need to improve the coverage and availability of data on the aid activities of Southern providers. Part of the challenge of measuring flows from Southern providers is linked to the difficulties of defining South-South cooperation (Besharati and MacFeely 2019). In this regard, there is a need for Southern providers to work towards a clear definition of activities and concessionality for their development finance, and to subsequently set standards for statistical reporting. Obviously, such data must be both produced by the South in accordance with standards they set and publicly available; it is promising that there is momentum for improving transparency and reporting. Without such data, it is impossible to empirically assess the full spectrum of development providers on their rationale for development assistance and to parse out potential discrepancies between the rhetoric and reality of allocations.

Third, there are opportunities for donors to create new mechanisms—or better utilise existing ones—to hold each other accountable to delivering principled aid in the national interest. This could include using the DAC peer review process to provide assessments of donor achievements towards the principled national interests while calling out those that are lagging behind. Among Southern providers, offices such as the United Nations Office for South-South Cooperation may be well placed to drive convergence towards such a normative standard of development cooperation provision. As providers continue to face domestic calls to align aid to their immediate national interest, cultivating relationships and developing mechanism that promote accountability between and across a broader spectrum of donors could foster collaboration towards aid that is principled and in the collective interest.

Lastly, ensuring that donors maintain focus on a principled narrative and allocation ultimately begins at home. In the vast majority of the world, inwardness and rising populism are making overseas development spending increasingly unpalatable. In these instances, documenting and illustrating the domestic benefits of long-term development engagement—for example, through the gains from fairer global trade, lower climate risks, and a better functioning rules-based international order—could reinforce the value of principled actions by development providers to their publics.

Distinguishing between a principled and a parochial national interest may provide a basis for converging a shared national interest narrative that is supportive of normative collaboration across the North and South. Such collaboration can ensure the promotion of shared values and foster greater dialogue on the role of national interests and agendas in relation to aid spending. Most importantly, collaboration based on a principled national interest can ensure that the actions of all donors are designed to support long-run developmental outcomes to promote prosperity, sustainability, and security for all.

Notes

1. While allocation based on country-needs or "merit" is sometimes associated as a third motivation for donor aid allocation decisions (Hoeffler and Outram 2011), "altruism" and "self-interest" remain the dominant dual motivational categories and, as such, we limit ourselves to an analysis centred on these two motivations. Furthermore, one might also view "merit" as a sub-category of need, and thus an expression of an altruistic motivation.
2. Calculations of the comparative size and terms of non-DAC development spending are inevitably provisional and further complicated by blurred distinctions between aid-like flows, other forms of soft financing, and other official flows (Bracho 2015, p. 19).
3. "EU institutions" are excluded on the basis that the factors influencing its motivation for aid allocation may differ from other donors by virtue of being funded by multiple EU states. Donors appear in the dataset in alignment with their accession to the OECD-DAC; Hungary is not included in the calculation prior to joining the DAC in 2016.
4. For more detailed information on indicator selection and development, please see Gulrajani and Calleja (2019).
5. A full and detailed description of the aggregation methodology is presented in Gulrajani and Calleja (2019).
6. Please note, data for Hungary is only reported for 2016 and 2017 in alignment with its DAC membership. As a result, scores for Hungary represent changes between 2016 and 2017 rather than over the full period beginning in 2013.

REFERENCES

Asmus, G., Fuchs, A., & Müller, A. (2017). *BRICS and foreign aid* (AidData Working Paper 42). Williamsburg, VA: AidData at William & Mary.

Benn, J., & Luijkx, W. (2017). *Emerging providers' international co-operation for development* (OECD Development Co-operation (Working Paper No. 33)). Paris: OECD Publishing.

Besharati, N. A., & MacFeely, S. (2019). *Defining and quantifying South-South cooperation* (UNCTAD Research Paper No. 30). Geneva: United Nations Conference on Trade and Development.

Black, D. R. (2016). Humane internationalism and the malaise of Canadian aid policy. In S. Brown, M. den Heyer, & D. R. Black (Eds.), *Rethinking Canadian aid* (2nd ed., pp. 17–36). Ottawa, ON: University of Ottawa Press.

Blodgett Bermeo, S. (2018). *Targeted development: Industrialized country strategy in a globalising world*. Oxford: Oxford University Press.

Bond (2016). *UK public attitudes towards development*. http://www.bond.org.uk/sites/default/files/resource-documents/bond-aid-tracker-online.pdf.

Bracho, G. (2015). *In search of a narrative for Southern providers: The challenge of the emerging economies to the development cooperation agenda* (DIE Discussion Paper 1/2015). Bonn: German Development Institute / Deutsches Institut für Entwicklungspolitik.

Carter, P. (2016). *Five ways to deliver UK aid in the national economic interest* (ODI Briefing Note). London: Overseas Development Institute.

Chandy, L., & Kharas, H. (2011). Why can't we all just get along? The practical limits to international development cooperation. *Journal of International Development, 27*(5), 739–751.

Collier, P. (2016). *The ethical foundations of aid: Two duties of rescue* (BSG Working Paper Series). Oxford: Blavatnik School of Government, Oxford University.

Dietrich, S. (2016). Donor political economies and the pursuit of aid effectiveness. *International Organization, 70*(1), 65–102.

Dreher, A., Eichenauer, V. Z., & Gehring, K. (2016). Geopolitics, aid, and growth: The impact of UN Security Council membership on the effectiveness of aid. *World Bank Economic Review, 32*(2), 1–25.

Fejerskov, A., Lundsgaarde, E., & Cold-Ravnkilde, S. (2017). Recasting the "new actors in development" research agenda. *European Journal of Development Research, 29*(5), 1070–1085.

Finnemore, M., & Sikkink, K. (2001). Taking stock: The constructivist research program in international relations and comparative politics. *Annual Review of Political Science, 4,* 391–416.

Fuchs, A., Dreher, A., & Nunnenkamp, P. (2014). Determinants of donor generosity: A survey of the aid budget literature. *World Development, 56,* 172–199.

Fukuda-Parr, S., & Shiga, H. (2016). *Normative framing of development cooperation: Japanese bilateral aid between the DAC and southern donors* (JICA Research Institute Working Paper 135). Tokyo: Japan International Cooperation Agency Research Institute.

Girod, D. (2008, November 14–15). *Cut from the same cloth? Bilateral vs. multilateral aid*. Paper presented at the Annual Meeting of the International Political Economy Society, Philadelphia, PA.

Girod, D. (2012). Effective foreign aid following civil war: The nonstrategic-desperation hypothesis. *American Journal of Political Science, 56*(1), 188–201.
Gov.UK. (2018, August 28). *PM's speech in Cape Town.* https://www.gov.uk/government/speeches/pms-speech-in-cape-town-28-august-2018.
Gulrajani, N. (2016). *Bilateral vs multilateral aid channels: Strategic choices for donors* (ODI Report). London: Overseas Development Institute.
Gulrajani, N. (2017). Bilateral donors and the age of the national interest: What prospects for challenge by development agencies? *World Development, 96,* 375–389.
Gulrajani, N., & Calleja, R. (2019). *Understanding donor motivations: Developing the Principled Aid Index* (ODI Working Paper 548). London: Overseas Development Institute.
Gulrajani, N., Mawdsley, E., & Roychoudhury, S. (2019). *The new development diplomacy in middle-income countries* (ODI Working Paper). London: Overseas Development Institute. Manuscript in preparation.
Gulrajani, N., & Swiss, L. (2017). *Why do countries become donors? Assessing the drivers and implications of donor proliferation* (ODI Report). London: Overseas Development Institute.
Gulrajani, N., & Swiss, L. (2018). Donor proliferation to what ends? New donor countries and the search for legitimacy. *Canadian Journal of Development Studies / Revue Canadienne D'études Du Développement, 40*(3), 1–21.
Gulrajani, N., & Swiss, L. (2019). Donorship in a state of flux. In I. Olivia & Z. Perez (Eds.), *Aid, power and politics* (pp. 199–222). London: Routledge.
Hoeffler, A., & Outram, V. (2011). Need, merit, or self-interest—what determines the allocation of aid? *Review of Development Economics, 15*(2), 237–250.
Kaul, I. (2017). *Providing global public goods: What role for multilateral development banks?* (ODI Report). London: Overseas Development Institute.
Keijzer, N., & Lundsgaarde, E. (2017). *When unintended effects become intended: Implications of "mutual benefit" discourses for development studies and evaluation practice.* (Ministry of Foreign Affairs of the Netherlands Working Paper No. 2017/7). The Hague: Ministry of Foreign Affairs.
Keijzer, N., & Lundsgaarde, E. (2018). When "unintended effects" reveal hidden intentions: Implications of "mutual benefit" discourses for evaluating development cooperation. *Evaluation and Program Planning, 68,* 210–217.
Kharas, H., & Rogerson, A. (2017). *Global development trends and challenges: Horizon 2025 revisited* (ODI Report). London: Overseas Development Institute.
Kilby, C., & Dreher, A. (2010). The impact of aid on growth revisited: Do donor motives matter? *Economics Letters, 107*(3), 338–340.
Kragelund, P. (2015). Towards convergence and cooperation in the global development finance regime: Closing Africa's policy space? *Cambridge Review of International Affairs, 28*(2), 246–262.
Lancaster, C. (2007). *Foreign aid: Diplomacy, development, domestic politics.* Chicago, IL: University of Chicago Press.
Lumsdaine, D. (1993). *Moral vision in international politics: The foreign aid regime 1949–1989.* Princeton, NJ: Princeton University Press.
Lumsdaine, D., & Schopf, J. C. (2007). Changing values and the recent rise in Korean development assistance. *The Pacific Review, 20*(2), 221–255.
Lundsgaarde, E. (2012). *The domestic politics of foreign aid.* London: Routledge.
Maizels, A., & Nissanke, M. K. (1984). Motivations for aid to developing countries. *World Development, 12*(9), 879–900.

Manuel, M., Desai, H., Samman, E., & Evans, M. (2018). *Financing the end of extreme poverty* (ODI Working Paper). London: Overseas Development Institute.

Mawdsley, E. (2015). Development geography 1: Cooperation, competition and convergence between "North" and "South". *Progress in Human Geography, 41*(1), 1–19.

Mawdsley, E. (2018). The "Southernisation" of development? *Asia Pacific Viewpoint, 59*(2), 173–185.

Mawdsley, E. (2019). South–South cooperation 3.0? Managing the consequences of success in the decade ahead. *Oxford Development Studies, 47*(3), 259–274.

Mawdsley, E., Murray, W. E., Overton, J., Scheyvens, R., & Banks, G. (2017). Exporting stimulus and "shared prosperity": Re-inventing foreign aid for a retro liberal era. *Development Policy Review, 36*(S1), 25–43.

McKinley, R. D., & Little, R. (1977). A foreign policy model of US bilateral aid allocation. *World Politics, 30*(1), 58–86.

McKinley, R. D., & Little, R. (1978a). A foreign policy model of the distribution of British bilateral aid. *British Journal of Political Science, 8*(3), 313–332.

McKinley, R. D., & Little, R. (1978b). A French aid relationship: A foreign policy model of the distribution of French bilateral aid. *Development and Change, 9*(3), 459–478.

McKinley, R. D., & Little, R. (1979). The US aid relationship: A test of the recipient need and the donor interest models. *Political Studies, 27*(2), 236–250.

Milner, H., & Tingley, D. (2013). *Introduction to the geopolitics of foreign aid*. Cheltenham, UK: Edward Elgar Publishing Ltd.

Morgenthau, H. (1962). A political theory of foreign aid. *American Political Science Review, 56*(2), 301–309.

Packenham, R. A. (1966). Political-development doctrines in the American foreign aid program. *World Politics, 18*(2), 194–235.

Pratt, C. (1989). Humane internationalism: Its significance and its variants. In C. Pratt (Ed.), *Internationalism under strain: The North-South policies of Canada, the Netherlands, Norway, and Sweden* (pp. 3–23). Toronto, ON: University of Toronto Press.

Pratt, C. (2000). Alleviating global poverty or enhancing security: Competing rationales for Canadian development assistance. In J. Freedman (Ed.), *Transforming development: Foreign aid in a changing world* (pp. 37–60). Toronto: University of Toronto Press.

Rabinowitz, G., & Greenhill, R. (2018). *Background paper: Aid in the national interest*. (Mimeo).

Schraeder, P. J., Hook, S. W., & Taylor, B. (1998). Clarifying the foreign aid puzzle. *World Politics, 50*(2), 294–323.

Steele, C. (2011). *Disease control and donor priorities: The political economy of development aid for health* (Ph.D. 3496673). Urbana, IL: University of Illinois at Urbana-Champaign.

Stone, R. W. (2010). *Buying influence: Development aid between the Cold War and the War on Terror* (University of Rochester Working Paper). Rochester, NY: University of Rochester.

UN News (2018, September 3). *In Beijing, UN chief urges win-win collaboration between China and Africa for "the future we want"*. https://news.un.org/en/story/2018/09/1018242.

UN News (2019, March 22). *UN conference agrees better ways for Global South countries to work together on sustainable development.* https://news.un.org/en/story/2019/03/1035271.

Van Dam, P., & van Dis, W. (2014). Beyond the merchant and the clergyman: Assessing moral claims about development cooperation. *Third World Quarterly, 35*(9), 1636–1655.

Van Heerde-Hudson, J., Hudson, D., & Morini, P. (2018). *Reasons for giving aid: A government policy in search of a public?* https://devcommslab.org/blog/reasons-for-giving-aid-a-government-policy-in-search-of-a-public.

Voeten, E., Strezhnev, A., Bailey, M. (2009). *United Nations General Assembly voting data: Harvard Dataverse.* https://dataverse.harvard.edu/dataset.xhtml?persistentId=hdl:1902.1/12379.

Wood, T., & Hoy, C. (2018). *Helping us or helping them? What makes aid appeal to Australians?* (Discussion Paper 75). Canberra: Development Policy Centre, Australian National University.

Yanguas, P. (2018). *Why we lie about aid: Development and the messy politics of change.* London: Zed Books.

Open Access This chapter is licensed under the terms of the Creative Commons Attribution 4.0 International License (http://creativecommons.org/licenses/by/4.0/), which permits use, sharing, adaptation, distribution and reproduction in any medium or format, as long as you give appropriate credit to the original author(s) and the source, provide a link to the Creative Commons license and indicate if changes were made.

The images or other third party material in this chapter are included in the chapter's Creative Commons license, unless indicated otherwise in a credit line to the material. If material is not included in the chapter's Creative Commons license and your intended use is not permitted by statutory regulation or exceeds the permitted use, you will need to obtain permission directly from the copyright holder.

CHAPTER 13

Monitoring and Evaluation in South-South Cooperation: The Case of CPEC in Pakistan

Murad Ali

13.1 Introduction

Among the six economic corridors envisaged under the BRI, CPEC is the only corridor that is already in the implementation phase, as work on a number of multi-sector infrastructure projects is already in progress. With a portfolio of about $62 billion for the 2015–2030 period, the leadership in both China and Pakistan has significant expectations for CPEC. In just a short time, the corridor has transformed the bilateral ties between the two countries. These ties have been cordial in the past but have been limited mainly to mutual cooperation in the areas of defence and security (Ali, 2017). Since the commencement of CPEC, the China–Pakistan relationship has expanded into a multi-dimensional partnership. Regular visits and meetings take place between the delegates of both countries. These meetings are not limited to political representatives and government officials—stakeholders from academia, business, think tanks, and the media also interact regularly. If successfully implemented and utilised, CPEC is expected to significantly enhance regional connectivity and trade and could facilitate the inter-regional movement of people, goods, and services.

The chapter examines the development partnership between both governments under CPEC to explore whether the official narrative of SSC is practised on the ground. It investigates whether SSC principles and features that China is advocating are being upheld while implementing projects in Pakistan. The chapter begins with an overview of CPEC and its potential contribution to the

---

M. Ali (✉)
Department of Political Science, University of Malakand, Chakdara, Pakistan

© The Author(s) 2021
S. Chaturvedi et al. (eds.), *The Palgrave Handbook of Development Cooperation for Achieving the 2030 Agenda*,
https://doi.org/10.1007/978-3-030-57938-8_13

2030 Agenda for Sustainable Development and the Sustainable Development Goals (SDGs) in Pakistan. A description of the analytical framework and its appropriateness to assess the quality of SSC constitutes the subsequent parts of the discussion. Based on the research findings, the chapter then discusses CPEC in the light of the five dimensions and 20 indicators that form the core of the SSC framework.

13.2 CPEC: A Catalyst for the 2030 Agenda and SDGs in Pakistan?

While the world has embraced the 2030 Agenda and the 17 SDGs, finding financial means to attain these goals remains an uphill task. Most countries, particularly those in the Global South, are faced with numerous challenges, and it is beyond their individual capacities to implement the 2030 Agenda without external financing. It is estimated that an aggregate of $3.3–$4.5 trillion is needed annually to implement the 2030 Agenda globally (World Bank, 2015). Although there are multiple sources of external financing that developing countries have access to, still "the annual SDG financing gap in developing countries is estimated at approximately $2.5 trillion" (Organisation for Economic Co-operation and Development [OECD], 2016, p. 69). The Addis Ababa Action Agenda has identified foreign direct investment (FDI) as an essential source to complement national development efforts (United Nations General Assembly [UNGA], 2015). It is argued that "investments in developing countries – and even in the least developed countries – are seen as business opportunities [...] companies provide jobs, infrastructure, innovation and social services" (OECD, 2016, p. 17).

In view of the strong link between external financing and its potential to contribute to socio-economic development, there are significant prospects associated with Chinese SSC in the form of CPEC in Pakistan. Three main components of CPEC are investments in the energy sector ($35 billion) as well as in communication infrastructure and special economic zones (SEZs) ($11 billion). Substantial investments in these areas have the potential to promote three SDGs, including Goals 7, 8, and 9. These three SDGs ensure access to affordable, reliable, sustainable, and modern energy for all (Goal 7), promote sustained, inclusive, and sustainable economic growth, full and productive employment, and decent work for all (Goal 8), and focus on building resilient infrastructure, promoting inclusive and sustainable industrialisation, and fostering innovation (Goal 9) (UNGA, 2015, p. 14). Thus, the execution of CPEC is expected to directly contribute towards attaining these three SDGs. If externalities regarding social and environmental costs are effectively addressed, Pakistan expects that CPEC will help in resolving the chronic issue of energy shortfalls, and people will have access to reliable and sustainable energy. Similarly, with the creations of SEZs, people will have better job opportunities and means of earning their livelihoods. With investments in the communication infrastructure, people are expected to have access to better roads and transport facilities. In sum, these three SDGs are directly related to CPEC projects, and Pakistan could significantly move ahead on these selected SDGs if various ventures planned under the corridor are successfully implemented.

Alongside contributing towards promoting the above SDGs directly, CPEC-related investments are likely to help in achieving various SDGs indirectly. For example, Goal 1 states to "end poverty in all its forms everywhere" (UNGA, 2015, p. 14). CPEC projects have created "more than 30,000 direct jobs for Pakistanis" (Government of Pakistan, 2018, p. 186), and the government estimates that it would generate two million jobs in the long run. This means if two million people secure employment, two million families will have a better means of livelihood and, subsequently, will achieve food security (Goal 2) as well as will have access to better health services (Goal 3), quality education (Goal 4), and clean water and sanitation (Goal 6). In sum, the effective execution of CPEC has enormous potential to contribute towards achieving a number of SDGs in Pakistan.

13.3 Analytical Framework for Assessing CPEC

The development partnership between Pakistan and China presents a compelling case to analyse the Chinese approach to SSC in Pakistan. China's modus operandi of project selection and execution is evaluated through an analytical framework developed by NeST. As presented in Table 13.1, the framework has five broad dimensions for assessing the effectiveness of SSC. It merits a mention here that the key themes identified in the SSC framework are largely the ones Beijing has endorsed in its official documents pertaining to foreign aid. As SSC is mostly dominated by government-to-government agreements with limited transparency, an assessment of China as the largest SSC provider is a very insightful case in the broader context of SSC. The aim is to critically evaluate Chinese-funded interventions in Pakistan and assess to what extent key features of SSC are actually adhered to. In analysing Chinese assistance to Pakistan, this chapter has two broad objectives. The first is to contribute to debates on the significance of SSC in the 2030 Agenda and its role in financing regional infrastructure projects. Second, by applying appropriate monitoring and evaluation (M&E) systems for SSC in the context of Pakistan, it is among a handful of research studies on this subject. The findings are of great significance to further refine and improve the analytical instruments for evaluating development cooperation between SSC actors. Also, the findings and lessons learnt are of equal importance for academics, researchers, practitioners, and policy-makers in the field of aid and development effectiveness, which is a critical area for the implementation of the 2030 Agenda.

The analytical framework consists of five dimensions and 20 indicators. The first element is inclusive national ownership, comprising four indicators. As SSC is mostly considered to be based on government-to-government

Table 13.1 Analytical framework for assessing China–Pakistan development partnership

Dimensions	Inclusive national ownership	Horizontality	Self-reliance and sustainability	Accountability and transparency	Development efficiency
Indicators	Multi-stakeholder partnerships	Mutual benefit	Capacity-building	Data management and reporting	Flexibility and adaptation
	People-centred inclusivity	Shared decisions and resources	Knowledge and technology transfer	M&E systems	Time and cost efficiency
	Demand-driven	Trust and solidarity	Use of country systems and human resources	Transparency and access to information	Internal and external coordination
	Non-conditionality	Global political coalitions	Domestic revenue generation	Mutual accountability and joint reviews	Policy coherence for development

Source Besharati et al. (2017)

relations, the framework stresses inclusive participation involving various stakeholders, including non-state actors and civil society organisations. Similarly, it focusses on people-centred inclusivity, which implies that SSC activities help in improving the socio-economic status of the poorest and most disenfranchised populations. The second aspect of the framework is horizontality, as SSC is considered to be a development partnership between equal partners. It means that instead of donors and recipients per se, SSC is for mutual benefit. Joint decision-making processes and mechanisms for sharing resources are among its key features. The third dimension is self-reliance and sustainability, which implies that SSC should aim to reduce external dependency. It can be achieved by various means, such as consistently enhancing and improving local capacity via the transfer of relevant knowledge and technology. The fourth element of the analytical framework is that SSC should be characterised by accountability and transparency. It elaborates that there must be sufficient data management and reporting systems. Also, there must be effective and quality M&E systems and tools so that various phases of the project cycle are properly evaluated against the project goals and targets. The fifth and last dimension of the framework is about the overall efficiency or impact of SSC endeavours in reaching the intended development targets.

The framework is very useful, as it has not only enshrined the key principles with which to evaluate the effectiveness of SSC, but the selected dimensions and respective indicators are also closely related to the main features advocated by Beijing in its foreign aid policy documents. However, the framework has its own limitations. By and large, the five dimensions resemble the discourse on aid effectiveness principles led by the Development Assistance Committee (DAC) of the Organisation for Economic Co-operation and Development (OECD). There is still no unanimous intergovernmental consensus among Southern aid providers on the use of such frameworks for assessing the impact of SSC. Besides, some of the indicators, such as "trust and solidarity", "global political coalitions", and "flexibility and adaptation", are quite broad concepts open to various interpretations. Hence, there is a need for further elaboration and refinement of the indicators regarding how these principles can be measured and used to assess the value of SSC. Despite these limitations, the framework is helpful, as it provides an effective and appropriate set of dimensions and principles with which to evaluate the quality of SSC.

There is another peculiar characteristic of the analytical framework: The five broad dimensions enshrined in the SSC framework are more or less the same as those that China has officially endorsed in its policy documents on foreign aid, with the exception of accountability and transparency. As per policy documents, China has vowed to adhere to such principles in the allocation of development cooperation. Beijing clearly mentions peaceful co-existence, respect for sovereignty, and mutual benefit as its guiding doctrines. Similarly, values such as mutual respect, equality, fulfilling promises, building local capacity, addressing the actual needs of partner countries, and adaptation and flexibility in development cooperation policy are some of the stated principles and features of development finance provided by China (People's Republic of China, 2014). Therefore, "while discussions around defining, accounting and reporting SSC flows are still inconclusive and present a vast diversity of views and approaches" (Besharati et al., 2017, p. 5), the analytical framework provides an appropriate set of indicators on which the quality and effectiveness of SSC partnerships can be measured.

13.4 CPEC IN THE SSC FRAMEWORK: FINDINGS AND DISCUSSION

As illustrated earlier, the analytical framework has five broad dimensions with 20 indicators. The following section discusses CPEC in the SSC framework in detail.

13.4.1 Inclusive National Ownership and CPEC

To assess the quality and effectiveness of SSC, the first aspect is inclusive national ownership. Rather than simply a state-to-state or government-to-government partnership, SSC initiatives should have policy frameworks and institutional mechanisms that involve various state and non-state actors to ensure the inclusive participation of a broad range of stakeholders (Indicator 1). When exploring which kinds of mechanisms and processes are in place to enable the participation of multiple stakeholders in CPEC projects, in the case of Pakistan, a number of stakeholders are involved in the identification, prioritisation, and recommendation of projects that are funded under CPEC. At the top, there is the Joint Cooperation Committee (JCC), co-chaired by the minister of Planning Development Reform (PDR) from the Pakistani side and the vice-chairman of the National Development and Reform Commission (NDRC) from the Chinese side. The JCC is the highest body, where all projects are discussed, reviewed, and approved. It comprises both political figures and administrative officials, such as heads of different departments and experts from various fields. Under the JCC, there are five joint working groups (JWGs), comprising experts from government agencies of both countries. Thus, at these two tiers, both Chinese and Pakistani officials are involved.

Within Pakistan, there are several actors involved in CPEC at various levels. First, projects are included in CPEC because of the financial and technical need, and all such projects are selected via existing government decision-making processes (personal communication with deputy director of CPEC, September 2017). The deputy director further stated that the Economic Coordination Committee, the Executive Committee of the National Economic Council, and the Central Development Working Party as well as other approving bodies and relevant ministries are involved in the identification and recommendation of projects to the JCC. Also, there is the CPEC Cabinet Committee, headed by the prime minister, comprising several ministers and secretaries/heads of key ministries engaged in CPEC projects. In addition, there is a Parliamentary Committee on CPEC comprising members from the ruling party as well as various opposition parties. In addition, there is a High-Powered Interprovincial Committee headed by the prime minister, with representation from all provinces and the federation. Thus, various national stakeholders and policy-making institutions are involved to ensure inclusive national ownership.[1]

Another indicator of the SSC framework is people-centred inclusivity (Indicator 2), which implies that SSC activities need to benefit the poorest and less advantaged people and that both SSC actors follow the "labour, land, safety, environmental and social standards of both partner countries" (Besharati et al., 2017, p. 13). Because about 75 per cent of CPEC's funding portfolio is for energy projects, access to an uninterrupted power supply could greatly benefit common people. An official in the Ministry of PDR stated that various roads planned under CPEC would enhance interprovincial connectivity and connect the less-developed areas of Baluchistan, Khyber Pakhtunkhwa, and Azad Jammu and Kashmir with the main corridor and help in bringing a new era of development to these parts (personal communication, September 2017). Similarly, almost all provinces have energy projects and industrial zones under CPEC. Hence, in terms of people-centred inclusivity, the expected socio-economic benefits would not be concentrated on certain groups of people or geographical areas, but would reach diverse segments of the population.

Regarding the protection of people and the environment, there are concerns about CO_2 emissions associated with coal-based thermal-power projects. Both Pakistani and Chinese officials stated during interviews that they have committed to adopt clean-coal combustion technologies that conform to international standards. Chinese deputy chief of mission in Pakistan stated that they are bringing to Pakistan the latest supercritical technology, which is used elsewhere in coal plants in the United States and Europe (personal communication, September 2017). Similarly, the deputy director of CPEC at the Ministry of PDR also asserted that Pakistan is conscious of the environmental repercussions of coal-based energy stations, and therefore consistent efforts are underway to minimise the costs to environment—the latest technology has been imported for coal power plants and offers reduced levels of CO_2 and other gas emission (personal communication, September 2017).

However, while interacting with a number of academics and civil society representatives in Pakistan, genuine concerns were raised that coal-based power plants could have serious environmental implications. A researcher from an Islamabad-based think tank stated that coal-fired power plants will prove harmful to the environment in the long run, particularly in Punjab, as the province is an agricultural hub of the country (personal communication, September 2017). Thus, although there are high hopes associated with huge investments being made in the energy sector, a paradigm shift towards coal-fired power plants could have serious long-term environmental implications for Pakistan, which is already quite vulnerable to climate-induced hazards (Isran, 2017; Saleem, 2017a; Zaman, 2016). According to the Global

Climate Risk Index 2017, which ranks countries based on impacts of extreme weather events, both in terms of fatalities as well as economic losses, Pakistan is among the 10 most-affected countries (Kreft et al., 2017). Greater dependence on coal-based power plants could further increase its vulnerability to environmental risks.

The element of inclusive national ownership also focusses on the demand-driven nature of the SSC, which asserts that SSC initiatives need to be clearly aligned to the needs and national priorities of partner countries (Indicator 3). In CPEC, the demand-driven nature of Chinese investment and cooperation is evident from the target sectors. For instance, investments in the energy sector are one of the main components of CPEC, as about 75 per cent of the investments are being made in power projects. This is due to the fact that Pakistan has been suffering from an acute energy shortfall. During times of acute need, particularly in the summer, the shortfall in energy reaches 7000 megawatts (MW), which "intensifies the woes of consumers, disrupts industrial and agricultural production and adds to costs making Pakistani products uncompetitive internationally" (Government of Pakistan, 2014, p. 16). According to policy documents, energy deficiency has a detrimental effect on the economy, causing an estimated 4–7 per cent loss to the country's gross domestic product (GDP) (Government of Pakistan, 2014).

In view of this, investments in the energy sector are a major component of CPEC. A total of 21 projects have been identified and planned in the energy sector, with a cost of more than $35 billion and having the capacity to generate 17,045 MW (CPEC Secretariat, 2017). Regarding the modus operandi of identifying energy and other infrastructure projects, the deputy director in the CPEC Secretariat stated that all Chinese assistance is demand-driven, as either the federal or provincial government identifies projects, which are then discussed as per existing procedures at different levels. After internal discussions, the projects are sent to the JCC, which decides whether to finance it under CPEC or not (personal communication, September 2017). Hence, as per government officials, it seems that all CPEC-related projects are demand-driven, whether they are in the energy sector or infrastructure.

In relation to Indicator 4 of this SSC principle—dealing with non-conditionality—there are some concerns in Pakistan. For example, a researcher from an Islamabad-based think tank stated that Chinese investment has a very high rate of return, up to 17 per cent, and CPEC is going to become a debt trap for the country (personal communication, September 2017). There is also a perception that Pakistan could be in serious financial trouble when it comes to the outflow of loan payments along with payable interest and profit remittances to Chinese companies. Hence, various economists and analysts have argued that this would put immense pressure on Pakistan's foreign reserves in the future once the repayment period begins (Ahmad, 2017; Isran, 2017; Saleem, 2017b). Some critics even argue that it is the colonisation of Pakistan by China, as CPEC is a Chinese project, for Chinese interests, and Pakistan just happens to be part of the geographical terrain (Khan and Hyder, 2017; Zaidi, 2017).

In contrast to this narrative, officials in policy-making institutions argue that the repayment of loans and outward flows of FDI and remittances would not pose a big financial challenge. An official in the Ministry of PDR stated that the interest rate was 2 per cent and Pakistan could easily repay loans, as CPEC projects would significantly boost productivity in various sectors (personal communication, September 2017). The official explained that CPEC would generate significant revenues, as there would be uninterrupted electricity and power for industries, which, in return, would lead to enhanced exports. Similarly, it was pointed out that the modernisation of transport infrastructure would result in greater inter-regional trade as well as in the generation of revenues in the form of a toll tax. In sum, there are two somewhat contrasting perceptions about whether there is any explicit or implicit form of conditionality from the Chinese side and what the long-term financial implications of CPEC are for Pakistan.

13.4.2   *CPEC in the Context of Horizontality*

The second aspect of the SSC framework is horizontality, as development partnerships between Southern actors are considered to be a mutual alliance between equal partners. It suggests that rather than being for the benefit of aid donors and recipients per se, SSC is for mutual benefit (Indicator 5), and there are joint decision-making mechanisms and resources (Indicator 6). Other key features of SSC under this dimension are trust and solidarity (Indicator 7) and global political coalitions or international alliances at different fora (Indicator 8) where Southern partners have shared interests.

Viewing CPEC within these parameters, there is a consensus—not only between the governments of both countries but also the intelligentsia from both Pakistan and China—that the corridor is mutually beneficial. Regarding its potential to enhance trade and regional connectivity, officials from both countries have stated that CPEC offers a win-win situation. The corridor presents a very viable alternate land-and-sea route via Pakistan's Gwadar Port to western regions of China. Thus, it has a number of mutual benefits concerning increased trade and regional connectivity.

Another dimension of the SSC is shared decision-making mechanisms for implementing development interventions. As mentioned earlier, to promote the construction of CPEC-related projects in Pakistan, the two countries set up the JCC, which is co-chaired by the minister of PDR from the Pakistani side and the vice-chairman of the NDRC from the Chinese side. The JCC is the highest body comprising both political figures and officials, such as heads of different departments. Under the JCC, there are five joint working groups, comprising experts from both countries, dealing with long-term planning, energy, transport infrastructure, industrial cooperation/SEZs, and the Gwadar Port. The JCC secretariats are within the NDRC in China and the Ministry of PDR in Pakistan, respectively. The two secretariats are responsible for communicating and coordinating with the respective line ministries related to the construction of CPEC. Thus, there exists a proper joint decision-making mechanism, which provides a platform for policy-makers and other stakeholders from both countries to discuss all CPEC projects and related issues.

Trust, solidarity, and broader political alliances are other key elements of the SSC framework under the domain of horizontality. In the context of SSC, it denotes that Southern partners have solidarity based on "common interest, objectives and principles" (Besharati et al., 2017, p. 14). China and Pakistan have a number of interests, including security concerns vis-à-vis India, geographical proximity, the role played by Islamabad in breaking the isolation of China in the 1960s, as well as backing China on issues such as Taiwan, Tibet, and Xinjiang (Ali, 2017; Hussain, 2016). The two countries have been cooperating in the field of defence and security for decades and have developed an "unusual level of mutual trust" (Small, 2015, p. 44). Thus, as far as trust, solidarity, and political alliances are concerned, it continues to remain unprecedented at the state or government level.

13.4.3 *Elements of Self-Reliance and Sustainability in CPEC*

To assess CPEC in the SSC framework, the third aspect is self-reliance and sustainability, which can be achieved through various means such as by consistently enhancing and improving local capacity (Indicator 9) as well as via the transfer of relevant knowledge and technology (Indicator 10). For accomplishing long-term and sustainable development outcomes, principles such as the use of local systems and resources (Indicator 11) and taking initiatives that could assist in domestic revenue generation (Indicator 12) are considered vital for SSC effectiveness.

For capacity-building and the transfer of knowledge and technology, various initiatives have been undertaken. These include offering scholarships to Pakistani students for studying in China as well as short-term scholarships for learning the Chinese language in Pakistan in order to prepare a well-trained labour force to properly implement CPEC projects (personal communication with officials in the CPEC secretariat, September 2017). Besides scholarships offered by the government, there are also funding opportunities from other sources. For example, the China Road and Bridge Corporation (CRBC)—one of the four large-scale, state-owned companies in China—is also implementing construction projects in Pakistan. In consultation with the Higher Education Commission, which is Pakistan's premier education body, the CRBC offered 30 fully funded scholarships to Pakistani students to study for their master's degree at Southeast University, China. Similarly, various other companies and organisations involved in CPEC are stated to have contributed to various social programmes in respective locations (personal communication with deputy chief of mission, Embassy of China, September 2017). Thus, to some extent, CPEC projects have been contributing towards capacity-building and the transfer of skills and technology in different areas.

In relation to the principle of untied aid, there has been a dominant perception that almost all procurement for CPEC projects is done from China. There has been criticism in the media that there is no competitive international bidding, as CPEC projects are implemented by Chinese companies without such bidding processes (Mustafa, 2018; Saleem, 2017b). A researcher in an Islamabad-based think tank stated that almost all the machinery and equipment employed in Pakistan has been brought from China, and that there has been no open bidding process (personal communication, September 2017). About 75 per cent of CPEC financing is in the form of FDI, loans obtained by Chinese companies from Chinese banks. According to Pakistani officials, these companies and investors are better placed to get the most relevant, affordable, and advanced technology for their projects (personal communication, September 2017). The fact remains that, in CPEC projects, almost all procurement has been done from China.

Another element of this dimension is the use of local systems and resources. In Pakistan, there are media reports that Chinese companies have been bringing most of the workforce from China rather than employing locals (Hussain, 2017; Saleem, 2017b). Among researchers that were interviewed in Islamabad, the prevailing perception is that China is bringing its own labour, and the use of Pakistani labour or other resources is minimal. In contradiction to this, Pakistani and Chinese officials have stated that thousands of locals have been employed in various projects, and that the local cement and construction industries have witnessed a significant boost on account of CPEC. An official at the CPEC secretariat stated that the ratio of Chinese nationals working in CPEC projects would be 20–30 per cent (personal communication, September 2017). Similarly, the senior vice-president of the Islamabad Chamber of Commerce & Industry stated that the cost of unskilled or semi-skilled labour is about $700 per month in China and about $200–270 in Pakistan, so it would not make sense for the Chinese to bring their own workers (personal communication, September 2017). The chairman of the Parliamentary Committee on CPEC was quoted in the media stating that, at present, about 9581 Chinese nationals are working on CPEC-related interventions, and around 10,000 are involved in non-CPEC projects (Haider, 2017). He explained that a total of about 20,000 Chinese are working as specialists and supervisors for all projects taking place with China's assistance, and he added that around 60,000 Pakistanis are working on CPEC projects. The deputy chief of mission at the Embassy of China in Islamabad stated that some elements have been spreading this misperception that China is coming up with its own workforce rather than giving opportunities to local people (personal communication, September 2017). He also questioned why China would bring its own labour, given that cheaper labour is available locally. The Chinese diplomat also stated that it would be illogical to bring raw materials or other resources that are already available in Pakistan. Thus, it seems to be an overstatement that Chinese companies are bringing their own workers and that there are few job opportunities for locals in CPEC projects.

Another important aspect of the analytical framework is domestic revenue generation and how SSC endeavours contribute to it in partner countries. There are significant prospects associated with CPEC and its potential for revenue generation. An official in the Board of Investment stated that the toll income alone generated by the CPEC route is hoped to be three times the national budget of the country once it becomes fully functional by 2030 (Board of Investment, 2017). However, a researcher calculated the potential of the CPEC toll and found that it seems highly unlikely that it could generate about $135 billion, an annual revenue stream that is two to three times the total CPEC portfolio (Khawar, 2017). Khawar argued that, based on China's total trade with Africa and the Middle East, if 30 per cent of it is diverted through the CPEC route, which is shorter than the current sea lane used by China for its exports and imports, Pakistan could generate an annual toll income of up to $4.8 billion. It must be clarified that those calculations are based on tolls from Chinese containers only. In its long-term plan, detailed in "Pakistan Vision 2025", the country has identified regional connectivity as a key element (Government of Pakistan, 2014). The policy document specifically mentions CPEC playing a vital role in achieving the potential of regional connectivity and trade with member states of the South Asian Association for Regional Cooperation, the Association of Southeast Asian Nations (ASEAN), the Central Asia Regional Economic Cooperation, and the Economic Cooperation Organization. A UN report has also stated that economic benefits of the corridor will go beyond participating countries and "will also benefit several neighbouring landlocked economies via access to sea through Pakistan" (United Nations Economic and Social Commission for Asia and the Pacific, 2017, p. 9). In that case, there is a significant potential for increased revenue generation in the form of tolls and other means of domestic financing once the corridor is fully operational and utilised to its true potential to connect various countries of the region.

13.4.4 Accountability and Transparency in CPEC Projects

The fourth aspect of the analytical framework in which CPEC is assessed is that SSC should espouse accountability and transparency. It is argued that there must be sufficient data management and reporting channels (Indicator 13) as well as M&E systems (Indicator 14) so that different phases of the project cycle are properly evaluated against the project goals and targets. Another key feature is that SSC providers (as well as receivers) need to be transparent regarding the sharing of data and information about the terms and conditions of financing (Indicator 15), and that such information must be accessible to civil society organisations, parliament, academia, and the media. Increased transparency regarding how SSC is provided and who the key decision-makers are would make the main stakeholders more responsible and accountable (Indicator 16). Thus, for enhanced reciprocal accountability and win-win situations, transparency is vital.

In relation to this dimension and associated indicators, some initiatives have been taken. There are interactive websites that share a significant amount of information about projects in various sectors as well as about the companies and organisations involved. For example, most information about the ongoing projects and those completed—or nearing completion—are given on the website of the CPEC secretariat, a dedicated government unit in the Ministry of PDR. The website also contains the geographical location of CPEC projects as well as their estimated costs and completion dates. Additionally, there is the CPEC Portal, which is jointly managed by the Pakistan-China Institute, a private think tank based in Islamabad, and China Radio International, China's state-level radio and television media organisation specialising in international communications (The CPEC Portal, 2017). This website also shares information, reports, media coverage, and events related to CPEC. In view of this, a former minister of PDR stated in an interview that nothing has been concealed regarding CPEC and all details are available on its website (Iqbal, 2017). This was also reiterated by various Pakistani and Chinese officials during interviews that CPEC projects are being implemented in a very transparent way and no data or information is kept secret.

Although the government has tried to come up with information-sharing mechanisms, there is still considerable scepticism about the general transparency of CPEC projects. There have been various critical op-eds in print media stating that the financial mechanism of CPEC is quite opaque, as the government has never shared any official policy document in this regard (Husain, 2017; Hussain, 2017; Isran, 2017; Khan and Hyder, 2017; Saleem, 2017b; Zaidi, 2017). Similar opinions were expressed by several academics during my field visit. Although government functionaries claim that everything is transparent and no information has been kept secret, there are perceptions in the media that the government has been hiding the terms and conditions of Chinese investment and concessional loans. For example, Pakistani and Chinese officials who were interviewed stated that the interest rate is 2–3 per cent (personal communication, September 2017). However, a request to an official in the Ministry of PDR for a copy of a memorandum of understanding (MoU) or agreement was not entertained, and it was stated that state-to-state agreements are exempt from the Right to Information Act (personal communication, September 2017). Although there is significant anecdotal information from various quarters, the fact remains that the government has not issued any policy document that specifically mentions Pakistan–China MoUs or agreements, nor the terms and conditions of development projects under CPEC.[2]

In view of this, it can be stated that there is a detailed step-by-step process in which different aspects of all CPEC projects are regularly reviewed by various groups and committees. It is too early to judge the efficacy of the process, as the real impacts of CPEC projects can only be evaluated once they are fully implemented. However, the presence of such mechanisms for decision-making and reviewing progress indicates that both sides have come up with appropriate measures to ensure reciprocal accountability for projects that are closely monitored not only by the independent media in Pakistan, but also by a number of international organisations.

13.4.5 Development Efficiency and the Role of CPEC

The fifth aspect of the SSC analytical framework is about its effectiveness in achieving development targets. There are four indicators to measure this dimension. Here, CPEC is assessed together in the light of flexibility and adaptation to local contexts (Indicator 17) and time and cost efficiency (Indicator 18). It is followed by a discussion of the two final indicators of SSC, including internal and external coordination and complementarity (Indicator 19) and policy coherence for development (Indicator 20) and how CPEC can be analysed according to these features.

Assessed in the light of "development effectiveness" and associated indicators, there are positive prospects associated with CPEC projects regarding power generation, creation of employment opportunities, and infrastructure upgradation. If viewed within the framework of specific indicators and principles such as time and cost efficiency, for example, an official in the Ministry of PDR stated that a coal-fired project in Sahiwal, Punjab—with a capacity of 1320 MW and costing $1.6 billion—was completed six months ahead of schedule (personal communication, September 2017). The official also stated that utilising cheap local labour and resources made this project more feasible and cost-efficient. In terms of its overall development impact, there is a broad consensus in Pakistan that CPEC is a win-win project for the entire region, as it will lead to greater regional connectivity and lower transport and communication costs. For instance, an aggregate of $11 billion has been allocated for numerous communication and transport projects along the CPEC route to connect China with the Indian Ocean via the Gwadar Port that will also increase interprovincial connectivity across Pakistan. The lack of efficient transport and communication networks cost the country's economy 4–6 per cent of GDP annually (Government of Pakistan, 2014). To overcome this, Vision 2025 aims to "ensure reduction in transportation costs, safety in mobility, effective connectivity between rural areas and markets/urban centres, inter-provincial high-speed connectivity" and to establish high-capacity transport corridors connecting major regional trading partners (Government of Pakistan, 2014, p. 86). Thus, if properly implemented, CPEC projects could bring significant socio-economic benefits for both countries.

In relation to internal and external coordination (Indicator 19), both countries have established various coordination mechanisms in the form of the JCC and JWGs. In these working groups and committee, both Pakistani and Chinese officials and experts from several areas discuss all CPEC-related plans and policies.

With regard to policy coherence for development (Indicator 20), the two countries have been enjoying strong diplomatic and military ties for decades.

However, trade and economic relations between the two countries were weak but intensified after the signing of the Free Trade Agreement (FTA) in 2006. Similarly, after the official launch of CPEC in 2015, multidimensional ties between the two countries have expanded significantly. An official in the Embassy of China stated that CPEC has accelerated cooperation between the two countries in other fields as well, especially in the education sector, as China is granting scholarships to hundreds of Pakistani students (personal communication, September 2017). The official also stated that there are about 22,000 Pakistani students in China. While all these are encouraging signs for greater people-to-people contact, research also shows that Pakistan has not benefited much from the FTA. According to Malik (2017), although bilateral trade has increased overall from about $85 million in 1952 to $17 billion in 2014, Pakistan's trade deficit has increased significantly, reaching $12 billion in 2014. The author argues that, along with other factors, one of the reasons for this huge trade deficit is that exporters from other regions and countries such as ASEAN, Australia, and New Zealand are offered more preferential treatment under the FTA than Pakistani businessmen and exporters (Malik, 2017). In view of this—and for greater policy coherence for development—it can be validly argued that Pakistani traders and exporters need to be provided the same set of concessions in Chinese markets as are provided to exporters from other countries that have FTAs with China. If that were the case, Pakistani businesspersons could compete on a level playing field, and there would be more exports and subsequent development at the country level.

Overall, there are positive developmental prospects from CPEC for Pakistan, but there is also some scepticism. According to government policy documents, "the country's outlook is brightened and looks promising on the back of agricultural recovery, rebound in industrial activities and inflow of investment under CPEC" (Government of Pakistan, 2017, p. vi). On account of early harvest CPEC projects, Pakistan expects that overall economic growth will substantially increase from the current rate of 5–6 per cent to "over 8 per cent between 2018 and 2025" (Government of Pakistan, 2014, p. 44). Thus, CPEC holds considerable potential for the development of the region in the context of regional connectivity, diverse investment opportunities, industrial cooperation, financial cooperation, tourism, people-to-people contact, and livelihood opportunities.

In Pakistan, however, there are somewhat divided opinions about the role of CPEC and its development effectiveness. Some economists and analysts have argued that CPEC would provide more benefits to China than to Pakistan (Ahmad, 2017; Isran, 2017; Saleem, 2017b). There is a perception that Pakistan will bear much of the environmental, social, and economic cost, whereas the corridor and allied infrastructure facilities will be used by China, primarily for its own exports and imports, with few trickle-down effects for the local population (Khan and Hyder, 2017).

There have been positive indicators offered by international organisations regarding CPEC, not only for Pakistan but for the whole region. If successfully implemented, the economic potential is significant for Pakistan and its neighbouring countries. In its report on Pakistan's economy, the International Monetary Fund mentioned the potential impact of CPEC. The report states that the economy is "benefitting from rising investment related to CPEC [...] over the medium term, growth is expected to increase to about 6 per cent on the back of CPEC and other energy sector investments" (International Monetary Fund [IMF], 2017, p. 7). However, the report also cautioned that "over the medium-term, external payment obligations from CPEC-related investments would lead to a reduction in foreign reserves coverage, underscoring the need to foster a strong and sustained pick-up in exports" (IMF, 2017, p. 23). Hence, while CPEC-related investments are expected to resolve the chronic problem of energy deficiency and upgrade transport and communication infrastructure, it is essential to establish policies and plans to maximise its benefits for people and to minimise its long-term undesirable social, environmental, and economic implications.

13.5 Conclusion

Based on the findings concerning Chinese-funded projects in the light of SSC principles, this chapter argues that the China–Pakistan development partnership under CPEC is an example of SSC. For example, CPEC is a blend of investments and concessional loans obtained by Chinese companies from Chinese banks for implementing projects in Pakistan. In this way, the financial instrument is not purely developmental, nor does it come as aid in the form of a grant, but there seems to be a mutual belief that it is a win-win situation. The findings are summarised in Table 13.2, as per the five main dimensions of the analytical framework.

To a large extent, elements of the SSC and Chinese foreign aid policy—comprising mutual respect, equality, fulfilling promises, building local capacity, and addressing actual needs—are adhered to in the context of CPEC projects. Findings show that decisions about inclusion and the approval of projects under CPEC are taken by the JCC and JWGs, thereby ensuring domestic ownership. Also, projects have been undertaken in specific areas to address the pressing needs of the country, including energy, infrastructure upgradation, and industrialisation. Initiatives are underway that aim to transfer skills, knowledge, and technology, which could help with long-term capacity-building and self-sustained economic development.

At the same time, there are certain issues with projects under the CPEC umbrella. For example, although considerable anecdotal information is available, there is still a significant lack of transparency and a dearth of data regarding the terms and conditions of Chinese investments and concessional loans as well as future sharing of the revenues from tolls and levies. Similarly,

Table 13.2 A brief assessment of CPEC within the NeST framework

Dimensions	Inclusive national ownership	Horizontality	Self-reliance and sustainability	Accountability and transparency	Development efficiency
Overall assessment	Institutional settings and mechanisms are in place to ensure effective ownership. However, there is little role for non-state actors/civil society in the policy formation, as negotiations are primarily between government-to-government agencies	Shared decision-making mechanisms have been established, and there is a broad consensus about the prospect of "mutual benefit". However, there are also reservations from some circles within academia and the media in Pakistan regarding the mutual "win-win" proposition	There has been considerable utilisation of local personnel and resources, but projects are mostly run and managed by Chinese counterparts with minimal use of local systems. Capacity-building initiatives have been undertaken for the transfer of knowledge and technology, which could help in promoting self-reliance and sustainability in the long run if properly absorbed and utilised	Although data management and M&E systems and mechanisms exist, there is not much transparency regarding the overall terms and conditions of financing, bidding, and procurement of projects. No project documents, MoUs, contracts, or agreements have been made public, so far	It is too early to prejudge projects and their development impact, but there have been considerable positive impacts from projects in the energy sector. Similarly, there has been an uptick in employment generation and an increasing demand for construction-related materials, giving a boost to local businesses and industries

Source Author

almost all the projects are being implemented by Chinese companies and state-owned enterprises without any competitive bidding. Thus, although there is no official document to confirm or deny it, there seems to be an understanding between the two governments that, in almost all projects, Chinese companies will implement projects without any external bidding. Considering this, it becomes clear that, although both governments have taken various initiatives and established platforms for joint decision-making and evaluation, there are still some issues, such as a lack of transparency and a prevalence of tied aid, in the CPEC financing mechanism.

Thus, it can be concluded that, as per the five broad dimensions of the SSC analytical framework, the China–Pakistan development partnership under CPEC has been doing well in the four areas of inclusive national ownership, horizontality, self-reliance and sustainability, and development effectiveness, but has lagged in accountability and transparency.

Notes

1. There is a perception among some members of the NeST that the SSC analytical framework has been developed by the South Africa (SA) chapter of NeST and therefore it is more appropriate to call it NeST SA or NSA framework. However, as the framework and its parameters and indicators have been taken from the study cited as NeST and not NSA, this study also uses NeST instead of NSA. Also, both in the NeST framework as well as in the Pakistani context, inclusive ownership is meant to include diverse government stakeholders, but there is no mention of private-sector actors. This work was supported by the Alexander von Humboldt Foundation under Grant No. 3.5 - 1162883 - PAK - GFHERMES-P.
2. The only document that has been released so far is the much-awaited "Long Term Plan for China-Pakistan Economic Corridor (2017–2030)", which was approved by both governments during the 7th JCC meeting held in Islamabad in November 2017. The policy document outlines CPEC's vision and key goals as well as its guidelines and basic principles of cooperation. The Long-Term Plan (LTP) lists seven major areas of focus: connectivity, energy, trade and industrial parks, agricultural development and poverty alleviation, tourism, cooperation in areas concerning people's livelihoods, and non-governmental exchanges and financial cooperation (Government of Pakistan and People's Republic of China, 2017). Overall, the LTP neither provides new information about CPEC nor assuages the concerns of critics.

References

Ahmad, S. I. (2017, September 3). CPEC is not a game-changer, it's game over. *The News on Sunday*. http://tns.thenews.com.pk/cpec-game-changer-game/.

Ali, G. (2017). *China–Pakistan relations: A historical analysis*. Karachi: Oxford University Press.

Besharati, N. A., Rawhani, C., & Rios, O. R. (2017). *A monitoring and evaluation framework for South-South cooperation* (Working Paper). Johannesburg: South African Institute of International Affairs.
Board of Investment. (2017). *CPEC toll income to be thrice the budget of Pakistan.* http://boi.gov.pk/ViewNews.aspx?NID=%201766.
CPEC Secretariat. (2017). *Updated energy projects.* http://cpec.gov.pk/energy.
Government of Pakistan. (2014). *Pakistan 2025: One nation one vision.* Islamabad: Ministry of Planning, Development and Reform.
Government of Pakistan. (2017). *Pakistan economic survey 2016–17.* Islamabad: Ministry of Finance.
Government of Pakistan. (2018). *Pakistan economic survey 2017–18.* Islamabad: Ministry of Finance.
Government of Pakistan, & People's Republic of China. (2017). *Long-term plan for China–Pakistan economic corridor (2017–2030).* Islamabad: Ministry of Planning, Development and Reform & People's Republic of China: National Development & Reform Commission.
Haider, M. (2017, November 28). Pakistan to get 9pc of Gwadar income, 15pc of FEZ: China. *The News International.* https://www.thenews.com.pk/print/249957-pakistan-to-get-9pc-of-gwadar-income-15pc-of-fez-china.
Husain, K. (2017, May 15). Exclusive: CPEC master plan revealed. *Dawn.* https://www.dawn.com/news/1333101.
Hussain, A. (2017, October 10). An open debate. *The News International.* https://www.thenews.com.pk/print/235858-An-open-debate.
Hussain, S. R. (2016). Sino-Pakistan ties: Trust, cooperation and consolidation. In T. Fingar (Ed.), *The new great game: China and South and Central Asia in the era of reform* (pp. 116–146). Stanford, CA: Stanford University Press.
IMF (International Monetary Fund). (2017). *Pakistan* (IMF Country Report No. 16/325). Washington, DC: Author.
Iqbal, A. (2017, May 17). CPEC most transparent project of Pakistan, says Ahsan Iqbal. *Pakistan Today.* https://profit.pakistantoday.com.pk/2017/05/17/cpec-most-transparent-project-of-pakistan-says-ahsan-iqbal/.
Isran, M. A. (2017, January 27). Six concerns PML-N government must address about CPEC. *The Express Tribune.* https://tribune.com.pk/story/1308699/six-concerns-pml-n-government-must-address-cpec/.
Khan, M., & Hyder, D. (2017, January 11). CPEC: The devil is not in the details. *Herald.* https://herald.dawn.com/news/1153597.
Khawar, H. (2017, October 26). CPEC toll income—Myth and reality. *The Express Tribune.* https://tribune.com.pk/story/1541404/6-cpec-toll-income-myth-reality/.
Kreft, S., Eckstein, D., & Melchior, I. (2017). *Global climate risk index 2017: Who suffers most from extreme weather events? Weather-related loss events in 2015 and 1996 to 2015.* Berlin: Germanwatch.
Malik, A. R. (2017). The Pakistan–China bilateral trade: The future trajectory. *Strategic Studies, 37*(1), 66–89.
Mustafa, K. (2018, May 9). Cost of CPEC coal power projects per MW 40pc higher. *The News International.* https://www.thenews.com.pk/print/314412-cost-of-cpec-coal-power-projects-per-mw-40pc-higher.

OECD (Organisation for Economic Co-operation and Development). (2016). *Development co-operation report 2016: The Sustainable Development Goals as business opportunities*. Paris: Author.
People's Republic of China. (2014). *China's foreign aid (2014)*. Beijing: Information Office of the State Council.
Saleem, F. (2017a, March 26). Coal power. *The News International*. https://www.thenews.com.pk/print/194527-Coal-power.
Saleem, F. (2017b, February 19). CPEC. *The News International*. https://www.the news.com.pk/print/235350-CPEC.
Small, A. (2015). *The China–Pakistan axis: Asia's new geopolitics*. New York, NY: Oxford University Press.
The CPEC Portal. (2017). *The CPEC portal*. http://www.cpecinfo.com/pci-cpec-fou nder.
United Nations Economic and Social Commission for Asia and the Pacific. (2017). *The Belt and Road Initiative and the role of ESCAP*. New York, NY: United Nations.
UNGA (United Nations General Assembly). (2015). *Transforming our world: The 2030 Agenda for Sustainable Development*. New York, NY: United Nations.
World Bank. (2015). *From billions to trillions: Transforming development finance post-2015*. Washington, DC: Author.
Zaidi, S. A. (2017, June 18). Has China taken over Pakistan? *The News on Sunday*. http://tns.thenews.com.pk/china-taken-pakistan-cpec/.
Zaman, M. H. (2016, December 27). Environment: Not for sale. *The Express Tribune*. http://tribune.com.pk/story/1276746/environment-not-sale/.

Open Access This chapter is licensed under the terms of the Creative Commons Attribution 4.0 International License (http://creativecommons.org/licenses/by/4.0/), which permits use, sharing, adaptation, distribution and reproduction in any medium or format, as long as you give appropriate credit to the original author(s) and the source, provide a link to the Creative Commons license and indicate if changes were made.

The images or other third party material in this chapter are included in the chapter's Creative Commons license, unless indicated otherwise in a credit line to the material. If material is not included in the chapter's Creative Commons license and your intended use is not permitted by statutory regulation or exceeds the permitted use, you will need to obtain permission directly from the copyright holder.

CHAPTER 14

The Implementation of the SDGs: The Feasibility of Using the GPEDC Monitoring Framework

Debapriya Bhattacharya, Victoria Gonsior, and Hannes Öhler

14.1 Introduction

Achieving the 2030 Agenda for Sustainable Development with its 17 Sustainable Development Goals (SDGs) requires significant behavioural changes on the global, regional, national, and sub-national levels from a variety of actors, including actors in development cooperation. Although significant progress was achieved in the era of the Millennium Development Goals—the predecessors of the SDGs—a wide variety of challenges remained; within the prevailing framework of the Millennium Development Goals, "development and sustainability aspirations were largely approached disjointly" (Kharas and Rogerson 2017, p. 18). Kharas and Rogerson (2017) list, for instance, the underdeveloped role of non-state and private actors, the inadequate concern for peace and institutions, and the strong emphasis on goals that were relatively easy to

---

D. Bhattacharya
Centre for Policy Dialogue (CPD), Dhaka, Bangladesh
e-mail: deb.bhattacharya@cpd.org.bd

V. Gonsior (✉)
German Development Institute / Deutsches Institut für Entwicklungspolitik (DIE), Bonn, Germany

H. Öhler
German Development Institute / Deutsches Institut für Entwicklungspolitik (DIE), Bonn, Germany
e-mail: hannes.oehler@die-gdi.de

measure. Today, the SDGs aim at addressing these shortcomings and introducing a narrative that is broader in scope and takes into account a diverse landscape of actors as well as development, in developing and developed countries alike (Fukuda-Parr 2017; Fukuda-Parr and McNeill 2019; The World in 2050 2018). In addition, the SDGs comprise—next to outcome targets—targets aiming at behavioural changes, such as targets addressing the means of implementation, SDG 17 (Partnerships for the goals), and targets focussing on processes and institutions (e.g. Engberg-Pedersen and Zwart 2018). These behavioural changes refer to a wide range of phenomena, including but not limited to empowering women, creating global partnerships, and building reliable and well-functioning institutions.

However—and as pointed out by the editors in the introduction of this book—as an implication of its broader nature, the SDGs do not address questions of responsibility and, subsequently, do not give guidelines or plans to review and follow up on the behavioural changes of specific actors. For example, the editors point out that SDG 17 is about promoting global partnerships, including public–private and civil society partnerships, but it does not provide concrete guidance for implementation. Arguably, the question of how to implement these envisaged behavioural changes in development cooperation is an important one for achieving the 2030 Agenda. This question is not covered by its follow-up and review (FUR) processes through a systematic approach. In fact, the United Nations (UN) does not have a global mechanism in place that steadily monitors the performance of all actors involved in development cooperation. According to Bexell and Jönsson (2017, p. 25), this might lead to unsystematic accountability and possibly encourage domestic political considerations and political will.[1] Within this context, it is open to question whether the Global Partnership for Effective Development Co-operation (GPEDC) can, through its monitoring framework, fill the gap and, thus, provide a significant contribution to the implementation of the SDGs.

The GPEDC, established in Busan in 2011, is a multi-stakeholder platform that brings together all types of development actors. The purpose of the GPEDC is to improve the practices of development cooperation partners, their means of implementation, processes, and institutions. The GPEDC's flagship product is the monitoring framework. The monitoring framework, consisting of 10 indicators, aims at enhancing the effectiveness of development cooperation and ultimately achieving development impact.[2] Following up on the effectiveness agenda agreed on in the Paris Declaration (2005) and the Accra Agenda for Action (2008),[3] the monitoring framework focusses on four effectiveness principles, that is, ownership, results orientation, inclusive development partnerships, and transparency and accountability. In order to implement these principles, development partners[4] and partner countries participating in the platform and its monitoring framework committed themselves to change the way they conduct development cooperation at the country level.

To answer the question whether the GPEDC, through its monitoring framework, can provide a significant contribution to the implementation of the SDGs, this chapter discusses critical political and technical factors that either positively or negatively influence the feasibility of such a contribution. The political factors strengthening the framework's potential contribution mainly comprise the complementarity of the GPEDC monitoring framework to the SDGs. On the contrary, the limited enthusiasm of development partners from the Global South, in particular China and India, as well as the limited amount of attention being paid by member countries of the Organisation for Economic Co-operation and Development (OECD) to the platform and the monitoring framework, can be seen as major political factors inhibiting a potential contribution.

Important technical factors benefitting a potential contribution are the significant share of behavioural changes envisaged by the SDGs that are applied by the monitoring framework to development cooperation and the large volume of empirical data that is generated biennially through the monitoring rounds. However, the empirical data is not being used as productively as it could be because interpretive evaluations of all stakeholders, especially of the performance of development partners, are largely missing. Hence, follow-up processes, most importantly at the national level, are limited. We conclude that making effective use of and developing the positive factors further, while taking into account and addressing, if possible, the negative factors, could lead to a significant contribution of the GPEDC, through its monitoring framework, to the implementation of the SDGs. We also discuss potential strategies in this regard.

This chapter is structured as follows: Sect. 14.2 embeds the GPEDC in a broader series of political events and presents the monitoring framework itself. In Sect. 14.3, we present critical political as well as technical factors that either positively or negatively influence the feasibility of a significant contribution to the implementation of the SDGs on the part of the GPEDC monitoring framework. In the last section, we discuss potential strategies to make effective use of positive factors and address negative ones.

14.2 The GPEDC Monitoring Framework[5]

14.2.1 Context: Emergence, Evolution, and Current Structure

The establishment of the GPEDC, in 2011 in Busan, is embedded in a broader series of political events, which all centre on the issue of how to enhance the impact of development cooperation (Abdel-Malek 2015). The GPEDC's origins may be traced back to the UN Financing for Development Conference held in Monterrey in 2002. Between 2002 and 2011, three High Level Fora on Aid Effectiveness—held in Rome (2003), Paris (2005), and Accra (2008)—provided a platform for international dialogue on the aid effectiveness agenda, which reached its climax with the adoption of the Paris Declaration in 2005.

Thereafter, at the High Level Forum in Busan in 2011, policy-makers discussed intensively the results of the "2011 Survey on Monitoring the Paris Declaration" and reviewed the progress made.[6] The outcome document postulated the establishment of the multi-stakeholder platform the GPEDC. The GPEDC aims at monitoring the implementation of effectiveness principles, which should mirror development effectiveness, rather than the narrower concept of aid effectiveness. Development effectiveness thereby refers to the overall achievement of development results and acknowledges a variety of actors in, and means for, achieving those (Kim 2013).

The post-Busan dialogue was carried forward in two high-level meetings (HLMs) that took place in Mexico City (2014) and Nairobi (2016).[7] These HLMs gave rise to a series of agreements that increasingly urged development partners to focus on nationally determined priorities and, at the same time, urged partner countries to take stronger leadership roles to guide development partners' efforts and facilitate approaches to development (Lundsgaarde and Keijzer 2016).

In 2011, the GPEDC was endorsed by 161 countries and 56 organisations. The GPEDC is led by a Steering Committee, which currently has 25 members, including representatives of development partners, partner countries, the multilateral system, the private sector, as well as public representatives and representatives from civil society. The Steering Committee has three Co-Chairs—a member country of the OECD, a development cooperation partner country, and a development partner of South-South cooperation (SSC). Most recently, a non-executive Co-Chair was appointed representing non-governmental stakeholders (e.g. non-governmental organisations (NGOs) and civil society organisations, private philanthropies, parliamentarians, the private sector, and trade unions). A Joint Support Team (JST) located at the OECD in Paris and the United Nations Development Programme (UNDP) in New York provides technical and administrative backup for the GPEDC.

14.2.2 *The Monitoring Exercise and Its Underlying Framework*

The GPEDC's flagship product, the global framework, monitors the implementation of four effectiveness principles: ownership, results orientation, inclusive development partnerships, and transparency and accountability. The monitoring takes place every two years (2014, 2016, and 2018, so far); the number of partner countries participating in the exercise rose in 2018 to 87 countries, which amounts to six more participating partner countries than in the previous round (2016) (Global Partnership for Effective Development Co-operation [GPEDC] 2019a). The monitoring focusses on official development assistance (ODA). However, in order to provide a more comprehensive picture of the development resources flowing into a partner country, development partners are encouraged to also report on other official flows, such as non-concessional loans.

The monitoring framework is based on 10 indicators that link to the four effectiveness principles (see Table 14.1). The monitoring framework adopted some of the indicators from the Paris and Accra agreements: results orientation [indicator 1], annual and medium-term predictability [indicator 5], on-budget

Table 14.1 GPEDC monitoring framework—effectiveness principles and indicators

Focus on results	Development efforts must have a lasting impact on eradicating poverty and reducing inequality and on enhancing developing countries' capacities so that they are in alignment with their own priorities.	Indicator: Countries strengthen their national results frameworks (1b) Indicator: Development partners use country-led results frameworks (1a)
Ownership of development priorities by developing countries	Partnerships for development can only succeed if they are led by developing countries that are implementing approaches, which are tailored to country-specific situations and needs.	Indicator: Development cooperation is predictable: annual predictability (5a) Indicator: Development cooperation is predicatable: medium-term predicatability (5b) Indicator: Quality of countries' public financial management systems (9a) Indicator: Development partners' use of country systems (9b) Indicator: Aid is untied (10)
Inclusive development partnerships	Openness, trust, mutual respect, and learning lie at the core of effective partnerships, which recognise the different and complementary roles of all actors.	Indicator: Quality of public-private dialogue (3) Indicator: Civil society organisations operate within an environment that maximises their engagement in and contribution to development (2)
Transparency and accountability to each other	Mutual accountability and accountability to the intended beneficiaries of development cooperation, as well as to respective citizens, organisations, constituents, and shareholders, is critical to delivering results. Transparent practices form the basis for enhanced accountability.	Indicator: Transparent information on development cooperation is publicly available (4) Indicator: Mutual accountability among development actors is strengthened through inclusive reviews (7) Indicator: Development cooperation is included in budgets subject to parliamentary oversight (6) Indicator: Countries have systems to track and make public allocations for gender equality and women's empowerment (8)

Source Authors' own graphical representation of the illustration in GPEDC (2018, p. 8)

development cooperation [indicator 6], mutual accountability [indicator 7], quality and use of the partner countries' systems [indicator 9], and delivery of untied aid [indicator 10]. Other indicators were newly introduced in 2012 to reflect the broader dimensions of development effectiveness. These include indicator 2 (focussing on civil society), indicator 3 (covering public–private dialogue), indicator 8 (targeting gender equality), and lastly indicator 4 (aiming at transparency). Each indicator is comprised of a subset of questions and measures that ultimately aim at providing evidence on the progress of the implementation of the effectiveness principles.

Throughout the past years, the GPEDC monitoring framework has undergone an extensive review process. In 2015, the GPEDC Co-Chairs and Steering Committee mandated the Monitoring Advisory Group, a body of 12 experts, to review, refine, and advise on the continued relevance of the Global Partnership's "Theory of Change", as well as on the 10 indicators of its global monitoring framework (Monitoring Advisory Group 2016). The revised framework, including updated guidelines and indicators, found traction within the latest GPEDC monitoring round in 2018.

Importantly, the responsibility for the monitoring exercise at the country level lies with the partner countries. Each partner country that chooses to participate designates a national coordinator, who coordinates the monitoring exercise among all relevant actors, including the data collection process. The national coordinator collates, validates, and passes the data on to the OECD/UNDP Joint Support Team of the GPEDC for consistency and completeness checks and aggregation. As such, participation in the monitoring exercise requires extensive investments, especially in terms of the partner countries' resources in the form of available time and staff capacities.

14.3 Contributing to the Implementation of the SDGs: Political and Technical Feasibility

To achieve the 2030 Agenda, behavioural changes from a variety of stakeholders on the global, regional, national, and sub-national levels are required. In this regard, the GPEDC, through its monitoring framework, can potentially provide a significant contribution to the implementation of the SDGs in the context of development cooperation. This section discusses critical political and technical factors that influence the feasibility of such a contribution.

14.3.1 Political Factors Influencing the Feasibility of a Significant Contribution of the Monitoring Framework to the Implementation of the SDGs

In recent years, the relevance and political interest in the effectiveness agenda have largely vanished (Abdel-Malek 2015; Mawdsley et al. 2018). According to Koch et al. (2017) and Booth (2012), the main reason for the agenda's lack of success was its sophisticated technocratic character, which failed to address the political economy in which development cooperation is embedded. Hence, when assessing the feasibility of a significant contribution of the monitoring framework to the implementation of the SDGs, it is crucial to assess not only technical aspects, in terms of the indicators, for instance. Instead, political factors that shape the context in which the framework operates and that could ultimately prevent the aforementioned contribution from materialising also need to be taken into account.

14.3.2 Factors Positively Influencing the Feasibility

Primarily, the complementarity and alignment of the monitoring framework to the principles and objectives of the 2030 Agenda positively influences the feasibility of a significant contribution of the monitoring framework to the implementation of the SDGs. The 2030 Agenda does not mention the GPEDC explicitly. Nevertheless, when comparing the 2030 Agenda and the effectiveness principles of the GPEDC, it becomes apparent that the 2030 Agenda very much reflects the understanding of the GPEDC. For instance, part of paragraph 60 under "Means of Implementation and the Global Partnership" reads as follows:

> We recognise that we will not be able to achieve our ambitious Goals and targets without a revitalised and enhanced Global Partnership and comparably ambitious means of implementation. The revitalised Global Partnership will facilitate an intensive global engagement in support of implementation of all the Goals and targets, bringing together governments, civil society, the private sector, the United Nations system and other actors and mobilising all available resources. (UN 2015, p. 28)

Although the term "Global Partnership" cannot directly be equated with the global partnership entailed in the name of the GPEDC—as it is a term coined during the United Nations Millennium Summit in 2000—a link to the GPEDC and how it envisions its contribution can be drawn through the notion of bringing multiple actors to the table. More specifically, the GPEDC presents its complementarity and alignment to the 2030 Agenda through its inclusion of emerging economies, the private sector, and civil society organisations, as well as through the creation of a multi-stakeholder platform (Coppard and Culey 2015). Furthermore, and in line with paragraph 63 of the 2030 Agenda, which emphasises the need for "cohesive nationally-owned sustainable development strategies, supported by integrated national financing frameworks" (United Nations [UN] 2015, p. 28), the GPEDC aims at increasing dialogue and encouraging the embedment of the principles of development effectiveness at various levels, including the national level. Only by doing so can its potential to provide a significant contribution to the implementation of the SDGs be "capitalised" (Coppard and Culey 2015, p. 3).

Importantly, the adoption of the SDGs calls for significant behavioural changes on the global, regional, national, and sub-national levels of a variety of actors, including actors in development cooperation. In particular, next to outcome targets, the SDGs comprise targets aiming at behavioural changes. However, as an implication of its broader nature, the 2030 Agenda does not give guidelines or plans to review and follow up on behavioural changes of specific development actors. Arguably, the question of how to implement these behavioural changes in development cooperation is an important one for the 2030 Agenda and its FUR processes.

The Global Accountability Surveys of the UN Development Cooperation Forum on progress in national mutual accountability and transparency—carried out biennially since 2008 by the UN Department of Economic and Social Affairs—are designed to incentivise behavioural changes and provide evidence on how development cooperation is conducted at the country level. These surveys are centred around the assessment of mutual accountability, thereby aiming at supporting government efforts to strengthen development partnerships at the country level.[8] However, these surveys mainly focus on the performance of government ministries and significantly less on development partners, calling into question whether the latter are held accountable in the context of the UN's own development cooperation monitoring and review mechanisms (United Nations Economic and Social Council 2018).

Within this context, the GPEDC monitoring framework can be seen as a valuable asset that could contribute to the monitoring of the SDGs. In fact, the monitoring framework is well-suited to facilitate behavioural changes in development cooperation and contribute to the monitoring framework of the SDGs, especially around the targets set under SDG 17. This could even be extended to the means of implementation for the targets of other goals (Coppard and Culey 2015).

Furthermore, the GPEDC seeks to instil mutual accountability among all actors engaged in development cooperation. With the inclusion of a wide range of actors in development cooperation—that is, governments of partner countries and development partner countries, multilateral organisations, civil society, the private sector, as well as other state and non-state actors—mutual accountability is created, even in the absence of an enforcement mechanism (Abdel-Malek 2015).[9] Information on the actors' performance with regard to the 10 indicators is publicly accessible, thereby exercising peer pressure on the actors involved. Given that mutual accountability is crucial for the implementation of the SDGs, the exploitation of synergies and complementarities between the established GPEDC accountability framework and the accountability concept envisaged for the 2030 Agenda would be beneficial (Mahn 2017).

These factors point in the direction that the GPEDC and its monitoring framework is well-positioned to make a significant contribution to the implementation of the SDGs (Constantine et al. 2015). From a strategic point of view, harnessing these beneficial factors could lead to an increase in the relevancy of the monitoring framework and the GPEDC itself and may even lead to a revivification of the effectiveness agenda in development cooperation.

14.3.3 Factors Negatively Influencing the Feasibility

However, not all political factors strengthen the feasibility of the framework's contribution to the implementation of the SDGs. One political factor that reduces its feasibility is the monitoring framework's limitations in covering the overall development cooperation landscape as well as in taking recent changes into account. Already before the establishment of the GPEDC and the development of the monitoring framework, the development cooperation landscape had begun to change significantly (Bhattacharya and Khan 2018b). The emerging landscape is, among other aspects, characterised by the rise of important new actors from the Global South, especially China and India (e.g. Organisation for Economic Co-operation and Development [OECD] 2018b). These countries are increasingly taking on a dual role in development cooperation and enhancing their contributions with regard to concessional financial flows to other developing countries.

The failure of the GPEDC to also include contributions of SSC development partners in its monitoring framework stems from the lack of enthusiasm among these emerging economies. In fact, from the perspective of the Global South, the GPEDC monitoring framework is largely an OECD Development Assistance Committee (DAC) driven exercise with very limited reflection on SSC approaches and the SSC paradigm (Abdel-Malek 2015; Li 2017).

Furthermore, limited consideration of the private sector, transnational NGOs, and private philanthropies in the monitoring framework have fuelled the perception that the framework does not measure the effectiveness of the overall international development cooperation landscape. This is especially the case because these actors are increasingly providing large volumes of development finance to partner countries. A thorough reflection on the effectiveness of the contributions of these actors is missing, with the acknowledgement that reflecting on such a diverse actor landscape with manifold interests is highly challenging (e.g. Wehrmann [2018] who discusses challenges of including private-sector actors in effective sustainable development initiatives, with a particular focus on the GPEDC).

Another political factor limiting the feasibility of the framework's contribution to the implementation of the SDGs lies in the fact that not only emerging economies but also OECD-DAC members do not seem to be particularly enthusiastic about the monitoring framework itself, and the GPEDC multi-stakeholder platform in general. Given the voluntary nature of the original commitments, traditional development partners have often shied away from the exercise and demonstrated a lack of consequential attention to the results. In particular, political challenges at headquarters are largely responsible for the lack of progress in those areas where development partners' efforts were most required (see Koch et al. [2017] for a discussion on the reasons why the backing for budget support has largely vanished in the last decade). Changing domestic politics have further contributed to the lack of progress. Throughout the past years, the emergence of the migration narrative, the rise of nationalism and populism, and a new demand to include "national interests" transparently on the development policy agendas of OECD countries have been at the centre of attention in traditional donor countries (Barder 2018; Hulme 2016; Keijzer et al. 2018; Mawdsley et al. 2018). In addition, the non-participation in the monitoring exercise by new key development actors from the South, such as China and India, has relaxed the pressure on the traditional development partners to stick to their commitments.

This factor is further intensified by the observation that the GPEDC monitoring framework does not address the funding commitments made by development partner countries at various international fora. In particular, achieving the targets of allocating 0.7 per cent ODA/GNI (gross national income) to developing countries, or 0.15 to 0.20 per cent of ODA/GNI to least-developed countries is not a subject of the monitoring framework. However, one could argue that the monitoring of international ODA commitments by development partners does not really fit into the monitoring exercise of the GPEDC, which is an exercise led by partner countries on how development cooperation is conducted at the country level. A more suitable platform for monitoring these commitments would be arguably the UN Financing for Development Conference.[10]

14.3.4 Technical Factors Influencing the Feasibility of a Significant Contribution of the Monitoring Framework to the Implementation of the SDGs

Besides political factors, there are also a number of technical factors that either positively or negatively influence the monitoring framework's feasibility of contributing to the implementation of the SDGs.

14.3.5 Factors Positively Influencing the Feasibility

From a technical point of view, the question arises as to what extent the GPEDC monitoring framework, in its present form, is designed to keep track of the behavioural changes in development cooperation that are envisaged by the SDGs. The SDGs, while encompassing a large number of outcome-related goals and targets, also include a number of targets related to behavioural changes, which are mostly also relevant for actors in development cooperation at the country level—the level of interest for the monitoring framework.[11] A detailed analysis shows that the monitoring framework with its 10 indicators fully applies to a significant number of SDG targets aiming at behavioural changes in development cooperation.[12] Thus, the monitoring framework is generally well set up to promote the behavioural changes envisaged by the

SDGs in development cooperation. Nevertheless, we also identify a number of targets that are only partly adopted by the monitoring framework, leaving some room for improvement.[13]

Another technical factor that could potentially enhance the framework's contribution to the SDGs is the fact that the monitoring framework regularly generates a large volume of empirical data on the country level on a global scale. Keeping track of these behavioural changes is crucial in the course of the implementation of the SDGs. In this regard, the monitoring framework generates data on a regular basis and in this way provides a large volume of empirical data on a global scale. The implementation of biennial monitoring rounds encourages development partners to follow a common methodology and standards for measuring development effectiveness, to disclose information about their development cooperation, and to smoothen the data collection process. The collected empirical data is ideally used to inform evidence-based decision-making at the global and local levels, and it enhances the pursuit of policy coherence for sustainable development in partner countries. Other attempts to address development effectiveness on a similar scale do not exist. Only a few alternative frameworks for the assessment of the quality of the contributions of development partners—such as the quality of ODA, which also relies to some extent on the GPEDC monitoring data, or the Commitment to Development Index—can be found.[14]

14.3.6 *Factors Negatively Influencing the Feasibility*

An aspect diminishing the feasibility of a significant contribution of the monitoring framework to the implementation of the SDGs is the lack of interpretive evaluations for all actors of the results of the respective monitoring rounds. Currently, the GPEDC monitoring framework collects data at the country level biennially and presents the aggregated data through a dashboard on their homepage.[15] Additionally, the JST provides a global report and short country briefs for participating partner countries.[16] However, the framework lacks an analysis of the results on the performance of development partners, including multilateral organisations, which are significantly contributing to the data collection exercise.

In addition, not only is the evaluation of the monitoring data limited, the monitoring framework also lacks respective feedback loops at the global and country levels to follow up on the rather extensive data collection process, inform stakeholders about the outcomes, and facilitate subsequently decision-making processes. As a result, no meaningful dialogue on follow-up commitments—bearing in mind the monitoring exercise's non-binding nature—is taking place, and the framework is proving to be insufficient at being able to profoundly inform and steer political debates on development effectiveness (Abdel-Malek 2015; Besharati 2013). Taken together, the last two aspects diminish the benefits of the monitoring exercise: especially at the country level, the results of the monitoring exercise are not being used as productively as they could be.

Not only from a political but also from a technical perspective, the framework's limitation in measuring the effectiveness of the overall changing development cooperation landscape is a factor that may hinder the feasibility of a significant contribution of the monitoring framework to the implementation of the SDGs. More specifically, the emerging SSC regime has been giving rise to a set of framework issues emerging from the fact that SSC is essentially different from traditional North-South and even trilateral cooperation relationships. These framework issues include, for example, monitoring indicators that do not sufficiently represent the evolution of thoughts within the SSC paradigm. At the same time though, a consensus regarding the need to assess the effectiveness of SSC is gradually emerging among the directly concerned stakeholders. Furthermore, discussions regarding distinguishing features of an assessment framework of South-South concessional flows are gathering momentum (Bhattacharya and Rashmin 2016).

Similar to the political and technical overlaps related to the SSC paradigm and traditional North-South development cooperation, a number of technical issues exist with regard to considerations about the contributions of the private sector, transnational NGOs, and private philanthropies in the monitoring exercise. In this regard, some emerging instruments in development cooperation, in particular blended finance (e.g. Attridge and Engen 2019; OECD 2018a), are trying to utilise the potential catalytic effect of ODA for mobilising additional resources, thereby involving a number of actors, especially from the private sector.[17] However, at the moment there is no GPEDC indicator that reflects the effectiveness of the catalytic potential of ODA. Finally, financial sources beyond ODA, such as non-concessional spending, are also not being assessed against the principles of ownership, results orientation, inclusive development partnerships, as well as transparency and accountability.

14.4 Discussion and Conclusion

To answer the question of whether the GPEDC, through its monitoring framework, can provide a significant contribution to the implementation of the SDGs, this chapter has discussed critical political and technical factors that either positively or negatively influence the feasibility of such a contribution. The political factors having a positive influence mainly comprise the complementarity of the GPEDC monitoring framework to the SDGs. On the other hand, the limited enthusiasm and participation by development partners from the Global South, in particular China and India, as well as the limited amount of attention being paid by member countries of the OECD to the platform and monitoring exercise, can be seen as major political factors that reduce the potential contribution of the monitoring framework. Important technical factors benefiting such a contribution can be identified in the significant share of behavioural changes envisaged by the SDGs that are applied by the monitoring framework to development cooperation and the large volume of empirical data that is generated with the monitoring rounds biennially. However, the generated data is not being used as productively as it could be because interpretive evaluations of all stakeholders, especially of the performance of development partners, are largely missing, thereby limiting the monitoring framework's potential contribution.

Drawing on these findings, we conclude this chapter by deriving potential strategies for "updating" the institutional setting of the GPEDC by making effective use of the factors that foster a significant contribution of the monitoring framework to the implementation of the SDGs. However, we also stress that the GPEDC needs to address the factors that negatively influence its contribution in order to minimise their effects.

With respect to the complementarity of the GPEDC monitoring framework to the SDGs, Bhattacharya et al. (2016) argue that the 2030 Agenda presents a unique opportunity for the GPEDC monitoring framework to reinvent itself by substantially contributing to the FUR process of the SDGs. The GPEDC itself identifies its contribution through the monitoring framework through two potential options. On the one hand, the GPEDC monitoring framework could be merged into the SDG monitoring framework. On the other hand, the GPEDC could provide a complementary approach that would address the quality of inputs for monitoring the implementation of the SDGs in a broad sense (Coppard and Culey 2015).

As discussed in this chapter, the GPEDC monitoring framework is currently one of the few global mechanisms available that seeks to instil mutual accountability in development cooperation processes. In addition, the framework is well-suited to facilitate behavioural changes, as its monitoring indicators mostly focus on processes and means of implementation. Hence, it would be favourable if the FUR process of the SDGs built on these existing mechanisms to further promote mutual accountability and behavioural changes among actors in development cooperation.

However, the voluntary national reviews (VNRs) of 2016 and 2017 show that neither the VNRs in OECD countries nor in developing countries extensively mention the results of the GPEDC monitoring framework. Consequently, the question of how to ensure better and broader use of GPEDC monitoring in the FUR process needs to be assessed. The most straightforward solution is that when VNRs are prepared, the governments of participating partner countries can use the GPEDC's country profiles, which include the country-specific results of the respective last monitoring rounds.[18] Moreover, these countries may utilise the findings of the monitoring exercise while drawing up their respective national SDG Action Plans. This would also provide the opportunity to subject the GPEDC output documents to scrutiny by a wider range of stakeholders and to improve the GPEDC monitoring framework further. In addition, it could stimulate important—currently missing—feedback loops of the results of the monitoring exercise.

Similarly, the UN Department of Economic and Social Affairs can also be sensitised regarding the use of the JST's global report when preparing the annual SDG Progress Report, particularly when reporting on SDG 17. In fact, the results of the GPEDC monitoring were not used in the 2018 SDG Progress Report (UN 2018). Importantly, the GPEDC has to open up to the High-Level Political Forum on Sustainable Development and make its monitoring report available as one of the resource documents. From a medium- to long-term perspective, the GPEDC HLMs may be included within the workflow of the High-Level Political Forum on Sustainable Development. This may lead to greater levels of acceptance of the GPEDC platform and its monitoring framework in the global development community—in particular among SSC development partners—as a global mechanism to promote development effectiveness and the implementation of the SDGs.

However, in order for the previously mentioned developments to materialise, the GPEDC needs to address the limited levels of enthusiasm among SSC development partners by opening up to the SSC paradigm and considering the demands and needs of SSC development partners in the context of an envisaged monitoring framework that covers the overall development cooperation landscape. For instance, the SSC development partners argue in favour of including a wide range of non-concessional finance and activities in the framework, as this would imply that the framework comprises certain key aspects of their development cooperation, that is, mutual economic benefits and development knowledge from their own experiences (Constantine et al. 2015). In addition, Southern scholars have produced a large body of interesting work on the assessment framework of SSC (Besharati et al. 2017). These resources may work as reference points for reflections on the GPEDC monitoring framework. Furthermore, open-ended, evidence-based discussions followed up by a couple of pilot projects may be able to break new ground in improving mutual understanding between Southern and OECD development partners. Simultaneously though, in order to overcome the weakness of data comparability with OECD development partners, Southern development partners would need to create comprehensive and real-time data on their development projects. The GPEDC is currently experimenting with a pilot framework on SSC whereby the consideration of both aspects is taken on board (GPEDC 2019b).

In addition, the non-consideration of financial contributions from the private sector, philanthropies, and NGOs appears to be a drawback in the current design of the monitoring framework. Lastly, the GPEDC monitoring framework in particular, and the GPEDC multi-stakeholder platform in general, would need to be revitalised through the infusion of political enthusiasm, in particular among OECD member countries. One promising path could be the addition of interpretive evaluations of monitoring results and feedback loops to inform evidence-based, multi-stakeholder dialogues and increase the monitoring exercise's added value.

The strategies present ideas for making effective use of the positive factors and diminishing the effects of the negative ones. Such efforts could increase the relevance of the monitoring framework, the GPEDC in general, and revive the effectiveness agenda on a global, regional, and local level.

NOTES

1. For further discussion on SDG accountability, refer next to Bexell and Jönsson (2017) and to Bowen et al. (2017).
2. Note that no rigorous quantitative analysis has been conducted attesting the assumption that effective practices of development partners lead to development impact. Rather, advocacy for compliance with the effectiveness principles is based on theoretical arguments and anecdotal and qualitative evidence (Knack 2012). Anecdotal evidence is provided, for instance, by the World Bank (2003). Leiderer (2015) offers a more in-depth descriptive study on health and education outcomes in Zambia. A qualitative evaluation by Wood et al. (2011) finds that the implementation of the Paris Declaration principles has contributed to better development results in the health sector in most of the 21 recipient countries taking part in the evaluation.
3. For further information, refer to the Paris Declaration on Aid Effectiveness and the Accra Agenda for Action: https://www.oecd.org/dac/effectiveness/34428351.pdf.
4. With development partners, we refer to the group of actors providing financial (and potentially non-financial) resources to partner countries.
5. The information presented in this section is based on key documents provided by the GPEDC itself, such as GPEDC/UNDP (2016) and GPEDC (2017), as well as Abdel-Malek (2015).
6. For further information, refer to the outcome document of the Fourth High Level Forum on Aid Effectiveness, in Busan, Republic of Korea, 29 Nov. to 1 Dec. 2011: https://www.oecd.org/dac/effectiveness/49650173.pdf.
7. For further information, refer to the outcome document of the first HLM of the GPEDC, in Mexico, 15–16 Apr. 2014: https://effectivecooperation.org/wp-content/uploads/2015/01/MEMORIA-FINAL.pdf, and the outcome document of the second HLM of the GPEDC, in Kenia, Nairobi, 1 Dec. 2016: http://effectivecooperation.org/wp-content/uploads/2016/12/OutcomeDocumentEnglish.pdf.
8. For further information please refer to: https://www.un.org/ecosoc/en/tracking-development-cooperation.
9. However, the fact that the members of the steering committee set the standards for accountability—but are at the same time part of the stakeholders held accountable—may threaten the GPEDC's credibility.
10. For more information, refer to: https://www.un.org/esa/ffd/ffdforum/.
11. Note that we refer to the targets of the SDGs, as they constitute about the same level as the GPEDC indicators. We do not consider the targets related to international commitments with respect to ODA funds, as it is not in the current mandate of the GPEDC to monitor whether the development partner countries comply with these commitments, as discussed in the previous section.

12. These targets refer to gender equality and women's empowerment (Target 5.C), public access to information, policy coherence (Target 17.14), the respect for each country's policy space and leadership (Target 17.15), enhancing the global partnership (Target 17.16), public–private and civil society partnerships (Target 17.17), and statistical capacity-building (Target 17.19).
13. These targets refer to the mobilisation of financial resources from a variety of sources (Targets 1.A and 17.3), pro-poor and gender sensitivity of national development frameworks (Target 1.B), quality of national procurement systems (Target 12.7), quality of institutions (Target 16.6), in particular the rule of law (16.3) and control of corruption (16.5), the participation of development countries in the institutions of global governance (Target 16.8), and knowledge cooperation in the form of North-South, SSC, and triangular cooperation (Target 17.6).
14. For further information refer to: https://www.cgdev.org/page/quality-oda-quoda and https://www.cgdev.org/commitment-development-index-2018.
15. The dashboard can be accessed here: http://dashboard.effectivecooperation.org/viewer.
16. The global report as well as the country briefs for the most recent monitoring round can be accessed here: http://effectivecooperation.org/monitoring-country-progress/country-and-territory-monitoring-profiles/.
17. The deployment of blended finance remains quite limited in the relatively less-developed countries (see e.g. Bhattacharya and Khan 2018a).
18. Up to date, only in three countries (Dominican Republic, Egypt, and Lao PDR), the 2016 monitoring results have been used for the preparation of VNRs.

References

Abdel-Malek, T. (2015). *The Global Partnership for Effective Development Cooperation: Origins, actions and future prospects* (DIE Studies 88). Bonn: German Development Institute/Deutsches Institut für Entwicklungspolitik (DIE).

Attridge, S., & Engen, L. (2019, April). *Blended finance in the poorest countries: The need for a better approach.* London: Overseas Development Institute.

Barder, O. (2018). *Aid in the national interest: When is development cooperation win-win?* https://www.cgdev.org/blog/aid-national-interest-when-development-cooperation-win-win.

Besharati, N. (2013). *A year after Busan: Where is the Global Partnership going?* (Occasional Paper 136). Johannesburg: South African Institute of International Affairs.

Besharati, N., Rawhani, C., & Rios, O. G. (2017, March). *A monitoring and evaluation framework for South-South cooperation* (NEST Working Paper). Johannesburg: South African Institute of International Affairs.

Bexell, M., & Jönsson, K. (2017). Responsibility and the United Nations' Sustainable Development Goals. *Forum for Development Studies, 44*(1), 13–29.

Bhattacharya, D., & Khan, S. (2018a). *Is blended finance trending in the LDCs? Perspectives from the ground* (Occasional Paper Series 49). (n.p.). Southern Voice.

Bhattacharya, D., & Khan, S. (2018b). *Why do we need to rethink development effectiveness?* http://southernvoice.org/why-do-we-need-to-rethink-development-effectiveness/.

Bhattacharya, D., & Rashmin, R. (2016). *Concessional financial flows among Southern countries: Conceptualising design principles, operational modalities and an assessment framework*. New York, NY: United Nations Development Programme.

Bhattacharya, D., Rashmin, R., & Mahfuze, A. H. (2016). *Strengthening accountability in development cooperation role of GPEDC monitoring indicators in the context of Agenda 2030 and AAAA* (Occasional Paper Series 29). (n.p.). Southern Voice.

Booth, D. (2012). *Development as a collective action problem: Addressing the real challenges of African governance: Synthesis report of the Africa Power and Politics Programme* (Synthesis Report). London: Africa Power and Politics Programme.

Bowen, K. J., Cradock-Henry, N. A., Koch, F., Patterson, J., Häyhä, T., Vogt, J., et al. (2017). Implementing the "Sustainable Development Goals": Towards addressing three key governance challenges—collective action, trade-offs, and accountability. *Current Opinion in Environmental Sustainability, 26–27*, 90–96.

Constantine, J., Shankland, A., & Gu, J. (2015). *Engaging the rising powers in the Global Partnership for Effective Development Cooperation: A framing paper*. https://effectivecooperation.org/wp-content/uploads/2016/08/GPEDC-Engagement-with-BRICS_IDS-Framing-Paper_New_June2015.pdf.

Coppard, D., & Culey, C. (2015). *The Global Partnership for Effective Development Co-operation's contribution to the 2030 Agenda for Sustainable Development*. http://devinit.org/wp-content/uploads/2015/12/Contribution-to-the-2030-Agenda-for-Sustainable-Development_FULL.pdf.

Engberg-Pedersen, P., & Zwart, R. (2018). *The 2030 Agenda and development co-operation results* (Development Policy Papers 9). Paris: Organisation for Economic Co-operation and Development.

Fukuda-Parr, S. (2017). *Millennium development goals: Ideas, interests and influence*. Abingdon: Routledge.

Fukuda-Parr, S., & McNeill, D. (2019). Knowledge and politics in setting and measuring SDGs. *Global Policy, 10*(S1), 5–15.

GPEDC/UNDP (Global Partnership for Effective Development Co-operation/United Nations Development Programme). (2016). *Making development cooperation more effective: 2016 progress report*. Paris: Organisation for Economic Co-operation and Development.

GPEDC. (2017). *2017 and 2018 programme of work*. https://effectivecooperation.org/wp-content/uploads/2017/05/2017-18-Global-Partnership-Work-Programme.pdf.

GPEDC. (2018). *2018 monitoring round. Mini guide for development partners*. http://effectivecooperation.org/pdf/2018MiniGuide_DevPartners.pdf.

GPEDC. (2019a). *3rd Global Partnership monitoring round: Update on process and preliminary findings*. https://effectivecooperation.org/wp-content/uploads/2019/03/Monitoring-Update-Session-2.pdf.

GPEDC. (2019b). *South-South cooperation effectiveness*. https://effectivecooperation.org/wp-content/uploads/2019/03/Monitoring-SSC-Session-3.pdf.

Hulme, D. (2016). *Should rich nations help the poor?* Cambridge: Polity Press.

Keijzer, N., Klingebiel, S., Örnemark, C., & Scholtes, F. (2018). *Seeking balanced ownership in changing development cooperation relationships* (EBA Rapport 2018:08). Stockholm: Expert Group for Aid Studies.

Kharas, H., & Rogerson, A. (2017, October). *Global development trends and challenges: Horizon 2025 revisited*. London: Overseas Development Institute.

Kim, E. M. (2013). Busan and beyond: South Korea and the transition from aid effectiveness to development effectiveness. *Journal of International Development, 25*(6), 787–801.

Knack, S. (2012). *When do donors trust recipient country systems?* (Policy Research Working Paper 6019). Washington, DC: World Bank.

Koch, S., Leiderer, S., Faust, J., & Molenaers, N. (2017). The rise and demise of European budget support: Political economy of collective European Union donor action. *Development Policy Review, 35*(4), 455–473.

Leiderer, S. (2015). Donor coordination for effective government policies? *Journal of International Development, 27*(8), 1422–1445.

Li, X. (2017). *Should China join the GPEDC? The prospects for China and the Global Partnership for Effective Development Co-operation* (DIE Discussion Paper 17/2017). Bonn: German Development Institute/Deutsches Institut für Entwicklungspolitik (DIE).

Lundsgaarde, E., & Keijzer, N. (2016, July). *Sustaining the development effectiveness agenda* (Policy Brief). Copenhagen: Danish Institute for International Studies.

Mahn, T. (2017). *Accountability for development cooperation under the 2030 Agenda* (DIE Discussion Paper 10/2017). Bonn: German Development Institute/Deutsches Institut für Entwicklungspolitik (DIE).

Mawdsley, E., Murray, W. E., Overton, J., Scheyvens, R., & Banks, G. (2018). Exporting stimulus and "shared prosperity": Reinventing foreign aid for a retroliberal era. *Development Policy Review, 2018*(36), O25–O43.

Monitoring Advisory Group. (2016). *Report to the tenth steering committee meeting, New York, July 14–15, 2016.* https://effectivecooperation.org/wp-content/uploads/2016/07/Final-July-6th-Monitoring-Advisory-Group-Report-for-SC.pdf.

OECD (Organisation for Economic Co-operation and Development). (2018a). *Making blended finance work for the Sustainable Development Goals.* Paris: Organisation for Economic Co-operation and Development.

OECD. (2018b). *Perspectives on global development 2019.* Paris: Organisation for Economic Co-operation and Development.

The World in 2050. (2018). *Transformations to achieve the Sustainable Development Goals.* Laxenburg: International Institute for Applied Systems Analysis.

UN (United Nations). (2015). *Resolution adopted by the General Assembly on 25 September 2015.* http://www.un.org/ga/search/view_doc.asp?symbol=A/RES/70/1&Lang=E.

UN. (2018). *The Sustainable Development Report 2018.* New York, NY: United Nations.

United Nations Economic and Social Council. (2018). *National mutual accountability and transparency in development cooperation: Study on the findings of the fifth DCF Survey 2018.* New York, NY: United Nations.

Wehrmann, D. (2018). *Multi-actor partnerships and private-sector engagement in development cooperation incentivising and regulating strategies* (DIE Discussion Paper 21/2018). Bonn: German Development Institute/Deutsches Institut für Entwicklungspolitik (DIE).

Wood, B., Betts, J., Etta, F., Gayfer, J., Kabell, D., Ngwira, N., & Samaranayake, M. (2011). *The evaluation of the Paris Declaration: Final report.* Copenhagen: Danish Institute for International Studies.

World Bank. (2003). *World Development Report 2004: Making services work for poor people.* Washington, DC: World Bank.

Open Access This chapter is licensed under the terms of the Creative Commons Attribution 4.0 International License (http://creativecommons.org/licenses/by/4.0/), which permits use, sharing, adaptation, distribution and reproduction in any medium or format, as long as you give appropriate credit to the original author(s) and the source, provide a link to the Creative Commons license and indicate if changes were made.

The images or other third party material in this chapter are included in the chapter's Creative Commons license, unless indicated otherwise in a credit line to the material. If material is not included in the chapter's Creative Commons license and your intended use is not permitted by statutory regulation or exceeds the permitted use, you will need to obtain permission directly from the copyright holder.

CHAPTER 15

Counting the Invisible: The Challenges and Opportunities of the SDG Indicator Framework for Statistical Capacity Development

Rolando Avendano, Johannes Jütting, and Manuel Kuhm

15.1 Introduction: Why Data Matters for the 2030 Agenda?

Better policies demand better data. High-quality and timely data is vital for governments, civil society, the private sector, and the public to make informed decisions on inclusive growth and public well-being, to hold governments and state actors accountable, and to ensure an accurate review of the progress and implementation of the global 2030 Agenda for Sustainable Development. Today, it is widely recognised that national statistical systems play a vital role in improving the collection, provision, and dissemination of official statistics to measure the achievements towards the Sustainable Development Goals (SDGs).

Tracking progress towards the SDGs requires collecting, processing, analysing, and disseminating an unprecedented amount of data and statistics at different levels, as well as considering new data sources such as citizen-generated and geospatial data. This represents a large challenge for

---

R. Avendano (✉)
Asian Development Bank, Manila, Philippines
e-mail: ravendano@adb.org

J. Jütting
PARIS21, OECD, Paris, France
e-mail: Johannes.jutting@oecd.org

M. Kuhm
University of Passau, Passau, Germany

© The Author(s) 2021
S. Chaturvedi et al. (eds.), *The Palgrave Handbook of Development Cooperation for Achieving the 2030 Agenda*,
https://doi.org/10.1007/978-3-030-57938-8_15

329

all countries, in particular low-income countries and Small Island Developing States (SIDS), where resource and capacity constraints widely prevail. Although countries need strong national statistical systems to live up to the high demands of the 2030 Agenda, many do not yet seem to have the required capacities to meet the data demands of the global SDG indicator framework and its premise to leave no one behind (Organisation for Economic Co-operation and Development [OECD] 2017).

The premise to leave no one behind starts with the need that everyone be counted. Yet, at present, more than 110 low- and middle-income countries lack functional civil registration and vital statistics systems, and they under-record—or completely fail to record—vital events of specific populations (World Bank 2018). Those living in poverty are most likely to be excluded; the poorest 20 per cent of the global population account for 55 per cent of unregistered births (Development Initiatives 2017). Furthermore, only 37 countries have statistical legislation that complies with the United Nations (UN) Fundamental Principles of Official Statistics. Making the invisible visible requires strengthening national statistical systems, developing required capacities and a supporting institutional infrastructure, and implementing data disaggregation strategies that are aligned with national development plans and the 2030 Agenda.

New data sources and providers are emerging as part of the data revolution, creating opportunities and challenges for national statistical systems. Transforming big data—such as mobile phone records and search engine queries, integrating geospatial information from GPS and satellite imagery, and considering crowdsourcing opportunities through citizen-generated data—presents valid complements to official statistics, eventually leading to cost savings and the efficient allocation of already scarce resources (Ginsberg et al. 2009; Gray et al. 2016; Lämmerhirt et al. 2018; Van Halderen et al. 2016). Broadening the production, dissemination, and use of data by integrating new data sources—while ensuring the highest quality possible, and mitigating risks of misuse and privacy violations—requires a fundamentally new vision for statistical capacity development that guides concerted action by all stakeholders in the new data ecosystem.

This chapter explores the main challenges and opportunities of the global SDG indicator framework, which was adopted to track progress towards the 2030 Agenda. It analyses three core problems in statistical capacity development identified in theory and practice, and it presents possible solutions associated with the new data demands of the SDG indicator framework.

First, the overburdening of national statistical systems, as one example of social systems, can be linked to resilience theory (Adger 2000; Holling 1973). Resilience has been a core aspect of most post-2015 international frameworks, such as the 2030 Agenda, as the international community recognised the predominant importance of capacity development within people, communities, states, and institutions to reduce, prevent, anticipate, absorb, and adjust to different risks and stressors in the process of sustainable development (OECD 2016). Ideally, the national statistical office (NSO) is developing established data collection methods and sharing agreements with system-wide providers, as well as sufficient training and staff to compile all required official statistics to meet users' needs—we define this state as the "business-as-usual" steady state. Once a disruptive external shock, risk, or stress—such as the SDG indicator framework and its requirement to compile 232 additional indicators—is introduced, the national statistical system faces three options. First, it can move to a new steady state that meets all data demands of the SDG indicator framework—it can rise to the challenge. Second, it can show sufficient resistance and persist in its current steady state, ignoring the global monitoring requirements and remaining in its "business-as-usual" steady state. Third, it can collapse. The compilation of a 100-indicator basket is already considered the upper limit by most countries' national statistical systems, irrespective of level of income (Sustainable Development Solutions Network [SDSN] 2015), thereby putting significant weight on the latter option. However, the following analysis shows that the voluntary nature of the SDG indicator framework, a lack of overall guidance in indicator compilation, and a persistent financing gap for statistical modernisation leave national statistical systems in a transitional state between the first two options: a sufficient will to commit but an absence of capacities to rise to the challenge.

Second, the increasing number of coordination failures between donors and countries, and within national statistical systems, are connected to game theory and cost-effectiveness (Bigsten and Tengstam 2015; Bourguignon and Platteau 2015). Coordination in development assistance recognises three different dimensions (World Health Organization [WHO] 2009):

- donor coordination (focus on better coordination in the development partners group),
- aid coordination (focus on effective use of provided resources for development),
- and development coordination (focus on government leadership and coordination in national systems)

– whereas a successful intervention likely requires a blended mixture of all three dimensions. Additionally, the coordination of national statistical systems is recognised to follow four main principles: validation, participation, harmonisation, and resource maximisation (United Nations Statistics Division [UNSD] 2015). All dimensions and principles require coordination mechanisms such as regional meetings and platforms, multilateral donor funds, or common standards and guidelines to result in "development effectiveness". As disruptive technologies and new data sources break the silo between data users and producers and affect the composition of stakeholders in national statistical systems, the SDG indicator framework's data demands require reformed and dynamic coordination mechanisms at all dimensions and levels (global, regional, national, subnational) so as to align the multitude of incentives in the new data ecosystem.

Third, a persistent lack of funding for statistical modernisation results from the political economy of statistical capacity development, the long-term nature of evidence-based policy-making outcomes, and the absence of compelling narratives with statistical insights (Dargent et al. 2018; OECD 2017; Taylor 2016). Taking into account the political economy of statistical capacity is a considerable aspect of successful development efforts in the area of data and statistics. Generally, there are two political-economic tensions at the heart of this lack of domestic investment in statistical capacity. First, better official statistics and data result—through public policies—in the efficient allocation of national resources, and thus to considerable society-wide welfare gains. Second, better official statistics and data reveal public policy deficiencies and are used to hold government representatives accountable, and thus better data can lead to demands for political change (Taylor 2016). Therefore, weakly performing national statistical systems, and NSOs in particular, are suitable indicators for weak state capacity in general, as the incentives of public policy-making are not aligned with the broader social welfare. Moreover, the long-term nature of statistical capacity-development outcomes further weakens the incentives of government representatives to invest in national statistical systems. For example, developing the capacities within an NSO to compile an indicator on food insecurity in rural areas that details the efficient allocation of seeds and fertiliser could take months to years before rural societies receive any beneficial outcomes. Considering short electoral cycles and voter behaviour, the government would have a greater incentive to invest in rural-agricultural development right away. Consequently, empowering NSOs and aligning socio-political incentives become crucial parts of (statistical) capacity-development financing. Lastly, the inability to turn statistical insights into compelling narratives—in the form of impact stories or case studies—further affects a rising distrust in numbers as well as the lack of investment in statistical modernisation.

The chapter concludes with an outlook on the role of development data in the context of "contested collaboration" and the future of development cooperation.

15.2 The SDG Indicator Framework: Data Gaps, Capacity Constraints, and Missing Alignment Between Global Requirements and National Needs

This section deals with the SDG indicator framework in general. It presents the main data gaps and capacity constraints faced by UN member states, which voluntarily agreed to track progress towards the 2030 Agenda. As supporting evidence for the missing alignment between global requirements and national needs, the section presents results from a survey conducted in 2018 by the Partnership in Statistics for Development in the 21st Century (PARIS21) and the High-Level Group for Partnership, Coordination and Capacity-Building for statistics for the 2030 Agenda (HLG-PCCB).

15.2.1 Persistent Sustainable Development Data Gaps

The SDG data framework, adopted on a voluntary basis in 2017, consists of 232 global indicators that build on the national and regional data of UN member states. National statistical systems are the main supporting structure for the compilation of the SDG indicators. The framework and its unprecedented ambition for global results-measurement towards a commonly defined global development agenda created a number of challenges for national statistical systems and the international statistical community alike.

An initial assessment of data availability indicates that the data revolution has not yet reached all countries. A recent assessment revealed that, on average, data for only 40 (20 per cent) of the adopted global SDG indicators are currently available, and another 47 global indicators (23 per cent) are considered "feasible" (i.e. data sources are available and the indicators could be compiled; United Nations Department of Economic and Social Affairs 2018). In other words, almost 60 per cent of SDG indicators lack most of the required data, are unavailable, or are methodologically undefined by the international statistical community. However, significant improvements in Tier I indicators (defined as conceptually clear, methodologically established, and regularly produced by at least 50 per cent of countries) are being achieved. In 2019, 101 SDG indicators were classified as Tier I, up from 82 indicators in 2017 (UNSD 2019).

On top of increasing demand, the 2030 Agenda requires data that is at least disaggregated by income, sex and gender, geography, age, and disability. Geographic disaggregation helps, for instance, in understanding the distributional impacts of poverty reduction policies, while gender-disaggregated data sheds light on the discrimination, exclusion, and marginalisation of social subgroups. However, several disaggregation dimensions lack benchmark definitions, standards, or classification criteria because concepts such as urban/rural or poor/non-poor concepts are not harmonised across countries. Likewise, most demographic and health surveys lack definitions for gender identity and disability, and they fail to adequately represent young (5–14 years) and old (over 49 years) age groups (OECD 2018). Allocated resources to data disaggregation are also scant: Only 13 per cent of countries worldwide have a dedicated budget for gender statistics. The evidence and modest progress made since the adoption of the SDG indicator framework suggests that national statistical systems are not yet fit to meet the data (and disaggregation) demands of the 2030 Agenda.

15.2.2 Capacity Constraints and Missing Alignment Between Global Requirements and National Needs

Statistical capacity can be defined as "the ability of a country's national statistical system, its organisations and individuals to collect, produce, analyse and disseminate high-quality and reliable statistics and data to meet users' needs" (Partnership in Statistics for Development in the 21st Century [PARIS21] 2018a). This definition stresses different levels (individual, organisational, and systemic) and the importance of considering a virtuous data life cycle in capacity-development efforts. It highlights a country-led, demand-driven, and long-term approach, in contrast to traditional supply-driven and external technical capacity-building efforts.

In 2017, PARIS21 and the HLG-PCCB designed a survey that aims to provide a better understanding of the current state of capacity-development efforts across national statistical systems, and the challenges, priorities, and plans NSOs have in view of SDG indicator framework implementation. This survey provides useful insights on untapped areas of capacity development, including individual non-technical skills, organisational practices, coordination between national agencies, and the mainstreaming of SDGs in national policies and reporting mechanisms. In 2017, the questionnaire was distributed to 193 UN member states and 2 non-members, of which 96 submitted a reply (around a 50 per cent response rate). The full results are published by PARIS21 (2018b).

The survey results indicate some regional discrepancies in the three most urgent SDG monitoring needs (see Table 15.1). Countries in Asia and the Pacific tend to prioritise indicators related to poverty, health, and well-being, whereas countries in Africa prioritise indicators related to poverty, food security, and water and sanitation. However, all regions stressed indicators related to poverty and its dimensions as a Top 1 capacity-development priority. A glance at the data by country income groups (low-income, lower-middle-income, upper-middle-income, and high-income) reveals a more nuanced picture of the most urgent SDG monitoring needs. Lower-middle-income countries tend to prioritise poverty indicators within their Top 3 priorities, whereas high-income countries express more interest in food security, gender equality, and education in their SDG indicator capacity-development efforts. Respecting expressed capacity-development needs against the backdrop of the SDG indicator framework in statistical capacity-development programmes offers great potential to produce the most sustainable results in the future.

The need for tailored SDG indicator production strategies becomes even more apparent when comparing regional disaggregation priorities (see Fig. 15.1). Disaggregation by income and geographical location is more important in Africa than anywhere else in the world. Disaggregation by migrant status needs immediate support in Asia and the Pacific, whereas disaggregation by disability is more important in Latin American and the Caribbean. These results illustrate that regional priorities vis-à-vis the 2030

Table 15.1 Survey results on regional SDG indicator prioritisation

Geographic region/Income group	Top 1	Top 2	Top 3
Global	1.1.1: Proportion of population below the international poverty line (disaggregated)	2.1.2: Prevalence of moderate or severe food insecurity in the population	1.2.2: Proportion of population living in poverty in all its dimensions
Africa	1.1.1: Proportion of population below the international poverty line (disaggregated)	2.1.2: Prevalence of moderate or severe food insecurity in the population	6.5.1: Degree of integrated water resources management implementation
Asia and Pacific	1.1.1: Proportion of population below the international poverty line (disaggregated)	1.2.1: Proportion of population living below the national poverty line (disaggregated)	3.2.1: Under-5 mortality rate
Eastern Europe	1.2.2: Proportion of population living in poverty in all its dimensions	2.c.1: Indicator of food price anomalies	None
Latin America and Caribbean	1.3.1: Proportion of population covered by social protection (disaggregated)	2.1.2: Prevalence of moderate or severe food insecurity in the population	None
Western Europe and Others	None	5.2.2: Proportion of female population subjected to sexual violence (disaggregated)	2.2.2: Prevalence of malnutrition among children under 5 years (disaggregated)
Low-Income	None	None	6.5.1: Degree of integrated water resources management implementation
Lower-Middle-Income	1.1.1: Proportion of population below the international poverty line (disaggregated)	1.2.1: Proportion of population living below the national poverty line (disaggregated)	1.2.2: Proportion of population living in poverty in all its dimensions
Upper-Middle-Income	1.2.2: Proportion of population living in poverty in all its dimensions	2.1.2: Prevalence of moderate or severe food insecurity in the population	6.2.1: Proportion of population using sanitation services
High-Income	2.1.2: Prevalence of moderate or severe food insecurity in the population	5.2.2: Proportion of female population subjected to sexual violence (disaggregated)	4.c.1: Proportion of teachers in primary and secondary education having received minimum training

Question 10: Considering your national priorities, what are the Top 3 Sustainable Development Goal indicators (please select only Tier II and I) that require immediate capacity building in your National Statistical Office?
Note "None" indicates that no SDG indicator was selected at least twice by two different countries in the same region/income group. Shade intensity represents the percentage of countries in the respective region/income group that selected the indicator (darker shade corresponds to higher percentage)
Source PARIS21 (2018b)

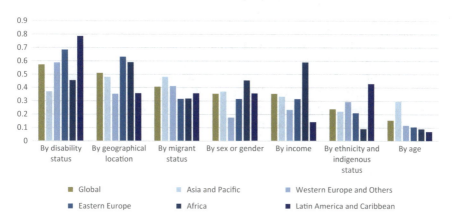

Fig. 15.1 Survey results on regional disaggregation requirements. Question 12: Please indicate what types of data disaggregation require the most immediate support (*Source* PARIS21 2018b)

Agenda are heterogeneous. Designing country-driven, localised SDG monitoring and disaggregation strategies in statistical capacity-development efforts will be an effective solution, given the immediate resource and capacity constraints.

15.3 SDG Indicator Framework Implementation: Main Challenges and Possible Solutions

This section outlines the three main challenges of the SDG indicator framework for national statistical systems, overburdening, coordination failures, and the lack of funding, and it presents possible solutions. Conclusively, Sect. 15.4 offers an outlook on the role of data in the future of development cooperation.

15.3.1 Lessen Overburdening of National Statistical Systems

The 2030 Agenda acknowledges the potential for reporting overburden and recommends that national statistical systems build on existing reporting mechanisms (WHO 2019). With follow-up and review processes being voluntary and country-led, several approaches are proposed to tackle the overburdening of national statistical systems. First, the statistical community could define a reduced set of indicators, thereby respecting global and key regional priorities. A 100-indicator basket is already considered to be an upper limit by most countries, irrespective of levels of income (SDSN 2015). Multi-purpose indicators could also be introduced to track progress towards different cross-cutting targets. Second, localised indicator frameworks incorporating "complementary indicators" that countries have chosen themselves for measuring particular national and/or regional concerns could be a valuable tool to reduce reporting burden. Most UN regional commissions are well-equipped to design illustrative national indicator frameworks to align regional and international monitoring needs. Third, designing new outreach strategies and incentives for collaboration with new actors is essential. Established platforms such as the World Business Council on Sustainable Development could be used to engage with the business community for designing complementary key performance indicators. Fourth, innovative planning tools can help in tracking reporting burden and presenting proper costing estimates for leveraging domestic and external financial resources (see Box 15.1).

> **Box 15.1 Improving planning and SDG readiness through ADAPT**
> The Advanced Data Planning Tool (ADAPT), developed by PARIS21, is an innovative web-based planning tool for NSOs to adapt their data production to the priority data needs of policy-makers. ADAPT is a consultative tool that brings data stakeholders together and defines the measurement context for relevant development plans in global and national contexts. ADAPT can be used for monitoring and analysing data gaps against the SDG indicator framework.
>
> Currently, ADAPT is being used by national agencies and international partners—notably the United Nations Statistics Division—in 21 countries worldwide. The new version of ADAPT features a costing module that provides statistical staff and policy-makers with detailed estimates of the required financial resources to close critical data gaps and meet national data needs.[1]

15.3.2 Avoiding Coordination Failures

A lack of coordination between beneficiaries, development partners, and donors funding statistical capacity development has led to duplication and unsustainable intervention results, as parties do not necessarily work together or strategies are poorly aligned with national data needs. Additionally, the new data ecosystem and its multitude of emerging providers requires innovative coordination mechanisms and strategies to foster effective data-sharing, integration, and quality assurance in the process.

Linked to the challenge of using national data for international monitoring is the need to better align national and international efforts to strengthen statistical capacity (PARIS21 2013). A coherent, inclusive, feasible, and politically backed national statistical plan can guide progress towards strengthened statistical capacity across the entire national statistical system. In 2018, 129 countries were implementing a national statistical plan—an increase of 26 per cent from 102 countries in 2017. Capacity-development strategies should emerge from an open and collaborative dialogue by local representatives from civil society and the political sphere as well as external partners and private stakeholders about their shared objectives and interests in addition to their respective contributions to the common goal.

Integrating emerging data providers into national statistical systems demands strengthening soft skills such as leadership and communication as well as establishing data partnerships and coordination mechanisms between all stakeholders to avoid critical failures and reduce risks (see Box 15.2). Integrative consultation platforms and processes for defining a set of nationally relevant indicators for data collection, open data principles to foster data collaboration efforts, and guidelines for leveraging innovative complementarities between traditional and new data sources (e.g. big data, citizen-generated data), as provided by private sector companies, will reduce costs and minimise levels of confusion related to data discrepancies. Furthermore, extended quality assurance frameworks will be needed to ensure the appropriate integration of new data sources while respecting confidentiality and privacy rights. Ultimately, successful coordination and collaboration in the new data ecosystem depend on fostering political will and establishing trust between all involved stakeholders.

> **Box 15.2 Effects of SDG data demands in Small Island Developing States**
> In the era of SDGs, SIDS face enormous statistical challenges due to the increased scope, depth, and level of detail of data needs for monitoring progress in achieving the SDGs. This was recognised early on by SIDS. Thus, in the cases of both the Caribbean and Pacific regions, it was agreed to produce a core set of SDG indicators relevant to their respective regions while taking into consideration the constraints of their overstretched national statistical systems (Caribbean Community 2018). It is important to note that SIDS national statistical systems vary considerably in terms of the size of NSOs, the available resources for statistics, technical capacity, institutional environments that support statistical work, political support, and data availability. Their capacity and readiness to address SDG data needs will largely depend on these factors as well as the extent to which the SDGs align with their national development policies and frameworks. Common SIDS challenges identified that relate to SDGs include, among others, funding insecurity, constraints in human resources, weak statistical systems, and missing alignment between global data collection requirements and existing national concerns.
>
> SIDS would need considerable funding to improve capacity and modernise national statistical systems. This would enable them to undertake the full range of statistical activities required to produce the data for monitoring the SDGs. As SIDS represent around 1 per cent of the global population, the unusually high per capita expenses for statistical activities preclude governments from allocating the necessary budget for statistics, which often results in the need for external financial support. However, dependence on external funding does not translate into a higher level of commitment to SIDS. In fact, external funding commitments to SIDS remain at a low level, with only about $33 million—or 5 per cent of total global commitments—for the period 2014–2016 (PARIS21 2018c). Only eight SIDS received funding of $1 million or over during the same period, which is unlikely to be sufficient in producing sustainable statistical capacity-development outcomes (PARIS21 2019b).
>
> *Source* Authors

15.3.3 Overcoming Funding Gap

Investing in national statistical systems needs to become a strategic priority for low- and lower-middle-income countries as well as providers of development cooperation (OECD 2017). The total estimated cost for 144 low- and middle-income countries to produce data for the SDG indicators (Tiers 1 and 2) is estimated at $2.8 to $3.0 billion per year until 2030 (Global Partnership for

Sustainable Development Data 2016), while the cost for the implementation of all Cape Town Global Action Plan objectives rises to $5.6 billion annually. Assuming an ambitious scenario of domestic resource mobilisation in low- and middle-income countries, closing the funding gap for SDG data demands and Cape Town Global Action Plan implementation requires doubling current external support for statistics—from 0.33 per cent (around $600 million) to 0.7 per cent per year (around $1.3 billion; PARIS21 2019a).

However, the level of financing for development is only part of the story. Simply increasing the amount of investment for statistical capacity-development efforts is unlikely to bring results without revising the delivery mechanisms behind them (PARIS21 2018c). An emerging consensus among development partners, agencies, and countries calls for more concerted action and coordination in the provision of capacity and technical support in the sector. Integrating new and better data sources in official statistics, improving the quality of financing for statistics, aligning country priorities for data with global monitoring demands, and creating compacts for country-led development data initiatives offer a promising vision for sustainable statistical capacity development in low- and lower-middle-income countries. The model of establishing a global partnership for managing financial resources for data could be extended to other areas. For example, to optimise capacity-development planning and the comparative advantages of capacity-development programmes among providers, alignment through established approaches—including strategic frameworks such as the National Strategies for the Development of Statistics, and planning tools such as ADAPT—will continue to ensure a strong basis for coordination (PARIS21 2019b).

15.4 The Changing Role of Data and Statistics in Development

Development cooperation paradigms are continually shifting and evolving because of the mismatch between predominant ideologies and accumulated experiences (Innis 1951). As development paradigms shift, so does the role of development data. The post-war era focussed on economic statistics and how they informed trade integration processes before moving on to social statistics in the 1970s and 1980s, which spawned various household survey initiatives. Advances in digital technologies in the 1990s facilitated the transition towards regular data-reporting systems to design and inform policy planning. Additionally, it entailed the introduction of the first data dissemination standards, thereby strengthening the international statistical community. The ambitious results-measurement frameworks of the Millennium Development Goals and the SDGs in the 2000s created an unprecedented imperative for more and better data on the national levels for informing development plans and Poverty Reduction Strategy Papers for achieving the 2030 Agenda. The subsequent sections present three emerging proposals for strengthening the role of data in development, created in an effort to rise to the challenges of the SDG indicator framework: triangular cooperation in statistical capacity development, a global financing facility for development data, and the power of humanising data through compelling stories.

15.4.1 Triangular Cooperation in Data and Statistics

The 2030 Agenda and its SDGs are broadening development efforts across the entirety of governments and societies worldwide while further diversifying the development cooperation landscape through the integration of new actors and partners. As a result, the management of development efforts and partner collaboration at the country level is fundamentally changed. These changes, in turn, affect the way government institutions organise themselves to manage development cooperation by putting specific coordination mechanisms and structures in place.

The engagement of new development partners needs to be effective and meaningful. Multi-stakeholder dialogues and inclusive consultations are needed to harness the full potential for building trust, the effective use of public resources, and the meaningful engagement of emerging donors and the private sector in development cooperation towards the 2030 Agenda. Furthermore, mutual accountability mechanisms between—and results-measurement frameworks of—the stakeholders involved need to be in place to manage the increasingly diverse landscape of partners engaged in statistical capacity development.

New forms of development cooperation in data and statistics are acknowledged and growing in importance. Triangular and South-South cooperation are considered an expression of multiple stakeholders and their desire to engage in practical and effective forms of cooperation in capacity-development efforts (Federal Ministry for Economic Cooperation and Development 2013). Typically, triangular cooperation in data and statistics involves the joint planning, financing, and implementation of capacity-development projects by an established Development Assistance Committee (DAC) donor, an emerging economy, and a beneficiary country. However, other forms of triangular cooperation in data and statistics exist as well. Typically, the collaboration involves a beneficiary NSO, an NSO from a DAC member country, and a funding agency. Rather than a new cooperation arrangement, triangular cooperation is considered as an additional instrument to foster mutual learning and knowledge exchange between all involved parties. PARIS21 has undertaken this collaborative approach with different development partners. The partnership between Statistics Canada, Global Affairs Canada, and PARIS21 has allowed for prioritising the beneficiaries' perspectives and aligning support with national priorities in order to identify synergies with Canada's overall development cooperation strategy. Similarly, the collaboration between the Department for International Development, the Office of National Statistics, and PARIS21 aims at identifying and leveraging UK policy experts to participate in development cooperation projects along the lines of international development priority areas. The results of these approaches are promising and should be further developed with other development providers.

15.4.2 Sustainable Financing for Development Data

Investing in data brings returns. Yet, national statistical systems in low- and lower-middle-income countries still face systematic underfunding and critical resource constraints. Quantitatively, the funding landscape for development data is confronting regional concentration and a high share of loan financing, posing challenges for project planning and implementation (PARIS21 2019b). Additionally, closing the funding gap for SDG reporting will require substantial resource mobilisation by leveraging domestic public finance or new pooled funding mechanisms. Qualitatively, development data is experiencing a lack of political awareness and low visibility, which has resulted from an insufficient understanding of data analysis and use (PARIS21 2019a). Additionally, the minimal harmonisation of support due to significant fragmentation, the poor alignment of external support to country systems and strategies, and poor sustainability and predictability prevent support from becoming effective. The possibility for data to be used as both a decision tool by public servants and an accountability tool by the public to hold policy-makers accountable weakens the incentives of government representatives to invest in better data, thus further limiting the public finance window.

Closing the development data funding gap and fulfilling these principles requires new mechanisms and instruments in order to improve donor coordination and the effectiveness of investments in statistical capacity development. The creation of a global financing facility or a global fund for sustainable development data could raise the political demand for data, improve alignment with national priorities, promote development partner coordination, and speed up access to finance at scale. Global funds have a greater capacity to address the challenges of funding statistical capacity development than other financial mechanisms, such as Multi-Donor Trust Funds, which are useful tools for emergency assistance (PARIS21 2019a). If designed properly, such a facility could match funding for national capacities with existent country-owned investment plans, and at the same time seed money for data innovation and new partnerships.

The concept of "aid as catalyst", which introduces public official development assistance as a leveraging force for private and further public resource mobilisation, is indeed already being observed in the data context. The prominence of emerging donors and philanthropic organisations in the data sector is noticeable. Between 2013 and 2015, nearly $574 million (2.4 per cent of all philanthropic support to development) can be linked to projects with a strong data and statistics component, in particular in medical and agricultural research (PARIS21 2018c). Current discussions on multilateral financing, in particular the World Bank International Development Association replenishment in 2019, aim at bringing additional financial resources to underfunded sectors, such as data and statistics. Current discussions could include the first-ever horizontal policy commitment for development data, which could serve as a catalyser for other actors to attract financial resources from the private and public sectors alike in the future.

However, there are still barriers preventing the public and private consolidation of financial resources for statistical capacity development. Development partners could rethink their role in the sector for attracting other forms of financial resources while providing "seed" financing for key areas of statistical development.

15.4.3 *The Power of Stories—Humanising Data*

Compelling narratives and reasons to invest in data need to be communicated to convince development partners to increase funding and efforts. For this purpose, stories of impact have to be well-documented and shared with the widest audience possible. In the past, data has proven to be able to save lives: For example, in the health sector, better data on maternal deaths and their causes during childbirth ensured that subsequent mothers did not have to die the same way during labour (WHO 2018). Additionally, data has proven to be able to improve lives: For example, in the financial sector, civil registration is a prerequisite to be eligible for access to credit and cash grants. The communication of new narratives wrapped in engaging case studies illustrating how SDG monitoring has saved and improved lives will be a means to an end of securing more and better funding for statistics and data.

Conclusively, the role of data in development presents one area of "contested collaboration" in development cooperation. First, global actors and, in particular, data partnerships contest existing institutions by elaborating new and flexible approaches to statistical capacity development (regime creation) and creating new mechanisms and instruments for development data financing (regime shifting). Second, the role of data in development fosters new and existing forms of collaboration through multi-stakeholder partnerships and new forms of cooperation (e.g. triangular), and by achieving cohesion between collective capacity-development efforts and national priorities (e.g. National Strategies for the Development of Statistics, "localised" SDG indicator frameworks). To attain these objectives, a revised approach to capacity development is needed that recognises elements such as leadership, management, and communication skills as effective vehicles for strengthening data systems. With a revised approach, development data can be a powerful driver and essential part in a new framing of data for development cooperation.

15.5 Conclusion

Providing an accurate review of the progress and implementation of the 2030 Agenda for Sustainable Development requires taking advantage of the "data revolution". Although there are opportunities to take advantage of, national statistical systems in developing countries still lack the necessary capacities to rise to the challenge and require more fundamental forms of support.

National statistical systems need to be modernised and strengthened significantly to meet the requirement for the sheer amount of data demanded by the global SDG indicator framework. The issues faced by statistical systems extend to three predominant themes: overburdening in data reporting, coordination failures in data partnerships, and inadequate funding.

Sustainable development strategies that are based on the global SDG indicator framework and incorporate key economic, social, political, and environmental aspects must be locally owned. Locally defined indicator frameworks and a reduced set of global indicators aligned with national and/or regional priorities present one opportunity to avoid the overburdening of national statistical capacities. Fostering collaboration platforms and political will—by strengthening trust and incentives in statistical capacity development—will be a prerequisite to avoid critical coordination failures in newly emerging multi-stakeholder data partnerships. Closing the development data funding gap requires a revised perspective on mechanisms and instruments so that they improve coordination and become more effective. Current discussions on a global financing facility for sustainable development data are leading in this direction.

Lastly, development is about human experiences. Humanising statistical capacity-development efforts by using compelling narratives and stories of impact about the power of data to save and improve lives will be a means to an end towards securing the necessary resources to ensure an accurate and quantifiable review of the progress and implementation of the global 2030 Agenda for Sustainable Development. Better policies demand better data, and better data demands better stories.

Note

1. For more information on ADAPT, please visit https://adapt.paris21.org/.

References

Adger, W. N. (2000). Social and ecological resilience: Are they related? *Progress in Human Geography, 24*(3), 347–364.

Bigsten, A., & Tengstam, S. (2015). International cooperation and the effectiveness of aid. *World Development, 69,* 75–85.

Bourguignon, F., & Platteau, J. (2015). The hard challenge of aid coordination. *World Development, 69,* 86–97.

Caribbean Community. (2018). *CARICOM core indicators for the Sustainable Development Goals (SDGs): Assessment of data availability in member states and associate members*. Georgetown, Guyana: Caribbean Community Secretariat.

Dargent, E., Lotta, G., Mejía-Guerra, J. A., & Moncada, G. (2018). *Who wants to know? The political economy of statistical capacity in Latin America*. Washington, DC: Inter-American Development Bank.

Development Initiatives. (2017). *P20 Initiative: Baseline report*. http://devinit.org/wp-content/uploads/2017/03/P20-Initiative-baseline-report.pdf.

Federal Ministry for Economic Cooperation and Development. (2013). *Triangular cooperation in German development cooperation*. Bonn: Author.

Ginsberg, J., Mohebbi, M. H., Patel, R. S., Brammer, L., Smolinski, M. S., & Brilliant, L. (2009). Detecting influenza epidemics using search engine query data. *Nature, 457*, 1012–1014.

Global Partnership for Sustainable Development Data. (2016). *The state of development data funding*. https://opendatawatch.com/wp-content/uploads/2016/09/development-data-funding-2016.pdf.

Gray, J., Lämmerhirt, D., & Bounegru, L. (2016). *Changing what counts: How can citizen-generated and civil society data be used as an advocacy tool to change official data collection?* http://civicus.org/thedatashift/wp-content/uploads/2016/03/changing-what-counts-2.pdf.

Holling, C. S. (1973). Resilience and stability of ecological systems. *Annual Review of Ecology and Systematics, 4*, 1–23.

Innis, H. A. (1951). Industrialism and cultural values. *American Economic Review, 41*(2), 201–209.

Lämmerhirt, D., Gray, J., Venturini, T., & Meunie, A. (2018). *Advancing sustainability together? Citizen-generated data and the Sustainable Development Goals*. http://www.data4sdgs.org/sites/default/files/services_files/Advancing%20Sustainability%20Together%20CGD%20Report_0.pdf.

OECD (Organisation for Economic Co-operation and Development). (2016). *Resilience systems analysis: Learning and recommendations report*. http://www.oecd.org/dac/conflict-fragility-resilience/docs/SwedenLearning_Recommendationsreport.pdf.

OECD. (2017). *Development co-operation report 2017: Data for development*. Paris: OECD Publishing.

OECD. (2018). *Development co-operation report 2018: Joining forces to leave no one behind*. Paris: OECD Publishing.

PARIS21 (Partnership in Statistics for Development in the 21st Century). (2013). *Strengthening national statistical systems to monitor global goals*. https://www.oecd.org/dac/POST-2015%20P21.pdf.

PARIS21. (2018a). *Proposing a framework for capacity development 4.0*. https://paris21.org/sites/default/files/inline-files/CD4.0-Framework_final.pdf.

PARIS21. (2018b). *Survey results: New approaches to capacity development and future priorities*. https://paris21.org/capacity-development-40/cd40-survey.

PARIS21. (2018c). *Partner report on support to statistics: PRESS 2018*. https://paris21.org/sites/default/files/inline-files/PRESS2018_BAT_web_v2.pdf.

PARIS21. (2019a). *Mobilising data for the SDGs* (PARIS21 Discussion Paper No. 15). Paris: Author.

PARIS21. (2019b). *Statistical capacity development outlook 2019.* http://statisticalcapacitymonitor.org/pdf/Statistical%20Capacity%20Development%20Outlook%202019.pdf.

SDSN (Sustainable Development Solutions Network). (2015). *Developing indicators for the Sustainable Development Goals: Reflections on the work of the IAEG-SDGs.* https://www.unsdsn.org/news/2015/06/23/reflections-on-the-iaeg-sdgs.

Taylor, M. (2016). *The political economy of statistical capacity.* Washington, DC: Inter-American Development Bank.

United Nations Department of Economic and Social Affairs. (2018). *The Sustainable Development Goals Report 2018.* New York, NY: Author.

UNSD (United Nations Statistics Division). (2015). *Coordination national statistical systems, global, regional.* https://unstats.un.org/unsd/nationalaccount/workshops/2016/Caribbean/Session_1_Dominica.pptx.

UNSD. (2019). *Tier classification for global SDG indicators.* https://unstats.un.org/sdgs/files/Tier%20Classification%20of%20SDG%20Indicators_13%20February%202019_web.pdf.

Van Halderen, G., Minchin, S., Brady, M., & Scott, G. (2016). Integrating statistical and geospatial information, cultures and professions: International developments and Australian experience. *Statistical Journal of the IAOS, 32*(4), 457–470.

WHO (World Health Organization). (2009). *Review of coordination mechanisms for development cooperation in Tajikistan.* http://www.euro.who.int/__data/assets/pdf_file/0013/106411/E93771.pdf.

WHO. (2018). *Maternal mortality.* https://www.who.int/gho/maternal_health/mortality/maternal_mortality_text/en/.

WHO. (2019). *How is progress towards SDGs measured and reported on?* http://www.euro.who.int/en/health-topics/health-policy/sustainable-development-goals/q-and-a-health-and-the-sustainable-development-goals/6.-how-is-progress-towards-the-sdgs-measured-and-reported-on.

World Bank. (2018). *Global civil registration and vital statistics.* https://www.worldbank.org/en/topic/health/brief/global-civil-registration-and-vital-statistics.

Open Access This chapter is licensed under the terms of the Creative Commons Attribution 4.0 International License (http://creativecommons.org/licenses/by/4.0/), which permits use, sharing, adaptation, distribution and reproduction in any medium or format, as long as you give appropriate credit to the original author(s) and the source, provide a link to the Creative Commons license and indicate if changes were made.

The images or other third party material in this chapter are included in the chapter's Creative Commons license, unless indicated otherwise in a credit line to the material. If material is not included in the chapter's Creative Commons license and your intended use is not permitted by statutory regulation or exceeds the permitted use, you will need to obtain permission directly from the copyright holder.

PART IV

Institutional Settings for Development Cooperation

CHAPTER 16

Building a Global Development Cooperation Regime: Failed but Necessary Efforts

André de Mello e Souza

16.1 Introduction

This chapter addresses two main questions. First, would a global development cooperation regime serve the purposes of global development better than current institutions and agreements? Second, how can recent failures to build such a regime be explained, given the attempts to render them more inclusive and legitimate?

Thus far, there is no overarching, truly global and functional development cooperation regime.[1] This is surprising from the viewpoint of international relations scholarship. Development, broadly conceived, is an issue-area where, perhaps more than any other in international negotiations, absolute gains prevail over relative ones.[2] No immediate or direct stakes for national security are involved, and, in contrast to regimes such as the United Nations (UN) Security Council or even the World Trade Organization, which implicate more clearly and directly the strategic and commercial concerns of members, development cooperation regimes are shaped by principled ideas and collective identities.[3] In other words, global discussions in the ambit of development cooperation regimes are much more centred on norms and principles than on instrumental interests, at least relative to those taking place in security or economic regimes.[4]

A. de Mello e Souza (✉)
Institute for Applied Economic Research (IPEA), Rio de Janeiro, Brazil
e-mail: andre.souza@ipea.gov.br

© The Author(s) 2021
S. Chaturvedi et al. (eds.), *The Palgrave Handbook of Development Cooperation for Achieving the 2030 Agenda*,
https://doi.org/10.1007/978-3-030-57938-8_16

Disagreements on principles of international development cooperation between high-income and emerging countries are well known and present significant implications for the practice of such cooperation. They involve the moral obligation of the former countries to compensate for the deleterious effects of colonialism and imperialism, as opposed to the mutual gains of partners proclaimed by the latter. In addition, the so-called emerging countries conceive of development cooperation as being much broader than the definition of official development assistance (ODA), including economic exchanges of various kinds. They also reject the purportedly vertical, paternalistic approach of high-income countries towards development cooperation, endorsing instead a horizontal relationship based on demand-driven practices, local ownership, and the self-reliance of partners. There are also opposing views on conditionalities related to human rights, good governance, or democracy, which emerging countries reject while Development Assistance Committee (DAC) members endorse. Additionally, there is divergence on the principles of transparency and accountability and the way they should be applied.[5] The aid effectiveness agenda closely associated with these principles has produced the Paris Declaration (2005) and the Accra Agenda for Action (2008) and has been a hallmark of the regime centred on the DAC, which can be considered the first major international development cooperation regime.

Since 1961 the DAC has proved capable of consolidating agreed norms and principles regarding development cooperation, and of generating considerable coherence, coordination, and even harmonisation in related practices, with institutionalised monitoring by means of annual reports with statistics and peer-review mechanisms. However, its members are limited to 23 high-income countries (plus the European Commission), which are all members of the Organisation for Economic Co-operation and Development (OECD). Furthermore, the increasing importance—in terms of the volume of resources, the range of modalities, and geographical reach—of the development cooperation offered by emerging economies as well as of non-state actors adds to the shortcomings of the DAC globally. Although the DAC has successfully courted many recipient developing countries to adhere to its aid effectiveness agenda, major emerging countries such as those in the BRICS group (Brazil, Russia, India, China, South Africa) have chosen to remain on the sidelines. They rejected the Paris Declaration as a normative or operational guideline for South-South cooperation.

After several unsuccessful attempts, the DAC finally managed in 2011 to lure Brazil, India, and China into signing the Busan outcome document that originated the Global Partnership for Effective Development Co-operation (GPEDC), a multi-stakeholder platform "to advance the effectiveness of development efforts" (Global Partnership for Effective Development Co-operation 2017). Talaat Abdel-Malek (2015, pp. 180–186) recalls that efforts to invite the participation of emerging economies – led by China, India and Brazil – [...] included visits to Beijing and other capitals by OECD officials; bilateral consultation by OECD ministers; joint studies, notably the OECD-China study; initiatives by Korean and Mexican officials; and exchanges between OECD and representatives of these countries during UN-sponsored events.

Its innovations in the governance of development cooperation notwithstanding, shortly thereafter, just before the kickoff of its first High Level Meeting in Mexico (2014), Brazil, India, and China left the GPEDC. These emerging countries condemned it for being a DAC-led initiative and for adopting approaches that are alien to South-South cooperation, while at the same time failing to effectively apply the principle of "common but differentiated responsibilities" (Besharati 2013, pp. 12–13).[6]

The other major international development cooperation regime is found in the UN Development Cooperation Forum (DCF), established in 2005 as a sub-organ of the UN Economic and Social Council. The DCF holds biennial sessions aimed at providing an all-inclusive channel of communication for development cooperation stakeholders to engage in mutual learning and knowledge sharing. The analytical work produced for the DCF—including the report of the Secretary-General on "Trends and Progress in International Development Cooperation" and policy briefs—is widely disseminated for use in UN processes and beyond. The forum thereby seeks to provide a platform for reaching widely shared and adopted principles, definitions, and norms of development cooperation.

Yet, the DCF has accomplished remarkably little since its creation, largely because member countries have failed to provide political and financial support for its operation. Whereas high-income countries have generally and historically distrusted the UN (Fues et al. 2012, p. 253), emerging countries have—at least in rhetoric, if not in practice—defended the role of the DCF as the appropriate regime for policy discussion and coordination regarding development cooperation. Not only do developing countries benefit from the majority of votes in the UN "one country one vote" decision-making system, but they have argued that the DCF is more inclusive and legitimate than the GPEDC (Abdel-Malek 2015, p. 180).

> When declining to engage in OECD-led processes, countries such as India and Brazil always refer back to the United Nations as the natural, legitimate and universal forum where most international issues, including development cooperation, should be discussed. Historically, in fact, the UN has always been an important platform for the nations of the South providing support services to the work of the G77. UN bodies such as UNDESA, UNCTAD, UNIDO, the FAO and UNDP all have units specifically dedicated to supporting [South-South cooperation]. (Besharati 2013, p. 48)

In addition to its lack of member support, the DCF has, as does the UN as a whole, negotiating and decision-making processes that are generally considered ineffective. Indeed, the DCF illustrates clearly the trade-off between legitimacy and efficiency, which is ubiquitous in the governance literature.[7] In particular, increased stakeholder participation and deliberation may be crucial to ensure legitimacy but tend to undermine efficiency by rendering the decision-making process more complicated and time-consuming, oftentimes leading to stalemate. In the words of Neissan A. Besharati (2013, p. 48):

> The massive UN bureaucracy has its limits because it operates very slowly and suffers from the influence of multiple political forces that pull it in different directions. The sheer number and diversity of stakeholders often make it difficult to reach consensus and to agree on clear and bold action for the future. This has led to a decrease in political interest in UN forums which are often characterized as mere "talk shops".

Indeed, these shortcomings of the DCF create incentives for the search of other development cooperation regimes, and the OECD member countries continue to promote their agenda even without the involvement of emerging countries (Mello e Souza 2014, p. 21). In parallel, the DCF continues to play a mostly technical role of generating and disseminating analyses and data.

The perceived lack of a common ground for building a stronger and all-inclusive global development cooperation regime and the deadlocks in burden-sharing negotiations between DAC members and some of the most important developing countries may put the very viability of such a regime in doubt. More fundamentally, it may lead one to consider whether it is necessary or even desirable, from a global perspective, to attempt to build a development cooperation regime. Failed efforts are costly in terms of resources and time, and probably also counterproductive in that they raise suspicion and scepticism towards future cooperation. Would such a regime serve the purposes of global development better than current plurilateral institutions and bilateral agreements? In the following section, I draw from mainstream regime theory and consider recent transformations in the nature of global development cooperation to address this question. I argue that an international development cooperation regime is necessary and preferable to the status quo due to the efficiency gains it provides and, in particular, the coordination and policy coherence requirements of the 2030 Agenda for Sustainable Development. The Sustainable Development Goals (SDGs) constitute evidence of common global interests that make this regime viable. This section therefore approaches the issue of the benefits of such a regime from a *systemic* perspective.

However, even if a global development cooperation regime is necessary and desirable, surely it will not come into force without efforts from countries and other stakeholders, whose particular interests and motivations often override global or collective concerns. Why have previous attempts at building such regimes failed, and what can be learnt from these failures? In particular, how can failures be explained in light of the attempts to broaden the membership base of the GPEDC and render it more inclusive? The results of recent efforts to bring together DAC members and emerging countries can be understood from the perspective of the regime's (perceived) lack of legitimacy, its costs, the opportunities for influence that it offers countries previously excluded from the DAC as well as its importance to those countries. In the third section, I resort to concepts and insights found in the literature on stakeholder participation in governance to try to shed light on these shortcomings. Hence, this section approaches the difficulties of building a development cooperation regime from an *agent* or *actor-centred* perspective. Hopefully, a better understanding of these difficulties may point to promising pathways for building a more inclusive, efficient, and legitimate global development cooperation regime.

The final section concludes the chapter by bringing together the main arguments presented beforehand and pointing to their implications for the global governance of international development cooperation. Notably, the main obstacle to building such governance is not an incompatibility of interests between emerging countries and DAC members, as often argued, but is rather related to the value countries place on global institutions and their opportunities and capabilities for effective participation and influence in these institutions.

16.2 Why Is a Global Development Cooperation Regime Important?

Why should DAC members, emerging countries, and other stakeholders strive to build a global and effective development cooperation regime? As already mentioned, there are costs involved in any such endeavour, and the record of previous failures is not encouraging. Furthermore, it is reasonable to question whether the enduring lack of convergence is so problematic. The continuation of the status quo of emerging countries independently setting their own standards and modus operandi on international development cooperation, all while DAC members continue to operate under their own consolidated framework, may not be such an undesirable outcome. This may be particularly the case if North-South and South-South cooperation are considered to be fundamentally different, though complementary.

Why is achieving a global development cooperation regime important? The main answers to this question have to do with efficiency. Building on the work of Robert O. Keohane (1984), mainstream theories of international regimes resort to a functionalist logic according to which such regimes are created precisely because they increase efficiency by helping members overcome collective action problems and "political market failures".

Regimes play this role whenever countries have shared—though not identical—interests. Global development certainly entails shared interests between countries. This is evidenced, for instance, in the agreed 2030 Agenda, even if countries disagree as to how to proceed in promoting it. Moreover, the experience of negotiating the GPEDC up until 2014, when Brazil, India, and China were still engaging members, suggests that there are commonalities of interests, notwithstanding these countries' later abandonment of the regime. In addition, though we cannot expect development cooperation regimes to be legally binding—as very few international regimes are—they may help "to establish stable mutual expectations about others' patterns of behaviour and to develop working relationships that will allow the parties to adapt their practices to new situations" (Keohane 1984, p. 89).

Regimes enhance efficiency mainly by reducing the costs for achieving common goals and providing public goods. By constructing issue linkages (Keohane 1984, p. 89), a development cooperation regime can promote policy coherence among members, making it less likely that they will pursue conflicting goals. More concretely, there are a plethora of trade-offs and conflicts in the global pursuit of the SDGs that need to be kept in check.

For instance, developing countries seeking to provide access to energy for all (SDG 7) may increase fossil fuel emissions, thus undermining the combat against climate change (SDG 13). Similarly, some countries' carbon-based, energy-intensive growth strategies may be effective in lifting large numbers of people out of poverty in the short term (SDG 1), but the emissions of carbon and other pollutants cause serious damage to health (SDG 3) across national borders.

Conversely, policies aiming to achieve one SDG may also help to attain others, as illustrated by the positive impact of trade and environmental protection on poverty alleviation and health, respectively. In short, promoting development in general—and particularly as agreed in the 2030 Agenda—requires aligning multiple policies within and across countries to maximise synergies of goals and minimise undesirable impacts from negative interlinkages.

Yet, such a global policy alignment can only be reached by means of a development cooperation regime. Insofar as each SDG or issue-area of development is approached independently between emerging countries and between them and the DAC members, it becomes much more difficult to have a holistic appreciation of global development challenges and needs. Similarly, bilateral agreements between partners or the parallel coexistence of numerous regimes—such as the DAC, the GPEDC, the DCF, and others—will be insufficient for the provision of global goods.

In addition, by making it possible to avoid the duplication of efforts or overlapping projects, a development cooperation regime may reduce the costs of achieving the 2030 Agenda. In other words, it may lead to a "division of labour",[8] so to speak, between development cooperation providers. Reduced costs are particularly important, given the concern over the availability of resources to finance this agenda.

Moreover, considering the abundance of specific policy issues that need to be addressed in order to effectively coordinate the practices of numerous actors of the development community, a regime would also help with the more prosaic task of making it easier and cheaper for these actors to meet and negotiate. Benefiting from economies of scale, once a regime is operational the marginal costs of negotiating each additional issue is reduced and becomes lower than it would be otherwise (Keohane 1984, p. 90). As a result, a regime can significantly reduce transaction costs.

Finally, a development cooperation regime would also play the crucial role of reducing problems of moral hazard and irresponsibility by increasing access to information (Keohane 1984, pp. 95–96). The moral hazard problem in particular arises quite prominently in financing for development, as partners may feel assured of foreign support under some circumstances, and hence adopt more risk-seeking or reckless policies. Partners may also fail to keep commitments or attempt to free-ride in any development cooperation agreement. A regime tends to mitigate these problems by reducing uncertainty and making monitoring easier.[9]

Both the need for an international development cooperation regime and its potential benefits, in terms of efficiency, have been significantly amplified by recent transformations in the nature of development cooperation itself, and the challenges it confronts. First, the number of stakeholders—and especially providers of development cooperation—has increased dramatically. Though emerging countries such as China, India, Brazil, South Africa, Mexico, Turkey, and others have been engaging in such cooperation for many decades, during the twenty-first century they have significantly increased the volume of resources directed to it, as well as the scope of modalities involved and the number of partners, which are increasingly from geographically distant regions (Mello e Souza 2012, pp. 89–90). Countries that were previously mostly or exclusively recipients of ODA have also become providers of development cooperation.[10] In addition, non-state actors such as private foundations, non-governmental organisations (Büthe et al. 2012, p. 572), and firms, have also become significant providers of development cooperation during the last two decades in ways that are unprecedented.

One significant implication of the entry of new actors is that, as already mentioned, the norms and principles set by the DAC regime apply to fewer providers of development cooperation. In other words, development cooperation is increasingly being implemented outside the purview of the DAC. The GPEDC can be seen as a deliberate, though failed, attempt to remedy this situation by bringing emerging countries into the agenda that they still see as largely being DAC-driven (Abdel-Malek 2015, p. 180).

Another major implication of the considerable growth in the number of development cooperation stakeholders and providers is that there is a greater need for a regime that will not only coordinate and bring coherence to their practices, but also better exploit their potentialities, comparative advantages, and complementarities, thereby enhancing the contributions that they can offer globally. As suggested by Mancur Olson's (1965) theory of collective action, the provision of global public goods by a large number of providers is much more difficult than by a small number of providers, because the incentives for not contributing towards the provision of these goods are greater and also because monitoring is harder. This helps to explain the successful institutionalisation of the DAC: among high-income countries, negotiations rarely depend on more than a few major participants. But it also points to the necessity of a regime for numerous actors to achieve mutually (and universally) beneficial outcomes.

Second, global development itself has changed significantly. Globalisation and associated technological changes have remarkably increased interdependence and interconnections among countries and across issue-areas.[11] This means that policies increasingly produce impacts that operate across national borders and issues, and that many of the most pressing and urgent tasks of contemporary development, such as combating climate change, reducing illicit financial flows, and promoting sustainable economic growth, can only be accomplished collectively and holistically. In Keohane's (1984, p. 79) words, the development "policy space" has become denser, meaning that different issues have become more closely linked, as illustrated by the previously mentioned SDG trade-off examples. As a result, the incentives to form an international regime are greater, "owing to the fact that ad hoc agreements in a dense policy space will tend to interfere with one another, unless they are based on a common set of principles and rules", and that there is greater demand for standards that will achieve greater consistency. Regimes will establish such principles, rules, and standards, hence reducing "the costs of continually taking into account the effect of one set of agreements on others" (Keohane 1984, p. 79).

Two caveats are in order here. First, SDGs vary greatly on the extent to which their achievement requires the operation of an international cooperation regime. Some SDGs—most notably the combating of climate change (SDG 13)—are clearly related to the provision of global public goods and, as such, cannot be achieved without the coordination and collaboration made possible by such a regime. In contrast, other SDGs such as ensuring inclusive and equitable quality education (SDG 4) can be achieved simply by employing adequate policies domestically. As noted by Ashoff and Klingebiel (2014, p. 21), international development cooperation thus far has "been overwhelmingly geared towards assisting a specific country in its development process, without necessarily producing a global good". While such cooperation may be valuable for upgrading some kinds of policies and institutions in partner countries, it is not suited for addressing global challenges, where it is most needed. Yet, making increased use of it to provide global public goods also "carries the latent risk of frustrating the original purpose of promoting development at the national level" (Ashoff and Klingebiel 2014, p. 21). A functional and truly global development cooperation regime will be useful in alleviating the tensions between national and global goals, both of which are crucial for fulfilling the 2030 Agenda.

The second caveat is that enhancing the efficiency of global development cooperation is not a purely functional challenge. The very concept of efficiency presupposes certain goals and beneficiaries. In other words, when a development cooperation agreement or regime is considered efficient, it is necessary to ask for which stakeholders it is efficient. Though the discussion in this section has focussed on the global efficiency of a development cooperation regime, or the overall benefits that this regime can potentially bring to global development, political and redistributive issues are also relevant.

Agreed principles, norms, and standards inevitably benefit some countries (or, more broadly, stakeholders) more than others. More fundamentally, the preferences (or "utility functions") of countries and their very notion of "development" vary significantly, which means that, even from a global perspective, desired outcomes may vary.[12] Finally, not only are different preferences in outcomes at stake in disputes between DAC members and emerging countries in international development cooperation regimes, but also processes. In other words, *how* goals are to be reached also matters. The political or normative dimensions implicit in any assessment of the efficiency of regimes leads to considerations of the viewpoints of particular countries and the choices they face in creating, joining, and maintaining such regimes. These questions are considered in the following section, which shifts the perspective to agents or actors.

16.3 Failed Attempts to Build a Development Cooperation Regime: What Can Be Learnt?

One of the most noteworthy recent transformations in global governance has been the undertaking of reforms in several institutions, across issue-areas, with the explicit objective of allowing for, or enhancing, the participation of previously excluded or marginalised stakeholders. The resulting institutional arrangements include trans-governmental networks, public–private partnerships, and entirely private bodies of technocrats, all of which provide a much broader membership base and access to stakeholder participation than traditional intergovernmental organisations. Greater inclusivity in governance is generally seen as favouring democratic ideals, hence being normatively desirable, and may also help to promote policy learning as well as compliance with established norms and principles (Pauwelyn et al. 2015).

Most notably, members of the DAC regime have attempted to bring emerging countries into the aid effectiveness agenda by launching the GPEDC, which in itself embodies many of the kinds of reforms that seek to ensure greater openness and access to stakeholder participation. In the words of Bracho (2017, p. 1):

> [The GPEDC] was intended to be more legitimate (with secretariat services not only from the DAC, but also from the United Nations Development Programme), more political (co-chaired by three acting ministers) [...]. Most of all, the GPEDC was to be more *inclusive*, involving not only the Southern providers, but also non-state actors. All these new players were expected to join a renewed commitments framework inherited from Paris, with commitments tailored to their specific circumstances. In short, the GPEDC was supposed to be a fundamentally new animal, capable of incorporating the Southern providers into the agenda.

These institutional novelties supposedly make the GPEDC more inclusive, legitimate, and therefore better equipped to deal with complex and rapidly evolving problems of development cooperation than the DCF regime nested in the UN, a most traditional international organisation.

In particular, historically underrepresented stakeholders may offer valuable context-specific information about development challenges, best practices, and unintended policy consequences that is unavailable elsewhere, due to their direct involvement. As a result, expanded stakeholder participation reduces uncertainty regarding the impact of development cooperation practices (DeMenno and Büthe 2018, pp. 19–20). GPEDC institutional innovations are therefore not only normatively desirable, but should also make it possible for crucial technical information that is provided by previously excluded or marginalised stakeholders to guide the partnership globally.

Moreover, by attempting to open space for the participation of important stakeholders, the GPEDC not only sought to become more efficient by reducing information asymmetries and collective action problems in ways similar to the ones discussed by Keohane (1984), but also by allowing for the possibility of "policy learning" via the provision of "political information" by such stakeholders:

> [P]olitical information comprises information about whom the policy impacts and the preferences of the affected. Stakeholders provide political information by identifying the relevant actors and signaling the degree of opposition or support for a proposed action or inaction. Political information can serve as a proxy for the relative value or weight that should be placed upon technical information and thus enables global governance bodies to prioritize changes and plan implementation and enforcement strategies. (DeMenno and Büthe 2018, p. 20)

Hence, policy learning, especially in development cooperation, also depends on political information provided by stakeholders.

Furthermore, Keohane's (1984, p. 100) analysis suggests that the existence of uncertainty and transaction costs makes regimes easier to maintain than create. It follows that it may make more sense for reluctant emerging countries to *join* the GPEDC and try to shape it in ways that conform to their preferences rather than to attempt to *create* an entirely new regime from scratch. Why have they not done so?

In a seminal book, Albert Hirschman (1970) analyses the conditions that underpin decisions by actors to address the causes of their dissatisfaction and engage with the governance institutions where they hold membership, thus exerting "voice" or, conversely, to abandon these institutions and take the "exit" option. Significantly, Brazil, India, and China for some time chose to exert voice instead of exit in the Busan negotiations leading to the creation of the GPEDC, but soon chose to exit, as Abdel-Malek (2015) and Bracho (2017) show.

Using Hirschman's (1970) concepts, and drawing from previous literature, Mercy DeMenno and Tim Büthe (2018) build a model of stakeholder participation in global governance institutions. They argue that the incentives for stakeholders to exert voice rather than exit depend both on (1) the importance of the institution for the stakeholder and (2) the stakeholder's capacity to participate. The importance of the institution depends on how much the issues it addresses are valued by the stakeholder as well as the availability of alternative institutions or other ways to influence global rules, norms, and practices, which constitute opportunities for exit. Stakeholder capacity to participate, in turn, is a function of stakeholder resources—including technical skills—and the ability to overcome collective action problems (DeMenno and Büthe 2018, pp. 3–4).

In the light of this model, the exit of Brazil, India, and China from the GPEDC can be understood in terms of the importance of the regime for them as well as of the capacities of these countries to shape the regime and benefit from it. How important is the GPEDC to emerging countries? First, Brazil, India, China, and other emerging countries—in sharp contrast to the DAC members—have not historically and traditionally enjoyed the benefits of a development cooperation regime. For this reason, they can be seen as having less to lose from the failures of the GPEDC, as for them this would mean maintaining the status quo. Accordingly, Li Xiaoyun (2017, p. 9) indicates that

> the importance of the GPEDC to China's own interests has not been recognized by the Chinese side for two reasons. The first is that the message of the GPEDC has not been presented properly within the Chinese foreign policy and think tank community, thus the GPEDC still lacks policy attention in China. Second, due to the fragmentation of the development cooperation policy process in China, the designated institution-to-institution approach routinely applied by development ministries to China does not sufficiently ensure the acknowledgement of the GPEDC by a wide range of institutions relating to decision-making in China.

Regarding the alternative regimes available to influence the global rules, norms, and practices of development cooperation, the DCF stands out, even if it lacks in efficiency what it offers in legitimacy. What is more important, however, is that emerging countries, and especially China, have decided to create their own financial institutions, such as the BRICS's New Development Bank and the Asian Infrastructure Investment Bank, to address the paucity of resources available to finance infrastructure investments in ways that they find appropriate. Increasingly, multiple alternative, competing regimes—none of which can act as focal points for the global governance of the 2030 Agenda—are to be expected given the diffusion of economic and political power without corresponding institutional change. This is the case despite the fact that emerging countries have not joined forces to propose or put in place an alternative development cooperation regime of their own. Moreover, as already mentioned, the status quo of implementing development cooperation by means of bilateral (or trilateral) agreements is not such an undesired outcome from the perspective of these countries.

To what extent do the capacities of emerging countries provide incentives for them to exert voice in the GPEDC? Clearly, among Brazil, India, and China, China is the country with greater capabilities. Yet, China's average gross domestic product per capita is still less than 30 per cent than that of the United States and other DAC members. The total amount of cooperation provided by 29 emerging countries in 2014, which would correspond to the ODA definition, was only about $32 billion (or 17 per cent of the total), compared to $150.8 billion (or 83 per cent of the total) of the 28 DAC members (Luijkx and Benn 2017, pp. 4, 23–24). Concerning financial capabilities, therefore, emerging countries are still falling behind. The abandoning of the "common but differentiated responsibilities" principle as the GPEDC negotiations evolved only compounded the gap in financial capabilities between emerging countries and DAC members.

What are the emerging countries' capabilities in terms of technical skills? Surely these skills are related to financial ones. Xiaoyun (2017, p. 8) also notes that these countries have a "weak knowledge base, compared to the strong voices of DAC-based research institutes". Crucially, joining the GPEDC entails costs in terms of building or maintaining technical capacities. In particular, the commitment to gather and process data, to build indicators, to follow pre-defined and somewhat rigid monitoring frameworks, and to meet particular targets[13] is much more costly for developing countries than for the DAC members. Emerging countries, in particular, are not eager to take on additional costly commitments given the much lower volume of resources they dispose for their own development cooperation and the view that these commitments reflect approaches which are from the DAC and alien to them. Needless to say, unlike other regimes, the GPEDC has no barriers to exit, and these countries had no loyalty whatsoever to the GPEDC.[14]

In this regard, it is crucial that, for all its merits, the GPEDC has been much more successful in promoting stakeholder *participation* than allowing for its *influence*.[15] In other words, greater stakeholder participation in the GPEDC has not allowed emerging countries to influence the main regime outcomes. As a DAC-driven endeavour, the GPEDC has an agenda that reflects the concerns of DAC members, while at the same time some of the core concerns of emerging countries are absent from the regime. Indeed, Xiaoyun (2017, p. 9) notes that the GPEDC also needs to realize that many topics listed in the working program are not the primary interest of the emerging powers. For instance, the GPEDC continues to focus on the "aid management" agenda, and a strong linkage between development cooperation and development is still missing.[16]

Equally important, Bracho sees the GPEDC monitoring framework as "the weak link" of the Busan promise of bringing OECD and emerging countries under the same regime. It evaluates compliance on the basis of 10 specific commitments, five of which are for providers. Yet, provider commitments "had been conceived by and for traditional donors. As the Southern providers had not committed to them and considered them inappropriate to their unique situation, they were opposed to being evaluated by these criteria".[17]

This is the case because much of the expanded participation allowed by the GPEDC's innovative governance structure is non-decisional.[18] It does not suffice to grant emerging countries a seat at the table if they lack actual decision-making power because the agenda has largely been set beforehand.[19] Conceptually, this can be seen as a problem of democratic accountability associated with the lack of both input and output legitimacy,[20] since the proclaimed enhanced input legitimacy of the GPEDC derived from greater stakeholder ability to exercise voice is not matched by stakeholder influence.

16.4 Conclusions

A global development cooperation regime is necessary from a systemic perspective. This is the case not just because of the efficiency gains expected from regimes in general, but also and primarily because the 2030 Agenda comprises a plethora of stakeholders and distinct, though intertwined, issue-areas that can hardly be linked and coordinated by means of bilateral agreements or several plurilateral ones. The existence of common goals regarding this agenda suggests that regime-building is possible.

Yet, efforts to this date to create a global development cooperation regime have failed. In the most noteworthy attempt, the GPEDC attempted to become an inclusive, legitimate, and global multi-stakeholder regime. But emerging countries, as key stakeholders, have preferred to exit the new GPEDC regime instead of trying to shape it through the channels provided for them to exercise voice. Though explanations for this outcome usually focus on the incompatibility of interests between emerging countries and DAC members, there is ample evidence of the existence of shared interests among them, including the fact that they worked together up until the Mexico High Level Meeting.

Rather, I resort to models of stakeholder participation in governance institutions to suggest that Brazil, India, and China exited the GPEDC for other reasons. First, because they did not value the regime much to begin with—to put it bluntly, they just did not care about the aid effectiveness agenda. Moreover, although the DCF could hardly be considered a very attractive alternative, given its shortcomings, the status quo was not such an undesired outcome.

Second, given their limited capabilities as well as the lack of channels for participation in decision-making afforded to them, emerging countries had no realistic possibilities of exerting *influence* in the GPEDC's pre-set agenda. GPEDC compliance came at a price they were not willing to pay, and by exiting the regime these countries refused to offer it a further veneer of legitimacy.

An important clarification is in order. The preceding analysis is not meant to suggest that a development cooperation regime without emerging countries is necessarily bound to fail, but only that such a regime could hardly be considered global, and would be sub-optimal to the extent that it excludes important stakeholders. Furthermore, Brazil, India, and China are not just accidental stakeholders, since arguably many of the principles, norms, and standards embraced by the GPEDC primarily and consciously target the international development cooperation of these countries.

What are the implications of the preceding analysis for future efforts to build a global development cooperation regime? First, as a strategy to increase the importance of the regime to key stakeholders, it is important that they own the regime (which is a way to create loyalty, in Hirschman's [1970] terms). For that purpose, building a new regime, even if more costly and uncertain, may be necessary. Second, these stakeholders need to have the capacity, in terms of resources as well as technical skills, to influence outcomes in the new regime. A challenge is to strike the balance between extending stakeholder decisional participation without compromising regime efficiency, at the risk of creating another regime similar to the DCF.

Notes

1. I adopt the highly influential definition of international regimes proposed by Stephan D. Krasner (1982, p. 185): "[I]mplicit or explicit principles, norms, rules and decision-making procedures around which actors' expectations converge in a given area of international relations".
2. For an overview of the absolute vs. relative gains debate in international regimes, see David A. Baldwin (1993).
3. The concept and role of principled ideas in foreign policy can be found in Judith Goldstein and Robert O. Keohane (1993). For an account of collective identities in international relations, see Alexander Wendt (1994).
4. This is not meant to suggest, obviously, that economic or even strategic interests are never involved in negotiations of global development cooperation regimes; nor that norms and principles cannot be used to dissimulate other ulterior motives and interests.
5. It is not the case that "Southern providers are against the principles of aid effectiveness as such, but they rather want to see those dimensions embedded in the broader context of 'development effectiveness'" (Fues et al. 2012, pp. 251–252).

6. For a historical analysis of how once promising negotiations in the ambit of the GPEDC broke down largely as a result of disagreements relating to this principle, see Gerardo C. Bracho (2017).
7. See, for instance, Robert A. Dahl (1999). Much has been written about this trade-off, particularly in the literature on the governance of the European Union. Alternatively, it can be conceptualised as a trade-off between input and output legitimacy.
8. This term is used by Fues, Chaturvedi and Sidiropoulos (2012, p. 255) to support their arguments in favour of "a new international framework for development cooperation".
9. Even though, as mentioned earlier, problems of burden-sharing also may prevent the regime from succeeding in the first place, as was arguably the case with the GPEDC. See Bracho (2017).
10. For a discussion of the great diversity and complexity of development cooperation stakeholders, see Besharati (2013, pp. 4–10).
11. Particularly relevant in this regard are transport, communication, and information technologies. For instance, industry 4.0 international integration in new supply chains, information networks, and data repositories will be critically linked to relevant knowledge in many countries. Accordingly, new cross-border challenges related to the application of such new technologies will involve legal, regulatory, and anti-trust jurisdictional issues. In particular, international norms regarding security and privacy concerns and protocols and procedures around upgrading, risk evaluation, monitoring, and data analysis in the digital space will become imperative. See Sachin Chaturvedi et al. (2019, p. 162).
12. This is the case even if, as discussed earlier, distributive and relative gains problems in global development are mitigated by the fact that national strategic and economic concerns are not directly impacted. A fundamental critique of functionalist theoretical approaches is precisely that they tend to downplay the role of power, politics, and relative gains in international relations. Furthermore, Bracho's (2017) analysis of the GPEDC as well as recent negotiations on the 2030 Agenda suggest that the distribution of the finance burden of global development motivates deadlocks in attempts to build or extend international regimes.
13. For a description of GPEDC indicators and targets, see Abdel-Malek (2015, pp. 282–286).
14. For a discussion of the impact of loyalty on exit and voice, see Hirschman (1970, pp. 77–86).
15. For a discussion of the conceptual distinction between participation and influence, see DeMenno and Büthe (2018).
16. See also Federal Ministry for Economic Cooperation and Development et al. (2017).
17. Bracho's chapter in this volume. See also Federal Ministry for Economic Cooperation and Development et al. (2017).
18. For a discussion of decisional participation, see Richard B. Stewart (2014, p. 213).
19. The GPEDC is led by three ministerial-level co-chairs and a fourth co-chair representing all non-executive constituencies. Bangladesh, Germany, Indonesia,

Malawi, Mexico, the Netherlands, Nigeria, Uganda, and the UK have all served as co-chairs. The GPEDC's governing body includes 25 representatives of national and local governments, civil society, the private sector, trade unions, parliaments, and philanthropy. It meets biannually to guide the work of the GPEDC.
20. For the origins of the concepts of input and output legitimacy, see Fritz W. Scharpf (1999, p. 6).

References

Abdel-Malek, T. (2015). *The Global Partnership for Effective Development Cooperation: Origins, actions and future prospects* (Study 88). Bonn: German Development Institute/Deutsches Institut für Entwicklungspolitik (DIE).

Ashoff, G., & Klingebiel, S. (2014). *Transformation of a policy area: Development policy is in a systemic crisis and faces the challenge of a more complex system environment* (Discussion Paper 9/2014). Bonn: German Development Institute/Deutsches Institut für Entwicklungspolitik (DIE).

Baldwin, D. A. (Ed.). (1993). *Neorealism and neoliberalism: The contemporary debate*. New York, NY: Columbia University Press.

Besharati, N. A. (2013). *Common goals and differential commitments: The role of emerging economies in global development* (Discussion Paper 26/2013). Bonn: German Development Institute/Deutsches Institut für Entwicklungspolitik (DIE).

Bracho, G. C. (2017). *The troubled relationship of the emerging powers and the effective development cooperation agenda: History, challenges and opportunities* (Discussion Paper 25/2017). Bonn: German Development Institute/Deutsches Institut für Entwicklungspolitik (DIE).

Büthe, T., Major, S., & de Mello e Souza, A. (2012). The politics of private foreign aid: Humanitarian principles, economic development objectives, and organizational interests in the allocation of private aid by NGOs. *International Organization*, 66(4), 571–607.

Chaturvedi, S., de Mello e Souza, A., & Besada, H. (2019). Forward and beyond. In Besada, H. (Ed.), *Cooperation beyond convention: Independent report on South-South and triangular cooperation* (pp. 153–181). New York, NY: UNOSSC.

Dahl, R. A. (1999). Can international organizations be democratic? A skeptic's view. In I. Shapiro & C. Hecker-Cordón (Eds.), *Democracy's edges* (pp. 19–36). Cambridge: Cambridge University Press.

DeMenno, M., & Büthe, T. (2018, January 11–12). *Voice and influence in global governance*. Paper presented at the Barcelona Workshop Access and Exclusion in Global Governance, Barcelona: ESADE & IBEI.

Federal Ministry for Economic Cooperation and Development, German Development Institute & Global Partnership for Effective Development Co-operation (GPEDC). (2017, November 24). Towards a shared understanding of effective development co-operation: Learning from different actors and approaches. *Informal exchange*. https://effectivecooperation.org/wp-content/uploads/2017/12/20171124_Informal_Exchange_with_Researchers_from_Emerging_Economies_summary.pdf.

Fues, T., Chaturvedi, S., & Sidiropoulos, E. (2012). Conclusion: Towards a global consensus on development cooperation. In T. Fues, S. Chaturvedi, & E.

Sidiropoulos (Eds.), *Development cooperation and emerging powers: New partners or old patterns?* (pp. 243–262). New York, NY: Zed Books.

Global Partnership for Effective Development Co-operation. (2017). *About the partnership*. http://effectivecooperation.org/about/about-the-partnership/.

Goldstein, J., & Keohane, R. O. (1993). *Ideas and foreign policy: Beliefs, institutions, and political change.* Ithaca, NY: Cornell University Press.

Hirschman, A. O. (1970). *Exit, voice and loyalty: Responses to decline in firms, organizations and states.* Cambridge, MA: Harvard University Press.

Keohane, R. O. (1984). *After hegemony: Cooperation and discord in the world political economy.* Princeton, NJ: Princeton University Press.

Krasner, S. D. (1982). Structural causes and regime consequences: Regimes as intervening variables. *International Organization, 36*(2), 185–205.

Luijkx, W., & Benn, J. (2017). *Emerging providers' international co-operation for development* (OECD Development Cooperation Working Paper 33). Paris: OECD Publishing.

Mello e Souza, A. de (2012). A cooperação para o desenvolvimento sul-sul: Os casos do Brasil, da Índia e da China. *Boletim de Economia e Política Internacional, 9*, 89–90.

Mello e Souza, A. de (2014). Repensando a cooperação internacional para o desenvolvimento. In A. de Mello e Souza (Ed.), *Repensando a cooperação internacional para o desenvolvimento* (pp. 11–29). Brasilia: Instituto de Pesquisa Econômica Aplicada.

Olson, M. (1965). *The logic of collective action: Public goods and the theory of groups.* Cambridge, MA: Harvard University Press.

Pauwelyn, J., Büthe, T., Maggetti, M., & Berman, A. (2015, February 26–27). *Rethinking stakeholder participation in global governance.* Paper presented at the Workshop for the Swiss Network for International Studies Project on Rethinking Stakeholder Participation in Global Governance: What are the Issues? What Works? Geneva: Graduate Institute.

Scharpf, F. W. (1999). *Governing in Europe: Effective and democratic?* Oxford: Oxford University Press.

Stewart, R. B. (2014). Remedying disregard in global regulatory governance: Accountability, participation, and responsiveness. *American Journal of International Law, 108*(2), 211–270.

Wendt, A. (1994). Collective identity formation and the international state. *American Political Science Review, 88*(2), 384–396.

Xiaoyun, L. (2017). *Should China join the GPEDC? The prospects for China and the Global Partnership for Effective Development Co-operation* (Discussion Paper 17/2017). Bonn: German Development Institute/Deutsches Institut für Entwicklungspolitik (DIE).

Open Access This chapter is licensed under the terms of the Creative Commons Attribution 4.0 International License (http://creativecommons.org/licenses/by/4.0/), which permits use, sharing, adaptation, distribution and reproduction in any medium or format, as long as you give appropriate credit to the original author(s) and the source, provide a link to the Creative Commons license and indicate if changes were made.

The images or other third party material in this chapter are included in the chapter's Creative Commons license, unless indicated otherwise in a credit line to the material. If material is not included in the chapter's Creative Commons license and your intended use is not permitted by statutory regulation or exceeds the permitted use, you will need to obtain permission directly from the copyright holder.

CHAPTER 17

Failing to Share the Burden: Traditional Donors, Southern Providers, and the Twilight of the GPEDC and the Post-War Aid System

Gerardo Bracho

17.1 INTRODUCTION

In November 2011, at a High-Level Meeting in Busan, Korea, all the main state actors of the international development cooperation agenda (traditional Development Assistance Committee [DAC] donors, new non-DAC donors, providers of South-South cooperation, and recipient partner countries) came together with other stakeholders to create a new platform to be run jointly by the Organisation for Economic Co-operation and Development (OECD)-DAC and the United Nations Development Programme (UNDP): the Global Partnership for Effective Development Co-operation (GPEDC).[1] The GPEDC was expected to be a place where traditional DAC donors (DDs) and emerging South-South cooperation (SSC) providers would work together to discuss and eventually adopt standards, norms, and commitments in order to improve their development cooperation and align it with the interests of

---

Gerardo Bracho is a Mexican diplomat and Associated fellow at the Centre for Global Cooperation Research. Mr. Bracho is a member of the Mexican Foreign Service, though he takes full responsibility for the views expressed in this paper, which should not be attributed to the Mexican government. He would like to thank Brian Atwood for his valuable comments on this subject as well as André de Mello e Souza, Heiner Janus, and Elizabeth Amann for their valuable corrections and suggestions.

G. Bracho (✉)
Paris, France

© The Author(s) 2021
S. Chaturvedi et al. (eds.), *The Palgrave Handbook of Development Cooperation for Achieving the 2030 Agenda*,
https://doi.org/10.1007/978-3-030-57938-8_17

recipient countries (RCs) and the "common good". In Busan, these two state actors seemed to reach a deal on an ad hoc "burden-sharing" framework based on "differential commitments". The GPEDC was set to incarnate a new *global* regime of effective development cooperation.[2]

By 2014, however, the *Busan agreement* laid in tatters as the main Southern providers (China, India, and Brazil) boycotted the first GPEDC High-Level Meeting (HLM) in Mexico City.[3] Since then, the GPEDC has followed an erratic course without them, and neither the UN Development Cooperation Forum nor any other institution has emerged to replace it. To gauge the fate and the potential of the GPEDC, it is important to understand why the Busan compromise fell short of its promise. Indeed, the episode illustrates the difficulties that new emerging powers (EPs) face when they attempt to join the post-war liberal order on terms that reflect their new status and potential. Are they capable and/or willing to join this order that is now in flux and also threatened from within by rising populism and nationalism? Is this order willing to make a proper space for them? Will at least some of them try to construct an alternative and competing order, as happened during the Cold War? The analysis of the relations between the GPEDC and the Southern providers can throw some light on these and similar questions.

In a recent essay (Bracho 2017), I reconstructed in some detail the history of the relations between Southern providers and the DAC-sponsored aid effectiveness agenda from the Paris Declaration (2005) to the GPEDC HLM meetings in Mexico City (2014) and Nairobi (2016). Building on this analysis, the first section of this essay briefly reconstructs the path to the Busan agreement. The second section presents an abstract "burden-sharing" model to highlight the issues at stake. The third section uses this model to explain why the Busan agreement collapsed. The final section offers conclusions based on this analysis.

17.2 The Promise and Failure of Busan[4]

Since its inception in 1960, the DAC has represented itself as a "standard-setting" institution: the place that created the concept of ODA and where the norms and "good practices" of donorship are established and administered. Like other OECD bodies, the DAC has a double task: It establishes standards for its members and, through "outreach", it attempts to recruit new members and encourage actors outside its membership to adopt its standards. In the last couple of decades, as "new donors" have appeared or re-emerged on the scene, the DAC has been relatively successful: It has eight new members and four "participants", while another 16 countries regularly report their ODA to the DAC (Gulrajani and Swiss 2017).

It has been much less successful, however, in convincing the other 10 or so "new donors" from the South—the "Southern providers"—to join the agenda. These include even OECD members, such as Mexico and Chile. These actors share two distinctive features. First, they are still recognised by the international system and the DAC itself as "developing countries".[5] For the most part, they are classified as upper-middle-income countries: Though relatively wealthy, they still face many development challenges and thus have a right to receive ODA[6] (Besharati 2013; Bracho 2015).

Second, as developing countries, they have been cooperating with peer countries for many decades under the SSC tradition born in Bandung in 1955. They have thus their own narrative about development (though with few codified standards and norms), which, in many ways, is opposed to that of the DAC. As was to be expected, co-opting or even cooperating with *these* actors as *donors* has turned out to be challenging.

Until recently, the DAC tried to cooperate with Southern providers, mainly through the effectiveness agenda. This is an "action agenda" in which all participants are expected to commit to specific tasks and policies to make the cooperation they provide or receive more transparent and effective. Its founding document—the Paris Declaration of 2005—embraced precise and quantifiable commitments for two state actors: donors and recipients. Some *new donors*—for example, the East Europeans—had no problem in accepting this. But the Southern providers, averse to being treated as "donors", refused to play along. After years of deliberating on how they might fit into an agenda devised for traditional donors and recipients, they finally agreed to participate in Busan as "providers of South-South cooperation" (Busan Article 14); that is, as a third bilateral actor seen as a *special kind* of donor and requiring differential treatment. Indeed, Busan was widely considered a success because it managed to bring the Southern providers on board (Atwood 2012; Eyben and Savage 2013; Kharas 2011; Kim and Lee 2013; Kindornay and Samy 2012; Lightfoot and Kim 2017).

The fact that the main Southern providers (China, India, and Brazil) signed the outcome document in Busan, along with all other countries that fit in this category (e.g. Mexico, Thailand, Turkey, Indonesia, South Africa, Chile), seemed to indicate that the Southern providers had finally found their place in the new Partnership. First, in contrast with Paris, they participated in the drafting of the Busan outcome document, in which they made a place for themselves, especially in Articles 2 and 14. Second, they were fully incorporated in the governing structure of the new GPEDC, represented in one of three ministerial co-chair slots and also in an extra one on the Steering Committee. Third, in joining, they recognised "common goals"— the Millennium Development Goals (MDGs)—and "shared principles", but on the understanding that SSC was different and that they would have "voluntary" and "differential commitments"; the latter concept being a proxy for common but differentiated responsibilities (CBDR), which Mexico originally introduced in the outcome draft, supported by the following argument:

> The concept (CBDR) is not meant to allow DAC donors to repudiate or dilute their responsibilities. It is neither meant to allow new large South-South providers to "do nothing". On the contrary, it is meant as a way to incorporate us, the latter ones, into the agenda, at a realistic and appropriate level given our middle-income countries' condition. (Working Party on Aid Effectiveness [WP-EFF] 2011)

The donors, however, were not happy with CBDR, which in climate change negotiations had been interpreted *negatively* as the absence of responsibilities. In this context, "differential commitments" emerged as a compromise concept, which, according to the Mexican rationale, implied that Southern providers were indeed willing to *commit*, though at a differentiated level. The idea was to put forward a positive interpretation of CBDR more closely linked to its literal meaning. The promise of Busan depended on this nuance.

The weak link, however, was the monitoring framework of the GPEDC, which evaluated compliance with 10 specific commitments: five for "providers", three for recipients, and two presumably for both. The "provider commitments" had been conceived by and for traditional donors. As Southern providers had not committed to them and considered them inappropriate to their unique situation, they were opposed to being evaluated by these criteria.

In an ideal world, Southern providers would have defined which, if any, of those commitments they could take on board and at what "differential" level; if unable to accept some, they would have been encouraged to propose alternative definitions and measures that better reflected their own circumstances. But the real world was very different. First, it was not clear which countries should belong to this new constituency of "Southern providers". Although there was a long-standing narrative about SSC, it had been developed at a very different time and encompassed *all* developing countries engaging in horizontal technical cooperation among *equals*—a narrative enshrined in the Buenos Aires Plan of Action (1978). Southern providers, however, were generally considered to be a smaller subgroup of EPs—generally richer and/or more capable of providing support to poorer/weaker developing countries and using a broader set of cooperation instruments. But which countries belonged to this subgroup exactly? This was not clear.

There was also little consensus about what counted as the cooperation they supplied. There was a shared perception that ODA was a "Northern flow", but there was no consensus as to how to define SSC. Would it involve only flows or also pro-development policies? And if the former, how would they be monetised given that much SSC was given in kind rather than in cash? The monitoring framework required indicators of performance, and these, in turn, required a clear definition of SSC in monetary terms. In sum, to participate properly in the Busan monitoring framework, Southern providers needed a new tailor-made narrative to underpin their new "differential commitments". This narrative did not exist, and it was not clear who and which institution should create it (Besharati 2013; Bracho 2015; Fues 2016, 2018; Quadir 2013).

To bridge the gap between the ideal and the real world, the Korean hosts (supported by Mexico, Brazil, and the DAC chair) came up with a deal on the "participation of South-South cooperation providers in the Busan Global Monitoring framework". Taking as a starting point "the different nature of South-South cooperation", the agreement stated:

> These new providers of assistance are not expected to participate in the global system proposed in this initial Partnership arrangement. Their future participation in aspects of the global system is a decision left to evolving and sovereign processes, and this will in no way inhibit their full participation in the Partnership as South-South partners. (WP-EFF 2012)[7]

The "Korean deal" was adopted by the GPEDC, but in order for it to endure two things had to take place. First, on the basis of their own "sovereign processes", the Southern providers had to develop their own narrative and their own "differential commitments". Second, while this was being sorted out, the GPEDC had to keep its word and leave the Southern providers temporarily out of the monitoring process.

Unfortunately, none of this happened. After Busan, a number of more or less legitimate Southern initiatives in search of a new narrative were initiated, but they produced few results.[8] At the same time, the Southern providers failed to work together in the GPEDC and made no effort to link those other discussions, however inconclusive, with the Partnership. On the eve of the GPEDC meeting in Mexico, their agenda had not advanced an inch.

Around the same time, the results of the first monitoring exercise of the GPEDC were made public. Though based on legitimate data provided by RCs, the report broke with the spirit of the Korean deal: The provider activities of China and India were monitored and subject to practically the same scrutiny as those of the traditional donors. Surprisingly, neither the traditional donors nor the Southern providers seemed to care or even notice. By then, both had withdrawn their support for the "differential commitments" formula that had underpinned the Busan promise and the Korean deal.

The collapse of this deal hollowed out the framework through which Southern providers were expected to participate in the GPEDC. As a result, the negotiations over the communiqué for the Mexico HLM started again from square one, as if Busan had never happened. Indeed, much of the substance of the negotiations between traditional donors and Southern providers—this time through a Mexican facilitator—was once again about "who should do what". Southern providers (China especially) complained that traditional donors intended to exaggerate the role of SSC; vice versa, traditional donors accused Southern providers of assuming no commitments and overemphasising the role of North-South cooperation. But now, with "differentiation" off the table, the middle ground had disappeared, and the negotiations went nowhere. In the end, dissatisfied with their whole GPEDC experience, the main Southern providers—China, India, and (partially) Brazil—decided not to participate in the first meeting of the Partnership in Mexico City (2014). They have not returned since. The Busan compromise collapsed and the GPEDC lost its global and inclusive character (Bracho 2017).

17.3 A Simple Burden-Sharing Model of the Bilateral Negotiations at the GPEDC

There are a number of papers on why and how the Southern providers left the GPEDC—or as some (wrongly) would have it, never *really* joined in the first place (Constantine et al. 2015; Li 2017; Li et al. 2018). Though these papers are weak in their historical narrative, most of the explanations that they have put forward are in one way or another relevant. There is one underlying factor, however, that has been overlooked in the literature and operated at a deeper level throughout the political negotiations in both Busan and Mexico City. As I suggest in my narrative above, this is the failure of traditional donors and Southern providers to compromise on the crucial issue of their *identities* and the *responsibilities* attached to them. In other words, the Busan compromise collapsed *mainly* on the question of *who does what* or, in other words, of *burden-sharing*.

To better analyse the issue, I present below an abstract model of a "burden sharing game". Before doing so, however, we need to understand how does burden-sharing play out in the development agenda. The starting point to answer this question, is to recognise that aid represents an *effort*, and thus a *burden* for donors. If supplying development aid is rarely a purely altruistic endeavour, this does not mean that there is no effort, and thus burden, involved. This burden is quite straightforward when we refer to quantity: As any other official flow, aid implies a budgetary effort. Matters are more complicated when we move to *quality*, since here the costs or burdens implied are *sui generis—as is the case of the costs of complying with the aid effectiveness agenda*.

First, there are administrative costs that arise from keeping with the effectiveness commitments.[9] But there are also costs at a deeper and more important level, because donor countries must "sacrifice" a degree of sovereignty, as when they join any international regime. In principle, donors could subordinate all the aid they give to their own political and/or economic interests and present it to the RCs as a "take it on these terms or leave it" proposition—though, of course, a degree of "mutual benefit" should be involved for aid to materialise at all.[10] In such case, they have an incentive to give more (though worse) aid, in their own (egoistic) terms, often in a "race-to-the bottom" competition with others—as was the case in the Cold War, and as I will argue is, to a certain extent, becoming the case again. The point of the GPEDC, with its commitments and monitoring framework, is to encourage donors to refrain at least in part from such behaviour and to adopt practices that directly further the *common good*, even at the expense of relegating their immediate national interests. To the extent that the benefits from aid accrue to all players, irrespective of their contribution (i.e. in reducing pollution, poverty, uncontrolled mass migration, terrorism, etc.), a system that encourages good aid can be perceived as a global public good (Kaul 2000). In this case, the usual mismatch between individual costs and global rewards brings up the issue of collective action and the problem of free riding (North 2005 [1990]; Olson 1965). When new players appear in an area in which established players are well organised and produce a public good through an implicit or explicit *burden-sharing agreement*, the latter will naturally try to encourage the former to follow the same rules in order to avoid unfair competition and free riding. This reasoning was, in fact, a crucial underlying driver that moved DAC donors to bring the Southern emerging powers into the GPEDC.

In the aid effectiveness context, moreover, burden-sharing is not straightforward because the burden to share is not fixed, as it is in the case of the costs to maintain a multilateral organisation (which is mostly a zero-sum game). As development has revealed itself to be a more complex and less tangible objective than the founding fathers of the development paradigm originally thought, the *aid burden* that must be divided among the various donors is not particularly fixed: All donors are expected to comply with the effectiveness standards and with the 0.7 per cent gross national income target, irrespective of what others do.

Now that some of the specificities of burden-sharing in the aid agenda have been explored, we are ready to move on. To the extent that development aid, both in its quantity and quality (effectiveness), represents an *effort*—and thus a *burden*—for donors, negotiations among donors and between donors and recipients often involve bargaining over burden-sharing. To better capture the logic of these negotiations in the aid effectiveness agenda, Table 17.1 presents an abstract burden-sharing game with four possible scenarios and three players: DAC donors, Emerging Powers, and Recipient Countries.[11] In each scenario, DDs and EPs incur *costs*, considered as foregone national benefits due to their compliance with the aid effectiveness agenda. These costs are (arbitrarily) set to five units for full responsibilities or commitments and only two for less-stringent, differentiated ones. Each level of costs is linked to a distinctive identity in the international cooperation architecture. These costs measure the effort of suppliers, but also the benefit of recipients and the common good: the greater the effort, the larger the benefits. In this respect, the model optimistically assumes: First, that by complying with the effectiveness agenda, providers generate matching benefits on the receiving end. Second, that the benefits directed to the RCs, usually to their standing governments, serve the common good. These assumptions, of course, often do not reflect reality.

The four scenarios with their corresponding outcomes are summarised in Table 17.1.

Scenario A represents the status quo of a North-South divide paradigm with just two players, in which Southern powers go unnoticed under the

Table 17.1 The burden-sharing game

Scenarios	DAC donors (DDs)		Southern emerging powers (EPs)		Recipient countries (common good)	North-South divide
	Identity	**Costs**	**Identity**	**Costs**	**Total benefits**	**Status**
A) Status quo with only responsibilities for DDs	Donor	5	SSC partner	0	5	Unchanged
B) Equal responsibilities for DDs and EPs	Donor	5	Donor	5	*10*	Unchanged
C) Differentiated responsibilities for EPs (with no change for DDs)	Donor	5	SSC *provider*	2	7	Nuanced (adapted to new realities)
D) Towards no responsibilities	Provider	→0	SSC partner	0	*→0*	Dissolved

Source Author

common identity of "developing countries" with a right to ODA and a tradition of providing (modest) SSC flows. In this scenario, the DAC donors bear all the responsibilities. Total costs/benefits amount to 5. **Scenario B** represents a situation in which Southern powers appear as donors *tout court* and have the same responsibilities as traditional donors. Total costs/benefits amount to 10. In **scenario C**, Southern powers appear with a new identity as *Southern providers*; they are now considered a special type of donor with a right to ODA but with *lower and/or fewer* tailor-made *differentiated responsibilities as providers*.[12] Meanwhile, the traditional donors retain their usual burdens. Total costs/benefits amount to 7. Finally, in **scenario D**, Southern EPs retain their traditional identity of developing countries with no responsibilities (as in scenario A), but now the traditional donors reinvent themselves as "providers" and begin to shed their historical responsibilities. Total costs/benefits tend towards 0.

The game starts with **scenario A**. Then a new set of players—the emerging Southern powers—arrive on the scene, disrupting the status quo and unleashing a burden-sharing game. The DAC donors will naturally try to co-opt these new players into their own regime. They will thus strive towards **scenario B**, in which all providers assume full responsibilities—the situation that generates the greatest benefits for RCs (10 units). But the Southern powers will consider this burden-sharing arrangement *unfair*, and thus unacceptable, since it does not recognise their situation as developing countries with their own development challenges. They would rather preserve the status quo of **scenario A**. But traditional donors now consider this old scenario—in which they bear all the responsibilities—to be outdated and also unfair. Moreover, **scenario A** generates fewer benefits for recipients (only 5 units). Two scenarios are now left. The first is **scenario C** with its *differentiated responsibilities*. This scenario is a *compromise* in which, unlike **scenarios A** and **B**, both traditional and Southern powers—now with the new identity of Southern providers—*gain something*, though not as much as they might like: Traditional donors incorporate the Southern powers into the effectiveness system, whereas the latter agree to join, but at a *differentiated* level. This is a burden-sharing agreement that both players can consider *just* and that generates greater benefits for recipients (7 units) than the status quo (5 units). Though not the first choice of any of the actors, it clearly represents the best collective outcome for this burden-sharing game. The other option is **scenario D**, which involves *no responsibilities*. This scenario of *no compromise* is the same as scenario A, but here the traditional donors, unhappy with the status quo, assume a new identity and begin to shed their own responsibilities: The quality or effectiveness of aid now begins to decline, moving towards 0. This is the worst outcome for recipients and for the common good as well.

17.4 Applying the Burden-Sharing Model to Better Understand the Collapse of the Busan Promise

I will now return to the historical narrative of Sect. 17.1 to show how this simple model helps to explain the dynamics of the negotiations among state actors in the effectiveness agenda and beyond. The status quo (i.e. scenario A) represents the workings of the post-war aid system that emerged in the 1950s and was based on only two types of state actors: *donors* with the responsibility to give aid, and *recipients* with the right to receive it. In this clear-cut, bipolar, North-South divide, the latter were expected to eventually leave underdevelopment behind, "graduate" (i.e. reach development), transform themselves in donors, and eventually join the DAC (or adopt its best practices), agreeing thus to "share the burden" with full donor responsibilities, as depicted in scenario B. As we saw in Sect. 17.1, a number of "emerging donors" have moved from scenario A to scenario B; the DAC has grown from eight members in 1960 to 30 members today.

The same strategy did not work with the Southern EPs, which by the early 2000s had begun to generate large amounts of cooperation. Refusing to be reclassified as donors when, according to the DAC's own rules, they still had the right to ODA, they rejected scenario B and joined the Paris Declaration in 2005 as recipients, as in scenario A. The Accra Action Agenda in 2008 took a step forward by recognising that developing countries not only receive aid from the North but also cooperate with one another under SSC rules and principles. This made SSC visible and gave nuance to the narrative of the RCs, but it did not change the status quo: the bipolar North-South divide of scenario A.

In 2011, the stakes rose in Busan. DAC donors, deeply affected by the financial crisis, were generally in dire straits. Moreover, global challenges, starting with climate change, were mounting. At the same time, Southern EPs, which had fared better during the crisis, had a larger and increasing share of the overall development cooperation portfolio. In this new context, DAC donors were increasingly dissatisfied with the status quo and the rigid North-South divide, in which they bore all the responsibilities. As EPs rejected scenario B and the traditional donors rejected scenario A, scenario C won the day in Busan. But it was a Pyrrhic victory that quickly unravelled, opening the way for scenario D, which, as we shall see, has taken root in different ways. The triumph of scenario D over C, which represented a fair formula of *burden-sharing* that could in principle be exported to more consequential regimes, suggests a defeat of international cooperation. In what follows, I will consider why C failed to gain acceptance and why D, the worst outcome, prevailed in the end.

17.4.1 *The Strategy of Traditional DAC Donors*

With hindsight, we can see that the consolidation of scenario C faced significant obstacles that went beyond the development cooperation agenda, both from the North and the South. As we have seen, in Busan traditional donors were uneasy with "differentiation" because they saw in it a synonym for "no commitments". But the most powerful donors had a deeper mistrust of scenario C, because even if it meant that the EPs were ready to somehow share the aid burden with them, it would help the latter to consolidate as a distinctive group of like-minded countries (i.e. as "Southern providers"). The rise of the "Global South", dragged by a group of Southern EPs, was beginning to reshape the world economy, fuelling fears that it could also derail the liberal post-war international order and its aid industry. As John Gray has observed, liberalism has always had two faces: a tolerant one ("the search for terms of peace among different ways of life") and an expansionist one ("a prescription of a universal regime") (Gray 2000, p. 8). The liberalism that underpins the post-war order is tilted towards this second, more problematic face, which has been well ingrained in the "crusader mentality" of US foreign policy since the Wilson administration (Anderson 2015; Kissinger 1994).

This latter mindset helps to explain the strong preference of key traditional donors for scenario B of co-optation and their uneasiness with scenario C based on differentiation—even in a weak regime such as development effectiveness, for the latter could create a "bad precedent". They feared that the rise of the Global South would reignite the North-South confrontations of the 1970s under new and more menacing circumstances.[13] To some extent, that danger was real: Though it never came to much, the idea of creating some sort of DAC for Southern providers, which would challenge the monopoly of the DAC on shaping the aid regime, lingered in the air, and there were even some vague attempts to put it into practice (Besharati 2013; Bracho 2015).[14]

In sum, key traditional donors were uneasy with the *differentiation* at the heart of scenario C, not only in its negative interpretation (no commitments), but also in its positive one of *different* commitments underpinned by a *different* SSC provider narrative. Finally, a scenario C—in defining different responsibilities for clearly identified groups of providers—incarnated a more structured and harder aid regime than the status quo of scenario A; this at a time when many traditional donors, due to financial stress and/or geopolitical considerations, were striving for a weaker aid regime. Indeed, some traditional donors were keener to move from the status quo of scenario A to the weaker aid regime of scenario D than to the "differentiated commitments" of scenario C.

17.4.2 The (Diverse) Strategies of the Emerging Powers

Although key traditional donors were uneasy with scenario C, they had, in principle, accepted it as a gesture to help bring the EPs into the GPEDC in Busan. As Li et al. put it, the concept of differentiated commitments on a voluntary basis was part of the compromise made by the DAC to "buy in more stakeholders, particularly China, India, and others" (Li et al. 2018, p. 149). Nonetheless, as the Korean deal stated, the EPs bore the main responsibility for implementing scenario C through their "sovereign processes", which, as we saw in Sect. 17.1, never really took off. Why did they let this compromise scenario lapse?

To begin, the emerging Southern powers were not clearly united behind scenario C (Bracho 2017). They were all in favour of "differentiation" (i.e. against assuming a donor identity), but they gave the term diverse meanings. Some had the standard negative view of CBDR as an (awkward) concept for *no commitments*. Others had a more positive one of *different commitments*. Both views eventually made it into the Busan outcome document, which included an Article (14) backed by Mexico and Brazil stating that the new "*providers* of South-South cooperation" would eventually participate in the monitoring framework under "differential commitments" (scenario C), and another Article (2), introduced by China and India, that stated that "South-South *partners*" would take on (Busan) commitments only "on a voluntary basis" (scenario A). But after Busan, the ad hoc alliance behind Article 14 disintegrated, while India and China, now partly joined by Brazil, moved even more forcefully towards scenario A and its traditional SSC narrative with no commitments. Entrenched in scenario A, the main EPs sent the message that they were not willing to participate *seriously* as *providers* in the GPEDC. But as they were not willing to do so as *recipients* either (and nobody expected them to), the message was that they were not willing to participate *at all*. Accordingly, they left the GPEDC at the eve of the Mexico meeting.

But why did some EPs insist on backing scenario A and others scenario C? At first sight, they all had few incentives for moving away from scenario A, in which—as SSC partners and keeping with their own decades-old SSC narrative—they had a great degree of freedom and no specific responsibilities. This narrative had for years allowed them to think of themselves as part of a "homogeneous South", in which they played a leading political and intellectual role, and with which they shared a common colonial or neo-colonial past and had collaborated in the struggles at the UN and other fora (Abdenur 2014; Bracho 2015, pp. 15–16; Esteves and Assunção 2014; Weinlich 2014). Finally, within the framework of the North-South divide, the rapid rise in the amount of SSC that they supplied could be presented as a purely quantitative phenomenon as opposed to a qualitative one, which would have required a shift in their role. In short, why should they take on *donor-like* responsibilities while they still faced important domestic challenges, their resources were scarce, and the risks of fracturing the political South or losing ODA in practice (whatever the formal rules) were high? These questions haunted—and continue to haunt—middle-income countries that toy with the idea of adopting a stronger provider identity.[15]

Nevertheless, the EPs also had incentives to move away from scenario A to embrace some version of scenario C (i.e. to shift from a partner to a provider narrative) and gave some signs that they were ready to so. In a recent study on new donors, Gulrajani and Swiss argue that a country is enticed to take on a donor identity "driven by the desire for state legitimacy as an advanced and influential nation" (Gulrajani and Swiss 2017, p. 8). More than prestige is at play. On the eve of the twenty-first century, the Southern EPs had integrated themselves more or less successfully into the whirlpool of globalisation and were eager to match their new economic status with a more relevant political one on the international stage. They signalled, in various ways, that they were ready to take on more responsibilities at the regional level, and some even at the global level—and development cooperation is indeed an ideal tool of *soft power* to do so (Nye 2011).

Moreover, the major EPs were not only offering much more cooperation, but also behaving *politically* as providers. Both China and India created institutional frameworks in which their leaders periodically met with their African counterparts to announce large "cooperation" programmes. Brazil and Turkey also took a visible political stand as providers. Finally, these powers were also giving signs that they no longer considered the traditional SSC framework (in terms of narrative and institutions) to be adequate for representing their new roles and the new reality, as when India launched the *Delhi process* for renovating SSC (Bracho 2015; Fues 2018), and China issued *white papers* on aid that were not clearly rooted in a traditional SSC narrative (Information Office of the State Council of the People's Republic of China 2011, 2014).

In sum, it is fair to say that the EPs had incentives to entrench themselves in scenario A but also incentives to move towards scenario C. The former option made headway in India, which was still a low-middle-income country marred by poverty. In contrast, China had fewer incentives to opt for scenario A in principle, but these were boosted by deep concerns with the DAC and the effectiveness agenda—a mix that gave way to a *defensive strategy*. Li et al. (2018) identify four such concerns, which they apply to the "rising powers", but which were especially relevant to China. These are: *political legitimacy, attribution of responsibilities, definition of the agenda, and trust* (Li et al. 2018, pp. 151–152).

The first concern—political legitimacy—is based on the fact that, despite the formal participation of the UNDP in its Secretariat, the GPEDC is not a universal UN body but rather one that is still presumably driven by the OECD-DAC. This concern was expressed from the outset, but had it been paramount, the EPs (which collaborate with the OECD on many other topics) would never have participated in the effectiveness agenda in the first place.

The second concern is in fact about "burden-sharing", which I have put at the centre of the whole story and which the EPs perceived in a negative way. As Professor Li argues, China perceived the GPEDC as a ploy of the DAC donors to share their "heavy burden accumulated over the decades" (Li 2017, p. 7), and thus dilute their own contributions to development—considering the aid burden as a zero-sum game (Weinlich 2014). In other words, the EPs did not perceive "burden-sharing" as an honest attempt to bring them into the agenda as providers; even when they were joining with "differential commitments", they remained suspicious of the project. They welcomed the inclusion of this concept as a "big compromise" (Li 2017, p. 7; Li et al. 2018, p. 149), but they did not take it seriously.

Li et al. (2018) identify the "definition of the agenda" as the EPs' third concern. I see this in a broader sense as a concern that the GPEDC would not be a venue where "differences" would be respected but rather a forum to pressure the EPs to accept the Western aid paradigm embedded in the post-war liberal regime. As we have seen, this was a well-grounded concern: The post-war liberal regime is indeed driven by a "crusader mentality" (Lind and Wohlford 2019).

The fourth and final concern was *trust*—a crucial ingredient for international endeavours to succeed (Messner et al. 2013). To a certain extent, most of the other concerns boil down to a lack of trust. The Busan compromise of scenario C portrayed the GPEDC as a neutral venue underpinned by the participation of the UNDP, which would respect *differences* among narratives, practices, and levels and types of commitments. The EPs were happy with this message, but some doubted that the DAC donors really *meant it*. Lacking trust, they perceived the GPEDC and its talk about transcending the North-South divide and transitioning from "aid to development effectiveness" as a smokescreen to coerce them into an unfair "burden-sharing" exercise and the liberal Western aid regime. As they lacked the intellectual and institutional resources of the North to be able to counter this with a modern *Southern narrative* of their own (a factor explored in Li 2017; Li et al. 2018), they preferred to adopt a *defensive strategy* and to stick to what they knew: the traditional SSC discourse. This allowed them to stay in the comfort zone of "no responsibilities" and the long-established discourse of the homogeneous South developed by the UN. They thus defended the status quo of scenario A rather than venture into the presumed "trap" of a new scenario C—though, in fact, as we have argued, the traditional donors were not so sure about the virtues of scenario C themselves.

Following this logic, the EPs that backed scenario C were those that did not share as much the concerns that haunted China and others. Take the case of Mexico (Villanueva Ulgard and López Chacón 2017; Bracho 2017). It was eager to participate in the effectiveness agenda, but like all other Southern EPs, it refused to be reclassified as a donor (i.e. it rejected scenario B) and considered itself part of the SSC community. Yet, in contrast with most other Southern countries and as a member of the OECD, an observer at the DAC, and a country that no longer belonged to the G77, Mexico had fewer political constraints and much less of a trust deficit. Therefore, it actively advocated for scenario C. Moreover, as it shared the values and policies of the post-war liberal order, the "costs" that Mexico might have had to pay by eventually joining the GPEDC and its monitoring framework as a provider were much lower. But being a modest provider and one too close to the North to have the required legitimacy, Mexico was not in a position to lead the South.[16] Without the support of the big Southern players, scenario C was bound to collapse—and eventually did.

17.4.3 The Strategy of Recipient Countries

I will now explore the position of RCs in the "burden-sharing battle" among traditional donors and EPs—acknowledging their limited clout due to the power asymmetries among these three actors. The model reckons that RCs are better off under scenario B (10 units) and thus predicts they would join the traditional donors in pressuring the EPs to adopt full donor identity and responsibilities. The model also suggests that recipients would prefer scenario C to the status quo of scenario A and would receive ever-diminishing benefits from scenario D. Nonetheless, the facts only partially confirm these predictions. Traditional donors have expected RCs to join them in "disciplining" the EPs. To some extent, the latter have done so, as when they have publicly asked the EPs to be more transparent and/or to untie more of their aid, or when they have reported the "donor activities" of those powers, as they did when they precipitated the collapse of the Korean deal.

But RCs have not advocated in a systematic way for scenario B—not even in the negotiations of the Busan outcome document and the Mexican communiqué, when they mostly stayed away from the negotiations between traditional donors and EPs. They had reasons to take this hands-off approach.

First, many RC's preferred to see traditional donors and EPs competing with each other rather than coalescing into a common donor group. This outcome was compatible with scenarios A, C, and D, but not with scenario B. This preference for competition can be explained in different ways: (i) one possibility is that RCs do not consider the Western aid regime to be well-aligned with their own interests[17]; (ii) another is that they gauge that Western donors and EPs have distinctive comparative advantages, and thus wanted to keep them separate to benefit fully from both (Bracho and Grimm 2016); and (iii) finally, it is possible that—independent of their assessment of Western donors and EPs as providers of aid—they prefer to keep them separate to increase their *own* negotiating power (Greenhil et al. 2016), much as they often did with Western and Soviet aid during the Cold War.

Second, RCs rejected scenario B out of their allegiance to the common house of the South. Just as the EPs hesitated to portray themselves as Southern providers, let alone donors, RCs—for deeply rooted historical reasons—are reluctant to demand that they do so. For both actors, path dependence reinforced the status quo of scenario A (North 2005).

The first argument for "competition" suggests why recipients would not be as keen for scenario B as the model suggests. But it does not rule out scenario C, in which the EPs retain their differences and comparative advantages, and thus continue to compete as providers while assuming well-defined responsibilities. Indeed, scenario C would fit into a framework of healthy, *structured competition* that avoids the *race-to-the-bottom* type exemplified by scenario D.

In contrast, the second argument—the allegiance to a "common Southern identity"—rules out not only scenario B but also C, and it leaves scenario A as the only strategy to follow, which is indeed what recipient continue to do, especially at UN fora. But if, as the game suggests, scenario A is suboptimal in terms of benefits, RCs, by keeping to a narrative of a homogeneous South, do not seem to be following the strategy that best represents their long-term interests and the common good. Moreover, by entrenching themselves in scenario A, both RCs and EPs have indirectly contributed to pushing the development cooperation agenda towards the overall weaker aid regime of scenario D.

17.4.4 Sliding into Scenario D of a Weak Aid System

Since the collapse of the GPEDC as a global forum, the weaker aid regime of scenario D has been gaining ground through three mutually reinforcing trends or processes: (i) the so-called *Southernisation* of the traditional donors' narrative and practices; (ii) the decline of the EP's agenda and the failure of the EP's to assume a coherent Southern provider identity; and (iii) the universalisation of the development cooperation agenda and the erosion of the North-South divide. I will consider each of these in turn.

As the literature has rightly observed, there has been a movement towards convergence between North-South cooperation and SSC through the so-called Southernisation of the Northern narrative, practices, and commitments (Bracho 2015; Fues 2015; Klingebiel and Esteves 2021; Mawdsley 2018). Instead of the DAC socialising the EPs (as in scenario B), the opposite has been taking place: Traditional donors have been co-opting the Southern narrative. DAC members do not consider themselves "donors" anymore, but rather "providers"; they now classify their assistance as "cooperation" rather than "aid"; they portray their aid relations as "horizontal partnerships among equals" rather than as "vertical relations among principals and clients"—as was the case, and often explicitly so, in the past; they now present their aid as stemming from "voluntary commitments" rather than from "historical responsibilities"; finally, they consider their assistance to be motivated by "mutual benefit" rather than "altruism".

To some extent, traditional donors have been co-opting Southern language to keep up with the more politically inclusive times, and this has had its positive effects. Thus, for example, partnership has not been an empty word, and developing countries now have a greater say in the aid industry than they did in the early days of the agenda. Moreover, by closing the gap between the narratives of the South and the North, Southernisation is contributing to a convergence that could help to re-create a global aid regime in the future (Janus and Tang 2021).

But more worryingly, *Southernisation* has also been about moving to a new, looser aid system, as with the one the Southern EPs enjoy in practice: a system with both lower and/or fewer commitments and weaker and more flexible rules. Since Gleneagles in 2005 and Accra in 2008, DAC donors have not made significant new collective commitments and have watered down earlier ones, including the 0.7 per cent of gross domestic product, the mother of all donor commitments.[18]

DAC donors have also loosened their own rules. For example, they have been tearing down the once stringent barrier between ODA and profit-making commercial flows—the crucial distinction on which their whole narrative and paradigm were built.[19] Here they are again following China, which often provides aid as part of "packages", mixing it with trade and investment and tying it to the use of its own companies' products and services (Bracho 2018b; Brautigam 2009, 2011).

Finally, and somehow paradoxically, by allowing countries to put their national interests above—or at an equal level with—development, Southernisation has been helping donor agencies to cope with the challenges of rising populism at home. Thus, it also has its silver lining (Gulrajani 2018; Kharas and Rogerson 2017).

Since the decline of the GPEDC as a *global* forum, developments in the South have also contributed to the move towards scenario D of a weaker and uncoordinated aid regime. Some Southern EPs have in *practice* reinforced their profile as providers. China, by far the most important, has continued to increase the volume and scope of the cooperation it provides, particularly through the Belt and Road Initiative. By launching a cooperation agency and spearheading the creation of new multilateral development banks, China has also engaged in institution-building. In a sense, it is creating the scaffolding for an alternative aid regime in competition with the West, reviving thus the possibility of a Cold War-like scenario in which two groups of donors compete for the allegiance of RCs (Bracho 2018b). Other Southern EPs, such as India and

Turkey, have also maintained or increased important volumes of development cooperation (DEVEX 2019).

But neither they nor China have assumed a coherent Southern provider identity and narrative. Indeed, their discourse often shifts radically according to the audience and/or the venue. Moreover, now that the economic boom of the early years of the century is over, the Southern provider agenda has actually moved backwards in some countries and regions, particularly in Latin America. The two main providers of the region have fallen into dire straits: The Venezuelan economy has collapsed entirely, and Brazil, now in a deep recession, has turned its back on Lula da Silva's activist policies towards the South. At the same time, Chile's and Uruguay's badly managed graduations from ODA have helped to push them and other upper-middle-income countries, including Mexico, into recipient mode.[20] Not only has the agenda of the Southern providers not advanced in Latin America, but it has also given way to a new narrative of *development in transition*, which is geared to justify why the high-middle-income countries of the region are still in need of development cooperation (Barcena et al. 2017; OECD et al. 2019).

All these trends came together in March 2019 at the recent Second High-Level UN Conference on SSC: the Buenos Aires Plan of Action plus 40 (BAPA+40). There were some expectations that BAPA+40 would *really* take stock of the massive changes that had occurred in the agenda since the first conference 40 years ago (Bracho 2018a; Klingebiel and Esteves 2018). But although the outcome document recognised the new role of triangular cooperation (Article 28) and advances in the institutionalisation of SSC (Article 26), it failed to acknowledge what arguably is the main novelty in the agenda: the emergence of the Southern provider. This concept appeared once in the original draft in a somewhat weak fashion but soon disappeared altogether. BAPA+40 failed to recognise differentiation among the countries of the South and did not integrate CBDR in its framework, as some important players (Faurie 2018) and observers expected (Klingebiel and Esteves 2018). In balance, BAPA+40 opted for the status quo narrative of scenario A, in which the Southern EPs assume no special responsibilities or commitments towards their poorer or less capable Southern brothers, and in so doing reinforced the downward slide of the whole agenda towards scenario D.

The third factor pushing towards a weaker aid system is *universalisation*. Unlike the MDGs, the Sustainable Development Goal (SDG) agenda is for all countries: poor and rich. This shift is the result of a powerful political narrative that regards all countries as being in the same boat, and which recognises that rich countries also face development challenges, and also that the South might be able to assist with the problems of the North (Longhurst 2017). This move towards universality received *universal* praise. Moreover, it was primarily the South—tired of the patronising North—that lobbied for universalisation. But now that the euphoria which accompanied its adoption in 2015 is dissipating, the SDG agenda is beginning to show a number of shortcomings. By deconstructing the North-South divide and treating all countries as "developing", the movement towards universalisation has lost focus on the *real* developing countries and has dissipated responsibilities, reinforcing the narrative and practices of the weaker aid system of scenario D (Bracho 2015; Esteves 2017).

17.5 Conclusions

This chapter has shown how the traditional and the Southern EPs briefly agreed on a rough framework on how to "share the burden" in the development effectiveness agenda in Busan. It has also put forward an explanation as to why and how the Busan promise of bringing together all major development cooperation providers under one tent rapidly collapsed. Finally, the essay describes how the collapse of this project could be considered part of the broader erosion of the traditional aid system and the decline of the liberal post-war order. Other authors evaluate these trends more positively. They consider the *erosion* of the aid system to be an *adaptation* to the challenges of new times: for example, the need to mobilise private capital or to counteract populism (Kharas and Rogerson 2017). Or they emphasise the benefits produced by competition from the Southern providers, who bring new resources, ideas, and practices (Greenhil et al. 2016). I do not deny that the erosion of the post-war aid system has to a certain extent been caused by good intentions, nor that it has led to some good outcomes. My main concern is that it is not giving way to an alternative global development cooperation regime.

In his piece in this volume, André de Mello e Souza makes a strong case for such a regime on the grounds of overall efficiency, including the need to tackle inconsistencies among different SDGs. Building on his analysis, I would argue that it is becoming a matter of *survival*. It is true that development cooperation—with or without a regime—contributed little towards achieving the MDGs, as most poverty reduction was achieved by China's ("dirty") economic growth. But development cooperation under a burden-sharing framework that clarifies "who should do what and how" will be crucial to tackling *climate change* and *inequality*, which are the main global challenges that are putting our planet and our civilisation at risk. These challenges cannot be confronted effectively without real collective action. Moreover, as the interdependence and "public bads" have multiplied, development cooperation has become part and parcel of a much broader international cooperation agenda. The principle of "self-differentiation" agreed in the Paris' climate negotiations, in which each country in "a responsible way" defines its own responsibilities, is clearly not enough (Liti Mbeva and Pauw 2016).

It is in this context that, even if development cooperation effectiveness plays a relatively minor role in this broad agenda, the story and analysis of the rise and fall of the Busan promise can provide useful lessons on the types of concerns and arguments that are keeping the International Community from *really* working together. Only thus can development cooperation realise its potential and contribute positively towards achieving the SDGs.

Notes

1. There is no consensual typology and nomenclature for the "actors" that participate in the development cooperation agenda. I herewith use the following ad hoc definitions: "Traditional DAC donors" stands for the members of the DAC of the OECD. "Recipient partner countries" (RC's) are countries included in the DAC list of RCs entitled to receive official development assistance (ODA). "Non-DAC" donors are countries that are not members of the DAC or included in the DAC list and offer meaningful volumes of development cooperation. "Providers of South-South cooperation" or "Southern providers" are countries that are still in the DAC list and, at the same time, offer meaningful volumes of development cooperation.
2. Following Stephen Krasner, "Regimes can be defined as a set of implicit or explicit, principles, norms, rules and decision making procedures around which actors' expectations converge in a given area of international relations" (Krasner 1983, p. 2).
3. In contrast to China and India, Brazil did attend the meeting, but publicly stated that it was not a member of the GPEDC.
4. For a comprehensive history of the Aid Effectiveness agenda, see Abdel-Malek (2015) for a firsthand account of the Busan meeting, see Atwood (2012) for a recount on Busan focussing on the role of the Southern Providers, see Bracho (2017), Eyben and Savage (2013), Kharas (2011), Mawdsley et al. (2014), as well as Villanueva Ulgard and López Chacón (2017).
5. This is no longer true for Chile and Uruguay. We will come back later to the issue of their recent graduation.
6. The conspicuous exceptions are India and Indonesia, which are still classified as low-middle-income countries.
7. The full text of the Korean deal and its rationale is reproduced as Annex 2 in Bracho (2017).
8. Among these processes and initiatives, three stand out: the Delhi process, the UNDESA initiative of a Core Group of Southern Partners, and the creation of a Network of Southern Think-Tanks (NEST) largely focussing in SSC (Besharati 2013; Bracho 2015; Fues 2018).
9. That is, the costs that donors incur with commitments such as: (i) compliance with recipients' priorities (Busan's 1st), or the cost to process and publish their information in order to be more transparent (Busan's 4th), or make multi-annual plans and be more predictable (Busan's 5th).
10. See the chapter in this volume by Nilima and Rachel, where they argue that the national interest and the common good do not necessarily conflict.
11. The exercise is inspired in basic game theory. In fact, as RCs have less power, and thus scarce agency, it could be to some extent re-casted as a prisoner's dilemma game with two players (DD and EP) and an equilibrium solution reached by cooperation among them. I am grateful to De Mello e Souza for pointing this out.

12. The differential commitments or responsibilities for Southern providers could be of the same type but implying a *lower* burden than those that apply for traditional donors—say provide 0.1 per cent instead of 0.7 per cent of GDP as official development aid, as Jeffrey Sachs has suggested (Sachs and Schmidt-Traub 2014). But they could also be *fewer*—say, exempt Southern providers from the commitment to untie their aid.
13. Some authors have seen the rise of the EPs in the development cooperation agenda as heralding the reconstitution of the political South striving—like in the 1970s—for an alternative world order. See Bockman (2015), Domínguez-Martín (2016, 2017), and Gosovic (2016).
14. Be it at the Heiligendamm process, at the G20, or at the GPEDC, Northern powers tried to discourage any prospect of the EPs forming a coherent group (Aranda Bezaury and Díaz Ceballos Parada 2010; Bracho 2015).
15. According to Li et al., middle-income countries will only (re)join the GPEDC as providers, when they "feel the security of showing international dominance as donors of development aid without fearing further decreases of ODA to their countries" (Li et al. 2018, p. 151).
16. Nonetheless, almost single-handedly, Mexico has continued to push forward the agenda of "adapting" the GPEDC principles and monitoring framework to SSC (Agencia Mexicana de Cooperación Internacional para el Desarrollo 2019).
17. Contrary to what the model assumes, as we warned, the cost of aid for donors will not automatically translate into benefits for recipients. One can argue that this happened during the 1980s and 1990s, when the aid regime was subordinated to push forward the Washington Consensus aligned to the interests of the North, but not generally speaking to those of the South (Fukuda-Parr 2014; Glennie 2008).
18. Since the Finance for Development summit in Addis Ababa (2015), every major international document stipulates that some DAC donors commit to the 0.7 target while others do not—a clear message that it is about a "voluntary commitment", not a "responsibility". Some donors have even turned away from previous commitments on ODA quantities that they had taken before, for example Australia (Organisation for Economic Co-operation and Development [OECD] 2018, p. 23).
19. Previous DAC chairs have rightly raised their concerns about the perils of this trend (Atwood et al. 2018; Manning 2013).
20. Chile and Uruguay graduated from the DAC list of ODA recipient countries in 2018. But rather than rejoicing, they complained, arguing that they still faced many development challenges and, rightly so, that income per capita was not (at least not anymore) a good indicator to gauge development.

REFERENCES

Abdel-Malek, T. (2015). *The Global Partnership for Effective Development Cooperation: Origins, actions and future prospects* (Studies 88). Bonn: German Development Institute/Deutsches Institut für Entwicklungspolitik (DIE).

Abdenur, A. E. (2014). Emerging powers as normative agents: Brazil and China within the UN development system. *Third World Quarterly, 35*(10), 1876–1893.

Agencia Mexicana de Cooperación Internacional para el Desarrollo. (2019). *Monitoring exercise in South-South cooperation effectiveness: Final report*. https://www.gob.mx/cms/uploads/attachment/file/447837/EJERCICIO_DE_MONITOREO_2019-eng.pdf.

Anderson, P. (2015). *American foreign policy and its thinkers*. London: Verso.

Aranda Bezaury, M., & Díaz Ceballos Parada, B. (2010). México y los cambios en la arquitectura económica internacional. In B. Torres & G. Vega (Eds.), *Los grandes problemas de México: Relaciones internacionales* (Vol. 7, pp. 651–673). Mexico: El Colegio de México.

Atwood, B. (2012). *Creating a Global Partnership for Effective Development Cooperation*. https://www.cgdev.org/sites/default/files/1426543_file_Atwood_Busan_FINAL_0.pdf.

Atwood, B. J., Manning, R., & Riegler, H. (2018, December 21). *Don't undermine the basic architecture of OECD/DAC statistics: A letter of warning*. https://www.brookings.edu/blog/future-development/2018/12/21/dont-undermine-the-basic-architecture-of-oecd-dac-statistics-a-letter-of-warning/.

Barcena, A., Manservisi, S., & Pezzini, M. (2017, July 3). Opinion: It's time to change the way we think about development policy. *DEVEX*. https://www.devex.com/news/opinion-it-s-time-to-change-the-way-we-think-about-development-policy-90605.

Besharati, N. A. (2013). *Common goals and differential commitments: The role of emerging economies in global development* (DIE Discussion Paper 26/2013). Bonn: German Development Institute/Deutsches Institut für Entwicklungspolitik (DIE).

Bockman, J. (2015). Socialist globalization against capitalist neocolonialism: The economic ideas behind the new international economic order. *Humanity: An International Journal of Human Rights, Humanitarianism, and Development, 6*(1), 109–125.

Bracho, G. (2015). *In search of a narrative for Southern providers: The challenge of the emerging economies to the development cooperation agenda* (DIE Discussion Paper 1/2015). Bonn: German Development Institute/Deutsches Institut für Entwicklungspolitik (DIE).

Bracho, G. (2017). *The troubled relationship of the emerging powers and the effective development cooperation agenda* (DIE Discussion Paper 25/2017). Bonn: German Development Institute/Deutsches Institut für Entwicklungspolitik (DIE).

Bracho, G. (2018a). Towards a common definition of South-South cooperation: Bringing together the spirit of Bandung and the spirit of Buenos Aires. *Development Cooperation Review, 1*(6), 9–13.

Bracho, G. (2018b). El CAD y China: origen y fin de la ayuda al desarrollo. *Revista CIDOB d'Afers Internacionals, 120*, 215–239.

Bracho, G., & Grimm, S. (2016). South-South cooperation and fragmentation: A nonissue. In S. Klingebiel, T. C. Mahn, & M. Negre (Eds.), *The fragmentation of aid: Concepts, measurements and implications for development cooperation* (pp. 121–134). London: Palgrave Macmillan.

Brautigam, D. (2009). *The dragon's gift: The real story of China in Africa*. Oxford: Oxford University Press.

Brautigam, D. (2011). Aid "with Chinese characteristics": Chinese foreign aid and development finance meet the OECD-DAC aid regime. *Journal of International Development, 23*(5), 752–764.

Constantine, J., Shankland, A., & Gu, J. (2015). *Engaging the rising powers in the Global Partnership for Effective Development Cooperation* (Working Paper). Sussex: Institute of Development Studies.

De Mello e Souza, A. (2021). Building a global development cooperation regime: Necessary but failed efforts. In: Palgrave this volume.

DEVEX (2019). *Emerging donors 2.0.* https://pages.devex.com/rs/685-KBL-765/images/Devex-Emerging-Donors-Report.pdf.

Domínguez-Martín, R. (2016). Cooperación financiera para el desarrollo, ADN de la cooperación Sur-Sur. *Iberoamerican Journal of Development Studies, 5*(1), 62–86.

Domínguez-Martín, R. (2017). En los pliegues de la historia: Cooperación Sur-Sur y procesos de integración en América Latina y el Caribe. *Estudios Internacionais Belo Horizonte, 4*(2), 57–78.

Esteves, P. (2017). Agora somos todos países em desenvolvimento? A Cooperacao Sul-Sul os ODS. *Pontes, 13*(2). https://www.ictsd.org/bridges-news/pontes/news/agora-somos-todos-pa%C3%ADses-em-desenvolvimento-a-coopera%C3%A7%C3%A3o-sul-sul-e-os-ods.

Esteves, P., & Assunção, M. (2014). South-South cooperation and the international development field: Between the OECD and the UN. *Third World Quarterly, 35*(10), 1775–1790.

Eyben, R., & Savage, L. (2013). Emerging and submerging powers: Imagined geographies in the new development partnership at the Busan Fourth High Level Forum. *Journal of Development Studies, 49*(4), 457–469.

Faurie, J. (2018). Next year BAPA+40 is a unique opportunity to forge a new global consensus for international development co-operation. In *OECD, development co-operation report 2018: Joining forces to leave no one behind* (p. 268). Paris: Organisation for Economic Co-operation and Development.

Fues, T. (2015). Converging practices and institutional diversity: How Southern providers and traditional donors are transforming the international system of development cooperation. In E. Sidiropoulos, J. A. Pérez Pineda, S. Chaturverdi, & T. Fues (Eds.), *Institutional architecture and development* (pp. 24–42). Johannesburg: South African Institute of International Affairs.

Fues, T. (2016, April 11). *South-South cooperation: Global force, uncertain identity* (The Current Column). Bonn: German Development Institute/Deutsches Institut für Entwicklungspolitik (DIE).

Fues, T. (2018). Convergence on South-South cooperation: The Delhi process after five years. *Development Cooperation Review, 1*(6), 3–8.

Fukuda-Parr, S. (2014). Should global goal-setting continue, and how, in the post-2015 era? In J. Alonso, A. Cornia, & R. Vos (Eds.), *Alternative development strategies in the post-2015 era* (pp. 35–67). London: Bloomsbury Press.

Glennie, J. (2008). *The trouble with aid: Why less could mean more for Africa.* London: Zed Books.

Gosovic, B. (2016). The resurgence of South-South cooperation. *Third World Quarterly, 37*(4), 733–743.

Gray, J. (2000). *Two faces of liberalism.* New York, NY: The New Press.

Greenhil, R., Prizzon, A., & Rogerson, A. (2016). The age of choice: Developing countries in the new aid landscape. In S. Klingebiel, T. Mahn, & M. Negre (Eds.), *The fragmentation of aid: Concepts, measurements and implications for development cooperation* (pp. 137–152). London: Palgrave Macmillan.

Gulrajani, N. (2018, January). *Merging development agencies: Making the right choice* (ODI Briefing Note). London: Overseas Development Institute.

Gulrajani, N., & Swiss, L. (2017, March). *Why do countries become donors?* London: Overseas Development Institute.

Information Office of the State Council of the People's Republic of China. (2011). *China's foreign aid*. http://english.gov.cn/archive/white_paper/2014/09/09/content_281474986284620.htm.

Information Office of the State Council of the People's Republic of China. (2014). *China's foreign aid*. http://english.gov.cn/archive/white_paper/2014/08/23/content_281474982986592.htm.

Janus, H., & Tang, L. (2021). Conceptualising ideational convergence of China and OECD donors: Coalition magnets in development cooperation. In: Palgrave this volume.

Kaul, I. (2000, June). What is a public good? *Le Monde Diplomatique* (English edition). https://mondediplo.com/2000/06/15publicgood.

Kharas, H. (2011). *Coming together: How a new partnership on development cooperation was forged at the Busan High Level Forum on Aid Effectiveness*. http://www.realinstitutoelcano.org/wps/portal/rielcano_en/contenido?WCM_GLOBAL_CONTEXT=/elcano/elcano_in/zonas_in/ARI%20164-2011.

Kharas, H., & Rogerson, A. (2017). *Global development trends and challenges: Horizon 2025 revisited*. https://www.odi.org/publications/10940-global-development-trends-and-challenges-horizon-2025-revisited.

Kim, E. M., & Lee, J. E. (2013). Busan and beyond: South Korea and the transition from aid effectiveness to development effectiveness. *Journal of International Development, 25*, 787–801.

Kindornay, S., & Samy, Y. (2012). *Establishing a legitimate development co-operation architecture in the Post-Busan era*. Ottawa: The North-South Institute.

Kissinger, H. (1994). *Diplomacy*. New York, NY: Simon and Schuster.

Klingebiel, S., & Esteves, P. (2018, September 12). *On the way to the 2nd UN conference on South-South cooperation* (The Current Column). Bonn: German Development Institute/Deutsches Institut für Entwicklungspolitik (DIE).

Klingebiel, S., & Esteves, P. (2021). Diffusion, fusion, and confusion: Development cooperation in a multiplex world order. In: Palgrave this volume.

Krasner, S. D. (1983). Structural causes and regime consequences: Regimes as intervening variables. In S. D. Krasner (Ed.), *International regimes* (pp. 1–21). Ithaca, NY: Cornell University Press.

Li, X. (2017). *Should China join the GPEDC? The prospects for China and the Partnership for Effective Development Cooperation* (DIE Discussion Paper 17/2017). Bonn: German Development Institute/Deutsches Institut für Entwicklungspolitik (DIE).

Li, X., Gu, J., Leistner, S., & Cabral, L. (2018). Perspectives on the Global Partnership for Effective Development Cooperation. *IDS Bulletin, 49*(3), 145–165.

Lightfoot, S., & Kim, S. (2017). The EU and the negotiation of global development norms: The case of aid effectiveness. *European Foreign Affairs Review, 22*(2), 159–176.

Lind, J., & Wohlford, W. C. (2019). The future of the liberal order is conservative. *Foreign Affairs, 98*(2), 70–82.

Liti Mbeva, K., & Pauw, P. (2016). *Self-differentiation of countries' responsibilities* (DIE Discussion Paper 4/2016). Bonn: German Development Institute/Deutsches Institut für Entwicklungspolitik (DIE).

Longhurst, R. (Ed.) (2017). Has universal development come of age? *IDS Bulletin, 48*(1A).

Manning, R. (2013, April 9). OECD is ignoring its definition of overseas aid. *Financial Times*. https://www.ft.com/content/b3d73884-a056-11e2-88b6-00144feabdc0.

Mawdsley, E. (2018). The "Southernization" of development. *Asia Pacific View Point, 59*(3), 173–185.

Mawdsley, E., Savage, L., & Kim, S.-M. (2014). A "post-aid world": Paradigm shift in foreign aid and development cooperation at the 2011 Busan High Level Forum. *The Geographical Journal, 180*(1), 27–38.

Messner, D., Guarín, A., & Haun, D. (2013). *The behavioural dimensions of international cooperation*. Duisburg: Käte Hamburger Kolleg/Centre for Global Cooperation Research.

North, D. C. (2005). *Understanding the process of economic change*. Princeton, NJ: Princeton University Press. (Original work published 1990.)

Nye, J. S. (2011). *The future of power*. New York, NY: Public Affairs.

OECD (Organisation for Economic Co-operation and Development). (2018). *OECD development co-operation peer reviews: Australia 2018*. https://doi.org/10.1787/9789264293366-en.

OECD, CAF, & UN ECLAC. (2019). *Latin American economic outlook: Development in transition*. https://doi.org/10.1787/g2g9ff18-en.

Olson, M. (1965). *The logic of collective action: Public goods and the theory of groups*. Cambridge, MA: Harvard University Press.

Quadir, F. (2013). Rising donors and the new narrative of "South-South" cooperation: What prospects for changing the landscape of development assistance programmes? *Third World Quarterly, 34*(2), 321–328.

Sachs, J. D., & Schmidt-Traub, G. (2014). *Financing sustainable development: Implementing the SDGs*. Sustainable Development Solutions Network. New York, NY: United Nations.

Villanueva Ulgard, R., & López Chacón, L. (2017). In search of making a difference: Mexico in the OECD international development co-operation architecture. *Development Policy Review, 35*(2), 287–302.

Weinlich, S. (2014). Emerging powers at the UN: Ducking for cover? *Third World Quarterly, 35*(10), 1829–1844.

WP-EFF (Working Party on Aid Effectiveness). (2011). *Compendium of written proposals received based on the third draft outcome document for HLF-4*. Paris: Organisation for Economic Co-operation and Development.

WP-EFF. (2012). *Note prepared by Korea on global monitoring: Participation of South-South cooperation providers in the Busan Global Monitoring framework (DCD-DAC-EFF-M [2012]3)*. Annex 2, pp. 20–21. Paris: Organisation for Economic Co-operation and Development.

Open Access This chapter is licensed under the terms of the Creative Commons Attribution 4.0 International License (http://creativecommons.org/licenses/by/4.0/), which permits use, sharing, adaptation, distribution and reproduction in any medium or format, as long as you give appropriate credit to the original author(s) and the source, provide a link to the Creative Commons license and indicate if changes were made.

The images or other third party material in this chapter are included in the chapter's Creative Commons license, unless indicated otherwise in a credit line to the material. If material is not included in the chapter's Creative Commons license and your intended use is not permitted by statutory regulation or exceeds the permitted use, you will need to obtain permission directly from the copyright holder.

CHAPTER 18

Should China Join the GPEDC? Prospects for China and the Global Partnership for Effective Development Cooperation

Li Xiaoyun and Qi Gubo

18.1 Introduction

Due to their continued reluctance—or even suspicious attitudes, which started right at the beginning of the Global Partnership for Effective Development Co-operation (GPEDC) process—four of the five BRICS (Brazil, Russia, India, China, and South Africa) were absent from the second forum, as only

---

Major parts of this paper were published in Discussion Paper 17/2017 of the German Development Institute (DIE).

Li Xiaoyun was a visiting fellow at the DIE. He holds a Distinguished Professorship of Development Studies at China Agricultural University in Beijing, China. He also chairs the China International Development Research Network (CIDRN), as well as the Network of Southern Think Tanks (NeST). Qi Gubo is a professor at the China Institute for South-South Cooperation in Agriculture/China Belt and Road Institute in Agriculture/College of Humanities and Development Studies, China Agricultural University.

X. Li (✉) · G. Qi
China Agricultural University, Beijing, China
e-mail: xiaoyun@cau.edu.cn

G. Qi
e-mail: qigupo@cau.edu.cn

Russia attended. This has had a big impact on the "global nature" of the partnership (Klingebiel and Li 2016).

After the First High-Level Meeting of the GPEDC—held in Mexico City on 15–16 April 2014 and attended by more than 1500 representatives from 130 countries—the second finally took place more than two years later in Nairobi, from 28 November to 1 December 2016. The GPEDC was launched at the Fourth High Level Forum on Aid Effectiveness, which was held in Busan, South Korea, in 2011, and proved to be a turning point for international development cooperation. It recognised the increasingly important role of South-South cooperation (SSC) and the existence and relevance of diverse actors and practices of development cooperation (Assunção and Esteves 2014). The first forum, in Mexico City, was aimed to kick off the agenda to transition from aid effectiveness to development effectiveness, whereas the second one came at a critical juncture. This was a moment to review the evidence and lessons learnt from the decade-long attempts to implement the aid- and development-effectiveness agendas, and to look ahead to the role of effectiveness in the new era of sustainable development, anchored in the 2030 Agenda for Sustainable Development (Blampied 2016). The core value of the GPEDC is to be more open in terms of its agenda and more inclusive in terms of its membership.

Although the Mexico City and Nairobi fora offered a diversified range of participants (developed countries, developing countries, international development organisations, non-governmental organisations, academic institutions, and think tanks), and the focus was changed from aid effectiveness to development effectiveness, the role of the GPEDC has been questioned by some countries and scholars (Ulfgard and Lopez 2016). Some suggest that, although various stakeholders involved in global development actively participated in the fora, the agenda was still under the control of developed countries (Ulfgard and Lopez 2016), which continued to try to bring in more countries to support their development approach, which had already been proven a failure (Li 2017). In addition, the absence of China and India in the two events—and the absence of Brazil and South Africa in the Nairobi forum—raised doubts as to the legitimacy of the fora. This signifies that the good intentions of starting an era in which traditional and emerging aid donors can hold talks on a level playing field in development cooperation have failed, and that the transformation of existing international development and cooperation architecture is still under way (Fues and Klingebiel 2014). Kharas (2014) argued during the Busan forum that the Busan meeting symbolised the paradigm shift from "aid effectiveness" to "development effectiveness", and that the increased diversity of participants could cause the further fragmentation of the cooperation plan or put at risk the internal consistency of the process. Besides, Day (2014) is concerned that launching such a negotiation outside the United Nations (UN) Development Cooperation Forum (DCF) will duly affect the legitimacy of the UN. Some have also questioned the effectiveness of the agenda and believe that it will fail to achieve salient results in the immediate future (Glennie 2014).

Contrary to these opinions, many have responded positively with regard to the shift in focus from aid to development towards more openness and inclusiveness. They consider it to be a perfect opportunity to develop a framework that is inclusive, sustainable, and comprised of diverse stakeholders (Atwood 2011, 2012). Chinese scholars are sceptical of the overall initiative, but they agree that the GPEDC provides a new space for China and other like-minded actors to influence global development through learning and sharing (Li et al. 2014). In fact, the GPEDC is one of the important outcomes of the changing global context. The agenda has been seen as a milestone in global development governance (Atwood 2012). It came during a critical era in which the role of new players in global development began to increase while the traditional players began to readjust their strategies. The GPEDC is certainly a new opportunity for all stakeholders to build a more inclusive global development platform, but a pertinent question is: Why did emerging powers decline to take part in it? This chapter aims to assess the reasons why emerging countries have been sceptical about the GPEDC by presenting China's case in particular. The chapter further analyses if the GPEDC is a useful platform for global development and whether all stakeholders can work together under this new structure. Finally, the chapter illustrates how—and under what conditions and circumstances—this can happen.

18.2 Critical Accounts of the History of the GPEDC

Some accused China and others of rejecting the opportunities offered by the GPEDC (Li 2017). Some even questioned those countries' commitments to global development, without acknowledging the fact that the emerging countries have been consistently sceptical of the legitimacy of the GPEDC: They do not consider the GPEDC to be a UN forum, as Bena summarised during the Nairobi forum (Bena 2017). The emerging countries have been very careful not to get trapped in the problems that the "Western" partners have, and therefore have avoided being brought into the system. The GPEDC is not just the outcome of the Fourth High Level Forum on Aid Effectiveness. Although the openness of the GPEDC is being brought into question less, it is still seen as an attempt by the partnership to remain relevant and merely an extension of the Development Assistance Committee (DAC) under a new label (Klingebiel and Li 2016). Therefore, to understand the perspective of the emerging countries on the GPEDC, it is relevant and useful to briefly review the history of the DAC first.

There was a mix of motives that blended the security and protection of US and European global/regional power interests with the "recognition" of a "moral imperative" to assist poor countries (Abdel-Malek 2015, p. 13) during the Cold War. Historically, after the economic rehabilitation of Western

Europe (with support from the Marshall Plan) and Japan, they joined the United States in providing development assistance. From the perspective of the United States, it was necessary to build a collective mechanism to coordinate the development aid provided by different countries (Adam 2018), international organisations, and non-governmental organisations. Due to this concern, the United States and its allies co-established the Development Assistance Group, which was set up in January 1960 and had 11 members, including the United States.[1] This marked the founding of the "Western"-led development cooperation system. It is viewed as the first expansion of the "Western"-led development cooperation system, into which the United States brought its allies to follow the interests of the United States (Li 2017).[2] In October 1961, the Development Assistance Group was integrated into the Organisation for Economic Co-operation and Development (OECD) with a different name—the Development Assistance Committee. To support the work of the DAC, the OECD established a department that consisted of the development financing branch and the technical assistance branch. The development financing office was renamed the Development Assistance Directorate in 1969, and then renamed again as the Development Cooperation Directorate in 1975, which, since then, has been serving as the permanent office and secretariat of the DAC.

The institutionalisation of the DAC marked the formal establishment of the international development cooperation system led by "Western" countries (Li 2017). The primary functions of the DAC are focussed on the following considerations. First, although different aid providers share the same goal, their activities can hardly be termed effective if aid is provided inconsistently or not coordinated among the different countries. Second, among group members that share the same goal, it is difficult for them to honour their promises to provide aid accordingly, without peer pressure. Finally, it is also a challenge to ensure the quality of the assistance programme without a universal standard. Therefore, the DAC adopted a series of standards in 1961 that all members should follow and required that "developed countries should spare 1 per cent of their GNP [gross national product] for development aid". The ratio was then modified to 0.7 per cent, based on the recommendation of the Pearson Report, issued in 1969. In 1993, GNP was replaced by gross national income, but the ratio stayed the same. In addition, the DAC conducted the first evaluation—called a "peer review" today—of its member countries in 1962. Meanwhile, the DAC, aiming to advance the peer review mechanism in a more effective way, established a statistical gathering and reporting system that can be used to compare different donors. However, the establishment of such a mechanism was not only a technical measure to ensure programme quality but, more importantly, a strategic effort to reinforce the political interests of the United States and its allies in the Cold War context (Li 2017).

Furthermore, the United States endeavoured to link the DAC's agenda with the First Development Decade of the UN with the aim of making the development assistance system global and, hence, more legitimate. In the same way, the adoption of the resolution by the UN in October 1970 that "developed countries should spare 0.7 per cent of their GNP as global development resources" further consolidated developed countries' economic power and gave them a more dominant role in international development policy. At the same time, with the support of the United States, the OECD established the Development Centre. Many developed countries hurriedly established think tanks on development issues to provide knowledge bases to make development assistance more technical and depoliticised in order to reduce potential political conflicts (Li 2017). Concepts such as "basic need strategy", "gender and development", "participatory development", "sustainable development", and "poverty reduction", among others, which have all been widely used since the 1970s, all fall into the category of "development knowledge". In the name of "shared values", similar concepts emerged, one after another, by claiming to be neutral—and even sympathetic—towards developing countries, and they won the hearts of a large number of loyal supporters. However, the metaphors about such knowledge could actually be argued as embodying the West's hegemony to a certain degree (Li 2017), and the bureaucratisation of development aid could be seen as covering up the political face and intentions of development aid (Mosse 2011). On the other hand, the development of the GPEDC is also closely related to a growing debate within the DAC member countries on the effect of the development aid provided by DAC members. To respond to the question, all development ministers of the DAC put forward the issue of how to measure aid effectiveness during the ministerial-level meeting in 1995, which later emerged as the "aid-effectiveness agenda". "Halving the global population under extreme poverty" was enacted after the meeting as the central element due to the report "Shaping the 21st Century: The Contribution of Development Cooperation", which was adopted later as a priority of the Millennium Development Goals by the UN.

Later on, at the International Conference on Financing for Development, held in Monterrey, Mexico, in March 2002, issues concerning the effectiveness of development aid started to draw attention, and the DAC quickly included aid effectiveness into its major work. In February 2003, the DAC held the First High Level Forum on Aid Effectiveness in Rome, Italy. At the forum, DAC members found that the reports they required from recipient countries were an additional burden to them and distracted them from focussing on studying their own development strategies. Therefore, the declaration adopted at the forum raised the concept of "harmonious aid" and established the Working Party on Aid Effectiveness. Meanwhile, the DAC also realised that, in order to improve aid effectiveness, their own efforts would not be enough. As a result, they called for the participation of bilateral institutions, multilateral institutions, governments of developing countries, emerging countries, social organisations, and the private sector (Organisation for Economic Co-operation and Development [OECD] 2018). This was the first time that the DAC extended its policy discussion range to the outside. The working group was eventually formed by 80 representatives from the above-mentioned institutions. This was different from the first expansion of the system, in which only the United States and its allies were members. This expansion is viewed as the second expansion of the US-led DAC to include a wide range of stakeholders, signifying that the DAC's influence in the decision-making of aid policies has started to decline (Li 2017).

After the Rome forum (2003), the Working Group on Aid Effectiveness held the Second High Level Forum on Aid Effectiveness, in Paris in 2005, and issued the Paris Declaration after the forum concluded. The declaration proposed 56 specific measures on issues, including ownership, aid alignment, aid harmonisation, management of results, and mutual accountability. From the author's observation, the most positive contribution to the forum was that the working group started to realise the asymmetric relation between aid and development and tried to fully mobilise recipient countries' initiatives in aid utilisation. Later, in September 2008, the Third High Level Forum on Aid Effectiveness was held in Accra, Ghana, where the Accra Agenda for Action was adopted. The attending parties reached a consensus on how recipient countries should make better use of aid, particularly on how they should rely on their own systems and resources. In November 2011, the working group held the Fourth High Level Forum on Aid Effectiveness in Busan, South Korea. More participating parties attended this forum than any of the previous fora. As a more marketable platform, this forum shifted its attention from aid effectiveness to development effectiveness, which posed unprecedented challenges to the influence and dominant position of the West in the field of international development. To cope with the challenges, the dominant parties, including the DAC, made big concessions in areas including forum documents, issues, and participation mechanisms. Meanwhile, they also hoped to hold their bottom lines by relying on the traditional buy-in approach. Therefore, the GPEDC is viewed as the one partnership agreement that symbolised the third expansion of the DAC-dominated development cooperation system (Ulfgard and Lopez 2016); in essence, it is an exercise of the hidden "buy-in" approach (Li 2017).

18.3 Different Views on the Role of the GPEDC

18.3.1 *A New Version of Historical Approach of Development Cooperation*

One critical perspective on the GPEDC states that it is unilateral in its approach to history (Li 2017). This examination probably unpacks one side of the story—that the DAC needs to sustain and renew its objective such as "leave no one behind" (OECD 2018). However, it also uncovers another fact: that the change in the global context has changed all global structures, and this change perhaps does not alter the role of international development cooperation, in which the DAC plays an important role in global development. Even in 1996, the DAC had already realised that the distinctions between "the West" and "the East" as well as between "the South" and "the North" were no longer relevant (Abdel-Malek 2015, p. 14). Justifying the legitimacy of the GPEDC is not the purpose of this chapter. Rather, it aims to provide a realistic account of the fact that the GPEDC will have to play an important role in global development, particularly to support the fulfilment of the Sustainable Development Goals (SDGs).

Firstly, the international development cooperation system has focussed on global development based on the ethics of global equality established since the Second World War, despite its political implications and "Western" domination. It has been, perhaps, the only means to transfer resources to balance the unequal wealth distribution between rich and poor countries, at least according to its stated intentions (Hynes and Scott 2013). In reality, the operationalisation of the 2030 Agenda, with its 232 indicators, relies heavily on the traditional concept of official development assistance (ODA) (Mahn 2017). Therefore, from a moral perspective, the system should be improved rather than undermined. This should be the basis upon which consensus can be reached among different parties; in fact, the emerging powers have endorsed it. A total of $4.02 trillion of ODA was contributed from DAC members from 1960 to 2016 in order to promote the economic development and welfare of developing countries, according to ODA data from the OECD (OECD 2019a).

Secondly, despite the argument on the effectiveness of development cooperation, it has a broad scope and wide domain, such as offering support for multilateral activities and institutions, including the UN, humanitarian assistance, food assistance, health, education, etc. It has been indispensable for poor countries. Furthermore, development cooperation also has helped the economic development of many countries such as Korea (from the 1950s to 1980s) and China: from 1980 up to the year 2000, China had become one of the largest recipients of support from bilateral and multilateral channels (OECD 2019b). This was in response to the fast-growing period in the country, although China's growth record alone cannot account for development cooperation's contribution. However, substantial support from the World Bank and Japan for infrastructure cannot be ignored. From 1979 to 2010, the World Bank (2019) had provided a total of $52.77 billion to China.

Thirdly, the DAC-based development cooperation system has accumulated rich experiences and lessons in almost all aspects of development assistance. Those experiences and lessons cover numerous critical issues such as recognition of knowledge-based programmes, local ownership, using local systems, country-led mechanisms, etc. Important lessons were also learnt about issues such as poor linkages with economic growth, the high costs of management, donor coordination, and fragmentation, among others.

Finally, the system has built up useful knowledge on production systems and also the system for international development-oriented human resources. It is clear that the DAC-based development cooperation system is the major part of the global governance system that has been developed over the last 60 years. It is expected to continue its vital role in global development with its strong comparative advantages because it has rich experiences and existing adaptive institutions.

18.3.2 The Complementary Role of Emerging Powers

There is also another narrative: that the emerging players should take a stake in—or even lead—the international development process due to its increasing economic role in the global system. However, this view does not account for the real capacity of emerging powers. Firstly, the economic capacities of all emerging powers[3] are still weak compared to those of the DAC members. Taking China as an example—the most developed country in the emerging group—its average gross domestic product per capita is still 30 per cent less than that of the United States and other DAC members. It is unrealistic to expect those countries to take a leading role in global development from a financial point of view. The total amount of ODA provided by 29 emerging countries in 2014 was only about $32 billion, compared to $150.8 billion of the 28 DAC members—although their contributions have increased (OECD 2019b). Secondly, the emerging powers (Benn and Luijkx 2017), in particular China, have provided alternative development experiences. This, however, can only be a complementary model because their engagement with other developing countries has not been as intensive and extensive as that of the traditional donors. They also have less experience in international development than the traditional donors. Thirdly, the emerging powers' engagement with other developing countries is less systematic than that of the traditional donors in terms of knowledge production, management, and human resources supply. Lastly, the emerging powers' approach to engaging with other developing countries is mainly through trade and investment rather than development cooperation. Therefore, the role of emerging powers in international development can only be complementary to the existing development cooperation structure.

18.3.3 The UN DCF and the GPEDC

Another argument for the GPEDC is the role of the UN DCF. There are two perspectives on this: One, from a political point of view, is that there is already a UN platform for discussing development cooperation issues. China, India, and Brazil believe that the UN forum is more internationally legitimate for discussing development cooperation than the "OECD-led" forum, which is not considered to be as globally inclusive (Abdel-Malek 2015, p. 180). Another perspective refers to the issue of efficiency (Janus et al. 2014).

Some argue that it wastes resources when two systems focus on the same issue. Synergies and complementariness between accountability mechanisms for development cooperation and those for the 2030 Agenda remain limited, and the established accountability frameworks for development cooperation, such as the GPEDC, are currently missing a linkage to global accountability (Mahn 2017). The debate from both perspectives is sensible, and the full utilisation of the UN platform for discussing development cooperation should be explored further.

We consider, indeed, it is true that the UN DCF is the legitimate platform, and that the GPEDC should not—and cannot—replace the role of the UN DCF. However, one should also take note that, historically, the DAC has provided strong support for the UN DCF and is very knowledgeable of the functions of the UN DCF through both its financial and knowledge support structures. It is due to this over-exercised role of the DAC in international development that many feel uncomfortable. Realistically—along with the consensus to make more viable reforms to strengthen the role of the UN platform in international development—by making the DAC more open and inclusive so that the DAC does not belong exclusively to the 28 DAC members, the GPEDC stands for its legitimacy.

However, the UN platform is often considered inefficient for consensus-making purposes, thus intermediate mechanisms would still be necessary in order to propose agendas and be attached to the UN as a functional mechanism. The GPEDC can be developed for this role. From a global development perspective—particularly from that of countries whose social and economic development still require financial support from the development cooperation modality—although the amount of development cooperation or ODA on balance is smaller than many other resources, it is the unique altruistic character of the intentional development of public resources (Strawson 2015, p. 6). The reality is that large parts of development cooperation can still—even for emerging powers—be channelled in a bilateral manner.

However, there is a need for a collective agenda and an agreement to ensure that both the strategy and implementation are more coordinated in order to ensure efficiency and effectiveness within development cooperation. Therefore, from all perspectives, instead of maintaining the DAC's hegemonic role, it is important to support the DAC-led development cooperation move towards more openness and inclusiveness—thus, the GPEDC is the first step in this direction.

18.4 Towards Genuine Partnership: What Can We Do?

Making the GPEDC more legitimate in terms of the participation of emerging powers requires efforts from both sides. In this regard, the first step is to reduce the suspicions about the intentions of the DAC on behalf of the emerging powers. The priority of creating mutual understanding should be conducted with further formal and close communication through a series of conferences and workshops. The OECD-DAC was seen by the emerging powers to have an inherent bias favouring OECD-DAC members and as being bent on applying its aid principles and modalities worldwide, as Abdel-Malek highlights (Abdel-Malek 2015, p. 180). Thus, they see the GPEDC as another form of the DAC's expansion of this historical process. The emerging powers think that the GPEDC is the strategic way to buy-in the emerging powers in order to share the heavy burden that the DAC has accumulated over the decades. Therefore, the emerging powers have been reluctant to join, or have even rejected the offer. The emerging powers need to recognise that the DAC has recognised the changing context, even since the middle of the 1990s, as reflected in the DAC's 1996 "21st Century Report". From the DAC's viewpoint—and according to the concessions made in the documents in Busan, Mexico City, and Nairobi—the principles for the emerging powers through "differentiated commitment" have been confirmed; SSC is only regarded as being complementary rather than being equally important, as with North-South cooperation. Those principles have helped remove the major obstacles preventing the emerging powers from taking part. Therefore, emerging powers—China in particular, because it has a larger capacity and extensive experience in SSC—should take the GPEDC as an opportunity to form a joint force to play a role in global development.

China has reiterated that it was and has been the creator, benefactor, as well as supporter of global governance. In the 1920s, China was the first country that appealed to the international community for financial and technical support. From 1929 to 1941, the League of Nations provided technical support to China (Ali and Zeb 2016). The GPEDC is certainly a part of the global governance structure, thus China should be a part of it; otherwise, China would not be able to be involved in policy-making conducted by the GPEDC. Secondly, despite the political arguments, the GPEDC originates from the High Level Forum on Aid Effectiveness. The agenda and main context presented in both fora still reflect aid-focussed issues and still largely reinforce the traditional donor–recipient model (Li 2017).

The relatively narrow OECD-DAC aid-effectiveness agenda is viewed as being inadequate to address the issues resulting from broad development cooperation (Abdel-Malek 2015, p. 180). Because of the limitations of the mandate and capacity of the DAC, it is also difficult—and unrealistic—to expect development ministries of the DAC members to move completely beyond an aid agenda.

The emerging powers also need to understand that aid is a business that involves many stakeholders. Changing the nature of aid-development cooperation would require changing the capacities of both institutional and individual structures as well as the whole portfolio structure within the DAC system. The difficulty is that, unless the agenda and context are focussed on development, the active participation of emerging powers is unlikely to happen.

The emerging powers, in particular China, believe that promoting development for developing countries requires different discussions that should relate to how development cooperation can promote trade, investment, agriculture, and industrialisation so that economic growth can be accelerated. Under this scenario, both sides would need to find consensus on how to move ahead.

The third issue varies slightly from the second issue. The original purpose of the World Food Programme was to strengthen the collective action and commitment of DAC members. Therefore, a series of requirements and indicators for data collection and reporting were enacted for monitoring and evaluation purposes. The GPEDC agreed that emerging powers would not need to follow these requirements. However, this privilege would demoralise the emerging powers if they were not able to present the data publicly.

Fourthly, even if they were to actively join the GPEDC, the emerging powers would feel that their development narratives could not be fully recognised because of their weak knowledge base, compared to the strong voices of DAC-based research institutes. Despite the changes made by the GPEDC agenda, conventional political and technical language still dominates the entire agenda.

Finally, the strength of emerging powers is also gradually being presented through those Global South-linked funding institutions such as the India–Brazil–South Africa Forum, the Asian Infrastructure Investment Bank (AIIB), and the New Development Bank (NDB). Active support and participation from OECD member states in these institutions could show a more sincere commitment towards more equal cooperation. However, from the case of the refusal of the United States and Japan to join the AIIB, it shows that the gap between traditional actors in international development assistance and the new players is still stubborn and cannot be filled automatically. However, this also presents another opportunity for DAC members to explore whether DAC-led development cooperation can be joined with those new development financing modalities. Concretely, the GPEDC should approach the NDB and the AIIB and invite them to take part in the forum to explore ways of how they could work together.

Based on the above analysis, one can see that there are various obstacles hindering the emerging powers from actively participating. However, the commitment made by all parties towards global development, in particular the SDGs, and the strong claims of the GPEDC to contribute to the SDGs (and also the agreement of a "common goal but differentiated responsibility" between the DAC members and the emerging powers envisaged in the GPDEC process) by making the GPEDC more inclusive and effective in supporting the SDGs should be the concrete step that encourages the participation of the emerging powers.

18.5 Recommendations for the GPEDC

The chapter offers China as the case example in order to provide the following recommendations for the GPEDC to move ahead. Although the emerging powers have behaved similarly towards the GPEDC, they are not coordinated in their foreign policy, and there is no common policy towards the GPEDC among them. The GPEDC should not categorise "the emerging powers" as being one and the same, but it should discuss the issues separately with each in order to understand their different viewpoints on the GPEDC.

Firstly, China has demonstrated a strong commitment to global development. It has claimed to be the creator, benefactor, and developer of global governance (Jiang 2017). China's SSC programmes have been increasingly more aligned with the model advocated, practised, and led by the DAC in terms of modalities. Taking part in the GPEDC should be the focus of China, rather than being brought in passively. China should take the GPEDC as an opportunity to exercise its "soft power". China's development experiences have been highly regarded by the GPEDC, and China can certainly make significant contributions to the paradigm shift of the GPEDC from aid to development. However, the importance of the GPEDC to China's own interests has not been recognised by the Chinese side for two reasons. Firstly, the message of the GPEDC has not been presented properly within the Chinese foreign policy and think tank community; thus, the GPEDC still lacks policy attention in China. Second, due to the fragmentation of the development cooperation policy process in China, the designated institution-to-institution approach routinely applied by development ministries to China does not sufficiently ensure the acknowledgement of the GPEDC by a wide range of institutions relating to decision-making in China. Therefore, it is important to strengthen the linkage via think tank research and policy advocacy to advertise the GPEDC in existing policy dialogue via separate DAC members with China, such as Sino-German and Sino-UK dialogues.

Secondly, the GPEDC should propose a concrete field that China might be interested in. For instance, for the next high-level forum, the topic on how development cooperation could better contribute to China's "Belt and Road Initiative" (BRI) could be suggested as one of the topics. China sees this programme as being a concrete measure to implement its global development commitment, and it has also asked for its own development cooperation programme to align with the BRI. The newly established China International Development Cooperation Agency, which was formally launched on 18 April 2018, also stated that it will support national foreign affairs strategy and BRI.

Thirdly, the GPEDC should realise that its legitimacy largely depends on the active participation of the emerging powers, thus the GPEDC should set up a working group to begin talks with the emerging powers to ensure their participation via process approaches rather than just event-based ones; the emerging powers'—even China's—capacities and human resources are limited, and they are not ready to provide an immediate response.

Lastly, the GPEDC also needs to realise that many topics listed in the working programme are not the primary interest of the emerging powers. For instance, the GPEDC continues to focus on the "aid management" agenda, and a strong linkage between development cooperation and development is still missing. The GPEDC needs further concessions to dispel the impression that it is another form of the DAC. Moreover, importantly, the GPEDC needs to highlight clearly how it can link with the UN DCF and other platforms such as the G20 Development Working Group.

18.6 Conclusions

The rapid development of emerging countries is not only changing the global political and economic landscape, but also reshaping the architecture of global development governance through initiatives such as the BRICS' NDB and AIIB. The emerging powers influence the global development agenda mainly via what they called the SSC approach, which emphasises trade and investment in development, whereas the GPEDC largely focusses on an aid-based development cooperation system, and its agenda is still largely to provide aid.

However, due to the fact that the GPEDC has moved towards a development-effectiveness agenda and the emerging powers have influenced global development via a developmental approach; there appears to be an opportunity to persuade different forces to contribute to the SDGs. To do this, both sides need to overcome difficulties via understanding the realities and demands of each side and take concrete steps towards a truly genuine partnership.

Notes

1. The members of the Development Assistance Group in 1960: Belgium, Canada, France, Germany, Italy, Portugal, the United Kingdom, the United States, the Commission of the European Economic Community, Japan, and the Netherlands.
2. These opinions were heard during the first and second fora as well as in informal discussions, inparticular during the Nairobi forum.
3. Emerging economies are the countries or regions with rapidly growing economies. There are two "groups" emerging in this way. One group is called BRIC, which includes China, Brazil, India, and Russia. Another group is called New Diamond, which includes Mexico, Korea, South Africa, Poland, Turkey, and Ethiopia.

References

Abdel-Malek, T. (2015). *The global partnership for effective development cooperation: Origins, actions and future prospects* (Studies 88). Bonn, Germany: German Development Institute/Deutsches Institut für Entwicklungspolitik (DIE).

Adam, F. (2018). What might international development cooperation be able to tell us about contemporary "policy government" in developed countries? *Administration & Society, 50*(3), 372–401.

Ali, M., & Zeb, A. (2016). Foreign aid: Origin, evolution and effectiveness in poverty reduction. *The Dialogue: A Quarterly Journal, XI*(1), 107–125.

Assunção, M., & Esteves, P. (2014). *The BRICS and the Global Partnership for Effective Development Cooperation (GPEDC)* (BPC Policy Brief V.4 N.03). Rio de Janeiro, Brazil: BRICS Policy Center.

Atwood, J. B. (2011). *The road to Busan: Pursuing a new consensus on development cooperation.* https://www.brookings.edu/wp-content/uploads/2016/07/2011_blum_road_to_busan_atwood.pdf.

Atwood, J. B. (2012, September 20–22). *Creating a global partnership for effective development cooperation.* https://www.cgdev.org/sites/default/files/1426543_file_Atwood_Busan_FINAL_0.pdf.

Bena, F. T. (2017). *The outcome of the 2nd high-level meeting of the global partnership for effective development co-operation and why it matters.* http://aidwatchcanada.ca/wp-content/uploads/2017/02/Final-GPEDC-HLM2-paper-Farida-T-Bena-with-Brian-Tomlinson-3Feb2017.pdf.

Benn, J., & Luijkx, W. (2017). *Emerging providers' international cooperation for development* (OECD Development Co-operation Working Papers No. 33). Paris: OECD Publishing.

Blampied, C. (2016, November). *Where next for development effectiveness? Recommendations to the GPEDC for Nairobi and beyond* (ODI Briefing). London: Overseas Development Institute (ODI).

Day, B. (2014, April 16). Paradigm shift or aid effectiveness adrift? Previewing the first high-level meeting of the global partnership. *DevPolicy Blog.* https://devpolicy.org/paradigm-shift-or-aid-effectiveness-adrift-previewing-the-first-high-level-meeting-of-the-global-partnership-20140416/.

Fues, T., & Klingebiel, S. (2014, April 17). *Unrequited love: What is the legacy to the first global partnership summit?* (The current column). Bonn, Germany: German Development Institute/ Deutsches Institut für Entwicklungspolitik (DIE).

Glennie, J. (2014, April 22). Development partnership conference: What did we learn? *The Guardian.* https://www.theguardian.com/global-development/poverty-matters/2014/apr/22/development-partnership-co-operation-conference.

Hynes, W., & Scott, S. (2013). *The evolution of official development assistance: Achievements, criticisms and a way forward* (OECD Development Co-operation Working Papers No. 12). Paris: OECD Publishing.

Janus, H., Klingebiel, S., & Mahn, T. (2014). *How to shape development cooperation? The global partnership and the development cooperation forum* (Briefing Paper 3/2014). Bonn, German: German Development Institute/ Deutsches Institut für Entwicklungspolitik (DIE).

Jiang, S. (2017, October 12). The role of BRICS in global governance. *People: Theory channel.* http://theory.people.com.cn/n1/2017/1012/c40531-29583869.html (in Chinese).

Kharas, H. (2014). *Improve aid effectiveness.* http://effectivecooperation.org/2014/04/improve-aid-effectiveness/.

Klingebiel, S., & Li, X. (2016, December 6). *Crisis or progress: Global partnership for effective development cooperation after Nairobi* (The current column). Bonn, German: German Development Institute/ Deutsches Institut für Entwicklungspolitik (DIE).

Li, X. (2017). Evolution and prospects of the global partnership for effective development cooperation. *Journal of Learning and Exploring, 6,* 107–113.

Li, X., Banik, D., Tang, L., & Wu, J. (2014). Difference or indifference: China's development assistance unpacked. *IDS Bulletin, 45*(4), 22–33.

Mahn, T. J. (2017). *Accountability for development cooperation under the 2030 Agenda* (Discussion Paper 10/2017). Bonn, Germany: German Development Institute/ Deutsches Institut für Entwicklungspolitik (DIE).

Mosse, D. (Ed.). (2011). *Adventures in aidland: The anthropology of professionals in international development.* Oxford and New York, NY: Berghahn Press.

OECD (Organisation for Economic Co-operation and Development). (2018). *Development co-operation report 2018: Joining forces to leave no one behind.* Paris: OECD Publishing.

OECD. (2019a). *Net ODA* (indicator). https://data.oecd.org/oda/net-oda.htm.

OECD. (2019b). *Country programmable aid* (CPA). https://stats.oecd.org/viewhtml.aspx?datasetcode=CPA&lang=en#.

Rome Forum. (2003). *Rome declaration on harmonization.* https://www.who.int/hdp/publications/1b_rome_declaration.pdf.

Strawson, T. (2015). *Improving ODA allocation for a post-2015 world: Executive summary.* New York, NY: United Nations.

Ulfgard, R. V., & Lopez, L. (2016). In search of making a difference: Mexico in the OECD international development co-operation architecture. *Development Policy Review, 35*(S2), O287–O302.

World Bank. (2019). *IBRD loans and IDA credits (DOD, current US$)/China.* https://data.worldbank.org/indicator/DT.DOD.MWBG.CD?end=2010&locations=CN&start=1970&view=chart. Accessed 22 Aug 2019.

Open Access This chapter is licensed under the terms of the Creative Commons Attribution 4.0 International License (http://creativecommons.org/licenses/by/4.0/), which permits use, sharing, adaptation, distribution and reproduction in any medium or format, as long as you give appropriate credit to the original author(s) and the source, provide a link to the Creative Commons license and indicate if changes were made.

The images or other third party material in this chapter are included in the chapter's Creative Commons license, unless indicated otherwise in a credit line to the material. If material is not included in the chapter's Creative Commons license and your intended use is not permitted by statutory regulation or exceeds the permitted use, you will need to obtain permission directly from the copyright holder.

CHAPTER 19

South Africa in Global Development Fora: Cooperation and Contestation

Elizabeth Sidiropoulos

19.1 Introduction

South Africa's engagement in global development mirrors the tensions between contestation and cooperation that have come to characterise development cooperation. South Africa is both an ardent proponent of a rules-based order and multilateralism and an advocate for system reform. The latter necessitates contestation not only in existing institutions regarding where norm- and rule-making power rests, but also contestation of the rules and the system taking place via the establishment of parallel processes or institutions.

South Africa has worked with the rest of Africa to build up African agency in international development. It participates in many traditional fora and it works with other, less formal (or new) institutions that focus on development. South Africa is present in many of the sites of contestation that the opening chapter of this volume refers to. It is also present in the new sites of contestation and institution formation.

First, this chapter provides a brief overview of the drivers and philosophy of South Africa's engagement in global development cooperation (for more detail, see Sidiropoulos [2019]). Second, it explores examples where the country has been engaged in regime- or institution-shifting and institution or regime creation. Third, it outlines what has driven South Africa's own development cooperation strategy since 1994 in the context of South-South cooperation (SSC). Fourth, the chapter documents Africa's growing agency

E. Sidiropoulos (✉)
South African Institute of International Affairs, Johannesburg, South Africa
e-mail: Elizabeth.sidiropoulos@wits.ac.za

in this field, which has created both greater contestation in some fora and the potential—through Africa's voice—to improve governance structures and make them more inclusive in a substantive rather than a token way. Finally, it argues that contested cooperation is an expected and necessary part of the process that the global system is undergoing, as it moves to reform and, in some instances, reconstruct new forms of global governance. In this interregnum, what role should middle powers such as South Africa play? In the past, South Africa's bridge-building role has been invaluable in overcoming impasses. Can it regain such a "pivot" role in a climate of global polarisation, which makes comprehensive coordination around global frameworks such as the 2030 Agenda for Sustainable Development more difficult?

19.2 Philosophy and Drivers of South Africa's Global Development Engagement

Post-apartheid South Africa regarded itself as an African state as well as a Global South state in terms of its identity. The governing African National Congress's (ANC) world view is that of a global contestation of forces, of which the untransformed global governance system is the prime example. In the global development terrain, the ANC still views the world as divided into two camps, with "imperialism [having] mutated into a sophisticated system in the globalised world" where "globalisation [… is] being shaped by the agenda of the dominant global forces" and where "an exploitative socio-economic system rules the world" (African National Congress [ANC] 2007, Introduction). Thus, priorities for the ANC are Southern solidarity, African development, and reform of global governance (Flemes 2009; Grobbelaar 2014).

These factors are considered to be undermining the system of global governance by eroding its legitimacy, which should derive from the integrity of the system to promote and protect a fair and level playing field. They explain the constant focus of both the ANC and the government it leads on global governance reform, which includes trade rules, the international financial institutions, and the UN Security Council. Yet, the new South Africa was also the poster-child of the post-Cold War "end of history" paradigm with its peaceful and negotiated transition to democracy and a human rights-based constitution.

For the ANC, the emerging Southern powers are important partners in this contestation. The ANC's national conference resolutions in 2017 note that the

> emergence of growing economic powers, especially China, India and Brazil have a perspective that is informed by their respective struggles. They are inclined to acting multilaterally and therefore share our commitment to rebuilding and transforming all the institutions of global governance. (ANC 2017, p. 58)

South Africa's own aspirations to African (and Southern) leadership, and the underlying world view of the political elite, chafed at a world, rules, and institutions that are shaped by the United States and Northern/Western dominance. Nevertheless, South Africa believed in international engagement to reform the system, rather than direct and outright confrontation. Considered as an emerging regional power, South Africa has been pragmatic in its engagement, often seeking to build consensus in international fora rather than adopting polarising positions.

A number of phases can be discerned in South Africa's global engagement since 1994. The first phase, lasting until the early 2000s, saw South Africa rejoin all the international governance fora, most notably the United Nations (UN), the International Monetary Fund, the World Bank, and the General Agreement on Tariffs and Trade. Its actions in those fora were intended to contribute to better outcomes in these institutions for developing countries, and specifically Africa. However, it was in the area of security that South Africa made an impression, working to ensure the Nuclear Non-Proliferation Treaty review is successful, and on the adoption of the Anti-Personnel Mine Ban Convention. During this period, South Africa was also an active player in the Millennium Declaration Summit. This was the phase of constructive engagement with the existing institutions, taking back its place after the decades of apartheid exclusion.

The second phase emerged in the early 2000s and was characterised by South Africa's exploration of the creation of additional mechanisms that reflected its Global South perspective—such as IBSA (India, Brazil, South Africa)—and coalitions within traditional global governance structures that enabled a push-back against the dominant Western perspectives and processes in bodies such as the World Trade Organization (where a group of developing countries that were also agricultural producers formed a negotiating coalition around the extent and ambition of agricultural trade reforms) (see Davies 2019). This was also accompanied by the creation of new African continental institutions such as the African Union (AU) and the New Partnership for Africa's Development (NEPAD). These institutions were intended to help Africa's voice be heard more clearly in the established global fora. As such, over the course of the subsequent decade, they became catalysts for driving some change in the way in which Africa was received at the global level (see below).

The third phase emerged from about the time of South Africa's joining of the BRICS (Brazil, Russia, India, China, and South Africa) in 2011.[1] The BRICS group was seen by many in both the developed and the developing world as a counterpoint to the G7. China's presence in the BRICS ensured that this grouping (as opposed to IBSA) would have much greater clout in global fora. In this third phase, South Africa, together with the other BRICS, pushed for reforms of the international financial institutes.

Until the mid-2000s, South Africa played a bridge-building role quite successfully. As a middle-sized developing country, South Africa's global influence can only be advanced through assiduous relationship-building across dividing lines around common interests (Schoeman 2015). That role was less in evidence in the Jacob Zuma period (Masters 2017). In the Zuma administration, there was much more foreign policy hype about South Africa's membership in the BRICS, although this was linked to its potential to help meet Africa's developmental challenges (Sidiropoulos et al. 2018).

During this period, South Africa was perceived to be ramping up its contestation in global fora, if only because its deepening political relations with the BRICS and China (and to some extent Russia), in particular, saw the country adopting positions in global fora that seemed to avoid upsetting its bigger partners—its position on the South China Sea dispute, in which it adopted the Chinese position on resolving issues bilaterally, or the annexation of Crimea, in which it chose to abstain from voting in the United Nations General Assembly (UNGA).

In the post-Zuma administration, South Africa faces specific challenges in its regime- and institution-creation actions. China's more assertive foreign policy and power projection, witnessed most illustratively in its 70th anniversary celebrations in September 2019, is seeing it chart a more independent path, not limited to its cooperation within the BRICS. The establishment of the Asian Infrastructure Investment Bank and the enunciation of the Belt and Road Initiative are two examples of China's own "outside options" beyond the BRICS, where the gap between it and developing economies widens, and concomitantly their respective interests diverge.

South Africa's commitment to the principles of SSC was strongly articulated at the Second High-level United Nations Conference on South-South Cooperation, also known as BAPA + 40 (Buenos Aires Plan of Action plus 40), held in Buenos Aires in March 2019. There, South Africa supported the point that SSC was complementary to North-South cooperation, while also recognising that triangular cooperation was a "beneficial, complementary modality of development cooperation with great potential for enriching partnerships" (Institute for Global Dialogue [IGD] 2019, p. 2.). The linkages made between the SSC agenda and the 2030 Agenda were also important, as was the reiteration of the principles of SSC agreed at the 2009 Nairobi Conference. The calls for accountability and impact assessment remained contentious in the light of the demand-driven nature of SSC, but South Africa

> supported the view that an impact assessment of SSC initiatives, as well as their monitoring and evaluation, should be undertaken as the need arises rather than imposing a common template, especially in view of the variations in configurations and patterns and the extent of the demands by partner countries. (IGD 2019, p. 3)

South Africa has also been a strong proponent of the view that SSC can only be driven by the countries of the Global South. It is a product of the South and should be respected as such (IGD 2019).

19.3 South Africa's Regime-/Institution-Shifting or Creation

From its early enunciations on the need for an African Renaissance and its seminal contribution to the adoption of NEPAD, and subsequently the establishment of a coordinating agency of the same name (NEPAD Planning and Coordinating Agency), South Africa identified the imperative of African development as central to many of its international engagements. South Africa was interested in both the substance of the global development debate to ensure that African positions were well-articulated, and its architecture, which it believed should provide greater space for developing economies in its decision-making processes.

As such, South Africa has been active in the various platforms focusing on development—from the High Level Forums (HLFs) of the Organisation for Economic Co-operation and Development (OECD)/Development Assistance Committee (DAC) (culminating in Busan in 2011) in the 2000s to the UN-led processes on sustainable development (including the hosting of the World Summit on Sustainable Development in 2002), Financing for Development, the Development Cooperation Forum, and the G20's Development Working Group (DWG). Development has also been on the agenda of two clubs to which South Africa belongs: IBSA and the BRICS.

In addition, since 2001, South Africa has been a provider of SSC via its African Renaissance and International Cooperation Fund (ARF). It was established with start-up funding of $30 million. Its goal was to promote democracy and good governance, socio-economic development and integration, and resolution of conflicts, among others, in Africa (Sidiropoulos 2012, p. 226).

This section focuses on a number of sites of contestation where South Africa is active in the global development discourse and divides them into those that can be termed regime- or institution-shifting and those that are regime- or institution-creating. South Africa's interaction with formal institutions such as the UN and the OECD-DAC High Level Forums and the Global Partnership on Effective Development Co-operation (GPEDC) is part of attempt at institution-shifting, whereas IBSA and BRICS mechanisms and institutions are institution-creating. Its own development cooperation initiatives have spanned peace-building (an area that traditionally has fallen outside SSC activities, but has been the focus of Northern development cooperation) and humanitarian relief and capacity-building, among others.

19.3.1 UN Processes

South Africa has always been unequivocal in stating that the "United Nations remains the most inclusive and transparent means to advance development cooperation". South Africa considers ECOSOC (United Nations Economic and Social Council) the "principal body for coordination, policy review, policy dialogue and recommendations on economic and social development [...]" (IGD 2013, p. 8). At the UN, South Africa's actions reflect its view that the UN requires reforms to ensure that developing countries have more say, but it does not question its legitimacy as the apex global governance body. In that sense, it is involved in regime- or institution-shifting with regard to the UN.

South Africa's major entry into the UN global sustainable development arena was its hosting of the World Summit on Sustainable Development (WSSD) in 2002. It was a high-water mark for the country's diplomacy.[2] An important outcome of the WSSD was the integration of the three pillars of sustainable development (social, economic, and environmental), with the country arguing strongly that poverty eradication needed to be at the heart of sustainable development (Mashabane 2018, p. 404; Schroeder 2002, p. 34).

South Africa's role on development matters in the UN has been projected often through its holding of various positions, most notably as chair of the G77 + China (2006 and 2015). In 2006, as chair of the G77 + China, South Africa "forcefully challenged" US efforts to water down the development proposals in the World Summit Outcome Document, while a decade later it played a constructive role in ensuring the 2030 Agenda was adopted by consensus (Mashabane 2018, p. 405). In a book on the inside story of the negotiations of the Sustainable Development Goals (SDGs), the authors note that "the chair of the G77 is perhaps the second most important multilateral post after the President of the UN General Assembly" because members in the UNGA usually look to the G77 to draft initial resolutions (Kamau et al. 2018, p. 10).

Earlier, in January 2013, the UNGA president appointed South Africa and Ireland to coordinate preparations for the Special Event scheduled for September 2013 to follow up on efforts made towards achieving the Millennium Development Goals (MDGs), which had been agreed at the UNGA High Level Plenary Meeting on the MDGs in 2010.

South Africa has been elected twice to serve as a member of the UN's ECOSOC (2004–2006 and 2013–2015). With regard to its latter term on ECOSOC, South Africa saw the period leading up to the post-2015 agenda as a crucial one and regarded ECOSOC's role in coordinating the various processes as key (IGD 2013, p. 8). South Africa has always advocated for the strengthening and further reform of ECOSOC so that it is better placed to tackle global challenges and the needs of developing countries (IGD 2013, p. 8).

South Africa was a strong proponent of the MDGs and what the Millennium Summit and Declaration promised, seeing it as carrying the potential to create a better life for all. President Thabo Mbeki said at the time: "The fundamental challenge that faces this Millennium Summit is that, credibly, we must demonstrate the will to end poverty and underdevelopment" (cited in Zondi 2017, p. 129). South Africa also championed the development of African capacity to generate its own data to monitor the MDGs. Nevertheless, a deficit in data to inform policy and track the SDGs continues to be a challenge for many African states in the post-2015 landscape.

Although South Africa worked constructively on the adoption of the SDGs, it has also argued strongly that the work of the MDGs still needs to be completed. The new set of goals and indicators should not supersede the MDG targets where these remain unfulfilled. Together with the other African countries, South Africa advocated that the "unfinished business" of the MDGs needs to be completed. At the 2013 UNGA, President Zuma set out South Africa's key concerns for both the content and the rules of a post-2015 agenda. These included the need to fully implement the MDGs and that this should remain a priority in the post-2015 landscape. He again emphasised that all three dimensions of sustainable development should be integrated: "eradication of poverty through economic development, social development and environmental sustainability" (Zuma 2013, para. 18). In addition, South Africa supported the principle of common but differentiated responsibilities between developed and developing economies. Zuma argued this in the context of what he explained as the "tendency to attempt to delegate some of these historical responsibilities to new emerging economies in the South". He said this was "unacceptable and unworkable as such emerging nations have their own historical challenges and backlogs to deal with" (Zuma 2013, para. 27).

South Africa was the co-facilitator of the UN Financing for Development Forum (FfD) in 2017 together with Belgium. The first forum in 2016 had produced a procedural text that had not covered all the chapters of the Addis Ababa Action Agenda (AAAA). When South Africa took over the co-facilitation together with Belgium, they aimed to get agreement on a substantive text in the UN Inter-Agency Task Force on Financing for Development (IATF) on financing for development that focused on a balanced approach to all chapters in the AAAA. South Africa believed that, if the forum was to advance development, the follow-up meetings could not only focus on certain elements but ignore others. Furthermore, South Africa's position in the negotiations was that this forum should not focus only on official development assistance (ODA) commitments— FfD was not about measurement but about financing. South Africa also stood firm against efforts by some countries to push the Busan principles into the document. The discussion on trade was also difficult. There had been a number of commitments in the AAAA, including those on strengthening the multilateral trading system, facilitating international trade, and promoting trade policy coherence. The IATF report was not able to significantly take these issues forward; rather, it resorted to the language that had been used in the AAAA. Overall, during its co-facilitation, South Africa was keen on strengthening the IATF report so that it provided concrete recommendations to member states to speed up implementation.

In advancing its cause of a greater voice for Africa and more inclusive global governance, South Africa has made use of a number of instruments—from hosting major global events to chairing groupings within the UN, and helping to shape the agendas.

19.3.2 The OECD and the DAC

For many countries in the South, the OECD is considered a rich man's club that has tried to assimilate emerging economies into its structures and encourage them to adopt rules and norms developed previously by its members. This outreach has been partially successful over the years, with a few developing economies joining its membership. The first of these was Mexico, but more recently, it has been followed by South Korea and Chile, with Costa Rica and Colombia on the candidate list for accession.

South Africa has been part of the OECD's enhanced engagement, or outreach, which includes four other emerging economies—China, India, Indonesia, and Brazil—and which began in 2007. Much of this engagement relates to domestic issues, such as macroeconomic policies and structural reforms; however, South Africa has worked with the OECD on its regional initiatives in sub-Saharan Africa, including as vice co-chair of the NEPAD-OECD African Investment Initiative. It is also active in the Southern African Development Community (SADC) Regional Investment Policy Framework and the OECD–African Development Bank Group initiative to support business integrity and anti-bribery efforts in Africa. South Africa is also an associate of the BEPS (base erosion and profit-shifting) project.

Yet, although South Africa recognises the technical value of its various engagements with the OECD, it has chosen not to join it. The developing countries that have joined it see their admission to the group as a mark of their developmental success.[3] South Africa and other developing countries, such as India, consider the OECD—and especially its Development Assistance Committee (DAC)—as a bastion of Western-created rules that should not be foisted upon developing countries, especially in relation to monitoring, measuring, and evaluating their SSC (Sidiropoulos 2012, p. 236).

In addition, the OECD's role in global economic governance has grown over the years, especially in its interaction and engagement with the G20, which often looks to it for technical support. Because the G20 does not have a formal Secretariat, the OECD partly fills that role in practice, positioning itself as a global policy network with wide-ranging expertise. Although this has proved extremely useful to G20 and other processes, a number of South African officials in the past have raised concerns that the absence of well-resourced institutions from the Global South means that policy advice and input into the G20 process is still shaped by Northern-dominated organisations, notwithstanding the fact that the G20—with its more diverse membership—should differentiate itself from the traditional orthodox global policy prescriptions.

Thus, South Africa objects to the dominance of a Northern-constructed and dominated organisation exercising a significant role both in the evolution of global public goods and in the development cooperation field.

South Africa is an emerging donor, but it does not report on its development cooperation to the OECD's Development Assistance Committee. Historically, after 1994, South Africa played an important role in the OECD-DAC meetings—and specifically the HLFs, starting with Rome and culminating in Busan in 2011—as a recipient.

In its dual role of being both a donor and a recipient, however, it has adopted an approach at the political level emphasising that the metrics created by the traditional aid donors to monitor and evaluate their development cooperation cannot be applied to SSC. South Africa argues that much of SSC is not financial, but technical, in-kind, or a contribution to global public goods (e.g. peace-building) (Klingebiel 2018; Lalbahadur and Rawhani 2017). The DAC system does not provide for the tracking and evaluation of that kind of cooperation through its focus on monetisation.

In 2015, the OECD spearheaded a process to develop a universal standard to track contributions to the SDGs—the Total Official Support for Sustainable Development (TOSSD). A number of developing countries opposed the OECD's engaging in this process. At a political level, the South Africa government prefers the UN's Inter-agency and Expert Group on SDG Indicators, and indeed at the UN in New York, TOSSD is perceived as a product of the DAC.[4] There is concern that TOSSD is another way of camouflaging ODA and reducing it overall.

In the OECD-DAC, South Africa in the early 2000s was instrumental in coordinating a more harmonised African voice in the HLFs that began with Rome in 2003 and ended with Busan in 2011.

19.3.3 Clubs—G20

Informal clubs are by their nature exclusive in terms of their input legitimacy, but they are increasingly being seen and used by countries as instruments of regime- or institution-shifting or regime- or institution-creating. When the G20 transformed into a leaders' summit at the onset of the global financial crisis in 2008, it was considered more inclusive than the G8 and thus better able to navigate the global challenges and develop new rules of engagement. Very soon afterwards, in 2010, the G20 established a Development Working Group, and South Africa has served as its co-chair since then. Both in that forum and in other G20 working groups, South Africa has lobbied for African concerns and for solutions to global challenges that also reflect Southern perspectives (Cooper 2013; Sidiropoulos 2019). Its above-mentioned concern about the inordinate influence on policy of the OECD in the G20 is one such example. South Africa has been a proponent of better coordination among the emerging market economies in the G20, recognising that the G7 operates as a much more effective caucus within the G20 because it already has established mechanisms and practices of coordination.

South Africa has strongly campaigned for the G20 to combat illicit financial flows (IFFs). In the DWG, South Africa was instrumental in pushing for the World Customs Organization to prepare a report on IFFs channelled via trade misinvoicing. By introducing it in the DWG, South Africa wanted to ensure that the development dimension would not be lost. South Africa has been particularly successful in drawing attention to the impact of IFFs on developing countries, particularly on African economies and development. South Africa was also active in the debates to tackle BEPS in the G20 and worked with the OECD in this regard.

Other issues that South Africa has keenly participated in, in the G20, are infrastructure and its asset class potential—an objective that NEPAD had also highlighted as important. The finance track has also been working on a set of G20 Principles for the Infrastructure Project Preparation Phase. These are intended to help "deliver a pipeline of well-prepared and bankable projects that are attractive to private investors by improving assessments of project rationale, options appraisal, commercial viability, long-term affordability, and deliverability" (Ministry of Finance Japan 2018, para. 4). For South Africa, project preparation in infrastructure is a neglected area. Another area that is relevant to Africa and development in the finance track is financial inclusion. This has also been part of the DWG mandate. South Africa is a co-chair of the subgroup on financial inclusion data and measurement[5] of the Global Partnership for Financial Inclusion, which was launched in December 2010 after the G20 Seoul Summit, where financial inclusion featured prominently in the Seoul Development Consensus. South Africa has also urged the International Monetary Fund to create a facility that meets the specific needs of countries in fragile situations that require financial support and have limited capacity to advance reforms to restore macroeconomic stability (International Monetary Fund 2016).

19.3.4 *Other Clubs—IBSA and the BRICS*

In the last two decades, a number of new informal groupings have emerged, especially in the developing world. South Africa played a key role in the establishment of the India–Brazil–South Africa Dialogue Forum in 2003 and joined the BRICS three years after it was established by the BRIC. These clubs are vehicles for contestation in existing institutional sites, as they enable South Africa and the other members to coordinate positions on a number of issues of global governance. They also help to spearhead new sites of institutional contestation, such as the New Development Bank (NDB).

IBSA's work in development cooperation is largely driven through the IBSA Fund and is regarded as a key pillar of SSC. The 2010 Brasilia Declaration of IBSA outlined the basic principles of SSC (India, Brazil, South Africa [IBSA] 2010). These were reaffirmed by the IBSA states in a declaration on SSC in June 2018. The declaration emphasised that at the core of SSC lies "[r]espect for national sovereignty […]. SSC is about interdependences and not 'new dependencies'. The partner countries themselves initiate, organise and manage SSC activities". It went on to note that the "primary responsibility towards development rests with the States themselves under their ownership and leadership". SSC is voluntary in nature and it is an expression of solidarity. The declaration emphasised that SSC was not aid, nor was it obligatory, as ODA was (IBSA 2018, Principles).

In 2004, IBSA established the India, Brazil, and South Africa Facility for Poverty and Hunger Alleviation (IBSA Fund), which was granted the MDG Award for its various successful and innovative projects in countries such as Burundi, Cambodia, Cape Verde, Guinea-Bissau, and Palestine. The fund, which had cumulative contributions amounting to $35.1 million, according to its 2018 report, worked with 19 partner states, nearly two-thirds of which were least-developed countries. The mandate of the fund is to "support projects on a demand-driven basis through partnerships with local governments, national institutions and implementing partners" (IBSA Fund 2018, p. 2).

The BRICS has been the preeminent South-South club for South Africa since it joined in 2011. In a speech in 2012, South Africa's international relations and cooperation minister highlighted that its membership had three objectives: to advance South Africa's national interests; to promote its regional integration programme and related continental infrastructure programme; and to partner with key players in the South on issues related to global governance and its reform (Department of International Relations and Cooperation, South Africa [DIRCO] 2012). It is clear that, for South Africa, the BRICS group provides an opportunity to leverage financing for Africa's infrastructure development in the priorities set out by NEPAD and Agenda 2063. The NDB is another important instrument for this objective. The Africa Regional Centre was established in Johannesburg in 2017, but the NDB's membership has not yet expanded beyond the five initial members to enable it to lend to other developing countries. In addition, South Africa and the other BRICS continued to engage constructively in global processes, the most notable of which were the Paris Agreement and the SDGs. But they also created new mechanisms or institutions such as the Contingency Reserve Arrangement and the NDB. There thus emerges a clear effort, only made possible by China's significant financial clout, to explore "outside options" (Roberts et al. 2018).

The global development agenda and the structures created to manage it form an important dimension of South Africa's foreign policy priorities. The country has played an active role in the most important development structures at various times and in various forms since the end of apartheid. It has recognised the impactful role that a host country can play in global summits when it hosted the WSSD. Equally, it has selected to chair important groupings of the Global South at critical junctures in global development debates. While respecting the legitimacy of agreements made in the formal multilateral bodies, South Africa has also been pragmatic in recognising that smaller informal clubs can play a significant role in advancing particular issues, especially where agreement among a few systemically important countries will make all the difference.

19.4 South Africa's Development Cooperation

South Africa's development cooperation since 1994 has focused largely on promoting peace, security, and economic development in Africa (Sidiropoulos 2012, p. 217). It was driven not only by the principle of Southern solidarity, but just as importantly by the country's own experiences in ending apartheid, regarded by the UN as a crime against humanity. Its political transition had been negotiated in a peaceful manner that brought all parties to the negotiating table and resulted in a government of national unity and a constitution that entrenched a Bill of Rights recognising both political and socio-economic rights. The new ANC-led government believed that this model of transformation could be applied to other conflicts in the continent. Equally, good governance and democracy were key pillars of conflict resolution, and over many years, its peace-building model, most notably in the Democratic Republic of Congo (DRC), reflected that (see Besharati and Rawhani 2016).

President Mbeki's African Renaissance vision, which morphed into NEPAD, included a component on a voluntary good governance mechanism, which became the African Peer Review Mechanism (APRM), the Secretariat of which is located in South Africa.[6] The African Renaissance vision was also apparent in the institutional reforms that South Africa championed in the SADC around democracy promotion and in the establishment of the AU (Lalbahadur and Rawhani 2017).

The ARF, which was established in 2000, reflected the importance that South Africa ascribed to these themes. Its aim was to "enhance cooperation between South Africa and other countries, in particular in Africa, through the promotion of democracy and good governance, socio-economic development and integration, humanitarian assistance and human resource development, and the prevention and resolution of conflict" (Parliamentary Monitoring Group [PMG] 2019b).

Start-up funding was $30 million in 2001. In more recent years, however, the disbursements have declined from nearly 190 million rand ($13.6 million) in 2014/5 to 57.6 million rand ($4 million) in 2016/7 (DIRCO, n.d.).

In the financial year 2018/9, the ARF disbursed 44.7 million rand (about $3.2 million) for humanitarian assistance, the promotion of democracy and good governance, and human resource development in Africa. Some of the countries and territories receiving the assistance included Namibia, Eswatini, Western Sahara, Lesotho, and Madagascar (PMG 2019a).

South Africa does not report on its development cooperation to the OECD's Development Assistance Committee. In its dual role of being both a donor and a recipient, its position is that the metrics created by the traditional aid donors to monitor and evaluate their development cooperation cannot be applied to SSC. Through its focus on monetisation, the DAC system does not provide for tracking and evaluating the cooperation undertaken by South Africa. The Department of International Relations and Cooperation (DIRCO) also argues that the metrics and models are not easy for developing countries to implement, nor are they necessarily pro-development.[7]

The Zuma administration took a decision to create the South African Development Partnership Agency, which would replace the ARF and ensure a more coordinated and accountable development partnership process (Sidiropoulos 2019). However, differences between the treasury and DIRCO about its governance apparently stalled the process. As of late 2019, there is still no indication if it will be established, although the need for an agency that can coordinate South Africa's development cooperation across all government actors remains crucial.

19.5 Africa's Growing Agency

In the section that follows, the paper focuses on how African states have sought to increase their voice in multilateral development fora through new institutions that have acted as catalysers (the AU and NEPAD/African Union Development Agency) and developed platforms and structures to advance development on the continent. First, in the early 2000s, Africa established an institution that was intended to be the continent's development agency, NEPAD; second, and under NEPAD, it established a development platform that would enable coordination and the articulation of common priorities through a united voice: the African Platform for Development Effectiveness; third, the AU adopted Agenda 2063 (Africa's 50-year vision for 2063) in 2013, which strengthened the conceptual coherence of Africa's priorities and provided a vision for the future; fourth, individual African countries and the continental institutions began to play a stronger role in global multilateral negotiations.

The African Renaissance idea of the late 1990s and early 2000s led to the establishment in 2001 of NEPAD. Its founding members were South Africa, Nigeria, Algeria, Senegal, and Egypt. The following year, the AU endorsed its adoption as a programme of the AU. In 2010, it was converted into the NEPAD Planning and Coordinating Agency (NEPAD Agency) as an outcome of the decision to integrate it into the AU structures and processes. Finally, at the 2018 mid-year AU Summit, it was formally converted into the AU Development Agency.

In his book *Africa's Critical Choices: A Call for a Pan African Roadmap*, the long-serving chief executive of the NEPAD Agency, Ibrahim Mayaki, explains that the NEPAD idea of the founding fathers was "to take back the developmental leadership of the continent with a pan-African point of view to give the continent its own path and an equal footing in its dealings with its international partners" (Mayaki 2018, p. 74).

From small beginnings, and while still facing funding constraints, the NEPAD Agency has grown in its role as the premier platform for African discussions on development and as a coordinator of African positions in global fora. The articulation of a new partnership and the establishment of the NEPAD Secretariat were accompanied by the transformation of the Organisation of African Unity to the African Union, while the APRM Secretariat, intended to focus on improving African governance, was an outgrowth of NEPAD and established in 2003.

NEPAD's role has been bolstered by the growing confidence and engagement on these issues by African countries individually, supported by the phenomenal economic growth that many experienced in the mid-2000s, which led to the moniker of "Africa Rising" or "Lions on the Move". As the socio-economic arm of the AU, NEPAD's priorities are human capital development; regional integration, infrastructure, and trade; industrialisation, science, technology, and innovation; and natural resource governance and food security. Since the adoption of the AU's Agenda 2063, NEPAD has served as its implementing body.

Projecting a common voice provides a stronger front in global debates that have traditionally been dominated by the big players; however, the continent is economically and politically diverse, making it difficult to carry through continental decisions to the national level, depending on the specific interests of each country. In an increasingly contested global terrain, African countries have become much more vocal in existing global development institutions. They are not turning away from those institutions, but are working to make their agendas better reflected in those contexts.

19.5.1 Adopting Common Positions: The Africa Platform for Development Effectiveness

Starting from the Accra HLF in 2008, the process of a more coherent and united voice for African issues began to form. The Africa Platform for Development Effectiveness (APDev) was endorsed at the 15th AU Summit in July 2010 and launched in March 2011. Managed by the NEPAD Agency, its focus was on providing coordination for a common voice for Africa's development perspectives, including SSC, aid effectiveness, and capacity development, which were the core focal areas of the platform.

By the time of the Busan HLF in 2011, Africa, for the first time, had a common position on development effectiveness, drawing on the outcomes of three regional meetings driven by the NEPAD Agency[8] under APDev that were held in Pretoria, Tunis, and Addis Ababa between March 2010 and September 2011.

This approach continued for other important global debates. The Africa Action Plan on Development Effectiveness[9] was adopted by the AU and its members in advance of the first HLM of the GPEDC in Mexico in April 2014. The action plan articulated, among other things, the challenges faced by middle-income countries, a broad definition of domestic resource mobilisation (going beyond tax), and the importance of regional organisations in development. It also proposed specific ideas to address them (NEPAD 2014). In the build-up to the adoption of the 2030 Agenda, the AU Summit in January 2014 adopted a Common African Position on the post-2015 Development Agenda (CAP). Africa and the rest of the developing world regarded these negotiations as a "unique opportunity to right the wrongs of the past and make any future development framework reflect the priorities and needs of the people most affected by poverty and inequality" (Nganje 2017, p. 61).

Formulating the common position was a difficult process. A number of issues that were to prove contentious in the UN process—both the Open Working Group (OWG) and the Intergovernmental Negotiations (IGNs)—played themselves out in the African context as well. For example, the peace and security pillar in the CAP elicited opposition from a number of African states. There were different interpretations of what this meant. South Africa's interpretation, for example, was based on the notion of human security, whereas Rwanda and Uganda regarded this as referring to state security (Nganje 2017, p. 75). SDG 16, which covers peace, justice, and strong institutions, was equally contentious within the UN process. Overall, however, the African process was fairly consultative and inclusive, with both state and non-state actors making inputs. There were also strong links with Agenda 2063 that had been developed earlier.

There have been other instances where Africa has adopted a common position (on climate change and on UN Security Council reform). Common positions on their own do not ensure that the continent's voice is stronger. It is also true that because the 54 states are so different, a common position may help to articulate shared priorities to guide negotiations but may be less able to shape outcomes or promote the continent's collective interest (Nganje 2017, p. 68). However, by working on a common voice, Africa has been systematic in its articulation of its priorities in all the development fora and, although traction is not easy, persistence has brought some outcomes. In the negotiations on the SDGs, most Africans working through the G77 + China stood their ground regarding SDG 16 on peace and security, which was key in ensuring that the G77 did not drop it and that the goal was eventually adopted (Kamau et al. 2018, p. 203).

African voice and participation have grown steadily in global development debates. The coordinating role of the AU and NEPAD in the preparation for global debates or initiatives has been key in this regard, but so too has the active role that certain African states and individuals have played. The section below discusses African involvement in the negotiations on the SDGs and the post-2015 development agenda as well as the Global Partnership process.

19.5.2 UN Processes

The SDGs were negotiated by the OWG, which comprises 70 members. Eleven African countries participated in the OWG: Algeria, Egypt, Morocco, Tunisia, Ghana, Benin, Kenya, Tanzania, Congo, Zambia, and Zimbabwe. The OWG was co-chaired by Kenya's Macharia Kamau and Hungary's Csaba Korosi. The process of selecting the co-chair from the South was quite fraught, with a number of developing countries (including Egypt) preferring Brazil. The reason for this is that most G77 + China countries believed that their interests would be better served by a co-chair from one of the emerging powers because they felt that African states (excluding South Africa) could be easily manipulated by the North. "Kenya was considered a Trojan horse for the Europeans and [the UN Environment Programme]" (Kamau et al. 2018, p. 60). Nevertheless, Kenya was able to deal with the concerns raised, and Kamau was nominated as co-chair by the G77.

The role that Kamau and Korosi played in driving the process of determining and adopting the SDGs, using a very open, transparent, and inclusive process, cannot be underestimated in ensuring a successful outcome and the overwhelming acceptance across the board of a set of goals.[10] Far from being a Trojan horse, Ambassador Kamau managed the process with his co-chair in a fair and non-partisan manner, ensuring that all views were heard and considered. It was equally significant that he was also made co-facilitator of the IGN process on the post-2015 development agenda by the president of UNGA, Uganda's foreign minister, after the OWG had completed its work.

Although in his position as co-chair and co-facilitator he was not representing Africa, his achievements were important in dispelling earlier myths that Africans could not be independent.

It is important to note that the IGN process on the post-2015 development agenda had three Africans in senior positions. The president of UNGA in 2015 was the Ugandan foreign minister, the co-facilitator was Kenyan, and the chair of the G77 + China was South Africa. Kamau et al. remarked that "often negotiations get into trouble when the chair of the G77 has a different agenda than the co-chairs or co-facilitators" (Kamau et al. 2018, p. 219). This was not so in the case of South Africa, and cooperation among the president, the co-facilitators, and the G77 was at the "highest level" (Kamau et al. 2018, p. 219).

South Africa's role as chair of the G77 + China was strategic, as it led the group in both the post-2015 development agenda negotiations and the Financing for Development process. South Africa supported the co-facilitators at the IGNs in advocating that the SDG discussions (once they had been finalised in the OWG) would not be reopened during the IGN process, as this would have upset the "delicate political compromise" (Kamau et al. 2018, p. 221). South Africa also argued on behalf of the G77 that the post-2015 agenda had to respect the national policy space of members.

Developing countries, and Africa in particular, were emphatic throughout the OWG process that the SDGs should not divert attention from the implementation of the MDGs, and that there should be a direct link between the two, including the post-2015 development agenda. The area of common but differentiated responsibilities (CBDR) was another point of emphasis that made it into the text.

In the OWG process, which was open to all UN members, irrespective of whether they had a formal seat on the working group or not, African states displayed a mixture of progressive and conservative approaches to issues. Kamau et al. (2018) identify Kenya, Botswana, Ghana, and South Africa among the former, especially on issues such as the green and the blue economy and renewable energy, whereas countries such as Uganda and Nigeria were far more conservative on LGBT (lesbian, gay, bisexual, transgender) rights and sexual and reproductive health (Kamau et al. 2018, p. 110). Kamau et al. recount that, at key moments, countries such as South Africa, Botswana, Tanzania, Rwanda, and Ethiopia were called on to support the chairs in keeping the momentum of the process going (Kamau et al. 2018, p. 158).

South Africa represented the G77 in the negotiations on FfD that led to the AAAA. South Africa emphasised from the outset in its interventions that this was a separate process and its scope needed to go beyond the discussion on financing the SDGs (Kamau et al. 2018, p. 232).

Overall, the final FfD document, the AAAA, did not reflect some of the biggest concerns of African states and the G77 + China. CBDR was not as explicitly set out, neither was the need by developed countries to honour the 0.7 per cent of gross national income commitments, or that climate financing had to be additional to ODA commitments. For South Africa and many other developing countries, the debate on IFFs was also not reflected adequately in the outcomes, and the failure to agree to upgrade the UN Tax Committee to an inter-governmental body was also a disappointment (Kamau et al. 2018, pp. 234–235).

19.5.3 The GPEDC Process

Since the establishment of the GPEDC, many African states and the AU have participated in it and regard it as an important platform for discussing development effectiveness. Egypt was the chair of the Post-Busan Interim Group (PBIG).[11] After Busan, Rwanda and Mali represented Africa in the PBIG and the AU, and its institutions were active in developing and projecting Africa's position in these discussions. Rwanda and the United Kingdom took the lead in finalising the indicators in the PBIG. These 10 indicators were approved in June 2012 at the final meeting of the Working Party on Aid Effectiveness.

When the GPEDC was launched in mid 2012, Nigeria became one of the co-chairs, together with the United Kingdom and Indonesia.[12] Chad was the other African country on the Steering Committee. The AU and NEPAD worked jointly to support the post-Busan implementation and to consolidate and coordinate African views. At the 19th AU Summit, it was agreed that the AU would request membership of the GPEDC (2012).

In 2014, Malawi became co-chair with the Netherlands and Mexico; Egypt, the AU, and NEPAD served on the Steering Committee. From 2015, Kenya also participated in the Steering Committee as host of the 2016 HLM, and Uganda became one of the co-chairs after the 2016 HLM. The other two co-chairs were Bangladesh, representing developing countries that were donors and recipients, and Germany, representing donor countries. An African country has always been one of the co-chairs. The rotation of African countries is managed through the AU, as is the election to the GPEDC co-chairmanship.

The NEPAD Agency is a permanent member of the Steering Committee and the official Secretariat of the GPEDC in Africa. Having NEPAD sit on the Steering Committee provides stability in terms of content, rather than the constant rotation among African states, which, while democratic, makes it extremely difficult to achieve continuity and a degree of expertise in the process. In 2016, Africa gained an extra seat on the Steering Committee. The continent now has four seats (one co-chair, the AU and NEPAD, and two African countries).

NEPAD and the African continent are part of a number of Global Partnership Initiatives (GPIs).[13] In 2015, the GPI on Results and Mutual Accountability piloted the Programme on Enhanced Use of Country Results Frameworks (CRFs). The initiative aims to reinforce improved use of country results frameworks to measure the impact of development cooperation in line with National Development Plans (NDPs), Agenda 2063, and the 2030 Agenda. The enhanced use of CRFs drawn from NDPs is essential in linking the critical functions of planning, budgeting, and implementation towards attaining sustainable developmental results.

Currently, the initiative has 10 African countries: Madagascar, Malawi, Benin, Burundi, the DRC, Uganda, Kenya, Rwanda, Mozambique, and Cameroon. Somalia requested to join as of 2018, which brings the total to 11 participating countries. The NEPAD Agency's Capacity Development and Monitoring and Evaluation divisions are collaborating to have a unified AU tracking and monitoring mechanism of development results for Agenda 2063 and the 2030 Agenda. In addition, Kenya, Malawi, Rwanda, and Uganda are among the 10 pilot countries on enhanced effectiveness at the country level that will feed into the Global Compendium of Good Practice (GPEDC 2018).

In 2018, the NEPAD Agency was conducting development finance assessments and integrated financing strategies and plans training to African countries to enhance capacities for the effective mobilisation of sustainable development finance.

Under the framework of the GPEDC, the NEPAD Agency and the UNDP Regional Service Centre for Africa are collaborating on the African South-South Cooperation Reporting Initiative. The programme aims to provide concrete evidence to inform policies and partnerships showing that South-South trade, partnerships, and investments have the potential to accelerate improvements in social and industrial sectors by harnessing technology, knowledge, and experience. This will help stimulate, foster, and enable sustainable South-South investments for the achievement of NDPs and Agenda 2063.

Africans on the GPEDC Steering Committee have consistently highlighted the importance of linking the GPEDC process to the UN processes—both the SDGs and FfD. For example, at the fourth Steering Committee meeting in Washington, DC, in October 2013, the Nigerian co-chair, Minister Okonjo-Iweala, indicated that work done within the Global Partnership on how effective development cooperation can mobilise domestic resources should be fed into post-2015 discussions, including the work of the Intergovernmental Committee of Experts on Sustainable Development Financing (GPEDC 2013).

As with the concern about abandoning the MDGs in favour of a new framework, so too have Africans in the GPEDC constantly reiterated the importance of not neglecting the unfinished business of the aid agenda, including use of country systems, transparency, untying aid, and predictability. The 15th meeting of the Steering Committee in 2018 endorsed a proposal to develop a Global Action Plan on Unfinished Business (GPEDC 2018).

African states also advocated for the establishment of an independent Monitoring Advisory Group. This proposal had emanated from a regional consultation that the AU and NEPAD had held in Kinshasa in November 2014 (GPEDC 2015). In 2015, the GPEDC established a Monitoring Advisory Group to provide technical expertise and advice to strengthen the Global Partnership monitoring framework and to ensure relevance to the post-2015 context.

Many Africans, both state and non-state actors, recognise that the GPEDC is a forum that gives them an opportunity to hold development partners to account. Among African states, Kenya has shown an increased level of engagement and leadership on global development and South-South discussions. In 2009, it hosted the High-level United Nations Conference on South-South Cooperation. In July 2016, Kenya hosted the fourteenth session United Nations Conference on Trade and Development, and in November 2016, it hosted the Second GPEDC HLM. At the announcement of its hosting, a senior official in the Ministry of Devolution and Planning said that "Kenya will lead the talks to ensure that a notable outcome for Africa and the developing world will be declared in Nairobi, which will shift relations between development partners and recipient countries" ("Kenya to host global aid coordination meeting", n.d.). During the 71st UNGA in 2016, Kenya expressed the view that the fact that international cooperation remained at the core of the SDGs highlighted the importance of global partnerships and, in particular, the Global Partnership for Effective Development Cooperation. This partnership has a special role in accelerating delivery of development outcomes as effectively, fairly and efficiently as possible, with particular attention to least developed countries. (Permanent Mission of the Republic of Kenya to the United Nations 2016, p. 3)

19.6 AFRICAN STATES AND SSC

For a long time, developing countries and civil society organisations have argued for greater accountability and transparency in not only aid provided by traditional donors, but also in SSC (Sidiropoulos 2015).[14] The latter topic has sometimes led to fraught discussions, as the South and its big players regard SSC as being underpinned by a different set of principles and moral imperatives; the North has to atone for its exploitation of the developing world—a responsibility that does not also accrue to the emerging economies. Although "Southern providers"—itself a contentious term—are still developing, the scale of their cooperation and its scope are now very different from those of the 1950s or 1970s, when the Buenos Aires Plan of Action was adopted. Debates among think tanks working in this field and also among the Network of Southern Think Tanks have highlighted this challenge, but also that SSC should not be seen through the prism of financial targets in the way OECD-DAC states do (German Federal Ministry for Economic Cooperation and Development/GPEDC/German Development Institute 2017; Research and Information Systems for Developing Countries, n.d.).

Regarding how African states view SSC, in APDev's submission to the OECD in April 2012, entitled "Africa's Response to the Global Partnership", Africa indicated that it supported the principle of a two-track approach—engaging with emerging economies through AU-sanctioned fora such as the Forum on China-Africa Cooperation, while the Global Partnership would complement this process rather than replacing it (Africa Platform for Development Effectiveness, n.d., p. 3). The importance of SSC in achieving development goals globally has been recognised by all stakeholders. However, in notes from the African representatives to the HLM in Mexico—made after an international workshop on the GPEDC in Seoul in November 2013 that focused on implementation strategies for effective development cooperation at country level[15]—they reported that development partners raised the "importance of establishing a framework of principles applicable to all stakeholders in the development environment". They further reported that China, Brazil, and South Africa, as South-South providers, emphasised that "the South-South relationship constituted a different mechanism with different rules and processes guiding it". The African representatives went on to add that at the Seoul workshop, all the South-South stakeholders reaffirmed their availability to "participate in discussions in respect of *diversified approaches in the partnership*" ("Note from the African representatives" 2013; emphasis added).

The Nairobi Outcome Document eroded the issues that especially the big Southern providers regarded as important, such as the differentiation between them and traditional donors. Bracho (2017, p. 2) argues that even in Mexico City

> some donors seemed uneasy with differentiation because they were dissatisfied with their own commitments, which they increasingly perceived as an unjustified burden made even worse by the "unfair competition" of new donor countries [Southern providers] that had no commitments at all.

The question that Africa should deliberate is whether the big Southern providers (China, India, and Brazil in particular) *do* have an obligation to commitments, not because of historical injustices perpetrated, but because they are now much more powerful economies. Such commitments, however, should be differentiated from those of the North because of the significant poverty challenges they still face in their own countries.

19.7 Conclusion

The chapter has argued that South Africa's approach to global governance, especially as it relates to development issues, has been defined by a willingness to cooperate with existing institutions to make them more responsive to African concerns. Its articulated foreign policy is one of advancing African interests on the global stage, and it has certainly executed that in a number of fora. However, South Africa has also become involved in the creation of new global institutions or groupings that can complement existing ones, or form the basis for alternative global structures. In this, it has worked most often with other emerging economies from outside the continent. Other African countries in the main have cooperated with existing institutions while seeking to build up their effectiveness and agenda-setting capacities therein.

Contested cooperation is an expected and necessary part of the process that the global system is undergoing, as it moves to reform and, in some instances, construct new forms of global governance in this interregnum, where relative power is shifting to actors from the Global South. As the country that had underpinned the post-1945 international order (the United States) seems less keen today to continue to uphold it and to reform the power balances, a number of emerging countries are exploring outside options beyond the current institutions. Although emerging countries such as South Africa are committed to the two key global development frameworks of recent years—the 2030 Agenda and the Paris Agreement—this polarisation and norm and institution contestation characterising the twenty-first century will make it very difficult to arrive at a comprehensive global monitoring, financing, and evaluation system on the road to achieving the 2030 Agenda.

The contestation of existing norms and structures is unavoidable, as it is only in this way that progress in reforming them can be made. In addition, the processes initiated by developing countries to create complementary but potentially parallel structures form part of the pressure that pushes the dominant states in the international order to concede certain points in the global architecture.

There is also a significant contestation of responsibilities between Northern and Southern states. As with institutions, not all developing countries are driving these or necessarily agree on the scale of responsibilities that the Global South should carry specifically. Countries such as China have much greater ability to choose their options and set the agenda than African countries, including South Africa. Although South Africa has aligned itself with large emerging powers in exploring alternatives to existing frameworks, it cannot solely rely on them to push reforms that are specifically pertinent to African countries. At the same time, South Africa and Africa have strength in their numbers and the legitimacy they can confer on any process that is driven or led by other bigger, more influential states. This leverage needs to be conferred judiciously.

Notes

1. South Africa only became a member of the BRICS in 2011 on the invitation of China, although the BRICS had been established in 2009, with its first summit in Yekaterinburg.
2. Interview with UN official, New York, May 2018.
3. When South Korea hosted the 4th High Level Meeting (HLM) in Busan in 2011, it sought to emphasise that it, too, had once been a poor, developing country that had been able to graduate to the ranks of developed countries.
4. Telephone interview with OECD Development Cooperation Directorate official, 2 August 2019.
5. There are four other subgroups: (i) regulations and standard-setting bodies; (ii) SME finance; (iii) financial consumer protection and financial literacy; (iv) markets and payment systems. The Global Partnership for Financial Inclusion is not limited to G20 members, and Kenya and Nigeria assisted with the work of the subgroup on principles and standard-setting bodies.
6. For further elaboration on the APRM and NEPAD, see Sidiropoulos and Hughes (2004).
7. DIRCO official at roundtable discussion, Pretoria, 5 August 2019.
8. NEPAD, in its 2001 base framework, proposed that Africa "establish a forum of African countries so as to develop a common African position on ODA reform, and to engage with the Development Assistance Committee (DAC) of the OECD and other partners in developing a charter underpinning the development partnership" (New Partnership for Africa's Development [NEPAD] 2001, para. 148).
9. The Action Plan was granted the status of official Global Partnership Initiative by the GPEDC. See http://www.nepad.org/nepad-oncontinent/capacity-development-programme-south-africa.
10. It has been documented in Kamau et al. (2018).
11. Egypt was also previously the co-chair of the WP-EFF.

12. Each of the co-chairs would represent a recipient country, a donor country, and a donor-recipient country.
13. The GPEDC's GPIs are voluntary initiatives led by national governments, civil society organisations, foundations, and members of the private sector, among others. They generate policy-relevant lessons and innovative solutions, sharing this knowledge to spur more effective development cooperation at the country, regional, and global levels.
14. See, for instance, the critique of SSC by a member of the Steering Committee of the GPEDC and head of Reality of Aid Africa, Vitalice Meja (2014).
15. Note from the African representatives (2013).

References

Africa Platform for Development Effectiveness. (n.d.). *Africa's response to the Global partnership*, April 2012. Unpublished document, author's hard copy.

ANC (African National Congress). (2007). *Resolutions by ANC, 20 December 2007, 52nd National Conference, Polokwane*. https://www.sahistory.org.za/archive/resolutions-anc-20-december-2007-52nd-national-conference-polokwane.

ANC. (2017). *54th National Conference: Report and resolutions*. http://joeslovo.anc.org.za/sites/default/files/docs/ANC%2054th_National_Conference_Report%20and%20Resolutions.pdf.

Besharati, N., & Rawhani, C. (2016). *South Africa and DRC: Evaluating a South-South partnership for peace, governance and development* (SAIIA Occasional Paper No. 235). https://saiia.org.za/research/south-africa-and-the-drc-evaluating-a-south-south-partnership-for-peace-governance-and-development/.

Bracho, G. (2017). *The troubled relationship of the emerging powers and the effective development cooperation agenda* (Discussion Paper 25/2017). Bonn: German Development Institute/Deutsches Institut für Entwicklungspolitik (DIE).

Cooper, A. F. (2013). Squeezed or revitalised? Middle powers, the G20 and the evolution of global governance. *Third World Quarterly, 34*(6), 963–984. https://doi.org/10.1080/01436597.2013.802508.

Davies, R. (2019). *The politics of trade in the era of hyperglobalisation: A Southern African perspective*. Geneva: South Centre.

DIRCO (Department of International Relations and Cooperation, South Africa). (2012). Speech by Minister of International Relations and Cooperation Maite Nkoana-Mashabane on the occasion of the New Age business briefing on South Africa's role in the BRICS and its benefits to job creation and the infrastructure drive in South Africa. http://www.dirco.gov.za/docs/speeches/2012/mash0911a.html.

DIRCO. (n.d.). *African Renaissance and International Cooperation Fund (ARF) revised strategic plan 2015–2020, annual performance plan 2018/19*. http://www.dirco.gov.za/department/african_renaissance2015_2020/arf_revised3_2015_2020.pdf.

Flemes, D. (2009). Regional power South Africa: Co-operative hegemony constrained by historical legacy. *Journal of Contemporary African Studies, 27*(2), 135–157. https://doi.org/10.1080/02589000902867238.

German Federal Ministry for Economic Cooperation and Development/GPEDC/German Development Institute. (2017, November 24). *Informal exchange on towards a shared understanding of effective development cooperation: Learning from different actors and approaches.* https://effectivecooperation.org/wp-content/uploads/2017/12/20171124_Informal_Exchange_with_Researchers_from_Emerging_Economies_summary.pdf.

GPEDC (Global Partnership for Effective Development Co-operation). (2012, December 5–6). *Global Partnership for Effective Development Co-operation, First Meeting of the Steering Committee.* http://effectivecooperation.org/wp-content/uploads/2016/08/Summary-First-Global-Partnership-Steering-Committee-5-6Dec12.pdf.

GPEDC. (2013, October 10–11). *Fourth meeting of the Global Partnership Steering Committee.* http://effectivecooperation.org/wp-content/uploads/2013/11/Summary-GPSteeringCommittee-Washington-Oct2013.pdf.

GPEDC. (2015, January 19–20). *Seventh meeting of the Global Partnership Steering Committee.* http://effectivecooperation.org/wp-content/uploads/2015/03/7th-SC-Meeting-Summary_Final-for-GPEDC-Website-5-March.pdf.

GPEDC. (2018, April 21–22). *Fifteenth meeting of the Global Partnership Steering Committee.* http://effectivecooperation.org/2018/04/15th-steering-committee-meeting-of-the-global-partnership-strategizing-for-2018-and-beyond/.

Grobbelaar, N. (2014). *Rising powers in international development: The state of the debate in South Africa* (IDS Evidence Report 91). https://www.gov.uk/dfid-research-outputs/rising-powers-in-international-development-the-state-of-the-debate-in-south-africa.

IBSA (India, Brazil, South Africa). (2010). *India-Brazil-South Africa dialogue forum: Fourth summit of heads of state/government Brasilia Declaration.* https://mea.gov.in/bilateral-documents.htm?dtl/4017/.

IBSA. (2018, June 4). *IBSA declaration on South-South cooperation.* Pretoria. http://www.dirco.gov.za/docs/2018/ibsa0605.htm.

IBSA Fund (The India, Brazil and South Africa Facility for Poverty and Hunger Alleviation). (2018). *2018 overview of the project portfolio.* https://drive.google.com/file/d/1zv2Z3Zl7raAHkpf0arqsLeN5nR1zYp00/view.

IGD (Institute for Global Dialogue). (2013). *Multilateral development cooperation: What does it mean for South Africa's foreign policy?* Opening address by Dr Sheldon Moulton, acting chief director DIRCO (Proceedings Report). Pretoria: Author.

IGD. (2019). *Appraising the dynamics of South-South cooperation and triangular cooperation: Lessons beyond the BAPA + 40 conference* (Proceedings Report). Pretoria: Author.

International Monetary Fund. (2016, April 16). *International monetary and financial committee: Thirty-third meeting.* Statement by Pravin Jamnadas Gordhan, Minister of Finance, South Africa. https://www.imf.org/External/spring/2016/imfc/statement/eng/zaf.pdf.

Kamau, M., Chasek, P., & O'Connor, D. (2018). *Transforming multilateral diplomacy: The inside story of the Sustainable Development Goals.* London and New York, NY: Routledge.

Kenya to host global aid coordination meeting in 2016. (n.d). *Coastweek.* http://www.coastweek.com/3808-%20Kenya-to-host-global-aid-coordination-meeting.htm.

Klingebiel, S. (2018). Transnational public goods provision: The increasing role of rising powers and the case of South Africa. *Third World Quarterly, 39*(1), 175–188.

Lalbahadur, A., & Rawhani, C. (2017). South Africa's peacebuilding in the DRC: Convergence and dissonance with the liberal model. *South African Journal of International Affairs, 24*(4), 523–545.

Mashabane, D. (2018). South Africa and the United Nations. In A. Adebajo & K. Virk (Eds.), *Foreign policy in post-apartheid South Africa: Security, diplomacy and trade* (pp. 395–410). London and New York, NY: I.B. Tauris.

Masters, L. (2017). Negotiating the North-South divide in the post-2015 development agenda: What role for SA? In S. Zondi & P. Mthembu (Eds.), *From the MDGs to Development Agenda 2030* (pp. 146–165). Pretoria: Africa Institute.

Mayaki, I. (2018). *Africa's critical choices: A call for a pan-African roadmap*. Malakoff: Armand Colin.

Meja, V. (2014). *Making South-South cooperation partnerships work for Africa: A situational analysis and policy recommendations*. http://www.realityofaid.org/wp-content/uploads/2014/12/4.Making-South-South-Cooperation-Partnerships.pdf.

Ministry of Finance Japan. (2018, July 21–22). *Communiqué, G20 finance ministers and central bank governors meeting*. https://www.mof.go.jp/english/international_policy/convention/g20/20180722.htm.

NEPAD (New Partnership for Africa's Development). (2001). *African consensus and position on development effectiveness*. http://www.effectivecooperation.org/wp-content/uploads/2016/03/african-consensus-english.pdf.

NEPAD. (2014). *Africa Action Plan on Development Effectiveness*. https://www.nepad.org/publication/africa-action-plan-development-effectiveness.

Nganje, F. (2017). The Common African Position on the post-2015 development agenda: A Western Trojan horse or catalyst to a new development era in Africa? In S. Zondi & P. Mthembu (Eds.), *From MDGs to Sustainable Development Goals: The travails of international development* (pp. 57–78). Pretoria: Institute for Global Dialogue.

Note from the African representatives to the High-Level Meeting in Mexico, Seoul. (2013, November 18–19). Emerging issues. Unpublished document, author's hard copy.

Permanent Mission of the Republic of Kenya to the United Nations. (2016, September 21). Statement by His Excellency Hon. William Sahoei Ruto, E.G.H. Deputy President of the Republic of Kenya during the General Debate of the 71st Session of the United Nations General Assembly, Wednesday. https://www.un.int/kenya/sites/www.un.int/files/Kenya/kenya_statement_during_the_71st_session_of_the_general_assembly_delivered_by_the_deputy_president_1_0.pdf.

PMG (Parliamentary Monitoring Group). (2019a, October 9). *DIRCO annual report 2018/19 with minister*. https://pmg.org.za/files/191009ARF.ppt.

PMG. (2019b, November 20). *DIRCO African Renaissance and International Cooperation Fund (ARF), 2019/20 quarter 1 and 2 performance information. Presentation to Portfolio Committee*. https://pmg.org.za/files/191120ARF.ppt.

Research and Information Systems for Developing Countries. (n.d.). *Delhi conference on South-South and triangular cooperation*, 24–25 August 2017, New Delhi (Background Note). http://ris.org.in/sites/default/files/concept2425.pdf.

Roberts, C., Armijo, L. E., & Katada, S. N. (2018). *The BRICS and collective financial statecraft*. Oxford: Oxford University Press.

Schoeman, M. (2015). South Africa as an emerging power: From label to "status consistency"? *South African Journal of International Affairs, 22*(4), 429–445. https://doi.org/10.1080/10220461.2015.1119719.

Schroeder, A. (2002). *Rio to Jo'burg and beyond: The World Summit on Sustainable Development.* https://www.africaportal.org/publications/rio-to-joburg-and-beyond-the-world-summit-on-sustainable-development/.

Sidiropoulos, E. (2012). South Africa: Development, international cooperation and soft power. In S. Chaturvedi, T. Fues, & E. Sidiropoulos (Eds.), *Development cooperation and emerging powers: New partners or old patterns?* (pp. 216–242). London: Zed Books.

Sidiropoulos, E. (2015, March). *SAIIA-NeST Africa workshop.* Midrand, South Africa (own notes).

Sidiropoulos, E. (2019). *South Africa's changing role in global development structures: Being in them but not always of them* (DIE Discussion Paper 4/2019). https://www.die-gdi.de/uploads/media/DP_4.2019.pdf.

Sidiropoulos, E., & Hughes, T. (2004). Between democratic governance and sovereignty: The challenge of SA's foreign policy. In S. Sidiropoulos (Ed.), *Apartheid past, renaissance future: South Africa's foreign policy 1994–2004* (pp. 61–84). Johannesburg: South African Institute of International Affairs.

Sidiropoulos, E., Prinsloo, C., Mpungose, L., & Grobbelaar, N. (2018). *BRICS-Africa cooperation: Achievements and opportunities* (Policy Briefing July/2018). Johannesburg: Global Economic Governance.

Zondi, S. (2017). The SA position on the post-2015 development agenda: An agenda for transforming power relations. In S. Zondi & P. Mthembu (Eds.), *From the MDGs to Development Agenda 2030* (pp. 124–145). Pretoria: Africa Institute.

Zuma, J. (2013). Statement of the President of the Republic of South Africa, His Excellency Mr Jacob Zuma, to the General Debate of the 68th Session of the UN General Assembly, UN Headquarters, New York, USA. http://www.dirco.gov.za/docs/speeches/2013/jzum0924.html.

Open Access This chapter is licensed under the terms of the Creative Commons Attribution 4.0 International License (http://creativecommons.org/licenses/by/4.0/), which permits use, sharing, adaptation, distribution and reproduction in any medium or format, as long as you give appropriate credit to the original author(s) and the source, provide a link to the Creative Commons license and indicate if changes were made.

The images or other third party material in this chapter are included in the chapter's Creative Commons license, unless indicated otherwise in a credit line to the material. If material is not included in the chapter's Creative Commons license and your intended use is not permitted by statutory regulation or exceeds the permitted use, you will need to obtain permission directly from the copyright holder.

CHAPTER 20

Middle Powers in International Development Cooperation: Assessing the Roles of South Korea and Turkey

R. Melis Baydag

20.1 INTRODUCTION

Fast-developing economies of the "Global South" have led to power shifts in international politics (Cornelissen 2009). It is believed that these rising, emerging, or latecomer countries play a pivotal role in future global governance (Cooper 2016; Okano-Heijmans 2012). They challenge "the Western-dominated patterns of international politics" (Schirm 2019, p. 2), as well as contribute to it (Grimm et al. 2009; Mawdsley 2012).

This chapter analyses the cases of South Korea (hereafter referred to as Korea) and Turkey as emerging powers in the field of development cooperation under the theoretical framework of Middle Power Theory (MPT). In international relations literature, they are considered as "emerging middle powers" (Bradford 2015; Cooper 2015b; Engin and Baba 2015; Jordaan 2003; Öniş and Kutlay 2017), which are members of the middle-power

---

R. Melis Baydag is currently a doctoral research associate and lecturer at the Chair of International Politics at Ruhr-University Bochum, Germany, melis.baydag@rub.de. This article benefits from the findings of Ms Baydag's master's thesis, titled *The Role of Foreign Aid in Middle Power Diplomacy: Comparative Analysis of South Korea and Turkey* (Baydag 2017) and defended on 16 June 2017.

R. M. Baydag (✉)
Ruhr-University Bochum, Bochum, Germany
e-mail: melis.baydag@rub.de

© The Author(s) 2021
S. Chaturvedi et al. (eds.), *The Palgrave Handbook of Development Cooperation for Achieving the 2030 Agenda*,
https://doi.org/10.1007/978-3-030-57938-8_20

grouping MIKTA (Mexico, Indonesia, Korea, Turkey, Australia), established in 2013 at the margins of the United Nations (UN) General Assembly. MIKTA members claim to be like-minded peers as democracies and free market economies. Moreover, they show cooperative behaviour through multipolar, mediation oriented foreign policy activism (Manicom and Reeves 2014, p. 30).

Korea and Turkey make use of their middle-power identity with the aim of increasing their presence around the globe, where development cooperation is used as an important foreign policy tool (Baydag 2017). Both countries locate their foreign aid approaches between those of traditional donors, that is, the Development Assistance Committee (DAC) of the Organisation for Economic Co-operation and Development (OECD), which is mainly composed of advanced Western economies,[1] and emerging donors, that is, developing countries of the Global South engaging with South-South Cooperation (SSC) based on a "horizontal cooperative relationship"[2] (Klingebiel 2014, p. 19; Woods 2008). Nevertheless, whereas Korea positions itself more in line with the DAC, Turkey adopts a Southern narrative.[3]

The comparative study of Korea and Turkey reveals their divergent approaches to foreign aid discourse,[4] which creates significant implications for global aid governance. Considering that effective international development cooperation based on a common framework depends on enhancing the dialogue between the DAC and the Southern providers (Fues et al. 2012, p. 144; Mawdsley 2012, p. 218), it is also crucial for Southern providers to reach common ground on their shared principles, which at the same time should lead towards efforts to fulfil the post-2015 agenda of the Sustainable Development Goals (Bracho 2018). As middle powers, Korea and Turkey have the capacity to contribute to the rapprochement between the traditional and the emerging donors as well as among the Southern providers. However, collaboration between the peers is seemingly being contested as a result of their divergent approaches to foreign aid, which stem from differing strategic and ideational paths in aid provision—the main focus of this chapter.

20.2 Locating Korea and Turkey in International Development Cooperation

Broadly speaking, the increasing weight of emerging powers in international politics is primarily the result of the rise of the BRICS (Brazil, Russia, India, China, and South Africa), which wish to change the distribution of power in the system by actively participating in different policy fields of global governance (Ferguson 2015; Hurrell and Sengupta 2012). Before designating Korea and Turkey in international development as donors, first it is necessary to briefly mention the aspects of their emerging power characteristics.

Korea and Turkey are mid-sized, emerging countries in terms of economy, population, and resources (Çağaptay 2013; Chin and Quadir 2013; Schirm 2019). In this respect, clustered among the second tiers, they are not expected to reach the BRICS level in terms of global ranking and are instead expected to remain regional players (Cooper 2015b). Nevertheless, Korea and Turkey combine their growing economic power with political power (Chin and Quadir 2013; Manning 2006; Woods 2008), that is, political power in the sense of active participation in global decision-making processes (Florini 2011; Klingebiel 2016, 2017). Additionally, they are not challengers of the liberal developed West[5] and remain integrated into the system of Western alliances (Hurrell 2006). Last but not least, they are expected to play an essential role in sharing the burden of global challenges such as financial crises, climate change, and development (Flemes and Habib 2009; Grimm et al. 2009).

The mainstream development cooperation agenda is largely dominated by Western practices and includes bilateral agencies, multilateral organisations, and even non-governmental organisations (Mawdsley 2012, p. 2). The term "mainstream" therefore refers to the foreign aid behaviours of the traditional donors, summarised as follows (Fues et al. 2012): traditional donors tend to emphasise altruistic motives in aid-giving by "concealing" their self-interest, unlike Southern providers, who frame their aid mostly in terms of mutual benefit based on solidarity and economic progress, resulting in a "win-win" situation (Fues et al. 2012, p. 139). In addition, traditional donors set political conditionality in their aid provision, especially regarding governance criteria such as the protection of human rights or the rule of law, which, in the past, has led to external interference in the political affairs of low-income countries. Although this started changing when many Western providers became more careful about not imposing culturally biased values, they still do not insist on the primacy of national sovereignty in all aspects of international relations as much as the Southern providers do. In this respect, the principle of non-interference, together with a pragmatic interest-based approach, is more visible in Southern foreign aid behaviour (Fues et al. 2012, p. 140).

On the one hand, Korea's and Turkey's aid discourses converge with those of traditional donors as a result of them being OECD members (i.e. Korea being a DAC member and Turkey regularly reporting to the Committee). In other words, they have traditionally been part of the mainstream aid agenda and do not significantly diverge from the Committee (Cihangir-Tetik and Müftüler-Baç 2018; Hausmann 2014; Stallings and Kim 2017).

On the other hand, their official discourses put emphasis on providing better approaches to development cooperation with insights from SSC. This has gained prominence among Southern providers as an alternative to traditional donor-recipient relations, which are based on "one-way giving", in order to eliminate the differentiation between partners (Davis and Taylor 2015, p. 154; Mawdsley 2012). The stress on eliminating differentiation in particular explains well how the official foreign aid discourses of both Korea and Turkey converge with those of the emerging donors of the South.

To illustrate, Korea focusses on "learning from experience" in its official motto and positions it as a model that is based on its own experience of receiving and using aid for poverty eradication—and most importantly in becoming a DAC donor as a result of its development success (Stallings and Kim 2017). Turkey, on the other hand, after a brief period of rapprochement with the OECD-DAC, has adopted a foreign aid discourse detached from the Committee, which envisages a global role for Turkey through its engagement with Southern partners, wherein Turkey will ideationally rebuild the historical and cultural ties of the Ottoman Empire (Donelli and Levaggi 2016).

Despite convergences with both camps, the foreign aid aspirations of Korea and Turkey can be further elaborated by referring to their mindset for following certain strategies in international development cooperation. In this respect, neither donor can be simply categorised as an emerging or traditional donor. The next section emphasises ideational aspects of their proactive role in employing the presumptions of the MPT as a significant cornerstone in positioning both countries within the international development cooperation system.

20.3 Middle-Power Theories

Middle powers are not as influential or powerful as great powers, but they still have a considerable amount of influence in promoting cohesion and stability in the international system (Chapnick 1999; Glazebrook 1947; Jordaan 2003). In other words, they are not powerful enough to act alone, but they are effective in collective action with either like-minded peers that have similar capacities or less powerful ones (Da Silva et al. 2016). They are also effective when acting through international organisations (Flemes and Habib 2009).

At first, the term "middle" evokes a positional understanding based on a hierarchy of states and material capabilities, for example size, population, or resources. Some scholars also emphasise their functional importance, whereby they either follow a great power or resort to niche diplomacy in international affairs (Chapnick 1999). Both approaches, however, do not reflect the assumptions of MPT in ideational terms. Of the different definitions, therefore, this chapter relies on the behavioural approach to MPT, with the following elements serving as the underlying determinants.

First, middle powers take positions in international disputes as mediators and pursue diplomacy by relying on the notion of "good international citizenship" (Cooper et al. 1993). Second, the state's will to—and capacity for—dedicating itself to becoming a middle power in accordance with good international citizenship is significant (Bélanger and Mace 1997; Hynek 2004). Third, middle powers are considered to be driven by "a role conception resting on the notion of a distinctive mode of statecraft" (Hynek 2004, p. 36).

Constructivist theory has strong foundations in behavioural approaches. It is assumed that the identity of a state—constructed by the country itself—determines its position in international politics. In that vein, non-material structures define actors' identities and form their interests (Finnemore and Sikkink 2001) in "how they think they should act, what perceived limitations on their actions are and what strategies they can imagine" (Reus-Smit 2005, p. 197). To that effect, middle-power identity is strategically constructed to justify actions and interests. Accordingly, Cooper (2015a) argues that using a flexible form of behaviour and strengthening the international system through diplomatic means are distinguishing characteristics of middle powers (Cooper 2015a, p. 35). They pursue multilateral solutions to global issues by affecting international outcomes (Cooper et al. 1993, p. 19; O'Neil 2015, p. 75) and being political representatives of "the social, environmental and human interests of humanity" (Bradford 2015, p. 9).

20.4 Like-Minded Peers or Counterparts?

Based on the theoretical framework of this chapter, the increasing influence of Korea and Turkey can be linked to their adopted middle-power identities. Hence, they are not simply second-tier emerging donors of growing political and economic importance. Their rise, in John's (2014) words, can also be considered as "a new discourse of [international relations] from the middle-power perspective as an alternative to the dominant narrative of great powers" (John 2014, p. 332).

Korea and Turkey claim to provide a better perspective based on their long history as aid recipients. Korea and Turkey also differ from some of the significant emerging donors, such as China and Russia, since they do not radically challenge the established system and have long been bound by Western institutions and practices (Hausmann 2014; Hausmann and Lundsgaarde 2015; Kim et al. 2013). Notwithstanding the above, their declarations of being like-minded peers in international cooperation do not seem to have led to converging perspectives on foreign aid.

Starting from this point, the chapter proceeds as follows. First, the official middle-power discourses of Korea and Turkey are introduced, and the role of foreign aid as a foreign policy tool is highlighted. Second, the foreign aid discourses of Korea and Turkey are discussed. Third, the section concludes with comparative results in relation to the OECD-DAC. In this respect, the OECD-DAC constitutes the main reference point for categorising the two donors for the purpose of comparing their discourses—not only to each other, but also to their traditional counterparts.

20.4.1 Global Visibility Through Middle-Power Strategies

Korea and Turkey take part in multilateral platforms that promote international commitments. Korea hosted the Fourth High Level Forum on Aid Effectiveness in 2011 in Busan. Following that, it has been actively engaging with the annual Busan Global Partnership for Effective Development Co-operation (GPEDC) since 2014 for encouraging and monitoring the country-level implementation of the Busan principles. Despite being a participant, Turkey has not been an active stakeholder in the GPEDC. In fact, Turkey's interests lay in humanitarianism from a least-developed country (LDC) perspective. Turkey hosted the Fourth UN Conference on the Least Developed Countries in 2011, promoting people-centred sustainable development (United Nations 2011). Turkey was also the first to host a UN humanitarian summit in 2016, urging for the delivery of foreign aid to end need (World Humanitarian Summit 2016).

More specifically, Korea launched the New Asian Initiative in 2009 under the Lee Myung-bak government, which attributed a leadership role to Korea as the leading voice of Asian countries in international platforms (O'Neil 2015, p. 84). Korea's membership in the OECD-DAC in 2010 has further reinforced its global position as the first country that went from being an LDC to a DAC donor (O'Neil 2015, p. 85). It was followed by the launch of the Global Korea initiative in 2012, in which official development assistance (ODA) is used as one of the policy instruments (Ko 2012, p. 296). Then-Vice Minister of Foreign Affairs and Trade, Sung-han Kim (2013), emphasised Korea's role as a middle power by stating that "[Middle powers] can lead a meaningful change in the world. They do so not by power, but through creative ideas, a smart and flexible strategy, and moral leadership" (Kim 2013).

In the case of Turkey, the current foreign minister, Mevlüt Çavuşoğlu, characterises Turkish foreign policy as "enterprising and humanitarian" (Republic of Turkey Ministry of Foreign Affairs [MFA Turkey] n.d.-a). The readings of former Prime Minister Ahmet Davutoğlu (2012) describe Turkey as a "central country with multiple regional identities" and presume that Turkey's identity will be transformed into a global power the more that it actively engages with global politics (Davutoğlu 2012, p. 83). Nevertheless, such an argument would be an unrealistic interpretation of Turkey's power because "there is no room in the existing international order for a medium-sized regional power to upgrade itself into a regional sub-superpower status" (Türkeş 2016, p. 211).

Although Turkey does not seem to be adopting a middle-power identity, the official discourse of the Turkish government comports with the theory's main assumptions. In fact, a middle power does not always have to behave in the way that the theory suggests (Gilley and O'Neil 2014). This chapter assumes Turkey to be a middle power because of its membership in MIKTA and as a result of the recent increase in its assertive of foreign policy matters (Cooper 2015b; Öniş 2011; Öniş and Kutlay 2017; Parlar Dal 2014). In official discourse, Turkey is identified as a humanitarian power that does not remain "indifferent to the developments in the world, assumes a reconciliatory, constructive and intermediary role in order to reach amicable solutions for the global problems" (Turkish Cooperation and Coordination Agency 2014, p. 2). Its middle-power role is based on an active regional and global involvement (Baba 2018; Meral and Paris 2010).

20.4.2 Foreign Aid Narratives

Generally speaking, Korea and Turkey emphasise their shared experiences with the developing world, thus differentiating their approaches to foreign aid from Western aid providers (Bilgic and Nascimento 2014, p. 2; Chun et al. 2010, p. 798). As mentioned in the joint statement of the Fourth MIKTA Foreign Ministers' Meeting, "MIKTA, as a consultative forum and innovative partnership, could play a bridging role between advanced countries and developing countries on key global issues" (MFA Turkey 2014).

Individual cases show that Korea's successful development story as a recipient is the primary aspect that the government highlights. Accordingly, Korea claims to base its foreign aid policy on "learning from experience" (Howe 2015; Stallings and Kim 2017). Korea's own history of economic development is the main source of its strength (Bradford 2015, p. 10), and Korea sees its OECD-DAC membership as a benchmark for measuring its level of achievement, since it gives Korea the chance to be recognised as a developed country (Chun et al. 2010).

In contrast to Korea, Turkey defines its development cooperation along the lines of the idealistic and cultural terms established through history and based on a humanitarian-sensitive generosity in aid-giving, particularly in neighbouring regions (Kardaş 2013; Kulaklıkaya and Nurdun 2010). The famine in Somalia in 2011 was the turning point for Turkey's rise as a humanitarian power that combined pure humanitarianism with "business ties, peace-building initiatives, education, infrastructure and development aid, and even military aid" and served as a model for its engagements with Africa (Gilley 2015, p. 39). The emphasis on solidarity and brotherhood in Somalia also signified its turn to the Global South (Donelli and Levaggi 2018; Stearns and Sucuoglu 2017).

The main divergence in the foreign aid discourses of the donors stems from how they position themselves as aid providers. Korea's attempt to distinguish itself as a DAC donor is basically done to gain more global reach and prestige. Korea realises its middle-power diplomacy by relying on its own development experience, and by emphasising the global characteristic of its development approach. Turkey focuses on cultural (as well as linguistic and religious) aspects, combined with a humanitarian stance. Turkey uses its geographical advantage and does not necessarily speak about a specific global development model. In this sense, its foreign aid discourse tends to be more region- and/or culture-specific.

20.4.3 Korea and Turkey in Relation to the OECD-DAC

The cases of Korea and Turkey offer both insider and outsider perspectives with regard to relations with the OECD-DAC. Korea and Turkey are insiders due to them being a DAC member and a DAC observer, respectively. When we look at it from the angle that both countries are emerging donors, how they seek to bring new perspectives to the provisioning of foreign aid becomes a relevant reference point. It is therefore significant to point out where Korea and Turkey—as both OECD members and Southern providers—stand in this picture.

20.4.4 Korea

The Korean foreign ministry highlights that Korea is a "recipient-turned-donor" country (Republic of Korea Ministry of Foreign Affairs n.d.). The Korean government stresses Korea's distinctive development achievement that started after the Korean War in the 1950s, when the only source of economic growth was based on foreign aid (Kim 2011). Korea's past experience as a recipient and its donor status achievement within the DAC are significant aspects. As Mawdsley suggested, "for South Korea, membership of the DAC represents another marker of international status" (Mawdsley 2012, p. 177). For some scholars, Koreans are proud of their achievement and ambitious to align their development programmes with the experiences of their own development (Chun et al. 2010). It is used as a way to distinguish Korea from traditional Western donors.

Korean aid can also be considered as being in a transition period. According to a scholar working on Korean development aid, some aspects of Korea's development cooperation reflect SSC "in spirit or in practice", while at the same time Korea is working with the DAC and "speaks the same language with it" (personal communication, 12 October 2016). In other words, although some aspects of Korea's donor behaviour still reflect an Asian model that was formerly represented by Japan (e.g. mixing aid and trade), Korea remains within the boundaries of the accepted norms and guidelines of the DAC (e.g. untying aid or increasing multilateral aid) (Stallings and Kim 2017, p. 97). Most importantly, governmental discourse does not refrain from associating Korean aid with Western aid.

20.4.5 Turkey

Turkey shares a long history of alliances and partnerships with the Western powers, which led its foreign aid policy to converge with Western practices (Donelli and Levaggi 2018; Mawdsley 2012). Turkey does not radically challenge the DAC principles. For instance, it is a participant of OECD-led platforms such as the GPEDC. However, the foreign policy shift since the early 2000s has led to an increasing Southern dimension in its foreign aid policy. Nowadays, Turkey officially considers itself to be one of the new aid providers actively engaging in SSC (MFA Turkey n.d.-b). As an official in the Turkish Cooperation and Coordination Agency assessed, joining the DAC does not seem to be one of its priorities in the near future (personal communication, 18 January 2017).

Table 20.1 Comparing Korea (KR) and Turkey (TR)

Middle-power approach				International	Development cooperation		
	Power	Identity	Membership	GDP ranking (current $) 2017[a]	Gross ODA ($, millions) 2017[b]	Approach	Behaviour
KR	Soft power	Good global citizen; bridge country	OECD G20 MIKTA GPEDC	12th	2201.35	Learning from development experience; global	Close to traditional donors
TR	Soft power	Good global citizen; bridge country	OECD G20 MIKTA GPEDC	17th	8120.92	Humanitarian; region-/culture-specific	Close to Southern donors

Sources [a]World Bank (2017); [b]See other years on OECD.Stat (Organisation for Economic Co-operation and Development 2017)

The interplay between external factors (e.g. rise of non-Western powers, 2008 financial crisis, and the aftermaths of the Arab uprising) and internal factors (the ideological orientation of the ruling party based on Islamic conservatism) has strengthened Turkey's Southern narratives (Donelli and Levaggi 2018, p. 95). In addition, the ruling party's status-seeking foreign policy strategy of "presenting itself as a regional order-builder to the surrounding regions" has further contributed to it (Donelli and Levaggi 2018, p. 58). Such a discourse seems to have alienated Turkey from a Western approach in development cooperation (Table 20.1).

20.5 Policy Implications

This chapter elaborates on the foreign aid behaviours of Korea and Turkey as emerging middle powers, broadly in international relations and specifically in development cooperation. Korea and Turkey are contributors to the new context in which development cooperation is taking place. They play active middle-power roles and are asserting their power to assume a moral stance as well as global responsibility. Despite claiming to be like-minded peers, they leave the issue of collaboration in international development cooperation contested by adopting an official discourse based on divergent narratives on development aid. In this regard, their role as significant aid providers should be studied carefully for further attempts at collaboration at the global level.

Today, a comprehensive partnership in international development is needed to address the visibly urgent global challenges. In the same vein, international development is in a transition period, whereby traditional donors are trying to maintain the status quo, and the emerging ones are challenging the established system. Middle powers play a role by either stabilising the system or decreasing the friction between clashing donor strategies. In this picture, Korea and Turkey could possibly be important binding stakeholders that contribute to the convergence between practices and values of different aid providers in the field. For that reason, their claim of being a bridge between the developed and the developing worlds should not be neglected by policy-makers and practitioners, despite the growing divergence in their approaches.

By the same token, we also see that the differing discursive stances of similar donors, such as Korea and Turkey, create a messier picture rather than positively contributing to the transformation of development cooperation as a policy area. In other words, global partners find it difficult to reach a global consensus in the presence of divergent approaches. Consequently, this contribution is significant in unveiling the core differences between seemingly similar aid providers, and therefore, it should be taken as a reminder of the challenges to global efforts to achieve international collaboration. Divergent foreign aid motivations of similar donors mentioned in this chapter might help us to formulate new ways of handling global aid governance, otherwise pledges for furthering cooperation remain mere lip service.

20.6 Further Research

Further studies on Korea and Turkey should focus on whether their development cooperation practices (actual aid flows) are compatible with their foreign aid discourses, because discourse does not always accurately reflect reality. More generally, a domestic politics perspective should not be neglected in studying foreign aid policy, as its political economy requires examining the domestic economic context in which aid decisions are made (Lundsgaarde 2013). It would be worth paying attention to the extent to which issue-specific controversies on the global level result from the heterogeneity of governmental preferences at the domestic level (Schirm 2013). This would also contribute to the discussions on the divergent/convergent approaches among different donors in global aid governance. Last but not least, the middle-power concept should be further clarified, since a wide range of states are now considered to be middle powers but are too diverse to identify a common pattern of middle-power behaviour (Jordaan 2017).

Notes

1. Among traditional DACdonors, Japan is the only Asian country. Korea became a DAC donor in 2010 and is therefore not yet considered a traditional donor.
2. The United Nations Office for South-South Cooperation defines SSC as "sharing knowledge, skills, expertise and resources to meet development goals

through concerted efforts" (United Nations Office for South-South Cooperation n.d.).
3. The term "narrative" is understood as "a representation of a particular situation or process in such a way as to reflect or conform to an overarching set of aims or values". The definition was retrieved from https://en.oxforddictionaries.com/definition/narrative.
4. The term "discourse" is understood as "written or spoken communication or debate". The definition was retrieved from https://en.oxforddictionaries.com/definition/discourse.
5. The majority of the BRICS countries are historically challengers of the liberal developed West, exemplified, among other things, by the *Revolutionism* of the Soviet Union and China, the *hard-revisionist Third Worldism* in post-1948 India, and the *soft-revisionist Third Worldism* of Brazil in the early 1970s and late 1980s (Hurrell 2006, p. 3). Most of the second tiers, on the contrary, have been part of an alliance led by a greater power. For instance, countries allied with the United States, such as Korea and Turkey (Wright 2015), have long benefited from its bilateral security and economic relations (Ikenberry 2004).

References

Baba, G. (2018). Turkey's multistakeholder diplomacy: From a middle power angle. In E. Parlar Dal (Ed.), *Middle powers in global governance: The rise of Turkey* (pp. 59–81). Cham: Palgrave Macmillan.

Baydag, R. M. (2017). *The role of foreign aid in middle power diplomacy: Comparative analysis of South Korea and Turkey*. Master's thesis, Middle East Technical University, Ankara, Turkey.

Bélanger, L., & Mace, G. (1997). Middle powers and regionalism in the Americas: The cases of Argentina and Mexico. In A. F. Cooper (Ed.), *Niche diplomacy: Middle powers after the Cold War* (pp. 164–183). New York, NY: St. Martin's Press.

Bilgic, A., & Nascimento, D. (2014, September). *Turkey's new focus on Africa: Causes and challenges* (Policy Brief). Oslo: Norwegian Peacebuilding Resource Centre.

Bracho, G. (2018). Towards a common definition of South-South cooperation: Bringing together the spirit of Bandung and the spirit of Buenos Aires. *Development Cooperation Review, 1*(6), 9–13.

Bradford, C. I. (2015). South Korea as a middle power in global governance: "Punching above its weight" based on national assets and dynamic trajectory. In S. A. Snyder (Ed.), *Middle-power Korea* (pp. 8–20). New York, NY: Council on Foreign Relations Press.

Çağaptay, S. (2013). Defining Turkish power: Turkey as a rising power embedded in the Western international system. *Turkish Studies, 14*(4), 797–811.

Chapnick, A. (1999). The middle power. *Canadian Foreign Policy Journal, 7*(2), 73–82.

Chin, G., & Quadir, F. (2013). Introduction: Rising states, rising donors and the global aid regime. *Cambridge Review of International Affairs, 25*(4), 493–506.

Chun, H.-M., Munyi, E. N., & Lee, H. (2010). South Korea as an emerging donor: Challenges and changes on its entering OECD/DAC. *Journal of International Development, 22*(6), 788–802.

Cihangir-Tetik, D., & Müftüler-Baç, M. (2018). Turkey's compliance with the European Union's development policy: A pattern of external differentiated integration? *Journal of European Integration, 40*(7), 939–959.

Cooper, A. F. (2015a). G20 middle powers and initiatives on development. In J. Mo (Ed.), *MIKTA, middle powers, and new dynamics of global governance* (pp. 32–46). New York, NY: Palgrave Macmillan.

Cooper, A. F. (2015b). MIKTA and the global projection of middle powers: Toward a summit of their own? *Global Summitry, 1*(1), 95–114.

Cooper, A. F. (2016). Testing middle power's collective action in a world of diffuse power. *International Journal, 71*(4), 529–544.

Cooper, A. F., Higgott, R. A., & Nossal, K. R. (1993). *Relocating middle powers: Australia and Canada in a changing world order*. Vancouver: UBC Press.

Cornelissen, S. (2009). Awkward embraces: Emerging and established powers and the shifting fortunes of Africa's international relations in the twenty-first century. *Politikon, 36*(1), 5–26.

Da Silva, A. L. R., Spohr, A. P., & da Silveira, I. L. (2016). From Bandung to Brasilia: IBSA and the political lineage of South-South cooperation. *South African Journal of International Affairs, 23*(2), 167–184.

Davis, R., & Taylor, I. (2015). "Africa rising" and the rising powers. In J. Gaskarth (Ed.), *Rising powers, global governance and global ethics* (pp. 152–172). New York, NY: Routledge.

Davutoğlu, A. (2012). *Stratejik derinlik: Türkiye'nin uluslararası konumu*. İstanbul: Küre Yayınları.

Donelli, F., & Levaggi, A. G. (2016). Becoming global actor: The Turkish agenda for the Global South. *Rising Powers Quarterly, 1*(2), 93–115.

Donelli, F., & Levaggi, A. G. (2018). From Mogadishu to Buenos Aires: The Global South in the Turkish foreign policy in the late JDP period (2011–2017). In E. Parlar Dal (Ed.), *Middle powers in global governance: The rise of Turkey* (pp. 53–76). Cham: Palgrave Macmillan.

Engin, B., & Baba, G. (2015). MIKTA: A functional product of new middle powerism. *Uluslararası Hukuk ve Politika, 11*(42), 1–40.

Ferguson, Y. H. (2015). Rising powers and global governance. In J. Gaskarth (Ed.), *Rising powers, global governance and global ethics* (pp. 21–40). New York, NY: Routledge.

Finnemore, M., & Sikkink, K. (2001). The constructivist research program in international relations and comparative politics. *Annual Review Political Science, 4*, 391–416.

Flemes, D., & Habib, A. (2009). Introduction: Regional powers in contest and engagement: Making sense of international relations in a globalised world. *South African Journal of International Affairs, 16*(2), 137–142.

Florini, A. (2011). Rising Asian powers and changing global governance. *International Studies Review, 13*(1), 24–33.

Fues, T., Chaturvedi, S., & Sidiropoulos, E. (2012). Towards a global consensus on development. In S. Chaturvedi, T. Fues, & E. Sidiropoulos (Eds.), *Development cooperation and emerging powers: New partners or old patterns?* (pp. 138–148). London: Zed Books.

Gilley, B. (2015). Turkey, middle power, and the new humanitarianism. *Perceptions, 20*(1), 37–58.

Gilley, B., & O'Neil, A. (2014). China's rise through the prism of middle powers. In B. Gilley & A. O'Neil (Eds.), *Middle powers and the rise of China* (pp. 1–22). Washington, DC: Georgetown University Press.

Glazebrook, G. D. (1947). The middle powers in the United Nations. *International Organisation, 1*(2), 307–315.

Grimm, S., Humphrey, J., Lundsgaarde, E., & De Sousa, S.-L. J. (2009). *European development cooperation to 2020: Challenges by new actors in international development* (Working Paper No. 4). Bonn: European Association of Development Research and Training Institutes.

Hausmann, J. (2014). *Turkey as a donor country and potential partner in triangular cooperation* (Discussion Paper No. 14). Bonn: German Development Institute/Deutsches Institut für Entwicklungspolitik (DIE).

Hausmann, J., & Lundsgaarde, E. (2015). *Turkey's role in development cooperation* (Working Paper). Bonn: United Nations University Centre for Policy Research.

Howe, B. (2015). Development effectiveness: Charting South Korea's role and contribution. In S. A. Snyder (Ed.), *Middle-power Korea* (pp. 21–43). New York, NY: Council on Foreign Relations Press.

Hurrell, A. (2006). Hegemony, liberalism and global order: What space for would-be great powers? *International Affairs, 82*(1), 1–19.

Hurrell, A., & Sengupta, S. (2012). Emerging powers, North-South relations and global climate politics. *International Affairs, 88*(3), 463–484.

Hynek, N. (2004). Canada as middle power: Conceptual limits and promises. *The Central European Journal of Canadian Studies, 4*(1), 33–43.

Ikenberry, G. J. (2004). Liberalism and empire: Logics of order in the American unipolar age. *Review of International Studies, 30*(4), 609–630.

John, J. V. (2014). Becoming and being a middle power: Exploring a new dimension of South Korea's foreign policy. *China Report, 50*(4), 325–341.

Jordaan, E. (2003). The concept of a middle power in international relations: Distinguishing between emerging and traditional middle powers. *Politikon, 30*(1), 165–181.

Jordaan, E. (2017). The emerging middle power concept: Time to say goodbye? *South African Journal of International Affairs, 24*(3), 395–412.

Kardaş, Ş. (2013). Turkey: A regional power facing a changing international system. *Turkish Studies, 14*(4), 637–660.

Kim, J. (2011). Foreign aid and economic development: The success story of South Korea. *Pacific Focus, 26*(2), 260–286.

Kim, S. (2013). *Global governance and middle powers: South Korea's role in the G20*. http://www.cfr.org/south-korea/global-governance-middle-powers-south-koreas-role-g20/p30062.

Kim, E. M., Kim, P. H., & Kim, J. (2013). From development to development cooperation: Foreign aid, country ownership, and the developmental state in South Korea. *The Pacific Review, 26*(3), 313–336.

Klingebiel, S. (2014). *Development cooperation: Challenges of the new aid architecture*. Basingstoke: Palgrave Macmillan, UK.

Klingebiel, S. (2016). Global problem-solving approaches: The crucial role of China and the group of rising powers. *Rising Powers Quarterly, 1*(1), 33–41.

Klingebiel, S. (2017). *Rising powers and the provision of transitional public goods: Conceptual considerations and features of South Africa as a case study* (Discussion Paper No. 3). Bonn: German Development Institute/Deutsches Institut für Entwicklungspolitik (DIE).

Ko, S. (2012). Korea's middle power activism and peacekeeping operations. *Asia Europe Journal, 10,* 287–299. https://doi.org/10.1007/s10308-012-033.

Kulaklıkaya, M., & Nurdun, R. (2010). Turkey as a new player in development cooperation. *Insight Turkey, 12*(4), 131–145.

Lundsgaarde, E. (2013). *The domestic politics of foreign aid.* New York, NY: Routledge.

Manicom, J., & Reeves, J. (2014). Locating middle powers in international relations theory and power transitions. In B. Gilley & A. O'Neil (Eds.), *Middle powers and the rise of China* (pp. 23–44). Washington, DC: Georgetown University Press.

Manning, R. (2006). Will "emerging donors" change the face of international co-operation? *Development Policy Review, 24*(4), 371–385.

Mawdsley, E. (2012). *From recipients to donors: Emerging powers and the changing development landscape.* London: Zed Books.

Meral, Z., & Paris, J. (2010). Decoding Turkish foreign policy hyperactivity. *The Washington Quarterly, 33*(4), 75–86.

MFA Turkey (Republic of Turkey Ministry of Foreign Affairs). (n.d.-a). *Turkey's enterprising and humanitarian foreign policy.* http://www.mfa.gov.tr/synopsis-of-the-turkish-foreign-policy.en.mfa.

MFA Turkey. (n.d.-b). *Turkey's development cooperation: General characteristics and the least developed countries (LDC) aspect.* http://www.mfa.gov.tr/turkey_s-development-cooperation.en.mfa.

MFA Turkey. (2014). *Joint statement of the 4th MIKTA foreign ministers' meeting, 15 November 2014.* http://www.mfa.gov.tr/joint-statement-of-the-4th-mikta-foreign-ministers_-meeting_-15-november-2014.en.mfa.

Okano-Heijmans, M. (2012). Power shift: Economic realism and economic diplomacy on the rise. In E. Fels, J.-F. Kremer, & K. Kronenberg (Eds.), *Power in the 21st century: International security and international political economy in a changing world* (pp. 269–286). Berlin and Heidelberg: Springer.

O'Neil, A. (2015). South Korea as a middle power: Global ambitions and looming challenges. In S. A. Snyder (Ed.), *Middle-power Korea* (pp. 75–89). New York, NY: Council on Foreign Relations Press.

Öniş, Z. (2011). Multiple faces of the "new" Turkish foreign policy: Underlying dynamics and a critique. *Insight Turkey, 13*(1), 47–65.

Öniş, Z., & Kutlay, M. (2017). The dynamics of emerging middle-power influence in regional and global governance: The paradoxical case of Turkey. *Australian Journal of International Affairs, 71*(2), 164–183.

Organisation for Economic Co-operation and Development. (2017). Total flows by donors (ODA+OOF+Private) [DAC1]. https://stats.oecd.org/.

Parlar Dal, E. (2014). On Turkey's trail as a "rising middle power" in the network of global governance: Preferences, capabilities, and strategies. *Perceptions, 19*(4), 107–136.

Republic of Korea Ministry of Foreign Affairs. (n.d.). *Korea's development: History of its transformation.* http://www.mofa.go.kr/ENG/policy/oda/Overview/index.jsp?menu=m_20_110_30.

Reus-Smit, C. (2005). Constructivism. In S. Burchill & A. Linklater (Eds.), *Theories of international relations* (3rd ed., pp. 189–212). New York, NY: Palgrave Macmillan.

Schirm, S. A. (2013). Global politics are domestic politics: A societal approach to divergence in the G20. *Review of International Studies, 39*(3), 685–706.

Schirm, S. A. (2019). In pursuit of self-determination and redistribution: Emerging powers and Western anti-establishment voters in international politics. *Global Affairs, 5*(2), 115–130.

Stallings, B., & Kim, E. M. (2017). *Promoting development: The political economy of East Asian foreign aid*. London: Palgrave Macmillan.

Stearns, J., & Sucuoglu, G. (2017). *South–South cooperation and peacebuilding: Turkey's involvement in Somalia* (Policy Insights No. 43). Johannesburg: The South African Institute of International Affairs.

Turkish Cooperation and Coordination Agency. (2014). *Turkish development assistance: From Turkey to the world*. http://www.tika.gov.tr/upload/2016/INGILIZCESITEESERLER/KALKINMARAPORLARI/DAReport2014.pdf.

Türkeş, M. (2016). Decomposing neo-Ottoman hegemony. *Journal of Balkan and Near Eastern Studies, 18*(3), 191–216.

United Nations. (2011). *Istanbul declaration*. http://www.un.org/wcm/webdav/site/ldc/shared/documents/SummaryofoutcomedocumentsofPCEs.pdf.

United Nations Office for South-South Cooperation. (n.d.). *What is South-South cooperation?* http://ssc.undp.org/content/ssc/about/what_is_ssc.html.

Woods, N. (2008). Whose aid? Whose influence? China, emerging donors and the silent revolution in development assistance. *International Affairs, 84*(6), 1205–1221.

World Bank. (2017). *World development indicators*. https://data.worldbank.org/indicator/NY.GDP.MKTP.CD.

World Humanitarian Summit. (2016). *Changing people's lives: From delivering aid to ending need*. https://consultations.worldhumanitariansummit.org/bitcache/1e8a030537b584bb62c7d75f71062383e24ff542?vid=575820&disposition=inline&op=view.

Wright, T. (2015). Middle powers and the middle pivot. In J. Mo (Ed.), *MIKTA, middle powers, and new dynamics of global governance* (pp. 13–31). New York, NY: Palgrave Macmillan.

Open Access This chapter is licensed under the terms of the Creative Commons Attribution 4.0 International License (http://creativecommons.org/licenses/by/4.0/), which permits use, sharing, adaptation, distribution and reproduction in any medium or format, as long as you give appropriate credit to the original author(s) and the source, provide a link to the Creative Commons license and indicate if changes were made.

The images or other third party material in this chapter are included in the chapter's Creative Commons license, unless indicated otherwise in a credit line to the material. If material is not included in the chapter's Creative Commons license and your intended use is not permitted by statutory regulation or exceeds the permitted use, you will need to obtain permission directly from the copyright holder.

PART V

Aligning National Priorities with Development Cooperation/SDGs

CHAPTER 21

The SDGs and the Empowerment of Bangladeshi Women

Naomi Hossain

21.1 Introduction

Changes in the lives of Bangladeshi women and girls have been held up as evidence that aid, political commitment, and partnerships with civil society can transform gender relations and empower women in the development process. The evidence of this transformation is visible. Bangladeshi women occupy a broader range of roles in their society—as factory workers, teachers and students, entrepreneurs, and explorers that have conquered Mount Everest, officials, prime ministers, models, journalists, protestors, international peacekeepers, migrant workers, police officers, as well as mothers, daughters, and wives—than could have been imagined at the country's birth, a mere couple of generations ago. The social transformation this new visibility implies is real. As the world gears up to meeting the Sustainable Development Goals (SDGs), it is worth understanding what Bangladesh has achieved, and how.

Bangladesh made surprisingly rapid and simultaneous progress on poverty and gender equality in the 1990s and 2000s. Women were included in the national development project in ways that recognised how their vulnerability and lack of power bred poverty and deepened gender inequalities; programmes and policies were designed to reach them in ways that amended, without radically transforming, gender relations. Lessons from Bangladesh's past development successes have already been widely shared in a growing body of literature[1]; this chapter looks forward, reflecting on the conditions under

N. Hossain (✉)
Accountability Research Center, American University, Washington, DC, USA
e-mail: hossain@american.edu

which Bangladesh made its gains on gender equality and women's empowerment during the Millennium Development Goals (MDGs) (1990–2015), and discusses how such inclusive policies became possible. It then builds on that analysis to assess the prospects for the achievement of the SDGs, with their stronger emphasis on inclusion, equality, and "leaving no one behind".

It should be noted that Bangladesh is no paradise of gender equality, and that women and girls face a broad range of discrimination and disadvantage because of their gender and its intersections with poverty and minority status. Violence against women and early marriage remain key concerns, and women and girls experience routine violations of their political, civic, and economic rights. Bangladesh faces significant challenges in meeting its SDG commitments, and these are being exacerbated by an apparent rise in the influence of political Islam (Nazneen 2018). Yet Bangladesh stands out in respect of women's empowerment and gender equality, in that it made relatively rapid gains from a low starting point—gains that could not be predicted from the country's social and gender relations at the time of its independence in 1971. At that time, it was a country with extensive poverty and a predominantly agrarian socio-economic structure, characteristics that do not usually facilitate rapid progress on gender equality (Mason and King 2001). It remains a Muslim-majority society situated within what Deniz Kandiyoti termed the belt of "classic patriarchy" (Kandiyoti 1988), which again are societal features believed to deter gender equality policies and programmes. Bangladesh is known to have performed "surprisingly" well in terms of reaching the most disadvantaged with health, education, and social protection services, and it is regarded as a "positive deviant" for having done so despite its overall low level of development and public spending (Asadullah et al. 2014; Chowdhury et al. 2013; Hossain 2017). Its performance on gender equality and women's empowerment is similarly surprising and merits explanation (Hossain 2018; Nazneen 2019).

The main argument of this chapter is that the relatively rapid improvements in the lives of, and opportunities for, Bangladeshi women owe in particular to comparatively strong elite commitment and increasing state capacity to reach and include women in the development process. As will be explained in the following, this elite commitment in turn grew out of a series of crises that highlighted the inadequate protections of patriarchal gender relations for many women. It led to their incorporation within the political settlement as citizens with rights as well as—through their reproductive roles—prime objects of, and vehicles for, governmental social policy.

In the aftermath of a brutal period of political violence and instability, a reasonably strong and enduring informal consensus emerged among the political, civil, military, economic, and social elites about the need to reach Bangladeshi women as integral to the larger project of national development (Hossain 2005, 2018). The elite were themselves a homogenous and close-knit group, and the crises of the early 1970s signalled a threat to the survival of the elite itself, and potentially even to national sovereignty. Forged in the shadow of economic disaster, famine, and assassination, the consensus included building better relationships with aid donors and accepting their conditionalities and priorities—for instance, around fertility control—where these were in line with the larger goal of development (Hossain 2017). The urgency of the need for economic stability and growth and for reaching the poor and vulnerable population licensed a range of innovative and experimental programmes and policies in Bangladesh, with creative partnerships and space for all manner of actors and ideas (Hossain 2017). From the 1970s to the 2000s, Bangladesh was a major recipient of foreign aid, including food aid. With economic growth, this relative dependence has declined significantly: Official development assistance comprised almost 6 per cent of annual gross domestic product in the 1980s, a figure that had dropped to around 1.5 per cent by the 2010s (Khatun 2018). At some point in the early 2020s, Bangladesh is expected to graduate from the category of "least-developed country" (LDC), the first large country to do so. It is widely seen as an example of effective aid, and a central focus on women was part of that (Abed 2013; Asadullah et al. 2014; Chowdhury et al. 2013).

From the 1990s onwards, this developmental focus on women could be seen in the rising number of girls enrolled in schools, women receiving health care and other services, and women in paid work in export factories or self-employment through micro-credit schemes (Kabeer and Hossain 2004). Laws, policies, and programmes to protect women and children against violence and to protect the most vulnerable from hunger and poverty were passed and implemented. Women played a growing role in politics through quotas and reservations, and they were employed in increasing numbers by the state, including as teachers, health workers, administrators, and the police (Nazneen and Sultan 2010; Nazneen et al. 2011).

But if elite commitment and state capacity were necessary elements of Bangladesh's unexpected success with women's empowerment and the MDGs, as is discussed further below, are they present and aligned in support of the SDGs? Can Bangladesh sustain its remarkable progress as it graduates out of the official LDC status of the United Nations (UN) in the early 2020s, with its implications for preferential trade and aid arrangements? How successfully will the country negotiate between a growing Islamist backlash against women's rights and the vocal demands of the country's robust women's movement (Nazneen 2018)? To answer these questions, the chapter first sets out the scale and nature of Bangladesh's success with gender equality, drawing attention to its MDG attainments and to debates about what worked in helping to achieve those. It then moves backward in time to explore the origins of elite commitment and state capacity to address (a limited range of) women's concerns, discussing the effects of a series of crises on how elites perceived women and their part in the development process around the time of the country's independence from Pakistan in 1971. It then returns to the challenges of the present—the early years of the SDGs—examining a select number of the gender equality targets on which Bangladesh faces an enduring challenge to transform its society and the lives of its female citizens. The analysis of the chapter focuses on exploring whether and to what extent the elite commitment and state capacity necessary to address the SDG challenges are in place, as they were for the MDGs, on which Bangladesh performed relatively well.

21.2 GENDER EQUALITY AND BANGLADESH'S UNEXPECTED DEVELOPMENT SUCCESS

21.2.1 Advances for Bangladeshi Women: From Independence to the MDGs

Since its liberation from Pakistan in 1971, Bangladesh has made comparatively rapid advances on gender equality, catching up with—and even overtaking—regional comparators on health, education, and life expectancy, among other dimensions (World Bank 2007). These gains were from a low base and at a low level of public and private expenditure (Asadullah et al. 2014). Bangladeshi women have benefited from policies and non-state social programmes that prevent hunger, improve livelihoods, extend life expectancies, expand access to basic reproductive and other health services (Chowdhury et al. 2013), get girls into school, and provide social protection for vulnerable women (Hossain 2017). According to the Global Gender Gap Index, which measures the disadvantage women face compared to men in health, education, the economy, and politics, the women of Bangladesh now score higher on some measures of gender equality than their South Asian sisters (see Fig. 21.1), but they lag behind on other important dimensions, notably early marriage (UNICEF [United Nations Children's Fund] 2014).[2] The Government of Bangladesh increasingly frames gender equality as central to its development successes in export production and human development, and as a goal in its own right (Wazed 2010).

With respect to the third MDG (promote gender equality and empower women), the Government of Bangladesh noted that it had achieved or made rapid progress towards key targets, including:

- successfully eliminating gender disparity in primary and secondary education,
- rapidly reducing gender disparities in tertiary-level enrolments,
- a (slow) rise in the proportion of women wage workers in non-agricultural employment, from 19 per cent in 1991–1992 to 32 per cent in 2013, and
- women taking a leading role in national politics.

In addition, Bangladesh made rapid progress on a number of other indicators with direct impact on women's lives and well-being, including:

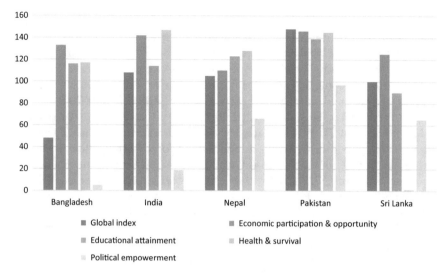

Fig. 21.1 Global Gender Gap Index rankings, South Asia, in 2018 (*Note* Lower scores indicate lower levels of gender inequality in the particular domain, that is, better scores. *Source* Author, based on data from the World Economic Forum [2018])

- halving the proportion of the population living in poverty (from 57 per cent in the early 1990s to 25 per cent in 2015) and in extreme poverty (from 25 per cent in 2005 to 13 per cent in 2015);
- rapid reductions in child mortality (under 5 years old—from 151 per thousand live births in 1990 to 36 in 2014) and infant mortality (from 94 per thousand live births in 1990 to 29 in 2015);
- a reduction in maternal mortality rates (from 472 per 100,000 live births in 1991 to 181 in 2015); and
- increases in maternal health care coverage (General Economic Division 2016).

In practical terms, this progress has meant the passage of laws to protect and advance women's rights within marriage, to property, personal safety and security, and political representation; the building of tens of thousands of schools, clinics, and hospitals; the recruitment of hundreds of thousands of health workers, teachers, and administrators—a rising proportion of them women; and the provision of services and social protection to tens of millions of women and their families through cash and food transfers, pensions, micro-credit, work, and income-generation schemes (Begum 2014).

It should be underlined that despite its good progress and general aura of success, Bangladesh did not meet all its MDG commitments on gender equality. In key areas of women's and girls' lives—in particular with respect to violence, poverty, and early marriage—signs of "empowerment" have been less evident than continuing powerlessness and discrimination, reflecting the persistence of certain patriarchal norms and practices, despite the significant changes marked by the MDG achievements. Whether incorporation into paid work in the export apparels industry or self-employment through microfinance is "empowering" for women—and if so, what that means for those women in those contexts—has also been the subject of much debate among feminist activists and scholars (Goetz and Gupta 1996; Heath 2014; Heath and Mobarak 2015; Hossain 2012; Kabeer 1999; Kabeer et al. 2018; Karim 2011; Siddiqi 2009). Women face a growing range of new challenges from their greater public civic, political, and labour force participation, including the rise of a new Islamic platform with influence over current politics. At the same time, the SDGs are widely understood to be a more challenging and broader index of development rooted in human rights and the analysis of the structural determinants of poverty, exclusion, and inequality, compared to the MDGs' narrower agenda, which was focused on income poverty and scaling up service provision (Esquivel and Sweetman 2016; Kabeer 2005). Can Bangladesh translate its (modest) successes in the MDGs into a strategy for achieving the SDGs? To understand the prospects for Bangladesh, we first need to understand how it achieved the change it did.

21.2.2 What Bangladesh Did Right

How were these comparatively rapid (if uneven) gains for women possible? We can draw on the analysis of Bangladesh's "surprisingly" inclusive development progress more generally by Asadullah et al. (2014) to identify the following determinants of women-oriented or gender-equitable policies in this context. First, Bangladesh had crafted "an inclusive development strategy involving various non-government stakeholders" including religious bodies, aid donors, and non-governmental organisations (NGOs), "which complemented public education and health interventions" (Asadullah et al. 2014, p. 151). Partnerships between state, international aid, and non-state actors helped bring about poverty reduction through services designed specifically to benefit impoverished and marginalised people, and in particular women; they also allowed new approaches to be innovated and tested as well as built on or scaled-up by the government (Hossain 2017).

Second, there were synergies between different forms of social progress so that, for instance, gains in health helped kick-start gains in education at different times. Fertility decline helped improve women's overall status, thereby improving their own health and enabling them to care for fewer children and undertake paid work and civic engagement. Girls' education meant more educated mothers, smaller families, and more investment in children's schooling (Asadullah et al. 2014, p. 151).

A third set of broad factors identified by Asadullah et al. included the very broad category of the geographical and sociocultural context. A small, densely populated landmass and a broadly shared cultural and linguistic heritage helped ensure that policies and programmes could be designed and rolled out with comparative ease and at a low cost. In addition, a strong political commitment to inclusive policies, including "[p]utting women in the forefront", featured in these gains (Asadullah et al. 2014, p. 151).

21.2.3 Ruptures in the Patriarchal Bargain and the Origins of Elite Commitment

These factors help to explain *how* Bangladesh transformed aspects of gender relations, thereby changing the relationship between Bangladeshi women and their state over a short space of a couple of generations. But they tell us little about *why* it overcame such strong gendered cultural and religious norms and traditions in order to do so. We know from political economy research that the broad factors driving inclusive development critically include elite commitment to inclusive policies and state capacity to enable their delivery (Hickey et al. 2015). So what drove elite commitment and state capacity to include women in the project of national development?

One explanation for Bangladesh's rapid progress on aspects of gender equality, despite its unpromising conditions in the early 1970s, was that the natural disasters, conflict, and humanitarian crises of the events surrounding that country's birth "marked a watershed in attempts to deal with women's issues" (Kabeer 1988, p. 110). The province of East Pakistan (soon to become Bangladesh) experienced a devastating cyclone in 1970, which triggered the Liberation War of 1971. It also established a strong political mandate for a nation state that would protect its citizens against such disasters. The war itself saw millions of Bangladeshis killed, displaced, or widowed, as well as the vast destruction of infrastructure and assets. Tens of thousands of women were raped by the Pakistani army and their collaborators, and they found it difficult to be re-integrated into a society in which sexual purity remained critical for gender relations. Not three years after independence, the country experienced a terrible famine in which 1.5 million people died. Women started to come out in their thousands looking for work—challenging norms of *purdah* (seclusion)—after being forced out by hunger and desperation (Hossain 2018).

These events surrounding the establishment of the new nation came on top of a longer period of decline in the old patriarchal-agrarian bargain, in which rising levels of landlessness and debt had impoverished the rural majority over a generation or more, affecting poor women most directly. In turn, each of these crises politicised the situation of Bangladeshi women in key respects. They meant that the rehabilitation of raped women into society was framed as a matter of national reconstruction and development, creating a precedent for state action and agencies to address women's concerns (D'Costa 2012; D'Costa and Hossain 2010; see in particular, Mookherjee 2008). The famine gave rise to new and pioneering programmes to reach the poorest women, such as Vulnerable Group Development, a food transfer scheme that has been run by the government and the World Food Programme since

1975. The spectre of famine firmed up a consensus between aid actors and domestic elites around the priority of population control; this meant that finding ways of reaching poor rural women in order to change their reproductive behaviour was crucial. The politics of the crises demanded that the Bangladeshi state develop the "biopower" to protect its citizens, rather than helplessly leaving them to the mercies of the markets or the elements (Hossain 2018). The Bangladesh women's movement, which had a long history of struggling with as well as alongside political elites, played a particularly important role in undertaking research, mobilising support, and framing women's issues as matters of rights and national development (Nazneen 2019; Nazneen and Sultan 2014).

21.2.4 From Commitment to Capacity

An elite consensus on the need for development to reach poor women made it possible to build state capacities to work with rural populations and licensed experimental models of governance and service delivery. This included creating space for non-state actors—in a context in which the emerging state lacked human and fiscal resources—as well as the physical outreach and flexibility of NGOs. The extent of the need meant the government of Bangladesh had little option but to seek assistance and build partnerships with NGOs. It is notable that the disasters of the 1970s were also moments when some of Bangladesh's NGOs (BRAC) and micro-credit institutions (Grameen Bank) were founded. Civil society leaders often explain their motivations for their innovative organisations as being due to having witnessed the hardships of the people, in particular of rural poor women, and becoming determined to make changes (Harvard Business School 2014; Yunus and Jolis 1999). Both BRAC and Grameen Bank have notably made women's empowerment and tackling poverty central to their work, and they have developed many innovative models that have been emulated—and criticised—around the world.

After the early 1970s crisis period, Bangladesh experienced a series of brutal political assassinations and coups, after which it embarked on a 15-year period of military rule that lasted till 1990. During this time, an elite consensus was forged on the need to open up to international aid and move towards economic liberalisation, while also creating space for civil society to operate and ensuring basic social provisioning (in particular, family planning and food security). This included a growing recognition of the centrality of women to development policy as well as the urgent need to reach the mass of female citizens in order to transform the population into a source of national wealth. International aid became a major influence through the introduction of new ideas and financing, often countervailing the push towards more regressive gender policies from Islamic allies in the Middle East and organised religious forces within the country (Hossain 2017).

At first, there was opposition from within the more conservative and traditionalist sections of society to birth control measures (viewed as un-Islamic), girls' schooling, and women attending public meetings. Micro-credit programmes were believed to be associated with raised levels of domestic violence, as some husbands resented women's growing control over household incomes. Yet, there was never an important constituency within the political, economic, or social elite, nor within organised politics or civil society to oppose such measures as scholarships for girls' secondary school, stipends for the mothers of primary schoolchildren, or food or cash transfers for elderly or destitute women. Political parties—even to some extent including those on the moderate religious right—broadly took the same view of the desirability of enabling women to be included in the development process (Nazneen 2009; Nazneen et al. 2011). Across the society, the appraisal of action to reach women was broadly pragmatic after the period of crisis, recognising that poor rural women in particular needed to be able to generate incomes and have the power to control their fertility in order to prevent extreme poverty for both themselves and their children. As the export garments industry took off after the 1980s, business leaders in particular recognised the advantages of policies promoting women's employment beyond the home, as they reaped the profits from an abundant supply of cheap female labour.

The advances in gender equality and women's empowerment of the MDG period were achieved during the country's (mainly) democratic period, in which the two main parties were routinely kicked out of office by the electorate, and in which competition for votes brought a broad range of policies and development performance into the public's political decision-making. For almost 30 years, the country has been ruled by women prime ministers from either party—a feature of Bangladeshi politics that arguably licensed a relatively strong focus on the "soft" social sectors of health, education, and social protection by the government. The women's movement mounted several effective campaigns, in key respects pushing party politics towards greater recognition of women voters. It seems unarguable that democratic competition played an important role in holding the elite consensus together and in creating space for civil society actors, both the women's movement and the service-providing NGOs. Since 2014, however, Bangladeshi politics has been increasingly dominated by a single party. Will that enable the government to sharpen its focus on women's empowerment and gender equality by ignoring claims from the Islamic right for policies to be in line with religion, and directing more resources towards building state capacity for gender equality policies? Or will it mean that the women's movement and popular feeling are suppressed by the increasing domination of the ruling party and the closure of the space for civil and political society? Will NGOs and civil society groups still be able to influence policies in positive ways? These are the key questions for the future achievement of the SDGs.

21.3 Next-Generation Challenges: Inclusion, Equality, and "Leaving No One Behind"

21.3.1 Intersectionality and Power in the SDGs

To properly understand the fresh challenge posed by the SDGs, it is necessary to understand where and why Bangladeshi women and girls continue to face significant challenges to their inclusion and equal participation, and in addition, the new challenges they face as a result of their changing social, economic, and political roles. Although all composite indices have their problems, the SDGs offer the promise of a better framework for analysing progress on gender equality and women's empowerment, for a number of reasons. As Esquivel and Sweetman (2016) argue, with 14 indicators addressing legal, political, economic, and social issues, the SDG indicators capture a broader range of dimensions of power at different stages of life and in multiple domains. As they also note, gender cuts across more of the other SDGs, and so it is mainstreamed in a way that was absent from the MDGs. Again, in contrast to the more minimal MDGs (which were set by donors and technocrats), SDG 5 was developed through extensive consultation with the women's movement and civil society activists and feminist scholars. This involvement can be seen in the more structural and intersectional approach taken to the measurement of progress towards women's empowerment in the SDGs, and it entails a recognition of the limitations of a narrow focus on economic empowerment, taking a human rights-based approach with a strong emphasis on equality (Razavi 2016). Such an approach makes possible:

> an intersectional analysis of power in which economic, political and social marginalisation based on identities clearly leads to the experience of "being left behind". If the Leave No-One Behind agenda is realised, it may help solve the problem of the limitations of simpler, goal-oriented development in the MDGs, which were able to realise targets because they had less ambitious goals, and therefore left the more difficult development challenges unaddressed … Leave No-One Behind highlights the fact that the issues facing women in poverty in the global South do not arise from gender inequality only; rather, they are at the intersection of different dimensions of inequality, including race and class. (Esquivel and Sweetman 2016, p. 7)

The SDGs are thus likely to prove to be a harder test of progress on gender equality and women's empowerment, and one which takes into account a broader range of dimensions of power in women's lives, and their intersection with each other. This means, among other things, an inherently more contested model of development cooperation, in which there may be fewer easy wins and more difficult choices and trade-offs.

21.3.2 The Problem of Early Marriage: SDGs 3 and 5

To assess the challenges posed by the SDGs, it helps to examine some of the enduring sources of gender inequality and women's disadvantage in Bangladesh, as well as to understand why they are so difficult to eradicate. The phenomenon of early marriage helps to illustrate the nature of the challenges particularly well.

It is notable that although Bangladesh scored well on the Global Gender Gap Index (see Fig. 21.1), the Gender Inequality Index (GII) of the UN Development Programme's Human Development Report tells a different—and for Bangladesh, a less promising—story. The GII measures the "loss in potential human development due to disparity between female and male achievements in reproductive health, empowerment and economic status". As with the Global Gender Gap Index, it aims to capture the effect of gender inequalities overall in society, but it includes in addition some indicators relating to other SDGs, such as health and education. Table 21.1 summarises the rankings of different South Asian countries on the GII. Ranked above only Pakistan of these major South Asian nations, Bangladesh is at or near the median score across most of the indicators. The exception is the adolescent birth rate (SDG target 3.7), which, at 83.5 per 1000, is 23 points higher than Nepal (the country with the next-worst adolescent birth rate), more than double that of Pakistan and India, and almost six times higher than in Sri Lanka.

Bangladesh's relatively poor overall performance within South Asia on the GII mainly reflects this extremely high proportion of adolescent births, which, in turn, reflects the very high rate of early marriage for girls in Bangladesh (Kamal et al. 2015; Streatfield et al. 2015). Despite its many gains on gender equality in education and other spheres of life, marriage remains routine for girls below the age of 18, and Bangladesh has one of the highest rates of early marriage in the world (UNICEF 2014). Both the adolescent birth rate (SDG target 3.7) and SDG target 5.3, which includes an indicator of the "Proportion of women aged 20–24 years who were married or in a union before age 15 and before age 18", aim to capture a core dimension of women's lives—whether they are able to make choices about when they marry and give birth, which is a decision with profound implications for their health and well-being, as well as for their chances of completing further or higher education and of getting paid work.

The stubborn problem of early marriage is a prime example of the nature of the challenge that Bangladesh is likely to face in attempting to attain the SDGs. It reflects, first, a relatively widespread social preference for girls to marry young. In turn, this reflects the absolute priority accorded to female sexual purity in Bengali Muslim culture, and the resulting pressure that parents perceive themselves to be under to ensure girls are married before they can develop independent romantic preferences and/or an undesirable social reputation. It also reflects the high degree of violence and harassment faced by

Table 21.1 Gender Inequality Index, South Asia

Country	Gender Inequality Index	SDG target 3.1 Maternal mortality ratio (deaths per 100,000 live births)	SDG target 3.7 Adolescent birth rate (births per 1000 women ages 15–19)	SDG target 5.5 Share of seats in parliament (% held by women)	SDG target 4.6 Population with at least some secondary education (% ages 25 and older)		SDG target Labour force participation rate (% ages 15 and older)	
	Rank				Female	Male	Female	Male
	2017	2015	2015–2020	2017	2010–2017	2010–2017	2017	2017
Sri Lanka	80	30	14.1	5.8	82.6	83.1	35.1	74.1
India	127	174	23.1	11.6	39.0	63.5	27.2	78.8
Bangladesh	134	176	83.5	20.3	44.0	48.2	33.0	79.8
Nepal	118	258	60.5	29.6	27.3	43.1	82.7	85.9
Pakistan	133	178	36.9	20.0	27.0	47.3	24.9	82.7

Source Author, based on United Nations Development Programme (n.d.)

Bangladeshi adolescents (Alam et al. 2010; Nahar et al. 2013) and the fear that harassment will cause the girls to be perceived as sexually active. The high rate of early marriage has also been linked to the prevalence of practices of grooms' families demanding substantial dowries; adolescents and young teenagers tend to be valued more highly than brides over the age of 18, and many parents prefer to marry their daughters off young in order to pay a smaller dowry (Amin and Huq 2008; Schuler et al. 2006).

Second, the persistence of early marriage against a backdrop of policy shifts to promote the educational and employment prospects of women and girls also reflects the extent to which the government has generally succeeded in advancing social agendas when those have been aligned with the popular will. There was a large unmet demand for reproductive health care and family planning, rising demands for universal basic education, and a growing push for access to work opportunities for those women who wanted or needed to earn (Kabeer 2001; Kabeer and Hossain 2004). By contrast, there remains such a strong societal preference for girls to be married young (or to be perceived as younger than 18 at the time of marriage) that many parents appear to prefer to lie about their daughters' ages in order to present them as being younger than they are, even though this means breaking the law (Streatfield et al. 2015). Put another way, the social pressures in favour of early marriage are stronger than the legal and civic pressures to ensure that daughters are over the legal age before they are married. In 2018, under pressure from Islamic clerics, among others, the government actually reduced the legal age at which girls can be married, from 18 to 16. Although the average age of marriage has been rising over time, it has done so very slowly, increasingly less than a year and a half between 1994 and 2003, a period otherwise known for its rapid progress on gender equality (and in particular for gains in girls' educational enrolment) (Kamal et al. 2015).

Third, the challenge of addressing early marriage has seen government policy not only run up against a widespread societal preference for girls to be married young, but also face relatively concerted and organised opposition from the Islamic right. The surprising volte-face of the government in reducing the age of marriage is believed to reflect the emergence of an influential and radical new Islamist platform (*Hefazat*), which has replaced the moderate Islamist parties of the past. In part, this group has emerged through virulent struggles against the adoption of the National Women's Development Policy, which had among its aims the equalisation of inheritance laws for men and women (Nazneen 2018). The government has also made concessions to this group regarding *madrassah* education; this, along with the relaxation of child marriage laws, indicates that, for the first time, development and gender equality policies are likely to face a coherent and organised opposition from the right.

A fourth factor to consider is that whereas the MDG period was characterised by partnerships between the government and aid, civil society,

NGOs, and community-based organisations, these more inclusive and innovative partnerships have been replaced by an increasingly government-driven agenda. From 1991 to 2014, the country featured highly competitive multi-party elections, and the media and civil society actors were relatively free to comment on and scrutinise public policy and the implementation of government programmes. In 2014, the present government "won" an uncontested election, which was boycotted by the opposition, who deemed it illegitimate. It went on to politicise the administration and restrict or co-opt civil society actors using a mixture of law, criminalisation, administrative measures, and stigmatisation, as well as outright intimidation and violence (Hassan and Nazneen 2017; Human Rights Watch 2017). The 2018 election is widely understood to have been thoroughly rigged to secure the position of the incumbent party. Civil society actors and the media have been cowed and threatened, and although they have not been entirely silenced or stopped, they are now forced to select their struggles carefully, at the risk of being de-registered or otherwise stopped. Women's movement actors are among those who have been silenced or co-opted.

Taken together, these factors signal that the conditions that enabled earlier—and in some respects, less radical—policy changes are no longer in place, or at least not for the stubborn problem of child marriage. The overall policy environment since 2014 has not been one of respect for human rights, although it has given an even stronger emphasis to service delivery and economic development than in the past. Yet, as the SDGs themselves indicate, women's empowerment and gender equality are not individual measures such as girls' enrolment in school or participation in non-agricultural wage work.

The critical question for Bangladesh as it strategises for achieving the SDGs is whether a strong political elite commitment to deliver services can overcome these features of the social and political environment that were absent during the MDG period. With respect to early marriage, these include a misalignment between societal and state goals; a lack of clear elite consensus over its importance; the presence of an increasingly organised opposition to gender equality policies, and in particular to stopping adult men from marrying girl children; and the increasingly state-dominated development process, which reduces the prospects for innovation through multi-stakeholder partnerships, accountability for achieving the SDGs, and in particular ensuring that no one is "left behind by development".

21.3.3 Women Workers' Rights: SDGs 1, 8, and 16

The past 30 years have seen dramatic changes in women's lives in Bangladesh. Among these is mass women's employment in export-sector garments production, which has, over the decades, brought millions of Bangladeshi women into formal industrial relations. At present, around 2 to 3 million women work in the industry, which accounts for 80 per cent of exports.

Incorporation into global value chains has undoubtedly been empowering for Bangladeshi women faced with the options of even lower-paid rural subsistence occupations or the rigours and uncertainties of family farming or domestic service (Hossain 2012; Kabeer and Mahmud 2004; Kabeer et al. 2018). Yet, wages have remained low, while living costs have risen, notably over the past decade. Evidence indicates that, even with two adults working, a household reliant on garment workers' wages would live below the poverty line (Moazzem and Arfanuzzaman 2018).

The new opportunities of ready-made garment employment have also seen women incorporated into global value chains on adverse terms, exposing them to new sources of discrimination and structural violence. The disastrous Rana Plaza factory collapse of 2013—the worst industrial disaster in the history of the global garments trade—graphically illustrated the effects of the lack of power of garment workers to resist pressures to turn up for work in unsafe factories in order to perform tough, but underpaid, labour. Since the calamity of 2013, which threatened the very existence of this overwhelmingly important industry in Bangladesh, garment workers have taken increasingly effective, if dangerous, collective action to demand safety at work and higher wages (Ashraf and Prentice 2019; Siddiqi 2015).

So although women have won some degree of economic empowerment through their precarious factory labour, this has chiefly been exercised in relation to the home and personal relationships. However, women workers remain deeply disempowered in relation to factory owners, the state, and the international buyers that source in Bangladesh. It has become increasingly evident that their empowerment and the achievement of decent work depend on their right to unionise and claim their rights. The Bangladeshi elite—and in particular the business elite—are not behind unionisation, in the belief that it would push wages infeasibly high and/or destroy the industry's competitive advantage. Under pressure from international trade regimes and international human rights institutions, the government is seeking ways of improving industrial relations without antagonising their important supporters in business.

Among the SDGs, the targets that are most at risk are SDG target 8.5 ("By 2030, achieve full and productive employment and decent work for all women and men, including for young people and persons with disabilities, and equal pay for work of equal value") and SDG target 8.8 ("Protect labour rights and promote safe and secure working environments for all workers, including migrant workers, in particular women migrants, and those in precarious employment"). Again, the SDGs mainstream gender across the set; with respect to Bangladesh's garment workers, it is clear that their disempowerment is by no means purely a result of their gender, but of how their gender intersects with class as well as political and economic power. The achievement of SDG 16 (peace, justice, and strong institutions) also speaks to these challenges, as they highlight the problem of violence and intimidation against trade union and labour activists, and its connections with the achievement of decent work, gender equality, and women's empowerment.

Bangladesh has been a (somewhat reluctant) host to a range of transnational multi-stakeholder initiatives to improve working conditions in garments factories ever since the Rana Plaza disaster (Donaghey and Reinecke 2018; Evans 2014; Khan and Wichterich 2015). In key respects, this has created an environment for experimentation with global governance that resembles the experimentation of earlier non-state innovations with service delivery and reaching women. The Bangladeshi labour movement remains weak and fragmented, however, and has been historically insufficiently attentive to women workers' concerns (Rahman and Langford 2012; Siddiqi 2017). Despite changes to the labour law, in practice, labour activism is dangerous and often violently suppressed. Women (and men) garment workers in Bangladesh are increasingly taking collective action nonetheless, and they are at times winning concessions over the minimum wage or other demands. Their struggles, while evidence of the growing desire to organise, are also evidence of the very high costs that many continue to pay to achieve their basic rights.

21.4 Conclusions

This chapter has reflected on Bangladesh's surprisingly rapid—if uneven and incomplete—progress on gender equality and women's empowerment. It explored both the scope and nature of that progress and how it came about. It also draws attention to the reasons why elites came to be committed to public action on some aspects of gender equality and women's empowerment (notably, social protection and income generation for poverty reduction, fertility control, and mass education), and therefore to building state—and indeed non-state—capacity to do so. Under conditions of multi-party competition and a flourishing civil society sector, Bangladesh made good progress on some of the MDGs—better than could have been expected because of its poverty, traditional patriarchal norms and institutions, and the predominantly Islamic faith of the population. The chapter notes the importance of ruptures in the old patterns and assumptions about gender relations around the country's tumultuous independent period. In particular, it notes recognition by elites that societal institutions such as marriage, the family, and the community were failing to protect Bangladeshi women against disasters, conflicts, and the grinding problems of poverty that so many millions faced. In a country without substantial natural resources, in which the main wealth was its people, addressing women's concerns became a matter of addressing the country's national development agenda and building a more productive—healthier, better nourished, better educated, and socialised—workforce. Governments developed inclusive partnerships with aid actors, civil society groups, and NGOs, and the women's movement played a critical role both in advancing an understanding of the instrumental importance of women's empowerment for national development as a whole and in sharing norms about women's rights and strategies for realising them.

What does Bangladesh's positive performance on the MDGs tell us about the prospects for the SDGs? The SDGs are more demanding, embedding an understanding of women's disadvantage not only concerning their gender, but also of how gender intersects with class, ethnicity and religion, and geography, among other factors. The SDGs draw attention to a broader range of factors affecting power in women's lives than the MDGs—and with greater attention being given to women and girls across their entire lives. The chapter analyses two enduring challenges facing women in Bangladesh in the light of the SDG emphasis on inclusion, equality, and "leaving no one behind" by development: early marriage and women workers' rights in global value chains. Each of these challenges is analysed in the light of what we have learnt about how Bangladesh succeeded (to the extent it did) in the MDGs. Several points stand out.

First, the "first generation" gains of girls' education and family planning services aligned closely with societal interests and concerns. By contrast, early marriage persists because of a broad societal preference (within highly constrained and gender-unequal conditions) for girls to be married young. The garments sector as a whole has been built on the low wages and presumed docility of women workers, and the interests in keeping it so are widespread and powerful.

The second point, which is related to the first, is that there is no elite consensus on these enduring and new challenges. Religious elites hold fast to their privileges, including having sex with girl children, even while the political and social elite decry the closely associated practices of dowry and child marriage, which are both fundamental to the violence faced by women and girls. State, political, civil society, and business elites are divided on the issue of unionisation in the industry, and so more powerful voices prevail. Issues of minimum wages and working conditions are proving to be topics of great contestation, in which cooperation or collaboration has to date proved elusive.

Third, whereas neither fertility control nor education or even micro-credit schemes have elicited much organised resistance from politically powerful groups, the rise of a new and more militant Islamic platform has successfully foisted a more Islamist agenda on the erstwhile secular ruling government. It is within this context that the law has been changed to *reduce* the legal age at which girls can marry. With respect to garments, women (and men) workers are prevented from realising their rights to form trade unions by a powerful business elite with strong and multiple connections to political power at both the local and national levels.

Fourth, political and civic spaces have been sharply curtailed just as the SDGs are being launched. The development process is increasingly being dominated by the state-party system of government under a party that has ruled (as of 2019) for a full decade. In theory, a more powerful government could build stronger capacity to implement important gender equality policies against the will of powerful religious or business actors. Yet, it may equally push out and silence the voices of the women's movement, NGOs, and civil society groups with knowledge, capacity, or access. The country's successes with development cooperation and effective aid during the MDG period may not easily be replicated amid the more widespread and polarised contention surrounding issues such as girl child marriage and minimum wages. Official development assistance is, overall, considerably less important to the policies Bangladesh is now designing and implementing. These are critical considerations for Bangladesh as it graduates from LDC status and takes its position as a middle-income country in its 50 year. The SDGs will provide a critical test for the "Bangladeshi model" of development.

Notes

1. See, for instance, Asadullah et al. (2014), Chowdhury et al. (2013), Hossain (2017), and Mahmud et al. (2008).
2. The UN Gender Inequality Index for 2017 ranked Bangladesh 134 out of 188 countries, compared to Sri Lanka at 80, Nepal at 118, India at 127, and Pakistan at 133, just above Bangladesh. This ranking, apparently at odds with other composite indices, appears to relate to the very high proportion of adolescent mothers in Bangladesh (between one-third and two-thirds higher than elsewhere in South Asia), which is one of five indicators measured. GII data is from UNDP (n.d.).

References

Abed, F. H. (2013). Bangladesh's health revolution. *The Lancet, 382*(9910), 2048–2049.

Alam, N., Roy, S. K., & Ahmed, T. (2010). Sexually harassing behavior against adolescent girls in rural Bangladesh: Implications for achieving Millennium Development Goals. *Journal of Interpersonal Violence, 25*(3), 443–456.

Amin, S., & Huq, L. (2008). *Marriage considerations in sending girls to school in Bangladesh: Some qualitative evidence*. New York, NY: Population Council.

Asadullah, M. N., Savoia, A., & Mahmud, W. (2014). Paths to development: Is there a Bangladesh surprise? *World Development, 62*, 138–154.

Ashraf, H., & Prentice, R. (2019). Beyond factory safety: Labor unions, militant protest, and the accelerated ambitions of Bangladesh's export garment industry. *Dialectical Anthropology, 43*(1), 93–107.

Begum, F. S. (2014). *Gender equality and women's empowerment: Suggested strategies for the 7th five year plan*. Dhaka: General Economics Division, Bangladesh Planning Commission, Government of the People's Republic of Bangladesh.

Chowdhury, A. M. R., Bhuiya, A., Chowdhury, M. E., Rasheed, S., Hussain, Z., & Chen, L. C. (2013). The Bangladesh paradox: Exceptional health achievement despite economic poverty. *The Lancet, 382*(9906), 1734–1745.

D'Costa, B. (2012). Women, war, and the making of Bangladesh: Remembering 1971. *Journal of Genocide Research, 14*(1), 110–114.

D'Costa, B., & Hossain, S. (2010). Redress for sexual violence before the International Crimes Tribunal in Bangladesh: Lessons from history, and hopes for the future. *Criminal Law Forum, 21*(2), 331–359.

Donaghey, J., & Reinecke, J. (2018). When industrial democracy meets corporate social responsibility—A comparison of the Bangladesh accord and alliance as responses to the Rana Plaza Disaster. *British Journal of Industrial Relations, 56*(1), 14–42.

Esquivel, V., & Sweetman, C. (2016). Gender and the Sustainable Development Goals. *Gender & Development, 24*(1), 1–8.

Evans, B. A. (2014). Accord on fire and building safety in Bangladesh: An international response to Bangladesh labor conditions notes & comments. *North Carolina Journal of International Law and Commercial Regulation, 40*(2), [i]-628.

General Economic Division. (2016). *Millennium Development Goals (MDGs): End-period stocktaking and final evaluation (2000–2015)*. Dhaka: General Economics Division, Bangladesh Planning Commission, Government of the People's Republic of Bangladesh.

Goetz, A. M., & Gupta, R. S. (1996). Who takes the credit? Gender, power, and control over loan use in rural credit programs in Bangladesh. *World Development, 24*(1), 45–63.

Harvard Business School. (2014, April 24). *Interview with Fazle Abed, interviewed by Tarun Khanna*. http://www.hbs.edu/businesshistory/Documents/emerging-markets-transcripts/Abed_Fazle_Web%20Copy.pdf.

Hassan, M., & Nazneen, S. (2017). Violence and the breakdown of the political settlement: An uncertain future for Bangladesh? *Conflict, Security & Development, 17*(3), 205–223.

Heath, R. (2014). Women's access to labor market opportunities, control of household resources, and domestic violence: Evidence from Bangladesh. *World Development, 57*, 32–46.

Heath, R., & Mobarak, A. M. (2015). Manufacturing growth and the lives of Bangladeshi women. *Journal of Development Economics, 115*, 1–15.

Hickey, S., Sen, K., & Bukenya, B. (2015). Exploring the politics of inclusive development: Towards a new conceptual approach. In S. Hickey, K. Sen, & B. Bukenya (Eds.), *The politics of inclusive development: Interrogating the evidence* (pp. 3–34). Oxford: Oxford University Press.

Hossain, N. (2005). *Elite perceptions of poverty in Bangladesh*. Dhaka: University Press Limited.

Hossain, N. (2012). *Exports, equity, and empowerment: The effects of readymade garments manufacturing employment on gender equality in Bangladesh*. Washington, DC: World Bank.

Hossain, N. (2017). *The aid lab: Understanding Bangladesh's unexpected success.* Oxford: Oxford University Press.

Hossain, N. (2018). Post-conflict ruptures and the space for women's empowerment in Bangladesh. *Women's Studies International Forum, 68,* 104–112.

Human Rights Watch. (2017). *Bangladesh: Events of 2016.* https://www.hrw.org/world-report/2017/country-chapters/bangladesh.

Kabeer, N. (1988). Subordination and struggle: Women in Bangladesh. *New Left Review, 168,* 95–121.

Kabeer, N. (1999). Resources, agency, achievements: Reflections on the measurement of women's empowerment. *Development and Change, 30*(3), 435–464.

Kabeer, N. (2001). Ideas, economics and "the sociology of supply": Explanations for fertility decline in Bangladesh. *The Journal of Development Studies, 38*(1), 29–70.

Kabeer, N. (2005). Gender equality and women's empowerment: A critical analysis of the third Millennium Development Goal 1. *Gender & Development, 13*(1), 13–24.

Kabeer, N., & Hossain, N. (2004). Achieving universal education and eliminating gender disparity in Bangladesh. *Economic and Political Weekly, 39*(36), 4093–4095, 4097–4100.

Kabeer, N., & Mahmud, S. (2004). Globalization, gender and poverty: Bangladeshi women workers in export and local markets. *Journal of International Development, 16*(1), 93–109.

Kabeer, N., Mahmud, S., & Tasneem, S. (2018). The contested relationship between paid work and women's empowerment: Empirical analysis from Bangladesh. *The European Journal of Development Research, 30*(2), 235–251.

Kamal, S. M. M., Hassan, C. H., Alam, G. M., & Ying, Y. (2015). Child marriage in Bangladesh: Trends and determinants. *Journal of Biosocial Science, 47*(1), 120–139.

Kandiyoti, D. (1988). Bargaining with patriarchy. *Gender & Society, 2*(3), 274–290.

Karim, L. (2011). *Microfinance and its discontents: Women in debt in Bangladesh.* London and Minneapolis, MN: University of Minnesota Press.

Khan, M. R. I., & Wichterich, C. (2015). *Safety and labour conditions: The accord and the national tripartite plan of action for the garment industry of Bangladesh* (Global Labour University Working Paper No. 38). Geneva: International Labour Organization.

Khatun, F. (2018). *Can Bangladesh do without foreign aid?* https://cpd.org.bd/wp-content/uploads/2018/11/Can-Bangladesh-do-without-Foreign-Aid.pdf.

Mahmud, W., Ahmed, S., & Mahajan, S. (2008). *Economic reforms, growth, and governance: The political economy aspects of Bangladesh's development surprise* (Working Paper No. 22). Washington, DC: World Bank.

Mason, A., & King, E. (2001). *Engendering development through gender equality in rights, resources, and voice.* Washington, DC: World Bank.

Moazzem, K. G., & Arfanuzzaman, Md. (2018). *Addressing the livelihood challenges of RMG workers: Exploring scope within the structure of minimum wages and beyond* (CPD Working Paper 122). Dhaka: Centre for Policy Dialogue.

Mookherjee, N. (2008). Gendered embodiments: Mapping the body-politic of the raped woman and the nation in Bangladesh. *Feminist Review, 88,* 36–53.

Nahar, P., van Reeuwijk, M., & Reis, R. (2013). Contextualising sexual harassment of adolescent girls in Bangladesh. *Reproductive Health Matters, 21*(41), 78–86.

Nazneen, S. (2009). Something is better than nothing: Political party discourses on women's empowerment in Bangladesh. *South Asian Journal, 24,* 44–52.

Nazneen, S. (2018). Binary framings, Islam and struggle for women's empowerment in Bangladesh. *Feminist Dissent, 3,* 194–230.

Nazneen, S. (2019). Building strategic relationships with the political elites. In S. Nazneen, S. Hickey, & E. Sifaki (Eds.), *Negotiating gender equity in the global South: The politics of domestic violence policy* (pp. 129–151). London: Routledge.

Nazneen, S., Hossain, N., & Sultan, M. (2011). *National discourses on women's empowerment in Bangladesh: Continuities and change.* http://www.ids.ac.uk/files/dmfile/Wp368.pdf.

Nazneen, S., & Sultan, M. (2010). Reciprocity, distancing, and opportunistic overtures: Women's organisations negotiating legitimacy and space in Bangladesh. *IDS Bulletin, 41*(2), 70–78.

Nazneen, S., & Sultan, M. (Eds.). (2014). *Voicing demands: Feminist activism in transitional contexts.* London: Zed Books.

Rahman, Z., & Langford, T. (2012). Why labour unions have failed Bangladesh's garment workers. In S. Mosoetsa (Ed.), *Labour in the global South: Challenges and alternatives for workers* (pp. 87–106). Geneva: International Labour Organization.

Razavi, S. (2016). The 2030 Agenda: Challenges of implementation to attain gender equality and women's rights. *Gender & Development, 24*(1), 25–41.

Schuler, S. R., Bates, L. M., Islam, F., & Islam, Md. K. (2006). The timing of marriage and childbearing among rural families in Bangladesh: Choosing between competing risks. *Social Science and Medicine, 62*(11), 2826–2837.

Siddiqi, D. M. (2009). Do Bangladeshi factory workers need saving? Sisterhood in the post-sweatshop era. *Feminist Review, 91,* 154–174.

Siddiqi, D. M. (2015). Starving for justice: Bangladeshi garment workers in a "Post-Rana Plaza" world. *International Labor and Working-Class History, 87,* 165–173.

Siddiqi, D. M. (2017). Before Rana Plaza: A history of labour organizing in Bangladesh's garments industry. In V. Crinis & A. Vickers (Eds.), *Labour in the clothing industry in the Asia Pacific* (pp. 60–79). Abingdon and New York, NY: Routledge.

Streatfield, P. K., Kamal, N., Ahsan, K. Z., & Nahar, Q. (2015). Early marriage in Bangladesh. *Asian Population Studies, 11*(1), 94–110.

UNDP (United Nations Development Programme). (n.d.). *Gender Inequality Index.* http://hdr.undp.org/en/composite/GII.

UNICEF (United Nations Children's Fund). (2014). *Ending child marriage: Progress and prospects.* New York, NY: Author.

Wazed, P. M. S. H. (2010). *High Level Plenary Meeting—Millennium Development Goals (MDGs): Statement by Her Excellency Sheikh Hasina, Prime Minister, Government of the People's Republic of Bangladesh.* https://pmo.portal.gov.bd/sites/default/files/files/pmo.portal.gov.bd/pm_speech/37621cb8_5c27_4133_9014_78fe61c8f25e/High%20Level%20Plenary%20Meeting_MDGs_20_220910.pdf.

World Bank. (2007). *Whispers to voices: Gender and social transformation in Bangladesh.* Dhaka: Author.

World Economic Forum. (2018). *Global gender gap report 2018.* https://www.weforum.org/reports/the-global-gender-gap-report-2018.

Yunus, M., & Jolis, A. (1999). *Banker to the poor: The autobiography of Muhammad Yunus, founder of the Grameen Bank.* London: Aurum Press.

Open Access This chapter is licensed under the terms of the Creative Commons Attribution 4.0 International License (http://creativecommons.org/licenses/by/4.0/), which permits use, sharing, adaptation, distribution and reproduction in any medium or format, as long as you give appropriate credit to the original author(s) and the source, provide a link to the Creative Commons license and indicate if changes were made.

The images or other third party material in this chapter are included in the chapter's Creative Commons license, unless indicated otherwise in a credit line to the material. If material is not included in the chapter's Creative Commons license and your intended use is not permitted by statutory regulation or exceeds the permitted use, you will need to obtain permission directly from the copyright holder.

CHAPTER 22

Russia's Approach to Official Development Assistance and Its Contribution to the SDGs

Yury K. Zaytsev

22.1 Introduction

In recent years, Russia's financial contributions to official development assistance (ODA)[1] have significantly increased and reflected Russia's growing interest in regional and global development cooperation. On 20 April 2014, the Government of the Russian Federation adopted the Concept of the Russian Federation's State Policy, in which national objectives and priorities were officially declared. The concept replaced the previous one, which had been approved in 2007 after Russia's first presidency in the G8 club of global donors. Russia's experience of hosting the G8 summit in 2006 influenced greatly the national ODA agenda and the first concept as well (Larionova 2007).

In spite of the ODA policy agenda—as formulated in the Concept of the Russian Federation's State Policy in the Area of International Development Assistance (2014) (hereafter ODA Concept 2014)—and its strong focus on debt relief, education, and health (Ministry of Foreign Affairs of the Russian

---

The paragraph was prepared as part of the research work of the state task of the Russian Academy of National Economy and Public Administration (RANEPA).

Y. K. Zaytsev (✉)
Moscow State Institute of International Relations (MGIMO University), Moscow, Russia

Russian Academy of National Economy and Public Administration, Moscow, Russia

© The Author(s) 2021
S. Chaturvedi et al. (eds.), *The Palgrave Handbook of Development Cooperation for Achieving the 2030 Agenda*,
https://doi.org/10.1007/978-3-030-57938-8_22

Federation [MoFA RF] 2014), the Russian government still has not fully articulated its national approach to ODA as a result of several issues associated with a lack of convergence of interests at the national level. In terms of its international development cooperation, the Russian government is slowly beginning to cooperate with the Organisation for Economic Co-operation and Development (OECD) Development Assistance Committee (DAC) by providing its ODA statistics. Moreover, it supports a dialogue with the Global South through the BRICS (Brazil, Russia, India, China, and South Africa) format, in which countries identify themselves as emerging donors. All of these trends, as well as the external pressures associated with Western sanctions against Russia and Russian counter-sanctions, challenge current Russian development aid politics.

Moreover, transforming the international architecture of ODA—as agreed upon in the 2030 Agenda for Sustainable Development—along with strengthening the role of new stakeholders, including businesses, present extra challenges for donors, including Russia. The challenges are associated with increasing competition for the markets of developing countries and developing new forms of partnerships.

The Russian government has not yet passed a special national law on compliance with the Sustainable Development Goal (SDG) commitments. However, some of the SDGs coincide with Russia's national priorities introduced by the Presidential May Decree of 2018 (Presidential Press and Information Office 2018) at the regional and country levels. The 2030 Agenda for Sustainable Development, adopted by the United Nations (UN) in 2015, puts a special focus on follow-up and review processes at the national and global levels. Thus, I argue that gradual achievement of the SDGs by 2030 as well as national priorities by 2024 requires strengthening the national ODA monitoring and evaluation (M&E) system to substantially increase the effectiveness and efficiency of Russian aid abroad as well as contribute towards decreasing excessive levels of bureaucracy.

In this chapter, research on Russia's development assistance is rooted in theoretical fields related to "systemic change" (Humphrey et al. 2014) and "scaling-up" approaches (World Business Council for Sustainable Development 2013). The "scaling-up" approach makes it possible to measure the scale of Russia's engagement in the markets of developing countries in terms of the amount of resources allocated, the number of people reached, geographic footprint, etc. Although economies of scale and returns on political investment are important for the Russian government, scale implies nothing specific about development impact. That is why the "systemic change" approach is useful for explaining how Russia's development cooperation activities align with the national goals and development goals of recipients and the SDGs. It implies transformation in the structure or dynamics of a system, which in turn leads to impacts on the material conditions or behaviours of large numbers of stakeholders. It aims to catalyse change with spillover effects that have broader direct and indirect impacts (Ruffer and Wach 2013). This approach helps to describe the complex nature of Russia's engagement in international development and reveals the issues, challenges, and impacts that have a "systemic change" effect (Harich 2010).

In order to reveal both the systemic change and scale-up effects of Russia's ODA projects, this chapter discusses M&E issues. Moreover, given the difficulties in achieving the SDGs, special emphasis is placed on changes that concern the scaling-up and systemic change approaches of Russia's ODA projects. Last but not least, Russian businesses are becoming increasingly empowered players that also contribute to systemic change and broadening the scale of Russia's ODA projects. All above-mentioned issues are addressed here from the perspective of both theoretical approaches and with the recognition that systemic change in progress is not straightforward, since it involves changes beyond just tangible outputs (Thorpe 2014).

Moreover, due to the changing nature of Russian ODA, its national projects are often associated with contested cooperation in order to overcome the challenges mentioned above. Contestation is present both at the national and international levels. At the national level in Russia, controversies have arisen among national governmental bodies, such as the Ministry of Finance (MoF) and the Ministry of Foreign Affairs, over Russia's financial and political influence in the context of ODA, which could potentially result in the creation of new national institutions that independently implement Russia's ODA policy. At the international level, contestation is due to Russia's participation in new institutions (New Development Bank, Asian Infrastructure Investment Bank, etc.) as a result of competition with international donors over the markets of developing countries.

To sum up, the chapter looks at Russia's evolving approach to ODA policy implementation. It places the emphasis on the background, the established modes of engagement by key sectors and channels, as well as new challenges concerning the implementation of the SDGs, such as Russia's M&E system and its engagement with businesses, which is also a challenge to the current ODA system.

22.2 Russia as a Global Donor

The Soviet mode of ODA engagement was mainly associated with the scaling-up approach, whereby the Soviet government injected financial resources into socialist countries and low-income economies for their political support in the international arena (Bartenev and Glazunova 2013). Russia's modern economic history can be characterised by the ups and downs regarding the significance ascribed to Russia as a partner in international development cooperation. In the 1990s, during a tumultuous transition period, Russia was included in the DAC recipient countries list and provided concessional credits to support its economy. In 1997, Russia was invited to join the G7/G8, in which it remained a member until 2013. In 2006, Russia officially became a global donor after accepting the presidency of the G8 and hosting the G8 summit in Saint Petersburg, where global donors made a set of commitments on fighting global poverty in such areas as education, energy, and health. This required the Russian government to adjust its ODA approach to the international development agenda. As a result, the process invoked a systemic transformation of national institutions for ODA policy implementation.

As was mentioned above, in 2007, immediately following Russia's G8 presidency, a decree on the "Concept of Russia's Participation in International Development Assistance" was approved by the Russian president (MoFA RF 2007). The 2007 decree made special reference to Russia's international commitments such as the Millennium Declaration, the Monterrey Consensus, and the Paris Declaration on Aid Effectiveness, among others. It reaffirmed Russia's multidimensional approach to development policy going beyond the previous focus on debt relief commitments, which Russia had made at the G8 summit in Gleneagles in 2005.

Russia has been gradually building up and broadening its international development assistance programmes: from about $100 million in 2004 to a peak of almost $1.3 billion annually by 2016 (Fig. 22.1). This is primarily associated with the government's efforts to create a national ODA system according to the geographical and sectoral priorities of the ODA Concept 2014. Although the amounts are modest by comparison with other donors, and also in relation to Russia's gross domestic product, they are nevertheless significant enough, especially at a time when the Russian economy is under severe stress from international sanctions, which undermine the national economy and decrease the overall level of governmental expenditures. For instance, ODA expenditures are comparable to the budgets of 10 of Russia's poorest regions and could be used to implement the Russian government's social commitments.

During the 2014–2017 period, which coincided with external and internal political and economic crises as a result of the imposition of Western sanctions against Russia and its counter-sanctions, the Russian Federation continued to strengthen its position as an international donor, supporting the annual financing of programmes and projects in the field of international development assistance at a level above $1 billion. A special priority was maintained with

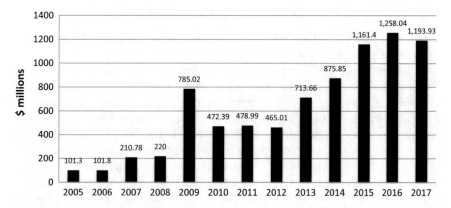

Fig. 22.1 Official development assistance provided by the Russian Federation in the period from 2005 to 2017 ($ millions) (*Source* Based on data provided by the OECD-DAC and the MoF of Russia [Knobel and Zaytsev 2018])

respect to the formation of a zone of good neighbourliness in the framework of economic support for countries in the Commonwealth of Independent States (CIS) (Knobel and Zaytsev 2017). Moreover, in 2014, after Crimea's annexation, a new presidential decree was issued for "Russia's State Policy in the Area of International Development Assistance" (MoFA RF 2014). The emphasis was kept on international commitments made between 2007 and 2014. The focus on supporting sustainable development outcomes was not changed. However, the ODA Concept 2014 reflected more active participation by Russia in ODA and referred to the significant roles of academia, civil society, and business. Moreover, a focus on the M&E component was also added. This trend is associated with the systemic change that the Russian government intended to make in the light of its new approach to foreign policy, which assumed a focus on enhanced cooperation with its Eastern neighbours.

According to recent statistics, in 2017, Russia allocated $1.19 billion for its ODA, which was 5 per cent less than in 2016. This correlates with the general downward trend of the global level of ODA, which, in 2017, was 0.6 per cent lower than the previous period and amounted to $146.6 billion (Organisation for Economic Co-operation and Development [OECD] 2017). The volume of Russian ODA does not exceed 0.1 per cent of its gross national income, whereas one of the UN's objectives for development financing is the annual allocation of donor assistance at the level of 0.7 per cent of gross national income (OECD 2019).

The enforcement of the ODA Concept 2014 also coincided with economic turmoil. The internal and external challenges for the Russian economy in the 2014–2017 period were mostly associated with sanctions, with the estimated impact for the Russian economy being between 1.0 per cent and 1.5 per cent of gross domestic product per year, and foreign direct investment outflow exceeding $150 billion (Central Bank of the Russian Federation 2018). Despite the economic decline, Russia managed to maintain its annual development aid allocations above $1 billion. This reflects both the scale-up and systemic changes of Russia's ODA policy. The "scale-up" is primarily associated with the resilience of the government to increase the volumes of ODA on an annual basis, whereas the "systemic change" effect of ODA programmes was ensured by the Presidential May Decree of 2018. This decree included the M&E component and a new approach to foreign policy that reinforces the new SDG agenda, all of which contribute to the transformation of the aid planning and aid delivery mechanisms.

22.3 Distribution of Russian ODA by Sector and Channel

Despite a wide range of priority sectors identified in Russia's ODA Concept 2014, the current practices concerning Russian ODA generally relate to multilateral and bilateral modes of engagement and are associated primarily with humanitarian aid and debt relief. The analysis of these priorities reveals the scope of Russia's engagement in international development cooperation and illustrates how these areas of engagement contribute to systemic change. Moreover, understating the current instrumental and sectoral modes of engagement in ODA helps to identify national priorities associated with achievement of the SDGs and M&E system establishment.

22.3.1 Multilateral Aid

The current mode of engagement for aid distribution is associated with an increase in the volume of bilateral aid. The main motivation of the Russian MoF is to raise the level of Russian aid effectiveness by developing bilateral channels with the Russian government, which could then exercise greater control over it.

However, in 2012, bilateral aid flows were almost at the same level as those for multilateral financing—and even in excess of them in 2013. Moreover, in the 2014–2017 period, the share of bilateral and multilateral assistance increased from 28.2 per cent in 2014 to 39 per cent (2016) and 38.5 per cent (2017), respectively, of total ODA (Fig. 22.2). This indicates the reliance of the Russian government on using international institutions as mechanisms for the provision of ODA.

The key multilateral partners for Russia in 2017 were UN institutions ($140.88 million), the World Bank ($61.3 million), and regional development banks ($225.12 million) (Table 22.1).

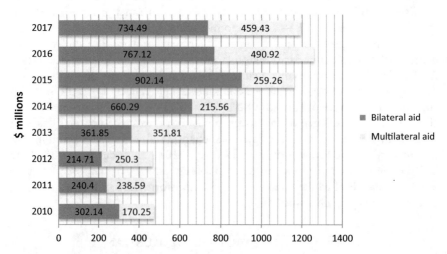

Fig. 22.2 Distribution of Russian ODA to bilateral and multilateral assistance ($ millions) (*Source* Based on data provided by the OECD-DAC and the MoF of Russia [Knobel and Zaytsev 2018])

Table 22.1 The amount of financial participation by Russia in international development institutions in 2017

International institute	The volume of financial participation by Russia ($ millions)
UN institutions	148.22
World Bank institutions (IDA, IBRD, IFC, IIGA)	61.3
Regional development banks	225.12
Montreal Protocol (1987)	3.55
Other international institutions	17.65
Total	455.83

Source Based on data provided by the OECD-DAC and the MoF of Russia (Knobel and Zaytsev 2018)

Despite the statements made in the framework of the spring annual meetings of the World Bank and the International Monetary Fund in 2018 on Russia's abstinence regarding the recapitalisation of the World Bank in the amount of $13 billion, the Russian government continues to use the bank's tools to implement aid programmes ("Russia and the United States" 2018). At the World Bank, the Russian Federation finances projects within the framework of the 21 established trust funds (World Bank 2019). The total cash contributions amounted to $62 million for the 2013–2017 period, earning Russia 25th place in the rankings of trust fund donors by the International Bank for Reconstruction and Development (IBRD) and the International Development Association (IDA) (World Bank 2018). As for the regional development banks, the main priority in 2017 was given to those that were implementing their projects in the Eurasian space (Knobel and Zaytsev 2018). The focus was set on the Eurasian Development Bank and its projects concerning regional infrastructure development (SDG 9) (Eurasian Development Bank 2017).

22.3.2 Bilateral Aid

As a part of its bilateral cooperation, Russia is implementing its scale-up approach and continues to focus on providing assistance to the CIS countries. In the cases of many post-Soviet countries, Russia became one of the largest donors. For example, according to the Russian Federal State Statistics Service (Rosstat) under the President of Tajikistan, Russia's share in overall development assistance amounted to 19.8 per cent ("What assistance does Russia provide" 2017). According to the deputy foreign minister, Alexander Pankin, Russia's priority regions in 2017 also included countries from Latin America, Africa, and Asia ("The volume of Russian assistance" 2018).

Yet, the majority of Russia's bilateral international development assistance is focussed on specific countries that are partners, friends, or neighbouring countries of Russia. Such country-specific programmes account for 40 per cent of all programmes and 80 per cent of all of Russia's current ODA financing (Annex A). The most prominent recipients are Kyrgyzstan, Tajikistan, Cuba, North Korea, Nicaragua, Guinea, Serbia, Mozambique, Syria, and Armenia, which together account for 95 per cent of Russian ODA directed at specific countries (Knobel and Zaytsev 2017).

Currently, Russian bilateral aid focusses mainly on debt relief (SDG 17), the environment (SDG 13), rural and infrastructure development (SDG 9), energy (SDG 7), health (SDG 3), water and sanitation (SDG 6), as well as budget support (SDG 17). Russia uses its multilateral mechanisms through the World Bank or the World Food Programme to assist CIS countries, while placing a special focus on the Kyrgyz Republic, Tajikistan, and Armenia for infrastructure development and the provision of food security. These activities are in line with Russia's specific national objectives in the Eurasian economic space (MoFA RF 2014) associated with economic integration at the sectoral and country levels.

As was mentioned above, Russia is also cooperating with the other BRICS countries. However, unlike the other members, it is not a part of the "Global South" nor a participant in South-South cooperation. BRICS countries do not have a common approach to ODA politics. ODA is one of the policy areas in which the only format of engagement for BRICS countries is dialogue.

22.3.3 *Humanitarian Aid and Debt Relief*

The ODA Concept 2014 identifies health, education, energy, and agriculture (food security) as the basic sectors for Russian aid provision. The main reasons for this are strong national competencies and, as a result, comparative advantages for Russia as a global donor. However, in practice, the bulk of Russian ODA is provided as humanitarian aid and debt relief. According to the Federal Customs Service, in 2017 Russia sent goods as humanitarian aid worth $23.3 million, which is 2.2 times more than in 2016. The key recipient of Russian humanitarian aid was the Syrian Arab Republic. The share of the charity aid provided to it made up 84 per cent of the total volume of Russian humanitarian aid, which, in value terms, is about $19.6 million (Federal Customs Service 2018). A significant share of Russia's ODA continues to be debt relief to developing countries. In 2017, the amount of debt forgiveness to this group of states amounted to $424.94 million (35.6 per cent of total ODA). For example, in June 2017, Kyrgyzstan had $240 million of its debt written off ("Russia has written off Kyrgyzstan's debt" 2017). This mechanism remains a traditional form of Russia's ODA. In 2017, for example, the Government of Russia issued a loan to the Republic of Belarus that amounted to about $700 million over a period of 10 years ("Belarus received from Russia a loan" 2017).

Cuba offers a special case in Russia's debt relief politics. On 7 June 2016, a special version of the Russian–Cuban intergovernmental agreement (of 25 October 2013) (Agreement between Cuba and Russia 2013) was agreed as a tool for the co-financing of projects implemented by Russian companies in Cuba (Ministry of Finance 2013). Funds in a special account are used to finance investment projects in the Republic of Cuba—including projects in the field of environmental protection—and selected by the Cuban Communist Party in accordance with the National Plan for Economic and Social Development of Cuba. As of 1 October 2017, the amount of funds deposited in a special account was $1.06 billion. This means that the Cuban government can attract these resources to finance its project with participation by Russian businesses. According to the agreement, the Cuban customer and the Russian contractor conclude a contract, under which the contractor implements the project approved by the parties (perform work, provide services, deliver goods, etc.). This also assumes public–private partnerships (PPPs), as long as the Cuban customer is represented by governmental bodies.

As an advantage, it provides access to a large amount of additional sources of project financing, reducing the need for loan funds. What is more, it provides a possibility for payment in the local currency for expenses incurred during the project. As a condition, the Government of Cuba should receive "priority project" status for such activities and include them in the National Plan for Economic and Social Development of Cuba. The disadvantage is that the Cuban government is only able to implement these projects in conjunction with Russian businesses. This mechanism is more about scale and return on investment rather than its importance for businesses. However, over a period of time, infrastructure and capacity-building project outputs may bring about systemic transformation.

Currently, the mechanism is also being used for financing parts of the "advanced" payments on the Cuban side for preparatory, construction, assembly, and other work being carried out by Cuban companies. This work is performed under existing contracts that are implemented through intergovernmental agreements on the provision of Russian state export credits (for projects such as the modernisation and construction of the Maksimo Gomez TPP East Havana and the metallurgical plant Antilla de Acero im José Martí).

It should be noted that the actual value of ODA provided by the Russian Federation exceeds the amounts published in OECD statistics. The first reason for this is the provision of assistance to countries that are not on the OECD-DAC list of beneficiaries. Russia continues to support the socio-economic development of South Ossetia, which is still considered by the international community to form part of Georgia. For example, the Russian government has allocated RUB 600 million for the construction of an operational-surgical complex at the Republican Hospital. This was a project included within the investment programme that relied on Russian financial assistance for the 2015–2017 period (Sineva 2018). Moreover, the Russian Federation, like other OECD-DAC countries, also allocates funds to combat international terrorism and provides military assistance. However, these areas of assistance are not taken into account in ODA statistics (Zaytsev 2013).

Thus, an appropriate accounting of Russian ODA would make it possible to provide more accurate assessments of the scale of Russia's official engagement into the markets of developing countries through bilateral and multilateral channels. Moreover, humanitarian aid and debt relief often reflect only the quantitative side of international development engagement. In order to make further qualitative judgements on the systemic change of Russian ODA and its impact, an evidence base is required. However, Russia's ODA politics currently lack substantive and qualitative impact assessments due to a concrete absence of ODA M&E practices.

22.4 Monitoring and Evaluation

Current trends reveal that Russia's ODA policy places a greater emphasis on tracing the government's actions in the field of development cooperation in order to raise the efficiency and effectiveness of Russian aid. Moreover, in the light of scarce budgetary resources, monitoring external and internal governmental policy implementation could raise Russia's accountability standards. That is why elaborating institutional models and establishing a national M&E system is essential, especially for external policies such as ODA (Boehmer and Zaytsev 2018). Moreover, as was mentioned above, M&E systems help to trace the progress of "systemic change" and evaluate the "scope" of engagement to fight global poverty.

From an expert point of view, there are several reasons for establishing an ODA M&E system in Russia.[2] The first reason is the provision of information to the public and the government, especially in time of budget constraints. The efforts should be undertaken in conjunction with a communication strategy, which requires the development of a clear narrative that speaks to key audiences and is based on factual data, combined with information on Russia's impact that stakeholders can relate to for further decision-making. This could take the form of an annual institutionalised report to the government and the public in the form of an easily understood brochure. These reports should incorporate simple indicators on what has been done on the global and country levels (Boehmer and Zaytsev 2018). They should be measurable and the data should be readily available. The successful examples of establishing ODA M&E systems are usually associated with the practices of the United Kingdom, Germany, Canada, Australia, etc. (Boehmer and Zaytsev 2019), where the efficiency of ODA projects is assessed against "systemic change" criteria.

The second reason is accountability to the Governmental Commission on International Development Assistance by providing data on Russia's ODA.[3] The main purpose of reporting to the commission is to show the value for money and the rationale for the spending of ODA.

The third reason is associated with G20 accountability, which assumes preparation of the National Action Plans to achieve the SDGs. As a member of the G20, Russia is committed to providing annual reports showing compliance with SDG targets. The international commitment coincides with Russia's national priorities on achieving the SDGs, which is reflected in the Concept of the Russian Federation's State Policy in the Area of International Development Assistance (MoFA RF 2014). Moreover, the usage of SDG indicators could strengthen the national ODA M&E system as well as optimise the efficiency and effectiveness of Russian development aid projects. Thus, SDG reporting for the G20 could be a part of national efforts towards ODA M&E.

According to Russia's MoF, Russia is accountable to the G20 and is in charge of preparing the National Action Plans to achieve the SDGs.[4] The report is supposed to be composed of two parts. The first part relates to national actions on internal politics. The second part deals with external actions associated with achievement of the SDGs. For this purpose, mainly SDGs 5 and 6 will be reported on at the G20. Many of the SDGs have cross-cutting points, and an SDG–Millennium Development Goal mapping should be done for the purpose of assessing the progress made.

Despite the inclusion of some M&E elements in the 2014 Presidential Decree, a little progress had been made in establishing an ODA M&E system. In part, this was due to the composition of Russia's aid with relatively few bilateral projects that would constitute a portfolio with the potential to draw lessons. Other reasons were more political, such as the decision-making process for the allocation of funding, which was associated with the divergent perspectives of the Ministry of Foreign Affairs and the MoF.

Shortly after the adoption of the 2014 Presidential Decree, the MoF was given full authority to develop a national ODA M&E system. However, given that Russia does not have a consolidated development assistance budget that is under the responsibility of a single line ministry, developing a national M&E system would inevitably involve cross-ministerial coordination and agreement on the key parameters (Boehmer and Zaytsev 2018).

The MoF first turned to other "Southern donors", including Brazil, to gain a better understanding of balancing domestic demands and international best practices. At the same time, multilateral organisations such as the World Bank and the United Nations Development Programme provided support in aligning national objectives with global agreements and practices. Although the 2014 Presidential Decree contained a long list of priorities, the MoF was unable to reach an agreement within the government on the purpose of the future M&E system. Pressure to make progress, however, continued to mount, with parliament expecting the Russian government—and specifically the MoF—to provide annual progress updates (Boehmer and Zaytsev 2018).

The emphasis on strengthening national ODA M&E systems has become one of the main prerequisites for the gradual achievement of the SDGs by 2030. The 2030 Agenda for Sustainable Development, adopted by the UN in 2015, puts a special focus on follow-up and review processes at the national and global levels. It should be informed by global and country-led evaluations and data that is high-quality, accessible, timely, and reliable (United Nations [UN] 2015) in order to inform stakeholders on the systemic changes and the scale of change.

With the launch of the SDGs, many governments are actively working to consider how they will address the SDG indicators and targets. It often makes them reconsider the main principles of the national M&E systems for addressing this challenge. Given that the Russian government is at the very early stage of establishing a national ODA M&E system, taking the SDGs into consideration could be a part of the process. This would also contribute towards raising the level of transparency of Russia's efforts in the field of international development cooperation. What is more, most of the SDGs assume long-lasting systemic change effects. To reveal these effects in the future, the M&E system should be created as fast as possible. Through the monitoring and assessing of appropriate SDG targets, the governmental bodies would be able to track their incremental efforts towards systemic change.

22.5 Russia's ODA Policy and the SDG Agenda

The SDGs have become a new challenge for the international community, especially in the light of the changing development agenda. Each SDG is subject to comprehensive efforts towards achieving and maintaining them, with all 17 SDGs being interconnected and interrelated. The relationships between the goals can be even more complex. Each goal is connected to other goals and sub-targets in different, often context-dependent ways (UN 2015). Moreover, the introduction of the SDGs into Russia's ODA politics addresses its systemic change approach, with spillover effects among the goals and targets that have direct and indirect impacts (Ruffer and Wach 2013). Currently, the systemic change with respect to SDG implementation is about altering functions and structures associated with Russian institutions and legislation. They relate primarily to ODA M&E system creation and the agency responsible for ODA provision.

In December 2016, a meeting of the State Council was held on the issue "On the environmental development of the Russian Federation in the interests of future generations" (Presidential Press and Information Office 2016). The government was instructed to consider "as one of the main goals of Russia's transition to a model environmentally sustainable development" to define and use a system of indicators for sustainable development—mechanisms for achieving the goals of the country's environmentally sustainable development policy by 2030, and thereafter by 2050. Other assignments for the government included: (1) the provision of the definition of target indicators of the energy efficiency of the economy and the implementation of a set of measures to increase it, including the development of renewable energy sources; (2) consideration of the impact of introducing environmentally sustainable development mechanisms.

The monitoring of Russia's achievement of the SDGs has been included in the Federal Statistical Work Plan since 2017 (Resolution of the Government of the Russian Federation 2017). Rosstat (2019) was assigned as the responsible body for the development of a national set of indicators of SDGs for Russia for their further implementation in state strategic documents.[5] It also coordinates the collection and provision of statistical information on SDG indicators to international organisations (Order of the Government of the Russian Federation 2017). In total, 90 SDG indicators have been collected, including 54 indicators (60 per cent) by Rosstat and 36 indicators (40 per cent) by ministries and departments. In 2017, the Rosstat portal created a "Sustainable Development Goals" section for downloading statistical information on monitoring the implementation of the SDGs at the national level (Rosstat 2015). Thus, the SDGs are shared by the Russian government with respect to its internal and external politics.

At the national level, the SDGs are partly expressed by a decree of the President of the Russian Federation "On the National Goals and Strategic Objectives of the Development of the Russian Federation for the Period up to 2024" (Presidential Press and Information Office 2018). The May Decree of 2018 sets strategic tasks for the government and determines the indicators for the results that are expected to be achieved in six years, thereby achieving the tasks of the SDGs.

The official version of the Presidential May Decree of 2018 encompasses nine national goals in the fields of demography, poverty eradication, income increases, housing improvements, technology development, digital economy, economic growth, and export expansion (Table 22.2).

From this, it can be seen that the SDGs are becoming priorities for Russia's social and environmental development (Presidential Press and Information Office 2016), with Rosstat having become the main stakeholder in identifying and monitoring the targets at the national level (Resolution of the

Table 22.2 List of national goals of the Presidential May Decree of 2018

a. ensuring sustainable natural growth of the population of the Russian Federation;
b. increase in life expectancy to 78 years (by 2030–up to 80 years);
c. ensuring a steady growth in the real incomes of citizens as well as an increase in pension amounts above inflation levels;
d. halving the level of poverty in the Russian Federation;
e. improvement of living conditions for at least 5 million families annually;
f. acceleration in the technological developments of the Russian Federation, and an increase in the number of organisations implementing technological innovations, up to 50 per cent of their total number;
g. ensuring the accelerated introduction of digital technologies in the economy and the social sphere;
h. contributing to the Russian Federation so that it becomes one of the five largest economies in the world, ensuring economic growth rates that are higher than global ones while maintaining macroeconomic stability, including inflation, at a level not exceeding 4 per cent;
i. job creation in the basic sectors of the economy, primarily in the manufacturing industry and the agro-industrial complex, for a highly productive export-oriented sector that is developed on modern technologies with highly qualified personnel.

Source Presidential Press and Information Office (2018)

Government of the Russian Federation 2017). However, it is still necessary to supplement the country's national strategic planning system for ODA with its Sustainable Development Strategy, as well as with the SDGs in order to contribute towards their achievement by 2030 (Bobylev and Grigoriev 2015).

The political goals for Russian ODA are also correlated with the SDGs and can be classified at the global, regional, and recipient country levels. Traditionally, Russia's priorities as a global actor covered the areas where the country possessed comparative advantages, such as health, education, and energy, as well as food security. All these areas are related to facilitating sustainable socio-economic development in partner countries, including post-conflict countries (SDG 1). Other goals of the ODA Concept 2014 at the global level—such as limiting the consequences of natural disasters or establishing a stable and equitable world order based on universally recognised norms of international law and relations between countries—can also easily be mapped (SDGs 11 and 17).

At the regional level, Russia's priorities are mostly associated with facilitating the integration processes among the CIS countries, with particular emphasis on the development of trade and economic cooperation (SDG 9) (Knobel et al. 2019). With respect to other neighbouring countries, Russia is primarily keen on facilitating the elimination of potential points of tension and conflict and sources of drug trafficking, international terrorism, and organised crime, as well as preventing their occurrence (SDG 16) (MoFA RF 2014).

At the level of recipient countries, the interests related to Russian ODA very often coincide with its global and regional priorities, so its ODA policy aims at overcoming the barriers at the national level in order to implement these priorities (Boehmer and Zaytsev 2018). Russia's national interest in supporting developing countries is translated into practice by boosting economic activity, creating conditions to involve the poorest groups of the population in economic activities (SDG 6 and 7), and providing access to vital resources, primarily water and electricity (SDG 9). In the case of Russia's Eurasian economic integration policy, all these measures help the recipients to improve conditions for their trade and investment activities in order to enhance their proactivity in the Eurasian economic space (Knobel et al. 2019).

Another angle of Russian national interest in ODA politics relates to the support of global partnerships (SDG 17), which is primarily associated with strengthening national health systems and social safety nets (SDG 3), raising the quality of education (SDG 4), and supporting efforts on post-conflict peace-building (SDG 16) (MoFA RF 2014). The partnerships are associated with institutional cooperation focussed in these areas at the international level in the framework of the G20, the UN system, etc.

Overall, most of the priority areas of Russia's ODA policy at the global, regional, and national levels correlate with the relevant SDGs. Given that the achievement of development objectives is not associated merely with a particular SDG or several SDGs, it is important to note that the priority areas and relevant objectives of Russia's ODA engagement should be mutually reinforcing and complement each other. Thus, the national priorities for Russia's ODA policy should result from considerations about the provisions of the ODA Concept 2014, the relevant SDGs discussed above, as well as the perspectives of stakeholders contributing to the implementation of ODA projects (such as the Ministry of Foreign Affairs and other sectoral federal governmental bodies, as well as civil society and business).

For a successful implementation of the objectives of the SDGs, it is necessary to adapt the SDG indicators at the national level. Existing tasks and activities within the framework of national socio-economic development programmes need to be analysed and compared with global goals and objectives to assess compatibility or conflicts as well as gaps in the content of national documents. Given the complex hierarchy of Russia's ODA priorities at different levels, it is essential to focus on areas where national interests coincide as well as on regional objectives and the SDGs as global priorities. So, in narrowing down the priority areas for the purposes of developing a simple M&E system, I suggest considering those areas where Russian national interests coincide directly with SDGs that support recipient countries. Those would be the goals of zero hunger (SDG 2), clean water and sanitation (SDG 6), affordable and clean energy (SDG 7), decent work and economic growth (SDG 8), as well as industry, innovation, and infrastructure (SDG 9) (Boehmer and Zaytsev 2018).

22.6 Russian Businesses and ODA

Russian businesses have been represented in the markets of developing countries since Soviet times. In essence, the economic assistance of the USSR served as a corporate social responsibility (CSR) programme for Soviet enterprises operating there. This form of cooperation was aimed at overcoming the negative externalities associated with the work of Soviet industrial enterprises, as well as at strengthening their positions. For ideological reasons, socially oriented programmes that accompanied the work of Soviet organisations could not conceptually and meaningfully intersect with the programmes of companies in capitalist countries. Nevertheless, in fact, they had a large number of points of intersection with the CSR projects of Western partners (Zaytsev 2018).

Notwithstanding that the current role ascribed to businesses as development actors goes far beyond their CSR practices, due to the lack of information on Russian private development engagement, this chapter only relies on open CSR data that is published by Russian companies as a part of their participation in the Global Reporting Initiative. The expenditures of Russian companies for external CSR practices are usually associated with development objectives in the field of infrastructure and human development.

The share of Russian businesses' foreign direct investment in the poorest countries of Africa, Latin America, and South-East Asia is still quite low. For example, the figure is less than 8 per cent in sub-Saharan Africa and less than 1 per cent in the Middle East and North Africa (RAS Institute 2014). In emerging and fast-growing markets, Russian investors are surpassed by their US, Chinese, EU, and Australian competitors in Africa, Latin America, and South-East Asia. The main reasons predominantly concern the relatively high levels of competition and support from national governments, which—in the cases of the United States and the European Union—often have more diversified and effective mechanisms of support. For example, in 2015, US companies spent more than $41.5 million for CSR projects in the African region. At the same time, Nigeria ($5.41 million) and Egypt ($6.14 million) are among the largest recipients of social investments (Chief Executives for Corporate Purpose 2016).

Russian companies are also represented in the region in the mining and services sectors, where CSR programmes accompany business processes. However, Russian companies' expenditures for external CSR are substantially lower. For instance, Lukoil Overseas implements its projects in Egypt, Ghana, Côte d'Ivoire, and Iraq. According to 2015 data, Lukoil Overseas spent more than $5 million for projects aimed at ensuring the company's CSR in foreign countries (Lukoil Overseas 2011).

However, the Russian private sector has an extended portfolio of CSR projects. CSR programmes implemented by Russian businesses abroad vary substantially, depending on the specifics of the business and terms of funding. For example, businesses from the industrial sector of the economy put special emphasis on infrastructure projects and the development of human capital and local communities, whereas businesses from the financial sector are implementing CSR projects, which mostly focus on environmental and social issues (Zaytsev 2018).

Russian businesses put a special emphasis on the projects that affect local communities when implementing CSR programmes. A prime example is the work of Russian companies from the mining sector, such as Alrosa, Lukoil Overseas, Rusal, Gazprom, and Rosneft, in the markets of developing countries and countries with rapidly growing economies.

Lukoil Overseas has become Russia's largest private company in terms of assets, sales, and spending on social-oriented projects in Africa, Latin America, and the Middle East. The company is ranked among the 10 largest non-financial transnational corporations that are represented in the markets of developing countries and countries with economies in transition.

One of the largest projects of the company in Africa is "Meleiha" (Western Desert), which will be implemented under the terms of a concession until 2024. The company owns a 50 per cent stake in the project. The Egyptian government and the Egyptian oil company EGPC are the holders of the rest of the shares. One of the conditions for the concession was the implementation of socially oriented projects aimed at ensuring the interests of local communities and the development of infrastructure. The company has implemented its CSR projects in Sierra Leone, Ghana, and areas around the Gulf of Guinea as part of its business activities. Most of the projects have focussed on the development of local communities.

The mining company Rusal is also among the key representatives of Russian companies implementing CSR projects in foreign countries where they operate, such as Guinea, Nigeria, Guyana, and Jamaica. The company is also leading in terms of financing social projects, which, for 2013, amounted to about $10 million (Rusal 2013a).

The social activities of the company relate to participation in infrastructure projects. In the city of Fria (Guinea) over the last 10 years, the company has been carrying out the construction of artesian wells, public schools, as well as the reconstruction of the city mosque and the Catholic Church. In Guyana, the company built a plant for the purification of drinking water for the Hururu village and carried out the electrification of the village—having supplied the electricity through the generating capacity of its plant (Rusal 2013b).

CSR practices have become an inevitable part of business activity portfolios and are often implemented as part of a corporate management programme. On the one hand, the practices are in line with governmental efforts to provide public goods. On the other hand, they do not always advance the core targets of the SDGs, but they do contribute to economic development and growth.

The integration of Russian businesses into the system of global economic relations means deeper involvement in value chains, which, in turn, suggests expanded production in developing markets, depending on the availability of critical production factors, which contribute to both scale and change. However, political risks and the inefficient system of state support to capital exporters—with a focus on companies with government participation—considerably complicate the invasion of foreign developing markets by Russian businesses. However, participation by Russian businesses in national ODA projects could substantially reduce such risks. What is more, commercial private capital could contribute towards financing the SDGs through blended mechanisms, with Russia as the official donor. Overall, development and related SDG projects are often not bankable for businesses. Consequently, private capital could be an alternative source to "turn the billions into trillions".

There are several mechanisms, including PPPs, that could increase the involvement of the Russian private sector in state ODA projects. PPPs have become an integral part of the SDG agenda and contain an enormous potential to contribute to the achievement of SDGs 8, 9, and 17, in particular.

Moreover, some Russian companies have already indirectly integrated the SDGs into their day-to-day activities. According to the Russian Union of Industrialists and Entrepreneurs, about 200 companies have implemented more than 500 projects to overcome social and environmental challenges, thereby contributing towards the achievement of the SDGs. Moreover, 25 of these companies—working in fields such as energy, oil and gas, metallurgical and mining, agriculture, and telecommunications—have streamlined their social and environmental practices with the SDGs of the 2030 Agenda (Russian Union of Industrialists and Entrepreneurs 2018). This approach is reflected in the company reports on CSR, in which particular activities are associated with the appropriate SDGs.

Despite Russia's economic decline, socially responsible projects should remain a priority for Russian corporations in the light of the environmental and social goals stipulated by the SDGs. This concerns not only the classic polluting companies, represented in the mining and manufacturing sectors, but also the businesses working in the services sector. Moreover, the development footprint of Russian business could be strengthened with governmental support, which is associated with PPP projects and political risk-reduction. Such cooperation is associated not only with a straightforward scale effect but also with long-lasting systemic changes.

22.7 Conclusions

In spite of the decline of the Russian economy and the instability of international relations with the United States and the EU since 2014, the government continues to develop its practices in the field of development assistance. As a result, it is impressive that Russia's commitment to international agreements remains solid, even as political actions, such as Western sanctions, push Russia into a more isolated position. Moreover, the government is trying to address the current challenges associated with both scale and change, such as the volumes of ODA provision, aid effectiveness, achievement of the SDGs, and business participation.[6] Thus, Russia's contribution to systemic change and the scale thereof may be associated with the factors against which the effectiveness and efficiency of its ODA politics may be assessed. However, the absence of an ODA M&E system at the national level makes it quite difficult to trace the progress.

The "scale-up" and "systemic change" theoretical approaches suggested for this chapter helped to reveal the modality of Russia's ODA provision. Russia has been incrementally increasing the volume of its ODA since it agreed to broaden the "scale" of the programmes and the number of regions covered by its ODA policy in its ODA Concept 2014. However, there is still a lack of evidence to help judge the "systemic change" of Russia's current efforts and results in the field of international development. The reason for this is the absence of a national ODA M&E system. The issues of Russia's ODA accountability commitment, along with problems about its effectiveness and efficiency, make the task of forming it even more urgent.

Moving forward with the establishment of a national ODA M&E system may result in more bureaucracy for decision-makers and implementers of ODA projects. However, the formation of such a system will help in solving other tasks related to the fulfilment of Russia's international obligations, including the achievement of the SDGs. In addition, it would inspire Russian businesses to become more significant development actors. Moreover, the concept of contested cooperation helps in assessing the current position of Russia as an international donor. On the one hand, Russia's ODA system is underdeveloped in comparison with other DAC countries. Cooperation with the DAC remains at quite a low level—Russia only reports to the DAC. On the other hand, Russia is also not a Global South country and has been isolated by the West from taking part in the fora of global donors, such as the G7 and G8 summits. This position requires the Russian government to look for other options for ODA system development.

As was revealed in the beginning, Russian development cooperation is often associated with contested cooperation, given the existing competition among national institutions over the implementation of Russian ODA. This is in addition to its activities that seek to shift the existing balance of international systems towards a new institutional order for development through the establishment of new institutions. The implementation of a new approach to Russia's foreign policy since 2014 (Concept of Foreign Politics) often implies the establishment of a new international institution as a way to challenge the existing system. Thus, the contested form of Russian development cooperation contributes to a proliferation of international institutions with the establishment of the New Development Bank and the Asian Infrastructure Investment Bank, as well as to the development of new national institutional practices that could contribute to aid effectiveness. Launching and operationalising an ODA M&E system as well as cooperating with private business would lead to increases in aid efficiency as well, which could lead to direct and indirect systemic changes in Russia's aid programmes and development results.

Notes

1. Official development assistance(ODA flows) is defined as flows to countries and territories on the DAC list of ODA recipients and multilateral development institutions as follows: (1) they are provided by official agencies, including state and local governments, or by their executive agencies; (2) each transaction is (a) administered with the promotion of the economic development and welfare of developing countries as its main objective; and (b) is concessional in character. For more details, see: https://www.oecd.org/dac/stats/officialdevelopmentassistancedefinitionandcoverage.htm.
2. This is according to outputs of the seminar "Towards the M&E Framework for Russian Development Aid", held by the World Bank on 15 March 2016 in Moscow.
3. The issues of international development assistance are currently being discussed at the governmental commission on economic development and integration (Governmental Commission 2019).
4. This is according to outputs of the seminar "Towards the M&E Framework for Russian Development Aid", held by the World Bank on 15 March 2016 in Moscow.
5. Of the 244 SDG indicators, 19 indicators (7 per cent) are in the process of development, 69 (28 per cent) are being developed, and 156 (71 per cent) are not being developed.
6. This is according to outputs of the seminar "Towards the M&E Framework for Russian Development Aid", held by the World Bank on 15 March 2016 in Moscow.

Annex A. Distribution of Russian bilateral assistance by recipient countries in 2012–2017 ($ millions)

Aid allocation	2012	2013	2014	2015	2016	2017
Bilateral aid (total)	214.71	361.85	660.29	902.14	762.06	733.77
Afghanistan	0.45	0	4.95	2.56	0.04	0.04
Armenia	5.79	5.26	5.86	37.37	40.33	15.63
Azerbaijan	1.73	–	0.48	0.01	0.05	2.49
Belarus	0.11	1.47	2.5	2.97	2.87	2.25
Burundi	0.14	–	–	–	–	0.04
Cambodia	0.09	–	–	–	0.15	0.37
Congo	0.28	–	–	1.21	–	1
Cuba	5.58	2.76	176.98	351.97	352	353.83
DPRK	15.5	33.61	68.42	59.77	58.63	57.71
Egypt	0.07	–	–	0.78	–	0.03
Fiji	–	–	0.13	–	0.02	0.01
Guinea	0.97	–	16.79	6.25	6.32	3.72
India	0.06	0.01	–	–	0.38	0.46
Iran	0.1	–	1.3	1.3	–	–
Iraq	0.41	0.55	1.07	0.23	1.58	1.59
Jordan	2.6	5.44	3	4.99	0.5	1.67
Kazakhstan	1.6	0.08	0.55	0.57	0.32	0.48
Kenya	2.88	2.19	2	–	–	1
Kiribati	–	–	–	–	–	0.01
Kyrgyzstan	37.92	76.73	202.87	322.81	198.81	129.81
Laos	0.23	–	–	–	–	0.17
Madagascar	0.06	–	–	–	9.89	8.89
Marshall Islands	–	–	–	–	–	0.01
Mongolia	7.92	0.01	–	0.23	0.21	1.16
Morocco	0.08	1.98	1.5	0.6	–	4.16
Mozambique	0.09	13.05	8	8	8	8
Myanmar	–	–	0.05	0.08	–	0.17
Namibia	0.09	0.46	–	0.06	–	1.5
Nepal	0.18	–	–	–	0.2	0.25
Nicaragua	10.86	36.4	17.24	5.56	12.04	14.01
Palau	–	–	–	–	–	0.01
Peru	–	–	–	–	–	0.4
Serbia	9.49	36.47	16.21	11.25	11.7	6.87
Somali	2.04	1	1	–	1	1
Sudan	0.01	2.56	0.05	1.54	0.01	1
Syria	11.17	12.95	7.33	22.1	4	20.53
Tajikistan	15.21	17.12	19.48	21.76	13.66	16.1
Tanzania	0.07	3.37	1.37	1.37	1.37	1.37
Tonga	–	–	–	–	–	0.01
Tunis	0.04	1.98	1.65	1.12	–	5.66
Ukraine	1.15	0.69	6.82	–	5.62	5

(continued)

(continued)

Aid allocation	2012	2013	2014	2015	2016	2017
Uzbekistan	0.92	0.34	1.15	0.52	0.05	2.98
Vietnam	2.56	0.4	–	0.16	0.2	6.93
Yemen	1.5	–	0.36	2.36	–	1

Source Based on data provided by the OECD-DAC and the MoF of Russia (Knobel and Zaytsev 2018)

REFERENCES

Agreement between Cuba and Russia. (2013). *Agreement on the settlement of the debt of the Republic of Cuba to the Russian Federation on loans extended in the period of the former USSR, signed on October 25, 2013.* http://asozd2.duma.gov.ru/addwork/scans.nsf/ID/31D1C5D3E102 245F43257D0A0052720C/$FILE/560637-6.PDF?OpenElement (in Russian).

Bartenev, V., & Glazunova, E. (2013). *International development cooperation: Set of lectures.* Moscow: World Bank.

Belarus received from Russia a loan of $700 million dollars. (2017, September 15). *Ukrop News 24.* https://ukropnews24.com/belarus-received-from-russia-a-loan-of-700-million/.

Bobylev, S. N., & Grigoriev, L. M. (2015). *The UN Sustainable Development Goals and Russia: Human Development Report in the Russian Federation.* http://ac.gov.ru/files/publication/a/11068.pdf (in Russian).

Boehmer, H. M., & Zaytsev, Y. (2018). *Monitoring and evaluation in Russia's international development assistance program.* Research paper for the 13-Biannual conference of the European Evaluation Society (EE18-0036). https://papers.ssrn.com/sol3/papers.cfm?abstract_id=3360461.

Boehmer, H. M., & Zaytsev, Y. (2019). Raising aid efficiency with ODA M&E systems. *Journal of MultiDisciplinary Evaluation, 15*(32), 28–36.

Central Bank of the Russian Federation. (2018). *Statistics of the Bank of Russia.* https://cbr.ru/eng/statistics/.

Chief Executives for Corporate Purpose. (2016). *Giving around the globe: 2016 edition.* https://cecp.co/wp-content/uploads/2016/11/2016_Giving_Around_the_Globe_web-1.pdf.

Eurasian Development Bank. (2017). *Eurasian fund for stabilization and development* (Annual report). https://efsd.eabr.org/upload/iblock/c5b/EABR_AR_2017_EFSD_EN-_1_.pdf.

Federal Customs Service. (2018). *Customs statistics of external trade.* Moscow: Author (in Russian).

Governmental Commission. (2019). *Governmental commission on economic development and integration.* Moscow: Government of Russia (in Russian).

Harich, J. (2010). Change resistance as the crux of the environmental sustainability problem. *System Dynamics Review, 26*(1), 35–72.

Humphrey, J., Spratt, S., Thorpe, J., & Henson, S. (2014). *Understanding and enhancing the role of business in international development: A conceptual framework and agenda for research* (IDS Working Paper 440). Brighton: Institute of Development Studies.

Knobel, A., & Zaytsev, Y. (2017). Russia's economic aid to other countries in 2016. *Economic Development of Russia, 24*(10), 17–21 (in Russian).

Knobel, A., & Zaytsev, Y. (2018). Russia as international donor in 2017. *Economic Development of Russia, 25*(12), 8–12 (in Russian).

Knobel, A., Lipin, A., Malokostov, A., Tarr, D. G., & Turdyeva, N. (2019). Deep integration in the Eurasian economic union: What are the benefits of successful implementation or wider liberalization? *Eurasian Geography and Economics, 60*(2), 177–210.

Larionova, M. (2007). G8 compliance with commitments, made at 2006 summit in St. Petersburg. *International Organizations Research Journal, 2*(3), 34–80 (in Russian).

Lukoil Overseas. (2011). *Annual report 2011.* http://www.lukoil.com/FileSystem/9/289069.pdf.

Ministry of Finance. (2013). *Presentation on the mechanism of using the special account funds for the purpose of financing supplies, works and services as part of projects in the Republic of Cuba in accordance with the Russian-Cuban Intergovernmental Agreement of October 25, 2013.* Moscow: Author.

MoFA RF (Ministry of Foreign Affairs of the Russian Federation). (2007, June 14). *The concept of Russia's participation in international development assistance (No. Pr-1040).* https://www.minfin.ru/common/img/uploaded/library/2007/06/concept_eng.pdf.

MoFA RF. (2014, April 20). *The concept of the Russian Federation's state policy in the area of international development assistance (PR-No. 259).* http://minfin.ru/common/upload/library/2007/06/concept_eng.pdf.

Montreal Protocol. (1987, September 16). *Montreal Protocol on ozone depleting substances.* http://www.un.org/ru/documents/decl_conv/conventions/montreal_prot.shtml.

OECD (Organisation for Economic Co-operation and Development). (2017). *Development aid stable in 2017 with more sent to poorest countries.* https://www.oecd.org/development/development-aid-stable-in-2017-with-more-sent-to-poorest-countries.htm.

OECD. (2019). *The 0.7% ODA/GNI target—A history.* http://www.oecd.org/dac/stats/the07odagnitarget-ahistory.htm.

Order of the Government of the Russian Federation. (2017). *On ensuring coordination of activities of subjects of official statistics on the formation and submission to international organizations of national statistical information on indicators of achievement of the Sustainable Development Goals (No. 1170-p).* http://docs.cntd.ru/document/436740030 (in Russian).

Presidential Press and Information Office. (2016, December 27). *Meeting of the State Council on the issue "on the environmental development of the Russian Federation in the interests of future generations".* http://kremlin.ru/events/president/news/53602 (in Russian).

Presidential Press and Information Office. (2018, March 7). *Decree of the president of the Russian Federation on national goals and strategic tasks of the development of the Russian Federation for the period up to 2024.* http://www.kremlin.ru/acts/bank/43027 (in Russian).

RAS Institute. (2014). *Investment from Russia stabilizes after the global crisis*. Moscow: RAS Institute of World Economy and International Relations.

Resolution of the Government of the Russian Federation. (2017). *Formation of official statistical information carried out by subjects of official statistical accounting* (Resolution No. 2033-r). Moscow: Government of Russia (in Russian).

Rosstat (Russian Federal State Statistics Service). (2015). *Sustainable Development Goals*. Moscow: Author (in Russian).

Rosstat. (2019). *Status of developing indicators for Sustainable Development Goals*. Moscow: Author (in Russian).

Ruffer, T., & Wach, E. (2013). *Review of M4P evaluation methods and approaches* (ITAD Report). Hove: Itad.

Rusal. (2013a). *Sustainable development report*. http://www.rusal.ru/upload/uf/ecd/EWF%20101.pdf (in Russian).

Rusal. (2013b). *Social programs abroad: Sustainability report of UC "Rusal"*. http://sr.rusal.ru/investments-in-development-of-local-communities/the-results-of-201 2.php (in Russian).

Russia and the United States refused to participate in the recapitalization of the World Bank. (2018, April 22). *RBC*. Moscow: RBC Group (in Russian).

Russia has written off Kyrgyzstan's debt of USD240 million. (2017, May 4). *UAWire*. https://www.uawire.org/news/russia-has-written-off-kyrgyzstan-s-debt-of-240-million-usd.

Russian Union of Industrialists and Entrepreneurs (2018). *Russian business and Sustainable Development Goals*. http://media.rspp.ru/document/1/b/2/b24091d44c9660fcf3a9fdad6551b88f.pdf (n Russian).

Sineva, O. (2018, July 11). *In South Ossetia, a surgical complex was built at the expense of the Russian budget*. https://vademec.ru/news/2018/07/11/v-yuzhnoy-osetii-otkryli-medkompleks-za-schet-finansovoy-pomoshchi-rossii/ (in Russian).

The volume of Russian assistance to developing countries in 2017 exceeded $1.2 billion. (2018, April 24). *Central Asian*. https://www.centralasian.org/a/291 89917.html (in Russian).

Thorpe, J. (2014). *Business and international development: Is systemic change part of the business approach?* https://opendocs.ids.ac.uk/opendocs/bitstream/handle/123456789/4307/ER92%20Business%20and%20International%20Development%20Is%20Systemic%20Change%20Part%20of%20the%20Business%20Approach.pdf.

UN (United Nations). (2015). *The United Nations 2030 Agenda for Sustainable Development*. https://sustainabledevelopment.un.org/content/documents/21252030%20Agenda%20for%20Sustainable%20Development%20web.pdf.

What assistance does Russia provide to Tajikistan? (2017, November 27). *TAJWeek*. http://news.tajweek.tj/view/kakuyu-pomosch-okazyvaet-rossiya-tadzhikistanu/ (in Russian).

World Bank. (2018). *2017 trust fund annual report*. http://documents.worldbank.org/curated/en/428511521809720471/2017-trust-fund-annual-report.

World Bank. (2019). *Russia and the World Bank: International development assistance*. https://www.worldbank.org/en/country/russia/brief/international-development.

World Business Council for Sustainable Development. (2013). *Scaling up inclusive business: Solutions to overcome internal barriers* (WBCSD Brief). Conches-Geneva: Author.

Zaytsev, Y. (2013). International development assistance programs in the context of supporting the investment activity of Russian business in developing countries: Opportunities and challenges. *Problems of National Strategy, 5*, 54–71 (in Russian).

Zaytsev, Y. (2018). Social investments of Russian businesses abroad. *International Trends, 16*(3), 189–201 (in Russian).

Open Access This chapter is licensed under the terms of the Creative Commons Attribution 4.0 International License (http://creativecommons.org/licenses/by/4.0/), which permits use, sharing, adaptation, distribution and reproduction in any medium or format, as long as you give appropriate credit to the original author(s) and the source, provide a link to the Creative Commons license and indicate if changes were made.

The images or other third party material in this chapter are included in the chapter's Creative Commons license, unless indicated otherwise in a credit line to the material. If material is not included in the chapter's Creative Commons license and your intended use is not permitted by statutory regulation or exceeds the permitted use, you will need to obtain permission directly from the copyright holder.

CHAPTER 23

US Multilateral Aid in Transition: Implications for Development Cooperation

Tony Pipa

23.1 Introduction

The United States, a progenitor of modern-day development cooperation, veered abruptly from its traditional role with the advent of the Trump administration. While the United States has a history of pushing for reforms at multilateral development institutions, it has also historically invested itself in the system and enjoyed significant benefits from its participation. President Donald Trump's scepticism of the effectiveness of development assistance and multilateral cooperation has increased the uncertainty about the role of US financial and political investment in the multilateral development system. He shows little patience and interest in engaging in the type of contested collaboration that this handbook explores, believing its institutions have shifted to such a degree that US political capital and power would be misused by trying to ensure its interests are adequately represented within the system.

Since 2017, the growing absence of proactive US leadership has severely complicated multilateral efforts to become fit for purpose in an ambitious and dynamic environment for global development, one marked by the global push to achieve the Sustainable Development Goals (SDGs). The abandonment by the United States of its traditional role is weakening its standing within multilateral settings, just as a "great power" competition with China continues to grow and is spilling into development cooperation. This chapter explores

T. Pipa (✉)
The Brookings Institution, Washington, DC, USA
e-mail: tpipa@brookings.edu

© The Author(s) 2021
S. Chaturvedi et al. (eds.), *The Palgrave Handbook of Development Cooperation for Achieving the 2030 Agenda*,
https://doi.org/10.1007/978-3-030-57938-8_23

these trends and their potential implications for the multilateral system and US development cooperation.

23.2 THE UNITED STATES AND MULTILATERAL DEVELOPMENT COOPERATION

Modern-day development cooperation has its roots in the US leadership that grew out of the Marshall Plan, a package of economic and humanitarian assistance provided by the United States to Europe in the aftermath of the Second World War. The Marshall Plan stressed local ownership and emphasised what modern development theory calls "country ownership": that, to be successful, the initiative for progress must come from the European countries themselves. It created bilateral institutions in each country, as well as a joint cooperative that eventually evolved into the Organisation for Economic Co-operation and Development (OECD). The scale was unprecedented: the United States provided $13.3 billion over four years or about $140 billion in 2017 dollars (Garret 2018).

Subsequent to their recovery, the recipient countries of the Marshall Plan transitioned into aid donors. Eventually, the United States led the formation of a Development Assistance Group (Fuhrer 1996), which grew into—and now comprises—the core of the Development Assistance Committee (DAC). The DAC's members provide economic and humanitarian assistance to developing countries, similar to how they once received it from the United States (Organisation for Economic Co-operation and Development [OECD] 2018).

The values and ideals of the United States thus provided the foundational principles of modern-day development cooperation. Granted, US political self-interest was a major factor—the Marshall Plan was part of a strategy to contain Soviet expansionism and help the United States build markets and economic relationships to strengthen its own prosperity and security. But George Marshall himself emphasised the importance of collective action grounded in compassion and humanitarian responsibility: "The program should be a joint one ... against hunger, poverty, desperation and chaos" (OECD, n.d.-a).

To this day, the OECD mission statement acknowledges that the "common thread of our work is a shared commitment to *market economies* backed by *democratic institutions* and focused on the well-being of all citizens" (OECD, n.d.-b, emphasis added). These are Western and American principles.

US leadership was central at the beginning of the OECD-DAC. Its first nine chairs were from the United States (OECD 2006). The United States was also the first convener of what has become an annual retreat of the development ministers of the DAC's members, named Tidewater after the location of the first gathering in eastern Maryland. With the election of Susanna Moorhead in December 2018, the UK just became the only other member to have seated more than one chair.

This history hints that American exceptionalism—the country's view of itself as the "indispensable nation", as former Secretary of State Madeline Albright termed it (US Department of State 1998)—has affected its perceived role within the multilateral system. Other countries see the United States as central to the multilateral system, serving as the catalyst for its creation and acting as its main funder and champion. At the same, while the United States promotes collective governance and shared leadership, other countries also see the United States as setting rules and using its informal authority to ensure that its interests are served (Lipscy 2017)—thus the view that US behaviour has given rise to contestation and struggles over governance within multilateral structures.

Yet, the United States gave up its chairmanship in 1999, just as the DAC was helping to incubate the Millennium Development Goals, which were adopted in 2001 at the United Nations (UN). Soon afterwards, the DAC became a key leader of a global discourse on aid effectiveness, beginning with the First High-Level Forum in Rome in 2003 and culminating in the Busan Partnership Agreement at the Fourth High-Level Forum in 2011 (Busan Partnership for Effective Development Cooperation 2011). The move by the United States to share leadership more equitably thus anticipated a move towards collective agreements to regularise development cooperation, defining standards that would be evenly applied.

The Marshall Plan remains a point of great national pride in the United States. It has been named by historians and social scientists as one of the greatest achievements of the US government in the last half of the twentieth century, and it continues to enjoy widespread recognition by the US general public. This nostalgia does not translate into an informed constituency for US foreign assistance. Polling regularly shows that the US public wildly overestimates the amount of development assistance that the United States makes available (Norris 2017) (perhaps the huge scale of the Marshall Plan has left a lingering imprint that influences perceptions even today) and suggests it ought to be reduced, even as it consistently demonstrates strong support for the United States to be involved in humanitarian and global development activities.

23.3 Trends of US Multilateral Development Aid

Not only have US values informed the foundational concepts of development cooperation—the United States has also been active in building and using multilateral institutions to implement development and humanitarian programmes. Working with like-minded allies, the United States played a major role in creating and leading what has grown into a system of diverse multilateral development organisations, including the financial institutions launched after Bretton Woods, such as the World Bank Group, the International Monetary Fund, and the regional multilateral development banks

(MDBs); the wide array of UN agencies working on humanitarian and development challenges; and newer purpose-specific funds such as the Global Fund for HIV/AIDS, Tuberculosis, and Malaria (the Global Fund), and GAVI, the Vaccine Alliance.

Its own use of this system has grown over the past decade. The United States is the world's largest bilateral donor, and its official development assistance (ODA) has steadily increased, growing more than 22 per cent from 2007 to 2016. As US ODA has increased, the share of US ODA channelled through multilateral institutions has also increased. More than a third of US ODA in 2016 went through multilateral channels, up from 20 per cent in 2005. In a recent analysis (McArthur and Rasmussen 2017) of the funding of 53 major multilateral development agencies between 2014 and 2016, the United States was the top funder of 24 organisations. The next highest-ranked donors—Japan and the UK—were the top funders for nine organisations each. This highlights the financial dominance of the United States in the multilateral development system (Fig. 23.1).

That said, US influence in the multilateral development system goes beyond just funding. It has an outsized role within key cornerstone institutions, giving

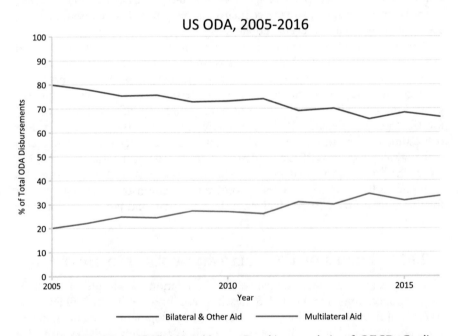

Fig. 23.1 US ODA, 2005–2016 (*Source* Brookings analysis of OECD Creditor Reporting System [CRS] ODA data [For more information on the data analysis, see "Note about the individual projects (CRS) database" under OECD. Stat on the OECD International Development Statistics (IDS) online databases website: https://www.oecd.org/dac/stats/idsonline.htm])

its "soft power" a reach and importance that is hard to quantify. It is the only member with veto power over structural changes at the World Bank (World Bank 2017),[1] for example, which is also located in the United States and has only had American presidents. The United Nations Children's Fund and the World Food Programme, two of the largest UN development agencies, have also traditionally had US leaders. As with development cooperation and the DAC, many of the norms and standards promoted within the multilateral development system reflect Western values and approaches to development, emphasising human rights and the rule of law.

Such a collective approach reflects how most Americans think the United States should conduct itself while pursuing global development priorities. In a 2017 poll by the Chicago Council of Global Affairs, a clear majority agreed that the United States should take an active role in world affairs, with 61 per cent suggesting that the best approach was to take a *shared* leadership role (Smeltz et al. 2017).[2] This is a consistent finding among polls on US global leadership; significant majorities are supportive of US participation and leadership in the multilateral system, and they are wary of the United States imposing its unilateral will (Kull et al. 2017).[3] On the other hand, they are sensitive to the United States playing a disproportionate role (Kull et al. 2017), a finding that suggests the Trump administration's priority to rebalance the "burden-sharing" within multilateral institutions resonates with the general public.

Although its use of multilateral channels has increased, US support has not been unqualified. Deeper analysis shows that the overwhelming majority of its support to UN agencies, for example, is restricted for specific purposes rather than core operations. The growth in its use of multilateral channels over the past decade is primarily due to increased investments in purpose-specific funds such as GAVI and the Global Fund, which focus on a particular issue or sector (Pipa et al. 2018). Both of these trends reflect a growing demand to exercise greater control and more directly attribute US investments to specific outcomes, even while benefiting from the leveraging of resources, knowledge, and political credibility that multilateral action offers.

The United States has also consistently kept a critical eye on organisational performance and effectiveness. Each of the last five US national security strategies, which span the presidential administrations of George W. Bush, Barack Obama, and Donald Trump, set out a reform agenda for both the UN system and the World Bank Group as a key priority. The annual report from the US Treasury to Congress on the International Monetary Fund and the MDBs also regularly outlines suggested reforms. Former senior US government officials at a 2017 Brookings roundtable acknowledged perceptions that many multilateral development organisations have become large, cumbersome bureaucracies in need of updating to perform at the highest level. Legislation proposed by Senators Corker (then-chairman of the Senate Foreign Relations Committee) and Coons surfaced in late 2017 to mandate a review to assess performance of the multilateral agencies that the US funds (US Senate—Foreign Relations 2017).

The increased ambitions of the global community around agreements like the SDGs and the need for global public goods are also forcing multilateral institutions to undertake their own reforms to ensure they are fit for purpose. These evolutions must adapt to the growing size and political influence of emerging economies, the enhanced agency of many developing countries, and an increasingly complex set of transnational issues that are reshaping the global context for development and humanitarian issues.

23.4 US Global Development and Multilateral Engagement in the Trump Era

President Trump has never articulated a clear personal vision for the role of the United States in global development. In his speech to the UN General Assembly in September 2018 (The White House 2018), he suggested that US foreign aid should go only to "friends", something he has often hinted but which, by mid-2019, had not resulted in a clear policy directive.

His foreign policy team has had to balance three tendencies of the president that have tested the coherence of US global development policy and challenged the multilateral development system far beyond anything advocated by his predecessors. He questions the effectiveness of aid, casting US foreign assistance as being expendable and transactional, which is an available point of leverage that he can use with countries in negotiations or interactions unrelated to development. He has an aversion towards collective action that reflects deep scepticism that the multilateral system serves US interests. And he exhibits a willingness to confront China directly, viewing it as a primary economic and political competitor to the United States.

These views have been balanced by trade-offs with other priorities, differing perspectives within the executive branch, and interactions with Congress. Global development has been one of the few issues to enjoy strong bipartisan support in a divided Congress, with 12 major pieces of legislation being passed in the 2016–2018 period alone.[4] Congress has disregarded the deep cuts to foreign assistance the president has proposed in his budgets, instead making appropriations that have generally maintained the funding of US aid at previous levels. In 2018 it also rejected proposed end-of-year rescissions for appropriated funds that had yet to be spent. The United States has continued to be the world's largest bilateral donor.

The Trump administration worked productively with Congress to enact the BUILD Act in late 2018, creating a new US development finance institution (Runde and Bandura 2018). This will multiply US capabilities to leverage private finance by expanding the authorities of the existing Overseas Private Investment Corporation (OPIC) and increasing the base of available capital. For many development professionals and advocates, this is a welcome step, one that positions the United States to continue its development leadership in today's dynamic financing environment, where the importance of private investment has risen significantly.

The administration suggested shutting down OPIC in its initial foreign affairs budget, then reversed its position and ultimately offered strong support for transforming OPIC into the new development finance institution. The reversal was as much for geopolitical reasons as anything else, based on a belief that it would enable the United States to offer an alternative to the infrastructure financing being extended by China through its Belt and Road Initiative (Pilling 2018).

Finding such areas of overlap among competing interests has produced other positive outcomes for global development cooperation. In 2018 the United States agreed to a capital increase at the World Bank, for example, by extracting a commitment for changes in salary and staffing structures that have long been a priority. In his first visit to the UN General Assembly, President Trump pledged support for the Secretary-General's reform agenda, which includes major changes to the UN development system, and convinced more than 100 other countries to adopt the same pledge (The White House 2017b).

United States Agency for International Development (USAID) Administrator Mark Green, who served from August 2017 to April 2020, pursued a reorganisation of the agency to improve its efficiency and effectiveness by bringing together policy, budget, and strategy; elevating the agency's focus on building resilience; and strengthening its top-of-class humanitarian assistance. His signature initiative at the agency focusses on a country's "Journey to Self-Reliance", an evidence-based assessment of a country's progress towards facilitating and funding its own development; its stated objective of making foreign assistance no longer necessary resonates with hard-line counterparts in the administration. He has kept USAID in the forefront of development practice among aid agencies worldwide (Timmons 2018).

On the policy side, however, US development cooperation during the Trump administration has come to reflect the scepticism towards multilateralism that is a norm of the president's America First foreign policy. Some of the headline shifts include pulling out from the Paris climate accord; withdrawing from the process to develop a Global Compact on Migration; stepping down from the UN Human Rights Council; and discontinuing funding for the UN Relief and Works Agency for Palestine Refugees in the Near East.

Many of these decisions have their basis in a policy dispute. The increasingly voluntary nature of these types of multilateral development agreements relies upon the reputational risk associated with mutual accountability, rather than the compliance mechanisms associated with international law or global regulations (Kaye 2013). US actions highlight the limits of this evolution. The administration's changes in policy direction placed the United States at such odds with the global consensus that administration officials deemed the potentially negative consequences for US credibility as being a worthwhile trade-off for withdrawal.

It was willing to risk a hit to the perceived dependability of the United States at future negotiating tables (Will the country follow through?) in service to stronger alignment with its change in policy. On the one hand, this weakens incentives for others to remain faithful to their own commitments under such agreements. In an era when high-profile agreements are based primarily on mutual accountability and reputational risk versus legal frameworks and compliance regimes, such moves from the United States—the system's historic champion—jeopardise the power and weight that future voluntary multilateral agreements will have. At the same time, the administration has a credible policy rationale for making such moves, based on its own policy positions.

Yet, the administration also seems to be avoiding multilateral settings even when its policy priorities align. A key example is the administration's quiet disregard of the SDGs. Rather than institution-creation or institution-shifting—the options outlined in this handbook's introduction—the Trump administration's default setting seems to be institution withdrawal.

The 2030 Agenda for Sustainable Development, which includes the SDGs as well as the Addis Ababa Action Agenda (AAAA) (which outlines ways to unleash the necessary financing for development), was agreed by all 193 Member States at the UN in 2015. Until 2030, they will serve as the common frame of reference for global development, for countries as well as a wide array of stakeholders with development interests.

Through the 2019 UN General Assembly, the United States and Austria are the only members of the OECD-DAC that have not done, nor signed up to do, a Voluntary National Review, the reports that countries voluntarily make at the UN to outline their progress and efforts to reach the SDGs. A 2018 study of G20 countries ranked the United States last in integrating the SDGs into its policies and institutions (Sachs et al. 2018).

In 2016 the United States created, and still maintains, an open-source reporting platform to provide national statistics based on the SDGs. Yet, the United States has not developed a national plan for implementation nor set up internal governance structures to monitor its success on the SDGs. Beyond the necessary diplomatic discourse at the UN, the SDGs are almost never mentioned by senior members of the Trump administration.

At the same time, the United States is undertaking policies that align with the SDGs. In USAID's focus on the "Journey to Self-Reliance", rolled out by Administrator Mark Green in 2018, many of the elements of development that USAID uses to determine a country's progress—captured in "country roadmaps"—are represented by one or more SDG targets. The agency acknowledges the overlap in a technical note and explains the relationship between the self-reliance metrics and the UN SDG indicators (USAID, n.d.).

There is little indication the agency will take advantage of the larger opportunity: to use a country's commitment to the SDGs as the basis for a frank development dialogue with the United States that the reliance metrics are designed to elicit. For example, the self-reliance indicators recognise the importance of government responsiveness and accountability, strength of governance, and citizens' right to a country's progress. SDG 16 also reinforces the centrality of these same elements—for the first time ever in a global agreement on development—to which all countries signed on. This offers the United States a significant opportunity to frame its bilateral interactions in terms of mutual accountability and partnership, with ambassadors pressing the presidents and prime ministers of partner countries to follow through on their commitments to SDG 16. Leaving it out of such development dialogues incurs a political opportunity cost and misses the chance to advance the administration's own policy.

The same dynamic recurs in USAID's 2018 Private-Sector Engagement Policy (USAID 2018e). Private-sector investment is one of the three streams of capital to be mobilised through the AAAA for financing the SDGs. Again, this frame of reference is shared by all countries, given the consensus agreement. Yet, the policy does not once mention the AAAA or the SDGs.

In 2017 the United States declined to pledge during the replenishment of the International Fund for Agricultural Development and withdrew its funding for the Global Agriculture and Food Security Program (Morris 2018). The Trump administration took this action despite its 2017 National Security Strategy elevating food security as a development priority (The White House 2017a).

The shift away from multilateralism occurs not just at the policy level, but also at the project level. In summer 2018, after an Inspector General report on multilateral humanitarian assistance to Syria and Iraq, USAID changed its multilateral procurement policies (USAID 2018f). Historically, USAID funding to public international organisations (PIOs)[5] has not required competition and enjoyed a favourable status. In the updated policy, USAID encourages—though does not require—competition. The policy also mandates that PIOs should be a partner of last resort:

> An agreement with a PIO should be the exception, not the rule, for our programming, and agreements with PIOs must provide a greater benefit to the U.S. Government and the people we serve than any other available transaction, as determined by USAID's Senior Obligation Alignment Review for an agreement. (USAID 2018c)

The USAID Administrator must now approve all awards to PIOs above $5 million. The threshold for Administrator approval on non-PIO awards is $40 million (USAID 2018b).

These actions represent a step away, not just a step back. The intentional narrowing of the use of multilateral channels, even when they offer a platform to advance US priorities, signals a dismissal of the system itself. During the Trump administration, the United States seems to have decided primarily to pursue its development priorities on its own or through bilateral agreements,[6] even when current multilateral efforts could be a force multiplier for the administration's own policies.

By intentionally ignoring the opportunities presented by the multilateral system, the United States is consciously limiting the impact of its aid. Today's most intractable development problems require resources and policy interventions that outstrip the financial and political capital of the United States acting alone. More importantly, its lack of confidence is posing an existential challenge to the multilateral development system while leaving a leadership vacuum.

It is unclear the extent to which these changes in US posture will persist past the Trump administration. Bipartisan congressional support for global development remains strong, but that does not always translate into support for multilateral institutions. Polls in 2018 showed increased public support for shared leadership on global challenges—perhaps a reaction to the administration's abrupt shift in policies (Smeltz et al. 2018).

Yet, changes made by the Trump administration might also be seen as a turbocharged acceleration of trends in US policy-maker attitudes, which were already reflecting increased ambivalence and dissatisfaction with multilateral development institutions, both with their effectiveness and the perceived dilution of US influence. The danger is that the administration has been willing to intensify US disregard for the traditional multilateral development system without a clear strategy or vision for what comes next—and who will lead it.

23.5 US Development Policy and China

The implications for multilateral cooperation are further complicated by emerging development "competition" between the United States and China. China's development investments, categorised as South-South Cooperation, do not conform to the standards of transparency; evaluation and measurement of impact; and accountability expected of ODA.

China chiefly provides development *finance*, which is different in character, scale, and uses from the development *aid* provided by the United States. Much of China's investments are offered as loans for infrastructure, versus the grants that the United States offers for social and humanitarian purposes such as health, education, and democratic strengthening. Even conservative estimates calculate that China's investments through its Belt and Road Initiative over the next several years could approach $1 trillion (Hillman 2018). This will create far-reaching economic relationships with many countries.

In summer 2018, USAID Administrator Green described China's investments as "mercantile authoritarian assistance programs… [that] secure conditions and indebtedness that I would argue essentially mortgage a country's future" (USAID 2018a). He reiterated these concerns in December, casting American and Chinese approaches as "two very different competing models of development" (USAID 2018d) that present recipient countries with a clear choice. A particular concern is that China is saddling countries with debt and substandard infrastructure while gaining undue influence, and even ownership of assets if countries struggle to repay them.

Vice President Mike Pence and former National Security Advisor John Bolton reiterated these themes in forceful terms. When El Salvador renounced

Taiwan in August 2018 to establish a relationship with China (which has since resulted in $150 million in Chinese aid), the United States considered reducing its foreign assistance and taking other punitive measures (Harris 2018).

Reservations about Chinese development activities are not new. The Obama administration declined to join the China-led Asian Infrastructure Investment Bank (AIIB), in part because of questions about growing Chinese influence and whether the new bank would adhere to high environmental and social standards (Etzioni 2016). Those concerns proved mostly unfounded as the AIIB adopted safeguards and policies similar to other MDBs (Asian Infrastructure Investment Bank 2016), and it was established with 57 founding country members—a full-fledged multilateral institution, much in the mould of US-led multilaterals (Weiss 2017).

At the same time, before the Trump administration, the United States also sought out areas of constructive engagement and collaboration on global development issues with China on areas where their interests overlap. The United States and China collaborated on global health security, jointly funding the creation of an African Centres for Disease Control and Prevention, modelled after the US Centers for Disease Control and Prevention. They also jointly funded agricultural programmes in Timor-Leste. Though a first-ever memorandum of understanding on global development, the two countries were exploring other joint projects (Zhang 2018).

Beginning in 2009, the OECD hosted the China-DAC Study Group (OECD, n.d.-c),[7] which provided the chance for high-ranking Chinese officials to experience and explore development practices reflective of development effectiveness principles. One of the DAC's motivations for establishing the study group was the prospect that exposure to best practices might encourage China to consider adopting them. Although Chinese interest was high, there is little evidence that the Chinese have modified their approach based on what they witnessed. This same opportunity is re-emerging with the launch by China of an official aid agency in 2018 (previous aid activity was overseen by the Ministry of Commerce). The United States, however, seems uninterested in trying to influence the new institution's structure and practices by constructively finding areas to work together.

Interestingly, the move by China to create the AIIB as well as the New Development Bank—a development institution created with Brazil, Russia, India, China, and South Africa (BRICS)—demonstrates a propensity for institution-creation and can be viewed as evidence of the value they place on multilateralism. In many ways, the two institutions are modelled after the traditional development banks created under the leadership of the United States. They incorporate tweaks to governance and operating structure in order to deliver their resources more efficiently and nimbly.

These new institutions are some of the highest profile examples of institution-creation within the multilateral system. It has led some to theorise that China may be strategising to create its own parallel multilateral development system, and these new entities provide China a platform for leadership and governance to a much larger degree than traditional multilateral institutions.

Yet, China's influence within the traditional multilateral system has also grown. It is now the second largest contributor (after the United States) to core operations within the UN. Its active participation in following through on SDG and climate commitments is seen by some observers as a move to promote and affirm the validity of its approach to development—that is, gain political cover for an approach to development that minimises a focus on human rights and the importance of responsive, democratic governance. Then-Treasury Under Secretary David Malpass, in testimony before Congress in December 2018, noted that "China has made substantial inroads into the multilateral development banks" (US Department of the Treasury 2018a). This is a warning about institution-shifting.

On the one hand, this could continue to alienate the United States from the multilateral system. Perceptions that China has "captured" the multilateral system and is gaining political affirmation of its approach to development—with its disregard for human rights and democratic expression—create real reputational risk for these institutions. That perception may worsen if China continues to advocate for—and is successful in gaining—changes to governance that would make these institutions more reflective of their share of the global economy.

This could also be the catalyst to bring the United States back in full diplomatic force. Indeed, Malpass suggested in late 2018 that the United States had begun to work with like-minded countries through the MDBs to counter China's perceived ambitions (US Department of the Treasury 2018b). With Malpass having been elected as World Bank president in April 2019, he now has the opportunity as leader of the institution to seek to stop the bank's willingness to lend to China—something he has advocated previously—and "play favourites" among key shareholders. The World Bank and the UN may end up a battlefront in a great power competition on development.

23.6 Conclusions

Despite the shifts in policy effected by the Trump administration, the United States continues to show leadership in advancing the practice of global development. US foreign assistance continues to flow at traditional levels. Yet, in an interconnected world where development progress depends upon shared responsibilities and global public goods, the United States is suddenly averse to using the current multilateral system, even to advance its own priorities. This is a reversal from its traditional role as a champion for collective approaches, even if it often retained certain privileges for itself. It is too early to tell the extent to which the changes in US posture are affecting the amount of US aid flowing through multilateral channels.

The United States will likely remain silent on the SDGs, both domestically and globally, during the Trump administration. Recent analyses show that the world is significantly off-track to reach the SDGs if business as usual continues (Kharas et al. 2018). Given the significant leverage the United States could wield to drive behaviour change, the disinterest of the world's largest donor leaves a substantial void in drawing attention and mobilising resources, policy changes, and new commitments from other stakeholders to advance the SDGs, even when its own development programming substantively aligns with SDG outcomes.

This does not mean that the SDGs will suffer from a total lack of US leadership. There are good examples of US cities, businesses, investors, philanthropies, and universities demonstrating serious commitments towards implementing the SDGs (Pipa 2017). New York City, for example, became the first city in the world to report to the UN its contributions to the SDGs (NYC Mayor's Office for International Affairs 2018).

This circle of emerging activity will only expand—a US microcosm of the diverse, growing global movement to reach the goals. The most important contribution of the United States—at least for the first third of the 15-year time frame of the SDGs—will come from these non-federal stakeholders.

Such activity raises interesting questions for the achievement of the SDGs. The leadership and dynamism of businesses, cities, universities, and philanthropies in contributing to the SDGs are welcome. Their appetite for advancing the SDGs may lead to new forms or models of cooperation as they seek to maximise their impact by aligning their policies and activities in a holistic manner. Their engagement also provides grist for a new narrative for US development assistance, but despite the substantial resources and capacities of these actors, their ability to advance the agenda remains secondary compared to the leadership of the federal government.

The US government will not be wholly missing in action; its aid and policies will continue to support issues key to SDG success. Yet, without its leadership in coordinating and mobilising action within the frame of reference of the SDGs, it seems more likely that the global community will fall short of the goals.

It also raises interesting questions for the future of global governance and multilateralism, and the extent to which global cooperation can or will adjust so as to integrate leadership and successfully extract accountability from stakeholders other than national governments (Wong 2014). Efforts to democratise global cooperation are finding expression through new platforms such as the Paris Peace Forum, convened in November 2018 by President Emmanuel Macron of France, and Urban 20, a network of major cities feeding into the G20.

Yet, the US retreat from the multilateral development system provides an opportunity for the OECD-DAC to renew its political relevance. Given the ambition of the SDGs, the DAC can act as the responsible caretaker to protect and promote accountability of the development effectiveness principles agreed at Busan. The Global Partnership for Effective Development Co-operation created in Busan never gained the necessary level of political traction, especially with key South-South providers such as China (Li 2017).

The DAC would also be a natural forum for the United States to attempt to build a serious diplomatic coalition to act as a counterpoint to China. On its own, the United States is unable to provide a viable alternative to China's development activities—if it is serious about countering those investments, it will need to do so by organising and inspiring like-minded donors to offer a collective response. However, the United States would have to reignite its inclination for collaboration as well as rebuild substantial political capital and credibility, with still uncertain prospects. Its traditional European allies may be hard to convince, since China's commitments on climate change are closer to their policy aspirations than those of the United States.

Yet, with a push, the DAC could reassert its combined political power—leveraging its shared values and developing a collective agenda—to engage diplomatically and politically with China and the other providers of South-South cooperation (as well as recipient countries), especially where debt crisis looms. The DAC has its distractions—the implications of Brexit as well as the mire of its current technical accounting debates—but the energy of a new chair could provide fresh momentum.

In addition to the great power geopolitical tug of war, there is a real political cost to the system that results from the current crisis of US confidence in multilateralism. Despite the United States, the global demand for multilateralism remains strong, and it continues to evolve. The SDGs and the Paris climate agreement embrace the concept of universality, breaking down the traditional dichotomy between developed and developing countries by having all countries commit to progress within their own borders. Yes, the wariness that larger, more politically powerful countries gain advantages within the system remains; but the newly agreed concept that every country is a developing country—just at different points on a continuum—provides additional rationale for more evenhanded structures.

Countries are coming to the multilateral arena to be treated as peers, with rules equitably applied and governance that is reflective of economic and political diversity. The serious reforms underway within the UN development system represent a major next step in this evolution—its progress will be closely watched by diplomats and policy-makers eager for a positive example of how multilateralism might evolve.

The pace of US policy change within the multilateral development system has been rapid and far-reaching since 2017. It remains to be seen whether it has been a momentary aberration or a permanent widening of fissures. Significant majorities of the US public, including significant majorities of US youth (UN Foundation 2018), continue to believe in the value of multilateralism. At the end of 2018, Secretary of State Mike Pompeo declared that the United States is on a "mission to reassert its sovereignty" while also "rallying the noble nations of the world to build a new liberal order" (US Department of State

2018). The full implications for the multilateral development system of these two contradictory impulses have yet to come.

Notes

1. See summary of the World Bank in the United States at https://www.worldbank.org/en/country/unitedstates/overview.
2. Versus being the dominant world leader (32 per cent) or playing no leadership role at all (7 per cent) (Chicago Council of Global Affairs 2017).
3. A January 2017 University of Maryland study found that overwhelming majorities agree that the United States should coordinate its power with other countries according to shared ideas of what is best for the world as a whole, repeating similar results from 2006 and 2004 (Kull et al. 2017).
4. Major foreign assistance bills enacted into law in the last two years include:

   (i) READ Act (H.R. 601—vehicle for a FY18 CR)
   (ii) Women, Peace, and Security Act (S. 1141)
   (iii) AGOA and MCA Modernization Act (H.R. 3445)
   (iv) BUILD Act (H.R. 302—part of the FAA Reauthorization)
   (v) Global Food Security Reauthorization Act (S. 2269)
   (vi) PEPFAR Extension Act (H.R. 6651)
   (vii) DELTA Act (H.R. 4819)
   (viii) Asia Reassurance Initiative Act (S. 2736)
   (ix) Global Health Innovation Act (H.R. 1660)
   (x) Women's Economic Empowerment Act (S. 3247)
   (xi) Protecting Girls' Access to Education in Vulnerable Settings Act (S. 1580).

5. USAID's terminology for multilateral development agencies.
6. This would be like the stance the United States has adopted on trade, where it is eschewing multilateral agreements such as the Trans-Pacific Partnership for bilateral trade agreements.
7. See http://www.oecd.org/dac/dac-global-relations/china-dac-study-group.htm for more explanation and background on the China-DAC Study Group.

References

Asian Infrastructure Investment Bank. (2016). *Environmental and social framework*. https://www.aiib.org/en/policies-strategies/_download/environment-framework/Final-ESF-Mar-14-2019-Final-P.pdf.
Busan Partnership for Effective Development Cooperation. (2011). Fourth High Level Forum on Aid Effectiveness. Busan, Republic of Korea, 19 November–1 December 2011. http://www.oecd.org/dac/effectiveness/49650173.pdf.
Chicago Council of Global Affairs. (2017). *What Americans think about America First*. https://www.thechicagocouncil.org/sites/default/files/ccgasurvey2017_what_americans_think_about_america_first.pdf.
Etzioni, A. (2016). The Asian Infrastructure Investment Bank: A case study of multifaceted containment. *Asian Perspective, 40*(2), 173–196.
Fuhrer, H. (1996). *A history of the Development Assistance Committee and the Development Cooperation Directorate in dates, names, and figures*. Paris: OECD Publishing.

Garret, A. (2018). Helping Europe help itself: The Marshall Plan. *Foreign Service Journal*, 95(1), 26–30.

Harris, G. (2018, September 29). U.S. weighed penalizing El Salvador over support for China, then backed off. *The New York Times*. https://www.nytimes.com/2018/09/29/world/americas/trump-china-taiwan-el-salvador.html.

Hillman, J. E. (2018, April 3). *How big is China's Belt and Road?* https://www.csis.org/analysis/how-big-chinas-belt-and-road.

Kaye, D. (2013). Stealth multilateralism: U.S. foreign policy without treaties—Or the Senate. *Foreign Affairs*, 92(5), 113–124.

Kharas, H., McArthur, J., & Rasmussen, K. (2018, September 14). *How many people will the world leave behind?* https://www.brookings.edu/research/how-many-people-will-the-world-leave-behind/.

Kull, S., Ramsay, C., Lewis, E., & Williams, A. (2017). *Americans on the U.S. role in the world: A study of U.S. public attitudes*. http://www.cissm.umd.edu/sites/default/files/PPC_Role_in_World_Report.pdf.

Li, X. (2017). *Should China join the GPEDC? The prospects for China and the Global Partnership for Effective Development Cooperation* (DIE Discussion Paper 17/2017). Bonn: German Development Institute/Deutsches Institut für Entwicklungspolitik (DIE).

Lipscy, P. (2017). *Renegotiating the world order: Institutional change in international relations*. Cambridge: Cambridge University Press.

McArthur, J., & Rasmussen, K. (2017, December 20). *Who funds which multilateral organizations?* https://www.brookings.edu/research/who-funds-which-multilateral-organizations/.

Morris, S. (2018, February 13). *The incredible shrinking US multilateralism*. https://www.cgdev.org/blog/incredible-shrinking-us-multilateralism.

Norris, J. (2017, August 15). Special feature: A history of American public opinion on foreign aid. *Devex*. https://www.devex.com/news/special-feature-a-history-of-american-public-opinion-on-foreign-aid-90732.

NYC Mayor's Office for International Affairs. (2018). *Voluntary local review: New York City's implementation of the 2030 Agenda for Sustainable Development*. https://www1.nyc.gov/assets/international/downloads/pdf/NYC_VLR_2018_FINAL.pdf.

OECD (Organisation for Economic Co-operation and Development). (2006). *DAC in dates: The history of the OECD's Development Assistance Committee*. Paris: OECD Publishing.

OECD. (2018). *Development co-operation report 2018: Joining forces to leave no one behind*. Paris: OECD Publishing.

OECD. (n.d.-a). *The "Marshall Plan" speech at Harvard University, 5 June 1947*. http://www.oecd.org/general/themarshallplanspeechatharvarduniversity5june1947.htm.

OECD. (n.d.-b). *Partner: Organisation for economic co-operation and development*. http://www.data4sdgs.org/partner/organisation-economic-co-operation-and-development.

OECD. (n.d.-c). *The China-DAC study group*. http://www.oecd.org/dac/dac-global-relations/china-dac-study-group.htm.

Pilling, D. (2018, September 23). US to set up $60bn agency to counter China in developing world. *The Financial Times*. https://www.ft.com/content/40d7eee4-bdc1-11e8-94b2-17176fbf93f5.

Pipa, A. F. (2017, November 17). *US non-federal stakeholders starting to fill the leadership gap on the SDGs.* https://www.brookings.edu/blog/up-front/2017/11/17/u-s-non-federal-stakeholders-starting-to-fill-the-leadership-gap-on-the-sdgs/.

Pipa, A. F., Seidel, B., & Conroy, C. (2018). *A U.S. multilateral aid review: Assessing the value of U.S. investments in the multilateral development system* (Global Economy & Development Working Paper 127). Washington, DC: The Brookings Institution.

Runde, D. F., & Bandura, R. (2018, October 12). *The BUILD Act has passed: What's next?* https://www.csis.org/analysis/build-act-has-passed-whats-next.

Sachs, J., Schmidt-Traub, G., Kroll, C., Lafortune, G., & Fuller, G. (2018). *SDG Index and Dashboards Report 2018.* New York, NY: Bertelsmann Stiftung and Sustainable Development Solutions Network.

Smeltz, D., Daalder, I., Friedhoff, K., & Kafura, C. (2017). *What Americans think about America First.* https://www.thechicagocouncil.org/sites/default/files/ccgasurvey2017_what_americans_think_about_america_first.pdf.

Smeltz, D., Daalder, I., Friedhoff, K., Kafura, C., & Wojtowicz, L. (2018). *America engaged: American public opinion and US foreign policy.* https://www.thechicagocouncil.org/sites/default/files/report_ccs18_america-engaged_181002.pdf.

The White House. (2017a, December 17). *National security strategy of the United States of America.* https://www.whitehouse.gov/wp-content/uploads/2017/12/NSS-Final-12-18-2017-0905.pdf.

The White House. (2017b, September 18). *Remarks by President Trump at the reforming the United Nations: Management, security, and development meeting.* https://www.whitehouse.gov/briefings-statements/remarks-president-trump-reforming-united-nations-management-security-development-meeting/.

The White House. (2018, September 25). *Remarks by President Trump to the 73rd session of the United Nations General Assembly.* https://www.whitehouse.gov/briefings-statements/remarks-president-trump-73rd-session-united-nations-general-assembly-new-york-ny/.

Timmons, H. (2018, September 26). The US is ranking which countries are most and least deserving of aid. *Quartz.* https://qz.com/1402646/unga-the-us-is-ranking-which-countries-deserve-aid/.

UN Foundation. (2018, September 20). *New poll: Young Americans favor an "America first, but not alone" approach to U.S. foreign policy.* https://unfoundation.org/media/new-poll-young-americans-favor-an-america-first-but-not-alone-approach-to-u-s-foreign-policy/.

US Department of State. (1998). *Secretary of State Madeleine K. Albright: Interview on NBC-TV "The Today Show" with Matt Lauer.* https://1997-2001.state.gov/statements/1998/980219a.html.

US Department of State. (2018, December 4). *Restoring the role of the nation-state in the liberal international order.* Remarks by Michael R. Pompeo, Secretary of State. https://www.state.gov/remarks-secretary-pompeo/.

US Department of the Treasury. (2018a, November 27). *Statement of Under Secretary David Malpass before the U.S. Senate Foreign Relations Subcommittee on multilateral international development, multilateral institutions, and international economic, energy, and environmental policy.* https://home.treasury.gov/news/press-releases/sm555.

US Department of the Treasury. (2018b, December 12). *Statement of Under Secretary David Malpass before the U.S. House Financial Services Subcommittee on monetary policy and trade.* https://home.treasury.gov/news/press-releases/sm572.

US Senate—Foreign Relations. (2017). *S. 1928— Multilateral Aid Review Act of 2017*. https://www.congress.gov/bill/115th-congress/senate-bill/1928.

USAID (United States Agency for International Development). (2018a, June 5). *Remarks by Administrator Mark Green at The Brookings Institution's "The Marshall Plan's 70th Anniversary and the Future of Development Cooperation" event*. https://www.usaid.gov/node/287696.

USAID. (2018b, June 27). *Senior obligation alignment review: Frequently asked questions: An additional help for ADS 300*. https://www.usaid.gov/sites/default/files/documents/1868/300sab_0.pdf.

USAID. (2018c, August 24). *ADS chapter 308: Agreements with public international organizations*. https://www.usaid.gov/sites/default/files/documents/1876/308.pdf.

USAID. (2018d, December 6). *US Agency for International Development Administrator Mark Green's remarks at the U.S. global leadership coalition 2018 tribute dinner*. https://www.usaid.gov/news-information/press-releases/dec-6-2018-usaid-administrator-mark-green-usglc-2018-tribute-dinner.

USAID. (2018e, December 12). *Private-sector engagement policy*. https://www.usaid.gov/sites/default/files/documents/1865/usaid_psepolicy_final.pdf.

USAID. (2018f, September 25). *Insufficient oversight of public international organizations puts U.S. foreign assistance programs at risk* (AUDIT REPORT 8-000-18-003-P). Office of Inspector General. https://oig.usaid.gov/sites/default/files/2018-09/8-000-18-003-P.pdf.

USAID. (n.d.). *The journey to self-reliance country roadmaps*. https://selfreliance.usaid.gov/.

Weiss, M. A. (2017). *Asian Infrastructure Investment Bank (AIIB)*. Congressional Research Service. https://fas.org/sgp/crs/row/R44754.pdf.

Wong, S. (2014). A power game of multi-stakeholder initiatives. *The Journal of Corporate Citizenship, 55*, 26–39.

World Bank. (2017). *The World Bank in United States*. https://www.worldbank.org/en/country/unitedstates.

Zhang, D. (2018). *US-China development cooperation: New bilateral dynamics?* (*Asia Pacific Bulletin Number 440*). Honolulu, HI: East West Center.

Open Access This chapter is licensed under the terms of the Creative Commons Attribution 4.0 International License (http://creativecommons.org/licenses/by/4.0/), which permits use, sharing, adaptation, distribution and reproduction in any medium or format, as long as you give appropriate credit to the original author(s) and the source, provide a link to the Creative Commons license and indicate if changes were made.

The images or other third party material in this chapter are included in the chapter's Creative Commons license, unless indicated otherwise in a credit line to the material. If material is not included in the chapter's Creative Commons license and your intended use is not permitted by statutory regulation or exceeds the permitted use, you will need to obtain permission directly from the copyright holder.

PART VI

The Contribution of SSC and Triangular Cooperation to the SDGs

CHAPTER 24

"The Asian Century": The Transformational Potential of Asian-Led Development Cooperation

Anthea Mulakala

24.1 INTRODUCTION

Twenty years ago, when I worked for the UK Department for International Development, no one talked about South-South cooperation (SSC). Discussions about Asian donors focussed exclusively on Japan. India was the largest recipient of the UK's official development assistance (ODA). Infrastructure development took a back seat to governance programmes—the new priority of ODA, as promoted by the Development Assistance Committee (DAC). Fast forward two decades and contemporary development discourse is obsessed with Chinese foreign aid and massive infrastructure schemes. India, Japan, and Korea also feature strongly in the landscape, followed by less-known actors such as Thailand, Indonesia, Malaysia, and Singapore.

This chapter presents current trends in Asian-led development cooperation, focussing on China and India, and explains why and how these trends—despite the controversy and contestation they generate—offer opportunities for new partnerships among diverse actors to achieve the Sustainable Development Goals (SDGs).

Section 24.2 provides background on Asian development cooperation, highlighting that Asia's rise and the decline of traditional aid have set the stage for a new era of cooperation. Section 24.3 examines significant trends in Asian development cooperation, specifically: large-scale connectivity and infrastructure schemes, increased multilateralism, and the increasing role

A. Mulakala (✉)
The Asia Foundation, Kuala Lumpur, Malaysia
e-mail: anthea.mulakala@asiafoundation.org

© The Author(s) 2021
S. Chaturvedi et al. (eds.), *The Palgrave Handbook of Development Cooperation for Achieving the 2030 Agenda*,
https://doi.org/10.1007/978-3-030-57938-8_24

of non-governmental organisations (NGOs) and the private sector. Finally, the chapter presents strategies and recommendations for Asian countries to improve their SSC, as well as for traditional donors, and other actors, to collaborate with Asian partners in aid and beyond-aid scenarios.

24.2 Contemporary Disrupters to Development Cooperation: Asia's Rise and Beyond Aid

There are many shifts and disruptors that shape and continue to shape twenty-first-century development cooperation, or "aid" (Kharas and Rogerson 2017). Asia's rise is one significant factor. In the last two decades, Asian (and other Southern) countries have increased their global might and influence—economically, politically, and socially—and this is transforming aid as we know it. In 1820, Asian countries produced more than 56 per cent of the world's output, which was overwhelmingly accounted for by China and India (excluding Japan from the calculation). By 1950, China and India's collective share of output had fallen to less than 9 per cent. To understand this aberration within the broader scope of history, this course correction began in the twenty-first century, which has been witness to a profound structural shift in the centre of economic gravity. Already, China and India account for at least one-quarter of global output.

Asians are also living longer, achieving higher levels of education, and earning more money. This has been reflected in rising scores in the Human Development Index since 1990: 22 per cent globally and 51 per cent in least-developed countries (United Nations Development Programme [UNDP] 2018). China has had the most remarkable ascent, having pulled nearly 850 million people out of poverty between 1981 and 2013, with the percentage of people living in extreme poverty falling from 88 to 1.85 per cent (Weiping 2018).

Consumption is also rising in Asia. The size of the "global middle class" will increase from 1.8 billion in 2009 to 3.2 billion by 2020 and 4.9 billion by 2030. The bulk of this growth will come from Asia: By 2030 Asia will represent 66 per cent of the global middle-class population and 59 per cent of middle-class consumption, compared to 28 and 23 per cent, respectively, in 2009 (Pezzini 2012). The developing world's "emerging middle class" is a critical economic, social, and environmental factor because of its potential as an engine of growth, particularly in the largest developing countries, such as China and India.

Given these global dynamics with the rise of "the South"—and particularly of Asia—the twentieth-century concept of "aid" has shifted as new forms of development partnership and finance have emerged to address global challenges. First, ODA has declined in term of its share of development finance in Asia. Today, development finance is less about aid and more about trade, foreign direct investment, export credits, and other resource flows, including remittances, broadly categorised by the DAC as "non-ODA". According to the most recent database of the Organisation for Economic Co-operation and Development (OECD)-DAC, Asia received just over $2 billion in ODA and more than $44.5 billion in non-ODA in 2015 (Organisation for Economic Co-operation and Development, n.d.). Much of this is what China and India (but also Indonesia, Thailand, Malaysia, Bangladesh, Mongolia) call South-South cooperation.

SSC predates traditional aid. The year 2015 marked the 60th anniversary of the historic 1955 Asian-African conference, held in Bandung, Indonesia, which laid the foundation for the solidarity in contemporary South-South cooperation. SSC approaches evolved during the twentieth century, as many countries in the region gained independence from former colonizers, struggled to rebuild from post-war situations, and faced acute poverty. Asia-to-Asia cooperation (one form of SSC) aimed to promote solidarity, collective self-reliance, and cooperation. It went far beyond monetary aid, encompassing trade, political and military support, as well as training, education, and cultural exchange.

However, as traditional aid was institutionalised from the 1960s onward, SSC levels fell significantly in the 1980s, as developing countries struggled with debt and inflation during the financial crisis fallout (Mulakala and Waglé 2015). Up until the twenty-first century, traditional aid and SSC rarely crossed paths; few observers or stakeholders compared or contrasted them because they shared so few similarities. SSC reappeared on the radar of most traditional donors in the last 15 years, and in the last 5-plus years, SSC has changed the discourse and practice of development cooperation as a whole. As Asia rises, SSC has increased in prominence as a form of partnership, with Asian countries taking the lead (Mulakala and Waglé 2015).

Today, SSC is big, bold, and SSC investments have predominantly a Chinese face. If we use DAC-like measures to measure the aid-like resources from SSC, Chinese aid would rank about 6th among DAC donors, with annual net disbursement in 2016 totalling $5.8 billion and gross disbursement totalling $6.6 billion (Kitano 2018). The net and gross disbursements of preferential buyer's credits are estimated to have totalled $8.1 billion and $9.3 billion, respectively, in 2016—much larger totals than the net and gross foreign aid flow totals for the same year (Kitano 2018). In comparison, India announced its foreign aid budget for 2019/20 as 90,693,400,000 Indian rupees, which converts to approximately $1.264 billion (Mitra 2019). Aid-like flows, however, are only one slice of the SSC pie. The big money is in investment, export credits, and non-concessional lending. The struggle to count these resources has led to the wild disparities in trying to count SSC. Lending from the China Development Bank (CDB) and China's Export-Import (EXIM) Bank dwarfs development finance from the World Bank or Asian Development Bank (ADB). Similarly, India's lines of credit are much larger than its "aid" totals. Lines of credit from India's EXIM Bank in 2014/2015 amounted to $40 billion, with 75 per cent going to African projects, mostly in the power and transport sectors.

Asian SSC is not homogeneous in evolution, form, or application. China and Indonesia are both SSC providers, but on a very different scale. South Korea and Japan are members of the OECD-DAC and share characteristics with Northern and Western donors as well as Asian SSC providers. The labels are historically important but presently constrain and limit us from recognising and shaping the evolving discourse.

The 2030 Agenda requires beyond-aid resources, strategies, and partnerships to achieve the SDGs. The role of SSC is critical. Asia's rise has generated some of these resources, launched new initiatives, and forged new partnerships. The rest of this chapter delves into some of these areas, identifying the opportunities they offer for the 2030 Agenda as well as the controversy and challenges they encounter.

24.3 Contemporary Features of Asian Development Cooperation

This section outlines three contemporary trends in Asian development cooperation, namely Asian investment in infrastructure and connectivity schemes, increased multilateralism, and the expansion of diverse partnerships with civil society and the private sector. I chose these themes because they represent twenty-first-century pivots in Asian development cooperation, provide significant opportunities to address multiple SDGs, and offer new opportunities for multi-stakeholder partnerships. I focus on China and India because they are leaders in the changing discourse and practice of SSC. Their approaches embody both traditional and new principles and practices of SSC. The section also discusses the challenges and contestations surrounding these developing approaches and where opportunities for improvements and collaboration exist.

24.3.1 Big-Ticket Schemes: Growth and Poverty Reduction Through Infrastructure

The principles and modalities of traditional aid have changed. The poverty and governance discourse that characterised aid in the 1990s and early 2000s has been taken over by a resurgence in economic growth priorities (especially inclusive growth) and a re-emphasis on the social and economic infrastructure necessary to stimulate growth and reduce poverty (Mawdsley 2018). Transformational investments have become the major emphasis of Chinese and Indian SSC, as well as of Korean and Japanese aid. These investments target the global infrastructure gap, which ADB in 2017 estimated to be at $459 billion per year for Asia (Asian Development Bank 2018).

The Belt and Road Initiative (BRI) is China's contribution to the infrastructure gap and global prosperity equation. The BRI is an economic and infrastructure corridor designed by China to promote development, trade, connectivity, policy coordination, financial integration, and people-to-people links. It involves about 65 per cent of the world's population, one-third of its gross domestic product, and it helps to move about a quarter of all its goods and services. As of March 2019, China has signed 171 cooperation documents with 29 international organisations and 123 countries as part of the BRI (Wenqian 2019). Most BRI investment has gone to South Asia and South-East Asia, strengthening trade and logistic connectivity between China and these regions. Among these projects is the $62 billion China–Pakistan economic corridor, a sprawling web of motorways, power plants, wind farms, factories, and railways that supporters say will spark an "economic revolution" and create up to one million jobs in Pakistan. Other high-profile schemes include the Hambantota port project in Sri Lanka (Oxford Business Group 2018), a high-speed rail link in Indonesia (Shuiyu and Zhong 2017), and an industrial park in Cambodia ("Exports from Chinese-invested industrial zone" 2019). China has signed more than 130 transport pacts with Belt and Road countries. For many countries, the BRI has been a boon, bringing much-needed resources quickly, without excessive conditions (Deloitte 2018).

The BRI is far more than infrastructure. Consistent with the principles of SSC, the BRI is intended to be mutually beneficial for China and its partners, without expressed political conditions ("Opportunities, outcomes" 2018), such as governance reforms, and delivered with speed (Deloitte 2018). As Wade Shepard aptly notes: "At root, developing physical infrastructure internationally is a way for China to establish and cement the long-term political relationships which are truly the beating heart of the BRI" (Shepard 2017). China has complemented the bridges, rails, and roads with soft infrastructure in the form of intergovernmental agreements, trade deals, customs pacts, and aid projects. Agreement and implementation are quick and relatively unencumbered (Deloitte 2018).

The sheer magnitude and scope of the BRI have made it a magnet for controversy and criticism on issues ranging from its financial viability to the economic, environmental, sociocultural, governance, and political impacts on partner countries and regions. Critics outside China claim China is driving the BRI for its own economic gain and accruing other benefits such as: finding more work for Chinese state-owned enterprises, exporting China's excess industrial capacity, expanding markets for Chinese goods, and boosting internationalisation of the renminbi (Deloitte 2018). The United States has argued that BRI projects are low-quality, self-serving for China, and a debt trap for partner countries (Rajah 2018). Limited adoption and absorption capacity, along with corruption and political constraints in partner countries, have slowed implementation. Unfortunately, China's no-strings approach to investment has fuelled corruption while allowing governments to burden their countries with unpayable debts. The Asian and international press has touted the BRI as "debt-trap diplomacy" (Lindberg and Lahiri 2018), with Sri Lanka's $1 billion Hambantota port being the most flaunted example (Limaye 2017). This situation has resulted in considerable anger towards China from citizens of many BRI countries, with some countries, such as Malaysia, initially stepping back from their agreements (Berger 2018), and then renegotiating more favourable terms (Parameswaran 2019).

24.3.2 Other Asian Initiatives

Unsurprisingly, other Asian and regional powers are not thrilled with the geopolitical implications of China literally bulldozing its way across their neighbourhood. In "response", India and Japan launched the Asia–Africa Growth Corridor (AAGC) in 2017. The main objective of the corridor is to enhance growth and connectivity between Asia and Africa in four areas: development cooperation projects, quality infrastructure and institutional connectivity, enhancing skills, and people-to-people partnerships (Research and Information Systems for Developing Countries 2017). During the 2018 India–Japan Summit, Prime Ministers Narendra Modi and Shinzō Abe identified Sri Lanka, Bangladesh, Myanmar, and Kenya as first-round priority countries for the AAGC (Baruah 2018). India hopes to further secure its toehold in its neighbourhood through two other initiatives. Since 1997, the Bay of Bengal Initiative for Multi-Sectoral Technical and Economic Cooperation (BIMSTEC)—which includes Bangladesh, India, Myanmar, Nepal, Sri Lanka, Bhutan, and Thailand and is established around regional connectivity and security cooperation—involves around 22 per cent of the world's population across the seven countries around the Bay of Bengal, with a combined gross domestic product close to $2.7 trillion. BIMSTEC is based on the SSC principles of sovereign equality, territorial integrity, political independence, non-interference in internal affairs, peaceful co-existence, and mutual benefit ("What is BIMSTEC" 2018). Unfortunately, apart from a few summits, the progress of BIMSTEC has suffered from poor coordination and a lack of resources (Subba 2018). The Bangladesh, Bhutan, India, and Nepal (BBIN) initiative provides unhindered road and rail transport across the borders of the four countries. Established in 2015, BBIN is making slow progress after a long ratification process (Subba 2018). Both BIMSTEC and BBIN aim to solidify Indian leadership and economic and strategic influence in the neighbourhood in the face of growing Chinese dominance.[1] Thailand and the United States are also setting up a regional infrastructure fund to offset Chinese dominance in the region (Jiangtao and Churchill 2019; Ono 2018). The Thailand fund is designed to support connectivity projects among Thailand, Cambodia, Laos, Myanmar, and Vietnam and reduce the dependence on Chinese resources. President Donald Trump's $113 million Asian investment programme fund is designed to support his Indo-Pacific strategy and will focus on technology, energy, and infrastructure (Jiangtao and Churchill 2019).

Despite these counter-efforts, the best approach to balancing the political power that infrastructure projects carry in the region may be to join China in the BRI rather than countering it with other initiatives. Long an opponent of the BRI, India, at the end of 2018, looked like it might join hands with China, perhaps realising that "sulking in the sidelines is not an option"

(Pahari 2018). Indeed, as a significant power in the region, India could shape the BRI to its own advantage, accessing trade routes through central Asia, stimulating the Indian private sector, and bringing India's sheer critical mass to balance the singular influence of China (Pahari 2018). Deloitte's recent analysis (2018) of the BRI assesses it as an ecosystem with expanding opportunities for multi-national corporations to invest and benefit in areas such as manufacturing, trading, and tourism. The United Nations Development Programme's (UNDP) comprehensive 2017 study of the BRI, in collaboration with the China Centre for International Economic Exchanges, contends that the BRI holds promising potential not only for global infrastructure development but also for global governance and the achievement of the SDGs. The study provides a roadmap for how China and collaborating partners can deliver the 2030 Agenda.

When seen in this optimistic light, the BRI—and accompanying big-ticket, Asian-led SSC initiatives—offer far more than infrastructure to the world. Although on the one hand they represent a significant shift in development emphasis and resources—from governance and social sectors favoured by traditional donors to infrastructure and connectivity priorities demanded by countries from the South—they also provide a framework for bringing these priorities together.

24.3.3 Increasing Multilateralism

A second recent trend in Asian SSC and development cooperation is increasing multilateralism. SSC historically has tended to be bilateral in nature. In contrast to the United States, which has become more nationalist, retreating from participation and support for multilateralism through the United Nations (UN) and other agreements such as the Paris Agreement, Asian countries—China and India in particular—are increasing their multilateral cooperation. There are several elements.

24.3.3.1 Multilateral Finance

Only a few years ago, a least-developed country without the credit capacity to borrow in international capital markets had no option but to go to a global financial institution such as the World Bank or to a regional multilateral bank for large-scale funding. Since the 2000s, China, India, and other Southern-based institutions have emerged as a major source of concessional and commercial development financing in Africa and Asia. Two new Southern-led multilateral banks—the New Development Bank (NDB) and the Asian Infrastructure Investment Bank (AIIB)—have increased the pool of multilateral finance but also changed the game in multilateral global governance. The AIIB has 93 members to date—six countries joined at the end of 2018 (Houston 2018)—and has approved loans worth $6.7 billion to more than 30 energy, transport, and urban projects (Suokas 2019). The NDB approved its third tranche of funding in May 2018. The project scope expanded to include urban development, water supply, and sanitation while keeping sustainable infrastructure development at the heart of its mandate (Vasquez 2018).

Despite these investments, multilateral finance still only makes up about 10 per cent of Asian infrastructure financing (United Nations Economic and Social Commission for Asia and the Pacific [UNESCAP] 2017). The AIIB finances about 1 per cent of the BRI (Deloitte 2018; UNDP 2017). The big money for infrastructure comes from public-sector funding, whether through direct government budgetary funding, ODA, or other concessionary loans at the sovereign level. Many of the loans are financed by the CDB, the EXIM Bank of China, the EXIM Bank of India, or commercial banks from the region (Deloitte 2018; UNDP 2017).

When the AIIB was launched, the critics were vocal about their concerns about governance, Chinese dominance, transparency, environmental and social safeguards, and competition with the World Bank and the ADB. However, this contestation was short lived. The AIIB's leaders come with extensive experience from other development banks. Both the World Bank and the ADB have co-financed AIIB loans in partner countries. The competition has been healthy, helping to fill the infrastructure gap, driving existing multilateral development banks to streamline their cumbersome operational procedures and processes, and forcing new multilateral development banks to strive to meet the expectations of partner countries regarding compliance as well as social and environmental safeguards (Rana 2018). With 93 members and an increasing voice of non-Chinese member states (Sun 2015), the AIIB has become a vehicle for increased collaboration among previously unlike-minded partners, "healthy competition and functional complementarity" as Rana calls it (Rana 2018). In December 2018, the UN granted permanent observer status to the AIIB (Suokas 2018), putting it on a par with other development organisations in the UN system such as the OECD, the African Development Bank, and the ADB. The NDB is also considering a sustainability framework drafted and presented by civil society members from BRICS countries (Brazil, Russia, India, China, and South Africa) (Vasquez et al. 2017).

24.3.3.2 UN and Other Multilateral Platforms

China and India are also stepping up their engagement with the UN, representationally and financially. China is now the third-largest contributor to the UN's regular budget, the second-largest contributor to the peacekeeping budget, and has committed more than 2500 personnel to UN peacekeeping operations as of 2018 (Center for Strategic and International Studies 2016). China has repeatedly expressed[2] its solidarity with other world leaders in support of multilateralism at the UN. This is in stark contrast to the US position. China has also set up funds to support the UN's mission, such as contributing $1 billion for the UN Peace and Development Trust Fund, and has committed to increase its contributions to the UN development system by $100 million by the year 2020. China's contributions, in kind and cash, expand its influence and extend its voice on international development issues.

This leverage is only likely to grow in the future. As Washington increasingly turns its back on multilateral platforms for development cooperation, perhaps China will become the main guarantor (Gowan 2018).

India has steadily increased its contributions to the UN and is one of the top contributors to the UN overall (Kinhal 2017). India has been successful in promoting global governance and international cooperation through the UN on issues of climate change and the 2030 Agenda. As Thakker (2018) points out, India was recognised as a drafting author of the climate change agreements and a leader within the Brazil–South Africa–India–China (BASIC) coalition as well as of the G77 during the Conferences of the Parties in Copenhagen and Paris. Significantly, following the United States pulling out of the Paris Agreement, Asian countries, including China, India, and Japan are stepping up. India established the international solar alliance with more than 120 countries and has contributed $30 million to its set-up in Delhi (Neslen 2015). China is expected to reach its reduced emissions targets well before 2030 (Gowen and Denyer 2017). India also sits on the Open Working Group on the SDGs, which is comprised of 30 member states (Thakker 2018). In June 2017, India signed a partnership agreement with the United Nations Office for South-South Cooperation (UNOSSC) to launch the UN Development Partnership Fund for $2 million, plus multi-year contributions of $100 million. There is also an India, Brazil, and South Africa Facility for Poverty and Hunger Alleviation (known as the IBSA Fund, which celebrated its 15th anniversary at the end of 2018) with $35 million in contributions (Akbaruddin 2018). These roles and resources signal India's commitment to a multilateral agenda for sustainable development, but also a recognition by other member states of the need to bring India's perspective to the table.

Outside of the UN, China was the chair of the G20 when its members adopted the G20 Action Plan on the 2030 Agenda for Sustainable Development in September 2016 (Risse 2017). The retreat of the United States from multilateralism and international engagements opens the space for China and India to step in, step up, and expand their influence.

24.3.3.3 New and Diverse Partnerships

Historically, nation-states initiated and led most Asian development cooperation and SSC programmes. Asian SSC did not involve civil society until recently (Mulakala 2017). East Asia's strong development states limited the emergence of domestic civil society and social activism while focussing on industrialisation and growth (Hirata 2002; Lee and Lee 2016; Zhang 2003). This was true in varying degrees for China, Japan, and Korea. Overall, civil society organisation (CSO) engagement in development cooperation remained limited in scale and scope. South Asia saw a somewhat different evolution. India and Bangladesh, for example, have longstanding, vibrant CSO sectors that have contributed to national development for decades. India and Bangladesh have long advocated for partnerships with civil society to address the countries' welfare and social development needs (Mulakala 2017).

The pivotal condition enabling Asian CSOs to engage (or not) in external development cooperation hinged on state facilitation. Both Japan and Korea are members of the OECD-DAC, which encourages diverse partnerships for ODA. In both countries, the government support for NGO/CSO partnerships contained in its overseas aid was an impetus for growth in the NGO/CSO sector (Hirata 2002; Lee and Lee 2016).

Though partnership with CSOs is a newer concept in China, China has now recognised CSOs as important partners in its expanding SSC and is implementing a facilitative and supportive regulatory and funding framework for CSO engagement abroad (Ministry of Foreign Affairs of the People's Republic of China 2016). China's largest and most influential poverty-reduction CSO—the China Foundation for Poverty Alleviation—had carried out projects in 17 countries and regions valued at more than $17 million (China Foundation for Poverty Alleviation 2017), as of the end of 2016.

In 2015, China announced the establishment of the South-South Cooperation Aid Fund, which has a current value of $3 billion (China International Development Cooperation Agency 2018). Chinese CSOs may apply to this fund for their programmes in other countries. These measures demonstrate a facilitative and supportive regulatory and funding framework for Chinese CSO engagement abroad. Indian CSOs (with a few exceptions) have not figured prominently in their country's official SSC, largely because India has preferred state-to-state relations and has a restrictive regulatory framework for CSOs (Forum for Indian Development Cooperation [FIDC] 2015; Mawdsley and Roychoudhury 2016). The exception is in service delivery. Where the Indian state has enabled CSOs to work outside the country—for example by engaging the Self-Employed Women's Association in Afghanistan for women's economic-empowerment programmes—positive impacts have followed ("Women empowerment" 2017). In terms of policy dialogue, India established the Forum for Indian Development Cooperation in 2014 to engage the government, universities, and CSOs on Indian SSC priorities (FIDC 2015). Beyond these state-facilitated partnerships, Indian CSOs, although vibrant and influential domestically, have limited activities outside of India. However, this is bound to change, given the expansion of Indian SSC and India's prioritisation of international people-to-people partnerships.

Asian private-sector companies and corporations (often state-owned or government-linked) have played a significant role in Asian-led economic cooperation for decades. Public–private partnerships, often facilitated by Asian states, have supported partner countries in developing infrastructure and extracting resources. For example, since 1987, Korea's Economic Development Cooperation Fund has committed $13.1 billion to 53 countries with 373 projects. Most of these projects aim to develop the transport sector in Asia and are implemented in cooperation with Korean companies (Lee 2017). Similarly, the line of credit is India's fastest-growing cooperation instrument[3] and is used to forge public–private partnerships in partner countries. The value of India's line of credit exceeded $40.108 billion, reaching 66 countries in 2014–2015

(Saxena 2016). Across South-East Asia, Chinese companies have increased their stake in infrastructure development, particularly in investment, transport, and real estate (Cheok 2017). These corporate efforts have received criticism due to sluggish implementation, preference for hiring their own nationals, lack of community engagement, and collusion with local officials (Guo and Zuan 2017; Kynge et al. 2016; Saxena 2016).

This adverse scenario is developing positively, however. As with the CSO sector, the role of the private sector in Asian-led SSC has evolved. As Asian companies become part of the "development cooperation" equation with partner countries, they increasingly look for ways to improve the social impact of their investments. Business is no longer seen as peripheral to discussions on how to reduce poverty and create positive community impact. Rather, Asian companies have expanded their exploration of responsible investment, corporate social responsibility activities, and shared-value strategies through their foreign direct investment and SSC.

Alongside the massive infrastructure investments, companies founded in Asia, such as AirAsia, Tata Group, CJ Cheil Jedang, Samsung, LG Electronics, and Alibaba, have altered traditional ways of doing business, bringing new technologies and innovation to markets, and creating additional jobs and opportunities that have brought millions out of poverty. Asian government facilitation has helped to promote socially responsible corporate investing. Chinese chambers of commerce and industry associations have developed standards of social responsibility for Chinese engineering contractors, requiring member companies to balance resource development with environmental protection and social development in partner countries (Liang 2016). The Chinese China Textile Information Center is implementing leadership development, health, and safety programmes for women employees in Chinese-invested companies in Pakistan, Bangladesh, Vietnam, Myanmar, and Cambodia (The Asia Foundation 2017). In 2013, India introduced a law requiring companies with an annual profit of 10 billion Indian rupees or more to contribute 2 per cent of their profits annually to corporate social responsibility efforts. This law has the potential to unlock $2.5–$3 billion in funding from around 16,000 eligible companies for social impact projects (Ghuliani 2013). So far, the law applies only in India, but it may expand internationally in the future. Korean food and entertainment conglomerate CJ Cheil Jedang embeds the SDGs into its business practice and measures its success against an SDG compass (CJ Cheil Jedang 2018). In Vietnam, CJ Cheil Jedang partnered with the Korean International Cooperation Agency to develop a shared-value strategy to improve the company's food manufacturing and distribution activities by enhancing the capabilities of local farmers and developing a sustainable agricultural community in Vietnam (CJ Cheil Jedang 2014). SCG, a Thai conglomerate more than 100 years old focussing on cement-building materials, chemicals, and packaging, has an impressive award-winning comprehensive sustainability strategy and approach that extends to its investments outside Thailand (SCG, n.d.). The increasing participation of Asian CSOs and the private sector adds new contours and possibilities to the landscape of Asian-led development and SSC.

24.4 ADVANCING ASIAN SSC: STRATEGIES AND COLLABORATIVE OPPORTUNITIES

This section outlines strategies (some already being implemented) for improving the effectiveness[4] of Asian SSC to deliver the SDG agenda in the pivotal areas raised in the preceding section, namely sustainable and responsible infrastructure schemes (SDG 9), diverse partnerships with civil society and the private sector, and multilateral engagements (SDG 17).

Develop sustainable and responsible infrastructure: Deloitte's publication "Embracing the BRI Ecosystem", like its title, expresses considerable optimism and opportunity for China's grand initiative. It regards the BRI to be a way to create a more equitable global ecosystem. The report takes the long-horizon (10–15 year) approach to the BRI, stating that, over that period, the BRI will diversify from infrastructure into multiple sectors, including, trade, manufacturing, internet, and tourism. It also states that, in this expanded scope, there are multi-year opportunities for developed and developing nations and multi-national corporations (Deloitte 2018). If we trust the long-term game proposed by Deloitte, the short-term (3–5 year) jitters voiced by critics, sceptics, and partner countries need to be addressed and mitigated.

Pursue multilateral approaches to manage debt: Debt risk is perhaps the most sensationalised concern. The risk is not good for China or its partners. Over the four years of BRI implementation, China has gradually taken the issue of currency and bank exposure more seriously. The China Banking Regulatory Commission is urging greater risk controls over external lending from the CDB and EXIM banks (Hurley et al. 2019). The government has improved scrutiny over deals and is placing more restrictions on state-owned enterprises and companies about where and how they can invest. China's state council is also holding state-owned enterprises accountable for bad investments (Deloitte 2018). China's more cautious approach is welcome, necessary, and should provide some reassurances to prospective partner countries. An increase in multilateral financing will also mitigate the debt risk. The Center for Global Development recommends that China can work in partnership with the multilateral development banks (World Bank, ADB, AIIB) to agree on a set of lending standards that will apply to all BRI projects regardless of lender (Hurley et al. 2019). This makes sense if China is committed to sustainable infrastructure, increased multilateralism, and debt sustainability, as articulated in SDG 17. China's lead in this area could encourage India to follow suit regarding its lines of credit.

Engage communities: The big-ticket connectivity projects (BRI, AAGC) encourage people-to-people links. Their benefits are intended to improve people's lives by providing roads, electricity, access to markets, telecommunications, and other services. But people and communities are often not consulted before, during, or after these projects (Buertey et al. 2016). This is old news to the World Bank and the ADB, whose portfolios of infrastructure projects created the demand for environmental and social safeguards.

Today the success of Asian partners' large infrastructure development projects require stakeholder accountability and engagement, particularly with local communities (Guo and Zuan 2017; UNESCAP 2019), including women. This is a pressing issue for the Chinese government, enterprises, and policy specialists, all of whom wish to see Chinese investments achieve higher levels of sustainability and acceptability in partner countries. Chinese enterprises, although accustomed to implementing infrastructure projects, are not familiar with direct community engagement. Infrastructure project implementation in China involves close coordination between enterprises and local government bodies, but not local communities. As such, understanding the demands and needs of local communities and navigating the community engagement process in partner countries is unfamiliar territory for Chinese enterprises. Partner governments also contribute to poor community accountability, often negotiating loans and projects without local stakeholder consultation. Recent studies by The Asia Foundation (2019) in Pakistan and Cambodia reveal that communities around two BRI projects (one bridge in Cambodia and one special economic zone in Pakistan) receive little information about these projects, neither from their local governments nor the implementing companies. They have had their livelihoods affected by the projects (both negatively and positively) and would value stronger ties with the project partners through small community-based infrastructure improvements, employment opportunities, and enhanced communication. Women's voices and needs were particularly missing, despite the fact that the majority of households around the Cambodian bridge were led by women, with males absent due to migration. Infrastructure is not a gender-neutral space. It is too late to consider women after the bridge is built.

Guo and Zuan (2017) echo these sentiments in their analysis of Chinese responsible investment and indicate how one Chinese palm oil company, Julong Group, is addressing these challenges in an Indonesian plantation by investing in local infrastructure, collaborating with local farmers, and hiring more Indonesian staff. Saxena's assessment of India's lines of credit (2016) also recommends that better engagement with local stakeholders at all levels will improve both the speed of implementation and the sustainability of Indian investments in partner countries.

24.4.1 Strengthen Civil Society and Private-Sector Partnerships

Complementary community initiatives will become critical in balancing the social, economic, and political objectives of the BRI, the AAGC, and other regional connectivity programmes. CSO/NGO private-sector partnerships offer beyond-aid answers to sustainability and scale by combining complementary resources and capabilities to address development challenges. The

BRI offers an opportunity for closer cooperation between Chinese CSOs and enterprises. Chinese companies lack the skills and experience to engage with communities, yet investment sustainability depends significantly on strengthened community impact. Partnerships with CSOs help in such cases. Perhaps with support from China's South-South Cooperation Assistance Fund, a new model of Chinese SSC will emerge—one where Chinese businesses, government, CSOs, and partner-country interests coalesce.

However, Asian governments can enable or stifle the ability of their national CSOs and NGOs to engage in international work. Whether through funding, regulations, or institutional mechanisms, Asian states exert significant power and influence over the extent of civil society participation in overseas development. At the same time, civil society participation enhances the impact of Asian SSC and can contribute to the sustainability of the big-ticket schemes. Governments can maximise these partnerships if they (i) offer capacity-building, particularly in project management and implementation, (ii) streamline institutional architecture for clear and dedicated coordination with CSOs/NGOs, (iii) ease rather than tighten the regulatory environment, and (iv) enhance policy dialogue and knowledge-sharing with CSOs on development cooperation strategies. Western and Northern donors have considerable experience to share in these areas, having worked for decades in partnerships with their national NGOs on development cooperation. This rich experience provides an opportunity for practical knowledge-sharing and exchange with Asian countries and their civil societies.

Similarly, we have seen that there are valuable skills and experiences in responsible investment, creating shared value, and aligning business practices with the SDGs in the Asian private sector. At the 2018 Global South-South Development Expo in New York, The Asia Foundation and UNOSSC facilitated a panel on Asian private-sector approaches to addressing the SDGs. Corporate panellists from Korea, China, Thailand, and Sri Lanka remarked that opportunities to share their experiences of responsible investment with others in Asia's corporate sector—as well as to learn from them—are rare. Knowledge-sharing initiatives can bridge this gap and support more responsible investment across Asia.

24.4.2 Expand Triangular and Multi-nodal Cooperation

Triangular cooperation is making a comeback, largely due to China's and India's increasing developmental impacts and influence in partner countries. Resources that China and India bring to the table are dwarfing contributions from traditional donors. Traditional donors have less leverage in partner countries because of their limited resources and the conditions attached to them. Triangular cooperation, previously seen as cumbersome and questionably effective, now provides an avenue for traditional donors to engage, and possibly influence, rising Asian contributors, and to stay relevant in partner countries, where traditional aid is diminishing in value and impact.

For example, Australia has found useful common ground and results tackling malaria with China in Papua New Guinea. Broader (beyond project) triangular cooperation is also growing in popularity. The UK's Department for International Development is investing $15.9 million to facilitate the transfer of agricultural technology to several countries in Africa, with China providing expertise ("DFID, China" 2012). Since 2014, the UK has collaborated with India on the Supporting Indian Trade and Investment for Africa project, which enhances South-South trade and investment cooperation between India and five East African countries (Ethiopia, Kenya, Rwanda, Uganda, and the United Republic of Tanzania), and across several priority sectors: pulses, spices, sunflower oil, coffee, information technology, leather and textiles, and apparel ("UK pledges additional funding" 2018). The United States has triangular cooperation projects with India in 18 partner countries in Asia and Africa (United States Agency for International Development 2019).

More recently, traditional donors have been signing multi-sectoral memorandums of understanding with China and India to better leverage and influence the resources and skills these countries bring to the development cooperation table. The UK recently launched the UK Indian Development Partnership Programme, which will provide up to £18 million during the 2018–2023 period to support India's contribution to delivering the SDGs in other developing countries and advancing global public goods. The aim is to unlock an additional $5.8 billion of financial resources ($1 billion grant + $4.8 billion concessional loans) per year from India for international development (Department for International Development 2019). For other Asian countries such as Indonesia, Mongolia, Thailand, and Malaysia with fewer resources but skills and knowledge to share, triangular cooperation with traditional donors such as Japan, Australia, or the United States has provided a vehicle for them to contribute to the SSC ecosystem. Mongolia's modest International Cooperation Fund, established in 2013, shared Mongolia's experience of democratisation with diverse countries, including Myanmar and Kyrgyzstan, with the help of triangular cooperation. The plans for the fund were supported by multilateral professional advice and expertise support from the International Republican Institute, UNDP, and The Asia Foundation (Jambaldorj and Lindberg 2016), demonstrating that triangular and multi-nodal partnerships offer opportunities for expanding SSC.

Such collaborations, which draw on the strengths and resources of diverse actors (North, South, government, non-government, private sector), require time and resources to organise. At present, these collaborative exchanges are rare, suggesting a greater potential scope for enabling organisations—such as The Asia Foundation, the UN, and others—to build bridges of knowledge and cooperation.

24.4.3 Establish Purposeful and Efficient Institutional Infrastructure

As Asian SSC expands and diversifies, countries have realised they need better institutional arrangements to manage it. The strategies and modalities discussed above will rely on sound institutional support. China, India, and other Asian countries have taken steps to improve their institutional architecture for SSC. India established the Development Partnership Administration within its Ministry of External Affairs in 2012 to oversee India's cooperation programmes. The administration, which has divisions responsible for lines of credit, capacity-building, and geographic regions, is more of a coordinating agency rather than a policy body. Decisions relating to Indian SSC policy still exist in a vague space between the Ministry of External Affairs and policy think tanks such as the Research and Information System for Developing Countries. In 2019, India, in partnership with the UK, will establish a Global Development Centre, whose mission will be to share Indian development experience and technical expertise with the rest of the world (Research and Information System for Developing Countries 2017). Korea and Thailand have dedicated aid agencies—the Korea International Cooperation Agency, established in 1991, and the Thailand International Cooperation Agency, set up in 2004—that oversee their grants and technical training. Both also have separate agencies that deal with loans and export credits (Kim 2016; Wajjwalku 2011). Indonesia has established an inter-ministerial task force on SSC, as a preliminary step towards creating a single SSC agency, which has been in the making for several years (Muhibat 2016). China established the China International Development Cooperation Agency in 2018. As a vice-ministerial agency—independent of the Ministry of Commerce or the Ministry of Foreign Affairs—it has responsibility for the formulation of foreign aid policies, regulations, and plans; the coordination of foreign aid across ministries; the reform of foreign aid modalities; the examination and approval of foreign aid projects; as well as monitoring and evaluation. The BRI's management sits elsewhere, line ministries still retain responsibility for project implementation, and triangular cooperation lies with the Department of International Trade and Economic Affairs (Rudyak 2018). More time is needed to see if the recent reform and establishment of the China International Development Cooperation Agency will decrease the fragmentation and bring more transparency to China's development cooperation.

The value of these institutional efforts lies in their aim to consolidate and improve the quality of development initiatives. The risk lies in these institutions becoming rigid bureaucracies that may stifle the flexible, fast, and situationally responsive nature of SSC that has long made it effective. In this connection, one might note that Canada, Australia, and New Zealand (all DAC members) have all collapsed their once-distinct aid departments within their ministries of foreign affairs and trade, reflecting the closer ties between aid and foreign policy ("Federal budget" 2013; Special Broadcasting Service 2013; Tran 2013), but not necessarily increasing efficiency or impact. Development partners from the North and South, Asia, and the rest should reflect on and share their knowledge and experience of development administration. No one seems to have found the right institutional formula to date.

24.5 Conclusion

The twenty-first century has been called the Asian century. Asian countries, led by China, are improving the prospects for global prosperity and the achievement of the SDGs. The transformational potential of Asian-led development cooperation extends beyond the state and beyond aid. Connectivity schemes such as the BRI and the AAGC, which involve mega-infrastructure investment projects and people-to-people partnerships, loom large on the global development horizon, producing both excitement for the connectivity they promise and fear about their geopolitical implications, financial risk, and potential harmful social and environmental impacts. Multilateral partnerships between government, civil society, and the private sector can improve the quality of Asian development cooperation and avert these challenges. This chapter has highlighted opportunities for strengthening civil society and private-sector partnerships, engaging communities for more sustainable infrastructure, multilateralising debt to avert risk, establishing purposeful and efficient development institutions, and strengthening triangular cooperation. These reforms, policies, and practices will usher in an era of more sustainable and accountable Asian development cooperation.

Notes

1. SAGAR (Security and Growth for All in the Region) is another maritime initiative, which prioritises peace, stability, and prosperity for the Indian Ocean ("SAGAR programme" 2018).
2. See UNGA speech of Chinese State Councillor and Foreign Minister Wang Yi addressing the General Debate of the 73rd session of the United Nations General Assembly at UN headquarters in New York, NY, on 28 September 2018.
3. Lines of credit are one of the modalities of India's development compact, which includes capacity-building, trade and investment, development finance, grants, and technology (Chaturvedi and Mulakala 2016).
4. Asian SSC tends not to adopt the OECD-DAC standards of development effectiveness. I refer to effectiveness in terms of increased accountability, transparency, delivery on the SDGs, and strategic partnerships.

References

Akbaruddin, S. (2018). *The India, Brazil and South Africa facility for poverty and hunger alleviation*. https://www.pminewyork.gov.in/pdf/uploadpdf/statements__1856867687.pdf.

Asian Development Bank. (2018). *Closing the financing gap in Asian infrastructure*. https://www.adb.org/sites/default/files/publication/431261/swp-057-financing-gap-asian-infrastructure.pdf.

Baruah, D. M. (2018, November 2). Tokyo and Delhi: Expanding strategic collaborations in the Indo-Pacific. *The Economic Times*. https://economictimes.indiatimes.com/news/defence/tokyo-and-delhi-expanding-strategic-collaborations-in-the-indo-pacific/articleshow/66477370.cms.

Berger, B. H. (2018, August 27). Malaysia's canceled Belt and Road Initiative projects and the implications for China. *The Diplomat*. https://thediplomat.com/2018/08/malaysias-canceled-belt-and-road-initiative-projects-and-the-implications-for-china/.

Buertey, J. I. T., Amofa, D., & Atsrim, F. (2016). Stakeholder management on construction projects: A key indicator for project success. *American Journal of Civil Engineering, 4*(4), 117–126.

Center for Strategic and International Studies. (2016, March 7). Is China contributing to the United Nations' mission? *China Power*. https://chinapower.csis.org/china-un-mission/.

Chaturvedi, S., & Mulakala, A. (2016). *India's approach to development cooperation*. London: Routledge.

Cheok, M. (2017, August 17). *China is increasing its share of Southeast Asia's infrastructure pie: Chinese corporations are acquiring major stakes in projects*. Bloomberg. https://www.bloomberg.com/news/articles/2017-08-17/china-s-growing-its-share-of-southeast-asia-s-infrastructure-pie.

China Foundation for Poverty Alleviation. (2017). *Love without border—CFPA's internationalization (internal document)*. Beijing: Author.

China International Development Cooperation Agency. (2018). *South-South Cooperation Assistance Fund*. http://en.cidca.gov.cn/southsouthcooperationfund.html.

CJ Cheil Jedang. (2014). *CJ Cheil Jedang: Sustainable agricultural development in rural Vietnam. Shared value initiative*. https://www.sharedvalue.org/sites/default/files/resource-files/SharedValueinAction_CJCorp_08-15-14_0.pdf.

CJ Cheil Jedang. (2018). *Sustainability report 2017*. https://www.cj.co.kr/cj_files/2017%20Sustainability%20Report_ko.pdf.

Deloitte. (2018). *Embracing the BRI ecosystem in 2018*. https://www2.deloitte.com/content/dam/insights/us/articles/4406_Belt-and-road-initiative/4406_Embracing-the-BRI-ecosystem.pdf.

Department for International Development. (2019). *The India–UK global partnership programme on development: Business case and summary*. https://devtracker.dfid.gov.uk/projects/GB-1-205142/documents.

DFID, China to improve farming in Africa. (2012, August 12). *The East African*. https://www.theeastafrican.co.ke/news/DfID-China-to-improve-farming-in-Africa-/2558-1639726-mas8tj/index.html.

Exports from Chinese-invested industrial zone in Cambodia up 68 pct in 2018. (2019, May 6). *Xinhua*. http://www.xinhuanet.com/english/2019-01/12/c_137737133.htm.

Federal budget folds CIDA into foreign affairs. (2013, March 21). *Canadian Broadcasting Corporation.* http://www.cbc.ca/news/politics/federal-budget-folds-cida-into-foreign-affairs-1.1412948.

FIDC (Forum for Indian Development Cooperation). (2015). *DAC members and engagement with CSOs: Emerging experiences and lessons.* http://www.ris.org.in/fidc/sites/default/files/4.pdf.

Ghuliani, C. (2013, November 22). *India companies act 2013: Five key points about India's "CSR Mandate".* BSR Blog. https://www.bsr.org/en/our-insights/blog-view/india-companies-act-2013-five-key-points-about-indias-csr-mandate.

Gowan, R. (2018, September 24). China fills a Trump-sized vacuum at the U.N. *Politico Magazine.* https://www.politico.com/magazine/story/2018/09/24/china-trump-united-nations-220529.

Gowen, A., & Denyer, S. (2017, June 1). As U.S. backs away from climate pledges, India and China step up. *The Washington Post.* https://www.washingtonpost.com/world/asia_pacific/as-us-backs-away-from-climate-pledges-india-and-china-step-up/2017/06/01/59ccb494-16e4-4d47-a881-c5bd0922c3db_story.html?noredirect=on&utm_term=.74f97111e3ef.

Guo, P., & Zuan, Z. (2017). Community engagement by Chinese companies investing overseas. In A. Mulakala (Ed.), *Partners in Asian development cooperation: The role of the NGOs and the private sector* (pp. 123–150). Sejong: Korea Development Institute.

Hirata, K. (2002). *Civil society in Japan: The growing role of NGOs in Tokyo's aid and development policy.* New York, NY: St. Martin's Press.

Houston, C. (2018, December 20). AIIB approves membership applications of six new countries. *GBTIMES.* https://gbtimes.com/aiib-approves-membership-applications-of-six-new-countries.

Hurley, J., Morris, S., & Portelance, G. (2019). *Examining the debt implications of the Belt and Road Initiative from a policy perspective.* https://www.cgdev.org/sites/default/files/examining-debt-implications-belt-and-road-initiative-policy-perspective.pdf.

Jambaldorj, T., & Lindberg, M. (2016). Knowledge-sharing in democratization: Mongolia's international cooperation. In A. Mulakala (Ed.), *Contemporary Asian perspectives on South-South cooperation* (pp. 139–161). Sejong: Korea Development Institute.

Jiangtao, S., & Churchill, O. (2019). US competes with China's "Belt and Road Initiative" with US$113 million Asian investment programme. *South China Morning Post.* https://www.scmp.com/news/china/economy/article/2157381/us-competes-chinas-belt-and-road-initiative-new-asian-investment.

Kharas, H., & Rogerson, A. (2017). *Global development trends and challenges: Horizon 2025 revisited.* London: Overseas Development Institute.

Kim, S. (2016). Tracing the roots and domestic sources of Korea's ODA: Aid as a Cold War statecraft for a middle-income country. *Journal of International Cooperation Studies, 24*(1), 87–102.

Kinhal, V. (2017, April 25). Top countries contributing to the United Nations. *World Atlas.* https://www.worldatlas.com/articles/top-countries-contributing-to-the-united-nations.html.

Kitano, N. (2018). *Estimating China's foreign aid using new data: 2015–2016 preliminary figures—Contribution to AIIB significantly increased China's aid volume*. https://www.jica.go.jp/jica-ri/publication/other/l75nbg00000puwc6-att/20180531_01.pdf.

Kynge, J., Haddou, L., & Peel, M. (2016, September 9). FT investigation: How China bought its way into Cambodia. *Financial Times*. https://www.ft.com/content/23968248-43a0-11e6-b22f-79eb4891c97d.

Lee, J. (2017, May). *Public–private partnerships for urban infrastructure development: The role of EDCF in PPPs*. PowerPoint presentation at the meeting of The Asia Foundation and Korea Development Institute, Manila, Philippines.

Lee, S. J., & Lee, K. S. (2016). The complex relationship between government and NGOs in international development cooperation: South Korea as an emerging donor country. *International Review of Public Administration, 21*(4), 275–291.

Liang, G. (2016, August). *Chinese government's policies to promote sustainable investment overseas (PowerPoint slides)*. San Francisco, CA: The Asia Foundation.

Limaye, Y. (2017, May 26). *Sri Lanka: A country trapped in debt*. BBC. https://www.bbc.com/news/business-40044113.

Lindberg, K., & Lahiri, T. (2018, December 28). From Asia to Africa, China's "debt-trap diplomacy" was under siege in 2018. *Quartz*. https://qz.com/1497584/how-chinas-debt-trap-diplomacy-came-under-siege-in-2018/.

Mawdsley, E. (2018). The "Southernisation" of development? *Asia Pacific Viewpoint, 59*(2), 173–185.

Mawdsley, E., & Roychoudhury, S. (2016). Civil society organisations and Indian development assistance: Emerging roles for commentators, collaborators, and critics. In S. Chaturvedi & A. Mulakala (Eds.), *India's approach to development cooperation* (pp. 79–94). London: Routledge.

Ministry of Foreign Affairs of the People's Republic of China. (2016). *China's National Plan on implementation of the 2030 Agenda for Sustainable Development*. https://www.fmprc.gov.cn/mfa_eng/topics_665678/2030kcxfzyc/P020161012716447531526.pdf.

Mitra, D. (2019, July 28). Six charts to make sense of India's budget for foreign policy. *The Wire*. https://thewire.in/diplomacy/budget-mea-foreign-policy-charts.

Muhibat, S. (2016). Charting the path to development effectiveness: Indonesia's SSC challenges. In A. Mulakala (Ed.), *Contemporary Asian perspectives on South-South cooperation* (pp. 118–139). Sejong: Korea Development Institute.

Mulakala, A. (2017). From state-led development cooperation to state-facilitated partnerships for development cooperation. In A. Mulakala (Ed.), *Partners in Asian development cooperation: The role of the NGOs and the private sector* (pp. 1–9). Sejong: Korea Development Institute.

Mulakala, A., & Waglé, S. (2015). The rise of the South and a new age of South-South cooperation. In A. Mulakala (Ed.), *Contemporary Asian perspectives on South-South cooperation* (pp. 118–139). Sejong: Korea Development Institute.

Neslen, A. (2015, November 30). India unveils global solar alliance of 120 countries at Paris climate summit. *The Guardian*. https://www.theguardian.com/environment/2015/nov/30/india-set-to-unveil-global-solar-alliance-of-120-countries-at-paris-climate-summit.

Ono, Y. (2018, June 4). Thailand plans regional infrastructure fund to reduce China dependence. *NIKKEI Asian Review*. https://asia.nikkei.com/Politics/International-relations/Thailand-plans-regional-infrastructure-fund-to-reduce-China-dependence.

Opportunities, outcomes of BRI to benefit world: Xi. (2018, September 8). *Xinhua.* http://www.xinhuanet.com/english/2018-04/10/c_137099836.htm.

Organisation for Economic Co-operation and Development. (n.d.). *Resource flows beyond ODA in DAC statistics.* http://www.oecd.org/dac/stats/beyond-oda.htm.

Oxford Business Group. (2018). China's Belt and Road Initiative reshapes Sri Lanka. *The Report: Sri Lanka 2018.* https://oxfordbusinessgroup.com/sri-lanka-2018.

Pahari, S. (2018, December 11). India stands to gain by joining the Belt and Road Initiative: Statesman contributor. *The Straits Times.* https://www.straitstimes.com/asia/south-asia/india-stands-to-gain-by-joining-the-belt-and-road-initiative-statesman-contributor.

Parameswaran, P. (2019, April 23). Malaysia's evolving approach to China's Belt and Road Initiative. *The Diplomat.* https://thediplomat.com/2019/04/malaysias-evolving-approach-to-chinas-belt-and-road-initiative/.

Pezzini, M. (2012). An emerging middle class. *OECD Observer.* http://oecdobserver.org/news/printpage.php/aid/3681/An_emerging_middle_class.html.

Rajah, R. (2018, August 3). An emerging Indo-Pacific infrastructure strategy. *The Interpreter.* https://www.lowyinstitute.org/the-interpreter/emerging-indo-pacific-infrastructure-strategy.

Rana, P. B. (2018, December 22). Healthy competition and cooperation for Asian development finance. *East Asia Forum.* http://www.eastasiaforum.org/2018/12/22/healthy-competition-and-cooperation-for-asian-development-finance/.

Research and Information System for Developing Countries. (2017). *Asia-Africa Growth Corridor: Partnership for sustainable and innovative development.* http://www.eria.org/Asia-Africa-Growth-Corridor-Document.pdf.

Risse, N. (2017, October 19). *G20 Development Group workshop considers 2030 Agenda implementation.* http://sdg.iisd.org/news/g20-development-group-workshop-considers-2030-agenda-implementation/.

Rudyak, M. (2018, November 2). *Through the looking glass: The institutions behind Chinese aid.* http://www.eastasiaforum.org/2018/11/02/through-the-looking-glass-the-institutions-behind-chinese-aid/.

SAGAR Programme (Security and Growth for All in the Region), Indian Medical Association, DigiShala. (2018, June 18). *Civilsdaily.* https://www.civilsdaily.com/prelims-spotlight-sagar-programme-security-and-growth-for-all-in-the-region-indian-medical-association-digishala/.

Saxena, P. (2016). India's credit lines: Instrument of economic diplomacy. In S. Chaturvedi & A. Mulakala (Eds.), *India's approach to development cooperation* (pp. 60–79). London: Routledge.

SCG. (n.d.). *SCG sustainable development policy.* https://www.scg.com/en/05sustainability_development/INDEX-1.html.

Shepard, W. (2017, October 17). China's challenges abroad: Why the Belt & Road Initiative will succeed. *Forbes.* https://www.forbes.com/sites/wadeshepard/2017/10/17/chinas-challenges-abroad-5-reasons-why-the-belt-road-will-succeed/#5233151d4a82.

Shuiyu, J., & Zhong, N. (2017, April 6). Indonesian rail project kick off. *China Daily.* http://global.chinadaily.com.cn/a/201704/06/WS59bb4697a310d4d9ab7e22f4.html.

Special Broadcasting Service. (2013, September 18). *AusAID to be absorbed into Department of Foreign Affairs and Trade.* https://www.sbs.com.au/news/ausaid-to-be-absorbed-into-department-of-foreign-affairs-and-trade.

Subba, M. B. (2018, December 8). Govt. to reconsider BBIN. *Kuensel*. http://www.kuenselonline.com/govt-to-reconsider-bbin/.

Sun, Y. (2015, July 31). How the international community changed China's Asian Infrastructure Investment Bank. *The Diplomat*. https://thediplomat.com/2015/07/how-the-international-community-changed-chinas-asian-infrastructure-investment-bank/.

Suokas, J. (2018, December 21). UN grants permanent observer status to China-led AIIB. *GBTIMES*. https://gbtimes.com/un-grants-permanent-observer-status-to-china-led-aiib.

Suokas, J. (2019, January 9). AIIB launches $500 m fund to invest in infrastructure company bonds. *GBTIMES*. https://gbtimes.com/aiib-launches-500m-fund-to-invest-in-infrastructure-company-bonds.

Thakker, A. Y. (2018, March 29). *India at the United Nations: An analysis of Indian multilateral strategies on international security and development*. https://www.orfonline.org/research/india-at-the-united-nations-an-analysis-of-indian-multilateral-strategies-on-international-security-and-development/.

The Asia Foundation. (2017). *Asian approaches to development cooperation: Focus on women and girls' empowerment*. https://asiafoundation.org/wp-content/uploads/2017/10/AADC_MG-Focus-on-Women-and-Girls-Empowerment.pdf.

The Asia Foundation. (2019). *Strengthening community engagement strategies in Belt and Road Initiative projects*. Manuscript in preparation.

Tran, M. (2013, September 18). Australian plans to merge aid agency with foreign affairs: A retrograde step. *The Guardian*. https://www.theguardian.com/global-development/2013/sep/18/australia-aid-foreign-policy.

UK pledges additional funding to expand ITC's SITA project. (2018, February 7). *International Trade Centre News*. http://www.intracen.org/news/UK-pledges-additional-funding-to-expand-ITCs-SITA-project/.

UNDP (United Nations Development Programme). (2017). *The Belt and Road Initiative: A new means to transformative global governance towards sustainable development*. https://www.undp.org/content/dam/china/docs/Publications/UNDP-CH-GGR%202017.pdf.

UNDP. (2018). *Human development indices and indicators 2018 statistical update*. http://hdr.undp.org/sites/default/files/2018_human_development_statistical_update.pdf.

UNESCAP (United Nations Economic and Social Commission for Asia and the Pacific). (2017). *Asia-Pacific countries with special needs development report 2017*. https://www.unescap.org/sites/default/files/publications/Final%2028CSN%29%206%20June.pdf.

UNESCAP. (2019). *Stakeholder engagement in the regional road map for implementing the 2030 Agenda for Sustainable Development in Asia and the Pacific*. https://www.unescap.org/apfsd/6/document/APFSD6_INF5E.pdf.

United States Agency for International Development. (2019, April 26). *U.S.–India triangular cooperation*. https://www.usaid.gov/india/us-india-triangular-cooperation.

Vasquez, K. C. (2018, July 25). *Can the BRICS propose a new development paradigm?* Aljazeera. https://www.aljazeera.com/indepth/opinion/brics-propose-development-paradigm-180718121646771.html.

Vasquez, K. C., Roychoudhury, S., & Borges, C. (2017). *Building infrastructure for 21st century sustainable development: Lessons and opportunities for the BRICS-led New Development Bank.* Delhi: Jindal School of International Affairs.

Wajjwalku, S. (2011). Thailand: An emerging donor? In W. Lim (Ed.), *Emerging Asian approaches to development cooperation* (pp. 79–94). Seoul: Korea Development Institute.

Weiping, T. (2018). *Chinese approach to the eradication of poverty: Taking targeted measures to lift people out of poverty.* https://www.un.org/development/desa/dspd/wp-content/uploads/sites/22/2018/05/15.pdf.

Wenqian, Z. (2019, March 7). *China has signed 171 B&R cooperation documents.* https://eng.yidaiyilu.gov.cn/qwyw/rdxw/81686.htm.

What is BIMSTEC and why is it important for India? (2018, August 30). *Hindustan Times.* https://www.hindustantimes.com/india-news/what-is-bimstec-and-why-is-it-important-for-india/story-SPT8asnufTPmW1kxG5PLaP.html.

Women empowerment crucial for peace in Afghanistan: India. (2017, March 16). *Indian Express.* http://indianexpress.com/article/world/women-empowerment-crucial-for-peace-in-afghanistan-india-4571083/.

Zhang, Y. (2003). *China's emerging civil society.* Washington, DC: Brookings Institution.

Open Access This chapter is licensed under the terms of the Creative Commons Attribution 4.0 International License (http://creativecommons.org/licenses/by/4.0/), which permits use, sharing, adaptation, distribution and reproduction in any medium or format, as long as you give appropriate credit to the original author(s) and the source, provide a link to the Creative Commons license and indicate if changes were made.

The images or other third party material in this chapter are included in the chapter's Creative Commons license, unless indicated otherwise in a credit line to the material. If material is not included in the chapter's Creative Commons license and your intended use is not permitted by statutory regulation or exceeds the permitted use, you will need to obtain permission directly from the copyright holder.

CHAPTER 25

South-South Development Cooperation as a Modality: Brazil's Cooperation with Mozambique

Jurek Seifert

25.1 Introduction

Countries such as Brazil, India, China, and South Africa (the BICS countries) have enhanced their cooperation programmes significantly and present their development cooperation as a different modality[1] that takes place between countries of the "Global South" (UN General Assembly [UNGA] 2018). Both scholars and Southern cooperation providers ascribe a notion of solidarity and horizontality to South-South development cooperation (SSDC), which ostensibly distinguishes it from the relationship patterns commonly associated with North-South cooperation. They frame SSDC as being normatively different from its Northern counterpart, since it claims to only attend to the recipient's demand, to create win-win situations for both cooperation partners, and to be based on the exchange of specific, "Southern" knowledge, which is better suited for overcoming development challenges (Bergamaschi and Tickner 2017; Mawdsley 2012, p. 153; Piefer 2014).

The international development cooperation (IDC) community has come to understand SSDC as a separate, complementary cooperation modality that is different from its Northern *pendant*, as consolidated, for instance, through the Busan Outcome Document of the Fourth High Level Forum in 2011 or, more recently, the Second High-level United Nations Conference on South-South Cooperation (BAPA+40) in Buenos Aires in March 2019 (Organisation for Economic Co-operation and Development/Development Assistance Committee [OECD-DAC] 2011; UNGA 2019). Historically, SSDC, as a

J. Seifert (✉)
International Development Cooperation, Bonn, Germany

© The Author(s) 2021
S. Chaturvedi et al. (eds.), *The Palgrave Handbook of Development Cooperation for Achieving the 2030 Agenda*,
https://doi.org/10.1007/978-3-030-57938-8_25

common endeavour of developing countries, can be traced back to the 1950s. The ever more important role of emerging economies such as the BICS countries, however, has led to a significant increase in the scope, quantity, and importance of Southern cooperation since the end of the 1990s.

As a re-emerging modality in the context of a changing development landscape, SSDC is a challenge to the cooperation provided by the so-called traditional donors: The "new development partners" claim that cooperation can be delivered differently, that is, in a horizontal manner, implying that their cooperation is morally—and to some extent practically—superior. The re-emergence of SSDC has given rise to new institutions such as the Development Cooperation Forum of the United Nations (UN DCF) (Bracho 2015; Esteves 2018; Verschaeve and Orbie 2015). As a consequence, some question whether the Organisation for Economic Co-operation and Development's (OECD) Development Assistance Committee (DAC) will continue to be the predominant institution for setting norms and standards in IDC and whether its standards for official development assistance (ODA) will define development cooperation in a post-2015 world (Janus et al. 2015; Mawdsley et al. 2014).

The 2030 Agenda for Sustainable Development mirrors this shift, among others, in the landscape of international cooperation and among multilateral development institutions. To implement the agenda, Sustainable Development Goal (SDG) 17 promotes new, inclusive partnerships that bring various stakeholders and their different approaches together. SSDC providers will play a crucial role in implementing the agenda (Renzio et al. 2015; United Nations 2013). However, the cooperation practices of new development partners such as the BICS countries, Mexico, Indonesia, and others have only been investigated to a comparatively small degree (Fejerskov et al. 2016). This makes it difficult to determine what de facto characterises SSDC as a cooperation modality, how the claims made for the characteristics of this modality are reflected in practice, and in how far it can be understood as a modality that contests practices commonly ascribed to "traditional" North-South cooperation.

This chapter tackles these questions by investigating the technical cooperation between Brazil and Mozambique. Brazil was one of the most prominent SSDC providers under President Luiz Inácio Lula da Silva (2003–2010) and was the first mandate of his successor, Dilma Rousseff (2011–2014)— although Brazil's enthusiasms decreased during this second period. Although official cooperation volumes increased from around $2 million in 2003 to almost $38 million in 2010 (and were then gradually cut back to $7.1 million in 2014) (Agência Brasileira de Cooperação [ABC] 2015b), figures—including contributions from sectoral institutions and Brazil's contributions to international organisation—reached an estimated total cooperation volume of around $4 billion between 2005 and 2016 (Instituto de Pesquisa Econômica Aplicada [IPEA] 2018) and of $1.5 billion between 2011 and 2013 (IPEA 2016). The country has foregrounded its role as an SSDC provider and explicitly pointed out the differentness of its cooperation from what is being offered by Northern donors. Due to the heterogeneity of SSDC providers, Brazil cannot be seen as a representative example. However, investigating the country's approach to SSDC serves to illustrate the extent that the characteristics ascribed above to the modality are reflected in cooperation practices.

As with the other BICS countries, Brazil has been strongly engaged in SSDC with partner countries in Africa (ABC 2015a; Burges 2012). Here, Mozambique has been one of Brazil's most important cooperation partners, receiving a significant share of Brazil's cooperation provided to the region (around $32 million in 2011; ABC 2015c). Therefore, the case of the cooperation between the two countries provides insights into the dynamics of SSDC practices and the narrative around it, helping to better understand how established forms of cooperation are being challenged.

The analysis of the case focusses on the central sectors of Brazilian–Mozambican cooperation—health, agriculture, and education/food security (ABC 2013, 2015c), as explained below. It shows the varying degree to which the characteristics alleged by Southern cooperation are "institutionalised" in Brazil's approach, such as the extent to which the characteristics ascribed to SSDC are embedded in cooperation practices through binding principles and guidelines, monitoring, and evaluation.[2] By investigating cooperation practices and asking in how far the narrative constructed around the differentness of Southern cooperation is perceived by its practitioners and reflected in its implementation, this chapter shows that SSDC does not always hold up to its claim to be a different, horizontal cooperation modality.

The following section briefly looks at the discussion on SSDC in international development cooperation. Subsequently, the characteristics ascribed to SSDC are explained before presenting the case study. The conclusive section analyses to what degree the characteristics of SSDC can be found in Brazilian–Mozambican cooperation and what this implies regarding the relevance of SSDC for implementing the 2030 Agenda.

25.2 SOUTH-SOUTH DEVELOPMENT COOPERATION IN THE INTERNATIONAL CONTEXT

South-South cooperation refers to various dimensions of cooperation—for instance political, financial, economic, and even cultural cooperation. These dimensions often overlap in practice and are sometimes used differently by Southern cooperation providers (Amanor 2013a; Kornegay 2013). This chapter understands SSDC as a *pendant* of Northern cooperation (i.e. cooperation provided by the OECD-DAC members) that can be delimited from these dimensions (Bracho 2015; Milani 2014) and comprises *technical cooperation among developing countries* (UN Development Programme [UNDP] UNDP 2016a). Within international cooperation, SSDC has increasingly gained importance. Particularly the High-level UN Conference on South-South Cooperation in Nairobi in 2009 (UN Office for South-South Cooperation

[UNOSSC] 2010) and the Busan High-Level Forum on Aid Effectiveness in 2011 contributed to the recognition and consolidation of SSDC as a modality in international cooperation (Eyben and Savage 2012; Mawdsley et al. 2014). This chapter focusses on technical SSDC to investigate the specific characteristics of the modality.

Many of the Southern cooperation providers have made a point of foregrounding the difference of their cooperation from "traditional" development cooperation and rejected being labelled as "donors" (Mawdsley 2011). They claim that (i) their cooperation is part of the historical solidary efforts among developing countries that aim to join forces against the "Global North", and that (ii) the relationship with their respective partner countries is different, since SSDC occurs between equal partners and is horizontal.

The rhetoric that frames the (re-)emergence of the new development partners is based on the historical trajectory of SSDC and presents it as a political endeavour to improve the common standing of the developing countries vis-à-vis the Global North. In this sense, the notion that SSDC is "different" is highly political. As Muhr (2015, p. 3) points out, in the discussion about the (renewed) relevance of SSDC, the argument is often put forth that it occurs merely on a rhetorical level, implying that this would reduce the de facto relevance of SSDC. However, what is called "rhetoric" is an important element of SSDC and should not be considered marginal. According to Mawdsley (2011, p. 10):

> The discourses mobilised by Southern donors around their development cooperation activities are not mere window-dressing, a gloss over the geostrategic and commercial ambitions that "truly" motivate such ties. Rather, they serve as a means of persuading, symbolising and euphemising claims to particular identities and social relations.

In this sense, a Southern identity is created through discourse by delimiting a community of countries, a "we" in the sense of a collective self from the "other", in this case, the Global North. Hence, as Cabral (2015, p. 1) puts it, "discourse is an expression of the political".

On a practical level, the efforts of Southern providers to establish their cooperation as a separate modality led to the founding in 2007 of the UN DCF, which holds biennial meetings to foster various modalities of development cooperation. The founding of the DCF has been interpreted as a challenge to the DAC as the central institution for IDC processes and has raised the question of who defines approaches such as *effectiveness* (Eyben 2012, p. 85; Glennie 2014). Several years after its founding, the relevance of the DCF and its relationship with the DAC have yet to be defined. However, the DCF can be perceived as a counterpart to the DAC and shows the (renewed) relevance of Southern cooperation. The effort of Southern providers to establish such an institution under the roof of the UN further illustrates a continuation of the historical trajectory of SSDC (Bergamaschi and Tickner 2017). With the establishment of the DCF, Southern providers emphasised that they do not want to participate in DAC processes and that they aim to establish alternative fora for a more balanced interaction of development partners (Besharati 2013; Bracho 2015; Verschaeve and Orbie 2015).

In an attempt to institutionalise the dialogue between Northern donors and Southern development partners, and as a follow-up to the Busan Forum, the Global Partnership for Effective Development Co-operation (GPEDC) was founded in 2012 (Abdel-Malek 2015; Kharas 2012; OECD-DAC 2011). It consists of a Secretariat led by the DAC and the UN Development Programme and three Co-Chairs from the country groups of "donors", "recipients", and "providers/recipients" (Fues 2012). However, the responses to the GPEDC among Southern providers were heterogeneous. The BICS countries have been either reluctant towards the partnership initiative or have explicitly renounced it as a "Northern"—that is, OEDC-driven—initiative (Constantine et al. 2014; Fejerskov et al. 2016, p. 13). On the other hand, countries such as

> Colombia, Egypt and Thailand keep a distance from the BRICS group (Brazil, Russia, India, China, and South Africa) and seek proximity to the DAC [i.e. the GPEDC]. Emerging market countries like Mexico, South Korea and Chile, who have joined the OECD, also do not have issues with the DAC. (Fues 2012, p. 301)

Against this background of ongoing shifts in IDC, the question arises as to what constitutes the "Southernness" of SSDC.

25.3 Characteristics of South-South Development Cooperation

The concept of SSDC and the question of what constitutes its differentness from "traditional" cooperation from the DAC donors remain disputed. Referring to the historical evolution of both cooperation modalities, the discourse around SSDC uses different symbolic regimes for framing each modality. Accordingly, the DAC donors would provide cooperation as a form of "charity" and based on a "moral obligation" to the less fortunate as well as their "expertise based on superior knowledge, institutions, science and technology". This also implies that this form of cooperation is not reciprocal (Mawdsley 2012, p. 153). SSDC providers claim that, in contrast to "Northern cooperation", their cooperation is a solidary endeavour between developing countries. Therefore, the main characteristics they attribute to their modality are that SSDC is (i) based on horizontality, (ii) non-interventionist and demand-driven, (iii) creating mutual benefits for cooperating partners, (iv) based on cultural proximity, and (v) focussing on knowledge exchange (Bracho 2015; Mawdsley 2012, p. 162; Piefer 2014).

First, the claim of SSDC being based on horizontality points at a central difference between Northern and Southern cooperation. To be horizontal, the relationship between cooperation partners would have to be equal in terms of political and economic power—despite possibly existing asymmetries between the two countries (Cesarino 2012, p. 522; De Morais 2005, p. 13)—or, if this is not possible, the cooperation would have to explicitly address and intend to overcome power disparities. From the notion of horizontality, the other, aforementioned characteristics ascribed to SSDC can be deduced.

The narrative around SSDC most often does not define clearly what is meant by horizontality but implies that it refers to power (im)balances between the cooperation partners. However, similar to North-South cooperation, power constellations between many Southern providers—such as the BICS—and their partner countries are often asymmetric. Therefore, when looking at the claim of *horizontality*, SSDC can be considered to be horizontal if an equal relationship *in spite of* possibly (or probably) existing power asymmetries between the cooperation partners is guaranteed. The providing party would have to transfer a degree of control to the recipient, make sure that the recipient's interests are reflected in the conceptualisation and implementation of the cooperation, and agree to establish mechanisms to monitor the horizontality of the cooperation.

SSDC would be less horizontal when SSDC providers explicitly adopt a position of superiority towards their counterparts in other countries, in the sense that they present themselves as more powerful and superior and do not take into account their partners' interests. Corrêa (2010, pp. 95–96) admits that, because of these power asymmetries in SSDC, there is a risk for Southern providers to reproduce similar asymmetries or paternalist patterns, as in North-South cooperation in asymmetric constellations. This would lead to a vertical relationship, which would, in turn, be the negation of the very concept of SSDC itself. Thus, political will on the provider's side would not be enough to guarantee a power equilibrium in the cooperation relationship.

SSDC providers thus face the same challenges as DAC donors when operating in partner countries with a significant lack of technical and institutional capacities. For instance, the question arises of how the process cycle of a cooperation project would have to be designed to maintain a power equilibrium between the cooperating parties if the recipient's intermediating agencies do not have the same capacities as the providing country. A lack of horizontality during the implementation could lead to "delicate situations" (Corrêa 2010, p. 96) on the political level (Secretaría General Iberoamericana 2008, p. 22).

Second, SSDC providers claim that their cooperation is *non-interventionist and demand-driven* (Bracho 2015, p. 7; Milani 2014, pp. 6–7). This means that it is based on mutual respect for the sovereignty of both countries and that, therefore, the provider does not interfere with the domestic politics of the recipient. SSDC claims to only focus on needs articulated by the recipient and to be free of any conditions. However, it is important that the discourse around SSDC often fails to specify which types of conditions are avoided: Northern cooperation has been making significant efforts to untie aid from economic strings, but it often strives to achieve political changes (e.g. democratisation, gender, decentralisation) (Chung et al. 2015; Dijkstra 2004). To provide demand-driven cooperation, SSDC providers do not "intervene" on the political level, but often attach economic conditions to their cooperation in praxis (Quadir 2013, p. 333), with China being a prominent example of this approach (Aidoo and Hess 2015). This can make SSDC an attractive option for recipient countries and challenge the model of "traditional" donors (Hernandez 2016).

The claim of non-interventionism helps promote SSDC as normatively "better" than the development cooperation provided by the OECD-DAC by referring to the idea of "collective self-reliance". This idea gained importance for the cooperation among developing countries in the context of the Non-Alignment Movement as a means to achieve independence from former colonisers through Southern solidarity (Alden et al. 2010, p. 60; Mawdsley 2012, p. 62). It also denounces—rather implicitly—"traditional" development cooperation as a form of illegitimate intervention in the developing countries that have fought (sometimes until recently) for their independence. "Traditional" North-South cooperation is hereby often ascribed a notion of paternalism and depicted as an instrument for influencing and maintaining continued control over the recipient country. DAC donors are presented as former colonising powers that continue to intrude in the domestic politics of the sovereign recipients, whereas SSDC providers highlight that their cooperation is to be seen as a continuation of historical South-South solidarity (Amanor 2013b, p. 3).

On a practical level, the concept of non-interventionism translates into *demand-driven* cooperation. SSDC providers argue that their cooperation is not pre-designed and driven by what the provider determines the recipient's needs to be, but rather that it is based on the demand for cooperation that the recipient articulates. The demand-driven approach is not only linked with the idea of non-interventionism and an emphasis on respect for recipient sovereignty. It can also be seen as an indirect critique of North-South cooperation, which has often been criticised for promoting a "one size fits all" approach towards its recipients (Africa Renewal 2015; UN Department of Economic and Social Affairs 2014), including by the movements of the Global South (Deen 2007). More recently, SSDC providers have also used the term "ownership", which is used in North-South cooperation to point out the importance of the active engagement of the recipient party (Buffardi 2013; Piefer 2014).

Third, SSDC is presented as a modality that creates *mutual benefits* for both cooperating parties, that is, "win-win" situations (Elsinger 2011; Lundsgaarde 2011; Mawdsley 2012, p. 145). By emphasising mutual benefits in SSDC, cooperation provided by the OECD-DAC is presented as an altruistic form of cooperation (and therefore as aid or assistance) that is given to the recipient without expecting anything in return (Kragelund 2015), implying that the benefits of Northern cooperation are not mutual. By emphasising that North-South cooperation is altruistic and non-reciprocal whereas Southern cooperation is mutually beneficial, Southern development partners imply that the former establishes a relationship of superiority and inferiority between the party providing the cooperation and the receiver. In SSDC, both parties "give and take", thus cooperation takes place on the same level (De la Fontaine et al. 2014; Naylor 2011). However, the questions of what is meant by "win-win", whether obtained benefits are actually mutual, and whether they occur at different levels or at the same level for both partners (e.g. gaining technical knowledge vs. international reputation) are seldom explicitly addressed in SSDC. In addition, it is important to note that, during recent years, the agencies of many DAC donors have openly assumed the importance of their national interests in development cooperation (e.g. market access) (Browne 2006, p. 113; Lancaster 2007, p. 21). Mawdsley explains that although both Southern cooperation providers and Northern donors will primarily follow their respective interests when providing cooperation, both use different symbolic regimes to present their cooperation,

> [w]hereas the West deploys a symbolic regime of charity and benevolence to obscure this truism [of national interests], the Southern donors invoke a rhetoric of solidarity, mutual benefit and shared identities. Moreover, assertions of "win–win" outcomes are founded on a simplistic construction of "national interest" (of both partners). (Mawdsley 2011, p. 11)

Fourth, some providers emphasise that SSDC is a common endeavour that is based on cultural proximity and a shared colonial past of both cooperating parties. *Cultural proximity* is emphasised to a varying degree by SSDC providers as a facilitating factor for cooperation. Brazil, for instance, has close ties to some countries in South America and has emphasised the historical bonds with Africa that stem from extensive slave trade during colonial times (Ferreira 2016; Milhorance de Castro 2013; Saraiva 2010). Where it applies, the notion of speaking a *common language* is also foregrounded (as in, for instance, the case of Brazil and its lusophone partners). India points out historical relations with countries in East Africa and highlights the importance of its diaspora to the continent (De la Fontaine 2009; Reddy 2008). China, however, puts less emphasis on cultural similarities in South-South cooperation—at least with its African partner countries—as there are fewer historical ties to refer to. South Africa holds a special position within its own region, since it mostly provides cooperation to other countries on the continent.

Despite often being highlighted on a rhetorical level, cultural proximity remains vaguer than most other aspects that allegedly distinguish SSDC from its Northern counterparts when it comes to the question of how this proximity translates into advantages over North-South cooperation in concrete cooperation practices. Sharing the same language might be considered an "obvious" advantage, but it will seldom be acknowledged officially as a strategic advantage of a cooperation modality. In addition, the claim of cultural similarities refers mostly to informal, subtle codes and nuances of human interaction (Alves 2013; Burges 2012). Thus, it can hardly be proven to be the cause of a better relationship, nor can it be measured. Nevertheless, it holds a prominent position in the SSDC narrative.

For constructing the notion of solidarity and horizontality in SSDC, references to the common position during colonial times and the ensuing development state are crucial (Burges 2012). By highlighting that their historical past puts them closer to the recipients of cooperation than the Northern donors, SSDC providers are also capable of underpinning the claim to non-interventionist and demand-driven cooperation, as described above.

Fifth, Southern development partners often foreground that their cooperation focusses on *knowledge exchange*. Sometimes, this implies that the understanding of how development should be conceptualised is different (Quadir 2013). Even if the notion of a different path to development is not explicitly foregrounded, it is often argued that new development partners face similar development challenges as their partners. They would therefore have more specific or more adequate knowledge on these challenges and could approach them with more consideration of their recipients' needs. Their expertise with regard to specific socio-economic developments would be "closer" to the problems that their cooperation partners face (Bilal 2012). The focus on knowledge exchange is often owed to the fact that, although many agencies of Southern providers have only small budgets, they have access to a high level of expertise from sectoral institutions in their countries. In the case of Brazil, the country's agricultural research cooperation, the Brazilian Agricultural Research Corporation (Embrapa), and the Oswaldo Cruz Foundation (Fiocruz), which conducts healthcare research and projects, are well-known examples of high-profile institutions with a strong focus on knowledge exchange in SSDC (Esteves et al. 2015). Although the claim of providing more adequate knowledge is prominent in South-South cooperation and has led the World Bank to foster High Level Meetings on the issue (UNOSSC 2016; World Bank 2016), it has to be asked to what extent "different" knowledge translates into different cooperation practices.

25.4 Brazil's Development Cooperation in Mozambique

The claims made about the characteristics of Southern cooperation point, on the one hand, to a modality that is conceptually different from "traditional" development cooperation. On the other, these claims often refer to a rather abstract level of cooperation and remain vague in how far they translate into different cooperation practices between Southern providers and their partners.

Brazil has been one of the most prominent *emerging powers* and has amplified its SSDC with developing countries. Under former President Lula da Silva (2003–2010) and during the first mandate of his successor, Dilma Rousseff (2011–2014), Brazil has framed its cooperation explicitly as "Southern" and as an endeavour that is based on the solidarity among developing countries (Cervo and Lessa 2014; Fellet 2013). Brazil has also been turning towards Africa as an important partner region throughout this period (Cabral et al. 2014; Esteves et al. 2015). The rise of Brazil was based on impressive economic growth, an even greater ascribed further potential, a comparatively high degree of political stability, and a significant decrease in external debt (Mineiro 2014, p. 25), rather than on "hard power" such as military strength (Lustig 2016). The main institution for carrying out technical SSDC projects is the Brazilian Cooperation Agency (ABC), a department of the Ministry of Foreign Affairs, but sectoral institutions—namely Embrapa in agriculture and Fiocruz in health—participate significantly in Brazil's cooperation.

In contrast to Brazil, Mozambique is one of the poorest and least-developed countries in the world that suffered from being a "playground" for the East and West during the Cold War. The country is highly dependent on external aid. As the UN pointed out, Mozambique is one of the countries with the strongest donor presence in Africa, with ODA financing a significant share of government expenditure (UNDP Mozambique 2010, p. 7). Since the devastating civil war (1975–1992) that followed its independence from Portugal, Mozambique has received development aid/cooperation, and its political actors have made an effort to implement the various policies and to abide by the rules brought on by the donors. This rather high degree of "compliance" has led to the country being called a "donor's darling" (Hanlon and Smart 2008, p. 122; Monge Roffarello 2015).

With Brazil being an emerging power with significant regional and international weight, and with Mozambique being a recipient country that, to a large extent, depends on external support, the relationship between the two is strongly asymmetric in terms of economic and political power. The case is therefore helpful to investigate the characteristics ascribed to SSDC, since these claims are based on the notion of horizontality, as outlined above. It is assumed here that in an asymmetrical constellation, there will be little or no necessity for Brazil, as the providing party, to adhere to the principle of horizontality in order to pursue its interests in cooperation or in the case of conflicts during the interaction. Therefore, due to the existing asymmetries between both countries, Brazil is very unlikely to conduct its SSDC in a horizontal manner in the case of Mozambique. In this sense, the case serves as a "hard test"—a *least likely case* (Flyvbjerg 2006, p. 231)—for the horizontality of Brazilian cooperation, as it will depend on Brazil's political will to put the characteristics it claims to be present in its cooperation into practice.

In Mozambique, Brazil has conducted cooperation in a variety of fields that range from strengthening institutional capacities to urban development to improving labour standards, based on an official cooperation agreement that was signed as early as 1981 (ABC 2013). For the sake of limiting its scope, this chapter focusses on the main areas of the cooperation between the two countries: health, agriculture, education, and food security (ABC 2015c). The cooperation portfolio is difficult to track over the course of time because ABC's database does not allow for a search structured via time period. A 2010 publication listed 16 planned projects (with a strong focus on health and agriculture), but it provided no information about implemented or concluded activities (ABC 2010, p. 108). According to a 2013 retrieval from ABC's database (ABC 2013), the agencies administered 16 bilateral projects in Mozambique in that year (5 in health, 5 in education, 1 in agriculture, and 5 cross-sector projects: food security, social development, capacity-building). Mozambique was the main recipient of Brazilian cooperation between 2005 and 2010, when counting the number of projects—16 per cent of all programmes were conducted in Mozambique (Marcondes de Souza Neto 2013, p. 9), and it received the biggest share of all Portuguese-speaking countries in Africa (Cabral and Shankland 2012, p. 8).

In the health sector, Brazil's health foundation Fiocruz has developed a structural approach that it applies in Mozambique with the objective of strengthening the national health system rather than targeting specific issues or diseases (Esteves et al. 2015). The foundation's structural approach explicitly builds on the notion of horizontality in SSDC. Fiocruz explains that it aims to strengthen institutional capacities through knowledge exchange, with the objective of improving the recipient's health system rather than focussing on specific health issues (Almeida et al. 2010, pp. 27–28).

The health cooperation portfolio between the two countries included projects such as the creation of a maternal milk bank in Maputo, capacity-building for oral health care, cancer prevention, communal therapy, HIV prevention, and health care for women (ABC 2010, pp. 108–114; 2013). One project that stands out as an example of Brazil's structural approach to health cooperation is the creation of an antiretroviral drug plant in Matola, close to the capital, Maputo. The plant is prominent in Brazilian health cooperation (beyond bilateral cooperation with Mozambique), as HIV/aids is one of Mozambique's most serious health problems. The project was presented with direct support from former President Lula da Silva in 2003 and has largely been financed by Brazil, but Mozambique has provided a counterpart (BBC Brasil 2008; Cabral et al. 2014, p. 192). The importance of the drug plant is also based on the fact that, by providing a means for medicament production, Brazilian cooperation would contribute to the increased structural independence of Mozambique's health system. The project was originally designed to expand production to a regional (eastern African) market, but production was delayed because of administrative challenges (Marcondes de Souza Neto 2013, p. 10; Esteves et al. 2015, pp. 25–26).

In agriculture, Brazil's cooperation portfolio covers a variety of agricultural issues, "such as support to production, training of extension agents, development of value chains, strengthening of public sector institutions, support to rural associations and cooperatives, sanitary and phytosanitary regulation, amongst others" (Cabral and Shankland 2012, p. 9). In Mozambique, the portfolio consists of projects such as support for establishing a seed bank, capacity-building in the use of seeds, support for the use of traditional seeds in small-scale agriculture (*agricultura familiar*) (ABC 2013), support for the development of small-scale agriculture and fishing, and technical support for food security in schools (ABC 2010). Additionally, Brazil has promoted a regional project for the production of cotton in Benin, Burkina Faso, Chad, Mali, and Togo, which led Mozambique's National Cotton Institute to procure expertise and capacity-building measures from Embrapa's cotton research unit in 2006 (Embrapa 2006). Brazil's agricultural research cooperation Embrapa has been central to turning large areas in the centre and the north of Brazil into productive agricultural regions (Embrapa 2015b), and it often grounds its cooperation in Mozambique on these domestic experiences. One prominent example here is ProSavana, a trilateral project with Japan that aims to transfer the experiences from developing Brazil's *cerrado* regions to Mozambique by scaling-up Brazil's experiences with Northern cooperation partners and making use of the acquired knowledge in its own cooperation (Funada Classen 2013; Japan International Cooperation Agency 2013; Mello 2013; ONGs Mozambicanas 2013).

In education, cooperation projects with universities have been at the forefront. Brazil has carried out projects with Brazilian professors teaching in Mozambique and Mozambican professors attending courses in Brazil so that Mozambican students can be taught at home and via online courses. Food security is a cooperation sector that often overlaps with education, since many projects are carried out in Mozambican schools. This sector is important in Brazil's cooperation portfolio due to the country's own socio-economic structure and the historic challenge of supplying its own population with sufficient amounts of food (Costa Leite et al. 2013, p. 19). In accordance with the ascent of South-South cooperation in Brazilian foreign policy, the transfer of knowledge and expertise in food security became an important factor for the country's SSDC. Former President Lula's Zero Hunger (Fome Zero) programme—with its famous conditional cash-transfer component, Bolsa Família—strongly contributed to his popularity at home and his reputation abroad. It is often mentioned as an example of knowledge sharing when analysing Brazil's increased level of engagement in international cooperation (Bartelt 2005; Seitenfuß 2007). Another important programme in this context is the Programa de Aquisição de Alimentos (Food Purchase Programme), which is also integrated into the Fome Zero programme (Bruyn 2013, p. 18; Costa Leite et al. 2013, pp. 19–20) and has achieved significant success in Brazil by involving the most relevant stakeholders in the multifaceted questions surrounding food security and purchasing power. In addition, Brazil's portfolio in Mozambique included a project to maintain a centre for professional capacity-building in Maputo; a project for capacity-building for work safety and work relation inspectors; the above-mentioned programme for food security and nutrition in schools; the cooperation with Eduardo Mondlane

University in Maputo on long-distance teaching; a project for capacity-building in the judicial sector; and a programme for capacity-building for diplomats (ABC 2013).

Throughout this portfolio, Brazil's approach to SSDC foregrounded the concept of horizontality and the ensuing characteristics of Southern cooperation. ABC, for instance, explicitly stated that Brazilian cooperation should (i) use joint "diplomacy based on solidarity", (ii) use "action in response to demands from developing countries", (iii) acknowledge "local experience" and "adapt Brazilian experience", (iv) not impose conditions, (v) not be associated with commercial interests, and (vi) not interfere with domestic issues of the recipient (ABC 2011, p. 6). Embrapa subscribed to the same principles and points out the necessity for a formal agreement under the auspices of ABC for conducting cooperation. In addition, the company highlighted its structural approach to cooperation and its focus on institutional development and capacity-building (Embrapa 2015a). The same principles can be found in the concept of "structural cooperation" in health developed by Fiocruz (Almeida et al. 2010). In this sense, the discourse that Brazil promoted on the foreign policy level is strongly reflected in its cooperation. However, the practitioners involved in the interaction evaluated the practices rather differently. Based on data from field research conducted between 2012 and 2014 in Brazil and Mozambique with high-ranking representatives from the Mozambican and Brazilian governments and experts from sectoral institutions and civil society[3] on the specific characteristics of SSDC, a rather mixed picture can be found.

First, to be horizontal, the cooperation design and the implementation would have to address which actors are involved on both sides, who exerts control over cooperation projects and to which degree, whether the procedures of decision-making and conflict resolution involve both sides equally, and whether the achieved objectives are in line with the interests of both sides. The field research showed that some practitioners highlighted the trustful atmosphere and perceived the cooperation to be horizontal (or at least that honest efforts were made towards horizontality). Others were clearly disappointed with Brazilian cooperation in this regard. In health, for example, Brazil's structural approach was perceived positively and as a differential to most "traditional" donors in the country. In agriculture, Mozambican respondents recognised Brazil's effort to conduct horizontal cooperation but stated that the notion of who provided cooperation to whom was still present. In education, respondents from both sides agreed that the relevant actors were involved in the cooperation, but Mozambicans felt that their interests were not being considered sufficiently, both during project planning and implementation.

Across the sectors, the practitioners involved pointed out that the fact that Brazil does not directly transfer financial means (budget support) and does not attach political conditionalities to its cooperation contributed strongly to the cooperation being perceived as rather horizontal by both sides. On the other hand, both Brazilian and Mozambican respondents pointed out that the importance of horizontality in the cooperation depended in most cases on the individuals involved rather than on the institutional guidelines and policies. In addition, the asymmetric setting between the two countries was perceived to be present in the cooperation in spite of the efforts to achieve horizontality.

Second, the notion of demand-driven cooperation features prominently between Brazil and Mozambique both in conceptualisation and praxis (ABC 2014). For Brazil, the idea of attending to the officially and formally articulated demands of the recipient is important throughout the cooperation. Brazilian practitioners indicated that they need to adhere to this as a political requirement in praxis. Mozambican respondents had the impression that they were able to articulate their demand for structural approaches in health through negotiations between Fiocruz and Mozambique's Ministry of Health. This resulted in cooperation projects that were aimed at strengthening the country's institutions rather than being subject to current trends focussing on single issues—a challenge that is sometimes perceived in Northern cooperation. Practitioners from Mozambican cooperation institutions saw these opportunities as adding to the sustainability of the cooperation, enabling the recipient to maintain control over the cooperation. It can therefore be assumed that the possibility to adapt the cooperation in accordance with Mozambican demands added significantly to the trustful atmosphere between the cooperation partners, according to respondents from both the Brazilian and Mozambican sides of the cooperation.

However, the data collected indicates that Brazilian cooperation tends to not be concerned with whether all relevant stakeholders are involved in the articulation of the demand. Beyond the necessity of a formal request from the partner government to initiate the cooperation, no mechanisms were established to guarantee the inclusion of the partner's demands—for instance from civil society—throughout the course of the cooperation. It is important that Brazil does not claim to have an inclusive approach to cooperation, but instead explicitly aims to cooperate with the partner government. However, namely Mozambican practitioners criticised this as a lack of participation and pointed at the risk of the cooperation attending (primarily) to the demands of elites and not necessarily to the target groups of the cooperation.

Third, when looking at the principle of mutual benefits, responses from both sides indicated—rather surprisingly—that these tend to be of minor relevance when conceptualising and implementing projects. Both cooperating parties were aware of the fact that while benefits were created for each respective partner, these often occurred on different levels of the cooperation. Respondents stated that additional gains, such as the international reputation that Brazil would gain by presenting itself as a provider of cooperation, were not included in the conceptualisation of the project. These benefits were not linked to the practical level of cooperation and were therefore not reflected in project conceptualisations. The project design instead put a focus on gains in technical knowledge.

However, respondents pointed out that programmes were designed to create imminent benefits for Mozambique, but not for Brazil. In this sense, the data suggests that the dyad of a cooperation provider and a recipient was maintained with one main beneficiary, and not with a horizontal partnership from which both sides profit. Respondents indicated that the benefits resulting from the cooperation for Brazil were not included in the programme design. It can be argued that this is understandable for the benefits outside of the scope and objective of a particular project, but not for benefits on a technical level if the notion of mutual benefits was to be a central aspect of the cooperation.

Fourth, and rather unexpectedly, despite being rather "soft" indicators that, at first glance, appear to have little influence on the power structures of cooperation, Brazilians and Mozambicans foregrounded both a common language and cultural similarities as relevant factors for creating a trustful atmosphere and a better understanding between cooperation partners, which, in turn, was decisive in the cooperation being perceived as (more) horizontal. For almost all respondents, both *cultural proximity* and a *common colonial past* influenced the perception of Brazil being a "Southern" provider and *not* a member of the Global North. The fact that Brazil was seen to be an emerging or middle country (between Mozambique and the Global North) was perceived to be an advantage, as Brazil could offer more adequate solutions (for instance in agriculture) and, according to Mozambicans, often showed a better understanding of development challenges. However, respondents also pointed out that a common language and cultural similarities do not eradicate all cultural differences between the cooperation partners. On the contrary, practitioners from cooperation agencies, ministries, and sectoral institutions highlighted that it was still necessary to adapt to different cultural settings and understandings, and to be aware of—and sensitive to—different social codes. As a result, even with both sides sharing a common language and similar cultural backgrounds, trust between cooperation partners still had to be built up over time. Conclusions drawn from the data on the importance of language and culture in SSDC are, however, case-specific, since most SSDC providers do not speak the same primary language as most of their cooperation partners. This also holds for many cases of Brazilian cooperation—and it can also be seen as one factor that potentially contributed to Brazil's focus on the lusophone countries (the PALOP community). It also has to be noted that both aspects of SSDC were not included in the project design or conceptualisation.

Fifth, the idea of knowledge exchange—often in the context of mutual benefits and cultural proximity—is prominent in Brazil's cooperation with Mozambique. Mozambican practitioners positively highlighted this aspect. In the health sector, knowledge exchange contributed towards attending to the recipient's demand, since capacity-building strengthens the recipient's sectoral institutions rather than addressing a specific issue. In this sense, capacity-building is a rather structural approach. In agriculture, knowledge previously obtained and adapted in Brazil—in some cases through North-South cooperation—proved useful for Mozambique's demand. Practitioners from both sides perceived the focus on knowledge exchange (or transfer) as a differential from Northern cooperation. Horizontal knowledge exchange and mutual learning were noted to be a *responsibility* for providers in SSDC.

25.5 Conclusions—The "Institutionalisation" of Southern Cooperation

The characteristics that constitute Southern cooperation are strongly present in Brazil's discourse around its cooperation with Mozambique and often in the conceptualisation of the cooperation projects. However, the case indicates that the relevance of these characteristics in cooperation practices tends to vary, depending to a significant degree on the individual practitioners. In this sense, Brazil, under the presidencies of Lula da Silva and Rousseff, "institutionalised" the notion of horizontality and the incurring characteristics that are so prominently foregrounded in the country's approach to cooperation only to a low degree: the policy appears to be implemented rather less rigidly than the solidarity rhetoric would imply, according to the experts of both countries.

The case study presented is not representative of Brazilian cooperation in general, and even to a lesser degree for SSDC provided by other emerging powers. On the one hand, Mozambique is a country that is highly dependent on external aid and highly accustomed to adopting policies from cooperation providers. This is likely to influence the perception of horizontality and further characteristics of SSDC, whereas cooperation with a partner that holds more bargaining power might be structured differently. On the other hand, other SSDC providers choose different approaches in their cooperation. For instance, China does not distinguish as clearly as Brazil between economic and technical cooperation (Bräutigam 2011). As a result, the importance of the SSDC characteristics investigated here will most likely vary.

In addition, the dynamics of *emerging powers* with strong influence on the international agenda have changed in recent years. Cooperation among the BICS has been less prominent and has received far less attention due to—among other factors—domestic reasons that have led some of these countries (such as Brazil, India, and South Africa) to focus more on internal affairs, or to pursue their international ambitions either unilaterally or in the context of other alliances, as China has done. On the other hand, emerging powers such as Turkey and Mexico continue to strive for international influence while putting less emphasis on their "Southern identity".

Nevertheless, the relationship between the discourse around SSDC and the cooperation practices deserves attention: the low degree of "institutionalisation" raises the matter of common standards, which would have to be established in SSDC if the modality continues to be presented as a cooperation that challenges and contests "traditional" development cooperation. Otherwise, Southern cooperation runs the risk of maintaining a dyad of a "provider" and a "recipient" (or beneficiary) (Esteves 2018). It can be assumed that if SSDC does not overcome the separation between provider and recipient, structures similar to the ones between DAC donors and their partner countries might either be established or consolidated, and recipients would have to continue to strive for greater independence and more bargaining power.

The question of whether the OECD's DAC will continue to be the central institution that sets the most important standards for development cooperation, or whether institutions such as the UN DCF will become more important in the arena where development cooperation agendas are defined, is still ongoing (Gulrajani and Swiss 2017). There is, however, no doubt that efforts from both "traditional" donors and new development partners will be necessary to implement the 2030 Agenda (UNGA 2018). Most importantly, the SDGs and the 2030 Agenda have been accompanied by different understandings of the relation between donors or providers of cooperation on the one hand, and recipients and beneficiaries on the other. The fact that not only Southern cooperation providers but also private foundations, the private sector, and civil society have become increasingly important actors in international development cooperation has added to the complexity of the IDC landscape (Esteves 2017).

Nevertheless, the engagement of Northern and Southern cooperation providers is far from being aligned, and the different framing of the cooperation modalities continues to hold its political connotation. For instance, the BICS have not joined the GPEDC but decided to discuss matters of effectiveness in the UN context. It is likely that the question that will become ever more central to the difference between Northern and Southern cooperation modalities and the relationship between donors and providers is the one concerning the effectiveness of cooperation and whether SSDC can make a relevant contribution here. Southern development partners such as the BICS continue to present their cooperation as being different from North-South cooperation, and the allocation of their cooperation follows different criteria. In this sense, SSDC continues to contest the established paradigm of cooperation being provided by the Global North. There is, however, little reason to doubt that the contributions from the South will be crucial for the implementation of the 2030 Agenda. Against this background, it is important to note that significant advances have been made in how SSDC can be monitored and evaluated (Esteves 2018; UNDP 2016b, c), and it is here that further development is most likely to be expected.

Notes

1. The term "modality" is often used differently and is sometimes controversial. Both the UN and the OEDC, however, have come to use the term to distinguish between North-South and South-South cooperation in the context of international development, emphasising the complementarity between both modalities (UNGA 2018).
2. This chapter is based on the author's PhD thesis, *Power and Horizontality in South-South Development Cooperation—The Case of Brazil and Mozambique*,

University of Duisburg-Essen (Logos, Berlin, 2020). The final version of the chapter was sent to the editors in November 2019.

3. A total of 38 qualitative, semi-structured interviews served to examine whether the cooperation projects were designed in accordance with the SSDC characteristics. In addition, they contained questions on the perceptions of these experts on the horizontality of the cooperation and the practical relevance of the characteristics of SSDC described above. In order to secure a high level of confidentiality with the interview partners and to take into account the political sensitiveness of some of the issues discussed in the interviews, the interviewees were granted anonymity.

References

ABC (Agência Brasileira de Cooperação). (2010). *A cooperação técnica do Brasil para a África*. http://www.abc.gov.br/abc_por/Conteudo/CatalogoABCAfrica2010_I.pdf.

ABC. (2011). *Brazilian technical cooperation*. http://www.abc.gov.br/api/publicacaoarquivo/47.

ABC. (2013). *Projetos em Moçambique em execução*. http://www.abc.gov.br/projetos/pesquisa.

ABC. (2014). *Manual de gestão da cooperção técnica Sul-Sul*. http://www.abc.gov.br/Content/ABC/docs/Manual_SulSul_v4.pdf.

ABC. (2015a). *África – execução financeira (2000–2014)*. http://www.abc.gov.br/Gestao/AfricaExecucaoFinanceira.

ABC. (2015b). *Evolução da execução financeira dos projetos da ABC*. http://www.abc.gov.br/Gestao/EvolucaoFinanceira.

ABC. (2015c). *Moçambique – acordo geral de cooperação*. http://www.abc.gov.br/Projetos/CooperacaoSulSul/Mocambique.

Abdel-Malek, T. (2015). *The global partnership for effective development cooperation: Origins, actions and future prospects* (Studies 88). Bonn: German Development Institute/Deutsches Institut für Entwicklungspolitik (DIE).

Africa Renewal. (2015). *For development finance, there is no one-size-fits-all solution*. http://www.un.org/africarenewal/magazine/august-2015/development-finance-there-no-one-size-fits-all-solution.

Aidoo, R., & Hess, S. (2015). Non-interference 2.0: China's evolving foreign policy towards a changing Africa. *Journal of Current Chinese Affairs, 44*(1), 107–139.

Alden, C., Vieira, M. A., & Morphet, S. (2010). *The South in world politics*. Basingstoke and New York, NY: Palgrave Macmillan.

Almeida, C., Campos, R. P. d., Buss, P., Ferreira, J., & Fonseca, L. (2010). A concepção brasileira de "cooperação Sul-Sul estruturante em saúde". *Revista Eletrônica de Comunicação, Informação & Inovação em Saúde – RECIIS, 4*(1), 25–35.

Alves, A. C. (2013). *Brazil-Africa technical co-operation: Structure, achievements and challenges (Policy Briefing 69)*. Johannesburg: South African Institute of International Affairs.

Amanor, K. S. (2013a). South-South cooperation in Africa: Historical, geopolitical and political economy dimensions of international development. *IDS Bulletin, 44*(4), 20–30.

Amanor, K.S. (2013b). *South-South cooperation in context: Perspectives from Africa.* http://citeseerx.ist.psu.edu/viewdoc/download?doi=10.1.1.433.3544&rep=rep1&type=pdf.

Bartelt, D. (2005). Szenen einer Ehe: Die Regierung Lula in Brasilien und ihre linken Kritiker. *Jahrbuch Lateinamerika: Analysen Und Berichte, 29,* 18–40.

BBC Brasil. (2008). *Brasil "tem compromisso moral" com África, diz Lula.* http://www.bbc.com/portuguese/reporterbbc/story/2008/10/081017_lulaencerramocambiquedg_ba.shtml.

Bergamaschi, I., & Tickner, A. B. (2017). Introduction: South-South cooperation beyond the myths: A critical analysis. In I. Bergamaschi, P. Tickner, I. Bergamaschi, P. V. Moore, & A. B. Tickner (Eds.), *South-South cooperation beyond the myths: Rising donors, new aid practices?* (pp. 1–27). London: Palgrave Macmillan.

Besharati, N. A. (2013). *A year after Busan: Where is the global partnership going?* http://www.saiia.org.za/doc_download/12-a-year-after-busan-where-is-the-global-partnership-going.

Bilal, S. (2012). *What is the rise of South-South relations about? Development, not aid.* http://ecdpm.org/wp-content/uploads/2013/10/What-is-Rise-South-South-Relations-about-Development-not-Aid-Bilal.pdf.

Bracho, G. (2015). *In search of a narrative for the Southern providers: The challenge of the emerging economies to the development cooperation agenda* (Discussion Paper 1/2015). Bonn: German Development Institute/Deutsches Institut für Entwicklungspolitik (DIE).

Bräutigam, D. (2011). Aid "with Chinese characteristics": Chinese foreign aid and development finance meet the OECD-DAC aid regime. *Journal of International Development, 23*(5), 752–764.

Browne, S. (2006). *Aid and influence: Do donors help or hinder?.* London: Earthscan.

Bruyn, T. D. (2013). *Adding new spices to development cooperation: Brazil, India, China and South Africa in health, agriculture and food security.* https://ghum.kuleuven.be/ggs/13-de-bruyn-afs-24032014.pdf.

Buffardi, A. L. (2013). Configuring "country ownership": Patterns of donor-recipient relations. *Development in Practice, 23*(8), 977–990.

Burges, S. W. (2012). Developing from the South: South-South cooperation in the global development game. *Brazilian Journal of Strategy & International Relations – Revista Brasileira de Estratégia e Relações Internacionais, 1*(2), 225–249.

Cabral, L. (2015). *Priests, technicians and traders? The discursive politics of Brazil's agricultural cooperation in Mozambique* (Future Agricultures Working Paper 110). https://www.future-agricultures.org/publications/working-papers-document/priests-technicians-and-traders-the-discursive-politics-of-brazils-agricultural-cooperation-in-mozambique/.

Cabral, L., Russo, G., & Weinstock, J. (2014). Brazil and the shifting consensus on development cooperation: Salutary diversions from the aid effectiveness trail. *Development Policy Review, 32*(2), 179–202.

Cabral, L., & Shankland, A. (2012). *Brazil's agriculture cooperation in Africa: New paradigms?* http://www.iese.ac.mz/lib/publication/III_Conf2012/IESE_IIIConf_Paper23.pdf.

Cervo, A. L., & Lessa, A. C. (2014). O declínio: inserção internacional do Brasil (2011–2014). *Revista Brasileira de Política Internacional, 57*(2), 133–151.

Cesarino, L. M. C. d. N. (2012). Anthropology of development and the challenge of South-South cooperation. *Vibrant, 9*(1), 508–537.

Chung, S., Eom, Y. H., & Jung, H. J. (2015). Why untie aid? An empirical analysis of the determinants of South Korea's untied aid from 2010 to 2013. *Journal of International Development*, *28*(4), 552–568.

Constantine, J., Shankland, A., & Gu, J. (2014). *Engaging the rising powers in the Global Partnership for Effective Development Cooperation: A framing paper*. https://effectivecooperation.org/wp-content/uploads/2016/08/GPEDC-Engagement-with-BRICS_IDS-Framing-Paper_New_June2015.pdf.

Corrêa, M. L. (2010). *Prática comentada da cooperação internacional: Entre a hegemonia e a busca de autonomia*. Brasilia: Author.

Costa Leite, I., Suyama, B., & Pomeroy, M. (2013). *Africa-Brazil co-operation in social protection: Drivers, lessons and shifts in the engagement of the Brazilian Ministry of Social Development* (Working Paper No. 2013/022). Helsinki: World Institute for Development Economics Research.

De la Fontaine, D. (2009, June). Indian foreign development assistance to Africa: Interests, actors and issues. ECAS—European Conference on African Studies 2009. http://www.uni-leipzig.de/~ecas2009/index.php?option=com_docman&task=doc_download&gid=556&Itemid=24.

De la Fontaine, D., Müller, F., & Sondermann, E. (2014). "Emerging donors": Current dynamics in international development cooperation from the perspective of gift theory. *Politische Vierteljahresschrift*, *48*, 249–289.

De Morais, M. G. (2005). *South-South cooperation, policy transfer and best-practice reasoning: The transfer of the solidarity in literacy program from Brazil to Mozambique* (Working Paper Series No. 406). The Hague: International Institute of Social Studies of Erasmus University Rotterdam.

Deen, T. (2007). *South faults one-size-fits-all approach*. https://www.globalpolicy.org/social-and-economic-policy/social-and-economic-policy-at-the-un/un-high-level-panel-on-systemwide-coherence/32349-south-faults-one-size-fits-all-approach.html.

Dijkstra, G. (2004). The effectiveness of policy conditionality: Eight country experiences. In J. P. Pronk (Ed.), *Catalysing development? A debate on aid* (pp. 89–115). Oxford: Blackwell UK.

Elsinger, M. (2011). *Just B(R)ICS in the wall? The impact of the financial and economic crisis on emerging powers and their weight in global governance structures*. Marburg, Germany: DVPW Conference.

Embrapa. (2006). *Instituto do Algodão de Moçambique envia técnicos a Embrapa Algodão*. http://www.cnpa.embrapa.br/noticias/2006/noticia_20060926.html.

Embrapa. (2015a). *Atuação internacional – portal Embrapa*. https://www.embrapa.br/atuacao-internacional.

Embrapa. (2015b). Quem somos – portal Embrapa. https://www.embrapa.br/quem-somos?p_auth=QGONlW4y&p_p_id=82&p_p_lifecycle=1&p_p_state=normal&p_p_mode=view&_82_struts_action=%2Flanguage%2Fview&_82_languageId=en_US.

Esteves, P. L. (2017). Agora somos todos países em desenvolvimento? A cooperação Sul-Sul e os ODS. *Pontes*, *13*(2). https://www.ictsd.org/bridges-news/pontes/news/agora-somos-todos-pa%C3%ADses-em-desenvolvimento-a-coopera%C3%A7%C3%A3o-sul-sul-e-os-ods.

Esteves, P. L. (2018). *How governments of the South assess the results of South-South cooperation: Case studies of South-led approaches*. https://www.iass-potsdam.de/de/ergebnisse/publikationen/2018/how-governments-south-assess-results-south-south-cooperation-case.

Esteves, P. L., Fonseca, J. Da, & Zoccal, G. (2015). *Brazilian health and agricultural cooperation in Mozambique: An overview* (BPC Papers, Vol. 2, No. 5). Rio de Janeiro: BRICS Policy Center.

Eyben, R. (2012). Struggles in Paris: The DAC and the purposes of development aid. *European Journal of Development Research, 25*(1), 78–91.

Eyben, R., & Savage, L. (2012). Emerging and submerging powers: Imagined geographies in the new development partnership at the Busan Fourth High Level Forum. *The Journal of Development Studies, 49*(4), 457–469.

Fejerskov, A., Lundsgaarde, E., & Cold-Ravnkilde, S. (2016). *Uncovering the dynamics of interaction in development cooperation: A review of the "new actors in development" research agenda* (Working Paper 2016:1). Copenhagen: Danish Institute for International Studies.

Fellet, J. (2013, February 20). Mais "fria" com a África, Dilma faz 2ª visita ao continente. *BBC Brasil*. http://www.bbc.co.uk/portuguese/noticias/2013/02/130219_dilma_africa_apresentacao_jp_jf.shtml.

Ferreira, W. (2016, March 19). Política externa brasileira para a África nos governos FHC, Lula e Dilma: reflexões sobre mudanças e incertezas. *Mundorama*. http://www.mundorama.net/2016/03/19/politica-externa-brasileira-para-a-africa-nos-governos-fhc-lula-e-dilma-reflexoes-sobre-mudancas-e-incertezas-por-walace-ferreira/.

Flyvbjerg, B. (2006). Five misunderstandings about case-study research. *Qualitative Inquiry, 12*(2), 219–245.

Fues, T. (2012). At a crossroads. *D + C—Development and Cooperation, 7*, 301–303. http://www.dandc.eu/articles/220599/index.en.shtml.

Funada Classen, S. (2013). Analysis of the discourse and background of the ProSAVANA programme in Mozambique—Focusing on Japan's role. https://pdfs.semanticscholar.org/87cf/dfafc5fb61744dc16a484631b00e40fc3a67.pdf.

Glennie, J. (2014, April 11). Will competing UN and OECD partnerships stymie aid effectiveness? *The Guardian*. http://www.theguardian.com/global-development/poverty-matters/2014/apr/11/un-oecd-partnerships-aid-effectiveness.

Gulrajani, N., & Swiss, L. (2017). *Why do countries become donors? Assessing the drivers and implications of donor proliferation*. London: Overseas Development Institute.

Hanlon, J., & Smart, T. (2008). *Do bicycles equal development in Mozambique? Woodbridge, UK, and Rochester*. NY: James Currey.

Hernandez, D. (2016). Are "new" donors challenging World Bank conditionality? *World Development, 96*, 529–549.

IPEA (Instituto de Pesquisa Econômica Aplicada). (2016). *Cooperação Brasileira para o desenvolvimento internacional 2011–2013*. http://www.ipea.gov.br/portal/images/stories/PDFs/livros/livros/161017_livro_cobradi_2011_2013.pdf.

IPEA. (2018). *Cooperação Brasileira para o desenvolvimento internacional: Levantamento 2014–2016*. http://www.ipea.gov.br/portal/images/stories/PDFs/livros/livros/181219_cobradi_2014-2016.pdf.

Janus, H., Klingebiel, S., & Paulo, S. (2015). Beyond aid: A conceptual perspective on the transformation of development cooperation. *Journal of International Development, 27*(2), 155–169.

Japan International Cooperation Agency. (2013). *Japanese CSO statement on ProSAVANA: Call for an immediate suspension and fundamental review*. http://www.cadtm.org/spip.php?page=imprimer&id_article=9609.

Kharas, H. J. (2012). *The global partnership for effective development cooperation* (Policy Paper 2012-04). Washington, DC: The Brookings Institution.

Kornegay, F. (2013). *Africa and developmental diplomacy in the Global South: The challenge of stabilisation.* Pretoria: Institute for Global Dialogue.

Kragelund, P. (2015, May). *Looking ahead: South-South cooperation in the next decade: Workshop on South-South cooperation.* Keynote speech. Cambridge: Newham College.

Lancaster, C. (2007). *Foreign aid: Diplomacy, development, domestic politics.* Chicago, IL: University of Chicago Press.

Lundsgaarde, E. (2011). *"New" actors and global development cooperation. European development co-operation to 2020.* http://www.edc2020.eu/fileadmin/publications/EDC2020_-_Policy_Brief_No_19_-_New_Actors_and_Global_Development_Cooperation.pdf.

Lustig, C. M. (2016). Soft or hard power? Discourse patterns in Brazil's foreign policy toward South America. *Latin American Politics and Society, 58*(4), 103–125.

Marcondes de Souza Neto, D. (2013, July). A cooperação Sul-Sul brasileira na área de saúde: o caso de Moçambique e a interação com novos atores? 4. Encontro Nacional ABRI, Belo Horizonte, MG, Brasil. http://www.encontronacional2013.abri.org.br/conteudo/view?ID_CONTEUDO=855.

Mawdsley, E. (2011). The changing geographies of foreign aid and development cooperation: Contributions from gift theory. *Transactions of the Institute of British Geographers, 37*(2), 256–272.

Mawdsley, E. (2012). *From recipients to donors: Emerging powers and the changing development landscape.* London and New York, NY: Zed Books.

Mawdsley, E., Savage, L., & Kim, S.-M. (2014). A "post-aid world"? Paradigm shift in foreign aid and development cooperation at the 2011 Busan High Level Forum. *The Geographical Journal, 180*(1), 27–38.

Mello, F. (2013, March 22). O que quer o Brasil com o ProSavana? *Verdade.* http://www.verdade.co.mz/economia/35642-o-que-quer-o-brasil-com-o-prosavana.

Milani, C. (2014). *Brazil's South–South co-operation strategies: From foreign policy to public policy.* https://saiia.org.za/research/brazils-south-south-co-operation-strategies-from-foreign-policy-to-public-policy/.

Milhorance de Castro, C. (2013). Brazil's South-South foreign policy post-Lula: Where does Africa fit in? *Afrique Contemporaine, 4*(248), 45–59.

Mineiro, A. (2014). *Brazil: From cursed legacy to compromised hope? Chapter two* (TNI Working Papers). Amsterdam: Transnational Institute.

Monge Roffarello, L. (2015). *Country brief for Mozambique.* https://www.mz.undp.org/content/dam/mozambique/docs/Poverty/Mozambique-Country-Brief-2015.pdf.

Muhr, T. (2015). Beyond "BRICS": Ten theses on South-South cooperation in the 21st century. *Third World Quarterly, 37*(4), 630–648.

Naylor, T. (2011). Deconstructing development: The use of power and pity in the international development discourse. *International Studies Quarterly, 55*(1), 177–197.

OECD-DAC (Organisation for Economic Co-operation and Development/Development Assistance Committee). (2011). *The Busan Global Partnership: A new milestone for effective development cooperation: Conference proceedings.*

https://www.oecd.org/dac/effectiveness/HLF4%20proceedings%20entire%20doc%20for%20web.pdf.

ONGs Mozambicanas. (2013). *Carta aberta para deter e reflectir de forma urgente o programa ProSavana*. https://www.farmlandgrab.org/uploads/attachment/Carta%20Aberta%20das%20organizac%cc%a7o%cc%83es%20e%20movimentos%20sociais%20para%20Detere%20Reflectir%20de%20Forma%20Urgente%20o%20Programa%20ProSavana-corrected.pdf.

Piefer, N. (2014). *Triangular cooperation – bridging South-South and North-South cooperation?* Paper prepared for the "Workshop on South-South Development Cooperation", University of Heidelberg, September 26th–27th 2014. https://www.uni-heidelberg.de/md/awi/ssdc_piefer.pdf.

Quadir, F. (2013). Rising donors and the new narrative of "South-South" cooperation: What prospects for changing the landscape of development assistance programmes? *Third World Quarterly, 34*(2), 321–338.

Reddy, G. (2008). Role of Indian diaspora in promoting India's trade and commerce relations with South Africa. In V. S. Sheth (Ed.), *India-Africa relations: Emerging policy and development perspective* (1st ed., pp. 227–234). Delhi: Academic Excellence.

Renzio, P. d., Zoccal, G., Assunção, M., & Alves, A. L. (2015). *A agenda do desenvolvimento internacional pós 2015: Que papel para os BRICS?* (BPC Policy Brief). Rio de Janeiro: BRICS Policy Center.

Saraiva, J. F. S. (2010). The new Africa and Brazil in the Lula era: The rebirth of Brazilian Atlantic policy. *Revista Brasileira De Política Internacional, 53*(spe), 169–182.

Secretaría General Iberoamericana. (2008). *II informe de la cooperación Sur-Sur en Iberoamérica*. https://www.segib.org/wp-content/uploads/sur_sur_web_ES.PDF.

Seitenfuß, R. (2007). O Brasil e suas relações internacionais. *Carta Internacional, 2*(1). http://cartainternacional.abri.emnuvens.com.br/Carta/article/view/405.

United Nations. (2013). *"Group of 77" nations key to shaping post-2015 development agenda, say UN officials*. https://news.un.org/en/story/2013/09/450882-group-77-nations-key-shaping-post-2015-development-agenda-say-un-officials.

UN Department of Economic and Social Affairs. (2014). *ECOSOC convenes symposium on development cooperation*. http://www.un.org/en/development/desa/news/ecosoc/dcf-high-level-symposium.html.

UNDP. (UN Development Programme) (2016a). *Background on South-South cooperation*. http://ssc.undp.org/content/ssc/about/Background.html.

UNDP. (2016b). *Brazilian triangular cooperation in social protection: Contribution to the 2030 Agenda*. https://www.undp.org/content/undp/en/home/librarypage/development-impact/Brazilian_triangular_cooperation.html.

UNDP. (2016c). *Monitoring and evaluation mechanisms for South-South and triangular development cooperation: Lessons from Brazil for the 2030 Agenda*. https://www.undp.org/content/dam/undp/library/development-impact/SS%20Research%20Publications/11875%20-%20Monitoring%20and%20evaluation%20mechanisms%20for%20South%20-%2006_Web%20Version(2).pdf.

UNDP Mozambique. (2010). *UN system aid effectiveness in Mozambique*. http://www.mz.undp.org/content/dam/mozambique/docs/Millennium_Development_Goals/UNDP_MOZ_UN_Aid%20Effectiveness%20in%20Mozambique.pdf.

UNGA (UN General Assembly). (2018). *The role of South-South cooperation and the implementation of the 2030 Agenda for sustainable development: Challenges and opportunities*. Report of the Secretary-General. https://www.unsouthsouth.org/2018/09/17/role-of-south-south-cooperation-and-the-implementation-of-the-2030-agenda-for-sustainable-development-challenges-and-opportunities-report-of-the-secretary-general/.

UNGA. (2019). Buenos Aires Outcome Document. https://www.unsouthsouth.org/2019/04/15/buenos-aires-outcome-document-adopted/.

UNOSSC (UN Office for South-South Cooperation). (2010). High-level United Nations Conference on South-South Cooperation: Nairobi Outcome Document. http://ssc.undp.org/content/dam/ssc/documents/Key%20Policy%20Documents/Nairobi%20Outcome%20Document.pdf.

UNOSSC. (2016). United Nations Office for South-South Cooperation—World Bank. http://ssc.undp.org/content/ssc/un_entities_space/WB.html.

Verschaeve, J., & Orbie, J. (2015). The DAC is dead, long live the DCF? A comparative analysis of the OECD Development Assistance Committee and the UN Development Cooperation Forum. *The European Journal of Development Research, 28*(4), 571–587.

World Bank. (2016). South-South knowledge exchange. https://www.worldbank.org/en/region/lac/brief/south-south-knowledge-exchange-latin-america-caribbean-region.

Open Access This chapter is licensed under the terms of the Creative Commons Attribution 4.0 International License (http://creativecommons.org/licenses/by/4.0/), which permits use, sharing, adaptation, distribution and reproduction in any medium or format, as long as you give appropriate credit to the original author(s) and the source, provide a link to the Creative Commons license and indicate if changes were made.

The images or other third party material in this chapter are included in the chapter's Creative Commons license, unless indicated otherwise in a credit line to the material. If material is not included in the chapter's Creative Commons license and your intended use is not permitted by statutory regulation or exceeds the permitted use, you will need to obtain permission directly from the copyright holder.

CHAPTER 26

South Africa as a Development Partner: An Empirical Analysis of the African Renaissance and International Cooperation Fund

Philani Mthembu

26.1 Introduction

An intriguing dynamic within the contemporary global political and economic landscape involves the growing role of Southern powers, which have increasingly important roles within their own regions, while also expanding their influence in various international jurisdictions. Global fora such as the G20 and the BRICS (Brazil, Russia, India, China, and South Africa) grouping have assumed prominence as a result of the growing influence of Southern powers within a changing global landscape. There is also growing literature on a shift in global power—from a largely unipolar world order to a multipolar world order (Mthembu 2018). This shift creates various points of contestation, including in the international development cooperation landscape, where coordination and responsibilities remain contested areas.

Within the broader rise of Southern powers, an area of increasing importance is their growing roles as sources of development cooperation. Although some researchers have labelled them as new development partners, they are actually not new to development cooperation, as many of them possess programmes that have been in existence for decades, even though the scale of those programmes has expanded more rapidly in recent years. However, as the roles they play have increased, so too have a lot of questions arisen. These range from disagreements on what constitutes development cooperation from Southern powers to how they disburse their development cooperation,

---

P. Mthembu (✉)
Institute for Global Dialogue, Pretoria, South Africa
e-mail: philani@igd.org.za

© The Author(s) 2021
S. Chaturvedi et al. (eds.), *The Palgrave Handbook of Development Cooperation for Achieving the 2030 Agenda*,
https://doi.org/10.1007/978-3-030-57938-8_26

why they have expanded their development cooperation, and why they use varying strategies while adhering to similar principles regarding development cooperation. South Africa is itself not immune to these questions (Mthembu 2018).

Despite an abundance of normative-based analyses on development cooperation, there remains a gap in systematic analysis based on comprehensive empirical evidence. This often leads to contestation within and among countries as they debate the contested responsibilities to fulfilling the Sustainable Development Goals (SDGs). As stated in the introductory chapter, state actors and non-state actors must find ways to work together to address the twin challenges of coordination and contested responsibilities in order to eradicate poverty and achieve the SDGs. Development cooperation in this handbook is thus seen as an example of contested multilateralism and contested global governance. This chapter must be located within this broader conceptual framework.

This chapter assesses empirically what insights can be learnt from South Africa's African Renaissance and International Cooperation Fund (ARF) and whether the budget allocations and disbursements over a period of 12 years show a Southern power allocating a growing amount of resources in line with its rhetoric or one that is increasingly learning to live within its means under tough economic times. If allocations and disbursements have consistently grown, one can conclude that the country's financial contributions on the African continent have increased in line with its policy of promoting the African agenda; however, if the disbursements are shrinking, then it is arguable that South Africa's development cooperation architecture is still working out its own capabilities while learning to live within its means. Both scenarios have an impact on the manner in which scholars can interpret South Africa's development diplomacy, especially in the context of the SDGs. However, although the findings may open a small window into South Africa's broader international development activities, they only apply to the ARF, which—although it is among the country's most visible tool for disbursing its development cooperation—still accounts for less than 5 per cent of the country's overall activities.

As South Africa looks to consolidate its role as a development partner, it thus remains an open question whether the country can maintain a strong presence on the African continent when it also faces significant challenges at home. With the economy struggling to reach pre-global financial-crisis growth levels and the government increasingly under pressure to cut expenditure at home, one has to wonder whether these cutbacks are translating into a reduction of its role as a development partner on the African continent. With the eagerly awaited South African Development Partnership Agency (SADPA) in mind, this chapter examines data from the ARF covering the years 2003 to 2015. It shows empirically that, despite increasing allocations and disbursements in the initial years following its inception, the global financial crisis, domestic challenges, and uncertainly over the operationalisation of SADPA have taken their toll on the ARF's activities. Given the centrality of the African continent to South Africa's foreign policy priorities, it is important to keep in mind the limited capability of the country for engagement beyond the continent in the area of development cooperation.

The summary of the foreign policy review panel, published in 2019 and led by former Deputy Minister of Foreign Affairs, Aziz Pahad, and ongoing processes to improve the training of the country's diplomatic corps through the Foreign Service Bill provide opportunities for the country to navigate a contested landscape, both domestically and internationally. The chapter seeks to contribute to the ongoing discussions and processes in South Africa on positioning the country's development cooperation and architecture in line with its regional and global aspirations. It also makes clear that an inability to operationalise SADPA will lead to mixed messages and irregular allocations and disbursements of the country's development cooperation resources.

26.2 Methodology

This chapter relied on the use of primary and secondary literature to assess the current state of research on the topic while identifying gaps. This meant making use of official legislation related to South Africa's foreign and development policy and participating in stakeholder meetings and round-table discussions involving foreign policy practitioners from the Department of International Relations and Cooperation, South Africa (DIRCO) in Pretoria and the Parliamentary Committee on International Relations and Cooperation in Cape Town. These engagements, which often involve participation from scholars and researchers engaged in the topic of South Africa's foreign policy, assist in locating the research of this chapter within its broader context while incorporating the most relevant and contemporary aspects related to South Africa's role as a development partner.

The empirical data used to answer the main research question relied on the use of annual reports published by the ARF, which show total budget allocation and expenditure, and to which country and project funds were channelled. This allows for assessing whether spending has been on an upward trajectory or whether less funding has been allocated in previous years, especially with the onset of the global financial crisis as well as challenges in the South African economy.

The strength of the methodology is that it offers an accurate profile of one of the most important institutions in South Africa's international development architecture. However, an important weakness stems from the reality that the ARF is only responsible for a limited amount of South Africa's overall allocation and disbursement of development cooperation. This allows for a limited generalisation that is applicable to the ARF but not to South Africa's overall development cooperation architecture, which involves many different line ministries. Despite this limitation, it makes an important empirical contribution towards understanding an institution that may subsequently be replaced by SADPA once it is operational.

26.3 Contextualising South Africa's Role as a Development Partner

South Africa's role as a development partner sits within the broader context of its foreign policy, especially in relation to what it refers to as the African agenda. Adebajo et al. (2007, p. 17) begin their analysis of South Africa's role in Africa in the post-apartheid era by asking the following questions:

> Can a country that has brutalized and exploited its own people, and those of surrounding countries, go on to become a credible champion of human rights, democracy and sustainable development on the African continent, even after a remarkable political transformation? To what extent has South Africa been liberated to play a leading role in Africa, and to what extent is it still crippled not only by the past, but by the widely varying priorities of its 47 million people? How have these dynamics played out in the years since the "rainbow" nation stepped out of its own shadow in 1994?

In a similar sentiment, an article in South Africa's *Financial Mail* (SA tops Africa's investors' list 2007) posed the following question: "Will the nations of Africa be able to look back and say that the SA [South African] companies played a critical role in the recovery? Or will they be regarded as exploitative neo-colonialists?" Grobbelaar (2005) states that, during the transition from pariah to legitimate player, South Africa has asserted its presence in Africa through corporate and parastatal investments, which have generated trade. In doing so, South Africa has become central to the flow of capital, goods, and people on the continent. He states that outside of the mining and energy sectors, South Africa's businesses have emerged as the leading investors on the continent and are involved in a number of sectors, including retail, property, construction, manufacturing, tourism, transport, telecommunications, and financial services.

Between 1994 and 2000, South African foreign direct investment into the Southern African Development Community (SADC) region amounted to $5.4 billion, which was more than the combined British and American foreign direct investment in the sub-region (SA tops Africa's investors' list 2007), whereas *Business Day* estimated that South African companies invested an average of $435 million a year in SADC countries between 1994 and 2003 (Stoddard 2005).

Since 1910, when the current nation-state of South Africa was established as a Union, the country's then white rulers did not see themselves and the country as a part of the rest of Africa. The government in Pretoria saw the continent and especially its immediate neighbours as places for exploitation and destabilisation, areas where cheap labour could be sought for the purpose of work in mines, farms, and industry for a pittance: essentially making the continent an extension of its domestic policy (Adebajo et al. 2007, p. 18). It was during the apartheid era that the white minority regime's "marauding military bombed Mozambique, Angola, Lesotho, Botswana, Zambia and Zimbabwe in a campaign of awesome destructiveness that eventually resulted in a million deaths and an estimated $60 billion in damages between 1980 and 1988" (Adebajo et al. 2007, p. 9).

Given the institutionalised racism in the country, "South Africa's apartheid governments saw themselves culturally and politically as very much a part of the West, with the country having been part of the 'white dominions', with Australia, Canada and New Zealand" (Adebajo et al. 2007, p. 18). Such attitudes were echoed through the words of one of the chief architects of the apartheid system, Hendrik Verwoerd, when he said: "[w]e look upon ourselves as indispensable to the white world [...] we are the link. We are white, but we are in Africa. We link them both, and that lays on us a special duty" (Barber and Barret 1990, p. 6).

It is therefore hardly surprising that much of post-apartheid foreign policy-making in South Africa has sought to affirm the country's identity as an African state. With so many people from the continent and the African diaspora having withstood much hardship and sacrifice for the liberation of South Africa from the tyranny of apartheid, it would be essential for the now legitimate government to demonstrate gratitude to its neighbours and seek to play a constructive role within Africa.

When the African National Congress (ANC) came into power in 1994, new policies were put in place based on the previous assertions of President Nelson Mandela (1993, p. 87) that democracy, human rights, and the interests of the African continent were to be the cornerstone of the new government's foreign policy. In the post-apartheid era, South Africa has thus sought to position itself as a peacemaker within Africa, in stark contrast to the destructiveness of the apartheid regime. Under President Thabo Mbeki, a key theme of South Africa's foreign policy became the promotion of the "African Renaissance", which sought to address the cultural, political, social, and economic renewal of a continent recovering from centuries of foreign domination. At the launch of the African Renaissance Institute in Pretoria, President Mbeki (1999, p. 2) made the following comments:

> The question has been posed repeatedly as to what we mean when we speak of an African Renaissance. As all of us know, the word "renaissance" means rebirth, renewal, springing up anew. Therefore, when we speak of an African Renaissance, we speak of the rebirth and renewal of our continent. This idea is not new to the struggles of the peoples of our continent for genuine emancipation. It has been propagated before by other activists for liberation, drawn from many countries. But it has been suggested that when this perspective was advanced in earlier periods, the conditions did not exist for its realisation. Accordingly,

what is new about it today is that the conditions exist for the process to be enhanced, throughout the continent, leading to the transformation of the idea from a dream dreamt by visionaries to a practical programme of action for revolutionaries.

The history and evolution of the South African state and its role on the African continent have thus had an important impact in shaping contemporary policy. The stated centrality of the African continent to the country's foreign policy is thus a theme that permeates across the different post-1994 administrations, even if each has shaped it in their own manner. Although the Jacob Zuma administration paid close attention to strengthening relations with Southern powers, it also sought to project South Africa's foreign policy as being centred on the African continent's revival within an evolving global political and economic order characterised by multi-polarity. This has also meant that, as South Africa continues to strengthen its relations with Southern powers in global politics, it must consolidate its role as a development partner on the African continent, especially in the context of a changing global development landscape and the SDGs. The ARF and the long-awaited SADPA present an important avenue for the country to consolidate its role as a development partner in South-South and triangular cooperation.

26.4 An Empirical Analysis of the African Renaissance and International Cooperation Fund

South Africa's development cooperation programme can be traced to largely ineffectual attempts by the apartheid regime to gain support in a few African countries such as Lesotho, Gabon, Ivory Coast, Equatorial Guinea, and Comoros, while support was also sought from Paraguay. The apartheid regime thus sought to overcome diplomatic isolation and buy votes at the United Nations. However, as the political context changed, the Development Assistance Programme, situated within the Department of Foreign Affairs, was wound down, and at the end of 2000 it was replaced by the African Renaissance and International Cooperation Fund (Sidiropoulos 2012, p. 220).

To further consolidate South Africa's role as a source of development cooperation, participants of the governing ANC's policy conference in June 2007 endorsed the creation of a SADPA, which would be tasked with controlling and coordinating the country's outward-bound development cooperation (Braude et al., 2008, p. 9). Sidiropoulos (2012, pp. 218, 226) further notes that, in her budget speech of April 2010, South Africa's Minister of International Relations and Cooperation, Maite Nkoana-Mashabane, announced that the department would present a bill to parliament to establish SADPA:

> The ARF is the most visibly structured component of South Africa's development cooperation. Regulated by the African Renaissance and International Cooperation Fund Act of 2000, its aim is to enhance cooperation between

South Africa and other countries, in particular in Africa, through the promotion of democracy and good governance, socio-economic development and integration, humanitarian assistance and human resource development, and the prevention and resolution of conflict. [...] The Fund utilizes both concessionary loans and grants, although the latter makes up the bulk of its operations.

Some of the activities that the ARF has been involved in over the years include the following (National Treasury 2009, p. 15):

- Funding for two infrastructural projects in Lesotho—the Sani Top to Mokhotlong road project, which would create a major trading link between Lesotho and the Port of Durban, and the Metolong Dam project in the Maseru district of Lesotho—for sustainable utilisation of water resources;
- A donation of 6.6 million South African rand (ZAR) to geochemical and hydrological projects of the Lesotho Ministry of Natural Resources;
- ZAR 10 million to help Zimbabwe in its 2007/8 local, parliamentary, and presidential elections;
- ZAR 31 million to train Comorian armed personnel to provide security during the presidential elections, and a technical team of electoral experts to assist the electoral commission in the same year;
- ZAR 22 million for a water supply scheme in Katanga province in the Democratic Republic of the Congo (DRC);
- ZAR 172 million for trilateral cooperation with Vietnam on efficient rice production in Guinea.

Other examples of the broad nature of the ARF's focus in Africa include the funding of cultural activities such as the preservation of ancient manuscripts in Timbuktu in Mali, and the writing off of almost ZAR 44 million in long-term loans made to mainly African countries in previous decades (ARF 2004/5, 2005/6).

Despite the establishment of the ARF, a majority of South Africa's development cooperation programmes are still conducted through a range of government departments, parastatal bodies, government agencies, and other statutory bodies outside of DIRCO; it is thus quite a decentralised system. In fact, although the ARF forms the most visibly structured part of South Africa's development cooperation architecture, it only comprises a small percentage of the total amount of South Africa's development cooperation, estimated at between 3.3 per cent and 3.8 per cent (Braude et al. 2008, p. 5).

The departments that are involved in the majority of activities include Defence, Education, the South African Police Service, Trade and Industry, Justice and Constitutional Development, Arts and Culture, Public Service and Administration, Public Enterprises, Science and Technology, and Agriculture. Some of the activities that these departments have been involved in include the following (Sidiropoulos 2012, pp. 230–231):

- training and technical assistance to Namibia, Botswana, Zambia, Sudan, and the DRC through the Department of Justice and Constitutional Development;
- schools as centres of care and support for pilot programmes with Swaziland, Zambia, Sudan, Rwanda, Burundi, Mali, and Lesotho through the Department of Education;
- operational police training in the DRC by the Department of Police's criminal asset recovery account fund;
- support through the Department of Public Service and Administration for the DRC's public service census project, anti-corruption initiatives, and the establishment of a national public administration training institute.

Langeni (2011) further states that since 2005, the South African government, acting through the University of South Africa, has trained more than a thousand South Sudanese officials on diplomacy, public service administration, public financial management, and disciplines such as legal affairs.

Indirectly forming part of South Africa's development cooperation architecture are the two development finance institutions: the Development Bank of Southern Africa (DBSA) and the Industrial Development Corporation, which both have units charged with supporting the objectives of the New Partnership for Africa's Development (NEPAD). They are indirect players because most of the development financing provided by them is at competitive market-related rates instead of explicit concessional loans or grants. These institutions play a critical role as sources of finance, especially in various infrastructure development projects (World Bank 2008). Between 2006 and 2009, the DBSA funded projects worth ZAR 60 billion, focussing on sectors such as energy, telecommunications, mining, transport, water, manufacturing, and health. This was facilitated through an extension of its mandate in 1997, allowing it to expand and fund projects in the SADC (Development Bank of Southern Africa [DBSA] 2006–2009).

In January 2011, the DBSA concluded a loan agreement of $262 million with the Zambian National Road Fund Agency for the rehabilitation of five priority roads. This would open economic trade routes between Angola, Botswana, the DRC, and Namibia. In 2011, the DBSA's annual Africa investment approvals were expected to exceed $1 billion, with transport infrastructure expected to absorb the bulk of the financing (DBSA 2011).

Like the DBSA, the Industrial Development Corporation also had its mandate extended in 2001 "for the benefit of the Southern African region specifically and the rest of Africa generally" (Industrial Development Amendment Act 2001). This expansion is in line with South Africa's foreign policy of supporting NEPAD.

Some of the programmes that have been funded include the following (Sidiropoulos 2012, p. 232):

- ZAR 361 million investment in a Namibian cement plant in 2010;
- ZAR 850 million majority stake (together with the Mozambican government, the South African power utility Eskom, and the DBSA) in the Cahora Bassa hydroelectric plant on the Zambezi River in Mozambique in 2008;
- collaboration with Healthshare Health Solutions in funding a new private hospital in Lusaka, Zambia, in 2009.

Development cooperation and development finance from Southern powers have thus increasingly played a crucial role as part of the overall flow of goods and services among developing countries, and its significance has grown more important as they have expanded their development cooperation programmes. Unlike the official development assistance provided by members of the Organisation for Economic Co-operation and Development's Development Assistance Committee, Southern powers such as South Africa state that they promote "win-win" relations, showing clearly that the act of disbursing development cooperation is not seen as a one-way action on the part of the donor, or as an act of charity, but as an effort to promote mutual benefits.

With development cooperation from "Southern" development partners growing as an instrument of promoting South-South cooperation, South Africa will be looking to ensure that its development cooperation can achieve positive impacts within Africa. Another challenge includes sustaining its development cooperation in times of economic difficulty at home and abroad. Using data from annual reports, Table 26.1 shows just how much has been

Table 26.1 ARF allocation and expenditure (2003–2015)

Year	Funds allocated from DIRCO (ZAR millions)	Expenditure from ARF (ZAR millions)
2003/4	50	62
2005/6	100	59
2006/7	150	392
2007/8	300	352
2008/9	699	476
2009/10	631	331
2010/11	401	4
2011/12	450	270
2012/13	517	1070
2013/14	485	41
2014/15	277	189
Total	4060	3246

Source Author, using data from annual reports of the ARF (2003–2015). The figures have been rounded off

allocated to the ARF between 2003 and 2015, while also showing the expenditure on development projects in that same time period. This allows for highlighting empirically the financing trends over a period of 12 years.

The table shows that in the 12 years under scrutiny in this chapter, a total of just over ZAR 4 billion was allocated to the ARF from DIRCO, while a total of just over ZAR 3 billion was utilised for a myriad of development projects throughout that time period. The highest allocations made were in the years 2008/9 and 2009/10, which saw totals of approximately ZAR 699 million and ZAR 631 million, respectively, whereas the highest level of expenditure from the ARF was in the year 2012/13, with just over ZAR 1 billion disbursed for various projects. When one excludes 2012/13, which varies quite a lot in comparison with other years, it was the year 2008/9 that witnessed the next highest level of expenditure at ZAR 476 million. This correlates with the period that also witnessed the highest allocation of funds.

What is of interest here is that between the years 2003/4 and 2008/9, allocations into the fund only grew, before starting with a gradual decline in allocations the following year up until 2015. With regard to the expenditure from the fund, what is of interest is that only during the years 2003/4, 2006/7, 2007/8, and 2012/13 did the fund spend more than what was allocated to it. The rest of the financial years is characterised by under spending on what has been allocated. Figures 26.1 and 26.2 reveal the allocation and expenditure trends from the ARF, showing the peaks and troughs on the respective graphs in order to better highlight what happened in that period of time.

Figure 26.1 highlights that although the allocation of funds to the ARF from DIRCO witnessed an upward trend from 2003/4 to 2008/9, it is generally a downward trend from thereon, even though there is a slight recovery

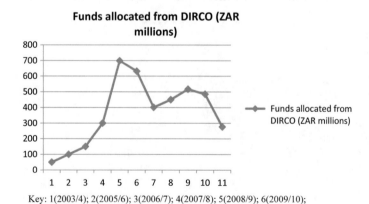

Key: 1(2003/4); 2(2005/6); 3(2006/7); 4(2007/8); 5(2008/9); 6(2009/10); 7(2010/11); 8(2011/12); 9(2012/13);10(2013/14); 11(2014/15).

Fig. 26.1 Allocation trends between 2003 and 2015 (*Source* Author, using data from annual reports of the ARF [2003–2015])

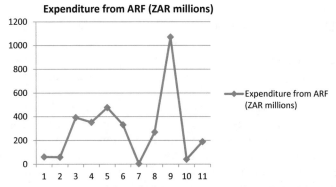

Fig. 26.2 Expenditure trends between 2003 and 2015 (*Source* Author, using data from annual reports of the ARF [2003–2015])

between 2010/11 and 2012/13. The allocations have just not recovered to anywhere near their peak levels, and the downward trend thus persists. This raises important questions to the research community and shows that, during the period under scrutiny, its peak coincided with the beginning of the global financial crisis, and that spending has just not recovered from that initial period, which saw an upward trend in the early years of the fund. One could certainly interpret this downward trend as South Africa cutting down on its development activities when it comes to the most distinct component of its development cooperation architecture and could have been motivated by several domestic and international factors.

However, although this interpretation does have some merit—given South Africa's domestic challenges and a general cutback in expenditure within the government—one should also be aware that, prior to the setting up of the long-proposed SADPA, the activities of the ARF will have to be wound down; this was, in fact, alluded to in the 2014/15 annual report (ARF 2014/15, p. 23) of the fund, which states:

> Slow disbursement of funds relates to the scale on which projects are funded or recommended. The department has commenced with the transitional arrangements for the establishment of the South African Development Partnership Agency (SADPA) through the enactment of the Partnership for Development Fund. The surplus retained will be transferred to SADPA.

Besides this, one must also be aware of the limitations of the generalisation that one can draw about South Africa's allocation patters as a whole, given the reality that ARF allocations do not even account for 5 per cent of South Africa's overall spending on development cooperation. To have a more conclusive picture, one would thus have to have data from many different government departments involved in South Africa's development cooperation. This would indeed go beyond the focus and scope of the current chapter. However, focussing on a small yet important component of South Africa's development cooperation architecture does allow us to draw concrete conclusions about the ARF, especially when one takes into account the imminent creation and operationalisation of SADPA.

Figure 26.2 shows that expenditure has been rather erratic in nature, with no consistent patterns. This seems to be more related to the management side of the fund rather than the availability of funds, since there are many years where the fund was not able to spend all of the money it was allocated. However, the 2012/13 financial year is something of an anomaly, as total expenditure shot up to just over ZAR 1 billion shortly after reaching a low of ZAR 4 million in 2010/11.

In explaining the anomaly in expenditure during the 2012/13 financial year, the annual report (ARF 2012/13, p. 10) states that "the Fund was seized with requests for humanitarian assistance, which were unprecedented, due to the scale and magnitude of intervention required". This subsequently led to large, irregular spending totals, as supply chain prescripts were not adhered to. It is further explained in the annual report that the irregular expenditure was partly caused by the absence of an emergency relief policy and strategy (ARF 2012/13, p. 10). The question thus remains whether the future SADPA will be a flexible fund, responding to policy-level demand.

The 2010/11 annual report also explains the reasons for having only spent ZAR 4 million. Although the advisory committee of the ARF had, in fact, recommended projects to the value of ZAR 141 million for approval by the Minister of International Relations and Cooperation and concurrence by the Minister of Finance, concurrence letters from the Minister of Finance had not yet come by the end of the financial year. In fact, this has been one of the key areas of deadlock in operationalising SADPA, with Treasury and DIRCO not reaching agreement for a prolonged period of time on the relative autonomy of the envisioned SADPA. This meant that in complying with "the principle of accrual accounting these projects ha[d] not been recognized as expenditure against the Fund" (ARF 2010/11, p. 6). It is quite striking that, since the anticipated conversion of the fund was already expected to be completed by the 2011/12 financial year, it is mentioned in every subsequent annual report as something that is imminent and important for the government. One can thus infer that this uncertainty and transition must also be having an impact on how much is being allocated and spent by the ARF, thus leading to declining allocation levels and consistent underspending on budgets. Domestic constraints have no doubt also led to this, as South Africa's economic growth has not been able to recover to the levels that existed prior to the global financial crisis. This is no doubt putting a strain on the resources that are allocated to meeting South Africa's development agenda on the African continent.

26.5 Conclusion

Chaturvedi et al. (2012, p. 5) opine that

> [d]evelopment cooperation in the various forms it assumes among the new participants is clearly an instrument of foreign policy; indisputably it may be used as part of alliance building and as a tool for advancing a country's "soft" power, hence its regional and global standing. These aspects of realpolitik may not appear in marketing brochures, but such nations are in the business of asserting their leadership credentials whether at the regional or international level.

The ARF is an example of this, as it has from the beginning formed an integral part of South Africa's foreign policy centred around the African Renaissance. Indeed, Southern powers have consistently elevated the idea of "win-win" and mutually beneficial relations in South-South cooperation instead of the aid–recipient narrative that has increasingly come under criticism.

In the post-apartheid era, it was thus essential for the South African government to re-establish closer ties within Africa by using the state apparatus in a constructive manner while seeking to play a positive role, and thus essentially giving back to countries that had played critical roles in supporting the anti-apartheid movement. This continues to be important in establishing post-apartheid South Africa's credentials as a peacemaker within the African continent.

The research undertaken for this chapter has showed that, although South Africa continues to be engaged on the continent, the amounts being committed to and disbursed by the ARF are not necessarily growing in line with its stated African agenda and have instead been declining since the onset of the global financial crisis. However, one must also take note of the reality that, although the ARF is certainly the most distinct part of South Africa's development cooperation architecture, it is only responsible for less than 5 per cent of the country's total commitments on the African continent. The chapter did not have such a wide scope and only interested itself with the ARF, in the hope that this would open a small window into South Africa's development cooperation. It is quite evident that, until SADPA comes into operation, the ARF will not be in a position to project the idea of a Southern power punching above its weight due to this uncertainty, which will affect the level of resources that are committed to the fund and those disbursed from the fund to South Africa's development partners. This is especially pertinent provided that the ARF will cease to exist once SADPA is operational.

One of the key tasks of the new portfolio committee on international relations will be to oversee the operationalisation of SADPA in order to position South Africa within a contested international development landscape where South-South and triangular cooperation play an increasing role as catalysts for achieving the SDGs. This process will have to address the domestic and international tensions related to contested responsibilities and coordination challenges. SADPA will thus have to address these questions as the country seeks to reposition itself despite serious constraints to its international development diplomacy.

References

Adebajo, A., Adedeji, A., & Landsberg, C. (Eds.). (2007). *South Africa in Africa: The post-apartheid era*. Scottsville: University of Kwa-Zulu Natal Press.

ARF (African Renaissance and International Cooperation Fund). (2003–2015). *Annual financial statements*. http://www.dirco.gov.za/department/report/index.htm.

Barber, J., & Barret, J. (1990). *South Africa's foreign policy*. Cambridge: Cambridge University Press.

Braude, W., Thandrayan, P., & Sidiropoulos, E. (2008). *Emerging donors in international development assistance: The South Africa case*. Ottawa: International Development Research Centre.

Chaturvedi, S., Fues, T., & Sidiropoulos, E. (Eds.) (2012). *Development cooperation and emerging powers: New partners or old patterns?* London: Zed Books.

DBSA (Development Bank of Southern Africa). (2006–2009). *Annual reports*. https://www.dbsa.org/EN/InvestorRelations/Pages/DBSA-Annual-Reports.aspx.

DBSA. (2011). *DBSA and Zambian RDFA sign a historic road development loan of USD 262 million to support economic development and regional integration*. Press release. https://www.dbsa.org/EN/DBSA-in-the-News/NEWS/Media%20Archives/2011.1.26%20DBSA%20Zambia%20RDFA%20Agreement.pdf.

Grobbelaar, N. (2005, June 1). *SA's influence a mixed blessing*. Business Day. https://www.businesslive.co.za/bd/.

Industrial Development Amendment Act. (2001). *Government gazette*. https://www.gov.za/sites/default/files/gcis_document/201409/a49-010.pdf.

Langeni, L. (2011, January 5). *Southern Sudan referendum in spotlight*. Business Day. https://www.businesslive.co.za/bd/.

Mandela, N. (1993). South Africa's future foreign policy. *Foreign Affairs, 72*(5), 86–97.

Mbeki, T. (1999, October 11). *Speech at the launch of the African renaissance institute, Pretoria*. Thabo Mbeki Foundation. https://www.mbeki.org/2016/06/09/speech-at-the-launch-of-the-african-renaissance-institute-pretoria-19991011/.

Mthembu, P. (2018). *China and India's development cooperation in Africa: The rise of Southern powers*. Basingstoke: Palgrave Macmillan.

National Treasury. (2009). *Estimate of expenditure 2009/2010*. http://www.treasury.gov.za/documents/national%20budget/2009/ene/0%20title.pdf.

SA tops Africa's investors' list. (2007, February 7). *Financial mail*. https://www.businesslive.co.za/fm/.

Sidiropoulos, E. (2012). South Africa: Development, international cooperation and soft power. In S. Chaturvedi, T. Fues, & E. Sidiropoulos (Eds.), *Development cooperation and emerging powers: New partners or old patterns?* (pp. 216–239). London: Zed Books.

Stoddard, E. (2005, May 11). *SA's economic growth shows way for the rest of Africa*. Business Day. https://www.businesslive.co.za/bd/.
World Bank. (2008). *Global development finance 2008: The role of international banking*. http://documents.worldbank.org/curated/en/docsearch/report/44981.

Open Access This chapter is licensed under the terms of the Creative Commons Attribution 4.0 International License (http://creativecommons.org/licenses/by/4.0/), which permits use, sharing, adaptation, distribution and reproduction in any medium or format, as long as you give appropriate credit to the original author(s) and the source, provide a link to the Creative Commons license and indicate if changes were made.

The images or other third party material in this chapter are included in the chapter's Creative Commons license, unless indicated otherwise in a credit line to the material. If material is not included in the chapter's Creative Commons license and your intended use is not permitted by statutory regulation or exceeds the permitted use, you will need to obtain permission directly from the copyright holder.

CHAPTER 27

Triangular Cooperation: Enabling Policy Spaces

Geovana Zoccal

27.1 Introduction

Since the turn of the twenty-first century, the architecture of the international system has undergone important changes in different areas. In the development cooperation system, new modalities, new actors, and the new relationship dynamics among them have changed the framework and definition of legitimate practices of this system. These changes are consolidating new institutional arrangements that are guiding stakeholders' relations in international development cooperation.

Triangular cooperation (TrC) is among those new arrangements. Around 40 years ago, the Plan of Action for Promoting and Implementing Technical Cooperation among Developing Countries (TCDC), known as the Buenos Aires Plan of Action (BAPA), recommended that traditional donors should act as catalysts for cooperation between developing countries (United Nations [UN] 1978). Currently, there is still no common understandings of TrC. The United Nations (UN) working definition for TrC is "southern-driven partnerships between two or more developing countries, supported by a developed country(ies) or multilateral organization(s), to implement development cooperation programmes and projects" (UN 2016, p. 5). The Organisation for Economic Co-operation and Development (OECD) characterises the modality as an arrangement "when countries, international organizations, civil society, private sector, private philanthropy and others work together in groups of three or more, to co-create flexible, cost-effective and innovative solutions

G. Zoccal (✉)
BRICS Policy Center, Rio de Janeiro, Brazil

© The Author(s) 2021
S. Chaturvedi et al. (eds.), *The Palgrave Handbook of Development Cooperation for Achieving the 2030 Agenda*,
https://doi.org/10.1007/978-3-030-57938-8_27

for reaching the [Sustainable Development Goals] (SDGs)" (Organisation for Economic Co-operation and Development [OECD] 2018a, p. 3).[1]

There is also no consensus on the term used to define the modality. The most often used term is "triangular cooperation", present in analyses and negotiations at, for instance, the UN, the OECD, and the Ibero-American General Secretariat (SEGIB). Nevertheless, there are also other terminologies, such as trilateral cooperation and tripartite cooperation. Professionals from the international cooperation of Brazil, China, and the United States frequently use the term "trilateral" instead of "triangular" (Milani 2017). Despite the fact that various analyses and studies use these variants as synonyms, there is contestation regarding the indiscriminate use of the term. These contestations are linked to the definition of principles and practices of this modality. The contestation relates, for instance, to questions of coordination and responsibility highlighted by the editors of this handbook (see Introduction in Chapter 1).

When reflecting on this clash, different stakeholders involved in international development cooperation understand it as being a matter related to linguistic lexicon and translation dilemmas, suggesting that "triangular" and "trilateral" are different terms used to characterise the same arrangement (IO#6 2017).[2] Building upon the idea that the corners of a triangle would inevitably be seen as hierarchical, professionals involved in Brazilian cooperation, for instance, argue that ignoring the difference between these terminologies would be capturing South-South cooperation (SSC) within the scope of the terms established by the Development Assistance Committee (DAC), reflecting vertical relations of North-South cooperation.

The definition, principles, and practices of this modality have raised great attention in international debates and academia. In the past decade, much research and analysis have been produced around TrC. In the international arena, many multilateral organisations have published reports on this topic, such as the OECD through the DAC, SEGIB, the GPI on Effective Triangular Co-operation,[3] and the United Nations Development Programme (UNDP) (Jones 2016; GPI on Effective Triangular Co-operation 2019; Ibero-American General Secretariat [SEGIB] 2017, 2018; OECD 2013a, 2018a; United Nations Development Programme 2016; World Food Programme 2016). The DAC has conducted two broad surveys (2012 and 2015) to collect data specifically on this modality, and the DAC has collected data on TrC through the official development assistance (ODA) reporting system since 2017.[4] From this, the OECD developed an online repository covering almost 800 TrC projects.[5]

In March 2019 the Second High-level United Nations Conference on South-South Cooperation took place (known as BAPA+40, in celebration of the 40th anniversary of the BAPA), held in Buenos Aires and hosted by the United Nations Office for South-South Cooperation (UNOSSC). The outcome document of the conference broadly covered this modality, highlighting its value added to the efforts towards achieving the 2030 Agenda for Sustainable Development.

In academia, the transformations of the international cooperation system since the 2000s are a constant subject of analysis. Due to TrC being a dynamic issue that has gained momentum in the development cooperation agenda in the past years, it has been a hot topic for chapters, articles, dissertations, and theses (Bandstein 2007; Langendorf 2012; Milani 2017; Seifert and Renzio 2014; Stahl 2018). These publications commonly present TrC as a tool or modality[6] for identifying and making use of comparative advantages and knowledge of DAC donors and emerging providers of the Global South[7] to implement development programmes and projects. Besides the project dimension, TrC is also analysed from a political perspective and portrayed as an arrangement that traditional donors make use of to learn from and influence SSC, bridging these two modalities (Abdenur and Fonseca 2013).

To advance the guiding question of this handbook, ("How can different narratives and norms in development cooperation be reconciled to achieving the 2030 Agenda?"), this chapter focusses on TrC and analyses the value added of this modality towards achieving the 2030 Agenda. The guiding question of the chapter is: "How does this cooperation modality strengthen partnerships between different actors in the policy field of development cooperation?" To answer this question, the chapter goes beyond the technical features of development projects. I argue that TrC became an enabler of policy spaces, without directly confronting contested political positions and jeopardising the dialogue and negotiation processes. The modality has allowed both traditional donors and Southern providers to create not only joint development projects, but also common strategies, guidelines, and principles. To advance this argument, the chapter has been divided into three sections following this introduction.

The following Sect. 27.2 covers the conditions that led to the emergence and strengthening of TrC as a modality. The increasing diversity of stakeholders involved in international cooperation for development built up new principles and practices in the field and created tension in the framework that had been established by the 1970s, mainly by DAC donors. Different stakeholders such as civil society organisations and the private sector also became agents of this system. The strengthening of SSC contested the established cooperation framework of the OECD-DAC. To convey some sort of accommodation among the cooperation principles, different formal and informal approaches came into place. TrC emerged as a modality enabling the intersection of established and emerging practices.

The Sect. 27.3 deepens the analysis of TrC and goes beyond the technical features of this modality, understanding it as an enabler of policy spaces for negotiations on practices and principles among stakeholders. Southern providers such as China and Brazil do not follow internationally established OECD norms, for example measuring ODA or reporting their cooperation initiatives to the DAC. Nonetheless, agents from the North and the South find in TrC a space to negotiate their principles and practices in the continually evolving international development cooperation system. This section identifies TrC as a strategic modality to create those negotiation spaces, both for traditional donors and for Southern providers.

The final Sect. 27.4 investigates how—despite the contestation of practices and principles among the different actors in the political spaces—TrC strengthens the collaboration among stakeholders. During the first initiatives of the modality, TrC was foremost conceived as a way for traditional donors to socialise and engage with the Southern providers and catalyse SSC. This perspective has evolved, and stakeholders now aim to go beyond the divisions on cost-sharing. The modality sometimes struggles not to be seen as an end in itself. Nevertheless, alleviating the contestations between traditional donors and Southern providers, through TrC different stakeholders have created room for policy dialogue and created common operation manuals, guidelines, and processes.

27.2 From the Establishment of ODA to the Emergency of New Modalities

27.2.1 Development Cooperation: A Revolving Field

The setting of an internationally agreed framework, practices, and categorisation of the stakeholders participating in the system for international development cooperation was mainly based on the definition of ODA, first agreed in 1969 by the DAC members. This was eight years after the establishment of the OECD and the DAC, under its umbrella—both of which were established in September 1961.

ODA defined assistance flows as those between a developed country or multilateral organisation and a developing country, in a vertical relationship of transferring concessional resources and development knowledge. The ODA definition has been under constant negotiation and opens room for interpretation. From 2010 to 2016, there was the implementation of clarified rules, which were related, for instance, to in-donor refugee costs. More recently, in early 2019 (reporting on 2018 data), there was a shift in the methodology for recording ODA data, and "ODA grant equivalent" replaced the "flow basis". However, in general terms, the ODA concept has remained the same since 1972, currently laid out as

> flows to countries and territories on the DAC List of ODA Recipients and to multilateral development institutions that are: i. provided by official agencies, including state and local governments, or by their executive agencies; and ii. each transaction of which: a) is administered with the promotion of the economic development and welfare of developing countries as its main objective; and b) is concessional in character. (OECD 2019, p. 6)

The direction of ODA flows defined which agent occupied the position of donor and recipient in this system, establishing a binary dividing North/developed countries/donors and South/developing countries/recipients. However, if initially this binary divided actors engaged in international cooperation, transformations in international politics during the turn of the twenty-first century also implicated changes in the development cooperation system. Currently, a much more diverse group of actors is part of this system, which includes providers from the Global South and non-governmental actors such as civil society organisations and the private sector.

Initiatives of cooperation among countries of the Global South have existed since the 1950s, with the Non-Alignment Movement frequently being identified as its embryo. After the BAPA in 1978, the outcome document agreed on during the 1978 UN Conference on Technical Cooperation among Developing Countries, TCDC was recognised as a modality of international development cooperation. Nevertheless, it gained strength mainly after the 1990s, when the South Commission published the report "The Challenge to the South" (South Centre 2015). Since then, emerging powers such as Brazil, China, and India have significantly increased their engagement in international cooperation for development and hence expanded their presence and influence in this system.

In 1978, the BAPA mainly disputed the vertical flows between donors and recipients, as envisaged by ODA, and put forward horizontal flows. Different stakeholders recognised horizontal relations among the agents as being complementary practice in the international development system. However, the donor–recipient binary continued to guide the framework previously established by DAC members.

Three decades later—endorsed during the Third High-Level Forum on Aid Effectiveness in 2008—the Accra Agenda for Action recognised SSC as an important complement to traditional cooperation. In 2009, in a context of significant economic growth of a few countries in the Global South and the deepening of a Southern identity narrative, the first High-level United Nations Conference on South-South Cooperation happened in Nairobi. Southern providers presented SSC as an alternative modality to North-South cooperation, building up dimensions allegedly opposed to traditional donors. The outcome document presented six principles of SSC: (i) respect for national sovereignty; (ii) national ownership and independence; (iii) equality (horizontality); (iv) non-conditionality; (v) non-interference in domestic affairs; and (vi) mutual benefits (UN 2009).

At that moment, the outcome document pointed to a "Northernised" agenda of SSC, which incorporated key terms such as ownership that were established by DAC donors during the Paris Declaration on Aid Effectiveness in 2005 (Zoccal 2018). However, in the Fourth High-Level Forum on Aid Effectiveness—guided by the DAC-hosted Working Party on Aid Effectiveness and held in 2011 in Busan—the transformations on the international cooperation for development framework were deeper than the ones that had happened since the BAPA of 1978. During the Busan Forum, the imagined geographical cleavage defining which agent is part of the North and which agent is part of the South defined the dynamics among them. It was also clear that, despite the obvious division between these two groups, neither traditional donors nor Southern providers are homogeneous groups (Eyben and Savage 2012).

Most Southern providers do not report to the DAC, and there is a diversity of standards and mechanisms to measure SSC volumes.[8] However, a number of reports have been published about the development cooperation initiatives of emerging providers in the past years. In 2015, the estimate of SSC participation in international development cooperation was 15.8 per cent, according to the OECD's "Development Co-operation Report 2017" (OECD 2017). The "Financing for Sustainable Development Report 2019" of the UN Department of Economic and Social Affairs indicates that 74 per cent of developing countries provided some form of development cooperation in 2017 (United Nations Department of Economic and Social Affairs 2019). Despite the lack of official, verified, and comparable data, these figures give an estimate of the current importance of SSC within the development cooperation agenda (Zoccal and Esteves 2018).

The categorisation of Southern providers broke the limits of the donor–recipient binary. Likewise, other groups of stakeholders such as civil society organisations and the private sector became active in the development agenda. In this context, the creation of the Global Partnership for Effective Development Co-operation (GPEDC)—a result of the High-Level Forum on Aid Effectiveness in Busan in 2011—aimed at building a platform encompassing a more complex constellation of agents than the one of the DAC members. The GPEDC Secretariat is shared between the OECD and UNDP. Even so, important Southern providers such as China, Brazil, and India contest this process, arguing that it was driven by the DAC's traditional normative framework. Without the support of these countries, the GPEDC did not succeed in fully integrating SSC and lost relevance.[9]

New approaches and arrangements guiding relations among different stakeholders have been consolidated. Besides platforms such as the GPEDC, new measures such as Total Official Support for Sustainable Development are examples of the complex constellation of the development cooperation system. In this context, TrC has perceptibly grown as a modality capable of bridging different initiatives, for example practices and frameworks of DAC members and Southern providers.

27.2.2 *Triangular Cooperation as a Development Cooperation Modality*

The first implicit reference to this modality was made already during the BAPA of 1978, recommending that developed countries and UN organisations should act as catalysts for cooperation between developing countries (UN 1978). The first use of the term "triangular cooperation" came two years later in the report "North-South: A Programme for Survival" of the Brandt Commission (Independent Commission for International Development Issues 1980; OECD 2013a).

On the UN scope, the term "triangular cooperation" was recognised 15 years later in the document "New Directions Strategy on Technical Cooperation among Developing Countries" in 1995. TrC arrangements were those "under which donors would agree to fund exchanges among developing countries" (UN 1995, p. 2).

> The concept of triangular cooperation, which involves the participation of developed countries in the TCDC process, has the potential to make a significant contribution to the realization of the objectives of TCDC. Under such arrangements, donor countries can utilize the services of developing countries with the requisite capacity to deliver a technical cooperation input to another developing country on a cost-effective basis. (UN 1995, p. 21)

The document identifies countries such as Brazil, China, and India as "pivotal countries", catalysts of the new modalities presented to the development cooperation system (UN 1995). The perception of key SSC countries as pivotal countries when engaging in TrC increased years later and is present in various publications produced mainly within the OECD scope.

TrC becomes an important modality to foster development cooperation projects based on the comparative advantages of different agents. The GPI on Effective Triangular Co-operation developed the typology "facilitating", "pivotal", and "beneficiary" partners to categorise the stakeholders involved in TrC (OECD 2018a; TRD#10 2019). Southern providers, mainly typified as the "pivotal" countries, would have a better understanding of beneficiary countries' local realities and the expertise needed to become adapted to each development project. DAC donors would have greater funding capacity and years of knowledge on international development cooperation, hence acting mostly as "facilitators" of the cooperation between developing countries. Despite not being commonly accepted and used, this typology has been advanced by a number of agents, including the OECD, Canada, and Mexico. However, it makes an implicit assumption of a division of labour based on each agent's capacities. This categorisation focusses on the comparative advantages for project implementation, and in this way it clouds the political and power relations between high-income countries and emerging economies.

At first, TrC would be carried out by combining the cultural, scientific, and technological resources of a developing country with the financial resources of a traditional donor. However, there has been an effort to move away from the idea that TrC is the traditional donor transferring resources and financing SSC (IO#8 2017; SSC#7 2019). Negotiations around this modality, within the scope of the OECD and the GPI on Effective Triangular Co-operation, sustain that all agents can potentially assume any of these three roles—facilitating, pivotal, and beneficiary. Nevertheless, the data presented by the two broad surveys on TrC applied by the DAC Global Relations Secretariat in 2012 and 2015, and also by the recent GPI report "Triangular Co-operation in the Era of the 2030 Agenda: Sharing Evidence and Stories from the Field", show that "facilitating" partners are traditional donors (whether they are high-income countries or international organisations), "pivotal" partners are Southern providers, and "beneficiaries" are countries regarded as traditional recipients of cooperation (GPI on Effective Triangular Co-operation 2019; OECD 2013b, 2016a).

In the past decade, studies about this modality spread throughout many international organisations (Langendorf et al. 2012; OECD 2016a). Under the OECD umbrella, there were more than 20 publications on this topic—the first of which was published in 2009. Four years after the Paris Declaration on Aid Effectiveness in 2005, "Triangular Co-operation and Aid Effectiveness" (OECD 2009) attempted to submit the new practices presented by SSC to the normative framework followed by the DAC at that time, using principles of the aid effectiveness agenda to systematise TrC.

Also in 2009, the final report of the Heiligendamm Process—a dialogue platform between G8 members and "Outreach 5" (China, Mexico, India, Brazil, and South Africa)—indicated that TrC was a strategic link between North-South and South-South cooperation (Group of 8 2009). Beyond its technical features related to development effectiveness and performance of the various projects, the modality is also understood as a sort of unofficial platform through which DAC donors and providers of SSC interact and negotiate principles and practices of international cooperation for development.

For many DAC donors, TrC is a strategic tool for maintaining cooperative relations with Southern providers that have graduated from the OECD-DAC list of recipient countries and are no longer eligible for receiving ODA (TRD#9 2019). That is the case, for instance, of the TrC projects (i) "Greater Rural Opportunities for Women (GROW) in Ghana", between Canada, Ghana, and Israel, (ii) "Strengthening of the Secretary of Public Affairs in Paraguay", between Paraguay, Chile, and Spain, and also (iii) "Mirada Ciudadana—Good Governance in Mercosur Municipalities", between the European Union, Uruguay, Chile, Argentina, Brazil, and Paraguay[10] (GPI on Effective Triangular Co-operation 2019).

There are an increasing number of TrC projects being systematised by different initiatives, for example the efforts of the GPI on Effective Triangular Co-operation and OECD, as well as of other organisations such as SEGIB, in addition to the countries themselves. These reports indicate a growing proportion of TrC in overall ODA and SSC initiatives (GPI on Effective Triangular Co-operation 2019; SEGIB 2017, 2018). However, both for traditional donors and for Southern providers, this modality is still small when compared to other initiatives. Additionally, TrC has different levels of importance within strategies followed by different actors.

For instance, the TrC initiatives of Germany—the champion of the modality in terms of the number of projects systematised by the DAC Global Relations Secretariat—account for less than 0.1 per cent of total German net ODA. This comparison is based on the 157 German TrC projects reported to the OECD and on Germany's net ODA reported to the DAC in the same period. In 2017, bilateral cooperation represented almost 80 per cent of the German portfolio, and multilateral cooperation represented around 20 per cent (German Federal Ministry for Economic Cooperation and Development [BMZ] 2019). Brazil, also among the champions of the modality, presents a different reality. Between 2014 and 2016, trilateral cooperation represented 4.7 per cent of total federal government expenditures, and multilateral cooperation represented 80.5 per cent, whereas bilateral cooperation represented 9.1 per cent during the referred period (Institute of Applied Economic Research and Brazilian Cooperation Agency 2018). It is important to highlight that TrC is very likely underreported (IO#8 2017; SSC#6 2019; TRD#10 2019). However, this comparison gives a sense of the importance of the modality relative to the totals of development cooperation initiatives (SSC#7 2019; SSC#8 2019).

The next section analyses how TrC arrangements fit into the international development cooperation system and enable policy spaces for collaboration between South-South and North-South cooperation. Beyond the technical dimension, this chapter understands that the modality has grown as a policy instrument between traditional donors and Southern providers—representing a negotiating space of practices and principles—and as a strategy to increase the level of influence on the international development system.

27.3 TRIANGULAR COOPERATION: FROM DEVELOPMENT PROJECTS TO ENABLER OF POLICY SPACES

TrC was frequently understood as a modality involving at least one traditional donor—either a DAC member or an international organisation—and two other developing countries, with one acting as a Southern provider and one as beneficiary (OECD 2016a). This would shadow other possible arrangements that do not involve a traditional donor, such as the Chile–Mexico Mixed Fund for Triangular Cooperation or other Chilean projects, for instance with Belize and El Salvador or with Brazil and Suriname (Chilean International Cooperation Agency 2014). Although it was at first atypical, TrC only among developing countries is increasingly producing more examples.

Additionally, a contemporary perspective also includes actors beyond national governments—for example civil society, subnational governments, and the private sector—developing a multi-stakeholder approach (GPI on Effective Triangular Co-operation 2019). The number of TrC initiatives involving more than three partners is also increasing (IO#9 2019). Despite these numerous arrangements, TrC is mainly perceived and debated as a modality bridging North-South and South-South cooperation. According to the UNOSSC, TrC is a different modality than North-South or South-South cooperation; nevertheless, it has to have at least one component of SSC to be considered TrC. As a reflection of this, many of the projects between two traditional donors and one recipient country—for example the partnership between the United Kingdom and the Food and Agriculture Organization of the United Nations for promoting climate-smart agriculture in Zimbabwe (FAO 2015)—are not considered TrC.

A number of professionals linked to traditional donor countries indicate that the relationship with emerging countries is among the main motivations of DAC members to engage in TrC, which is considered to be a way of showing the world that there is a strengthening of North and South relations (IO#6 2017; IO#8 2017). Arising from a technical need, TrC has become an important tool that has enabled development cooperation policy spaces between North-South and South-South cooperation, without engaging in political debate and challenging these positions up front. This modality has been used as an instrument for the informal negotiation of practices and principles among agents. According to a high-ranking professional working on this modality,

> using the excuse of triangular cooperation to build this political dialogue can be a first step [for North and South] to discuss impact, results and a distinct framework. For example, in the DAC sphere we are discussing whether a project is tied aid or not. In triangular cooperation there is no such discussion. It is also a space for donors, who feel more comfortable to create information and discuss. I think this is easier in a technical partnership, with no political focus, because politics have a lot of history. (IO#6 2017, own translation)

> Politically, what is the comparative advantage of triangular cooperation? We are not discussing tied aid, we are not discussing reporting logic. What we are discussing is: How can we find together the solution to that problem? We accept that there are different ways of responding to certain problems. There are different technical tools for reaching that problem. (IO#6 2017, own translation)

> An interesting point to think about is how we can encourage developing countries to make more use of this modality. And, by getting developing countries rooting this tool, how this modality can be used to transform mentality and convey change within the political divide. (IO#6 2017, own translation)

During the first TrC initiatives, DAC members called countries such as China, India, and Brazil "anchor countries", since they were anchors of the regional expansion of cooperation. However, the increasing relevance that Southern providers have on the international cooperation for development system has changed the dynamics between those agents, and these countries are now considered "development partners" by some of those DAC members (TRD#2 2017). According to a professional of the Brazilian Cooperation Agency, during the 5th International Meeting on Triangular Co-operation, held in Lisbon in October 2019, the UK and Brazil were developing a "Partnership for Global Development", a long-term strategy to go beyond their TrC initiatives.

In 2018, the advocacy working stream of the GPI on Effective Triangular Co-operation started to elaborate voluntary principles for TrC, accelerating a debate on the different terminologies used by the array of stakeholders involved, for instance "beneficiary country", which would not reflect the idea of mutual benefits (OECD and Camões 2018), which is a key principle of SSC.

During BAPA+40, the GPI on Effective Triangular Co-operation presented voluntary guidelines for effective TrC:

(i) Country **ownership** and **demand-driven** co-operation; (ii) Shared commitment; (iii) Focus on **results-oriented approaches** and solutions; (iv) Inclusive partnerships and multi-stakeholder dialogues; (v) Transparency and **mutual accountability**; (vi) Innovation and co-creation; (vii) **Joint-learning** and **knowledge-sharing** for sustainable development; (viii) Advance gender equality and the empowerment of women and girls; and (ix) Leaving no one behind. (GPI on Effective Triangular Co-operation 2019, p. 15; emphasis added)

Ownership, results-oriented approaches, and mutual accountability are principles agreed upon in the Paris Declaration on Aid Effectiveness. On the other hand, demand-drivenness and joint learning as principles were advanced by SSC. The debate surrounding TrC indicates a mix of otherwise contested principles and practices between Southern providers and traditional donors, strengthening the partnerships between North-South and South-South cooperation.

Even though SSC presents different principles than traditional cooperation, many professionals of North-South cooperation indicate that the practices on the ground are not so different. Hence, besides fostering development projects, the development of TrC as a modality also emphasises the policy space that allows traditional donors and Southern providers to overcome the differences of narratives through joint practices. Stakeholders from both the DAC and Southern providers point to TrC as a mechanism of influence—whether of the OECD-DAC principles on Southern providers or of the SSC principles on traditional donors (IO#6 2017; SSC#5 2017; TRD#1 2017).

In the case of Brazil, the principles guiding its engagement on trilateral cooperation—following the term used by its representatives—are the same as those followed by Brazilian SSC, that is, the ones established during the first High-level United Nations Conference on South-South Cooperation in Nairobi in 2009 (SSC#5 2017). The "Brazilian-German Trilateral Cooperation Program: Operational Handbook" exemplifies the blend of principles among a DAC donor and a Southern provider (Brazilian Cooperation Agency and Deutsche Gesellschaft für Internationale Zusammenarbeit 2019). After a long period of negotiation, the memorandum of understanding signed in 2010—the basis for the processes described in the manual—points to the operational principles debated during the Heiligendamm Process as a reference for the modality, indicating a commitment to the implementation of the principles of ownership and alignment (IO#8 2017).

Already in 2009, during the Policy Dialogue on Development Cooperation, organised by the OECD in Mexico City, the Brazilian representative emphasised that,

> as Brazil does not consider itself as an "emerging donor", the South-South components present in triangular cooperation schemes with developed partners are based on **different standards compared to the North-South cooperation**. But such differences should not be a major challenge, because we believe that both modalities are **convergent** in the promotion of local **ownership, alignment** with national development policies and **coordination** and transparency among partners.
>
> For the success of triangular partnerships, it is essential that **traditional donor countries and international organizations get familiar with the basic elements of South-South cooperation**. It is important to stress that triangular cooperation should not be seen as a different way of doing North-South cooperation. Triangular cooperation is complementary to South-South cooperation. (Corrêa 2009; emphasis added)

Curiously, Brazil did not endorse the Paris Declaration on Aid Effectiveness, established at the Second High-Level Forum on Aid Effectiveness in 2005, claiming that the aid effectiveness agenda and its principles—ownership, alignment, harmonisation, management for results, and mutual accountability—represent a vertical view of donor–recipient relations. Consequently, it should be applied only in the logic of North-South cooperation. At the Fourth High-Level Forum on Aid Effectiveness, held in Busan in 2011, the Brazilian delegation pointed out that "triangular cooperation gives the opportunity for donor countries to get in touch with South-South cooperation practices, promoting changes in 'calcified' ODA practices" (Brazilian Delegation 2011).

A closer look into the efforts to strengthen TrC as a development cooperation modality indicates two dimensions of this struggle. On the one hand, it is possible to identify an attempt to capture Southern providers into the aid effectiveness agenda. On the other, through TrC it is also possible to identify a Southernisation[11] of traditional donors, incorporating principles and practices of SSC. Both Southern providers and DAC donors negotiate and operate their terms through this modality, which earned value as a smoother space of interaction among agents. This policy space, enabled through TrC, does not carry the burden of a political debate with a history of already embedded contestations.

27.4 CONCLUSIONS: STRENGTHENING PARTNERSHIPS FOR DEVELOPMENT COOPERATION

Previous sections present how TrC has become more complex over the years and drawn greater attention in the past decade. There have been increasing efforts towards creating a greater number of studies on this topic as well as numerous international meetings that are completely or partially dedicated to this modality, under the umbrella of, for example, SEGIB, the European Union, the OECD, the GPEDC, and the UN. Nevertheless, in the context of fragmented norms and narratives highlighted by the editors and authors of other chapters in this handbook, the diversity of stakeholders has not agreed on a common perspective, nor on the practices, assessment mechanisms, or even the definition of the term to characterise this modality.

The analysis of not only the broad range of academic work, but also the publications and events dedicated to TrC indicates there is no internationally agreed guiding mechanism. However, this chapter shows that, because the modality is broad, dynamic, and flexible, it enables policy spaces through which the cleavage between the North and South is loosened. According to a professional from a DAC country highly involved in the TrC debate, "the modality is shifting and not doing what [traditional donors] used to do years ago. It is bridging the gap between the North and the South and could be a shift in a way we approach development challenges" (TRD#10 2019).

> If we can encourage a model that does not become institutionalised in such a way that it is restrictive, it can be viable. The new world is about partnerships in a more equal level than the previous model. [...] DAC members will have to find a way to codify the way triangular cooperation operates. It allows dynamics. We cannot afford to box ourselves too much. (TRD#10 2019)

Various participants of the 5th International Meeting on Triangular Cooperation, held in October 2019 in Lisbon, stressed the recent shift in the way that TrC was understood and being used. This shift is reflected in the BAPA+40 Outcome Document. In the BAPA of 1978, the term did not exist. In the 2009 Nairobi Outcome Document, the modality was mentioned 14 times. The outcome document of the BAPA+40 refers 73 times to TrC, also mentioning the voluntary efforts of the GPI on Effective Triangular Cooperation.

During the meeting, both the UNOSSC director, Jorge Chediek, and the director of the OECD Development Co-operation Directorate, Jorge Moreira da Silva, highlighted BAPA+40 as being a paradigm shift for TrC. For the first time, TrC was broadly discussed in an internationally agreed document. If some years earlier TrC was considered a niche, it has become a mainstream tool for development dialogue.

The remarks of the G77+China on the draft of the BAPA+40 Outcome Document—and also the outcome document itself—indicate that TrC should be "aimed at facilitating, supporting and enhancing South-South initiatives" (Group of 77 2019, p. 1) and "complements and adds value to South-South cooperation" (UN 2019, p. 2), respectively. Efforts of some Northern donors during the negotiations for the BAPA+40 Outcome Document to incorporate TrC as a modality that also adds value to North-South cooperation have not succeeded. Even so, the document reflects TrC as a "blank space for G77 and the UN and even the DAC" (TRD#13 2019). The modality has enabled policy debates not only among North-South and South-South cooperation, but also between the UN and the OECD, for example the joint work of the core group of the GPI on Effective Triangular Cooperation that both the UNOSSC and the OECD are part of. According to a professional of a DAC country involved in TrC, when reflecting on these changes, "five years ago, OECD and UN were not speaking to each other" (TRD#13 2019).

The strengthening of SSC and the consolidation of the Southern providers as stakeholders of the system of international cooperation for development broke the limits of the donor–recipient binary. In a context of contestation between North-South and South-South cooperation, TrC not only bridges these modalities by socialising the different agents, but it also creates spaces for dialogue and sheds light upon the contestation of principles and practices of different stakeholders. However, the policy space created by TrC is protected from the clashes of political debate. Numerous recent reports and guidelines mentioned in this chapter show TrC carrying principles from both the aid effectiveness agenda and SSC.

SDG 17 of the 2030 Agenda, adopted in 2015, aims to "strengthen the means of implementation and revitalize the global partnership for sustainable development" (United Nations General Assembly 2015). Beyond being a means of implementation of development projects and programmes, TrC is also a means for increasing the policy dialogue between the North and the South. Agents that present contested narratives in institutionalised political platforms—and hence do not agree on sharing principles, practices, or assessment mechanisms—can coordinate action towards achieving the 2030 Agenda through TrC.

Despite involving different stakeholders from the field, TrC is a modality that is fundamentally based on the relations between traditional donors and Southern providers. At first glance, as a technical mechanism that is based on the comparative advantages of the different stakeholders in the system of international cooperation for development, TrC enables policy dialogue but is not advanced as being a space for political confrontation.

The dynamics of this modality make evident the differences between North-South and South-South cooperation. How does TrC strengthen collaboration among traditional donors and newcomers, most specifically with key Southern providers that, as a matter of principle, do not agree with the DAC narrative, for example, the aid effectiveness agenda? Despite the different interests involved, collaboration between the North and the South through this modality alleviates the contestations concerning different principles and practices that are abundantly present in formal political negotiation spaces. Not only is there the joint execution of projects, but also the development of joint operation manuals, guidelines, and processes.

To strengthen TrC as an effective modality, stakeholders are trying to move away from two ideas: (i) that TrC arrangements are those in which the traditional donor transfers resources and finances SSC, and (ii) that TrC is an end in itself. Traditional donors often mention mutual learning as being a motivation for their involvement in TrC. On the one hand, Southern providers have a comparative advantage relating to domestic development experience and, hence, technical knowledge. On the other hand, traditional donors' experiences are focussed on managing international cooperation for development. Nevertheless, North-South cooperation professionals are often hesitant when questioned about the benefits gained through partnerships with developing partners. Learning is mostly connected to the TrC process itself and how to engage with Southern providers (IO#6 2017; IO#8 2017; TRD#1 2017; TRD#2 2017).

Considering the array of stakeholders involved and the perception that TrC should not be an end in itself, it is key to have a clear comparative advantage to justify the use of TrC as an effective means of implementation. When reflecting on TrC projects, different stakeholders mentioned initiatives emerging not at first from a necessity or demand of the developing country, but from, for example, good relations between ambassadors or professionals of development cooperation serving in the beneficiary country (IO#8 2017; TRD#10 2019).

There has been an effort to clarify statements that doubt the effectiveness of TrC, for example, the understanding that TrC development projects are small-scale in terms of duration, resources, and impacts, and that the modality lacks a particular strategic vision, clear added value, or defined implementation mechanisms. The OECD report "Dispelling the Myths of Triangular Co-operation" argues that there is a wide variety of programmes and projects, both small- and large-scale, and TrC should not be understood as homogeneous. The report also argues that stable partnership arrangements can compensate for high transaction costs, which is often indicated as one of the main challenges to this modality (OECD 2016a, b).

Some actors have developed strategies for this modality and signed agreements with different partners to simplify implementation and reduce transaction costs, concurrently establishing common guidelines. Examples of this are a strategy paper on TrC in German development cooperation (BMZ 2013), the management guidelines for implementing TrC in Ibero-America (Ibero-American Programme for the Strengthening of South-South Cooperation 2015), the toolkit for identifying, monitoring, and evaluating the value added of TrC (OECD 2018b), and the Brazilian general guideline for the design, coordination, and management of trilateral technical cooperation initiatives (Brazilian Cooperation Agency 2019). These new arrangements are constituted by—and also constitute—the current transition period redefining development practices. The broad definition of TrC opens room for the coordination of policy dialogues among different stakeholders towards achieving the 2030 Agenda, without directly confronting contested political positions and jeopardising partnerships.

Notes

1. The OECD's definition of TrC is close to a multi-stakeholder partnership, which is understood as "a type of cooperation when stakeholders from at least three different sectors work together as equals through an organized, and long-term engagement in order to contribute to the common good" (Partnerships 2030 2019). Nevertheless, even if the diversity of stakeholders that might be involved in TrC initiatives is recognised, OECD publications and repositories of projects indicate that TrC is a modality led by governments and international organisations, which is then different from being a multi-stakeholder partnership.
2. This chapter is based not only on analysis of official documents and reports, but also on anonymous interviews with different stakeholders of the international development agenda, such as academics, multilateral organisations, and high-ranking professionals who are linked both to traditional and South-South cooperation, among others. Thirty-six interviews were conducted between 2017 and 2019 and focussed on South-South and triangular cooperation. To retain the anonymity of the interviewees, the references are here categorised as follows: representatives of DAC donors are identified as TRD; representatives of South-South cooperation are identified as SSC; representatives of international organisations are identified as IO.
3. The GPI on Effective Triangular Co-operation was created during the Second High-Level Meeting of the GPEDC in 2016, led by Mexico, along with 28 other global partnership initiatives covering different thematic areas of international cooperation for development. Besides Mexico, core group members of the GPI on Effective Triangular Co-operation are Canada, Chile, SEGIB's Ibero-American Programme for the Strengthening of South-South Co-operation, Japan, UNOSSC, the Islamic Development Bank, and the OECD. So far, 51 other countries and international organisations, civil society organisations, representatives from the private sector, and research institutions have joined this GPI.
4. Which means data since 2016, as countries report ODA data from the previous year to the DAC.
5. The OECD TrC project repository is constantly being updated. This number refers to the total number of projects at the time of this publication, accessed in August 2019.
6. Different stakeholders refer to triangular co-operation as a tool, instrument, mechanism, initiative, or other terms. There is no common systematisation of aid modalities, yet many donors often use this general term to encompass initiatives such as project support, budget support, and sector programme support (Bandstein 2007), usually implemented bilaterally. On the other hand, initiatives such as South-South cooperation and triangular cooperation are also often referred to as modalities and presented as an alternative and complement to traditional North-South cooperation (UN 2019). Accordingly, this chapter recognises North-South cooperation, South-South cooperation, and Triangular cooperation as different basic modalities of development cooperation.

7. The "The Challenge to the South: The Report of the South Commission" indicates a world divided by an imagined geography that is based not on the equatorial line, but on levels of prosperity and development. I consider that the Global South, as indicated by the South Commission, comprises populations and governments of developing countries that are, for the most part, more vulnerable to external factors (South Centre 2015).
8. As of July 2019, 20 countries that are not DAC members reported their aid flows to the OECD. Among them are Israel, Turkey, and Thailand.
9. The UN Development Cooperation Forum (UN DCF) is frequently mentioned as another platform with a universal character that could serve as a global platform of international cooperation for development. For a deeper analysis of this debate on the GPECD and the UN DCF, see Bracho (2017), Esteves and Assunção (2014), and Janus et al. (2014).
10. Israel was removed from the DAC List of ODA Recipients in 1997; Chile and Uruguay were removed in 2018.
11. The term "Southernisation" originated in the mid-1990s (Shaffer 1994) and was recently associated with the system of international development cooperation after analysis by the new statistical measure Total Official Support for Sustainable Development (Chaturvedi et al. 2016).

References

Abdenur, A. E., & Fonseca, J. M. (2013). The North's growing role in South-South cooperation: Keeping the foothold. *Third World Quarterly, 34*(8), 1475–1491.

Bandstein, S. (2007). *What determines the choice of aid modalities?—A framework for assessing incentive structures* (SADEV Report). Karlstad: Swedish Agency for Development Evaluation.

BMZ (German Federal Ministry for Economic Cooperation and Development/Bundesministerium für wirtschaftliche Zusammenarbeit und Entwicklung). (2013). *Triangular cooperation in German development cooperation* (BMZ Strategy Paper 5). Berlin and Bonn: Author.

BMZ. (2019, January 19). *Entwicklung der bi- und multilateralen Netto—ODA 2012–2017*. http://www.bmz.de/de/ministerium/zahlen_fakten/oda/leistungen/entwicklung_2012_2017/index.html.

Bracho, G. (2017). *The troubled relationship of the emerging powers and the effective development cooperation agenda: History, challenges and opportunities* (Discussion Paper 25/2017). Bonn: German Development Institute/Deutsches Institut für Entwicklungspolitik (DIE).

Brazilian Cooperation Agency. (2019). *General guidelines for the design, coordination and management of trilateral technical cooperation initiatives* (1st ed.). Brasília: Ministry of Foreign Affairs.

Brazilian Cooperation Agency & Gesellschaft für Internationale Zusammenarbeit. (2019). *Brazilian-German trilateral cooperation program: Operational handbook* (2nd ed.). Brasília: Brazilian Cooperation Agency.

Brazilian Delegation. (2011). *Brazil's views on the Busan's IV HLF*. Busan: IV High Level Forum on Aid Effectiveness.

Chaturvedi, S., Chakrabarti, M., & Shiva, H. (2016, November). *TOSSD: Southernisation of ODA* (FIDC Policy Brief No. 9). New Delhi: Forum for Indian Development Cooperation.

Chilean International Cooperation Agency. (2014). *Chile's role as a triangular partner for development cooperation* (Working Paper). Santiago: Author.

Corrêa, M. L. (2009, September 28–29). *Policy dialogue on development co-operation: Session II—Triangular co-operation.* http://www.oecd.org/dac/dac-global-relations/43876987.pdf.

Esteves, P., & Assunção, M. (2014). South-South cooperation and the international development battlefield: Between the OECD and the UN. *Third World Quarterly, 35*(10), 1175–1790.

Eyben, R., & Savage, L. (2012, December 19). Emerging and submerging powers: Imagined geographies in the new development partnership at the Busan Fourth High Level Forum. *The Journal of Development Studies, 49*(4), 457–469.

FAO (Food and Agriculture Organization of the United Nations). (2015). *United Kingdom and FAO: Partnering to build sustainable livelihoods and food security.* Rome: Author.

GPI on Effective Triangular Cooperation. (2019). *Triangular co-operation in the era of the 2030 Agenda: Sharing evidence and stories from the field.* Paris: Author.

Group of 8. (2009). *Concluding report of the Heiligendamm process.* http://www.g8.utoronto.ca/summit/2009laquila/2009-g5-g8-1-hdp.pdf.

Group of 77. (2019, January 31). Remarks on behalf of the Group of 77 and China by Ambassador Riyad Mansour (state of Palestine), chair of the Group of 77, at the third informal consultations on the Draft Outcome Document of the Second High-Level United Nations Conference on South-South Cooperation—BAPA+40. http://www.g77.org/statement/getstatement.php?id=190131b.

Ibero-American Programme for the Strengthening of South-South Cooperation. (2015). *Management guidelines for implementing triangular cooperation in Ibero-America.* Buenos Aires: Ibero-American General Secretariat (SEGIB).

Independent Commission on International Development Issues. (1980). *North-South: A programme for survival.* Cambridge: Independent Commission on International Development Issues.

Institute of Applied Economic Research & Brazilian Cooperation Agency. (2018). *Cooperação brasileira para o desenvolvimento internacional: Levantamento 2014–2016.* Brasilia: Authors.

Janus, H., Klingebiel, S., & Mahn, T. (2014). *How to shape development cooperation? The global partnership and the Development Cooperation Forum* (Briefing Paper 3/2014). Bonn: German Development Institute/Deutsches Institut für Entwicklungspolitik (DIE).

Jones, A. (2016, December 2). Three is company. *Thomson Reuters Foundation News.* http://news.trust.org/item/20161202120830-hizst/.

Langendorf, J. (2012). Triangular cooperation as a complementary strategy for development. In J. Langendorf, N. Piefer, M. Knodt, U. Müller, & L. Lázaro (Eds.), *Triangular cooperation: A guideline for working practice* (pp. 21–32). Bonn and Eschborn: Nomos.

Langendorf, J., Piefer, N., Knodt, M., Müller, U., & Lázaro, L. (2012). Introduction. In J. Langendorf, N. Piefer, M. Knodt, U. Müller, & L. Lázaro (Eds.), *Triangular cooperation: A guideline for working in practice* (pp. 15–20). Bonn and Eschborn: Nomos.

Milani, C. R. (2017). *ABC 30 anos: História e desafios futuros.* Brasília: Brazilian Cooperation Agency.

OECD (Organisation for Economic Co-operation and Development). (2009, September 28–29). *Policy dialogue on development co-operation: Triangular co-operation and aid effectiveness: Can triangular co-operation make aid more effective?* Paris: Author.

OECD. (2013a). *Triangular co-operation: What's the literature telling us?* (DAC Global Relations). Paris: Author.

OECD. (2013b). *Triangular co-operation: What can we learn from a survey of actors involved?* (DAC Global Relations). Paris: Author.

OECD. (2016a). *Dispelling the myths of triangular co-operation: Evidence from the 2015 OECD survey on triangular co-operation* (OECD Secretary-General). Paris: Author.

OECD. (2016b). *Triangular co-operation: Promoting partnerships to implement the Sustainable Development Goals: International meeting on triangular co-operation.* Lisbon: Author.

OECD. (2017). *Development co-operation report 2017.* Paris: Author.

OECD. (2018a). *Triangular co-operation: Why does it matter?* Paris: Author.

OECD. (2018b). *Toolkit for identifying, monitoring and evaluating the value added of triangular co-operation.* Paris: Author.

OECD (2019). *What is ODA?* https://www.oecd.org/dac/financing-sustainable-development/development-finance-standards/What-is-ODA.pdf.

OECD & Camões. (2018). *Making better use of the value added of triangular co-operation: Summary of discussions.* Lisbon: Organisation for Economic Co-operation and Development.

Partnerships 2030. (2019, January 22). *What is an MSP?* https://www.partnerschaften2030.de/en/was-ist-eine-map/.

SEGIB (Ibero-American General Secretariat/Secretaría General Iberoamericana). (2017). *Relatório da cooperação Sul-Sul na Ibero-América 2017.* Madrid: Author.

SEGIB. (2018). *La cooperación Sur-Sur y triangular en los escenarios globales y regionales (2012–2016).* Madrid: Author.

Seifert, J., & Renzio, P.d. (2014, April–May). *Além da divisão Norte-Sul: a cooperação triangular na nova cooperação para o desenvolvimento* (Policy Brief). Rio de Janeiro: BRICS Policy Center.

Shaffer, L. (1994). Southernization. *Journal of World History, 5*(1), 1–21.

South Centre. (2015). *About the South Centre.* http://www.southcentre.int/about-the-south-centre/.

Stahl, A. K. (2018). *EU-China-Africa trilateral relations in a multipolar world: Hic sunt dracones.* Basingstoke: Palgrave Macmillan.

UN (United Nations). (1978). Report of the United Nations conference on technical cooperation among developing countries: Buenos Aires 30 August to 12 September 1978 (A/CONF.79/13/Rev.1). New York, NY: United Nations Publications.

UN. (1995, November 13). *New directions for technical cooperation among developing countries: High-Level Committee on the review of technical cooperation among developing countries.* http://unossc1.undp.org/sscexpo/content/ssc/about/faq.htm.

UN. (2009). *Outcome document of the High-Level United Nations Conference on South-South Cooperation 2009* (A/RES/64/222). New York, NY: Author.

UN. (2016). *Framework of operational guidelines on United Nations support to South-South and triangular cooperation: High-level Committee on South-South Cooperation* (Nineteenth session). https://digitallibrary.un.org/record/826679.

UN. (2019). *Buenos Aires Outcome Document of the Second High-Level United Nations Conference on South-South Cooperation* (A/CONF.235/3). Buenos Aires: Author.

United Nations Department of Economic and Social Affairs. (2019). *Financing for sustainable development report 2019: Inter-agency task force on financing for development.* New York, NY: UN.

United Nations Development Programme. (2016). *Monitoring and evaluation mechanisms for South-South and triangular development cooperation: Lessons from Brazil for the 2030 Agenda.* New York, NY: Author.

United Nations General Assembly. (2015). *Transforming our world: The 2030 Agenda for Sustainable Development* (A/RES/70/1). New York, NY: Author.

World Food Programme. (2016). *South-South and triangular cooperation for food security and nutrition.* Rome: Author.

Zoccal, G. (2018). *Fronteiras Esgarçadas: Mobilização de capitais transformando fronteiras e prática dóxica da coope-ração internacional para o desenvolvimento.* Ph.D. thesis. Rio de Janeiro.

Zoccal, G., & Esteves, P. (2018, July). The BRICS effect: Impacts of South–South cooperation in the social field of international development cooperation. *IDS Bulletin, 49*(4), 129–144.

List of Interviews

IO#6. (2017, June 28). Semi-structured interview (G. Zoccal, Interviewer). Paris.
IO#8. (2017, July 5). Semi-structured interview (G. Zoccal, Interviewer). Phone.
IO#9. (2019, September 17). Semi-structured interview (G. Zoccal, Interviewer). Phone.
SSC#5. (2017, October 31). Semi-structured interview (G. Zoccal, Interviewer). Brasília.
SSC#6. (2019, October 11). Semi-structured interview (G. Zoccal, Interviewer). Bonn.
SSC#7. (2019, August 27). Semi-structured interview (G. Zoccal, Interviewer). Phone.
SSC#8. (2019, October 7). Semi-structured interview (G. Zoccal, Interviewer). Phone.
TRD#1. (2017, June 14). Semi-structured interview (G. Zoccal, Interviewer). Bonn.
TRD#2. (2017, June 16). Semi-structured interview (G. Zoccal, Interviewer). Bonn.
TRD#9. (2019, September 9). Semi-structured interview (G. Zoccal, Interviewer). Phone.
TRD#10. (2019, October 1). Semi-structured interview (G. Zoccal, Interviewer). Phone.
TRD#13. (2019, September 17). Semi-structured interview (G. Zoccal, Interviewer). Phone.

Open Access This chapter is licensed under the terms of the Creative Commons Attribution 4.0 International License (http://creativecommons.org/licenses/by/4.0/), which permits use, sharing, adaptation, distribution and reproduction in any medium or format, as long as you give appropriate credit to the original author(s) and the source, provide a link to the Creative Commons license and indicate if changes were made.

The images or other third party material in this chapter are included in the chapter's Creative Commons license, unless indicated otherwise in a credit line to the material. If material is not included in the chapter's Creative Commons license and your intended use is not permitted by statutory regulation or exceeds the permitted use, you will need to obtain permission directly from the copyright holder.

CHAPTER 28

Achieving the SDGs in Africa Through South-South Cooperation on Climate Change with China

Moritz Weigel and Alexander Demissie

28.1 Introduction

The Paris Agreement under the United Nations Framework Convention on Climate Change (UNFCCC) (United Nations [UN] 2015a) and the United Nations 2030 Agenda for Sustainable Development (2030 Agenda) with its 17 Sustainable Development Goals (SDGs) (UN 2015b) represent unprecedented multilateral commitments to a prosperous and sustainable future for life on Earth. There is a growing recognition that progress on achieving the 2030 Agenda and the SDGs is inextricably linked to progress on the implementation of the Paris Agreement and vice versa (German Development Institute/Deutsches Institut für Entwicklungspolitik [DIE] 2019; NewClimate Institute [NCI] 2018; Stockholm Environment Institute [SEI] 2017; United Nations Executive Office of the Secretary-General [UN EOSG] 2017; United Nations Framework Convention on Climate Change [UNFCCC] 2016; World Resources Institute [WRI] 2016). While climate action constitutes one of the SDGs, it is also interconnected with all other SDGs. Therefore, climate action offers a catalytic solution to all SDGs.

South-South cooperation (SSC)[1] on the SDGs and climate change is recognised by the SDGs and the Paris Agreement as an important means of support in addition to developed countries' obligations. Specifically, SDG 17 includes

M. Weigel (✉) · A. Demissie
The ChinaAfricaAdvisory, Cologne, Germany
e-mail: weigel@chinaafricaadvisory.com

A. Demissie
e-mail: demissie@chinaafricaadvisory.com

© The Author(s) 2021
S. Chaturvedi et al. (eds.), *The Palgrave Handbook of Development Cooperation for Achieving the 2030 Agenda*,
https://doi.org/10.1007/978-3-030-57938-8_28

targets on finance, technology, and capacity-building that refer to SSC as a way of strengthening the means of implementation and revitalising the global partnership for sustainable development (UN 2019a). The Paris Agreement makes indirect reference to SSC in its Article 9.2 by encouraging developing countries to "provide or continue to provide [financial resources to assist developing-country Parties with respect to both mitigation and adaptation] voluntarily" (UN 2015a).

In this chapter, we argue that SSC on climate change (SSCCC) with China has a tremendous potential for African countries to realise their climate action priorities, as outlined in their nationally determined contributions (NDCs) under the Paris Agreement (UNFCCC 2019), and through this enable the achievement of the SDGs on the continent. Our analysis proceeds as follows.

First, we look at the linkages between climate action and the SDGs. Second, we review the overall evolution of SSCCC between China and African countries, based on which we apply the concept of "contested cooperation" (please refer to the introductory chapter of this book) by showcasing how China is using existing bilateral and multilateral channels for SSCCC with African countries as well as creating new platforms for cooperation with African partners in this context. China cooperates with multilateral institutions such as United Nations organisations on SSCCC with African countries by providing both financial and technical support, and through that gradually, but steadily, increasing the SSCCC portfolio of those organisations. At the same time, China contests existing cooperation mechanisms by expanding its bilateral support for SSCCC with African countries as well as by driving the establishment of new multilateral financial institutions that support low-emission, climate-resilient development as an alternative to the traditional development finance architecture (Cooper and Farooq 2015). Third, we look at African countries' climate action priorities and show how they tally with China's current SSCCC and pledges in this area. We conclude by looking at challenges for realising the full potential of SSC between China and African countries for low-emission, climate-resilient development and the achievement of the SDGs in Africa and offer recommendations on how to address these challenges, including through triangular cooperation with developed countries.

28.2 Achieving the SDGs in Africa Through Climate Action

There is a growing recognition by countries (UNFCCC 2016) and in research (DIE 2019; NCI 2018; SEI 2017; UN EOSG 2017; WRI 2016) that the implementation of the NDCs is inextricably linked to the achievement of the SDGs and vice versa. For example, "NDC-SDG Connections" (DIE 2019), which is a joint initiative of the German Development Institute/Deutsches Institut für Entwicklungspolitik and the Stockholm Environment Institute, shows the various connections and synergies between the NDCs and the 17 SDGs with their 169 targets. This tool aims to support policy-makers in identifying potential entry points for more coherent policies and action (see Fig. 28.1).

Another example of an analysis on linkages between climate action priorities of countries under the Paris Agreement and the SDGs is the recently published "SDG Climate Action Nexus" tool, which showcases hundreds of specific linkages between climate action and SDG targets (NewClimate Institute 2018). To date, the most comprehensive analysis on linkages between the NDCs and the SDGs with a focus on developing countries is a report jointly published by the United Nations Executive Office of the Secretary-General and the UNFCCC Secretariat. The report finds that more than three-quarters of developing countries' NDCs have clear linkages to 10 of the 17 SDGs—namely SDGs 2, 6, 7, 8, 9, 11, 12, 13, 15, and 17—and more than half of the NDCs have linkages to SDGs 3, 4, and 14. Examples of how the SDG targets can be achieved through the implementation of activities spelt out in developing countries' NDCs include: SDG 2 (zero hunger) through climate-resilient agriculture; SDG 6 (clean water and sanitation) through ensuring water access and integrated water management, improvement of sewerage systems, and wastewater treatment; SDG 7 (affordable and clean energy) through the proliferation of renewable energy and energy-efficiency technologies; SDG 9 (industry, innovation, and infrastructure) through improvement in production processes and the development of low-emission infrastructure; and SDG 15 (life on land), which is addressed by more than 90 per cent

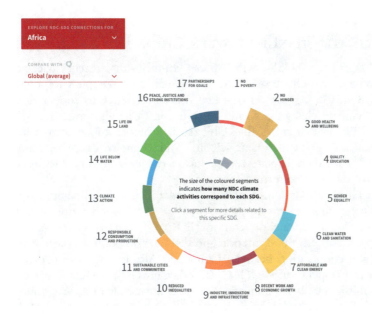

Fig. 28.1 "NDC-SDG Connections"—overview of linkages between African countries' NDCs and the SDGs (*Source* DIE [2019])

of the NDCs from developing countries that indicate actions on forest and land management issues. The report also includes case studies of South-South and triangular cooperation from those areas that feature most prominently in developing countries' NDCs, namely energy, land-use, transport, waste, agriculture, and water, showcasing how the achievement of specific SDGs is supported in each case (UN EOSG 2017).

The Fifth Assessment Report of the Intergovernmental Panel on Climate Change (IPCC)[2] presents strong evidence for the adverse effects of climatic change—particularly on the health, livelihoods, and food security of people in African countries—and concludes that climate change poses a significant threat to socio-economic development in Africa (Intergovernmental Panel on Climate Change [IPCC] 2014a). Therefore, achieving the SDGs in Africa will not be possible without addressing climate change. With regard to low-emission development, the IPCC report states that African countries have abundant opportunities to adopt clean, efficient, low-emission technologies and practices while avoiding inefficient, fossil fuel-dependent infrastructure that more developed countries are locked into (IPCC 2014b). Utilising these opportunities will provide generous gains in economic productivity, human development, and quality of life (IPCC 2014b). As we show in the following sections, SSCCC has become an important part of African countries SSC with China. In this chapter, China thus serves as an example to illustrate the potential of SSCCC for achieving the SDGs in Africa.

28.3 Evolution of South-South Cooperation on Climate Change Between China and Africa

China has a long history of SSC with African countries that reaches back to the 1950s (Information Office of the State Council of the People's Republic of China [IOSC] 2011). However, the first official reference to cooperation on addressing climate change can only be found in "China's Africa Policy", published in 2006, which states that China will promote cooperation with Africa on climate change by increasing scientific and technological cooperation (IOSC 2006).[3] Since then, climate change has increasingly become a focus of China's SSC with African countries.

In 2009, China and African countries agreed to include cooperation on addressing climate change as one of the new areas for cooperation under the Forum on China–Africa Cooperation (FOCAC),[4] which serves as the main platform for collective consultation and dialogue on political, economic, and sociocultural cooperation between China and African countries (Forum on China–Africa Cooperation [FOCAC] 2009). China's first white paper on foreign aid, published in 2011, confirmed the prominent role of African countries in China's SSC and highlighted climate change as a new area of China's foreign aid (IOSC 2011).

At FOCAC's fifth ministerial meeting in 2012, China and African countries expressed satisfaction with the progress in cooperation in protecting the environment and addressing climate change in recent years and underscored the willingness to continue exchanges and cooperation in these areas. China pledged to continue to support African countries in building capacity for climate change adaptation and mitigation as well as for sustainable development (FOCAC 2012). China's latest white paper on foreign aid includes a dedicated section on SSCCC, with Africa stating that China has "actively helped African countries improve their ability to cope with climate change, and strengthened cooperation with them in meteorological satellite monitoring, new energy development and utilization, desertification prevention and control, and urban environmental protection" (IOSC 2014).

Furthermore, China's second Africa policy paper, published shortly before the 2015 FOCAC summit in Johannesburg, stipulated cooperation on climate change as being one of the six areas for which China's assistance would be primarily used, and that China will boost and consolidate cooperation with African countries under the UNFCCC ("China's second Africa policy paper" 2015). In the FOCAC Johannesburg Declaration and Action Plan, China and African countries acknowledged that climate change is exacerbating existing development challenges in Africa and is placing additional burdens on the national budgets and efforts of African countries to achieve sustainable development. China and participating African countries reiterated their intentions to strengthen their policy dialogue on climate change as well as deepen cooperation in tackling climate change, in particular as regards climate change monitoring; climate risk and vulnerabilities reduction; strengthening resilience; promoting adaptation, support for mitigation in terms of capacity-building, technology transfer, as well as financing for monitoring and implementation (FOCAC 2015a, b).

The vision for China's Belt and Road Initiative, also published in 2015, by China's National Development and Reform Commission—the supreme macroeconomic planning and management body—together with the ministries of Foreign Affairs and Commerce, also includes provisions on "tackling climate change" and pursuing low-emission and climate-resilient infrastructure construction and operation (National Development and Reform Commission [NDRC] 2015a). This is of importance, as 37 of the 53 African countries that have diplomatic relations with China had already joined the Belt and Road Initiative by September 2018 ("China signs MOUs with 37 African countries" 2018).

The outcome documents of the latest FOCAC summit, held in 2018, reaffirmed this commitment to further deepening "pragmatic cooperation with African countries under the framework of Climate Change South-South Cooperation, and help African countries strengthen climate change adaption capabilities through providing assistance in kind and capacity-building training to jointly meet the challenge posed by climate change". In particular, China will help increase African countries' resilience to climate change by advancing sustainable agriculture, forest management, and organic farming, and through the efficient management of natural resources as well as supporting disaster prevention and raising public awareness (FOCAC 2018a, b).

28.4 CONTESTED COOPERATION: OLD AND NEW CHANNELS OF CHINA'S SOUTH-SOUTH COOPERATION ON CLIMATE CHANGE WITH AFRICAN COUNTRIES

Over the past decade, China has emerged as one of the leading developing countries on SSCCC (Ha et al. 2015; Weigel 2016). China's SSCCC with African countries has not only increased through established bilateral and multilateral channels, but also through China's creation of new bilateral and multilateral mechanism, as described below. This leads to "regime shifting" (Morse and Keohane 2014) within international climate change cooperation through the adjustment of existing—and the introduction of new—approaches, in line with China's aid principles (Weigel 2016).

Since 2008, China's SSCCC projects in Africa are listed in an annual report titled "China's Policies and Actions on Addressing Climate Change" and in China's two white papers on foreign aid published in 2011 (IOSC 2011) and 2014 (IOSC 2014). For example, China has signed bilateral agreements on "Complimentary Supplies for Addressing Climate Change" with Benin, Burundi, Cameroon, Egypt, Ethiopia, Ghana, Madagascar, and Nigeria. It has also implemented projects on bioenergy with Guinea, Sudan, and Tunisia; on solar and wind power with Ethiopia, Morocco, and South Africa; and on capacity-building on low-emission industrial development and energy policies, water resources management and conservation, forestry, desertification prevention and control, early warning systems, and satellite weather monitoring in many African countries (IOSC 2014).

Most significantly, in 2015, China's president, Xi Jinping, announced the establishment of a $3.1 billion (20 billion Chinese yuan) South-South Cooperation Climate Fund. This pledge is significant, not only because it is the largest single pledge for supporting climate action in developing countries made by any country to date, but also because it represents a significant increase from China's previous spending on SSCCC of about $30 million per year (Weigel 2016). Even if it were spent over 15 years, the pledge would equal a more than sixfold increase per annum. Figure 28.2 illustrates the significance of this pledge based on 5-year, 10-year, and 15-year spending scenarios.

The establishment of the fund is also part of China's climate action pledge under the Paris Agreement, as spelt out in its NDC (NDRC 2015b). However, due to administrative challenges and changes in institutional arrangements—including the establishment of China's new Ministry of Ecology and Environment (MEE), which now includes the SSCCC portfolio—the fund has not yet become fully operational. Until China's recent ministerial reshuffling in 2018, the National Development and Reform Commission (NDRC)[5] was in charge

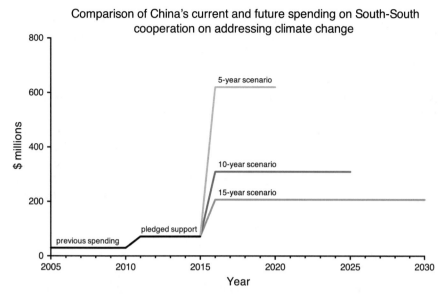

Fig. 28.2 Current and future spending scenarios on China's SSCCC (*Source* Weigel [2016])

of bilateral SSCCC projects, with project implementation being led by the NDRC-affiliated National Center for Climate Change Strategy and International Cooperation. SSCCC is now under the responsibility of China's MEE in coordination with China's new aid agency, the China International Development Cooperation Agency. There seems to be consistency in bilateral SSCCC projects as the National Center for Climate Change Strategy and International Cooperation continues its implementation role under MEE leadership.

In addition to its bilateral channels, China has been increasingly using existing multilateral channels under the umbrella of the United Nations for advancing SSCCC with African countries. For example, China established dedicated funds and programmes on climate-resilient agriculture with the Food and Agriculture Organization of the United Nations (FAO)[6] (FAO 2019), on climate change adaptation with the United Nations Environment Programme (UNEP)[7] (UNEP 2014, 2015a, b, 2019), and on broadly advancing SSCCC within the United Nations System together with the United Nations Office for South-South Cooperation (UNOSSC) (2019b). For example, China provided $6 million to the United Nations Executive Office of the Secretary-General (Ministry of Foreign Affairs of the People's Republic of China 2014), which was used to establish the Southern Climate Partnership Incubator (SCPI), also known as the United Nations Climate Partnerships for the Global South. The SCPI was launched on the margins of the signing of the Paris Agreement in 2016 to foster, support, and promote South-South and triangular cooperation for climate action by facilitating network and partnership-building, assist with policy exchange, technical assistance, and capacity-building between countries of the Global South, and accelerate access to green technologies to Southern countries on favourable terms. The SCPI has been instrumental in developing the first United Nations Action Plan on South-South Climate Cooperation (2017–2021), which was adopted in November 2017 (UNOSSC 2019c). China has also been increasingly engaging on triangular cooperation with United Nations entities and African countries to address climate change, for example with the United Nations Development Programme (UNDP) on sharing expertise and technologies for renewable energy generation in Burundi, Ghana, and Zambia and supporting drought management and desertification control in Ethiopia and Kenya (UNDP 2015).

While China has been increasingly using existing bilateral and multilateral channels for advancing SSCCC with African countries, it has also created new channels for this purpose, most prominently the already mentioned South-South Cooperation Climate Fund. Following the announcement of the $3.1 billion fund by President Xi in September 2015, he specified in his speech at the United Nations Climate Change Conference in Paris in November 2015 that China will pursue a "10-100-1000" South-South cooperation initiative, which aims to implement 10 low-carbon development demonstration projects, 100 climate mitigation and adaptation projects in developing countries, as well as provide climate change capacity-building opportunities for 1000 representatives from developing countries. He also said that China will continue to promote international cooperation in such areas as clean energy, disaster prevention and mitigation, ecological protection, climate-smart agriculture, and low-carbon and smart cities ("Full text of President Xi's speech" 2015).

In the same year, China also established the South-South Cooperation Assistance Fund and pledge $2 billion to the fund, which has the overall objective of supporting developing countries to achieve the SDGs and therefore also has strong relevance for SSCCC. The fund has been operational since 2016, and grant applications are required to demonstrate clearly how the proposed project supports the achievement of specific SDGs, SDG targets, and indicators. To date, there has not been a public call for applications, but internal calls for proposals were received by government-affiliated entities and multilateral organisations based in China.

In addition to the two funds that are, so far, mainly focussed on expanding bilateral cooperation, China has also spearheaded the establishment of two major new development banks, namely the New Development Bank (NDB)[8] and the Asian Infrastructure Investment Bank (AIIB),[9] which are both committed to supporting low-emission, climate-resilient development. These new multilateral development finance institutions are often perceived as challenging existing institutions (Callaghan and Hubbard 2016), but they can equally be seen as a response to the growing financing gaps for development, including climate finance, which has not been provided adequately to developing countries (De Haan and Warmerdam 2017). The NDB makes it clear that it was established "to support infrastructure and sustainable development efforts in BRICS [Brazil, Russia, India, China, South Africa] and other underserved, emerging economies for faster development through innovation and cutting-edge technology" (New Development Bank [NDB] 2019a). Addressing climate change is among the core principles of the bank's Environmental and Social Framework, which commits the bank to promote mitigation and adaptation measures by pursuing the development of a green economy; promoting the conservation of natural resources, including energy and water; supporting sustainable land-use management and urban development; and "climate proofing of its infrastructure financing and investments". The coverage of the environmental impact assessment explicitly includes the assessment of "both the potential impacts of the project on climate change as well as the implications of climate change on the project", the development of "both mitigation or adaptation measures as appropriate", and the identification of "opportunities for no- or low-carbon use, where applicable, and for reducing emissions from the project" (NDB 2016). The Environmental and Social Framework also requires the integration of "principles of cleaner production into product design and production processes with the objective of conserving raw materials, energy and water" (NDB 2016). Furthermore, efforts need to be made to reduce project-related greenhouse gas (GHG) emissions during design and operation, and projects with significant GHG emissions are encouraged to quantify direct and indirect emissions, in line with national protocols (NDB 2016). So far, South Africa is the NDB's only African member state, but the bank foresees opening up membership beyond its five founding members in the future. The NDB has already provided a total of $680 million for the financing of energy and transport projects in South Africa (NDB 2019b).

The AIIB is also committed to addressing climate change and makes specific reference to supporting the implementation of the Paris Agreement by contributing to "mitigation, adaptation and the redirection of financial flows" (Asian Infrastructure Investment Bank [AIIB] 2016). In particular, the bank "stands ready [...] to assist its Clients in achieving their nationally determined contributions" and with the formulation of long-term, low GHG-emission development strategies (AIIB 2016). The AIIB aims to "prioritize investments promoting greenhouse gas emission neutral and climate resilient infrastructure, including actions for reducing emissions, climate-proofing and promotion of renewable energy" (AIIB 2016). The bank's environmental and social standards include a dedicated section on climate change, which calls for the development of mitigation or adaptation measures to reduce climate change-related risks and an assessment of the impacts of any project on climate change, including emissions, as well as the implications of climate change for the project (AIIB 2016). Furthermore, projects should identify opportunities for reducing GHG emissions, enhancing adaptive capacity, strengthening resilience, and reducing vulnerability to climate change, including through incorporating climate-proofing into the project and promoting the use of renewable energy (AIIB 2016). The AIIB also "promotes the conservation of energy, water and other resources; supports sustainable land use management; and encourages making best use of green growth and low-carbon technologies, renewable energy, cleaner production, sustainable transport systems and sustainable urban development" (AIIB 2016). Furthermore, the AIIB supports "reporting on greenhouse gas emissions for implementation of the Paris Agreement" by financing measures to quantify and report to national authorities direct and indirect project-related emissions (AIIB 2016). Eleven African countries are already either Members[10] or Prospective Members[11] of the AIIB, and the bank is already co-financing renewable energy (AIIB 2017) and sustainable rural sanitation projects (AIIB 2018) in Egypt, providing a total of $510 million as long-term debt financing.

In the context of how cooperation with these new multilateral development banks can contribute to climate action—and through this support the achievement of the SDGs—it is important to note that the strengthening of implementation rules for the banks' Environmental and Social Frameworks, including public access to information, will be key for ensuring that the banks' aspirations on addressing climate change and fostering development are met in practice (GEGAfrica 2017; Germanwatch 2019; Heinrich Böll Foundation 2019).

As explained in more detail in the introductory chapter of this book, contested cooperation describes the current development cooperation landscape that is being shaped by "ongoing processes of institution shifting and institution creation within established forms of development cooperation and new types of collaboration". In the context of China's SSCCC with African countries, we see institution-shifting through China's contribution to the relative expansion of SSCCC with African countries under FAO, UNDP, UNEP, and UNOSSC, as well as institution-creation through the expansion of China's bilateral SSCCC channels with African partners and the drive to establish new multilateral financial institutions that support climate action. As illustrated in Table 28.1, contested cooperation leads to a certain level of re-focussing of the work of existing institutions, such as the aforementioned United Nations organisations, and the establishment of new institutions in this context, such as the Southern Climate Partnership Incubator. At the same time, within the concept of contested cooperation, either existing institutions incorporate new types of collaboration, such as South-South and triangular cooperation in the case of the United Nations organisations, or new types of collaboration are pursued by newly created institutions, such as the AIIB, the NDB, or China's emerging South-South Cooperation Climate Fund.

Table 28.1 Contested cooperation matrix for China's South-South cooperation on climate change with African countries

Contestation			
		Institution-shifting	*Institution-creation*
Cooperation	Established cooperation	Updating international institutions *Re-focussing the work of United Nations organisations on SSCCC with African countries*	Proliferating international institutions *Creation of AIIB and NDB*
	New types of collaboration	Collaborating in international institutions *Establishing the Southern Climate Partnership Incubator*	Piloting collaboration *Collaboration under the China South-South Cooperation Climate Fund*

Source Authors

28.5 African Countries' Climate Action Priorities

African countries' NDCs include specified goals or targets for reducing GHG emissions as well as adaptation components that describe how the country is adversely impacted by climate change and what the country intends to do to adapt to these impacts (UNFCCC 2019). An analysis of all NDCs submitted by African countries to the UNFCCC under the Paris Agreement found that agriculture, land-use and forestry, water, energy, and transport range among the priority areas for climate action on the continent (Weigel and Demissie 2017). The above section on China's SSCCC with African countries has shown that cooperation is already taking place in all of these priority areas. In the areas of agriculture, land-use and forestry, there is not only bilateral cooperation between China and African countries on introducing practices and technologies that increase climate-resilience (Bräutigam 2015; FOCAC 2009, 2012, 2015a, 2018b; IOSC 2011, 2014), but also increasing cooperation through partnerships with multilateral organisations, for example with the FAO (2019) and the International Bamboo and Rattan Organisation (2019). In the area of water, there are also many examples of bilateral and multilateral cooperation, for example under the UNEP–China–Africa Cooperation Programme. This programme includes cooperation on the planning, development, and demonstration of new technologies for safe water supply, water quality, and ecosystem monitoring; the demonstration of new wastewater treatment technologies, drought early warning systems, and adaptive technologies; the development and demonstration of water-saving techniques for dry land agriculture and agricultural mapping; and the development and demonstration of technologies for combating desertification (UNEP 2014, 2015a, b). There is a broad spectrum of SSCCC projects between China and African countries in the area of energy, ranging from supporting the development of renewable energy policies to providing technical support for the planning, development, and operation of renewable energy projects (UNFCCC 2018b), the donation of energy-efficient equipment (NDRC 2013), the financing of large-scale renewable energy projects (Ismail 2018), as well as support for setting up local production facilities (Ismail 2018). Finally, in the area of transport, cooperation between African countries and China has brought about pioneering low-emission transport systems, such as through renewable energy-powered Light Rail Transit in Ethiopia's capital, Addis Ababa, as well as the electrified railway line between Addis Ababa and Djibouti (UNFCCC 2018b). We have seen that addressing climate change is a prerequisite for achieving the SDGs and the 2030 Agenda in Africa. We have also seen that China has emerged as an important partner for African countries on SSCCC by using existing, and creating new, bilateral and multilateral channels of support. We have further seen that China's past and current SSCCC with Africa tallies with African countries' climate action priorities, and that pledges made by China on future support hold a tremendous potential for supporting Africa's climate action priorities.

28.6 Unlocking the Full Potential of South-South Cooperation on Climate Change Between China and African Countries

In order to unlock the full potential of SSCCC between China and African partners, the following should be considered by Chinese, African, and other decision-makers in this area:

- A global survey on China's SSCCC undertaken by UNDP in 2015 (Weigel 2016) found that many African countries are not fully aware of how to enter into SSCCC with Chinese partners. In order to address this challenge, China should publish a comprehensive overview of its bilateral and multilateral support for SSCCC, including information on how African countries can access support. Such an overview should include SSCCC and related activities under all FOCAC funds and mechanisms and be carried out by all relevant ministries, including the Ministry of Agriculture, the Ministry of Commerce, and the Ministry of Science and Technology, among others.
- China should fully operationalise its South-South Cooperation Climate Fund and make information on the fund's access, operational modalities, and activities publicly available. Given the size of the fund, with a pledged amount of $3.1 billion, its operation could significantly contribute to further unlocking the full potential of SSCCC. Activities of the fund should include direct support for the development and implementation of SSCCC projects in African countries. Access to the fund should be

quick, unbureaucratic, and transparent to serves as an efficient and effective complement to the often complex access requirements for climate finance provided by developed countries, for example through the Green Climate Fund.[12]

- The South-South Cooperation Climate Fund should contribute to ensuring that the new development finance architecture emerging under China's leadership through the AIIB and the NDB is living up to its commitment of fostering low-emission and climate-resilient development. Such work could have a catalysing effect and support developing countries in integrating climate change aspects into their socio-economic programmes, far beyond the scope of the South-South Cooperation Climate Fund. Furthermore, the enforcement of strong environmental safeguards in the operation of the new institutions would help ensure that the efforts of the South-South Cooperation Climate Fund are not undermined by other funds through, for example, the financing of coal-fired power plants.
- African countries should build on pledges made by China under the Belt and Road Initiative and FOCAC regarding SSCCC and proactively identify concrete ways of implementing their climate action priorities with support from Chinese partners. For example, as the "10 low-carbon development demonstration projects" are still being identified, African countries pursuing the development of sustainable special economic zones, such as Ethiopia, Kenya, Rwanda, and South Africa, could present a concrete cooperation proposal in this regard.
- African countries should also get actively involved with the AIIB and the NDB and seek ways to use these institutions for implementing their NDCs, in particular with regard to low-emission, climate-resilient infrastructure development and renewable energy projects. The NDB is only now opening up to a broader membership, which should be used by African countries to influence, and benefit from, these new development finance institutions for implementing their NDCs. Such an involvement should be pursued as a complement to existing engagements with other multilateral financial institutions.
- Multilateral climate funds should follow the successful example of the Adaptation Fund to provide SSC grants that foster peer-to-peer learning between developing countries on the successful application and management of funds (Adaptation Fund 2019).
- Developed countries should support SSCCC between China and African countries through triangular cooperation, in line with agreed targets and indicators of SDG 17 as well as the outcome document of the Second High-level United Nations Conference on South-South Cooperation (UN 2019b), which was adopted by all United Nations Member States in April 2019 as a blue print for future South-South and triangular cooperation for the achievement of the SDGs. In particular, existing pledges in this area should be realised, such as by the European Union,

which already committed itself in 2016 to turn "what is often perceived as EU-China competition in Africa into greater cooperation" and to pursue "joint approaches" to "speed up the implementation of the Paris Agreement wherever possible, including the implementation of Nationally Determined Contributions" (European Commission 2016).[13] Germany is also well-positioned to spearhead triangular cooperation on climate change with Chinese and African partners by building on its triangular cooperation strategy (Federal Ministry for Economic Cooperation and Development 2013) and fully utilising the recently established Sino-German Center for Sustainable Development (2019), which inter alia aims to support low-emission, climate-resilient infrastructure development in African countries.

Notes

1. For the purpose of this article "South-South cooperation" is understood as a broad framework for collaboration among developing countries in political, economic, social, cultural, environmental, and technical domains, through which developing countries share knowledge, skills, expertise, and resources to meet their development goals through concerted efforts (UNOSSC 2019a). South-South cooperation on climate change is therefore defined as any of the above-listed collaborations between developing countries that aim to reduce GHG emissions or support the adaptation to the adverse effects of climate change.
2. The IPCC is a body of the United Nations dedicated to providing the world with an objective, scientific view of climate change; its natural, political, and economic impacts and risks; and possible response options.
3. However, China has already been engaged in renewable energy projects with African countries since the 1980s, for example in the area of biogas, and started undertaking small-scale hydro, solar, and wind power projects and training programmes on climate change, forest management, and desertification in many countries in the 1990s and 2000s (IOSC 2011).
4. Following proposals from Benin, Ethiopia, Madagascar, and Mauritius, FOCAC was established in 2000 by China in collaboration with African countries (Li 2012). FOCAC ministerial meetings take place every three years. The ministerial meetings were elevated to summits with the participation of heads of state and government in the years 2006, 2015, and 2018. Further information on FOCAC is available at: http://www.focac.org.
5. Theoretically the NDRC needed to be involved in any work on international cooperation on climate change-related matters. However, in practice, this was not always the case due to the broad scope of climate change-related work and the absence of a clear definition of what constitutes SSCCC (Weigel 2016).
6. China has been actively involved in, and largely contributed to, FAO's SSC Programme since its launch in 1996. In 2008, China donated $30 million to FAO to establish an SSC Trust Fund, which funds the FAO–China SSC Programme, which supports many African countries to promote climate-smart agriculture. In 2014, China added $50 million to the Trust Fund (FAO 2019).

7. The UNEP–China–Africa Cooperation Programme focusses on enhancing the capacity of African countries to address climate change through technology transfer and capacity-building, in particular with regard to ecosystem management, disaster reduction, climate change adaptation, and renewable energy generation.
8. The NDB was established in 2015 with an initial subscribed capital of $50 billion and initial authorised capital of $100 billion. The five founding members—Brazil, China, India, Russia, and South Africa—hold equal shares and voting power. The NDB is headquartered in Shanghai, China. Its first Regional Center is located in Johannesburg, South Africa.
9. Following a proposal by China in 2013, the AIIB was established in 2015 with an initial subscribed capital of $100 billion. The allocated shares are based on the size of each member country's economy. Voting power is divided into basic votes, share votes, and founding member votes. China has, by far, the largest voting power, with about 27 per cent of the total votes (AIIB 2019). The AIIB is headquartered in Beijing, China.
10. Egypt, Ethiopia, Madagascar, and Sudan (AIIB 2019).
11. Algeria, Ghana, Kenya, Libya, Morocco, South Africa, and Togo (AIIB 2019).
12. Established in 2010, the Green Climate Fund launched a Readiness and Preparatory Support Programme (Readiness Programme) in 2014 to help developing countries fulfil its complex requirements for receiving financial support. However, in practice, even accessing the Green Climate Fund Readiness Programme is challenging for many developing countries and requires support from Northern providers to become "ready" for the Readiness Programme (UNFCCC 2018a).
13. In the EU–China Leaders' Statement on Climate Change and Clean Energy, published in July 2018, both sides stated their commitment to "explore possibilities for triangular cooperation on promoting sustainable energy access, energy efficiency and low greenhouse gas emission development in other developing countries and assist them to increase the capacities in combating climate change, with particular focus on least developed countries, small island developing states and African countries, as reflected in these countries' national climate plans, strategies and policies" (European Union 2018).

References

Adaptation Fund. (2019). *South-South cooperation grants*. https://www.adaptation-fund.org/readiness/readiness-grants/south-south-cooperation-grants/.

AIIB (Asian Infrastructure Investment Bank). (2016). *Environmental and social framework*. https://www.aiib.org/en/policies-strategies/_download/environment-framework/20160226043633542.pdf.

AIIB. (2017). *Egypt Round II Solar PV Feed-in Tariffs Program*. https://www.aiib.org/en/projects/approved/2017/egypt-round-II-solar-pv-feed-in-tariffs-program.html.

AIIB. (2018). *Program document of the Asian Infrastructure Investment Bank: Arab Republic of Egypt Sustainable Rural Sanitation Services Program*. https://www.aiib.org/en/projects/approved/2018/_download/egypt/document/egypt-sustainable-rural.pdf.

AIIB. (2019). *Members and prospective members of the bank.* https://www.aiib.org/en/about-aiib/governance/members-of-bank/index.html.

Bräutigam, D. (2015). *Will Africa feed China?* New York, NY: Oxford University Press.

Callaghan, M., & Hubbard, P. (2016). The Asian Infrastructure Investment Bank: Multilateralism on the Silk Road. *China Economic Journal, 9*(2), 116–139.

China signs MOUs with 37 African countries, AU on B&R development. (2018, September 7). *Xinhuanet.* http://www.xinhuanet.com/english/2018-09/07/c_137452482.htm.

China's second Africa policy paper. (2015, December 5). *ChinaDaily.* http://www.chinadaily.com.cn/world/XiattendsParisclimateconference/2015-12/05/content_22632874.htm.

Cooper, A. F., & Farooq, A. B. (2015). Testing the club dynamics of the BRICS: The New Development Bank from conception to establishment. *International Organizations Research Journal, 10*(2), 1–15.

De Haan, A., & Warmerdam, W. (2017). China's foreign aid: Towards a new normal? *ResearchGate.* https://www.researchgate.net/publication/311992075_China%27s_Foreign_Aid_Towards_a_new_normal.

DIE (German Development Institute/Deutsches Institut für Entwicklungspolitik). (2019). *NDC-SDG connections.* https://klimalog.die-gdi.de/ndc-sdg/country/Africa.

European Commission. (2016). *Joint communication to the European Parliament and the Council: Elements for a new EU strategy on China.* http://eeas.europa.eu/archives/docs/china/docs/joint_communication_to_the_european_parliament_and_the_council_-_elements_for_a_new_eu_strategy_on_china.pdf.

European Union. (2018). *Joint statement of the 20th EU–China summit.* https://eeas.europa.eu/delegations/china_en/48424/Joint%20statement%20of%20the%2020th%20EU-China%20Summit.

FAO (Food and Agriculture Organization of the United Nations). (2019). *FAO–China South-South cooperation programme.* http://www.fao.org/3/a-i4700e.pdf.

Federal Ministry for Economic Cooperation and Development. (2013). *Triangular cooperation in German development cooperation: Position paper* (BMZ Strategy Paper 5). Bonn: Author.

FOCAC (Forum on China–Africa Cooperation). (2009). *Forum on China–Africa cooperation Sharm El Sheikh Action Plan.* https://www.focac.org/eng/zywx_1/zywj/t626387.htm.

FOCAC. (2012). *The Fifth Ministerial conference of the Forum on China–Africa cooperation Beijing Action Plan (2013–2015).* https://www.focac.org/eng/zywx_1/zywj/t954620.htm.

FOCAC. (2015a). *Declaration of the Johannesburg Summit of the Forum on China–Africa cooperation.* https://www.focac.org/eng/zywx_1/zywj/t1327960.htm.

FOCAC. (2015b). *The Forum on China–Africa Cooperation Johannesburg Action Plan (2016–2018).* https://www.focac.org/eng/zywx_1/zywj/t1327961.htm.

FOCAC. (2018a). *Beijing Declaration—Toward an even stronger China–Africa community with a shared future.* https://www.focac.org/eng/zywx_1/zywj/t1594324.htm.

FOCAC. (2018b). *Forum on China–Africa Cooperation Beijing Action Plan (2019–2021).* https://www.focac.org/eng/zywx_1/zywj/t1594297.htm.

Full text of President Xi's speech at opening ceremony of Paris climate summit. (2015, January 12). *China Daily*. http://www.chinadaily.com.cn/world/Xiattends Parisclimateconference/2015-12/01/content_22592469.htm.

GEGAfrica. (2017). *The New Development Bank as an advocate of country systems*. https://www.saiia.org.za/wp-content/uploads/2017/08/GA_Th1_PB-pri nsloo_20170831.pdf.

Germanwatch. (2019). *Aligning the Asian Infrastructure Investment Bank with the Paris Agreement and the SDGs: Challenges and opportunities*. http://www.german watch.org/sites/germanwatch.org/files/AIIB_Report_web_0.pdf.

Ha, S., Hale, T., & Ogden, P. (2015). Climate finance in and between developing countries: An emerging opportunity to build on. *Global Policy, 7*(1), 102–108.

Heinrich Böll Foundation. (2019). *The Asian Infrastructure Investment Bank: A multilateral bank where China sets the rules*. https://th.boell.org/sites/default/files/boell_aiib-studie_en_web_v01.pdf.

International Bamboo and Rattan Organisation. (2019). *Dutch-Sino-East Africa Bamboo Development Programme*. https://www.inbar.int/project/dutch-sino-east-africa-bamboo-development-project/.

IOSC (Information Office of the State Council of the People's Republic of China). (2006). *China's Africa policy*. http://en.people.cn/200601/12/eng20060112_234894.html.

IOSC. (2011). *China's foreign aid*. http://english.gov.cn/archive/white_paper/2014/09/09/content_281474986284620.htm.

IOSC. (2014). *China's foreign aid*. http://english.gov.cn/archive/white_paper/2014/08/23/content_281474982986592.htm.

IPCC (Intergovernmental Panel on Climate Change). (2014a). *AR5 climate change 2014: Impacts, adaptation and vulnerabilities*. https://www.ipcc.ch/report/ar5/wg2/.

IPCC. (2014b). *AR5 climate change 2014: Mitigation of climate change*. https://www.ipcc.ch/report/ar5/wg3/.

Ismail, A. (2018, May 10). *Egypt signs MOU with China's GCL for $2 billion solar panel factory*. Reuters. https://www.reuters.com/article/us-egypt-solar/egypt-signs-mou-with-chinas-gcl-for-2-billion-solar-panel-factory-idUSKBN1IB1WI.

Li, A. (2012). *The Forum on China–Africa cooperation: From a sustainability perspective*. http://awsassets.panda.org/downloads/the_forum_on_china_afr ica_cooperation_1.pdf.

Ministry of Foreign Affairs of the People's Republic of China. (2014). *Zhang Gaoli attends UN Climate Summit and delivers speech*. https://www.fmprc.gov.cn/ce/ceun/eng/chinaandun/economicdevelopment/climatechange/.

Morse, J. C., & Keohane, R. O. (2014). Contested multilateralism. *The Review of International Organizations, 9*(4), 385–412.

NCI (NewClimate Institute). (2018). *NDC update report special edition: Linking NDCs and SDGs*. https://newclimate.org/2018/05/07/ndc-update-report-spe cial-edition-linking-ndcs-and-sdgs.

NDB (New Development Bank). (2016). *New Development Bank: Environmental and social framework*. https://www.ndb.int/wp-content/uploads/2017/02/ndb-enviro nment-social-framework-20160330.pdf.

NDB. (2019a). *Mission*. https://www.ndb.int/about-us/essence/mission-values.

NDB. (2019b). *Projects*. https://www.ndb.int/projects/list-of-all-projects.

NDRC (National Development and Reform Commission). (2013). *China's policies and actions for addressing climate change*. http://en.ndrc.gov.cn/newsrelease/201311/P020131108611533042884.pdf.

NDRC. (2015a). *Vision and actions on jointly building Silk Road economic belt and 21st-century maritime Silk Road*. http://en.ndrc.gov.cn/newsrelease/201503/t20150330_669367.html.

NDRC. (2015b). *Enhanced actions on climate change: China's intended nationally determined contributions*. https://www4.unfccc.int/sites/ndcstaging/PublishedDocuments/China%20First/China%27s%20First%20NDC%20Submission.pdf.

SEI (Stockholm Environment Institute). (2017). *Exploring connections between the Paris Agreement and the 2030 Agenda for Sustainable Development*. https://mediamanager.sei.org/documents/Publications/SEI-PB-2017-NDC-SDG-Connections.pdf.

Sino-German Center for Sustainable Development. (2019). *Trilateral cooperation projects*. https://sg-csd.org.

UN (United Nations). (2015a). *Paris Agreement*. https://unfccc.int/sites/default/files/english_paris_agreement.pdf.

UN. (2015b). *Transforming our world: The 2030 Agenda for Sustainable Development*. A/RES/70/1. https://sustainabledevelopment.un.org/content/documents/21252030%20Agenda%20for%20Sustainable%20Development%20web.pdf.

UN. (2019a). *Sustainable Development Goals knowledge platform: Sustainable Development Goals*. https://sustainabledevelopment.un.org.

UN. (2019b). *Buenos Aires Outcome Document of the Second High-level United Nations Conference on South-South Cooperation*. https://digitallibrary.un.org/record/3802251?ln=en.

UNDP (United Nations Development Programme). (2015). *Fast facts—Climate change in China*. http://www.cn.undp.org/content/dam/china/docs/Publications/UNDP-CHFast%20Facts%20on%20Climate%20Change%202.pdf.

UN EOSG (United Nations Executive Office of the Secretary-General). (2017). *Catalysing the implementation of nationally determined contributions in the context of the 2030 Agenda through South-South cooperation*. https://unfccc.int/sites/default/files/ssc_ndc_report.pdf.

UNEP (United Nations Environment Programme). (2014). *New China–UNEP agreement to boost South-South cooperation on climate change adaptation*. https://www.unenvironment.org/news-and-stories/press-release/new-china-unep-agreement-boost-south-south-cooperation-climate.

UNEP. (2015a). *The UNEP–China–Africa cooperation programme: Enhancing the role of ecosystem management in climate change adaptation report*. https://www.unenvironment.org/news-and-stories/press-release/unep-china-africa-cooperation-programme-enhancing-role-ecosystem.

UNEP. (2015b). *UNEP–China–Africa cooperation on the environment*. http://www.unep.org/rso/portals/118/documents/unep_china/unep-china-africa.pdf.

UNEP. (2019). *China Trust Fund. Strengthening strategic cooperation on environmental conservation*. https://wedocs.unep.org/bitstream/handle/20.500.11822/22316/Chinese%20Trust%20Fund%20Brochure%20Phase%20II%20Eng.pdf?sequence=1&isAllowed=y.

UNFCCC (United Nations Framework Convention on Climate Change). (2016). *Aggregate effect of the intended nationally determined contributions: An update*. Synthesis report by the Secretariat. http://unfccc.int/resource/docs/2016/cop22/eng/02.pdf.

UNFCCC. (2018a). *Adaptation Committee workshop on accessing the readiness and preparatory support programme of the Green Climate Fund for adaptation*. https://unfccc.int/sites/default/files/resource/SB48.AC_.1.pdf.

UNFCCC. (2018b). *Potential of South-South and triangular cooperation on climate technologies for advancing implementation of nationally determined contributions and national adaptation plans*. http://unfccc.int/ttclear/misc_/StaticFiles/gnwoerk_static/brief9/7a74a2f17f204b6ba17f1ec965da70d7/f4e361cd56d4463a8daa4ab29a1254db.pdf.

UNFCCC. (2019). *NDC registry*. https://www4.unfccc.int/sites/NDCStaging/Pages/All.aspx.

UNOSSC (United Nations Office for South-South Cooperation). (2019a). *About South-South and triangular cooperation*. https://www.unsouthsouth.org/about/about-sstc/.

UNOSSC. (2019b). *Southern climate partnership incubator*. https://www.unsouthsouth.org/our-work/partnership-building/southern-climate-partnership-incubator/.

UNOSSC. (2019c). *United Nations Action Plan on South-South Climate Cooperation (2017–2021)*. https://www.unsouthsouth.org/south-south-cooperation-action-plan-for-climate-change-engagement-strategy-2017-2021/.

Weigel, M. (2016). *More money, more impact? China's climate change South-South cooperation to date and future trends*. http://www.cn.undp.org/content/china/en/home/library/south-south-cooperation/more-money-more-impact-china-s-climate-change-south-south-coop.html.

Weigel, M., & Demissie, A. (2017). *A new climate trilateralism? Opportunities for cooperation between the EU, China and African countries on addressing climate change* (DIE Discussion Paper 8/2017). Bonn: German Development Institute/Deutsches Institut für Entwicklungspolitik (DIE).

WRI (World Resources Institute). (2016). *Examining the alignment between the intended nationally determined contributions and Sustainable Development Goals*. https://www.wri.org/sites/default/files/WRI_INDCs_v5.pdf.

Open Access This chapter is licensed under the terms of the Creative Commons Attribution 4.0 International License (http://creativecommons.org/licenses/by/4.0/), which permits use, sharing, adaptation, distribution and reproduction in any medium or format, as long as you give appropriate credit to the original author(s) and the source, provide a link to the Creative Commons license and indicate if changes were made.

The images or other third party material in this chapter are included in the chapter's Creative Commons license, unless indicated otherwise in a credit line to the material. If material is not included in the chapter's Creative Commons license and your intended use is not permitted by statutory regulation or exceeds the permitted use, you will need to obtain permission directly from the copyright holder.

CHAPTER 29

India as a Partner in Triangular Development Cooperation

Sebastian Paulo

29.1 Introduction

Triangular cooperation has attracted growing attention as a feature of the current transformations in the global development landscape. The changing role of rising powers and other middle-income countries as development partners has contributed to a growing diversity of development cooperation approaches (Zimmermann and Smith 2011). In this context, triangular cooperation presents opportunities to shape new types of partnerships that create synergies between North-South and South-South cooperation. As a modality to promote knowledge-sharing among developing countries, triangular cooperation has existed for several decades. The 40th anniversary of the Buenos Aires Plan of Action plus 40 (BAPA+40), celebrated at the Second High-Level United Nations Conference on South-South Cooperation in March 2019, is a reminder of the long history of support for technical cooperation among developing countries. However, the concept has gained additional traction in recent years as transformations in the global development landscape have accelerated and the implementation of the 2030 Agenda for Sustainable Development has been raising new challenges for global collective action.

The debate on the "means of implementation" for the 2030 Agenda refers to triangular cooperation as a modality to achieve the Sustainable Development Goals (SDGs). SDG 17 stresses the role of triangular cooperation for the sharing of knowledge and technology as well as capacity-building

S. Paulo (✉)
Independent Researcher, Berlin, Germany
e-mail: mail@sebastianpaulo.net

© The Author(s) 2021
S. Chaturvedi et al. (eds.), *The Palgrave Handbook of Development Cooperation for Achieving the 2030 Agenda*,
https://doi.org/10.1007/978-3-030-57938-8_29

(United Nations [UN] 2015a). The Addis Ababa Action Agenda of the Third International Conference on Financing for Development mentions triangular cooperation "as a means of bringing relevant experience and expertise to bear in development cooperation" (UN 2015b). All major international platforms with a mandate to shape international development cooperation—the Global Partnership for Effective Development Cooperation, the United Nations Development Cooperation Forum, and the Development Assistance Committee (DAC) of the Organisation for Economic Co-operation and Development (OECD)—endorse and support triangular cooperation as a complementary modality.

Although understandings and terminologies of triangular cooperation[1] vary, the concept generally refers to projects and other initiatives that combine the comparative advantages of Northern donors[2] and providers of South-South cooperation to share knowledge and address challenges among developing countries. Conventional definitions distinguish between the roles of three different types of actors: "pivotal" countries (especially as contributors of knowledge and development experience), "facilitators" (which support cooperation, e.g. through funding and their experience in managing development cooperation), and partner countries (where the results of cooperation are to be achieved) (Organisation for Economic Co-operation and Development [OECD] 2017). The UN, for instance, defines triangular cooperation as "Southern-driven partnerships between two or more developing countries, supported by a developed country (or countries) or multilateral organization(s) to implement development cooperation programs or projects" (UN 2012).

India has often been highlighted as a country that would be particularly suited to act as a pivotal country in triangular partnerships, given the relevance of its development experience. The idea of India assuming the role of pivotal partner has always evoked high expectations of stronger Southern leadership in triangular cooperation. However, the analysis of the growing global practice of triangular cooperation has given little attention to India's role as a partner so far. India's preference for bilateral action within the framework of South-South cooperation has long prevented a stronger engagement in triangular cooperation. However, India's reluctance to participate in this modality has turned into more openness for alternative partnerships. India has shown leadership in shaping UN-managed funds to support South-South cooperation, such as the India, Brazil, and South Africa Facility for Poverty and Hunger Alleviation (IBSA Fund). Moreover, various types of Indian partners have increasingly cooperated with traditional bilateral donors from the OECD/DAC, such as Norway, the United Kingdom (UK), and the United States, to implement projects in Africa and Asia. The Indo-Japanese initiative for an Asia-Africa Growth Corridor (AAGC) shows growing levels of ambition to work in triangular partnerships. Similarly, Indo-French cooperation to set up the International Solar Alliance (ISA) indicates that India's global action on development issues is no longer exclusively determined by traditional conceptions of the North-South divide.

This chapter aims to advance the understanding of India's emerging practice of triangular cooperation.[3] To this end, the chapter provides a systematic overview and discussion of the main types of triangular cooperation in which India has been engaging. First, the chapter outlines the changes in India's position that have enabled India's growing involvement in triangular cooperation. Second, the chapter presents the two main types of triangular cooperation in which Indian participation has been the most visible so far: UN-supported funds and brokering mechanisms promoted by Northern donors. Third, the chapter discusses possible explanations for India's engagement in these types of triangular cooperation against the background of this volume's conceptual framework of contested cooperation. Finally, the chapter advances the argument that the main push of India's growing practice of triangular cooperation is coming in the form of a third type, referred to here as "triangular platforms" and illustrated through the examples of the AAGC, the ISA, and the Global Forum on Cyber Expertise (GFCE).

The chapter argues that India's emerging practice of triangular cooperation does not fit easily with established definitions and concepts. India's special brand of engagement in triangular cooperation has the potential to reshape important aspects of the global architecture of development cooperation and make significant contributions to achieving the SDGs. Accordingly, the Indian experience should inform the analysis and international practice of triangular cooperation more strongly than in the past.

29.2 India's Changing Position Towards Triangular Cooperation

India has long been sceptical of triangular cooperation. The analysis of India's position towards this modality should nevertheless acknowledge that triangular cooperation can be said to have been part of the early history of India's development cooperation. Examples of cooperation with industrialised nations in developing countries date back to the 1950s, when India cooperated with the United States in road and telecommunication projects in Nepal (Chaturvedi 2012a, p. 172). In general, however, India has been reluctant to engage with Northern donors in other developing countries throughout a long period of its post-independence history. India's framing of development cooperation in terms of Southern solidarity, non-alignment, and anti-colonialism has largely stood in contrast to engagement in triangular cooperation, at least as far as cooperation with Northern donors is concerned.

India has shaped its identity as a development partner within the framework of South-South cooperation, explicitly distinguishing its approach from Northern donors. Put differently, "Indian policy reflects a lack of comfort with the prevalent DAC narrative" (Mohanty 2016, p. 2). India's self-image as a demand-oriented development partner mirrors its criticism of Northern donors, which are seen as inadequately addressing the needs of developing countries, applying conditionality, and reinforcing asymmetric relationships. Thus, triangular cooperation has constituted a certain reputational risk for India's standing as a leader and benign influence in the Global South. This position continues to influence the rhetoric through which India aims to differentiate itself from the "top-down" or prescriptive approaches of Northern donors. Viewed from the conceptual perspective of this volume, India's scepticism towards triangular cooperation can be seen as an expression of contestation of the Northern donor-led architecture of development cooperation. This contestation forms an integral part of the way in which India has been constructing its identity as a development partner.

Given the absence of an explicit policy document for India's development cooperation in general, India's position and approach towards triangular cooperation are not formalised. The principles of South-South cooperation provide the general framework for India's development partnerships, including India's engagement in triangular cooperation (i.e. respect for national sovereignty, national ownership and independence, equality, non-conditionality, non-interference in domestic affairs, and mutual benefit). Chaturvedi (2016, p. 7), for instance, analyses the larger framework of India's development cooperation through the concept of "development compact", which denotes relations between actors of the South based "on the principles that govern SSC [South-South cooperation]". In line with these principles, triangular cooperation should be demand-driven, triggered by specific requests, and decided on a case-by-case basis for sector-specific projects that yield tangible results for partner countries. These elements are, for instance, strongly reflected in the understanding of India's development cooperation in terms of Mohanty's (2016) "mission approach".

In India's engagement as a partner in triangular cooperation, these principles are naturally enshrined in the UN-based funds supported by India. Moreover, official declarations of intent through which India endorses triangular cooperation with partners such as the British Department for International Development (DFID) contain references to compatibility with key principles of South-South cooperation. For example, the India-UK "Statement of Intent on Partnership for Cooperation with Third Countries" emphasises the "wholly demand-driven manner" of cooperation (Ministry of External Affairs India [MEA India] and Department for International Development [DFID] 2015). Overall, India's approach to triangular cooperation remains vague and flexible, implicitly defined based on the main principles of its development cooperation in general.

India's long-standing distance from triangular cooperation reflects the critical view that, in the absence of genuinely Southern-led initiatives, triangular cooperation perpetuates power imbalances and strengthens Northern influence over South-South cooperation (Abdenur and Marques da Fonseca 2013). Given concerns over Northern domination of triangular cooperation, some Southern partners—wary of being "socialised" into existing patterns of development cooperation and co-opted as cheap contractors—have remained reluctant partners. According to some observers, such concerns about equal partnership account for the long absence of major Southern players, especially China and India, from triangular cooperation (McEwan and Mawdsley 2012, p. 1198).

The continued evolution of India's position towards triangular cooperation has to be seen in the context of broader foreign policy shifts in the post-Cold War and post-liberalisation period. According to a common interpretation of these shifts, India has been relaxing its emphasis on "idealism" in favour of a more pragmatic approach to using foreign policy in support of its political and economic emergence on the global stage (Mohan 2003). However, critiques of this perspective caution against overstating the pragmatic turn from "Nehruvian" ideals towards economic interest in India's foreign policy. According to this view, India's foreign policy is the result of "incremental shifts [...] that still pay homage to entrenched institutionalized ideas and ideational frameworks" (Miller and Sullivan de Estrada 2017, p. 49). In a similar vein, analysts of India's development cooperation have been pointing out the continued relevance of the discourse of Southern solidarity for India's development partnerships (Harris and Vittorini 2018). India's position on triangular cooperation can therefore be said to be influenced by the two parallel features of increasing pragmatism, which facilitates stronger engagement with Northern donors, and the enduring pertinence of Southern solidarity as an ideational framework, which continues to feed traditional scepticism towards this type of engagement.

India's position on triangular cooperation also needs to be seen in the context of the evolution of its broader development cooperation architecture. In this regard, India has substantially expanded resources and capacity to forge development partnerships. The financial volume of India's development cooperation saw a fivefold increase during the two decades following the end of the Cold War (Mohanty 2016, p. 6). Geographically, India's bilateral development partnerships expanded to comprehensively cover the Global South, going well beyond the traditional focus on South Asia. India's development cooperation has also matured in terms of instruments and modalities. India's "development compact" provides a broad range of tools and instruments for engagement with other developing countries (trade and investment; technology exchange; training, human capacity and skills development (Indian Technical and Economic Cooperation Programme); lines of credit; and grants) (Chaturvedi 2016). Finally, the institutional architecture of India's development partnerships has evolved, leading to the creation of the Development Partnership Administration (DPA) within the Ministry of External Affairs India (MEA India) in 2012 (Chaturvedi 2015). Based on this institutional development, India's capacity to act as a "pivotal" partner in triangular cooperation has been growing. Especially, the focus of India's development cooperation on capacity-building, skills, and human resource development makes India a suitable fit for the activities typically associated with this modality. At the same time, the evolution of India's development cooperation has also increased opportunities for bilateral cooperation, which remains India's preferred option under the framework of South-South cooperation.

As a parallel outcome of India's growing global role as a development partner, India has become increasingly active in shaping alternative platforms and partnerships to complement bilateral action. Since the 2000s, India has been actively shaping new groupings such as IBSA and Brazil, Russia, India, China and South Africa (BRICS), and has forged relationships with regional and continental frameworks, for instance in Africa. Increasing engagement in triangular cooperation, which originated during the same time, can be seen as part of this trend towards a diversification of India's engagement to complement bilateral ties.

Overall, India's gradual openness for (or decreasing scepticism against) triangular cooperation has been facilitated by the softening of the reasons that led to India's initial reluctance. In a more heterogeneous Global South, the foundation of the traditional North-South divide has weakened. Becoming a net provider of development cooperation has put India on a more equal footing with Northern donors. Overall, India's stance on triangular cooperation has changed from reluctance to a discreet form of openness:

> India should collaborate with and learn from other donor countries; at the same time, the Indian core mission remains unchanged – empowering developing countries under the SSC [South-South cooperation] umbrella, continuing to play the role of a "partner" as opposed to a "donor" in development assistance initiatives. (Mohanty 2016, p. 8)

29.3 THE PRACTICE OF INDIA'S ENGAGEMENT IN TRIANGULAR COOPERATION

Identifying or quantifying India's engagement in triangular cooperation is difficult, as India does not specifically report cooperation under this label. The analysis in this chapter is limited to the most systematic examples of India's engagement in triangular cooperation. The examples highlighted in this chapter can essentially be divided into two main categories: fund mechanisms in the UN system and brokering mechanisms promoted by Northern donors in India, most importantly DFID and the United States Agency for International Development (USAID). The choice of this distinction does not preclude the existence of other, more isolated examples of triangular cooperation that might not fit into these two categories.

29.3.1 Fund Mechanisms

India has shown a preference for triangular cooperation with the UN, which it perceives as a neutral partner promoting Southern-led cooperation. UN organisations have increasingly integrated "South-South and Triangular Cooperation" into their mandates. In 1974, the UN General Assembly endorsed the creation of a Special Unit for South-South Cooperation within the United Nations Development Programme (UNDP), now renamed the United Nations Office for South-South Cooperation (UNOSSC). Working with these structures, India has shown leadership in the multilateral sphere by shaping funds for triangular cooperation. These funds can also be seen in the context of India's long-standing support for the BAPA+40 process.

One example is the IBSA Fund, which was established in 2004 and became operational in 2006 (IBSA n.d.). The fund has the objective to share experiences from IBSA countries with least-developed countries and post-conflict countries. It emphasises the importance of capacity-building, local procurement, and the use of Southern expertise. India, Brazil, and South Africa each contribute $1 million per year. Interested governments initiate discussions on projects and can request support with IBSA representatives around the world. Proposals that receive a favourable opinion from one or more of the IBSA Focal Points in the three capitals are forwarded to the IBSA Fund Board of Directors, which meets quarterly to approve projects, monitor implementation, and provide strategic direction. The UNOSSC acts as the fund manager and the secretariat for the Board of Directors. It initiates contact with potential executing agencies and supports implementation.

As an example of a project, the IBSA Fund financed the building of a centre for HIV/AIDS prevention, testing, and treatment in Burundi. Implemented from January 2010 to December 2012, the project had the objective to support government capacity for the implementation of its HIV/AIDS prevention and care strategy, and to improve the provision of healthcare services related to reproductive health, prenatal care, and family planning. The project budget amounted to $1,145,630, with project partners being the Ministry of Health; the Society of Women and AIDS in Africa, Burundi; the UNDP, Burundi; and the United Nations Population Fund (UNFPA), Burundi. Overall, the 2018 overview of the IBSA Fund's project portfolio includes 30 completed, ongoing, or recently approved projects (IBSA and United Nations Office for South-South Cooperation [UNOSSC] 2018).

Another example is the India-UN Development Partnership Fund (DPF), launched on 8 June 2017. The DPF supports the 2030 Agenda for Sustainable Development, prioritising poverty reduction and hunger, health, education, and access to clean water and energy. The DPF's objective is to "support Southern-owned and -led, demand-driven, and transformational sustainable development projects across the developing world" (UNOSSC 2017a). It focuses on least-developed countries and Small Island Developing States. The DPF's first project, for instance, deals with improving resilience to natural disasters in seven Pacific small-island states. The UNOSSC acts as the fund's manager and serves as a secretariat for its Board of Directors. In this role, the UNOSSC coordinates the implementation of projects through UN agencies, governments, and other stakeholders in coordination with partner countries. At the launch, India made an initial contribution of $5 million, which has since been increased by an additional pledge for a multi-year contribution of $100 million (UN 2018).

The DPF's first project has been dealing with improving resilience to natural disasters in seven Pacific small-island states (UNOSSC 2017b). Another example is the project Reinforce the Resilience of the Vulnerable Populations in the Regions of the Kanem and Lake Chad. The project aims to restore degraded lands and improve water and sanitation. In addition to supporting sanitation infrastructure, the project builds the capacity of local committees for water management, hygiene, and sanitation, including through training in administrative and financial management. It has a budget of $600,000 and is implemented by the UNDP and Chad's Ministry of Energy, Water, and Fishing (UNOSSC 2019).

Overall, the two UN-based funds show that India's role in triangular cooperation is not necessarily limited to being a typical pivotal country that provides knowledge and experience. In fact, Indian partners are not mainly involved in the implementation of the projects mentioned in this section. Instead, India has assumed different roles, notably in conceptualising the funds' structures and approaches, and by providing funding.

29.3.2 Brokering Mechanisms

The second main form of Indian engagement in triangular cooperation consists in partnerships among actors from India and other developing countries, with Northern donors acting as brokers of knowledge partnerships and other initiatives. As brokers, Northern donor agencies assume roles that can conceptually be understood as a form of "orchestration" (Abbott et al. 2015). The Northern donor agencies do not implement projects directly but enlist (especially non-governmental) partners from India and other developing countries. To this end, they help connect partners from India and other countries with each other and support their cooperation through facilitative measures, including administrative support, expertise, support for capacity development, and funding. Individual examples of this type of engagement by Indian partners can already be found in the early 2000s, when Norway conducted a programme for "Triangular Institutional Cooperation". In this programme, Norway facilitated cooperation between non-governmental organisations from Ethiopia and India to strengthen their capabilities in the management of natural resources in semi-arid areas (Rajasekaran 2006).

More systematic approaches to engaging Indian partners in triangular cooperation have subsequently been emerging as part of UK and US strategies to reduce and phase out traditional aid programmes. India's global development partnerships with the United States and the United Kingdom have been instrumental in shaping a model for Indian engagement in triangular cooperation. Both the United States and the United Kingdom stress India's potential as a source of pro-poor innovations that could be applied to different contexts across the developing world (Mitchell 2011; United States Agency for International Development [USAID] n.d.-a). This model focuses on leveraging the strengths of India's diverse landscape of non-state and parastatal actors (private sector, civil society organisations, research institutes, the Exim Bank of India, the Federation of Indian Chambers of Commerce and Industry, etc.) to address development challenges in India and other countries. To this end, DFID and USAID draw on technical assistance to build the capacity of partners in India and other partner countries, and facilitate their relationships.

Triangular cooperation in the India-UK partnership has been implemented in several partner countries in South Asia and Africa, covering a broad range of sectors, including nutrition, health, gender equality, trade and investment, and clean energy.[4] As an example, the Innovative Ventures and Technology for Development Programme aims to tap the innovative potential of the Indian private sector to make technological and business solutions available to the poor in low-income states in India and other countries. Another example, the Global Research Partnership on Food and Nutrition Security, Health and Women, is designed as a "trilateral collaborative research programme". The programme promotes the generation, testing, and use of research conducted by consortia of institutions from India, the United Kingdom, and developing countries. As a final example, Supporting Indian Trade and Investment for Africa (SITA) is a South-South aid-for-trade and value-chain programme. The programme supports higher-value exports from Ethiopia, Kenya, Rwanda, Tanzania, and Uganda to India and other countries by leveraging Indian know-how, technology, and investment to upgrade exports in partner countries. In international comparison, DFID's triangular programmes with Indian partners stand out, in that they have above average durations (ranging from four to seven years) and higher budgets (from £9 to £38 million), when compared to other cases of triangular cooperation (OECD 2017; Paulo 2018).

Triangular cooperation in the framework of the India-US development partnership has been implemented in a growing number of countries in Asia and Africa, for example Afghanistan, Cambodia, Laos, Ghana, Tanzania, and Zambia (USAID n.d.-b). Projects cover food security and nutrition, access to quality health care, women's empowerment, and clean energy. Triangular projects have been implemented, for example, under the US presidential initiative "Feed the Future", in which the United States cooperates with India as a strategic partner. In one example, the Feed the Future India Triangular Training Program, USAID cooperates with the National Institute of Agricultural Extension Management (MANAGE), a research institute affiliated with the Indian Ministry of Agriculture. The project trains agricultural practitioners from 17 countries across Africa and Asia on specialised farming practices to improve productivity and incomes (USAID n.d.-b). Another example is the Global Linkages project that facilitates the sharing of Indian innovations and best practices in family planning as well as child and maternal health care with other countries. As a final example, the United States works with Indian institutions in the South Asia Regional Initiative for Energy Integration to promote cross-border electricity trade in South Asia by facilitating energy relations between India and neighbouring countries.

DFID and USAID programmes are often structured around a lead partner that has the required management experience and sector-specific expertise. Examples of lead partners include the International Trade Centre in the case of SITA and MANAGE in the Feed the Future India Triangular Training Program. Lead partners often already have experience in working in other countries and have relevant networks. For instance, the Energy and Resources Institute (TERI)—the lead partner in the completed DFID-TERI Partnership for Clean Energy Access and Improved Policies for Sustainable Development—has a track record and presence in Africa.

Compared to approaches that work through given structures of bilateral cooperation or permanent funds, brokering mechanisms are more flexible. This way of working corresponds to an explorative and demand-searching approach that allows room for innovative ideas. At the same time, brokering mechanisms rely strongly on donor agencies to overcome and manage start-up and transaction costs, and to facilitate cooperation as hubs for expertise, knowledge, and partnership-building throughout the duration of programmes (Paulo 2018). This changing profile of requirements has also led to organisational innovations, allowing donor agencies to assume the role of identifying potential areas of cooperation, convening partners, and establishing relationships. The Global Partnership Team in DFID India is an example.

The design of triangular cooperation as brokering mechanisms is also a consequence of large differences in development cooperation approaches between India and Northern partners. As a result, this type of triangular cooperation has remained operationally relatively disconnected from India's and Northern partners' respective bilateral programmes with partner countries. Overall, these brokering mechanisms correspond to what is called a "broad" definition of triangular cooperation. Views differ with regard to how the three main actor types in triangular cooperation ("facilitator", "pivotal country", partner country) should be involved throughout the various phases of cooperation. Some countries and organisations distinguish between "strong"/"narrow" and "weak"/"broad" definitions (OECD 2013, p. 14). According to the former, all partners are involved at each step of the project cycle, from planning, financing, and implementation to evaluation. The German Ministry for Economic Cooperation and Development, for instance, defines triangular cooperation as being "jointly planned, financed and implemented" by all partners together (German Ministry for Economic Cooperation and Development 2013). The broader definition, in contrast, is more flexible and can therefore grasp a wider range of examples. From this perspective, actors can have varying degrees of involvement throughout the project or programme cycle (e.g. planning and funding by the Northern donor, implementation by partners from the pivotal and partner countries).

29.4 Why Does India Engage in Triangular Cooperation?

India's motivations for engaging in triangular cooperation cannot be considered separately from determinants of India's development cooperation in general. Throughout different phases of its history, India's development cooperation "has always been driven by a mix of strategic and prestige-related motives" (Mukherjee 2015, p. 180). In addition to Southern solidarity and the desire to acquire international prestige, motivating factors also include a range of economic and political interests (Fuchs and Vadlamannati 2013). Similarly, a mix of all these factors is likely to influence India's engagement in triangular cooperation. For instance, it would be plausible to assume that India's support of UN-based funds is closely related to motives around Southern solidarity, global responsibility, and international prestige (also in view of achieving ambitions such as a permanent seat in the United Nations Security Council).

However, determining the reasons behind India's engagement in triangular cooperation in a more consistent manner is difficult, as this modality is still only a minor aspect of India's role as a global development partner. Referring to the limited role of triangular cooperation in India's development cooperation is not necessarily only a quantitative argument. Triangular cooperation is usually not a dominant expenditure item for any development actor, not even for countries that have a reputation for being highly active users of this modality. A more important impediment to identifying motivating factors is that India has not prominently showcased triangular cooperation as part of its development partnerships until now, at least not when it comes to such partnerships with Northern donors.

Part of the reason why India has been reluctant to engage with Northern donors for so long is a lack of clear incentives. Interestingly, India and China, which both avoided triangular cooperation with Northern donors until recently, are now becoming more active in this modality at the same time. China engages in partnerships with Northern donors to address critical perceptions of its growing external footprint and to demonstrate that it is a reliable international actor willing to learn from other partners (United Nations Development Programme 2016). Mutual learning and assuming growing global responsibilities are equally relevant to India's engagement in triangular cooperation. In view of growing global demands on India as a rising power, cooperation with international partners can help bridge gaps in India's capacity to deliver development partnerships. Observers of India's development cooperation expect "enormous potential gains to be made through improved trilateral donor cooperation" (Chaturvedi 2012b, p. 575). For India, triangular cooperation is therefore an option to satisfy growing demand for cooperation and assume global responsibility without straining the capacity of its own official development partnerships.

Bolstering capacity to act as a development partner also matters for India in the context of a challenging geopolitical environment. India's recent political endorsement of triangular cooperation correlates closely with China's announcement of the "Belt and Road Initiative" (BRI) in 2013. India is among the most vocal critics of China's flagship infrastructure and connectivity initiative, having raised concerns about the BRI's political and security implications in its neighbourhood (Baruah 2018). Since 2015, India has endorsed triangular cooperation (or references to cooperation in third countries) at the highest political level with partners such as the United States, Japan, the United Kingdom, the European Union, and France.[5] Moreover, triangular cooperation with the United Kingdom and the United States has acquired a more official dimension through the adoption of guiding documents. The MEA India and USAID signed a "Statement of Guiding Principles on Triangular Cooperation for Global Development" in 2014 (MEA India 2014). Moreover, the US Millennium Challenge Cooperation and the DPA signed a "Joint Statement on Cooperation" in 2017 to strengthen regional integration and connectivity, especially in the areas of energy, trade, and investment (US Millennium Challenge Cooperation and Development Partnership Administration 2017). In 2015, the MEA India and DFID signed the "Statement of Intent on Partnership for Cooperation in Third Countries" (MEA India and DFID 2015). Overall, triangular cooperation has increasingly been integrated as an appendix to broader political, security, and economic relationships with like-minded partners, with China's growing global footprint being a relevant—but not the only—factor in the international context.

Against this background, India aims to construct its own global role by differentiating its approaches from the "top-down" approaches of both Northern donors and China, while at the same time seeking cooperation with both. India's positioning has become more pragmatic, drawing on different partnership geometries depending on the strategic context and the issue concerned. In some cases, India seeks to distance itself from Northern donors by cooperating with China in the BRICS framework, for instance by creating new development finance institutions, such as the New Development Bank and the Asian Infrastructure Investment Bank. At the Wuhan summit in 2017, India and China evoked the possibility of Indo-Chinese triangular cooperation with Afghanistan (Varma 2018). In other cases, India has projected criticism at China that it usually voices against Northern donors. In these cases, India constructs partnerships, including triangular cooperation with Northern donors, to offer developing countries additional options to China's growing global footprint as a development partner.

This fluid positioning between contestation and cooperation raises the question to what extent India's growing engagement in triangular cooperation can be interpreted through this volume's main theme of contested cooperation. Some aspects of India's global engagement, such as the establishment of the New Development Bank and the Asian Infrastructure Investment Bank in the BRICS framework, have already been analysed from similar perspectives, such as "contested global governance" (Zürn 2018) or "contested multilateralism" (Morse and Keohane 2014). In a similar vein, India's engagement in triangular cooperation could be considered as a strategy to reshape existing institutions of development cooperation or create new ones. However, as far as the cases of Indian participation in triangular cooperation discussed above are concerned, they do not lend themselves as clear-cut examples of contested cooperation. For instance, India's UN-based triangular funds are clearly not an attempt to challenge the UN. On the contrary, these funds are an expression of India's support for the UN system and a demonstration of its willingness to assume more global responsibility.

In the case of triangular cooperation with Northern donors, India does not yet have a sufficiently strategic approach to be able to draw on triangular cooperation as a means of contested cooperation. In other words, there is no strong evidence to suggest that India actively steers triangular relationships with donors such as USAID or DFID to achieve specific strategic objectives. In the mentioned examples, the Indian government's operational support for the implementation of triangular projects outside of India remains weak, given line ministries' focus on domestic concerns and capacity limitations in the foreign service. As a consequence, the role of Northern donor agencies as brokers of cooperation is still driving these partnerships. Rather than India actively drawing on triangular cooperation to change the norms, ideas, and institutions of development cooperation, Northern donors hope to integrate India into the existing architecture of development cooperation. However, the overall weak government-to-government dimension of this type of triangular cooperation limits influence in both ways. Northern donors do not substantially influence India's development cooperation, nor does India actively use triangular cooperation to challenge and reshape global institutions of development cooperation. In short, triangular cooperation between India and Northern donors has so far had little mutual influence on their approaches to development cooperation.

29.5 Shaping Narratives and Institutions Through Triangular Platforms

Although contested cooperation cannot provide a convincing explanation for the current practice of India's engagement in triangular cooperation, it might still help in understanding other innovative aspects of India's cooperation with Northern donor countries. One such aspect is the emergence of larger cooperation frameworks, which will be described here as "triangular platforms", to (re)shape narratives and institutions of global development. Three examples illustrate how India has been initiating or engaging in such platforms: the AAGC, the ISA, and the GFCE.

This chapter uses the term "triangular platform" as an analytical perspective through which important aspects of India's global engagement as a development partner can be understood and interpreted. However, the use of this term does not suggest that the examples in this chapter constitute a new empirical reality in global affairs. Nor does the term replace other concepts that already grasp the mentioned examples as empirical phenomena. As an inter-governmental treaty-based organisation headquartered in India, the ISA, for instance, is conceptually already covered as an international organisation. The nature of the GFCE can be understood with concepts such as "multi-stakeholder partnership" or "polycentric institutions" with the participation of both public and private actors in global governance (e.g. Ostrom 2012). Finally, the AAGC could simply be considered as a bilateral statement of intent between Japan and India. The term "triangular platform" is therefore not necessary to establish the empirical existence of these different examples. However, drawing on this new term—based on the underlying logic of triangular cooperation—highlights certain main characteristics that all these examples have in common.

These platforms share basic characteristics with triangular cooperation, notably the combination of different types of actors. Similar to a conventional understanding of triangular cooperation, triangular platforms combine the comparative advantages of Northern and Southern providers of development cooperation to address challenges in developing countries. They all provide space for collaboration among different actor types, including rising powers, developing and industrialised countries, as well as international organisations and various non-state actors.[6]

With the AAGC, for instance, India and Japan aim to link economies from Asia and Africa through physical infrastructure as well as institutional, regulatory, and digital connectivity (Research and Information System for Developing Countries [RIS] et al. 2017). Combining the comparative advantages of India, Japan, and other international partners, the AAGC aims to facilitate the sharing of development experience among Asian and African countries. Similarly, the ISA was launched under the leadership of India and France. It provides a platform for cooperation to promote the use of solar energy and reduce dependency on fossil fuels in developing countries. The ISA aims to address the particular set of challenges that solar resource-rich countries face with regard to energy access, energy equity, and affordability. To this end, ISA member countries and other stakeholders cooperate on a voluntary basis in programmes and activities that facilitate the use of solar energy, including access to finance, sharing of solar technologies and innovations, research, and capacity-building (International Solar Alliance 2016). Finally, the GFCE is a multi-stakeholder platform for cooperation among countries, international organisations, and private companies to strengthen cyber capacity and expertise globally. In its early phase, the GFCE was strongly driven by European countries, especially the Netherlands. However, India's engagement as a member country, hosting the GFCE in November 2017, has added triangular features to the platform. As such, the platform aims to support developing countries in reaping the benefits of digital development while managing risks related to cyberspace. To this end, the GFCE aims to promote more effective international cooperation in the area of cyber capacity-building (Global Forum on Cyber Expertise [GFCE] 2017).

The perspective of triangular platforms constitutes a fundamental change from conventional definitions of triangular cooperation, which focuses on the level of specific projects, programmes, or other activities, especially as a modality for the implementation of development cooperation. In contrast, triangular platforms shift the perspective from implementation to a higher level of analysis. To be sure, the inclusive composition of these platforms beyond traditional North-South divides opens up new space for triangular projects, programmes, or other activities in the traditional sense. However, this is not their main purpose, as their implementation can also be realised through the usual bilateral or multilateral channels. The first initiatives of the ISA, for instance, consisted of an announcement by the Indian government to extend more than $1 billion of Indian lines of credit to partner countries; that is, the implementation phase draws on a tool from India's normal bilateral cooperation (MEA India 2018). Such examples raise questions about the relevance of the conventional understanding of triangular cooperation as projects and programmes for India and other developing countries. The specific geometry of triangular cooperation—bringing together diverse actors from the North and the South—can yield more significant opportunities than the limited exchange of knowledge and experiences. Most importantly, these platforms embody an innovative way of shaping policy narratives and institutional frameworks in specific issue areas.

In this sense, triangular platforms can be understood in terms of contested cooperation. However, the target is not the global aid architecture as such. The Delhi Communiqué, agreed at the GFCE meeting in 2017, is instructive in this regard (GFCE 2017). The communiqué, which outlines general principles to enhance cooperation on cyber capacity-building, is one of the rare documents in which India has subscribed to the development effectiveness principles of the Global Partnership for Effective Development Cooperation. Rather than countering the global aid architecture in general, triangular platforms aim to influence issue-specific norms, standards, and institutions in areas such as connectivity, clean energy, and digital development.

The AAGC, for instance, can be understood as an attempt to shape narratives and institutions of connectivity. The global landscape of connectivity is currently strongly influenced by China's important role in this area of cooperation. India has expressed reservations about China's approach to connectivity, especially the BRI, being concerned that such initiatives might unilaterally determine a connectivity model and undercut international standards (Saran 2018). India's criticism is rhetorically mirrored by the AAGC's emphasis on quality infrastructure and people-centred connectivity (RIS et al. 2017). Although the AAGC should not be considered as an effort to compete with China's connectivity initiatives, it represents an attempt to shape a different connectivity paradigm.

The cases of the ISA and the GFCE illustrate how India and Northern partners shape new institutions in issue areas where the interests and needs of developing countries have so far not been met by the multilateral system. For instance, Northern donors and the global climate regime have yet to live up to their commitments towards the Global South in terms of access to finance and technology transfer for clean energy. The ISA's geographical definition (with a focus on countries located between the Tropic of Cancer and the Tropic of Capricorn) symbolises a re-balancing from Northern countries as the sources of finance and technology, towards developing countries as the sources of the largest growth in demand for energy in the coming decades. The Indian prime minister's description of the ISA as the "OPEC [Organization of the Petroleum Exporting Countries]" of the future underlines the general idea of empowering developing countries to become major actors in the field of clean energy (Mohan 2018).

Finally, India's increasing engagement with the GFCE is shifting global narratives on Internet governance and standards in cyber capacity-building. As a "swing state" in the debate about Internet governance, India rallies with Western partners to support the model of a free and open Internet governed by a multi-stakeholder approach. At the same time, India promotes the right of developing countries to close the digital divide and develop digital economies that leave room for domestically grown digital solutions and are not subject to technological domination from large global companies.

29.6 Conclusion

India's growing presence in triangular cooperation gives new weight to this niche modality of development cooperation. It also opens up opportunities to address global development challenges in new types of partnerships. India's role in triangular cooperation holds the promise of substantially scaling-up knowledge-sharing among developing countries as a contribution to achieving the SDGs.

India's practice also spearheads new trends. The triangular programmes supported by DFID and USAID, for instance, demonstrate innovative approaches to strengthening the role of non-state actors in triangular cooperation. In the case of IBSA and the DPF, India has taken on roles that go far beyond the sharing of knowledge and experience usually associated with pivotal countries by conceptualising Southern-driven funds and providing (co-)funding. Overall, however, India's experience does not fit easily with narrow definitions that prevail in the international debate around this modality. In particular, the emergence of triangular platforms in key areas of global development, such as connectivity, clean energy, and digital development, provides larger frameworks for collective action beyond small-scale knowledge-sharing. These innovations challenge existing analytical perspectives on triangular cooperation.

The Indian experience should therefore inform the theoretical and practical debate on triangular cooperation more strongly. India's long absence from this debate can partly be explained by its reluctance to engage in triangular cooperation. However, Indian experiences also lack visibility in the analysis of triangular cooperation because they are not yet adequately accommodated by existing definitions and concepts. The emerging practice of India's engagement in triangular cooperation cannot be easily grasped by the predominantly technocratic discourse around mechanisms, operational guidelines, etc. India's practice of triangular cooperation calls into question the emphasis on narrow definitions as the "gold standard" for identifying triangular cooperation.

Most importantly, India's experience calls into question the dominant focus on particular models of designing and implementing projects, programmes, and other activities as the central criteria for identifying triangular cooperation. This chapter proposes to include a higher level of analysis on which Northern and Southern partners engage in shaping narratives and institutions of global development. The AAGC, the ISA, and the GFCE illustrate how the rationale of triangular cooperation can be reframed as providing platforms to facilitate the participation of developing countries in creating the global environment on which their development trajectories depend. Implementation under these larger frameworks does not necessarily need to be triangular, and it can be done in the way that is most effective. Being jointly engaged in every single phase of projects or programmes—as per conventional concepts of triangular cooperation—can improve mutual learning and knowledge-sharing. But it is not an end in itself and does not automatically lead to increased ownership of developing countries. Fulfilling the promises of triangular cooperation also depends on the extent to which triangular cooperation facilitates Southern influence on norms, rules, and institutions of global development. Understood in this way, the modality would gain more traction in India and other developing countries.

Finally, this volume's conceptual perspective on cooperation and contestation sheds light on important dynamics behind India's evolving practice of triangular cooperation. India's positioning has become more flexible than in the past, drawing on different partnership geometries, depending on the strategic context and the issues concerned. Triangular cooperation with Northern donors is one element of these dynamics. However, not every aspect of India's engagement in triangular cooperation can be understood through the prism of cooperation and contestation. Above all, India's approach is not yet entirely guided by a strategy, but it still happens largely by default, driven by broader foreign policy shifts, path dependencies, and capacity constraints. However, given India's growing role as a global development actor, there is a strong case for India's foreign policy and development community to adopt a more active stance in leading and shaping triangular cooperation.

Notes

1. This chapter uses the term "triangular" synonymous with "trilateral". Although a case can be made for distinguishing the two terms, discussions around terminology are not the main objective of this chapter.
2. This chapter uses the term "Northern donors" to refer to member countries of the OECD/DAC.
3. This chapter builds on Paulo (2018) and research conducted by the author during his stay at the Observer Research Foundation in New Delhi.
4. The examples are based on Paulo (2018) and drawn from the business cases and annual reviews published on the DFID Development Tracker: https://devtracker.dfid.gov.uk/.
5. See, for instance, India–US Joint Statement "The United States and India: Enduring Global Partners in the 21st Century", Washington DC, 7 June 2016. India–Japan Joint Statement during the state visit of Prime Minister Narendra Modi, Tokyo, 11 November 2016. Joint Statement during the visit of UK Prime Minister Theresa May to India, "Indi a–UK Strategic Partnership Looking Forward to a Renewed Engagement: Vision for the Decade Ahead", New Delhi, 7 November 2016.. Joint Statement of the 14th India–EU Summit, New Delhi, 6 October 2017. India–France Joint Statement during state visit of president of France to India, 10 March 2018.
6. It could of course be argued that this characteristic is present in most international organisations, such as the UN and the World Trade Organisation, as these organisations also bring together countries of different income levels from the North and the South. However, this chapter uses the term "triangular platforms" for organisations, partnerships, and other initiatives that are (1) not universal (i.e. not covering close to all countries in the world) and (2) co-created or co-shaped by collaboration between a (or several) Northern donor(s) and an (or several) emerging country (countries) with the main objective to support developing countries in a specific issue area.

References

Abbott, K., Genschel, P., Snidal, D., & Zangl, B. (2015). Orchestration: Global governance through intermediaries. In K. Abbott, P. Genschel, D. Snidal, & B. Zangl (Eds.), *International organizations as orchestrators* (pp. 3–36). Cambridge: Cambridge University Press.

Abdenur, A. E., & Marques da Fonseca, J. M. E. (2013). The North's growing role in South-South cooperation: Keeping the foothold. *Third World Quarterly, 34*(8), 1475–1491.

Baruah, D. (2018, August). *India's answer to the belt and road: A road map for South Asia* (Carnegie India Working Paper). Washington, DC: Carnegie Endowment for International Peace.

Chaturvedi, S. (2012a). India's development cooperation: Expressing Southern solidarity. In S. Chaturvedi, T. Fues, & E. Sidiropoulos (Eds.), *Development cooperation and emerging powers: New partners or old patterns?* (pp. 169–189). London and New York, NY: Zed Books.

Chaturvedi, S. (2012b). India's development partnership: Key policy shifts and institutional evolution. *Cambridge Review of International Affairs, 25*(4), 557–577.

Chaturvedi, S. (2015). The emerging institutional architecture of India's development cooperation. In E. Sidiropoulos, et al. (Eds.), *Institutional architecture and development: Responses from emerging powers* (pp. 138–154). Johannesburg: South African Institute of International Affairs.

Chaturvedi, S. (2016, June). *The development compact: A theoretical construct for South-South cooperation* (RIS Discussion Paper #203). New Delhi: Research and Information System for Developing Countries.

Fuchs, A., & Vadlamannati, K. C. (2013). The needy donor: An empirical analysis of India's aid motives. *World Development, 44*(C), 110–128.

German Ministry for Economic Cooperation and Development. (2013). *Triangular cooperation in German development cooperation* (BMZ Strategy Paper 5/2013e). Bonn: Author.

GFCE (Global Forum on Cyber Expertise). (2017, November 24). *Delhi communiqué on a GFCE global agenda for cyber capacity building*. https://www.thegfce.com/binaries/gfce/documents/publications/2017/11/24/delhi-communique/Delhi+Communiqu%C3%A9.pdf.

Harris, D., & Vittorini, S. (2018). Taking "development cooperation" and South-South discourse seriously: Indian claims and Ghanaian responses. *Commonwealth and Comparative Politics, 56*(3), 360–378.

IBSA. (n.d.). *The IBSA fund*. http://www.ibsa-trilateral.org.

IBSA & UNOSSC (United Nations Office for South-South Cooperation). (2018). *2018 overview of project portfolio*. http://www.ibsa-trilateral.org/images/IBSA_Fund_Report_2018.pdf.

International Solar Alliance. (2016). *Framework agreement on the establishment of the international solar alliance (ISA)*. http://isolaralliance.org/docs/Framework%20Agreement%20of%20ISA-English%20Version.pdf.

McEwan, C., & Mawdsley, E. (2012). Trilateral development cooperation: Power and politics in emerging aid relationships. *Development and Change, 43*(6), 1185–1209.

MEA India (Ministry of External Affairs India). (2014, November 3). *India and US expand development cooperation in Asia and Africa*. https://mea.gov.in/press-releases.htm?dtl/24184/India+and+US+Expand+Development+Cooperation+in+Asia+and+Africa.

MEA India. (2018, March 11). *List of solar projects under GoI-LOCs for announcement at ISA founding conference*. https://mea.gov.in/bilateral-documents.htm?dtl/29606/List_of_solar_projects_under_GoILOCs_for_announcement_at_ISA_Founding_Conference.

MEA India & DFID (Department for International Development). (2015, November 10). *Statement of intent on partnership for cooperation in third countries*. http://mea.gov.in/Images/pdf1/statemet_2015_11_12.pdf.

Miller, M. C., & Sullivan de Estrada, K. (2017). Pragmatism in Indian foreign policy: How ideas constrain Modi. *International Affairs, 93*(1), 27–49.

Mitchell, A. (2011, February 15). *Emerging powers and the international development agenda*. Transcript of a speech delivered at Chatham House, London. https://www.chathamhouse.org/sites/default/files/public/Meetings/Meeting%20Transcripts/150211mitchell.pdf.

Mohan, R. (2003). *Crossing the rubicon: The shaping of India's new foreign policy*. New Delhi: Viking.

Mohan, V. (2018, October 3). ISA could replace OPEC as key global energy supplier in future: PM Modi. *The Times of India*. https://timesofindia.indiatimes.com/

india/isa-could-replace-opec-as-key-global-energy-supplier-in-future-pm-modi/art icleshow/66044985.cms.

Mohanty, S. K. (2016). Shaping Indian development cooperation: India's mission approach in a theoretical framework. In S. Chaturvedi & A. Mulakala (Eds.), *India's approach to development cooperation* (pp. 1–13). London and New York, NY: Routledge.

Morse, J. C., & Keohane, R. O. (2014). Contested multilateralism. *The Review of International Organizations, 9*(4), 385–412.

Mukherjee, R. (2015). India's international development program. In D. M. Malone, R. Mohan, & S. Raghavan (Eds.), *The Oxford handbook of indian foreign policy* (pp. 173–187). Oxford: Oxford University Press.

OECD (Organisation for Economic Co-operation and Development). (2013, May). *Triangular cooperation: What's the literature telling us? Literature review prepared by the OECD development co-operation directorate*. Paris: Author.

OECD. (2017, May). *Dispelling the myths of triangular co-operation—Evidence from the 2015 OECD survey on triangular co-operation* (OECD Development Policy Papers No. 6). Paris: Author.

Ostrom, E. (2012). Nested externalities and polycentric institutions: Must we wait for global solutions to climate change before taking action at other scales? *Economic Theory, 49*(2), Special Issue on Economic Theory and the Global Environment, 353–369.

Paulo, S. (2018, March). *India as a partner in triangular development cooperation: Prospects for the India-UK partnership for global development* (ORF Working Paper). New Delhi: Observer Research Foundation.

Rajasekaran, N. (2006, May). *External evaluation of the triangular institutional co-operation II phase 2003–2005*. Oslo: Development Fund.

RIS, ERIA, & IDE-JETRO (Research and Information System for Developing Countries, Economic Research Institute for ASEAN and East Asia, and Institute for Developing Economies/Japan External Trade Organization). (2017, May 22–26). *Asia Africa growth corridor: Partnership for sustainable and innovative development*. http://www.eria.org/Asia-Africa-Growth-Corridor-Document.pdf.

Saran, S. (2018, April 12). Why regional connectivity in South Asia should be a strategic priority for India. *Hindustan Times*. https://www.hindustantimes.com/analysis/why-regional-connectivity-in-south-asia-should-be-a-strategic-priority-for-india/story-F54OnZRLWM22kbr2LmS7BM.html.

UN (United Nations). (2012, May). *Framework of operational guidelines on United Nations support to South-South and triangular cooperation SSC/17/3 (2012)*. Note by the Secretary-General, High-level Committee on South-South Cooperation, 17th session. New York, NY: Author.

UN. (2015a). *Transforming our world: The 2030 agenda for sustainable development (A/RES/70/1)*. New York, NY: Author.

UN. (2015b). *Addis Ababa action agenda of the third international conference on financing for development*. Final text of the outcome document, endorsed by the General Assembly in resolution 60/313 on 27 July 2015. https://www.un.org/esa/ffd/wp-content/uploads/2015/08/AAAA_Outcome.pdf.

UN. (2018, June 8). *India-UN fund gets 22 development projects off the ground in first year*. https://news.un.org/en/story/2018/06/1011791.

United Nations Development Programme. (2016, August). *Trilateral cooperation with China. Sharing China's development experience through innovative partnerships* (UNDP Discussion Paper). Beijing: Author.

UNOSSC (United Nations Office for South-South Cooperation). (2017a, July 14). *India intensifies South-South collaboration through the United Nations.* https://www.undp.org/content/undp/en/home/presscenter/pressreleases/2017/07/14/india-intensifies-south-south-collaboration-through-the-united-nations.html.

UNOSSC. (2017b, October 5). *India to support reconstruction and rehabilitation efforts in hurricane affected countries.* https://www.unsouthsouth.org/2017/10/05/india-to-support-reconstruction-and-rehabilitation-efforts-in-hurricane-affected-countries/.

UNOSSC. (2019, January 11). *India-funded project garners praise for livelihood improvements in Chad.* https://www.unsouthsouth.org/2019/01/11/india-funded-project-garners-praise-for-livelihood-improvements-in-chad/.

US Millennium Challenge Corporation & Development Partnership Administration. (2017, January 13). *Joint statement on cooperation between the millennium challenge corporation of the United States of America and the development partnership administration of the ministry of external affairs of India.* https://mea.gov.in/bilateral-documents.htm?dtl/27937/Joint_Statement_on_Cooperation_between_the_Millennium_Challenge_Corporation_of_the_United_States_of_America_and_the_Development_Partnership_Administra.

USAID (United States Agency for International Development). (n.d.-a). *USAID/India: Country development cooperation strategy 2012–2016.* http://pdf.usaid.gov/pdf_docs/pdacx592.pdf.

USAID. (n.d.-b). *US-India triangular cooperation.* https://www.usaid.gov/india/us-india-triangular-cooperation.

Varma, K. J. M. (2018, April 28). Wuhan summit: India, China to undertake joint economic project in Afghanistan. *LiveMint.* https://www.livemint.com/Politics/ETJ8tht0aj3TOX4ZEX3GyI/Wuhan-summit-India-China-to-undertake-joint-economic-proje.html.

Zimmermann, F., & Smith, K. (2011). More actors, more money, more ideas for international development co-operation. *Journal of International Development, 23*(5), 722–738.

Zürn, M. (2018). Contested global governance. *Global Policy, 9*(1), 138–145.

Open Access This chapter is licensed under the terms of the Creative Commons Attribution 4.0 International License (http://creativecommons.org/licenses/by/4.0/), which permits use, sharing, adaptation, distribution and reproduction in any medium or format, as long as you give appropriate credit to the original author(s) and the source, provide a link to the Creative Commons license and indicate if changes were made.

The images or other third party material in this chapter are included in the chapter's Creative Commons license, unless indicated otherwise in a credit line to the material. If material is not included in the chapter's Creative Commons license and your intended use is not permitted by statutory regulation or exceeds the permitted use, you will need to obtain permission directly from the copyright holder.

PART VII

The Role of Non-state Actors to the SDGs

CHAPTER 30

Partnerships with the Private Sector: Success Factors and Levels of Engagement in Development Cooperation

Jorge A. Pérez-Pineda and Dorothea Wehrmann

30.1 INTRODUCTION

Practitioners and researchers alike increasingly regard the private sector[1] as a crucial partner for development cooperation (e.g. Nelson and Prescott 2008; Pingeot 2014). Also, international agreements such as the Monterrey Consensus (2002), the Busan Declaration (2011), the Rio+20 outcome document (2012), and the Addis Ababa Action Agenda (2015) all encouraged the formation of public–private partnerships (PPPs) (Pérez-Pineda 2017). With the 2030 Agenda for Sustainable Development, the private sector is considered to be more important than ever. It is a widespread narrative that states need to cooperate with the private sector in order to access knowledge (such as technical expertise) (The North-South Institute 2013) and to fill financial gaps of up to $2.5 trillion annually to implement the Sustainable Development Goals (SDGs) (United Nations Conference on Trade and Development [UNCTAD] 2015, p. 7; United Nations Development Programme 2017). Particularly international organisations such as the Organisation for Economic Co-operation and Development (OECD), the World Bank, and numerous agencies and programmes affiliated with the United Nations (UN) have focussed on the means to incentivise and better include the private sector in

---

J. A. Pérez-Pineda (✉)
Universidad Anáhuac México, Huixquilucan, Estado de México, México

D. Wehrmann
German Development Institute / Deutsches Institut für Entwicklungspolitik (DIE), Bonn, Germany
e-mail: Dorothea.wehrmann@die-gdi.de

© The Author(s) 2021
S. Chaturvedi et al. (eds.), *The Palgrave Handbook of Development Cooperation for Achieving the 2030 Agenda*,
https://doi.org/10.1007/978-3-030-57938-8_30

the development agenda—however, the success so far has been limited (United Nations 2009; Organisation for Economic Co-operation and Development [OECD] 2011; International Labour Organization 2017).

The overall forms of engagement and the contributions of private-sector actors are often not clear. Moreover, researchers have reviewed arrangements with "the business and/or philanthropic sector" often negatively, for example, as providing "limited means to secure the mandated responsibilities of the UN, and [as being] far from transformative in terms of long-term development" (Adams and Martens 2015, p. 113). Instead, actors from the private sector are often considered to be trying to polish their reputations via their engagements in development cooperation (Beisheim and Liese 2014; Said et al. 1995). Particularly partnerships with more powerful multi-national companies are seen to be potentially reproducing patterns of domination, exclusion, and geographical asymmetry (Pattberg and Widerberg 2014). Without regulatory oversight, "progressive, just development outcomes" thus seem uncertain (Mawdsley 2015, 2018).

Others hope that the inclusion of private-sector actors in policy dialogues may influence the negotiation of priorities—ideally, such dialogues may also inspire changing behaviours as a result of "mutual appreciation and learning" (Altenburg 2005, p. 4). Similarly, the more private-sector actors that become involved, discourses and peer-pressure are also seen as means to further "stimulate business solutions that contribute to development" (Davis 2011, p. 17; see also Kindornay and Reilly-King 2013, p. vii, and Tienhaara et al. 2012, p. 47).

Specifically in development cooperation at the country level, however, in many cases private-sector engagement had not proven to be effective (Beisheim and Liese 2014; Romero 2015), as companies focussed on their profits, while some used the SDGs primarily to sell new products and access new markets (Abshagen et al. 2018, p. 7). Still, national development agencies often pursue the strategy of multi-stakeholder approaches that include actors from the private sector in order to reach development goals (Altenburg 2005). This has also been a common practice in the context of South-South cooperation, which has been ascribed a salient role for achieving the 2030 Agenda (United Nations General Assembly 2018), but the quality of these partnerships are being discussed more often in recent years.[2] At the Development Cooperation Forum Argentina High-Level Symposium, for example, the participants agreed on five areas for further work in the preparations for BAPA+40 (the 40th Anniversary of the Buenos Aires Plan of Action on the promotion and implementation of technical cooperation among developing countries). They stated, among other things: "South-South and triangular cooperation must take inclusiveness to a new level. They can help shift the focus *beyond expanding partnerships, to fostering quality multi-stakeholder engagement* that can improve the livelihoods and wellbeing of people" (Development Cooperation Forum 2017, p. 6, emphasis added).

While arguing in favour of multi-stakeholder partnerships, at the same time they demanded more *quality* to meet the shared objective of BAPA+40 and the 2030 Agenda: to transform the world for the better. In this regard, previous research has shown that strategies to incentivise and enhance partnerships with the private sector need to be context- and actor-specific to be successful. Country-specific regulations, the capacities and internal structures of private-sector actors (e.g. between state- and shareholder-owned businesses), as well as the political intentions linked to their engagement in development cooperation differ (Byiers et al. 2015; Chan 2014; Wehrmann 2018). Multi-stakeholder approaches that consider such individual factors may foster their quality (understood here as success in terms of envisioned outcomes) by enhancing the identification and agreement on shared objectives, responsibilities, and monitoring mechanisms, while limiting the possibilities to dominate cooperation in multi-stakeholder partnerships for the sake of individual benefits. But how can this be done in practice?

Concepts of indirect governance, such as the approach of orchestration, guide different actors that share a similar goal and thus support the consideration of individual factors (Abbott et al. 2016; Chan and Pauw 2014). Orchestrators (e.g. multi-stakeholder platforms) provide ideational and material support to like-minded intermediaries (e.g. multi-actor partnerships or partnering countries), who then address individual targets or target groups (e.g. private-sector actors). In this chapter, we apply this concept by considering different levels of engagement for private-sector actors under the current development agenda: We show that it matters whether it is envisioned to incentivise and regulate private-sector engagement *at the global level* (e.g. in multi-stakeholder platforms) or *at the country level* (e.g. with development agencies). Under consideration of these different levels, this chapter examines the question of how partnerships with private-sector actors can become more successful to achieve the 2030 Agenda.

Specifically, this chapter cites two cases of multi-stakeholder partnerships that aim at advancing the implementation of the SDGs at the global level or at the country level by enhancing the engagement of actors from the private sector. This is done in order to show how partnerships apply different strategies to use opportunities and meet challenges that result from their scope. First, we shed light on the case of the Global Partnership for Effective Development Co-operation (GPEDC), a multi-stakeholder platform and multi-actor partnership that intends to be inclusive and global in scope. Different from the majority of multi-actor partnerships, which mainly focus on the means to co-finance sustainable development initiatives when engaging with the private sector, the GPEDC is one of the very few partnerships intending to enhance public–private dialogue and knowledge-sharing (Global Partnership for Effective Development Co-operation [GPEDC] 2018). Due to its global approach, however, it faces the challenge of remaining either rather general or too specific to apply to every SDG partnership (Wehrmann 2018). In this regard, the cases considered at the national level, on the other hand, provide a better understanding of context-specific particularities. The Alliance for Sustainability (AS) serves as one such example: It was one of the first formal initiatives of the Mexican Agency for International Development Cooperation (Agencia Mexicana de Cooperación Internacional para el Desarrollo, AMEXCID) that incorporates the private sector in its strategy to implement the 2030 Agenda. A central challenge that the AS has been facing is to advance institutional capacities to implement projects of the AS and to support its sustainability (Agencia Mexicana de Cooperación Internacional para el Desarrollo [AMEXCID] 2018; Pérez-Pineda 2017). Considering the cases of the GPEDC and of the AS allows us to identify the different challenges and related potentials of private-sector engagement when contributing to development initiatives as knowledge or resource providers at the national and global levels.

This work builds on a desk-based analysis of policy papers, reports, and secondary literature. It also considers information gained from interviews with researchers who focus on multi-stakeholder networks and from political practitioners engaged in the GPEDC and in South-South cooperation. First, this chapter introduces the more general debate on private-sector engagement in development cooperation and discusses the different types of—and relevance ascribed to—multi-actor partnerships. Second, we differentiate between internal and contextual challenges, and we introduce the means to support the success of private-sector engagement in development cooperation in this regard. Third, by investigating specific cases (the GPEDC and the AS), this chapter cites the diversity of private-sector actors and their potentials for engaging at different levels in development cooperation. Based on these cases, this chapter further investigates how the concept of orchestration may enhance the impact of private-sector engagement to achieve the 2030 Agenda. It is important to say that since the current analysis is based on a qualitative approach, there is not a ranking for which the achievements or accomplishments within the framework can be graded. Instead, the cases are helpful for illustrating how internal and contextual challenges in partnerships are adapted and overcome. The last and concluding section summarises the central results for paving the way towards more successful private-sector engagement in development cooperation.

30.2 Classification and Relevance of Partnerships with Actors from the Private Sector in the Context of the SDGs

In the context of the SDGs, the inclusion of the private sector in development cooperation is still contested: Although some hope that companies will address social and environmental challenges and still make a profit (OECD 2018b), others fear that private-sector actors may hijack the 2030 Agenda to access new markets (GPEDC 2019). This fear is also spurred by the multiplicity and diversity of partnerships that exist at present: The UN Sustainable Development Knowledge Platform, for example, currently lists 3828 partnerships for the SDGs. All these partnerships aim to contribute to at least one of the SDGs, and they differ with regard to target groups and main focus areas. Thus, even though partnerships with private-sector actors are nothing new, in addition to the number of partnerships, the forms of cooperation have also multiplied over the past decades. It can be traced back to the Marshall Plan (1948) that governments and the private sector have worked jointly in so-called public–private partnerships on large-scale (infrastructure, reconstruction) projects in which sharing risks and resources was an efficient way to tackle big challenges (Sorel and Padoan 2008). Since the launch of the Millennium Development Goals, it has been recognised at different summits and in declarations related to aid effectiveness and financial development agendas that the current challenges of the world cannot be addressed without partnerships that include actors from the private sector.

Before the SDGs, however, in the context of the Millennium Development Goals, the way to engage with the private sector was still incipient. Prior to the 2030 Agenda, the way to achieve multilateral development objectives, which was a common concern related to private-sector engagement, was to find out which forms of cooperation with actors from the private sector could be proposed beyond PPPs. Until then, PPPs, as a term, was predominantly used in bilateral cooperation—it "originates from the sphere of public procurement, and refers to the transfer of responsibility for performing a public task to a private-sector actor" (Federal Ministry for Economic Cooperation and Development [BMZ] 2011, p. 9). In the literature, corporations are mostly related to the provision of goods and services, investments, employment, and technology (UNCTAD 2005), and by extension through PPPs. Moreover, partnerships with actors from the private sector more generally are envisioned to contribute to the achievement of international development agendas by sharing responsibilities, resources, and costs through different channels such as policy dialogues, value chains, knowledge-sharing, technical cooperation, advice, social investment, and finance (Di Bella et al. 2013). In this way, at least six different forms of cooperation with actors from the private sector have been recognised by practitioners in the field of development cooperation and realised by development agencies in the "Global North" and "Global South" (BMZ 2011, p. 6)[3]:

- sponsoring and co-financing (such as philanthropies),
- multi-stakeholder dialogues and formal networks (such as consultative processes, institutionalised public–private dialogues, multi-stakeholder platforms),
- development partnerships with the private sector (such as strategic alliances, round tables),
- public–private partnerships[4] (such as service contracts, management contracts, leasings, concessions),
- mobilisation and combination of private and public capital (such as structured funds, securitisation, equity participation),

- financial and advisory services for private investment in developing countries (such as loans for manufacturing industries, finance for private infrastructure, and finance for small and medium-sized enterprises).

All these types of engagement with the private sector have acquired relevance in recent years (i.a. OECD 2018a). Thus, it comes as no surprise that multi-actor partnerships with private-sector actors are often considered "as important new mechanisms to help resolve a variety of current governance deficits" (Pattberg and Widerberg 2014, p. 9)—irrespective of the form they may take.

30.3 Means to Support the Success of Private-Sector Engagement in Development Cooperation

In the 2030 Agenda, multi-actor partnerships with actors from the private sector are seen as crucial instruments for implementing the SDGs (SDG 17). The heterogeneity of partnerships and the respective roles that private-sector actors may take in such partnerships matter even more as a determining factor for the success of partnerships directed towards the SDGs when considering the global scope of the 2030 Agenda and the number of different goals that are summarised under the SDGs. Given the different *contextual and internal challenges* they have to deal with, the question of how partnerships with actors from the private sector can be more successful is of central relevance in the debate on how to achieve the 2030 Agenda.

Both the more policy-oriented literature and the global governance literature found that the success of partnership initiatives with the private sector very much depends on the institutional oversight provided, among other things, by governmental development agencies and international organisations. We argue that also the different levels at which development agencies and international organisations operate matter greatly. The strategies developed at these different levels are not necessarily aligned. Legal frameworks, development priorities, and the respective mandates differ and shape cooperation with private-sector actors in various ways.

We thus propose to differentiate between the contextual and internal challenges at three levels of engagement for actors from the private sector that contribute to the implementation of the SDGs (either directly or indirectly): global, national, and individual. The global level involves, among other things, companies collaborating in cross-border initiatives with other non-state and state actors. At the national level, the actor's commitment is in a particular country with actions that matter primarily at the national level. Finally, at the individual level, a company decides on its own to undertake a corporate social responsibility strategy or to adopt a sustainable business model that will align its core business to the 2030 Agenda without being linked, allied, or partnered with someone else. The first two formats of cooperation can be identified as models of cooperation with actors from the private sector, such as multi-stakeholder dialogues, development partnerships, and PPPs.

When investigating these different levels of engagement and looking at the transnational level of engagement, for example, the case of the GPEDC illustrates that—due to its governance structure and the absence of security for private-sector actors—the potentials and benefits arising from their cooperation in such kinds of partnerships have not been clear. Engaging at the national level[5] instead seems to provide more advantages for private-sector actors, allowing, among other things, for better knowledge-exchange on regulating frameworks and potentials for cooperation. In this way, the example from Mexico shows how concrete initiatives such as the AS can promote common goals and incentives among private and public actors. This case, however, also illustrates that—judging from the many actors categorised under the term "private sector"—it is still most often multi-national and large local companies that are addressed by development agencies.

When focussing explicitly on internal challenges in partnerships, more policy-oriented research recommends four central actions to support the success of partnerships with private-sector actors in development cooperation—regardless of the distinct objectives, focus areas, modalities of cooperation, or the actors engaged in different forms of multi-stakeholder cooperation (i.a. Brouwer et al. 2015; Prescott and Stibbe 2017; Tennyson 2011; United Nations Global Compact 2013; see also Wehrmann 2018):

1. to clarify the roles that private-sector actors are expected to perform,
2. to encourage transparent and inclusive dialogues,
3. to clarify and specify regulating frameworks early on, and
4. to select the most suitable private-sector actors when considering the overall objectives of the partnership.

To address contextual challenges, researchers from the field of global governance, on the other hand, have often argued in favour of strategies that derive from context-specific, case-by-case assessments and outlined the heterogeneity of partnerships and networks and the difficulties in comparing them (see i.a. Treichel et al. 2016). Following their analysis of the main factors of success for transnational multi-stakeholder partnerships with private-sector actors in the area of sustainable development, Pattberg and Widerberg (2014) further identify three main categories and nine key aspects that contribute to a successful outcome of partnerships (see Table 30.1).

Table 30.1 Elements contributing to the success of partnerships

Categories	Key aspects
Actors	1. Leadership 2. Partners
Process	3. Goal-setting 4. Funding 5. Management 6. Monitoring, reporting, evaluation, and learning
Context	7. Meta-governance 8. Problem structure 9. Political & social context

Source Based on Pattberg and Widerberg (2014, p. 22)

30.4 Engaging with Private-Sector Actors at the Global Level

As an SDG partnership, the GPEDC focusses on the implementation of SDG 17. It aims at enhancing knowledge-exchange and capacity-building on a global scale (its members currently include 161 countries and 56 international organisations). To engage with private-sector actors in this regard, the GPEDC implemented a business-leaders caucus (to advise on the GPEDC's guidelines for private-sector engagement) and organised specialised policy dialogues and country-level workshops (e.g. in Bangladesh, Egypt, El Salvador, and Uganda) that were guided by studies conducted under the auspices of the GPEDC. All these activities fall into the category of public–private dialogue and relate to the GPEDC's mandate to achieve the 2030 Agenda by "promoting effective development co-operation geared towards ending all forms of poverty and reducing inequality, advancing sustainable development and ensuring that no-one is left behind" (GPEDC 2016, p. 27; Working Party on Aid Effectiveness 2012).

Private-sector actors that engage with the GPEDC are able to participate in events organised by the GPEDC and to learn from and contribute to knowledge-sharing in this regard. Private-sector actors thus receive access to information provided by the members (primarily governments) of the GPEDC, with whom they potentially seek to collaborate as partners in other initiatives (e.g. when entering dialogues with emerging economies). At the same time, they may share their experiences and (knowledge) resources when engaging in dialogues with the members of the GPEDC. More specifically, the GPEDC's monitoring framework, for example, is based on voluntary and country-led reports and provides information on "how effectively governments put in place a conducive environment to maximise the impact of development co-operation and enable contributions from nongovernmental actors" (OECD and United Nations Development Programme 2016, p. 16). Such information can be of help to identify new partners or possibilities for the implementation of initiatives.

The monitoring framework has been criticised, however, for not reflecting the realities in which the GPEDC's partnering actors operate (German Development Institute [DIE] et al. 2017). An exemplary problem that also relates to the GPEDC's limited scope of action when trying to incentivise and regulate private-sector engagement in development cooperation (particularly when considering the four central actions to address the internal challenges outlined above) is that, due to the GPEDC's global scope and membership, the GPEDC integrates very different approaches to development cooperation. A comprehensive and sound monitoring framework has to reflect these differences (specifically via the indicators applied for the respective assessments). Similarly, strategies developed under the auspices of the GPEDC to enhance private-sector engagement in development cooperation need to encompass context-specific particularities in its partnering countries. Such strategies thus seem to face the dilemma of either remaining rather general (which contradicts the preferences of private-sector actors to engage in concrete and short-term activities with predictable outcomes) or being too specific to apply to every country.

To deal with this dilemma and to scale-up the impact of partnerships with private-sector actors by addressing the internal and contextual challenges mentioned before, the GPEDC may act as an orchestrator (see Wehrmann 2018). In general, orchestrators and intermediaries cooperate to achieve a shared goal that they are unable to achieve on their own (such as the implementation of the 2030 Agenda). Instead of determining one strategy that is shared by all collaborating partners, the concept of orchestration supports the integration of different approaches and processes (Caplan 2013). It thus recognises that partners have different visions and means for reaching a common goal and enhances the consideration of different contextual challenges (also with regard to the broader field of development cooperation and global governance) as well as the internal challenges arising from the constellation of cooperating actors in the multi-actor partnerships referred to above. As it is up to the orchestrators to set the goal and the related agenda, however, orchestrators are not apolitical or impartial and obtain a more powerful position if compared to the individual and collaborating intermediaries. Although in some regards the GPEDC already operates as an orchestrator (e.g. by providing ideational and material support to like-minded members that also aim at contributing to the implementation of the 2030 Agenda), a main difference is that the GPEDC develops and recommends the use of specific strategies (e.g. to incentivise private-sector engagement) to reach the common goal. An orchestrator, in contrast, facilitates the knowledge-sharing on strategies but leaves it up to the intermediaries to develop different context-specific approaches to advance the shared goal (Fig. 30.1).

When considering the internal challenges and four suggested actions introduced above (to clarify the roles that private-sector actors are expected to perform, to encourage transparent and inclusive dialogues, to clarify and specify regulating frameworks early on, to select the most suitable private-sector actors when considering the overall objectives of the partnership), for a global actor such as the GPEDC, however, several limitations and potentials arise from the application of this concept.

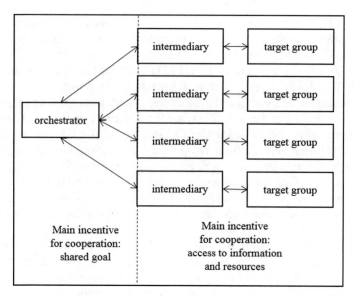

Fig. 30.1 Concept of orchestration (*Source* Wehrmann [2018])

Firstly, regarding the clarification of the roles that private-sector actors are expected to perform, the GPEDC, as an orchestrating actor, is not in the position to assign whether private-sector actors shall contribute, for example, as resource or knowledge providers to (transnational) multi-actor initiatives or in a specific country setting. However, it can contribute to the suggested clarification in this regard by enhancing transparency on the structures and needs of collaborating partners. To also address the related contextual challenges, the GPEDC, as an orchestrator, can improve the "process" (see Pattberg and Widerberg 2014) of incentivising and regulating private-sector engagement in multi-actor initiatives by informing about (discussing and providing) minimum standards for private-sector engagement (such as the Private-Sector Engagement Principles developed under the auspices of the GPEDC) and by encouraging reflection concerning the goal-setting, funding, management, monitoring, and learning in multi-actor initiatives (as aspects considered in the monitoring provided by the GPEDC).

Secondly, encouraging transparent and inclusive dialogues shall help collaborating partners to adapt and balance priorities, allowing private-sector actors, for example, to better classify the potentials and risks of their engagement. However, as an orchestrating actor, the GPEDC cannot interfere in such dialogue. Still, the country workshops organised under the auspices of the GPEDC provide evidence that the GPEDC is able to enhance such dialogue and to address a central internal challenge in this regard. Via its monitoring framework, it further provides institutional oversight that may improve the effectiveness of such dialogue and thus contributes to the establishment of a meta-governance and problem structure, as summarised under the "context" category identified by Pattberg and Widerberg (2014). The country workshops and different summits organised by the GPEDC further encourage knowledge transfers across multi-actor initiatives and contribute to a better understanding and reflection of different political and social contexts.

Thirdly, if regulating frameworks are clarified and specified early on, private-sector actors are more likely to contribute to SDG partnerships. This allows them to develop avenues for balancing different priorities in their endeavours and to justify their cooperation towards their shareholders. Although it is equally important that the GPEDC clarifies and specifies its monitoring framework to avoid any misunderstandings, it is not up to an orchestrating actor to clarify and specify regulating frameworks from partnering countries. Thus, the GPEDC cannot determine the conditions under which its partnering countries collaborate with private-sector actors. This is an internal challenge to be solved at the national levels. However, as mentioned before, the GPEDC can demand and provide transparency on contextual "process" challenges in this regard, for example, concerning the different regulating frameworks that state actors are bound to in their cooperation.

Fourthly, strategies to incentivise private-sector engagement in multi-actor partnerships are more successful if they are adapted towards the specific actor desired to take part in the partnership. It is beyond the scope of the GPEDC to develop such individualised strategies due to the different contexts, the heterogeneity of its partners, and the different functions that private-sector actors may have (e.g. for-profit and state-owned companies). Furthermore, the GPEDC does not obtain the authority to develop such strategies because of the principles to which it is committed. Thus, also this internal challenge cannot be solved at the global level but needs to be addressed at the national level. However, the GPEDC can contribute to the selection process of "actors" by developing recommendations and non-binding guidelines based on experiences from collaborating partners—as it is currently aiming at with its Business Leaders Caucus.

30.5 Engaging with the Private Sector at the National Level

The case of the AS, on the other hand, illustrates how, at the national level, private-sector engagement can be fostered by multi-stakeholder platforms and how they may contribute through alliances with other actors towards the achievement of the SDGs. The AS was founded in 2013, when AMEXCID, the Mexican cooperation agency created in 2011, developed its own "Private-Sector Collaboration Framework", supported by the Deutsche Gesellschaft für Internationale Zusammenarbeit (GIZ). Its main action principles since then have been: (1) to promote platforms of dialogue that consider inclusive business models and corporate social responsibility, (2) to align PPPs with development policies, and (3) to become more cooperation-oriented to improve human capital (Martin et al. 2015).

Although actors from the private sector were not included as relevant actors in the 2011 Mexican Law on International Development Cooperation, the creation of the agency, the launch of the International Development Cooperation Programme 2014–2018 (Programa de Cooperación Internacional para el Desarrollo, PROCID), and later, the narratives promoted by the 2030 Agenda spurred the need to include other non-state actors, such as the private sector, in Mexican development cooperation. The Mexican PROCID 2014–2018, for example, recognised explicitly that the private sector must be included in development cooperation activities of the Mexican government and cites PPPs as one of the main models of engagement (Diario Oficial de la Federación 2014, p. 11).

Accordingly, the AS launched in May 2016 by AMEXCID was designed as a strategic dialogue and cooperation platform with actors from the private sector that may collaborate with civil society, academia, and others. Its purpose has been to promote cooperation projects to achieve the 2030 Agenda in Mexico, Latin America, and the Caribbean. The AS provides contributions (projects oriented towards 5 of the 17 SDGs, as mentioned above) from the local level (a particular country: Mexico) to the regional level (considering the target region that the AS focusses on) by collaborating in particular with the private sector. AMEXCID formed the AS around six principles to guide the effectiveness of cooperation with actors from the private sector to face the challenges of the SDGs in a better way (AMEXCID 2017): (1) shared responsibility in the implementation of the 2030 Agenda, (2) mutual benefits, (3) priority regions, (4) impartiality, (5) transparency and accountability, and (6) replicability. Originally, the AS was supported by 61 firms, 9 entrepreneurial organisations, 12 private foundations, and 4 development agencies.[6]

To make this alliance work and to align efforts towards the SDGs, the participants decided to create five working committees, each of which related to one main SDG: affordable and clean energy (SDG 7), sustainable cities and communities (SDG 11), responsible production and consumption (SDG 12), quality education (SDG 4), and social inclusion (SDGs 8 and 10). AMEXCID saw these issues in particular to be areas where actors from the private sector and AMEXCID could contribute jointly in a more strategic way to cope with two main issues: environmental and social problems in the country.

Even though there is not a quantitative way to measure the degree of achievement so far, following the conceptual framework introduced above, the case of the AS illustrates how it addressed the four proposed actions to overcome internal challenges at the national level (to clarify the roles that private-sector actors are expected to perform; to encourage transparent and inclusive dialogues; to clarify and specify regulating frameworks early on; and to select the most suitable private-sector actors when considering the overall objectives of the partnership) by operating as an orchestrator in parts.

First, the AS succeeded in defining *clear roles* for all involved actors. AMEXCID—the orchestrator—provides support and governance around the sharing of benefits, resources, and risks as well as on the identification of needs; the catalysing of resources for projects; the promotion, design, and coordination of projects; and visibility for the AS. The AS can be considered the intermediate channel to engage the private sector. The private sector is mainly expected to contribute with its technical, financial, and innovative capacities, resources, and infrastructure (AMEXCID 2017, p. 8; 2018, pp. 24, 41–42).

Second, the AS is based on reciprocity (in the sense of what actors from the private sector may bring and take from multi-actor development initiatives). Actors from the private sector that cooperate in strategic alliances with development agencies—as in the case of the AS—benefit from cost-sharing (as a result of the public co-financing), increased legitimacy (minimising the usual prejudice against the private sector related to the negative effects of their activity), and access to complementary specialisation (such as organising stakeholder dialogues or facilitating government contacts), helping them to deal with the public administration and governments (see also Altenburg 2005, pp. 2–4). Furthermore, reciprocity is useful to encourage *transparency in both sides and inclusive dialogue*. In that way, it was proposed, for example, at the fourth meeting of the AS to create a webpage to share best practices and relevant information, as reported by AMEXCID, aligning Mexican cooperation to the principles of "aid effectiveness", transparency, and accountability. This implies that AMEXCID and the private sector, as well as other partners of the AS, are committed to exchanging information, managing cooperation activities jointly, and supporting decisions, thereby facilitating better and more efficient outputs, shared responsibility, and mutual gains (AMEXCID 2017, pp. 5–6).

Third, the AS is based on *clear rules and frameworks* for cooperation, such as the "Collaboration Framework to Engage with the Private Sector" (AMEXCID 2015, pp. 23–42) and PROCID 2014–2018, which is mandated by Mexican law. According to the theoretical elaborations outlined above, the definition of clear roles, the encouragement of transparency, and inclusive dialogue contribute to the success of partnerships. In addition, given these, there may be a "call effect", that means if the incentives are clear, and if there is reciprocity, the multi-stakeholder dialogue will be transparent, efficient, and accountable; in that regard it will generate trust among others, who will see the AS as a good space to be supported and to collaborate with. The improvement of a partnership will be reflected in its success. This also applies to the AS and, when considering the elements that are considered as contributing to the success of multi-stakeholder partnerships (see Table 30.1), the AS shows that it already includes these elements: The objectives and partners of the AS are clear (actors), as are the leadership, contributions, and the management of the process through the five working committees (process), and its governance is aligned with the framework of the SDGs (context).

Finally, for the fourth point, when considering AMEXCID as performing the role of an "orchestrator", it pushes the AS in various ways: By providing the space to meet with other actors, it enhances cooperation in development initiatives and the establishment of strategic links with the public, civil society, foreign governments, international organisations, and particularly with *the most suitable private-sector actors,* offering all of them national and international resources (AMEXCID 2017, p. 8; 2018, pp. 20–35). Up to now, however, most of the private-sector actors collaborating in the AS are transnational companies with branches in Mexico or large firms that seem to have the initiative, interest, resources, and capacity to engage in an ambitious agenda such as the 2030 Agenda. Here we refer to companies such as ABB, AXA, BBVA, Danone, Deloitte, EY, Gruma, Scotiabank, Nestlé, Pepsico, Pfizer, Schneider, Volkswagen, and Volvo, among others (AMEXCID 2017, p. 6). In that line, the AS operates as an intermediary to achieve the 2030 Agenda at the national level by engaging the private sector (target group). Considering the elements around the way the AS works, it is noticeable that this alliance is not based on a hierarchical structure, since, as was explained above, they work around five committees and are thus based on horizontal dialogue.

Based on the latter, AMEXCID, as an orchestrator, facilitates the implementation of the four actions above. At the same time, the AS can be considered as a case that already successfully applies the central actions to regulate and enhance private-sector engagement outlined above (encouraging transparency and inclusive dialogues, defining regulating frameworks and roles for actors from the private sector, as well as selecting the most suitable private-sector actors). However, when examining the Mexican case in light of the orchestration approach, it is not clear whether there is a need for an actor to operate as orchestrator. In the case of the AS, modes of indirect governance do not seem necessary, as there is such close proximity among actors and good relations that the influence can be almost direct. Moreover, the types of actors (companies, countries, or multilateral platforms) facilitate the relationships among themselves, which allows for regular contact due to the good relationships. However, the approach can be useful to map the way actors could be related to each other and the channels of influence needed to enhance the effectiveness of cooperation platforms, since the AS has shown a specific model of cooperation that leads to the achievement of the SDGs.

In sum, the AS works as a platform of cooperation for different actors. It provides a particular "model" of cooperation to integrate the interests, demands, and concerns of the private sector with local problems that are aligned to the 2030 Agenda. In this way, national development agencies such as AMEXCID aim at providing a more inclusive and strategic cooperation beyond borders, particularly in the five SDGs targeted by the AS. Self-assessments of the processes that have been realised through the experience, such as the 2018 "Prototype of the AS" (AMEXCID 2018), provide initial evaluations to improve the process and enhance the quality of private-sector engagement.

30.6 Conclusions and Policy Recommendations

By focussing on different levels of engagement, the cases of the AS and of the GPEDC illustrated how cooperation with private-sector actors in development cooperation can be improved. At the national level, the case of the AS showed that, although guidance provided by a partner with more experience with private-sector engagement stimulated the national development agency to form an alliance with private-sector actors, once it was established, no further indirect governance seemed necessary to keep these actors engaged in the initiative. Instead, horizontal dialogue facilitated the identification of topics that all the engaged actors were interested in working on. In the AS, AMEXCID can be seen as an "orchestrator-light". Even though it implemented the respective committees and has been evaluating the AS, thus taking over institutional responsibilities, AMEXCID does not use intermediaries in its collaboration with private-sector actors but addresses them directly. In contrast, at the global level, the GPEDC would benefit from scaling-up its orchestrating capacities, particularly by providing more institutional regulation to overcome very general approaches that neglect context-specific particularities, thus remaining very vague and not allowing private-sector actors to identify the benefits arising from such collaborations at first glance. However, the GPEDC already operates as an orchestrator when considering its mode of cooperation with national development agencies, which act as intermediaries when providing, for example, all necessary information for the monitoring provided by the GPEDC.

The following lessons emerge from the case of the AS and can be transferred to international dialogues and platforms such as the GEPDC:

1. The case of the AS exemplifies that, at the national level, private-sector actors are already engaged in development initiatives to achieve the 2030 Agenda. In the case of the AS, however, these are mostly multi-national or large local companies and not smaller firms.
2. As a multi-actor partnership, the AS already applies the four central actions often suggested to enhance private-sector engagement in development cooperation. These central actions can be considered as having contributed to the success of the AS in its collaboration with private-sector actors.
3. The AS seems to have also benefitted from the guidance provided by a leading institution (AMEXCID) and its regulatory framework that legitimated the leadership and cooperation with other official, private, social, and international actors.[7]
4. At least in a middle-income country such as Mexico (which plays a dual role in terms of international cooperation as a provider and recipient), it is important that the leading institution (in this case AMEXCID) had the support of development partners with more experience (in this case GIZ), which contributed to the development of responses to the multiple

challenges that come along with the 2030 Agenda requiring collaboration at different levels, not only locally. This is key in a country where there may be some other local priorities and a lack of human resources to develop collaboration frameworks in a short period of time.
5. The case of the AS shows that it is important to work closely with the private sector to define the relevant topics of interest and to align them with the SDGs in a horizontal dialogue so that they make sense to the involved actors and mirror local needs.
6. To advance the implementation of the 2030 Agenda through the engagement of private-sector actors in development initiatives, the AS process provides evidence that clear rules and incentives matter greatly as well as the commitment to acknowledge local needs.

We do not claim that the cases of the AS and of the GPEDC are representative for all multi-actor partnerships. Further evidence and research are needed to investigate whether the identified factors of success are transferable to partnerships in other countries. However, despite the differences also among the two cases examined, from our analysis of internal and contextual challenges at the different levels of engagement in development cooperation, we derived two results that seem central for the success of partnerships with private-sector actors:

1. The cases of the AS and of the GPEDC have shown that, at the national level, it seems to be easier to enhance and maintain the engagement of private-sector actors in development initiatives because the terms of cooperation are more specific. This is particularly relevant in the context of the 2030 Agenda to specify expected outcomes according to local needs and to generate ownership in the process. Thus, national development agencies are important focal points whose efforts need to be strengthened when aiming at incentivising private-sector engagement in development cooperation.
2. To scale-up the impact of multi-stakeholder initiatives with private-sector actors, both at the global and national levels, monitoring frameworks are needed. Although they should be aligned with the 2030 Agenda in order to evaluate the expected outcomes of such initiatives, it is necessary to differentiate between the different formats of multi-actor partnerships and the settings in which they operate. The GPEDC and the AS, for example, try to enhance private-sector engagement for different purposes, as both partnerships are driven by different objectives. Ideally, the evaluation results deriving from such frameworks are used as a basis for further dialogue across the different levels of engagement—for example among AMEXCID and other development agencies in emerging economies or the GPEDC—to enhance knowledge transfer and the identification of unused potentials and challenges for international and South-South initiatives.

Although these results imply responsibilities particularly for governing actors in multi-actor partnerships, there is no doubt that the success of partnerships with private-sector actors depends on the commitment of all involved actors, including private-sector actors. In this way, it is crucial that private-sector actors feel a responsibility to contribute to the implementation of the 2030 Agenda, but at the same time that they acknowledge the principle of country ownership and do not undermine related processes, for example, by not providing access to information that is relevant for monitoring and evaluation mechanisms. However, this is also a matter of communication for which, following the principle of country ownership, governments should be held responsible.

Notes

1. Despite its heterogeneity, scholars and practitioners often relate to "the private sector" or "the business sector" in general terms without specifying the kind of for-profit actor they are referring to. The possibilities and roles of private-sector actors in development cooperation initiatives, however, differ and also depend on their size, structure, and ownership—as do the knowledge, innovations, and investments they may be able to provide to implement the SDGs. In general, particularly small and medium-sized enterprises, multinational corporations, state-owned enterprises, as well as business-related private foundations operating on a non-profit basis are regarded as important partners in sustainable development partnerships. In this chapter, we relate to all these actors when using the term "private sector".
2. When considering the different formats of cooperation that are summarised under the umbrella of South-South Cooperation, it becomes clear that neither practitioners nor researchers share a similar understanding of what South-South cooperation actually (can) encompass(es) (Fues 2016; Renzio and Seifert 2014). It is, however, a widespread perception that collaboration with partners from "the South" is less paternalistic than with traditional partners. This supports the understanding that partnerships are to a greater extent motivated by the notion of solidarity (Argente-Linares et al. 2013; Finance Center for South-South Cooperation 2017; Renzio and Seifert 2014, 1861f.; Stijns 2011; United Nations Executive Office of the Secretary-General and United Nations Framework Convention on Climate Change 2017).
3. For a brief summary of private-sector engagement in the context of the 2030 Agenda and public–private forms of collaboration, see Pérez-Pineda (2017, pp. 97–99), and for a guide to integrate the SDGs through the private sector, see Global Reporting Initiative et al. (2015).
4. Within PPPs, variants can be found that are shaped by a different degree of strategic engagement and number of actors. Hence, authors such as Gómez-Galán and Sainz (2014) and Casado (2007) consider three types: (1) In the context of public–private collaborations, for example, one common format of engagement between the public and private sectors relates to public procurement or subcontracting; (2) public–private partnerships are based on a service or management contract, or joint investments, according to which risks are shared. These two models usually build on a client–provider relationship among

the public and private sectors; (3) public–private partnerships for development (PPPDs) are understood as initiatives in which, apart from actors from the public and private sectors, civil society and academia are involved with joint action, sharing risks, benefits, and targets oriented to development (Mataix et al. 2008, pp. 10–12). PPPDs can be considered as being more consistent with the multi-actor dialogue approaches.

5. The individual level of engagement (potentials and challenges of private-sector actors to collaborate in partnerships) is also of great significance when discussing different levels of engagement, but it is not systematically considered in the chapter, as these internal matters do not directly relate to the question of how multi-stakeholder initiatives can be improved. It is, however, noticeable that companies more often use the 2030 Agenda as a reference point—especially transnational companies that engage in international markets and face the respective competition.

6. Its main objectives are: to share and spread successful cases of using the SDGs into business models; to identify strategic priorities and activities that are pro-SDG between the public and private sectors; to design and implement sustainable development projects in Mexico, Central America, and the Caribbean; to develop capacities for the private sector to implement the SDGs into their business models; to create strategic alliances for development with civil society as well as local and state governments; to define and execute financial plans through development banks, private funds, and other development funds; to build tools for monitoring the advancement of the 2030 Agenda (see: https://www.gob.mx/amexcid/es/acciones-y-programas/alianza-por-la-sostenibilidad).

7. Some of these lessons coincide with findings of Abbott and Bernstein (2015) that are related to conditions for the success of an orchestration strategy, particularly legitimacy and focal institutional position.

References

Abbott, K., & Bernstein, S. (2015). The high-level political forum on sustainable development: Orchestration by default and design. *Global Policy*, 6(3), 222–233.

Abbott, K. W., Genschel, P., Snidal, D., & Zangl, B. (2016). Two logics of indirect governance: Delegation and orchestration. *British Journal of Political Science*, 46(4), 719–729.

Abshagen, M.-L., Cavazzini, A., Graen, L., & Obenland, W. (2018). *Analysis: Hijacking the SDGs? The private sector and the sustainable development goals (Analysis 78)*. https://www.globalpolicy.org/images/pdfs/GPFEurope/Hijacking_the_SDGs.pdf.

Adams, B., & Martens, J. (2015). *Fit for whose purpose? Private funding and corporate influence in the United Nations*. https://sustainabledevelopment.un.org/content/documents/2101Fit_for_whose_purpose_online.pdf.

Altenburg, T. (2005). *The private sector and development agencies: How to form successful alliances. Critical issues and lessons learned from leading donor programs* (DIE Discussion Paper). Bonn: German Development Institute / Deutsches Institut für Entwicklungspolitik (DIE).

AMEXCID (Agencia Mexicana de Cooperación Internacional para el Desarrollo). (2015). "Marco de Colaboración con el Sector Privado para la Cooperación Internacional para el Desarrollo". In J. Martin, D. Angelino, & L. López, *Construcción de una estrategia de colaboración de AMEXCID con el sector privado* (pp. 23–42). Proyecto de Cooperación para el Fortalecimiento Institucional de la AMEXCID (Documento 4). https://www.gob.mx/cms/uploads/attachment/file/124687/160530_Documentacion_Sector_Privado_AMEXCID-_GIZ_Copy_VF.pdf.

AMEXCID. (2017). *Alianza por la sostenibilidad: Visión para la vinculacion con el sector privado.* https://www.gob.mx/cms/uploads/attachment/file/273197/Visi_n_de_la_AxS.pdf.

AMEXCID. (2018). *La alianza por la sostenibilidad: Un prototipo de la AMEXCID para la vinculación con el sector privado.* Ciudad de México: SRE, Author, AxS, GIZ.

Argente-Linares, E., López-Pérez, M. V., & Rodríguez-Ariza, L. (2013). Organizational structure and success of international joint ventures in emerging economies: The case of Spanish-Moroccan SMEs. *Review of Managerial Science, 7*(4), 499–512.

Beisheim, M., & Liese, A. (Eds.). (2014). *Transnational partnerships: Effectively providing for sustainable development?* London: Palgrave Macmillan.

BMZ (Federal Ministry for Economic Cooperation and Development). (2011). *Forms of development cooperation involving the private sector.* https://www.bmz.de/en/publications/archiv/type_of_publication/strategies/Strategiepapier306_05_2011.pdf.

Brouwer, H., Woodhill, J., Hemmati, M., Verhoosel, K., & van Vugt, S. (2015). *The MSP guide: How to design and facilitate multi-stakeholder partnerships.* Wageningen, NL: Centre for Development Innovation.

Byiers, B., Guadagno, F., & Karaki, K. (2015). *From looking good to doing good: Mapping CSO business partnerships* (Discussion Paper No. 182). Maastricht: European Centre for Development Policy Management.

Caplan, K. (2013). *Taking the mythology out of partnerships—A view from the ground up.* http://www.bpdws.org/web/d/DOC_359.pdf?statsHandlerDone=1.

Casado, F. (2007). *Las alianzas público privadas para el desarrollo* (Documento de trabajo no. 9). Madrid: Fundación Carolina- CeALCI.

Chan, S. (2014). *Partnerships for sustainable development emergence: Adaptation and impacts in global and domestic governance contexts.* Dissertation, Amsterdam: Universiteit Amsterdam.

Chan, S., & Pauw, P. (2014). *A global framework for climate action (GFCA): Orchestrating non-state and subnational initiatives for more effective global climate governance* (DIE Discussion Paper 34). Bonn: German Development Institute / Deutsches Institut für Entwicklungspolitik (DIE).

Davis, P. (2011). *The role of the private sector in the context of aid effectiveness.* Consultative findings document. http://www.oecd.org/dac/effectiveness/47088121.pdf.

Development Cooperation Forum. (2017). *DCF Argentina high-level symposium.* https://www.un.org/ecosoc/sites/www.un.org.ecosoc/files/files/en/dcf/dcf-argentina-summary.pdf.

Diario Oficial de la Federación. (2014, April 30). *Decreto por el que se aprueba el Programa de Cooperación Internacional para el Desarrollo 2014-2018.* http://sre.gob.mx/images/stories/marconormativodoc/nor2014/dof300414.pdf.

Di Bella, J., Grant, A., Kindornay, S., & Tissot, S. (2013). *How to engage the private sector for development*. Ottawa: The North-South Institute.

DIE (German Development Institute), Federal Ministry for Economic Cooperation and Development, & Global Partnership for Effective Development Co-operation. (2017). *Towards a shared understanding of effective development co-operation: Learning from different sectors and approaches*. Informal exchange. https://www.die-gdi.de/uploads/tx_veranstaltung/20171124_Informal_Exchange_with_Researchers_from_Emerging_Economies_summary.pdf.

Finance Center for South-South Cooperation. (2017). *South-South cooperation report. Changing roles of South-South cooperation in global development system: Towards 2030*. Hong Kong: Author.

Fues, T. (2016, April 11). *Süd-Süd-Kooperation: Globaler Akteur mit unklarer Identität* (DIE Die aktuelle Kolumne). Bonn: German Development Institute / Deutsches Institut für Entwicklungspolitik (DIE).

Global Reporting Initiative, United Nations Global Compact, & World Business Council for Sustainable Development. (2015). *SDG compass*. https://sdgcompass.org/.

Gómez-Galán, M., & Sainz, H. (2014). *Alianzas público-privadas para resultados de desarrollo: Una guía para la gestión*. Madrid: Fundación CIDEAL.

GPEDC (Global Partnership for Effective Development Co-operation). (2016). *Nairobi outcome document*. http://effectivecooperation.org/wp-content/uploads/2016/12/OutcomeDocumentEnglish.pdf.

GPEDC. (2018). *Agenda 2030: Promoting effective private sector engagement through development co-operation*. http://effectivecooperation.org/wp-content/uploads/2018/01/Private-Sector-Engagement-Concept-Note.pdf.

GPEDC. (2019). *Private sector engagement through development co-operation*. https://effectivecooperation.org/our-work/2017-2018-programme-of-work/private-sector-engagement-through-development-co-operation/.

International Labour Organization. (2017). *Tripartite declaration of principles concerning multinational enterprises and social policy*. Fifth Edition. http://www.ilo.org/wcmsp5/groups/public/—ed_emp/—emp_ent/—multi/documents/publication/wcms_094386.pdf.

Kindornay, S., & Reilly-King, F. (2013). *Investing in the business of development: Bilateral donor approaches to engaging with the private sector*. http://www.nsi-ins.ca/wp-content/uploads/2013/01/2012-The-Business-of-Development.pdf.

Martin, J., Angelino, D., & López, L. (2015). *Construcción de una estrategia de colaboración de AMEXCID con el sector privado*. Proyecto de Cooperación para el Fortalecimiento Institucional de la AMEXCID (Documento 4). https://www.gob.mx/cms/uploads/attachment/file/124687/160530_Documentacion_Sector_Privado_AMEXCID-_GIZ_Copy_VF.pdf.

Mataix, C., Sánchez, E., Huerta, M. A., & Lumbreras, J. (2008). *Cooperación para el desarrollo y alianzas público-privadas: Experiencias internacionales y recomendaciones para el caso español* (Documento de trabajo no. 20). Madrid: Fundación Carolina-CeALCI.

Mawdsley, E. (2015). DFID, the private sector and the re-centring of an economic growth agenda in international development. *Global Society, 29*(3), 339–358.

Mawdsley, E. (2018). "From billions to trillions": Financing the SDGs in a world "beyond aid". *Dialogues in Human Geography, 8*(2), 191–195.

Nelson, J., & Prescott, D. (2008). *Business and the millennium development goals: A framework for action*. London and New York, NY: United Nations Development Programme and the International Business Leaders Forum.

OECD (Organisation for Economic Co-operation and Development). (2011). *OECD guidelines for multinational enterprises*. Paris: OECD Publishing.

OECD. (2018a). *Global outlook on financing for sustainable development 2019: Time to face the challenge*. Paris: OECD Publishing.

OECD. (2018b). *Development co-operation report 2018: Joining forces to leave no one behind*. Paris: OECD Publishing.

OECD & United Nations Development Programme. (2016). *Making development co-operation more effective: 2016 progress report*. Paris: OECD Publishing.

Pattberg, P., & Widerberg, O. (2014). *Transnational multi-stakeholder partnerships for sustainable development: Building blocks for success*. http://dx.doi.org/10.2139/ssrn.2480302.

Pérez-Pineda, J. A. (2017). El sector privado en el cumplimiento de los ODS: La experiencia Mexicana. *Revista Española de Desarrollo y Cooperación, 40*, 93–103.

Pingeot, L. (2014). *La influencia empresarial en el proceso post-2015: Cuadernos 2015 y más. Obeservatorio de Multinacionales en América Latina*. http://omal.info/IMG/pdf/cuaderno_4_digital.pdf.

Prescott, D., & Stibbe, D. (2017). *Better together: Unleashing the power of the private sector to tackle non-communicable diseases. A guidebook for collaboration between non-profit organisations and businesses*. Oxford, Geneva, and London: The Partnering Initiative, Union for International Cancer Control, and Bupa.

Renzio, P. d., & Seifert, J. (2014). South-South cooperation and the future of development assistance: Mapping actors and opinions. *Third World Quarterly, 35*(10), 1860–1875.

Romero, M. J. (2015). *What lies beneath? A critical assessment of PPPs and their impact on sustainable development*. http://eurodad.org/files/pdf/559e6c832c087.pdf.

Said, A. A., Lerche, C. O., Jr., & Lerche, C. O., III. (1995). *Concepts of international politics in global perspective*. Englewood Cliffs, NJ: Prentice Hall.

Sorel, E., & Padoan, P. C. (2008). *The marshall plan: Lessons learned for the 21st century*. Paris: OECD Publishing.

Stijns, J.-P. (2011). Africa's emerging partnerships. *OECD Observer, 285*(Q2), 17–18.

Tennyson, R. (2011). *The partnering toolbook: An essential guide to cross-sector partnering*. https://thepartneringinitiative.org/wp-content/uploads/2014/08/Partnering-Toolbook-en-20113.pdf.

The North-South Institute. (2013). *Mapping private sector engagements in development cooperation*. http://www.nsi-ins.ca/wp-content/uploads/2013/09/Mapping-PS-Engagment-in-Development-Cooperation-Final.pdf.

Tienhaara, K., Orsini, A., & Falkner, R. (2012). Global corporations. In F. Biermann & P. Pattberg (Eds.), *Global environmental governance reconsidered* (pp. 45–68). Cambridge, MA: The MIT Press.

Treichel, K., Höh, A., Biermann, S., & Conze, P. (2016). *Multi-Akteurs-Partnerschaften im Rahmen der Agenda 2030: Eine praxisorientierte Analyse von Potentialen, Herausforderungen und Erfolgsfaktoren*. https://www.partnerschaften2030.de/wp-content/uploads/2017/09/Viadrina_Governance_MAP-Studie_WEB.pdf.

UNCTAD (United Nations Conference on Trade and Development). (2005). *UNCTAD: Positive corporate contributions to the economic and social development of host developing countries, TD/B/COM.2/EM.17/2.* https://unctad.org/en/Docs/c2em17d2_en.pdf.

UNCTAD. (2015). *UNCTAD: Investing in sustainable development goals: Action plan for private investments in SDGs.* https://unctad.org/en/PublicationsLibrary/osg2015d3_en.pdf.

United Nations. (2009). *Guidelines on cooperation between the United Nations and the business sector.* http://www.un.org/ar/business/pdf/Guidelines_on_UN_Business_Cooperation.pdf.

United Nations Development Programme. (2017). *Impact investment to close the SDG funding gap.* https://www.undp.org/content/undp/en/home/blog/2017/7/13/What-kind-of-blender-do-we-need-to-finance-the-SDGs-.html.

United Nations Executive Office of the Secretary-General & United Nations Framework Convention on Climate Change. (2017). *Catalysing the implementation of nationally determined contributions in the context of the 2030 agenda through South-South cooperation.* https://www.un.org/sustainabledevelopment/wp-content/uploads/2017/05/Download-Report.pdf.

United Nations General Assembly. (2018). *Role of South-South cooperation and the implementation of the 2030 agenda for sustainable development: Challenges and opportunities.* http://www.un.org/ga/search/view_doc.asp?symbol=A/73/383&Lang=E.

United Nations Global Compact. (2013). *UN-business partnerships: A handbook.* https://www.unglobalcompact.org/docs/issues_doc/un_business_partnerships/UNBusinessPartnershipHandbook.pdf.

Wehrmann, D. (2018). *Incentivising and regulating multi-actor partnerships and private-sector engagement in development cooperation* (DIE Discussion Paper 21). Bonn: German Development Institute / Deutsches Institut für Entwicklungspolitik (DIE).

Working Party on Aid Effectiveness. (2012). *Proposed mandate for the global partnership for effective development co-operation.* Paris: United Nations Educational, Scientific and Cultural Organization.

Open Access This chapter is licensed under the terms of the Creative Commons Attribution 4.0 International License (http://creativecommons.org/licenses/by/4.0/), which permits use, sharing, adaptation, distribution and reproduction in any medium or format, as long as you give appropriate credit to the original author(s) and the source, provide a link to the Creative Commons license and indicate if changes were made.

The images or other third party material in this chapter are included in the chapter's Creative Commons license, unless indicated otherwise in a credit line to the material. If material is not included in the chapter's Creative Commons license and your intended use is not permitted by statutory regulation or exceeds the permitted use, you will need to obtain permission directly from the copyright holder.

CHAPTER 31

The Role and Contributions of Development NGOs to Development Cooperation: What Do We Know?

Nicola Banks

31.1 INTRODUCTION

A long and rich history of academic scholarship on development non-governmental organisations (NGOs) reveals much about their shape and strategy, their diverse priorities and modalities, and their operations and impact, among other things. One consistent question that has been asked in NGO research across the past three decades is whether and how NGOs can live up to their civil society functions alongside their successes in service delivery. Whereas one section of academic literature applauds NGOs for their impact across a number of diverse sectors and in diverse contexts (see the systematic review of Brass et al. [2018]), another body of literature takes a much more critical stance in asking whether this is enough, given the transformative ideologies and principles and the pursuit of social justice that underpin their motivations (see Banks et al. 2015). An increasingly managerial-driven aid system has fostered an increasingly professionalised cadre of development NGOs internationally, pulling them away from these more political roots and roles.

Although we know a lot qualitatively about the roles and contributions of development NGOs from existing literature, we know less quantitatively about their overall contribution to development cooperation. This is a problem rooted in the methodological approach that most academic literature takes. Nationally and internationally, data is not compiled in ways that can give us

N. Banks (✉)
University of Manchester, Manchester, UK
e-mail: Nicola.banks@manchester.ac.uk

© The Author(s) 2021
S. Chaturvedi et al. (eds.), *The Palgrave Handbook of Development Cooperation for Achieving the 2030 Agenda*,
https://doi.org/10.1007/978-3-030-57938-8_31

a complete picture of the contributions of development NGOs in a donor country's overall foreign aid efforts, or of their holistic contributions in the countries where they operate. Research has a tendency to be based on small samples of (typically the largest) NGOs, within one country or internationally. Within such an approach, we lack knowledge on diversity and scale within the sector. A stronger methodological approach that seeks a sector-wide understanding of development NGOs within any given context would not only allow us to measure the added value of development NGOs to foreign aid, but would also allow us to explore their integration within the broader system of development cooperation. One key example here would be to explore the ways in which donor funding shapes and influences NGO sectors to prove or disprove common assumptions around NGO dependence on donor funding and the challenges that accompany this.

We seek to make advances in these new directions here, drawing upon recent research to extend our knowledge of the contributions of development NGOs to foreign aid efforts, and the implications that we can draw from this regarding their roles and relationships with development cooperation. We also explore the innovative ways in which the Dutch government has tried to respond to the challenges facing NGOs in the aid chain in its radical new policy for funding the political roles of NGOs, Dialogue and Dissent. This is an important precedent for a major donor to begin unpicking the managerialist ideology that underpins civil society funding. This policy is rooted in academic evidence and critiques of the sector, highlighting an important message for NGO researchers to maintain a radical stance rather than embrace the technical language and priorities of donors. This is a trend highlighted by Marberg et al. (2019) that risks buying into and prolonging the principles and ideologies held up by neoliberal regimes.

We first seek to define and summarise what we know about development NGOs. This focusses particularly on long-standing criticisms (Hulme and Edwards 1997) that highlight an increasingly professionalised but "watered-down" sector when it comes to generating and pursuing transformative social and political change. It also highlights limitations to our knowledge because of a lack of systematically compiled and analysed data on development NGOs within donor countries. The following two sections then advance our existing knowledge by looking at new innovations in policy and research. First, we explore recent innovations in Dutch foreign policy that have confronted these challenges, exploring their new policy that seeks to promote NGOs as vehicles of direct political action. We then look at new research in the UK and Canada that has taken a much broader methodological approach to understanding development NGO sectors. Section 31.5 then concludes with how these new studies have added to our understanding of the roles of development NGOs in development cooperation.

We find that although there is strong evidence of increased development cooperation from NGOs as key development actors, long-standing critiques of the extent to which they have been able to expand their political roles alongside this means that the NGO sector can be seen as a good example of "contested cooperation". Although measuring their roles and operations against progress made towards each of the Sustainable Development Goals (SDGs) is beyond the scope of this chapter, we finish with some reflections for what this means for SDG 17 (Partnerships for the goals).

These case studies—the Netherlands, the UK, and Canada—give us diverse insights into NGO sectors (and their influences) across different contexts. Their selection has been predominantly due to availability. With regard to policy, this is the first attempt to promote the political roles of NGOs by a Development Assistance Committee (DAC) donor (DAC 2018); with regard to research, these are the only attempts the author is aware of in terms of systematically analysing development NGO sectors in Northern contexts.

Before we move on, it is also important to define what is meant by "development NGOs". This is not as easy as it may seem. Academic literature has in fact struggled to "define" development NGOs, given the breadth and diversity within and among them (see Vakil 1997). There is great heterogeneity in development NGOs across the Global North and South for example, or in terms of their size and spheres of operation, and in their motivations, among other things. Yet, despite this, there has been increasing recognition of development NGOs as a "sector" (Marburg et al. 2016), and by this, we mean those NGOs working in the field of international development who pursue "development alternatives" that offer more people-centred and grassroots approaches to development than those pursued by the state and market.

31.2 What Do We Know About Development NGOs?

An increasing proliferation of research on development NGOs has accompanied the "meteoric" rise of NGOs in international development over the past three decades (Brass et al. 2018). This research highlights the dramatic transformation of NGOs as they have become increasingly prominent actors in development: They are bigger, more numerous, and more sophisticated, receiving larger sums of development finance than ever before (Banks et al. 2015). Funding channelled to, or through, development NGOs by DAC donor governments has increased from $17.4 billion in 2010 to $19.8 billion in 2016 (DAC 2018).

This makes them rightly deserving of an increasing research profile. Yet— and perhaps this may seem a controversial statement—despite this expanding empirical knowledge base, research has stayed within a relatively confined range of themes and theories, development contexts, and "types" of development NGOs. There remains, for example, a distinctive bias of research and knowledge production towards the biggest NGOs (Banks and Brockington 2018) and towards more populous or politically important countries (Brass et al. 2018). Another hugely significant blind spot when it comes to NGO research is understanding how particular NGO "sectors" are structured and operate—those based in a particular country or working on a particular theme, for example. This means that while we know a lot about development NGOs, we know a lot less about their overall contributions to development cooperation. Rarely are they discussed in the questions or the measurement and analyses of "foreign aid", or development cooperation more broadly,[1] for example. Many underlying assumptions or narratives of the sector (e.g. as being the pawn of donor governments, overly dependent on their funding and priorities) would perhaps indicate that their contributions are not significant enough to include in such discussions. But these assumptions are not grounded in research or evidence. In fact, the problem has been that research has not been systematic enough to measure this.[2]

Here we look at what we know about development NGOs, theoretically and empirically. A systematic review of 35 years of scholarship on NGOs and international development (Brass et al. 2018) is critical reading for anyone interested in a broader discussion of this than we can do justice to. It is certainly not something worth duplicating here. One research gap that becomes prominent when looking at the six overarching research questions that categorise this wealth of development NGOs is exactly the one stated above. Looking from a more sector-wide perspective, how do the contributions of development NGOs "add up"? What do they contribute to development cooperation more generally? Until recently, these two questions have been unanswerable because of methodological issues. No pre-existing databases systematically collect NGO data on incomes and expenditures at the country level, let alone globally. It is no surprise then that research on NGOs has been primarily qualitative, rather than quantitative (Brass et al. 2018). But this means our awareness of NGOs as core development stakeholders making significant contributions to development cooperation is vastly limited.

Let us first review this pre-existing literature before moving on to look at two recent studies that have made the methodological advances necessary to start understanding the size, structure, and mechanics of development NGO sectors in the UK (Banks and Brockington 2018) and Canada (Davis 2019).

Brass et al. (2018) find that the literature on NGOs is framed around six key issues regarding (i) the nature of NGOs, (ii) their emergence and development, (iii) how they conduct their work, (iv) their impacts, (v) how they relate to other actors, and (vi) how they contribute to the (re)production of cultural dynamics and power asymmetries through their operations. The systematic nature of their work is also revealing of the bias within existing research in terms of the countries (focussing on the most populated or most politically salient countries) and sectors (focussing primarily on governance and health sectors) that it overwhelmingly focusses on, and in terms of its authorship, with Northern academics creating most of the published knowledge (Brass et al. 2018). A lack of voices from the Global South in NGO research is also highlighted by Kareithi and Lund's (2012) review. Banks and Brockington (2018) reveal one further important bias—that of a clear preference towards the largest international NGOs in case study methodologies, which, as Brass et al. highlight, dominate 54 per cent of academic papers on

NGOs. We know little about whether these largest NGOs are representative of the many more development NGOs operating across the Global North and South, and as Brass et al. (2018) highlight, there is often no clear rationale laid out for choosing particular cases; in many instances, it is because of practitioner involvement with them.

One recurring concern throughout the research on NGOs is whether—and to what extent—NGOs are able to live up to their perceived comparative advantages and their promise of being genuine development alternatives, given the context of the hierarchical aid chains they are situated within. The work of David Hulme and Michael Edwards (1997) is seminal here. Their early work argued that while NGOs rose to prominence and "favour" for the roles they could play in strengthening good governance agendas and pursuing more people-centred approaches to development to fill in service delivery gaps, in fact many of these justifications were based on ideological grounds rather than on evidence. They highlighted the closeness of NGOs to the donors that funded them, asking whether this dependence undermined the strengths that justified their roles in the first place.

Eighteen years later, with the original authors, I found that research on NGOs across that period largely pointed to very similar conclusions. Despite significant growth and changes in the NGO landscape internationally, the ability of NGOs to meet their long-term transformative goals remains undermined by their weak roots in civil society and by a rising tide of technocracy and professionalisation that has swept through the world of foreign aid (Banks et al. 2015).

A critique of whether the modus operandi of NGOs enables them to pursue social justice as well as to meet the service delivery needs of disadvantaged groups is both widespread in the literature and consistent over time (Atia and Herrold 2018; Banks et al. 2015; Mitlin et al. 2007; Suarez and Gugerty 2016). The Buthe et al. (2012) study of 40 US development NGOs is an interesting addition to this literature because it analyses how development NGOs allocate their *privately* financed resources across the countries they operate within. Taking away the influence of donors from the analysis still reveals remarkably similar findings: A humanitarian discourse rooted in service provision based on objective need is the primary driver of how these NGOs allocate their privately sourced finances globally. There is only weak support in their sample that a stronger "development" discourse that seeks to tackle the deeper roots of poverty and to secure longer-term transformation influences their allocation (Buthe et al. 2012).

Perhaps a rather stark warning to researchers of NGOs comes from Marberg et al. (2019), who use topic-modelling to explore the language used by academic research into NGOs across the 1990–2010 period. This shows a clear trend of researchers beginning to take on the buzzwords used by donors and displays a clear dilution of the original principles identified in Drabek's (1987) original call to action for NGOs. Research in the early 1990s could be categorised along the lines of establishing purpose, doing good, and change.

But this moved on to focus on effectiveness and accountability in the late 1990s, management and globalisation into the early to mid-2000s, education and being "more like businesses" in the late 2000s, and then turned to the language of strategy and regulation in 2010. They highlight that NGO researchers themselves also point to an increasing inclination towards professionalisation, warning that this should not come at the cost of upholding a critical stance on the language that maintains the governance system within neoliberal systems: keep contesting the system or adopt the language and uphold it (Marberg et al. 2019).

Against this rather sceptical theorising of NGOs in existing research, does it come as a surprise to also find that, on the whole, research also assesses the outcomes of NGO activities and interventions as having favourable effects, as the Brass et al. (2018) review also highlights? These things are not necessarily irreconcilable. Hulme and Edward's original criticism was not that NGOs do not have impact, but that positive impact in terms of measurable outputs such as service delivery or infrastructure provision does not equate to social justice. In this, too, we can argue that the focus of the SDGs themselves "fits in" to a measurement of NGO effectiveness in terms of benchmarking their progress towards the many targets and indicators nestled within the 17 goals.[3] With the exception of SDG 17 on partnerships (which is discussed in the conclusions), there is little scope for assessing what the unique value-added role of NGOs (versus other actors) is in their contribution to meeting the goals. This is not something amenable to the measurable targets and indicators upon which goal-setting depends. *What* development NGOs contribute to the SDGs may be measurable in terms of outputs and indicators, but not *how* they do it, and it is this issue of process that is the heart of academic debate and the interest surrounding it.

If we prioritise the processes through which NGOs operate and the longer-term outcomes of social and political transformation that they aim for through these, then we are assessing a different kind of impact. Academic criticisms of development NGOs do not seek to demerit their contributions and successes in service delivery, but to highlight the fact that their operational modalities do not necessarily reconfigure the relationships between the state, the market, and civil society—as originally intended—in ways that lead to more pro-poor development. NGOs have to negotiate difficult accountabilities on two sides that pull them away from this more transformative role and from the grass-roots populations that they are meant to represent. This includes the donors that fund them and the ways in which a managerial, project-based, and results-focussed aid system has led to increasingly professionalised organisations that are far-removed from the communities they represent and the modes of operation necessary to pursue incremental—but transformative—development. In Ghana and Indonesia, Kamstra and Schulpen (2015), for example, highlight the managerial forces through which donor funding leads to the homogenisation of NGOs; this is in stark contrast to the importance they attach to tailor-made approaches and the complexities of local contextual factors.

At the same time, organisational survival also means negotiating and fitting in with government regulations that dictate whether and how NGOs operate. Across the Global South, there are many harsh examples of shrinking civil society space, creating complex challenges to NGO activities (Dupuy et al. 2016). Where governments equate civil society (often viewed synonymously with NGOs) with political opposition, creating regulations to dampen or repress it is widespread. The collapse of highly politicised NGOs working in areas of democracy promotion and politics is often a harsh warning to other NGOs seeking to stray into more democratic arenas (Ulvila and Hossain 2002). Instead, NGOs interested in organisational survival must persuade the state that they are non-political—a process that is incompatible with trying to reconfigure state–civil society relationships in order to advance the interests of marginalised social groups (Dicklitch and Lwanga 2003). Together, these influences—both from donor governments and governments in countries of operation—vastly restrict the ability of NGOs to seek more radical, political action and change. Yet, there are bright glimmers of hope due to one recent advancement. We see in the following section how one major donor—the Dutch government—has drawn upon this academic literature to design a radical new policy for funding the political roles of NGOs. This takes into account these major constraints on the ability of NGOs to act politically and sets important precedents in terms of focus and flexible funding arrangements.

31.3 Innovation and Influence in Donor Strategies for Civil Society

As the previous section has illustrated, the aid chain raises multiple tensions and pressures that have constrained the ability of NGOs to work more politically towards goals of social justice and transformation. NGOs have become increasingly professionalised, and project-based approaches have dominated. This managerial approach has come at the direct cost of their transformative abilities (Yanguas 2018). These theoretical constructs and the empirical analyses that have pursued and affirmed them have a tendency to see donors like-for-like. There has been little academic research that looks at different donor approaches to civil society funding and whether and how differences in processes and procedures may influence these processes of professionalisation and the dilution of transformative principles that have accompanied these. This leads Kamstra and Schulpen (2015) to argue that future research should differentiate between different types of donors, recognising that there may be vast differences in flexibility and focus here.

One recent example is an innovative and radical new strategy for civil society funding by the Dutch government called Dialogue and Dissent: Supporting Civil Society's Political Role. They have directly sought to address the limited scope for political action for NGOs, drawing on diverse academic evidence in its rationale for, and design of, the policy. Through this, the Dutch Ministry of Foreign Affairs is dedicating one-quarter of its civil society funding (totalling close to €1 billion over the period 2016–2021) to political activities seeking to expand civil society through its flagship policy (Ministry of Foreign Affairs of the Netherlands 2017). Twenty-five Strategic Partnerships (of Dutch NGOs or Dutch NGO consortia and their global networks of Southern NGO and community-based organisation partners) have been funded to directly tackle lobbying and advocacy activities in low- and lower-middle-income countries around the world in partnership with local Dutch Embassies, offering new scope for NGOs to work on the more transformative ideologies in which they are rooted.

These Strategic Partnerships represent a strong shift from a managerial to a social transformative approach to funding development NGOs, recognising that development as broader transformation cannot be fostered through discrete and disparate projects or through the hierarchical relationships that have characterised the aid chain to date. The new policy explicitly recognises the original founding strengths of NGOs in its priorities, reconceptualising development as an indigenous process of changing power relations that must be locally owned to be effective and sustainable (Van Wessel et al. 2017). Consequently, funding must be spent on efforts that promote lobbying and advocacy, or on capacity-building and networking activities that fulfil explicitly political roles.

Within this new approach, there has been a complete shift in how the roles and value-added of international NGOs are conceptualised in the aid chain. Dutch NGOs are no longer the main vehicle in pursuing transformative change globally. Their roles are legitimated by the value they can add to local civil society organisation (CSO) partners in strengthening their capacity to pursue lobbying and advocacy work via training, resources, capacity-building, and network-building, among other things. This represents a movement towards the "bridge-building" role that Banks et al. (2015) advocate if NGOs are to get more serious about pursuing longer-term transformative and more inclusive development. Early evaluations of the Dialogue and Dissent policy highlight that Dutch NGOs and local civil society partners globally have applauded these changes, embracing the partnership approach, the more flexible funding and monitoring regime, and the fact it has opened up new possibilities in programming and action (Van Wessel et al. 2017).

At a 2019 stakeholder workshop I attended, the policy was described as "an island in a sea of managerial-driven international cooperation" by one civil society delegate. Likewise, the policy has been highlighted by the DAC (2018) as an "innovative and bold shift for the Netherlands" that is significant due to the precedents that it sets for other donors.[4] Two are of particular significance. One highlights the returns to a shift from a managerial to a social transformative approach to development cooperation that recognises poverty is a political, rather than a technical, problem, and requires bold political approaches to tackle it—and more flexible regulations and monitoring requirements that enable this. The second highlights the possibilities of and returns to a new form of development cooperation that brings together bilateral donors, international NGOs, and local civil society in partnerships, rather than the strict hierarchical relationships that have characterised the aid chain to date. The Dutch Ministry of Foreign Affairs is no longer simply a funder of development projects, but a key ally and development partner in the 25 Strategic Partnerships, facilitating and protecting NGOs and their local partners in a context of shrinking civil society space globally. NGOs see added value in this partnership in the capacity of the ministry (via local embassies globally) to open doors, act as an ally for partners, assert greater leverage in their lobby and advocacy activities, and its ability to protect NGOs and their partners in difficult working environments (Van Wessel et al. 2017).

Flexibility is key to meeting the transformative goals of these Strategic Partnerships. Dialogue and Dissent provides space and flexibility that allows the partnerships to make their own choices and advance their own objectives without having to design programmes along donor priorities or to report heavily throughout the design, implementation, and evaluation phases. It offers opportunities for partnerships to negotiate adjustments in interventions and budgets in response to new opportunities, challenges, or learnings (CARE Netherlands 2017). Relationships with the ministry as donor have shifted away from one of *reporting to*, to one of *collaborating with*.

While offering an exciting potential for development NGOs, it is also important to highlight that structural changes like this to the funding system are also a huge challenge and trigger for change for development NGOs (Schulpen et al. 2018). As well as opening new opportunities, this can raise new challenges. Discussions at the 2019 workshop I attended, for example, suggested that NGOs had struggled to pass on this flexibility in funding that is afforded to them under Strategic Partnerships to local NGO partners in the Global South. This makes the approach taken throughout this first phase of the policy—including regular multi-stakeholder interactions and dialogue and a significant investment into academic research projects "testing" the assumptions upon which the policy is founded—critical to learning from the lessons experienced so that they can be addressed moving forwards.

A monitoring tool designed in collaboration with the Strategic Partnerships has replaced rigid management tools such as Results Based Frameworks and Logical Framework Analyses. This unique "outcome-harvesting" approach to monitoring outcomes explores the impact the partnerships have had along a number of benchmarks, but in much more fluid ways that recognise which social and political changes are harder to capture in rigid monitoring and evaluation frameworks. Evaluation looks for outcomes that represent political change: new policies or laws created or implemented; the number of spaces created for seeking political change; the number of people trained in capacity-building for political participation; the number of instances of participation in local governance processes; the number of CSOs with increased lobbying and advocacy capacities; the number of institutions strengthened to become more responsive, among other things. These are verified externally and uploaded to become publicly accessible through the global aid reporting standard of the

International Aid Transparency Initiative d-portal database, making the data both accessible and comparable.

Just one example: An external mid-term review of CARE Netherlands' Every Voice Counts programme highlights that it "has, in a relatively short period of time [...] managed to advance the promotion of inclusive and effective governance processes" (CARE Netherlands 2017, p. viii). That this is a programme seeking inclusive and pro-poor development in fragile and post-conflict settings in which certain segments of society are structurally excluded from local, district, and national governance processes makes this even more striking. With this Strategic Partnership, the Dialogue and Dissent programme has enabled CARE to design and implement a political programme of action and broad networks that would not traditionally fit into donor requirements and frameworks (Lori Cajegas, personal communication, 2019).

To recap, this policy innovation displays two important shifts for donor–NGO relationships in ways that are critical to the heart of long-standing academic critiques of development NGOs. One is a shift away from a technical and managerial approach to funding development NGOs to a social transformative approach. The second is a shift away from seeing NGOs as service delivery organisations to reconceptualising their role as bridge-builders whose key roles are to strengthen and connect locally rooted CSOs with national- and local-level institutions and processes in their countries of operation. These two shifts are imperative if NGOs are to fulfil their potential in pursuing longer-term transformation and social justice.

31.4 What Does a Sectoral Approach to Development NGOs Contribute to Our Understanding?

Above we highlighted a lack of systematic analysis of NGO sectors as a major constraint on our understanding of development NGOs. Lacking this more representative sector-wide understanding of how NGO sectors look or perform in any given country (or thematic sector) makes it impossible to accurately explore their contributions to development cooperation. Although research on development NGOs alludes to development NGOs as a collective—as a group thought of for their cumulative consequences and influences—it has tended to focus on individual or small collectives of NGOs and to concentrate on the largest (Banks and Brockington 2018).[5] This means we know much less about the size, composition, and contributions of diverse sectors globally, or about how they are financed, structured, and operate. Here, in fact, we know surprisingly little.

Those funding, working in, or researching the sector would no doubt all agree that NGOs play an important, if not sometimes contentious, role. But, until recently, there has been no data systematically compiled that allows us to measure accurately how major or minor they are as actors. Donors may now be requiring government-funded projects to report to global standards databases such as the International Aid Transparency Initiative d-portal database, but NGOs receive income from multiple sources that do not have to be reported through these channels. This is also a critical issue for policy. How can civil society policies be evidence-based if decision-makers lack stronger empirical knowledge bases? New methodological advances made recently in NGO research are beginning to answer these questions.

Two recent studies in the UK (Banks and Brockington 2018) and Canada (Davis 2019) offer revealing sector-wide insights. Through creating databases of UK-based and Canadian development NGOs and measuring their incomes, expenditures, and sources of income, both studies highlight that the financial contribution of NGOs to international development is hugely significant. In 2015, British development NGOs spent the equivalent of 55 per cent of all UK official development assistance (ODA) for that year (Banks and Brockington 2018). In Canada, this figure increases to around 60 per cent; 14 ODA-eligible countries receive more aid from Canadian NGOs than they do from Canadian ODA (Davis 2019). These new databases reveal that NGOs are far from being secondary or minor development actors. Increasing levels of funding from multiple sources (including the general public as the biggest financial supporter) have elevated their contributions to such an extent that they are major players globally. That development NGO sectors and their contributions have been unquantifiable until this new methodological approach means that their roles in, and contributions to, domestic foreign aid efforts have been underestimated.

Such a systematic approach can also enable important insights beyond these headline figures, allowing new analyses to shed light on theories or widespread assumptions about the sector. As those familiar with NGO research are aware, NGO positioning between donors and their local Southern partners leads to questions around their autonomy, accountability, and grassroots orientation. As Sect. 31.2 details, questions over whether NGOs are "too close for comfort" have been a long-standing concern of academic research (Hulme and Edwards 1997). In fact, it was this assumption and widespread criticism in Canada—that non-governmental "aid" was not "non"-governmental at all because of a dependence on government funding—that inspired Davis (2019) to compile his database to test this. This dominant narrative is unjustified, he finds, with only 13 per cent of Canadian NGOs receiving any form of government funding. These insights are critical to working towards a more nuanced narrative that reflects the complex realities of domestic NGO sectors. It also allows us to identify those organisations that do rely somewhat (or heavily) upon government funding in order to explore in more depth whether and how this influences their vision, direction, and activities.

Likewise Banks and Brockington's (2018) research reveals that the British public have been by far the biggest supporters of Britain's development NGO sector, contributing 40 per cent of the sector's income across the 2009–2014

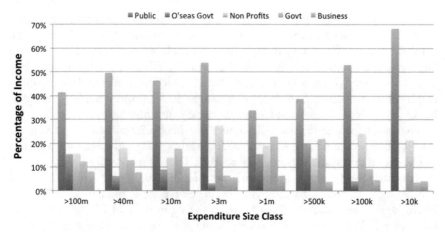

Fig. 31.1 Sources of income for British development NGOs (2009–2014) (*Source* Banks and Brockington 2018)

period. In comparison, the British government provided just 17 per cent (Fig. 31.1).[6]

This is the case for all size classifications of development NGOs. The smallest development NGOs receive almost 70 per cent of their income from public donations and negligible funding direct from the UK government.[7] Government funding becomes more prominent when NGOs hit the £100,000 expenditure mark. Here still, however, the government provides less than 10 per cent of income, on average. It is the mid-size categories of NGOs (between £500,000 and £3 million) that must be singled out for their higher proportion of government funding as an income source. Both receive more than 20 per cent of their funding from the UK government. In the size class above this (NGOs spending between £3 m and £10 m), funding from other charities becomes a core component of funding, reducing the relative dependence of this group on government funds.

Looking at the structural composition of the sector over time also provides important new insights into trends and pressures within the sector. The research compared the sector's structural composition in 2009 and in 2014, that is, the "share" of the sector's expenditure held by different size classes of development NGOs. Here we see evidence that changes to UK government spending have led to increasing levels of intermediation within the UK's development NGO sector (Banks and Brockington 2018). Despite a huge 45 per cent increase in funds to the sector over this period, structural unevenness across the sector—with only 8 per cent of organisations dominating around 90 per cent of expenditure—has remained remarkably stable (Banks and Brockington 2018).

This is because, despite the fact that expenditure growth has taken place across all size classes of NGOs, it has been strongest for the largest, allowing them to maintain this dominance (Banks and Brockington 2018). One of the key shifts here has been mentioned above—that government funds have shifted away from the smallest NGOs and rapidly expanded in volume towards the biggest.

Through this sectoral analysis, we can see the importance of applying the concept of intermediation—most commonly investigated within the broader aid chain, with NGOs holding an intermediary position between donors and local counterparts or beneficiaries—to the domestic sector itself (Banks and Brockington 2018). This process introduces new links within the UK aid chain, with money passing through additional UK-based development NGOs before reaching development partners internationally.

As the biggest NGOs have been receiving increasing volumes of government funding, a new pattern of spending it through other British-based charities has emerged. This is evidenced by an increase in funds from "other non-profits" among smaller size classes. The smallest NGOs, for example, have experienced average losses of government funding of 13 per cent across the period above, at the same time as almost doubling their income from other non-profits (Banks and Brockington 2018). Amidst austerity pressures, the benefits of these funding arrangements are clear (Gulrajani 2017). Although ODA levels have increased with the 0.7 per cent commitment written into law, staffing levels and operating budgets have remained under pressure from austerity measures (Evans 2018). Within this context, smaller NGOs are unable to process the volumes of funds that the Department for International Development (DFID) needs to shift.

In broader analyses of intermediation, funding relationships with donors—and the donor priorities that influence the projects that are designed and implemented by NGOs—are seen as problematic because they have the potential to pull NGOs away from the local realities and beneficiaries that they represent. These findings, however, suggest interesting and important new questions to explore, including (i) how this new form of intermediation affects the efficiency of these new sectoral mechanics, and (ii) whether any negative side-effects are generated as a result. For smaller NGOs now receiving funds through other charities, for example, there is little means through which they can build relationships with DFID, nor positive feedback loops through which they can demonstrate the strength of their approaches and potentially secure more funds. It also eliminates the channels through which DFID can learn from new innovations. There are potentially damaging losses to this on both sides (Evans 2018).

31.5 Conclusions

As we have seen, despite a burgeoning literature on development NGOs globally, there remain striking knowledge gaps and "blind spots" that act as significant barriers to making more informed civil society policies. One of these is a striking lack of research from a sector-wide perspective, with research being dominated by case study approaches rooted in the largest organisations. This means that we know little about the contributions of development NGOs in the broader system of development cooperation. New methodological advances in Britain (Banks and Brockington 2018) and Canada (Davis 2019) highlight the new insights and findings that can be revealed through a more systematic compilation and analysis of NGO data. They also reveal that common concerns theorised in the literature—such as a heavy dependence on government funding constraining NGO independence and shifting their focus away from the grassroots—may not be as big a concern as commonly conceptualised. Both studies reveal a surprisingly small volume of government funds in relation to the overwhelming and increasing levels of support for development NGOs from private individuals. This sector-wide perspective in Britain also illuminates what we can learn about sectoral mechanics, revealing that processes of intermediation—commonly conceptualised globally within the aid chain—are beginning to occur even domestically, before funds reach international partners. Only through this systematic methodology can we begin to trace and understand how changes in funding and finance influence the sector and how it operates. This is a critical first step in understanding the effectiveness of these mechanics and operations.

These new insights and policies have implications for our understanding and progress towards SDG 17 (Partnerships for the goals). New methodological advancements in NGO research that take a systematic, sector-wide approach to understanding the contributions of development NGOs in Britain and Canada can also begin to shed light on the true extent of civil society's contributions towards meeting these goals. In the UK, in particular, this research also highlights the increasing volumes of financial support for development that development NGOs have been able to mobilise from non-state actors in these efforts.

We also highlight another success story, looking at the ways in which conceptually grounded research has influenced government policy for civil society funding in the Netherlands. This radical new policy that promotes the political roles of NGOs moves far beyond the "business as usual" approach of traditional donors and, as such, has important implications for SDG 17. Moving away from managerialist to transformative ideologies and principles has formed the basis of new relationships that offer flexibility, core funding, and a partnership model that goes beyond simply funding. Such an approach is critical if we seek to catalyse a much stronger and more deeply-rooted, transformative value-added role for development NGOs in meeting the global goals. Importantly, this highlights that not only must we focus on progress made towards targets and indicators, we must also focus on modalities—*how* NGO operations are funded and executed, and whether this enables NGOs to be political as well as professional organisations, generating social and political change alongside their admirable impacts on the ground in service delivery. The ways in which international NGOs manage their local partnerships in the countries where they operate is also critical here in terms of building capacity and offering the flexibility and security of funding that enables greater political action.

Often—and understandably—academic research that talks conceptually about NGOs in ways that undermine diversity serves to irritate, rather than engage with, NGO practitioners. I speak from experience here—our work on NGOs and development is brought up by Duncan Green on his widely-read "Poverty and Power" blog every time he has a frustration to be aired about academic research. This does not mean that NGOs and those working for them are not sympathetic to the core concerns this critical work represents; often these parallel discussions are going on behind closed doors, as Kloster's (2018) recent discussion on the dilemmas of "going global" and losing touch with core civil society values richly illustrates. But, as outsiders, drawing upon a broad range of academic sources of evidence in an effort to test core assumptions or build theories, it can perhaps seem far-removed from—or a too simplified version of—the complex realities and challenges that NGOs grapple with on a daily basis. That this rich body of work can feed into radical new policies that enable NGOs to move back to old roots highlights the importance of academics maintaining a radical stance on development NGOs who continue to fight for the genuine development alternatives they seek to offer.

Notes

1. AidData, for example—a project compiling and analysing data on foreign aid—does not include NGOs in their database.
2. In fact, it appears that donors have been more proactive here than researchers. Many donors, including DFID and the Dutch Ministry of Foreign Affairs, ensure that all NGOs funded through ODA input their data online with the International Aid Transparency Initiative in an attempt to make NGO expenditures more transparent and accountable. Currently, however, it is not possible to search this data in ways that allow for a more sector-wide perspective, that is, one cannot search for "all British NGOs funded by DFID". Even if this were possible, this would not necessarily include all British NGOs that are independent of government funds.
3. Although beyond the scope of this chapter, the ways in which NGOs report on their contributions to meeting the SDGs and their responsibilities in holding governments to account through Shadow Reports is an interesting issue. See Long (2018) and International Forum of National NGO Platforms (2018), for example.

4. Of course, this new policy change is best understood within the recent history of broader changes to the Netherland's foreign aid policy and the institutions that drive it. This is beyond the scope of this chapter here, but Schulpen (2016) and Schulpen et al. (2018) give an excellent overview of these changes while analysing their influence on Dutch development NGOs.
5. There are some excellent exceptions here, as with the analysis of Buthe et al. (2012) on how 40 leading transnational NGOs in the United States allocate their *privately* collected finances across their countries of operation. The methodological choice for this is clearly defined given the study's scope and objectives, but by excluding government and multilateral funding within these organisations (and given the fact that it studies a sample of some of the largest organisations), this still means that we have a far from complete picture of NGO contributions to development cooperation from this data. Likewise, an earlier study by Koch et al. (2009) analysed the distributional choices of international NGOs operating across several OECD countries. Diversifying the number of countries under study means looking at fewer organisations within them—and consequently, the biggest. There are no insights, as a result, into the activities and decision-making of international NGOs spending less than €10 million, of which there are many.
6. The legal commitment to spend 0.7 per cent of gross national income on ODA, enshrined in law in 2015, increases the relative importance of government funding in relation to the sector's overall income, from 17 to around 20 per cent.
7. Recent changes and additions to DFID's civil society portfolio may have influenced this finding, opening up opportunities for smaller NGOs through the Small Charities Fund.

References

Atia, M., & Herrold, C. E. (2018). Governing through patronage: The rise of NGOs and the fall of civil society in Palestine and Morocco. *VOLUNTAS: International Journal of Voluntary and Non-Profit Organizations, 29*(5), 1044–1054.

Banks, N., & Brockington, D. (2018). *Mapping the UK's development NGOs: Income, geography and contributions to development* (GDI Working Paper 2019-035). Manchester: University of Manchester.

Banks, N., Hulme, D., & Edwards, M. (2015). NGOs, states and donors revisited: Still too close for comfort? *World Development, 66*, 707–718.

Brass, J., Longhofer, W., Robinson, R. S., & Schnable, A. (2018). NGOs and international development: A review of 35 years of scholarship. *World Development, 112*, 134–149.

Buthe, T., Major, S., & de Mello e Souza, A. (2012). The politics of private foreign aid: Humanitarian principles, economic development objectives and organizational interests in the allocation of private aid by NGOs. *International Organization, 66*(4), 571–607.

CARE Netherlands (2017). *From participation to influence: Lessons learned from inclusive governance programming in fragile settings* (CARE Netherlands Policy Briefing). The Hague: Author.

DAC (Development Assistance Committee). (2018). *Aid for civil society organisations: Statistics based on DAC members' reporting to the Creditor Reporting System Database (CRS), 2015–2016*. Paris: Organisation for Economic Co-operation and Development.

Davis, J. M. (2019). Real "non-governmental" aid and poverty: Comparing privately and publicly financed NGOs in Canada. *Canadian Journal of Development Studies/Revue Canadienne D'études Du Développement*. https://doi.org/10.1080/02255189.2019.1556623.

Dicklitch, S., & Lwanga, D. (2003). The politics of being non-political: Human rights organisations and the creation of a positive human rights culture in Uganda. *Human Rights Quarterly, 25*(2), 482–509.

Drabek, A. G. (1987). Development alternatives: The challenge for NGOs. An overview of the issues. *World Development, 15*, ix–xv.

Dupuy, K., Ron, J., & Prakash, A. (2016). Hands off my regime! Governments' restrictions on foreign aid to non-governmental organisations in poor and middle-income countries. *World Development, 84*, 299–311.

Evans, R. (2018). *Whose problems? Whose solutions? The role of for-profit contractors as managers of British development challenge funds* (master's thesis). Amsterdam: University of Amsterdam, International Development Studies.

Gulrajani, N. (2017). Bilateral donors and the age of the national interest: What prospects for challenge by development agencies? *World Development, 96*, 375–389.

Hulme, D., & Edwards, M. (1997). *NGOs, states and donors: Too close for comfort?*. London: Palgrave Macmillan.

International Forum of National NGO Platforms. (2018). *Guidelines for CSO shadow reports: Monitoring the implementation of Agenda 2030 at the national level*. http://forus-international.org/en/resources/8.

Kamstra, J., & Schulpen, L. (2015). Worlds apart but much alike: Donor funding and the homogenization of NGOs in Ghana and Indonesia. *Studies in Comparative International Development, 50*(3), 331–357.

Kareithi, R. N. M., & Lund, C. (2012). Review of NGO performance research published in academic journals between 1996 and 2008. *South African Journal of Science, 108*, 36–44.

Kloster, M. O. (2018). Why it hurts: Save the Children Norway and the dilemmas of "going global". *Forum for Development Studies, 46*(1), 109–130.

Koch, D. J., Nunnekamp, P., & Thiele, R. (2009). Keeping a low profile: What determines allocation of aid by non-governmental organizations? *World Development, 37*(5), 902–918.

Long, G. (2018). *How should civil society stakeholders report their contribution to the 2030 Agenda for Sustainable Development?* (Technical paper for the Division of Sustainable Development, UN-DESA). https://sustainabledevelopment.un.org/content/documents/18445CSOreporting_paper_revisions_4May.pdf.

Marberg, A., Korzilius, H., & van Kranenburg, H. (2019). What is in a theme? Professionalization in nonprofit and nongovernmental organizations research. *Nonprofit Management and Leadership*. https://doi.org/10.1002/nml.21355.

Marburg, A., van Kranenburg, H., & Korzilius, H. (2016). NGOs in the news: The road to taken-for-grantedness. *VOLUNTAS: International Journal of Voluntary and Non-Profit Organizations, 27*(6), 2734–2763.

Ministry of Foreign Affairs of the Netherlands. (2017). *Dialogue and dissent theory of change 2.0: Supporting civil society's political role*. The Hague: Ministry of Foreign Affairs Civil Society Unit.

Mitlin, D., Hickey, S., & Bebbington, A. (2007). Reclaiming development? NGOs and the challenge of alternatives. *World Development, 35*(10), 1699–1720.

Schulpen, L. (2016). *The NGO funding game: The case of the Netherlands*. Cidin: Radboud University.

Schulpen, L., van Kempen, L., & Elbers, W. (2018). *The changing Dutch NGO: Exploring organisational, strategic and financial changes between 2010–2016*. Cidin: Radboud University.

Suarez, D., & Gugerty, M. K. (2016). Funding civil society? Bilateral government support for development NGOs. *VOLUNTAS: International Journal of Voluntary and Non-Profit Organizations, 27*(6), 2617–2640.

Ulvila, M., & Hossain, F. (2002). Development NGOs and political participation of the poor in Bangladesh and Nepal. *Voluntas: International Journal of Voluntary and Non-Profit Organizations, 13*(2), 149–163.

Vakil, A. C. (1997). Confronting the classification problem: Toward a taxonomy of NGOs. *World Development, 25*(12), 2057–2070.

Van Wessel, M., Schulpen, L., Hilhorst, D., & Biekart, K. (2017). *Mapping the expectations of the Dutch Strategic Partnerships for lobby and advocacy*. Wageningen: Wageningen University and Research, Radboud University Nijmegen and Institute of Social Studies, Erasmus University.

Yanguas, P. (2018). *Why we lie about aid: Development and the messy politics of change*. London: Zed Books.

Open Access This chapter is licensed under the terms of the Creative Commons Attribution 4.0 International License (http://creativecommons.org/licenses/by/4.0/), which permits use, sharing, adaptation, distribution and reproduction in any medium or format, as long as you give appropriate credit to the original author(s) and the source, provide a link to the Creative Commons license and indicate if changes were made.

The images or other third party material in this chapter are included in the chapter's Creative Commons license, unless indicated otherwise in a credit line to the material. If material is not included in the chapter's Creative Commons license and your intended use is not permitted by statutory regulation or exceeds the permitted use, you will need to obtain permission directly from the copyright holder.

CHAPTER 32

Southern Think Tank Partnerships in the Era of the 2030 Agenda

Andrea Ordóñez-Llanos

32.1 Introduction

More than ever, there is a growing realisation of the importance of global issues—specifically those that go beyond national borders, either because they are not divisible or because they are persistent across diverse countries and regions. With a global policy agenda in the form of the 2030 Agenda for Sustainable Development, the central questions relate to how these decisions will be made and the type of knowledge that will inform such an agenda. This chapter focusses on the emergence of Southern think tanks as actors in the debates on global development and examines their engagement with global policy debates.

Southern think tanks are important actors that generate evidence for policy debates and create spaces for dialogues on difficult policy choices by becoming brokers of diverse perspectives. Through these strategies, Southern think tanks have in many instances successfully influenced policy processes and outcomes (Ordóñez et al. 2012). These institutions, by their very definition, work within the intersection of policy and knowledge and bridge connections between diverse actors through policy debates. With the 2030 Agenda and the new impetus towards working through partnerships, think tanks have the potential of becoming key actors that enable these collaborations. This chapter explores the relationships between think tanks from the Global South with each other,

---

A. Ordóñez-Llanos (✉)
Southern Voice, Lima, Peru
e-mail: andrea@southernvoice.org
URL: http://www.southernvoice.org

© The Author(s) 2021
S. Chaturvedi et al. (eds.), *The Palgrave Handbook of Development Cooperation for Achieving the 2030 Agenda*,
https://doi.org/10.1007/978-3-030-57938-8_32

their Northern peers, and the broader international community. The final objective is to explore how think tanks are positioned to engage in partnerships and to determine the critical factors that can enable their participation in such collaborations.

The Sustainable Development Goals (SDGs) are part of the consolidation of global policy-making processes ever since the creation of the United Nations and other multilateral organisations. Stone uses the metaphor of "agora" to describe global policy-making because it refers to the "growing global public spaces of fluid, dynamic and intermeshed relations of politics, markets, culture and society. This public space is brought about by the interactions of its actors" (Stone 2013, p. 17). Thinks tanks have become important actors in these processes. This relational view of global policy-making processes highlights the disconnect between the national policy-making processes and the global ones. The global processes cannot be considered an aggregation of the national-level policy ones, but rather distinct processes in themselves. Stone also notes the differences in the actors involved compared to those in the national policy-making processes, including what she calls "internationalised public sector officials", "international civil servants", and "transnational policy professionals", all of whom interact to shape global policy. The exchanges among these actors are fluid and do not follow national divisions. For example, a delegation to the United Nations in country A may reach out to experts from country B for advice or respond to pressures from an international non-governmental organisation in a different country. This is not to say that there are no lines of accountability—especially from the "internationalised public sector officials"—to their respective governments and citizens, but that these other drivers are also at play at the global level. In this context, think tanks themselves are evolving as organisations with the capacity to navigate both national and global contexts and to talk to a diversity of global actors, not only those within their national policy context.

Think tanks are a growing group of actors engaged in policy debates worldwide. As of 2018, the Open Think Tank Directory accounts for 2714 think tanks worldwide.[1] In Africa, there are 106; in Latin America and the Caribbean 624; and 520 in Asia—in total representing 46.06 per cent of the total entries in the database.[2] Although the think tank tradition was born in "Western" democracies such as the United States and the UK, their presence in the Global South is significant. Among them, there are varying types of organisations, ranging from well-established with a long tradition of working on policy issues, to newer and more nimble ones. From the total universe of think tanks, a smaller number of organisations work on development issues or engage with the global debates on development. However, because of the diverse and fluid nature of these organisations, it is hard to classify them purely along their thematic or geographic reach.[3] Nonetheless, some of these think tanks—and among these some specific researchers and policy experts—act as what Stone defines as "transnational policy professionals", meaning experts that provide policy advice to diverse countries, multilateral organisations, and other global institutions.

Think tanks located in the Global North that work on development issues traditionally had more access to global policy processes, such as debates held at the United Nations, the World Trade Organization, and multilateral organisations. They have developed presence and reputation in these debates, thanks in part to being located in or close to the cities where global debates take place, such as New York or Geneva, and having access to financing opportunities from countries in the Global North. Stone (2001) identifies some key factors that enable think tanks to engage in global debates: (i) a vibrant and critical national scene for think tanks, (ii) funding opportunities, (iii) freedom of speech, and (iv) "pull" factors, such as the demand from institutions such as the European Union or the United Nations. Staff members of these think tanks can easily move between their organisations within the multilateral or diplomatic sphere in what is usually referred to as the revolving door (Stone 2007). Although think tanks from the Global South have traditionally had less prominence in global development debates, new technologies—as well as the new framing of the 2030 Agenda, an inclusive global development plan of action—create opportunities for more proactive participation. The next section explores how the framing of the 2030 Agenda may shape the knowledge produced by think tanks and other policy experts. The following three sections explore in detail how Southern think tanks relate to each other and other actors involved in global policy-making, such as their Northern peers, civil society, governments, and the private sector. A final reflection focusses on how think tanks from the Global South can collaborate more with others.

32.2 The Implications of the 2030 Agenda for Think Tanks

Although criticisms about the viability and technical soundness of the 2030 Agenda and the SDGs abound, the agenda remains a powerful tool to re-frame how different knowledge actors engage in the "global agora" of development debates.[4] The first aspect of the SDGs that shapes the research agendas is their universality. This shift also affects the primary locus of research on development. Before the 2030 Agenda, development was perceived as an agenda for developing countries only; research on development focussed mainly on countries in the Global South. This focus somewhat expanded beyond the Global South through research on international cooperation and also through research on policy coherence for development. The effectiveness of development cooperation research, for example, explores the challenges of cooperation between donor and recipient countries, which may include issues of the recipient as well as of the provider of cooperation (Howes 2014). The research on policy coherence went beyond development assistance; it explored how a diversity of other policies by donor countries (trade, intellectual property, or migration) affect—directly or indirectly—the success of development programmes and policies in developed countries (Ashoff 2005). However, the shift in focus of development from being an agenda only for the

Global South to one that includes all countries is different since, in a universal agenda, domestic policies in developed countries also become relevant areas of research. This is particularly true in the context of the degree of progress on different social, environmental, and economic indicators, which show a growing convergence across countries, but more extensive divergence within countries (Horner and Hulme 2019). Although the differences between countries remain, the normative divisions between "developed" and "developing" lose ground, as goals and targets are expected to be reached by all countries, independent of their level of economic development.

Furthermore, the differences among countries from the Global South are growing, and referring to them as one group of developing countries is becoming less useful in practical terms. Geopolitically, however, it has been useful for nations to have a joint group (such as the G77) for development debates to strengthen their presence globally (Perkins 2013). In short, the 2030 Agenda changes the paradigm—from a focus on the Global South to an understanding of development as a global agenda across countries of all income levels. As a result, the knowledge required to inform the implementation of such an agenda is also broader.

For development research and policy analysis, this may be summarised in what Horner and Hulme (2019) have labelled a shift from international to global development. For think tanks, a universal agenda may entail the expansion of their reach beyond national settings. Indeed, "Western" think tanks have been experiencing these changes through the expansion and internationalisation of their work while seeking out new horizons beyond their national borders and establishing offices in important capitals of the world as they pursue new audiences, funding, and networks (Niblett 2018). Think tanks of the Global South have less experience internationalising their presence. Some of the possible reasons for this is that these think tanks are newer institutions with research agendas that are predominately focussed on national issues. Furthermore, the disconnect among countries in the Global South has allowed for fewer interactions among researchers across regions.

Nonetheless, the SDGs create the opportunity to engage further in global debates by bringing particular perspectives to dialogues on what an international agenda means for diverse national and subnational realities (Bhattacharya and Ordóñez-Llanos 2016). Part of the challenge of a global agenda is to make it relevant in different contexts. For this challenge, think tanks from the South can provide nuanced research that is grounded in the reality of different contexts and can bridge national and global debates.

The second aspect of the SDGs that impacts the research agendas is that they incorporate environmental, social, and economic dimensions of well-being. The broadening of the development agenda means that knowledge that focusses on coming to a better understanding of the interconnected nature of societal change will become more valuable. At the same time, it means that policy processes and spaces will transform from being sector-specific to becoming inter-sectoral. A think tank that worked in a particular policy area may find itself working with actors well beyond its original scope to include others that were not previously involved in a given issue. What does this mean for think tanks in the Global South?

By putting partnerships and non-state actors at the centre of its approach (SDG 17), the 2030 Agenda emphasises a change that the world has already begun to experience: multi-level, multi-actor governance. This third aspect encompasses a change from centralised, government-led policy processes to an interconnected network of various actors making decisions and implementing them. The shift began already before the adoption of the 2030 Agenda; however, it is now an official global policy document. These changes in the processes of global policy-making also affect the traditional work of think tanks around the world. The traditional approach of think tanks was to talk directly to policy-makers and provide specific ideas and advice. However, this model does not fit anymore, given that there are many more actors involved in the policy-making processes. Formal and informal consultations with civil society, the influence of lobby groups, and decentralised policy-making are some of the factors that have led more actors to become involved. In this context, it is essential to ask: To whom do the think tanks speak to? How do they conduct their research? And for whom is their policy analysis relevant? This chapter focusses mainly on how think tanks engage in these processes through the formation of different types of partnerships and collaborations.

In summary, the 2030 Agenda, as a normative proposition, shifts the work of think tanks: towards a global understanding of development issues, towards a more interdisciplinary research agenda, and towards new strategies to reach and inform policy. Despite the stated partnership approach, it is essential to note that inherited power asymmetries in the global debates persist. These asymmetries shape the extent to which these partnerships can be horizontal. They also represent the variety of interests these partnerships bring together and whether they reproduce power asymmetries, thus promoting primarily the interests of those who have more power to begin with.

A parallel phenomenon is occurring thematically. The 2030 Agenda explicitly states that all the dimensions of sustainable development—economic, social, environmental, institutional—are equally relevant. Nonetheless, this does not necessarily translate into a balanced approach at the time of planning and implementing policy. Having a holistic approach that takes into consideration all of these dimensions requires better coordination in policy-making—explicitly interdisciplinary research. For think tanks and policy experts, this also means that their approaches to research should also evolve.

The 2030 Agenda sets the goals for more collaboration and partnerships. As explored before, however, inherited power asymmetries cannot be overlooked. The following section analyses the respective relationships that are emerging among think tanks from the Global South and beyond.

32.3 COLLABORATION AND CONTESTATION WITH AND AMONG THINK TANKS: "THE FOUR-C'S MODEL"

The 2030 Agenda has proposed significant normative changes to what development is and how it should be achieved, including a strong emphasis on partnerships. In practice, a variety of relationships will emerge, and the different actors will need to adapt to them. In this context, it is relevant to understand the relationships that emerge, how the actors share power, and what enables vital partnerships.

Najam (2000) explains the nature of relations between non-governmental organisations (NGOs) and governmental organisations and proposes a conceptual framework denominated the Four-C's model. This model is based on a theory of strategic institutional interests, and it proposes that relations boil down to a question of ends and means. This framework can also be useful for exploring relations among a variety of actors. In this case, it will be used to explore the nature of the relationships between think tanks and the diversity of actors involved in the global policy debates of the SDGs.

There are four types of relationships that are based on the strategies and goals each actor has in a given policy process (Najam 2000): (i) cooperation, (ii) confrontation, (iii) complementarity, or (iv) co-optation. Cooperation occurs when NGOs and government agencies share similar strategies for achieving similar policy goals. Hence, there is a convergence of preferred ends as well as means. Confrontation happens when NGOs and governmental agencies perceive the other's strategies and goals to be antithetical to their own. Some scholars consider this to be the natural order of things because NGOs and governments often find themselves—explicitly or implicitly—in adversarial relationships. Najam's model defines confrontation as encompassing not just acts of coercive control by the government but also policy defiance and opposition by NGOs. Complementarity occurs when two actors prefer different strategies but share similar goals. Najam describes this type of relationship as a function of goals. When both parties share similar goals, it is more likely that they can reach an agreement in which they complement each other in the achievement of a shared outcome. Finally, Najam mentions co-optation as another type of relationship. This is when both parties prefer different goals but share similar strategies; such situations are often transitory. Najam (2000, p. 389) points out that

> as each side tries to change the goal preference of the other side, the discomfort is likely to be directly proportional to the power asymmetry. It is the power asymmetry that will decide whether, and which, side gives in or gives up – the instability is resolved as the relationship moves to one of the other three boxes.

As discussed in the previous section, there are a diversity of actors and policy areas in play—a perfect scenario for complex relationships. The following sections explore how think tanks from the Global South interact among themselves and with other key actors and analyse the extent to which they can engage in partnerships and other cooperation strategies.

32.4 Collaboration Among Think Tanks in the Global South

Analysing the relationships between think tanks from the Global South through the Four-C's model reveals that the think tanks remain collaborative in the context of the global development agenda. They have identified both the common goals and the strategies that foster collaboration. Networks of think tanks emerging from the Global South serve various purposes: they support the shaping of a common agenda among countries, sustaining spaces for informal diplomacy as an alternative to delicate official diplomacy when obstacles emerge, and they can position Southern think tanks vis-à-vis their Northern peers.

The Association of Southeast Asian Nations (ASEAN) Institutes of Strategic and International Studies network is one such example. Although it was formally launched as an association in 1988, it emerged from earlier conversations and dialogues among think tanks from core ASEAN countries. Through informal diplomacy, joint research efforts, and constant dialogue, the network has been able to establish regional positions and develop a collaborative research agenda. The network filled an existing gap in providing knowledge and policy advice to the ASEAN Secretariat, and it has had an essential role in setting an agenda for ASEAN collaboration (Stone 2013). The ASEAN Secretariat now officially seeks out input and collaborations with think tanks from the region (Association of Southeast Asian Nations 2019). Furthermore, with the creation of the ASEAN+3 forum, which includes China, Japan, and South Korea, the Network of East Asian Think-Tanks was established as a recommendation from the East Asia Vision Group in 2003 with organisations designated by the respective governments. It is conceived as a space for "Track 2" diplomacy to support the forum (Council on East Asian Community, n.d.). The experiences of ASEAN countries exemplify not only the interest of think tanks to collaborate but also the interest of governments to promote this collaboration and engage with think tanks. However, all of these networks emerged and were conceived before the 2030 Agenda. With ASEAN becoming an effective platform for the SDGs in the region, different networks may emerge as ASEAN engages with other development actors and think tanks that go beyond international relations towards more development policy. In order to lead on sustainable development, ASEAN will need to strengthen its policy-research capacity at the regional and national levels (Parks et al. 2018). This model of cooperation shows an evolution from a focus on diplomatic brokerage to more in-depth policy discussions.

The BRICS (Brazil, Russia, India, China, and South Africa) Think Tanks Council was created in 2013 as an extension of the summit of the emerging powers with objectives of "forming a platform for the exchange of ideas among researchers, academia and think tanks; convening the annual BRICS Academic Forum; and making policy recommendations and giving guidance to the BRICS Leaders for consideration" (Department of International Relations and Cooperation Republic of South Africa 2013). Similar to the Network of East Asian Think-Tanks, the BRICS Think Tanks Council emerged from an official mandate, which may put pressure on the independence of the networks and their flexibility to adapt and evolve. In this model of cooperation, as with the ASEAN model, it is essential to note the relevance of the support from governments and the clear mandate for collaborating.

Another collaboration among think tanks from the Global South is the Network of Southern Think Tanks (NeST),[5] which works to generate and consolidate knowledge on South-South cooperation (SSC). It was launched during the Mexico High-Level Meeting on Effective Development Cooperation in 2014, at a time when the debates on development cooperation were at a difficult stage. At this point of the global process, the Global Partnership for Effective Development Co-operation was created with the expectation of bringing new actors into the debates on development cooperation—mainly countries with emerging economies, since they were not engaged in the previous debates on effective development cooperation. Given the lack of formal agreement between governments, it was important, in this context, for government and non-government think tanks to initiate a network to shape SSC at a technical level (Shankland and Constantine 2014). NeST was convened by think tanks from India, South Africa, Brazil, and China. Two Northern-based think tanks were also invited as observers, signalling an interest of further engaging with Northern peers in the debates on cooperation. Using technical information, the research from the network backs the political discussions on SSC, mainly through the lenses of SSC providers. The network also fills an existing gap, as SSC processes have received much less attention than those for North-South cooperation in terms of global norm-setting. The NeST model showcases an example of a hybrid space between government and non-government think tanks that enables the co-production of research while maintaining a close connection with inter-governmental processes.

Southern Voice, a network of 51 think tanks from Africa, Asia, and Latin America, was founded in 2012. The founding members of the network were all part of the Think Tank Initiative, a multi-donor programme managed by the Canadian government's International Development Research Centre that aimed to strengthen think tanks' capacities in various countries. Meetings across regions for the first time created a unique opportunity to identify alternatives to collaborate and influence global debates. The main goal of the network remains repositioning research and policy analysis from developing countries and serving as an open platform for the debates on the SDGs.

Southern Voice "informs global discussions by bringing national and regional knowledge, along with a sense of realism and pragmatism, to the table" (Bhattacharya and Ordóñez-Llanos 2016, p. 4). Since its inception, Southern Voice has generated evidence around a variety of topics related to the SDGs, from its design and implementation to the data required for its proper evaluation. Southern Voice's contribution is to create an independent space for thinking strategically about long-term policy changes as well as issues that may not be a priority in current debates. Although independence is important, this model has the challenge of continually finding the links to the policy arena.

These models of networks and collaborations among think tanks from the Global South show that they can identify similar strategies and goals, which lead to collaborations, as described in the Four-C's model. The objectives may be to strengthen a regional or thematic position, to facilitate a technical dialogue among diverse groups, or to create new policy ideas and narratives. These networks all respond to an asymmetry of knowledge and power between the North and the South in global debates and the realisations that, for Southern governments, having a stronger position on global policy dialogues requires up-to-date knowledge and evidence as well as innovative ideas and propositions. Think tanks can play a role, either by building bridges among themselves or with governments and regional bodies.

32.5 North-South Think Tank Collaborations

As the 2030 Agenda requires broader consensus-building across countries of different regions and at different levels of economic development, new partnerships may emerge for this purpose. Think tanks and academic institutions can promote action by "addressing the North-South divide that often plagues these discussions by enabling more South-South partnerships and by coming together beyond such divides to take the Agenda forward" (Jha et al. 2016, p. 2). Can such partnerships emerge that go beyond the North-South divide?

Collaborations among think tanks from the North and South for working on development are not new and may be seen as mechanisms to increase the reach of think tanks from the Global North and improve the capacities of peers in the Global South (Kimenyi 2013). But these collaborations have focussed more on research and capacity-building than informing global policy-making. The fact that the previous development agenda did not have a global reach may help explain the limited opportunities for more formal global think tank networks to emerge.

The process of the Think 20 (T20) network may be evolving in nature to include a broad range of think tanks from diverse regions to inform this global policy-making space. T20 originated in 2012 and is part of the engagement mechanisms of the G20. There are several engagement groups for businesses, civil society, and labour unions, among others, and together they comprise the consultative processes of the G20 process. No clear set of rules define the participation or decision-making processes—these change every year due to the rotating G20 presidency. Each government defines the co-chairs of the different engagement groups. As a result, the legitimacy of the composition and the importance of each group changes with the host country (Alexander and Löschmann 2016). In 2017, during the German presidency, the presence of the engagement groups and the levels of diversity increased. Under the presidency of Argentina in 2018, the T20 network expanded further, with the Argentinean co-chairs explicitly aiming to increase the reach of the network to include think tanks beyond the G20 countries. They acknowledged that G20 policies have an impact beyond the national borders of G20 countries. The regional representation of Africa in these engagement groups is particularly limited, as South Africa is the only formal African member of the G20. Within the T20 process, which is relatively fluid and changing, the T20 Africa Standing Group emerged as a permanent space of engagement for African scholars. It is a network that brings together more than 30 think tanks from Africa and G20 countries to collaborate specifically on informing the policy-making process of the G20 in relation to its impacts on Africa (Leininger 2017). The group aims to have a consistent presence and mechanisms of communication as well as to follow-up on the recommendations proposed by the group (Begashaw et al. 2018). Among its members in the United Nations Economic Commission for Africa, the T20 Africa Standing Group includes an interlocutor to advance a regional agenda. The existence of this sub-network within a broader global network may be a symptom of the difficulty of creating horizontal partnerships among Northern and Southern peers in the context of persistent asymmetries in power, capacity, and funding. Following Najam's model (2000), the T20 Africa Standing Group is a mechanism to prevent co-optation, which happens when actors have similar strategies but different objectives. In this case, the particular concerns of experts in Africa may have particular positions that are different to those of experts focussed more broadly on the G20 countries. Having a group that thinks of the particular needs of a region prevents these interests from being overshadowed by the broader G20 agenda.

What the previous two sections point to is to an emerging community of think tanks engaged in the global policy space of the 2030 Agenda. By having a national focus and a global reach, the 2030 Agenda allows for a broader range of actors to engage and to share lessons. Although some of the networks analysed emerge from a tradition of international studies and informal diplomacy, a new wave of networks is developing from the broader community of think tanks working on policy issues and agendas. In practice, networks between think tanks will emerge as constellations. Constellations is a valuable metaphor, as they are not fixed entities—they are open and can provide flexible arrangements, whereby a think tank is not just part of one network but can engage in diverse networks, each with specific purposes. What enables collaboration among think tanks, whether North-South or South-South, is a common purpose. Most of the networks described in the previous sections are relatively new and still establishing themselves as well as their purposes, audiences, and operating modalities. But what will happen as they become stronger? Or as their agendas begin to diverge? Following Najam's (2000) model, co-optation of these spaces and networks may occur. Whether the stronger parties try to absorb or take over the others has yet to be seen.

32.6 Southern Think Tank Engagement with Other International Actors

As discussed in the first section, the global policy space includes a diversity of other actors that think tanks can potentially relate to, such as NGOs, international NGOs, international and multilateral organisations, actors from the private sector, and governments, particularly the offices of the ministries of foreign affairs. Given the relative newness of the SDGs, these relationships are emerging and will most likely include a variety of actors in different partnership compositions.

Relationships between NGOs and think tanks can be complementary if common goals are identified. NGOs and think tanks tend to differ in their strategies for outreach and advocacy. Although NGOs use their values and relationships with broader society as legitimacy tools to engage in policy debates, think tanks base their legitimacy on the findings of their research. In the current context, NGOs can benefit from more support in making sense of the complex 2030 Agenda (Shankland and Constantine 2014) as well as identifying policy options that achieve the goals of NGOs but that are also grounded in research and evidence. At the same time, think tanks may find it valuable to reach out to NGOs to share their policy ideas and recommendations, as NGOs are also relevant actors in development, and their buy-into policy reforms is important. To further these relationships, think tanks and NGOs may need to overcome the mistrust that may emerge from their distinct approaches, even when they have similar goals.

Collaborations with actors from the private sector and governments are challenging, primarily for independent think tanks in the Global South that wish to set clear boundaries on the external influence on their research agendas. In the global space, think tanks can engage with governments beyond their own. In these relationships, funding becomes a key question: Does receiving funds from governments or the private sector undermine a think tank's independence? In the global space, does it undermine the sovereignty of the think tank's own country? There are significant debates on whether think tanks are vehicles for foreign powers to intrude in domestic politics or advocacy fronts for corporations (Baertl Helguero 2018). The global nature of policy debates may accentuate this discussion and the related challenges for think tanks. Transparency becomes an important ingredient for maintaining the independence of think tanks.

Through the Four-C's model, the previous sections explored the relationships of Southern think tanks with each other and with other actors. Think tanks are organisations with a strong capacity to facilitate partnerships and dialogues. Collaboration among think tanks from the Global South enables not only a sharing of knowledge among them, but also the opportunity to build bridges between countries. Partnerships involving peers from the Global North are also feasible, but the possibility of co-optation is present in the context of asymmetries of power, capacities, and resources. With other actors, there are also opportunities for cooperation, particularly when the final goals (or ends in the Four-C's model) are aligned. Even then, however, actors would require building trust so that common goals guide these partnerships, even if the strategies (or means) are different.

32.7 Think Tanks in the Age of Partnerships

"All countries and all stakeholders, acting in collaborative partnership, will implement this plan", states the declaration of the 2030 Agenda in its second paragraph, setting the tone of global development policy moving forward (United Nations 2016, preamble). Turning these partnerships into practice, however, remains a challenge. This chapter has explored the relationships between think tanks from the Global South with each other, with their Northern peers, and with the broader international community. It shows that collaborations may drive relationships with others, given that some conditions are met.

First, think tanks need to rethink their business models for the age of partnerships. As described in Sect. 32.2 on the implications of the SDGs on think tanks, the 2030 Agenda poses challenges to the work of think tanks—both in how they do research and how they support policy reform. The diversity of actors in the policy debates makes it hard for think tanks to approach only governments—and alone. They need to be working alongside them and collaborating with other organisations that are active in global debates, including NGOs and actors from the private sector. This may require changes to how they carry out research, how they communicate it, and how they engage in policy debates, publicly and behind closed doors. Think tanks also need to be able to develop trust with other actors. Besides, think tanks will need to embrace research strategies and methods that reflect the multi-dimensional challenges of sustainable development.

Second, partnerships need to gain legitimacy, which depends on the extent to which they are inclusive, deliberative, and effective at accomplishing their goals (Verschaeve and Orbie 2016). The participation of more actors from the Global South, including think tanks, may increase the inclusivity of partnerships, which is one key element of legitimacy. The second dimension—being deliberative—requires not only the inclusion of actors, but also their active engagement in the debates and decision-making processes. Applying the Four-C's model highlights a challenge of inclusive partnerships when there is an asymmetry of power: the possibility of co-optation. Maintaining a deliberative partnership is more challenging and requires acknowledging and tackling the power asymmetries described in previous sections.

Finally, partnerships will have to be effective and able to deliver on their mandates. However, partnerships that become more inclusive and deliberative may struggle to make decisions and achieve results. Keeping in mind these aspects can help Southern think tanks and other actors to engage in collaborative partnerships.

Notes

1. For more information, see https://ottd.onthinktanks.org/directory/.
2. It is quite difficult to account for the total number of think tanks in the world, given their fluid nature. Some organisations that carry out the activities of think tanks in research, policy analysis, and outreach may not consider themselves to be think tanks.
3. Think tanks are research centres that produce research related to policy and conduct outreach and communications activities to share policy ideas and recommendations with policy experts and the broader public.
4. The MDGs had focussed primarily on how to alleviate poverty in developing countries, the role of aid, and more broadly the international community. Now development debates are framed around the SDGs and include economic, social, and environmental dimensions. The discussions are no longer focussed on developing countries but are universal.
5. For more information, please go to http://southernthinktanks.org.

References

Alexander, N., & Löschmann, H. (2016, December 9). *The solar system of G20: Engagement groups*. https://www.boell.de/en/2016/12/08/solar-system-g20-engagement-groups.

Ashoff, G. (2005). *Enhancing policy coherence for development: Justification, recognition and approaches to achievement* (Studies 11). Bonn: German Development Institute/Deutsches Institut für Entwicklungspolitik (DIE).

Association of Southeast Asian Nations. (2019, February 22). *ASEAN think-tanks meet to discuss achieving ASEAN vision and ASCC Blueprint 2025* (ASEAN Secretariat News). https://asean.org/asean-think-tanks-meet-discuss-achieving-asean-vision-ascc-blueprint-2025/.

Baertl Helguero, A. (2018). *De-constructing credibility factors that affect a think tank's credibility* (Working Paper 4). https://medium.com/@info_92670/de-constructing-credibility-722ade1f731b.

Begashaw, B., Onubedo, G., Hui, M., & Chakrabarti, M. (2018). *Cooperation with Africa—T20 Africa, G20 and Africa: Assessing our impact and influence*. https://t20argentina.org/wp-content/uploads/2018/08/T20-Africa-Monitoring-and-Evaluation-v6.pdf.

Bhattacharya, D., & Ordóñez-Llanos, A. (2016). *Southern perspectives on the post-2015 international development agenda*. Abingdon: Routledge.

Council on East Asian Community. (n.d.). *NEAT and EAF*. http://www.ceac.jp/e/neat.htm.

Department of International Relations and Cooperation Republic of South Africa. (2013, November 12). *Mid-term meeting of the BRICS Think Tanks Council.* http://www.dirco.gov.za/docs/2013/brics1112a.html.

Horner, R., & Hulme, D. (2019). From international to global development: New geographies of 21st century development. *Development and Change, 50*(2), 347–378.

Howes, S. (2014). A framework for understanding aid effectiveness determinants, strategies and tradeoffs: Understanding aid effectiveness. *Asia & the Pacific Policy Studies, 1,* 58–72.

Jha, A., Kickbusch, I., Taylor, P., & Abbasi, K. (2016). Accelerating achievement of the Sustainable Development Goals. *BMJ, 352*(i409), 1–2.

Kimenyi, M. (2013, August 14). *Creating global reach: Brookings's partnerships with think tanks in Africa.* https://www.brookings.edu/blog/up-front/2013/08/14/creating-global-reach-brookingss-partnerships-with-think-tanks-in-africa/.

Leininger, J. (2017). "On the table or at the table?" G20 and its cooperation with Africa. *Global Summitry, 3*(2), 193–205.

Najam, A. (2000). The four C's of government third sector-government relations. *Nonprofit Management and Leadership, 10*(4), 375–396.

Niblett, R. (2018). Rediscovering a sense of purpose: The challenge for Western think-tanks. *International Affairs, 94*(6), 1409–1429.

Ordóñez, A., Bellettini, O., Mendizabal, E., Broadbent, E., & Muller, J. (2012). *Influencing as a learning process: Think tanks and the challenge of improving policies and promoting social change.* https://idl-bnc-idrc.dspacedirect.org/bitstream/handle/10625/50230/IDL-50230.pdf.

Parks, T., Maramis, L., Sunchindah, A., & Wongwatanakul, W. (2018). *ASEAN as the architect for regional development cooperation; advancing ASEAN centrality and catalyzing action for sustainable development.* http://hdl.handle.net/11540/8970.

Perkins, R. (2013). Sustainable development and the making and unmaking of a developing world. *Environment and Planning C: Government and Policy, 31*(6), 1003–1022.

Shankland, A., & Constantine, J. (2014). Defining the post-2015 world: What roles for inclusive rights-based partnerships? In B. Tomlinson (Ed.), *Beyond lip service on mutual learning: The potential of CSO and think-tank partnerships for transforming rising powers' contributions to sustainable development* (pp. 105–116). East Sussex: Institute of Development Studies.

Stone, D. (2001). Think tanks, global lesson-drawing and networking social policy ideas. *Global Social Policy: An Interdisciplinary Journal of Public Policy and Social Development, 1*(3), 338–360.

Stone, D. (2007). Recycling bins, garbage cans or think tanks? Three myths regarding policy analysis institutes. *Public Administration, 85*(2), 259–278.

Stone, D. (2013). *Knowledge actors and transnational governance: The private–public policy nexus in the global agora.* Basingstoke: Palgrave Macmillan.

United Nations. (2016). *Transforming our world: The 2030 Agenda for Sustainable Development.* https://sustainabledevelopment.un.org/post2015/transformingourworld.

Verschaeve, J., & Orbie, J. (2016). The DAC is dead, long live the DCF? A comparative analysis of the OECD Development Assistance Committee and the UN development cooperation forum. *European Journal of Development Research, 28*(4), 571–587.

Open Access This chapter is licensed under the terms of the Creative Commons Attribution 4.0 International License (http://creativecommons.org/licenses/by/4.0/), which permits use, sharing, adaptation, distribution and reproduction in any medium or format, as long as you give appropriate credit to the original author(s) and the source, provide a link to the Creative Commons license and indicate if changes were made.

The images or other third party material in this chapter are included in the chapter's Creative Commons license, unless indicated otherwise in a credit line to the material. If material is not included in the chapter's Creative Commons license and your intended use is not permitted by statutory regulation or exceeds the permitted use, you will need to obtain permission directly from the copyright holder.

CHAPTER 33

Conclusion: Leveraging Development Cooperation Experiences for the 2030 Agenda—Key Messages and the Way Forward

Sachin Chaturvedi, Heiner Janus, Stephan Klingebiel, Li Xiaoyun, André de Mello e Souza, Elizabeth Sidiropoulos, and Dorothea Wehrmann

The chapters in this volume have all addressed the challenges of contested cooperation in moving towards collaboration in ways that contribute to implementing the 2030 Agenda for Sustainable Development. They focus on the evolving and conflicting normative views on development cooperation, on the roles of specific and important stakeholders, on technical issues involved in that agenda, and on the needs and challenges of institution-shifting and of

---

S. Chaturvedi (✉)
Research and Information System for Developing Countries (RIS), New Delhi, India
e-mail: sachin@ris.org.in

H. Janus · S. Klingebiel · D. Wehrmann
German Development Institute / Deutsches Institut für Entwicklungspolitik (DIE), Bonn, Germany
e-mail: heiner.janus@die-gdi.de

S. Klingebiel
e-mail: stephan.klingebiel@die-gdi.de

D. Wehrmann
e-mail: dorothea.wehrmann@die-gdi.de

X. Li
China Agricultural University, Beijing, China
e-mail: xiaoyun@cau.edu.cn

A. de Mello e Souza
Institute for Applied Economic Research, Brasília, Brazil
e-mail: andre.souza@ipea.gov.br

© The Author(s) 2021
S. Chaturvedi et al. (eds.), *The Palgrave Handbook of Development Cooperation for Achieving the 2030 Agenda*,
https://doi.org/10.1007/978-3-030-57938-8_33

newly created platforms. In the process, the handbook also takes up Agenda 2063 with its seven aspirations that Africa wants to achieve, highlighted in the chapter by Sidiropoulos, and the Paris Agreement, noted in chapters by Chan, Iacobuta, and Haegele as well as Weigel and Demissie. Both were incidentally adopted in 2015.

The handbook sets out to answer the question of how different narratives and norms in development cooperation can be reconciled towards achieving the 2030 Agenda. We propose a three-step approach for reflecting on this guiding question. First, we provide a more detailed overview of the narratives and norms shaping distinct approaches in the realm of policy for development cooperation. Second, we explore persisting and new institutional sites of contestations. Third, we also explore how international governance structures can better address contestations and enhance collaboration and cooperation.

By mapping the evolving and increasingly complex multi-stakeholder landscape of development cooperation actors, the chapters in this volume contribute to a deeper knowledge of the various norms and narratives guiding the practices in the field of development cooperation. Furthermore, the chapters shed light on what we called "persisting and new sites of contested cooperation, particularly in the areas of setting narratives and norms, institutional architecture and international governance structures". These sites include the negotiation processes among states and non-state actors within international and multilateral organisations, multi-stakeholder partnerships, bilateral and multilateral cooperation, and other development cooperation-related platforms. As an example of this global landscape of contested cooperation, in his chapter, Swiss describes how the globalisation of aid unfolds as a cyclical dynamic of the coming and going of vogues of different aid priorities.

Notably, the Sustainable Development Goal (SDG) framework only offers little guidance on how these different actors and platforms can coordinate their contributions towards achieving the 2030 Agenda. In addition, the consensus underlying the SDGs is permanently contested by changing political dynamics, including the rise of nationalist policies and a decreasing readiness for global collective action. Against this background, several chapters explore how existing global governance structures may be further improved for dealing with contestations and avoiding gridlock; these include the chapters of Chan, Iacobuta, and Haegele; Mello e Souza; Li and Qi; Engberg-Pedersen and Fejerskov; Kloke-Lesch; and Weigel and Demissie. The two critical categories for these examples are actors voluntarily taking on greater responsibilities for international cooperation and actors piloting new forms of cooperation under the SDG framework.

E. Sidiropoulos
South African Institute of International Affairs, Johannesburg, South Africa
e-mail: Elizabeth.sidiropoulos@wits.ac.za

Several examples from the chapters illustrate these points. The financing of Sustainable Development, as defined in the 2030 Agenda, is a key concern that has been taken up across this volume by different authors. This issue assumes special significance in this handbook because the 2030 Agenda and its 17 SDGs are far more ambitious than the Millennium Development Goals, and so far, the expected financing mechanisms have not been able to deliver what was expected. Very few donor countries provide the 0.7 per cent of gross national income to finance official development assistance (ODA), including debt relief. Although efforts are required to continue to press for the 0.7 per cent of gross national income commitment, it is important to supplement efforts for a large quanta of resource mobilisation for the timely achievement of the SDGs. In this regard, the concept of Total Official Support for Sustainable Development is aimed at complementing ODA and is addressed in this volume. Various chapters acknowledge the growing role that emerging economies are playing in supporting multilateralism, among other ways by promoting two new multilateral institutions, viz. the New Development Bank (NDB) (popularly known as the "BRICS bank") and the Asian Infrastructure Investment Bank (AIIB); this is discussed at length in the chapters by Paulo; Seifert; and Zaytsev.

Next, several chapters analyse how development cooperation actors have taken on greater responsibilities in promoting the 2030 Agenda across different regions. Janus and Tang, for example, illustrate how China promoted the 2030 Agenda during its G20 presidency and enhanced national development commitments. In addition to these examples, there are four cross-cutting contributions of this handbook that emerge from the chapters and represent key findings on the evolution of the policy field of development cooperation: (1) the primacy of the SDGs, (2) new theoretical frameworks, (3) contestations and cooperation, and (4) going beyond contestations.

33.1 Primacy of the SDGs

Achieving development goals has been, both historically and theoretically, a complex and elusive task. In the context of globalisation, the imperative of providing global public goods and addressing the increasing cross-border effects of domestic policies render international development cooperation indispensable. The SDGs cannot be successfully achieved in the absence of some sort of cross-border cooperation, as discussed in the introduction of this volume as well as throughout several subsequent chapters.

As they emerge, two profound and relatively recent developments in world politics can be expected to make international collaboration in the ambit of the 2030 Agenda more challenging: first, significant shifts in the world distribution of power, marked by the emergence of multipolarity and the increasing role of rising powers such as Brazil, Russia, India, China, and South Africa (BRICS)—especially China; second, and related, increasing institutional fragmentation that is caused by shifts in existing institutions and the creation of new institutions. Fragmentation trends go well beyond development cooperation topics (Klingebiel et al. 2016). This has been visible, for example, in the emerging structure on global environmental governance over the last few decades (Zelli and van Asselt 2013). Such fragmentation generates, in turn, greater challenges for policy coordination, coherence, and efficiency on all levels. Globally, it leads to a proliferation of institutions and platforms.

Simple coordination problems are usually easier to solve than those that involve distributional issues or normative contestation, which often refer to the very notion of development itself. More generally, cross-border cooperation can assume different degrees of stakeholder involvement and commitment, which largely depend on the different kinds of collective action problems to be addressed.

Burden-sharing and joint risk-taking are characteristics of deeper forms of cooperation that we call collaboration. We found indications that the SDG framework has a much greater chance of succeeding if multiple actors are engaged in related processes, especially when including non-state and subnational actors. Given the fact that the SDGs and climate governance are polycentric in nature, the chapter by Chan, Iacobuta, and Haegele focusses on three interlinkages, viz. sustainable and climate-resilient development, emerging polycentricity, and coordination tools. The polycentric structure holds the promise of more effective governance and, in a scenario in which contestations have multiplied, this may help even in the absence of hierarchy.

This may become possible with new modalities, which may include greater convergence of various modes of engagement. Fejerskov and Engberg-Pedersen, on the other hand, argue that the extent to which global norms diffuse as a recognisable, homogeneous understanding is crucial for their broader acceptability across countries and in their differing social milieus and contexts. They introduce a "situated approach to global norms" to explain why the SDGs have not uniformised development discussions around the world yet.

The challenge of collaboration can be summarised as one of reconciling the need for inclusive and legitimate norms and institutions with efficiency, as argued by Mello e Souza, as notably a development cooperation regime becomes necessary from a systemic perspective. The chapter uses models of stakeholder participation in governance institutions to understand the exiting of Brazil, India, and China from the attempted global multi-stakeholder regime of the Global Partnership for Effective Development Co-operation (GPEDC).

This problem is compounded by the absence of any mechanism for prioritising the SDGs, which are numerous and arguably comprise all issues that relate to development, broadly conceived. As a result, the 2030 Agenda risks not bringing about significant change, but rather serving to legitimise policies that national governments planned to adopt regardless of the SDGs, but which can be presented as a response to the SDGs.

On a global level, Mawdsley, in her chapter, warns that the SDGs cannot resolve the existing contradictions between economies, societies, and environments that persist under the hegemony of finance capital. The regional connect at times is very strong when it comes to specific actors, as Zaytsev presents in his chapter on aid flows from Russia. As it has emerged, Russia's priorities are mostly associated with facilitating the integration processes within the realm of the Commonwealth of Independent States, with a particular emphasis on the development of trade and economic cooperation (SDG 9).

Moreover, the fact that voluntary national reviews (VNRs) on the implementation of the 2030 Agenda at the United Nations (UN) High-level Political Forum on Sustainable Development are the cornerstone of the follow-up and review framework of the 2030 Agenda further weakens this framework institutionally. However, the efforts to bring in accountability through measurement are a ray of hope. Collective efforts would be required to bring out the majority of indicators appearing in the "Tier III" category for precision in implementation gaps with no clear data sources or methodologies. In their chapter, Avendano, Jütting, and Kuhm argue that the alignment of global requirements with national priorities, new forms of inclusive cooperation, and a global financing facility for development data are possible solutions to overcome key challenges of the SDG indicator framework.

Schwachula in this volume has analysed German science policy for cooperation between Germany and the Global South. She suggests that, as we are moving forward with the SDGs, the possibilities for bilateral understanding and/or agreement between the Global North and South may be explored, bringing in different stakeholders, scales of cooperation, and themes for sustainable cooperation. The need for collective cooperation is captured in the chapter by Chakrabarti and Chaturvedi, who call for the creation of global public goods in order to achieve the SDGs.

33.2 Theoretical Frameworks

The volume addresses several theoretical frameworks across different chapters. Some of the key frameworks that are theoretically important and practically relevant are discussed below for facilitating a broader discussion on possible choices for parallel frameworks.

33.2.1 *The Globalisation of Aid and Diffusion of Norms*

Swiss applies sociological theories drawing on the World Society literature towards studying the globalisation of foreign aid at the macro- and micro-levels. At the macro-level, donors are influenced by the behaviour of other states, embedded in the global networks of international organisations, and aim to comply with global agendas such as the SDGs. At the micro-level, the literature on policy and norm translation describes how officials act to translate and adapt ideas into aid agencies. Pedersen and Fejerskov add to this analysis by arguing that diffusion of the 2030 Agenda and the SDGs is not only challenging due to contemporary political circumstances, but also because of the fundamentally situated nature of how actors engage with global norms. They highlight that global norms are at the core of the SDGs and have an "inter-subjective nature", which means that they are addressed, reproduced, or changed during social interactions and cannot be understood as existing outside such processes. Complementing these two theoretical perspectives on norms, Gulrajani and Calleja undertake an empirical mapping of aid allocation patterns of "Northern" donors, showing to what extents norms of "self-interest" and what they call "principled interest" in furthering the security, stability, and prosperity of the world prevail.

33.2.2 Discursive Institutionalism

Discursive institutionalism is a framework that helps to move away from a static perspective. Instead, the framework draws attention to the contexts in which agents think, speak, and act, for example, as part of an institution rather than being external to it. By considering this framework and the concept of coalition magnets, Janus and Tang analyse three areas of engagement, viz. the 2030 Agenda, mutual benefit, and development results. As per the discussions in other fora, this framework encourages "the North" to learn from "the South" and to adopt some of the best practices that are prevalent across "the South" for advancing the 2030 Agenda. These examples, however, largely focus on governmental actors, whereas the key success of South-South cooperation (SSC) is the multiplicity of actors engaged.

There is a need to evolve a framework that includes the considerations of non-state actors and encourages social mobilisation around some of the select features. While selecting coalition magnet ideas, one may also, of course, evolve frameworks that bring in specific endogenous variables from two contesting entities for better convergence as they move towards implementing a global agenda. For instance, mutual benefit is actually not a feature of the Organisation for Economic Co-operation and Development (OECD) Development Assistance Committee (DAC) approach of Official Development Assistance (ODA); putting that as a coalition magnet may not be relevant for many of their members.

Further work with these new approaches and contexts would certainly trigger a greater move towards more broadly acceptable approaches. In this volume, an initial effort in this direction is made by Ali in examining the China–Pakistan Economic Corridor (CPEC) using the South Africa SSC framework of the Network of Southern Think Tanks. Though the author recognises the data limitations, the lack of transparency, and the lack of competitive bidding in the Chinese financing of CPEC, on a broader level he notes that CPEC reflects the underlying principles of SSC comprising mutual respect and building local capacity.

Additionally, India's theoretical framework of the Development Compact is also enumerated in the chapter by Chakrabarti and Chaturvedi, who call for better convergence between the SDGs and SSC. The chapter analyses some newer experiments in the institutionalisation of cooperation in providing global public goods that would facilitate the achievements of SDGs.

33.2.3 Orchestration, the Theory of Middle Powers, and the Four-C's Model

The concept of orchestration, on the other hand, facilitates the integration of different approaches and considerations brought forward by state and non-state actors that are geared towards achieving a shared goal. Orchestrators (e.g. international organisations) define an agenda (such as the 2030 Agenda) that is shared by intermediaries (states) who engage with individual targets or target groups (e.g. actors from the private sector) to reach the shared goal. The chapter by Pérez-Pineda and Wehrmann shows that when engaging with individual targets or target groups at different (global or national) levels, it is important that intermediaries consider context-specific particularities and adapt their aims and strategies, respectively. Their investigation of the cases of the Alliance for Sustainability and the GPEDC further illustrates that the success of different types of actors that cooperate in multi-actor partnerships also depends on how orchestrators perform in their role.

Middle Power Theory (MPT) focusses on countries that have considerable influence, but not as much as super powers. The chapter by Baydag presents an MPT-based approach with the case studies of South Korea and Turkey in international development cooperation. Both have enhanced their visibility through their aid and development projects. MPT helps in understanding the role of middle powers in reducing possible conflicts between the established actors and the emerging actors. Middle powers help to bring possible convergences and can thus also be perceived as intermediaries.

Furthermore, Ordóñez-Llanos introduces the "Four-C's model" as a concept that illuminates the relationships that emerge among different actors, and particularly how actors share power and contribute to vital partnerships. She applies this model to investigate the relationships between think tanks from the "Global South" with their "Northern" peers as well as with the broader international community. In her chapter, she classifies these relationships according to the strategies and goals that actors have in a given policy process, namely the "Four-C's": cooperation, confrontation, complementarity, or co-optation. From this classification, Ordóñez-Llanos concludes that the possibility for co-optation is the challenge of developing inclusive partnerships when there is an asymmetry of power.

33.3 Contestations and Cooperation

The rise of right-wing nationalism and populism worldwide poses challenges of its own to international development cooperation, and especially collaboration. Most notably, leaders in the United States, the UK, Russia, Turkey, Brazil, India, Israel, Austria, Hungary, Poland, Italy, the Philippines, and elsewhere have produced different outcomes in this regard. Some of them have rejected multilateralism, globalism, and international cooperation, whereas others have stood in favour of these approaches. However, there seems to be a greater degree of convergence when it comes to nationalism and domestic-growth-related approaches. In this context, the purposes of achieving the SDGs may not be free from several fragmentation-related challenges.

While the political pendulum does not swing back, governments unwilling to take on the burden of development finance are increasingly pointing to private-sector investments as a major source of such finance. Yet, relying on such a source requires developing strategies that enhance and regulate private-sector engagement by considering national heterogeneities and differences between the national and global levels, as demonstrated by Pérez-Pineda and Wehrmann in their chapter. This risk tends to be accentuated with the expansion of blended finance and all the challenges it poses for transparency and accountability, as shown in the chapter of Mawdsley. Instead of funding activities designed to fulfil the SDGs, there is a risk that the main role of ODA will be to leverage investment from business, venture capital, sovereign wealth funds, and other non-state sources.

Other private actors and stakeholders are also increasingly relevant in the efforts to achieve the SDGs by means of international development cooperation, by simultaneously contesting cooperation and engaging in cooperation. The role of Southern think tanks in providing the technical and specialised knowledge required to pursue the SDGs is examined by Ordóñez-Llanos. Banks investigate the role and contributions of development non-governmental organisations (NGOs) to development cooperation, pointing to the need for NGOs to maintain a radical stance rather than embrace the technical language and priorities of donors. Banks call for a transformative value-added role for development NGOs in meeting the SDGs by not only focussing on progress made towards targets and indicators, but also on modalities, the ways in which NGO operations are funded and executed, and whether this enables NGOs to be political as well as professional organisations, generating social and political change alongside their admirable impacts on the ground in service delivery.

The volume also reveals striking variations not just between South-South and North-South cooperation, but also between SSC itself, as discussed in the case studies provided in the chapters by Sidiropoulos, Baydag, Zaytsev, Pipa, and Mthembu. Furthermore, regional variations are also examined in the chapters by Mulakala and by Janus and Tang. Arguably, defining and clarifying the role of SSC in the 2030 Agenda requires building a minimally common narrative that will, in turn, require bridging these different approaches of the South.

Finally, there is variation in the very notions of development and development aid, assistance, and cooperation across time, as examined by Esteves and Klingebiel in their chapter. Several other chapters also look into specific sectors or modalities of international development cooperation and their relations with the SDG agenda, such as climate governance in Chan, Iacobuta, and Hägele as well as in Weigel and Demissie, and gender equality in Fejerskov and Engberg-Pedersen as well as in Hossain.

In addition to political and normative forms of contestation, there remain significant technical challenges to the achievement of the SDGs by means of international development cooperation. Three chapters illustrate that seemingly technical questions of measuring cooperation have deeper underlying conceptual dimensions of contested global governance. Mitchell looks into how we can measure the effort and quality of international development cooperation in his chapter and demonstrates the insufficient conceptualisation of measuring contributions to global public goods. The problems and possible solutions for the data demands of the SDG framework are examined by Avendano, Jütting, and Kuhm. Kloke-Lesch argues in favour of a functional approach to development cooperation that "would not start with the question whether countries, or people in countries, are needy, but rather whether there is a necessity or interest felt to impact on developments in countries, irrespective of whether they are listed as 'developing' or 'developed' countries". Kloke-Lesch highlights that the "means of implementation", as operationalised in the SDGs, still have a bias towards "North-South" cooperation and neglect the potential of a more universally oriented global development agenda.

There are several chapters in the handbook that refer to the GPEDC as a central example for "contested cooperation". The GPEDC has piloted new forms of cooperation and collaboration, for instance, by transitioning to a multi-stakeholder partnership itself and by forming a platform for other multi-stakeholder initiatives. At the same time, several areas of contestation, especially due to their links to the OECD, persist. As Li and Qi begin their chapter with a quote saying that, "Due to their continued reluctance – or even suspicious attitude, which started right at the beginning of the [GPEDC] process – four of the five BRICS [...] were absent from the second forum, as only Russia attended. This has had a big impact on the 'global nature' of the partnership".

Against this context, several chapters attempt to analyse related contestations. The analysis by Bracho on the failure of the GPEDC to bring together OECD members and the main emerging powers under the same institutional framework shows this greater difficulty in overcoming burden-sharing deadlocks in international negotiations. In addition, Mello e Souza points to the failure in promoting the decisional participation of emerging powers in the GPEDC. In turn, Li and Qi illustrate how China has contested many of the norms contained in the GPEDC, both implicit and explicit.

However, there are now efforts by OECD-DAC members to follow the principles of SSC on a selective basis. Reference is to be made here to the SSC principle of mutual gain, which is receiving greater acceptance in the OECD sphere. Gulrajani and Calleja have rightly captured a statement by UK Prime Minister Theresa May in South Africa in 2018, on her first trip to the continent, when she said, "I am unashamed about the need to ensure that our aid programme works for the UK". A net positive return to both donor and recipient is now a legitimate expectation and politically acceptable rationale for international aid provision.

Whether the GPEDC fills the gap through its monitoring framework—thus providing a significant contribution to the implementation of the SDGs—is the question that Bhattacharya, Gonsior, and Öhler respond to in this handbook. They suggest that this can be accomplished if UN VNRs bring in the GPEDC monitoring framework.

33.4 Going Beyond Contestations

Among the possible options for a way forward, the chapters by Zoccal and by Paulo examine triangular cooperation (TrC) as a modality that may reshape important aspects of the global architecture of development cooperation and make significant contributions to achieving the SDGs, also contributing to the promotion of greater normative convergence between South-South and North-South cooperation. Mulakala, in her chapter, observes that TrC is making a comeback, largely due to China's and India's increasing developmental impacts and influence in partner countries. Traditional donors may find TrC as a way to engage with—and possibly influence—Southern actors, and as a way to stay relevant in partner countries, whereas traditional aid is diminishing in value and impact. Paulo highlights that India's emerging practice of TrC has unique characteristics and is making significant contributions towards achieving the SDGs.

The other instrument for moving beyond contestations is common but differentiated responsibilities (CBDR), placed on a high pedestal by the Busan process at the Fourth High Level Forum on Aid Effectiveness (2011). Bracho, in his chapter, analyses at length the constraints that are evident with the application of CBDR at a practical level. According to him, this may require a new approach and a new articulation. The chapter on CBDR even suggests that those countries most in need should be doing a better job of holding all providers accountable.

Furthermore, the authors in the volume also identify areas where the development cooperation of different countries and regions is coming together. Globalisation may have led to a convergence in development norms—at least with respect to the development cooperation offered by high-income donors—by means of isomorphic processes taking place between aid institutions, as noted by Swiss.

Several chapters across the handbook discuss the evolving global convergence of approaches in the realm of development cooperation for promoting the 2030 Agenda. As may be expected, reference to the GPEDC has once more come up as a possible choice. There are views in favour and against this platform about its ability to play a global role that is acceptable to all. In the context of the GPEDC, one important recommendation from the chapter by Li and Qi is that it should not categorise "the emerging powers" as one and the same, but should rather differentiate between them and discuss the issues separately with each in order to understand their different viewpoints on the GPEDC. This is important for the global narrative to go beyond the idea of contestations. The chapter also offers interesting theoretical insights on why the GPEDC should go beyond aid-based structures and get closer to what emerging countries are arguing for—a "development compact", whereby modalities of engagement bring in coherence across trade and investment, apart from just aid-based transactions.

Next, several chapters highlight the prevailing importance of multilateral institutions. Pipa emphasises how the United States continues to promote collective governance and shared leadership, although the Trump administration has given rise to contestation and struggles over governance within multilateral structures. Whereas the United States represents an example of contestation in the form of "politicisation of international authorities" (also called regime-shifting or institution-shifting), there is also a second type of contestation in the form of "counter-institutionalisation" (also called regime-creation or institution-creation). Here, the creation of new institutions such as the AIIB or the NDB does not necessarily have to undermine multilateralism as such, but it can create new opportunities for collaboration, as explored in the chapter on SSC in addressing climate change by Weigel and Demissie.

One interesting formulation that has emerged in the handbook is the role that the middle powers may play in minimising the confrontations and enhancing convergence. However, an issue that has also emerged is that the middle-power concept requires further sharpening for easily identifying the possible countries that may be placed in this category and, with their divergence, a common pattern of middle-power behaviour can be identified.

Polycentric governance, as discussed in the handbook, may also help us move towards the 2030 Agenda and avoid contestations. The suggested tools eventually may help in understanding synergies and trade-offs. This may help in ensuring transparency about the types of actions and actors by using integrated assessment models and mapping interlinkages between goals.

Overall, our handbook applied contestation as a key concept throughout the chapters. Contested global governance (Cooper 2014; Zürn 2018) has become a main feature in international relations. Interestingly, the policy field of development cooperation is no exception and has demonstrated increased levels of contestation, despite prevailing cooperation norms. In this context, the 2030 Agenda for Sustainable Development is a source for contestation and consensus at the same time. In development cooperation, the agenda is used extensively by actors and provides an overarching narrative, while also defending or scrutinising different narratives and norms. Exploring this duality of contested global governance in development cooperation further, therefore, remains key for future research.

References

Cooper, A. F. (2014). The G20 and contested global governance: BRICS, middle powers and small states. *Caribbean Journal of International Relations and Diplomacy, 2*(3), 87–109.

Klingebiel, S., Mahn, T., & Negre, M. (2016). Fragmentation: A key concept for development cooperation. In S. Klingebiel, T. Mahn, & M. Negre (Eds.), *The fragmentation of aid: Concepts, measurements and implications for development cooperation* (pp. 1–18). London: Palgrave Macmillan UK.

Zelli, F., & van Asselt, H. (2013). Introduction: The institutional fragmentation of global environmental governance—Causes, consequences and responses. *Global Environmental Politics, 13*(3), 1–13.

Zürn, M. (2018). Contested global governance. *Global. Policy, 9*(1), 138–145.

Open Access This chapter is licensed under the terms of the Creative Commons Attribution 4.0 International License (http://creativecommons.org/licenses/by/4.0/), which permits use, sharing, adaptation, distribution and reproduction in any medium or format, as long as you give appropriate credit to the original author(s) and the source, provide a link to the Creative Commons license and indicate if changes were made.

The images or other third party material in this chapter are included in the chapter's Creative Commons license, unless indicated otherwise in a credit line to the material. If material is not included in the chapter's Creative Commons license and your intended use is not permitted by statutory regulation or exceeds the permitted use, you will need to obtain permission directly from the copyright holder.

INDEX

A

access, 28, 37, 77, 78, 92–98, 100–102, 106, 107, 109, 110, 169, 173, 225, 258, 266, 267, 290–292, 295, 300, 324, 341, 342, 354, 355, 357, 456, 465, 470, 483, 488, 530, 550, 551, 607, 612, 614, 616, 617, 619, 631, 633, 638, 640, 649, 650, 652, 656, 661, 665, 691
accountability mechanisms, 53, 340, 401
Accra Action Agenda, 375
actor-centred perspective, 353
Agencia Mexicana de Cooperación Internacional para el Desarrollo (AMEXCID), 171, 177, 178, 386, 652, 659–664
2030 Agenda (for sustainable development), 1–4, 6, 8–11, 13–15, 25, 26, 29, 31, 35, 39, 42, 43, 51–53, 60, 64, 66, 72–74, 78, 92, 110, 113, 117, 119, 120, 122, 127–132, 136–147, 149, 150, 165–168, 170, 173, 179, 180, 185, 187, 218, 219, 223, 224, 227, 229–231, 233–235, 248, 249, 290, 291, 309, 310, 314–316, 321, 329, 330, 332, 333, 336, 339, 340, 343, 352–354, 356, 360, 361, 363, 394, 399, 401, 410, 412, 414, 423, 426, 429, 476, 485, 491, 506, 522, 525, 527, 544, 545, 559, 584, 585, 589, 596, 598, 605, 616, 625, 631, 649–654, 656, 657, 660, 662–666, 689, 691–695, 697–700, 705–712, 715
agenda-setting, 67, 76, 77, 114, 117, 188, 223, 235, 429
aid agencies, 114, 117, 118, 121, 133, 136, 171, 176–178, 505, 509, 534, 611, 710
aid allocation, 117, 225, 233, 258, 273, 277, 284, 479, 494, 495, 710
aid burden, 373, 376, 379
aid effectiveness, 3, 15, 116, 121, 199–201, 233, 253, 255–257, 261, 293, 311, 312, 350, 357, 361, 362, 368, 373, 394, 397, 398, 422, 480, 492, 493, 501, 590, 594, 596, 653, 661
Aid Effectiveness agenda, 385
aid funds, 113, 227
alternative approaches, 118, 120
alternative development experiences, 400
alternative model, 217, 220
altruism, 273, 284, 382
ambiguity, 170, 223
ambitious agenda, 110, 166, 662
analytical framework, 3, 92, 93, 131, 209, 219, 222, 290–294, 300, 302, 304, 306

Asian Infrastructure Investment Bank (AIIB), 3, 5, 12, 150, 218, 359, 403, 405, 412, 477, 493, 509, 525, 526, 530, 612–615, 617, 619, 636, 707, 715
autonomy, 31, 71, 75, 117, 189, 195, 578, 681

B
Bandung Conference, 186, 191, 224
behavioural changes, 38, 309–311, 314, 316, 318–321
Beijing World Conference on Women, 116
Belt and Road Initiative (BRI), 5, 218, 226, 229, 289, 382, 404, 412, 505, 508, 522–526, 530, 531, 534, 535, 609, 617, 636, 639
best practice, 110, 116, 118, 121, 257, 358, 375, 485, 509, 633, 661, 710
bilateral agreements, 352, 354, 361, 507, 610
bilateral aid donors, 113
Bill & Melinda Gates Foundation (BMGF), 97, 98, 152
billions to trillions, 51, 204
Blended Finance Taskforce, 52
Brazil, Russia, India, China and South Africa (BRICS), 4, 5, 69, 186, 207, 218, 225, 350, 359, 393, 405, 411–413, 418, 419, 430, 436, 437, 445, 476, 482, 509, 526, 567, 613, 630, 636, 696, 707, 713
Buenos Aires Plan of Action (BAPA), 5, 12, 147, 186, 200, 208, 209, 283, 370, 383, 412, 428, 543, 583, 584, 587, 588, 593, 595, 596, 625, 631, 650, 651
burden-sharing, 208, 230, 231, 352, 363, 368, 372–376, 379, 380, 384, 503, 708, 713
Busan agreement, 368
Busan high-level forum on aid effectiveness, 546, 588
Busan outcome document, 350, 369, 377, 380, 543
buy-in approach, 398

C
capacity development, 60, 63, 64, 70, 78, 203, 330, 332, 334, 337, 339–343, 422, 632
capital flight, 52
causal pathways, 273
certification process, 120
China–Pakistan Economic Corridor (CPEC), 289–291, 294–306, 523, 710
civil society groups, 117, 461, 469, 470
civil society partnerships, 7, 310, 324
climate change, 3, 26, 28, 32, 41, 52, 56, 66, 78, 91, 106, 110, 116, 118, 143, 179, 271, 277, 279, 354, 356, 370, 376, 423, 437, 512, 527, 605, 606, 608–619, 715
climate governance, 27, 30–34, 36, 38, 44, 708, 713
coalition magnets, 219, 222–224, 227, 229, 231–235, 710
co-existence, 293, 524
co-financing policy, 98, 99
coherence, 26–30, 36–44, 60, 69–71, 75, 76, 78, 119, 120, 137, 144, 147, 174, 199, 233, 258, 292, 302, 303, 319, 324, 350, 352, 354, 355, 415, 421, 504, 691, 708, 715
Cold War, 8, 187, 197, 198, 274, 275, 368, 372, 381, 382, 395, 396, 410, 552, 629
collaboration, 12, 13, 16, 27, 28, 102, 105, 116, 120, 121, 153, 179, 193, 199, 247, 250, 260, 271, 283, 284, 332, 336–338, 340, 342, 343, 356, 436, 443, 444, 469, 499, 509, 512, 522, 525, 526, 533, 575, 586, 591, 596, 614, 615, 618, 638, 642, 663–665, 679, 689, 693, 695–700, 705–708, 712, 713, 715
collective action problems, 6, 7, 16, 353, 358, 359, 708
collective commitment, 91, 382
colonialism, 53, 93, 192, 350
colonial times, 61, 62, 64, 550, 551
commercial interests, 12, 232, 253, 555
Commitment to Development Index (CDI), 257, 258, 319

common goals, 101, 202, 337, 354, 361, 369, 403, 655, 657, 695, 699, 700
common good, 2, 9, 13–15, 131, 151, 368, 373, 375, 381, 385, 598
communication infrastructure, 290, 291, 304
comparison, 10, 114, 146, 188, 218, 247, 248, 252, 254, 255, 258, 261, 478, 492, 521, 576, 590, 591, 633, 682
competition, 3, 14, 15, 26, 167, 168, 176, 190, 209, 233, 257, 275, 372, 373, 380–382, 384, 429, 461, 468, 476, 477, 490, 493, 499, 507, 508, 510, 526, 618, 666
complementarity, 200, 254, 302, 311, 315, 320, 321, 526, 559, 694, 711
compromise, 28, 38, 42, 132, 368, 370, 372, 375, 377, 379, 425
concessional finance, 250, 252, 253, 255, 256, 261, 262
consensus-making, 401
constellation of actors, 186
constructivist approach, 61, 218
contestation, 2, 4–6, 8–14, 33, 120, 121, 127–134, 165, 167, 175, 177, 234, 409, 410, 412, 413, 418, 429, 430, 469, 477, 501, 519, 522, 526, 567, 568, 584, 586, 594, 596, 615, 628, 636, 641, 706–708, 713–715
contested collaboration, 179, 332, 342, 499
contested cooperation, 2, 6, 10–15, 113, 120–122, 185, 410, 429, 477, 492, 493, 606, 614, 615, 627, 636, 637, 639, 673, 705, 706, 713
convergence, 33, 151, 218, 219, 223, 226, 228–235, 276, 282, 283, 353, 381, 382, 438, 444, 476, 692, 694, 708, 710–712, 714, 715
coordination failures, 7, 331, 336, 343
coordination tools, 27, 708
Copenhagen Climate Change Conference, 32
Copernican turn, 129, 139
cost-effectiveness, 109, 331, 583, 589
country policies, 69, 259

credibility, 61, 132, 171, 172, 201, 323, 503, 505, 512
critical development studies, 131
cultural models, 114

D

Danish International Development Agency (DANIDA), 171, 175, 180
data, 3, 8, 10, 40, 41, 73, 74, 79, 98, 199, 204, 206, 228, 252, 254–257, 261, 276–280, 283, 284, 292, 293, 300, 301, 304, 305, 311, 314, 319, 321, 322, 329–334, 336–343, 352, 360, 363, 371, 399, 403, 415, 418, 470, 480, 481, 484, 485, 489, 490, 495, 502, 555–557, 568, 569, 575, 577, 584, 586, 588, 589, 598, 671, 672, 674, 680, 684–686, 697, 709, 710, 713
decision-making, 3, 6, 41–43, 67, 109, 222, 293, 294, 297, 298, 301, 305, 306, 319, 351, 352, 359, 361, 362, 398, 404, 413, 437, 461, 484, 485, 555, 686, 697, 700
decolonisation, 190, 192
deeper collaboration, 247
demand-driven practices, 334, 350
deterioration, 195, 282
developed countries, 32, 35, 65, 67, 127, 129, 131, 138–142, 144, 146, 147, 149–152, 190–193, 195, 196, 201, 204, 205, 207, 290, 310, 318, 394, 396, 397, 400, 419, 425, 428, 430, 441, 583, 586, 588, 589, 605, 606, 608, 617, 619, 626, 631, 691, 692
development agenda, 2, 76, 77, 128, 204, 333, 372, 405, 419, 424, 425, 469, 477, 486, 578, 588, 598, 650, 651, 653, 692, 695, 697, 713
development aid, 43, 372, 373, 386, 396, 397, 441–443, 476, 479, 485, 508, 552, 713
developmental disparities, 93
Development Assistance Committee (DAC), 3, 4, 10, 12, 55, 74, 92, 116, 120, 121, 130, 133, 134, 144, 147, 152, 167, 186, 188, 192–194,

197–204, 206, 207, 210, 217–219,
223–229, 232, 233, 235, 236, 252,
254, 256–258, 263, 264, 274, 275,
277–279, 283, 284, 293, 317, 340,
350, 352–357, 359–361, 367–371,
373–382, 385, 386, 395–405, 413,
416, 417, 421, 430, 436–442, 444,
476–478, 480, 481, 483, 492, 493,
495, 500, 501, 503, 506, 509,
511, 512, 519–522, 528, 534, 535,
543–550, 559, 575, 584–596, 598,
599, 626, 627, 642, 673, 678, 710,
714
development compact, 10, 92–95, 535, 628, 629, 711, 715
Development Cooperation Forum (DCF), 121, 351, 352, 354, 358, 359, 361, 362, 394, 413, 546, 650
development cooperation regime, 349–357, 359–362, 384, 708
development finance, 5, 15, 52, 53, 55, 91, 95, 186, 204, 206, 250–256, 258, 259, 261, 262, 283, 294, 317, 426, 504, 505, 508, 520, 521, 535, 574, 575, 606, 612, 617, 636, 673, 712
development paradigm, 62, 77, 186, 231, 339, 373
development priorities, 26, 100, 113, 118, 254, 263, 334, 341, 503, 507, 654
development research, 59, 60, 67, 131, 187, 188, 209, 692
differential responsibilities, 196, 202, 208
digital financial technologies, 54
diplomacy, 134, 274, 414, 438, 441, 555, 568, 574, 580, 695, 698
disaggregated accounts, 253
disagreement, 186, 350, 363, 567
discursive institutionalism, 221, 223, 231, 235, 710
discursive power, 61
dispossession, 189–191, 208
divergences, 165, 230, 234, 350, 441, 444, 692, 715
diversity, 5, 151, 170, 254, 294, 352, 363, 394, 512, 585, 588, 595, 598,
625, 652, 672, 673, 685, 690, 691, 694, 695, 698–700
division of labour, 16, 145, 354, 589
domestic constituency, 177, 273
domestic resource mobilisation (DRM), 52, 259, 339, 423
domestic spending, 95
donor–recipient relationship, 130
donor motivations, 225, 271–273
donors, 44, 52–54, 79, 113–122, 133, 146, 168, 171, 186, 190, 192–199, 201, 202, 204, 206–210, 217–219, 224–229, 232–236, 247, 255, 257, 258, 261, 271–278, 280–284, 293, 297, 331, 337, 340, 341, 361, 367–382, 385, 386, 394, 396, 400, 417, 421, 426, 428, 429, 436, 437, 439, 441, 442, 444, 455, 458, 462, 475–478, 481, 485, 493, 500, 502, 512, 519–522, 525, 532, 533, 544–552, 555, 559, 583, 585–598, 626–630, 632, 635–637, 640–642, 672, 675–678, 680, 681, 683–685, 709, 710, 712, 714

E

East-West conflict, 133
economic growth, 28, 52, 62, 67, 74, 96, 152, 217, 220, 290, 303, 356, 384, 399, 403, 422, 442, 455, 487, 489, 522, 552, 578, 587
economic system, 56, 410
emerging economies, 3, 10, 69, 144, 179, 225, 230, 259, 315, 317, 340, 350, 351, 405, 415, 416, 428, 429, 504, 544, 589, 613, 656, 664, 696, 707
emerging global consensus, 113
emerging powers (EPs), 65, 201, 202, 208, 361, 368, 370, 373–384, 386, 395, 399–405, 424, 430, 435, 436, 551, 558, 587, 696, 713, 715
employment, 96, 103, 257, 290, 291, 302, 305, 456, 461, 465, 467, 468, 531, 653
enforcement mechanism, 316
engagement, 14, 28, 31, 32, 36–39, 42, 96, 101, 109, 133, 166, 167,

169, 170, 172, 173, 177–179, 206, 217–220, 225, 226, 233, 235, 256, 273, 283, 284, 315, 340, 400, 409, 411, 413, 416, 417, 422, 427, 438, 441, 458, 476, 477, 479, 480, 482, 484, 489, 509, 511, 526–531, 549, 554, 559, 569, 587, 593, 598, 617, 626–630, 632, 635–638, 640, 641, 650–660, 662–666, 697, 698, 700, 710, 712, 715
enlightened self-interest, 14, 133, 220, 233, 276
entrepreneurs, 169, 178, 179, 207, 222–224, 226, 227, 229, 231–236, 453
equitable cooperation, 60
expansion, 5, 193, 204, 206, 220, 396, 398, 402, 487, 522, 528, 574, 592, 614, 692, 712
external dependency, 293
external policies, 484

F
feasibility, 311, 314, 315, 317–320
feedback loops, 275, 319, 321, 322, 683
fields of knowledge, 27
financial inclusion, 54, 418, 430
financial instruments, 53, 104, 304
financial sector, 52, 342, 490
Financing for Development (FfD) Forum, 4, 283, 415, 425, 427
fiscal austerity, 274
flows of public money, 55
follow-up and review (FUR), 142, 230, 310, 316, 321, 336, 476, 485, 709
footprint, 208, 248, 476, 492, 635, 636
foreign aid, 3, 52, 113, 121, 188, 217–220, 224–228, 232, 233, 272, 274, 291, 293, 304, 436–444, 455, 504, 519, 521, 534, 608–610, 672, 674, 675, 681, 685, 686, 709
Forum on China-Africa Cooperation, 271, 428
fragmentation, 30, 33, 134, 185, 202, 203, 257, 341, 359, 394, 399, 404, 534, 707, 708, 712
functional approach, 127, 136, 713
functionalist logic, 37, 353

G
game theory, 7, 331, 385
gender, 28, 96, 113–117, 121, 142, 145, 168, 169, 171, 172, 174–179, 314, 324, 333, 334, 397, 425, 453–457, 459–466, 468–470, 549, 593, 633, 713
generosity, 56, 272, 441
genuine partnership, 405
geopolitical interests, 276
geospatial information, 330
global challenges, 3, 26, 30, 31, 36, 179, 204, 282, 356, 376, 384, 414, 417, 437, 443, 508, 520
global consensus, 94, 113, 114, 208, 444, 505
global debates, 60, 422, 423, 690–693, 696, 697, 700
global development, 52, 59, 76–78, 132, 137, 149, 152, 165, 179, 218, 224, 231, 276–278, 283, 322, 333, 349, 352–354, 356, 357, 361–363, 384, 394, 395, 397, 399–405, 409, 410, 413, 419, 422, 423, 427, 429, 441, 475, 499, 501, 503–506, 508–510, 535, 572, 625, 632, 635, 637, 640, 641, 689, 691, 692, 695, 700, 713
Global Development Centre, 534
global financial market, 55
global financing facility (GFF), 340, 341, 343, 709
global goals, 30, 51, 56, 120, 262, 356, 489, 684
global governance, 4, 5, 10, 11, 13–15, 60, 68, 69, 72, 74, 76, 78, 144, 186, 188, 324, 353, 357–360, 400, 402, 404, 410, 411, 414, 416, 418, 419, 429, 435, 436, 468, 511, 525, 527, 568, 638, 654, 655, 657, 706, 713, 715, 716
globalisation, 2, 9, 16, 113–122, 131, 356, 378, 410, 676, 706, 707, 709, 714
global mechanism, 310, 321, 322
global nature, 394, 699, 713
global norms, 60, 68, 75, 166–173, 177, 178, 180, 273, 708, 710
Global Partnership for Effective Development Co-operation (GPEDC),

4, 11, 60, 64, 72–74, 76–78, 187, 202–204, 206, 209, 247, 254, 255, 257, 261–263, 310–323, 350, 351, 353–355, 357–364, 367–373, 377, 379–382, 385, 386, 393–395, 397–405, 413, 423, 426–428, 430, 431, 439, 442, 512, 547, 559, 588, 595, 598, 651, 652, 655–659, 663, 664, 696, 708, 711, 713–715
global public goods (GPG), 5, 7, 9, 15, 91–93, 96, 133, 135, 137, 145, 147, 220, 226, 233, 235, 250–252, 259–262, 265, 277, 355, 356, 373, 417, 504, 510, 533, 707, 709, 711, 713
Global Reporting Initiative (GRI), 249, 489, 665
global requirements, 332, 709
global scientific networks, 65
global sustainability politics, 30
global warming, 26, 41
good practices, 368
governance system, 33, 36–38, 95, 676
government-to-government, 291, 294, 305, 637
grand challenges, 118
greenhouse gas emissions, 26, 28, 248, 260, 265, 613, 614, 619
growth strategies, 91, 354

H

harmonisation, 203, 207, 331, 341, 350, 398, 594
Health system strengthening (HSS), 98, 99, 101
high-income countries, 143, 144, 150, 334, 350, 351, 356, 589, 590
High Level Forum on Aid Effectiveness, 190, 199, 323, 394, 395, 397, 398, 402, 439, 587, 594, 714
High-Level Panel, 128
high-level principles, 253
holistic assessment, 511, 693
homogenisation, 113, 169, 178, 676
horizontality, 3, 195, 275, 292, 293, 297, 298, 305, 306, 543, 547, 548, 551–553, 555, 556, 558, 560, 587

I

idealistic, 273, 441
ideational convergence, 218
ideologies, 54, 165, 166, 339, 671, 672, 678, 684
imperialism, 350, 410
implementation levels, 28
inclusive development, 73, 91, 310, 312, 320, 458, 459, 678
inclusive development partnerships, 73, 203, 310, 312, 320
inclusive growth, 329, 522
income growth, 53
incompatibility of interests, 353, 361
India, Brazil and South Africa (IBSA), 4
influence, 3, 8, 11, 39, 44, 61, 68, 70, 101, 114–117, 119, 136, 167–170, 172, 173, 175–180, 186, 187, 189, 191, 197, 199, 209, 222, 232–234, 259, 273, 275, 311, 314, 315, 318, 320, 321, 352, 353, 359–363, 395, 398, 405, 412, 418, 438, 439, 454, 458, 460, 461, 477, 501, 502, 504, 508–510, 520, 524–527, 532, 533, 557, 558, 567, 585, 587, 591, 593, 617, 628, 635, 637, 639, 641, 650, 662, 672, 673, 675, 677, 680, 681, 683, 684, 686, 693, 696, 699, 711, 714
innovative solutions, 79, 200, 431, 583
innovative sources, 91
institutionalisation, 5, 35, 73, 141, 173, 177, 356, 383, 396, 558, 711
institutional structures, 10, 92, 94, 97, 98, 101, 102, 104, 106, 108, 109, 146, 218
integrity, 39, 42, 130, 132, 191, 410, 416, 524
interconnections, 6, 61, 68, 276, 356
intergovernmental process, 128, 696
interlinkages, 7, 25, 31, 40, 44, 64, 141, 354, 708, 715
internalisation, 117, 119
international cooperation, 2, 11, 42, 43, 67, 68, 71, 75, 76, 127–129, 131, 139, 141, 149–151, 179, 186, 229, 230, 235, 356, 373, 376, 384, 427, 439, 527, 544–546, 554, 584–587,

590, 592, 596–599, 612, 618, 639, 663, 678, 691, 706, 712
international development cooperation (IDC), 43, 170, 219, 223, 234, 273, 317, 350–353, 355–357, 362, 367, 394, 396, 399, 436, 438, 443, 476, 477, 480, 486, 543–547, 559, 567, 583–589, 591, 626, 660, 707, 711–713
International Finance Facility for Immunisation (IFFIm), 97–99
international funding, 95
internationalisation, 68, 70, 71, 523, 692
international regimes, 33, 39, 353, 354, 356, 362, 363
international relations (IR), 13, 30, 127, 136, 187, 188, 207, 209, 218, 220, 221, 226, 272, 349, 362, 363, 385, 419, 435, 437, 439, 443, 492, 579, 695, 715
International Solar Alliance (ISA), 92, 96, 101–106, 110, 527, 626, 627, 637–641
inter-regional movement, 289
interrelationship, 187
inter-subjective, 167, 710
Iran nuclear deal, 220
Islamic Relief Worldwide, 171, 174, 178
isomorphism, 113–115, 118, 121

J
Joint Cooperation Committee (JCC), 294, 296, 297, 302, 304, 306
Joint Support Team (JST), 312, 314, 319, 322

K
key features, 127, 149, 185, 291, 293, 297, 300
knowledge, 3, 5, 6, 10, 15, 27, 60–68, 71–74, 76–79, 93, 104, 135, 140, 143, 176, 199, 251, 259, 260, 263, 273, 292, 298, 304, 305, 322, 324, 340, 363, 397, 400, 401, 403, 427, 431, 444, 470, 503, 533, 535, 543, 547, 550, 551, 553, 554, 556–558, 585, 586, 589, 597, 618, 625, 626, 632, 634, 639, 640, 649, 652, 656, 658, 659, 664, 665, 672–674, 681, 684, 689, 691, 692, 695–697, 700, 706, 712
knowledge-based programmes, 399
knowledge sharing, 64, 74, 134, 351, 532, 554, 593, 625, 640, 641, 651, 653, 656, 657
Korean deal, 371, 377, 380, 385
Kyoto Protocol (KP), 32

L
lack of funding, 67, 78, 332, 336
leakage, 258
learning and sharing, 395
leaving no one behind (LNOB), 93, 179, 454, 469, 593
legacies, 166, 274
legitimacy, 39, 168, 172, 176, 197, 198, 201, 207, 222, 223, 225, 228, 229, 231, 352, 353, 359, 361–364, 378–380, 394, 395, 399, 401, 404, 410, 414, 417, 420, 430, 661, 666, 698–700
lessons learnt, 291, 394
limiting factor, 251
local contexts, 60, 118, 302, 676
local ownership, 350, 399, 500, 594
low-income countries (LIC), 8, 53, 133, 149, 274, 330, 437

M
macro-level, 114–116
mainstream development approaches, 174
market-based resources, 274
Marshall Plan, 5, 190, 396, 500, 501, 653
means of implementation (MoIs), 35, 43, 73, 127, 130, 137–142, 147, 249, 250, 310, 315, 316, 321, 596, 597, 606, 625, 713
measurement, 3, 9, 31, 79, 172, 204, 247, 248, 261, 333, 337, 339, 340, 415, 418, 462, 508, 674, 676, 709
mercantile, 272, 276, 508

Mexico, Indonesia, Korea, Turkey and Australia (MIKTA), 4
micro-level, 114, 117
middle-income countries (MIC), 52–55, 133, 150, 199, 255, 259, 274, 330, 334, 338, 339, 341, 369, 370, 378, 383, 385, 386, 423, 470, 625, 663, 678
migration, 3, 11, 132, 133, 135, 248, 250, 251, 258–261, 266, 318, 373, 505, 531, 691
Millenniums Development Goals (MDGs), 2, 51–53, 117, 119, 128, 130, 133, 139, 151, 165, 177, 369, 383, 384, 414, 415, 425, 427, 454–456, 458, 462, 468, 469, 701
mimicry, 114, 115
modernisation, 38, 62, 190, 297, 331, 332, 483
monitoring and evaluation (M&E), 232, 233, 291–293, 300, 305, 403, 412, 426, 476, 477, 479, 480, 484–486, 489, 492, 493, 534, 665, 679
monitoring framework, 255, 310–323, 360, 361, 370–372, 377, 380, 386, 427, 656–659, 664, 714
moral imperative, 395, 428
multi-actors, 29, 43
multi-dimensionality, 29
multi-dimensional partnership, 289
multilateralism, 4, 11, 167, 218, 231, 234, 409, 505, 507, 509, 511, 512, 519, 522, 525–527, 530, 568, 637, 707, 712, 715
multimodal, 134, 149
multi-modality approach, 92, 95
multi-stakeholder meetings, 51
multi-stakeholder participation, 638
multi-stakeholder platform, 199, 202, 310, 312, 315, 317, 322, 350, 638, 651, 653, 659
mutual, 10, 16, 36, 67, 77, 78, 134, 149, 191, 200, 203, 220, 225, 226, 266, 271, 276, 289, 293, 297, 298, 304, 314, 316, 321, 322, 340, 350, 354, 398, 401, 505–507, 548, 550, 593, 594, 661, 710, 714
mutual benefits, 3, 10, 147, 191, 195, 196, 205, 207, 219, 223–227, 229, 231–235, 250, 274, 292, 293, 297, 305, 372, 382, 437, 524, 547, 549, 550, 556, 557, 575, 587, 593, 628, 660, 710
mutual learning, 64, 78, 256, 340, 351, 558, 597, 635, 641

N
narratives, 2–4, 6, 10, 13–15, 54, 55, 128, 173, 187, 219, 272, 276, 277, 282, 342, 343, 379, 382, 403, 443, 585, 593, 595, 596, 637, 639–641, 660, 674, 697, 706, 716
national development agencies, 52, 117, 650, 662–664
National Development and Reform Commission (NDRC), 294, 297, 609, 610, 616, 618
national interest, 113, 114, 132, 218, 220, 225, 226, 232, 271, 272, 275–278, 280, 282–284, 318, 373, 382, 385, 419, 488, 489, 550
Nationally determined contributions (NDCs), 26, 33, 40, 42, 44, 606–608, 613, 615, 617, 618
national needs, 272, 277, 296, 333, 659, 664
national security, 189, 349, 503
national sovereignty, 10, 94, 191, 419, 437, 454, 587, 628
national statistical office (NSO), 331, 332, 335, 340
national statistical systems, 329–334, 336–338, 341, 343
neo-colonial, 378
Network of Southern Think Tanks (NeST), 291, 305, 306, 393, 428, 696, 710
networks, 32, 38, 68, 93, 95, 114, 115, 169, 224, 302, 357, 363, 634, 652, 653, 655, 678, 680, 692, 695–699, 709
new actors, 73, 130, 133, 317, 336, 340, 355, 583, 696
New Development Bank (NDB), 3–5, 12, 103, 218, 359, 403, 405, 418, 419, 477, 493, 509, 525, 526, 612–615, 617, 619, 636, 707, 715

INDEX 725

new donors, 116, 120, 368, 369, 378, 429
new global regime, 368
non-DAC (Development Assistance Committee) donors, 120, 218, 367, 385
non-governmental, 1, 8, 10, 43, 114, 122, 134–136, 139, 149, 152, 171, 205, 235, 306, 312, 355, 394, 396, 437, 458, 520, 587, 632, 671, 681, 690, 694, 712
non-hierarchical institutions, 31
Non-Proliferation Treaty, 188, 411
normative collaboration, 283, 284
normative conceptualisation, 129, 130
normative support, 166
norm-diffusion, 167, 178, 187–189, 198, 207–209, 709
norm-making, 187, 208
norms, 2–4, 6, 10, 13–16, 31, 34, 36, 38, 62, 68, 71–76, 78, 116, 120, 121, 128, 129, 135, 136, 142, 167–169, 171–175, 177–180, 186–190, 194, 202–204, 206–210, 218, 221, 224, 226, 234, 260, 267, 275, 349–351, 355, 357, 359, 362, 363, 367–369, 385, 416, 429, 442, 458, 459, 468, 469, 488, 503, 544, 585, 595, 637, 639, 641, 706, 708–710, 713–716
norm-taking, 187
Northern flow, 370
North-South, 5, 12, 59, 62, 67, 72, 78, 129, 136, 148, 149, 151, 195, 199, 230, 276, 278, 283, 320, 324, 353, 371, 373, 376, 402, 412, 543, 544, 548–550, 557, 559, 584, 587, 588, 590–594, 596–598, 625, 696, 698, 712–714
North-South divide, 230, 283, 373–376, 378, 379, 381, 383, 627, 630, 639, 697
North-South knowledge transfer, 60

O

OECD Development Centre, 397
official development assistance (ODA), 3, 5, 8, 10–12, 14, 15, 52, 53, 55, 69, 71, 72, 74–76, 79, 92, 94, 119, 120, 133, 134, 147, 152, 185–190, 192–198, 200, 202–209, 217, 225, 228, 232, 233, 235, 236, 252, 256, 257, 259, 263, 265, 274–276, 279, 280, 312, 318–320, 323, 341, 350, 355, 360, 368–370, 374, 375, 378, 382, 383, 385, 386, 399–401, 415, 417, 419, 425, 430, 440, 443, 455, 470, 475–480, 482–486, 488, 489, 491–493, 502, 508, 519–521, 526, 528, 544, 552, 575, 584–587, 590, 594, 598, 599, 681, 683, 685, 686, 707, 712
openness, 201, 357, 395, 401, 626, 630
Open Working Group (OWG), 35, 128, 151, 230, 423–425, 527
organisational culture, 171–173, 176
organisational field, 8, 176
Organisation for Economic Co-operation and Development (OECD), 3, 4, 12, 14, 27, 29, 43, 53, 54, 72–74, 79, 80, 92, 94, 95, 115, 130, 134, 143–145, 152, 167, 168, 179, 185–188, 192, 193, 196, 197, 199–202, 204–210, 217–219, 223–235, 247–250, 252–257, 261, 263, 279, 280, 284, 290, 293, 311, 312, 314, 317, 318, 320–322, 330–333, 338, 350–352, 361, 367, 368, 379, 380, 383, 385, 386, 396–400, 402, 403, 413, 416–418, 421, 428, 430, 436–443, 476, 478–481, 483, 495, 500, 502, 506, 509, 511, 521, 522, 526, 528, 535, 543–545, 547, 549, 559, 575, 583–586, 588–591, 593–599, 626, 633, 634, 642, 649, 650, 652, 654, 656, 686, 710, 713, 714
other official flows (OOF), 192, 252, 284, 312
overlap, 68, 71, 101, 139, 218, 250, 320, 354, 505, 506, 509, 545, 554
ownership, 9, 10, 62, 67, 73, 75, 76, 99, 186, 200, 203, 207, 209, 254, 291, 292, 294–296, 304–306, 310, 312, 320, 398, 419, 500, 508, 549, 587, 593, 594, 628, 641, 664, 665

Oxfam Great Britain (Oxfam GB), 171, 175, 176

P
Pakistan, 108, 289–291, 294–300, 302–306, 455, 456, 459, 463, 464, 470, 523, 529, 531
paradigm, 38, 60, 78, 79, 129, 132, 149, 295, 317, 320, 322, 339, 373, 379, 382, 394, 404, 410, 559, 595, 639, 692
Paris Agreement, 25, 26, 33, 35, 40, 42, 116, 143, 220, 230, 419, 429, 525, 527, 605–607, 610, 611, 613–615, 618, 706
partnerships, 4–7, 10, 13, 35, 37–39, 42, 52, 55, 67, 70, 72–76, 92, 96, 104, 107, 119, 185, 203, 204, 209, 254, 292, 294, 297, 310, 312, 316, 320, 337, 341–343, 357, 382, 412, 419, 427, 428, 442, 453, 455, 458, 460, 465, 466, 469, 476, 488, 519, 522, 524, 527, 528, 530–533, 535, 544, 583, 585, 593–595, 597, 598, 615, 625, 626, 628–630, 632, 635–637, 640, 642, 650–657, 659, 661, 664–666, 673, 676, 678, 679, 685, 689, 693–695, 697–701, 706, 711
path dependencies, 7, 66, 641
peer pressure, 316, 396
peer reviews, 116, 256, 283, 396, 420
people-centred inclusivity, 292, 293, 295
Planning Development Reform (PDR), 294, 295, 297, 301, 302
platform for global development, 395
plurilateral institutions, 352
policy coherence, 26–29, 40, 42, 43, 60, 70, 71, 75, 76, 119, 136, 137, 144, 147, 258, 292, 302, 303, 319, 324, 352, 354, 415, 691
policy entrepreneurs, 222–224, 226, 227, 229, 231–236
political behaviour, 221
political-economic tensions, 332
political practice, 127, 149
political will, 34, 310, 338, 343, 548, 552

politicisation, 11, 715
pollution, 41, 260, 275, 373
polycentric governance, 27, 30, 31, 33, 34, 36, 37, 43, 44, 715
polysemic idea, 222, 224, 229
poor countries, 259, 263, 395, 399
populism, 2, 167, 231, 272, 274, 284, 318, 368, 382, 384, 712
post-Busan dialogue, 312
poverty reduction, 5, 41, 52–54, 133, 225, 261, 272, 274, 333, 384, 397, 458, 468, 631
power imbalances, 67, 227, 628
power relations, 7, 8, 62, 141, 189, 208, 209, 222, 225, 232, 589, 678
pragmatic, 273, 411, 420, 437, 461, 609, 629, 636
pre-2015, 127, 129, 139, 141, 142, 147, 148, 150
principled aid, 283
private foundations, 9, 355, 559, 660, 665
problem-solving, 2, 28, 31, 32, 67
processes and institutions, 310
provider commitments, 361, 370
public money, 53, 55
public well-being, 329

Q
quality, 3, 15, 26, 28, 91, 98, 102, 106, 109, 142, 252, 255–259, 290, 293, 294, 314, 319, 321, 324, 330, 334, 337–339, 356, 372, 373, 375, 396, 488, 524, 534, 535, 608, 615, 633, 639, 650, 651, 662, 713
quality of development cooperation, 3, 15
quantity, 252, 253, 255, 257, 259, 261, 372, 373, 544

R
recipient countries, 44, 98, 118, 201, 210, 225, 227, 232, 233, 257, 263, 264, 277, 323, 368, 371–374, 385, 386, 397, 398, 427, 431, 477, 488, 489, 494, 500, 508, 512, 549, 552, 590, 591, 691

recipient partner countries, 367, 385
reciprocity, 193, 196, 274, 275, 661
refugee movements, 275
regime theory, 352
relative average income, 249
repercussions, 129, 295
research, 3, 6, 8, 10, 11, 13, 27, 59, 60, 62, 64–80, 97, 98, 102, 106, 113–116, 118, 120, 129, 146, 168, 170, 171, 187, 188, 208, 209, 218, 219, 225, 235, 254, 257, 259, 260, 262, 266, 273, 290, 291, 303, 341, 360, 403, 404, 459, 460, 476, 551, 554, 555, 569, 577, 579, 584, 598, 606, 633, 638, 642, 651, 655, 664, 671–677, 679–682, 684, 685, 691–693, 695–697, 699–701, 716
resilience, 26, 38, 479, 505, 609, 613, 631, 632
resilience theory, 330
resource allocation, 168
resources, 15, 16, 27, 30, 34, 35, 41, 44, 52, 54, 61, 66, 72, 92–99, 101, 102, 104, 106–110, 119, 140, 143, 145, 149, 152, 166, 172, 173, 189, 190, 195–197, 204, 206, 209, 222, 261, 267, 274–278, 292, 293, 297–299, 302, 305, 312, 314, 315, 320, 322–324, 330–333, 336, 338–340, 342, 343, 350, 352, 354, 355, 359, 360, 362, 378, 379, 384, 397–401, 404, 420, 422, 423, 427, 436, 438, 444, 460, 461, 468, 476, 477, 483, 484, 488, 503, 508, 509, 511, 520–525, 527–529, 531–533, 568, 569, 573, 578, 579, 586, 589, 597, 606, 610, 613, 614, 618, 629, 632, 652, 653, 656, 658, 661, 662, 664, 675, 678, 700, 707
respect for sovereignty, 191, 293
responsibilities, 5–8, 10, 14, 16, 30, 32, 43, 53, 60, 69, 72, 108, 109, 137, 140, 147, 166, 192, 193, 195, 196, 202, 203, 205, 226, 230, 247–249, 258, 260, 275, 310, 314, 351, 360, 367, 369, 370, 372–384, 386, 403, 415, 419, 428, 430, 443, 485, 489, 500, 510, 529, 534, 558, 567, 568, 580, 584, 611, 635, 637, 650, 651, 653, 654, 659–661, 663, 665, 685, 706, 707
results orientation, 310, 312, 320
retroliberalism, 225
review process, 142, 314
Rio+20 conference, 128, 151, 152
rising power, 12, 201, 202, 217, 378, 625, 635, 638, 707
rules of production, 61, 62

S
Science, 7, 59–62, 64–70, 72–80, 174, 219, 271, 422, 547
science policy, 60, 65, 68, 69, 72, 75, 79, 709
sector-specific approaches, 30
security, 7, 26, 66, 75, 107, 108, 114, 121, 135, 191, 197, 206, 225, 226, 250, 251, 258, 260, 261, 266, 272, 275, 278, 283, 284, 289, 291, 298, 334, 349, 363, 386, 395, 411, 420, 422, 423, 445, 457, 460, 482, 488, 500, 503, 507, 509, 524, 545, 553, 554, 573, 608, 633, 636, 655, 685, 710
self-interest, 14, 132, 133, 220, 221, 233, 273, 274, 276, 284, 437, 500, 710
selfishness, 132, 136, 272, 276
self-reliance, 37, 189, 195, 292, 293, 298, 305, 306, 350, 505, 506, 521, 549
set of targets, 119
shared interests, 283, 297, 353, 361
shared principles, 369, 436
shared values, 284, 397, 512, 529, 532
short-term gains, 277
sinocentric, 226
situated approach, 169, 708
Small Island Developing States (SIDS), 103, 330, 338, 619, 631
smart economics, 172
social action, 170, 178
socio-economic development, 290, 413, 420, 483, 488, 489, 551, 573, 608
sociological, 114, 117, 221, 709
soft power, 186, 220, 378, 404, 443, 503

Southern agents, 203, 207
Southern providers, 255, 272, 275, 283, 358, 361, 362, 368–372, 374–376, 381, 383–386, 428, 429, 436, 437, 442, 546–548, 551, 585–594, 596, 597, 638
Southern scientific knowledge, 64
South-North cooperation, 5, 13, 149
South-South cooperation (SSC), 3, 62, 79, 92, 120, 121, 147, 153, 185, 199, 200, 204, 208, 210, 223, 224, 226–229, 233, 256, 275, 283, 312, 340, 351, 353, 367, 369, 371, 374, 375, 377, 383, 385, 393, 394, 409, 412, 427, 436, 444, 482, 508, 512, 519, 521, 527, 528, 543, 545, 550, 551, 554, 559, 575, 579, 584, 587, 590–594, 596–598, 605, 609–612, 615–618, 625–628, 630, 631, 650, 652, 665, 696, 710
spillovers, 9, 140, 248–250, 252, 265–267, 275, 476, 486
spread of ideas, 188
stakeholders, 4, 6, 28, 29, 33–35, 38, 40, 41, 43, 55, 60, 77, 79, 94–97, 99, 101, 102, 104–107, 109, 119, 128, 141, 142, 172, 176, 177, 201, 202, 227–229, 289, 292–295, 298, 300, 306, 311, 312, 314, 319–321, 323, 330, 331, 337, 338, 340, 351–353, 355, 357–363, 367, 377, 394, 395, 398, 402, 428, 440, 444, 458, 468, 476, 484, 485, 487, 489, 506, 511, 521, 531, 544, 554, 556, 569, 583–589, 593, 595–598, 631, 638, 652, 655, 661, 674, 678, 700, 705, 708, 709, 712
stalemate, 352
standard-setting, 4, 33, 368, 430
statistical capacity, 324, 330, 332, 334, 336, 337, 339–343
Steering Committee, 312, 314, 323, 369, 426, 427, 431
structuration, 189
sustainability, 1, 6, 12, 13, 25–27, 30, 31, 34, 36, 37, 39, 40, 42, 53, 60, 65–69, 79, 98, 99, 128, 131, 198, 207, 222, 249, 284, 292, 293, 298, 305, 306, 309, 341, 415, 526, 529–532, 556, 652
Sustainable Development Goals (SDGs), 2–8, 11–14, 25, 26, 29, 34, 35, 37–40, 42, 43, 51–53, 55, 56, 63, 72–74, 77, 91–94, 96, 101, 107, 110, 117, 119, 120, 122, 128, 129, 132, 137, 140–144, 146, 147, 149, 165–173, 175, 177–180, 185, 223, 228–230, 233, 234, 248–250, 253, 256, 258, 262, 275, 283, 290, 291, 309–311, 314–322, 329, 334, 335, 338–340, 352, 354, 356, 383–385, 399, 403, 405, 414, 415, 417, 419, 423–425, 427, 436, 453–455, 458, 461–463, 466–470, 476, 477, 480, 484–489, 491, 492, 499, 504, 506, 507, 511, 512, 519, 522, 525, 527, 529, 532, 533, 535, 544, 559, 568, 572, 579, 584, 605–608, 612, 614, 616, 617, 625, 627, 640, 649–654, 659–662, 664, 673, 676, 690–692, 694–696, 699, 700, 706–714
synergies, 6, 27–29, 36, 37, 39, 40, 42, 97, 199, 316, 340, 354, 401, 458, 606, 625, 715
systemic risk, 55

T

tax evasion, 52
technical factors, 310, 311, 314, 318–320
technology transfer, 43, 64, 78, 95, 292, 609, 619, 640
terrorism, 275, 373, 483, 488
the Vaccine Alliance (GAVI) (originally: Global Alliance for Vaccines and Immunization), 92, 96–102, 253, 502, 503
Total Official Support for Sustainable Development (TOSSD), 3, 134, 204–206, 209, 232, 252, 261, 417, 588, 599, 707
trade, 5, 7, 11, 91, 95, 132, 134, 136, 139, 140, 146, 149, 193, 196, 204, 220, 225, 235, 248, 250, 251, 258, 259, 261, 274, 275, 277, 279, 284, 289, 297, 300, 303, 306, 312, 339,

354, 382, 400, 403, 405, 410, 411, 415, 418, 422, 427, 442, 455, 467–469, 488, 513, 520–523, 525, 530, 533–535, 550, 570, 574, 629, 633, 634, 636, 691, 709, 715
trade-offs, 6, 26–30, 37–39, 41, 42, 67, 68, 233, 260, 262, 352, 354, 356, 363, 462, 504, 505, 715
traditional donors, 153, 197, 199, 202, 204, 206–209, 247, 275, 318, 361, 369–372, 374–377, 380–382, 386, 400, 402, 428, 429, 436–438, 443, 444, 520, 521, 525, 532, 533, 544, 583, 585–597, 684, 714
transformation, 14, 25, 26, 59, 65, 66, 68, 109, 131, 133, 141, 146, 166, 168, 169, 187, 195, 258, 273, 352, 355, 357, 394, 420, 422, 444, 453, 476, 477, 479, 483, 570, 572, 585–587, 625, 673, 675–678, 680
transformative change, 66, 150, 678
transmission chains, 275
transnational research cooperation, 59, 60, 66, 73, 75
transparency, 42, 55, 73, 200, 203, 228, 232, 233, 254–256, 264, 266, 275, 283, 291–293, 300, 301, 304–306, 310, 312, 314, 316, 320, 350, 427, 428, 486, 508, 526, 534, 535, 593, 594, 658–662, 699, 710, 712, 715
transport facilities, 291
tripartite structure, 189
Truman Doctrine, 190

U

umbrella concept, 185
UN's Business & Sustainable Development Commission, 52, 55
UN Conference on Trade and Development (UNCTAD), 193, 194, 207, 351, 649, 653
underprovision, 96
UN Development Cooperation Forum (DCF), 4, 121, 187, 199–201, 209, 316, 351, 368, 394, 400, 401, 405, 544, 546, 559, 599, 626

UN Development Programme (UNDP), 4, 51, 63, 73, 74, 103, 104, 145, 187, 202, 279, 312, 314, 323, 351, 367, 379, 427, 463, 470, 520, 525, 526, 533, 545, 547, 552, 559, 584, 588, 612, 614, 616, 631, 632
UN Financing for Development Conference, 311, 318
unilateralism, 166
United Nations Security Council, 349, 410, 423, 635
United Nations (UN), 2, 15, 28, 33, 51, 63, 64, 96, 109, 128, 186, 195, 218, 247, 271, 310, 315, 330, 332–334, 336, 349, 351, 394, 411, 414, 428, 436, 440, 455, 476, 485, 501, 525, 544, 572, 583, 592, 605, 606, 611, 612, 614, 618, 626, 649, 690, 691, 700, 709
United Nations (UN) Fundamental Principles of Official Statistics, 330
universality, 5, 137, 138, 142, 143, 147, 149, 230, 248, 383, 512, 691
UN Peacekeeping (UNPK), 96, 107–109, 266, 526

V

values, 3, 62, 71, 136, 166, 174–176, 180, 188–190, 194, 208, 224, 262, 272, 282, 293, 380, 437, 444, 445, 500, 501, 503, 685, 699
voluntary basis, 39, 333, 377, 638
Voluntary National Reviews (VNRs), 6, 12, 13, 44, 73, 142, 152, 321, 324, 506, 709, 714
voter behaviour, 332

W

Western domination, 399
win-win collaboration, 271
women's empowerment, 145, 168, 169, 171, 177, 324, 454, 455, 460–462, 466, 468, 469, 633
Working Party on Aid Effectiveness (WP-EFF), 186, 187, 210, 370, 371, 397, 425, 430, 587, 656
World Bank, 10, 63, 79, 98, 103–105, 143, 171, 172, 178, 249, 257, 258,

263, 290, 323, 330, 399, 411, 456, 480–482, 485, 493, 501, 503, 505, 510, 513, 521, 525, 526, 530, 531, 551, 574, 649

World Society, 114–116, 709

Z

zero-sum game, 373

Printed in the United States
By Bookmasters